A HANDBOOK
on
THE GOSPEL OF MATTHEW

The Handbooks in the **UBS Handbook Series** are detailed commentaries providing valuable exegetical, historical, cultural, and linguistic information on the books of the Bible. They are prepared primarily to assist practicing Bible translators as they carry out the important task of putting God's Word into the many languages spoken in the world today. The text is discussed verse by verse and is accompanied by running text in at least one modern English translation.

Over the years church leaders and Bible readers have found the UBS Handbooks to be useful for their own study of the Scriptures. Many of the issues Bible translators must address when trying to communicate the Bible's message to modern readers are the ones Bible students must address when approaching the Bible text as part of their own private study and devotions.

The Handbooks will continue to be prepared primarily for translators, but we are confident that they will be useful to a wider audience, helping all who use them to gain a better understanding of the Bible message.

D1603440

Helps for Translators

A HANDBOOK ON

The Gospel of Matthew

by Barclay M. Newman
and Philip C. Stine

UBS Handbook Series

United Bible Societies
New York

Books in the series of **Helps for Translators** may be ordered from a national Bible Society or from either of the following centers:

United Bible Societies
European Production Fund
W-70520 Stuttgart 80
Postfach 81 03 40
Germany

United Bible Societies
1865 Broadway
New York, New York 10023
U.S.A.

L.C. Cataloging-in-Publication Data

Newman, Barclay Moon, 1931-
    [Translator's handbook on the Gospel of Matthew]
    A handbook on the Gospel of Matthew / by Barclay M. Newman and Philip C. Stine.
        p.   cm. — (UBS helps for translators) (UBS handbook series)
        Originally published: A translator's handbook on the Gospel of Matthew. c1988.
        Includes bibliographical references and index.
        ISBN 0-8267-0155-8
        1. Bible. N.T. Matthew—Translating. 2. Bible. N.T. Matthew—Criticism, interpretation, etc. I. Stine, Philip C., 1943-   .
II. Title. III. Series. IV. Series: UBS handbook series.
BS2575.5.N47 1992
226.2'077—dc20   92-25802
                                                                  CIP

ABS-2/94-400-2,900-EB-5-102725

Contents

CONTENTS

Preface

A Handbook on the Gospel of Matthew has been in preparation for more than five years, and we are happy to add this volume to the series of Handbooks in the United Bible Societies' Helps for Translators series. Special attention has been given to the ways in which the various kinds of discourse relate to each other, so that the translator will be able to trace the emphases and the thought patterns as they develop and move along, all contributing to the total message of the Gospel of Matthew.

The Revised Standard Version (RSV) and the Today's English Version (TEV) translations are shown at the beginning of each section, so that the translator may compare the two approaches to overall discourse structure and paragraph division. They are shown again at the beginning of the comments on each verse, so that they may be compared in detail. However, the discussion follows RSV, and references to words and phrases from the verse under discussion are printed in underlined boldface so that the translator can easily locate desired information. TEV is kept before the translator as a possible model for a meaningful translation. References to TEV from the passage being discussed are in boldface with quotation marks, while references to other versions and to quotations from elsewhere in RSV and TEV are simply displayed within quotation marks.

This Handbook follows the tradition of the series by concentrating on exegetical matters that are of prime importance for translators, and it attempts to indicate possible solutions for translational problems that may arise because of language or culture. In this respect the Handbook attempts to deal with the full range of information important to translators. However, the authors do not attempt to provide help that other theologians and scholars may be seeking but which is not directly useful for the task of translating. It is assumed that such information is available elsewhere.

A limited Bibliography is included for the benefit of those who are interested in further study. Furthermore, a Glossary is provided that explains technical terms according to their usage in this volume. The translator may find it useful to read through the Glossary in order to become aware of the specialized way in which certain terms are used. An Index gives the location by page number of some of the important words and subjects discussed in the Handbook, especially where the Handbook provides the translator with help in rendering these concepts into the receptor language.

A special word of thanks is due to Kevin Jarrett of the Summer Institute of Linguistics, who read the exegetical draft and provided comments that arose from his use of the draft in checking a translation of the Gospel of Matthew.

The editor of Helps for Translators is happy to receive comments from translators and others who use these books, so that future volumes may benefit and may better serve the needs of the readers.

Abbreviations Used in This Volume

General Abbreviations, Bible Texts, Versions, and Other Works Cited
(For details see Bibliography)

AB	Anchor Bible	MACL	Malay common language version
A.D.	*Anno Domini* (in the year of our Lord)	Mft	Moffatt
AT	American Translation	NAB	New American Bible
B.C.	Before Christ	NASB	New American Standard Bible
BJ	*Bible de Jérusalem*		
Brc	Barclay	NEB	New English Bible
CLT	common language translation	NIV	New International Version
DUCL	Dutch common language version	NJB	New Jerusalem Bible
		Phps	Phillips
FRCL	French common language version	RSV	Revised Standard Version
		Seg	Segond
GECL	German common language version	TC-GNT	A Textual Commentary on the Greek New Testament
INCL	Indonesian common language version	TEV	Today's English Version
		TNT	Translator's New Testament
JB	Jerusalem Bible	TOB	*Traduction œcuménique de la Bible*
KJV	King James Version		
LB	Living Bible	UBS	United Bible Societies
Lu	Luther revised (German)	Zür	*Zürcher Bibel*

Books of the Bible

Gen	Genesis	Dan	Daniel
Exo	Exodus	Hos	Hosea
Lev	Leviticus	Zech	Zechariah
Num	Numbers	Matt	Matthew
Deut	Deuteronomy	Rom	Romans
Josh	Joshua	1,2 Cor	1,2 Corinthians
1,2 Sam	1,2 Samuel	Gal	Galatians
1,2 Kgs	1,2 Kings	Eph	Ephesians
1,2 Chr	1,2 Chronicles	Phil	Philippians
Neh	Nehemiah	Col	Colossians
Est	Esther	1,2 Thes	1,2 Thessalonians
Psa	Psalms	1,2 Tim	1,2 Timothy
Isa	Isaiah	Heb	Hebrews
Jer	Jeremiah	Rev	Revelation
Ezek	Ezekiel		

PALESTINE IN THE TIME OF JESUS

Miles 0 — 40

Kms 0 — 40

MEDITERRANEAN

SEA

PHOENICIA

LEBANON MTS.

SYRIA

Sidon

Zarephath

Tyre

Abila
ABILENE

Damascus

▲ *MT. HERMON*

Caesarea Philippi

Ptolemais

GALILEE

Chorazin
Capernaum

Bethsaida

Lake

Magadan

Cana   Tiberias

MT. CARMEL▲

Galilee

Nazareth

▲ *MT.
TABOR*

Nain

Gadara

Caesarea

TEN TOWNS

SAMARIA

Salim

Aenon

Samaria

▲ *MT. EBAL*

Gerasa

MT. GERIZIM▲ Sychar

Joppa

Jordan River

PEREA

Arimathea?

Ephraim

Jericho

Emmaus

Bethany

Azotus

Jerusalem

Qumran

Ascalon

JUDEA

Bethlehem

Gaza

Hebron

Dead

Sea

IDUMEA

NABATEA

© United Bible Societies, 1976

ix

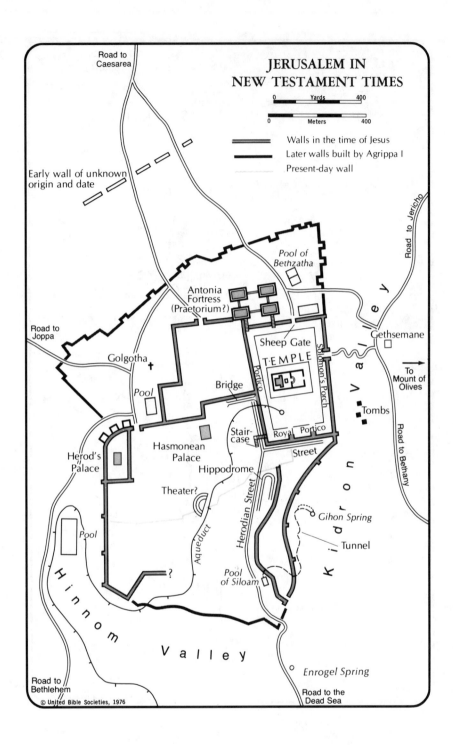

JERUSALEM IN NEW TESTAMENT TIMES

Road to Caesarea

Early wall of unknown origin and date

Road to Jericho

Yards 0 400
Meters 0 400

Walls in the time of Jesus
Later walls built by Agrippa I
Present-day wall

Pool of Bethzatha

Antonia Fortress (Praetorium?)

Road to Joppa

Golgotha

Sheep Gate

TEMPLE

Solomon's Porch

Gethsemane

To Mount of Olives

Pool

Bridge

Portico

Tombs

Stair-case

Royal Portico

Road to Bethany

Herod's Palace

Hasmonean Palace

Street

Hippodrome

Theater?

Herodian Street

Gihon Spring

Tunnel

Pool

Aqueduct

?

Pool of Siloam

K i d r o n V a l l e y

H i n n o m V a l l e y

Enrogel Spring

Road to Bethlehem

Road to the Dead Sea

© United Bible Societies, 1976

Translating the Gospel of Matthew

There are many things a translator should know about the Gospel of Matthew before attempting to translate even the first word. This brief introduction to the Gospel is intended to make the translator aware of some of the more important things, and alert for some of the hints that the authors provide in the discussion of each chapter and verse.

Special Features of the Gospel of Matthew
One important literary feature of the Gospel of Matthew is its relation to the Old Testament. In the first place, as Matthew attempted to recount the sayings and teachings and the story of Jesus in a coherent manner, he had, as did all the Gospel writers, the example of the Jewish Bible (later called the Old Testament), which mixed narrative, law and poetry. Secondly, and much more important, Matthew always treats the Old Testament material as true and valid, but acts on the premise that it is not complete. One writer has pointed out that the relation of the Gospel of Matthew to the Old Testament is like the relation of the second part of lines of Hebrew parallelism to the first part. The second part affirms that the first part is true, but then adds something more, and this extra or excess of the second part over the first is what transforms it and fulfills it.

This is particularly true in the way Matthew handles the Jewish Law. Take for example 5.17-18: "Think not that I have come the abolish the law and the prophets; I have come not to abolish them but to fulfill them. For truly, I say to you, till heaven and earth pass away, not an iota, not a dot, will pass from the law until all is accomplished." Thus Matthew assumes that even the smallest letter and most minute detail of the Law is sacred. But for the Law to be fulfilled it must be transformed, and in the case of Matthew's Gospel, transformation involves observing the Law even more strictly than the Jews supposed. In fact, excess is the mark of transformation. Thus it is not enough to be simply innocent of murder or adultery; one should not even contemplate these things. In the Sermon on the Mount, one finds over and over the statements "You have heard . . . but I say," with an added admonition which has the effect of actually keeping the Law to excess.

Some phrases that will be very important to translators, then, include the one we have just listed above, "You have heard . . . but I say," and also the continuing question, "How much more . . . ." Another phrase that relates to the theme is "All this took place to fulfill what the Lord had spoken by the Prophet."

These particular phrases constitute an important part of the structure of the Gospel. Also related to this will be certain words, in particular "fulfill" (1.22; 5.17), "law" (5.17), and "righteous" (3.15).

These expressions and terms are discussed at some length in this Handbook at their first occurrences in the Gospel. In addition to these, there are several other

1

terms that we have found it necessary to discuss at length the first time they occur. These include "Son of Man" (8.20), "Kingdom of Heaven" (3.2), "Messiah/Christ" (1.1), and "prophet" (1.22).

Another feature of the Gospel is the large number of references to the Old Testament. Some citations are fairly obvious, as where Matthew says "as the prophet wrote." But in many other places he cites passages from the Old Testament without necessarily identifying them as citations. His readers would have recognized what they were, but often modern readers will not. We have taken note of this problem in this Handbook as well.

We now turn to the way in which Matthew structured his Gospel, since it is important for the translator to understand just what is the author's intention as he moves from one section of his Gospel into another.

The Structure of Matthew's Gospel

It was at one time maintained that the Gospel of Matthew consists solely of five discourses, preceded by the nativity narrative, and with the passion narrative added as a conclusion. While this is no longer fashionable, it is just as impossible to deny either the existence or the significance of the summary statements with which each of these five sections concludes (7.28; 11.1; 13.53; 19.1; 26.1). Thus it may reasonably be argued that the Gospel of Matthew contains at least five major discourses embedded in a larger framework of narrative and other collections of Jesus' teachings. Moreover, from both a chronological and a theological perspective, the nativity and passion narratives are properly placed within this structure.

With these considerations in mind, and remembering that Jesus Christ is the central figure about whom all else revolves, the following outline will provide a broad perspective from which to view the overall flow of Matthew's Gospel:

I. The Origin and Person of Jesus Christ
(1.1-4.17)

By way of genealogy (1.1-17), nativity narrative (1.18-25), testimony of John the Baptist (3.1-12), and the voice from heaven (3.13-17), Jesus is variously identified as the Messiah, the Suffering Servant, and the Son of God. Then, following upon the heels of his temptation (4.1-11), which also serves to define who he is, Jesus initiates his Galilean ministry in fulfillment of the words of the prophet Isaiah (4.12-16). Verse seventeen of chapter 4 may be understood as either a summary of what has taken place or as an anticipation of what is to come.

II. The Ministry and Message of Jesus Christ
(4.18-16.20)

Jesus' public ministry begins with the call of his first four followers (4.18-22), whose response sets the pattern for discipleship as it is found elsewhere in the Gospel (see 9.9-13, which is also pattern-setting). After a successful preaching and healing ministry (4.23-25), Jesus instructs his disciples in the ways of his kingdom and contrasts its values with those of traditional Judaism (5.1-7.28). On his return from the mountain, Jesus immediately acts in numerous ways which demonstrate his authority over disease and demons, as well as over people and nature (8.1-9.34).

The second major block of teaching in the book (10.1-11.1) is preceded by a summary section similar to that which set the stage for the Sermon on the Mount

2

(compare 4.23-25 with 9.35-38). The "Twelve"—who in a sense represent all followers—are sent forth with the message about the kingdom, warned of persecution, told whom they must fear, and promised a reward worthy of their calling.

Chapters 11 and 12 consist mainly of questions and controversies concerning the person and authority of Jesus: John the Baptist, now in prison, has doubts and sends messengers with questions (11.2-19), the towns of Chorazin and Bethsaida, where he had performed many miracles, turn their backs on him (11.20-24), the Pharisees and the teachers of the Law have already decided that anyone who desecrates the Sabbath (12.1-14) must be under the control of Beelzebul (12.22-32), and even the members of Jesus' own family come to have a talk with him (12.46-50). Jesus is indeed the enigmatic Servant of the Lord (12.15-21), who offers rest to all who accept him, but promises a severe judgment to those who reject him (12.33-45).

At this juncture in Jesus' ministry—when doubt and unbelief are rampant among the masses—Matthew introduces the chapter on parables to explain the reason for this negative reaction to the message of the kingdom: the people have closed their minds, stopped up their ears, and shut their eyes to the truth (13.15). And so the necessity for the use of parables (13.13).

After teaching in parables beside Lake Galilee, Jesus immediately enters his hometown of Nazareth, where he does not perform any miracles because of the people's lack of faith (13.53-58). John the Baptist, whose destiny is similar to that of Jesus and whose death foreshadows that of his Lord, is also rejected and executed by Herod Antipas, the son of Herod the Great (14.1-12).

Having withdrawn to a desert region after the death of John, Jesus miraculously feeds a crowd of five thousand (14.13-21) and later walks on the stormy surface of Lake Galilee (14.22-33). Most probably the two miracles are intended to be reminiscent of the crossing of the Red Sea (Exodus 14) and the provision of manna during the desert wanderings of the Israelites (Exodus 16).

When Jesus returns to the west bank of the Jordan, he is met by throngs of people who have heard about him and who bring to him their sick, whom he cures (14.34-36). Then from Jerusalem there arrives a delegation which challenges him on the issue of what defiles a person in the sight of God (15.1-20). But a woman—who is a foreigner and thus "defiled"—expresses unusual faith (15.21-28), following which Jesus again heals many people (15.29-31) before feeding a crowd of four thousand (15.32-39).

The demand by the Pharisees and the Sadducees for a miraculous sign (16.1-4) provides Jesus with an opportunity to warn his disciples against the hypocrisy of the Pharisees and Sadducees (16.5-12), which brings to conclusion his ministry among the masses and makes way for the confession of Peter, which serves as a bridge to Jesus' revelation of himself to his small band of followers (16.13-20).

III. The Mystery and Revelation of Jesus Christ
(16.21–20.34)

Following the declaration of Peter (16.13-20), Jesus privately instructs his disciples on three occasions concerning the fate that awaits him in Jerusalem—specifically, his rejection by the religious authorities and his subsequent death and resurrection (16.21-28; 17.22-23; 20.17-19). Six days after the first prediction of his death, Jesus is transformed in the presence of Peter, James, and John, and a voice from heaven affirms him to be the Son of God (17.1-13).

3

As soon as Jesus comes down from the mountain (compare 8.1-4), he is met by a man whose demon-possessed son he cures (17.14-20). Matthew then narrates the incident of the payment of the temple tax (17.24-27), which once again raises the question of the relation of the Christian faith to Judaism. Between the second and third references to his impending suffering, Jesus instructs his disciples on the nature of true greatness and the necessity of forgiveness (18.1–19.1).

During this period of withdrawal from the crowds, Jesus also teaches his disciples concerning other issues that are central to his message of the kingdom: marriage (19.1-12), humility and greatness (19.13-15; 20.20-28), possessions (19.16-30), and God's generosity (20.1-16). The two blind men at Jericho (20.29-34) reveal greater insight than will the people of Jerusalem, whose enthusiastic reception will swiftly shift to hostility.

IV. The Death and Resurrection of Jesus
(21.1–28.20)

Though Jesus is welcomed into Jerusalem (21.1-11), his activity in the temple (21.12-17), leads to the challenge of his authority by the chief priests and the Jewish elders (21.23-27), against whom he reacts with three parables (21.28-32; 33-46; 22.1-14). After being questioned on several other key issues (22.15-22; 23-33; 34-40), Jesus himself raises the problem of the relation between David and the Messiah (22.41-46) and then denounces the hypocrisy of the Pharisees and the teachers of the Law (23.1-36).

When alone with his disciples, Jesus employs his teaching about the destruction of Jerusalem and the coming of apocalyptic events (24.1-31) as a summons to watchfulness (25.1-13) and faithfulness (25.14-30) on the part of his followers (24.32-51). But above all else, Jesus' depiction of the final judgment (25.31-46) is intended to awaken the readers of the Gospel to the realities of when and where they encounter the Son of Man and the weight that their response will carry on the day of judgment.

Finally, after being betrayed by Judas (26.47-56), denied by Peter (26.69-75), and rejected by his nation (26.57-67), Jesus is crucified (27.32-44). But even his death has miraculous effects (27.45-56), and no less miraculous is his resurrection (28.1-10). The account closes with Jesus' commissioning of his followers to proclaim his message to all the world and with his promise to be with them always (28.16-20).

Acknowledgments

The Bibliography provides a general list of references used by the authors of this Handbook, as well as suggested works that will be useful for the translators themselves. However, certain scholars influenced the writers of this Handbook more than others, even though credit for their ideas is not mentioned explicitly in the text. Included among them are Walter Grundmann, David Hill, Ernst Lohmeyer and Werner Schmauch, and Eduard Schweizer. Jack Kingsbury's monograph on the parables has been especially helpful.

Title

The Gospel According to Matthew: **Gospel** is usually translated "Good News" or "Good Word." When one of the four Gospels is being referred to, as here, some translators specify "The Good News about Jesus Christ."

According to Matthew: although nowhere in the book itself does it say who wrote it, tradition attributes it directly or indirectly to the Apostle Matthew, and the traditional title in the Greek text calls it his Gospel. However, to say "of Matthew," a possible rendering of the Greek which some translations follow, can be misunderstood to mean that the book is about Matthew. This is why "according to" is a better translation. It is possible to say "as Matthew wrote it," so that the full title of the book would be "The Good News about Jesus Christ as Matthew wrote it" or "The Good News as Matthew wrote it."

Chapter 1

1.1-17

REVISED STANDARD VERSION

TODAY'S ENGLISH VERSION

The Ancestors of Jesus Christ

1 The book of the genealogy of Jesus Christ, the son of David, the son of Abraham.

2 Abraham was the father of Isaac, and Isaac the father of Jacob, and Jacob the father of Judah and his brothers, 3 and Judah the father of Perez and Zerah by Tamar, and Perez the father of Hezron, and Hezron the father of Ram,^{a} 4 and Ram^a the father of Amminadab, and Amminadab the father of Nahshon, and Nahshon the father of Salmon, 5 and Salmon the father of Boaz by Rahab, and Boaz the father of Obed by Ruth, and Obed the father of Jesse, 6 and Jesse the father of David the king.

And David was the father of Solomon by the wife of Uriah, 7 and Solomon the father of Rehoboam, and Rehoboam the father of Abijah, and Abijah the father of Asa,^{b} 8 and Asa^b the father of Jehoshaphat, and Jehoshaphat the father of Joram, and Joram the father of Uzziah, 9 and Uzziah the father of Jotham, and Jotham the

1 This is the list of the ancestors of Jesus Christ, a descendant of David, who was a descendant of Abraham.

2-6a From Abraham to King David, the following ancestors are listed: Abraham, Isaac, Jacob, Judah and his brothers; then Perez and Zerah (their mother was Tamar), Hezron, Ram, Amminadab, Nahshon, Salmon, Boaz (his mother was Rahab), Obed (his mother was Ruth), Jesse, and King David.

6b-11 From David to the time when the people of Israel were taken into exile in Babylon, the following ancestors are listed: David, Solomon (his mother was the woman who had been Uriah's wife), Rehoboam, Abijah, Asa, Jehoshaphat, Jehoram, Uzziah, Jotham, Ahaz, Hezekiah, Manasseh, Amon, Josiah, and Jehoiachin and his brothers.

12-16 From the time after the exile in Babylon to the birth of Jesus, the following ances-

father of Ahaz, and Ahaz the father of Hezekiah, 10 and Hezekiah the father of Manasseh, and Manasseh the father of Amos,^{c} and Amos^c the father of Josiah, 11 and Josiah the father of Jechoniah and his brothers, at the time of the deportation to Babylon.

12 And after the deportation to Babylon: Jechoniah was the father of Shealtiel,^{d} and Shealtiel^d the father of Zerubbabel, 13 and Zerubbabel the father of Abiud, and Abiud the father of Eliakim, and Eliakim the father of Azor, 14 and Azor the father of Zadok, and Zadok the father of Achim, and Achim the father of Eliud, 15 and Eliud the father of Eleazar, and Eleazar the father of Matthan, and Matthan the father of Jacob, 16 and Jacob the father of Joseph the husband of Mary, of whom Jesus was born, who is called Christ.

17 So all the generations from Abraham to David were fourteen generations, and from David to the deportation to Babylon fourteen generations, and from the deportation to Babylon to the Christ fourteen generations.

tors are listed: Jehoiachin, Shealtiel, Zerubbabel, Abiud, Eliakim, Azor, Zadok, Achim, Eliud, Eleazar, Matthan, Jacob, and Joseph, who married Mary, the mother of Jesus, who was called the Messiah.

17 So then, there were fourteen generations from Abraham to David, and fourteen from David to the exile in Babylon, and fourteen from then to the birth of the Messiah.

^{a}Greek *Aram*
^{b}Greek *Asaph*
^{c}Other authorities read *Amon*
^{d}Greek *Salathiel*

SECTION HEADING: "**The Ancestors of Jesus Christ**" (Today's English Version [TEV]): for this section heading, if the translators follow TEV they should use the normal word for "ancestors," which in some languages is "fathers" or "grandfathers." Translators can also say "The people who were the fathers of Jesus Christ" or "The people from whom Jesus Christ descended." Some translators put the emphasis on the fact that this is a genealogy, that is, a list of ancestors, and say "The list of Jesus Christ's ancestors."

There are languages where even section headings need to be complete sentences, so that translators say something like "This is the list of Jesus Christ's ancestors" or "These are the names of Jesus Christ's ancestors."

In this Handbook we will comment on the section headings of TEV. However, translators should not feel they have to use these necessarily. They may find that in their translation some headings should be dropped or others added. Generally, good section headings help readers understand the text.

"**Jesus Christ**": see notes on "Christ" and on names in 1.1. "Christ" is used here with "Jesus" as a name and will be transliterated, not translated.

The record of Jesus' ancestors (1.1-17) is closely connected with the story of Jesus' birth (1.18-2.23). Both the genealogy and the story of Jesus' birth begin with introductory sentences (1.1; 1.18) in which the word "genealogy" or words related to it are used. In this first section of his Gospel (1.1-2.23), Matthew answers two questions: "Who is Jesus Christ?" and "Where does he come from?" In particular the record of Jesus' ancestors is intended to prove that the entire history of Israel finds its fulfillment in Jesus Christ. He is a descendant of Abraham, to whom God

6

made the promise that he would bless all families on earth (Gen 12.3). But at the same time he is a descendant of David and so has claim to be the expected Messiah, the rightful heir to the promises made to David (2 Sam 7.12-16).

Matthew states that the list of Jesus' ancestors falls into three groups of fourteen names each. Although it is difficult to find more than thirteen names in the third group, at least two solutions to this problem are possible: (1) in verse 16 "Jesus" may be considered the thirteenth name and "Christ" the fourteenth name; or (2) the division of names in verse 17 may be understood to include "David" as the final name of the first group and the first name of the second group, yielding the following arrangement: from Abraham to David (verses 2-6a), from David to the Babylonian Exile (verses 6b-11), and from the time of the Exile to the birth of Jesus, the Promised Savior (verses 12-16). In this way Matthew indicates the high point of Israel's sacred history (the time when David was king) as well as its low point (the Babylonian Exile) and its fulfillment (Jesus Christ). The result is three lists of fourteen names each:

1	2	3
(Abraham—David)	(David—Exile)	(Exile—Jesus)
1. Abraham	1. David	1. Jechoniah
2. Isaac	2. Solomon	2. Shealtiel
3. Jacob	3. Rehoboam	3. Zerubbabel
4. Judah	4. Abijah	4. Abiud
5. Perez	5. Asa	5. Eliakim
6. Hezron	6. Jehoshaphat	6. Azor
7. Ram	7. Joram	7. Zadok
8. Amminadab	8. Uzziah	8. Achim
9. Nahshon	9. Jotham	9. Eliud
10. Salmon	10. Ahaz	10. Eleazar
11. Boaz	11. Hezekiah	11. Matthan
12. Obed	12. Manasseh	12. Jacob
13. Jesse	13. Amos	13. Joseph
14. David	14. Josiah	14. Jesus

Jewish genealogical lists generally did not normally include women. Tamar (verse 3; see Gen 38.24), Rahab (verse 5; see Josh 2.1; Heb 11.31; James 2.25), and Ruth (verse 5; see Ruth 1.4) are all listed in the first section; in the second section the wife of Uriah is mentioned (verse 6; see 2 Sam 11.1-13), while in the final section Mary is named (verse 16). Tamar, Rahab, and Ruth were all non-Israelites, and Bathsheba (the wife of Uriah) may also be considered "non-Israelite" because of her marriage to a non-Israelite man.

Matthew's genealogical list down through Zerubbabel in verse 12 is apparently based on the Septuagint text of 1 Chronicles 1-3 (verse 2: 1 Chr 1.34; 2.1; verse 3: 1 Chr 2.4,5,9; verses 4-11: 1 Chr 2.10-13; 3.5,10-15; verse 12: 1 Chr 3.17-19). The source, or sources, used for verses 13-16 are unknown, but the names are well-attested Jewish names.

It goes without saying that translators should translate what Matthew says when he gives the three sets of fourteen generations, even though, as we pointed out above, it may not be immediately evident to readers how Matthew arrives at the number fourteen in every case. It would be wrong to change the numbers he gives or to add other names from the Old Testament.

1.1   RSV   TEV

The book of the genealogy of   **This is the list of the ancestors**
Jesus Christ, the son of David, the   **of Jesus Christ, a descendant of**
son of Abraham.   **David, who was a descendant of**
                                                Abraham.

Book of the genealogy (TEV "**list of the ancestors**") translates a phrase which clearly has its origin in Genesis 2.4a: "These are the generations of the heaven and earth." Similar use of this expression occurs in Genesis 5.1; 6.9; 10.1; 11.10,27, showing clearly that the phrase reflected in Matthew may include not only a list of ancestors but narrative as well.

The book of the genealogy may be interpreted in three different ways: (1) It may be limited to mean "a list of the ancestors" (TEV, French common language version [FRCL], German common language version [GECL]; Jerusalem Bible [JB] "A genealogy"; New English Bible [NEB] "A table of the descent"; New American Bible [NAB] "A family record"; Moffatt [Mft] "The birth roll"; American Translation [AT] "The ancestry"; Phillips [Phps] "This is the record of the ancestry"; Barclay [Brc] "This is the family tree").

(2) Following the pattern of Genesis, one may enlarge the phrase to include not only a list of the ancestors of Jesus Christ, but the events surrounding his birth and childhood as well (1.1–2.23). No translations appear to state this explicitly, though it is possible to take the ambiguous phrase **The book of the genealogy** in this sense (so also *Zürcher Bibel* [Zür]; see *Traduction œcuménique de la Bible* [TOB] "The book of the origin of Jesus Christ"). However, it may as easily be assumed that these translations have done nothing more than to perpetuate a literal rendering of the Greek phrase.

(3) It is also possible to take this phrase to include the whole Gospel of Matthew, which may be the intention of Luther Revised (Lu): "This is the book of the story of Jesus Christ . . . ."

On the whole, the second of these three possibilities seems to be the best choice in light of the way that this phrase is used in Genesis; though, as can be seen from the translations quoted, most translators apparently prefer the first of these possibilities.

Translators who choose the second interpretation of the phrase **The book of the genealogy**, and understand it to include the events surrounding Jesus' birth and childhood as well as the list of his ancestors, can use a phrase such as "This is the story of the ancestors of Jesus Christ and his birth." (For "ancestors," see comments on the section heading.) In some languages "story" is usually reserved for some tale that is not true. In such cases a better sentence will be "This writing (or, book) is about the ancestors of Jesus Christ and his birth."

"Birth" will in some cases be translated by a noun, as in the above examples, and in others by a verb, as in "and how he was born."

Those who follow the third interpretation, which suggests that **book of the genealogy** refers to all of Matthew, will use sentences such as "This book (or, writing) is the story of Jesus Christ" or ". . . is about Jesus Christ."

Most translators, however, will follow the first interpretation and understand **book of the genealogy** to refer to a list of ancestors. Then, like TEV, they may say "This is the list of the ancestors of Jesus Christ." In languages where there is no word "list," or in which it would be awkward to use that word in this context, translators can say "These are the ancestors," or "These are the names of the ancestors."

This verse may be restructured in a variety of ways. But if the exegesis followed by the majority of translators is accepted, then GECL gives a more natural order: "Jesus Christ is a descendant of David and Abraham. Here is the list of his ancestors: . . . ." This restructuring has a twofold advantage: (1) It introduces at the very first the information about Jesus' ancestry from David and Abraham, which is so important to the Gospel of Matthew; and (2) the list of ancestors is given immediately following the mention of the list.

Note that even though **The book of the genealogy** is not a complete sentence, all the solutions we are suggesting are. ("These are . . . ," "This is . . . ," etc.) Many readers will find complete sentences easier to follow.

The word **Jesus** is a Greek equivalent of a well-known Hebrew name. It is constructed from two Hebrew words which mean "Lord" and "save," and it is probably best taken in its root meaning: "O Lord, save." In 1.21 the angel indicates to Mary the true and full significance of the name Jesus—he will save his people from their sins. However, even though the meaning of the name is significant, translators should not try to translate **Jesus**, but write it as a proper noun.

Most translators and commentators are apparently in agreement that the word Christ in this verse is used as a proper name, not with the force of "the Christ," as in verses 16 and 17. The Greek word "Christ" is a translation of the Hebrew "Messiah," meaning "the Anointed One." In New Testament times it was a technical term used to describe the promised Savior-King, and it generally had political and military overtones. However, when used of Jesus by Matthew and the other New Testament writers, it is used exclusively in a spiritual sense. The complete name **Jesus Christ** is rare in the first three Gospels. It occurs here and in Mark 1.1 for certain; in 1.18 and 16.21 the Greek manuscripts vary between "Jesus" and "Jesus Christ."

It is difficult in a Handbook to advise translators on writing proper nouns, since the problem is wider than just the specific names in any one book. It is important for translators to agree on the principles to follow fairly early in their work. (They can discuss this with their Translation Consultant.) In areas where a major language such as Spanish, French, English, or Portuguese dominates, translators often take the pronunciation of names in that language and adapt them so that they follow the phonological and orthographic patterns of their own language. Exceptions are sometimes made for well-known names in common usage in the area, such as Peter, John, or James.

A further problem is the case of several variants of one name in the Scriptures themselves, as we see with "Ram" in verse 3. Translators will have to consider what will be best for their readers. Certainly those preparing common language translations (CLTs) will find that following the lead of TEV will help avoid confusion with this problem.

For translators, there are two basic decisions that have to be made about "Christ" and "Messiah." As we said, the two terms mean the same thing, but whereas "Messiah" is always used as a title ("the Messiah"), "Christ" is sometimes a title ("the Christ") and sometimes a name or part of a name ("Jesus Christ"). This can be very confusing to readers. Since "Messiah" in English now is understood very much as in the biblical text, TEV has followed the policy in the Gospels of using "Messiah" whenever the title is involved, whether the text has "the Christ" or "the Messiah." TEV then reserves "Christ" for its usage as a name. Many translators will want to consider doing the same thing.

A second decision to make is whether to transliterate "Messiah" or to translate it. Some translators have said "God's promised Savior," "God's chosen Savior," or simply "the One God promised (or, chose)." There are those who both transliterate and translate, saying "the Messiah, God's chosen Savior."

Christ as a name (as here) will be written in accordance with the principles followed for names.

Jesus Christ is specified as **the son of David, the son of Abraham**. Most languages have a noun that means "**descendant**" (TEV), and translators either use a sentence similar to TEV or use a construction such as "He descended from David and from Abraham" or "He descended from David, who descended from Abraham."

In languages which use "son" to mean "descendant," the sentence must be constructed so that it is clear that David was not the biological father of Jesus, and that Abraham was neither David's father nor the father of Jesus. Sentences such as "one of his fathers of long ago was David and another was Abraham" or "One of his fathers of long ago was David, and one of David's fathers was Abraham" will also be good ways to handle the phrase.

Matthew's readers knew that **David** was the famous king of Israel's history, but many readers today will not know that, particularly in languages that do not have an Old Testament. Translators in these languages may want to supply that information in a footnote or in the glossary, or they can insert it directly into the text by saying "King David."

Similarly, not all modern readers will know that **Abraham** was the great founder of the nation of Israel, and translators sometimes say "Our founder Abraham" or "Abraham, who founded our nation."

1.2	RSV	TEV
	Abraham was the father of Isaac, and Isaac the father of Jacob, and Jacob the father of Judah and his brothers,	From Abraham to King David, the following ancestors are listed: Abraham, Isaac, Jacob, Judah and his brothers;

Abraham was the father of Isaac: notice that TEV restructures verses 2-16 (2-6a, 6b-11, 12-16) on the basis of the information given in verse 17: "So then, there were fourteen generations from Abraham to David, and fourteen from David to the exile in Babylon, and fourteen from then to the birth of the Messiah." That is, at the beginning of each list (2a; 6a; 12) TEV provides a summary of the ancestors to be mentioned: "From Abraham to King David . . . From David to the time when the people of Israel were taken into exile in Babylon . . . From the time after the exile in Babylon to the birth of Jesus . . . ." This has the advantage of presenting the lists in a way that is natural in English. However, if the reader looks for the fourteen generations (see verse 17) in each of these lists, he may still be at a loss as to what persons are to be included, because this information is still not immediately evident. Therefore the following restructuring may be helpful in making all the relevant information immediately evident for the reader:

This is the list of the ancestors of Jesus Christ, who was a descendant of David, who was a descendant of Abraham.

There were fourteen generations from Abraham to David:
1. Abraham
2. Isaac
3. Jacob, the father of Judah and his brothers
4. Judah, the father of Perez and Zerah (their mother was Tamar)
5. Perez
6. Hezron
7. Ram
8. Amminadab
9. Nahshon
10. Salmon
11. Boaz (Rahab was his mother)
12. Obed (Ruth was his mother)
13. Jesse
14. King David

There were fourteen generations from David to the time when the people were carried away to Babylon:
1. David
2. Solomon (his mother had been Uriah's wife)
3. Rehoboam
4. Abijah
5. Asa
6. Jehoshaphat
7. Jehoram
8. Uzziah
9. Jotham
10. Ahaz
11. Hezekiah
12. Manasseh
13. Amon
14. Josiah, the father of Jehoiachin and his brothers, at the time when the people of Israel were carried away to Babylon.

There were fourteen generations from the time the people were carried away to Babylon to the birth of the Promised Savior:
1. Jechoniah
2. Shealtiel
3. Zerubbabel
4. Abiud
5. Eliakim
6. Azor
7. Zadok
8. Achim
9. Eliud
10. Eleazar
11. Matthan
12. Jacob
13. Joseph, the husband of Mary, who was the mother of Jesus
14. Jesus, the Promised Savior (the Messiah).

In many societies it is common to give the lists of the ancestors of people. But even in those societies where it is not often done, there will generally be ways to do it that people can follow easily. When translating these lists in verses 2-16, it is important to keep in mind what is normal and what the readers will follow easily. It may be that putting a restatement of the summary in verse 17 at the beginning will be helpful. This can be done as in TEV, or as we suggested above: "There were 14 generations from Abraham to King David." Other suggestions are "The descendants Abraham had up to the time of King David are these" or "These are the names of the descendants of Abraham until the time of King David."

This type of summary introductory statement may not be helpful or necessary in all languages. But those translators who do find it helpful will not only use one here in verse 2, but also in verses 6b and 12.

Some languages will normally use the formula "Abraham was the father of Isaac, Isaac was the father of Jacob . . ." throughout the genealogy, much as Matthew did it. Translators will then follow the text quite closely. Other languages have formulas that mention the sons, as in "Abraham, his son was Isaac. Isaac, his son was Jacob . . . ." There are also languages that find it more natural to say "Isaac, his father was Abraham. Jacob, his father was Isaac . . . ."

Isaac the father of Jacob, and Jacob: in 1 Chronicles 1.34 the Hebrew text has "Israel," whereas the Greek translation has **Jacob**, which indicates that Matthew is following the Septuagint rather than the Hebrew text. Matthew then takes the name **Judah** from 1 Chronicles 2.1 and summarizes with the phrase **and his brothers**, whereas in the Septuagint the names are listed individually.

Judah and his brothers: readers who do not know the Old Testament at all find it strange to add "and his brothers." These readers suggest that of course Jacob was also the father of Judah's brothers, or they would not be his brothers! The important historical information is that the twelve of them founded Israel's twelve tribes, and this information should be given in a footnote.

Some languages normally use a word which means "siblings," which covers both brothers and sisters. Since the text is speaking here of twelve specific brothers, then in those languages translators need to say "his male siblings" or "Jacob was the father of Judah and of the other sons."

1.3 RSV TEV

and Judah the father of Perez and Zerah by Tamar, and Perez the father of Hezron, and Hezron the father of Ram,[a]

then Perez and Zerah (their mother was Tamar), Hezron, Ram,

[a] Greek *Aram*

The first clause is from 1 Chronicles 2.4 ("and Tamar his wife [Hebrew: daughter-in-law] gave birth to Perez and Zerah").

Many languages have to make **by Tamar** a separate sentence: "Their mother was Tamar."

In 1 Chronicles 2.9 **Ram** is mentioned as one of the sons of **Hezron**. For **Ram** the Septuagint has Aram (see the RSV footnote), but **Ram** is obviously the person who is meant, and many modern translations follow this spelling (Phps, NEB, NAB, New Jerusalem Bible [NJB], Translator's New Testament [TNT]), though others maintain the Septuagint spelling (TOB, Zür, Brc, Mft, AT). The advantage of using **Ram** is that it avoids confusion with the several Arams mentioned in the Old Testament (see Gen 10.22,23; 22.21; Num 23.7; 2 Sam 8.6; 15.8; 1 Chr 1.17; 2.23; 7.34; Hos 12.12; Zech 9.1), some of which are people and the others are places, but none of which are the person intended by Matthew. See the comments on names in 1.1.

1.4 RSV TEV

and Ram[a] **the father of Amminadab, and Amminadab the father of Nahshon, and Nahshon the father of Salmon,**

Amminadab, Nahshon, Salmon,

[a] Greek *Aram*

In 1 Chronicles 2.10 **Amminadab** is listed as the son of **Ram**, and in 1 Chronicles 2.11 **Nahshon** and **Salmon** are mentioned.

1.5-6a RSV TEV

and Salmon the father of Boaz by Rahab, and Boaz the father of Obed by Ruth, and Obed the father of

Boaz (his mother was Rahab), Obed (his mother was Ruth), Jesse, and King David.

Jesse, and Jesse the father of David
the king.

In 1 Chronicles 2.11 **Salmon** is listed as the father of **Boaz**, though Rahab is not mentioned. **Obed** and **Jesse** are Septuagint forms and come from 1 Chronicles 2.12. The names of the women **Rahab** and **Ruth** are not listed in the genealogy of 1 Chronicles.

David the king: there are several ways to translate this naturally: "**King David**" (TEV) or "David who was (or, became) king." Some languages have to specify the people over whom he was king. These translations can say "the king of Israel."

1.6b	RSV	TEV

And David was the father of Solomon by the wife of Uriah,	From David to the time when the people of Israel were taken into exile in Babylon, the following ancestors are listed: David, Solomon (his mother was the woman who had been Uriah's wife),

Those translators who used a short summary at the beginning of verse 2 to introduce the list of ancestors will do a similar thing here. "These are the descendants of David until the people of Israel were taken into exile in Babylon" or "After David, and until the people of Israel were taken into exile in Babylon, these are the names of his descendants."

For TEV's "**Babylon**" and "**deportation**" (or, "exile"), see comments on verse 11.

Solomon is listed in 1 Chronicles 3.5,10. As with Rahab and Ruth, the **wife of Uriah** is not given in the Chronicles list, either by name or by indirect allusion.

By the wife of Uriah: as with "by Tamar" in verse 3, this phrase may need a separate sentence: "His mother was Uriah's wife." In many cases it is important to specify that she was not Uriah's wife at the time of Solomon's birth but had been his wife previously. Translators can follow TEV or even say "His mother had been the wife of Uriah before."

1.7	RSV	TEV

and Solomon the father of Rehoboam, and Rehoboam the father of Abijah, and Abijah the father of Asa,[b]	Rehoboam, Abijah, Asa,

[b] Greek *Asaph*

Rehoboam, **Abijah**, and **Asa** are mentioned in 1 Chronicles 3.10. Although "Asaph" is the earliest form of the text, the name **Asa** apparently is used in most translations. The name Asaph occurs in the headings of some Hebrew psalms, while Amos is the name of the prophet. For further comment on the textual problem, see verse 10.

1.8-9   RSV   TEV

8 and Asa*b* the father of Jehosha-phat, and Jehoshaphat the father of Joram, and Joram the father of Uz-ziah, 9 and Uzziah the father of Jo-tham, and Jotham the father of Ahaz, and Ahaz the father of Hezekiah,	Jehoshaphat, Jehoram, Uzziah, Jo-tham, Ahaz, Hezekiah,

b Greek *Asaph*

Jehoshaphat is listed in 1 Chronicles 3.10, while **Joram** and **Uzziah** are mentioned in the Septuagint text of 3.11. Where Matthew has the shorter text ("Uzziah was the father of Jotham"), the Septuagint has the longer, "Uzziah was the father of Joash; Joash was the father of Amaziah; Amaziah was the father of Azariah; Azariah was the father of Jotham." So then, for whatever reason, whether textual (the accidental omission of these three names) or thematic (the intentional omission of names to maintain the schematic arrangement of three groups of fourteen names), Matthew has omitted three names: Joash, Amaziah, and Azariah.

1.10   RSV   TEV

and Hezekiah the father of Manas-seh, and Manasseh the father of Amos,*c* and Amos*c* the father of Jo-siah,	Manasseh, Amon, Josiah,

c Other authorities read *Amon*

This verse is based on 1 Chronicles 3.13,14. The translations are divided between **Amos** (RSV, Brc, TNT, Zür, NAB) and "**Amon**" (TEV, Phps, GECL, Lu, Segond [Seg], FRCL, TOB, Mft, AT, NEB, NJB) because there is a textual variant in the Greek text. This variant probably goes back to the Septuagint, which had **Amos** in some manuscripts and "**Amon**" in other manuscripts. The United Bible Societies' (UBS) Greek New Testament accepts the reading **Amos** because of the strong manuscript evidence in its favor, although the majority of modern translations seemingly prefer "**Amon**." See the comments on names in 1.1. However, TEV uses "**Amon**" because of the principle of consistency between the Old and the New Testaments when referring to the same person. This is true also with "Jechoniah" and "Jehoiachin" in verse 11.

and Josiah the father of Jechoniah   **and Jehoiachin and his brothers.**
and his brothers, at the time of the
deportation to Babylon.

Jechoniah and "**Jehoiachin**" (TEV) are the same person, but TEV has adopted
the principle of following the more familiar name of a person rather than maintaining both names for the same individual (see, for example, the following verses, where
Jehoiachin is referred to as Jechoniah in the Old Testament: 1 Chr 3.16,17; Est 2.6;
Jer 24.1; 27.20; 28.4; 29.2). See the comments on names in 1.1.

The phrase **and his brothers** is perhaps based on the text of 1 Chronicles 3.15,
where the names of Jechoniah's brothers are listed. The brothers of Jechoniah are
not as important in the tradition of the people of Israel as the brothers of Judah in
verse 2. In languages that have one word for both brothers and sisters, translators
should say "Jehoiachin and his male siblings" or "Josiah was the father of Jehoiachin
and other sons."

At the time of the deportation to Babylon is rendered "**when the people
of Israel were taken into exile in Babylon**" by TEV and introduced earlier
(verse 6b). GECL ("This was at the time when the inhabitants of Jerusalem were
carried off to Babylon") and FRCL ("at the time when the Israelites were deported
to Babylon") provide a dynamic restructuring of the last part of this verse. The
mention of the Babylonian exile closes the second division of the genealogical list.

Deportation is a concept many cultures understand far too readily and for
which they have a way of speaking. In many cases the word for it is understood to
mean "carried into slavery." If possible the real emphasis should be on exile rather
than on slavery. There are languages where the idea is expressed with two or more
verbs, as in "At the time when the Israelites were conquered and forced to go live
in Babylon" or "At that time, the Babylonians forced the Israelites to go live in their
country." Of course, translators must make sure that it does not sound as if the
Israelites were literally picked up and carried to Babylon.

Most CLTs make it clear who was deported, that is, the people of Israel, and
some languages also have to indicate who did it, by saying "the Babylonians forced
. . . ."

Babylon refers to both the city and the country around it. In modern writings
the city is commonly referred to as "Babylon," while the country of which it is the
capital is called "Babylonia." Translators should use terms that are consistent for
their own languages. Since not all the Israelites were made to live in the city, it may
be best to say "the country of Babylonia" or, as above, "in their country."

1.12   RSV   TEV

And after the deportation to   **From the time after the exile in**
Babylon: Jechoniah was the father of   **Babylon to the birth of Jesus, the**
Shealtiel,^{d} and Shealtiel^d the father of   **following ancestors are listed: Je-**
Zerubbabel,   **hoiachin, Shealtiel, Zerubbabel,**

And after the deportation to Babylon (TEV **"From the time after the exile in Babylon"**) is based on 1 Chronicles 3.17. This verse clearly indicates that Matthew is basing his genealogical references on the Septuagint rather than on the Hebrew, since the Hebrew text lists **Zerubbabel** as the son of Pedaiah (1 Chr 3.19), while the Septuagint lists him as the son of **Shealtiel**.

Translators who choose to introduce each section of the genealogy with a summary from verse 17, as in verses 2 and 6b, will do the same here: "From the time after the people of Israel were carried away to Babylon until Jesus was born, these were his ancestors" or "These are the names of Jesus' ancestors who were born (who lived) after the time the people of Israel were taken into Babylon (right up) until his own time."

For **deportation** and **Babylon**, see comments on verse 11.

1.13-15 RSV	TEV
and Zerubbabel the father of Abiud, and Abiud the father of Eliakim, and Eliakim the father of Azor, 14 and Azor the father of Zadok, and Zadok the father of Achim, and Achim the father of Eliud, 15 and Eliud the father of Eleazar, and Eleazar the father of Matthan, and Matthan the father of Jacob,	Abiud, Eliakim, Azor, Zadok, Achim, Eliud, Eleazar, Matthan, Jacob,

Matthew was dependent on unknown sources for the names listed in these verses and gives only ten names (**Zerubbabel** of verse 13 to **Jacob** of verse 16) for the five-hundred-year period.

1.16 RSV	TEV
and Jacob the father of Joseph the husband of Mary, of whom Jesus was born, who is called Christ.	and Joseph, who married Mary, the mother of Jesus, who was called the Messiah.

Joseph the husband of Mary, of whom Jesus was born, who is called Christ: the focus is on legal rather than physical descent. According to Jewish teaching, if a man acknowledged a son as his own, then he was considered that man's son, without any further question. Matthew can thus show that Jesus was a descendant of David through Joseph and at the same time emphasize the unique aspect of Jesus' birth through the virgin Mary (1.18-25).

For **the husband of Mary**, some languages say "Joseph, who married Mary."

There are several things to consider before translating this verse. It is important to structure the verse so that it is clear that Jesus is Mary's child, not Joseph's.

Secondly, translators do not want to give the impression that Joseph married Mary after Jesus had been born. A third problem for some translators is that **of whom Jesus was born** must be rendered by an active sentence, such as "She gave birth to" or "She was the mother of Jesus." A further concern is that in many languages it is not possible to separate "Jesus" from "who is called the Christ" by the phrase "was born" unless a new sentence is started. Keeping all these things in mind, some translators have sentences such as "Jacob was the father of Joseph. He married Mary, who gave birth to Jesus, who is called Christ," or "Jacob was the father of Joseph. Joseph's wife was Mary who was the mother of Jesus. Jesus is called Christ."

Who is called Christ: the present tense, **is called**, indicates that this is what people continue to call him. Here, "called" does not mean he is named "Christ," but refers instead to the fact that people have applied the title of "Christ" to him, that is, "People call him the Christ" or "People say, 'He is the Christ.' "

For **Christ** (TEV **"the Messiah"**) see comments at verse 17 and verse 1.

1.17 RSV	TEV
So all the generations from Abraham to David were fourteen generations, and from David to the deportation to Babylon fourteen generations, and from the deportation to Babylon to the Christ fourteen generations.	So then, there were fourteen generations from Abraham to David, and fourteen from David to the exile in Babylon, and fourteen from then to the birth of the Messiah.

It is not always easy to speak of **generations**. Some languages use the same word as for ancestors. The translation may then be "So from Abraham to David there were fourteen ancestors of Jesus" or "From David back to Abraham there were fourteen ancestors." Another way would be to use the word "descendant," as in "Abraham had fourteen descendants until David." But it would be very important to make sure that such a sentence was understood in the sense of a line of generations, and not, for example, that one man had fourteen sons.

For notes on other parts of the verse, see verses 2, 6b, and 12.

To the Christ is translated as **"to the birth of the Messiah"** by TEV. Both here and in verse 16 there is a problem related to the translation of the word rendered **Christ** by RSV and **"Messiah"** by TEV. In the Greek text there is no definite article before the word in verse 16, though there is in verse 17. The problem then is whether in both places or in either of these places the term **Christ** is used in the technical sense of **"the Messiah"** or simply as part of the proper name of Jesus. TEV, together with a few other translations (NEB, NAB, Brc, FRCL), understands this to be the technical term referring to the promised Savior-King, and so translates "Messiah." All of these translations have "Messiah" in verse 16 and "the Messiah" in verse 17, maintaining a formal rendering of the Greek text. The Greek word **Christ** is, of course, simply the equivalent of the Hebrew word **"Messiah."**

See verse 1 for comments on the translation of **Christ**.

1.18-25

RSV   TEV

The Birth of Jesus Christ

18 Now the birth of Jesus Christ[f] took place in this way. When his mother Mary had been betrothed to Joseph, before they came together she was found to be with child of the Holy Spirit; 19 and her husband Joseph, being a just man and unwilling to put her to shame, resolved to divorce her quietly. 20 But as he considered this, behold, an angel of the Lord appeared to him in a dream, saying, "Joseph, son of David, do not fear to take Mary your wife, for that which is conceived in her is of the Holy Spirit; 21 she will bear a son, and you shall call his name Jesus, for he will save his people from their sins." 22 All this took place to fulfil what the Lord had spoken by the prophet:

23   "Behold, a virgin shall conceive and bear a
                son,
        and his name shall be called Emmanuel"

(which means, God with us). 24 When Joseph woke from sleep, he did as the angel of the Lord commanded him; he took his wife, 25 but knew her not until she had born a son; and he called his name Jesus.

[f] Other ancient authorities read *of the Christ*

18 This was how the birth of Jesus Christ took place. His mother Mary was engaged to Joseph, but before they were married, she found out that she was going to have a baby by the Holy Spirit. 19 Joseph was a man who always did what was right, but he did not want to disgrace Mary publicly; so he made plans to break the engagement privately. 20 While he was thinking about this, an angel of the Lord appeared to him in a dream and said, "Joseph, descendant of David, do not be afraid to take Mary to be your wife. For it is by the Holy Spirit that she has conceived. 21 She will have a son, and you will name him Jesus—because he will save his people from their sins."

22 Now all of this happened in order to make come true what the Lord had said through the prophet, 23 "A virgin will become pregnant and have a son, and he will be called Immanuel" (which means, "God is with us").

24 So when Joseph woke up, he married Mary, as the angel of the Lord had told him to. 25 But he had no sexual relations with her before she gave birth to her son. And Joseph named him Jesus.

SECTION HEADING: "The Birth of Jesus Christ." Many languages will be able to use a short phrase like this for a section heading, or something such as "The story of how Jesus Christ was born" or "How Jesus Christ was born." But in many languages a complete sentence is much clearer: "Jesus Christ was born" or "This is the story of how Jesus Christ was born."

This is the first in a series of five narratives dealing with the birth and infancy of Jesus: (1) The birth of Jesus (1.18-25), (2) the visitors from the East (2.1-12), (3) the escape to Egypt (2.13-15), (4) the killing of the children (2.16-18), and (5) the return from Egypt (2.19-23). One commentator divides the first of these five narratives into three sections: (1) The first section relates the conflict which developed in Joseph's mind because of the pregnancy of Mary, to whom he was engaged (18-19). (2) In verses 20-23 the conflict is resolved: an angel of the Lord appears to Joseph in a dream and tells him that it is by the Holy Spirit that she has conceived. The angel's words are followed immediately by an Old Testament quotation, which is intended to verify the divine origin of the child and to indicate that God is in control in all of these events. (3) The final section (24-25) describes Joseph's response to the resolution of the conflict and his obedience to the divine command. Three basic themes are interwoven throughout the narrative: (1) the conception by the Holy Spirit, (2) the birth through the virgin Mary, and (3) the giving of the name, Jesus.

1.18 RSV TEV

Now the birth of Jesus Christ*f* took place in this way. When his mother Mary had been betrothed to Joseph, before they came together she was found to be with child of the Holy Spirit;

This was how the birth of Jesus Christ took place. His mother Mary was engaged to Joseph, but before they were married, she found out that she was going to have a baby by the Holy Spirit.

f Other ancient authorities read *of the Christ*

In Greek the first sentence of this verse serves two functions: it ties the story of the birth of Jesus Christ to the genealogy, and it functions as a topic sentence to introduce the narrative which follows. Note, for example, GECL: "As to the birth of Jesus Christ, it took place as follows: . . . ."

Most languages have words or phrases that function like **Now**, to show the connection between the paragraphs, and the translators should use what is most natural for them.

It is important that **in this way** ("how" in TEV) not be translated to mean the physical details of labor and birth. The expression refers to the broader context of events around the birth. Some translators say "This is what happened when Jesus Christ was born" or "This is the story of how Jesus Christ was born." This is a good solution, too, for languages which do not have a noun **birth** but must use a verbal phrase.

As the RSV footnote indicates, some ancient authorities read "the Christ" in place of **Jesus Christ**, which is the basis for NEB: "the birth of the Messiah." *A Textual Commentary on the Greek New Testament* (TC-GNT) reports that the committee for the UBS Greek text had a choice that was "exceedingly difficult," though it favors the reading followed by RSV, TEV, and most other translations.

Betrothed . . . came together (TEV "**engaged . . . married**"): though the Jews did distinguish engagement from marriage, the dissolution of an engagement was considered the equivalent of divorce, and an engaged woman whose husband-to-be had died was regarded as a widow. Consequently, any sexual relations between an engaged woman and another man was viewed as adultery, and the woman was punished accordingly.

Betrothed: some languages find "promised" as the closest equivalent to "engaged," as in "Jesus' mother was Mary. She was promised in marriage to Joseph." Other ways to speak of it might be "had promised to marry" or "was going to marry."

There are languages that have to introduce Joseph as a participant in the discourse. These cannot say simply that Mary was engaged "to Joseph," but rather "to a man named Joseph."

In some cases, putting the statement that Mary was Jesus' mother before the statement that she was engaged to Joseph makes it seem that Jesus was born before the engagement. To avoid that, translators say "Mary was Jesus' mother. At the time she was engaged (or, promised in marriage) to a man named Joseph, before they came together . . . ," or even "Mary was Jesus' mother. Before that, at the time she was engaged to Joseph . . . ."

Before they came together: although this verb most frequently means "come together," it is also used in papyri contracts with the meaning of "marry," which is the basis for TEV "**before they were married**." Matthew is obviously referring to marriage, and there is no particular advantage in translating by a verb which is not specific. Although in many respects (as mentioned above) engagement was considered as binding as marriage, the two words are distinguished from one another. Marriage actually took place only as the bridegroom took his bride to his home and consummated the marriage with her.

Some translators have taken **come together** to mean specifically "sexual intercourse," but "married" is more accurate here. Translators can also use expressions such as "live together as husband and wife."

She was found to be with is transformed by TEV to read "**she found out**" (similarly NEB). However, most all modern English translations maintain the impersonal force of the Greek passive verb, as does RSV.

In many languages, "it was seen that," or "one saw that," or "they found that" are ways to keep it impersonal, that is, not saying specifically who found out the information.

The problem is that frequently it is difficult to translate impersonally without sounding somewhat indelicate. GECL is sensitive in its restructuring: "but before the couple entered marriage, it turned out that Mary was expecting a child through the working of the Holy Spirit."

Another expression that can be used is "it happened that . . . ."

To be with child of the Holy Spirit (TEV "**she was going to have a baby by the Holy Spirit**"): although the virginity of Mary is assumed throughout the narrative, it is not in focus. What is in focus is that this birth is brought about by God himself, through his Holy Spirit. There is rarely a problem in using a normal term for pregnancy here: "She was pregnant" or "with child." But translators must be sure that the term they use is considered polite. Perhaps "she was going to be a mother."

As for **of the Holy Spirit**, a few translators have used a phrase which made it seem the Holy Spirit had sexual intercourse with Mary. This should be avoided. It would be better to say "It was the Holy Spirit that caused her to be pregnant," or "The Holy Spirit had brought this about," or "The power of the Holy Spirit had made this happen."

There are two problems in finding a good translation of **Holy Spirit**. First, translators need to study the understanding of spiritual powers and forces their own people have, and then choose a word in their language for "spirit" that conforms most closely to the idea of a vital principle or animating force within living beings.

As translators study the concepts of "holy" in various contexts, it becomes apparent that "holy" involves things that somehow relate to God. Things or people can be called "holy" if they belong to God, are consecrated to him, are like him, or if he is in them, and so forth. In some cases there will be a word in a language to cover "holy" that will fit well with this idea in most contexts. Translators can then use it. But very often translators find that "God" should actually be used in the translation. Thus the Holy Spirit can be translated "God's Spirit."

It is especially important to avoid words for "holy" that in fact mean "taboo," or words such as "white" or "good" or "clean" which do not adequately show the God-ness of "holy."

1.19	RSV	TEV

and her husband Joseph, being a just man and unwilling to put her to shame, resolved to divorce her quietly.	**Joseph was a man who always did what was right, but he did not want to disgrace Mary publicly; so he made plans to break the engagement privately.**

Her husband Joseph is rendered simply "**Joseph**" by TEV, GECL 1st edition, NEB; Brc has "her intended husband," and Phps "her future husband." Having said in verse 18 that she was engaged to Joseph, to put "husband" here would be confusing. But translators who cannot say simply "Joseph" will do well to follow Brc or Phps with "intended" or "future," or perhaps "promised husband."

The Greek adjective **just** is translated in TEV by the clause "**who always did what was right**." There is, however, much difference of opinion regarding its precise meaning in the context, and at least three possibilities present themselves: (1) "one obedient to the commands of God, an upright man, a man of character"; (2) "kind" or "compassionate" (see 25.37-40; 10.41); (3) "good" (see Psa 145.17). The adjective is a key term in the Gospel of Matthew and is discussed more fully in conjunction with the noun form at 5.6, "righteousness." But see also 5.45, which may be the best commentary on the word. Although there is some overlap, the meaning of "good" (Phps) or "compassionate" seems most appropriate for the present context. TEV's "**who always did what is right**" is close, if taken in the sense of Micah 6.8. It is interesting that many languages have less difficulty with this word than English does, since they have ways of referring to people who treat others "correctly," by which they include the idea of "compassion" as well as "legal correctness." Sometimes "straight" covers this, or "good" or "true."

Unwilling to put her to shame: the relation between this clause and what precedes it depends in large measure upon the interpretation given the adjective rendered **just** by RSV. If it is understood to mean Joseph kept the Law, that would normally imply that of course he would not follow through with the marriage plans; however, then the fact that he was unwilling to disgrace Mary is unexpected, so "but" would be appropriate, as in TEV: "**but he did not want to disgrace Mary publicly**." But if the meaning is taken to be "good," then there is no need to signify a contrast. One may then follow the restructuring either of Phps ("who was a good man and did not want to see her disgraced") or of JB ("being a man of honour and wanting to spare her publicity"). Apparently it is the rather rigid interpretation of this adjective with the meaning of "just" that leads many translators to introduce this clause which follows by the conjunction "but."

The verb **put . . . to shame** (TEV "**disgrace . . . publicly**") occurs only here and in Colossians 2.15 in the New Testament. Joseph had two courses of action open to him. He could either have brought charges against Mary in court or else have divorced her privately in the presence of two witnesses. Joseph chose the more merciful course of action. Strictly speaking, the punishment for adultery was death by stoning, although the penalty in New Testament times may have been less severe. Most translators find that the idea of "publicity" is an important part of "shame," and therefore do something similar to TEV. "He did not want her to suffer public shame," or "He did not want to cause shame to come on her," or "He did not want other people to see her in disgrace."

Resolved means "decided," "made up his mind to . . . ," or "planned."

Divorce: if there is a word for this in their language, translators must find out first whether it can be used for what is essentially the breaking of an engagement. Perhaps "call off the marriage" or "break the promise to marry."

The adverb **quietly** (so also Phps, NEB, NAB; TEV, AT "**privately**") in other contexts may carry the meaning "secretly" (TNT, Mft, Brc). But in the present context the meaning is not "secretly" (that is, "without witnesses"), but "without bringing charges" or "without a public trial and without statement of the cause."

Some translators say "without accusing her before others," or "without making her case public (or, known to everyone)," or "without telling other people." Sometimes it is necessary to make explicit the source of her shame (as Joseph saw it, at least), as in "He did not want to accuse her of adultery in front of other people when he broke the engagement."

1.20	RSV	TEV

But as he considered this, behold, an angel of the Lord appeared to him in a dream, saying, "Joseph, son of David, do not fear to take Mary your wife, for that which is conceived in her is of the Holy Spirit;	**While he was thinking about this, an angel of the Lord appeared to him in a dream and said, "Joseph, descendant of David, do not be afraid to take Mary to be your wife. For it is by the Holy Spirit that she has conceived.**

Verse 20 is normally taken to contrast with verse 19, as shown by **But**. Not all languages need such a word, since the context shows the contrast clearly. Here **as** has the sense of "while," as in "(But) while he was thinking . . . ."

The verb **considered** (TEV "**thinking about**") appears in the New Testament only here and in 9.4 in the construction "thinking such evil things" (TEV). Translators can do something similar to TEV with phrases such as "planning this," "planning to do this," "putting his mind to this thing," or "trying to decide what to do."

Behold in Greek is related to the imperative form of the verb "Look!" It translates a Semitic form which may be rendered a number of ways, depending on the context. Quite often it is impossible to render it by any equivalent word in English. It may serve to enliven a narrative, to introduce new events, or even to add stress or emphasis. Perhaps it is best to think of it as an "attention-getter," a device for calling attention to what follows.

Many languages do not use words like **behold** in this context. In such cases translators should not try to translate it here either. But in other languages, as for example in most African languages, such particles are an essential part of the discourse, and translators should use them not only here, but in many places where the text does not have them. The purpose here is to attract the attention of the readers: "Pay attention" or "Note this."

The expression **an angel of the Lord** is used by Matthew also in verse 24; 2.13,19; 28.2. An angel regularly represents God, either by bringing a message or by performing an action. The rendering of **angel of the Lord** can be affected by the manner translators have chosen to translate "angel." For example, if "angel" has been translated elsewhere as "messenger of God," then it will be strange to say in effect "a messenger of God of the Lord." "Messenger of the Lord" will suffice in this context. If "spirit messenger" or "heavenly messenger" is the usual translation used, the phrase in this verse can be "spirit messenger of the Lord" or "heavenly messenger of the Lord." In some languages the translation of "angel" is simply "messenger." Then the expression "an angel (or, messenger) of the Lord" may unintentionally coincide with the term used for "preacher" or "prophet." It is most likely that since in this verse the angel appears in a dream, readers will probably not think it was one of these human messengers. However, if testing shows that they do, translators will have to say here "heavenly (or, spirit) messenger of the Lord."

It is sometimes necessary to indicate that **of the Lord** means it was the Lord who sent the angel, as in "an angel who came from the Lord" or "an angel whom the Lord sent." If **Lord** is frequently used in a language for Jesus Christ, then translators can say "angel from God" in this verse.

In a dream is found only six times in the New Testament: Matthew 1.20; 2.12,13,19,22; 27.19. In Judaism, dreams were acceptable means of divine revelation. Many languages distinguish between an ordinary dream and one that has a vision or supernatural oracle in it. The latter term would be the one to use here. It may be that instead of **appeared . . . in a dream**, it would be more natural to say "came to him while he was dreaming," "came to him in the form of a dream," or "showed himself to Joseph while he was dreaming."

As indicated by the form of address, **son of David**, what is in focus here is the legal fatherhood of Joseph by which Jesus becomes a legitimate descendant of David. In some languages **son of David** will be correctly understood to mean a descendant, but in others, this phrase will make it seem that Joseph was the biological son of David, contrary to verse 16. In these languages translators can say "descendant of David," "you who are descended from David," "you who are from David's family," or "you whose ancestor was David." Since the emphasis is on the fact that Joseph is from the royal line of David, it may be helpful to say "King David."

Do not fear to take Mary your wife is ambiguous because in English it may seem to say that Mary is already his wife. The meaning is "do not be afraid to take Mary as your wife." TEV renders "**do not be afraid to take Mary to be your wife**," and NEB "do not be afraid to take Mary home with you as your wife." The reference, of course, is to the final phase in the marriage arrangement, whereby the husband takes his wife to his home. Brc renders "do not hesitate to marry Mary."

For that which is conceived in her is of the Holy Spirit is rendered by TEV as "**For it is by the Holy Spirit that she has conceived.**" GECL translates "since the child which she is expecting comes from the Spirit of God." NEB and NAB render "It is by the Holy Spirit that she has conceived this child." The most natural thing in some languages may be "It is the Holy Spirit that has caused her to be pregnant" or "She will have this baby because the Holy Spirit caused her to be pregnant."

Although in Greek the definite article **the** is lacking before **Holy Spirit**, this is of no significance, because in the Greek of the New Testament it is difficult to establish clear rules for the use of the article. Moreover, the context clearly indicates that the reference is to God's Spirit, that is, "the Holy Spirit."

1.21	RSV	TEV
	she will bear a son, and you shall call his name Jesus, for he will save his people from their sins."	She will have a son, and you will name him Jesus—because he will save his people from their sins."

She will bear a son, and you shall call his name Jesus: the first of these clauses simply gives information, as RSV and TEV indicate, but the second clause is better rendered as an imperative: "and you are to name him Jesus" (NAB). Note GECL, "she will have a son; you must name him Jesus"; and Brc, "she will have a son, and you must call him by the name Jesus." **She will bear a son** can be translated fairly easily in most languages. "She will give birth to a son (or, baby boy)" is usually possible, or "The baby she will bear will be a boy."

Except for the name **Jesus**, this sentence is a direct quotation from the Septuagint of Isaiah 7.14, which suggests that the name is in focus. For this reason the use of the imperative ("you are to [or, you must] name . . .") is more satisfactory than the simple future. It is not correct in many languages to say **you shall call his name**, since this will mean calling out loud rather than naming. Translators should use the natural way to speak of naming a child; for example, "The name you are to give him will be Jesus" or "You should name him Jesus." **You** is singular here, meaning Joseph.

On the meaning of the name **Jesus**, see comments on verse 1.

For he will save his people from their sins is in part a quotation from Psalm 130.8 ("he [the Lord] will save his people Israel from all their sins," TEV). The forgiveness of sins summarizes the concept of salvation, both in the Old Testament and in the New Testament. It includes much more than the mere pardon of individual wrongs; it indicates that the barrier between God and people has been removed.

It is important to translate the notion of cause in the word **for**. In some languages translators will not start a new sentence after "name him Jesus" but will continue with the same sentence as using "for" or "because," ". . . call his name Jesus, because . . ." or, if a separate sentence is used, "The reason you will give him this name is that . . . ."

Save has sometimes been translated as "rescue," as in "He will rescue his people from their sins." Another way has been "redeemed" or "set free," as one may perhaps buy a slave his freedom: "He will set his people free from their sins." It would be wrong, however, to give the idea that his people will stop committing sin. Better would be "He will rescue them from the situation of sin" or "from the effects (or, results) of their sins." Since these results are God's punishment, translators can even say "from the punishment because of their sins." These solutions are also useful in languages where the concept of rescuing from sins does not make sense because sins are not seen as the type of situation from which one needs to be rescued or can be rescued. It would not be right, either, to translate **save** as "forgive." Jesus will not forgive his people, but rather will bring about God's forgiveness.

Sins itself is a concept that has been translated in many different ways. Of course, many languages are familiar with the concept and have no problem translating it. The word used indicates a violation of the teachings, laws, and traditions of that culture. But in other languages the closest equivalent is "bad actions," "wrong actions," or "forbidden actions." Translators have sometimes found it necessary to make clear that sins are actions against God's teaching, and have used phrases such as "acts that disobey God." The translation of this sentence will then be something like "He will rescue his people from the effects of their disobeying God."

In the Gospel of Matthew, **his people** means "Israel." But this information is probably best put in the footnotes, leaving **his people** or "his own people" in the text.

1.22	RSV	TEV

All this took place to fulfil what the Lord had spoken by the prophet:	**Now all of this happened in order to make come true what the Lord had said through the prophet,**

"**Now**" of TEV and NJB is not a temporal marker; its function is purely transitional, and it represents a Greek particle left implicit in RSV. Again, as with "behold" in verse 20, translators will use or not use a transitional particle or phrase like "**Now**," depending on what would be most natural in the discourse of their language. But note that this particle shows a logical relation: "The reason all this happened was . . ." or "Now then, all this happened because . . . ."

It is no longer the angel speaking, and translators will probably begin a new paragraph or will mark clearly in some other way that it is the narrator, Matthew, who is speaking. As above, "Now then . . ." or "In fact . . ." are possible.

All this took place refers to the events mentioned in verses 18-21. The same expression is found in 26.56, while "This took place" is used in 21.4. It is now the author of the Gospel who is speaking. Nowhere in the Bible does an angel appeal to Scripture as the basis of his proclamation.

All this may have to be plural in some languages, as in "These things happened . . . ."

To fulfil (TEV "**in order to make come true**") is found as a quotation formula only in the Gospel of Matthew, and it occurs in several variant forms: 2.15,17,23; 4.14; 8.17; 12.17; 13.35; 21.4; 27.9. See also 26.56, which is parallel to Mark 14.49. Similar formulas are also known in Jewish writings. None of the quotations which Matthew introduces by these formulas conforms exactly to the Septuagint text. For the most part they are rather free renderings of the Old Testament and are sometimes composite in nature. Through the use of these quotations, Matthew indicates the inseparable ties that exist between Israel's past and present, brought to fulfillment in the person of Jesus Christ.

To fulfil expresses purpose, as seen in TEV, and some languages use "so that." There are languages where purpose is expressed at the beginning of the sentence; for example, "The reason all this took place was to fulfill . . . ."

Fulfil in this context means **"to make come true"** (TEV) or "to cause to happen." Some languages express this "to make happen what the Lord by the prophet said should happen."

Prophet is a word for which translators need to find a good translation early in their work. Certainly the best solution is not "seer" or "future teller." Rather, the prophets were God's spokesmen. Sometimes the message God gave them dealt with the future, but it was in their capacity as his spokesmen that the prophets brought these messages. Many languages say simply "spokesman" or "God's spokesman." In some societies there are spokesmen who serve chiefs or other authorities and who have titles in the languages. In these places, translators can use the titles but add "of God." Still other societies have town criers who carry important messages from authorities, and in these situations, "prophets" can be translated "God's town criers."

By the prophet is a good example of the role of the prophets. They spoke what God gave them to speak, and their words were therefore God's words. Some translations say "what the Lord said by means of the prophet." Others have used "what the Lord said through (or, by) the mouth of the prophet." Other solutions are "what the prophet said when the Lord gave him the words" or "what the prophet said when he spoke the words the Lord told him." But in sentences like these latter ones, it is important to be sure that the readers see that the real agent or speaker is the Lord, and the prophet is the instrument.

Before **the prophet** some ancient manuscripts include "Isaiah," since he is obviously the prophet indicated by the following verse. But the name "Isaiah" is not mentioned in the original text.

1.23	RSV	TEV

"Behold, a virgin shall conceive and bear a son, and his name shall be called Emmanuel" (which means, God with us).

"A virgin will become pregnant and have a son, and he will be called Immanuel" (which means, "God is with us"). .

The quotation in this verse comes from Isaiah 7.14; it agrees with the Septuagint text, except that Matthew substitutes "they will call you" for "you will call" of the Septuagint. TEV **he will be called** (so also GECL 1st edition) is a translational adjustment, taking Matthew's rendering in an impersonal sense, without specific reference to any given person.

In the Septuagint text of Isaiah 7.14, the translators use a Greek word which normally means "virgin." The Hebrew word used, however, has a wider meaning than "virgin." Although occasionally the Septuagint translator may use the same word to refer to a girl who is no longer a virgin (twice in Gen 34.3), it is obvious that in the present context Matthew intends for the word to be taken in its root meaning of "virgin." More important for Matthew, however, is the significance of the name **Emmanuel**, which means "God is with us."

Some languages must introduce quotations with a phrase such as "He said," "When he said," "saying," or even "This is what he said." Translators will follow the rules of their own languages in this.

Behold: see comments on verse 20.

Since Matthew means by **virgin** specifically a young woman who has not yet had sexual relations, translators should find the most natural and at the same time polite way of saying this, whether with a word or a phrase. In some languages it is actually best to say "A young woman who has not been with men" or "a young woman who has not slept with a man." Actually, "young woman" is a problem in some languages where "woman" means a married woman and everyone else is called "girl." The context should make it clear that the "girl" is of marriageable age here, but that she has not yet slept with a man, as a wife and her husband do.

As in verse 18, translators express **conceive** in the most natural way, whether with "conceive" or with a phrase such as "will become pregnant," "will be with child."

For **bear a son**, see comments on verse 21.

The phrase **his name shall be called** is impersonal here and not imperative, as the similar phrase was in verse 21. **Called** means "named," so translators should find the natural, impersonal way of saying "He will be named." Perhaps "They (or, one) will name him," or "His name will be," or "People will call him."

Emmanuel should be written as a name, not translated here.

Since the phrase **which means, God with us** is not part of the quotation from the prophet, many translators will find it necessary to begin a new sentence: "This name means 'God is with us' " or "The meaning of this name is 'God with us.' "

1.24   RSV   TEV

When Joseph woke from sleep, he   So when Joseph woke up, he
did as the angel of the Lord com-   married Mary, as the angel of the
manded him; he took his wife,   Lord had told him to.

When can also be translated "after": "After Joseph woke up . . . ."

Woke translates a Greek verb which is also found with this same meaning in the Septuagint (Gen 28.16; Judges 16.14). Here it is followed by the phrase **from sleep**. In the structure of TEV, however, it is not explicitly mentioned, since this information is clearly implicit in the text and more natural in English without it. The same is true in many other languages. Translators must ask themselves whether they would say "Wake up" or "Wake up from sleep," and then use the appropriate phrase.

He took his wife (TEV "**he married Mary**") represents the same expression discussed in verse 20, and translators should translate the phrase here in a way similar to what they did there: "He married Mary," or "He took Mary to be his wife," or "He received her as his wife."

For **the angel of the Lord**, see comments on verse 20.

Notice that TEV has reversed the order of the last two phrases in this verse. This is perhaps more natural in English, and other translators should do what is natural in their languages. A further problem is that in some translations it sounds as if he married Mary immediately after waking up. So it may be necessary to have sentences such as these: "When Joseph woke up, he did what the angel of the Lord had told him to do when he said he should marry Mary," or "Joseph woke up. After that, he married Mary, because that was what the angel of the Lord had commanded him to do."

1.25	RSV	TEV
	but knew her not until she had borne a son; and he called his name Jesus.	**But he had no sexual relations with her before she gave birth to her son. And Joseph named him Jesus.**

Knew her not: the Hebrew verb "to know" is frequently used in the Old Testament in the sense of "have sex with" (Gen 19.8; Num 31.17; 1 Sam 1.19). Thus the basis for "**he had no sexual relations with her**" of TEV.

This direct way of speaking is used in many translations besides TEV. However, there are languages in which it is not polite to speak directly of sexual relations, although generally some indirect way is acceptable: "to lie with," or "to be with her as a man with his wife," or something similar. Rarely is the Hebrew "to know" understood in other cultures, however, as having this meaning.

Until (so also NEB, TNT, AT, Phps, Brc, Mft) represents a Greek adverbial construction rendered "**before**" by TEV and "at any time before" by NAB. JB translates the two clauses "and, though he had not had intercourse with her, she gave birth to a son," and adds a footnote: "literally 'and he did not know her until the day she gave birth.' " Catholic scholars do not attempt to support the doctrine of the perpetual virginity of Mary on the basis of this verse, as may be seen by the JB footnote: "The text is not concerned with the period that followed and, taken by itself, does not assert Mary's perpetual virginity which, however, the gospels elsewhere suppose and which the Tradition of the Church affirms." The NAB footnote is certainly correct: "The evangelist emphasizes the virginity of the mother of Jesus from the moment of his conception to his birth. He does not concern himself here with the period that followed the birth of Jesus, but merely wishes to show that Joseph fully respected the legal character of the paternity imposed on him by the divine will." In other words, most commentators, Catholic and Protestant alike, agree that the period in focus is the time from the conception until the birth of Jesus. Matthew is not really concerned to make any statement regarding the marital relations between Joseph and Mary after the birth of Jesus. So then, it is best to translate in such a way as to leave open the possibility for either understanding of the subsequent marital relationship between Joseph and Mary. That is perhaps the basis for TEV's "**before**," since it represents a more neutral interpretation of the text than does **until**, which definitely implies sexual relations after the time of the birth of Jesus. Translators can convey the meaning with something such as "before the time that . . ." or "before she gave birth."

Some languages have a single word for **son**, but others say "male baby" or "male child." Whether to say "a son" or "her son" depends on the individual language. In the context the meaning is the same.

And he called his name Jesus: the Greek construction is simply the third person singular verb form without indication as to whether the subject is "he" or "she." However, in the Jewish setting it would have been the father who gave the name (see Luke 1.63); TEV makes this information explicit: **"And Joseph named him Jesus."**

We have already discussed the expression **called his name** in verse 21. In addition to the TEV way of expressing it, translators may say "The name he gave him was Jesus" or "Joseph said the baby's name should be Jesus."

Chapter 2

RSV | TEV

Visitors from the East

1 Now when Jesus was born in Bethlehem of Judea in the days of Herod the king, behold, wise men from the East came to Jerusalem, saying, 2 "Where is he who has been born king of the Jews? For we have seen his star in the East, and have come to worship him." 3 When Herod the king heard this, he was troubled, and all Jerusalem with him; 4 and assembling all the chief priests and scribes of the people, he inquired of them where the Christ was to be born. 5 They told him, "In Bethlehem of Judea; for so it is written by the prophet:

6   'And you, O Bethlehem, in the land of Judah,
    are by no means least among the rulers of Judah;
    for from you shall come a ruler
    who will govern my people Israel.' "

7 Then Herod summoned the wise men secretly and ascertained from them what time the star appeared; 8 and he sent them to Bethlehem, saying, "Go and search diligently for the child, and when you have found him bring me word, that I too may come and worship him." 9 When they had heard the king they went their way; and lo, the star which they had seen in the East went before them, till it came to rest over the place where the child was. 10 When they saw the star, they rejoiced exceedingly with great joy; 11 and going into the house they saw the child with Mary his mother, and they fell down and worshiped him. Then, opening their treasures, they offered him gifts, gold and frankincense and myrrh. 12 And being warned in a dream not to return to Herod, they departed to their own country by another way.

1 Jesus was born in the town of Bethlehem in Judea, during the time when Herod was king. Soon afterward, some men who studied the stars came from the East to Jerusalem 2 and asked, "Where is the baby born to be the king of the Jews? We saw his star when it came up in the east, and we have come to worship him."

3 When King Herod heard about this, he was very upset, and so was everyone else in Jerusalem. 4 He called together all the chief priests and the teachers of the Law and asked them, "Where will the Messiah be born?"

5 "In the town of Bethlehem in Judea," they answered. "For this is what the prophet wrote:

6   'Bethlehem in the land of Judah,
    you are by no means the least of the leading cities of Judah;
    for from you will come a leader
    who will guide my people Israel.' "

7 So Herod called the visitors from the East to a secret meeting and found out from them the exact time the star had appeared. 8 Then he sent them to Bethlehem with these instructions: "Go and make a careful search for the child; and when you find him, let me know, so that I too may go and worship him."

9-10 And so they left, and on their way they saw the same star they had seen in the East. When they saw it, how happy they were, what joy was theirs! It went ahead of them until it stopped over the place where the child was. 11 They went into the house, and when they saw the child with his mother Mary, they knelt down and worshiped him. They brought out their gifts of gold, frankincense, and myrrh, and presented them to him.

12 Then they returned to their country by another road, since God had warned them in a dream not to go back to Herod.

SECTION HEADING: **"Visitors from the East**." In some parts of the world, "**Visitors**" are called "strangers." Other languages say "People who came to visit." Sometimes the object of their visit must be specified, as in "People who came to see Jesus (or, the baby Jesus)." Other translators take their cue from verse 1 and say "Wise men" or "Wise men from the east," or even "Men who studied the stars."

"**East**" in many languages is "the direction where the sun rises." Since this makes a very long phrase, it is sometimes dropped from the section heading.

Some languages will need complete sentences for section headings; for example, "There were visitors who came from the east (to see Jesus)" or "Some men who studied the stars came from the east (to see Jesus)."

The story of the visitors from the East may be divided into six brief scenes: (1) The visitors from the East arrive in Jerusalem (1-2); (2) Herod and the teachers of the Law (3-6); (3) Herod and the visitors from the East (7-8); (4) The visitors on their way to find the child (9-10); (5) The visitors worship the child (11); (6) The visitors on their journey home (12).

2.1　　　　　　　RSV　　　　　　　　　　　　　TEV

Now when Jesus was born in Bethlehem of Judea in the days of Herod the king, behold, wise men from the East came to Jerusalem, saying,	Jesus was born in the town of Bethlehem in Judea, during the time when Herod was king. Soon afterward, some men who studied the stars came from the East to Jerusalem

Now is a word that indicates a new section is starting and does not indicate time. TEV does not find it necessary in English to have such a word or expression, but many other languages will, as in "Now then."

Matthew identifies **Bethlehem** as the one in **Judea** (there was another Bethlehem in Zebulun); GECL 1st edition further identifies Bethlehem as "a place," and TEV as "**the town of**." Herod the Great is the king referred to. The Roman Senate appointed him king in 40 B.C., but he actually reigned only from 37 B.C. to 4 B.C. Neither **Bethlehem** nor **Judea** will be known to many readers, and translators can help these readers by using classifiers, as in "the town of Bethlehem in the region of Judea."

When translates a participial construction in Greek, which may also mean "After" (NJB) or "**Soon afterward**" (TEV, GECL). Some languages will say "After Jesus was born . . ." or "When Jesus was born . . . ," but others will find it more natural to do it this way: "Jesus was born in the town of Bethlehem in Judea when Herod was the king. After that . . . ." However, **when** needs to be examined in its relationship with the word **behold**. This word will not be expressed at all in some languages, but in others the ideas "behold" and "when" come together in a phrase like "**Soon afterward**" as in TEV, or "And it happened that . . . ," or simply as "Then."

In the days of Herod the king may be "during the time when Herod was the king there." But in some languages a separate sentence will be better, as in "At that time, Herod was king there" or "At that time, the king there was named Herod."

Wise men translates a Greek noun which originally referred to Persian priests who were experts in astrology and in the interpretation of dreams. But the word may also be used in a derogatory sense of "magician" or "charlatan," a meaning which it has in its only other New Testament occurrences outside Matthew's nativity narrative (Acts 13.6,8). Matthew most likely has Babylonian astrologers in mind. "Astrologers" (NAB, NEB, Phps) is perhaps the nearest technical term, but in light of its intended readership TEV has chosen the more lengthy phrase: **"some men who studied the stars."** Note also Brc ("scholars who were students of the stars"), which is very good because in the present context the word is not intended to have a derogatory or negative meaning such as "astrologers" may have. Mft's "magicians" misses the target in the present context, though it is well suited for the passage in Acts. It may not be sufficient to say **"studied the stars,"** since this would mean the wise men were astronomers, and translators in these languages will have to add "to know things." This is even expressed sometimes as "men who knew things from studying the stars."

What is meant by **the East** is not known precisely, though most commentators assume Babylonia is intended (present-day Iran).

East: "from the direction where the sun rises" is a very common way to express this, or "from a country that is in the direction where the sun rises."

Jerusalem, as with "Bethlehem," will not be known to some readers. In those languages the translators will specify "the city Jerusalem."

Saying: "They said" or "When they reached Jerusalem, they asked people . . . ." But it can mean "they asked the authorities (or, responsible people)."

2.2   RSV   TEV

"Where is he who has been born king of the Jews? For we have seen his star in the East, and have come to worship him."

and asked, "Where is the baby born to be the king of the Jews? We saw his star when it came up in the east, and we have come to worship him."

Born king of the Jews is translated sometimes as "the king of the Jews who was born recently." Note that their question does imply that this future king was born recently, so that specifying "baby" is accurate. However, this does not mean they thought the baby was king immediately, that is, king at the time of his birth, but was rather "the baby born to be king" or "the baby who will become king."

For indicates that the wise men are giving the reason they are asking where this baby is. Some languages need a phrase such as "We ask because . . ." or "We want to know because . . . ." In others, such as English, the relation is understood without being explicit.

His star is thought by some scholars to be a heavenly counterpart of the newborn king. However, the phrase most probably means simply "the star which announced his birth." As far as translation is concerned, it is not necessary to identify specifically what star or constellation is indicated. In many languages, to say **his star** would make it seem that he possessed it. Then translators will find "the star which announced his birth" helpful. Other ways may be "the star that relates to him" or ". . . tells us about him."

In the East is translated as a complete statement by TEV: **"when it came up in the east**." With regard to this phrase, a few commentators state that the meaning "in the east" can be arrived at only with great difficulty, and that the meaning must be "at its rising." Nevertheless, other commentators and lexicographers supply references where the Greek noun does mean "east" (see Rev 7.2; 16.12; 21.13). The translations are divided. RSV, Phps, Zür translate **in the East**. TOB also follows this translation, but with a note giving the alternative possibility. In favor of the meaning "at its rising" are GECL ("We have seen his star rise"), Brc, TNT, Mft, NEB. JB also accepts this rendering but gives the alternative translation in a footnote, basing it on the Vulgate. On the basis of the evidence available, it seems that either translation is possible, and TEV has attempted to maintain the best of both worlds by including each of the two elements: **"when it came up"** and **"in the east."** Since either translation is possible, the real question is what would the astrologers themselves most likely have said. It seems more likely that people coming from the east would have said something like "in our own land" in place of "in the east." If this is the case, then it is quite possible that this is a technical term referring to the beginning of the phenomenon observed by the astrologers. Following these interpretations, then, translators can say "his star in our country (in the direction of the east)" or "his star as it came from the east."

The same term for **east** should be used as in verse 1.

The word translated **worship** is used thirteen times in Matthew as compared with two times in Mark and three in Luke. In the context it may mean either divine worship or homage paid to a king; however, in the final analysis it is difficult to draw a sharp line between these two meanings. Many languages use "pray to" for **worship**, which would not really be best here. "Pay homage to," "pay our respects to," or "honor because he is king" is better.

2.3   RSV   TEV

When Herod the king heard this, he   When King Herod heard about
was troubled, and all Jerusalem with   this, he was very upset, and so was
him;   everyone else in Jerusalem.

In Greek **heard** has no object, though an object is clearly implied. RSV has supplied **this** and TEV **"about this"** to make more natural English structures. **Heard this** is sometimes more naturally rendered "When people told these things to King Herod." Some languages need an object of "heard" more specific than "this" and say "heard what the wise men were saying" or "heard about the wise men."

He was troubled (TEV **"he was very upset"**) translates the same Greek verb used of the disciples in 14.26, its only other occurrence in Matthew's Gospel. Phps translates "deeply perturbed"; NEB "greatly perturbed"; NAB "greatly disturbed"; and Brc "alarmed." Many languages have expressions such as "his peace left him" or "his heart became troubled."

He was troubled and all Jerusalem with him translates a Semitic Greek construction. The adjective **all** is used here, as frequently in the Old Testament, in the sense of "a large portion of," and the reference is specifically to people. One may then translate "He was upset, and many people in Jerusalem were also upset." In many languages the exaggeration of Matthew's style is quite normal, as in phrases such as "and everyone in Jerusalem was also upset" or "and the people who lived in Jerusalem were upset as well as he was." But other languages will find "many people" more natural.

2.4	RSV	TEV

RSV	TEV
and assembling all the chief priests and scribes of the people, he inquired of them where the Christ was to be born.	He called together all the chief priests and the teachers of the Law and asked them, "Where will the Messiah be born?"

And indicates a continuation of the narrative. Some languages do not need any marker like this, but others will say "So," "Therefore," or "Then."

Assembling can be "**He called together**" (TEV) or "he held a meeting of," or "he asked them to come meet with him."

The word list of GECL defines **chief priests** as "the executive committee within the Jewish Council, which consisted of the High Priest, the officer in charge of the temple guard (Acts 4.1), several leading priests of high rank, and three influential laymen." It is probable also that they were "members of the families from which the high priests were at that time appointed."

Many translators use a term such as "sacrificers" for **priests** and "chief (or, big) sacrificers" for **chief priests**. This certainly emphasizes the main role of the priests and works especially well if translators use "house of sacrifice" to translate "temple." Other translators construct a short phrase such as "one who goes before God (for the people)" or "mediator between God and the people" for translating "priest," and for "chief priest" add "chief" or "big," or whatever word means "leader."

The scribes were experts in Jewish religious law; TEV uses the less technical term "**the teachers of the Law**," in which "Law" means "the Jewish religious Law." Certainly translators should avoid translating **scribes** simply as "writers," since this would not indicate the true role the scribes played for the Jewish people at that time, which was to be teachers and experts in the Law. Some translators cannot say "of the Law" without specifying which law, as in "of the Law of Moses" or "of the Jewish Law." In Matthew **the people** always refers to the Jews, and so in the present context the equivalent would be "the Jewish people" (NEB). Phps translates the entire phrase as "all the Jewish chief priests and scribes," while Brc follows TEV in leaving **of the people** implicit. If translators have already modified **priests** or **scribes** with "of the Jews" as in "Jewish sacrificers" or "teachers of the Jewish law," then they can either leave **of the people** implicit, as in TEV, or say "of those people."

The word **inquired** (TEV "**asked**") occurs only here in Matthew's Gospel. It is used by John in 4.52; all of its other occurrences are found in the Lukan writings (Luke 15.26; 18.36; Acts 4.7; 10.18,29; 21.33; 23.19,20, and 34).

For **the Christ** (TEV "**the Messiah**") see the discussion at 1.17 and 1.1. In the present context the term refers back to the king of the Jews of verse 2. But readers who are not familiar with the meaning of this term may not see the connection, so

GECL translates "the Promised King" (Indonesian Common Language Version [INCL] "the Promised Savior King").

Some languages must use direct speech, as in "Where will the one be born who is the Messiah?" or "When the Messiah comes, where will he be born?"

2.5	RSV	TEV

RSV	TEV
They told him, "In Bethlehem of Judea; for so it is written by the prophet:	**"In the town of Bethlehem in Judea," they answered. "For this is what the prophet wrote:**

On the expectation of the Messiah from **Bethlehem**, see John 7.41-42. TEV marks Bethlehem as a "**town**." See comments on 2.1.

In some languages it will be necessary to answer Herod's question with a full sentence, as in "He will be born in the town of Bethlehem in Judea."

Note that the phrase which introduces the reported speech, **They told him**, is at the beginning of all they said in RSV, but has been inserted in the middle of the quote itself in TEV. In English, as in many languages, this is perhaps a matter of style. But in other languages this is completely unnatural, so that the translator can only do something similar to the RSV form.

The Greek passive construction **for so it is written by the prophet** is transformed by TEV into an active construction: "**For this is what the prophet wrote**." The same "quotation formula" (**it is written**) is also found in 4.4,6,7,10; 11.10; 21.13; 26.24,31.

The causative **for** can be handled in many ways: "We know this because of what the prophet wrote," or "This is how we know this thing: the prophet wrote . . . ," or even in some languages, "The prophet wrote that it would be in the town of Bethlehem in Judah. He said . . . ." Of course, other languages will do something very similar to TEV.

For **prophet**, see comments on 1.22. In languages where there is already an Old Testament, it is good to indicate in the footnotes that this is a quotation from the book of the prophet Micah, but it will not be necessary to put this information in the text.

2.6	RSV	TEV

RSV	TEV
'And you, O Bethlehem, in the land of Judah, **are by no means least among the rulers of Judah;** **for from you shall come a ruler** **who will govern my people Israel.' "**	**'Bethlehem in the land of Judah,** **you are by no means the least of the leading cities of Judah;** **for from you will come a leader who will guide my people Israel.' "**

The quotation in this verse comes from Micah 5.2 (5.1 in Hebrew), except for the last clause (**who will govern my people Israel**), which apparently is assimilated from 2 Samuel 5.2. The Septuagint text is not followed here and, in part at least, the quotation appears to be an independent rendering of the Hebrew text. For a detailed discussion of the problem, consult the commentaries.

O Bethlehem: as we indicated above, the prophet is speaking on behalf of God. Many translations make this explicit by saying "God said, 'You Bethlehem . . . .'" Of course, **O** is not used in current English, nor in many languages, and can be dropped without losing the meaning that the speaker is addressing **Bethlehem** directly. It will be strange in some languages to speak to a town. Translators can then say "You people of Bethlehem, in the land of Judah, your town is by no means the least . . . ."

Languages that make a distinction between "country" and "region" or "province" should use one of these latter two words. Judah was only one region of the country.

Least among the rulers of Judah is interpreted by TEV and GECL to mean "**least of the leading cities of Judah**." NEB has a different interpretation ("least in the eyes of the rulers of Judah"), while others (Phps, NAB) take "leaders" in the technical sense of "princes." The problem for the translator is that he is dealing with a mixed metaphor. The town of Bethlehem is addressed as though it were a person, a leader in the country of Judah. TEV and GECL have unscrambled the mixed metaphor, while NEB has interpreted "least among" to mean "least in the eyes of."

Many languages do not use the same word for "least in size" and "least in importance." The latter is the better one in this case. "You are not the least important of the leading cities of Judah." It will be much easier in many languages to change the double negative ("not the least") into a positive statement, as in "You are one of the most important" or "You are among the greatest of the cities of Judah."

If translators do understand **rulers** to mean "the people who rule" (instead of "**leading cities**"), a possible translation will be "The rulers of the area of Judah do not think you are the least important of the towns" or "The rulers of Judah know you are one of the most important towns in their region."

From you: "from among your people" or "one of your people" are possibilities. The translators who have had to say "people of Bethlehem" above can put here simply "one of you."

A ruler who will govern appears in GECL as "the man who will protect and guide," and in TEV as "**a leader who will guide**." The Greek verb literally means "to shepherd" (see NJB, NAB, NEB, Phps, Brc). Since the verb "to shepherd" is rare in English and certainly does not have the biblical connotation of ruling, NEB has restructured: "a leader to be the shepherd of my people Israel." Elsewhere, especially in the Septuagint, the verb often has the extended meaning of "lead," "guide," or "rule," which gives support for the renderings of RSV and TEV. The prophesy is about one specific leader, so many translators have "One of your people will be the leader of my people Israel," or "The person who is going to lead my people Israel will come from you," or "Someone from your town will be the one who leads my people Israel."

If "lead" is used in a language in the restricted sense of "lead in a particular direction," then "govern" or "rule" is better here.

In its original context the possessive pronoun **my** (in the construction **my people**) referred to God, not the prophet, which seems also to be the case in the setting of Matthew. Many readers will think **my people** means "Micah's people" or even "Matthew's people." To avoid this, some translators say "Israel, God's people" or "Israel, the people God says are his." Of course, if translators put "God said" at the beginning of the verse, it is usually clear that "my" means "God's."

2.7   RSV   TEV

> **Then Herod summoned the wise men secretly and ascertained from them what time the star appeared;**

> So Herod called the visitors from the East to a secret meeting and found out from them the exact time the star had appeared.

Then (TEV "**So**") translates a particle which Matthew uses some ninety times. It is usually translated "then" but has a number of different functions, depending upon the context in which it is used. NEB translates "Next," while NAB leaves the force of the particle implicit in the text. There are languages where one of these English solutions to **Then** will be acceptable, but many others will need a transitional phrase such as "When (or, after) Herod heard that . . . ."

The wise men is here translated "**the visitors from the East**" by TEV, though it was translated in verse 1 by TEV as "some men who studied the stars." This is merely an attempt to avoid the use of the technical term "astrologers" and at the same time to find a phrase which fits in naturally with English discourse structure. Similarly other translators should use a phrase that is natural in the discourse of their language, one that clearly shows these are the same wise men as in verse 1. It may be necessary to repeat the phrase used there, but translators may also say "those wise men," "those men who were seeking the newborn king," or "those men who studied the stars."

Summoned . . . secretly is restructured by TEV to read "**called . . . to a secret meeting.**" NJB translates "Then Herod summoned the wise men to see him privately," and NEB has "Herod next called the astrologers to meet him in private." **Summoned . . . secretly** has been translated by some in such a way that it seems Herod called the wise men to a meeting no one else knew about. This may be true, but generally the emphasis is on the fact that no one else was there, as in "Herod asked the wise men to come to a meeting at which no one else was present" or ". . . to meet with him by himself."

Ascertained (so also NEB) translates a Greek verb used only here in the New Testament. As RSV indicates, the **time** is object of the verb, and since the idea of "exactness" is actually contained in the verb itself, TEV renders "**found out . . . the exact time.**" Brc translates "carefully questioned them" without stating explicitly that Herod learned the information. AT, Phps, NAB have the same wording as TEV. One standard lexicon suggests the meaning "inquire carefully" for this passage. Some translators will use a phrase such as "asked them about what time the star appeared" or "about the time when the star appeared." But others will be closer to TEV with phrases such as "learned from them when the star appeared."

In many languages it will be more natural to use direct discourse, as in "Herod asked them, 'Exactly when did the star appear?' " or " 'Tell me all about the time when the star appeared.' "

RSV	TEV
and he sent them to Bethlehem, saying, "Go and search diligently for the child, and when you have found him bring me word, that I too may come and worship him."	**Then he sent them to Bethlehem with these instructions: "Go and make a careful search for the child; and when you find him, let me know, so that I too may go and worship him."**

And he sent them . . . saying is represented by TEV by "**Then he sent them . . . ,**" or it may be rendered "After that, he told them to go . . . ." There are languages where it must be made explicit that the wise men answered Herod's questions before he sent them to Bethlehem. In these, translators will add "The wise men answered his questions, and then Herod sent them to Bethlehem."

As a way of translating **saying**, some languages say "He said to them . . ." or "He told them that they should go and search . . . ."

In some languages it will be better to make **to Bethlehem** a part of the direct discourse of what Herod said: "After that, Herod said to them, 'Go to Bethlehem. There, look carefully for the child . . . .' "

Go and search translates a participle followed by an imperative. However, this is a common structure in Semitic Greek and is best translated in English by two imperatives, as RSV, TEV, and most other English translations have done. GECL has the same structure as the English.

Search translates a verb which is used only two other times in the New Testament (Matt 10.11; John 21.12). In itself the verb means "to search carefully," though in the present context its meaning is intensified by the inclusion of the adverb **diligently**. NAB translates "Go and get detailed information about the child," and Phps "search for this little child with the utmost care." TEV has "**make a careful search for the child.**" A simple phrase may prove easiest in some languages: "Look everywhere for this child."

The Greek word translated **child** may mean "very young child" or "infant," as is indicated by its usage of an eight-day-old child in the Septuagint of Genesis 17.12. In John 16.21 it has the meaning "baby." However, the word normally means "child," without reference to its age. The context implies that Jesus is no longer a baby at the time the men arrive; they seem not to have set off from their homeland in the east until the star signifying his birth had appeared. The same word is used of Jesus in verses 9,11,13,14,20,21. In verse 16 it is the equivalent of a masculine plural form and is translated "male children" by RSV and "boys" by TEV.

When you have found him may be "When you have found where he is."

Bring me word can be "Come and tell me (about it)" or "You should come back here to tell me where the place is."

In Greek the pronoun **I** is emphatic, as is indicated by the inclusion of the intensifier **too** in RSV and TEV.

That clearly indicates purpose. Herod wants the wise men to tell him where the new king is, "So that I also can worship . . . ." "When you tell me where he is, I also will be able to worship . . ." is another way, or "I want you to tell me so that I will be able to worship . . . ."

Herod is in Jerusalem as he speaks. Many languages cannot have him say that he will **come** to Bethlehem, but rather that he will "go" there.

Worship is the same verb used in verse 2.

2.9	RSV	TEV

When they had heard the king they went their way; and lo, the star which they had seen in the East went before them, till it came to rest over the place where the child was.	9-10 And so they left, and on their way they saw the same star they had seen in the East. When they saw it, how happy they were, what joy was theirs! It went ahead of them until it stopped over the place where the child was.

TEV places verses 9-10 together in order to effect a more logical sequence of events for the English reader. "**When they saw it . . . what joy was theirs**" of TEV translates verse 10 of the Greek text. TEV makes this restructuring in order to show an immediate connection between the seeing of the star and the joyful response of the men. Then TEV picks up the information about the movement of the star to the place where the child was, which in Greek is the last part of verse 9. Other translators who follow this interpretation might say "When they saw the star again, they were very happy . . ." or "It made them very happy to see the star again."

However, GECL reflects naturally the joyful response of the men without reordering the information in verses 9-10. This is achieved through translating the first part of verse 10 "as they saw it there." In other words, in GECL their joyful response is occasioned by seeing the star stop over the place where the child was, not, as TEV suggests, by the sight of the star after leaving King Herod. This seems more in keeping with the Greek text and with the movement of the story itself. Translators who follow this interpretation can use sentences such as "When they saw the star at that place, they became very happy," or perhaps "When they saw where the star was, it gave them happiness." See also the comments on verse 10.

When they had heard the king they went their way is restructured by TEV to read "**And so they left, and on their way . . . .**" NEB translates "They set out at the king's bidding," and GECL "after they had received these instructions, they set out on their way." Other ways may be "After the king told them this . . ." or "When they heard what they king said, they left."

And lo translates the same Greek construction discussed in 1.20 (see comments there under "behold"). As in that verse, translators may use an expression such as "and then" or "now then." The meaning can also be included in a sentence such as "As they were going" or "As they were on the way."

In the East translates the same construction discussed in verse 2. Here, depending on the flow of the discourse, the star can be referred to as "that star they had seen when it appeared (or, rose)" or as "the star they had seen in their country."

In many languages it will be necessary to make explicit that the star appeared again. That is, it would sound strange to say the star went before them without first indicating that it appeared again and the wise men saw it. Thus, "They saw the same star . . . and it went . . ." or "The star appeared again . . . and it went . . . ."

Before them. Some translators feel it would be hard for the wise men to perceive a star actually moving the short distance of eight kilometers (five miles) between Jerusalem and Bethlehem. As a result they translate "before" with the sense of "before in time." But the text seems to describe a star moving in the sky "in front of them" or "leading their way."

The star **came to rest**, that is, it "stopped moving" or "stood still."

Over can be translated as "above" or "on top of," although the translation should not make it seem the star was touching the house.

The place where the child was. Some languages have to use something more specific than "place," and say "house" or "building." Also, some cannot say "was" and must say "was staying."

Child is the same word used in verse 8.

2.10	RSV	TEV

When they saw the star, they rejoiced exceedingly with great joy;

. . . When they saw it, how happy they were, what joy was theirs! . . .

In very strong terms Matthew describes the response of the men when they saw the star: **they rejoiced exceedingly with great joy**. It is impossible to overtranslate the reaction of the men to the seeing of the star; the translation should express the greatest possible joy. TEV has "**how happy they were, what joy was theirs**" and NEB "they were overjoyed." NJB reads "The sight of the star filled them with delight."

Every language has its own way of expressing happiness or joy, and translators should use the most natural expressions they have. Some languages refer to parts of the body, as in "their hearts (or, their stomachs) were happy (or, sweet)," and so forth. Others say something like "happiness seized them" or "happiness came to them." Another way may be "their happiness was too great to measure."

2.11	RSV	TEV

and going into the house they saw the child with Mary his mother, and they fell down and worshiped him. Then, opening their treasures, they offered him gifts, gold and frankincense and myrrh.

They went into the house, and when they saw the child with his mother Mary, they knelt down and worshiped him. They brought out their gifts of gold, frankincense, and myrrh, and presented them to him.

The opening of this verse with **and** reflects Semitic structure. Some languages will use a similar transition, but others will start a new sentence, either as TEV has or with a phrase such as "Then (or, So) they went into the house."

Mary his mother. Some languages will naturally use the same expression as the text, but others will more likely say "his mother Mary." Some will make it a separate sentence or phrase: "He (or, who) was with his mother Mary."

They fell down and worshiped him (NEB "bowed to the ground in homage to him"; Phps "fell on their knees and worshipped him"; Brc "knelt down and did him homage") is represented by TEV as "**they knelt down and worshiped him.**" The problem with the literal rendering **they fell down** is that it might imply accidental falling, as though the men had tripped and fallen over something, or perhaps been so struck with awe they literally fell down. NJB attempts to resolve this difficulty by translating "falling to their knees," but in most languages it is more natural to say "**they knelt,**" as in TEV, or "they bowed to the floor," "they bowed low," or "they prostrated themselves."

Worshiped: this is the same word as in verses 2 and 8.

Opening their treasures is a rather literal rendering of the Greek text. The word translated **treasures** may refer either to something that is stored away or to the place or object in which something is stored away. It is used in the Septuagint in Deuteronomy 28.12 (TEV "storehouse"), Ezekiel 28.4 (TEV "treasures"), and Psalm 135.7 (Septuagint 134.7; TEV "storeroom"). In the present context the translations are divided between the meaning "treasure" and "treasure container"; and even where the second of these interpretations is followed, commentators do not agree as to the nature of the container. For example, some suggest "treasure box," while others deny this meaning and argue for "sack." In light of the many possibilities, none of which is conclusive, the best solution is simply to translate in a way which is most natural in the receptor language yet does not contradict the biblical culture. Some examples of things that contradict the biblical culture would be "suitcases," "trunks," or "safes." These should be avoided. Many translators have used general words such as "baggage" or "sacks (or, containers) they carried their valuable things in."

It may not be necessary to speak of "opening." An example of this is "They took out their gifts from their baggage." Some translators find that it is easier not even to mention the containers. They do something very similar to TEV, as in "They took out their gifts." But on the other hand, many languages will require that all the action be specified, as in "They opened their baggage and took out gifts for the baby."

In some languages the use of **gifts** requires naming who is to get the gift, as in "their gifts for the baby." It is important, however, either by using the words "valuable," "gift," or "treasure," to indicate they had something of value they were bringing to offer.

The gifts of **gold, frankincense, and myrrh** are not to be given individual symbolic significance. These are royal gifts, worthy of a king (see Psa 72.10-11,15; 45.7-9; Isa 60.6). **Frankincense**, a valuable incense made from the sap of a certain tree, was probably imported from Arabia. **Myrrh** is a sweet smelling resin of an Arabian shrub; it was used both for medicinal purposes (Mark 15.23) and for preparing bodies for burial (John 19.39). And the value of **gold** has been universally acknowledged for centuries.

Gold is generally well known, but in languages where it is not, translators will have to say something like "a very valuable metal (called gold)." In some languages it is natural to say simply that one of the gifts was "gold," but in others it is better to speak of "gold objects," "things made from gold," or possibly even "gold coins (or, pieces)."

Frankincense is less well known, but translators can try to find some general word such as "incense" or "sweet smelling powder," and then modify it by adding "valuable" and possibly "called frankincense." Thus they would have "a valuable incense (called frankincense)." In a similar way, **myrrh** can be "another sweet-smelling thing called myrrh" or "a valuable medicine (from a tree,) called myrrh."

It must be clear from the structure that the gold, frankincense, and myrrh are the gifts. In some languages a literal translation of the text means they gave him four things: gifts, gold, frankincense, and myrrh. Another matter of structure is when to mention what these gifts are. In the text they are listed after "gifts," but in many languages, it is more natural to reverse this, for example, "They took out from their treasure boxes gold, frankincense, and myrrh, and they gave these to him as gifts."

2.12	RSV	TEV

And being warned in a dream not to return to Herod, they departed to their own country by another way.	Then they returned to their country by another road, since God had warned them in a dream not to go back to Herod.

TEV reverses the order of the two clauses as they appear in the Greek text (compare RSV and TEV), thereby destroying the chronological sequence. For most languages the Greek order, retained by RSV, will be more natural.

Being warned translates one word in Greek; TEV restructures as an active, indicating subject and indirect object: "**since God had warned them.**" This is legitimate, since the Greek verb refers specifically to a revelation which originates from God, and several other translations also make this information explicit (Mft "they had been divinely warned"; Brc "because a message from God came to them . . . warning them"; GECL "God commanded them"). This verb is used once again in verse 22, but nowhere else in the Gospel.

Being warned will be expressed in some languages with indirect speech, as in "God told them in a dream they should not go back to Herod." But others will use direct speech: "God spoke to them while they dreamed, and said, 'You should not go back to Herod.' "

In a dream is the same expression used in 1.20. Here some possibilities are "God appeared to them in a dream," "God gave them a dream and said to them . . . ," or "God showed himself to them while they slept and warned them . . . ." Others will have "God warned them . . . Therefore (or, As a result) they departed."

The verb translated **return** is rare in the New Testament; other than here it occurs only in Luke 10.6; Acts 18.21; and Hebrews 11.15; it is also found in some manuscripts in 2 Peter 2.21. It can be translated "go back to" or perhaps "go back to see."

For **departed to their own country**, translators can say "they went back" or "they went to their own country," or "they left there to go to their own country."

Their own country can be "the region where they lived."

Another way means a route or road different from the one by which they had come from their country: "They took a different road" or "They followed a road they had not taken when they came."

2.13-15

RSV   TEV

The Escape to Egypt

13 Now when they had departed, behold, an angel of the Lord appeared to Joseph in a dream and said, "Rise, take the child and his mother, and flee to Egypt, and remain there till I tell you; for Herod is about to search for the child, to destroy him." 14 And he rose and took the child and his mother by night, and departed to Egypt, 15 and remained there until the death of Herod. This was to fulfill what the Lord had spoken by the prophet, "Out of Egypt have I called my son."

13 After they had left, an angel of the Lord appeared in a dream to Joseph and said, "Herod will be looking for the child in order to kill him. So get up, take the child and his mother and escape to Egypt, and stay there until I tell you to leave."

14 Joseph got up, took the child and his mother, and left during the night for Egypt, 15 where he stayed until Herod died. This was done to make come true what the Lord had said through the prophet, "I called my Son out of Egypt."

SECTION HEADING: "**The Escape to Egypt**." Many languages require that the subject of the escaping be named. That is, they must say who escaped. Further, it is often necessary to render section headings with complete sentences. Therefore translators may say "Joseph goes with Mary and Jesus to Egypt."

Although this section is entitled "**The Escape to Egypt**," Matthew's basic concern is not with the threatening events themselves but with divine providence. As one commentator observes, the entire passage (2.13-23) is similar in style to a Greek epic poem: short sentences are solemnly repeated in similar form; compare "an angel of the Lord appeared to Joseph in a dream and said" of verse 13 with "an angel of the Lord appeared in a dream to Joseph in Egypt, saying" of verse 20; compare also "rise, take the child and his mother" of verse 13 with "rise, take the child and his mother" of verse 20. "And he rose and took the child and his mother," verse 14, is repeated word for word in verse 21. Three times in this brief narrative, more frequently than anywhere else, Matthew states "this was to fulfill what the Lord had spoken by the prophet" (verses 15,17,23).

Traits of popular story telling may also be found in the use of the historical present (verses 13,19,22), so frequently found in Mark and John, but rarely in Matthew.

Finally, the narrative contains echoes of the childhood of Moses (persecution through a king hostile to God, the death of the children, Egypt). Verse 20 is reminiscent of Exodus 4.19: "Go back to Egypt, for all those who wanted to kill you are dead." Verse 15 recalls the exodus experience.

2.13   RSV   TEV

Now when they had departed, behold, an angel of the Lord ap-

After they had left, an angel of the Lord appeared in a dream to

44

peared to Joseph in a dream and said, "Rise, take the child and his mother, and flee to Egypt, and remain there till I tell you; for Herod is about to search for the child, to destroy him."

Joseph and said, "Herod will be looking for the child in order to kill him. So get up, take the child and his mother and escape to Egypt, and stay there until I tell you to leave."

Since **when they had departed** is clearly implied in the preceding verse ("they departed to their own country by another way"), GECL omits this clause and introduces this section with "In the following night Joseph had a dream . . . ." Whether to keep or omit the clause will depend on what will be most natural in a language. Since this is the beginning of a new section, in many languages it will be a natural translation to repeat the phrase, as in "After the wise men departed" or "The wise men departed. After that . . . ." In other languages a shorter phrase such as "After that" or "After all these things happened" will be acceptable, or even something similar to what GECL has done.

Also because the sentence begins a new section, it will be better in many cases to repeat the subject rather than use the pronoun **they**: "After the wise men left," "After the visitors from the east left," or "After the men who studied the stars departed."

The Greek particle translated **behold** is perhaps best left untranslated. Its function here is to focus attention upon the angel. See comment at 1.20. Also see 1.20 for **angel of the Lord**. We do not know from the Greek if it is the same angel as the one that appeared earlier, so it would not be right to use "that angel" or "the angel." It should still be **an angel of the Lord**.

Appeared translates a Greek present tense, known as the historical present, which is characteristic of narrative style. One primary function of the historical present is to make vivid the events narrated, as though they were happening at the time of the storytelling itself. Many languages use the historical present in telling stories, but when and how to use it will vary from language to language. In some languages, for example, it is only used in very colloquial, nonliterary situations. In others it is used to mark a change of focus, and so on. Therefore before going very far in their work, translators should study what is natural in their case, perhaps with the help of their translation consultant, and then use the historical present or various past tenses as would be normal, regardless of what tense actually appears in the text.

For **appeared**, see also its use in 1.20. Perhaps "an angel of the Lord showed himself to Joseph" or "Joseph had a dream (or, vision) and saw an angel of the Lord."

Rise may here be taken in its literal sense of "**get up**" (TEV). However, there are many places in the Old Testament where such a construction merely indicates the initiation of an action described in the verb which follows **rise**. In the present context the verb is not redundant, as some commentators suggest, since Joseph is evidently lying down asleep!

Take . . . and flee to Egypt. There are languages where it will be better not to have two separate verbs, but instead to have sentences with a single verb, as in "Flee to Egypt with the child and his mother," or "You and the child and his mother should all flee to Egypt." Other languages may use two verbs, but have sentences more like "Go with the child and his mother and flee to Egypt."

The expression **the child and his mother** also appears in verse 4 and in verses 20 and 21. Obviously it is a feature of Matthew's style, and translators should try to follow it. To say "Jesus and Mary" or "Mary and Jesus" would not reflect that at all.

Flee may be "run away," "go to find safety," "escape," or "leave at once."

For those readers who are unfamiliar with **Egypt**, it may be necessary to say "the land (or, country) of Egypt."

Till I tell you is incomplete; the full meaning is either "**until I tell you to leave**" (TEV) or "until I tell you that you can come" (GECL).

Herod is about to search should not be translated so as to imply that Herod himself will do the searching. Matthew clearly implies that Herod will send men (most probably soldiers) to do the searching in his behalf. In some languages it is clearly understood that since Herod is a monarch, he would have someone else do the searching. But in others, better sentences may be "Herod will send people (or, his soldiers) to search for the child" or "Herod will order a search to be made for this child."

To destroy him obviously means "**to kill him**" (TEV). It may be necessary to specify who would kill the child. Again, it would not be Herod himself. Thus, "so that they would kill him."

Notice that **for** indicates a reason. In many languages the reason usually comes first, as in TEV. Others mark it strongly with a phrase such as "The reason you should do that is . . ." or "I tell you this because . . . ."

2.14   RSV   TEV

And he rose and took the child and his mother by night, and departed to Egypt,

Joseph got up, took the child and his mother, and left during the night for Egypt,

As we have mentioned before, **And** will be omitted in some languages, but in others it will be translated by something such as "And so," "So," or "Therefore."

In the Greek text **he** refers to Joseph. To avoid confusion because of the several persons mentioned in the narrative (the angel, Joseph, Herod, the child), TEV makes the pronominal reference explicit.

Rose: "got up." See also comment in verse 13.

His mother refers to Mary, the mother of Jesus, not to Joseph's mother. This information is, of course, clear to the good reader, but the translation should leave no possibility of ambiguity. Some languages will have to say "the child and the mother" or "the child and the child's mother."

By night means "during the night" or "while it was still night." Note that as in TEV, "**left during the night**" is probably better than "took by night."

Departed: they set out on the journey that same night. The translation should not intimate that they arrived there in the same night.

Took . . . departed is similar to "take . . . flee" in verse 13. It can be expressed by "He went with the child and his mother and they left," or simply "He left with the child and his mother."

There are languages where **departed to Egypt** will have to be expressed by two verbs, as in "They left during the night to go toward Egypt" or "They left during the night. They went toward Egypt."

2.15	RSV	TEV

and remained there until the death of Herod. This was to fulfil what the Lord had spoken by the prophet, "Out of Egypt have I called my son."	where he stayed until Herod died. This was done to make come true what the Lord had said through the prophet, "I called my Son out of Egypt."

Remained is singular in Greek, with "he" (Joseph) as the understood subject. But although Joseph is in focus, it may be necessary in some languages to say "they remained," including Jesus and Mary as well. It may be better in some languages to start a new sentence here, as in "They stayed there until Herod died."

Death is often best expressed as a verb, as in "until Herod died." **Herod** died shortly before Passover in 4 B.C.

On the formula **This was to fulfil**, see comments on 1.22. **This** can be translated as "This happened," "These things took place," or even in some languages, "The reason they went to Egypt and stayed there was . . . ."

To fulfil, as in 1.22, can be "to make come true" or "so that the things would take place that the Lord by means of the prophet said would happen."

The Lord: as in 1.20, this is God.

By the prophet: see suggestions under 1.22.

The quotation **Out of Egypt have I called my son** is from Hosea 11.1, where the Septuagint reading is "out of Egypt I called his children," which is not suitable for Matthew's purpose. Matthew either made a fresh translation from the Hebrew or else quotes an early Christian form of the Hosea Septuagint text. In Hosea the equivalent of **my son** refers to Israel (see Exo 4.22); in Matthew the application is made to Jesus. The Jews frequently interpreted the coming Messianic salvation in light of the exodus experience, and early Christians often spoke in these same terms of the salvation brought by Jesus.

Translators in many languages find it necessary to use what is for them a more natural order: "I called (or, have called) my son out of Egypt." **Out of Egypt** means that the son will come from Egypt. **Called**, then, means "summoned," not "named" or "called to." Thus, "I called my son to come from (or, out of) Egypt."

2.16-18

RSV	TEV

The Killing of the Children

16 Then Herod, when he saw that he had been tricked by the wise men, was in a furious rage, and he sent and killed all the male children in Bethlehem and in all that region who were two	16 When Herod realized that the visitors from the East had tricked him, he was furious. He gave orders to kill all the boys in Bethlehem and its neighborhood who were two years old and

years old or under, according to the time which he had ascertained from the wise men. 17 Then was fulfilled what was spoken by the prophet Jeremiah:

18   "A voice was heard in Ramah,
      wailing and loud lamentation,
      Rachel weeping for her children;
      she refused to be consoled,
      because they were no more."

younger—this was done in accordance with what he had learned from the visitors about the time when the star had appeared.

17 In this way what the prophet Jeremiah had said came true:

18   "A sound is heard in Ramah,
      the sound of bitter weeping.
      Rachel is crying for her children;
      she refuses to be comforted,
      for they are dead."

SECTION HEADING: "**The Killing of the Children:**" many languages do not have a noun like "**Killing**" but must say "are killed," or "Herod kills," or "Herod has the children killed."

It may be necessary to specify that "**the Children**" were in fact male babies less than two years old: "baby boys." Also, it may in some languages be necessary to specify which particular babies were killed, by adding "in Bethlehem." Thus, "The baby boys in Bethlehem are killed" or "Herod has the baby boys in Bethlehem killed."

This brief section consists of two sentences in Greek, each of which begins with the word **Then** (verses 16,17). The first sentence (verse 16) narrates, while the second sentence (verses 17-18) interprets.

2.16 RSV	TEV
Then Herod, when he saw that he had been tricked by the wise men, was in a furious rage, and he sent and killed all the male children in Bethlehem and in all that region who were two years old or under, according to the time which he had ascertained from the wise men.	When Herod realized that the visitors from the East had tricked him, he was furious. He gave orders to kill all the boys in Bethlehem and its neighborhood who were two years old and younger—s was done in accordance with what he had learned from the visitors about the time when the star had appeared.

The single Greek sentence (as in the RSV text) has been made into three sentences in TEV (the first two are separated by a period, while the second and third are separated by a dash).

Notice that **Then** is often not translated. This is a new section, and many languages will either not have a transition or will use a phrase such as "Now . . ." or "Later . . . ."

Saw can be translated "realized," "became aware of," or "learned."

The verb translated **tricked** appears elsewhere in Matthew's Gospel only in connection with the mockery made of Jesus (20.19; 27.29,31,41 "make fun of," TEV). In the context here, it is usually translated in the sense of "deceived" or "fooled."

For **wise men**, see comments on 2.1.

TEV translates the Greek passive construction **he had been tricked by the wise men** by an active form: "**the visitors from the East had tricked him.**" TEV also simplifies the structure by placing subject and verb close to one another:

compare **"When Herod realized . . . he was furious"** of TEV with **Then Herod, when he saw . . . was in a furious rage**. Some languages will make this long Greek sentence into even more than the three of TEV. For example, "Herod realized the wise men had tricked him. Then he became furious. So he gave orders . . . ."

Was in a furious rage translates a verb ("to be angry") followed by an adverb "very." Although the noun meaning "anger" occurs a number of times in the New Testament, this is the only occurrence in the New Testament of the verb itself. Brc follows the form of the Greek ("was very angry"), while Mft and Phps translate "was furiously angry"; TEV has **"was furious."** As the translations indicate, extremely strong emotion is intended. Translators should not be misled by RSV's **rage** and picture Herod as having something like a rabid fit. Very strong anger or fury should be indicated.

It is necessary in many languages to have an object of **sent**. In those cases translators can say "He sent some soldiers" or "He ordered his soldiers to go." It is then made explicit that it was the soldiers who **killed**. "He sent his soldiers to kill" or "He sent his soldiers to Bethlehem. They killed . . . ." Of course other languages find it natural to omit the idea of "sending" and have, as in TEV, "he gave orders to kill" or "he ordered that the boy babies should be killed."

Sometimes direct discourse is necessary, as in "Herod said to his soldiers, 'Go and kill . . . ' " or " 'Go to Bethlehem and kill . . . .' "

Male children (TEV **"boys"**) translates the masculine plural form of the noun translated "child" in verse 8; see comments there.

Two years old or under implies that the astrologers had seen the star no earlier than two years previous. The phrase can be translated as "the boy babies who were less then two years old," or "those boy babies who were not more than two years old," or even, in some languages, "those boy babies who were not up to three years old."

Ascertained translates the same verb used in verse 7.

According to the time. This often requires a new sentence, as in "This was in accordance with what the wise men had told him about when they saw the star" or "He chose babies of that age because he had learned from the wise men it had been two years since they had first seen the star."

2.17-18	RSV	TEV
	17 Then was fulfilled what was spoken by the prophet Jeremiah:	17 In this way what the prophet Jeremiah had said came true:
	18 "A voice was heard in Ramah, wailing and loud lamentation, Rachel weeping for her children; she refused to be consoled, because they were no more."	18 "A sound is heard in Ramah, the sound of bitter weeping. Rachel is crying for her children; she refuses to be comforted, for they are dead."

Then was fulfilled contrasts with "to fulfill" of 1.22 and 2.15. In 2.23 the subjunctive form ("might be fulfilled") is employed. TEV translates **Then was fulfilled** as **"In this way . . . came true."** Other ways that could be used are "Then came true what . . ." or "And so what the prophet Jeremiah said would happen took place."

The quotation in verse 18 is from Jeremiah 31.15. Scholars debate whether it is a translation of the Hebrew rather than taken from the Septuagint, or whether the author cites the passage from his memory of the Septuagint text, or whether Matthew quotes a source completely different from either the Hebrew we have or the Septuagint. Scholarly opinion is clearly divided, and no dogmatic conclusion is possible. One may only surmise that Matthew felt a great deal of freedom in his choice and use of Old Testament texts, as did, in fact, most writers at that time.

What was spoken by the prophet Jeremiah is made into an active construction by TEV: "**what the prophet Jeremiah had said.**" The full meaning is "what the Lord had spoken through the prophet Jeremiah," and some translators use a sentence very much like that. Although "the Lord" is not in the text, it is clearly understood (see comments in 1.22 on "prophets"). A possible translation for this verse, then, is "And so took place what God had said through the prophet Jeremiah would happen." This may be better in many languages if the order is reversed: "God had spoken through the prophet Jeremiah about what would happen. And now it came true like this."

It may be necessary in some languages to introduce the quotation in verse 18 with "He said" or "This is what he had said."

Ramah is an Ephraimite town about eight miles north of Jerusalem (see Judges 19.13 and 1 Sam 1.1). In some languages it may be helpful to say "the town of Ramah."

Voice may be "the voice of someone," "someone crying," or as in TEV, "**sound.**"

In many languages the passive, **a voice was heard**, is better handled by an active sentence, as in "People heard a voice," or "People heard the voice of someone crying," or "There is a sound coming from Ramah."

Rachel was the mother of Joseph and Benjamin, and Ephraim was Joseph's son. The picture in Jeremiah 31.15 is that of the Ephraimites (Rachel's descendants) going into exile in Babylon.

Wailing and loud lamentation is compressed by TEV to "**the sound of bitter weeping.**" The reference is to Rachel's **weeping for her children**, as the next line makes clear. Radical restructuring may be necessary in order to make evident the relation between all the parts:

> "The sound of bitter crying is heard in the town of Ramah.
> It is Rachel, crying for her children.
>   They are dead,
>   and she refuses to be comforted."

But other structures can work, too. Some translators will be able to make clear the relation between **voice** (or, "sound") and **wailing and loud lamentation** in two lines, as there are in the text. For example, they might have:

> "People heard a voice in Ramah;
> it was someone crying bitterly."

or: "People heard the voice of someone crying in Ramah;
they heard bitter weeping there."

or: "There is a sound coming from the town of Ramah;
the sound of someone weeping bitterly."

Rachel weeping may be introduced, then, by a phrase such as "It is Rachel," or "What they hear is Rachel," or "The crying is coming from Rachel. She is weeping for her children."

She refused to be consoled: "She refuses to be comforted," "She cannot be comforted," or "There is no one who can comfort her."

Because they were no more means "**they are dead**" (TEV). GECL 1st edition and TNT also indicate explicitly that death is intended, while most translations prefer to remain ambiguous; for example, "because they were gone" (AT).

There are different ways languages mark the causal relationship seen in **because**. Some will put the phrase at the end, as in RSV and TEV, and use "because," "for," "the reason was that they are dead," or something similar. Other languages will find it more natural to put this clause first, as in our example above: "They are dead, and she refuses to be comforted" or "They are dead. That is why she refuses to be comforted."

2.19-23

The Return from Egypt

RSV   TEV

The Return from Egypt

19 But when Herod died, behold, an angel of the Lord appeared in a dream to Joseph in Egypt, saying, 20 "Rise, take the child and his mother, and go to the land of Israel, for those who sought the child's life are dead." 21 And he rose and took the child and his mother, and went to the land of Israel. 22 But when he heard that Archelaus reigned over Judea in place of his father Herod, he was afraid to go there, and being warned in a dream he withdrew to the district of Galilee. 23 And he went and dwelt in a city called Nazareth, that what was spoken by the prophets might be fulfilled, "He shall be called a Nazarene."

19 After Herod died, an angel of the Lord appeared in a dream to Joseph in Egypt 20 and said, "Get up, take the child and his mother, and go back to the land of Israel, because those who tried to kill the child are dead." 21 So Joseph got up, took the child and his mother, and went back to Israel.

22 But when Joseph heard that Archelaus had succeeded his father Herod as king of Judea, he was afraid to go there. He was given more instructions in a dream, so he went to the province of Galilee 23 and made his home in a town named Nazareth. And so what the prophets had said came true: "He will be called a Nazarene."

SECTION HEADING: "**The Return from Egypt**." It is often necessary to identify who returned, as in "Joseph, Mary, and Jesus returned from Egypt" or "Joseph returns from Egypt with Mary and Jesus."

If it is necessary to say where they returned to, translators can put "returned to the land of Israel from Egypt."

> But when Herod died, behold, an angel of the Lord appeared in a dream to Joseph in Egypt, saying,

> After Herod died, an angel of the Lord appeared in a dream to Joseph in Egypt

In Greek the structure **when Herod died** is similar to the structure "when Jesus was born" (2.1). As can be seen by the two TEV renderings ("**After Herod died**" and "Jesus was born"), it is possible to translate these structures by either dependent or independent clauses. The determinative factor is the structure that is most natural in the receptor language. Some languages will have to use two independent sentences, as in "Herod died. After that an angel of the Lord . . . ."

For **Behold, an angel of the Lord appeared in a dream**, see comments on 1.20.

2.20   RSV   TEV

> "Rise, take the child and his mother, and go to the land of Israel, for those who sought the child's life are dead."

> and said, "Get up, take the child and his mother, and go back to the land of Israel, because those who tried to kill the child are dead."

The command to return to Palestine parallels exactly the command to leave in verse 13.

Rise, take translates a participle followed by an imperative. However, the structure is the equivalent of two imperatives, and almost all translations render in it this way.

For suggestions on translating **Rise, take the child and his mother**, see comments on verse 13. Other suggestions are "Get up and go with the child and his mother to the land of Israel" or "Get up, take the child and his mother, and go with them to the land of Israel."

Land of Israel is used here and in verse 21, but nowhere else in the New Testament. Translators in some languages will not be able to use **land** but will have to make a choice between "country" or "region." Probably the former would be better.

Earlier Matthew mentions only the king as the one who is seeking the child (verse 13). But now he very strikingly introduces a plural structure: **those who sought the child's life**. However, the reference here would be to Herod and his advisors, not to the soldiers whom Herod would have sent, as noted in verse 13.

Those will have to be "those people" in many languages.

Sought the child's life may be "who wanted to kill the child" or "who were trying to kill the child."

For again indicates a causal relationship, and this may be handled in different ways. A simple "for" or "because" as in RSV or TEV is often acceptable. Other languages will use a sentence such as "I tell you this because" or "Do this because." Others will start the verse with the cause: "The people who were trying to kill the child are dead. Therefore, get up and take the child and his mother to the land of Israel."

2.21	RSV	TEV

And he rose and took the child and his mother, and went to the land of Israel.	And he rose and took the child and his mother, and went to the land of Israel.

He refers to Joseph, and so TEV makes the identification for its readers: "**Joseph got up.**"

Rose and took translates a participle (the same form mentioned in verse 20) followed by a finite verb. Most translations use two finite verbs, as RSV and TEV have done. See also comments at verse 14 for suggestions on translating **rose . . . took . . . went . . .** , and verse 20 for **land of Israel**.

2.22	RSV	TEV

But when he heard that Archelaus reigned over Judea in place of his father Herod, he was afraid to go there, and being warned in a dream he withdrew to the district of Galilee.	But when Joseph heard that Archelaus had succeeded his father Herod as king of Judea, he was afraid to go there. He was given more instructions in a dream, so he went to the province of Galilee

But when: this may be "However, when . . ." or "But he heard that Archelaus reigned . . . . Therefore he was afraid."

The pronominal subject **he** is once again identified by TEV: "**Joseph**."

Reigned over Judea in place of his father Herod is restructured by TEV to read "**succeeded his father Herod as king of Judea**." After Herod's death the land of Israel was divided into several provinces and placed under the authority of Herod's sons. **Archelaus** was given the title of king and ruled over the provinces of Judea, Samaria, and Perea from 4 B.C. to A.D. 6. He was a cruel and despotic ruler.

Reigned over may be expressed by a phrase such as "was king of Judea in place of" or "had become king of Judea after his father Herod died."

It may be necessary to specify that **Judea** was a province, as in "the region (or, territory) of Judea."

And being warned in a dream, a participial construction in Greek, is rendered "**was given more instructions in a dream**" by TEV. The agent of the passive structure **being warned** would be either the Lord or an angel of the Lord. In light of verses 13,19,20, the meaning most likely intended is "an angel of the Lord gave Joseph more instructions." **Warned** translates the same verb used in verse 12. **Being warned in a dream** can be translated by a passive in some languages, as TEV has done. Another example is "He had a dream and was told what to do." Other translators will prefer an active construction, as in the above paragraph, where "an angel" is stated explicitly. Perhaps "an angel appeared to him in a dream and told him not to go there."

Withdrew is generally translated as "went" or "moved."

2.23	RSV	TEV

RSV	TEV
And he went and dwelt in a city called Nazareth, that what was spoken by the prophets might be fulfilled, "He shall be called a Nazarene."	and made his home in a town maned Nazareth. And so what the prophets had said came true: "He will be called a Nazarene."

According to the Gospel of Matthew, Bethlehem is assumed to be the home of Joseph (see 2.1). It is only at the command of the angel that Joseph moves with his family to **Nazareth**. The climax of the story is reached by the quotation **He shall be called a Nazarene**.

Dwelt means "established as a home," "resided," or "settled." Thus, TEV has "**made his home**." Some languages can get this across with a phrase such as "went to live.

Nazareth is located about twenty-seven kilometers (seventeen miles) west of the southern end of Lake Galilee.

That carries the idea "in order to" or "so that." They settled in Nazareth in order to fulfill the words of the prophets.

What was spoken refers normally to oral speech rather than to written information, although what the prophets spoke was normally preserved in writing. There is no record in the Old Testament of this prophecy, and there is no clear explanation as to where it comes from.

Prophets is plural and can be understood to refer to the prophets in general or even to their writings, as in "what the prophets had written" or "what was written in the books of the prophets."

For suggestions on **fulfilled**, see 1.22.

The word translated **Nazarene** in Greek is somewhat of a puzzle, though Matthew obviously takes it as a fulfillment of the prophecy that Jesus moved to Nazareth. Accordingly, **Nazarene** can be translated as "a citizen (or, person) of Nazareth."

Called does not mean here "named." Some languages have to say "He will be known as a citizen of Nazareth" or "People will know (or, say) he is from Nazareth."

He in the scripture quotation refers to Jesus, not to Joseph, as the pronominal referent might suggest. In place of **he** one may translate "the Messiah." Translators who do this should refer to the comments on "Messiah" in 1.1.

Translators should render the verse as naturally as possible in their languages. Often this requires two sentences, as in the following:

> So he went to Nazareth and made his home there. In this way (or, When he did this) what the prophets had said about the Messiah came true (or, the prophets' words came true). They had said the Messiah would be known as a person from Nazareth.

Chapter 3

RSV

TEV

The Preaching of John the Baptist

1 In those days came John the Baptist, preaching in the wilderness of Judea, 2 "Repent, for the kingdom of heaven is at hand." 3 For this is he who was spoken of by the prophet Isaiah when he said,

"The voice of one crying in the wilderness:
Prepare the way of the Lord,
make his paths straight."

4 Now John wore a garment of camel's hair, and a leather girdle around his waist; and his food was locusts and wild honey. 5 Then went out to him Jerusalem and all Judea and all the region about the Jordan, 6 and they were baptized by him in the river Jordan, confessing their sins.

7 But when he saw many of the Pharisees and Sadducees coming for baptism, he said to them, "You brood of vipers! Who warned you to flee from the wrath to come? 8 Bear fruit that befits repentance, 9 and do not presume to say to yourselves, 'We have Abraham as our father'; for I tell you, God is able from these stones to raise up children to Abraham. 10 Even now the axe is laid to the root of the trees; every tree therefore that does not bear good fruit is cut down and thrown into the fire.

11 "I baptize you with water for repentance, but he who is coming after me is mightier than I, whose sandals I am not worthy to carry; he will baptize you with the Holy Spirit and with fire. 12 His winnowing fork is in his hand, and he will clear his threshing floor and gather his wheat into the granary, but the chaff he will burn with unquenchable fire."

1 At that time John the Baptist came to the desert of Judea and started preaching. 2 "Turn away from your sins," he said, "because the Kingdom of heaven is near!" 3 John was the man the prophet Isaiah was talking about when he said,

"Someone is shouting in the desert,
'Prepare a road for the Lord;
make a straight path for him to travel!' "

4 John's clothes were made of camel's hair; he wore a leather belt around his waist, and his food was locusts and wild honey. 5 People came to him from Jerusalem, from the whole province of Judea, and from all over the country near the Jordan River. 6 They confessed their sins, and he baptized them in the Jordan.

7 When John saw many Pharisees and Sadducees coming to him to be baptized, he said to them, "You snakes—who told you that you could escape from the punishment God is about to send? 8 Do those things that will show that you have turned from your sins. 9 And don't think you can escape punishment by saying that Abraham is your ancestor. I tell you that God can take these rocks and make descendants for Abraham! 10 The ax is ready to cut down the trees at the roots; every tree that does not bear good fruit will be cut down and thrown in the fire. 11 I baptize you with water to show that you have repented, but the one who will come after me will baptize you with the Holy Spirit and fire. He is much greater than I am; and I am not good enough even to carry his sandals. 12 He has his winnowing shovel with him to thresh out all the grain. He will gather his wheat into his barn, but he will burn the chaff in a fire that never goes out."

SECTION HEADING: "**The Preaching of John the Baptist**." Many languages will not normally express the action of preaching with a noun, as English does. They may say "What John the Baptist preached" or "The message John the Baptist proclaimed." Many translators will need to use a complete sentence such as "John the Baptist preaches (in the wilderness)" or "John the Baptist proclaims a message." For "**Baptist**," see comments on verse 1.

Matthew proceeds immediately from the birth narratives to the account of the preaching of John the Baptist (3.1-12) and the baptism of Jesus (3.13-17).

Verses 1-3 hint at the significance that the appearance and activity of John the Baptist held for the early Christian community. In particular, the use of the Greek historical present in these three verses underscores the continuing importance of John for the believing community to which Matthew addresses himself. John's significance is further emphasized by the observation that his coming is described as the fulfillment of the prophetic message of Isaiah 40.3.

Verses 4-6 use words similar to those of Mark (1.4-6) to describe the external appearance and the public activity of the Baptist. This section is introduced very abruptly in Greek, with the result that the immediate connection with the Isaiah quotation is almost obscured (compare Mark 1.2-3).

Finally, the content of John's repentance preaching and Messianic preaching are summarized in verses 7-12.

3.1	RSV	TEV
	In those days came John the Baptist, preaching in the wilderness of Judea,	At that time John the Baptist came to the desert of Judea and started preaching.

Matthew introduces his account of **John the Baptist** with echoes of Old Testament language. Note the following examples: (1) **In those days** (TEV "**At that time**") reflects the Septuagint text of Judges 18.1 and Daniel 10.2. Similar also is "in those many days" of Exodus 2.11. In the New Testament this phrase is found in at least the following passages: Matthew 24.19,38; Mark 1.9; 8.1; 13.17,24; Luke 2.1; 4.2; 5.35; 9.36; 23.7; 24.18; and Acts 1.15. (2) The Greek verb translated **came** (NEB "appeared"; NAB "made his appearance"; Phps "arrived"; Brc "appeared on the scene") is found frequently in the Septuagint and in the Gospel of Luke. In Matthew it appears elsewhere only in 2.1 and 3.13. (3) Finally, the term **wilderness** falls also into this category of biblical language. The full expression (**the wilderness of Judea**) appears only twice in the Old Testament (Judges 1.16 and in the superscription of Psa 63). For Matthew the significance would be as much theological as geographical.

In those days does not refer to the time Joseph returned from Egypt, described at the end of chapter 2. Rather it is an expression of an indefinite time, referring to the beginning of the ministry of Jesus, perhaps thirty years after the return. Translators may say "Some years later," "Some time later," or even "The time came when John the Baptist came . . . ."

In many languages, **came** can only be used if John the Baptist went to where the listeners or readers of the text actually were, so that "went" will be more appropriate. However, many translators will do something similar to the examples given above from NEB, NAB, or Brc, and say "appeared in the desert" or "arrived in the desert." (Of course, if translators do use "appeared," it must not seem as if John suddenly appeared like a vision, but rather that he began to make public appearances.)

The verb **came** is before the subject in RSV, but TEV has reversed this to a more normal English expression, "**John the Baptist came . . . .**"

The title **the Baptist** is also used of John in 11.11-12; 14.2,8; 16.14; 17.13; Mark 6.25; 8.28; Luke 7.20,33; 9.19. In the parallel to the present passage, Mark 1.4, and in 6.14, Mark refers to him by the descriptive participle "the baptizing one."

John the Baptist is introduced as though he were someone already known to the readers. This was true of Matthew's original readers. But many modern readers of the Gospel will not know of him, and he has not been previously mentioned in the book. Therefore, very often it is helpful to say "the man named John the Baptist appeared . . . ."

Some translators have treated **Baptist** as a proper name, and simply written it as it would be pronounced in their language. Others have tried to translate it as "the one who baptizes" or "the one they called 'the Baptizer.' " Such translations depend on how "baptize" itself is translated, and this can be a major problem. In many cultures baptism is completely unknown. Where it has been introduced by the churches, different denominations have often disagreed on method and theological implications, and have even introduced these differences into the terms they have used to translate; for example, "sprinkling," or "immersing." To avoid these problems, translators have either borrowed the Greek word "baptize" or used expressions like "putting on water," "putting on God's water," "washing," or "God's washing." Translators should always consider this problem carefully, keeping in mind the terms used by the churches in their area and the practice of the ritual itself.

Preaching (a participle in Greek) is translated "announced" by GECL and "**started preaching**" by TEV. Other languages say "announced (or, proclaimed) God's word," "proclaimed his message," or "told the people this message."

Wilderness or "**desert**" (TEV) has been difficult for translators who live in places where dry regions of sparse vegetation are simply not known. Some have said "sandy region," but that may make readers think of a seashore or a sandy river bank. It is better in these situations to emphasize the fact that the "wilderness" is a remote area where no one lives, as in "that area (of Judea) where no one lives" or "the area (in Judea) far away from where people stayed."

Some translations will put the phrase "in the wilderness" after "appeared" or "came," and others after "preaching." This does not matter as long as the sentence is structured in the most natural way in the language.

3.2	RSV	TEV
	"Repent, for the kingdom of heaven is at hand."	"Turn away from your sins," he said, "because the Kingdom of heaven is near!"

It may be necessary to start the verse with a phrase such as "This is what he was saying," "He was telling the people," or "He was preaching that . . . ." What he was saying will be either in direct speech (as in TEV and RSV) or indirect, as in "He was preaching that people should repent." It depends on what is more natural.

Repent. The root meaning of the Old Testament word for "repent" is "turn away from sin," and so the basis for TEV **"Turn away from your sins."** NAB translates "Reform your lives!" which is similar to the rendering of GECL. When translating **Repent**, it is important to realize that it does not mean simply "to be sorry about" or "to regret," but rather involves a change of both attitude (or heart) and of conduct. This is why translators have used expressions such as "Turn your back on your sinning," "Change your way of living," or "Turn away from your bad actions."

Kingdom of heaven: most biblical scholars would agree with the statement in the new Oxford Annotated Bible: "The Kingdom of heaven is Matthew's usual way of expressing the equivalent phrase, 'the Kingdom of God,' found in parallel accounts in the other Gospels." Fortunately, as far as translation is concerned, it is not important to decide on which was the original term, so long as it can be agreed that the two terms are identical in meaning. A number of CLTs have already adopted the policy of rendering both phrases in the same way. NAB in a number of places translates "the Kingdom of Heaven" as "the Reign of God," and here, at the first occurrence of the term in the New Testament, gives a note: ". . . literally, 'the Kingdom of heaven.' 'Heaven' is a conventional expression which avoids using the divine name. The term invokes God's sovereign authority over the human race. It announces that a new intervention of God is beginning in history which invites Israel to accept the prophetic manifestation of his will through the baptizer." Dutch common language translation (DUCL) sometimes translates "Kingdom of God" instead of "Kingdom of heaven," while still other translations utilize a glossary to make the identity clear: FRCL, INCL, and TEV.

It is also fairly well accepted among biblical scholars that the term "Kingdom of God," both in the Old Testament and in the New Testament, has as its primary meaning "God's kingly rule." That is, the basic emphasis is on the actual rule of God as an activity, rather than on the realm or territory over which he rules.

Although the central meaning of these two phrases is the kingly rule of God, the focus may be different in various contexts. For example, in the New Testament it is used in at least the following ways: (1) Focus on the activity of God in bringing about his rule in the world. An example of this is the present verse. Here the emphasis is on the fact that God will soon begin (or has already begun) his rule in this world. (2) Focus on the acceptance of God's rule in one's life. An illustration of this use is found in 19.23-26 (parallels Mark 10.23 and Luke 18.24), which RSV translates "it will be hard for a rich man to enter the kingdom of heaven." The meaning of this verse is "it will be hard for a rich man to submit himself to God's rule." (3) Focus on the enjoyment of the blessings or quality of life experienced under God's rule. Matthew 5.3 falls under this category. (4) Focus on the consummation of God's activity in bringing about his rule in this world. (5) Focus on the idea of the community of God's people, as in "enter the kingdom."

Too often, translators have chosen a way of translating **kingdom** which emphasizes the territory of a king. If a word can be found which means "rule," "reign," or "kingship," it will be better. Many translators have found it best to use a verb; for example, "God rules." In these cases the translation of "Kingdom of God (or, of heaven)" varies greatly as translators construct different sentences for the various contexts of the phrase. We will discuss these as we come to them throughout the Gospel.

In most areas it will not be readily seen that "heaven" represents "God" in this expression. Further, it seems odd to speak of "the rule (or, reign) of heaven" or to say "heaven rules." Therefore most translators will use "kingdom of God" or "rule of God," and so forth, as in Mark and Luke.

The kingdom of heaven is at hand may be discussed together with 4.17 (parallel Mark 1.15), since the passages are identical and so present the same exegetical and translational problems. Matthew 4.17 repeats Matthew 3.2 word for word, and Mark 1.15 is the same except that he has "kingdom of God" in place of "kingdom of heaven." The basic exegetical problem in this statement relates to the interpretation of the Greek verb **is at hand** (literally "has approached"); that is, whether it indicates that the Kingdom of God has already arrived or that it is soon to arrive. Most modern translations and commentators seem to prefer the second of these two alternatives, and it is the recommended meaning to accept (NEB "is upon you"; NJB "is close at hand"; Mft "is near"; AT "is coming"; Brc "is almost here"). RSV and NAB are ambiguous ("is at hand"), but Phps follows the first exegesis ("has arrived"). GECL evidently also accepts the exegesis that God's rule is imminent, though not yet present, and restructures the verse entirely: "God will now accomplish his work and establish his rule." Malay Common Language (MACL) has "God will soon establish his rule." In cultures where the concept of a rule connotes something evil or oppressive, one may want to translate "the time is near when God will come to save his people," since salvation, as opposed to judgment, is primary in the meaning of God's kingly rule.

Some languages can leave the sentence abstract, as in "God's reign will begin soon" or "God's rule will soon be established." Others will make "God" an active agent, as in the examples above from GECL and MACL, "God will soon establish his reign (or, rule)." Other translations say "God will soon rule" or "The time is near when God will rule."

In many languages, however, it is necessary to specify over who or what God will rule, as in "rule over the world," "rule over us," or "rule over people."

The relationship between the two things John was saying is shown by the word **for**. John tells the people that the reason they should repent is that soon God's rule will be established. Presumably, if they do not repent they will not be a part of that rule. Most translators will show this relation in a way similar to TEV or RSV, with "for" or "because." Other languages, however, will more naturally say "God's rule will soon be established. For that reason, you should repent."

3.3 RSV	TEV
For this is he who was spoken of by the prophet Isaiah when he said,	John was the man the prophet Isaiah was talking about when he said,
"The voice of one crying in the wilderness: Prepare the way of the Lord, make his paths straight."	"Someone is shouting in the desert, 'Prepare a road for the Lord; make a straight path for him to travel!' "

As may be gathered from the more literal rendering of RSV (**For this is he who**), John is not actually mentioned by name in the Greek text. TEV and GECL mention the name explicitly for stylistic reasons. Actually, most translators will find that doing this will help their readers to follow the flow of the passage better. Another way may be "It was John that the prophet Isaiah was talking about."

For does indicate that John's ministry was a fulfillment of the prophecy of Isaiah. TEV showed this relation with the expression "**John was the man . . . ,**" without using the word "for." Another way to do this may be "In fact, John was the person . . . ."

There are languages which more naturally start this verse with "Isaiah." But translators must make sure that the focus is still on John: "Isaiah the prophet had spoken about someone and said, 'Someone is shouting . . . for him to travel.' That person he spoke of was John."

For comments on **prophet**, see 1.22.

The quotation of Isaiah 40.3, which Matthew has taken over from Mark (1.2-3), differs from the quotations in chapters 2 and 3 in that the "to be fulfilled" is lacking. At this point Matthew clearly adopts the Septuagint, in which the phrase **in the wilderness** is connected with **crying** (TEV "shouting") rather than with the imperative **prepare**, as in Hebrew.

There is, however, one important distinction between the Septuagint text and the quotation in Matthew and Mark: in place of **make his** (the Messiah's) **paths straight**, the Septuagint follows the meaning of the Hebrew: "make a straight path for our God to travel." In other words, both the Hebrew and the Septuagint consider "the Lord" to refer to God, while Matthew interprets "the Lord" as referring to the expected Messiah.

TEV has translated clearly the meaning of the ambiguous expression **his paths** by "**path for him to travel.**"

It is difficult in many languages to speak of a **voice** shouting. Instead translators may say "The voice of someone" or just "Someone." Another possibility is to say "People hear the voice of someone shouting . . . ."

Crying does not mean "weeping" here, but "**shouting.**"

The same word for **wilderness** is used here as in verse 1. Translators should use the same word in both verses so that the connection between them is clear.

Many languages must introduce what the voice said, with "He (or, that person) said" or "saying," or even "He was saying."

Prepare the way means "Get a road ready," "Make a road," or even "Cut a path." Of course Isaiah is not speaking literally of a road but is actually speaking about providing the right circumstances so that the Lord can come. However, translators should keep the figure Isaiah used, if at all possible.

The way **of the Lord** is a road "for the Lord," a road "on which the Lord can travel," or "for him to travel on."

The second command, to **make his paths straight**, has essentially the same meaning as the first one, as in "Make straight paths for him" or "Prepare straight paths for him (to travel on)."

Since it is understood that this path or road is for the Lord to travel on as he comes to us, some translators say something like "to travel on to us" or "to come to his people."

> Now John wore a garment of camel's hair, and a leather girdle around his waist; and his food was locusts and wild honey.

> John's clothes were made of camel's hair; he wore a leather belt around his waist, and his food was locusts and wild honey.

The description of John in verse 4 is not part of the quotation from Isaiah. Readers in many languages can tell this by the use of the quotation marks. However, in many societies where people are not very accustomed to reading, it is still normal to have some word or phrase to indicate the end of the quotation; for example, "That is what he said." In still others a transition word such as **Now** in RSV is used to show that the quotation is finished and something new has started. The important thing is that the transition be smooth and natural in the translation.

According to Malachi 4.5 the return of Elijah is to precede the coming of the Messiah. John is identified as Elijah in Matthew 17.10-13, but in the present passage the similarity between John and Elijah exists only in the allusion to John's clothes: **a garment of camel's hair, and a leather girdle around his waist** (see 2 Kgs 1.8).

John **wore** habitually the clothes described: "John used to wear," "was wearing," or "wore all the time."

In many areas **camels** are unknown, and likewise the rough cloth made from camel's hair. Translators in such areas can say "John's clothing was made from the hair of a domestic animal (or, hair of an animal called camel)," or possibly "John's clothing was made of a rough cloth made from the hair of an animal called camel."

For **garment** sometimes a general word like "clothing" or "clothes" is available, but in other languages a specific term has to be named. In these cases translators should use a word for a tunic, or shirt, or a wrap that a man might commonly wear.

The **leather girdle** can be translated as in TEV, **"leather belt,"** but also as "belt of dried animal skin" or "a strip of dried animal skin around his waist to hold his clothing."

Food translates a noun which literally means "nourishment"; but here and elsewhere in Matthew the meaning is "food" (see 6.25; 10.10; 24.45). Just as the clothing referred to was his usual clothing, by **food** is meant his customary or habitual nourishment. "He used to eat" or "His usual food was" are ways to handle this.

The mention of **locusts** and **wild honey** does not belong to a part of the description of Elijah. **Locusts** were recognized as clean food by the Jews and are still eaten by Arabs of the Near or Middle East. There is no basis for the identification of this word as "carob," or "cakes," or "milk."

It should be noticed that Matthew's rearrangement of the Marcan order by placing the information of Mark 1.6 (Matt 3.4) before that of Mark 1.5 (Matt 3.5-6) achieves a much smoother transition. Matthew 3.4-6 and Mark 1.5-6 are without parallel in the Lukan account.

Wild honey is honey found in natural beehives, out in the fields or wilderness perhaps, as distinguished from honey from beehives kept by people. However, this distinction is simply unknown in areas where people do not keep bees, and translators can then say either "honey" or "honey found in the wilderness (or, in the forest)."

3.5	RSV	TEV

Then went out to him Jerusalem and all Judea and all the region about the Jordan,

People came to him from Jerusalem, from the whole province of Judea, and from all over the country near the Jordan River.

The verb **went out** is in the imperfect tense in Greek and suggests repeated action. In Greek the subject of the verb **went out** is **Jerusalem and all Judea and all the region about the Jordan** (that is, the region near where the Jordan River empties into the Dead Sea). What is meant, of course, is that the people of these regions went out. The use of **all** in both occurrences is a typical idiomatic expression in Hebrew; the meaning here is "many of the people from . . . ."

The requirements of the receptor language will determine whether the form **went out to him** or "**came to him**" (TEV) is better. Translators in many languages will find it natural to retain the sense of repeated action that is carried by the imperfect tense of **went**. They might have "people in Jerusalem used to go out" or "were going out." **To him** may be "to where he was." Also it is sometimes necessary to say why they were going out, as in "to hear him" or "to listen to him."

No translator wants to give the impression that it was the city of **Jerusalem** or the province of **Judea** that went to see him. It was the people from there. Whether to say "all the people," "many of the people," or just "people" will depend on what expression the language will normally have.

Since **Jerusalem** has already been mentioned several times in the Gospel, it may not be necessary to say "the city of Jerusalem," but the province in which Jerusalem was located, **Judea**, will be sufficiently unfamiliar to many readers that translators will need to say "region (or, province) of Judea."

Similarly, **Jordan** is a river, so translations often follow the example of TEV, with a phrase such as "people from all over the region near the Jordan River."

3.6	RSV	TEV

and they were baptized by him in the river Jordan, confessing their sins.

They confessed their sins, and he baptized them in the Jordan.

TEV restructures this verse chronologically, placing the act of confession before that of baptism. In Greek **baptized** translates an imperfect tense (parallel to the imperfect of **went out** in verse 5), while **confessing** translates a participle (a present participle in Greek may refer to an action preceding that of the main verb). But these represent formal features of the Greek, and the translator must decide what form is most adequate for the needs of the receptor language. GECL, among others, restructures in chronological sequence in TEV tradition. It should be noted that the gift of forgiveness came later from Jesus (see Matt 26.28); there is no connection between baptism and forgiveness as in Mark. Here the work of the Baptist relates solely to the matter of confession.

Some scholars believe that **were baptized by him** may rather have the meaning "were baptized under his supervision" or "baptized themselves under his supervision." No translations go in this direction.

Some suggest that John took over his rite of baptism from Jewish proselyte baptism; one scholar, for example, affirms without hesitation that it was taken from the Qumran community (the Essenes), but given a "far more profound meaning." For a summary discussion of the differences between the baptism of the Qumran community and that of John the Baptist, see the modern commentaries. Regardless of the source of John's baptism, the meaning that he gave to it is clear in the context. For a discussion of **baptized**, see verse 3.1. Here "they had John baptize them" or "John baptized them."

The word **confessing** is often translated as "They declared openly the wrong things they had done" or "They admitted in public (or, before God) their sins."

Whichever action, confessing or baptizing, is given first, the important thing is that the relationship between them be clear. Chronologically, the confessing preceded their being baptized. It was the people who confessed and John who baptized them. It should not sound as if John was confessing. This can be expressed as "They declared before all the sins they had done, and John baptized them in the Jordan River" or "The people were baptized by John in the Jordan River after they confessed their sins."

3.7	RSV	TEV

But when he saw many of the Pharisees and Sadducees coming for baptism, he said to them, "You brood of vipers! Who warned you to flee from the wrath to come?	**When John saw many Pharisees and Sadducees coming to him to be baptized, he said to them, "You snakes—who told you that you could escape from the punishment God is about to send?**

Verses 7-10 agree word for word with Luke 3.7-9, except for the introduction in verse 7 and a few minor changes (Matthew "fruit" for Luke "fruits" in verse 8, and Matthew "do not presume to say" for Luke "do not begin to say" of verse 9). Both Matthew and Luke reproduce in the same way what John the Baptist said, but they direct his message to two entirely different audiences. According to Luke (3.7-9), God's wrath is directed against all Israel, whereas Matthew makes a distinction within Israel: God's wrath is directed against **the Pharisees and Sadducees**. The TEV word list provides a description of these two religious groups. For Matthew both are "representative of disbelief and opposition to Jesus." And it is probably best to agree with those scholars who conclude that these two groups in Matthew's Gospel represent the collective leadership of Israel in its opposition against Jesus.

The important thing in translating **Pharisees** is to indicate to readers that they were members of a group or sect. Too often the translation makes it seem they were people from some place called "Pharisee." Thus translators can say "Many people from the group Pharisee" or "Many members of the religious group that is called Pharisee." Where the Pharisees are mentioned several times in the passage, it should not be necessary to use such a complete translation in every place. After the first occurrence it may be sufficient to say "Pharisees" or "Pharisee people" in the rest of the passage.

Similarly with **Sadducees**, "members from the group Sadducee" or "people from the religious group Sadducee" are common translations.

For both **Sadducees** and **Pharisees**, it is important to have a fuller definition in a word list.

The Greek word construction **for baptism** means "in order to be baptized" or "in order to get themselves baptized." It can be translated as "coming to him to be baptized," "coming to him so he would baptize them," or "coming to receive the baptism he was giving." These phrases make it explicit that it was John's baptism they were seeking.

You brood of vipers! John addresses his audience in words that are sharper than those of any Old Testament prophet. So sharp are his words that elsewhere in Matthew's Gospel (12.34; 23.33) only Jesus himself uses them. The employment of such a figure of speech is almost without parallel, although the group of pious Jews who withdrew to the desert did refer to the "dragon's venom and viper's poison" of unfaithful Israelites. According to the Old Testament and Israelite popular thought, the snake is the most cunning of all beasts, a demonic creature who leads people astray (Gen 3.1; Job 20.16; Psa 58.4; 140.3; Sirach 39.30).

Many translators try to translate **brood of vipers** literally as "family (or, group) of vipers." If there are no vipers in their area, they substitute some other venomous snake. However, it is better to recognize that John is using a metaphor to call the Pharisees and Sadducees clever and wicked deceivers, hypocrites who lead people astray. It is more important in the translation to have something that is insulting and vivid than to have a literal translation of **brood of vipers**. It may be enough to say "You snakes" or "You deceiving snakes." In some cases a simile can be used, as in "You are like a bunch of wicked (or, clever) snakes" or "You are as clever as snakes."

Who warned you to flee from the wrath to come? is rendered somewhat more dynamically by TEV: **"Who told you that you could escape from the punishment God is about to send?"** Both **who** and **you** are emphatic, and "the tone is one of ironical surprise," so one commentator notes, and he translates "Can it actually be the case that you have been persuaded to believe that the divine judgment is near, and stirred to endeavor to escape from it?" The notion of "**could escape**" (TEV) or "endeavor to escape" is not explicitly marked out in the Greek text, but it is clearly implicit in the overall context.

It is important in translation to realize that **Who warned you** is a rhetorical question. It is not asking for information about who it was that actually warned the Pharisees and Sadducees, or how they came to learn of the impending judgment. Further, the literal expression in English can give the impression that someone told them that they should try to escape. Rather, as we pointed out above, the phrase is actually expressing ironical surprise: "Where did you get the idea God's judgment is near? What roused you to escape it?"

Although the phrase **the wrath to come** does not mention God by name, **the wrath** refers to God's wrath. All commentators agree that this is the meaning, and

GECL has made it explicit: "the imminent judgment of God." It is important not to speak of the wrath of God and the emotion of anger as if they were the same thing. Although God is totally and constantly opposed to evil, what is indicated is not God's anger, but rather the reaction of a holy and loving God toward sin which defiles and destroys his creation. This always results in judgment. Thus the sentence can be translated "Where did you get the idea you needed to escape the punishment God will bring soon?" "What? You, too, have decided you need a way to escape God's judgment?" or "I'm surprised to see you have decided you need to escape the punishment God will carry out."

3.8 RSV TEV

Bear fruit that befits repentance, Do those things that will show that you have turned from your sins.

Bear fruit that befits repentance: "fruit" as a metaphor is typical of the Bible. Fruit simply grows naturally out of a fundamental disposition of the heart; it is not something that can be done by human plan. The translations attempt a wide variety of dynamic equivalent renderings: Phps "Go and do something to show that your hearts are really changed"; Brc "prove the sincerity of your repentance by your life and conduct"; TNT "Show by your conduct that you have truly repented"; NAB "Give some evidence that you mean to reform"; GECL "show first of all through your deeds that you really want to change!"

Whereas in verse 2 the verb "to repent" is used, here the noun **repentance** is used in the Greek construction "worthy of repentance." Both RSV (**befits repentance**) and TEV ("**that will show that you have turned from your sins**") make the shift to a verb phrase.

In addition to the examples cited above, other phrases translators may try include "Do what is required to show you have repented," "Live the life that people who have repented should live," or "Live in such a way people will know you have turned from your sins."

For comments on **repentance**, see verse 2.

3.9 RSV TEV

and do not presume to say to your-selves, 'We have Abraham as our father'; for I tell you, God is able from these stones to raise up chil-dren to Abraham.

And don't think you can escape pun-ishment by saying that Abraham is your ancestor. I tell you that God can take these rocks and make descen-dants for Abraham!

TEV has rather radically restructured this verse. First, on the basis of verse 7, **do not presume to say** has been given its full form: "**don't think you can escape punishment by saying.**" Then the direct discourse of the Greek (**We have Abraham as our father**) appears as indirect discourse in TEV. Both of these translational techniques have been adopted by GECL, though with a different result:

"You imagine that nothing can happen to you because Abraham is your ancestor. Do not fool yourselves . . . ." **Abraham** is the famous ancestor of the Jews with whom God made his covenant, and it was evidently quite common for the Jews of John's day to rest their hopes for salvation on the claim that Abraham was their ancestor. See John 8.33-41.

Translators will often find that following the example of TEV in this verse is very helpful. Other translators have "Do not give yourself false hopes by saying . . ." or "Do not think it will save you to claim . . . ."

As we pointed out, **father** here means "ancestor." For a discussion of this word, see comments on the section heading of 1.1. Some translators may also say "It is Abraham who is our ancestor" or "We are descendants even of Abraham."

The word **for** indicates a relation between the two parts of the verse. John tells the Pharisees and Sadducees they should not expect salvation simply because they are descendants of Abraham, for, John says, that does not mean a thing in God's sight. God could provide all the descendants of Abraham he needed, even making them from these stones if necessary. In some languages, to make this flow of ideas clear, translators say "Believe me" or "I tell you this because . . . ."

These stones (TEV "rocks") is an evident allusion to the stones of the Judean desert. The general interpretation is that **from these stones** means that God will use them as the material for making descendants for Abraham, as seen in TEV.

In Hebrew there is a play on words between **children** (*banim*) and **stones** (*abanim*). In the context **children** has the extended meaning of "**descendants**" (TEV). In most languages it will be well to use "descendants" so no one will think it means actual children.

As witnessed by Deuteronomy 18.15,18, the expression **raise up** is here equivalent to "cause to be born." TEV translates **raise up children to Abraham** as "**make descendants for Abraham**." Translators can say "produce descendants" or "cause descendants to be born."

The phrase **to Abraham** is not natural English, and "**for Abraham**," as in TEV, is certainly better in most languages. Other suggestions are "God can use these stones to make descendants of Abraham" and "God can make descendants of Abraham out of these stones."

3.10   RSV   TEV

Even now the axe is laid to the root of the trees; every tree therefore that does not bear good fruit is cut down and thrown into the fire.	The ax is ready to cut down the trees at the roots; every tree that does not bear good fruit will be cut down and thrown in the fire.

The theme of judgment binds together verses 10-12, and in each of these three verses the word "fire" is explicitly mentioned. Although Jeremiah 46.22 speaks of men who go into the forest to chop down trees, the figure of **the axe** that **is laid to the root of the trees** is best understood as drawn from the experience of either a gardener or a person who takes care of grapevines. The **trees** referred to here are useful trees or grapevines from which one could expect to gather **good fruit**. The background for the words of John the Baptist may be found in Ezekiel 15.1-8, where the prophet compares the people of Jerusalem to the wood of the grapevine. Once the vine has ceased bearing fruit it is useless, and there is nothing that can be done with its wood, except to burn it. John the Baptist does not speak of someone who comes to prune the vine with a knife, but of one who comes to "**cut down the trees at the roots**" (TEV), after which they will be **thrown into the fire**.

Even now can be "Already," or the meaning can be included in a phrase such as "God is ready" or "The ax is ready."

For the ax to be **laid to the root of the trees** does not make sense in many languages, and the idea that everything is prepared to cut down the trees needs to be made explicit. Further, in many languages one cannot say that the ax is ready. The person who is going to use the ax must be mentioned. Thus one can say "God has the ax ready to cut down the trees at the roots." If "ax" is difficult to translate, one can even say "God is ready to cut down . . . ."

Cut down and thrown is a passive construction, but it is God who does this. Translations can have "God will cut it down and throw it into the fire."

Every tree may be "any tree that does not . . ." or "If a tree does not . . . ."

To bear good fruit may be translated "bear fruit that is edible (or, sweet)" or "bear fruit like it should." In some cases it will be enough to say "produce fruit."

The fire is a symbol of hell, the place of punishment. It is not normally advisable to say "hell" in the translation, but many translations make "fire" definite (that is, "the fire") and not indefinite ("a fire").

<u>3.11</u> RSV	TEV
"I baptize you with water for repentance, but he who is coming after me is mightier than I, whose sandals I am not worthy to carry; he will baptize you with the Holy Spirit and with fire.	I baptize you with water to show that you have repented, but the one who will come after me will baptize you with the Holy Spirit and fire. He is much greater than I am; and I am not good enough even to carry his sandals.

Note that the present tense **I baptize you** does not mean "I am baptizing you at this moment" but rather "when (or, as) I baptize you people."

For comments on **baptize**, see 3.1.

The phrase **with water** (so most translations) may also be rendered "in water" (AT, NAB, NJB). The problem is that one normally thinks of baptizing a person "in" something, but according to the last part of this verse the one **who is coming** will baptize people "in (or, with)" the Holy Spirit. Therefore in order to make the analogy carry through, it seems best to translate in both instances as "with." Translators can say simply "with water," or they may say "I use (or, take) water when I baptize you" or "When I baptize you, I do it with water." It is important that the same construction be used for the baptism by John, with water, and for the baptism by the one to come, with the Holy Spirit and with fire.

TEV translates the Greek noun phrase **for repentance** as "**to show that you have repented**." Phps and TNT have "as a sign of your repentance"; AT "in token of your repentance"; NAB "for the sake of reform"; Brc "to make you repent"; GECL

1st edition "Because you want to change your life." If translators accept the interpretation of TEV, then they can say "as proof (or, evidence) that you have repented" or "so people will see you have repented." On the other hand, if they follow the interpretation of Brc, for example, they might say something like "so that you will repent" or "to bring about your repentance." For comments on **repentance**, see 3.2.

Translators need to make sure that the ideas are correctly combined. A sentence such as "When I baptize you, I do it with water to show that you have repented" could give the impression that John could also use other materials to baptize with to show something other than repentance. In other words, it could appear that it is the water that shows the repentance. A better sentence would be "When I baptize you to show you have repented, I use water" or "The baptism I give you to show you have repented is a baptism with water."

John speaks of **he who is coming after me**. This does not mean a disciple of John, nor someone chasing John, but rather "the man who will proclaim his message after I do" or "the man who will appear later." Another way to structure it is to say "Someone will appear later on, and he . . . ."

This person who is coming later is **mightier** than John. This does not refer to physical strength. Rather "He has more authority than I have" or "He is more important than I am."

The Jewish expectation of Jesus' day looked for "the Coming One" to be both a mighty leader (see Isa 9.1-6) and the world judge (see Dan 7.13). John does not consider himself worthy enough even to be the slave of the one who follows after him: "**I am not good enough even to carry his sandals**" (TEV). Mark (1.7) and Luke (3.16) have "to untie" in place of "carry his sandals," a variation which may reflect two translations of an Aramaic original. **Sandals** are soles, usually made of leather, fastened to the feet with strings, thongs, or straps, and used as shoes for walking.

For **not worthy**, translators can use "not important enough" or phrases such as "I don't deserve" or "I don't qualify even to be a person who can carry his sandals."

TEV has somewhat radically restructured the remainder of this verse in order to make the sequence of events and the contrast clearer for the readers. This is accomplished by bringing together the contrast between the baptism with water and the baptism with the Holy Spirit and fire, which appears as the last clause in the Greek text of this verse (compare RSV). Some few scholars rather dogmatically affirm that the phrase **with the Holy Spirit and with fire** forms a hendiadys, meaning that the reference is not to two different objects (**Holy Spirit . . . fire**), as the conjunction "and" might suggest, but rather one (**Holy Spirit**) which is modified by the other (**fire**). These scholars would then translate "with the fire of the Holy Spirit." In support of this interpretation they appeal to the evidence of the Dead Sea literature. If this structure is to be understood as a hendiadys, then **fire** must be taken in a positive sense. See, for example, the NJB footnote: "In the Old Testament fire, a purifying element more refined and efficacious than water, was already a symbol of God's supreme intervention in history and of his Spirit which comes to purify hearts."

On the other hand, the translators of TOB indicate in their footnote that, although it is possible to translate the phrase as "the Holy Spirit which purifies as fire," they prefer to see here the meaning of judgment, especially in light of verses 11-12 (see also verse 7). **Fire** is often used in Jewish apocalyptic literature to describe the final judgment, and in this context fire obviously refers to judgment in its other two occurrences (see verses 10,12). It therefore is proper to conclude that judgment is primary in this passage. Note GECL: "With the fire of judgment."

He will baptize you with the Holy Spirit and with fire. As we mentioned earlier, the construction used here should be parallel to that used in speaking of the baptizing John did: "He will use (or, take) the Holy Spirit and fire when he baptizes you" or "When he baptizes, he will do it with the Holy Spirit and with fire." For comments on **Holy Spirit**, see 1.18.

Translators will note that TEV has restructured the verse to mark clearly the comparison between the two kinds of baptisms in the verse. One can also follow the RSV order but break it up into several sentences: "When I baptize you to show you have repented, I do it using water. But there is someone coming later on, someone more important than I. I am not worthy even to carry his sandals. He will baptize you using the Holy Spirit and fire." There are many ways it can be done, but translators should always look for the order that is most natural in their language.

<hr>

3.12	RSV	TEV

RSV	TEV
His winnowing fork is in his hand, and he will clear his threshing floor and gather his wheat into the granary, but the chaff he will burn with unquenchable fire."	He has his winnowing shovel with him to thresh out all the grain. He will gather his wheat into his barn, but he will burn the chaff in a fire that never goes out."

In Greek this verse is one sentence consisting of four coordinate clauses. See RSV for a representation of the formal structure of the Greek. TEV divides the verse into two sentences and does some further restructuring as well.

The **winnowing fork** (TEV "**winnowing shovel**") was used to throw grain into the air so that the wind could blow away the **chaff**, which is the loose covering from around the grain and is lighter than the grain itself. A **winnowing fork** or "shovel" is not known in many parts of the world. Translators can say "a tool for winnowing grain" or "a tool for separating grain from chaff." To say he has the winnowing fork in his hand means he is ready to use it. Some translations say "He has his winnowing fork ready to use" or "He is ready to begin separating the grain from the chaff with his winnowing fork."

To **clear his threshing floor** probably means to clear all the chaff from the area where he threshes the grain. Thus "He will clear all the chaff from the place where he threshes (or, where he beats the grain to separate it from the chaff)." Brc has "He will clear every speck of rubbish from his threshing floor."

In areas that do not have **wheat**, "grain" can be used. Some languages do not have this generic word "grain," and use "seed" or "fruit" even for crops that have grains and need threshing.

The word **granary** can be translated as "**barn**" or "store house."

Whatever the interpretation given to **fire** in the previous verse, it is obvious that the **fire** referred to here is that of judgment: "**but he will burn the chaff in a fire that never goes out**" (TEV).

It is good to retain the metaphor of this passage, but for readers in some languages, similes are easier to comprehend since they make explicit the basis of the comparison of the metaphor. This verse is actually speaking about the judgment of God, where he will separate the good from the bad people. If necessary, then, translators can do something like this:

> He is ready to judge and separate the good people from the bad, like the farmer who is ready to separate the grain from the chaff with his winnowing fork; he will keep safe the good, like the farmer puts wheat into his granary, and just as the farmer clears his threshing floor of the chaff and burns it in a fire, he will cause the bad people to burn in a fire that never goes out.

3.13-17

RSV	TEV
	The Baptism of Jesus
13 Then Jesus came from Galilee to the Jordan to John, to be baptized by him. 14 John would have prevented him, saying, "I need to be baptized by you, and do you come to me?" 15 But Jesus answered him, "Let it be so now; for thus it is fitting for us to fulfil all righteousness." Then he consented. 16 And when Jesus was baptized, he went up immediately from the water, and behold, the heavens were opened[g] and he saw the Spirit of God descending like a dove, and alighting on him; 17 and lo, a voice from heaven, saying, "This is my beloved Son,[h] with whom I am well pleased."	13 At that time Jesus arrived from Galilee and came to John at the Jordan to be baptized by him. 14 But John tried to make him change his mind. "I ought to be baptized by you," John said, "and yet you have come to me!" 15 But Jesus answered him, "Let it be so for now. For in this way we shall do all that God requires." So John agreed. 16 As soon as Jesus was baptized, he came up out of the water. Then heaven was opened to him, and he saw the Spirit of God coming down like a dove and lighting on him. 17 Then a voice said from heaven, "This is my own dear Son, with whom I am pleased."

[g] Other ancient authorities add *to him*
[h] Or *my Son, my* (or *the*) *Beloved*

SECTION HEADING: "**The Baptism of Jesus**" can be "Jesus is baptized." There are languages that cannot use a passive construction and must instead supply the agent: "John baptizes Jesus."

This brief narrative falls into three parts: (1) introduction (verse 13), (2) the dialogue between Jesus and John the Baptist (verses 14-15), and (3) the baptism itself and the miracle connected with it (verses 16-17). Verses 13 and 16-17 are similar to Mark 1.9-11, except for the differences which will be noted in the discussion of the individual verses.

3.13 RSV TEV

Then Jesus came from Galilee to the Jordan to John, to be baptized by him.	**At that time Jesus arrived from Galilee and came to John at the Jordan to be baptized by him.**

Most scholars assume that Matthew is dependent upon Mark for this account. However, the choice of words and the phrase and clause structure differ so much from the Marcan text that there is a strong argument in favor of its being an independent oral or written tradition.

Then (TEV "**At that time**") translates one of Matthew's favorite particles; see comment at 2.7. Here a phrase such as "A short time later," "Soon afterward," or "About that time" will be acceptable.

As in 3.1, instead of **came**, many languages will have to say "went."

Galilee refers to the region or province. Some languages will need to specify this: "region of Galilee."

It may or may not be necessary to specify that **Jordan** here is the river, since that fact has already been mentioned.

Jesus went **to John**, that is, to where John was at that time.

Notice the way TEV has restructured. Whether it is better to say "to John at the Jordan" or "to the Jordan to John" will depend on the normal structure of the language of the translator.

To be baptized by him differs from the Marcan wording "and was baptized by John." Thus Matthew shows purpose and intent on the part of Jesus. This can be expressed by phrases such as "so that John would baptize him," "to have John baptize him," "to ask John to baptize him," or "because he wanted John to baptize him."

3.14 RSV TEV

John would have prevented him, saying, "I need to be baptized by you, and do you come to me?"	**But John tried to make him change his mind. "I ought to be baptized by you," John said, "and yet you have come to me!"**

Would have prevented translates one word in Greek, literally "was preventing," which is followed by the object **him**. However, in the present context the verb indicates action attempted but not achieved (technically a connotative imperfect), which may be rendered "wanted to prevent, tried to prevent" (TEV "**tried to make him change his mind**"). GECL translates "tried to dissuade him" (so also NEB, NJB); NAB "tried to refuse him with the protest"; Phps "tried to prevent him"; and Brc "tried to stop him." This could even be expressed in direct speech if necessary, as in "John said, 'You should not do this.' "

Translators can express **saying** with "by saying" or "He said."

John felt that the more important one, Jesus, should not be baptized by the lesser, himself. "It is I who should be baptized by you." "I am the one who should be asking you to baptize me," or "You should baptize me."

John then continues with a rhetorical question, **and do you come to me?** This is transformed into a statement by TEV: **"and yet you have come to me."** NJB and NAB also change the question to a statement. Although retaining the question form, TNT structures in such a way as to help its readers: "Why do you come to me?" Many translators can retain the form of a question: "Why ask me to baptize you?" or "How can you ask me to baptize you?" TEV has shown the thrust of the question by changing it into a statement. A similar example is "But you are the one asking me to do this."

3.15 RSV TEV

RSV	TEV
But Jesus answered him, "Let it be so now; for thus it is fitting for us to fulfil all righteousness." Then he consented.	But Jesus answered him, "Let it be so for now. For in this way we shall do all that God requires." So John agreed.

But Jesus answered him (so most modern translations) differs from the formal structure of the Greek, which has a participle connected with a finite verb: "but having answered, Jesus said to him." It is a common semitic expression which is not natural in many other languages.

Jesus says to John, **Let it be so now**, which means "Do as I am asking this time," "Don't object this time," or "For now, do as I am asking." In fact he agrees that John is right, but asks John to comply with his request at this occasion.

There is a significant problem that relates to the interpretation of the phrase **to fulfil all righteousness**, which TEV represents by **"do all that God requires."** In this interpretation TEV has the support of a number of modern translations (TNT, GECL 1st edition, FRCL, DUCL, NAB, NEB, Mft). Phps relates it specifically to the fulfillment of God's Law ("It is right for us to meet all the Law's demands"), while Brc is even more general: "for the right thing for us to do is to do everything a good man ought to do." One scholar affirms that the key to understanding the meaning of **righteousness** in the Gospel of Matthew is its usage in the Old Testament. There the phrase "the righteousness of God" refers to "God's acts of righteousness" by which he brings about salvation for his people. "Righteousness" in fact becomes a synonym for "salvation," and the Messiah may be referred to as "the Lord is our righteousness" (Jer 23.6; 33.16; see Isa 11.1-4). By obedience to God, his people themselves become involved in God's redemptive activity: "do righteousness, for soon my salvation (my righteousness) will come" (Isa 56.1). If this idea is followed through in the Old Testament, the conclusion must then be reached that "we can no longer make a sharp distinction between God's actions with respect to men and the human actions that spring from God's. The question is only one of emphasis. . . . In our passage the doing of God's will is certainly intended."

Other scholars concur with this opinion: for example, one of them defines the meaning of **to fulfil all righteousness** as "to leave nothing undone that had been revealed as the righteous will of God." Another scholar points out that the concept of "righteousness" grows out of the Old Testament notion of God's faithfulness to the covenant that he made with Israel. It is also used of the obedience that is demanded by God of the people who accept this covenant relation with him. By this act of baptism, Jesus at once identifies himself with the whole people of God and at the same time does what God demands of him.

In an important study of the term **righteousness**, it is concluded that **righteousness** is a peculiarity of Matthew's linguistic usage (seven times in Matthew, but elsewhere in the Synoptic Gospels only in Luke 1.75). The scholar who made the study states: "It is a case of a completely uniform use: it denotes the conduct of a man which is in agreement with God's will, which is well pleasing to him and right, rightness of life before God." Further support is offered by another scholar who believes that righteousness "must be seen as the whole purpose of God for his people, and not . . . as a moral quality only." He therefore takes the phrase **to fulfil all righteousness** to mean "the fulfillment not only of the demands of God upon his people, but also the fulfillment of those Scriptures in which those demands are set out—law, prophets, writings. In any event, the baptism administered by John was a direct response to the will of God, and so the Messiah must submit to it."

The above scholars have been referred to in some detail for the sake of pointing out that there is wide agreement regarding the meaning of **righteousness** in the Gospel of Matthew. The basic notion is that of doing the will of God. It is in no way a legalistic term, but describes the natural and inevitable response to God by his people. In the present context Jesus interprets baptism at the hands of John the Baptist as a means by which both he and John must react to God's will and grace.

Thus in Matthew it is fitting to render righteousness generally with a term such as "doing what God requires" or "doing God's will." The actual expression will vary according to the structure of the individual sentence in which it occurs.

In a large number of languages, translators have found that the translation of **fulfil all righteousness** in TEV has been a useful model. "In this way we will be doing what God requires" or ". . . what God wants done," or "will be fulfilling God's righteous plan."

In the short sentence **Then he consented**, the Greek text does not explicitly mention John by name; TEV (and other translations) explicitly identify him on the basis of the requirements of the respective receptor languages. This sentence can be translated "So he agreed" or "So John did what Jesus asked."

3.16	RSV	TEV

And when Jesus was baptized, he went up immediately from the water, and behold, the heavens were opened[g] and he saw the Spirit of God descending like a dove, and alighting on him;

As soon as Jesus was baptized, he came up out of the water. Then heaven was opened to him, and he saw the Spirit of God coming down like a dove and lighting on him.

[g] Other ancient authorities add *to him*

Immediately translates the adverb rendered "**as soon as**" by TEV. This is a favorite transitional marker in the Gospel of Mark where it is used forty-one times; Matthew uses it much less frequently (13.20,21; 14.27; 21.2,3; 26.74).

From the RSV text one can see that there are two transitions, the one translated **and when**, and the other translated **immediately**. These can be handled in several ways. Some translations will find a solution modeled on TEV very helpful: "As soon as John baptized Jesus . . ." or "Right after being baptized, Jesus . . . ." In other languages it will not be possible to say "As soon as Jesus was baptized" without having first said that he was baptized. Translations in these languages will use something like "Jesus was baptized and straight away (or, afterward) came up out of the water." There are also translations that will have something very near RSV: "After Jesus was baptized, he immediately came out of the water."

To describe Jesus' actions in leaving the water, Matthew uses a different preposition than does Mark (1.10); he employs one that would normally mean **from** (NJB "up from"), whereas the preposition which Mark uses normally means "out of." In light of the fact of the many differing church traditions, it seems best to translate in such a way as not necessarily to imply immersion, but to allow for it. Matthew is certainly not as much interested in the form as he is in the meaning which he indicates quite clearly. Therefore most translations will say simply something like "came out of the water."

And behold is the same form rendered "and lo" in verse 17; see comment at 1.20.

The heavens were opened and he saw, except for the shift from "I saw," repeats almost exactly the words of Ezekiel 1.1; while in place of **the Spirit of God descending**, Ezekiel 2.2 has "and a spirit came on me." In this context the pronoun **he** most likely refers to Jesus, the person just mentioned, and so translators should retain the information that it was Jesus who saw the heavens opened. Whether John saw it is not mentioned in this Gospel.

In place of the verb "to open," Mark uses the more graphic "to split" (1.10); however, translations generally have something like "to open" for both verbs. The use of the passive **were opened** may imply divine agency ("God opened"), while "to him" (see below) may mean either that Jesus alone witnessed the event or else that it was for his benefit alone.

In very many languages the plural form **heavens** makes little sense, and translators use the singular, **"heaven"** (TEV).

The strangeness in many languages of speaking of heaven being "open" is compounded by the passive **were opened**, so that many translators find it better to say "God opened heaven."

As the RSV footnote indicates, the phrase **"to him"** (TEV) is doubtful in the text. TC-GNT recognizes the strength of the manuscript evidence in favor of its inclusion, but also realizes that copyists may have omitted the phrase as unnecessary. Therefore the UBS Greek text encloses the words (one word in Greek) within square brackets to indicate that the presence of these words in the text is disputed. The phrase **"to him,"** if translated, will be expressed as "for him to see" or simply "for him," depending on which interpretation is chosen.

The Spirit of God is mentioned elsewhere in Matthew's Gospel only in 12.28. For comments on the translations of the **Spirit**, see 1.18.

One commentator, on the basis of Luke's interpretation (Luke 3.22: "in bodily form like a dove"), states that the phrase **like a dove** "must mean like a dove in appearance." However, on the basis of the Greek text, it is more appropriate to connect the phrase **like a dove** with the participle **descending**. In this case the meaning is "descending in the way that a dove descends." Regardless of the Lukan interpretation, we are here translating the Gospel of Matthew. Matthew's concern is different from that of Luke, and it is extremely doubtful if anyone would ever have thought to interpret his words in this manner, had it not been for the Lukan parallel. The phrase can be translated "Coming down in the way a dove does" or "Coming down on him the way a dove flies down."

Alighting can be "landed on him," "sat on him," or "rested on him." Thus the sentence can be "He saw God's Spirit coming down and landing on him in a manner a dove would."

3.17   RSV   TEV

and lo, a voice from heaven, saying,   Then a voice said from heaven, "This
"This is my beloved Son,*h* with whom   is my own dear Son, with whom I am
I am well pleased."   pleased."

h Or *my Son, my* (or *the*) *Beloved*

For a translation of **and lo**, see 1.20.

As with the opening of the heavens and with the descent of the Spirit (verse 16), so the **voice from heaven** also has its counterpart in Ezekiel 1.28–2.1.

It may be possible to say "A voice was heard coming from heaven" or "A voice in heaven spoke." If it is not possible to use a passive construction like this, translators can say "He (or, they) heard a voice speaking in heaven." If at all possible it is best to avoid saying specifically that it was God speaking.

The words of the heavenly voice agree with those spoken at the transfiguration (17.5). The quotation may be described as composite, with reflections of Psalm 2.7 ("You are my son, today I have begotten you") and Isaiah 42.1 ("Behold my servant, whom I uphold, my chosen in whom my soul delights; I have put my Spirit upon him . . .").

According to Mark (1.11), the voice is addressed directly to Jesus ("You are"), while in Matthew it is a public proclamation (**This is**). **This** refers to Jesus. It may be necessary to say "This man" or "This one."

Beloved (TEV "**dear**") is understood by a number of translations as an attributive adjective, modifying **Son** (so RSV, TEV, NAB, Phps, TNT, Lu). The punctuation selected for the UBS Greek New Testament supports this interpretation. However, a contrary view is held by some scholars who maintain that it is a separate title, in apposition. This would then become an independent title equivalent to the Messiah: "my Son, my (or, the) Beloved" (RSV footnote). Among the translations, this interpretation is adopted by Mft, NEB, Brc, AT. Both interpretations have the support of sound scholarship. But if this phrase is given the meaning of a separate title, equivalent to that of Messiah, then some improvement must be made over what has traditionally been done in English translations. The reader will not usually see in the phrase "the Beloved" a Messianic title unless a footnote is used. If one feels strongly that this is the meaning, then that meaning should be made clear in the translation itself.

Translators who accept the first interpretation will generally have something like "My Son whom I love." If the second interpretation is followed, then some formula should be used that would show that **Beloved** is a title, as in "My Son, the one called (or, known as) the Beloved."

With whom I am well pleased or "on whom my favour rests" (NEB) is representative of the way that most translations have rendered the last clause of verse 17. However, the clause may also be understood as a reference to the divine election of the Messiah: "I have chosen him" (GECL). **With whom I am well pleased** can be translated "I am very pleased with him," "who pleases me very much," or "He gives me much pleasure." The declaration from heaven may have to be expressed by more than one sentence. "This is my Son. I love him, and he gives me much happiness."

Chapter 4

4.1-11

RSV	TEV
	The Temptation of Jesus

1 Then Jesus was led up by the Spirit into the wilderness to be tempted by the devil. 2 And he fasted forty days and forty nights, and afterward he was hungry. 3 And the tempter came and said to him, "If you are the Son of God, command these stones to become loaves of bread." 4 But he answered, "It is written,

'Man shall not live by bread alone,

but by every word that proceeds from the mouth of God.' "

5 Then the devil took him to the holy city, and set him on the pinnacle of the temple, 6 and said to him, "If you are the Son of God, throw yourself down; for it is written,

'He will give his angels charge of you,'

and

'On their hands they will bear you up,

lest you strike your foot against a stone.' "

7 Jesus said to him, "Again it is written, 'You shall not tempt the Lord your God.' " 8 Again, the devil took him to a very high mountain, and showed him all the kingdoms of the world and the glory of them; 9 and he said to him, "All these I will give you, if you will fall down and worship me." 10 Then Jesus said to him, "Begone, Satan! for it is written,

'You shall worship the Lord your God

and him only shall you serve.' "

11 Then the devil left him, and behold, angels came and ministered to him.

1 Then the Spirit led Jesus into the desert to be tempted by the Devil. 2 After spending forty days and nights without food, Jesus was hungry. 3 Then the Devil came to him and said, "If you are God's Son, order these stones to turn into bread."

4 But Jesus answered, "The scripture says, 'Man cannot live on bread alone, but needs every word that God speaks.' "

5 Then the Devil took Jesus to Jerusalem, the Holy City, set him on the highest point of the Temple, 6 and said to him, "If you are God's Son, throw yourself down, for the scripture says,

'God will give orders to his angels about you;

they will hold you up with their hands,

so that not even your feet will be hurt on the stones.' "

7 Jesus answered, "But the scripture also says, 'Do not put the Lord your God to the test.' "

8 Then the Devil took Jesus to a very high mountain and showed him all the kingdoms of the world in all their greatness. 9 "All this I will give you," the Devil said, "if you kneel down and worship me."

10 Then Jesus answered, "Go away, Satan! The scripture says, 'Worship the Lord your God and serve only him!' "

11 Then the Devil left Jesus; and angels came and helped him.

SECTION HEADING: "**The Temptation of Jesus**." This often needs to be expressed as a short sentence, as in "Jesus is tempted by the Devil" or "The Devil tries to make Jesus do wrong." As we point out below (4.1), the word translated here as "tempted" can be translated as "tested." The section heading will then be "The Devil puts Jesus to the test" or "The testing of Jesus."

The first part of this chapter divides easily into five sections: the three temptation accounts (verses 3-4; 5-7; 8-10), which are held together by a narrative introduction (verses 1-2) and a conclusion (verse 11).

It should be noticed that the shorter temptation account of Mark (1.12-13) is quite different in its outlook than the accounts of Matthew (4.1-11) and Luke (4.1-13). According to Mark, the angels took care of Jesus' needs throughout the entire period, and there is no suggestion of fasting. Matthew contains essentially the same material as Luke, except that the order of temptations differs. In translation each of the three accounts should be allowed to make its own unique emphasis, and the order of the temptations should be allowed to stand, without an attempt to harmonize one Gospel with another. See further at 4.8.

4.1   RSV   TEV

Then Jesus was led up by the Spirit into the wilderness to be tempted by the devil.

Then the Spirit led Jesus into the desert to be tempted by the Devil.

Then indicates that the events described here occurred immediately after the baptism described in chapter 3. Translators can use "Next" or "After that."

Then Jesus was led up by the Spirit is transformed into an active construction by TEV: **"Then the Spirit led Jesus."** Mark (1.12) uses an active form and a stronger verb: "the Spirit made him go." It is characteristic of Matthew that he changes Mark's active voice into a passive (see 9.25; 14.11; 16.26; 18.8; 19.13; 24.22 [twice]; 26.57; 27.38; and 28.6); however, this stylistic feature of Matthew's Gospel must not be carried over automatically into translation. Instead the translator must choose in each instance the form that is most satisfactory for his own language (whether active or passive), rather than following the form of either Matthew or Mark.

The root meaning of the verb used by Matthew is "to lead up" (see RSV, TNT, Phps). However, most translations do not render the verb literally, even though from the Jordan River valley one would have to go "up" to get into the Jordan wilderness.

The word translated **was led up** is not as strong as the one used in Mark ("was made to go"), but it is nevertheless important to avoid a word that means simply that the Spirit "went before him" or "showed him the way." Translators should use "was taken" or "was conducted," or if the active form is used, "took" or "conducted."

GECL explicitly identifies **the Spirit** as the "Spirit of God." In fact, there are many languages where it will be necessary to do the same thing, or perhaps to use "Holy Spirit." Otherwise, in cultures where everyone is believed to have a spirit in him, it could appear that it was Jesus' own spirit that led him, or that he went entirely at his own inclination.

Translators should use the same word for **wilderness** here that they did in 3.1.

Matthew sees divine purpose involved in Jesus' going to the wilderness, as is indicated by the structure **to be tempted** (see comment at 3.13). Although **to be tempted** is the rendering represented by most translations, the context seems better satisfied by "to be put to the test" (GECL, TNT). In the same way that God put his son Israel to the test during the days of Moses, so now his son Jesus is put to the test in the wilderness. However, in keeping with later Jewish thought, it is the Devil, rather than God, who now puts Jesus' loyalty to the test.

When translating **to be tempted**, it is first necessary to find a solution for "tempted." As we pointed out, "put to the test" is probably closer to the meaning in this context. Brc has "to undergo the ordeal of temptation." Some translations have "prove" or "test to see how strong he was." Others have used "to be tried" (but in the sense of testing, not in a juridical sense of being on trial). There are translators who have followed the more traditional understanding of "tempted" and said "so the Devil could try to make him do wrong."

The construction shows purpose. He was led into the wilderness "in order to be tested" or "so that he could be tested." Often an active sentence is better than a passive one: "so that the Devil could put him to the test" or "so that there the Devil would test him."

The devil is the translation of the Greek word that means "the accuser, opponent." This is one of the titles for "Satan"—which is just one of his names. As part of the same exercise that translators go through to find a good way to translate "Holy Spirit," a word is usually discovered that can be used for "spirits," supernatural beings that have the power to act in the world in various ways. Sometimes these are seen by people as inherently evil, so that the word can stand alone to translate "evil spirits," "demons," and "unclean spirits." In other cultures, these spirits are thought to do both bad and good, and the adjective "evil" or "bad" must be used with the noun in translation. Often there will be a name for one evil spirit that is the source of evil or the source of power for the other evil spirits, and this name can then be used for "Devil." Otherwise, the word "chief" or "head" is used with the word chosen for "evil spirits," so that "Devil" is "chief (or, head) evil spirit." If possible, translators should then use this title in places where the text has "Devil," and reserve "Satan" for the places where that proper name is used.

4.2	RSV		TEV

And he fasted forty days and forty nights, and afterward he was hungry.

After spending forty days and nights without food, Jesus was hungry.

Jesus spends forty days in the wilderness, as Moses spent forty days on Mount Sinai, where he received the Law.

And is a transition leading on from verse 1. Translators might use "After" or "Then," or perhaps no transition will be needed at all.

Jesus **fasted**. "To fast" means to voluntarily go without food. It is sometimes done as a religious duty. The custom is known in many parts of the world and poses no translation problem, but where it is not known, the voluntary aspect of it should be included in the translation so that it does not appear Jesus did not eat simply because there was no food. Brc has that "he had deliberately gone without food." "He refrained from eating" would be another possibility.

In some languages it is more natural to say simply "forty days" than **forty days and forty nights**. Other languages would say "forty full days" or "forty days and nights." The impression must not be given that he fasted only in the daytime (and ate at night).

Afterward can be "after that time," "at the end of the forty days and nights," or "after he had fasted for forty days and nights, he became hungry."

4.2

He was hungry translates a Greek aorist tense which may well be translated "He got hungry" or "and so he was hungry." Brc has "he was attacked by pangs of hunger."

4.3 RSV TEV

RSV	TEV
And the tempter came and said to him, "If you are the Son of God, command these stones to become loaves of bread."	Then the Devil came to him and said, "If you are God's Son, order these stones to turn into bread."

The tempter (so most translations) is changed by TEV to **"the Devil"** for the sake of its intended readers, since the same being is first referred to as "the Devil" in verse 1. That he comes "to tempt" is clear from verse 1, and so TEV uses the same title here as in verse 1, so that the readers will not think a different person is involved. For **"Devil"** see verse 1. If **tempter** is used, then translators can say "the One who tempts people" or "the One who tries to get people to do wrong." Also possible is "the Devil came to tempt him."

As in other cases of **came**, some languages have to say "went." In addition, the destination may be necessary, as in "went to him" or "came to where he was."

In the Old Testament the term **Son of God** may be used of angels or of divine beings (Gen 6.2; Job 38.7), of the Israelite nation (Hos 11.1), or of the chosen king (Psa 2.7). The Jews rarely used Son of God as a Messianic title. But when they did, the primary reference was to "the moral relationship of love and filial obedience which should exist between a father and his son." In the present passage the title calls attention to Jesus' unique relation to God, as well as to his divine powers. See also 5.9 and discussion.

The Devil is probably not wondering whether or not Jesus is God's Son. He assumes he is. The word **If** here is better translated "Since you are God's Son," "In that you are God's Son," or "You are God's Son, and therefore . . . ." However, it is also possible to understand him to be saying "If you are God's Son, prove it by . . . ."

Command these stones to become loaves of bread represents the temptation for Jesus "to misconstrue divine sonship as the power to do miracles." But it also recalls the wilderness experience of Israel. It is the temptation to make bread from the stones of the wilderness in a similar way to which God miraculously provided manna and water for the Israelites during their wilderness journey. It is also closely related to the events narrated in John 6, when the people wanted to make Jesus the Messianic King, because he had miraculously fed the crowds.

Luke 4.3 has the singular "this stone." The use of the plural **stones** is characteristic of Matthew's style. For example, he frequently uses "crowds" in place of "the crowd" of Mark. Compare also the following passages with their Marcan parallels: 8.26 ("winds" for "wind"); 13.11 ("secrets" for "secret"); and 26.15 (Matthew uses the Greek plural for "silver," while Mark uses the singular). **These stones** refers to the stones lying about where Jesus and the Devil were: "these stones here" or "some of these stones lying here."

The Devil suggests Jesus command the stones **to become loaves of bread**. In some languages direct speech may be necessary: "Say to these stones 'Turn into bread (or, Become loaves of bread).' "

But he answered, "It is written, 'Man shall not live by bread alone, but by every word that pro- ceeds from the mouth of God.' "	But Jesus answered, "The scripture says, 'Man cannot live on bread alone, but needs every word that God speaks.' "

But he answered: see comment at 3.15.

For many readers, making "**Jesus**" explicit as TEV has done will prove helpful. Otherwise "he" might be understood to refer to the Devil.

Some languages have to specify whom he answered: "answered the Devil" or "answered him."

It is written refers to scripture, and so TEV has "**The scripture says**," and GECL translates "In the Holy Scripture it stands." Most translations need to make it clear that **it is written** introduces a quote from scripture. They can say "In God's book it says" or "In God's writing it says." Translators should be careful not to use the word "Bible" or any expression which would be understood to mean "the Bible," that is, both the Old and the New Testaments, since the New Testament had not yet been written. They can try "In the holy book of us Jews, it says . . ." or "In our holy book . . . ."

The quotation which follows is from Deuteronomy 8.3 in the language of the Septuagint. Most translations render the quotation rather literally, but compare Brc ("It takes more than bread to keep a man alive; man's life depends on every word that God speaks") and NEB ("Man cannot live on bread alone; he lives on every word that God utters"). In the context **man** means "people," "humanity," and it is interesting to note how Jesus identifies with humanity in this quotation. For Jesus to be Son of God does not deny his humanity, but it does mean "that he can hear and obey God totally, leaving everything up to him."

For **man**, many translations will say "people" or "human beings," or whatever expression refers to mankind and not just human males.

Bread is here used in a general sense, in reference to the basic food of the Israelites. It is generally translated as "food" so that readers do not think specifically of bread when they read the passage. However, since in verse 3 the reference is to bread, some translators will retain that even here.

As seen by the examples above, **live** really means more than physical existence here. "Man's life does not depend only on food" or "Man's existence does not depend only on having food." Rather, for man to have real life, he must have **every word that proceeds from the mouth of God**, that is, "what God speaks" or "what God commands."

Above we cited several ways this quote has been translated, including those of Brc and NEB. Other ways translators may try are "Man's existence does not depend only on food, but on what God has spoken," "For man to have real life, he needs more than food; he needs also the words that God speaks," or "In order to really live, man needs every word from God. Food alone is not enough to sustain him."

4.5	RSV	TEV

Then the devil took him to the holy city, and set him on the pinnacle of the temple,	**Then the Devil took Jesus to Jerusalem, the Holy City, set him on the highest point of the Temple,**

Then: "Next" and "After that" are possible translations.

Throughout verses 5-10 Matthew uses a number of the so called "historical presents," which is a vivid way of narrating past events. See comment on "appeared" at 2.13.

Took could give the impression that the Devil used physical force to take Jesus to the holy city. Translators should make sure they do not give this impression. They can use instead words such as "led," "went with," or "made him go."

Whether translations have **him** or "Jesus" depends on what would be most natural in those languages.

The Greek text of this verse reads **the holy city**, which TEV identifies as **"Jerusalem, the Holy City,"** assuming that some readers of TEV may not know what city is intended. Most translations render merely "the Holy City," while GECL 1st edition simply has "Jerusalem." In the Lukan parallel (4.9) only "Jerusalem" is used. For Jerusalem as the Holy City see Matthew 27.53; Revelation 11.2; 21.2,10; 22.19. If translators render **the holy city** literally as in the text, it is a real possibility that many of their readers will not realize that Jerusalem is the city being referred to. For this reason they should consider either "Jerusalem" or **"Jerusalem, the Holy City"** (as in TEV).

Set him could give the impression the Devil carried Jesus to the pinnacle and set him down there. A better translation is "had him stand there" or "caused him to stand there."

The precise meaning of the word translated **pinnacle** (TEV "highest point") is in dispute. It literally means "little wing," and the only other time it is used in the New Testament is in the Lukan parallel (4.9). The word may possibly mean "little tower" or "parapet," and at least one scholar tentatively identifies it with "an eminence on the royal cloister on the south side of the temple enclosure, which consisted of four rows of Corinthian columns." Most translations have **pinnacle**, and a few others have "parapet" (NJB, NEB, NAB); Brc has "the highest spire." In the following verse Psalm 91.11-12 is quoted, and one commentator notes that in the Septuagint of Psalm 91.4 there appears the word "wings," which sounds very similar to the word used in this account. It is therefore quite possible that the word in Psalm 91.4 has influenced the usage here, especially since this psalm was used in the Temple worship and occasionally linked with Israel's wilderness wandering. Whatever exact part of the temple is being referred to by **pinnacle** or "parapet," it is clear that it is a very high place. Translators can say "the highest place," "a very high place," or "the very top."

When translators look for a way to translate **temple**, they need to consider "synagogue" and "church" in its modern usage, to be sure the three terms do not overlap too much. Of course, in the New Testament, "church" was not a building at all, but referred to the community of believers. "Synagogue" is often translated as "a meeting house" or "a prayer house," and "Temple" as "house of God." If this term coincides with the term people use for a modern church, then in order to keep "Temple" distinct, translators sometimes say "House of God of the Jews" or "Jewish House of God." Another way is to emphasize the Temple's function as the place where sacrifices were offered. This is done with a phrase such as "House of sacrifice," "House of sacrifice of the Jews," or "House of sacrifice to God."

The Temple was actually a complex of buildings and courtyards, so "place" is sometimes better than "house" or "building."

TEV regularly uses upper-case for the first letter of "**Temple**" when it refers to the Temple in Jerusalem, to keep the reference distinct from other temples. Translators should do whatever is appropriate in their own language.

It is worth noting that many translators find that an excellent way to show the relationship between "priest" and "Temple" is to translate the one as "sacrificer" and the other as "place of sacrifice."

4.6 RSV TEV

and said to him, "If you are the Son of God, throw yourself down; for it is written,	and said to him, "If you are God's Son, throw yourself down, for the scripture says,
'He will give his angels charge of you,'	'God will give orders to his angels about you;
and	they will hold you up with their hands,
'On their hands they will bear you up,	so that not even your feet will be hurt on the stones.' "
lest you strike your foot against a stone.' "	

The narration continues from verse 5, so that **and said to him** is part of the same sentence. However, many translators begin a new sentence at this point.

The use of **If** in the clause **If you are the Son of God** is like that in verse 3: "Since you are God's Son" or "Seeing that you are God's Son," as well as "**If you are God's Son.**"

Throw yourself down means "Jump down" or "Fling yourself," or possibly "Let yourself fall." In some languages it may be necessary to add "to the ground" or "to the bottom."

The relation shown by **for** is usually indicated by a similar word in the translation; for example, "because." However, there are languages where it is better to make more explicit the connection between what the Devil suggests Jesus should do and the scriptural justification for it. For example, translations may have "You can do that because of what it says in the scripture. It says . . . ."

For the expression **it is written**, see comments on verse 4.

The quotation from Psalm 91.11-12 closely follows the Septuagint, except that here the second line of verse 11 ("to guard you in all your ways") is omitted, since it has no relevance for the context. Quite possibly this psalm was chosen because verse 11 tells how God appointed his angels to protect the faithful believer, and verse 13 tells how the believer will triumph over wild animals.

He: in the quotation from the psalm, both TEV and GECL specifically identify the subject **He** as "**God**."

The phrase **give his angels charge of you** can be "God will have his angels be responsible for you" or "God will tell his angels to take care of you."

On their hands they will bear you up expresses the idea that the angels would actually hold Jesus on his way down, as in "They will hold you (in their hands) on your way down" or "They will hold you safe as you fall."

They will do that **lest you strike your foot against a stone**, that is, "so that you won't be hurt at all, you won't even hurt your foot on the stones," or simply "so you won't even hurt your foot on a stone." TEV does only slight restructuring: "**so that not even your feet will be hurt on the stones**." Although the text mentions the foot, here the foot probably represents the whole body, and the idea is that he will escape all injury. But translators should try to retain the image of the foot, so that this quotation will be close to an eventual translation of the psalm.

As we pointed out above, this quotation is from Psalm 91.11-12, but part of verse 11 has been left out. For this reason, RSV has treated it as two quotations, separated by **and**. Translations that follow this lead may even introduce the second part of the citation with "It is also written" or "And it also says." Other translations, among them TEV, feel that it is better to show this as one quotation. These translations drop the **and** altogether, with a transition such as "so that." For example, "God will tell his angels to take care of you so that they will hold you in their hands . . . ."

4.7 RSV TEV

Jesus said to him, "Again it is written, 'You shall not tempt the Lord your God.' "

Jesus answered, "But the scripture also says, 'Do not put the Lord your God to the test.' "

Again it is written is similar in form to the structure in verse 4; TEV has "**But the scripture also says**." Other possibilities are "In another place the scripture says" or "Another passage of scripture says."

You shall not tempt the Lord your God comes from the Septuagint of Deuteronomy 6.16.

The **You** in the quotation does not refer to the Devil but to the people of Israel, to whom this statement was originally made. The translator should take care that the reader will not be confused about this. Translators may have "You people," "None of you," or the impersonal "One."

Tempt translates a compound form of the verb made from the same root as the one used in verse 1; either may mean "put to the test" or "tempt," depending upon the context. Elsewhere in the New Testament this compound form of the verb appears only in Luke 4.12; 10.25; and 1 Corinthians 10.9, where it is used in parallel with the verb of 4.1. The Deuteronomy passage refers to the time when the Israelites put God to the test at Massah (see Exo 17.1-7). They were thirsty and demanded that God work a miracle, but here Jesus refuses to put God to the test by demanding a miracle of him. The sense of **tempt** that people first think of is "to try to get someone to do wrong," an idea that would certainly not fit in this context. Translators will do better to follow TEV, "**Don't put the Lord your God to the test**," or to use an expression such as "Don't try to force God to prove himself," "Don't try to test God," or, as in Brc, "You must not try to see how far you can go with the Lord your God."

It is not possible here to give a complete discussion of how to translate **Lord**. Translators look for a term used for someone to whom others owe allegiance. This is sometimes the same term as "chief" or "elder brother." In some languages it is "the owner of the people" or even "our owner." (Translators can discuss this with their translation consultant.)

It is used here with **your God**. The "your" in the quotation meant the God the people of Israel worshiped. Therefore "you" should not refer to the Devil. But translations can say "the Lord, the God of Israel" or "the Lord who is God." It can also be in the third person, as in "No one must put the Lord his God to the test."

4.8	RSV	TEV

Again, the devil took him to a very high mountain, and showed him all the kingdoms of the world and the glory of them;	**Then the Devil took Jesus to a very high mountain and showed him all the kingdoms of the world in all their greatness.**

As noted in the introduction to this section, the sequence of the second and third temptations differs in Matthew and Luke. Luke's arrangement avoids the double change of scene that is found in Matthew: desert to Jerusalem, Jerusalem to a high mountain.

Again (TEV "**Then**") translates the same adverb used in verse 7; there it was equivalent to "also," while the meaning here is "next in sequence." A literal rendering may lead to the faulty conclusion that this is the second time that the Devil had taken Jesus to a very high mountain: "Once again, the devil took him to a very high mountain" (NEB). A number of translations have attempted to avoid this erroneous impression; for example: "Next, taking him to a very high mountain" (NJB). Translators can also use "After that." In some languages it may not be necessary to use any transition word at all.

Instead of **took . . . to a very high mountain**, Luke (4.5) has simply "took . . . up." But a number of scholars are convinced that Matthew intends a parallel between this experience and that of Moses, when he was taken up to a high mountain to see "all the land" (Deut 34.1-4). Matthew places several other important events of Jesus' ministry on a mountain top: the sermon (5.1), the transfiguration (17.1), and the ascension (28.16).

For a translation of **took**, see comments on verse 5.

If translators are working in areas where mountains are unknown, they usually say "where the land was very high" or "to where the land was high so a person could see a great distance." Of course, no mountain is high enough so that someone could see all over the world from that spot. But translators should retain this exaggerated style in any case.

Kingdoms here means "countries," "nations," or "lands," not just areas ruled over by kings.

And all their glory, a Hebraism, is rendered "**in all their greatness**" by TEV; GECL has "in their greatness and beauty"; NEB "in their glory"; NAB "in their magnificence." Translations can also use "all their powers" or "all their wealth." They can also make this a separate sentence: "He showed him how great and beautiful they were."

4.9   RSV   TEV

and he said to him, "All these I will   "All this I will give you," the Devil
give you, if you will fall down and   said, "if you kneel down and worship
worship me."   me."

In the clause **and he said to him**, the pronoun **he** refers to the Devil (see TEV). Many translations will find it better for their readers, too, if they say "The Devil said to him."

All these, emphatic in the Greek text, may be translated collectively as in TEV ("**All this**"); Mft has "all that," and Phps "everything there." Since the plural form "all these" is purely stylistic, having no theological significance, one should then choose the structure which best suits the receptor language. In the Lukan parallel (4.6) a different construction is used: "all this authority and all their glory." Other ways to express this may be "all these countries" or "all you can see."

The phrase **All these** is given emphasis by its placement before the subject. The Devil is claiming he controls and can give to Jesus all the countries on earth. Many translations will not be able to use this RSV order, but they should nevertheless try to retain the emphasis that is there. Sentences such as "What you see, I will give it all to you" or "I will give to you all these things here" may carry the correct emphasis in some languages. Translators can also say "You can have all this that you see."

The meaning of **fall down** is not to fall accidentally, but rather to "bow down low to the ground," or "prostrate yourself," or "kneel down" for worship or to show great respect. See comments on 2.11.

For comments on **worship**, see 2.11. Here what the devil is asking is that Jesus "acknowledge me as your master (or, God)" or "respect me in the way you do God."

4.10   RSV   TEV

Then Jesus said to him, "Begone,   Then Jesus answered, "Go
Satan! for it is written,   away, Satan! The scripture says,
    'You shall worship the Lord   'Worship the Lord your God and
    your God   serve only him!' "

> and him only shall you
> serve.' "

Begone (TEV "**Go away**") is the same verb used in 16.23, where it is followed by the pronoun construction "from me." A few ancient manuscripts include the words here, a translational device that may be necessary in some languages. In both instances the command is given to persons (here the Devil, later Peter) who attempt to lead Jesus in a path that would avoid suffering. Translators should try to find an expression for **Begone** that is some kind of sharp retort or rebuke, as in "Leave!" or "Leave me alone!" "Get away from me" may be acceptable, although slang should be avoided.

Whereas the word "Devil" is of Greek origin, the word **Satan** is of Hebrew origin, but the reference is to the same being. Originally he was conceived of by the Jews as an almost neutral being, with the responsibility of pointing out to God the failures of his people. However, by New Testament times he was described as a totally evil being in complete opposition to God. As we pointed out in verse 1, **Satan** is used as a proper noun and should be written in the way it would be pronounced in the language of the translation.

Again, as in verses 4 and 7, we see the formula **it is written**, as Jesus once more quotes from scriptures in replying to the Devil. Translations should have the same formula here as in those verses. **It is written** (TEV "**The scripture says**") is a reference to Deuteronomy 6.13. In the Septuagint the word **only** is omitted, and the verb **worship** appears as "fear" in the major Septuagint tradition (the word "worship" is a favorite in Matthew: 2.2,8,11; 4.9; 8.2; 9.18; 14.33; 15.25; 18.26; 28.9).

Translators must not mistake **you shall worship** for a simple future tense. It is an imperative, as is clearly seen in TEV. As with the second person "your" in verse 7, **you** meant Israel in the quotation from Deuteronomy. If "you" in the translation will make readers think the command was addressed to Satan, then it can be changed to an impersonal "one should worship" or "a person should worship."

For comments on **worship**, see 2.11. Here it can be translated as "to acknowledge as divine," "to pray to," "to respect greatly," or "to accept as Lord."

The idea that Israel was to worship only the Lord is emphasized by putting **him only** before the verb. This same emphasis can be done in several ways: "Worship the Lord your God. He is the only one you should serve" or "Worship the Lord your God; serve no one but him."

Serve translates a verb which may be used in the technical sense of "the carrying out of religious duties, especially of a cultic nature." However, in the present context **worship** and **serve** are used with the same meaning, the second verb forming a parallel to the first.

4.11	RSV	TEV

Then the devil left him, and behold, angels came and ministered to him.

Then the Devil left Jesus; and angels came and helped him.

To avoid ambiguity in the phrase **left him**, TEV and GECL identify **him** as "**Jesus**."

Left means "went away from him." The translators must not take it to mean that he deposited Jesus somewhere.

For comments on **and behold**, see 1.20. "And then it happened that . . ." or "and then."

For comments on **angels**, see 1.20. In keeping with the promise of protection in Psalm 91.11-14, **angels came and ministered to him**. GECL 1st edition identifies these angels as "the angels of God." According to Matthew, angels come to help Jesus only at the end of the period of forty days, whereas Mark describes them as helping him throughout the entire period of the temptation (Mark 1.13).

The verb **ministered** (TEV "**helped**"; GECL 1st edition "served") is used elsewhere in the Gospel at 8.15; 20.28 (twice); 25.44; 27.55. For **ministered**, translators usually use a phrase such as "took care of him," "helped him," "took care of his needs," or "gave him what he needed."

4.12-17

RSV	TEV
	Jesus Begins His Work in Galilee
12 Now when he heard that John had been arrested, he withdrew into Galilee; 13 and leaving Nazareth he went and dwelt in Capernaum by the sea, in the territory of Zebulun and Naphtali, 14 that what was spoken by the prophet Isaiah might be fulfilled:	12 When Jesus heard that John had been put in prison, he went away to Galilee. 13 He did not stay in Nazareth, but went to live in Capernaum, a town by Lake Galilee, in the territory of Zebulun and Naphtali. 14 This was done to make come true what the prophet Isaiah had said,
15 "The land of Zebulun and the land of Naphtali, toward the sea, across the Jordan, Galilee of the Gentiles—	15 "Land of Zebulun and land of Naphtali, on the road to the sea, on the other side of the Jordan, Galilee, land of the Gentiles!
16 the people who sat in darkness have seen a great light, and for those who sat in the region and shadow of death light has dawned."	16 The people who live in darkness will see a great light. On those who live in the dark land of death the light will shine."
17 From that time Jesus began to preach, saying, "Repent, for the kingdom of heaven is at hand."	17 From that time Jesus began to preach his message: "Turn away from your sins, because the Kingdom of heaven is near!"

SECTION HEADING: "**Jesus Begins His Work in Galilee**." "**Work**" here refers to the ministry or mission of Jesus. Perhaps translators can say "Jesus begins his ministry in Galilee," "Jesus goes to Galilee to begin his ministry," or "Jesus goes to Galilee and begins preaching his message."

4.12   RSV   TEV

Now when he heard that John had been arrested, he withdrew into Galilee;

When Jesus heard that John had been put in prison, he went away to Galilee.

Throughout this section only pronouns are used of Jesus, thus suggesting a close connection in the Greek text between it and the story of the temptation. Mark (1.14-15) too begins his account of Jesus' ministry immediately following the temptation, but he does not make specific reference to Capernaum as the place where Jesus settled (Matt 4.13). However, Matthew is concerned to show that Jesus' activities are the fulfillment of God's purpose, and that his ministry takes place among the "heathen" of Galilee, not in Jerusalem and Judea, and so he identifies the place where Jesus went to live.

Now when shows that the text is moving on to a new episode but, as we said, one that follows closely after the temptation story. At the same time the phrase indicates that the readers were already familiar with the fact of John's arrest. Translators can do several things to introduce this passage: "Shortly after, Jesus heard that John had been put in prison," "John had been arrested. When Jesus heard of it, he . . . ," "At that time, John was arrested. When people told Jesus about it . . . ."

He heard may need to be expressed in some languages as "When people told Jesus."

John is John the Baptist, and there are translators who have found it helpful to say that.

Had been arrested (TEV "**had been put in prison**") translates a verb which has as its first meaning "to be handed over (to police or court)." King James Version (KJV) translates "was cast into prison," and Brc "had been committed to prison." Most translations apparently prefer the less specific rendering "had been arrested." It is the same verb used of the betrayal of Jesus by Judas (26.15), and it is also used of the arrest of believers (see 10.17,19,21; 24.9,10). **Had been arrested** often needs to be made into an active sentence: "The authorities put John in prison" or "King Herod sent soldiers to arrest John."

Withdrew (so also NEB, NAB) is the same verb translated "departed" (TEV "returned") in 2.12. But "withdrew" may have negative connotations; TEV has "**went away**," and GECL "returned." Translations can also put "he went" or "he traveled."

This is the second mention of **Galilee** in the Gospel (see 2.22). To avoid confusion with Lake Galilee, many translations put "the province (or, region) of Galilee."

4.13 RSV	TEV
and leaving Nazareth he went and dwelt in Capernaum by the sea, in the territory of Zebulun and Naphtali,	He did not stay in Nazareth, but went to live in Capernaum, a town by Lake Galilee, in the territory of Zebulun and Naphtali.

Nazareth is spelled "Nazara" in the Greek text of this verse, as opposed to the usual spelling "Nazareth" (2.23; 21.11). It is obvious that the two variant spellings point to the same place, and most all translations follow the common spelling **Nazareth**. After leaving Nazareth, Capernaum evidently becomes Jesus' permanent home (see Mark 2.1).

Dwelt (TEV "**live in**") is rendered "settled in (or, at)" by several translations (NEB, NJB, TNT), while Brc has "made his home in." The verb is used extensively in the New Testament, with the basic meaning "make one's home in." Elsewhere Matthew uses it in 2.23; 12.45; 23.21.

Capernaum by the sea. In the quotation from Isaiah, which follows in verses 15-16, the original meaning was probably the Mediterranean Sea. But in the context of Matthew's Gospel the meaning is clearly Lake Galilee, and TEV has made this information explicit for its readers. Also, since this is the first time Capernaum is mentioned in the Gospel, TEV defines it fully as "**a town**."

The town of Capernaum is on the northern edge of Lake Galilee just to the west of where the Jordan River empties into it. The territory of Naphtali is immediately west of Lake Galilee, extending up north as far as the city of Dan. South and west of the territory of Naphtali is the territory of Zebulun. These were the territories where the two Israelite tribes by these names settled during the days of Joshua. In New Testament times both of these territories were in the geographical region of Galilee.

Nazareth and **Capernaum** are both towns. The context may make this clear, but some will find that it will help their readers if they say "the town of Nazareth" and "the town of Capernaum."

Most translations will find it useful to follow the lead of TEV in translating **by the sea**: "This town was on the shore of Lake Galilee" or "the town of Capernaum which is beside Lake Galilee." If readers of the translation live far from any lake or sea, then the translation may have "the big water" or something similar for **sea**.

The construction **and leaving . . . dwelt** poses a problem in languages where it is impossible to say he left a place if the information is not given that he had gone there. In such languages, translations have sometimes had "He went to Nazareth, then left there and went to live in Capernaum." However, it is more likely that the verse reflects the fact that up till this time, Jesus' home had been Nazareth, where his family lived, and he moved now to establish his home in Capernaum. A sentence such as in TEV would indicate this. Another way to do it is "He moved his home from Nazareth to Capernaum and lived there."

Zebulun and Naphtali can be treated as the names of regions, as in the phrase "in the territories of Zebulun and Naphtali" or, as some translations have it, "in the region of the tribes of Zebulun and Naphtali."

4.14	RSV	TEV
	that what was spoken by the prophet Isaiah might be fulfilled:	This was done to make come true what the prophet Isaiah had said,

In most languages translators will start a new sentence here as TEV does. This will render the passage more readable for many readers.

Spoken by the prophet Isaiah, may need to be expanded to "what God said through the prophet Isaiah."

Might be fulfilled is similar in form to the quotation formula used in 1.22. The words of the quotation do not come from the Septuagint but are rather a free rendering of portions of Isaiah 9.1-2. See commentaries for details. Scriptural support for this move is not supplied by either Mark (1.14-15) or Luke (4.14-15).

Translators are referred to the comments at 1.22. Here they can follow TEV or say "He did this so that the thing the prophet Isaiah said would actually take place," or "Jesus went to live in Capernaum so that the thing would take place as the prophet Isaiah had said it would," or "Jesus went to live in Capernaum to make come true what the prophet Isaiah had said about that."

4.15-16	RSV	TEV
15	"The land of Zebulun and the land of Naphtali, toward the sea, across the Jordan, Galilee of the Gentiles—	15 "Land of Zebulun and land of Naphtali, on the road to the sea, on the other side of the Jordan, Galilee, land of the Gentiles!
16	the people who sat in darkness have seen a great light, and for those who sat in the region and shadow of death light has dawned."	16 The people who live in darkness will see a great light. On those who live in the dark land of death the light will shine."

Zebulun and **Naphtali** are placed in apposition with **Galilee**, and they are located **toward the sea** (TEV "**on the road to the sea**"), **across the Jordan**. This last phrase (**across the Jordan**) normally refers to the east bank of the Jordan River, seen by someone standing on the west bank; here, however, the reference is to the western side, where the territories of Zebulun and Naphtali are located.

The land of Zebulun and the land of Naphtali, as in verse 13, may be translated as "the regions of," "the territories of," or "the territory of the tribes of Zebulun and Naphtali."

These areas are **toward the sea**. Translators may have to specify which sea. If so, they should say "toward the sea of Galilee" or "on the way to the sea of Galilee."

For **across the Jordan**, translators often put "across the Jordan River" or "on the other side of the Jordan River," or they can say "on the west side of the Jordan River."

Galilee of the Gentiles is translated "**Galilee, land of the Gentiles**" by TEV. The noun **Galilee** comes from the Hebrew, which means "circle" or "district." In New Testament times "Galilee of the Gentiles" meant "the district of the non-Jews." Galilee was on the edge of Israelite territory. **Galilee of the Gentiles** can be expressed as "Galilee, where the non-Jews live" or "Galilee, the territory where the non-Jews stay." Note that "non-Jews" is the usual translation of "Gentiles." There were also Jews living there—it was not an area exclusively for Gentiles. It may be good to say "where there are non-Jews living" or "where non-Jews also live."

All of this verse is talking about the same place. The territories of Zebulun and Naphtali are the same area as the territory of Galilee where the non-Jews live. In some languages, to avoid giving the impression that they are different territories, translators have "territories of the tribes of Zebulun and Naphtali, which are on the way to the sea of Galilee, on the other side of the Jordan River, that territory of Galilee where there are non-Jews."

A more difficult problem for many translators is that it is often impossible to address territories as if they were people. Translators can say "You who live in the territories of Zebulun and Naphtali . . . ." But it may be necessary to use indirect speech: "The prophet spoke to the people who live in the territories of Zebulun and Naphtali, on the way to the sea of Galilee, on the other side of the River Jordan, that territory where the non-Jews live. He said, 'The people who sat in darkness . . . .' "

The people (verse 16) are the Jews. Verse 15 refers to Jesus' ministry to the non-Jews, whereas verse 16 indicates that he brings light to his own people who live in darkness.

Light, which signifies salvation, is now applied by Matthew to Jesus. Among the Jews both concepts (**light** and **dawned**) would have held a saving significance.

Some translators have wanted to say "you people who sat in darkness . . . ." However, since the people of verse 16 are the Jews, then it should say "The people who . . . ." **Sat** means "lived" or "were located."

Darkness does not refer to physical darkness like night, but rather to spiritual and moral darkness. Not all cultures use or understand this figure of speech, and translators say "moral darkness," "darkness of sin," or "The people who lived like they were in darkness, they couldn't see the right way to live."

Light, it then follows, is the salvation God brings to his people. Again, for languages where the lightness and darkness figures of speech are not known, translators will say "have seen the light of God's salvation," "the light God gives," or "God has shown them a new life which is like a light to them."

To live (or sit) in **the region and shadow of death** refers to the condition of people who are spiritually dead. To live apart from God is like having no life at all: "For those who were living without having real life" or "For those people whose lives didn't have the life God gives."

As we pointed out, **light** and **dawn** would both refer to the salvation God gives: "God's salvation has come to them like the light of dawn," "God has brought them light," "God's light has risen in them."

4.17   RSV   TEV

From that time Jesus began to preach, saying, "Repent, for the kingdom of heaven is at hand."

From that time Jesus began to preach his message: "Turn away from your sins, because the Kingdom of heaven is near!"

Almost all translations begin a new paragraph with this verse, as does the UBS Greek text. However, because of the absence of section headings in many translations, it is often difficult to determine whether this verse is understood as the conclusion to the previous section or as the beginning of a new section. NAB, NJB, GECL, and TEV clearly consider it the conclusion to the previous section, and this decision finds support among the commentators.

But others see here the beginning of a new section in the Gospel; one commentator, for example, states that "it marks the beginning of a new stage in his narrative, the public preaching of Jesus." In still another commentary this is designated a new section in the Gospel ("The Master and His Work," 4.17-9.34), which is then subdivided into two parts: (1) The Teaching of the Lord (4.17-7.27), and (2) The Healing Deeds of the Lord (8.1-9.34). Yet another scholar, who would begin a new section here, brings it to a conclusion at 11.30. He entitles the entire section: "The Messiah, His Message, Ministry, and Disciples." Within this larger unit he believes that 4.17-25 functions as a prologue, while the other divisions are Message (5.1-7.29), Ministry (8.1-9.38), and Disciples (10.1-11.30).

Obviously no final decision is possible; all of these alternatives have scholarly support, and one must make a choice. Unless one feels strongly convinced to the contrary, it may be wise to follow the decision represented by the UBS Greek text.

From that time translates a Greek phrase which appears also in 16.21 and 26.16. The phrase does not mean from the time of Isaiah's words, but from the time Jesus began his work in Galilee (verse 12). Some translations say "From the time Jesus went there" or "From the time Jesus began to preach there, he was saying."

In the Greek sentence structure the name **Jesus** is in focus. It was John the Baptist who had been preaching. Now that Jesus had been baptized and tested, John had been arrested, and Jesus had located himself in the place he wanted to work, it is he who took up preaching. Translators can indicate this emphasis with a phrase such as "From that time, it was Jesus who began to preach" or "From that time, Jesus himself started preaching."

Began to preach, saying is represented in TEV by "**began to preach his message.**" **Preach** is the same verb used to describe the activity of John the Baptist (3.1). Elsewhere in the Gospel of Matthew it appears in 4.23; 9.35; 10.7,27; 11.1; 24.14; and 26.13. **Preach** can be "proclaimed (or, announced) this message." See comments on 3.1.

The message of Jesus in this verse is word for word the same as that of John the Baptist (3.1). Translators should therefore refer to the comments on 3.1 and 3.2 for discussions of **repent** and **the kingdom of heaven is at hand**.

4.18-22

RSV | TEV

Jesus Calls Four Fishermen

18 As he walked by the Sea of Galilee, he saw two brothers, Simon who is called Peter and Andrew his brother, casting a net into the sea; for they were fishermen. 19 And he said to them, "Follow me, and I will make you fishers of men." 20 Immediately they left their nets and followed him. 21 And going on from there he saw two other brothers, James the son of Zebedee and John his brother, in the boat with Zebedee their father, mending their nets, and he called them. 22 Immediately they left the boat and their father, and followed him.

18 As Jesus walked along the shore of Lake Galilee, he saw two brothers who were fishermen, Simon (called Peter) and his brother Andrew, catching fish in the lake with a net. 19 Jesus said to them, "Come with me, and I will teach you to catch men." 20 At once they left their nets and went with him.

21 He went on and saw two other brothers, James and John, the sons of Zebedee. They were in their boat with their father Zebedee, getting their nets ready. Jesus called them, 22 and at once they left the boat and their father, and went with him.

SECTION HEADING: "**Jesus Calls Four Fishermen.**" This can be translated "Jesus invites (or, commands) four fishermen to serve him (or, to be his disciples)." "**Fishermen**" is discussed at verse 18 below.

4.18	RSV	TEV

RSV	TEV
As he walked by the Sea of Galilee, he saw two brothers, Simon who is called Peter and Andrew his brother, casting a net into the sea; for they were fishermen.	As Jesus walked along the shore of Lake Galilee, he saw two brothers who were fishermen, Simon (called Peter) and his brother Andrew, catching fish in the lake with a net.

Translators need to consider restructuring this verse, since languages present information about characters or participants in narratives in different ways. Translators therefore are required to choose the order of presenting this information that would be the most natural in their languages.

Matthew begins this verse with a participle (**As he walked**) in which the name Jesus is not explicitly mentioned. But since this introduces a new section, it is helpful to mention the subject (Jesus) by name, as translations such as TEV, NEB, GECL, and Brc have done.

By (so NEB, NJB), a preposition in Greek, is rendered "**along the shore of**" by TEV. It can also be translated "near," "along," or "beside."

Walked may be "was walking" in some translations. Whatever is natural is what the translation should have.

Sea or "**Lake**" is sometimes difficult in areas that do not have lakes and which are too far inland for the people to know the ocean, either. Translations in these cases use "big water," "wide river," or something similar. This lake is about 20 kilometers long by 13 kilometers wide.

In some languages **he saw two brothers** could mean they were his brothers, that is, the brothers of Jesus himself, certainly an erroneous impression. Secondly, there are only two men whom Jesus sees here. But if translators do not restructure the information as their languages require, it may seem that there are four people: the two brothers, and Simon and Andrew.

Simon was a common Greek name; it is found in Sirach 50.1, in Josephus, and in the New Testament. The Hebrew form of the name is "Shimeon."

Matthew includes the information **called Peter**, which is not found in the Marcan parallel (1.16). According to Mark (3.16), this was the name Jesus later gave to Simon, but Matthew probably uses it from the beginning of his Gospel because it was the name by which his readers knew Simon. Translators can say "Simon, who was also called Peter," or "Simon, whose other name was Peter."

Andrew is a Greek name and not uncommon. As early as 169 B.C. it appears as the name of a Jew on an inscription in Olympus.

Many languages do not have a word for **brother**, but have one word for "younger brother" and another for "elder brother." We can guess that Peter was the elder since he was named first, but this cannot be proved. If a decision must be made, however, then Andrew should be called "his younger brother."

Casting a net into the sea is represented in TEV by "**catching fish in the lake with a net.**" The **net** referred to was probably a circular net with weights and a draw rope around its edge.

It is important in many areas to indicate that they were **casting a net** in order to catch fish. Translations can have "they were fishing by throwing a net into the lake (or, water)" or "they were throwing a net into the lake to catch fish."

Note that both of them were fishing, not just Andrew, as some translations have made it appear.

Fishermen here indicates that this was their profession, their regular way of making a living. The word some languages have will indicate this, but others will have to say "for that was what they did for their living (or, as their occupation)."

For they were fishermen is restructured as a relative clause by TEV ("**who were fishermen**") and placed immediately following **Peter and Andrew his brother**. Other possibilities of restructuring also exist; for example, ". . . he saw two fishermen catching fish in the lake with a net. They were brothers. The older one was Simon (called Peter) and the younger was Andrew." Another example is ". . . he saw two men. One was Simon, whose other name is Peter, and the other was his brother Andrew. They were fishermen, and were throwing their nets into the lake to catch fish."

4.19	RSV	TEV
	And he said to them, "Follow me, and I will make you fishers of men."	Jesus said to them, "Come with me, and I will teach you to catch men."

And he said to them. Once again Jesus is not mentioned by name in the Greek text, but TEV and other translations do so at the beginning of this verse for the sake of clarity.

Follow me (so most modern English translations) is translated "**Come with me**" by TEV, GECL 1st edition, and FRCL. The call is a call to discipleship. The Jewish rabbis had disciples who went with them, observing their actions and listening to their words in all possible circumstances. This now becomes the responsibility of Jesus' disciples to him.

Some translations make the meaning of **Follow me** completely explicit with "Come be my disciples." It is important not to give the impression that Jesus is suggesting they simply walk behind him, which is one of the meanings of "follow."

A number of translations have attempted a dynamic equivalent of **I will make you fishers of men**. For example, AT and Mft render "I will make you fish for men"; Brc "I will make you fishermen who catch men"; and Phps "I will teach you to catch men." One problem in English is that the construction of **fishers of men** is an extremely awkward one. The idea of "catching men" usually had negative connotations in rabbinic and Greek literature, as it does in Jeremiah 16.16, but Jesus changes it to the positive concept of bringing men to salvation. **Men**, of course, refers to both men and women, and so "people" may be a better equivalent.

In different languages the literal sense of "fisher" is one who catches, traps, or even kills fish. When used with "men" as the object, it can seem that Jesus wants Simon and Andrew to catch, trap, or kill men. Very often, therefore, translators use a simile to escape the dilemma, as in "I will teach you to bring people to salvation (or, to follow me) in the same way you have been catching (or killing, or trapping) fish," or "just as you now catch fish, I will teach you how to catch people's hearts so they follow me."

4.20 RSV TEV

Immediately they left their nets and followed him. **At once they left their nets and went with him.**

The adverb **Immediately** is in focus here as it is in verse 22. It represents a form of the adverb which is favored by Matthew, who uses it twelve times (see 8.3; 13.5; 14.22,31; 20.34; 24.29; 25.16; 26.49,74; 27.48), as compared to six times by Luke, three times by John, and none by Mark. It should be translated "At once," "Right away," or "Without delay."

They left their nets, that is, "they left their nets right there," "they abandoned their nets," or "they quit working with their nets."

The Greek expression translated **followed** is different from the verb used in verse 19 but has the same meaning in this context. As used in the New Testament, it frequently has the extended meaning of "follow as a disciple." A good example of this shift may be observed in John 1.37-38, where the literal meaning of "follow" is intended. But in verses 40 and 43 of that same chapter the extended sense of "be a disciple" comes into focus.

Followed here may well be translated "they became his disciples (or, followers)" or "**they . . . went with him,**" as in TEV.

4.21 RSV TEV

And going on from there he saw two other brothers, James the son of Zebedee and John his brother, in the boat with Zebedee their father, mending their nets, and he called them. **He went on and saw two other brothers, James and John, the sons of Zebedee. They were in their boat with their father Zebedee, getting their nets ready. Jesus called them,**

The Greek participial construction **and going on from there** is translated as a finite verb by TEV: "**He went.**" It may also be translated "He went on" or "As they proceeded from there."

Two other brothers, James the son of Zebedee and John his brother is restructured somewhat more naturally for English speakers by TEV: "**two other brothers, James and John, the sons of Zebedee.**" TEV also has attempted to make the verse more easily understood by breaking it up into shorter sentences, as compared with the single sentence of RSV.

Since James is mentioned first, he may have been the older brother and John the younger; however, this is not certain. Some translators may have to say "two men, same father same mother."

Many translations that have followed the RSV order too closely have given some incorrect impressions to readers. For example, **two other brothers** means another set of men who were brothers to each other, not, as some have translated, brothers to Simon and Andrew. Some translations make it seem that John is Zebedee's brother, with "his" or **his brother** referring to Zebedee instead of to James.

Another error has been with translations that make it seem Jesus saw five people, not three. This happens when it is not made clear that the two brothers are James and John. Again, as in verse 18, translators need to structure the verse according to the normal way their language would present information. Some examples are "he saw two other men named James and John. They were also brothers, and their father was Zebedee. They were in their boat with their father . . . ," "he saw two other men who were brothers. Their names were James and John, and their father's name was Zebedee," or "he saw two of the sons of a man named Zebedee. The names of these brothers were James and John."

The Greek verb translated **mending** may have the specific meaning of "repair" (see Phps, NJB). But it may also have a more general meaning of "**getting . . . ready**" (TEV); AT has "putting their nets in order"; Brc "servicing their nets"; NEB "overhauling their nets."

It must be made clear that when Jesus **called** them, he "called them to follow him" or "said to them, 'Come with me.' " He only called James and John, not Zebedee.

4.22   RSV   TEV

Immediately they left the boat and their father, and followed him.

and at once they left the boat and their father, and went with him.

In this verse, as in verse 21, Matthew connects the adverb **Immediately** with the fact that they left. However, in the Marcan parallel "immediately" is not connected with their leaving but with Jesus' call: "and immediately he called them" (Mark 1.20). Care should be taken not to follow the example of the Living Bible (LB), which forces the Marcan text to agree with Matthew: "He called them too, and immediately they left their father Zebedee in the boat . . . ." Here, as elsewhere, the translator should never force one Gospel to agree with another.

As in verse 20, **Immediately** will be translated as "Right away," "At once," or "Without delay."

For **left**, see also verse 20. "They left the boat and their father there," or "they abandoned the boat and left their father to go with Jesus (or, to become Jesus' disciples)." (See verse 20 for other comments on **followed**.)

4.23-25

RSV   TEV

Jesus Teaches, Preaches, and Heals

23 And he went about all Galilee, teaching in their synagogues and preaching the gospel of

23 Jesus went all over Galilee, teaching in the synagogues, preaching the Good News about

the kingdom and healing every disease and every infirmity among the people. 24 So his fame spread throughout all Syria, and they brought him all the sick, those afflicted with various diseases and pains, demoniacs, epileptics, and paralytics, and he healed them. 25 And great crowds followed him from Galilee and the Decapolis and Jerusalem and Judea and from beyond the Jordan.

the Kingdom, and healing people who had all kinds of disease and sickness. 24 The news about him spread through the whole country of Syria, so that people brought to him all those who were sick, suffering from all kinds of diseases and disorders: people with demons, and epileptics, and paralytics—and Jesus healed them all. 25 Large crowds followed him from Galilee and the Ten Towns, from Jerusalem, Judea, and the land on the other side of the Jordan.

SECTION HEADING: "**Jesus Teaches, Preaches, and Heals.**" For a discussion of "**Teaches,**" "**Preaches,**" and "**Heals,**" see below under verse 23. Often languages require that there be objects with these verbs, as in "Jesus teaches people (about God), proclaims his message, and heals people."

4.23   RSV   TEV

And he went about all Galilee, teaching in their synagogues and preaching the gospel of the kingdom and healing every disease and every infirmity among the people.

Jesus went all over Galilee, teaching in the synagogues, preaching the Good News about the Kingdom, and healing people who had all kinds of disease and sickness.

And may not be natural at the beginning of a new section. Some translations, for example TEV and Brc, do not have any transition word. Others have an expression such as "At that time."

Also, since it is a new section, it will often be better to say "**Jesus**" instead of **he**.

Went about occurs in the New Testament only here and 9.35; 23.15; Mark 6.6; Acts 13.11; 1 Corinthians 9.5. It is emphatic in the Greek text. The sphere of this activity is defined as **all Galilee**. Matthew thereby affirms that Jesus is the fulfillment of Isaiah 9.1-2 and so is the eschatological messenger of good news.

TEV has made this point clear by saying that Jesus went "**all over Galilee.**" It can be translated "he traveled (or, went) throughout the territory of Galilee" or "everywhere in Galilee."

Teaching in their synagogues and preaching the gospel of the kingdom and healing every disease and every infirmity among the people is repeated word for word in 9.35. Therefore several scholars conclude that these two verses summarize the contents of chapters 5–9. If this conclusion is valid, then chapters 5–7 may be said to tell of the Messiah's teaching ministry and chapters 8–9 of his healing ministry. One commentator characterizes the entire section 4.23–9.34 as "the work of Jesus Christ in word and deed."

The two verbs **teaching** and **preaching** appear together in Matthew's Gospel elsewhere only in 9.35 and 11.1. It has already been noted that 9.35 is parallel to the present passage; 11.1 is also similar in that it too is a summary of Jesus' activity. The verb "teach" is used elsewhere in 5.2,19 (twice); 7.29; 9.35; 11.1; 13.54; 15.9; 21.23; 22.16; 26.55; 28.15,20; "preach" is found in 3.1; 4.17; 9.35; 10.7,27; 11.1; 24.14; 26.13.

Some scholars attempt to differentiate between "teaching" and "preaching" on the grounds that teaching relates primarily to the polemical dialogues that took place between Jesus and the religious leaders in the synagogues, while preaching is essentially the proclamation of the Good News. But such a distinction is difficult to maintain, since the Sermon on the Mount is introduced by the form "and he began to teach them" (5.2, TEV). A valid distinction may, however, be found at the level of form rather than content. Whether teaching or preaching, Jesus is the promised herald of good news, which he proclaims both in synagogues and along the roadside. Yet the form of this message may be different in the synagogue than at other places.

As we said above concerning the section heading, it may not be possible to say **teaching** without specifying whom he taught, as in "teaching the people."

It is important to avoid a word for "teaching" that would convey a narrow sense of teaching in a classroom. Many translations have to give some indication of what he was teaching about by using sentences such as "teaching people about God" or "teaching people about the rule of God."

Synagogues were places of public worship and of teaching; any Jewish man capable of teaching was permitted to do so in the synagogue. Notice how Matthew separates between his Jewish readers and the Jews of the synagogues: **their synagogues**.

Synagogues was mentioned briefly in the discussion of "temple" at 4.5. They are usually called "houses of prayer" or "meeting houses." Occasionally translators add "of the Jews." In many parts of the world today, there are buildings that serve a very similar function to that of the synagogues. For example, in parts of West Africa, village palaver huts are used for meetings and religious and traditional teaching. In such cases translations often have "palaver hut of the Jews" for "synagogue."

Since it says here **their synagogues**, translations sometimes have "the synagogues of those people" or "that were there."

Preaching has been discussed in 3.1 and 4.17. Here one can say "proclaiming (or, announcing) the Good News."

The gospel of the kingdom is translated less ambiguously by TEV ("**the Good News about the Kingdom**") and GECL 1st edition ("the Good News that God would now accomplish his work"). By means of this phrase Matthew means that Jesus had announced the arrival of God's reign, and so MACL translates "the Good News that God would soon establish his reign."

Gospel: see comments on the title of this book.

For comments on **kingdom**, see 3.2. The **gospel of the kingdom** is then "the Good News about God's rule" or "the Good News that God would soon establish his reign (or, rule)." GECL and MACL cited above are other possibilities.

Every disease and every infirmity appears again in 9.35 and 10.1, but nowhere else in the New Testament. The first of these terms means "sickness" or "illness"; the second word has the root meaning of "softness" or "weakness." However, in the present passage there seems to be no real distinction intended. In Deuteronomy 7.15 of the Septuagint, these two words appear together, but in inverse order from the way they appear here.

In some languages one cannot say **healing every disease** but instead must say "healing people of every kind of disease" or "healing people of all the diseases they had."

Some translations have a phrase like "physical weaknesses" for **infirmities**, which is acceptable if this refers to physical handicaps or disorders. But in other languages there is no real distinction made between "disease" and "infirmities." Since the use of the two words together in the text has the effect of covering all kinds of physical ailments, translators should use an expression that would in fact do the same thing in their languages.

4.24	RSV	TEV

So his fame spread throughout all Syria, and they brought him all the sick, those afflicted with various diseases and pains, demoniacs, epileptics, and paralytics, and he healed them.

The news about him spread through the whole country of Syria, so that people brought to him all those who were sick, suffering from all kinds of diseases and disorders: people with demons, and epileptics, and paralytics—and Jesus healed them all.

So indicates that as a result of what he is described as doing in verse 23, his fame spread. Some translations, for example TEV, indicate the link by the structure and do not need a specific word or phrase to mark this relation. Others say "As a result" or "Consequently."

The text says his **fame spread**, that is, "his reputation spread," "**news about him spread**" (as in TEV), or "people began to hear (or, talk) about him more and more."

Syria probably denotes the region north of Galilee, although in the first century it was sometimes used of Palestine as well. In the New Testament "Syria" usually denotes the Roman province of that name, which included Palestine (Luke 2.2; Acts 15.23,41; Gal 1.21, etc.), but it probably means here the area to the north of and bordering on Galilee, that is, "Syria" according to the Jewish usage. To the Jew, this "true Syria" did not include Phoenicia.

Translators can say "through the whole province of Syria" or "from there and into the province of Syria as well." They can then put a footnote to explain more precisely the relation of Syria to Galilee.

In Greek the subject of the verb **brought** is **they**, for which TEV has substituted "**people**" (GECL uses a German idiom: "one brought"). It may be necessary to indicate that **brought** means "brought so he would heal them" or "brought to him for healing."

Matthew mentions a lengthy list of illnesses and sufferings, to make certain that the healing aspect of Jesus' ministry is not underestimated. As TEV's restructuring suggests, the word **sick** is a general term, qualified by the five disorders that follow. **Diseases** translates the first noun discussed in verse 23. **Pains** (TEV "**disorders**") is a word most frequently used of severe pain or torture; here it refers to some sort of physical disorder. NAB renders "racked with pain," as does NEB. NJB translates "painful complaints of one kind or another." In the New Testament the word is used elsewhere only in Luke 16.23,28.

It is not always possible to have words that correspond exactly to **sick**, **diseases**, and **pains**. But that is not really too important as long as a way can be found to cover every kind of physical suffering: "people brought to him all the people who were sick or in pain" or "all who were suffering from sickness and physical ailments (or, disorders)."

Demoniacs refers, of course, to people who were demon possessed. Languages have different ways of speaking of **demoniacs**, that is, people who are possessed by demons or evil spirits. Some speak of "being in the power of an evil spirit" or "having an evil spirit on (or, in) one." For "evil spirit" see comments on verse 1. It would be wrong to insert a modern or a medical point of view and say "insane people."

Epileptics has the root meaning of "moon struck," which NAB renders "lunatics." But in modern English "lunatics" is used exclusively of insane people, who in the Gospels would be the demon possessed. Elsewhere in the New Testament this word appears only in Matthew 17.15, where it also refers to epilepsy. The footnote of JB is misleading: "Lit. 'moon-struck, lunatic' (cf. 17.15)."

Epilepsy is a widespread disorder, although it is not well understood. For example, in many societies **epileptics** are considered to be suffering from some spirit possession. If there is a specific name for this disorder in a language, it should be used; otherwise translations can say "people who had a kind of nervous disorder" or "people with a disorder which caused them to have fits."

Paralytics can be translated as "people who were paralyzed" (see NEB, NAB), "people who could not walk," or "people who could not move their legs."

People with all these ailments were brought to Jesus, and **he healed them**, that is, "he cured all their diseases" or "he cured all the people of those diseases and ailments."

4.25	RSV	TEV

And great crowds followed him from Galilee and the Decapolis and Jerusalem and Judea and from beyond the Jordan.	Large crowds followed him from Galilee and the Ten Towns, from Jerusalem, Judea, and the land on the other side of the Jordan.

And: "As a result," "Therefore," or "After that."

Great crowds, or simply "crowds," are frequently mentioned as following Jesus. These same people are perhaps to be identified with the disciples of 5.1 (see comments there). Only toward the end of the Gospel, under the influence of the religious leaders, do the crowds become hostile to Jesus.

The crowds were **from Galilee** and the other places mentioned. It does not say that Jesus went to those places. "Great crowds of people came from Galilee and the Ten Towns, from Jerusalem and Judea, and from the region on the other side of the Jordan River, and they went with Jesus where he went."

Here **followed** does not mean "became his disciples" but rather "went with him" or "went where he went."

The Decapolis (TEV "**The Ten Towns**") was a league of Greek-speaking (and largely pagan) city-states. All except the city of Bethshan (Scythopolis) were east of the Jordan. Included among these cities were Damascus, Gadara, Pella, Gerasa, and Philadelphia. Most translations follow the example of TEV and translate **Decapolis** as "**the Ten Towns**" rather than writing the word in their language as it might be pronounced.

Chapter 5

5.1-2

RSV   TEV

The Sermon on the Mount

1 Seeing the crowds, he went up on the mountain, and when he sat down his disciples came to him. 2 And he opened his mouth and taught them, saying:

1 Jesus saw the crowds and went up a hill, where he sat down. His disciples gathered around him, 2 and he began to teach them:

SECTION HEADING: **"The Sermon on the Mount."** It may be necessary to identify who delivered the sermon, "Jesus," and also possibly to whom he delivered it. The heading can be, therefore, "The sermon of Jesus on the mountain," "The sermon Jesus preached on the mountain (to the people)," or "Jesus preaches on the mountain to the people." Of course, "sermon" does not appear in the text, and it is only a tradition to call it that. "Jesus teaches (people) on a mountain" may be quite acceptable.

Matthew 5–7 is the first in a series of five discourses in the Gospel, each of which is concluded by what is essentially the same formula. (7.28; 11.1; 13.53; 19.1; 26.1). All five of these discourses generally follow the Marcan arrangement, though sometimes Matthew expands his text (see in particular chapters 8–9) to give more complete examples of what is to be included in the discourse.

The composition of this section, as well as its location in the Gospel, is clearly a unique feature of Matthew's Gospel. Some of the material is found in Luke's "Sermon on the Plain" (6.20-49) and in his "Travel Narrative" (9.51–18.14), but both Matthew and Luke each reflect their own unique features of composition. In the exegesis to follow, attention will occasionally be called to the differences between the Matthean and Lukan arrangements, particularly in passages where this information may be important for interpretation and translation.

5.1   RSV   TEV

Seeing the crowds, he went up on the mountain, and when he sat down his disciples came to him.

Jesus saw the crowds and went up a hill, where he sat down. His disciples gathered around him,

Seeing (so also NJB) translates a participle which Matthew elsewhere uses to introduce something unexpected that leads to further action (3.7; 9.2,4,22,23,36; 21.19; 27.24). A number of translators give it the temporal sense of "when he saw"

102

(Mft, AT, NAB, Brc, Phps, NEB, GECL), while TEV simply translates it as a finite verb, coordinate with the one which follows: "**Jesus saw . . . and went up.**" Some scholars ascribe to the participle a causative force, on the assumption that Jesus went up the mountain where he could avoid the crowd and instruct his disciples without being disturbed. But Matthew intimates that the whole crowd heard (7.28-29), and so it seems doubtful that a causative force is intended.

Since chapter 5 is treated as beginning a new section, some translations have introduced **the crowds** as if new information. "There were crowds following Jesus. He saw them and went up . . . (or, When he saw them, he went up . . .)." However, the participle **Seeing** indicates that the narration is continuing from 4.25 (as would the phrase "When he saw"). That is, the crowds have already been introduced to the readers. Therefore it may be better to use a sentence that does in fact follow on from 4.25. For example, translators can say "When he saw the crowds that were following him" or "He saw all those crowds following him and went up."

Crowds is the object of the participle **seeing**; this noun often carries an important meaning in Matthew's Gospel. Matthew uses the plural form about thirty times, and on most occasions the "crowds" are receptive to the person and teaching of Jesus; the religious leaders are the ones who reject him. Thus in this context it is rather likely that the "crowds" of 4.25 and 5.1a are to be equated with the disciples of 5.1b. In 4.25 the crowds were great groups of people coming from different places to follow Jesus. Here, although the text still has **the crowds**, they have obviously come together into one large crowd. Translations can have "the large group (or, crowd) of people" or "all the people."

The place where Jesus went up can be either a **mountain** or a "**hill**," since the Greek word can mean either. Some commentators see here an intended contrast to Sinai, where the Law was given. However, there are no grounds, implicit or explicit, for identifying the mountain as a "New Sinai."

The Greek noun, whether translated "mountain" or "hill," has the definite article before it, which leads several scholars to believe that it signifies a well-known location (see also 8.1; 14.23; 15.29; 24.3; 28.16; and especially 17.1, where there is no definite article). At least one commentator thinks that the reference is to the hill country that rises from the western shore of Lake Galilee, while according to the NJB footnote it is: "one of the hills near Capernaum." But the evidence is too inconclusive to be dogmatic. Modern translations vary in their renderings: RSV, AT have **mountain**; NAB "mountainside"; NEB, Mft, Phps, JB, Brc have either "hill" or "hillside."

Jesus **went up on** the mountain or hill. There is no reason to use a word like "climb." The normal word "went" or "went up" is all the translation needs.

A Jewish rabbi usually **sat down** to teach his disciples (see 13.2; 23.2; 24.3), as did teachers in the synagogue (Luke 4.20). So then the Sermon on the Mount actually reflects a teaching situation, and this is confirmed by Matthew's choice of verbs.

In many languages the phrase **when he sat down** is too elliptical or shortened. In these languages one cannot speak of when he sat down without first having said that he did it. Translators will therefore do something like TEV, "**where he sat down**," or say "he sat down there."

"Disciple" means "one who learns from another," but in the special context of the New Testament the **disciples** are those persons whom Jesus called, not only to learn his teachings, but to share his life and his destiny. Usually, as here, they are spoken of as **his disciples**, thus intimating something of the closeness of the relation between the Lord and those whom he called to follow him. In the Gospels the term may refer to the limited circle of the twelve or to Jesus' followers in general. Although the context here is not specific in its usage of the term, taken in light of 4.25 and 5.1, the larger group seems to be intended.

For **disciples** most translators have tried to avoid a word that simply means "students," but it has often been possible to use "apprentices." Some have used "followers." "Apprentices" and "followers" are especially appropriate translations in languages where these words are actually used to speak of people who stay with and learn from a teacher, doctor, skilled craftsman, or a person known in Asia as a guru. Other translations have used "companions," but this is far too general a word to be a good translation of "disciples." "Helpers" is sometimes acceptable.

Came translates the same verb discussed in 4.3. It is quite possible that the meaning "gather for a formal teaching session" is to be preferred here (see NEB "had gathered round"), especially if the "crowds" of verse 1 and the "disciples" of verse 2 are thought to constitute the same group. Some scholars see here a parallel with the men who stood around Ezra when he read the Law (Neh 8.4), and with the priests who gathered around the High Priest at the offering of sacrifice (Sirach 50.11-21). This intimates that the scene is that of a solemn hour of worship: God's people stand in his presence to hear his teachings from the one who teaches with God's own authority. As in 4.3, **came** might have to be "went." Here it can be translated "**gathered around him**" (TEV), or "went close to him to listen to him."

5.2	RSV	TEV

And he opened his mouth and taught them, saying: **and he began to teach them:**

He opened his mouth is the literal rendering of a formula that is found in classical literature and in Jewish rabbinical sources. Scholars classify it as both "a Semitic idiom" (Dan 10.16; Job 3.1; 33.2) and "a traditional formula" (Acts 8.35; 10.34). On the basis of its usage in Daniel 10.16 and Job 3.1, at least one commentator believes that it functions to give emphasis to what follows, and that may well be its function here. However, the more acceptable solution is that which understands the expression to mean "begin (verb of) discourse" (see TEV "**began to teach**").

Taught them. The verb "teach" may have as its object either the person who is taught or the content of the teaching; in certain contexts it may be followed by both objects. But in Matthew the content of the teaching appears as an object of the verb only in 15.9, which is within a quotation from Isaiah 29.13. Interesting also is the location of Jesus' teaching in this Gospel; it is always done away from the crowded places, whether on a hill or along the shore of Lake Galilee.

The nearest antecedent to **them** is "his disciples" (verse 1). It may be necessary in the receptor language to make explicit the persons intended by the pronoun. Some translators interpret **them** in a wider sense by saying "all the people," "the people," or "the crowd." But it is probably better to leave it as "them" or "his disciples," as we said above.

The use of the participle **saying** also reflects Semitic style in which the participle serves merely to indicate that direct discourse is to follow. It then becomes equivalent to quotation marks at the beginning of direct discourse in English. **He opened his mouth and taught them, saying** is best represented in English as "**he began to teach them,**" followed by quotation marks. Accordingly NEB restructures as ". . . he began to address them. And this is the teaching he gave"; Phps has "Then he began his teaching by saying to them." Brc seems to have overtranslated the expression: "He opened his mind and heart to them, and this was the substance of his teaching." Luke begins his discourse with a different, yet equally challenging structure: "he lifted up his eyes" (6.20).

5.3-12

RSV	TEV
	True Happiness

RSV		TEV
3 "Blessed are the poor in spirit, for theirs is the kingdom of heaven.	3	"Happy are those who know they are spiritually poor; the Kingdom of heaven belongs to them!
4 "Blessed are those who mourn, for they shall be comforted.	4	"Happy are those who mourn; God will comfort them!
5 "Blessed are the meek, for they shall inherit the earth.	5	"Happy are those who are humble; they will receive what God has promised!
6 "Blessed are those who hunger and thirst for righteousness, for they shall be satisfied.	6	"Happy are those whose greatest desire is to do what God requires; God will satisfy them fully!
7 "Blessed are the merciful, for they shall obtain mercy.	7	"Happy are those who are merciful to others; God will be merciful to them!
8 "Blessed are the pure in heart, for they shall see God.	8	"Happy are the pure in heart; they will see God!
9 "Blessed are the peacemakers, for they shall be called sons of God.	9	"Happy are those who work for peace; God will call them his children!
10 "Blessed are those who are persecuted for righteousness' sake, for theirs is the kingdom of heaven.	10	"Happy are those who are persecuted because they do what God requires; the Kingdom of heaven belongs to them!
11 "Blessed are you when men revile you and persecute you and utter all kinds of evil against you falsely on my account. 12 Rejoice and be glad, for your reward is great in heaven, for so men persecuted the prophets who were before you.		11 "Happy are you when people insult you and persecute you and tell all kinds of evil lies against you because you are my followers. 12 Be happy and glad, for a great reward is kept for you in heaven. This is how the prophets who lived before you were persecuted.

SECTION HEADING: "True Happiness." The translation of this section heading will depend on how one translates **Blessed** or "Happy" (TEV) in the beatitudes that follow. It may not be possible in a language to use an abstract noun such as "**Happiness,**" especially if it stands alone without being part of a clause or sentence. The section heading may be "People who are truly happy" or "Jesus tells what makes people really happy."

Luke has four beatitudes (6.20-22), but how many are contained in Matthew 5.1-12? There is no justification for making the beatitudes number seven (a sacred number among the Jews) by regarding verses 10-12 as transitional. And it is no less arbitrary to make them number ten, following the pattern of the Ten Commandments, by making verses 11 and 12 two separate beatitudes. Verse 12, which lacks the affirmation **Blessed are** . . . , must be taken as a continuation of the beatitude begun in verse 11. Had Matthew intended a series of ten beatitudes, he could easily have accomplished it without leaving any doubt in the reader's mind, for he includes similar structures at other places (11.6; 13.16; 16.17; 24.46).

But how does verse 10 fit into the pattern of the beatitudes? And are verses 11-12 to be interpreted as a separate beatitude or as an expression of the one in verse 10? Some scholars have raised the objection that verse 10 should not be considered a beatitude, because the happiness referred to in it arises from persecution, whereas the happiness of verses 3-9 grows out of internal conditions under the believer's control. But this is a false distinction. In the context of the Sermon on the Mount, persecution is viewed as inevitable for one whose life is regulated by the Spirit of Christ. Persecution may arise from without, but it is a response to what is within the believer. Nor is the argument that the reward of verse 10 is the same as that promised in verse 3 a valid argument against the inclusion of this as a separate beatitude; the parallelism between verse 10 and verses 3-9 is too definite to be overlooked.

But the more difficult question concerns the relation of verses 11-12 to the entire series of beatitudes. Do these verses contain a separate beatitude, thus resulting in a series of nine? Or are the verses to be considered an expansion of verse 10, thus resulting in only eight beatitudes?

Either conclusion is possible. In defense of the verses as a separate beatitude is its opening, **Blessed are** . . . , which parallels the other beatitudes. On the other hand one may argue to the contrary, on the basis of the shift from the third person "they" of the previous beatitudes to the second person "you." No firm decision is possible, though the majority of scholars today interpret verses 11-12 as a separate beatitude, parallel to those of verses 3-10.

In terms of structure, it should be noted that verses 3-6 and 7-10 form two parallel divisions, even to the point of having the same number of words in the Greek text. And finally, the first group of four (verses 3-6) is parallel to the Lukan series (6.20-23), while the second group of four (verses 7-10) is unique to Matthew's Gospel. In place of this last series of four beatitudes, Luke has four "woes" (6.24-26).

Blessed (TEV "**Happy**") translates a Greek word which is used quite frequently in the Septuagint as a translation of a Hebrew word meaning "Oh the happiness of." In the Old Testament this word is used most often in the Psalms and in the Wisdom literature; elsewhere in Matthew's Gospel it appears in 11.6; 13.16; 16.17; 24.46.

The religious usage of the word may have had its origin in the pronouncement by the worship leader upon the pilgrims who came to ascend the sacred hill in Jerusalem. It perhaps meant something like "You are the fortunate recipients of God's mercy and blessing." In the present passage a number of English translations have **Blessed** (KJV, RSV, AT, Mft); NEB and NAB have "How blest"; Brc "Oh the bliss"; Phps, JB "How happy" then "Happy"; Anchor Bible (AB) "Fortunate are." What these translations do not indicate clearly is that the one doing the good is God.

In the Old Testament, beatitudes are most generally in the third person. Here verses 3-10 follow the third person form, though the shift is made in verses 11-12 to the less frequent second person form (see also 13.16; 16.17). Beatitudes found in Greek literature are similar to those of the Old Testament in that they too occur in series and are usually given in the third person: "Blessings on him who . . . !"

Blessed has been a very difficult problem for translators, as seen by the variety of ways it has been handled. "Blessed" or "blessing" are simply not common events in all societies. Further, the word used in some languages refers to a superficial happiness or good thing rather than to a right and harmonious relationship in which one party, usually the superior, does good to the other. "Happy" has as its primary meaning an emotional state. "Fortunate" too often is understood to mean "to have good luck." And yet each of these words can have the intended meaning in some contexts. The same is true of expressions such as "to be well off." One translation that has often worked is "to be in a good position," that is, "to be favorably placed to receive something good."

In many languages translators find that it is more natural not to start the sentence with the notion of blessed or happiness. Instead they use a construction such as "People who are poor in spirit (or, who mourn) are in a good position (or are well off, or are truly fortunate), because . . . ."

The beatitudes say that certain people are well placed (or, happy) **for**, that is, "because" of something that God will do for them. Some languages do not use a word or phrase to indicate this relation. TEV is an example in English. Others will use "for" or "because," and still others will start a new sentence with "The reason for that is . . ." or "These people will receive . . . ."

5.3	RSV	TEV

RSV	TEV
"Blessed are the poor in spirit, for theirs is the kingdom of heaven.	"Happy are those who know they are spiritually poor; the Kingdom of heaven belongs to them!

Poor in spirit is understood by some few interpreters to mean "poor for the sake of their spirit." The reference would then be to persons who impoverish themselves for the sake of strengthening their spiritual condition. But it is more natural to take the Greek phrase following "poor" with the meaning "in the realm of," after the analogy of such expressions as "pure in heart" (Matt 5.8) or "humble in spirit" (Psa 34.18 RSV: "crushed in spirit"), rather than with the meaning of "for the sake of."

TEV translates **poor in spirit** as "**who know they are spiritually poor**" (AT "who feel their spiritual need"). Almost all commentators agree that there are two Hebrew words which provide the background for this saying; these words are synonymous, and each one may mean either "poor" or "humble." For example, the word **poor** is essentially synonymous with the word translated "meek" ("humble") in verse 5, and there is scholarly agreement that the meanings should not be too neatly distinguished. The word here translated **poor** is used in the Septuagint to translate Hebrew words which mean not only "poor" and "needy," but also "broken in spirit" and "humble." During the time for which Isaiah 40–55 was written, the term "poor" was used of all Israelites who were living in exile without a land of their own. Later the lower social classes used this term to distinguish themselves from the upper classes, who lorded over them and oppressed them. By Jesus' day it had become a kind of "title of honor" for the faithful of God's people, who had accepted the difficult way of life that he had marked out for them.

In Jesus' thinking, the "poor" are most probably those people whose outward circumstances force them to look to God for everything, but who also receive from God the gift of the spirit (faith) to look to him for everything. Therefore, the "poor" of Luke 6.20 and Matthew's "poor in spirit" are the same trusting, though afflicted, poor people; but Matthew has made the sense explicit by adding "in spirit." But by this slight alteration Matthew introduces a significant safeguard, which leads away from the thought that poverty in itself is automatically a sign of closeness to God. Jesus' words may not be interpreted legalistically. True "blessedness" comes only as God's Spirit is capable of leading the human spirit to trust absolutely in God.

It may be that the renderings of TEV and AT are too narrow and represent a modern overinterpretation. For the meaning is not so much that people recognize their spiritual need as separate from any other needs, but rather that they stand before God and recognize their absolute need of him. NEB translates "who know their need of God" (Phps "who know their need for God"). Brc translates "who realize the destitution of their own lives," and GECL 1st edition is strikingly picturesque, "who stand with empty hands before God," symbolizing absolute dependence on him.

In addition to the examples we have cited here, other possible ways of expressing the meaning are "who place all their hope in God" and "who stand before God knowing how (or, how much) they need him."

Theirs is the kingdom of heaven is typical of most translations: JB "theirs is the kingdom of heaven"; NEB, Phps "the kingdom of Heaven is theirs"; NAB "the reign of God is theirs"; Mft "the Realm of heaven is theirs." In fact some scholars assume, and rightly so, that this is the best sense for the present passage. But whether one interprets the meaning to be "belong to" or "consist of," the emphasis is on the benefits or blessings shared by those persons who experience the rule of God in their lives. Only a few translations have really taken seriously the meaning of this part of the verse. GECL 1st edition translates "they will be God's people when he completes his work"; Brc has "for the blessings of the Kingdom of Heaven are theirs here and now." The Greek text is actually in the present tense ("the kingdom of heaven is . . ."), and so the basis for Brc's rendering; but it is possible to take the present with a future force and translate as GECL 1st edition has done. Both Brc and GECL have obviously realized the difficulty, if not the impossibility, of rendering "the kingdom of heaven belongs to them"; for if the kingdom refers to God's rule, how can it be spoken of as "belonging to" someone? This is one of those passages where the focus is actually on the benefits shared by persons who experience God's rule, and both translations have attempted to make this meaning explicit. MACL translates "they enjoy the blessings of God's rule." In some cultures the idea of a rule always conveys negative connotations, suggesting coercion, oppression, and violence. And there are some few cultures which do not know the meaning of strong or powerful rulers. In such language situations one may want to translate "God accepts (or, will accept) them as his own people" or "they enjoy (or, will enjoy) the blessings that God gives his people."

There are other cultures where the idea of a rule generally conveys positive connotations, so that to say "they are a part of God's kingdom (or, rule)" is enough to be considered happy or well off. Translators can also say "God accepts them in his kingdom." Otherwise translators may need to make explicit these positive benefits of being in God's kingdom, much as MACL (cited above) has done; for example, "They enjoy the benefits that come to those who are under God's rule" or "The good things God gives to those who are a part of his reign are for them." For a fuller discussion of **kingdom**, see 3.2.

5.4	RSV	TEV
	"Blessed are those who mourn, for they shall be comforted.	"Happy are those who mourn; God will comfort them!

The original order of verses 4-5 is not certain; manuscripts dating from the second century differ in the order of presentation. The manuscript evidence, though rather certain, is not conclusive (the UBS Greek New Testament gives its choice of text a "B" rating). The argument that verse 5 may have been placed prior to verse 4 by an early scribe is suggested by the possibility that the scribe may have tried to make a type of antithetical parallelism between verse 3 (mention of heaven) and verse 5 (mention of earth). On the other hand, there seems to be no obvious reason for suggesting why he may have placed verse 4 before verse 5, had verse 5 originally come first, unless this was an attempt to place verses 3-4 together on the basis of their common background in Isaiah 61.1-2. Among the translations, NJB, *Bible de Jérusalem* (BJ), and TOB (with a footnote) depart from the traditional order; NAB retains the order but places verse 5 in square brackets.

Those who mourn points in the same direction as the previous beatitude; taken together, verses 3 and 4 are an allusion to Isaiah 61.1-2.

"To comfort those who are mourning" is one of the promises of the anticipated Messianic salvation (see Luke 2.25). In the Septuagint the verb **mourn** is used both for mourning in behalf of the dead and for the sins of others. It is a common verb in biblical Greek and cannot be confined to the idea of mourning for sin. According to Matthew, one hates sin and forsakes it; one does not mourn it. In the present context the idea is best interpreted as a contrast between the "mourning" of the present age and the "comfort" of the coming age. At least this is highly probable in light of its connection with the words from Isaiah. Translators can show this contrast with a phrase such as "people who are mourning now (or, at this time)."

As we said, no reason for the mourning is given, nor should it be in the translation. If a language does require some kind of reason for the mourning, translators should try to be indefinite or use a phrase such as "because they need God." This is not ideal, however.

It would have been immediately evident to any Jewish reader of Matthew's Gospel that **shall be comforted** was merely a way of affirming the result of divine activity: "**God will comfort them**" (TEV). Such a so-called "divine passive" construction was typical of Semitic language usage, and the theological outlook of Judaism expected that God himself would save and comfort his people. **Comforted** means "consoled" or possibly "made happy again." Thus translations can have "God will restore their happiness" or "God will console them."

5.5 RSV TEV

"Blessed are the meek, for they shall inherit the earth.

"Happy are those who are humble; they will receive what God has promised!

In the same way that verses 3-4 are based on Isaiah 61, so verse 5 finds its background in Psalm 37.11. As the psalm indicates, the metaphor was taken over from the possession of Canaan by the Israelites. The **meek** (TEV "**humble**") of this verse and the "poor" of verse 3 are the same people viewed from a different perspective (see comment at verse 3). In fact, in the language of Jesus the word could hardly be distinguished from "poor." It contained echoes of "insignificant, lowly," and may even be rendered "powerless." These people possess no power because they do not need it; they rest their entire hope on God. Instead of trying to overpower others, they serve him. Phps translates "those who claim nothing," and Brc "whose strength is in their gentleness." Once again GECL 1st edition is dynamic: "who renounce the use of force." Elsewhere in the New Testament the word **meek** is used only in Matthew 11.29; 21.5; and 1 Peter 3.4, where TEV renders either "gentle" or "humble."

Meek in modern English has negative connotations of someone who is submissive and easily imposed on. Words such as "gentle," "humble," or "nonaggressive" are perhaps better. One good translation is "who don't trust in their own power."

They shall inherit the earth. The verb translated **inherit** carries the more general meaning of "to receive as one's possession" or "to share in" (see 19.29; 25.34; 1 Cor 6.9-10; 15.50; Gal 5.21; Heb 1.14). To translate with the equivalent of the English word **inherit** may intimate that someone has died (in this context, God!) and has left someone else his possessions.

The promise of possessing the land was originally limited to the land of Canaan (see Gen 17.8) but then was extended to include the entire earth, over which God would someday rule. In essence, then, this is simply another expression for the Kingdom of heaven of verse 3 (TOB note). Both of these ideas existed side by side in Israel's expectation for the future. The God of heaven has given earth to mankind as a place for their existence. But the time would come when God's people would enjoy the benefits of heaven and the joys of a redeemed earth. TEV completely spiritualizes this promise ("**they will receive what God has promised**"), while GECL attempts to maintain some of the imagery ("since God will give them the earth for their possession"). NEB ("they shall have the earth for their possession") and Phps ("for the whole earth will belong to them") are similar to GECL, except that they have maintained the passive rather than making God the explicit subject.

Those translators who follow the interpretation of TEV may need to use an active construction instead of a passive one. Further, they may have to specify what God is going to give; for example, "the blessing" or "the good things." Consequently, possible translations are "God will give them what he has promised" or "God will give them all the blessings (or, good things) he has promised." But other translators who want to retain the image of "earth" will find GECL 1st edition a useful model, as in "God will give them the whole earth to possess."

5.6	RSV	TEV
	"Blessed are those who hunger and thirst for righteousness, for they shall be satisfied.	"Happy are those whose greatest desire is to do what God requires; God will satisfy them fully!

Hunger and thirst for righteousness. Hungering and thirsting are figures for longing after God, both in the Old Testament (Isa 55.1; Psa 42.2; Baruch 2.18) and in the New Testament (John 4.13; 7.37; Rev 21.6; 22.17). The meaning of the figure is to seek something with all one's heart, to desire it above all else. Most translations maintain the original figure of speech, but those that do away with it include TEV ("**whose greatest desire is to do**") and GECL ("who burn as they wait for God's will to be done").

The parallel passage in Luke reads "Blessed are you that hunger now, for you shall be satisfied" (6.21). But Matthew moves from a literal, physical hunger to that of hungering after **righteousness**, a term which is not easily defined (see comments at 3.15). Some translations reflect the meaning as "the desire to do right" (AT "uprightness"; Mft "goodness"; Phps "true goodness"; and NAB "holiness"). TEV renders "what God requires," while GECL prefers "that God's will may be done."

In many cases translators have felt that the metaphor **hunger and thirst** will be clearly understood by their readers. Other translators have felt that a simile is better, as in "those who desire righteousness as if they were hungering and thirsting" or "who long for God's will to be done like people who are hungry and thirsty long for food and drink." This can make for a rather long and awkward construction, so many translators do find it better to drop the image altogether, as TEV and GECL have done. Other examples of this are "who want more than anything else to do God's will" or "who seek with all their heart to do God's will."

As we pointed out, another acceptable translation of **righteousness** here is "to see God's will done." Thus translators can say in this verse "whose greatest desire is for people to do what God tells them to do" or "whose greatest desire is that people do what God wants."

Translators will probably not translate **satisfied** with a word that only means to be full from eating enough, especially if they have dropped the image of hungering and thirsting. The idea of getting what one desires, however, can be used: "God will give them what they desire" or "God will satisfy them completely."

| **5.7** | RSV | TEV |

"Blessed are the merciful, for they shall obtain mercy.

"Happy are those who are merciful to others; God will be merciful to them!

This beatitude is best interpreted in light of a passage such as the fifth petition of the Lord's Prayer ("forgive us the wrongs that we have done, as we forgive the wrongs that others have done us") or of Jesus' prayer on the cross in Luke 23.34 ("Forgive them, Father! They don't know what they are doing"). The same teaching is also reflected in other New Testament passages, as well as in a familiar rabbinic saying: "as God is merciful, so you must be merciful." This beatitude is in contradiction to traditional Pharisaic theology, which would have affirmed "Happy are those who are righteous, for God will be merciful to them." For Matthew the point is that a person who does not show mercy cannot count on God's mercy. Occasionally this verse has been wrongly understood to mean that the believer is to be merciful towards others so that they will treat him in the same way. This is not the meaning, and no Jew of Jesus' day would have understood it in this way; it is imperative for the translator to make the meaning explicit, as TEV has done (**"God will be merciful to them!"**).

Mercy is defined as having a feeling of sorrow over someone's bad situation and trying to do something about it. People who are **merciful** can be said to be "kind" or "forgiving," or to be "people who take pity on others," "people who show mercy to others."

Similarly, then, "God will take pity on them," "will forgive them," or "will show mercy to them." Some translators may have to specify when people will obtain this mercy from God; for example, "on the Judgment Day." In that case the translation can be "on the Day when he judges the world, God will show mercy to them."

| **5.8** | RSV | TEV |

"Blessed are the pure in heart, for they shall see God.

"Happy are the pure in heart; they will see God!

According to Psalm 24.3-4 "clean hands and a pure heart" are demanded of persons who would come into the presence of God in his Temple. In this context the **heart** represents more than the seat of emotions; it refers to one's innermost being, that which shapes a person's life. The purity referred to means singleness of motive and of devotion, as opposed to a divided motive, without specific reference to either moral perfection or sexual purity. In Hebrew thought the **heart** is used as a symbol of one's mind or thoughts, and here the reference is to thoughts or to a mind concerned solely to please God. For example, it is applicable to one's attitude toward people of the opposite sex (5.28), or money (6.20-21), or even toward one's own words (5.37). NAB translates "single-hearted" with a note: ". . . those who serve God loyally for his own sake and not primarily out of self-interest."

People who are **pure in heart**, can be "people whose only interest is to serve God," "whose lives are directed only to serving God," "whose devotion to God is complete (or, total)," or "who are completely devoted to God (or, to serving God)."

To **see God** is a gift which is impossible for humans to experience in this life. It is available only in the coming age. Perhaps the best way to translate **see God** is to say "be where he is, to see him" or "to see God in his presence."

5.9 RSV	TEV
"Blessed are the peacemakers, for they shall be called sons of God.	"Happy are those who work for peace; God will call them his children!

Who are the **peacemakers** spoken of in this verse? Are they people who make peace between man and God or between man and man? Either interpretation is possible, but both the nonbiblical Jewish literature and the biblical writings themselves support the idea that the peace spoken of is that which is established among people. (See especially Heb 12.14; Eph 2.15; James 3.18.) Brc translates "those who make men friends with each other." Some other ways to speak of **peacemakers** are "those who cause people to be friends," "those who help people to live in peace," "those who make peace between people," or "those who work to stop people from being enemies."

They shall be called sons of God translates a Greek passive structure which presupposes that God is the actor. Therefore TEV has "**God will call them his children.**" "To be called" means "to become," as the Old Testament examples in Genesis 21.12 and Isaiah 56.7 indicate. GECL translates "They will be children of God." Brc renders "for they shall be ranked as the sons of God" (see also Mft). Phps translates "for they will be known as sons of God!"

Sons does not here refer only to male offspring, but means "children."

In addition to the examples cited above, there are many ways translators have handled this passive construction **shall be called**. Some translators keep the idea of **called** with phrases like "God will say to them, 'You are my children,' " "God will say that they are his children," or "God will consider them his children." Or translators can do the same as TEV: "**God will call them his children.**" Others put the emphasis on the idea of becoming, and say "they will become God's children" or "God will make them his children."

The phrase **sons of God** (or, children of God) causes a problem in cultures where readers would not understand this phrase to be figurative and, further, would not accept the idea of God having physical offspring. Translators in these cases sometimes use similes, as in "God will say they are like children to him," "God will consider them as if they were his children," or "God will have a relationship with (or, will care for) them like a father with his children."

Only with great reserve does the Bible refer to people as **sons** (better "children") **of God**. This is a status established solely as an act of God's mercy and grace. In the context the reference is to the final judgment, and verses 44-45 are the best commentary on the verse. See also 4.3 and comments.

5.10	RSV	TEV

"Blessed are those who are persecuted for righteousness' sake, for theirs is the kingdom of heaven.

"Happy are those who are persecuted because they do what God requires; the Kingdom of heaven belongs to them!

Theirs is the kingdom of heaven occurs in both the first and the eighth beatitudes. This signals the beginning and the end of a section, and it is an example of a literary device known as "inclusion," found elsewhere as well in Matthew. One can easily see the differences between the form of these beatitudes and the form of the last one, verses 11-12.

Are persecuted translates a perfect participle in Greek, which suggests that as Matthew writes, the church of his day is suffering persecution. Most translations, such as TEV ("**who are persecuted**"), give something of a timeless force to the participle; only Phps and NEB take seriously the perfect tense ("who have suffered persecution"). **Are persecuted** is often translated "receive suffering," so that this phrase can be "the people whom other people make suffer (or, persecute)." (Of course, any of these can be rendered as past or future if translators prefer those interpretations.)

For righteousness' sake is translated "**because they do what God requires**" by TEV. GECL and FRCL translate as TEV does, and Brc renders "for their loyalty to God's way of life." Other translations are similar: NEB "for the cause of right"; NAB "for holiness' sake" (with note: "fidelity to the divine precepts through which holiness is attained is deepened by the test of persecution"); JB "in the cause of right" and Mft "for the sake of goodness!" (Phps "for the cause of goodness"). See comments at 3.15 and 5.6 on "righteousness." Many translations have had "because they do what is right" as a translation of **for righteousness' sake**. But as we pointed out above, what is right is in fact that which conforms to God's will, so that the phrase can also be as in TEV, "**because they do what God requires**," or "because their lives are right before God," or "because they live as God wants people to."

See verse 3 for comments on **theirs is the kingdom of heaven**.

5.11	RSV	TEV

"Blessed are you when men revile you and persecute you and utter all kinds of evil against you falsely on my account.

"Happy are you when people insult you and persecute you and tell all kinds of evil lies against you because you are my followers.

Verses 11-12 form a parallel to verse 10; they apply verse 10 specifically to the persecuted disciples and the Church. In the face of opposition and oppression, Jesus' promise becomes a reality here and now. This explains the shift to the second person pronoun **you**, which also anticipates the transition to verses 13-16.

When here means "on those occasions," "at those times when," or "whenever."

Revile (TEV "**insult**") is used of strong verbal abuse (see 27.44; 1 Peter 4.14). One commentator notes that the Jews considered verbal abuse to be extremely vicious. The rabbis considered it as evil as idolatry, fornication, and bloodshed all combined. By defamation of character a person lost his place in the community and, according to the circumstance of that day, almost the possibility of continuing his life. The insulting word itself was believed to have a power of its own. **Revile** can be translated "say evil about" or "say you are bad." Many translators in West Africa use the idiom "spoil your name."

For **persecute**, see comments on verse 10. Here translations can have "whenever people make you suffer" or "when people harm you."

There is a textual problem regarding the adverb **falsely**. The UBS Greek text includes the word within square brackets, and the reason, according to TC-GNT, is that it may not have been an original part of the text. On the one hand, its absence may be accounted for as a scribal attempt to make the passage resemble the Lukan form (Luke 6.22). On the other hand, scribes would have been tempted to insert the word in order to limit an overgeneralization of Jesus' teaching, and to express specifically what was believed to be implied by the very nature of Jesus' words. But whether it is regarded as an integral part of the text or a later addition, it does explain the true meaning of the text, and this information must somehow be conveyed through translation. So then, whether on textual or translational grounds, it has been retained in a number of translations. For example, it is found in RSV, GECL, and TEV ("**tell all kinds of evil lies**"), though omitted by NEB and Phps.

To translate **utter all kinds of evil against you falsely**, phrases such as "say bad things about you that aren't true" or "tell all kinds of wicked lies about you" can be used.

The phrase **on my account** is taken by TEV to mean "**because you are my followers**." Most translations follow the text literally, while GECL translates "because you belong to me."

A translation of **on my account** such as "for my sake" is also literal, but many translations have used it. "Because they are against me" is less so, although the clearest translation would be very similar to either TEV or GECL: "because you follow me" or "because you are my people."

This sentence is longer than those in verses 3-10, but it can still be made to flow smoothly: "Whenever people say evil about you and do harm to you, and tell all kinds of wicked lies about you simply because you follow me, then you are in a good position," or ". . . you are fortunate," or ". . . you are happy."

5.12	RSV	TEV
	Rejoice and be glad, for your reward is great in heaven, for so men persecuted the prophets who were before you.	**Be happy and glad, for a great reward is kept for you in heaven. This is how the prophets who lived before you were persecuted.**

Matthew uses the command **Rejoice** in the present tense to encourage the disciples to be happy and to keep on being happy in the face of difficult circumstances. The verb is the same one used of the wise men in 2.10; elsewhere Matthew employs it in 18.13; 26.49; 27.29; 28.9.

Matthew includes a second verb, **be glad**, not found in Luke's Gospel. Commentators differ in their evaluation of its meaning. For example, one commentator notes that it is a "strong word of Hellenistic coinage" which means "to leap much, signifying irrepressible demonstrative gladness." On the other hand, another commentator affirms: "Matthew's word for 'be glad' . . . does not contain the idea of the physical expression of joy, such as is contained in Luke's 'leap for joy.' " However, it seems to express extreme joy, especially as it is used in the Septuagint (in particular see Isa 12.6; 25.9; 29.19; 35.1,2; 41.17; 49.13; 61.10; 65.14,19). One of the standard lexicons gives the following definitions: "exult, be glad, overjoyed." And in 1 Peter 4.13, where both these verbs occur together, this same lexicon translates "that you might shout for joy." Elsewhere in the New Testament the word occurs in Luke 1.47; 10.21; John 5.35; 8.56; Acts 2.26; 16.34; 1 Peter 1.6,8; 4.13; and Revelation 19.7. The related noun form is found in Luke 1.14, 44; Acts 2.46; Hebrews 1.9; and Jude 24.

Most translators will treat **rejoice** and **be glad** together. They are close in meaning, and one gets the impression that the two terms together simply emphasize the point being made here that people should really be happy. Besides, many languages simply do not have two separate words they would use together in this kind of context. Therefore translators will use an expression that means to be very happy, to exult, to be overjoyed. They may use an imperative, as in "Be really happy," "Make this an occasion for rejoicing," or "Rejoice." Or they may have a sentence with "should," such as "You should rejoice greatly" or "You should rejoice and celebrate."

The concept of a **reward** may be difficult for many readers. The main idea is that of a compensation which is valuable and special. If the idea of a reward sounds strange, one should realize that it is a reward of God's grace, that is, a reward not merited but which God wills to give to those who serve him faithfully. It is not a compensation for work done, but rather a gift which far exceeds any service rendered.

The Greek passive construction, **for your reward is great in heaven**, is given an active form in GECL: "God will reward you richly." This is a legitimate and perhaps even necessary restructuring, since heaven was a frequent synonym for God. One commentator warns: "It is important not to read into this phrase the notion of 'going into heaven,' but rather 'with God.' "

Some translations will use "gift" for **reward**, or even "great (or, valuable) gift." This is kept **in heaven**, which means that it is God who will give it, as we pointed out. Thus the translation can be "God is keeping a valuable reward for you in heaven," "God will reward you greatly in heaven," or "the gift God is keeping for you in heaven is great."

For so men persecuted the prophets who were before you: the Old Testament tells how prophets like Elijah, Amos, and Jeremiah were persecuted. In addition the Jews of the first century A.D. believed that the prophet Isaiah had been sawn in two, after he had hidden himself in a hollow tree. Hebrews 11.37 may be a reference to this event. Moreover, Jesus was certainly familiar with the tradition that the prophets were persecuted by the people of their own generation (Matt 23.29-36).

For comments on **persecuted**, see verse 10. The prophets who were persecuted **were before you**, that is, "they lived long ago" or "they lived back before your own time."

So means "in the same way." Thus this whole clause can be translated "people made the prophets of long ago suffer in the same way."

It may be necessary to reorder this verse, since as the text stands, it is possible to take "**This is how men persecuted the prophets who lived before you**" (TEV) as a reference to "**for a great reward is kept for you in heaven**" (TEV). To avoid this ambiguity, one need merely to reverse the order of the two sentences: "They persecuted the prophets who lived before you in this way. Be glad and happy, because there is a big reward which the Lord has prepared for you." Another way to handle it is to say "Be happy and glad, because God is keeping a great gift for you in heaven. In fact, people persecuted the prophets of long ago in the same way they now persecute you."

5.13-16

RSV	TEV
	Salt and Light
13 "You are the salt of the earth; but if salt has lost its taste, how shall its saltness be restored? It is no longer good for anything except to be thrown out and trodden under foot by men.	13 "You are like salt for all mankind. But if salt loses its saltiness, there is no way to make it salty again. It has become worthless, so it is thrown out and people trample on it.
14 "You are the light of the world. A city set on a hill cannot be hid. 15 Nor do men light a lamp and put it under a bushel, but on a stand, and it gives light to all in the house. 16 Let your light so shine before men, that they may see your good works and give glory to your Father who is in heaven.	14 "You are like light for the whole world. A city built on a hill cannot be hid. 15 No one lights a lamp and puts it under a bowl; instead he puts it on the lampstand, where it gives light for everyone in the house. 16 In the same way your light must shine before people, so that they will see the good things you do and praise your Father in heaven.

SECTION HEADING: "**Salt and Light**": as in the case of all section headings, this may need to be a complete sentence: "Jesus says his followers are like salt and light" or "The followers of Jesus are like salt and light."

The sayings about salt and light refer to discipleship; for parallels to these sayings see Mark 9.50; Luke 14.34-35 (salt); Mark 4.21; Luke 8.16 (light). There is a formal connection between this passage and the beatitudes by the continuing use of "you," which was introduced in verses 11-12.

5.13 RSV	TEV
"**You are the salt of the earth; but if salt has lost its taste, how shall its saltness be restored? It is no longer good for anything except to**	"**You are like salt for all mankind. But if salt loses its saltiness, there is no way to make it salty again. It has become worthless, so it**

be thrown out and trodden under foot by men.	**is thrown out and people trample on it.**

Whereas in Mark 9.50 the disciples are told to have salt in themselves (TEV "Have the salt of friendship among yourselves"), here they themselves are identified as **the salt of the earth**. TEV transforms the metaphor **you are the salt** into a simile, **"you are like salt."** In English, as in many other languages, the use of a simile ("X is like Y") is clearer and more straightforward than a metaphor ("X is Y").

As it stands, the genitive expression **of the earth** is difficult to understand because it leaves ambiguous the relation between salt and earth. NEB is an improvement ("You are salt to the world"), and TEV has ". . . for all mankind." GECL entirely restructures ("What salt is for food, this is what you must be for the world"), and INCL has "You are like salt that is needed by this world."

In many languages it will be necessary to specify in what way you are like salt. Some translations have felt the basis of the comparison is that in the same way salt gives flavor or savor to food, you must give flavor to the earth. But this is probably not what is meant here. It is more likely that you are to preserve or save the earth as salt preserves food. However, because of the variety of ways the expression can be interpreted, a large number of translations have preferred to say in the text "You are like salt for men," and to discuss what it means in a footnote.

Of the earth, as we pointed out, means "for all people" or "for people everywhere."

Has lost its taste is difficult to interpret. Salt that is used for food does not lose its taste or its saltness even if unused for a long period of time. This expression must therefore refer to the salt being diluted or somehow mixed with other substances so that it becomes ineffective. The root meaning of the verb is "make foolish" or "show to be foolish" (1 Cor 1.20), and in the passive, "become foolish" (Rom 1.22). Only in this verse and in Luke 14.34 do the lexicons give the meaning for the passive as "become tasteless."

Scholars have suggested many possible explanations. One is that Jesus is referring to salt being mixed with other substances so that it is no longer effective. Another is that the salt retrieved from the Dead Sea contains other substances, and that if the salt is washed out and lost, only those worthless substances are left. AB has "If the salt is of low grade," and the authors in this way reflect their interpretation of the verb "become foolish" as referring to the salt becoming "insipid" by being mixed and thus weakened. Others suggest that a play on words was involved, in which the Hebrew word for "be foolish" resembles the Aramaic word for "seasoned, salty." Another suggestion is that salt has been a symbol of wisdom, and that Jesus is warning his disciples not to become "foolish," as indicated by the use of the Greek verb. Another possibility, of course, is that Jesus knew perfectly well that salt does not change, but that he simply used this unreal and surprising figure of speech in order to teach a lesson more effectively.

We must not assume that Jesus and his disciples knew nothing of the properties of salt. Instead, it is important to recognize the function of this saying of Jesus. First, it is better to regard the figure of salt as referring to preservation of food rather than to improving the taste, although both may be involved. Although JB follows RSV with "become tasteless," most of the modern translations settle for the meaning "loses its strength" (TEV, GECL, AT, Lu). Second, he is saying that the disciples are the people who have the spiritual knowledge, wisdom, and way of life by which to preserve this world in a proper condition, and it is not the religious leaders or government officials who can do it. Third, he is warning his followers against a useless discipleship, one that is weak or diluted so as to become ineffective.

Because salt is known wherever Bible translations are prepared, there is no difficulty preparing a translation that preserves **salt** as a figure of speech. However, the translator should take care that the structure of the sentence will not cause undue difficulty for the practical application of the figure in the life of a Christian. Few translations choose the interpretation "be foolish" for **lost its taste**. More common are those who say "no longer tastes like salt," "no longer does what salt should do," or "if the salt becomes so impure that it is no longer really salt." But "loses its strength" will be the most common.

The sentence continues by asking **how shall its saltness be restored?** The translation will depend on how "lost its taste" was translated, since it should be similar. Following the above examples, the clause can be "how can it be made to taste like salt again?" "how can it once more do what salt should do (or, once more act like salt)?" "how can it become salt again?" or "how can it regain its strength?"

It is no longer good for anything (TEV "**It has become worthless**") is more literally "It no longer has strength for anything." GECL has "One can no longer use it for anything." Other options are "People have no further use for it," "It is no longer good for anything," or "You can do nothing with it," as in Brc.

Thrown out may have to be "thrown outside" or "thrown out of doors."

Trodden (TEV "**trample**") is also used in Matthew 7.6 and Luke 8.5 with the same meaning. Elsewhere in the New Testament it is found only in Luke 12.1 and Hebrews 10.29. **Trodden under foot** does not mean people will deliberately walk on it or somehow try to stamp it into the ground. The idea is it will be out on the ground where people walk, perhaps even on a road.

Taking these things into account, the sentence can be translated "It is no longer good for anything, so it will just be thrown outdoors where it will be walked on," or "You can do nothing with it except throw it out, and there it will get walked on (or, people will walk on it)."

5.14	RSV	TEV

"You are the light of the world. A city set on a hill cannot be hid.

    "You are like light for the whole world. A city built on a hill cannot be hid.

You are the light of the world is made into a simile by TEV: "**You are like light.**" And TEV understands **of the world** to mean "**for the whole world.**" GECL translates, "You are the light for the world." INCL renders, "You are like light that is needed by everyone in this world."

As with "salt" in the previous verse, many translations have used a simile to translate **You are the light of the world**. TEV and INCL are examples cited above. Those translations which have tried to show the basis of the comparison, in what way the disciples are like light, have said "You show people the way (to God) as a light does," "You help people to see God as if you were a light," or "People can see their way to God because of you who are like a light for them."

Again, **world** means "all the people of the world" or "people everywhere."

The saying about **a city set on a hill** may originally have been a secular proverb which could have been used in a variety of contexts. Here the meaning is clear: light is certain to be noticed.

The city on a hill **cannot be hid**, that is, "cannot remain unseen," "people can easily see it."

Some translations tie the two statements in this verse closely together with sentences such as "You are the light of the world that people cannot fail to see, just as they cannot fail to see a city built on a hill," or "People cannot fail to see the way to God (or, way of life) because you are a light for them which they can see as easily as they see a city on a hill."

5.15   RSV   TEV

| Nor do men light a lamp and put it under a bushel, but on a stand, and it gives light to all in the house. | No one lights a lamp and puts it under a bowl; instead he puts it on the lampstand, where it gives light for everyone in the house. |

Nor do men light a lamp and put it under a bushel. A lamp would be placed under a bushel (TEV **"bowl"**) solely in order to hide it. It would be totally absurd for someone to light a lamp for the purpose of supplying light for a one-room Palestinian house, and then immediately hide it.

Nor indicates a continuation of the thought from the previous verse. Translators sometimes say "further" or "similarly."

Men may be "people," but when the negative component from **Nor** is added, it may be translated as **"No one,"** as in TEV. If the singular **"No one"** is used, then English will normally speak of lighting **a lamp**. However, if "people" or "men" is used, it will be more natural to speak of lighting "lamps."

A **lamp** may be a "lantern" or "light." But "candle," used by some, would be wrong, since candles were not in use in Palestine at that time.

The word translated **bushel** is a Latin loan word which originally referred to a grain measure containing about 8.75 liters, or almost exactly one peck. Elsewhere in the New Testament it occurs only in Mark 4.21 and Luke 11.33. In this passage the size of the vessel is not so important as its function, that is, to hide the light of the lamp. If there is no exact equivalent of a **bushel** in an area, then translators may use some other kind of container that would effectively hide a lamp were it placed over it. Such objects include "basket," "calabash," or "large bowl."

The light is placed on a **stand**, "a place where lamps are placed," "a high table for the lamp," or "a shelf for the lamp."

All means all the people, as TEV shows.

It gives light to all in the house presupposes a one-room structure in which a lamp is placed in a position where it can give light to the entire area. The context allows for **light** to be taken as a reference to the disciples, the preaching of the disciples, Jesus himself, or the preaching of Jesus. Fortunately, this is something the translator need not and should not make explicit. The sentence can be translated "it is placed on a stand where it lights up the house for everyone" or "it is put in its place so that everyone in the house can have light."

5.16

RSV	TEV
Let your light so shine before men, that they may see your good works and give glory to your Father who is in heaven.	**In the same way your light must shine before people, so that they will see the good things you do and praise your Father in heaven.**

This verse is closely related to verses 13-15. **Before men** echoes "by men" of verse 13, while **light** is a central theme both here and in verses 14-15.

Let your light so shine translates a third person imperative, which is difficult to express in many languages. Most contemporary English translations use some structure with "must" (see TEV "**your light must shine**") rather than the traditional **Let** of KJV and RSV. In many languages it may be necessary to switch either to a second person imperative ("Shine your light") or to some other less difficult form (for example, "Be sure that your light shines").

Your light may be "the light you produce," "the light that shines from you," or "the light you are."

So means "in such a way." Here it refers back to the lamp on the lampstand in verse 15. TEV makes this clear with "**In the same way.**" Translators can also say "Similarly," "Just so," or "The light you produce should also be like that. Let it shine before people . . . ."

Before men can be translated "so everyone can see it" or "for all to see."

That they may see is the purpose of letting your light shine before people. Translations may use "so that" or "in order that people can see."

The Greek noun construction **your good works** is represented as a verb construction by TEV: "**the good things you do.**" The focus now shifts from the character of the disciples to their good works which result from this character. What the disciples are must be evident to all, but in such a way that it reveals the true origin of the **good works** that they do. These works may be characterized as deeds of mercy and of reconciliation, a conclusion supported both by the Gospel itself (see 5.38-48; 25.31-46) and by the Jewish concept of good works. The phrase **good works** is found only one other time in Matthew's Gospel; it appears in 26.10 in the singular "good work." More frequently the expression "good fruit" is used (3.10; 7.17-19; 12.33). **Your good works** may be translated "your good actions" or "your good deeds." Brc has translated "the lovely things you do."

Give glory to (TEV "**praise**") is similar to the expression used in 9.8 and 15.31, where the meaning is clearly "give praise to." The thought is parallel to Isaiah 49.3 ("Israel, you are my servant; because of you, people will praise me") and to the Testament of Naphtali 8.1 ("Do what is good, my children. Then men and angels will praise you, and God will be honored among the heathen"). But it contrasts with the thinking of the hypocrites, who perform their religious duties to receive praise from people (6.2).

When men see your good actions, they will **give glory to your Father who is in heaven**. "Men will see the good things you do and therefore praise your Father in heaven." If there is not a good way of saying **give glory to** or "praise" in a language, it may be necessary to say "so that men will say good things about (or, will honor) your Father in heaven."

Your Father who is in heaven and related expressions with "my" or "our" is used some twenty times in Matthew, but only once in Mark (11.25) and not at all in Luke. Evidently this reflects a common usage in Jewish rabbinical literature, as the commentators note.

The expression **your Father who is in heaven** is not necessarily understood by all readers to refer to God. Translators can say "God, who is your Father in heaven" or "God, your Father who lives (or, stays) in heaven." We have mentioned before that there are cultures where it would not be normal to use figures of speech such as "father" when speaking of God. The phrase is then understood literally, which may further disturb the readers who react against the idea of God having human offspring. Or they might assume that "father in heaven" refers to one's dead ancestor. In either case, a simile may be helpful, as in "God who is like a father to you," "God who created you and cares for you like a father," or "God in heaven whom you call your Father."

5.17-20

<table>
<tr><td>RSV</td><td>TEV</td></tr>
<tr><td></td><td>**Teaching about the Law**</td></tr>
<tr><td>

17 "Think not that I have come to abolish the law and the prophets; I have come not to abolish them but to fulfil them. 18 For truly, I say to you, till heaven and earth pass away, not an iota, not a dot, will pass from the law until all is accomplished. 19 Whoever then relaxes one of the least of these commandments and teaches men so, shall be called least in the kingdom of heaven; but he who does them and teaches them shall be called great in the kingdom of heaven. 20 For I tell you, unless your righteousness exceeds that of the scribes and Pharisees, you will never enter the kingdom of heaven.

</td><td>

17 "Do not think that I have come to do away with the Law of Moses and the teachings of the prophets. I have not come to do away with them, but to make their teachings come true. 18 Remember that as long as heaven and earth last, not the least point nor the smallest detail of the Law will be done away with—not until the end of all things.[a] 19 So then, whoever disobeys even the least important of the commandments and teaches others to do the same, will be least in the Kingdom of heaven. On the other hand, whoever obeys the Law and teaches others to do the same, will be great in the Kingdom of heaven. 20 I tell you, then, that you will be able to enter the Kingdom of heaven only if you are more faithful than the teachers of the Law and the Pharisees in doing what God requires.

</td></tr>
</table>

[a] the end of all things *or* all its teachings come true.

SECTION HEADING: "**Teaching about the Law**." The "**Law**" is "the Jewish Law," "the Law of Moses," or "the Law Moses gave." Many translators will prefer a short sentence for this section heading, such as "Jesus teaches about the Law (or, the Law of Moses)" or "Jesus talks about the laws Moses gave the people."

Except for the parallel to verse 18 in Luke 16.17 (see also Mark 13.31), this passage is unique to Matthew. Its function is probably to serve as an introduction to the series of contrasts which follow (verses 21-48) and at the same time to prevent a misunderstanding of Jesus' teaching in these verses.

5.17	RSV	TEV
	"Think not that I have come to abolish the law and the prophets; I have come not to abolish them but to fulfil them.	"Do not think that I have come to do away with the Law of Moses and the teachings of the prophets. I have not come to do away with them, but to make their teachings come true.

Think not that I have come is repeated word for word in 10.34. "**Do not think**" (TEV) or "You should not think" are natural ways to express **Think not** in English.

Jesus does not mean by **I have come** simply that he had gone to the mountain at that particular time. He is referring to his ministry in the world, so translations can have "I have come to the world" or "I have come teaching and preaching."

The Greek verb **abolish** (TEV "**do away with**") has the root meaning of "to destroy"; it is found in 2 Maccabees 2.22 and 4 Maccabees 5.33 with precisely the same meaning that it has here.

To translate **abolish**, translators have used "put an end to," "render (or, make) useless," "cancel," "say the Law has no value," or "say you don't have to obey the Law anymore." The term used should fit both the Law and the prophets as direct objects.

The law and the prophets is translated in TEV as "**the Law of Moses and the teachings of the prophets**." In the Greek text **and** here is literally "or"; elsewhere Matthew uses this phrase with the Greek for "and" (7.12; 11.3; 22.40), as it also occurs elsewhere in the New Testament (Luke 16.16; 24.44; John 1.45; Acts 13.15; 28.23; Rom 3.21). The use of "or" here in place of the usual "and" is probably caused by the negative construction; most translations have "and"; no difference in meaning is to be sought between the two forms.

One approach to translating **the law and the prophets** has been to use an expression such as in TEV and say "the Law (or, laws) given by Moses and the teachings given by the prophets (or, written in the books of the prophets)." Another way has been to use a general word to cover both, such as "the teachings of the Scriptures" or "the teachings in the holy writings."

I have come translates the first of five "I came" sayings of Matthew's Gospel (5.17 [twice]; 9.13; 10.34,35); all are aorist in Greek.

The meaning of **to fulfil** is hotly disputed. The Greek verb means literally to fill up something, as to fill a jar with water. The use here is figurative, and it can have two basic meanings: 1) "fulfill" in the sense of actions or events that are required by the Law or predicted by the prophets; and 2) "fill up" in the sense of making complete what was not yet complete.

The first meaning is represented by those translations that use **fulfill** (RSV, NAB, Brc). TEV **"to make their teachings come true."** The advantage of this interpretation is that it fits the use of the term elsewhere in Matthew (as in 1.22; 2.15,17,23; 3.15).

The second meaning can refer to bringing the Law and the prophets themselves to completion, as if they were not yet completely set forth. This interpretation has the advantage of tying verse 17 closely to verses 21-48, where Jesus gives the fuller implications of certain commands in the Law. Or this second meaning can refer to bringing to completion the understanding people should have about the Law and the prophets. Several commentators understand it in this sense, "to bring into clear light the true scope and meaning," and one can understand verses 21-48 in that light as well. Similarly TOB translates the verb as "accomplish," but in the sense of making complete; the TOB footnote concludes that the meaning in this context is that of bringing the Law to perfection by giving it its true sense. So also GECL 1st edition, "to give them their true meaning." Some commentators trace the verb back to the Aramaic mother tongue of Jesus and maintain that the meaning is "to bring into effect" or "to confirm" by means of teaching, which is also accomplished in verses 21-48. It is possible to see a relation between these two variations, since the meaning "to complete," as in NEB, Phps, NJB, carries the sense of "to set forth in its true meaning" (see JB footnote).

The better interpretation seems to be that of TEV, which follows the first meaning. This interpretation is consistent with the use of the term in Matthew. However, if a translator has reason to disagree, a variation of the second meaning will be appropriate. No one has provided final proof for either interpretation.

If translators accept the interpretation that **fulfil** here means "complete," then they can say "to make them perfect (or, the way they should be)." If they prefer the idea seen in GECL 1st edition, "to give them their true meaning," they can have "to make the Law and the prophets understood properly," "to make the Law and the prophets have their true sense," or "to show people what the Law was really saying."

As we pointed out, however, there is good evidence to prefer the interpretation of TEV (**"to make their teachings come true"**) and to have a sentence such as "to cause to happen what those teachings said would happen." See also comments on 1.22.

In this verse, a very strong contrast is given between false assumptions about why Jesus came and the real reasons. Some languages have to express this in a style that almost overemphasizes the contrast: "Don't think that the reason I have come to the world is to do away with the Law of Moses and the teachings of the prophets. I have not come to do away with them at all. On the contrary, the reason I am here is to make them come true." Translators should keep this contrast in mind and express it in the way that will be most natural for them.

5.18 RSV TEV

For truly, I say to you, till heaven and earth pass away, not an iota, not a dot, will pass from the law until all is accomplished.

Remember that as long as heaven and earth last, not the least point nor the smallest detail of the Law will be done away with—not until the end of

all things.^a

> ^a the end of all things *or* all its teachings come true.

For truly, I say to you translates a solemn formula which appears in the Gospels only in the mouth of Jesus. It denotes a solemn assertion of divine truth. GECL translates "I assure you" (so TEV in 10.15), and TEV has "**Remember.**" Translators can also say "I tell you the truth," "I declare to you in truth," or "Remember, the fact (or, truth) is."

Till heaven and earth pass away may reflect the Jewish conviction that the Law and all of its parts were eternal and possessed eternal value. After the destruction of Jerusalem this developed into an unshakable affirmation of faith, held to firmly by the homeless Jewish people. TEV states this negative affirmation in a positive form: "**as long as heaven and earth last**." Other translations that can be used include "till heaven and earth are destroyed (or, come to an end)," "till the whole universe is gone," "till the end of the world," or "as long as there is a heaven and an earth."

Iota (TEV "**the least point**") is the name of the smallest letter in the Greek alphabet. It substitutes here for *yod*, the smallest letter in the Hebrew alphabet. The **dot** (TEV "**the smallest detail of the Law**") is generally taken to refer to a tiny mark (literally "horn") attached to some Hebrew letters to keep them from being confused with others. But some scholars affirm that we cannot know for certain whether this is the reference or not, since archaeological evidence is inconclusive. NEB translates "not a letter, not a stroke." GECL combines the two terms into "the dot of an i." Brc has "not the smallest letter, not the smallest part of a letter."

Translators have found different ways to express this. Some prefer to keep the image of the text and say "not one letter or part of a letter" or "not even a part of the writing of one word." Others have used expressions such as "not one part of the Law," "not one detail of the Law," or "not in any way at all." This is less vivid and not as good, since the imagery Jesus uses here tends to dramatize forcefully the point he is making.

To **pass from the law** means that it "will be removed from the law," "be changed," "will stop being valid," or "be destroyed."

Much controversy surrounds the interpretation of the clause **until all is accomplished**. TEV translates this clause as "**not until the end of all things**," with an alternative rendering in the margin ("until all its teaching come true"). The Greek expression is literally "until all things happen," which basically offers two possibilities of interpretation:

(1) "All things" may be interpreted as a reference to events which must happen before the end of time; this seems to be the approach taken by most translations: "until all that must happen has happened" (NEB), "until history comes to an end" (Brc), "not before the end of this world" (GECL 1st edition). The TOB footnote qualifies this as a "difficult expression" but prefers the meaning "until the end of the world."

(2) "All things" may also be interpreted as a reference to the demands of the Law: "until all its teachings come true" (TEV alternative rendering), "before all that it stands for is achieved" (NEB alternative rendering), "until its purpose is complete"

(Phps), "until all its purpose is achieved" (NJB). Mft ("until it is all in force"), and AT ("until it is all observed") seem also to accept this exegesis.

It is difficult to believe that the first of these possibilities is what is meant, for this would simply be repeating what is said at the first of the verse. Moreover, the contextual demands are met much better by the second of these alternative possibilities.

Taking this second interpretation, translators can have "until everything in the Law is fulfilled," "until everything the Law speaks of comes true," "until the whole purpose of the Law is achieved," or "until everything happens as the Law says it will."

Translators may structure this verse in different ways: "For I assure you, until the very end of the world, not even one part of one word of the writing of the law will be done away with until everything in it is fulfilled," or "For I tell you in truth, not one part of the writing of the law will be destroyed before everything happens as the law says it will, not as long as heaven and earth last."

5.19

RSV	TEV
Whoever then relaxes one of the least of these commandments and teaches men so, shall be called least in the kingdom of heaven; but he who does them and teaches them shall be called great in the kingdom of heaven.	So then, whoever disobeys even the least important of the commandments and teaches others to do the same, will be least in the Kingdom of heaven. On the other hand, whoever obeys the Law and teaches others to do the same, will be great in the Kingdom of heaven.

Relaxes (TEV "**disobeys**") literally means "to loose," "set free," "untie"; here it probably means "to set aside" (see NEB) or "to weaken the authority of" (Brc). The concept would be related to the rabbinic idea of declaring a certain law no longer valid, and this in fact gives us a good pointer on how to translate. The translation can be "says is not valid" or "decides it does not need to be obeyed anymore."

The least of these commandments may be a reference to the Law (verse 18) or to the teachings of Jesus which follow. The rendering of TEV ("**the least important of the commandments**") sounds as if the Ten Commandments may be the point of reference, and NEB is explicit: "the least of the Law's demands." One scholar believes that the saying, as used by Matthew, "probably refers to the commandments taught by Jesus, which follow."

From a purely grammatical point of view, neither interpretation is completely satisfactory. Some commentators note, for example, that the Greek participle **then** (TEV "**So then**") is normally used to draw an inference from what precedes, which makes it difficult to interpret the commandment of this verse as a reference to the teachings of Jesus that follow. On the other hand, if a reference were to the Law of verse 18, one would normally expect a singular pronoun ("its commands") in place of the Greek plural pronoun ("these commands"). Although neither interpretation is absolutely satisfactory, it is proposed that one of the two choices mentioned be followed in translation, since both of them have the support of standard commentaries and translations. The other option may be given in a footnote.

Translations that follow the first interpretation will have "these laws God has given" or "these laws that you have had."

Those translators who follow the second interpretation will have "these commandments I give you" or "these commandments I tell you now."

Note that if the second interpretation is followed, **then** cannot really be translated, unless one says "Therefore" or "So I tell you now."

The text specifies **one of the least of these commandments**, which is to say "even one of the smallest," "even one of the most unimportant" of the commandments.

There is an intended contrast between **relaxes . . . teaches** and **does . . . teaches**. Matthew is not primarily concerned with traditional arguments regarding the importance or lack of importance of a particular command; he is concerned with the practical matter of obedience to the commands of God and the teaching that results from this obedience.

Teaches men so may be "teaches people that it is not valid," "teaches people not to obey," or "teaches people not to pay attention to them."

Shall be called least is represented in TEV by "**will be least.**" As in 5.9, **shall be called** means "will be." Both GECL and FRCL have the same form as TEV.

The adjectives **least** and "little" hold a significant place in Matthew's Gospel. In 25.40,45 "the least of these my brethren" is used as a reference to the disciples, while in 10.42; 18.6,10,14 "one of these little ones" is used with the same meaning. The contrast is between the world's evaluation of Jesus' followers and God's evaluation of them. Since the temporal reference is the end of the world, GECL translates "in God's new world," and MACL "when God establishes his rule."

The phrase **called least in the kingdom of heaven** is often difficult for translators. As we pointed out, **called least** is sometimes translated "will be the least." But other translations prefer to say "God will call (or, consider) him the least." To say "least in importance (or, in the lowest position) in the kingdom of heaven (or, of God)" is a good solution for translators that use "kingdom." For those that use "rule" or "reign," however, the problem is more acute, since "least in God's rule" does not make much sense. In these cases translators can say "least important of the people under God's rule" or "least important of those who are a part of God's reign." A translation should not imply they are among those ruling, but rather are subjects ruled over by God.

The verse goes on to speak of the person who **does them and teaches them**, which is to say "who obeys the commandments and who also teaches people to obey them." The text speaks of **he who**, that is, "whoever" or "any person who." It does not refer only to males.

To be **great** here means "to be important" or "to have high status." **Shall be called great in the kingdom of heaven** should be treated in the same way as **shall be called least** (but using "great" instead of "least," of course).

For I tell you, unless your righteousness exceeds that of the scribes and Pharisees, you will never enter the kingdom of heaven.	I tell you, then, that you will be able to enter the Kingdom of heaven only if you are more faithful than the teachers of the Law and the Pharisees in doing what God requires.

For I tell you is an emphatic transitional which serves to tie this verse with the preceding and to draw attention to the words that follow. TEV inverts the order of the final two clauses in Greek, thus avoiding the more difficult "unless . . ." structure (see RSV). GECL has adopted the same order as TEV.

You is plural here, and in some translations appears as "you people" or "you all."

Unless your righteousness exceeds appears in TEV as "**only if you are more faithful . . . in doing what God requires**," and in GECL as "If you do not fulfill his will more perfectly than do the teachers of the Law and the Pharisees." Full discussion has already been given to the word **righteousness** (see comments on 3.15; 5.6,10). A proper understanding of this **righteousness** is extremely important: it does not mean they are to adopt a greater number of commandments and prohibitions—Matthew in fact reduces all the commandments to one, the double commandment to love God and one's fellow man. Jesus means that people must think in terms of a new and far more comprehensive righteousness. GECL renders "If you do not fulfill his will more perfectly than the teachers of the Law and the Pharisees." In general the other translations follow along the same lines that they did in the earlier verses where "righteousness" was used. TOB, in its footnote on this verse, points out that the meaning is the same here as in 5.6,10; it is the faithfulness of the disciples to the Law of God, a new faithfulness rendered possible and urgent by the authoritative interpretation which Jesus gives to that Law (7.29).

Both TEV and GECL provide useful models for the phrase **unless your righteousness exceeds**. Similar sentences are "unless you make a greater effort in doing God's will" or "unless you are more careful to do what God requires."

Scribes (TEV "**teachers of the law**") were first mentioned in 2.4. The word is here used in conjunction with **Pharisees**, and it should be kept in mind: Scribes and Pharisees are overlapping but not identical groups. Among the scribes or experts in the law were found both Pharisees and Sadducees, and only a small proportion of the Pharisaic party was composed of scribes. Elsewhere they are mentioned together in 12.38; 15.1; 23.2,13,14,15. See 2.4 for a discussion of **scribes**, and 3.7 for **Pharisees**.

It is very important that **enter the kingdom of heaven** not be understood or translated as "go to heaven." Of course, if "kingdom of heaven" is being translated as "rule (or, reign) of God," the misunderstanding is not likely to arise. But on the other hand, it may be difficult to speak of "entering the rule." Translators can say "will be one of those over whom God rules," "will be one of the people under God's reign," or "God will not be able to make them part of his reign." Another approach is to see the expression as meaning to become a part of the community of people over whom God rules: "become one of the people under God's rule."

As we pointed out above, TEV and GECL have restructured the verse to avoid what would be a rather complex sentence if "unless" were used. Every language is different, and translators must restructure in ways that are natural. Some other examples may include "For I tell you all, that you will never be among those under God's reign if you are not more careful to fulfill God's will than the teachers of the Law and the Pharisees are," or "There's no way you can be some of those people who are ruled over by God if you are not more faithful than the teachers of the Law and the Pharisees in doing what God requires."

5.21-26

RSV | TEV

Teaching about Anger

21 "You have heard that it was said to the men of old, 'You shall not kill; and whoever kills shall be liable to judgment.' 22 But I say to you that every one who is angry with his brother* shall be liable to judgment; whoever insults*^j his brother shall be liable to the council, and whoever says, 'You fool!' shall be liable to the hell^k of fire. 23 So if you are offering your gift at the altar, and there remember that your brother has something against you, 24 leave your gift there before the altar and go; first be reconciled to your brother, and then come and offer your gift. 25 Make friends quickly with your accuser, while you are going with him to court, lest your accuser hand you over to the judge, and the judge to the guard, and you be put in prison; 26 truly, I say to you, you will never get out till you have paid the last penny.

ⁱ Other ancient authorities insert *without cause*
^j Greek *says Raca to* (an obscure term of abuse)
^k Greek *Gehenna*

21 "You have heard that people were told in the past, 'Do not commit murder; anyone who does will be brought to trial.' 22 But now I tell you: whoever is angry^b with his brother will be brought to trial, whoever calls his brother 'You good-for-nothing!' will be brought before the Council, and whoever calls his brother a worthless fool will be in danger of going to the fire of hell. 23 So if you are about to offer your gift to God at the altar and there you remember that your brother has something against you, 24 leave your gift there in front of the altar, go at once and make peace with your brother, and then come back and offer your gift to God.

25 "If someone brings a lawsuit against you and takes you to court, settle the dispute with him while there is time, before you get to court. Once you are there, he will turn you over to the judge, who will hand you over to the police, and you will be put in jail. 26 There you will stay, I tell you, until you pay the last penny of your fine.

^b whoever is angry; *some manuscripts have* whoever without cause is angry.

SECTION HEADING: "**Teaching about Anger**." Again, many languages will use complete sentences for the section heading, as in "Jesus teaches about anger." If the language does not normally speak of "anger," an abstract noun, then the heading may be "Jesus teaches about people who get angry" or "Jesus teaches about when people are angry."

Although some commentators begin a new section with verse 20, most commentators view 5.21-48 as a unit under the general heading "The New Righteousness." Contained within this section are six "contrasts" or "antitheses." The first two and the fourth (21-26; 27-30; 33-37) are alike in that in each instance Jesus takes up one of the Ten Commandments and goes beyond it, by forbidding not only the deed itself but the attitude which lies behind the deed. The remaining three contrasts invalidate popular interpretations of commands relating to divorce (31-32), retaliation (38-42), and love (43-47).

The contrasts between Jesus' teaching and three of the Ten Commandments (21-26; 27-30; 33-37) are unique to Matthew, while the teaching about divorce (31-32) grows out of Jesus' remarks on adultery (27-30). Luke has parallels to the teaching about divorce (16.18), retaliation (6.29-30), and love for one's enemies (6.27-28,32-36). All this suggests that the entire section is a Matthean construction made from traditional sayings. Some scholars interpret these verses as a "New Law," "The Law of the Messiah." And all agree that the overall purpose is to stress the real meaning of the word of God in the Old Testament and to affirm its fulfillment in Jesus Christ.

5.21

RSV	TEV
"You have heard that it was said to the men of old, 'You shall not kill; and whoever kills shall be liable to judgment.'	"You have heard that people were told in the past, 'Do not commit murder; anyone who does will be brought to trial.'

You have heard that it was said to the men of old is restructured by TEV as "**You have heard that people were told in the past**." GECL translates "You know that it has been said to our ancestors" (JB "You have learnt how it was said to our ancestors"; NAB "You have heard the commandment imposed on your forefathers"). The impersonal passive form of **it was said** can possibly mean "people of the past said"; however, in the New Testament such a passive always introduces a divine utterance or a scriptural quotation. One may therefore translate "You know that God said . . . ." Many translations will therefore use a sentence such as "You know God said to your ancestors" or "People have told you what God said to your fathers of long ago."

The men of old refers primarily to the "Sinai generation." However, all subsequent generations are also included. The same construction occurs in verse 33. The phrase is usually translated as "your ancestors" or "your fathers of long ago." Note that it refers to all those people, not just to the males.

You shall not kill comes from Exodus 20.13, while **whoever kills shall be liable to judgment** echoes Deuteronomy 17.8. TEV correctly translates "**murder**" as the meaning of **kill**. Both the Hebrew and the Greek verbs mean murder or assassination, not just any form of taking life.

The distinction between "murder" and "kill" has often proved a problem for translators. "Murder" specifically means killing that is not legal or sanctioned by the community, nor is it accidental. Thus killing in battle or sanctioned executions are not included in the commandment **You shall not kill**. Usually a language will have a way of referring to murder, either with a specific word or with a phrase such as "killing from anger" or "killing of one's own volition." Such expressions should also exclude killing accidentally.

The **shall**, of course, is not a simple future reference but an imperative: "you must not" or "I forbid you." **You** is in the singular in the text.

Whoever means "anyone who," "any person who," or "that person who."

Liable to judgment (TEV "**brought to trial**") is translated "answer for it before the court" by NJB and "stand his trial" by Phps. The verb may, however, mean "guilty," as it does in 26.66. One commentator, accepting the meaning "guilty" (that is, "condemned by the properly constituted authority"), is convinced that it is here equivalent to "be put to death." In this case the properly constituted authority would be the twenty-three members of the local sanhedrin. See comments at verse 22 for coordinating the translation of this term with its use there.

Translators who follow the first interpretation, the one in TEV, will use the normal expression in their language for being brought to trial: "accused before the judge," "will be taken to court to be tried (or, judged)," and so forth.

Other translations will follow the second interpretation, whereby **judgment** implies "guilt." They might say "found guilty by the judge" or "the judge will declare him guilty." A common West African expression is "the judge will cut the case against him."

5.22	RSV	TEV

But I say to you that every one who is angry with his brother[i] shall be liable to judgment; whoever insults[j] his brother shall be liable to the council, and whoever says, 'You fool!' shall be liable to the hell[k] of fire.	But now I tell you: whoever is angry[b] with his brother will be brought to trial, whoever calls his brother 'You good-for-nothing!' will be brought before the Council, and whoever calls his brother a worthless fool will be in danger of going to the fire of hell.

[i] Other ancient authorities insert *without cause*
[j] Greek *says Raca to* (an obscure term of abuse)
[k] Greek *Gehenna*

[b] whoever is angry; *some manuscripts have* whoever without cause is angry.

But I say to you is best understood as a contrast to the last clause of verse 21 ("whoever kills shall be liable to judgment") rather than to the entire command. What is significant and unprecedented is the phrase **But I say**, in which **I** stands in an emphatic position, thus placing the authority of Jesus parallel with the hidden name of God in the phrase "it was said to the men of old."

TEV has shown this emphasis on the first person **I** with "**now**" in the phrase "**But now I tell you.**" Translators can also say "But what I tell you is . . . ."

As the RSV footnote indicates, **every one who is angry** is found in some manuscripts in the expanded form ". . . angry without cause." The UBS Greek text reflects the opinion that "without cause" was added by scribes in order to soften Jesus' remark (so TC-GNT). Apparently none of the modern standard translations include it in their text, though several of them provide a footnote, indicating the alternative possibility (for example, RSV, TEV, NEB).

Every one can be "any person who" or "whoever."

The frequent usage of **brother** throughout this passage in particular and throughout the Sermon as a whole suggests that the ethical concern is not about general rules for human behavior; in this context the concern may be for disciples in their relations to one another. Certainly, the use of **brother** for people not physically related was distinctively Christian.

Many languages use **brother** to mean a close friend, associate, or fellow member of some group. In these cases "brother" will be understood correctly. In languages where the word is understood only to refer to a blood brother, or where it means one's fellow men in general, then a better translation may be "fellow disciple" or "fellow believer" (but not "fellow Christian"!).

Shall be liable to judgment translates the same expression used in verse 21 (see comments there). Several scholars affirm without hesitation that in each instance the reference is to God's final judgment, "for carrying out a death sentence according to the Law of Moses is the same as executing God's final judgment. The Pentateuch did not think in terms of a judgment after death, and God's judgment can only be performed in this world." The confusion arose "when the continuation was added with its mention of the Council (the Sanhedrin or supreme judicial body in Palestine)," at which time the meaning of the first judgment was restricted to that of the local authority.

Some scholars see an ascending scale of sins: anger, the accusation "Raca," and the accusation "you fool." However, it is difficult to see how **judgment** can refer to human courts, since human courts judge a person according to one's deeds, not one's attitude. Although this conclusion may nullify the possibility of discovering here a neatly marked-out ascending scale of sins and their corresponding punishments, it does seem to be the most valid interpretation in light of what the text itself says.

For these reasons, then, **judgment** here should probably be translated "be brought before God for judgment," "God will judge him," or "will be a person to come before God and be judged."

Insults: the term *Raca* (see RSV footnote) is generally assumed to be of Aramaic origin, with the root meaning "empty." Several scholars indicate that it may have meant something like **"good-for-nothing"** (so TEV) or "fool." Some translations have followed the RSV fairly closely when translating **insults**, and said "whoever says insults (or, bad things) to his brother" or "whoever calls his brother bad names." Others have chosen to use direct speech as TEV does, and say something like "whoever calls his brother, 'You worthless person' or 'You no-good.' " This can also be in indirect speech, as in "whoever calls his brother a worthless person (or, a no-good)." Most languages have an insulting expression from their language which they can use. The important consideration is to be sure a term with a strong emotive force is used.

The **council** was the supreme judicial body of the Jews. In cultures where it is the elders who judge violations of tradition or religion, this can be translated as "the elders of the Jews" or "the Council of our elders." Other translations may say "the highest court of our people" or "the most senior judges in our land." Thus **be liable to the council** means "will be taken to be judged by the council" or "they will carry that person before our senior elders so they can judge him."

Fool (TEV **"worthless fool"**), in addition to the usual meaning of "senseless," would probably have suggested "religious impiety" as well. Several scholars interpret it to mean "one who rebels against God." **Fool** is used in the Old Testament primarily of the godless (Psa 14.1; 94.8; Isa 32.6; Deut 32.6; Jer 5.21).

In translation, both "Raca" and **fool** should be given the component of "foolishness," with the second term somewhat stronger, possibly implying impiety as well. Elsewhere in the Gospel of Matthew, the word is used in 7.26; 23.17,19; 25.2,3,8. No other Gospel writer uses it, though it is found four times in 1 Corinthians (1.25,27; 3.18; 4.10), and once each in 2 Timothy (2.23) and Titus (3.9). **Fool** has sometimes been translated as "godless," "you don't know God at all," or "you are a wicked fool."

The hell of fire (TEV "the fire of hell") is literally "the Gehenna of fire" (see RSV footnote). Gehenna was the name of a valley southwest of Jerusalem, where human sacrifices had once been offered and where garbage from the city was constantly burning. Later this picture was combined with the idea of God's judgment, and so the notion of a fiery hell developed. Most commentators assume that the reference is to hell, and a number of translations make this information explicit. However, some few interpreters dogmatically deny that Gehenna was equated with hell in New Testament times. Therefore AB has "merits a fiery death." See comments on "hell" in verse 29.

The person who is **liable to the hell of fire** can be said to be a person "who will be sent to hell (or, the fires of hell)."

Hell is sometimes an unknown concept. There are contexts where "the place of the dead" is a good translation, but not here. "The place of torture (or, punishment)" would be better, or possibly "the place of torture of the dead." Here, then, translations can have "the place of fiery punishment."

5.23	RSV	TEV
	So if you are offering your gift at the altar, and there remember that your brother has something against you,	So if you are about to offer your gift to God at the altar and there you remember that your brother has something against you,

Verses 23-24 describe a situation where someone has a just claim against the person here spoken to, but where the guilty person does not feel hostile toward the one who has this claim against him. This is the first application of the principles given in verse 21-22, and it is concerned with reconciliation.

So indicates the relation between what has just been said and what Jesus is going on to say. "As a result," "Consequently," "Therefore," or "Because of this" are common translations.

You is singular, as if Jesus is speaking to each individual among the disciples.

The **gift** is some sort of sacrifice. The Greek text does not specify the recipient, but "God" is obviously intended (TEV, FRCL, GECL). **Offering your gift** is speaking of "offering a sacrifice to God" or "making an offering to God."

The **altar** is "the place for making sacrifices" or "the platform (or, place) on which offerings to God are given." It may be necessary to add "in the Temple."

That your brother has something against you indicates that the person who is bringing the sacrifice is the one at fault. This may be translated as "that your brother has a grievance (or, complaint) against you (for something you did)," or "is angry because of what you did." Note also the comments on "brother" in verse 22.

In several languages this whole verse should be restructured to be more natural. For example, "So if you are about to offer a gift to God on the altar, but remember that there is a brother who has a grievance against you . . . ." or "So if, as you are coming to offer your gift to God on the altar, you remember that your brother has a complaint with you . . . ."

5.24 RSV   TEV

leave your gift there before the altar   leave your gift there in front of the
and go; first be reconciled to your   altar, go at once and make peace
brother, and then come and offer   with your brother, and then come
your gift.   back and offer your gift to God.

Leave your gift must not be translated in a way that would give the impression it was left as a sacrifice. On the contrary, the instruction is to not complete the offering. This can be "put your gift aside in front of the altar" or "leave your gift in front of the altar without offering it to God."

Go can be "go from there," but it is probably better to combine it with the next clause, as in "go find your brother" or "first go to your brother."

First . . . and then is translated "**At once . . . and then**" by TEV, and "First . . . and only then" by NEB. Other ways translations can express this are to say "only after you have first reconciled yourself to your brother should you come and offer your gift" or "you should be reconciled to your brother first before you come back and offer your gift to God."

Be reconciled (NJB, NAB "be reconciled with") is translated "**make peace with**" by TEV and "make your peace with" by Phps and NEB. The reference is to a broken relationship which must be healed; here it is the responsibility of the guilty person to take the initiative. **Be reconciled to** can therefore be translated as "do what is necessary to be friends with your brother again" or "become friends again."

And then come back and offer your gift. Again TEV, FRCL, and GECL specify God as the one to whom the gift is offered (see verse 23).

5.25 RSV   TEV

Make friends quickly with your ac-   "If someone brings a lawsuit
cuser, while you are going with him   against you and takes you to court,
to court, lest your accuser hand you   settle the dispute with him while
over to the judge, and the judge to   there is time, before you get to court.
the guard, and you be put in prison;   Once you are there, he will turn you
                                                  over to the judge, who will hand you
                                                  over to the police, and you will be
                                                  put in jail.

This brief parable concerning going before the judge is also found in Luke 12.57-59, though in an entirely different context. Here it warns of the necessity for being quickly reconciled with one's legal adversary, lest one wind up in jail! Luke places the parable in an eschatological context, with the meaning, just as you would try to settle a case out of court, in the same way, the time to get reconciled with God is now. But several scholars interpret the real focus to be God's final judgment in Matthew as well, concerning which the disciples are warned of the urgency to be reconciled with their brothers, without which it is impossible to be reconciled with God.

At the first of the verse, TEV includes a clause which places the saying in its proper context: "**If someone brings a lawsuit against you and takes you to court**." Support for TEV's restructuring is provided from at least two directions: (1) the noun **accuser** (TEV "**someone** [who] **brings a lawsuit against you**") represents the injured party in a legal action. (2) The Greek "while you are with him in the way" actually means **while you are going with him to court** (see also Phps, NEB, NAB, and others which specify "to court"). Many translators have found this model of TEV very helpful. Other examples are "If someone is taking you to the judge to accuse you" or "If someone is accusing you of things, while you are going with him to court (or, to the judge) . . . ."

Make friends . . . with (TEV "**settle the dispute**") focuses on the need to resolve the differences with one's legal adversary before getting to court; NEB, NJB have "come to terms with"; NAB renders "settle with." Other translations have said "make an agreement with," "settle the matter," or "find a solution to your differences."

Quickly (TEV "**while there is time**") is also translated in a number of ways: NEB "promptly"; JB "in good time"; NAB "Lose no time."

"**Once you are there**" of TEV provides a necessary transitional in the English structure. A number of other translations use the word "otherwise" (NAB, NEB, Phps). Brc translates "if you do not" (so also TNT). RSV has the word **lest**, which means literally "so that not." It can also be expressed as "so that your accuser won't . . . ." or "in order to prevent him from . . . ."

Judge is the preference of most translations for the first of the two officials. But the noun translated **guard** is more difficult. The primary meaning is "servant, helper, assistant"; but since the reference here is specifically to the servants of the court, RSV has **guard**, and TEV "**police**." Mft and TNT translate "jailer"; Brc "court officer"; NJB "officer." In 26.58 the reference is to the Temple guards.

In many cultures it seems odd to speak of handing someone over to a judge. Translators have to say "give you to the judge so he can deal with you," "ask the judge to deal with you," or "charge you before the judge so he decides your case."

However, when the judge hands someone over to the guard, that is so that the guard can administer the punishment determined by the judge—in this case, to be put in prison. Thus the translation can have "and the judge will give you to the guard" or "will tell the guard to take you and put you in prison."

For **guard** translators may say "soldier," "police," "official," or whatever term normally designates the person who is responsible to put someone in jail.

A **prison** or "**jail**" is well known now in most parts of the world. In some places it may be necessary to say "the building where they guard you and you can't leave" or "the building where they punish people by making them stay there."

5.26   RSV   TEV

truly, I say to you, you will never get out till you have paid the last penny.	There you will stay, I tell you, until you pay the last penny of your fine.

Truly, I say to you (TEV "**I tell you**") translates a strong emphatic statement similar in impact to "For truly, I say to you" of verse 18.

Penny is the rendering of most translations. The name of the coin in Greek represents a Latin loan word. According to Mark 12.42, this coin has the value of the two coins given by the widow. The Lukan parable (12.59) uses the name of one of the coins given by the widow, Mark 12.42.

Many translations will use the least valuable coin or piece of money used in their country today. However, the expression **last penny** means "all that must be paid before you can be set free." Some translations have thought this referred to paying off the debt you owed your accuser, but it is more likely that it means "paid off all the money the judge fined you (or, said you must pay)."

5.27-30

RSV   TEV

Teaching about Adultery

27 "You have heard that it was said, 'You shall not commit adultery.' 28 But I say to you that every one who looks at a woman lustfully has already committed adultery with her in his heart. 29 If your right eye causes you to sin, pluck it out and throw it away; it is better that you lose one of your members than that your whole body be thrown into hell.[k] 30 And if your right hand causes you to sin, cut it off and throw it away; it is better that you lose one of your members than that your whole body go into hell.[k]

27 "You have heard that it was said, 'Do not commit adultery.' 28 But now I tell you: anyone who looks at a woman and wants to possess her is guilty of committing adultery with her in his heart. 29 So if your right eye causes you to sin, take it out and throw it away! It is much better for you to lose a part of your body than to have your whole body thrown into hell. 30 If your right hand causes you to sin, cut it off and throw it away! It is much better for you to lose one of your limbs than to have your whole body go off to hell.

[k] Greek *Gehenna*

SECTION HEADING: "**Teaching about Adultery**." This must not be translated so it seems Jesus is teaching how to commit adultery. Rather, he defines it and teaches about the laws that pertain to it. Translators can say "Jesus teaches about adultery" or "Jesus teaches about the laws against committing adultery."

Adultery is often mistranslated. (See discussion below under verse 27.) It may be necessary to say here "Jesus teaches about people who sleep with someone else's wife."

This section is related to the previous, in that it also deals with an elaboration of one of the Ten Commandments.

5.27   RSV   TEV

"You have heard that it was
said, 'You shall not commit adultery.'

"You have heard that it was
said, 'Do not commit adultery.'

You have heard that it was said translates the same formula that is used to introduce verse 21, except that the phrase "to the men of old" does not appear here. According to Jewish law, the term "adultery" referred to sexual intercourse with the wife or the betrothed of a Jew. Both the commandment itself (Exo 20.14; Deut 5.18) and the Jewish interpretation of the commandment condemned adultery, because it involved the taking of another man's wife. That is, it was considered the illicit use of another man's property.

Many translators have used a word for **adultery** that is too broad for the Jewish use of the word. Either they have used a word that included all sexual relations between people not married to each other (really fornication), or they have used the word that would apply to such actions where at least one of the people involved was married, whether it was the woman or the man. This is the way the word is generally used in English today, for example. However, as we pointed out above, for the Jews, the word "adultery" was restricted to situations where the woman was married to someone else.

In those cases where the word normally used in the language is a general word for illicit sex, then translators can add the phrase "with a married woman" or "with someone else's wife." Or they can use the normal word for sexual relations and add the same phrase "with someone else's wife."

Translators must be sure that whatever word they use for sexual relations is acceptable in polite company. They must avoid words that would be shocking or offensive. Many languages use a euphemism such as "sleep with."

Again, as in verse 21, a commandment is being cited. **Shall** is not being used as a simple future but marks an imperative.

5.28   RSV   TEV

But I say to you that every one who
looks at a woman lustfully has already committed adultery with her in
his heart.

But now I tell you: anyone who looks
at a woman and wants to possess
her is guilty of committing adultery
with her in his heart.

But I say to you is the same statement that introduces verse 22.

Everyone who looks at a woman lustfully is translated in a number of different ways. For example, TEV "**anyone who looks at a woman and wants to possess her**"; Mft "anyone who even looks with lust at a woman"; and Brc "if anyone looks at a woman in such a way as deliberately to awaken within himself the forbidden desire for her."

It is important to note that this verse does not just refer to noticing a woman as attractive, or even to a brief recognition that she is sexually appealing. It refers instead to actually contemplating having sex with her, that is, to having the intention of doing so. Thus, for **looks . . . lustfully** translators can say "wants to sleep with her," "wants sex with her," or "looks at her with the intention of sleeping with her."

Has already committed adultery with her (so also NEB, NAB, NJB) translates a Greek aorist; but for English speakers the perfect tense adequately and accurately expresses the meaning.

Since **heart** refers to the realm of thought, GECL translates **in his heart** as "in thought." In many cultures, **in his heart** would only be understood to refer to the emotions, so that "in his thought" or "in his thinking" are better translations.

Some translators have used a translation like "it is as if he is already guilty of committing adultery with her." This would be wrong because Jesus does not say it as if he were guilty, but affirms that he is guilty already. Thus the sin of adultery is not in the act but in the lust or desire to do so.

5.29	RSV	TEV

| If your right eye causes you to sin, pluck it out and throw it away; it is better that you lose one of your members than that your whole body be thrown into hell.*k* | So if your right eye causes you to sin, take it out and throw it away! It is much better for you to lose a part of your body than to have your whole body thrown into hell. |

k Greek *Gehenna*

This and the following verse are applications of the statement regarding adultery. Even if a man's eye, which should keep him from stumbling, causes him to sin, it should be taken out and thrown away! Commentators agree that the **right eye** is chosen as an illustration on the analogy of the "right hand" (verse 30), which is generally regarded as more useful than the left. Quite often translators find it odd to speak of one particular eye causing sin, since we see with both. Therefore some say "your eye" or "your eyes."

Causes . . . to sin translates a verb frequently used in Matthew's Gospel (5.30; 11.6; 13.21,57; 15.12; 17.27; 18.6,8,9; 24.10; 26.31,33). The root meaning is "cause to stumble," and the specific nature of the "stumbling," whether physical or otherwise, is determined by the context. In Matthew the focus is generally upon the doing of something that may lead another to give up his faith. **Causes . . . to sin** can be translated as "causes you to do wrong," "makes you sin," or "makes you think about doing wrong so that you sin."

The phrase needs to be restructured in many languages, as in "if, because of what your eye has seen, you sin" or "if you are led to do sin because of your eyes (or, because of what you have seen with your eyes)."

If translators have used the plural "your eyes," then they will say "pluck them out" rather than **pluck it out**.

Of course, Jesus is using very exaggerated language to impress on his hearers the seriousness of what he is saying. There have been translators that have wanted to tone it down, or to make the application clear in the translation, as in "You must not let anything prevent you from entering the kingdom and send you to hell instead.

Even your vision is less important." But translators should retain the language of Jesus at this point.

One of your members means "one part of your body." Some translations make it clear that the eye is the part of the body being spoken of here, as in "your eye, which is only one part of your body."

Lose means "deprived of." The sentence can be "It is better not to have one of the parts of the body" or "It is better to have one of the parts of your body missing." "Lose" in the sense of "not able to find" would be wrong in this context.

Hell is the rendering of most modern translations (NJB, NEB, Brc, GECL, FRCL, DUCL). AT translates "the pit!" and Phps "the rubbish-heap." RSV follows the translation **hell** with a note "Greek *Gehenna*"; both Mft and NAB translate "Gehenna." The word "Gehenna" is merely a transliteration of the Greek, which itself is a Grecized form of the Hebrew. See comments at verse 22, where the word is first used.

The phrase **thrown into hell** is a passive construction. Many translations use an impersonal construction such as "they throw your body into hell" or "they force you to go to hell." Others make God the indirect agent, as in "God has your body thrown." Another way would be to say simply that you "go to hell."

Some translations use a sentence with "worse" rather than "better," as in "It is bad to lose a part of your body, but it is worse if the whole body gets thrown into hell."

5.30 RSV	TEV
And if your right hand causes you to sin, cut it off and throw it away; it is better that you lose one of your members than that your whole body go into hell.*ᵏ*	If your right hand causes you to sin, cut it off and throw it away! It is much better for you to lose one of your limbs than to have your whole body go off to hell.

ᵏ Greek *Gehenna*

The structure of this verse is basically the same as that of verse 29. Here the **right hand** is used in place of the right eye as an application of the teaching about adultery, and there is a shift in the verb from "be thrown into" to **go into**. Both verbs are very common, and they generally are translated similarly to the way that RSV has done. In some languages it may be necessary to shift the first three verbs to an active form. If the meaning of "hell" is accepted for Gehenna, then God may be made the subject of the active verb. One should not assume that the reference is to the valley outside of Jerusalem and to the individual's body being thrown into that after death. This would make little sense in the context, for then the verse would lose its impact, which is the threat of punishment for the offender. In order for this verse to carry through its full impact, the reference must be to hell as a place of punishment, rather than to the garbage pile outside of Jerusalem, where the worst that can happen is for the person's body to be consumed after death.

Translators will generally translate this verse very much as they did verse 29. As with "right eye," **right hand** may in some languages be "one of your hands," "your hand," or "your hands."

One slight difference from verse 29 is that here the text says **go into hell**, not "be thrown," but the meaning is essentially the same. Thus the phrase may be "than that your whole body go to hell (or, be sent to hell, or, be sent by God to hell)" or "than that God send you to hell."

5.31-32

RSV	TEV
	Teaching about Divorce
31 "It was also said, 'Whoever divorces his wife, let him give her a certificate of divorce.' 32 But I say to you that every one who divorces his wife, except on the ground of unchastity, makes her an adulteress; and whoever marries a divorced woman commits adultery.	31 "It was also said, 'Anyone who divorces his wife must give her a written notice of divorce.' 32 But now I tell you: if a man divorces his wife for any cause other than her unfaithfulness, then he is guilty of making her commit adultery if she marries again; and the man who marries her commits adultery also.

SECTION HEADING: "**Teaching about Divorce**." This can be "Jesus teaches about divorce." As with the teaching on adultery, Jesus is not talking about how to divorce but about the commandment that relates to it, as in "Jesus talks about the commandments that concern divorce."

The reference in this section is not to any of the Ten Commandments, but to the regulations of Deuteronomy 24.1-4. In verse 28 Jesus' purpose was the protection of the woman, which is precisely the original purpose of the Deuteronomy passage.

5.31	RSV	TEV

"It was also said, 'Whoever divorces his wife, let him give her a certificate of divorce.'	"It was also said, 'Anyone who divorces his wife must give her a written notice of divorce.'

According to Deuteronomy 24.1, a man may divorce a woman "because he finds something about her that he doesn't like." However, in the case of Deuteronomy the man was required to write out divorce papers before sending the woman away from his house. Previous to this time, it was possible for a man to divorce the woman without any action other then the mere statement that he had divorced her. As an attempt to regulate and restrain this tendency, Deuteronomy required a written statement of divorce. However, according to Matthew 19.8 Jesus teaches that even this was an allowance made by Moses because men were not willing to live according to God's Law.

As we have pointed out, **It was also said** is a way of introducing a citation from the Scriptures. "God also said in the Scriptures" or "God's Scriptures also said" are ways to handle this here. Another method may be to say "You were also taught" or "Another thing people taught you."

Whoever can be "Anyone who," but in this context it can even be "Any husband who," since the verse clearly is speaking about divorcing a wife.

For **divorces**, translators can use the normal way that their language speaks of divorce; perhaps "Whoever returns his wife to her family," "sends his wife away," or "puts an end to the marriage."

Let him give her can be "he should give her" or "he must give her."

The **certificate of divorce** can be translated "a piece of paper saying he had divorced her," "a paper stating he had put an end to the marriage," or "a paper saying that the marriage was over."

5.32   RSV   TEV

But I say to you that every one who divorces his wife, except on the ground of unchastity, makes her an adulteress; and whoever marries a divorced woman commits adultery.	But now I tell you: if a man divorces his wife for any cause other than her unfaithfulness, then he is guilty of making her commit adultery if she marries again; and the man who marries her commits adultery also.

But I say to you places the declaration of Jesus in contrast to that of the Old Testament; this is the same formula used in verse 22.

The text has **every one**, but it is often more natural to say "anyone" or "whoever."

Unchastity (so also NEB, Mft, TNT) was translated "fornication" by JB and "lewd conduct" by NAB, since the Greek word may refer to any illicit sexual relations, although it would be assumed to mean adultery here. TEV and GECL have "unfaithful" (Phps, AT "unfaithfulness"). However, sociological studies of New Testament times have led some scholars to suggest that a better rendering would be "an unlawful marriage," as for example between people of certain blood or legal relationships who were forbidden to marry each other by Mosaic Law. NJB and TOB, for example, have "except for the case of an illicit marriage," and the revised New Testament of NAB has "unless the marriage is unlawful."

Translations which follow the first interpretation can have "unless she had committed adultery," "unless she had been unfaithful," or "unless she had slept with other men." Those who follow the second will have a sentence similar to NJB, TOB, or revised NAB, cited above.

In many languages, translators have to restructure this sentence slightly to cover the meaning of **except**. Examples are "anyone who divorces his wife for any reason except . . ." or "anyone who divorces his wife, but the reason was not because she . . . ."

The Old Testament commandment allowing for a bill of divorce to be given accepted divorce as legitimate. However, Jesus is denying this by saying that unless the marriage was illegal (or possibly unless the woman had been unfaithful), then the divorce is not legal, and the woman is guilty of adultery if she marries again. Moreover, the assumption is that she will probably marry again. Therefore the inclusion of "if she marries again" (TEV, FRCL, GECL 1st edition, DUCL) is necessary for the reader; otherwise the point of what Jesus is saying will be missed completely.

To say **he makes her an adulteress** means that "he makes her guilty of adultery" or "he is the one responsible for making her commit adultery." Since this will only be the case if she marries again, something in the possible future, then translators can say "then if she marries again, he is the one responsible for her committing adultery in that way," or "when she remarries and in doing so becomes guilty of adultery, then he is the one who has caused this adultery."

And whoever marries a divorced woman commits adultery is also based on the logic that in principle—though not legally—the divorced woman is still married to her first husband. Some Greek manuscripts omit this clause. But the UBS Greek New Testament favors the opinion that its omission is due to the overzealousness of certain scribes who may have regarded these words as unnecessary in light of the previous statement, **makes her an adulteress** (so TC-GNT).

The last clause can be expressed as "the man who marries a divorced woman is committing adultery" or "it is adultery also for the man if he marries a divorced woman."

5.33-37

RSV	TEV
	Teaching about Vows
33 "Again you have heard that it was said to the men of old, 'You shall not swear falsely, but shall perform to the Lord what you have sworn.' 34 But I say to you, Do not swear at all, either by heaven, for it is the throne of God, 35 or by the earth, for it is his footstool, or by Jerusalem, for it is the city of the great King. 36 And do not swear by your head, for you cannot make one hair white or black. 37 Let what you say be simply 'Yes' or 'No'; anything more than this comes from evil.*[l]*	33 "You have also heard that people were told in the past, 'Do not break your promise, but do what you have vowed to the Lord to do.' 34 But now I tell you: do not use any vow when you make a promise. Do not swear by heaven, because it is God's throne; 35 nor by earth, because it is the resting place for his feet; nor by Jerusalem, because it is the city of the great King. 36 Do not even swear by your head, because you cannot make a single hair white or black. 37 Just say 'Yes' or 'No'—anything else you say comes from the Evil One.

[l] Or *the evil one*

SECTION HEADING: "**Teaching about Vows**." Translators may say "Jesus teaches about making vows (or, promises) to God" or "Jesus teaches about the commandments concerning promises before God."

5.33   RSV   TEV

"Again you have heard that it was said to the men of old, 'You shall not swear falsely, but shall perform to the Lord what you have sworn.'	**"You have also heard that people were told in the past, 'Do not break your promise, but do what you have vowed to the Lord to do.'**

Matthew now returns to his exposition of the Ten Commandments. The words about swearing deal with the commandment in the Decalogue concerning false witness, following those concerning murder and adultery.

Again (first used in 4.7,8) translates an adverb which is used when a speaker takes up a formula previously used and continues. In GECL it is left implicit, where the first sentence of verse 33 is "You know that our ancestors were told . . . ." TEV has translated this as "**also.**" Brc has tried to show the meaning with "To take another example . . . ."

Have heard (so most English translations) renders an aorist tense in Greek, which may be rendered "heard." NEB, JB render "have learned," and NAB has "heard the commandment imposed on . . . ." As noted above, GECL has "You know . . . ." It is important that the translation imply that the hearers are familiar with the command, rather than that it is merely hearsay to them, as may be suggested to some by the use of the verb "to hear." Translators should refer to verse 21 for **have heard**. Here, this can be "Another thing you know God said to your ancestors is that . . ." or "Another thing people have told you God said to the men of long ago."

To the men of old is also found in verse 21, but nowhere else in the Sermon on the Mount.

As in verses 21 and 27, **You shall not** is a formula for a command and should not be translated as a simple future.

Neither the negative command (**shall not swear falsely**) nor the positive command (**shall perform to the Lord what you have sworn**) is a direct quotation from any Old Testament passage. The two commands constitute a summary of Leviticus 19.12; Exodus 20.7; Deuteronomy 5.11; Numbers 30.3; and Deuteronomy 23.22.

Swear falsely translates a Greek verb which may mean either "break an oath" or "commit perjury." This is its only occurrence in the New Testament, and both meanings are possible for the context. A related noun form is used in 1 Timothy 1.10 (TEV "those who . . . give false testimony"). Translations are divided rather sharply on the meaning. TEV, NEB, NJB have "break promise (or, oath)"; while others go in the direction of "to perjure" (for example, Mft, Phps, "forswear"; NAB "take a false oath"; RSV, AT, GECL 1st edition "swear falsely"). AB has "make vows rashly." As one may expect, New Testament scholars are also divided on their interpretation of this verb, though several commentators note that the meaning "break an oath" goes better with the last clause of the verse.

Translators who choose the first interpretation can have phrases such as "Do not fail to do what you promised (before God)," "Always do what you promised (before God)," or "Don't promise (or, swear) to do something when in fact you do not intend to do it." Those who choose the second interpretation will have translations such as "Don't swear (by God) something is true when you know it isn't." But the first interpretation does seem to fit the context of the passage better, particularly since **perform to the Lord** does imply a promise. Of course, languages that have a word that covers both meanings, as the Greek does, will do best to use that word. See notes below for a discussion of "swear."

What you have sworn (TEV "**what you have vowed**") alters the Greek noun phrase "your vows" to a relative clause with a verb describing the action.

The meaning of the clause **shall perform to the Lord what you have sworn** is seen in TEV. You are commanded "to do the things you vowed to the Lord you would do."

Some languages have difficulty with the distinctions between "promise," "vow," "swear," and "oath." To promise simply means to affirm that you will do something. However, to vow is to make a sacred promise in front of witnesses. Usually the person making the vow will invoke a deity's punishment if he fails to do what he is saying. To make an oath is very similar to vowing. It is to make a pledge to do something while calling upon God or a sacred object as a witness. In swearing, one makes a solemn declaration stating something is true, and invokes a deity or sacred object to confirm that what is said is in fact true.

As can be seen, these terms are similar and in fact overlap a great deal in actual usage. Most languages have a word for "promise," so that word poses no problem to translators. A problem sometimes arises with the other words when translators are reluctant to use the traditional words that would be the closest natural equivalents. In their cultures oaths or vows are made before idols or involve other ceremonies that the translators consider inappropriate to include in Christian Scriptures. But these translators should realize that formally these customs in their cultures are similar to what the Jews did, and the main difference is in the deity or spirit power involved.

If there are no close expressions in the language, translators can find various other solutions. For example, "vow" can often be translated "make a promise using God's name," and "oath" can be handled in the same way. "Swear" can be "to declare as true," or "declare before God that something is true," or "declare in God's name (or, by God) something is true." However, translators should always look to the context to see what is most appropriate in each case.

5.34   RSV   TEV

But I say to you, Do not swear at all, either by heaven, for it is the throne of God,	But now I tell you: do not use any vow when you make a promise. Do not swear by heaven, because it is God's throne;

But I say to you repeats the formula first used in 5.22; it also occurs in verse 32.

Do not swear at all represents a literal rendering of the Greek. From the context it is clear that Jesus' objection is not to the use of promises in religion, but to the false distinctions made by Jewish teachers between different formulas used in taking vows. TEV therefore follows the negative command with words of clarification: **"when you make a promise."**

Heaven . . . earth . . . Jerusalem. The last half of this verse and the first half of verse 35 contain an allusion to Isaiah 66.1, where the Lord declares "Heaven is my throne, and the earth is my footstool." Some Jewish teachers taught that an oath was not binding if made in the name of **heaven** or **earth**. But Jesus teaches that whether the name of God is used or not, a person has to deal with God when he makes a vow.

In line with our discussion in verse 33, translations can begin the statement of Jesus like this: "When you declare something is true, don't use the name of God or anything at all," or "Don't make declarations before God or before any other thing when you say something is true." The translation can then continue: "Don't use heaven (in your declaration)," "Don't make your declaration before heaven," "Don't use heaven to make your declaration (or, statement) true," or "Don't ask heaven to give authority to your declaration."

Heaven is **the throne of God**, that is, "where God sits to rule" or "the place from which God rules."

5.35	RSV	TEV

or by the earth, for it is his footstool, or by Jerusalem, for it is the city of the great King.	nor by earth, because it is the resting place for his feet; nor by Jerusalem, because it is the city of the great King.

The Greek noun **footstool** is translated by a phrase ("**the resting place for his feet**") in TEV. The picture is that of God as king; he is seated upon his throne (verse 34), with his feet resting upon a **footstool**. See Isaiah 66.1 and 1 Chronicles 28.2.

According to at least one source, the Jews are known to have taken vows **by Jerusalem**, though not oaths. However, the principle would be the same, since **it is the city of the great King**, that is, of God. In the Greek text the preposition used before **Jerusalem** is not the same as that used before **heaven** and **earth**, though most all translations translate it **by**. It literally means "toward," and so one scholar suggests that it may reflect the rabbinic teaching that a vow made "by Jerusalem" is not valid unless it is sworn "toward Jerusalem" (that is, while facing in the direction of Jerusalem). The reference to Jerusalem as **the city of the great King** is an allusion to Psalm 48.2. The **great King** is, of course, God.

By the earth and **by Jerusalem** will be translated the same way as "by heaven" in verse 34. Even though the text has "toward Jerusalem," the sense is still that one swears "in the name of or by Jerusalem."

The **footstool** can be "the small stool where he rests his feet" or "the place for resting his feet."

The city of the great King can be "the city where the great King rules (or, lives)." Two sentences that may be better are "the city where God the great King rules" or "the city that belongs to God, the great King."

5.36	RSV	TEV

And do not swear by your head, for you cannot make one hair white or black.	Do not even swear by your head, because you cannot make a single hair white or black.

And do not swear translates a Greek negative particle, literally "nor," with the verb **swear** implied. This is its fourth occurrence in this passage (once in verse 34, twice in verse 35, and once in verse 36); when used in sequence it means "neither . . . nor . . . nor . . . ." Its four occurrences in TEV are rendered: "Do not swear . . . nor . . . nor . . . . Do not even swear." A similar restructuring is found in GECL.

To **swear by your head** has sometimes been difficult to express. Some translators have said here "Do not even use your own head as authority when you declare something is true" or "When you declare something true, don't even refer to your head to confirm it."

For you cannot make one hair black or white reveals that God is called into the situation even when one invokes one's own head. Even the color of one's hair is determined by God. The translation can be "you can't even make one hair change color (from white to black)." The translation should not mean one hair is first made white then black or that some hairs will be made one color and others the other color. Some translations have had to say "because you do not even have enough authority over your head to make one hair white or black (or, to change the color of one hair)."

5.37   RSV   TEV

Let what you say be simply 'Yes' or   Just say 'Yes' or 'No'—anything else
'No'; anything more than this comes   you say comes from the Evil One.
from evil.*

¹ Or the evil one

Let what you say be simply 'Yes' or 'No' is literally "But let your word be 'yes, yes' or 'no, no.' " In light of a similar passage in James 5.12 and the interpretation given this verse in the early church, the meaning is that every "Yes" must be simply "Yes," every "No" simply "No." The translations concur with this conclusion: NIV "Simply let your 'Yes' be 'Yes,' and your 'No,' 'No' "; Brc "when you mean yes, say yes—nothing more; when you mean no, say no—nothing more"; NJB "All you need say is 'Yes' if you mean yes, 'No' if you mean no."

The examples of Brc and NJB have proved particularly helpful as models to translators. But it is important that the translation does not seem to be talking about ways of answering questions. Rather, Jesus is still discussing affirming that one will or will not do something. Therefore one possible translation is "When you are going to do something, just say yes, you will do it, or no, that you are not going to do it."

Evil (AB "of evil origin") translates a noun which may be either neuter or masculine (TEV **"the Evil One"**; so also NJB, Brc, NAB, NIV, RSV footnote; NEB, GECL "the devil"). The same ambiguity exists in 5.39; 6.13; and 13.38. Scholars argue in both directions. For example, one commentator believes "evil" to be the more likely translation, even though in 13.19 the reference must be to "the Evil One" in light of the parallel with Mark 4.15, which has "Satan." Another commentator argues in favor of "the Evil One" on the basis of 19.17, where God is referred to as "the Good One." This interpretation, **"the Evil One,"** seems to satisfy best the demands of the present context.

The words **anything more** refer to adding to your declaration any confirmation or guarantee beyond your own word. The feeling that you need to do this **comes from**, that is, "is inspired by," "is caused by," or "has as its source" **the Evil One**."

"**The Evil One**" is not always easily understood. Translators may say "that One who is the source of evil" or "the Devil, who is the Evil One."

The last part of this verse may be restructured as "The idea that you need to say any more (or, do more than give your word) comes from the Devil, the Evil One," "It is the Devil, who is the Evil One, who makes you think you need to do more than that when you declare something true," or "Any statement more than that is caused by the Evil One, the Devil."

5.38-42

RSV	TEV
Teaching about Revenge
38 "You have heard that it was said, 'An eye for an eye and a tooth for a tooth.' 39 But I say to you, Do not resist one who is evil. But if any one strikes you on the right cheek, turn to him the other one also; 40 and if any one would sue you and take your coat, let him have your cloak as well; 41 and if any one forces you to go one mile, go with him two miles. 42 Give to him who begs from you, and do not refuse him who would borrow from you.	38 "You have heard that it was said, 'An eye for an eye, and a tooth for a tooth.' 39 But now I tell you: do not take revenge on someone who wrongs you. If anyone slaps you on the right cheek, let him slap your left cheek too. 40 And if someone takes you to court to sue you for your shirt, let him have your coat as well. 41 And if one of the occupation troops forces you to carry his pack one mile, carry it two miles. 42 When someone asks you for something, give it to him; when someone wants to borrow something, lend it to him.

SECTION HEADING: "**Teaching about Revenge**." This heading can be expressed in several ways; for example, "Jesus teaches about the commandments that are about getting revenge," "Jesus teaches what we should believe about seeking revenge on someone," "Jesus teaches that people should not look for revenge." "**Revenge**" may be "getting back at people" or "doing harm to someone because they harmed you."

In place of the law of retaliation (verse 38), Jesus presents the principle of self restraint, which he illustrates with four specific situations (verses 39-42).

5.38	RSV	TEV
"You have heard that it was said, 'An eye for an eye and a tooth for a tooth.'	"You have heard that it was said, 'An eye for an eye, and a tooth for a tooth.'

The law of **an eye for an eye and a tooth for a tooth** is mentioned in Exodus 21.24; Leviticus 24.20; and Deuteronomy 19.21; its original intent was humanitarian, to prevent unrestrained blood vengeance (Gen 4.23 is an example). However, its purpose was later reversed, and people began to appeal to it primarily as the means of making their own claims prevail.

5.38

For a discussion of **You have heard that it was said**, see verse 27.

It is important in translations that the phrase **an eye for an eye and a tooth for a tooth** be understood in the context of vengeance or retaliation. It is not a matter of "you can give an eye to get an eye," that is, an exchange, but rather the idea is that "If you cause someone to lose an eye, your eye should be taken out also, and if you cause someone to lose a tooth, your tooth can be taken out." This can also be "If a person destroys someone's eye (or tooth), then he should have his eye (or tooth) destroyed." Whether to use "you" or "someone" depends on what will be best understood by readers of a particular language.

5.39	RSV	TEV

But I say to you, Do not resist one who is evil. But if any one strikes you on the right cheek, turn to him the other one also;

But now I tell you: do not take revenge on someone who wrongs you. If anyone slaps you on the right cheek, let him slap your left cheek too.

But I say to you repeats the emphatic formula frequently used throughout this passage (see verse 22 and comments there).

Resist is the rendering of most English translations (so AT, Mft, Brc, AB, NIV, NJB; NAB "offer . . . resistance"); NEB translates "set yourself against." A literal translation of the verb is to "stand against." The context, as well as the parallels found in rabbinic sources, suggests that the word has a specifically legal connotation: "resist" in a court of law, or "oppose" before a judge. The TOB footnote indicates that the verb carries the sense of a retort or of a payment in kind, be it immediate and personal or before a court of law; in the footnote attention is called to the following verses: Luke 21.15; Acts 13.8; Romans 13.2; Galatians 2.11; James 4.7; 1 Peter 5.9.

For these reasons it is important that **resist** not be translated so as to refer to physical resistance. Some translations (for example, TEV) have used a fairly general expression such as "Don't try to pay back," "Don't go seeking revenge," or "Don't try to do something in return." Others follow more strictly the interpretation that puts "resist" in a legal context here, and say "Don't try to get a judge to help you get revenge" or "Don't take someone who wrongs you to court to get revenge."

One who is evil (TEV "**someone who wrongs you**") in the Greek is simply the adjective "evil" used as a noun. It presents the same problems of interpretation as does "evil" in verse 37. AB follows RSV; NEB has "the man who wrongs you"; NIV translates "an evil person"; JB has "the wicked man." Other translations take the word in an impersonal or abstract sense: "evil" (Brc, GECL) or "injury" (Mft, AT, NAB). But the context favors the interpretation represented in RSV and TEV. And it is erroneous to force modern psychology on the text by affirming that the reference is to "evil in the abstract," which becomes visible through a person's actions. The commentator is perhaps correct who narrows the meaning to "one who wishes to do injury." Thus translators will translate **one who is evil** as "the one who wrongs you," "does something bad to you," or "who harms you."

148

Note that **But** indicates a contrast: "Instead," or even "Instead, the way you should behave is."

If anyone strikes you on the right cheek has reference to an injury of insult, not of violence. In the near East, both in Jesus' day and in the present, the most insulting physical blow that one can give another is a slap with the back of the hand against the right cheek. Luke, on the other hand, substitutes a different verb (6.29), suggesting "a violent act."

If possible, translators should use a word that means "slap" for **strikes**. Some have used "one cheek" for **right cheek**, but as we explained, it was in fact the right cheek that was slapped as an insult, and the biblical form should be retained if possible. Translators may consider saying "hits you on the cheek to insult you."

Turn to him implies "let him slap" (TEV) and **the other** obviously has reference to "the left cheek" (see TEV, GECL, FRCL). The translation can be "turn the left cheek for him to slap as well" or "turn so he can also slap your left cheek."

5.40	RSV	TEV
	and if any one would sue you and take your coat, let him have your cloak as well;	And if someone takes you to court to sue you for your shirt, let him have your coat as well.

Most all modern translations take this verse in the context of a lawsuit, though the restructuring is in each case somewhat different. For example, NEB has "If a man wants to sue you for your shirt," and NIV "and if someone wants to sue you and take your tunic." JB renders "if a man takes you to law and would have your tunic," and NAB "If anyone wants to go to law over your shirt."

For **would sue you**, translations can have "**takes you to court**," as in TEV, "wants to take you before the judge," or "goes before the judge to ask the judge to give him your coat."

He takes you to court to **take your coat**, that is, "to make you give him your coat," "so that the judge makes you give him your coat."

The words rendered **coat** and **cloak** require comment, since they reflect a unique aspect of Israelite Law. The outer garment (**cloak**) was both an article of clothing and a covering for the night. Israelite law did not permit it to be kept from its owner overnight; therefore the legal adversary was actually after the man's **coat**, a garment worn under the outer **cloak**. In Luke 6.29 the two garments are mentioned in reverse order. There, however, the context is not that of a lawsuit, but of a robbery in which one man forcibly tears away another's outer garment. The **coat** was a long, close-fitting garment worn next to the skin; it was used by both sexes.

Coat will be difficult for some translators, because it is distinguished from the outer garment or **cloak**. If there are terms that distinguish from the outer garment, they can usually be used, much as TEV has used "**shirt**" and "**coat**." Otherwise, translators will look for general or descriptive phrases such as "the clothing you wear under your outer wrap (or, near your body)," and "the clothing that covers the outer clothing."

However, to help readers realize the difference in value of the two garments, something Jesus' hearers would have understood immediately, translators may prefer to say "your garment that is of little value" and "your outer garment that is more valuable."

5.41

RSV	TEV
and if any one forces you to go one mile, go with him two miles.	And if one of the occupation troops forces you to carry his pack one mile, carry it two miles.

Any one is translated "**one of the occupation troops**" by TEV. The basis for this rendering is the verb **forces**, which in Greek is a technical term used of pressing into service, whether military or civil. Elsewhere in the New Testament the verb is used only of Simon from Cyrene, whom the Roman soldiers forced to carry Jesus' cross to the place of execution (27.32; Mark 15.21). Most translations use **forces**, but others attempt to reflect the cultural situation: JB ("And if anyone orders you to go one mile"), NEB ("If a man in authority makes you to go one mile"), NAB ("Should anyone press you into service for one mile"), and Brc ("And if a Roman officer commandeers you to act as a baggage-porter for one mile").

In addition to these models, other ways to handle **forces** include "if anyone makes you help him on the road" or "if anyone makes you carry his things."

The **mile** referred to is a Roman mile (equal to 4,854 feet or 1,478.5 meters). Many translations have apparently maintained the literal mile, even in situations where the metric system is employed. However, in place of **one mile . . . two miles** GECL translates: "a far distance . . . twice as far." **One mile** was presumably the distance a Roman soldier could force a Jew to carry his equipment. What is important here is not the exact distance, but the relation between **one mile** and **two miles**. Even if readers do not know exactly how far a mile is, they may well seize the intent of what Jesus is saying even if "mile" is translated literally. Nevertheless, many translators have said "one kilometer" and "two kilometers" simply to avoid introducing an unknown word, "mile."

5.42

RSV	TEV
Give to him who begs from you, and do not refuse him who would borrow from you.	When someone asks you for something, give it to him; when someone wants to borrow something, lend it to him.

Who begs from you . . . who would borrow from you: **Begs** means to ask someone to give something (so also AT, Mft, NAB). The second verb has the meaning **borrow** or "ask a loan." The response to the first request is stated positively (**give**), while the second response is stated negatively (**do not refuse**).

It is important not to use a word for **begs** that refers only to common begging. Translators may use "**asks you for something**" (as in TEV) or "asks you for something you have."

Many languages require a direct object of **give**, so that the sentence can be "give whatever someone needs when they ask you" or, probably better, "when someone asks for something from you, give it to him."

Do not refuse can be "don't refuse to give" or "don't say 'No' when someone asks . . . ."

Again, as with "give," **borrow** is a verb that often requires an object. People may want to borrow "something" or "something you have."

The second part of the verse may be structured like this: "When someone asks you to loan him something, don't refuse to help," "When someone asks if he can borrow something from you, don't say 'No,' " "When someone asks to borrow something from you, lend it to him," or "Don't refuse to help the person who asks to borrow something from you."

5.43-48

RSV	TEV
	Love for Enemies
43 "You have heard that it was said, 'You shall love your neighbor and hate your enemy.' 44 But I say to you, Love your enemies and pray for those who persecute you, 45 so that you may be sons of your Father who is in heaven; for he makes his sun rise on the evil and on the good, and sends rain on the just and on the unjust. 46 For if you love those who love you, what reward have you? Do not even the tax collectors do the same? 47 And if you salute only your brethren, what more are you doing than others? Do not even the Gentiles do the same? 48 You, therefore, must be perfect, as your heavenly Father is perfect.	43 "You have heard that it was said, 'Love your friends, hate your enemies.' 44 But now I tell you: love your enemies and pray for those who persecute you, 45 so that you may become the sons of your Father in heaven. For he makes his sun to shine on bad and good people alike, and gives rain to those who do good and to those who do evil. 46 Why should God reward you if you love only the people who love you? Even the tax collectors do that! 47 And if you speak only to your friends, have you done anything out of the ordinary? Even the pagans do that! 48 You must be perfect—just as your Father in heaven is perfect.

SECTION HEADING: "**Love for Enemies**." "Jesus teaches that we should love our enemies," "Jesus talks about loving people who hate us."

5.43 RSV	TEV
"**You have heard that it was said, 'You shall love your neighbor and hate your enemy.'**	"**You have heard that it was said, 'Love your friends, hate your enemies.'**

You have heard that it was said. See comments on verses 21 and 27.

The command **love your neighbor** comes from Leviticus 19.18, and it was always interpreted so as to apply to fellow Israelites, not to aliens. NAB translates "You shall love your countryman," and TEV "**Love your friends**."

It would be wrong to use a word for **neighbor** that meant only someone who lived in the immediate area, such as in the same section of town. Some translations follow NAB with "your countryman" or "your own people." This is probably the best rendering. Others follow TEV, **"your friends,"** or "the people you like," or even "the people who like you." Note that "neighbor" may be singular or plural, depending on which is more natural.

Love is extraordinarily difficult to translate in many parts of the world. In those languages which do not have a real equivalent, different ways of speaking of love are used, including "be concerned for their welfare," "care for," "treat (or, think of) with affection," "have sweet (or, hot or cool, etc.) stomach (or, liver or heart) for," and so on. The term from the Old Testament always implies a sense of faithful loyalty, not mere emotion, so that expressions which approach this idea are to be preferred over those meaning merely to like someone very much.

As in verse 21, **shall** is an imperative.

The command **hate your enemy** has puzzled scholars. It cannot be found as a quotation, nor can it be considered as a fair interpretation of Jewish ethics of the time. But although the command is not specifically mentioned in the Old Testament, there are many passages which not only permit but even encourage hatred and revenge against one's enemies. Moreover, groups such as the scribes and the Qumran sect, which thrived on absolute devotion to God and strict observance to his laws, did despise and even hate people of less dedication. Therefore it is quite likely that Jesus' words reflect popular attitudes of his day, if not actual teachings.

Some languages will express **hate** as "despise" or "wish evil toward."

If there is no word for **enemy** in a language, then translators use a phrase such as "the person who hates you" or "who opposes you."

5.44	RSV	TEV

But I say to you, Love your enemies and pray for those who persecute you,	But now I tell you: love your enemies and pray for those who persecute you,

But I say to you repeats a formula of emphasis used several times throughout this discourse; it first appears in verse 22.

Love your enemies is the rendering of most all English translations. Following this command, some late manuscripts of the New Testament insert "bless those who curse you, do good to those who hate you" (so KJV; see the footnotes of NEB and NIV). This addition comes from the parallel account in Luke 6.27-28. As TC-GNT indicates, the omission of these exhortations from the earliest representatives of the different text types "would be entirely unaccountable," had they originally been a part of Matthew's Gospel. **Love your enemies** is an exhortation or a command: "You must have love for" or "You are to show love for." See the comment at verse 34 on "love." **Enemies** was discussed in the previous verse.

Both Matthew and Luke (6.27-28) indicate that the disciples are to **pray** for those who oppose them. The verb translated **pray** occurs a total of eighty-six times in the New Testament, including sixteen times in this Gospel; it is the most general verb used of prayer, and any specific meaning (whether petition, request, or any other) will depend entirely upon the context in which it is used. Here **pray** can be translated "ask God to bless" or "pray to God to help."

The inclusion of **persecute** in Matthew, as opposed to the more general terms in Luke ("hate . . . curse . . . abuse"), intimates to some scholars that Matthew is thinking of a realistic situation in which the disciples are now undergoing persecution. The verb **persecute** is found also in 5.10,11,12; 10.23; 23.34; it generally refers to religious persecution. **Persecute** was discussed in verse 10. Here it can be "those who cause you to suffer," "who harm you," or "who mistreat you."

5.45	RSV	TEV
	so that you may be sons of your Father who is in heaven; for he makes his sun rise on the evil and on the good, and sends rain on the just and on the unjust.	so that you may become the sons of your Father in heaven. For he makes his sun to shine on bad and good people alike, and gives rain to those who do good and to those who do evil.

To be **sons** (or, children) of God in the biblical sense is to reflect the character and likeness of God, for which the second half of the verse provides specific illustrations. For example, the Father in heaven provides sun and rain for all people, without discriminating between the bad and the good. In the same way, if Jesus' followers are to prove that they are sons of God, they must show love to their enemies and pray for those who persecute them. **Sons** is meant to include both men and women.

So that you may be sons of your Father who is in heaven is a fairly literal rendering of the Greek text. AB is barely one step away from a literal rendering by beginning a new sentence with this verse: "In this way you will become sons of your heavenly Father . . . ." The more precise meaning of the verb **be** in the context is "will show that you are." This is the basis of NAB ("This will prove that you are sons of your heavenly Father"), AT ("so that you may show yourselves true sons of your Father in heaven"), and GECL ("So you will prove yourselves to be children of your Father in heaven"). Another way is to say "so that people will know (or, see) that you are children of God, your Father in heaven."

Your Father in heaven is the same expression used in verse 16.

For further notes on the phrase "son of God" or "child of God," see verse 9. Here translators may also say "that you are like children to God" or "that God considers you his children." However, it may be best to show the real meaning of the phrase with a translation such as "so that you may show that you are like God, your Father in heaven."

Evil . . . unjust are synonyms, as are **good . . . just**, as the illustration below will demonstrate. Such an arrangement is called a chiastic arrangement, after the name of the Greek letter *chi*, which is in the shape of an "X." A similar structure is also used in 6.24 and 7.6.

In translation it may be advisable to rearrange the order so that the parallelisms will show up more clearly; for example, "evil and unjust" in one line, with "good and just" in the other. Or, the entire structure may be translated "For he provides sunshine and rain for good people and bad people alike."

The adjective **just** is first used in 1.19 (see comments there); **unjust** is its opposite, as **evil** is the opposite of **good**. Elsewhere in Matthew **good** is used in 7.11 (twice),17,18; 12.34,35 (twice); 19.16,17 (twice). The adjective **evil** was used in verses 11,37,39; elsewhere in the Sermon on the Mount it is used in 6.13,23; 7.11,17,18.

The expression **his sun** may have to be expressed as "the sun he created." The phrase **makes his sun rise** can be translated literally, or as "he provides the sun" or "he gives sunshine."

The evil and **the good** are "evil (or, bad) people" and "good people," and similarly, **the just** and **the unjust** are "people who do right" and "people who do evil," or "people who obey God's law" and "people who disobey God's law."

We suggested above that translators often restructure the passage so that their readers can follow the thoughts more easily. For example, it may be rendered "for he makes his sun rise and the rain fall on the evil people who do not obey God's law just as he does on the good people who are faithful to obey." Another way is "As far as providing the blessings of sunshine and rain to people, he treats all alike, both the good people and the bad, both those who obey his laws and those who do not."

5.46	RSV	TEV
	For if you love those who love you, what reward have you? Do not even the tax collectors do the same?	**Why should God reward you if you love only the people who love you? Even the tax collectors do that!**

What reward have you. On the notion of rewards see verse 12. The question actually means "what reward can you expect?" (NEB, Brc). But it is God from whom one expects to receive the reward, and GECL follows TEV in making this explicit ("How can you expect a reward from God . . ."); FRCL is similar.

The question **if you love those who love you** should give the idea of loving only those who love you: "If you love only the people who love you . . . ."

This is a rhetorical question. Jesus is not asking what the reward is, but is rather pointing out forcefully that loving those who love you will not bring a reward. This may be expressed as a statement, as in "to love only those people who love you does not bring any reward," "God isn't going to reward you because you love people who love you also," "you should not expect a reward for loving those people who love you," or "God should not reward you for loving people who love you." Another way is to use a rhetorical question like that in TEV, **"Why should God reward you . . . ?"**

Do not even the tax collectors do the same? translates a question form in Greek which expects a positive reply (note JB "Even the tax collectors do as much, do they not?"). Several translations (GECL, NEB, FRCL, DUCL) restructure by a statement, as does TEV: **"Even the tax collectors do that!"**

The **tax collectors** referred to in the Gospels are probably the Jewish employees of the chief collectors. The Roman system for gathering taxes made for inequality and oppression, and that is one reason that in the Gospels tax collectors are quite often grouped together with sinners. To emphasize the derogatory connotation of the term, Brc translates "the renegade tax collectors."

Many translations have fairly literal renderings of **tax collectors**. They have, for example, "people who collect money for the government" or "people who make everyone pay money to the government." Some say "to the Roman government" or "to the emperor (or, king) in Rome." Other translations reflect the low esteem in which tax collectors were held by saying "those unpatriotic (or unscrupulous, or oppressive) tax collectors."

5.47	RSV	TEV
	And if you salute only your brethren, what more are you doing than others? Do not even the Gentiles do the same?	And if you speak only to your friends, have you done anything out of the ordinary? Even the pagans do that!

And if you salute only your brethren. It is important to note that in the Jewish context the salutation is more than a gesture or greeting; it expresses a desire for the peace and welfare of the one greeted. GECL renders the sentence dynamically: "And what is so special if you are friendly only with your brothers?" For most English speakers **salute** refers to a formal military greeting; the meaning is "greet" or "**speak to**" (TEV). AT has "And if you are polite to." Some have said "greet politely" or "show courtesy by greeting."

It is fairly well agreed among the commentators that **brethren**, as used here, means "fellow members of a religious community." Mft, Brc, together with TEV, translate the noun as "**friends**." Phps translates the clause, "And if you exchange greetings only with your own circle . . . ." A common way to translate this has been to say "people of your own group." See also comments on verse 22.

What more are you doing than others? assumes the answer "Nothing more!" It is possible to shift to a declaration, "you are not doing anything more than what people ordinarily do." Modern translations represent the question in many different ways: "what is there remarkable in that?" (AT), "what is special about that?" (Mft), "what is so praiseworthy about that ?" (NAB), and "are you doing anything exceptional?" (NJB).

This question can also be expressed as a statement, as we have suggested. Other examples are "you are only doing the same as everyone else" or "you have not done anything more than other people do."

Gentiles is rendered "**pagans**" by NIV, Mft, NAB, JB, Phps; "the heathen" is the translation of AB, NEB, Brc (AT "the very heathen"). GECL renders: "Those who do not know God." Etymologically the Greek word meant "national," then "foreign" or "Gentile," when used in contrast to Jews. However, in many occurrences of **Gentiles** in the New Testament it is the religious rather than the racial contrast which is intended, and for this reason such a rendering as **Gentiles** is inadequate. Elsewhere in the New Testament the word is used in Matthew 6.7; 18.17 (TEV "pagans") and in 3 John 7 (TEV "unbelievers"). Some later manuscripts of the New Testament substitute "tax collectors" for **Gentiles**. But TC-GNT indicates that this was merely an attempt "to bring the statement into closer parallelism with the preceding sentence," as with the final sentence of verse 46.

The translation of GECL, "those who do not know God" for **Gentiles**, has often been a useful model. A similar expression is "those who do not believe in God." However, a problem can arise in cultures where it is accepted that everyone knows and believes in God, but Gentiles are those who either "don't know him as he really is" or "don't know him to worship him."

Do not even the Gentiles do the same? expects a "yes" answer, and so may be represented by a statement: "**Even the pagans do that!**" (TEV).

5.48 RSV TEV

You, therefore, must be perfect, as your heavenly Father is perfect. **You must be perfect—just as your Father in heaven is perfect.**

This verse is a summation in which Jesus bases the call to discipleship upon the nature of God who is perfect. The verse is best taken, not merely as a conclusion to verses 43-47, but to the whole series of antitheses as well (verses 21-48).

In the statement **You . . . must be perfect**, the pronoun **You** is strongly emphasized.

Perfect in the Greek has the meaning of having come to completion or wholeness; it can refer to maturity or to moral and ethical integrity, that is, to being flawless. **Perfect** is the rendering of most translations. But NEB attempts a dynamic rendering: "There must be no limit to your goodness, as your heavenly Father's goodness knows no bounds."

One scholar observes that **perfect** is used in the Greek Old Testament "to translate a Hebrew concept that refers to what is whole, intact, undivided." The sect at Qumran used it in a somewhat different sense. For them it became a description of their own community, "referring to its way of life totally devoted to God's Law, although of course with the knowledge that this way of life is always a gift from the Lord himself . . . ." Matthew also uses it of devotion to God, rather than of flawlessness of character. In his Gospel "such devotion means doing right," and this is the same sense it has in James 1.4; 3.2. Jesus refers to God as **perfect**, because he is "totally, undividedly devoted to man; he is faithful to his covenant; he is totally given to those he loves."

Following this idea, then, translators could say "you must be perfect (or, flawless or, completely faithful) in your devotion to the Lord, just as God your heavenly Father is perfect (or, flawless or, completely faithful) in loving you," or "you must be completely devoted to doing what God requires in the same way that God your Father in heaven is completely devoted to the people he loves."

For comments on **your heavenly Father**, see verse 16.

Chapter 6

RSV

TEV

Teaching about Charity

1 "Beware of practicing your piety before men in order to be seen by them; for then you will have no reward from your Father who is in heaven.

2 "Thus, when you give alms, sound no trumpet before you, as the hypocrites do in the synagogues and in the streets, that they may be praised by men. Truly, I say to you, they have received their reward. 3 But when you give alms, do not let your left hand know what your right hand is doing, 4 so that your alms may be in secret; and your Father who sees in secret will reward you.

1 "Make certain you do not perform your religious duties in public so that people will see what you do. If you do these things publicly, you will not have any reward from your Father in heaven.

2 "So when you give something to a needy person, do not make a big show of it, as the hypocrites do in the houses of worship and on the streets. They do it so that people will praise them. I assure you, they have already been paid in full. 3 But when you help a needy person, do it in such a way that even your closest friend will not know about it. 4 Then it will be a private matter. And the Father, who sees what you do in private, will reward you.

SECTION HEADING: "**Teaching about Charity**." The section heading will be expressed as a complete sentence in many languages, indicating clearly who is doing the teaching and possibly who is being taught. The word "charity" means to give help to people in need. Thus this heading may be "Jesus teaches about giving help to needy people," "Jesus teaches people about how they should help those who are in need," or "Jesus teaches how to give help to needy people."

For purposes of discussion, several commentators place together verses 1-6 and 16-18. Verse 1 may be regarded as an introduction, followed by three similarly constructed passages (2-4; 5-15; 16-18), each containing two refrains: (1) "they have received their reward" (verses 2,5,16), and (2) "your Father who sees in secret will reward you" (verses 4,6,18). To the second passage (verses 5-15), which deals with prayer, are added special sayings on prayer (verses 7-8; 14-15) and the Lord's Prayer (verses 9-13).

6.1   RSV

TEV

"Beware of practicing your piety before men in order to be seen by them; for then you will have no reward from your Father who is in

"Make certain you do not perform your religious duties in public so that people will see what you do. If you do these things publicly, you

heaven.   **will not have any reward from your Father in heaven.**

Some Greek manuscripts begin chapter 6 with the conjunction "But," which some scholars interpret as a scribal attempt to balance the preceding demand for absolute righteousness with the warnings that accompany the discussion of that righteousness. In any case, the use of the conjunction in translation will depend entirely upon the requirements of the receptor language.

The chapter is a continuation of the discourse begun in chapter 5, so it may not need any particular transition or introduction. But there are translators who have found it useful to say something like "Jesus continued by saying" or "Jesus continued to speak to the crowds."

Beware of (so also Phps) represents the translation of an imperative (TEV "**Make certain**") plus a negative ("**not**"). English translations represent the verb in a variety of ways: "Be careful" (NEB, NJB, NIV), "Take care" (Brc, AT, Mft), and "Be on guard" (NAB). Elsewhere in Matthew this verb is used in 7.15; 10.17; 16.6,11,12. This imperative may be expressed as "Be sure that you don't," "Don't ever," or "You must never."

Piety (TEV "**religious duties**") translates the noun earlier rendered "righteousness"; see 3.15; 5.6,10,20. Here it serves as a summary term for almsgiving, prayer, and fasting, which were for Judaism the three most important expressions of one's religious duties. Accordingly TOB translates "practice of your religion." NEB translates the first sentence "Be careful not to make a show of your religion before men"; NAB has "Be on guard against performing religious acts for people to see." Other translations tend to utilize more general terms for the noun: "good deeds" (AT, Phps, JB), "righteous deeds" (AB), and "acts of righteousness" (NIV). In the Greek manuscript followed by KJV, the word "alms" appears in place of "righteousness"; however, this wording is so poorly attested that it does not even appear as an alternative possibility in the UBS Greek text. Moreover, this would make "alms" in verse 2 almost redundant.

Practicing your piety has proved quite difficult for many translators, primarily because many languages do not have a convenient word for "religion" or "religious." A common way to handle "religion" has been "way of worshiping God," so that "practicing your piety" can be expressed as "doing the things you must as part of your worshiping God" or "doing the things that you have to do because your way of worshiping God requires them."

Before men in order to be seen by them is presented somewhat more dynamically by TEV: "**in public so that people will see what you do.**" FRCL has "for all the world to notice you"; and GECL 1st edition reads "to be admired by people." Other ways to say it are "in front of people so they can see that you do these things" or "in front of people so they will notice what you are doing." The first part of this sentence can be "Don't make a public show of doing the things you must because of your way of worshiping God" or "It is wrong to perform the things that are a part of your worship of God in public just so people can see you."

For then (NEB "If you do") translates a series of four Greek particles, which TEV fills out as "If you do these things publicly." Translations employ a wide variety of literary devices, all of them designed to relate the second half of the verse to the first half.

Reward was first used in 5.12. Elsewhere in Matthew's Gospel it is found in 5.46; 6.2,5,16; 10.41,42; 20.8.

Father who is in heaven: see comments on 5.16.

Ways of expressing the last part of the verse include "If you do that, God your Father in heaven will have no great gift to give you," "If you do, God your heavenly Father will not give you any reward (or, valuable gift)," and "Because then you will be unable to receive a great gift from God your heavenly Father."

<u>6.2</u> RSV	TEV
"Thus, when you give alms, sound no trumpet before you, as the hypocrites do in the synagogues and in the streets, that they may be praised by men. Truly, I say to you, they have received their reward.	"So when you give something to a needy person, do not make a big show of it, as the hypocrites do in the houses of worship and on the streets. They do it so that people will praise them. I assure you, they have already been paid in full.

Thus, when you give alms is given in more contemporary language by TEV: "**So when you give something to a needy person**." NEB ("Thus, when you do some act of charity") and Brc ("When you are going to perform an act of charity") are similar. GECL translates "When you help someone." However, this and Phps ("So, when you do good to other people") may not emphasize enough that what is involved here is giving help to the needy. Other than in Matthew 6.2,3,4 the word **alms** is found in the New Testament only in the Lukan writings: Luke 11.41; 12.33; Acts 3.2,3,10; 9.36; 10.2,4,31; 24.17.

The transition **Thus** can be "Therefore," or "So then."

When is "on those occasions," "whenever," or "at any time when."

Many languages have a word which means **give alms**. This is particularly true in areas where a religion such as Islam predominates, which encourages this practice. In other cases translators can use a phrase similar to that in TEV, such as "give something to people who are in need (or, who are poor)."

Sound no trumpet before you is translated nonfiguratively by TEV: "**do not make a big show of it**." This figure of speech is probably not to be taken literally, but as a metaphor for attracting notice. However, it may contain a reference to the practice of blowing trumpets in the Temple at the time of collecting alms for some special need. It was the custom to sound trumpets during public fasts on the occasions of drought. During these times prayers were frequently offered in the streets, and some commentators believe that collections for the poor may also have been made during these public fasts. Whether the expression is taken to be figurative or literal, it should be rendered in the receptor language in such a way as to make a dynamic impact. Note, for example, GECL: "Don't hang it on the great bell!" In German this expression means something like "Don't make a big fuss about it" or "Don't broadcast it all around." Several English translations maintain the trumpet imagery with forceful impact: "do not announce it with trumpets" (NIV), "do not announce it with a flourish of trumpets" (NEB), and "don't hire a trumpeter to go in front of you" (Phps).

Translators who prefer to keep the image of the trumpet may say "Don't have someone blow a trumpet to draw attention to what you are doing." Others may use another image, as in "Don't beat the drums to tell everyone about it." Translators who use no image at all will say something like "Don't do it in such a way that everyone will know about it," "Don't attract attention to what you are doing," or "Don't make a big noise (or, fuss) about it."

Hypocrites is the translation (rather transliteration) of a Greek word originally used of an actor who played a role (Phps: "play actors"). In the Septuagint it is employed as a term for the godless. In the Psalms of Solomon, which are of Pharisaic origin, it is applied to the Sadducees, since they were considered worldly by the Pharisees (Psalms of Solomon 4.7,25). Although the word itself may indicate self-delusion, in the context conscious deception is evidently intended. This interpretation is supported by the terrible accusations brought against hypocrisy in the following verses. The word is quite frequently used in Matthew's Gospel: 6.2,5,16; 7.5; 15.7; 22.18; 23.13,(14,)15,23,25,27,29; 24.51. Outside the Gospel of Matthew it occurs only four times in the New Testament: Mark 7.6; Luke 6.42; 12.56; 13.15.

Hypocrisy is probably something known in every culture in the world, so many languages will have a word that means exactly **hypocrites**. Others, however, will speak of such people as "those who appear to be one thing but are really the opposite" or "people who pretend to be good and are really bad." In this verse, translators should not identify the hypocrites as Pharisees or as any other specific group.

Synagogues were the Jewish **"houses of worship"** (TEV); see comments on 4.23.

Streets follows the Greek text and is the rendering of most translations; AB has "market places." In some languages it may sound odd to have the people standing out in the middle of busy streets praying; any place where large crowds of people normally gather for daily activities, such as market places or street corners, would seem a most satisfactory rendering. Thus translators may have "out in the middle of town" or "in the busy parts of the towns."

The word **as** means "just like" or "in the same manner." This sentence can be structured in two or three ways; for example, "When you give to needy people, don't do it the way the hypocrites do. They have someone blow a trumpet in the synagogues and in the streets to draw attention to what they are doing" or "When you give something to needy people, don't have someone blow a trumpet to announce it. That is what the hypocrites do in the synagogues and in the streets."

The passive form of the Greek text (**that they may be praised by men**) is changed into an active by TEV's **"so that people will praise them."** NAB has "looking for applause"; Brc "to win popular applause"; NJB "to win human admiration"; NEB "to win admiration from men"; GECL: "they want only to be honored by men." Translations have also said "so that people will say how good they are" or "because they want people to praise them."

Truly, I say to you. See 5.18, where almost the same form is used. The Greek verb translated **received** by RSV occurs frequently in written materials from those days as a technical term in drawing up a receipt. Matthew uses it with this same meaning in verse 16; elsewhere it occurs in the Gospel in 14.24 and 15.8, though with a different meaning.

Reward: although the word has "wages" as its first meaning, it may also mean "reward" as a special gift given either by humans or by God. Elsewhere in Matthew it occurs in 5.12 (see comments there); 5.46; 6.1,16; 10.41,42; and as "wages" in 20.8. It is sometimes translated "gift for what they have done," or simply "gift."

Jesus is saying here "They have received already all the reward they are going to receive" or "They will not get any more reward than that." It may be helpful to indicate that any further reward or gift would have come from God. This can be done with a phrase like "God won't give them any gift beyond that (or, that praise)." The "that" refers, of course, to the praise of men. Another way to express the thought is "When people praise them, that is the only reward they will receive."

6.3	RSV	TEV
	But when you give alms, do not let your left hand know what your right hand is doing,	**But when you help a needy person, do it in such a way that even your closest friend will not know about it.**

When you give alms translates the same structure used in verse 2.

Do not let your left hand know what your right hand is doing. GECL is similar to TEV: "so that your best friend will not know about it." A number of commentators believe that Jesus is speaking of a generosity that even one's most intimate friend must not know about, and at least one commentator notes that the interpretation as a reference to one's closest friend finds support in a current Arabic proverb. But whether the reference is to one's best friend or to one's self, the focus is on the secrecy of the action. Jesus is here calling upon his followers to disregard self in the giving of gifts for the needy. Giving is to be for the sake of the poor and not for personal satisfaction. In giving, one is not to seek praise from God or from people; a person who truly loves God and others does not think of self.

Many translators have felt that their readers will have no trouble understanding a literal translation of this verse. The idea of the secrecy of the action is clear. Others have felt that the idiom needs clarification. Some have followed the model of TEV, where the reference is to one's best friend, but many prefer to be more general, as in "do it so that no one else will know about it." The sentence may be "When you give to help some needy person, do it in such a way that no one will know what you have done" or "When you give to people who don't have all they need to live, give help to them in secret."

6.4	RSV	TEV
	so that your alms may be in secret; and your Father who sees in secret will reward you.	**Then it will be a private matter. And the Father, who sees what you do in private, will reward you.**

So that your alms may be in secret, as RSV indicates, is a continuation of the sentence begun in verse 3. TEV begins a new sentence: "**Then it will be a private matter.**" GECL does not render this clause expressly in verse 4. However, the meaning is carried by the inclusion of "so inconspicuously that" in verse 3: "³When you help someone, do it so inconspicuously that not even your best friend will know of it. ⁴Your Father, who sees even the most secret things, will reward you."

The meaning of **in secret** (TEV "**a private matter**") is not altogether clear. It may refer to deeds that are known only to God and to the person who does them. Or it may refer to deeds that are done so naturally, without conscious effort, that only God knows them, since even the doer himself is unaware. The term apparently is repeated intentionally in verse 6, perhaps for emphasis, and the translator should take the expression there into account.

Translators will do well to work on verses 3 and 4 together so that the translation flows naturally. Some will construct verse 3 in such a way that the first phrase of verse 4, **so that your alms may be in secret**, does not need to be rendered explicitly. This is what GECL, cited above, has done. Those languages that do express the phrase explicitly can follow TEV or use a phrase like "then no one else will know about what you have given," "then the fact that you gave will be a secret," or "your giving won't be something people know about."

Father, as in 5.48, is God.

For comments on **reward**, see 5.12.

Although the text does not explicitly state when **your Father . . . will reward you**, it is best understood as a reference to the final judgment. Here again KJV includes the word "openly" after **will reward you**; this inclusion, however, has no basis in the best Greek manuscripts.

Translators can express the last part of the verse in various ways: "And God your Father, who sees what you do in private, will give you a reward," "God your Father sees these secret things and he will reward you," or "It is God your Father who will reward you for the things you do in private."

6.5-15

RSV   TEV

Teaching about Prayer

5 "And when you pray, you must not be like the hypocrites; for they love to stand and pray in the synagogues and at the street corners, that they may be seen by men. Truly, I say to you, they have received their reward. 6 But when you pray, go into your room and shut the door and pray to your Father who is in secret; and your Father who sees in secret will reward you.

7 "And in praying do not heap up empty phrases as the Gentiles do; for they think that they will be heard for their many words. 8 Do not be like them, for your Father knows what you need before you ask him. 9 Pray then like this:
    Our Father who art in heaven,
    Hallowed be thy name.
10   Thy kingdom come,
    Thy will be done,
       On earth as it is in heaven.
11   Give us this day our daily bread;ᵐ

5 "When you pray, do not be like the hypocrites! They love to stand up and pray in the houses of worship and on the street corners, so that everyone will see them. I assure you, they have already been paid in full. 6 But when you pray, go to your room, close the door, and pray to your Father, who is unseen. And your Father, who sees what you do in private, will reward you.

7 "When you pray, do not use a lot of meaningless words, as the pagans do, who think that God will hear them because their prayers are long. 8 Do not be like them. Your Father already knows what you need before you ask him. 9 This, then, is how you should pray:
    'Our Father in heaven:
    May your holy name be honored;
10   may your Kingdom come;
    may your will be done on earth as it is in
       heaven.

12   And forgive us our debts,
       As we also have forgiven our debtors;
13   And lead us not into temptation,
       But deliver us from evil.*n*
	11 Give us today the food we need.*c*
	12 Forgive us the wrongs we have done,
	       as we forgive the wrongs that others
	       have done to us.

14 For if you forgive men their trespasses, your heavenly Father also will forgive you; 15 but if you do not forgive men their trespasses, neither will your Father forgive your trespasses.

13   Do not bring us to hard testing,
       but keep us safe from the Evil One.*x*
14 "If you forgive others the wrongs they have done to you, your Father in heaven will also forgive you. 15 But if you do not forgive others, then your Father will not forgive the wrongs you have done.

m Or *our bread for the morrow*
n Or *the evil one.* Other authorities, some ancient, add, in some form, *For thine is the kingdom and the power and the glory, for ever. Amen.*

c we need *or* for today *or* for tomorrow.
x *Some manuscripts add* For yours is the kingdom, and the power, and the glory forever. Amen.

SECTION HEADING: "**Teaching about Prayer**." This may be "Jesus teaches how people should pray (to God)" or ". . . how people should talk to God."

6.5	RSV	TEV

"**And when you pray, you must not be like the hypocrites; for they love to stand and pray in the synagogues and at the street corners, that they may be seen by men. Truly, I say to you, they have received their reward.**"

"**When you pray, do not be like the hypocrites! They love to stand up and pray in the houses of worship and on the street corners, so that everyone will see them. I assure you, they have already been paid in full.**"

There is quite a variety of ways that churches have translated **pray**. In some traditions the words used have really referred to ritual recitations or incantations. In other places a word that really means "beg" has been used. Translators should avoid both these ideas and concentrate instead on the idea of "speak with God" or "talk to God."

When will normally be rendered as "On those occasions when" or "Whenever."

In Greek the "you" of verse 1 is plural, while in verses 2-4 "you" is singular. Verses 5 and 7-14 use the plural form, but verse 6 is in the singular. This alternation between singular and plural takes place throughout the Sermon on the Mount and is apparently of no exegetical significance. Translators should use the form of the second person that is most natural in their language.

On **hypocrites**, see comments on verse 2. Jesus says, whenever you pray, **you must not be like the hypocrites**, which can also be expressed "you must not pray as the hypocrites do."

TEV starts a new sentence to mark the transition shown by **for** in RSV. Other translators can say "Because what they do is . . ." or "They are the kind of people who . . . ."

Love to in this context means "like to," that is, they very much enjoy doing it. It should be noted that the object of **love** is the entire construction **to stand and pray**, not just the verb **to stand**. NJB and NEB render "they love to say their prayers standing up," which may make the connection between verb and object clearer. In addition there are two or three ways that the clause **they love to stand and pray** can be restructured. Translators may say "They love to stand in the synagogues or on the street corners to pray," "They love to make their prayers when standing in the synagogues and on the street corners," or "They love to do their prayers by standing in the synagogues and on the street corners and saying them." Of course, in many languages translators can follow RSV quite closely with no difficulty.

Synagogues: see comments on 4.23; 6.2.

Street corners renders a Greek phrase which is different from "streets" of verse 2. **Street corners** would presumably be even more crowded with people than the streets. **Street corners** may not be readily understood by many rural readers, so translators may say "where streets cross each other in a town" or "where several paths come together in a town."

The passive construction **that they may be seen by men** appears as an active formation in TEV: "**so that everyone will see them.**" NAB renders "in order to be noticed." Brc is dramatic: "Their idea is to be seen praying by as many people as possible." Another rendering is "They want many people to see them. That's why they do that."

Notice that **men** is translated as "everyone" or "many people."

Truly, I say to you is the same expression used in verse 2; a similar form is used in 5.18.

They have received their reward translates the same statement made in verse 2.

6.6   RSV   TEV

But when you pray, go into your room and shut the door and pray to your Father who is in secret; and your Father who sees in secret will reward you.

But when you pray, go to your room, close the door, and pray to your Father, who is unseen. And your Father, who sees what you do in private, will reward you.

But when can be "For your part, on those occasions when . . ." or "Instead, whenever . . . ."

Room translates a Greek word that refers to a small storeroom attached to the Jewish house. It would have been the only room provided with a door, and at least one commentator observes that it had become almost a proverbial expression for a place where one could go and not be seen. Elsewhere in the New Testament it occurs only three times: Matthew 24.26; Luke 12.3,24. Some commentators note that **go into your room and shut the door** is almost a verbal assimilation to the Septuagint of Isaiah 26.20; only in Isaiah the context is that of a threat to hide from the Lord's anger. These same commentators also call attention to 2 Kings 4.33, where Elisha "went in and shut the door upon the two of them and prayed to the Lord."

For many translators, **go into your room and shut the door** poses no problem. Sometimes **your room** becomes "a room," "a part of the house," or "a part of your compound (or, living quarters)." In languages where houses perhaps normally do not have rooms with doors, then the way to say this is "Go into a room where you can be alone" or "Go to a place (in your house) where you will be alone."

Father here, as throughout the passage, is God. Some translations will say "God, who is your Father." See comments on 5.16.

The meaning of the Greek structure translated **who is in secret** is unclear. Compare the expression as it occurs in verse 4. A number of translations maintain the literalism of the Greek text, but others try to make some meaning of the strange expression. TEV and NIV have "who is unseen"; others go in the direction of NJB: "who is in that secret place" (see NEB, FRCL). NAB translates "pray to your Father in private." In favor of the interpretation given in NJB and NAB is the clause **who sees in secret**, which suggests that the emphasis is upon the Father's ability to see what takes place, because he is there in that private place. If translators follow the lead of TEV and NIV in translating **who is in secret**, they may say "whom nobody can see" or "that no one sees." Those who follow the interpretation of NJB and NAB will have a phrase such as "who is in that private place" or "who is there (where you are praying)."

The translation of **who sees in secret** will then be similar: "Your Father who sees what you do in secret (or, private)," "who sees what others can't see" or "your Father who sees what you do there (or, in that private place)."

Will reward you repeats the last part of verse 4.

6.7-13: The "Lord's Prayer" is contained in verses 7-13; the prayer proper is found in 9b-13, with 7-9a providing the contextual setting. Both in Matthew and in Luke (11.1-4) it appears as the ideal Christian prayer, although the two contexts are different. The Lukan context sets it in contrast to the prayers that John the Baptist taught his disciples to pray. The prayer also occurs in the Didache, a Christian document of great authority during the early Christian centuries. The form of the prayer in the Didache is practically identical with that of Matthew, and questions regarding the original form, whether to be found in Matthew or Luke, remain unresolved. Scholars have often argued in favor of the originality of the Lukan form, since it reflects less of a liturgical structure. On the other hand, Matthew is more eschatologically oriented, while Luke's interests seem to have shifted to the affairs of everyday living. Here, as elsewhere, the role of the translator is to reproduce the meaning of the text according to the unique emphasis given it by the author of the particular Gospel that is being translated.

6.7	RSV	TEV
	"And in praying do not heap up empty phrases as the Gentiles do; for they think that they will be heard for their many words.	"When you pray, do not use a lot of meaningless words, as the pagans do, who think that God will hear them because their prayers are long.

And in praying (TEV "**When you pray**") translates a Greek participle. NEB and NJB render "In your prayers" and Brc "When you say your prayers." It is translationally sound, of course, to render the participle as a finite verb (so TEV), drawing the subject "you" from the main verb in the clause.

Most translations will begin this verse very much as they did verses 5 and 6, or they may have "The way you should pray, it is not by using . . . ."

Heap up empty phrases (TEV "**use a lot of meaningless words**") translates one verb in Greek. It occurs only here in the New Testament, and apparently there is only one known occurrence of its usage in Greek literature outside the New Testament. The meaning is somehow related to **for their many words** at the end of the verse. Some scholars see in the verb the meaning "speak stammeringly, say the same thing over and over again." At least one scholar understands the verb to be onomatopoeic, that is, it sounds like its referent. In Greek the verb consists of two parts, a stem meaning "speak," and a prefix *batta*, which is not a meaningful word. If the verb is taken to be onomatopoeic, the sense will then be "go on and on saying *batta, batta, batta.'* " Others see a probable connection between this word and a word found in an Aramaic papyrus from Qumran which means "without effect." Several scholars follow yet another interpretation. Inasmuch as the prayers of pagans (and not hypocrites) is in focus, they take this as a reference to the pagan practice of heaping up names or terms for God to insure that the correct name of God would not be omitted during their prayers. Since it is impossible to be conclusive, the translator is advised to follow one of the standard translations. For example: "do not go babbling on like the heathen" (NEB), "do not babble as the pagans do" (JB), "do not rattle on like the pagans" (NAB), and "don't use a lot of words like the heathen do" (GECL 1st edition). Other models translators can follow include "Don't use a lot of words that don't make sense," "Don't go on repeating strange sounds (or, words)." This sentence may be restructured in some translations: "The way you should pray, it is not by using a lot of words that don't make sense. That is what the pagans do."

Gentiles (TEV "**pagans**") was first used in 5.47 (see comments there).

"**God will hear them**" of TEV is an active transform of the Greek passive structure **they will be heard** with the subject (God) explicitly expressed. When used of prayer the verb "**hear**" means "answer." Therefore "**God will hear them**" means "God will answer their prayers." GECL translates "They think that they can get something from God." This can also be "They think that God will pay attention to their prayers" or "They think that God will give them what they pray for."

For their many words refers specifically to prayer, and so TEV has "**because their prayers are long.**" NAB renders "by the sheer multiplication of words." NEB restructures entirely: "who imagine that the more they say the more likely they are to be heard." Brc translates "Their idea is that God will hear their prayers because of their length." Translators may also render **for their many words** as "because they said many words when they prayed," or "because they prayed for such a long time." Or they may well have "they imagine that using so many words will make God give them what they pray for."

Do not be like them, for your Father knows what you need before you ask him.

Do not be like them. Your Father already knows what you need before you ask him.

Do not be like them is rendered "Do not imitate them" by a number of translations (NEB, NAB, FRCL). The intent of this command is not to discourage prayer, but to remind the worshiper that God cannot be coerced into action merely because one piles up words with this purpose in mind.

Thus **Do not be like them** is more often translated "Don't pray like they do," "Don't be like them when you pray," "Don't use the kinds of prayers they do," or "Don't talk to God in that way."

The last half of this verse (**for your Father knows what you need before you ask him**) is rendered similarly in most all translations.

For comments on **Father**, see 5.16; "God your Father" is possible.

What you need may be "the things that it is necessary to have," "the things you should have but don't have them now," or "the things you need him to give you."

The first occurrence in this Gospel of the verb translated **ask** is 5.42; though the verb may be used of prayer, its use is not confined to prayer. **Ask him** is elliptical, that is, it is a shortened form of "ask him for it" or "ask him to give it to you."

Pray then like this:
   Our Father who art in heaven,
   Hallowed be thy name.

This, then, is how you should pray:
   'Our Father in heaven:
   May your holy name be honored;

Pray then like this is rendered similarly by most translations. Note, for example, NEB ("This is how you should pray") and NJB ("So you should pray like this"). At least one commentator points out that the meaning is "in this way," not "in these words."

Following this interpretation, translators may have "When you pray, you should pray in this way," "Your praying should be like this," or "When you pray, this is the kind of prayer you should make."

There is one practical problem in translating the Lord's Prayer that we should mention. The version used in liturgy is often different from the text of Matthew. Translators should not try to make their translation of the version of it in Matthew conform to the version that is already in use in the Church. They must do the best they can to translate the prayer meaningfully as they find it in Matthew. In any case, Luke's version is different, and the usual church version contains an ending not found in the New Testament text, so total conformity will never be possible.

The form of address in Matthew (**Our Father who art in heaven**) appears in Luke simply as "Father" (Luke 11.2). The modifier **Our** reminds us that no believer stands alone, while **in heaven** serves both to differentiate the heavenly Father from earthly fathers and at the same time to preserve the distance between God and man.

Note **Our** refers to those of us here on earth praying. Some languages have two words for "our," one that includes the person with whom one is talking (inclusive) and one that does not (exclusive). The latter should be used, since here God is being addressed, that is, being spoken to.

Father has been discussed in 5.16. Here there are many translations that say "God, our Father in heaven" to avoid any possibility that readers think the prayer is addressed to an earthly father who has died and gone to heaven. Others say "God in heaven, who is (like) a Father to us." Other ways to structure this phrase include "God our Father, you who live in heaven" and "Our Father God, whose place is heaven."

With regard to the last part of this verse and the entirety of the following verse, commentators observe that the three petitions are parallel in thought, and both the passive form and the use of "name" reflect the attitude of reverence found in Jewish prayers.

The archaic **Hallowed be thy name** is translated "may your name be honoured" by Phps and "May your name be held in reverence" by Brc. NJB translates "may your name be held holy." Together with RSV, a number of so-called modern English translations perpetuate the archaic **hallowed** (NIV, NEB, NAB), which translates a Greek verb meaning "make holy." TEV incorporates the idea of holy, but the restructuring is quite different: "**May your holy name be honored.**"

Through the use of the noun **name**, Matthew is able to refer to God without mentioning him. In the Bible, **name** is often a substitute for the person spoken of. It is a way of referring to God as he has revealed himself in history, and it indicates the very presence of God himself. Scholars note that the passive form of the verb is used to avoid giving God a direct command. The petitioner is asking God to cause people to honor his sacred name, that is, to honor God himself.

We discussed "**holy**" under 1.18. If translators have a good word for "holy," then they can say "may people honor your holy name," much as in TEV, or "we pray that people will treat your name as holy." However, where there is not an acceptable single word for "holy," where people have usually translated the term with a phrase that includes "God," then here the translations may have to use "honor." One way is "May people really honor your name." But much better may be "May people give the honor to your name which they should because you are God."

In many cultures, readers will readily understand that to honor his name is a way of saying to honor him. But in others this will not be understood, and people will use "you" directly. Thus they may have in the translation "may people show you great honor," "may people show the honor due you as God," or "may people recognize you as God."

6.10　　　　RSV　　　　　　　　　　　　　TEV

Thy kingdom come,
Thy will be done,
　On earth as it is in heaven.

may your Kingdom come;
may your will be done on earth
　as it is in heaven.

Thy kingdom come is parallel to the first petition. The reference is to the final establishment of God's reign on earth. And, as one commentator observes, the prayer requests that God establish his reign for us, not that we establish it for him.

For a discussion of the term **kingdom**, see 3.2. GECL 1st edition effectively restructures, "You are the Lord! Come and accomplish your work." INCL translates "May you rule here," and MACL reads "Establish your reign (or, rule) on earth." Most translations will be similar to INCL and MACL: "May your rule (or, reign) be established," "We pray you will establish (or, begin) your rule (or, reign) on earth," "We pray that you will soon rule over people," or "May you bring all people under your rule."

The next petition, **Thy will be done, On earth as it is in heaven**, is not found in Luke's presentation of the Lord's Prayer. This petition is an exact parallel to the first petition concerning the honoring of God's name, and as such it also stands parallel with the second petition. The meaning of the petition may be expressed in a variety of ways: "May people obey you as you are obeyed in heaven" (MACL), "May you be obeyed all over the earth as you are obeyed in heaven" (INCL), and "What you will, may it be done not only in heaven, but also among us" (GECL 1st edition).

Thy will be done is a passive and does not specify who is to do God's will. Many translations have to say "may people do what you will" or "the things you want, may people carry them out." In some languages the idea of people doing God's will is acceptable for here on earth, but it does not fit as well with people when heaven is also considered. In those cases, phrases like this can be used: "The things you will, may people carry them out on earth, just as those (beings) in heaven do (or, just as the angels in heaven do or, just as your servants in heaven do)."

Some translations have understood the prayer to be asking that God's will be done on earth and be done in heaven, whereas it is probably better to assume that his will is already done in heaven, and that the prayer is that people on earth carry out his will just as it is already carried out in heaven.

6.11	RSV	TEV
	Give us this day our daily bread;*m*	Give us today the food we need.*c*

m Or *our bread for the morrow*   *c* we need; *or* for tomorrow.

This verse is short but difficult to interpret. The difficulty can best be demonstrated from the RSV rendering (**Give us this day our daily bread**), which represents a fairly literal rendering of the Greek. The problem concerns the meaning of the word rendered **daily**. The word appears only in Christian literature (perhaps also once in a non-Christian papyrus), and its origin and meaning have never been explained to the satisfaction of all. Several solutions have been offered and are summarized in the commentaries. One of the standard Greek lexicons presents them in the following order:

(1) "Necessary for existence." This is the choice of TEV ("**Give us today the food we need**"), GECL ("Give us what we need for life today"), and FRCL ("Give us today the necessary food"). Some commentators say that this interpretation makes

the petition less than spiritual. But Jesus and his followers took seriously the needs of the body.

(2) "For the current day, for today." This seems to be the interpretation favored by translations which render "daily" (see NIV, NJB, NAB, NEB, RSV). AT ("Give us today bread for the day") and Phps ("Give us each day the bread we need for the day") also favor this interpretation.

(3) "For the following day." This would refer to the daily ration of bread, given for the next day; therefore, "Give us today our daily portion." Mft translates "give us to-day our bread for the morrow," while Brc renders "Give us today our bread for the coming day." This interpretation offers several possibilities of meaning. If the prayer is said in the morning, the "coming day" would be the day in progress. If prayed in the evening, the petition would also include the following day. But the future reference would permit an eschatological interpretation as well, in which case the "coming day" could be the coming Messianic banquet. However, in this context such an interpretation is highly unlikely.

(4) "Bread for the future." This is discussed under (3) above; it is the so-called eschatological interpretation.

There is really no significant difference of meaning between the first two alternatives. Moreover, the third alternative, if taken as a reference to the present day, comes to mean essentially the same as the first two possibilities. The fourth interpretation, though attractive, does not seem to be in focus in the present passage.

Give may be "provide" or "make sure we have."

Since an eschatological interpretation of **daily** should be rejected, the translation of **this day** should not be "in these days" or "in this age." It means simply "today," although it can be "each day" or "day by day" in some constructions, depending on how **daily** is dealt with.

The Greek word for **bread** is here used with the wider meaning of "food." In very few cultures would the figure "bread" be understood to mean food in general, and therefore almost all translations say "food" or "things to eat."

Some have wanted to take **bread** to mean more than "food," feeling it represents all our needs, spiritual and physical. They have had translations like "everything we need for true life" or "for our souls (or, spirits) and bodies." This would be incorrect, as would an interpretation like "everything we need for a living," which covers all physical needs. It is best here to limit the interpretation of "bread" to "food," as we said.

Most translators will follow the examples listed under the first two interpretations: "Give us each day (or, today) the food we need," "Give us today the food for living," "Give us what food we need to live each day," or "Give us the food to satisfy our needs each day," and so forth.

6.12 RSV	TEV
And forgive us our debts, As we also have forgiven our debtors;	Forgive us the wrongs we have done, as we forgive the wrongs that others have done to us.

Forgive has proved remarkably difficult to translate in many languages in which there is no one word that can be used. However, there is usually an idiom or some figure of speech that can express the concept of forgiveness. "Forget the wrong," "no longer see the wrong," "put the wrong behind one's back," "lift the wrong from between us"—these are just a few ways we have seen "forgiveness" expressed.

Debts (so most translations) represents a literal rendering of the Greek word. However, commentators note that the word is here used figuratively for "sins," and one standard lexicon gives the meaning "sin" (in this passage the plural form "sins" is used). GECL renders "Forgive us our guilt as we also pardon each one who has done us wrong." The translator must not translate Luke in place of Matthew; however, it may be worth noting that in the parallel passage Luke uses the word for "sins." Both NEB and NAB have **"wrongs,"** as does TEV. If translators render **debts** literally, it is entirely likely readers will think of debts we owe people, what we have to pay back because we borrowed something. Therefore "sins" or "wrongs" will be much better.

These are wrongs against God, and some translations have had to make this clear, as in "forgive our wrongs against you." (Of course, if translators use "sins," it may not be necessary to add "against you," since in many languages sins are by definition wrongs against God.) It may be necessary to expand "wrongs" to **"wrongs we have done,"** as TEV has done. Other languages might say "our wrong actions."

In the clause **As we also have forgiven**, the pronoun **we** is emphatic. The verb **have forgiven** represents an aorist indicative in Greek. A number of translations give it an habitual or timeless force (TEV **"as we forgive"**). Others specify that the action is past in reference to the petition for God to forgive (see RSV). But the function of the aorist indicative is not simply to indicate past action. And so it may then be used here as a means of emphasizing that the act of forgiveness is an accomplished fact. This means translators do have the choice between "as we have already forgiven" and "as we generally (or, habitually) forgive."

The word **as** is important. Some translators have taken it to mean "because" or "since." But it is better to have "in the same way" or "just as." That is, we ask God to forgive us in the same manner we forgive others.

Note, also, that we forgive others for their wrongs against us. They are **our debtors.** This can be expressed "for the wrongs they have done to us," "for the bad things they have done to us," or "for the wrongs against us they have committed."

6.13 RSV	TEV
And lead us not into temptation, But deliver us from evil.*n*	Do not bring us to hard testing, but keep us safe from the Evil One.*x*
n Or *the evil one.* Other authorities, some ancient, add, in some form, *For thine is the kingdom and the power and the glory, for ever. Amen.*	*xSome manuscripts add* For yours is the kingdom, and the power, and the glory forever. Amen.

This final petition is especially difficult to interpret. The Greek word translated **temptation** may also mean "trial, persecution." A number of commentators interpret it in light of the Jewish and early Christian belief that a period of trial and persecution would come upon the faithful immediately before the end of the world. But as one scholar observes, the lack of the definite article before **temptation** is a strong argument against this particularized interpretation. A more general interpretation of **temptation** seems best in light of the absence of any specific reference to "the" one great and final period of temptation. See further at 26.41.

The Greek verb translated **lead . . . into** by RSV and **"bring . . . to"** by TEV is a verb which may be used in a wide range of contexts (see Luke 5.18,19; 11.4; 12.11; Acts 17.20; 1 Tim 6.7; Heb 13.11). There is a dilemma here. According to the Old Testament, God does put people to the test to find out if they will obey him (for example, Gen 22.1-2; Exo 16.4), and according to 1 Corinthians 10.13 it is God who creates both the source of testing and the strength to endure it. But one commentator suggests that the original Aramaic was either causative ("and causes us not to enter") or permissive ("allow us not to enter"), in which case the question of God's directing people toward temptation is not really of concern. In either case, the question whether God sends temptation is not really of concern here, if either cause or permission is a valid interpretation.

For a discussion of **temptation**, see 4.1. As we pointed out there, the sense here can be either "to tempt to do wrong" or "to test or try." If translators follow the former interpretation and at the same time use the causative or permissive interpretation of **lead . . . into**, then the sentence can be "Don't cause us to enter into temptation" or "Don't let it happen that we are tempted to do wrong."

Translations that follow the second interpretation, translating "temptation" as "testing," will have a rendering much like that of TEV, possibly saying "Don't put us through the ordeal of testing," "Don't cause us to undergo testing," or "Don't cause us to be tried too hard."

Deliver . . . from (TEV **"keep . . . safe from"**) translates a verb which may mean either "rescue from" or "protect against." A number of translations render "save . . . from" (NEB, NJB, AT, Phps); Brc has "rescue . . . from" and GECL "protect . . . from." Translators who prefer the first meaning, "rescue from," will have a rendering such as "save us from" or "take us out of the hands of." Those who choose the other possible meaning, "protect against," will have expressions such as "protect us from," "keep us safe from," or "do not let us be conquered by."

Evil translates a noun which may also mean "the evil one" (RSV footnote). New Testament scholars are divided on their judgment. Some are of the opinion that the word is neuter, inasmuch as neither Hebrew nor Aramaic uses "the evil one" to denote Satan. Others, basing their judgment upon 13.19, believe that the phrase may refer to the Evil One, that is, the Devil. In either case, whether evil or the Evil One, the power of evil is here spoken of as a reality. See comments at 5.37,39.

Many translators prefer to interpret **evil** as the Devil, and have either "the Evil One" or "the Devil, the Evil One." But others will keep "evil" as an abstract idea or force, as in "take us out of evil" or "protect us from evil."

A number of manuscripts, but not the best or most ancient, include a benediction at the close of the Lord's Prayer, as TC-GNT notes. For English speaking readers the most familiar of these is that of KJV: "For thine is the kingdom, and the power, and the glory, forever. Amen." Another ancient source simply has "For yours is the power forever and ever." Several late manuscripts even have "For yours is the kingdom and the power and the glory of the Father and of the Son and of the Holy Spirit forever. Amen." One scholar argues for including the doxology because it is impossible to imagine that either Jesus or Matthew would have ended a prayer without a doxology, since Jewish prayers traditionally concluded in this manner. However, it must be borne in mind that the best textual traditions do not include a doxology. It is unlikely that a scribe would have omitted a doxology when copying the text, but it is far more likely that he would add one to the original text. We assume that it was not in the original text, in light of all the evidence. None of the standard modern translations include the doxology.

6.14-15 RSV	TEV
14 For if you forgive men their trespasses, your heavenly Father also will forgive you; 15 but if you do not forgive men their trespasses, neither will your Father forgive your trespasses.	14 "If you forgive others the wrongs they have done to you, your Father in heaven will also forgive you. 15 But if you do not forgive others, then your Father will not forgive the wrongs you have done.

The same truth is stated in each of these two verses, first negatively (verse 14), then positively (verse 15). A parallel to the positive form appears in Mark 11.25, and some commentators call attention to the similarity between these two verses and Matthew 7.1 (see Luke 6.37), and to their agreement with Matthew 5.22,45,48.

Jesus here adds a short comment on the words about forgiveness in verse 12. RSV has the transition **For**. Some languages will not need any transition. For example, TEV in English does not have one. Others will say something like "You can pray like that because."

We discussed **forgive** in verse 12.

The Greek word translated **trespasses** (TEV "**wrongs**") is found in Matthew only in these two verses. Elsewhere in the Gospels it is used only once (Mark 11.25; and in some manuscripts in 11.26). Outside the Gospels it appears only in the letters of Paul (Rom 4.25; 5.15,16,17,18,20; 11.11,12; 2 Cor 5.19; Gal 6.1; Eph 1.7; 2.1; 2.5; and Col 2.13). The word literally means "stepping aside" and is rendered "false step, transgression, sin" by one of the standard lexicons. **If you forgive men** (TEV "**others**") **their trespasses** is translated "For if you forgive men when they sin against you" by NIV. NAB uses "faults" and NJB "failings" (Phps "failures"). However, in the present context a wrong or sin against someone is definitely indicated. This is made clear by **your trespasses**, which clearly means "your wrongs against your (heavenly) Father." **Trespasses** that people commit against you can be "wrongs" or "harm they do you." **Your trespasses**, as we explained, refers to "the wrongs you commit against God," or "your sins." Translators should find TEV or NIV (cited above) helpful models. "If you forgive people when they do wrong to you" or "If you forgive people for the wrongs they do to you."

For God to forgive you depends on your forgiving others. This must be clear, as in "then in his turn God your Father in heaven will forgive you your sins" or "then in the same way, your heavenly Father will forgive you your sins." The same relation holds true in verse 15: "But if you fail to forgive other people when they do wrong to you, your heavenly Father will not forgive you either for your sins against him."

For comments on **heavenly Father**, see 5.16.

6.16-18

RSV   TEV

Teaching about Fasting

16 "And when you fast, do not look dismal, like the hypocrites, for they disfigure their faces that their fasting may be seen by men. Truly, I say to you, they have received their reward. 17 But when you fast, anoint your head and wash your face, 18 that your fasting may not be seen by men but by your Father who is in secret; and your Father who sees in secret will reward you.

16 "And when you fast, do not put on a sad face as the hypocrites do. They neglect their appearance so that everyone will see that they are fasting. I assure you, they have already been paid in full. 17 When you go without food, wash your face and comb your hair, 18 so that others cannot know that you are fasting—only your Father, who is unseen, will know. And your Father, who sees what you do in private, will reward you.

SECTION HEADING: "**Teaching about Fasting**." For comments on **Fasting**, see 4.2. This section heading can be "Jesus teaches about fasting" or "Jesus teaches about how people go without food to worship (or, honor) God."

6.16

RSV   TEV

"And when you fast, do not look dismal, like the hypocrites, for they disfigure their faces that their fasting may be seen by men. Truly, I say to you, they have received their reward.

"And when you fast, do not put on a sad face as the hypocrites do. They neglect their appearance so that everyone will see that they are fasting. I assure you, they have already been paid in full.

For the Jewish community of Jesus' day, the three primary expressions of piety were charity, prayer, and fasting. In verses 16-18 the matter of fasting is discussed. The only official Jewish day of fasting was the Day of Atonement, when eating, drinking, bathing, and anointing with oil were forbidden. The Jews would also fast in connection with the celebration of days of national disaster, and it was frequently done on a private and individual basis as well.

As we said in the discussion of 4.2, **fast** means to deliberately go without food, usually as a way of honoring God or as part of a period of meditation and prayer. The custom is known in many parts of the world and poses no translation problem in such places. Where it is not known, translators can say "Whenever you go without food to honor God" or "On those occasions when you do not eat so you can worship God."

Dismal (TEV "**sad face**") translates a word used in the New Testament only here and in Luke 24.17. It may be used of one who looks angry, sullen, or sad. In the Septuagint it is used to describe the chief baker and the wine steward of the king

(Gen 40.1). A number of translations render it with the meaning "gloomy" (NJB, NEB, AT, Mft, Brc). To **look dismal** can be "to go about looking pitiful (or, sad or, gloomy)."

The word **hypocrites** is first used in verse 2 (see comments there). The real point is that the hypocrites are intentionally acting in such a manner as to draw attention to themselves. Translators may say "that is what the hypocrites do" or "that is how the hypocrites show (or, present) themselves."

Disfigure their faces (so also NIV, Brc) is translated "**neglect their appearance**" by TEV and "neglect their personal appearance" by AT. JB renders "pull long faces" and NEB "make their faces unsightly." One commentator notes that the Greek verb translated **disfigure** appears not to be used elsewhere with "face" as its object, and he suggests that it was chosen here because it rhymes with the Greek verb rendered **may be seen**. For other occurrences of the Greek verb for **disfigure**, see verses 19,20 ("consume") and Acts 13.41 ("perish"). Some commentators limit **disfigure their faces** to the matter of leaving them unwashed. Others extend the meaning to include leaving their faces unwashed and their hair uncombed and the strewing of ashes on their heads. For English speakers the problem with **disfigure** is that it may imply a permanent action, whereas the reference is limited to things done during days of fasting.

It is important to show that when the hypocrites **disfigure their faces**, it is a deliberate thing. Thus the phrase can be rendered "they deliberately go with dirty faces (or, unkempt appearances)," "they make themselves appear to be suffering," or "they allow themselves to look terrible."

That their fasting may be seen by men is inverted by TEV: "**so that everyone will see that they are fasting**." In the context **men** is used inclusively of "people," and so NEB translates "so that other people may see that they are fasting" (NAB "so that others may see they are fasting").

Some translations make this a new sentence, as in "They do that so everyone can see they are fasting" or "They do that to make sure people know they are fasting."

Truly, I say to you: see 5.18, where almost the precise form is used; see 5.20 for the exact words.

They have received their reward: see comments on verse 2.

6.17   RSV   TEV

RSV	TEV
But when you fast, anoint your head and wash your face,	When you go without food, wash your face and comb your hair,

But when you fast. The meaning is "When you go without food for a period of time in order to worship God in a special way."

When can be "whenever" or "on those occasions that."

TEV rearranges the two commands in a manner that is more natural for American readers: "**wash your face and comb your hair**." FRCL and GECL follow TEV in this, whereas most English translators retain the literal **anoint your head**. Some few attempt to update "anoint" by rendering "put oil on your head" (JB, NIV), while NAB renders "groom your hair," and AT has "perfume your hair." One commentator observes that when the disciples fast, they are to give the impression of persons going to a feast. But it may be, as other commentators suggest, that the disciples are simply commanded to look the same when they are fasting and when they are not fasting.

Many translations that have retained **anoint your head** have in fact misled their readers, who have identified this anointing with that done to those chosen to be kings in the Old Testament, or even to Christ. ("Christ" means "anointed.") It is better to do something similar to TEV or NAB and use a normal term for grooming or combing hair.

In translation it is not necessary to make a distinction between the use of the plural "you" in the Greek text of verse 16 and the singular "you" in verses 17 and 18.

6.18   RSV   TEV

that your fasting may not be seen by men but by your Father who is in secret; and your Father who sees in secret will reward you.	so that others cannot know that you are fasting—only your Father, who is unseen, will know. And your Father, who sees what you do in private, will reward you.

RSV retains the formal structure of the Greek text, which continues in this verse the sentence begun in verse 17. Translators can also begin a new sentence, as in "Do that so that people won't notice that you are fasting" or "You should do this so no one will know when you are fasting."

Who is in secret . . . **who sees in secret**. The Greek noun used here for **secret** differs from that of verses 4 and 6. But there is no difficulty in interpreting the two nouns as synonymous. Problematic, however, is how God may be spoken of as the one **who is in secret**. TEV resolves the problem by translating "**who is unseen.**" This interpretation finds support in the Septuagint of Jeremiah 23.24. The same phrase is used there (except in the plural), where the text reads, "Can anyone hide himself in secret places where I cannot see him?" In the Jeremiah passage the phrase is easily equivalent to "in places where he cannot be seen" or "in places where he is unseen." NAB translates the two clauses as "who is hidden . . . who sees what is hidden," and NJB translates the two of them "who sees all that is done in secret." NEB has "your Father who is in the secret place . . . your Father who sees what is secret."

Translators most often do something similar to what they did in verses 4 and 6. They can say "Your Father who is in that private place will see (or, know about) your fasting, and he will reward you" or "Your Father whom men (or, you) can't see will see what you do and will reward you." Few translators will find it natural to repeat the phrase **in secret**, although TEV has done it in English. Those who do will render the verse "So that no one will know when you are fasting except your Father whom no one can see. He sees all that is done in private, and will reward you."

Father, as in 5.16, is God.

Will reward you: see comments on 5.12 and 6.4, where the same expression is used.

6.19-21

Riches in Heaven

19 "Do not lay up for yourselves treasures on earth, where moth and rust*⁰* consume and where thieves break in and steal, 20 but lay up for yourselves treasures in heaven, where neither moth nor rust*⁰* consumes and where thieves do not break in and steal. 21 For where your treasure is, there will your heart be also.

19 "Do not store up riches for yourselves here on earth, where moths and rust destroy, and robbers break in and steal. 20 Instead, store up riches for yourselves in heaven, where moths and rust cannot destroy, and robbers cannot break in and steal. 21 For your heart will always be where your riches are.

⁰ Or *worm*

SECTION HEADING: "**Riches in Heaven**." Some translators will use a sentence such as "Jesus teaches about riches in heaven." Others will have "Jesus teaches about the kinds of riches we should store up." See below under verse 19 for a discussion of "**riches**" or **treasures**.

The entire section (6.19-34) is concerned with an absolute loyalty to God, a loyalty that prevails over worldly concerns and results in a wholeness of life. Nothing in this section is found in Luke's Sermon on the Plain, which takes up again with Matthew 7.1 (see Luke 6.37). However, Luke does include in other contexts everything except Matthew 6.34. One commentator believes that the section dealing with the accumulation of riches (verses 19-24) may be said to be directed more toward the rich, while the section dealing with anxiety (verses 25-34) is directed more toward the poor.

6.19   RSV   TEV

"**Do not lay up for yourselves treasures on earth, where moth and rust*⁰* consume and where thieves break in and steal,**

"**Do not store up riches for yourselves here on earth, where moths and rust destroy, and robbers break in and steal.**

⁰ Or *worm*

In Matthew's Gospel the repeated contrast in verses 1-18 between reward from men and reward from God leads to this saying; in Luke 12.33 the saying appears in the form of a general command to the disciples to sell their property and give the money to the poor.

On the basis of Aramaic language features, scholars have demonstrated the poetical character of verses 19-21. Verses 19 and 20 each consist of three lines with three stresses in each line, with verse 19 pointing out the wrong way and verse 20 indicating the right way. Verse 21, consisting of one four-stress line, states a general truth and rounds off the structure.

The imperatives in verse 19 are in the plural in contrast to the use of the singular in verse 18; in verse 21 the singular form of "your" is used. However, as indicated earlier, the shifts between singular and plural in the Sermon seem only to deal with the form in which the sayings were originally circulated, and apparently make no exegetical significance.

Do not lay up (TEV "**store up**") **for yourself treasures on earth** is a fairly literal translation of the Greek, as are most other translations. **Lay up** can also be "gather for yourself." GECL translates, "Gather no riches here on earth!" The negative command can be translated in a negative or positive form. "You should not store up (or, save)" and "Do not accumulate" are examples of the negative. "Store up for yourself no riches" is an example of a positive command.

Treasures has often been rendered "riches." It refers to expensive things, wealth, or valuable things that people can own, and it can be translated by any one of these terms.

The word rendered **rust** is literally "eating." It may refer to food (John 4.32; 6.27,55), to a meal (Heb 12.16) or even to the act of eating (Rom 14.17). In the present context it is generally taken to mean "corrosion, rust." However, the word may refer to an insect, as it does in the Septuagint of Malachi 3.11, where it translates a Hebrew word which RSV translates "devourer," with marginal note "devouring locust." In the Malachi passage TEV has "insects," NEB "pests," and NJB "locust." In the present passage most modern translations have "rust," but TOB has "worms" (RSV alternative rendering), and JB "woodworms." But, as scholars note, the impact is essentially the same; "rust" eats away metal, while "worms" eat away cloth.

This sentence also mentions the **moth**, which is an insect that destroys cloth and similar material. If translators follow RSV and TEV and choose to render "eating" as **rust**, then valuable items of both metal and cloth are shown to be vulnerable in the verse. This is one reason many translators prefer "rust" to "worm" and have phrases such as "here on earth where things can be destroyed by moths or rust."

However, if "worm" is used, then the sentence will be "Here on earth, where moths and worms destroy (or, eat things)." As we said, the point is essentially the same with either interpretation.

The word **consume** (TEV "**destroy**") translates the same verb rendered "disfigure" in verse 16. The verb covers a wide range and may mean either "make unrecognizable" or "destroy, ruin." **Consume** in this passage is often translated "ruin" or "make so it no longer has value." In many West African languages the figure of "consume" or "eat" is a natural expression to use here. Another expression that has the sense of destroy in some languages is "spoil."

Surely every language has a word for **thieves**. However, there are languages that make distinctions between people who steal in different ways. That is, they use one word for people who steal by using weapons or force, and another for those who break into a house, perhaps still another for someone who uses guile, and so on. Obviously, in this verse translators should use the word that would be appropriate for people who break into houses to steal.

The verb **break in** is literally "dig through." TOB translates "break through the walls," with a note that the allusion is to the rural Palestinian home where a thief would dig through the wall in order to get into the house (see Job 24.16). The allusion may even be applied to the act of tunneling under a house into the place where the treasure is stored, since the Greek verb used here is related to the Greek noun which means "canal." The reference may also be to the uncovering of treasure hidden in the ground (see 13.44 and 25.25). Another possibility is that the reference may be that of "forcing a hole through a wall," either of a house (see 24.43) or, more likely, of a storeroom, where the activity would be less easily noticed. In one standard lexicon the verb is connected with the activity of digging through the "sun-dried brick" wall of a house.

Whatever the exact reference of the word, in this context it seems best to use an expression for forcefully entering a house or building in order to steal, and probably without the owner knowing it. It may be necessary in many languages to add an object for "break in"; for example, "into houses" or "into places where you store things."

6.20

RSV	TEV
but lay up for yourselves treasures in heaven, where neither moth nor rust^o consumes and where thieves do not break in and steal.	**Instead, store up riches for yourselves in heaven, where moths and rust cannot destroy, and robbers cannot break in and steal.**

^{o} Or *worm*

Most translations will start a new sentence here. The **but** marks a contrast which TEV has indicated by "**Instead**."

As indicated in the introduction to this section, this verse states positively what was stated negatively in the preceding verse. One commentator warns that "a man can be just as selfishly and greedily devoted to riches stored up in heaven as to earthly riches." GECL renders the first clause of this verse as "Rather store up riches with God."

Many languages will do the same as GECL and render **heaven** as "God." There will be cases where the notion of gathering things of value in heaven or with God will not be understood to refer to storing up things of spiritual value. Often in these cases a literal translation makes no sense. ("How can we ask God to store things for us?" people ask.) In such cases translators will have to say something like this: "Instead, the things that should be valuable for you (and which you want a great deal of) are the experiences you have with God in heaven. Moths and rust can't destroy those and thieves can't break in and steal them." However, if at all possible translators should try to retain the figure of "treasures in heaven," to show the contrast with "earth" in verse 19. Also, Jesus does not indicate here what the treasures in heaven really are.

6.21

RSV	TEV
For where your treasure is, there will your heart be also.	**For your heart will always be where your riches are.**

Jesus does not give an indication how one stores up treasures in heaven or what they consist of; he does indicate that it is a matter of the proper orientation of one's heart. The real question is whether God or riches rules a person's heart, and behind Jesus' words stands the demand for singleness of devotion. TEV reverses the order of the two Greek clauses by translating **"For your heart will always be where your riches are."** The same order is followed by GECL.

Heart here refers to your concerns, interests, your feelings about things. The idea, then, is that you devote time and concern to the things that are valuable to you. Thus the verse can be rendered "For your devotion will be to what is valuable to you," "Make the things in heaven the ones you value, because the thing you always think of is the place where your valuables are," or "Because if the things of greatest value to you are the things of God, then those are what you will always be concerned with."

6.22-23

RSV   TEV

The Light of the Body

22 "The eye is the lamp of the body. So, if your eye is sound, your whole body will be full of light; 23 but if your eye is not sound, your whole body will be full of darkness. If then the light in you is darkness, how great is the darkness!

22 "The eyes are like a lamp for the body. If your eyes are sound, your whole body will be full of light; 23 but if your eyes are no good, your body will be in darkness. So if the light in you is darkness, how terribly dark it will be!

SECTION HEADING: **"The Light of the Body."** This can be "Jesus teaches about what gives light to the body," "Jesus tells people what gives them light," or "Jesus teaches how the eyes are like lamps for us."

6.22-23   RSV   TEV

22 **"The eye is the lamp of the body. So, if your eye is sound, your whole body will be full of light; 23 but if your eye is not sound, your whole body will be full of darkness. If then the light in you is darkness, how great is the darkness!**

22 **"The eyes are like a lamp for the body. If your eyes are sound, your whole body will be full of light; 23 but if your eyes are no good, your body will be in darkness. So if the light in you is darkness, how terribly dark it will be!**

The interpretation of verses 22-23 is difficult, and their place in the context is not easily defined. But they seem to make the most sense if taken as references to whatever distracts a person from full devotion to God, whether wealth (6.19-21,24) or anxiety (6.25-34).

The eye is the lamp of the body is ambiguous; it may indicate either that the eye betrays what an individual is like inwardly, or that the eye gives light to the body. Scholars quote Jewish sources in support of the first interpretation. However, the closing sentence of verse 23 shows that more is intended than mere knowledge of a man's heart through looking into his eye. TEV therefore follows the second interpretation.

The Greek singular **eye** may be rendered as a plural, **"eyes"** (TEV), and the equational statement, **The eye is the lamp**, can be restructured as a simile (TEV

"the eyes are like a lamp"). GECL 1st edition translates "The eye gives light to a person," while the later GECL has "The eye mediates light to a person." Translators will find it useful to do something very similar to TEV or either edition of GECL. Some use full comparison, a combination of these two versions, and say "The eye is like a lamp that gives light to a person." The order can be reversed: "A person's eye provides light for his whole body (like a lamp)."

Sound is the word used by most translations, but the precise meaning is difficult to determine. By itself it contrasts with the Greek term for "twofold," as if to say "singlefold." It thus has the idea of simplicity, straightforwardness, or purity, and depending upon context it can mean "single," "simple," or "sincere," that is, with no ulterior motive. In this context it contrasts with **not sound**, which is literally "if your eye is *bad* or *evil*." In this sense the two expressions can describe eyes that are medically in good or in bad condition, the **sound** eye being "clear" or "healthy," and the one that is **not sound** being unhealthy. But it is clear that in this context the terms are used figuratively for something else.

Since an "evil eye" is a Jewish metaphor for stinginess, some scholars argue that this "good eye" fits the metaphor for generosity. Note that in 20.15 the expression "evil eye" clearly means "greedy" (TEV "jealous"). The context of verses 19-21 favors this understanding here. Brc translates in a way that retains both the figure and this meaning: "sound and generous . . . diseased and grudging."

Other scholars point out that in the Septuagint this word and its cognates represent a Hebrew word which means "singleness of purpose" or "undivided loyalty," especially toward God. And the Aramaic counterpart to the Hebrew may mean both "undivided commitment" and "health." The passage is then understood to mean that, just as blindness makes a person's entire life one of darkness, so distraction by earthly riches blinds a person to God and leads to total darkness.

Matthew frequently uses parts of the body figuratively: verses 21-23 speak of the heart and eye, while 5.28,30 speak of the eye, heart, and hand, 6.3 speaks of the hand, and 15.11 of the mouth. As the eye goes, so goes the entire person. If the eye is sound, one can see the light; if it is not sound, the entire individual walks in darkness. This means that if one's eye for God is darkened, the total person gropes around in darkness. If a person lacks the ability to perceive the presence of God, how terribly dark it is!

Translators will do well to follow this interpretation. To say that an eye is **sound** means that it is healthy, that it is free from defect, or that it works properly. The eye that **is not sound** will be unhealthy, it will have defects, or it will not see as an eye should.

With a sound eye, then, **your whole body will be full of light**. This can probably be translated literally in many languages. It can also be stated as "Thus all of your body (or, being) will see the light" or "You will have light in your whole body (or, whole being)." In some cases, where the figure or image of a light means nothing, people will say "You will know (or, see) clearly what you are doing in every aspect of your life."

Similarly, with unsound eyes, **your whole body will be full of darkness**. If a literal translation means nothing in a language, then translators may say "then all of you will see nothing, as if you were in darkness," "your entire being will be in darkness," or "you won't know what you are doing in any aspect of your life."

If then the light in you is darkness is practically a literal rendering of the Greek and results in a zero meaning. A few translations, however, do attempt to make some meaning of the text. For example, NEB ("If then the only light you have is darkness, the darkness is doubly dark"), Brc ("If the light that ought to be in you has turned to darkness, what a terrible darkness that darkness is!"), and GECL 1st edition ("If what was supposed to give you light has become dark, how terrible then will that darkness be!"). The meaning seems to be "The eye is the organ through which light is supposed to come into the body. However, if the organ which was supposed to bring light into the body has gone bad, then the whole body is in terrible darkness." This sentence is perhaps the key to the interpretation of verses 22-23: an analogy is made between the eye, which is intended to bring light into the body, and the "spiritual eye," through which a person is supposed to perceive the light of God's revelation.

Most translators will be able to use a sentence like those examples listed above: "If the thing that is supposed to give you light is instead darkness, how great your darkness is (or, how great is the darkness in which you are)," "If the thing that is supposed to bring understanding to you, like a light, is dark, then you can't understand anything, and the darkness in which you live is great."

6.24-34

RSV

TEV

God and Possessions

24 "No one can serve two masters; for either he will hate the one and love the other, or he will be devoted to the one and despise the other. You cannot serve God and mammon.^{x}
25 "Therefore I tell you, do not be anxious about your life, what you shall eat or what you shall drink, nor about your body, what you shall put on. Is not life more than food, and the body more than clothing? 26 Look at the birds of the air: they neither sow nor reap nor gather into barns, and yet your heavenly Father feeds them. Are you not of more value than they? 27 And which of you by being anxious can add one cubit to his span of life?^{p} 28 And why are you anxious about clothing? Consider the lilies of the field, how they grow; they neither toil nor spin; 29 yet I tell you, even Solomon in all his glory was not arrayed like one of these. 30 But if God so clothes the grass of the field, which today is alive and tomorrow is thrown into the oven, will he not much more clothe you, O men of little faith? 31 Therefore do not be anxious, saying, 'What shall we eat?' or 'What shall we drink?' or 'What shall we wear?' 32 For the Gentiles seek all these things; and your heavenly Father knows that you need them all. 33 But seek first his kingdom and his righteousness, and all these things shall be yours as well.

24 "No one can be a slave of two masters; he will hate one and love the other; he will be loyal to one and despise the other. You cannot serve both God and money.
25 "This is why I tell you: do not be worried about the food and drink you need in order to stay alive, or about clothes for your body. After all, isn't life worth more than food? And isn't the body worth more than clothes? 26 Look at the birds: they do not plant seeds, gather a harvest and put it in barns; yet your Father in heaven takes care of them! Aren't you worth much more than birds? 27 Can any of you live a bit longer^d by worrying about it?
28 "And why worry about clothes? Look how the wild flowers grow: they do not work or make clothes for themselves. 29 But I tell you that not even King Solomon with all his wealth had clothes as beautiful as one of these flowers. 30 It is God who clothes the wild grass—grass that is here today and gone tomorrow, burned up in the oven. Won't he be all the more sure to clothe you? What little faith you have!
31 "So do not start worrying: 'Where will my food come from? or my drink? or my clothes?' 32 (These are the things the pagans are always concerned about.) Your Father in heaven knows that you need all these things. 33 Instead, be

34 "Therefore do not be anxious about tomorrow, for tomorrow will be anxious for itself. Let the day's own trouble be sufficient for the day.

x *Mammon* is a Semitic word for money or riches

p Or *to his stature*

concerned above everything else with the Kingdom of God and with what he requires of you, and he will provide you with all these other things. 34 So do not worry about tomorrow; it will have enough worries of its own. There is no need to add to the troubles each day brings.

d live a bit longer; *or* grow a bit taller.

SECTION HEADING: "**God and Possessions.**" This can be expressed in several ways, including "Jesus teaches about God and the things we can own," "Jesus teaches about God and money," and "People cannot serve God and money too."

6.24   RSV   TEV

"No one can serve two masters; for either he will hate the one and love the other, or he will be devoted to the one and despise the other. You cannot serve God and mammon.*x*

"No one can be a slave of two masters; he will hate one and love the other; he will be loyal to one and despise the other. You cannot serve both God and money.

x *Mammon* is a Semitic word for money or riches

In the UBS Greek text verse 24 stands alone under the heading "God and Mammon." The Lukan parallel is found in Luke 16.13, where it forms the conclusion to the parable of the dishonest steward. Other than the difference in contextual setting, Luke has "No servant" where Matthew has "No one." The verse consists of three parts, and the first part has proverbial character.

No one can serve two masters is the proverbial part of the verse. Its background is the relationship between slave and master in the Roman world, according to which a slave's master had absolute rights of life and death over his slave. Given this situation it was impossible for a slave to have been at the same time the property of two owners. He would have belonged absolutely to one owner; he could not have belonged to two owners.

Some translations have wanted to say "No one can work for two employers," but that clearly is not true. Nowadays many people do work for more than one employer. TEV has thus made it clear that what is being discussed here is the relationship between slave and master, and other translations often find this a useful model. In other situations where this causes problems, perhaps because the concept of slave is not known, then the idea of being totally devoted to a master must be emphasized. Examples are "No one can devote all his services to two different people at the same time" or "No one can serve with his whole being two different employers at once."

The second part of the verse is linked to the first by **for**. The full relationship that is being expressed is "For if he does, the result will be." The context may make this clear without any word or phrase of transition. Other languages may require a phrase such as "Because" or "Because the result would be."

For either he will hate . . . and despise the other explains what would result if a slave ever got into the position of trying to serve two masters. The four verbs (**hate . . . love** and **be devoted to . . . despise**) are in a chiastic arrangement, in which the first and fourth members and second and third members respectively are parallel with one another (see comments on chiasm under 5.45). In many languages it will be more natural to invert the order of the second and third verbs so that a strict parallelism results. In 7.6 TEV has done precisely this sort of thing, in order to make all four members of the verse clear in their relationship one to the other.

The words **hate** and **love** do not relate primarily to feelings and emotions, but to a decision in behalf of one master as over against the other. In fact, what is at issue here are degrees of loyalty. Thus translators can say "He will not care for one of them but only for the other," "He will neglect one of them in favor of the other," "He will love one more than the other," or "He will be loyal to one and not to the other."

Notice that these last two examples actually reverse the order of **hate** and **love** in the text, which makes them parallel to **be devoted to** and **despise**. Translators should do whatever restructuring is necessary to make the whole verse natural in their language.

The Greek verb translated **be devoted to** occurs only three other times in the New Testament. It is found in the Lukan parallel (Luke 16.13), where the meaning is the same. In 1 Thessalonians 5.14 it is rendered "help (the weak)" by TEV, and in Titus 1.9 TEV translates "hold firmly to (the message)." Here NEB renders "be devoted to" (so Brc and NIV), while Mft and AT have "stand by."

Other than in the Lukan parallel at 16.13, the verb translated **despise** is found in seven other New Testament passages: Matthew 18.10; Romans 2.4; 1 Corinthians 11.22; 1 Timothy 4.12; 6.2; Hebrews 12.2; 2 Peter 2.10. One standard Greek lexicon gives the primary meanings as "look down on, despise, scorn, treat with contempt."

Be devoted to and **despise** have a similar meaning to **hate** and **love**. Translators can say "be devoted to one and look down on the other (or, and have no interest in the other)."

You cannot serve both God and mammon (TEV "**money**") is the third part of the verse, and it forms the conclusion to the first part. **Mammon**, a term that has no meaning in English, is the transliteration of the word used in the Greek text. The footnote in RSV explains its origin: "*Mammon* is a Semitic word for money or riches." Many modern translations render "**money**," as TEV has done (NEB uses a capital "M"). The word **mammon** is well attested in Jewish literature, with the meaning "money, profit, wealth." As used by the Jews it had no negative connotations, which makes the contrast in the present passage even more striking. Jesus' words are concerned with property in general, not with possessions obtained by evil means. TOB also translates with a capital, followed by a footnote indicating that "Money" is here personified as a power which enslaves the world. GECL translates the entire verse in the following way: "No one can serve two masters at the same time. He will neglect the one and prefer the other. He will be loyal to one and cheat the other. You cannot serve them both: God and money."

For some, the main problem is how to speak of serving money, since men can only serve a person or God. Possible solutions are to say "You cannot love and be devoted to both God and money" or "You cannot give your service to God and to gaining money at the same time."

RSV	TEV
"Therefore I tell you, do not be anxious about your life, what you shall eat or what you shall drink, nor about your body, what you shall put on. Is not life more than food and the body more than clothing?	"This is why I tell you: do not be worried about the food and drink you need in order to stay alive, or about clothes for your body. After all, isn't life worth more than food? And isn't the body worth more than clothes?

Matthew 6.25-34 forms a unit in itself and calls for absolute commitment to God and his Kingdom (verse 33) rather than to earthly possessions. It continues the main theme of the preceding paragraph, that is, the necessity for complete devotion to the service of God. There is a parallel in Luke, but it appears in a different context (12.22-34).

Therefore (TEV "**This is why**") forms only a loose connection in the context. The presence of the complete formula (**Therefore I tell you**) in both Matthew and Luke (12.22) suggests that the words were taken over from the special source shared by Matthew and Luke, where **Therefore** may have had a closer connection with the context. In this verse translators most often indicate a rather loose connection, with transitions such as "And so I tell you," "I tell you, then," or "So I tell you."

Anxious about is translated by the equivalent of "worry about" in TEV, NAB, NJB, AT, Brc, Phps. Either translation is an accurate rendering of the Greek. One commentator expresses the meaning as "You must not be distracted by cares." The verb occurs four more times in this passage (verses 27,28,31,34) and in 10.19. There are several ways languages express the meaning of **anxious about**. Some say "Don't be overly concerned," "Don't let the worries distract you," or "Don't allow the cares to bother you too much."

The Greek word rendered **life** literally means "soul." However, it is not here used in contrast to **body**, but appears as a word that is nearly synonymous, since both terms really refer to one's own self. The use of the word in this verse, as elsewhere in the Bible, indicates that the "soul" is not to be understood as an eternal part in man, but as his entire being. In the Jewish sense, "soul" is the basic element in a person's vitality, requiring food for sustenance, and is thereby essentially synonymous with **life**. TEV interprets with this same meaning but with considerable restructuring: "**do not be worried about the food and drink you need in order to stay alive.**" A number of other modern translations are also dynamic. For example, "Stop worrying about what you are going to eat and drink to keep you alive" (Brc), "don't worry about living—wondering what you are going to eat or drink" (Phps), "do not worry about your life, what you will eat or drink" (NIV). GECL ties this clause with the next: "Do not worry about food and drink and your clothing. Life is more than food and drink, and the body is more than clothing." The use of "stop worrying about" (Brc) is based on the observation that the Greek verb tense is a present imperative, implying a command to stop doing some action already in progress. Brc also uses this same form in the second half of the command: "Stop worrying about the clothes you are going to wear to keep your body warm."

Some translations have said "Don't be overly concerned about the things that relate to your life, such as what you're going to eat or drink" or "You should not always be preoccupied by (or, worrying yourself about) things to keep alive with, such as food or drink."

Nor about your body, what you shall put on is rather awkward for English speakers. A number of modern translations have restructured similarly to TEV: ". . . and clothes to cover your body" (NEB), ". . . or use for clothing" (NAB), and JB ". . . nor about your body and how you are to clothe it." This phrase can also be "nor about what clothes you'll cover your body with" or "nor about the clothing you need to protect your body."

TEV prefaces **Is not life more than food** with "**After all.**" This phrase does not represent any specific words in the Greek text; it is introduced in English because the need is felt for a transitional.

Is not introduces a rhetorical question in Greek which expects the answer "Yes." NJB changes the question form of the Greek text to a statement: "Surely life is more than food, and the body more than clothing!" NEB and GECL, among others, restructure similarly. In some languages, a question will be formed at the end of a sentence, as in "Life means more than food and the body means more than clothing, isn't that so?"

The concepts of **life** being **more than food** and the **body more than clothing** often need to be restructured if readers are to understand what is meant. Some ways will be to say "What is important in life is much more than food," "There is much more to life than just food," or "There is much more of importance to life than food." Similarly the second part may be "There are things more important to our bodies than clothing."

Of course, any one of these statements can be expressed as a question, as in the text: "Isn't there more to life than just food?" "Aren't there things more important to our bodies than clothing?" and so on.

6.26 RSV	TEV
Look at the birds of the air: they neither sow nor reap nor gather into barns, and yet your heavenly Father feeds them. Are you not of more value than they?	Look at the birds: they do not plant seeds, gather a harvest and put it in barns; yet your Father in heaven takes care of them! Aren't you worth much more than birds?

Look at is not really an order to look at the birds, but is Jesus' way of drawing attention to them by way of illustration. Some translators have said "Take for example the birds," or "Consider the birds."

Birds of the air is a typical Jewish expression; it merely means "birds." The parallel in Luke 12.24 has "crows"; according to Jewish teaching, crows were unclean birds. NJB and NAB have "the birds in the sky," GECL "the birds." Since **of the air** is simply a part of the idiomatic expression **the birds of the air**, referring to all birds, it is unnecessary to reproduce the full form in translation. The reference is not to birds that fly in contrast to birds that do not fly; it is an inclusive formula covering all birds.

Of course, in those languages where it is quite natural to say **birds of the air**, there will be no need to drop **of the air**. But translators should be sure that it is in fact natural and not just something they have become accustomed to from the Bible.

Sow may need an object, as in "sow seed," "plant crops," or "sow seeds in fields."

Similarly with **reap**, an object is often required: "harvest crops," "harvest the fields," or "gather the crops in when they are ripe (or, ready)."

And so, too, with **gather**, where it may be necessary to say "gather the crops into the barns" or "gather into barns what they've reaped."

In place of **heavenly Father** Luke (12.24) has "God." See the discussion in 5.16. It may have to be "God, your Father in heaven" in some languages.

Feeds may also have the less restricted meaning of "**takes care of**" (TEV). The context suggests that the wider meaning is intended. In the New Testament this verb occurs elsewhere in Matthew 25.37; Luke 4.16; 12.24; 23.29; Acts 12.20; James 5.5; Revelation 12.6,14. Translators can render **feeds** as "gives them what they need" or "makes sure they have what they need to live."

The rhetorical question, **Are you not of more value than they?** has a form in Greek which requires the answer "Yes." GECL utilizes an exclamatory sentence: "And you are worth much more than all birds!" The intent or thrust of the question can be carried in several ways, including "You are certainly of more value than they," "You are of more value than they, aren't you?" and "Don't you think you are worth more than they are?"

6.27	RSV	TEV

And which of you by being anxious can add one cubit to his span of life?[p]

Can any of you live a bit longer[d] **by worrying about it?**

[d]live a bit longer; *or* grow a bit taller.

[p] Or *to his stature*

Again there is a rhetorical question, one that requires no answer but makes a particularly strong statement. Jesus does not want to know which of his hearers can actually lengthen their lives, but he is saying "None of you can" or "No one can."

The word **anxious** here is the same as in verse 25. In this context it means "worrying about," "being concerned about," or "being distracted by the cares about."

Add one cubit to his span of life (TEV "**live a bit longer**"). As RSV's footnote indicates, **to the span of his life** may also be interpreted to mean "to his stature" (TEV footnote, "grow a bit taller"). One problem of interpretation is that the word which RSV renders **cubit** is normally used of distance rather than of time. However, it may also be used of time, and that meaning is much more satisfactory in the present context. Moreover, the Greek word given the meaning **span of life** is more frequently used as a measurement of time than height. Needless to say, scholarly opinion is divided, but modern translations tend to accept the meaning represented by RSV and TEV. If **span** is used as a measurement of time, it would mean a brief span, whereas if it is used of a person's height, it would be a significant amount (about 18 inches). NAB renders "add a moment to his life-span," and GECL has "lengthen his life only by one day."

As for translating **cubit**, those translators who follow the TEV model will generally have "add a little time to his life," "live a little longer," or "make his life last even a little longer." Some will indicate a specific amount of time, such as "even one day" or "even one hour."

6.28	RSV	TEV

And why are you anxious about clothing? Consider the lilies of the field, how they grow; they neither toil nor spin;	"And why worry about clothes? Look how the wild flowers grow: they do not work or make clothes for themselves.

And why are you anxious about clothing? is a fairly literal rendering of the Greek text. This question may also be phrased as a statement: "There is no need to worry about clothes." Or a question can be retained, as in "Is there any need to worry about clothing?"

For comments on **anxious**, see verse 25.

To worry **about clothing** means "to worry about having enough clothing."

Consider can be "think about" or "look at," or, as TEV has it, "**look how they grow.**"

Lilies of the field (so also NIV) is rendered "**wild flowers**" by TEV, NAB, AT, Phps. NJB has "flowers growing in the fields," and Brc has "wild lilies." There is some discussion regarding the precise reference intended by the Greek word used here and in Luke 12.27. Most commentators apparently prefer to take it as a reference to the anemone, a beautiful flower of bright colors. It is found on the Galilean hills, and it would undoubtedly have been observed by the people who listened to Jesus.

For this reason, then, most translations will not use **lilies** but will follow TEV or NJB, as cited above. They may have "flowers growing in the fields," "flowers growing wild," or "flowers growing in the forest."

Toil nor spin is translated "**make clothes for themselves**" by TEV. The picture is that of spinning fiber to make clothes. Both GECL and FRCL translate in the tradition of TEV. Some translations have had a slight change from this by saying "They don't work to make clothes" or "They don't work to make cloth for clothing themselves."

6.29	RSV	TEV

yet I tell you, even Solomon in all his glory was not arrayed like one of these.	But I tell you that not even King Solomon with all his wealth had clothes as beautiful as one of these flowers.

Solomon, son and successor to King David, was noted for his great wealth. Many readers will not know who **Solomon** was, so translators should say "King Solomon" or "the great King Solomon." More information about him can be put in the glossary.

In all his glory can be "in all his wealth" or "who was so rich."

Like one of these refers back to the noun translated "lilies" in verse 28. TEV has **"as one of these flowers"** because "flowers" was used there by TEV. The choice of a noun here will naturally be determined by the interpretation given in verse 28.

The text says that even Solomon **was not arrayed like one of these**. This means that "Even the clothing of King Solomon was not as splendid (or, as beautiful) as the clothing of one of these flowers" or "Even King Solomon didn't have clothes as beautiful as any of these flowers."

6.30	RSV	TEV

But if God so clothes the grass of the field, which today is alive and tomorrow is thrown into the oven, will he not much more clothe you, O men of little faith?	It is God who clothes the wild grass that is here today and gone tomorrow, burned up in the oven. Won't he be all the more sure to clothe you? What little faith you have!

In Greek this verse consists of one sentence; for the form of the sentence as it appears in Greek, see RSV. The particular form of the **if** clause in Greek indicates that the content of the clause is assumed to be true. That is why TEV translates it as a statement: **"It is God who clothes the wild grass . . . ."** The form of the argument, which moves from the lesser to the greater, is typically Jewish: God cares for the wild grass (the lesser) and, therefore, he will care for you (the greater). For this same form of argument, see 7.11.

In addition to the way TEV has restructured, translators may try "Just as God . . . so he will much more . . ." or "Since God clothes . . . therefore even more . . . ." This can also be made into a statement and a question: "God clothes the grass of the field like that, and the grass is alive today and burned up tomorrow. Don't you think he will be even more sure to clothe you?"

Grass of the field (TEV "**wild grass**"). The reference may well include, or be equivalent to, wild flowers.

Some languages will just have "grass," since they make no distinction between wild grass and any other. Or they may say "the grass growing everywhere."

The grass **today is alive**, that is, it is "living today" or "is here one day (and burned the next)."

Thrown into is translated "**burned up**" by TEV, which focuses upon the end result of the action and indicates what happens to the grass after it is thrown **into the oven**. In place of **into the oven**, NEB has "on the stove," and NAB renders "on the fire." The situation is that of an earthen oven into which dead grass and weeds were thrown and used for fuel. GECL equates "grass" of this verse with "wild flowers" of the previous verse and does not mention "oven": "If God so clothes the wild flowers which blossom today and tomorrow are burned up . . . ."

189

In many languages it is not normal to burn grass in an oven, and translators will do better to say simply "burned up" or "burned up in someone's fire."

Will he not much more clothe you represents one part of the Greek sentence, which is literally "(Will he) not much more (clothe) you." The restructuring of RSV necessitates the repetition of the verb **clothe**. In fact, even those translations which are generally rather formal have for the most part felt the need to repeat the verb. The question may be rendered as a strong affirmative statement; for example, "You can be sure then that he will clothe you."

God will **much more clothe you**. This can mean that he will give you better or more clothing, but most translators take it to mean he will more surely clothe you. Examples of possible translations include "Don't you think he is even more likely to clothe you?" "He is even more certain to provide clothes for you."

O men of little faith translates one word in the Greek text, a noun of address. TEV has "**What little faith you have**." GECL renders "Have more faith!" Elsewhere in the New Testament this word is used in Matthew 8.26; 14.31; 16.8; and Luke 12.28.

Many translators will make this a short sentence such as "You have so little faith!" or "Your faith in God is so small!" Jesus is rebuking the people, and this tone should be communicated, however the sentence is translated.

6.31	RSV	TEV

Therefore do not be anxious, saying, 'What shall we eat?' or 'What shall we drink?' or 'What shall we wear?'	"So do not start worrying: 'Where will my food come from? or my drink? or my clothes?'

Do not be anxious translates an aorist subjunctive in Greek which normally carries an ingressive force, focusing upon the beginning of the action. That is why TEV includes the helping verb "**start**" ("**Do not start worrying**"). Both NAB ("Stop worrying, then, over questions like . . .") and Brc ("So then, make up your mind to stop worrying, and to stop saying . . .") take the aorist subjunctive to have force other than its usual one of initiating an action. This probably is best in this context.

The word **anxious** itself will be translated as it has been elsewhere (see verse 25). Here it can be "Don't start being overly concerned" or "Don't now let yourself be distracted by the concerns of."

Following the command **do not be anxious** is a participle which RSV translates **saying**. NJB renders the entire construction "So do not worry; do not say," and NEB "No, do not ask anxiously."

For a literal rendering of the three questions (**What shall . . . eat . . . drink . . . wear?**) see RSV. Although the Greek has a first person plural in each instance, TEV follows with a first person singular, since this is a more natural form in English.

Another way to handle this verse is to say "Don't keep on worrying about where your food, drink, or clothes will come from" or "Don't let yourself be distracted with worries about how you will get something to eat and drink and clothing to wear."

6.32   RSV   TEV

For the Gentiles seek all these things; and your heavenly Father knows that you need them all. | (These are the things the pagans are always concerned about.) Your Father in heaven knows that you need all these things.

Gentiles (TEV, JB "**pagans**") is made from the same stem as the noun used in 5.47 (see comments there), and the two words mean the same. The more general use of the term simply means "Gentiles" as opposed to Jews. However, in the present context it is apparently used in a derogatory sense of people who have not learned to trust in the God of the Jews. Brc translates "the people who don't know God" (so also GECL); NAB has "The unbelievers"; NEB renders "the heathen."

Seek (TEV "**are . . . concerned about**") is given a dynamic translation by many: "running after" (NAB), "set their hearts on" (NJB), and "keep thinking about" (Brc). Elsewhere in the Gospel of Matthew this same Greek verb is found only in 12.39 and 16.4, where it is translated "ask for (of a miracle)" by TEV.

Seek can also be "worry about," "keep thinking about," or "preoccupied with." Many languages will use an idiomatic expression such as "Those things fill their hearts (or, minds)."

All these things is translated "**These are the things**" by TEV. But TEV includes the force of **all** by the rendering "**always**" in conjunction with the verb (so also NAB).

Some translators have rendered **all these things** as "These are the very things that Gentiles are always worrying about" or "It is all these kinds of things that concern the Gentiles."

Heavenly Father, as elsewhere in this passage, refers to God. He **knows that you need them all**, that is, "He knows that you should have these things" or "He is aware that it is necessary for you to have these things."

6.33   RSV   TEV

But seek first his kingdom and his righteousness, and all these things shall be yours as well. | Instead, be concerned above everything else with the Kingdom of God and with what he requires of you, and he will provide you with all these other things.

Seek translates the same Greek verb used in the previous verse, but without a prefix. Although it could be argued that the form with the prefix is stronger, it is better to conclude that the two verbs are here used synonymously. In fact, most translations make no difference in the way in which they render the two verbs.

The text says you are to seek God's kingdom **first**, that is, "above all else." In other words, God's kingdom should be "your primary concern" or "the thing you should be concerned with before anything else."

His kingdom is translated "**Kingdom of God**" by TEV. The words "of God" are not found in some manuscripts, and in other manuscripts the words **kingdom**

and **righteousness** are found in reverse order from what they appear in RSV and TEV. TC-GNT indicates that the UBS Greek text committee supports the order of RSV and TEV, but they are uncertain regarding "of God." However, the overall context of Matthew makes it clear that the **kingdom** referred to is God's kingdom, and so the implicit information may be included on translational grounds. RSV in fact does so by translating **his** (that is, God's) **kingdom**.

Both **kingdom** (see 3.2) and **righteousness** (see 3.15; 5.6,10) were previously discussed. In summary it may be recalled that "the kingdom of God" refers primarily to God's kingly rule, while "righteousness" is the doing of what God requires and of what pleases him. Most commentaries agree with the exegesis represented here, but most translations maintain a rather formal rendering. There are a few exceptions; for example, "Be concerned above all else that you submit yourself to his rule and do what he requires" (GECL), and "Above all else, strive to be a citizen of God's rule and do what he requires of you" (INCL). It is possible also to understand **his kingdom** and **his righteousness** to be essentially synonymous, as in NAB: "Seek first his kingship over you, his way of holiness."

Some, as we said, will follow the text quite closely with a phrase like "May your primary concern be that God's rule be established and that people do his will." This is rather impersonal. Others will make it more personal, as in "Be concerned above all else that God establish his rule over you and that you do what he requires" or "Your primary concern should be that you submit yourself to God's ruling and do all that he requires."

The passive structure of the Greek text (**and all these things shall be yours as well**) is transformed into an active construction by TEV, with God expressly indicated as the subject: **"He will provide you with all these other things."** It is important that God be explicitly indicated as the subject, otherwise the meaning may be entirely missed. For example, Phps misses the meaning: "and all these things will come to you as a matter of course."

The clause is introduced by **and**. Some translators mark the relationship between the two halves of the verse with an expression such as "If you do that, then God . . . ."

6.34   RSV   TEV

"Therefore do not be anxious about tomorrow, for tomorrow will be anxious for itself. Let the day's own trouble be sufficient for the day.

So do not worry about tomorrow; it will have enough worries of its own. There is no need to add to the troubles each day brings.

Do not be anxious. See verse 31 for the same construction.

For tomorrow will be anxious for itself is expressed more naturally in TEV: **"It will have enough worries of its own."** NAB renders "Let tomorrow take care of itself"; NJB and NEB are similar.

In some languages it is strange to speak of being concerned about **tomorrow**. The idea of the verse is that you should not be concerned about "what may happen tomorrow" or "what you will need tomorrow." For tomorrow to **be anxious for**

itself means "for there will be enough things to worry about tomorrow" or "tomorrow you should worry about those things."

Let the day's own trouble be sufficient for the day is translated "**There is no need to add to the trouble each day brings**" by TEV, and Phps has "One day's trouble is enough for one day." NEB translates "Each day has troubles enough of its own." The Greek word translated **trouble** is not a reference to objective moral evil, but rather describes those things which bring trouble to people; in fact it is frequently used in the Septuagint for a Hebrew word that means "trouble" in general.

The idea here can be expressed in several ways: "It's enough to be concerned each day with that day's problems," "Each day has enough problems without adding to them troubles from other days," or "Don't add to the troubles that are before you on any particular day." The examples cited in the previous paragraph may also be helpful.

Chapter 7

RSV

TEV

Judging Others

1 "Judge not, that you be not judged. 2 For with the judgment you pronounce you will be judged, and the measure you give will be the measure you get. 3 Why do you see the speck that is in your brother's eye, but do not notice the log that is in your own eye? 4 Or how can you say to your brother, 'Let me take the speck out of your eye,' when there is the log in your own eye? 5 You hypocrite, first take the log out of your own eye, and then you will see clearly to take the speck out of your brother's eye.

6 "Do not give dogs what is holy; and do not throw your pearls before swine, lest they trample them under foot and turn to attack you.

1 "Do not judge others, so that God will not judge you, 2 for God will judge you in the same way you judge others, and he will apply to you the same rules you apply to others. 3 Why, then, do you look at the speck in your brother's eye and pay no attention to the log in your own eye? 4 How dare you say to your brother, 'Please, let me take that speck out of your eye,' when you have a log in your own eye? 5 You hypocrite! First take the log out of your own eye, and then you will be able to see clearly to take the speck out of your brother's eye.

6 "Do not give what is holy to dogs—they will only turn and attack you. Do not throw your pearls in front of pigs—they will only trample them underfoot.

SECTION HEADING: "**Judging Others**." This section heading may be acceptable as "Judging other people." But many languages will need to identify the participants with sentences such as "We should not judge (or, condemn) people." This can also be "Jesus teaches about people judging each other" or "Jesus teaches we should not judge (or, condemn) other people."

For "**Judging**" see the discussion below.

This chapter is difficult to outline. One problem is that there is apparently no thought relation between 7.1-6 and what comes immediately before it. There is a similarity in theme between this passage and both the fifth petition of the Lord's prayer (6.12) and the teaching of 6.14-15. And a number of commentators note that this section comes logically after 5.48, as is supported by the observation that in Luke it is placed precisely in that context. Though the relation of these verses to the context is difficult, the theme is clear enough: if we are not willing to forgive others, God will not forgive us. Regarding the structure of these verses, commentators note that the form is that used by Jewish teachers of Jesus' day.

Verse 6, which TEV includes under this section heading, finds no parallel in any of the other Gospels. Both its interpretation and the reason for its inclusion here are problematic.

7.1   RSV   TEV

> "Judge not, that you be not   "Do not judge others, so that
> judged.   God will not judge you,

In Greek this verse reads **Judge not, that you be not judged**. In English the verb **judge** generally requires an object, and for that reason TEV has supplied the object "**others**." GECL, DUCL, and FRCL have done the same thing, as has Brc.

Most translators avoid rendering **Judge** as "criticize." Some use a word that means to examine the facts about someone and make a decision, very much as a judge might make a decision. More often, however, translators have felt the context indicates here that the idea is more "declare guilty" or "condemn." Thus, possible translations are "Don't pass judgment on people," "Don't decide other people are guilty," or "Don't condemn people."

The Greek passive **that you be not judged** is assumed by the majority of scholars to be a reference to God as judge. Most translations maintain the passive form and so are ambiguous. JB retains the passive, but with a footnote indicating the meaning: "Do not judge others if you do not wish to be judged by God." Several translations switch to the active, with God as the explicit subject (TEV, GECL, FRCL, DUCL). Phps obviously takes it as human judgment: "Don't criticize people, and you will not be criticized." In the solemn context of the Sermon on the Mount, it seems extremely doubtful that Jesus would be warning against the danger of reciprocal criticism from one's fellowman. The situation demands that God be the subject of the passive verb.

Failure to make "God" explicit in the second part almost invariably leads people to believe the verse is saying "Don't judge other people so they won't judge you." For this reason it is advisable to say "so God won't judge you," as in TEV and other dynamic translations, or "so God won't condemn you." Jewish writers used the passive to avoid pronouncing God's name, but the hearers understood that God was the agent. Few cultures today share this taboo, and there is no reason to maintain it, especially if the passive would not be correctly understood.

7.2   RSV   TEV

> For with the judgment you pro-   for God will judge you in the same
> nounce you will be judged, and the   way you judge others, and he will
> measure you give will be the mea-   apply to you the same rules you
> sure you get.   apply to others.

Parallels to this verse are found in both Mark and Luke; in Mark 4.24 it is applied to the new understanding that is constantly given to persons who obey the words of Jesus, while in Luke 6.38 it is applied to the reward for generosity. Matthew uses it of judgment, indicating that God will judge us with the same severity with which we judge others. The formula means that the same standard of measurement has been used for the goods received as for those which were given in exchange. A number of CLTs identify God as the one who judges and measures out in return (TEV, DUCL, FRCL).

Translators should not forget to link verses 1 and 2 with "for" or "because," as the text does.

We indicated above that to be judged **with the judgment you pronounce** refers to the severity with which we judge others. Again, the passive **you will be judged** involves God as the agent. This can be "God will judge you in the same manner as you judge other people" or "God will judge you as severely as you judge others."

Note that the examples we have given have reversed the order of the text. This seems easiest in many languages, but the order of the text can be retained with a sentence such as "For in the way you condemn other people, that's how severe God will be when he judges you."

The second part of the verse involves the **measure you give** and **will get**. This can be rendered as "God will condemn you in the same amount as you condemn others" or "God will use the same rules (or, standards) to judge you as you use for judging others."

7.3	RSV	TEV

Why do you see the speck that is in your brother's eye, but do not notice the log that is in your own eye?	**Why, then, do you look at the speck in your brother's eye and pay no attention to the log in your own eye?**

Verses 3-5 illustrate the principle enunciated in verse 1 and form the theological justification for the declaration of verse 2. **See** (so also Brc) is translated "**look at**" by TEV, NAB, NEB, NIV. The context indicates that the meaning is not merely that of casual observation, as **see** might suggest, but of paying attention to something. Some translators have had "Why do you remark about," "Why are you concerned about," or "Why do you bring attention to." "**Look at**" of TEV also works well in many languages.

Why do you see is often translated by a similar question, but the phrase can also be a statement such as "You should not pay attention to . . . ." Another way to render it is to say "you notice some speck of wood in your brother's eye, and fail to see the whole plank in your own. How can that be?"

The Greek word translated **speck** may refer to a small piece of straw, chaff, or wood; it signifies something quite insignificant. On the other hand, the word rendered **log** describes a piece of lumber used in building. This saying about the **speck** and the **log** is purposely ridiculous and is to be compared with the saying in 19.24. One scholar describes the figure as intentionally grotesque, since no one can in reality have a **log** in his eye. It is intended to contrast the insignificant wrongs that others do to us with the enormous sins that we commit against God, and so its real purpose is to exclude all condemnation of others. Indeed, this exaggerated language should be retained in the translation to make sure the readers get the point. **Speck** can be "small piece of dust (or, wood)" or "small splinter of wood." **Log** can be "a tree trunk," "a plank of wood," or "a big stick."

For comments on **your brother**, see 5.22.

7.4   RSV   TEV

RSV	TEV
Or how can you say to your brother, 'Let me take the speck out of your eye,' when there is the log in your own eye?	**How dare you say to your brother, 'Please, let me take that speck out of your eye,' when you have a log in your own eye?**

This verse essentially repeats the content of verse 3. The question may need to be restructured, however. Translators may say "Do you think it is right to say," "How can you possibly say," or "By what right can you say." The sentence may need indirect speech instead of direct, as in "How can you offer to take a speck from your brother's eye . . ." or "You shouldn't ask your brother if you can remove a speck . . . ."

It may be necessary to put the offer to help the brother at the end of the verse, as in "There you are with a whole plank in your eye, and you dare to say to your brother, 'Let me take the speck out of your eye,' " or "You have a log in your eye. How can you possibly offer to take the speck out of your brother's?"

7.5   RSV   TEV

RSV	TEV
You hypocrite, first take the log out of your own eye, and then you will see clearly to take the speck out of your brother's eye.	**You hypocrite! First take the log out of your own eye, and then you will be able to see clearly to take the speck out of your brother's eye.**

Hypocrite was first used in 6.2 (see comments there).

This verse also is essentially a repeat of verse 3. Again, however, it may need to be restructured, depending on what would be most natural in the language. For example, "You hypocrite, only if you take the log out of your own eye will you be able to see clearly enough to be able to take out the speck from your brother's eye" and "You hypocrite, you must first take out the log from your eye before you see clearly and be able to take the speck in your brother's eye."

7.6   RSV   TEV

RSV	TEV
"Do not give dogs what is holy; and do not throw your pearls before swine, lest they trample them under foot and turn to attack you.	**"Do not give what is holy to dogs—they will only turn and attack you. Do not throw your pearls in front of pigs—they will only trample them underfoot.**

This verse appears to have the order of a chiasm, as RSV shows by means of a literal translation (see the discussion of chiastic arrangements under 5.45). RSV makes it appear that the **dogs** do nothing, while the **swine** both **trample** and **attack**. This is, of course, possible, but it is more probable that the chiastic "A-B-B'-A' " arrangement intends to say that the **dogs** (A) will **turn to attack you** (A'), while the

swine (B) will **trample them under foot** (B'). A number of CLTs take this to be the meaning (TEV, GECL 1st edition, FRCL, DUCL), and they provide good examples of how the verse can be rendered meaningfully.

The term **dogs** is almost always translated literally. It is regularly used disparagingly in the Old Testament for street dogs, and in this context the meaning "unclean" seems to be implied, in contrast with **holy**. Thus **dogs** may well be rendered as "dogs, which are impure animals." Some cultures use the term to refer to people of certain immoral behavior, which would not apply here, and so translators can say in those languages "unclean animals" or "compound (or, household) dogs."

Translators often have to ask what things are being referred to as **holy**. Some have said "things that are for God" or "things that have to do with God." Scholars are of divided opinion concerning whom or what is referred to by **what is holy**, **dogs**, **pearls**, and **swine**. However, **what is holy** should not be identified any more specifically than that, since the intention seems to be to refer to things in general that may be classified as holy.

The phrase **do not throw your pearls before swine** needs to be carefully analyzed before it is translated. There are, first of all, several metaphors here. **Pearls** may not be known, in which case they can be translated as "valuable stones" or "beautiful beads," possibly with the addition "called pearls." No one agrees exactly what **pearls** stand for in this verse, but since they are something valuable or precious, some have thought it might be "your experiences with God" or "your teachings from God," or something similar. We do not recommend necessarily that this be included in the translation. We list it here merely to help translators have some idea of how to analyze the sentence before translating it. What may be helpful is to say "things that are precious to you like pearls."

Throw . . . before then may best be translated as "share with" or "let others have."

Swine (or, "**pigs**") is often understood to stand for people who have no appreciation of truly valuable things, much as pigs are thought to eat both garbage and good food with equal pleasure. Translators can say simply "pigs," "pigs who can't tell what is valuable and isn't," or "pigs that can't appreciate valuable things."

The whole phrase can be rendered "Don't share what is valuable to you, like pearls, with swine who can't tell the value" or ". . . with people who, like swine, can't tell what is of value." But to repeat our advice above, translators should not be more specific than this about what **pearls** and **swine** actually refer to.

The warning **lest they trample them under foot** may be expressed as "so they won't just trample them under foot" or "if you do, they will only trample them under their feet."

7.7-12

RSV

TEV

Ask, Seek, Knock

7 "Ask, and it will be given you; seek, and you will find; knock, and it will be opened to you. 8 For every one who asks receives, and he who

7 "Ask, and you will receive; seek, and you will find; knock, and the door will be opened to you. 8 For everyone who asks will receive, and

seeks finds, and to him who knocks it will be opened. 9 Or what man of you, if his son asks him for bread, will give him a stone? 10 Or if he asks for a fish, will give him a serpent? 11 If you then, who are evil, know how to give good gifts to your children, how much more will your Father who is in heaven give good things to those who ask him! 12 So whatever you wish that men would do to you, do so to them; for this is the law and the prophets.

anyone who seeks will find, and the door will be opened to him who knocks. 9 Would any of you who are fathers give your son a stone when he asks for bread? 10 Or would you give him a snake when he asks for a fish? 11 As bad as you are, you know how to give good things to your children. How much more, then, will your Father in heaven give good things to those who ask him!

12 "Do for others what you want them to do for you: this is the meaning of the Law of Moses and of the teachings of the prophets.

SECTION HEADING: "**Ask, Seek, Knock**." Other section headings here can be "Jesus teaches people to ask for things from God" or "Jesus teaches that we should ask God for what we need."

This entire passage also has its parallel in Luke. Verse 12 is found in Luke 6.31, where it appears as the conclusion to the Lukan parallel to Matthew 5.38-42. The first part of this section (verses 7-11) follows the parable about the friend who comes asking for bread in the middle of the night (Luke 11.9-13), which in turn comes immediately after Luke's presentation of the Lord's Prayer. It therefore becomes obvious that Matthew has placed this entire section (7.7-12) in the present context in order to serve as a conclusion to 5.17, indicating the true significance of the Law and the prophets.

7.7-8	RSV	TEV

7 "Ask, and it will be given you; seek, and you will find; knock, and it will be opened to you. 8 For every one who asks receives, and he who seeks finds, and to him who knocks it will be opened.

7 "Ask, and you will receive; seek, and you will find; knock, and the door will be opened to you. 8 For everyone who asks will receive, and anyone who seeks will find, and the door will be opened to him who knocks.

The three imperatives (**Ask** . . . **seek** . . . **knock**) are probably intended to be emphatic. In Greek they are present imperatives and may carry the force of "keep on asking . . . seeking . . . knocking" (so Brc). Commentators point out that the imagery of knocking on a door has associations in Judaism with the study of the Law and its interpretation and with prayers for God's mercy.

Many languages cannot say simply **ask** but must specify who is being asked, and possibly what is being asked for. They would then say "Ask God" or "Ask God for what you need." In this context **Ask** means to ask for, not to ask a question.

To **seek** means to look for, to try to find a particular thing. It is not God we are to seek in this verse, but rather we are to look to him for what we want. Thus it could be rendered "seek what you are looking for" or "seek from God what you are looking for."

Knock refers to a way of asking that a door be opened. One cannot say "knock on God," but it may be possible to say "knock on the door where God is" or "knock on the door that God opens."

In many African cultures people do not normally knock on doors to request the people inside to open them. Quite often, only thieves would knock on doors (waiting to hear any noise inside before entering to steal), so the translators need to say either "ask for the door to be opened" or "clap (or cough, or call) at the door." If the image of knocking at a door makes no sense, translators can add "to ask God's help."

The two passive structures (**will be given** . . . **you will find**) presuppose God as the subject: "God will give you . . . God will let you find." The last clause may be rendered accordingly: "Knock, and God will open the door for you."

Find in this context means to find on purpose, not by accident. The phrase may be translated as "you will have (or, obtain) it" or "God will let you obtain it."

As with "ask" and "seek," it may be necessary to provide objects for **will be given** and **you will find**. Thus "ask God for what you need and he will give it to you" or "seek what you are looking for and God will let you find it" are possible ways to restructure. Similarly, translators can say "knock on God's door and he will open it for you" or "knock on the door where God is, and he will open it and help you." The translation can also be "and he will open it so you can enter."

It should be noted that this teaching is not intended to make prayer into a magical ritual, nor is it to suggest that one can coerce God into acting. The real emphasis is upon the certainty that God will answer the prayer, and that it is a prayer that **every one** can pray.

Scholars observe that verse 8 is in the form of a proverbial saying, as is 6.34.

Translators should use the same expressions in verse 8 that they did in verse 7. Translators should not modify what Jesus says. The language is quite absolute. It does not say "will receive something" or "will receive things that God feels we need," but it says that God will give to those who ask (what they are asking for).

7.9-10   RSV   TEV

RSV	TEV
9 Or what man of you, if his son asks him for bread, will give him a stone? 10 Or if he asks for a fish, will give him a serpent?	9 Would any of you who are fathers give your son a stone when he asks for bread? 10 Or would you give him a snake when he asks for a fish?

The comparisons (**bread** with **stone** and **fish** with **serpent**) were used for perhaps two reasons: (1) bread and fish were the foods that would be most common near the Sea of Galilee, and (2) bread is shaped somewhat like a stone, and a fish has scales and other features similar to those of a snake. One commentator in fact notes that a certain species of fish (barbut) even has the appearance of a snake. Though most translations retain the question form of the Greek text, it is obvious that in many languages a statement would be more effective: "No father would give his son a stone when he asks for bread . . . ." This can also be rendered "Surely none of you who is a father would give" or "No father would give his son a stone . . . would he?"

The sentence may need to be reversed, as in "When a son asks his father for bread, do you think the father would give him a stone?"

All these ways of rendering verse 9 can be used in verse 10, too. In fact, it is probably a good idea to use the same structure.

Bread is widely known, but in areas where it is not, "food" or "something to eat" can be used, or possibly some local food that has a similar function to bread.

A **serpent** is a snake. The type of snake does not need to be specified. For the passage to be meaningful, it must be understood by the readers that the Jews did not eat snakes. It would be just as unlikely for a Jew to eat a snake as a stone. In areas where people do eat some kinds of snakes, translators can add a footnote saying that Jews were forbidden to eat snakes, or they can use the name of a type of snake that is not eaten. They can even add the phrase "which God forbids us to eat" in the translation itself, if they feel that otherwise the verse will make no sense.

7.11 RSV	TEV
If you then, who are evil, know how to give good gifts to your children, how much more will your Father who is in heaven give good things to those who ask him!	As bad as you are, you know how to give good things to your children. How much more, then, will your Father in heaven give good things to those who ask him!

Who are evil (TEV "**as bad as you are**") is not intended to be a philosophical statement regarding human nature; the comparison is between God and the human race, all of whom are sinful. The phrase **who are evil** may be expressed "Even though you are sinful (or, bad), you know how to . . . ."

In some languages it is redundant to speak of "giving gifts," but one can give "**good things.**" TEV has used this phrase.

How much more introduces an argument "from the lesser to the greater" (see 6.30 for this same form of argument): human fathers are evil, but they still give good things to their children; our Father in heaven is good, and so he is much more ready to give good things to those who ask him.

For **your Father in heaven**, see comments on 5.16.

In place of **good things** Luke has "the Holy Spirit" (Luke 11.13). One commentator suggests that **good things** are probably intended to include everything mentioned in the Lord's Prayer, though Matthew may be thinking of God's will in general.

The phrase **who ask him** is a shortened form of "who ask him for something (or, for what they need)." In some languages it may be necessary to use this longer form, or possibly "who ask him to give them good things."

Quite often, to render this verse easier for their readers to understand, translators will find it necessary to restructure. For example, they may break it up into two sentences, as in these examples: "You are sinful and yet you know how to give good things to your children. Think then how much better God your Father in heaven is able to give good things to those who ask him," or "Even though you are evil, you know how to give good things to your children. Surely God your heavenly Father will give things that are much better than that to those who ask him."

7.12   RSV   TEV

So whatever you wish that men would do to you, do so to them; for this is the law and the prophets.	"Do for others what you want them to do for you: this is the meaning of the Law of Moses and of the teachings of the prophets.

It is general knowledge that even before Jesus, the Jewish Rabbi Hillel gave the "Golden Rule" in its negative form: "Do not do to others what you would not want them to do to you; that is the entire Law, and all else is interpretation."

The word **So** would make it appear that this verse is summing up the previous passage. However, this is not the case. The preceding verses have been talking about a person's relation to God, but this verse talks about people's relation to each other. Therefore many translations, including TEV, do not put any transition here.

Men is translated "**others**" by TEV, since the reference is to people in general.

There are several ways to express this "Golden Rule." For example, translators can say "However you want people to treat you, that's how you should treat them" or "The things you want people to do to you, do those things first to other people." The sentence can also be reversed: "Treat other people the way you would like them to treat you."

For this is the law and the prophets. JB renders "that is the meaning of the Law and the Prophets," and NAB "this sums up the law and the prophets." Brc translates "This is a summary of the message of the Law and the Prophets," and GECL 1st edition "this is the content of the Law and the teachings of the Prophets." This can also be expressed as "this is what the Law and the prophets actually teach" or "this is what the Law and the prophets say."

For a discussion of **the law and the prophets**, see 5.17.

7.13-14

                    RSV   TEV

The Narrow Gate

13 "Enter by the narrow gate; for the gate is wide and the way is easy,[q] that leads to destruction, and those who enter by it are many. 14 For the gate is narrow and the way is hard, that leads to life, and those who find it are few.	13 "Go in through the narrow gate, because the gate to hell is wide and the road that leads to it is easy, and there are many who travel it. 14 But the gate to life is narrow and the way that leads to it is hard, and there are few people who find it.

[q] Other ancient authorities read *for the way is wide and easy*

SECTION HEADING: "**The Narrow Gate**." In many languages this short phrase will be acceptable as a heading. But translators in some languages need to indicate more precisely what the gate leads to, as in "The gate to life (or, real life) is narrow" or "The path to life is a narrow one."

The four concluding exhortations (7.1-12) are now followed by four concluding warnings (7.13-27). One commentator on the text believes that Matthew originally intended to bring the Sermon on the Mount to a conclusion with verse 23, but then added verses 24-27, which stood at this place in the sayings source used by him and Luke. He further comments that the composition of 7.13-23 is held together both by the repetition of the verb "to enter" (verses 13,21) and by the theme of the distinction between destruction and life, which is already experienced in man's earthly existence and will have its final fulfillment in the judgment (verses 13,14,19,22,23).

7.13 RSV TEV

"Enter by the narrow gate; for the gate is wide and the way is easy,[q] that leads to destruction, and those who enter by it are many.

"Go in through the narrow gate, because the gate to hell is wide and the road that leads to it is easy, and there are many who travel it.

[q] Other ancient authorities read *for the way is wide and easy*

Commentators note that the figure of two ways was a frequent one, not only in the Old Testament and Jewish world, but also in the Greek and Hellenistic world. It was also used widely in early Christian writings, and the Qumran sect speaks of the way of light and the way of darkness.

A literal translation shows the formal structure of the Greek of verses 13-14:

13 Enter through the narrow gate;
    for wide [is the gate] and easy is the way
        that leads to destruction
    and many are those entering it;
14 how narrow [is the gate] and hard is the way
        that leads to life
    and few are those finding it.

The first line gives the command, and in the remaining lines the section "for wide . . ." is followed by "how narrow . . ." in perfectly parallel form, with individual words contrasting with each other; for example, **wide** and **narrow**, **few** and **many**, **easy** and **hard**. Most translators will find it useful to retain such parallel contrasts, but they should feel free to make adjustments necessary for their own languages.

In the first line, in many languages one cannot simply say **enter** but must specify what one is to enter. In these cases translators can say "Enter life" or "When you look for a path to follow for life, go through the narrow gate." Another way is to say "When you go into life, go in through the narrow gate."

There is no problem in the contrast between the adjectives **narrow** and **wide**.

The Greek text uses the same word for **gate** in this and the following verse. However, GECL 1st edition uses "door" where the modifier "narrow" occurs, and "gate" where the modifier "wide" is used, since these are the appropriate words in German in this context. Scholars are of divided opinion regarding the relation between the **gate** and the **way**. Some believe that the order (**gate . . . way**) is inverted: the narrow way leads to the gate of the city of God, and the wide way leads to the gate of Hell. Others hold the two figures to be an example of hendiadys, that is, that the two figures represent a single idea. They find support for their argument in the observation that the same verb (**enter**) is used both of the gate and the way.

Gate does not usually pose many problems, but it sometimes is translated as "entrance." In the second occurrence, when the text speaks of the gate **that leads** to destruction, it may even be translated as "the way in" or "the place one passes through."

In some manuscripts **gate** is lacking in its second occurrence in this verse. (Note that the places where some manuscripts omit **gate** are marked with square brackets in the literal translation.) In Greek both **gate** and **way** are feminine, and so there is no problem as far as modifiers are concerned if **gate** is deleted from the text. For example, JB has "since the road that leads to perdition is wide and spacious," which follows the manuscript tradition that omits **gate** from the text. A similar textual problem exists in verse 14, and there Mft follows the textual tradition that drops the word **gate** ("But the road that leads to life is both narrow and close"). A number of translations follow the textual evidence that includes **gate** in both occurrences, but provide a footnote indicating the alternative possibility (NEB, RSV). TC-GNT is convinced that the textual evidence in favor of the inclusion of **gate** in both instances is overwhelming. They account for its omission as a deliberate act made by some copyists "who failed to understand that the picture is that of a roadway leading to a gate."

The Greek adjective rendered **easy** really means "broad, spacious, roomy" and is almost synonymous with **wide**. When used as a noun it may refer to a large and spacious room in which one can live comfortably. It will be good if a term can be used that will contrast with **hard** in verse 14. Although the sentence can be "the way is broad," the sense may be seen a little better in a sentence like "the way is easy to travel on."

Destruction (TEV "**hell**") is translated "perdition" by JB and NEB; it is "damnation" in NAB. Brc translates "ruin." Most translations agree with RSV in using the noun **destruction**, which is the literal meaning of the Greek noun. It may be used of destruction in general or of the final destruction, that is, hell. In verse 14 **life** certainly refers to eternal life, and by analogy **destruction** must be given the meaning "eternal destruction" or "eternal death," which would be equivalent to "hell."

Some translations will say "eternal destruction." If translators decide to use "hell," they must be sure that the term they are using does give the idea of something final and destructive. For example, "Place of the dead," an expression that is acceptable for hell in some contexts, may not be acceptable here, depending on how the culture perceives such a place.

And those who enter by it are many is translated "**and there are many who travel it**" by TEV. GECL has "many are traveling on it." It may also be possible to coordinate the translation with the expression for **Enter** in the first line.

Translators will notice that TEV has restructured this verse somewhat by putting "**to hell**" directly after "**gate.**" Many other translators will do the same thing. They may have, for example, "for the gate people go through to final destruction (or, hell) is a wide one, and the road that goes there is broad (or, easy for traveling)." TEV has then indicated that there are many people on this road, whereas in the text, the idea is more that there are many people who go through the wide gate. If translators have restructured as we suggested above, then they may need to repeat "gate," as in "and there are many people who go through that wide gate."

7.14	RSV	TEV

For the gate is narrow and the way is hard, that leads to life, and those who find it are few.

But the gate to life is narrow and the way that leads to it is hard, and there are few people who find it.

There is a textual problem regarding the first word of this verse, whether it should be the Greek word for **For** (meaning "because" or "but") or "How!" The UBS Greek New Testament highly favors the second alternative, which represents a Semitic exclamatory form. The restructuring of the translations make it difficult to determine precisely what textual tradition is followed. Only NAB clearly reflects the exclamatory form: "But how narrow is the gate . . . how rough the road . . . how few there are!"

Translators who accept the interpretation of **For** as "How!" may have something similar to NAB cited above, or a phrase such as "But that gate that leads to life, how narrow it is (or, it is really a narrow one)."

Narrow does not usually pose difficulties, but some translators have rendered it as "hard (or, small) to pass through." It should be possible to use the same expression as in verse 13.

Way can be "road" or "path," as in verse 13.

The Greek word rendered **hard** represents a participial form (literally "pressed together"), which carries the meaning "unspacious" or "crowded." NAB renders "rough," and Brc translates "beset with troubles." GECL 1st edition translates by an adjective which may mean "strenuous" or even "back-breaking."

When speaking of the way as being **hard,** in addition to the possible translations cited above, other things that can be said include "the way is difficult to travel on" and "it is full of difficulties (for people traveling on it)." In any case, it will be good if the expression will contrast with **easy** in verse 13.

As in verse 13, it may be necessary to restructure the verse slightly. For example, "the gate that leads to life is really narrow, and the road there is full of difficulties."

Life can refer to "real life" or "true life." From the context it seems clear that it is also acceptable to say "eternal life."

In the sentence **those who find it are few,** there is some question as to what **it** refers to, whether it is the gate, the way, or life. Probably the best interpretation is that it refers to the way, especially since it is parallel to **it** in verse 13. Thus translators can say "there are only a few people who find that way," or possibly ". . . that way to life."

When translating these two verses, 13 and 14, translators should treat them as a single paragraph. It may not be natural in some languages to follow the same structure as the text, which starts with the narrow gate, switches to the wide one, and then returns to the narrow one. Instead, it may be more natural to do something like this:

The gate you go through on the way to eternal destruction is wide, and the road you take there is easy to travel on. There are many people who take that way. But the gate that leads to life is really narrow, and the way there is full of difficulties. Few people find that way. But you should go through that gate to find life.

It should be noted, however, that the focus is on this narrow gate.

7.15-20

RSV	TEV
	A Tree and Its Fruit
15 "Beware of false prophets, who come to you in sheep's clothing but inwardly are ravenous wolves. 16 You will know them by their fruits. Are grapes gathered from thorns, or figs from thistles? 17 So, every sound tree bears good fruit, but the bad tree bears evil fruit. 18 A sound tree cannot bear evil fruit, nor can a bad tree bear good fruit. 19 Every tree that does not bear good fruit is cut down and thrown into the fire. 20 Thus you will know them by their fruits.	15 "Be on your guard against false prophets; they come to you looking like sheep on the outside, but on the inside they are really like wild wolves. 16 You will know them by what they do. Thorn bushes do not bear grapes, and briers do not bear figs. 17 A healthy tree bears good fruit, but a poor tree bears bad fruit. 18 A healthy tree cannot bear bad fruit, and a poor tree cannot bear good fruit. 19 And any tree that does not bear good fruit is cut down and thrown in the fire. 20 So then, you will know the false prophets by what they do.

SECTION HEADING: "**A Tree and Its Fruit**." If translators cannot use this same phrase, they may be able to say "The kind of fruit a tree produces." Or they may use the theme of verse 15 as a section heading, with a clause like "Jesus warns about false prophets."

7.15

RSV	TEV
"Beware of false prophets, who come to you in sheep's clothing but inwardly are ravenous wolves.	**"Be on your guard against false prophets; they come to you looking like sheep on the outside, but on the inside they are really like wild wolves.**

Beware of (so also NJB, NEB) translates a verb first used in 6.1; the verb is also used in 10.17; 16.6,11,12. TEV and NAB have "**Be on your guard against**," and Brc has "Be continually on your guard against." This can also be rendered "Watch out for" or "Be very careful to look for."

False prophets represents the rendering of most translations; Phps has "false religious teachers." It is important to note that the reference is not to the Pharisees or to any other group of outsiders, but to "false Christian prophets," as is indicated by 24.11,24. This interpretation of the text is also supported by the observation that the false prophets have the appearance of **sheep**, a figure used of God's people in the Old Testament. Matthew is stating that the Christian community of his day must be on guard against people from their own midst who have the appearance of speaking God's message to them, but in reality are **ravenous wolves**.

For **false prophets**, translators have said "people who pretend to be prophets (of God) but aren't" or "people who say they proclaim God's word, but don't really." For **prophet** see comments on 1.22.

Inwardly are ravenous wolves, a metaphor in the Greek text, is translated as a simile by TEV: "**but on the inside they are really like wild wolves**."

Ravenous (TEV "**wild**") in Greek means "greedy," "preying." It describes wolves as waiting to attack the flock and steal a lamb or a sheep. Note "savage" of NEB. GECL 1st edition translates the clause "They look as harmless as sheep, but in reality they are wild wolves."

This rendering of GECL 1st edition can be a helpful model for translators. The sentence **who come to you in sheep's clothing** should not be translated literally. It does not refer to someone wearing clothing belonging to a sheep or wearing sheep skin as clothing, but rather to someone who appears harmless and guileless like a sheep does. There are cultures where people do not necessarily associate ideas like guileless or harmless with sheep, nor the ideas of weakness or meekness. (Often sheep are only seen as stupid, for example.) In these cases it is certainly necessary to make one of the components, either harmless or guileless, explicit. The translation can be "looking as harmless as a sheep" or "pretending to be harmless like a sheep." It may be possible, although less forceful as a translation, to say simply "appear to be harmless (or, meek)."

The same is true of **ravenous wolves**. Translators may have "they are destructive like wolves" or simply "they are destructive." **Inwardly** can be expressed as "in fact," "in reality," or "the way they really are."

7.16	RSV	TEV
	You will know them by their fruits. Are grapes gathered from thorns, or figs from thistles?	You will know them by what they do. Thorn bushes do not bear grapes, and briers do not bear figs.

Know can be translated as "recognize" or "realize what they really are."

Fruits is a common figure for "actions" or "things people do." See 3.8 for a further example of this. The Semitic Greek structure **by their fruits** (TEV "**by their deeds**") is in the emphatic position in the Greek text. The plural **fruits** is here used symbolically of a person's deeds (NAB "You will know them by their deeds"). The meaning is that people are able to judge a person on the basis of what his life reveals him to be, rather than upon what a person claims to be. In verse 20 **by their fruits** is again translated "**by what they do**" in TEV. GECL follows TEV in its restructuring here, but in verse 20 the German translators prefer to retain the image ("So you can recognize the false prophets by their fruits").

In verse 20 the figure is not difficult for the reader to process, since the imagery of a tree and its fruit is discussed in verses 17-19. However, it may prove difficult in verse 16, where the imagery of the tree and its fruit has not yet been mentioned. For Jewish readers it probably would have occasioned no difficulty even in verse 16, because the figure would have been familiar to them.

Are grapes gathered from thorns, or figs from thistles? translates a rhetorical question which expects the answer "No." For many readers this is better represented as a statement: **"Thorn bushes do not bear grapes, and briers do not bear figs"** (TEV).

Thorns (TEV "thorn bushes") translates a noun which may be used of any thorny or prickly plant. **Thistles** (TEV "briers") may also refer to various prickly plants, including the water chestnut. Many varieties of thorns and thistles abound in the dry climate of Palestine, and it is not possible to determine precisely which variety is intended. What is important is that these represent plants which are weeds that cause problems rather than provide desirable fruit.

In many parts of the world, people are not familiar with **grapes**. However, in this figure of speech it is not too important if readers do not know any more about them than that they are a fruit. Translators can put "a fruit called grape" or "small round fruit (or, berries) called grapes" or even "a sweet fruit."

The same is true of **figs**. They can be rendered here "a fruit called fig" or "a sweet fruit."

If such general words are used to translate "grapes" and "figs," then translators should take care that **thorns** and **thistles** are translated by words for bushes that do not normally have edible fruits. If there are two different kinds of thorn bushes that grow in the wild and do not bear fruit, they can usually be used in the translation of this verse.

7.17-18	RSV	TEV

17 So, every sound tree bears good fruit, but the bad tree bears evil fruit. 18 A sound tree cannot bear evil fruit, nor can a bad tree bear good fruit.	17 A healthy tree bears good fruit, but a poor tree bears bad fruit. 18 A healthy tree cannot bear bad fruit, and a poor tree cannot bear good fruit.

So represents a Greek word that introduces the next stage in the teaching. Many languages will not use such a term, and TEV leaves it implicit. There is a shift from one figure, thorny plants, to the figure of good trees contrasted with decaying or rotting trees.

Here a **sound tree** (TEV **"healthy tree"**) is contrasted with a **bad tree** (TEV **"poor tree,"** literally a "decayed" or "rotting tree"), and **good fruit** is contrasted with **evil fruit** (literally **"bad fruit,"** as in TEV). To translate as **evil fruit** in English mixes the imagery of fruit with moral qualities, and most languages will not be able to mix figures effectively that way. NEB translates "good tree . . . poor tree" and "good fruit . . . bad fruit"; NJB has "sound tree . . . rotten tree" and "good fruit . . . bad fruit."

The text speaks of **every sound tree**, which can be rendered "healthy trees," "a healthy tree," or "any healthy tree."

Since we gather from verse 19 that this verse is not speaking about trees in the wild but rather trees someone has planted for fruit, perhaps in an orchard, some translators have said "any sound (or, bad) tree in an orchard (or, in a plantation)" or "every tree a farmer has planted."

The **good fruit** it bears can be expressed as "edible fruit," "fruit people can eat," or even "delicious fruit."

A **bad tree** is one that "is not healthy" or "is not growing properly." And the **evil fruit** is "fruit that no one can eat" or "fruit that tastes bad."

In some languages the idea of **bears** is not expressed directly. Translators may say instead "the fruit you get from the healthy tree, it is good." Similarly with the bearing of bad fruit, the sentence can be "the fruit you get from an unhealthy tree can't be eaten." In verse 18, then, the translation may be "and you cannot get fruit that is bad from a healthy tree or good fruit from an unhealthy tree."

Some translators have found it more natural to combine verses 17 and 18, putting the references in the two verses about the healthy tree together at one place and all information about the unhealthy tree in one place. An example of this is "A healthy tree only bears good fruit. It cannot produce bad fruit. And the unhealthy tree only produces bad fruit. It cannot bear good fruit."

7.19

RSV	TEV
Every tree that does not bear good fruit is cut down and thrown into the fire.	And any tree that does not bear good fruit is cut down and thrown in the fire.

A parallel to this verse is found also in the preaching of John the Baptist (Matt 3.10; Luke 3.9), though it is not found in the Lukan parallel to the present passage (Luke 6.43-45). It is a simple statement of what a farmer does to a tree that does not produce fruit over a period of time: "Any tree that does not bear good fruit is cut down and burned" (GECL). Mft, in fact, places verse 20 before verse 19, both to preserve the thought sequence and to make proper connection with the following paragraph: "*20* So you will know them by their fruit. *19* Any tree that does not produce sound fruit will be cut down and thrown into the fire."

This sentence, verse 19, is a passive construction. Many languages naturally use an active construction, which means that an agent must be supplied. Quite often this is something like "the farmer." Further, keeping in mind what is said under verse 17 about the trees being part of a plantation or an orchard, the verse can well be rendered "The farmer (or, A man) will cut down and burn in a fire any tree on his farm that does not bear good fruit."

Also see 3.10 for similar expressions.

7.20

RSV	TEV
Thus you will know them by their fruits.	So then, you will know the false prophets by what they do.

The conclusion drawn in this verse refers back to verses 15-18. In the same way that trees are recognized by the fruit that they produce, so false prophets are recognized by the things they do. RSV represents a literal rendering of the Greek text (**Thus you will know them by their fruits**), and most translations follow the tradition of RSV by failing to make explicit the pronominal reference of **them**. However, TEV, GECL, FRCL, and DUCL all make this information explicit, "**false prophets**"; Brc renders "As with trees, so with men—you can tell what kind of men they are by the conduct they produce."

This verse means exactly the same as the first part of verse 16. Even if translators do not want to do exactly what Brc has done, they can profit from his translation. **Thus** really indicates that as trees are recognized by their fruit, so are men. In particular, here the false prophets are being referred to. Therefore to translate **Thus**, it is possible to say "It is like that with men too" or "The false prophets are like those trees."

Know again means "recognize for what they are."

In many languages it will be necessary to replace **them** with "false prophets." Otherwise, the word will only be understood to refer to the trees.

As before, **fruits** means actions, behavior, or conduct.

7.21-23

RSV	TEV
	I Never Knew You
21 "Not every one who says to me, 'Lord, Lord,' shall enter the kingdom of heaven, but he who does the will of my Father who is in heaven. 22 On that day many will say to me, 'Lord, Lord, did we not prophesy in your name, and cast out demons in your name, and do many mighty works in your name?' 23 And then will I declare to them, 'I never knew you; depart from me, you evildoers.'	21 "Not everyone who calls me 'Lord, Lord' will enter the Kingdom of heaven, but only those who do what my Father in heaven wants them to do. 22 When the Judgment Day comes, many will say to me, 'Lord, Lord! In your name we spoke God's message, by your name we drove out many demons and performed many miracles!' 23 Then I will say to them, 'I never knew you. Get away from me, you wicked people!'

SECTION HEADING: "**I Never Knew You.**" This section heading often needs to be changed, since the participants need to be identified. Some translators say "Jesus says of some people 'I never knew you' " or "Jesus says who he will not recognize (as being his people)." It can also be "The day of judgment" or "The day when God will judge people." Still another way is to say "Jesus says who will enter the kingdom of God" or "Those who will be under God's rule (or, reign)."

Verses 21-23 describe what will happen on the day of judgment, when Jesus himself will become the judge.

7.21 RSV	TEV
"Not every one who says to me, 'Lord, Lord,' shall enter the kingdom of heaven, but he who does the will of my Father who is in heaven.	"Not everyone who calls me 'Lord, Lord' will enter the Kingdom of heaven, but only those who do what my Father in heaven wants them to do.

The construction **Not every one** may have to be expressed as "It will not be everyone," "Not all people," or "Even some people who say to me 'Lord, Lord' won't . . . ."

There is some disagreement regarding the precise meaning of **Lord** in this verse. The Lukan parallel (6.46) suggests the possible meaning of "teacher," and some scholars believe that originally the meaning was either "teacher" or "master." But apparently no translations follow this interpretation. The next verse is an obvious reference to the exalted Lord on the day of judgment, and this is surely the meaning that Matthew intends here. The majority of translations accept this interpretation.

The repetition of the noun of address, **Lord, Lord**, is somewhat unnatural following either the verb **says** or the verb **"calls"** (TEV). The meaning is "not everyone who is in the habit of saying that I am his Lord . . . ." Phps translates "It is not everyone who keeps saying to me 'Lord, Lord' . . . ." GECL 1st edition renders "Not everyone who constantly has my name in his mouth . . . ." TOB has "It is not sufficient to say to me: 'Lord, Lord!' " One way that closely reflects the meaning is "It won't be everyone who constantly says I am his Lord" or ". . . who is constantly acknowledging me as his Lord." Another way is "It is not enough to always be saying I am Lord. Not all those who do that will enter the kingdom of heaven." There will be languages where the idea will most easily be expressed as "Not all people who say to me 'You are the one I serve.' "

Kingdom of heaven is synonymous with "Kingdom of God" (NAB). Most translations reproduce a literal rendering of the Greek text, but a few are dynamic: ". . . will come into God's new world" (GECL), ". . . will become a member of God's people" (INCL), and ". . . will enjoy the blessings of God's rule" (MACL).

We discussed **enter the kingdom of heaven** at 5.20. In addition to the suggestions there and the ways that we cited above, other ways to express this phrase include "Will be among the people who receive the blessings of God's rule" or "Will be a part of God's reign."

The contrast signaled by **but** sometimes is shown by a new sentence, as in "It is (only) the person who does what God my Father in heaven wants who will be a part of God's reign."

Does the will means simply to do what God requires or wants done.

Note that as we have seen elsewhere, **my Father who is in heaven** refers to God. This fact may have to be made explicit as "God my Father."

7.22 RSV	TEV
On that day many will say to me, 'Lord, Lord, did we not prophesy in your name, and cast out demons in your name, and do many mighty works in your name?'	When the Judgment Day comes, many will say to me, 'Lord, Lord! In your name we spoke God's message, by your name we drove out many demons and performed many miracles!'

That day (see Isa 2.11,17; Zech 14.6) is specifically identified by TEV as "**the Judgment Day.**" Most scholars agree that this is the meaning, and some translations are explicit: "On the Day of Judgment" (GECL). JB supplies a footnote indicating that the reference is to "the day of the final Judgment." This can also be expressed as "On that day when God will judge the world (or, the people of the world)" or "When the day comes for God to judge everyone."

Did we not prophesy in your name translates a rhetorical question which expects the answer "Yes." For English readers a rhetorical question is not always easy to understand, especially when it is negative (**did we not**), and so TEV changes it to a statement: **"In your name we spoke God's message."** Phps and Brc retain the rhetorical question but simplify the construction by the use of more idiomatic English: "didn't we . . . ?" GECL, FRCL, and DUCL follow TEV in the use of a statement. There are also languages where a question is formed at the end of a statement, as in "Lord, Lord, we prophesied in your name, and . . . , didn't we (or, isn't that so)?"

In your name occurs three times in this verse. The phrase "in someone's name" may have various functions: (1) appealing to the person mentioned; (2) acting or speaking in that person's strength or authority; or (3) appealing to or mentioning one's relationship to that person.

Most translators follow the second interpretation of **in your name**, with a phrase such as "with your power (or, authority)" or "as you gave us power to do so." Some, however, follow the third interpretation and say "as your followers." Those who do prefer the first interpretation can say "Because we sought this ability from you."

Prophesy (so most translations) is represented in TEV by **"spoke God's message."** Phps translates "preach," and GECL "proclaim God's instructions." The basic meaning of the Greek word is that of proclaiming a divine revelation rather than of predicting the future. Although **prophesy** is a rather accurate transliteration of the Greek word, it fails as a translation because English speakers generally understand the verb **prophesy** to have primarily a predictive sense.

We discussed "prophet" at 1.22, and translators are referred there for comments on **prophesy**. This verb is usually translated "speak God's message" or "told people the message from God."

Cast out demons is translated "exorcised demons" by NAB. The Greek verb means "drive out" or "expel," generally with the notion of force. In the New Testament it is used especially of the exorcism of demons who have taken control of a person (see for example Matt 9.34; 10.1,8; 12.27; 17.19).

"Many demons" of TEV is literally **demons** (RSV, NJB, NAB); NEB, Phps, and Brc have "devils"; GECL, FRCL render "evil spirits."

Before translating **cast out demons**, translators should read the discussion at 4.24 on **demons**, since the way a language refers to casting out evil spirits depends on how spirit possession is spoken of. **Cast out** may be "chased spirits from people," "removed evil spirits from people," "took the evil spirits from behind people," or simply "made the evil spirits leave people." In some languages this phrase may be "freed people from the power of evil spirits."

Mighty works (one word in Greek) is translated **"miracles"** by TEV and a number of other translations. The Greek word emphasizes the notion of power (see its usage in 11.20,21,23; 13.54,58; 14.2; 22.29; 24.29; 25.15; 26.64).

Mighty works or "miracles" can be "mighty actions" or "wonderful actions." Sometimes the phrase "that only God could do" is added, or possibly "that normally couldn't be done." Another rendering is "great acts that show God's power."

7.23

RSV	TEV
And then will I declare to them, 'I never knew you; depart from me, you evildoers.'	Then I will say to them, 'I never knew you. Get away from me, you wicked people!'

And then translates a frequently used transitional in Matthew.

I will declare translates a Greek verb which has a wide variety of meanings; quite frequently it is translated "confess." Here the verb has its root meaning of "to speak openly and freely." Most translations prefer a somewhat strong affirmation: "I will pass judgment" (GECL), "I shall tell them to their faces" (NJB), "I will tell them straight" (Brc), and "I shall tell them plainly" (Phps). Many translators find that the Phps rendering is a helpful model. They have "I will tell them openly (or, directly)."

Several scholars note that the words **I never knew you** constitute a formula used by Jewish rabbis when pronouncing a ban against someone; it means "I have nothing to do with you" or "You mean nothing to me." Brc translates "You are complete strangers to me!" "I have nothing to do with you" or "You were not my people (or, my followers)" are the most common renderings.

Evildoers (TEV **"wicked people"**) is literally "who work lawlessness." The noun "lawlessness" is one of Matthew's favorite terms (see 13.41; 23.28; 24.12; it is not found in the other Gospels). In the Old Testament "lawlessness" means doing what is contrary to the Law of God, which is also true for Matthew. However, for him "lawlessness" is expressed in the failure to show love for one's neighbor, since "love" is the true fulfillment of God's Law. A number of translations are dynamic: "Out of my sight! Your deeds were sins!" (Brc), "out of my sight, you and your wicked ways!" (NEB), and "You have neglected to live according to the will of God; away with you!" (GECL).

Depart from me, you evildoers is an allusion to Psalm 6.8. A parallel passage is found in Luke 13.27. Neither Luke nor Matthew agree in all details with the Septuagint. Luke agrees with the Septuagint in its choice of the initial verb (TEV **"Get away"**), while Matthew's choice of a verb differs. On the other hand, Matthew agrees with the Septuagint in its use of the final noun ("lawlessness"), while Luke prefers another noun in its place ("wickedness").

The expression **depart from me** is certainly not very colloquial English. TEV **"Get away from me"** is much better. Other possibilities include "Leave!" or "Get out of my sight."

As for **you evildoers**, it is difficult to have an expression that is both accurate, in line with the explanations above, and also dynamic. NEB, GECL, and Brc are good attempts. Other translators have said "Disobedient people!" "You never did what God required," or "Your ways were contrary to God."

7.24-27

RSV	TEV
	The Two House Builders
24 "Every one then who hears these words of mine and does them will be like a wise man	24 "So then, anyone who hears these words of mine and obeys them is like a wise man who

who built his house upon the rock; 25 and the rain fell, and the floods came, and the winds blew and beat upon that house, but it did not fall, because it had been founded on the rock. 26 And every one who hears these words of mine and does not do them will be like a foolish man who built his house upon the sand; 27 and the rain fell, and the floods came, and the winds blew and beat against that house, and it fell; and great was the fall of it."

built his house on rock. 25 The rain poured down, the rivers flooded over, and the wind blew hard against that house. But it did not fall, because it was built on rock.

26 "But anyone who hears these words of mine and does not obey them is like a foolish man who built his house on sand. 27 The rain poured down, the rivers flooded over, the wind blew hard against that house, and it fell. And what a terrible fall that was!"

SECTION HEADING: "**The Two House Builders.**" This heading can also be "Two different kinds of houses," "Two men who built houses," or "The house on the sand and the house on the rock." If a complete sentence is required, "Two men build houses" will serve.

Verses 24-27, which distinguish between valid and invalid hearing, are entitled "What Hearing Really Means" by one commentator. Since valid hearing leads to action, this section forms a parallel with the two previous sections (verses 15-20 and 21-23). The parallelism between these three passages may further be seen in that, in the phrase "bear fruit" (used five times in verses 17-19), the verb "bear" is the same one translated "do" or "does" throughout verses 21-27.

This same parable also concludes Luke's Sermon on the Plain (6.47-49), but there is only slight verbal agreement between the two passages. Luke describes two houses built alongside a river; one has a foundation that reaches down to rock, but the other house is built without laying a foundation on the rock. Matthew, on the other hand, places the two houses in entirely different localities; one is built on the rock of a mountainside, the other on the sand of the valley.

While some scholars apply this parable to life's crises in general, the intense eschatological orientation of the context doubtless makes the last judgment the point of reference.

7.24   RSV   TEV

"Every one then who hears these words of mine and does them will be like a wise man who built his house upon the rock;

"So then, anyone who hears these words of mine and obeys them is like a wise man who built his house on rock.

As the books of Leviticus (26.1-46) and Deuteronomy (28.1-68; 30.15-20) draw to an end with the pronouncement of blessings and curses, so the Sermon on the Mount concludes with a promise (7.24-25) and a warning (7.26-27).

In Greek the pronoun **of mine** is emphatic. The demonstrative pronoun **these** (not found in Luke) indicates clearly that **these words** refer to the content of the Sermon which is now being brought to its conclusion.

There will be languages where some grammatical features will indicate that **these words** refer to the ones just spoken. However, it is important that the reference should be not only to the immediately preceding verses. It may be necessary to say "all these things I have said" or "what I have said here."

In the context **does** is the equivalent of "**obeys**" (TEV). Similarly in verse 26 "does not do" means "does not obey" (TEV).

It may not be possible to say one **does** or even "**obeys**" words. In such cases translators can have "does what I have said to do" or "obeys these instructions.

TEV and a number of other translations (GECL, NEB, Phps, NAB) see in the Greek future tense **will be like** a present meaning: "**is like.**" This is because, in English and in some other European languages, the present tense is used to describe something that is true whenever it may occur. Other languages may have their own ways of saying such things.

In place of the impersonal passive **will be like**, some manuscripts have a first person singular active form "I will liken." TC-GNT believes that the alternative reading may have been influenced by the scribes' familiarity with the Lukan form of the saying: "I will show you what he is like" (6.47).

Wise is a characteristic feature of Matthew's vocabulary (see 10.16; 24.45; 25.2,4,8,9). **Wise man** is a traditional and literal rendering. NEB ("who had the sense [to build]") and GECL ("who thought about what he was doing [and built]") are more dynamic. The phrase **wise man** is usually translated literally but can also be rendered as "a man of good judgment," "a sensible man," "a person who considered carefully what he was doing."

The rock (so also NIV). The use of the definite article **the** in this construction is unnatural for English speakers, though it is found in the Greek text. TEV "**on rock**" is a more natural equivalent. GECL has "on rocky [that is, rock-like] ground." See comment on "the sand" in verse 26.

To build a house **upon the rock** does not mean it was built on rocks, that is, that the builder used rocks as a foundation. It refers more to being built on a solid rock. This is a problem in many parts of the world where houses are built without foundations, and are in fact built on soil or sand quite frequently. (It is granaries that are built on rock so as to keep out termites.) In such places translators have often wanted to say "built his house in a solid way" or "built it on a high place." This does change the analogy of Jesus quite a bit, and it may be better to say "built his house on a rock to make it very strong."

7.25	RSV	TEV
	and the rain fell, and the floods came, and the winds blew and beat upon that house, but it did not fall, because it had been founded on the rock.	The rain poured down, the rivers flooded over, and the wind blew hard against that house. But it did not fall, because it was built on rock.

Some languages would not say that **the rain fell**, but rather "it rained" or "the rain came."

As for **floods**, it is often necessary to specify what was flooding, as in "the rivers flooded over." Other translations can say "the flood waters rose up."

The Greek verb rendered **beat upon** is different from the one translated "beat against" in verse 27. The verb used here literally means "fall against," while the one in verse 27 literally means "strike against." It is difficult to tell which, if either, of the two verbs is intended to be stronger than the other. Commentators do not agree, and no clues are given in the lexicons. Some translations do not distinguish between the two renderings, while others do. NJB reads: "gales blew and hurled themselves against that house . . . gales blew and struck that house." Brc translates "and the winds blew and battered that house, . . . and the winds blew and buffeted that house." NAB renders the verb in verse 27 "the winds blew and lashed against his house," while translating the first part of verse 25 "When the rainy season set in, the torrents came and the winds blew and buffeted his house." GECL, which gives the same rendering in each verse, has "Then, when there is a cloudburst, rivers overflood their banks, and the storm rages and shakes the house . . . ."

The phrase **the winds blew and beat upon that house** can be expressed "there were strong winds that blew against the house" or "strong winds came against that house."

But it did not fall, except for the negative, appears in the same form in verse 27. The normal word that is used for a building collapsing should be used here.

The translation of **founded on rock** will depend on how verse 24 was handled. It may be necessary to say "because the rock on which it was built gave it strength (or, made it strong)."

7.26   RSV   TEV

And every one who hears these   "But anyone who hears these
words of mine and does not do them   words of mine and does not obey
will be like a foolish man who built   them is like a foolish man who built
his house upon the sand;   his house on sand.

Every one can be rendered "Anyone," "Whoever," or "Those people who."

The phrase **hears these words of mine and does not do them will be like** is similar to verse 24 except for the negative "does not do them."

The Greek word translated **foolish man** was first used in 5.22. It is also used in 23.17 and in 25.2,3,8. See 5.22 for a discussion of the word. Here it can be "stupid person" or "person who has no sense."

Upon the sand would be more natural for English speakers without the use of the definite article **the**, which is found in Greek. TEV, NJB, and NEB omit the article, and NAB has "on sandy ground." See comment on "the rock" in verse 24.

As with "on the rock," **upon the sand** will pose a problem for people who do in fact build houses on sand. They may have to say "on top of sand so it was not strong" or "on sand with the result that nothing could give it strength."

7.27   RSV   TEV

and the rain fell, and the floods   The rain poured down, the rivers
came, and the winds blew and beat   flooded over, the wind blew hard
against that house, and it fell; and   against that house, and it fell. And
great was the fall of it."   what a terrible fall that was!"

The first part of this verse can be translated like verse 25. See comments there for a discussion of **beat against**.

And it fell; and great was the fall of it describes complete destruction, and this impact should be conveyed in translation. Brc renders "and it collapsed, and its ruin was complete." NAB translates "It collapsed under all this and was completely ruined."

7.28-29

RSV	TEV
	The Authority of Jesus
28 And when Jesus finished these sayings, the crowds were astonished at his teaching, 29 for he taught them as one who had authority, and not as their scribes.	28 When Jesus finished saying these things, the crowd was amazed at the way he taught. 29 He wasn't like the teachers of the Law; instead, he taught with authority.

SECTION HEADING: "**The Authority of Jesus.**" Translators should read the comments under verse 29 for a discussion of "**Authority.**" This section heading can be "Jesus teaches with authority" or "Jesus has authority when he teaches."

7.28	RSV	TEV

And when Jesus finished these sayings, the crowds were astonished at his teaching,

When Jesus finished saying these things, the crowd was amazed at the way he taught.

With verses 28-29 the Sermon on the Mount is concluded. **And when Jesus finished these sayings** is a formula which is used five times in the Gospel (11.1; 13.53; 19.1; 26.1). Here it is used solely as a conclusion, while in the remaining four passages it also functions as a transition to what follows. In each occurrence the only difference is the object of the verb **finished**: "these sayings" (7.28; 19.1), "instructing his twelve disciples (11.1), "these parables" (13.53), "all these sayings" (26.1).

Since this formula here functions solely as a conclusion and not as a transition (8.1 is the transition), this may suggest the special significance that this initial block of teaching material has in the framework of the Gospel.

This clause, **And when Jesus finished these sayings**, may be expressed as "After Jesus finished saying all these things," "Jesus finished saying these things. After that . . . ," or "Jesus said all these things, and after he had finished . . . ."

The crowds may be rendered in the singular as "the crowd" or perhaps as something like "all those people there."

The Greek verb translated **astonished** (TEV "**amazed**") is a very strong verb and may be used of either wonder or fear. In Matthew's Gospel it appears here and in 13.54; 19.25; 22.33. Elsewhere in the New Testament it is used in Mark 1.22; 6.2; 7.37; 10.26; 11.18; Luke 2.48; 4.32; 9.43; and Acts 13.12.

At his teaching, a noun structure in the Greek text, is translated "**at the way he taught**" in TEV. Some have said "at the things he taught," but this is not really correct. Verse 29 shows that it was his manner of teaching that astonished people, and not the content. TEV is thus a better rendering than RSV.

7.29	RSV	TEV

RSV	TEV
for he taught them as one who had authority, and not as their scribes.	He wasn't like the teachers of the Law; instead, he taught with authority.

RSV follows the order of the Greek text, but TEV inverts the order of the two clauses, thereby introducing the negative clause first and concluding with a positive statement: "**instead, he taught with authority.**"

Taught . . . authority contrasts the teaching of Jesus with that of the scribes. Elsewhere in the Gospel the noun **authority** is used in 8.9; 9.6,8; 10.1; 21.23,24,27; according to 28.18 the exalted Lord has been given "all authority."

The idea of teaching with authority has often been misunderstood. Many have translated it as "he taught with power," for example. However, this verse is contrasting the way Jesus taught with the way the teachers of the Law taught. Their manner was to take a scripture verse and cite what a variety of other rabbis or teachers had said about it. But Jesus taught directly without referring to other teachers. As Brc phrases it, "he taught as one who needed no authority beyond his own." Another way to express this may be "he taught as one who had authority himself to teach the truth."

Scribes (TEV "**the teachers of the Law**") is first used in 2.4 (see comments there), though it is also found earlier in the Sermon itself (5.20). They were teachers and interpreters of the Jewish Law, and one of their primary concerns was the perpetuation of traditional decisions based on it. Jesus, on the other hand, was more concerned with the plain meaning of Scripture than with the intricate legal system that had been developed from it.

Worthy of comment is Matthew's use of **their** in the phrase **their scribes**. Matthew probably intends to differentiate between the Jewish teachers of Scripture and a similar class of teachers who were interpreters of the Christian tradition. Therefore he uses "their teachers" as opposed to "the teachers" of Mark 1.22. Compare also 12.9, where Matthew refers to "their synagogue"; Mark 3.1 and Luke 6.6, in the parallel passage, have "the synagogue."

For **their scribes**, translators sometimes have to put "the teachers of the law of those people" or ". . . of the Jews." This makes it clear who **their** refers to.

As in TEV, it may be necessary to reverse the last part of the verse: "He didn't teach like their teachers of the Law. He needed no authority other than his own."

It is to be noticed that in the Gospel of Mark (1.22) this verse is set in a totally different context, thus giving it an entirely different meaning and function.

Chapter 8

Chapters 8 and 9, which contain ten miracle stories and three calls to discipleship, are considered by a number of commentators to be the next unit of Matthew's Gospel. This outline is suggested by 4.23-25, where the work of the Messiah is both that of teaching and healing. The Sermon on the Mount indicates the teaching activity of the Messiah, while the accumulation of miracles in these two chapters calls attention to the work of the Messiah, who heals all the diseases of his people. Accordingly, one commentator entitles chapters 8 and 9, "The Messiah of the Deed."

8.1-4

RSV	TEV
	Jesus Heals a Man
1 When he came down from the mountain, great crowds followed him; 2 and behold, a leper came to him and knelt before him, saying, "Lord, if you will, you can make me clean." 3 And he stretched out his hand and touched him, saying, "I will; be clean." And immediately his leprosy was cleansed. 4 And Jesus said to him, "See that you say nothing to any one; but go, show yourself to the priest, and offer the gift that Moses commanded, for a proof to the people."*r*	1 When Jesus came down from the hill, large crowds followed him. 2 Then a man suffering from a dreaded skin disease came to him, knelt down before him, and said, "Sir, if you want to, you can make me clean."*e*
	3 Jesus reached out and touched him. "I do want to," he answered. "Be clean!" At once the man was healed of his disease. 4 Then Jesus said to him, "Listen! Don't tell anyone, but go straight to the priest and let him examine you; then in order to prove to everyone that you are cured, offer the sacrifice that Moses ordered."
r Greek *to them*	
	e MAKE ME CLEAN: *This disease was considered to make a person ritually unclean.*

SECTION HEADING: "**Jesus Heals a Man**." In some languages it may be necessary to state clearly that the man was suffering from some illness or disease. A sentence such as "Jesus heals a sick man" or "Jesus cures a man of a disease" will show this. Some languages will even have to specify the illness, as in "Jesus heals a man of leprosy" or "Jesus heals a leper." But note our discussion of "leper" in verse 2. Whatever is used there should also appear in the title.

8.1　　　RSV　　　　　　　　　　TEV

When he came down from the
mountain, great crowds followed
him;

When Jesus came down from
the hill, large crowds followed him.

When he came down from the mountain serves as an editorial link between the Sermon on the Mount and the healing of the man. In Greek Jesus is not mentioned by name, but in many languages it is advisable to use the proper name when a new section is introduced.

In some languages one cannot say "When he came down" without having said first that he came down. Translators in such languages can say "Jesus came down the mountain, and when (or, as) he came . . . ."

Of course, whatever word was used for **mountain** in 5.1 should be used here too.

In general Matthew pictures the **crowds** as receptive to Jesus and his message. See comments on 4.25 and 5.1. He enjoys identifying them as **great crowds**.

Often the phrase **great crowds** makes it seem that there were separate groups of people. It may be better to say "a large crowd" or "very many people."

Here **followed** means "accompanied" or "went with." See comments on 4.25.

8.2　　　RSV　　　　　　　　　　TEV

and behold, a leper came to him and
knelt before him, saying, "Lord, if
you will, you can make me clean."

Then a man suffering from a dreaded
skin disease came to him, knelt
down before him, and said, "Sir, if
you want to, you can make me
clean."*e*

*e*MAKE ME CLEAN: *This disease was
considered to make a person ritually
unclean.*

In Greek this verse begins with **and behold**, which reflects Semitic language. Elsewhere in the Gospel this phrase is used with a special emphasis at 8.24,29,32; 9.2,3,10,20; 26.51. Scholars indicate that we cannot speak of a systematic usage of the idiom, even though Matthew enjoys using it to stress something that is important to him. See comment at 1.20. As there, it may be translated as "and then," "all of a sudden," or "it happened at that time."

Leper (so most translations) is translated "**a man suffering from a dreaded skin disease**" by TEV. As scholars note, the Greek word itself provides no real clue, since it can also cover elephantiasis, psoriasis, and vitiligo (depigmentation of skin). Today the term leprosy is properly applied to Hansen's Disease, which was first isolated in 1871. Although it is possible that the reference here is to what modern science terms leprosy, this is not a necessary conclusion. NEB translates "a leper" but follows with a note: "*The words* leper, leprosy, *as used in this translation, refer to some disfiguring skin disease which entailed ceremonial defilement. It is different from what* *is now called leprosy.*" For translation it is best to use a term which may include leprosy but which does not necessarily indicate leprosy.

It is also important to note that institutions that work with leprosy patients prefer that we avoid putting a stigma upon anyone by calling a person a "leper." It is better to refer to the disease, "leprosy," and then to state that someone "has leprosy," or "suffers from leprosy," or "is a leprosy patient," rather than marking the individual as a "leper." We cannot, of course, call it "Hansen's Disease," since it did not have that name at the time of Jesus, and to give it that name would be an anachronism.

Having said that, we should point out that in many languages this is hard advice to follow. Some languages can use a general word or phrase much like "**dreaded skin disease**" of TEV, and if so, translators should use it. But there are many languages that do not have a general word for "disease" or "skin disease" and must therefore always specify which disease. In such cases translators must either say "leprosy" or arbitrarily name some other disease. Some have used "skin fungus," for example. However, it is unlikely that such an ailment would ever render someone ritually unclean or make him a social outcast the way leprosy would, and for this reason translators may be forced (we hope with reluctance) to revert to using "leprosy," even though they know it may be incorrect.

Came to him may be "approached him" or "came to where Jesus was walking."

That the man **knelt before** Jesus is an acknowledgment of the power and authority of Jesus, since one normally knelt before gods and kings. And, as one commentator observes, in the Old Testament the expression "come and kneel down" often refers to a ritual form of religious adoration. Both Matthew and Mark (1.40) indicate that the man knelt before Jesus, though they each use a different term; Luke (5.12) states that the man "fell on his face." The word **knelt before** is the same as in 2.11. It may be translated here as "knelt down in front of him to show honor" or "knelt down in great respect in front of him."

Lord is translated "**Sir**" by TEV and a number of other modern English translations (JB, NEB, NAB, Brc, AT). This noun of address here is notable for two reasons. First, it is not found in the Marcan account, and Matthew has a tendency to abbreviate Mark. Second, elsewhere in Matthew's Gospel the noun is used only in the speech of those who believe in Jesus. It is quite likely, therefore, that the term carries the full significance of **Lord**. The real difficulty is that of the time perspective. It may well be that in the original situation the man meant "**Sir**." However, in the context of Matthew writing for the Christian community, the meaning is most probably **Lord**. In light of this, it seems best to use the term here that is used for **Lord** elsewhere, as for example when the disciples called Jesus "Lord" (8.25 is an example).

The Christian use of **Lord** has been handled in many ways. Often there is in a language a respectful term of address used only with chiefs or others to whom one owes allegiance. In many West African languages, Christians have found that the best equivalent is a term which means "Owner" or "Our Owner" or "Owner of the people." "Lord" is thus one who has authority over us, one to whom we owe allegiance. There are other languages which have a respectful term of address used only for God, and in some cases that works well for the Christian usage also.

For the more common use, the equivalent of "**Sir**" in English, translators usually use the polite term with which they address some elder or senior person.

If you will (NEB "if only you will"; AB "if you are willing") is translated by TEV in such a manner as to leave the false impression that the man was giving Jesus permission to make him well: "**If you want to.**" Some scholars indicate that the man's words must not be taken to suggest that he thought Jesus was unwilling to heal him; rather, he addresses Jesus in a complimentary way, because he views him as a miracle worker.

The use of a phrase such as **if you will**, "would you be willing," or "if it pleases you" as a very polite way of requesting something, is not uncommon, so many translators will be able to use a sentence similar to the text. In other languages a phrase such as "I would ask that you be willing" is appropriate.

You can make me clean is a literal rendering of the Greek text. As the footnote in TEV indicates, this was a reference to ritual purification. The laws concerning leprosy are found in Leviticus 13-14 and Deuteronomy 24.8. The notion of ritual purification may be difficult in some translations, and GECL has rendered "you can make me well!" JB has "you can cure me," as does NAB. Brc also goes in this direction: "if you want to cure me, you can." This seems to be a better solution than the retaining of the more difficult **you can make me clean**.

If translators retain the form of the text, **you can make me clean**, readers may think only of physical cleanliness, as if the man were washed. On the other hand, if they say "you can cure me," important cultural information is lost. Some translations have tried to convey both by using phrases such as "you can heal me and make me acceptable to mix with people (or, make me clean in regard to God's things)." But most translations have done something similar to TEV and put the cultural information in a footnote.

The idea of being ritually clean, whether expressed in the text or explained in a footnote, is itself difficult to communicate in many cultures. Some translations have said "to be seen as clean in regards to the things of God (or, in regards to ways of worshiping God)" or "to be free from things God (or, people) call unclean." Others have had to have a fairly extensive footnote, such as "There are some things that prevent a person from mixing with others and being able to worship God properly. These things are called unclean."

8.3   RSV   TEV

And he stretched out his hand and touched him, saying, "I will; be clean." And immediately his leprosy was cleansed.

Jesus reached out and touched him. "I do want to," he answered. "Be clean!" At once the man was healed of his disease.

One commentator calls attention to the striking parallelism between the man's actions ("came to him and knelt before him, saying") and Jesus' response (**stretched out his hand and touched him, saying**). Reaching out and touching the man are best interpreted as gestures of healing (see 2 Kings 5.11; Mark 8.22-23). According to Jewish law, physical contact with someone who had leprosy would also have made

Jesus unclean, yet all three of the Synoptic Gospels record this event (Mark 1.41; Luke 5.13). In Greek, Jesus' action of touching the man is in focus.

In some languages it is better to say "Jesus" instead of **he**, so that it does not seem that the man stretched out his hand. TEV is an example.

There are languages that can naturally say **he stretched out his hand**, but others will more likely say "stretched out and touched," "reached out," or simply "touched him with his hand."

I will (TEV "**I do want to**") should be rendered as emphatically as possible. NEB has "Indeed I will," and JB "Of course I want to!" But translators should check how they handled the question in verse 2, so that the reply of Jesus here is appropriate.

Be clean may be more effectively rendered "Be cured!" (JB). Of course translators will use either "Be cleaned" or "Be cured" according to what they used in verse 2. It may be difficult to use a passive imperative such as "Be cleaned" or "Be healed," so that a phrase such as "I make you clean" or "You are now clean" may be better, or "You are healed" or "I now cure you." But sentences such as these do not often have the same impact as the imperative, which should be used if at all possible.

And immediately is emphatic in the Greek sentence structure. Jesus' power is beyond doubt, and the cure is immediate and complete. "At that very moment," "Right that moment," "At once"—phrases such as these can indicate this.

Was cleansed translates the same Greek verb rendered "you can make me clean" (verse 2) and **Be clean!** TEV shifts from the use of the ceremonial term to "**was healed.**" NAB translates "Immediately the man's leprosy disappeared." This can also be expressed as "the man was cured" or "the man was cured of his leprosy (or, his disease)." Certainly in very few languages will one speak of the disease being cleansed or healed. Almost always it is better to say the man was healed of the disease.

8.4	RSV	TEV
	And Jesus said to him, "See that you say nothing to any one; but go, show yourself to the priest, and offer the gift that Moses commanded, for a proof to the people." [r]	Then Jesus said to him, "Listen! Don't tell anyone, but go straight to the priest and let him examine you; then in order to prove to everyone that you are cured, offer the sacrifice that Moses ordered."

[r] Greek *to them*

The function of this verse is not to confirm the miracle, but to present Jesus as an Israelite faithful to the Law. It also shows that Jesus wants the man to be fully accepted in the community.

Mark's Gospel contains frequent commands to silence, but most of them are omitted by Matthew. However, a few are retained (see 9.30; 12.16; 16.20; 17.9).

See that you say nothing to any one can be expressed "Make sure you don't talk about this to anyone," "Don't say anything about this," or "Don't let people know what happened." TEV further emphasizes the imperative with "**Listen!**" Translators can also say "Pay attention now" or "Look, I'm telling you."

Priest is often translated "sacrificer," "sacrificer to God (for the people)," or "the one who goes before God for the people." **The priest** would have been the one on duty in the Jerusalem Temple; only there could the purification ceremony have taken place (see Leviticus 14.1-32).

Jesus tells the man **show yourself**. This does not mean simply that he should let the priest see him or look at him, but rather that he should let the priest examine him. Thus it can be expressed "Go to the priest so he can examine you" or "Go have the priest examine you." It may be necessary to add "so he can see you are cured." Note that these examples combine **go** and **show** into one imperative.

According to Leviticus 14.1-7, **the gift that Moses commanded** consisted of two birds. One of the birds was killed during the ceremony; the other was released. Here **offer the gift** means "to make (or, offer) the sacrifice."

Moses refers to the Law of Moses or the book Moses wrote, so that the translation can be "as the Law of Moses commands" or "that the book of Moses says you should." It may be necessary to add "when you are cured of this disease."

For a proof to the people, a noun phrase consisting of three words in Greek, is translated more fully by TEV: **"then in order to prove to everyone that you are cured."** The basic problem of interpretation relates to the words **to the people**, which is literally "to them," as the RSV footnote indicates. It may refer to the people in general (TEV, RSV), to Jesus' critics, or to the priests. Both NEB ("that will certify the cure") and NAB ("That should be the proof they need") retain the ambiguity.

The ambiguity can also be retained with a phrase like "that will prove you are cured." However, in many languages it is necessary to say before whom the proof is offered, so that translators say "to prove to people" or "as evidence to all."

Note that it is the sacrifice that is the proof, not the examination by the priest. TEV expresses this relationship with the phrase **"in order to prove."** Another way is "this will prove" or "doing this will prove."

8.5-13

RSV   TEV

Jesus Heals a Roman Officer's Servant

5 As he entered Capernaum, a centurion came forward to him, beseeching him 6 and saying, "Lord, my servant is lying paralyzed at home, in terrible distress." 7 And he said to him, "I will come and heal him." 8 But the centurion answered him, "Lord, I am not worthy to have you come under my roof; but only say the word, and my servant will be healed. 9 For I am a man under authority, with soldiers under me; and I say to one, 'Go,' and he goes, and to another, 'Come,' and he comes, and to my slave, 'Do this,' and he does it." 10 When Jesus heard him, he marveled, and said to those who followed him, "Truly, I say to you, not even^s in Israel have I found such faith. 11 I tell you, many will come from east and west and sit at table with Abraham, Isaac, and Jacob in the kingdom of heaven, 12 while the sons of the

5 When Jesus entered Capernaum, a Roman officer met him and begged for help: 6 "Sir, my servant is sick in bed at home, unable to move and suffering terribly."

7 "I will go and make him well," Jesus said.

8 "Oh no, sir," answered the officer. "I do not deserve to have you come into my house. Just give the order, and my servant will get well. 9 I, too, am a man under the authority of superior officers, and I have soldiers under me. I order this one, 'Go!' and he goes; and I order that one, 'Come!' and he comes; and I order my slave, 'Do this!' and he does it."

10 When Jesus heard this, he was surprised and said to the people following him, "I tell you, I have never found anyone in Israel with faith like this. 11 I assure you that many will come from the

kingdom will be thrown into the outer darkness; there men will weep and gnash their teeth." 13 And to the centurion Jesus said, "Go; be it done for you as you have believed." And the servant was healed at that very moment.

s Other ancient authorities read *with no one*

east and the west and sit down with Abraham, Isaac, and Jacob at the feast in the Kingdom of heaven. 12 But those who should be in the Kingdom will be thrown out into the darkness, where they will cry and gnash their teeth." 13 Then Jesus said to the officer, "Go home, and what you believe will be done for you."

And the officer's servant was healed that very moment.

SECTION HEADING: **"Jesus Heals a Roman Officer's Servant."** The translation of this heading depends on how **"Roman Officer"** or <u>centurion</u> in verse 5 and **servant** in verse 6 are translated.

Luke 7.1-10 contains a parallel to this healing miracle, and there is almost a word-for-word agreement between Matthew 8.9-10 and Luke 7.8-9. But Luke 7.7a contains a remark of the Roman officer not recorded by Matthew (TEV "Neither do I consider myself worthy to come to you in person"). And the remainder of the narrative is also very different, except for the term used of the Roman officer and the mention of Capernaum. In general scholars agree that the major emphasis in the narrative is not on Jesus' power to heal, but on the way that a Gentile (a Roman military officer) comes to believe in Jesus and is praised by Jesus because of his faith.

<u>8.5</u> RSV	TEV

As he entered Capernaum, a centurion came forward to him, beseeching him	When Jesus entered Capernaum, a Roman officer met him and begged for help:

As he entered Capernaum: since this is a new section, TEV replaces the pronoun **he** of the Greek text with the noun **"Jesus."** This is the second mention of **Capernaum** in the Gospel; the town is first mentioned in 4.13. The name Capernaum literally means "village of Nahum," and it lies on the northwest coast of Lake Galilee near the northeast edge of the plain of Gennesaret. Translations usually retain the name **Capernaum** and do not translate it as "village of Nahum." As with many geographical places with which modern readers are not familiar, translators sometimes use a generic term with the name, as in "town of Capernaum."

The phrase **As he entered** presupposes some movement on the part of Jesus since the previous section. This does not always need to be mentioned, but in some languages the narrative will sound very awkward unless there is some phrase such as "Jesus went to Capernaum. As he entered the town . . ." or "Jesus traveled on. When he entered Capernaum . . . ."

Centurion is the traditional rendering of most English translations, but it is translated **"Roman officer"** by TEV. In the Roman army a man of this rank commanded one hundred men, and so the origin of the term **centurion**, which derives from a Latin noun meaning "one hundred." The man was probably a Gentile from Syria serving in the Roman army. Centurions were career soldiers, and as such they were often the most experienced and most highly regarded men in the Roman army. This centurion was probably stationed in Palestine for the sake of police duty. The Romans would not have allowed the governor of Galilee (Herod Antipas at this time) to maintain a Jewish army. Outside of this story the noun is used in Matthew's Gospel only in 27.54.

Centurion can be translated as "a Roman Officer," "officer of the Roman Army," "a man over one hundred Roman soldiers," or "a leader of a group in the Roman Army."

Came forward translates a verb used 51 times by Matthew; it is in fact the same verb translated "came" by RSV in verse 2. The problem with **"met** (him)**"** of TEV is that the reader may be left with the impression that this is a chance meeting. It is not; the officer intentionally approaches Jesus. Thus it can be translated as "came to meet" or "approached him."

Beseeching is translated **"begged for help"** by TEV. NEB renders "to ask his help," and NJB "pleaded with him." The verb itself may be used in a wide variety of contexts and so have a number of different meanings. Most frequently in Matthew it means either "beg," "request" (8.31,34; 14.36; 18.29), or "request help" (26.53). It can also be expressed as "he asked for his help" or "he made an earnest request."

8.6	RSV	TEV

and saying, "Lord, my servant is lying paralyzed at home, in terrible distress."	**"Sir, my servant is sick in bed at home, unable to move and suffering terribly."**

Lord is the same noun of address used in verse 2. Although the term may mean Lord, in the present context it may best be understood as a noun of polite address (TEV "Sir"). See comments at verse 2.

Servant (NAB "serving boy") may mean either "servant" or "boy" (that is, "son"). The Lukan parallel initially has a word which specifically means "servant" (7.2), though in Luke 7.7 a shift is made to the same word which Matthew uses here. The only place in the New Testament where the word clearly means "son" is John 4.51. The plural form is used in Matthew 21.15, where it included both male and female children. The plural form is also used in 2.16, but there it may mean either "boys" or "children." Here the word is probably used of the Roman officer's orderly, which seems to be the understanding reflected in GECL 1st edition. Hence the translation can either be "my servant" or "the man who serves me."

Lying paralyzed at home. TEV, GECL 1st edition, and DUCL further identify the place where his is **lying . . . at home** as **"in bed."** The Greek text does not specify the nature of the paralysis, and it is best to select a very general term such as **"unable to move"** (TEV).

As in TEV, it is probably good to indicate that he is paralyzed because of some illness, as in "he is sick and unable to move at all" or "he has an illness which makes him so he can't move. He is lying in bed at home."

In terrible distress translates an adverb, **terrible**, plus a participle, **in . . . distress**; the verb form for **distress** is used in verse 29, where it is translated "to torment." See also 14.24.

In terrible distress can be translated "he is suffering greatly," "he is in great pain," or "the pain is causing him great suffering."

8.7   RSV   TEV

And he said to him, "I will come and   **"I will go and make him well,"**
heal him."   **Jesus said.**

And he said to him: for stylistic reasons TEV identifies **he** as Jesus and transfers "**Jesus said**" to the end of the verse, though it comes first in the Greek sentence. However, in many languages (for example, most languages in Africa) it will be more natural to keep "Jesus said to him" at the beginning of the sentence.

The pronoun **I** is emphatic in Greek. The original Greek manuscripts did not have any punctuation, and it is possible to take **I will come and heal him** as a question: "Am I to come and cure him?" (NEB alternative rendering). Although a question is possible, most translations prefer a statement and do not even include a question as a possible alternative. Whether one translates as a statement or as a question, the main point of Jesus' response is that he is willing to associate with a Gentile.

Whether to use **come** or "**go**" will depend on the language. There may also be need for a destination, as in "I will come to your house" or "I will go there." Also possible is "I will go with you."

Heal can also be "cure" or "make well."

8.8   RSV   TEV

But the centurion answered him,   **"Oh no, sir," answered the**
"Lord, I am not worthy to have you   **officer. "I do not deserve to have**
come under my roof; but only say   **you come into my house. Just give**
the word, and my servant will be   **the order, and my servant will get**
healed.   **well.**

RSV here follows the word order of the Greek text, which TEV has somewhat rearranged for the sake of English style. Compare the two.

Lord is the same noun of address used in verses 2 and 6. As in verse 6, the polite form of address is to be preferred.

I am not worthy can be expressed as "I am not good enough," "I am not important enough," or, as in TEV, "I don't deserve." It may also be possible to say "you are too important to come into my house."

Under my roof represents an idiomatic expression which TEV translates "**into my house**." Many languages will have their own idiomatic ways of saying this same thing.

But only say the word. In the context **word** clearly means an order; NAB "Just give an order"; TEV "**Just give the order**." Other ways can be "Just say it shall be done" or "Just say for him to be healed."

The servant **will be healed**, that is, "he will become well" or "he will be well again."

Some ancient manuscripts omit the words **my servant** from the text, but translationally some subject must be given for the verb. In Greek, of course, the third person ("he" or "she") is automatically indicated by the verb ending. However, for English speakers either a noun or a pronoun must be included.

8.9 RSV	TEV
For I am a man under authority, with soldiers under me; and I say to one, 'Go,' and he goes, and to another, 'Come,' and he comes, and to my slave, 'Do this,' and he does it."	**I, too, am a man under the authority of superior officers, and I have soldiers under me. I order this one, 'Go!' and he goes; and I order that one, 'Come!' and he comes; and I order my slave, 'Do this!' and he does it."**

In Greek the pronoun **I** is in emphatic position. This is why TEV has "**I, too.**"

For I am a man under authority with soldiers under me reflects the compact style of the Greek. It is possible, as some scholars suggest, that the terseness of the officer's reply derives from his military background. For most readers of English it may be better to fill in the "blanks" with the words that are presupposed though not expressly stated. Compare TEV, for example, where several words are included that are not found in the Greek text:

> "**I, too, am a man under [the] authority [of superior officers], [and I] have soldiers under me.**"

To express the idea of being under the authority of superior officers, translators can say "I have leaders who can order me" or "I, too, have people who are bigger (or, more important) than I and who can tell me what I have to do."

To have **soldiers under me** can then be "and there are soldiers who have to obey my orders" or "there are soldiers who do what I command."

There are languages that will find the direct speech "Go" and "Come" very natural, but in other cases it will prove better to use indirect speech, as in "I tell one soldier to go, and he goes, and I say to another that he should come, and he comes. In the same way, if I tell my slave to do something, he does it."

Slave does not translate the same word rendered "servant" in verses 6 and 8. This Greek word normally means "slave" in the sense of a servant who is the property of the master. The question is whether or not it refers to the same person mentioned in verse 6. Most translations apparently differentiate between the two, though GECL and NJB translate by the same word in both verses. The word in verse 2 is more nearly a term of endearment than is this word, and it is valid to conclude that the word is used here solely as an illustration and without specific reference to any particular individual, as are **one** and **another**.

It may be necessary to say "a slave" or "one of my slaves" to indicate that the centurion is speaking in general terms.

　　　　RSV　　　　　　　　　　　　TEV

When Jesus heard him, he marveled, and said to those who followed him, "Truly, I say to you, not even*s* in Israel have I found such faith.	When Jesus heard this, he was surprised and said to the people following him, "I tell you, I have never found anyone in Israel with faith like this.

s Other ancient authorities read *with no one*

RSV has **heard him** and TEV "**heard this.**" It can also be "heard what the centurion said" or "heard these words."

Marveled is used of Jesus only here and in Mark 6.6. In the Marcan context it occurs as a negative reaction of Jesus toward the lack of faith on the part of the Jews; here, of course, the reaction is positive because of the faith of the Gentile soldier. This same verb appears elsewhere in Matthew in 8.27; 9.33; 15.31; 21.20; 22.22; 27.14.

To say Jesus **marveled** translators can use expressions such as "was surprised," ". . . astonished," or ". . . amazed." It is possible to tie the first two clauses of the sentence more closely together, as in "Jesus was amazed to hear what he said" or "Jesus was really surprised to hear this."

Those who followed him is probably a reference to the "great crowds" of 8.1. It may need to be expressed as "those people who were following him."

Truly, I say to you: this formula serves to make emphatic the words of Jesus which follow. See comment at 5.18. Here it may be "Believe me" or "It is the truth, I tell you."

Not even in Israel have I found such faith represents the words of some Greek manuscripts which TC-GNT believes to be influenced by the parallel in Luke 7.9. The UBS Greek New Testament supports the Greek text translated in the RSV footnote: "with no one in Israel have I found such faith" ("B" decision, signifying some degree of doubt). TEV, with slight restructuring, follows the UBS Greek text, "**I have never found anyone in Israel with faith like this.**" NEB adopts the same text as RSV and translates "Nowhere, even in Israel, have I found such faith." NAB apparently follows the same Greek text as RSV, though the translators seem to move in the direction of a compromise rendering, "I have never found this much faith in Israel."

Such faith obviously means "a person who has such faith as this" or "a person who trusts in God so much." In fact it is precisely because of this that most translators will translate the RSV and the UBS Greek text in the same way. Even if one follows RSV, it is unusual to speak of "such faith" by itself. "A person with faith like that" will generally be more natural. **Such faith** can refer to quantity, as in "who trusts God so much," or to manner, as in "who trusts in this way," although the two obviously overlap a great deal in this context. Another expression can be "who has such strong faith."

The phrase **even in Israel** indicates that normally Jesus would expect to find stronger faith among the Jews than among outsiders. This idea may be conveyed by a phrase like that in NEB cited above, or "I have never found anyone, not even one of the Jews, with faith like this."

8.11   RSV   TEV

I tell you, many will come from east and west and sit at table with Abraham, Isaac, and Jacob in the kingdom of heaven,	I assure you that many will come from the east and the west and sit down with Abraham, Isaac, and Jacob at the feast in the Kingdom of heaven.

I tell you is similar in form and function to "Truly, I say to you" of verse 10. It both adds emphasis and serves as a transitional. The phrase can be translated as "Let me tell you" or "Let me assure you." Jesus is still talking to the followers who are with him.

The **many** who **will come from east and west** are Gentile believers. In translation it may be necessary to say "many others who trust in God as this man does."

East and west are not to be taken merely as references to opposing geographical directions; the meaning is rather "from all over the world" or "from everywhere."

Sit at table (used again in 14.19) translates one word in the Greek text. The reference is to the coming Messianic feast, which is symbolic of the joys to be experienced **in the kingdom of heaven** (see 22.1-14; 25.10). It may be necessary to indicate that the reason these people will **sit at table** is to eat. TEV has indicated this with "**at the feast**." Other translations may have "sit to eat" or "come to feast (or, eat) with."

Many readers will not know who **Abraham, Isaac, and Jacob** were. It may be necessary to say "our great ancestors, Abraham, Isaac, and Jacob."

Kingdom of heaven was discussed in 3.2 and in chapter 5, and should probably be translated in a similar way here, perhaps as "when God establishes his rule."

GECL 1st edition renders the entire verse: "But this is the way it will be when God has completed his work: many will come from the east and the west to sit at the table with Abraham, Isaac, and Jacob." INCL renders "Many people will come from the east and west in order to rejoice together with Abraham, Isaac, and Jacob in God's New World." Another possibility is "Many people will come from all over the world to share in the feast with our great ancestors Abraham, Isaac, and Jacob when God begins his rule."

8.12   RSV   TEV

while the sons of the kingdom will be thrown into the outer darkness; there men will weep and gnash their teeth."	But those who should be in the Kingdom will be thrown out into the darkness, where they will cry and gnash their teeth."

Sons of the kingdom is a Semitic idiom meaning "people (here, the Jewish people) who belong to the kingdom." In 9.15 "sons of the bridechamber" means wedding guests, and the Jews could also speak of "sons of the city," "sons of the coming age," and "a son of the Law." GECL 1st edition translates **sons of the**

kingdom by "people who actually were appointed for God's New World." INCL renders "people who were supposed to have been God's people"; MACL has "people who were supposed to enjoy the blessings of God's rule"; and Brc has "those who were born to be members of the Kingdom." Translators will find all of these useful models.

In place of the passive for **will be thrown into**, some Greek manuscripts have the active form, "will go into." TC-GNT believes that the evidence favors the passive, and most all modern translations apparently accept this reading. NEB translates "will be driven out" (so also NAB), while JB renders "will be turned out." For those languages that do not normally use a passive construction, an agent must be supplied, as in "God will throw them" or "God will have his angels throw them."

The outer darkness is also used elsewhere by Matthew as a description of the doom that awaits people who reject God (22.13; 25.30). The figure of crying and gnashing teeth appears in conjunction with **the outer darkness** in 25.30 and is used without the figure of darkness in 24.51. Luke 13.28-29 is a parallel to verses 11-12, only in reverse order.

The outer darkness, obviously a reference to hell, represents what it is like where God is not found. Translators should try to retain this image, saying "the dark world where God is not (or, does not go)" or "the dark place away from God's rule." Some have said "the great dark place of hell." "Dark" or "darkness" may have to be rendered as "black" or "place with no light."

Men means people, not just males.

Gnash their teeth is a favorite Matthean formula; see 13.42,50; 22.13; 24.51; 25.30. Elsewhere it occurs only in Luke 13.28. It means to grind or strike the teeth together in rage or pain. It may be necessary to add "in great pain" to the phrase **gnash their teeth** if this expression is not known.

8.13   RSV   TEV

And to the centurion Jesus said,   Then Jesus said to the officer, "Go
"Go; be it done for you as you have   home, and what you believe will be
believed." And the servant was   done for you."
healed at that very moment.   And the officer's servant was
                                                          healed that very moment.

The sentence **And to the centurion Jesus said** is in a word order not possible in many languages. It serves to show that Jesus is now addressing the centurion and no longer the disciples around him. This may be shown clearly in sentences such as "Then Jesus turned to the Roman officer and said" or "Then Jesus spoke to the centurion. He said."

Go is translated "**Go home**" by TEV. Several translations render with the same meaning as TEV (NEB, NAB, GECL), though others are less specific: "Go back, then . . ." (NJB).

Be it done for you as you have believed: the Greek particle rendered **as** may either be comparative or causative. RSV is ambiguous, but NEB ("because of your faith") and NAB ("because you trusted") are explicitly causative. AT apparently believes the particle to be comparative: "you shall find it just as you believe!" The context seems to favor the causative force, and in some languages it may be necessary to be more explicit: "God will heal your servant because you believed that he would heal him" or "You believed that God would heal your servant, and so he will do it for you."

Be it done for you is another passive construction, but at the same time it expresses an imperative. If an agent has to be supplied, it should be "God," as in "May God do what you asked for." When combined with the causative **as** that we discussed above, the translation can be "Because you have believed God could heal your servant, may he do so" or "God will heal your servant, as I have asked, because you believed he would."

The servant is identified by TEV as **"the officer's servant."** **Servant** is the same noun used in verse 6.

At that very moment is literally "in that hour." But "hour" is here used idiomatically, and several translations have **"moment"** (TEV, NJB, NEB). Matthew elsewhere employs this expression in 10.19; 18.1; 26.55; Mark (13.11) and Luke (7.21) use it but once each.

Was healed is another passive that may need to be rendered as an active. It can be "And the servant got better at that very moment." It is also possible to have an agent, God, as in "And God healed that servant right then."

8.14-17

RSV	TEV
	Jesus Heals Many People
14 And when Jesus entered Peter's house, he saw his mother-in-law lying sick with a fever; 15 he touched her hand, and the fever left her, and she rose and served him. 16 That evening they brought to him many who were possessed with demons; and he cast out the spirits with a word, and healed all who were sick. 17 This was to fulfil what was spoken by the prophet Isaiah, "He took our infirmities and bore our diseases."	14 Jesus went to Peter's home, and there he saw Peter's mother-in-law sick in bed with a fever. 15 He touched her hand; the fever left her, and she got up and began to wait on him. 16 When evening came, people brought to Jesus many who had demons in them. Jesus drove out the evil spirits with a word and healed all who were sick. 17 He did this to make come true what the prophet Isaiah had said, "He himself took our sickness and carried away our diseases."

SECTION HEADING: **"Jesus Heals Many People."** In some languages this may have to be "Jesus heals many people of their diseases."

According to the context of Mark (1.29-34) and Luke (4.38-41), this scene took place on a Sabbath, immediately after Jesus had healed a man with an evil spirit. Matthew's account is much shorter than either that of Mark or Luke.

8.14 RSV	TEV
And when Jesus entered Peter's house, he saw his mother-in-law lying sick with a fever;	**Jesus went to Peter's home, and there he saw Peter's mother-in-law sick in bed with a fever.**

And when Jesus entered Peter's house is translated "**Jesus went to Peter's home**" by TEV. The most noticeable difference is that RSV uses a temporal clause, while TEV does not. The basis for this difference is the Greek verb form, which is a participle and may be rendered as either an independent ("**Jesus went**") or dependent (**when Jesus entered**) clause. NEB has "Jesus then went to Peter's house . . ."; NAB "Jesus entered Peter's house." NJB maintains the participial form of the Greek text: "And going into Peter's house . . . ." All of these different renderings are merely stylistic variations and do not represent any difference of exegesis.

The stylistic variations are important, however, in languages that do require some sort of transition. Such languages may have to say "Then Jesus went to Peter's house," or "Jesus went to Peter's house. When he went in . . . ."

In both Mark (1.29) and Luke (4.38) Peter is referred to by the name "Simon." But even more significant than the difference in names is the observation that in Matthew it is Jesus himself who takes the initiative in healing Simon's mother-in-law: **he saw his** (that is, Peter's) **mother-in-law lying sick with a fever**. In the Mark and Luke accounts, the people had to call Jesus' attention to the sick woman. Here, however, it is said that Jesus saw her and then took the initiative to heal her.

Saw may need to be translated "found," but the sentence should still reflect that Jesus was the one taking the initiative.

The **mother-in-law** is Peter's, as we indicated above. Translators must make sure it does not appear the woman is Jesus' mother-in-law. **Mother-in-law** is the meaning of the Greek word used here; there is no other meaning to the word, and all translations render it in this way. In 1 Corinthians 9.5 Peter's wife is mentioned.

Lying sick (TEV "**sick in bed**") translates the same participial form used in 9.2. The participle literally means "having been thrown down" or "lying." Here it is used without specification of the place where Peter's mother-in-law was lying, but the obvious conclusion is that she was lying on a bed. In 9.2 the place is specifically indicated as being on a bed. NEB renders "in bed with fever."

There has been some speculation regarding the nature of the **fever**, but the Greek text gives no hints, and the translation should not specify the nature of the fever.

There will be many quite natural ways to express **lying sick with a fever**. One can say "lying in bed with a fever" or "lying in bed because she had a fever."

8.15	RSV	TEV

he touched her hand, and the fever left her, and she rose and served him.	He touched her hand; the fever left her, and she got up and began to wait on him.

He touched her hand: the Greek verb may mean either **touched** or "took hold of" (NAB "He took her by the hand"). Mark specifically states that Jesus took hold of her hand and raised her up (1.31), information that is not included by Matthew. Here in Matthew the verse can be translated "He grasped (or, held) her hand," "He took hold of her hand," or simply "He touched her hand." There is no reason to specify which hand. The translators who cannot say "her hand" can always say "one of her hands."

As an immediate result of Jesus' touching her hand, **the fever left her, and she rose up and served him**. Although the Greek does not have the adverb "at once" (NAB), the implication is that she got up immediately. Some translations have said "the fever left her then."

Rose means that she "got up" or "got out of bed."

Served may also be translated so as to focus upon the initiation of the action, as in TEV, NJB, and NAB (**"and began to wait on"**). NEB has "and waited on . . . ." **Served** means here "waited on," "took care of his needs," or even "served him food and drink."

Matthew supplies **him** as the object of the verb **served**, but Mark gives "them" as its object. It is not legitimate to translate Matthew in light of Mark, and to give "them" as the object of the verb here, as does the Living Bible (LB).

8.16 RSV	TEV
That evening they brought to him many who were possessed with demons; and he cast out the spirits with a word, and healed all who were sick.	When evening came, people brought to Jesus many who had demons in them. Jesus drove out the evil spirits with a word and healed all who were sick.

Evening marks the beginning of a new day for the Jewish people. In the context of the story in Mark's Gospel, it serves the function of bringing the Sabbath to a close. Matthew does not indicate that it was a Sabbath on which Jesus performed these healings. Translators can use either RSV or TEV as a model, or put "In the evening" as long as it meant that evening, not just any evening in general. It can also possibly be "After sunset."

They brought is translated **"people brought"** in TEV. Since no antecedent is indicated in the context, it is more natural in English to use a noun (**"people"**) than a pronoun (**they**). GECL makes a similar alteration, employing a singular form ("one brought") which is the natural German idiom for such a context. Some languages will need "Some people brought."

Similarly, **many** may be "many people."

Possessed with demons translates a Greek participle. The meaning is "under the power of demons." NEB and NJB translate "who were possessed by devils." **Possessed with demons** should be translated in exactly the same way as the phrase in 4.24. **Demons** and **"evil spirits"** are generally translated in the same way. And "possessed by," "under the power of," or "had" are all ways of referring to the one phenomenon of spirit possession.

Cast out is the same verb used of the casting out of demons in 7.22; in its passive form it is used in 8.12, where RSV translates "will be thrown."

Spirits are qualified by TEV as **"evil spirits."** These are the same beings referred to earlier in the verse as **demons**, and it is important that the reader recognize this. GECL renders "As evening came, they brought Jesus many people who were possessed. Through the power of his word he cast out the evil spirits . . . ."

With a word is translated "through the power of his word" by GECL (see above paragraph). Other ways to handle this would be "threw out the evil spirits by commanding them (to go)," "he commanded the spirits to leave and they did," or "he threw the spirits out by telling them, 'Go out.' "

In the ancient world illnesses were frequently attributed to the power of demons and evil spirits. But the people **who were sick** are here distinguished from those who were possessed by demons. Most translations are careful to mark them out as two separate and distinct groups.

8.17   RSV   TEV

This was to fulfil what was spoken by the prophet Isaiah, "He took our infirmities and bore our diseases."

He did this to make come true what the prophet Isaiah had said, "He himself took our sickness and carried away our diseases."

Matthew discovers the significance of Jesus' healing ministry in the words of Isaiah 53.4. Both Mark (1.34) and Luke (4.41) give a different conclusion to this short narrative.

This was to fulfill what was spoken by the prophet Isaiah is essentially the same introductory formula used by Matthew in 4.14. GECL renders "In this way he did what the prophet Isaiah had said would happen."

This refers, of course, to casting out spirits and healing people. Some translations can follow TEV, **"He did this."** Others will say "He cured people like that because . . ." or "He did these things for people so that . . . ."

For suggestions on the rest of the formula, **what was . . . Isaiah**, see 1.22; 4.14.

He took our infirmities and bore our diseases comes from Isaiah 53.4 and is based on the Hebrew text. This is the only place in the Gospels where there exists an explicit reference to Isaiah 53, and it is noteworthy that it appears in relation to Jesus' acts of healing rather than to his suffering and exaltation. The Septuagint translators of Isaiah spiritualized the passage by making it refer to sin and hardship. Matthew's concern, however, is to relate it solely to the healing activity of Jesus. The two clauses are essentially synonymous: **took** and **bore** are parallel to one another, as are **infirmities** and **diseases**. Therefore GECL can translate "He has taken from us our sickness and our suffering." **Infirmities** derives from a root which means "weakness," but the noun is frequently used in the sense of sickness or disease. This is its only occurrence in the Gospel. The word translated **diseases** refers specifically to diseases or illnesses; it was first used in 4.23,24 ("disease"), and see also 9.35; 10.1.

Both **took** and **bore** signify here "carried away" or "took away," for purpose of removal, not merely "took upon himself." Translators can even say "freed us from."

Some translators will keep the parallelism of the text, as in "He freed us from our sickness and carried away our diseases." Others, however, will find it easier to collapse this into one line, as in "He took away all our diseases" or "He freed us from all sickness."

235

8.18-22

RSV	TEV
	The Would-be Followers of Jesus
18 Now when Jesus saw great crowds around him, he gave orders to go over to the other side. 19 And a scribe came up and said to him, "Teacher, I will follow you wherever you go." 20 And Jesus said to him, "Foxes have holes, and birds of the air have nests; but the Son of man has nowhere to lay his head." 21 Another of the disciples said to him, "Lord, let me first go and bury my father." 22 But Jesus said to him, "Follow me, and leave the dead to bury their own dead."	18 When Jesus noticed the crowd around him, he ordered his disciples to go to the other side of the lake. 19 A teacher of the Law came to him. "Teacher," he said, "I am ready to go with you wherever you go." 20 Jesus answered him, "Foxes have holes, and birds have nests, but the Son of Man has no place to lie down and rest." 21 Another man, who was a disciple, said, "Sir, first let me go back and bury my father." 22 "Follow me," Jesus answered, "and let the dead bury their own dead."

SECTION HEADING: "**The Would-be Followers of Jesus.**" This title may cause problems in some languages. Some have said "People who said they would follow Jesus, but didn't," or possibly "People (or, Two people) who said they would follow Jesus."

The Lukan parallel (9.57-62) is not found until the close of Jesus' Galilean ministry, as he prepares for the journey to Jerusalem. Luke mentions in addition a third would-be disciple (9.61-62). It is generally agreed among scholars that the verb "follow" here takes on the extended meaning of "become a follower" (see verses 19,22).

8.18   RSV   TEV

Now when Jesus saw great crowds around him, he gave orders to go over to the other side.	**When Jesus noticed the crowd around him, he ordered his disciples to go to the other side of the lake.**

The word **Now** indicates the start of a new unit. In some languages, style does not require such a word at all. In others a phrase such as "It happened" is natural, or possibly "On one occasion."

Saw has been translated as "**noticed**" in TEV. Translators should use whichever would be most natural in describing the scene.

In Greek the phrase **great crowds** does not have the definite article before it as in TEV "**the crowd.**" This suggests that the people mentioned in verse 16 may not be the same ones referred to here. But most translations are apparently based on the assumption that **great crowds** does at least include those mentioned earlier, though others would be added to the group as well. GECL seems not to agree with this: "When many people once again gathered around Jesus . . . ."

Another problem of exegesis relates to the verb **gave orders**, which does not have an object in the Greek text. It is quite possible, as some have suggested, that Jesus issued this order to everyone in the crowd, and that only those who obeyed him were really his followers. But the presence of the crowd seems in some way responsible for Jesus' giving the command, and a more logical conclusion is that

Jesus wanted to take his disciples away from the crowd for private instruction. Moreover, verse 23 explicitly states that his disciples got into the boat and went with him. Most translations are ambiguous, but TEV and Brc indicate that the command was given to his disciples.

For these reasons most translators will specify that Jesus **gave orders** "to his disciples" or "to his followers." Some translators will prefer direct speech, as in "He told his disciples 'Let's go to the other side.' " The order "Go to the other side" may make it seem they were to go without him, which would be incorrect.

The other side refers to the eastern shore of Lake Galilee; this construction appears in the Gospel in 8.28; 14.22; 16.5. Most translations will have "the other side of the lake."

8.19	RSV	TEV

RSV	TEV
And a scribe came up and said to him, "Teacher, I will follow you wherever you go."	A teacher of the Law came to him. "Teacher," he said, "I am ready to go with you wherever you go."

<u>Scribe</u>: see comment at 2.4. These men were expert in Jewish religious law. TEV usually translates "**a teacher of the Law.**"

This is the first time in the Gospel where Jesus is addressed as **Teacher**. It is quite natural that someone interested in the detailed interpretation of the Jewish Law should use this noun of address, and it seems strange that GECL should drop it from translation. Elsewhere in Matthew it is used as a noun of address for Jesus in 12.38; 19.16; 22.16,24,36. In 26.18 Jesus refers to himself as "the Teacher" when sending his disciples to prepare for the Passover meal. Some languages do not normally address someone with a title like **Teacher**, but if possible the term should be retained. It was a title of respect.

I will follow you: as stated in the introduction to verses 18-22, **follow** here takes on the extended meaning of "become a follower" or "become a disciple." The man is declaring his willingness to become one of Jesus' disciples, but as the next verse will reveal, he is not prepared to make the full commitment that discipleship involves. As we have pointed out before, it would be incorrect to use a term that merely meant "to follow behind." "Go with" or "accompany" would be better, but "become one of your disciples" or "become one of your people" may be even closer to the intended meaning. Then it will be necessary to add "and I'll go with you wherever you go."

8.20	RSV	TEV

RSV	TEV
And Jesus said to him, "Foxes have holes, and birds of the air have nests; but the Son of man has nowhere to lay his head."	Jesus answered him, "Foxes have holes, and birds have nests, but the Son of Man has no place to lie down and rest."

Foxes have holes, and birds of the air have nests is translated by GECL "The foxes have their holes, and the birds have their nests." The meaning is that wild animals and birds have their homes.

Foxes have holes can pose some problems. In areas where foxes are not known, some other similar animals such as jackals or wild dogs may have to be used. Since Jesus is using "foxes" here only as an example or illustration, this cultural substitution will not have any serious theological significance.

Holes refers to places where foxes live. Other terms can be "burrows" or "lairs." Some translations say simply "holes where they live." Similarly for **nests**, some translators will find it better to say "nests to stay in."

Birds of the air, a Hebraism, is redundant in most languages. In fact, for many languages it would imply the wrong meaning, "birds that can fly" as opposed to "birds that cannot fly." It is therefore better to render it simply as "**birds**."

But the Son of man has no place to lay his head is difficult to interpret. First, there is the problem of the meaning and translation of the phrase **Son of man**. Outside the Gospels it is used only once (Acts 7.56). In the Gospels it is used only by Jesus and as a reference to himself, always speaking of himself in the third person. New Testament scholars are not in agreement regarding the background for the interpretation of the phrase, but at least the following points can be made:

(1) It was sometimes used to refer to one who comes with and experiences divine authority.

(2) The notion of "human being" is not an essential or distinguishing component of this phrase except for its usage in the book of Ezekiel. We are all human beings, but what distinguishes the Son of Man is the authority given him. This is the view one has also in Ethiopic Enoch.

(3) The third person reference in Hebrew and in Aramaic was not as disturbing as it may be in many other languages. Many languages do use third-person reference for first person. In Malay, for example, it is often used of people of some high rank.

(4) Jesus' audience probably understood him to be referring to himself, but in light of the resurrection, the Christian community to whom Matthew and the other Gospel writers may have been writing understood the term as it is used in Daniel 7.13 and in 1 Enoch, that is, the one exalted with power. Exegetical support for the fact that Jesus was seen to be referring to himself may be found in those passages where one Gospel has "the Son of Man" (third person) and another Gospel has the first person singular ("I"). The most obvious example is Matthew 16.13, where Jesus asks, "Who do men say the Son of Man is?" Two verses later Matthew himself clears up any possible misunderstanding on the part of his readers by the additional question, "Who do men say I am?" In the parallel to Matthew 16.13, both Mark (8.27) and Luke (9.18) have the first person ("I").

As far as the translation of the term is concerned, the following guidelines may be beneficial:

(1) Since a literal rendering of **Son of man** is meaningless in a particular language, a dynamic equivalent term should be substituted. Central to the meaning is one who speaks and acts with divine power and authority. Some translations have tried an expression such as "the Man whom God has appointed," or "the Man whom God has chosen," or "the Man whom God has installed." Translators have to be very certain, however, that they do not use the same expression that they have for translating "Messiah."

(2) Many translators have started from the premise that the most important thing about the term is that it is a title, and they then use a formula in their language for titles. For example, many West African translators have used "the One called Son of Man" or "the One who is the Son of Man." Sometimes such an expression will have no meaning; in other cases it will be a common way to refer to a person or to any human being. But often the use of the title formula makes this expression seem to refer to one specific person, and he is somehow "special."

An important benefit from using a title formula is that often using a third-person form is more acceptable than would otherwise be the case. In some languages third person is used with titles for certain important figures such as potentates and kings, so that this title works exceptionally well in places like that.

(3) Obviously from what we have said so far, translators should attempt to find an expression with third person if at all possible, even though it is clear that Jesus was referring to himself. The fact that third person was used when first person could have been used means that in some sense the term was being set off and marked as a title, or to indicate that it was being used in some special way. But there will be languages in which the third-person reference will simply be impossible, and it may be obligatory to use a first-person reference. Even then, however, it is helpful to use this in conjunction with a title formula, as in "I, the one called Son of Man."

Another problem of exegesis concerns the phrase **has nowhere to lay his head**. The problem is that Jesus does seem to have a permanent home in Capernaum (Matt 9.1; Mark 2.1). Of course, the crowds give him no opportunity to rest, and this may also be a reason for his statement. In any case, the majority of translations remain fairly literal.

Lay his head may not be very clear, and translators may either add "and rest" or follow TEV, "**to lie down and rest.**" Another way is "nowhere where he can go and rest."

8.21   RSV   TEV

Another of the disciples said to him, "Lord, let me first go and bury my father."

Another man, who was a disciple, said, "Sir, first let me go back and bury my father."

Another of the disciples (TEV "**Another man, who was a disciple**"): some Greek manuscripts have "of the disciples of his," while others omit the possessive, since the definite article **the** carries the same impact. In many languages the possessive pronoun will be required, as in "another of his disciples." Brc has a rendering similar to TEV's: "Another man, one of his disciples."

Lord: the same problem exists here as in verse 6. Most translations seem to prefer "sir."

Let me go and bury my father: in Judaism the obligation to bury the dead, especially one's parents, has always held a high priority. The High Priest (Lev 21.11-12) and Nazirites (Num 6.6-7) were exempt from this regulation, but only because they were uniquely dedicated to God. Jesus is here indicating that the command to follow him has precedence over all other obligations, even the most binding family responsibilities.

The word **first** is an indication that probably Jesus had just then suggested to the man that he follow him. Some translators may feel that their languages require them to make this explicit by saying "Sir, before I follow you, first let me bury my father."

In many languages, when one speaks of burying him, one also has to mention that the father died, as in "Let me first go and bury my father, who has died" or "My father has died. Let me first go and bury him."

8.22	RSV	TEV

But Jesus said to him, "Follow me, and leave the dead to bury their own dead."

"Follow me," Jesus answered, "and let the dead bury their own dead."

Follow me is a command to discipleship and may be translated "Come and be my disciple." See comments on "follow" in verse 19.

Leave the dead to bury their own dead is best interpreted as a striking image like that of the log in the eye (7.3). One should not spiritualize by translating "Those who refuse to follow me are spiritually dead. Let them stay and bury the dead."

It may not be possible to say simply **the dead** unless they are specified as "dead people." It can be, therefore, "Let those who are dead bury their own dead (people)."

8.23-27

RSV

TEV

Jesus Calms a Storm

23 And when he got into the boat, his disciples followed him. 24 And behold, there arose a great storm on the sea, so that the boat was being swamped by the waves; but he was asleep. 25 And they went and woke him, saying, "Save, Lord; we are perishing." 26 And he said to them, "Why are you afraid, O men of little faith?" Then he rose and rebuked the winds and the sea; and there was a great calm. 27 And the men marveled, saying, "What sort of man is this, that even winds and sea obey him?"

23 Jesus got into a boat, and his disciples went with him. 24 Suddenly a fierce storm hit the lake, and the boat was in danger of sinking. But Jesus was asleep. 25 The disciples went to him and woke him up. "Save us, Lord!" they said. "We are about to die!"

26 "Why are you so frightened?" Jesus answered. "What little faith you have!" Then he got up and ordered the winds and the waves to stop, and there was a great calm.

27 Everyone was amazed. "What kind of man is this?" they said. "Even the winds and the waves obey him!"

SECTION HEADING: "**Jesus Calms a Storm**." This may be expressed as "Jesus makes a storm stop" or "Jesus commands a storm to stop (or, stop blowing)."

This section is parallel to Mark 4.35-41. The command to cross the lake (Mark 4.35) is included earlier by Matthew (8.8). The placement of this narrative in the structure of Matthew differs also from its position in Mark, where it follows Jesus' second stay in Capernaum. According to Matthew it is a further revelation of Jesus' authority; he has taught with authority, healed with authority, and now his authority is shown to extend over the forces of nature.

And when he got into the boat,   Jesus got into a boat, and his
his disciples followed him.   disciples went with him.

And when he got into translates a participial construction similar to "and getting into" of 9.1. Since a new section begins here, several translations identify Jesus as the subject (TEV, NEB, GECL). The **And** which helps mark the beginning of this new section will be unnecessary in many languages. Similarly, the **when** will often be unnatural. TEV has dropped both. Other translations say "At that time, Jesus got into the boat."

In some languages people get in boats, in others they go down to boats or up to them. Whichever way is normal in a language should be used.

The boat: there is a textual problem regarding the inclusion of the definite article **the** before **boat**. The UBS Greek text favors the inclusion of the article (so RSV, NEB, NJB), but it indicates that there exists a considerable degree of doubt regarding the text. Although the textual evidence is against the inclusion of the article, the internal evidence speaks in favor of it (more often than not Matthew uses the definite article before **boat** in his Gospel, and the omission of the article may be accounted for by scribes who followed the parallel in Luke 8.22). In translations such as TEV and GECL, where the article is omitted, it is hard to know whether the decision is based on textual evidence or on the expectations of the receptor languages. The last mention of a boat was in 4.21,22, which is probably not intended by Matthew to be the boat of this chapter. And even if it were, most readers would have forgotten that boat by now. Thus it seems proper to delete the article in an English translation.

Thus the translation will say "a boat." Those translators who want to retain the definite article but at the same time have the translation make sense can say "the boat they had" or "the boat that was there for them," but this would be a little forced.

Matthew specifically identifies Jesus' **disciples** as those who **followed him**. Since the entire narrative is concerned with the meaning of discipleship, the verb "follow" takes on more than a literal significance; it means to follow in the sense of discipleship. However, not all languages will be able to reflect the metaphorical significance.

In some languages, **followed** must have a destination, so translators may have to say "the disciples followed him into the boat" or "went with him in it."

And behold, there arose a great   Suddenly a fierce storm hit the lake,
storm on the sea, so that the boat   and the boat was in danger of sink-

was being swamped by the waves;   ing. But Jesus was asleep.
but he was asleep.

And behold (see comments on 1.20) is translated "**Suddenly**" by TEV. Both
JB and NAB render "Without warning," and NEB has "All at once."

A great storm (so also NEB) is translated "**a fierce storm**" by TEV and "a
violent storm" by NAB; NJB restructures: "a storm broke over the lake, so violent that
. . . ." The word rendered **storm** may also mean "earthquake," as it does in all of its
other occurrences in the New Testament (24.7; 27.54; 28.2; Mark 13.8; Luke 21.11;
Acts 16.26; Rev 6.12; 8.5; 11.13,19; 16.18), but of course in this context it can only
mean **storm**.

Arose . . . on (TEV "**hit**") is more literally "happened in (or, on)." The
meaning may be represented translationally in a number of ways; for example "broke
over" (NJB) and "blew up on" (Brc). Other ways are "came up on," "started to
blow," or "came suddenly."

Sea has usually been translated as "**lake**." See comments on 4.18.

So that the boat was being swamped by the waves appears in TEV as "**and
the boat was in danger of sinking**." Each language offers a variety of idiomatic
possibilities. Note "and the boat began to be swamped by the waves" (NAB) and "till
the waves were breaking right over the boat" (NEB; JB is similar).

Some translators begin a new sentence here: "The storm was so big that waves
were splashing into the boat" or ". . . were filling the boat with water," or ". . . so
that the waves were making the boat be close to sinking."

He of the Greek text is translated "**Jesus**" by TEV. But here again the choice
of a noun or pronoun is dependent upon the requirements of the receptor language
(NAB: "Jesus was sleeping soundly . . .").

8.25   RSV   TEV

And they went and woke him, saying, "Save, Lord; we are perishing."	The disciples went to him and woke him up. "Save us, Lord!" they said. "We are about to die!"

In some Greek manuscripts **they** is either "the disciples" or "his disciples."
However, regardless of one's evaluation of the manuscript evidence, many languages
will require either "the disciples," "his disciples," or even "Jesus' disciples."

In Greek **went** is a participle, dependent upon the main verb **woke**. However,
a number of translations render both verbs as finite forms in a parallel structure as
both RSV and TEV have done. Here again the choice of restructuring is dependent
purely upon the requirements of the receptor language. Those translations that do
not follow RSV in this will probably say "His disciples woke him up." Note that some
languages will use "came" instead of **went**.

They did not wake him by saying "Save us, Lord," which is the impression some
translators have received from the participle **saying**. A better rendering is "They
woke him and said, 'Save us, Lord.' "

In the better Greek manuscripts **save** does not have an expressed object (TEV
"**us**"). Since RSV slavishly omits the object, even though one is required by English

structure, one wonders why the translators did not follow the order of the Greek ("Lord, save").

Lord here should be taken in the Christian sense (see comments on verse 2).

For **save**, translators should use a term that is most natural in this context, such as "rescue," "deliver," or something similar. Most will use the object "us" as TEV has done.

The choice of an inclusive or exclusive **we** is not easy. This is a question which in all probability would not have arisen in the mind of Matthew, since neither Greek nor Aramaic requires the choice between these two forms. If a choice must be made, it seems best to use the inclusive form. This is not to deny the deity of Jesus, but it is to assume that at this point in Jesus' ministry the disciples did not fully recognize who Jesus was and so would have assumed that he also could have drowned.

We are perishing (Brc "we're drowning") translates a Greek verb tense which suggests action in progress. It may also be expressed "**we are about to die**" (TEV) or "we are going down" (JB). **Perishing** may refer to the destruction of either living beings or inanimate objects. When used of people it means "die," with the kind of death determined by the context. Here, of course, the form of death is drowning. GECL translates the plea of the disciples, "Rescue us, Lord, we are going under!" Some more examples are "we are drowning," "we are about to die," and "we are going to drown."

8.26	RSV	TEV
	And he said to them, "Why are you afraid, O men of little faith?" Then he rose and rebuked the winds and the sea; and there was a great calm.	"Why are you so frightened?" Jesus answered. "What little faith you have!" Then he got up and ordered the winds and the waves to stop, and there was a great calm.

And he said to them refers to Jesus, and it will be necessary in some languages to be specific (TEV "**Jesus answered**").

The sequence of events in Matthew differs from that of Mark (4.39-40) and Luke (8.24-25). According to Matthew, Jesus first rebukes the disciples and then he orders the storm to stop, which is a reversal of the order of events in Mark and Luke. Similarly, in 14.31-32 Jesus rebukes Peter for his lack of faith before the storm stops.

Why are you afraid? (TEV, NJB ". . . so frightened?") is translated "Why are you such cowards?" by NEB. This is a rhetorical question which expects no answer but implies "There is no reason for you to be afraid!" The adjective translated **afraid** is a very strong word, occurring elsewhere in the New Testament only in Mark 4.40 and Revelation 21.8 (TEV "cowards"). Thus it can be translated here as "scared," "terrified," or "fearful." In some languages the strength of the word is seen better in a construction like "You are really terrified. Why is that?" or ". . . There is no reason for that!"

Men of little faith translates one word in the Greek text. It is used by Matthew also in 6.30; 8.26; 14.31; 16.8, but elsewhere in the New Testament only in Luke 12.28. A related noun is used in Matthew 17.20. See 6.30 for a discussion of **men of**

little faith. Here the rebuke is very strong, as in "Your faith is so little," "You don't trust very much in God," "Don't you have any trust in God?" or "Your trust in God is so little. Is that good?"

Rose means "got up," or possibly even "stood up."

Rebuked (so NJB, NEB) is the basic meaning of the Greek verb, but it may even mean "warn" or "threaten" (GECL). NAB has "took . . . to task," and TEV **"ordered . . . to stop."** It is obvious from these examples that **rebuked** can be translated with either of two emphases. The stronger, more usual understanding requires a translation like "reprimand," "warn," or "speak severely to." Another way is to say "tell (or, command) to stop."

Perhaps it should also be noted that Matthew has the plural **winds**, where Mark 4.39 has the singular "wind." The preference for the plural mirrors a stylistic feature of Matthew's Gospel: the plural "crowds" is frequently present in place of the Marcan "crowd"; in 13.5 both "other" and "rocky ground" are plural forms (Mark has the singular); in 13.11 Matthew has "secrets" for the Marcan "secret"; in 26.15 Matthew has the plural "pieces of silver" and Mark has "silver" (meaning "money"). Translators should use singular or plural according to the normal form in their language.

Instead of **sea** it may be better to say "lake," but "water" or "waves" are also acceptable.

And there was a great calm is a literal rendering of the Greek text. JB renders "and all was calm again"; NAB retains a rather high level of language: "Complete calm ensued." Translators should use whatever phrase is natural to indicate that all was calm again; perhaps "everything was quiet again," or even "and the weather and lake became calm again."

It seems clear that this happened right after he spoke. Some translations add "right then" or "at once."

8.27　　　　　RSV　　　　　　　　　　　　　　TEV

And the men marveled, saying, "What sort of man is this, that even winds and sea obey him?"

Everyone was amazed. "What kind of man is this?" they said. "Even the winds and the waves obey him!"

In place of **the men** Mark has the pronoun "they"; Mark also has the verb construction "were terribly afraid," for which Matthew has substituted **marveled** (TEV **Everyone was amazed**). **The men** is best taken as a reference to the men in the boat with Jesus, that is, his disciples. The rendering of AB ("Men wondered . . .") broadens the reference too much. It is possible to translate impersonally, as GECL 1st edition has done: "The astonishment was great." However, most translations will have **the men** or "the men with him."

Marveled, as in verse 10, can be translated as "were surprised" or "were amazed," or even "spoke to each other in awe (or, amazement)."

The question of the disciples, **What sort of man is this?** is an expression of amazement. In Greek the last clause of this verse is a part of their question, as in RSV, **What sort of man is this, that even winds and sea obey him?** However, most modern English translations find it more effective to divide the response of the disciples into a question followed by a statement. Brc, on the other hand, handles the text in a slightly different but effective manner: " 'What kind of man is this,' they said, 'for even the winds and the waters obey him?' " In some languages it may even be more natural to invert the order of the clauses; for example, "Even the winds and the waves obey this man! What kind of man must he be?"

By the omission of the definite article before **winds** and **waves**, GECL includes all winds and waves within the scope of Jesus' power: "So that even winds and waves obey him."

The disciples do not ask who Jesus is, but ask what sort of man he is, thus indicating that they think he is somehow quite special. The translation should reflect that. Further, the use of a question here probably shows the extent of their wonder more than a statement or exclamation would, so it should be retained. Besides, the disciples do not yet know what type of man Jesus is.

8.28-34

RSV

TEV

Jesus Heals Two Men with Demons

28 And when he came to the other side, to the country of the Gadarenes,[f] two demoniacs met him, coming out of the tombs, so fierce that no one could pass that way. 29 And behold, they cried out, "What have you to do with us, O Son of God? Have you come here to torment us before the time?" 30 Now a herd of many swine was feeding at some distance from them. 31 And the demons begged him, "If you cast us out, send us away into the herd of swine." 32 And he said to them, "Go." So they came out and went into the swine; and behold, the whole herd rushed down the steep bank into the sea, and perished in the waters. 33 The herdsmen fled, and going into the city they told everything, and what had happened to the demoniacs. 34 And behold, all the city came out to meet Jesus; and when they saw him, they begged him to leave their neighborhood.

[f] Other ancient authorities read *Gergesenes*; some *Gerasenes*

28 When Jesus came to the territory of Gadara on the other side of the lake, he was met by two men who came out of the burial caves there. These men had demons in them and were so fierce that no one dared travel on that road. 29 At once they screamed, "What do you want with us, you Son of God? Have you come to punish us before the right time?"

30 Not far away there was a large herd of pigs feeding. 31 So the demons begged Jesus, "If you are going to drive us out, send us into that herd of pigs."

32 "Go," Jesus told them; so they left and went off into the pigs. The whole herd rushed down the side of the cliff into the lake and was drowned.

33 The men who had been taking care of the pigs ran away and went into the town, where they told the whole story and what had happened to the men with the demons. 34 So everyone from the town went out to meet Jesus; and when they saw him, they begged him to leave their territory.

SECTION HEADING: **"Jesus Heals Two Men with Demons."** For **"Demons"** see comments on 4.24. Instead of using **"Heals,"** some will say "Jesus throws evil spirits out of two men."

All three of the Synoptics include this event at this point in Jesus' ministry (Mark 5.1-20; Luke 8.26-39). But Matthew differs from the other two in several respects, the most noticeable being the mention of two demoniacs in place of one. Other differences are: the name given the demoniac (Mark 5.9; Luke 8.30) is not mentioned, no allusion is made to the transformed appearance of the healed man

(Mark 5.15-16; Luke 8.35-36), and the wish of the man to follow Jesus is omitted (Mark 5.18; Luke 8.38). Moreover, there is a rather significant difference in the place name (see verse 28). The details that Matthew omitted, however, enabled him to stress the authority of Jesus over demons without unnecessary adornment of details. It is perhaps significant that in verse 32 the destruction of the demons, rather than the healing of the men, is emphasized.

8.28	RSV	TEV

RSV	TEV
And when he came to the other side, to the country of the Gadarenes,[t] two demoniacs met him, coming out of the tombs, so fierce that no one could pass that way.	When Jesus came to the territory of Gadara on the other side of the lake, he was met by two men who came out of the burial caves there. These men had demons in them and were so fierce that no one dared travel on that road.
[t] Other ancient authorities read *Gergesenes*; some *Gerasenes*	

Since the text goes straight on from the scene in the boat, it will not be a problem in most languages to retain **when**. Compare how this differs from 8.23, for example. **And** does indicate it is a new unit, however, but whether to retain it or not depends on the receptor language.

He came: here again TEV identifies the pronoun of the Greek text as "**Jesus**," since a new section is introduced.

Came may also be rendered "arrived" or "reached."

The other side refers to the eastern shore of Lake Galilee. See comment at verse 18. As there, some will say "the other side of the lake."

There is a textual problem regarding the name **Gadarenes**. Other manuscripts have "Gergesenes," and still others have "Gerasenes." The best textual evidence is in favor of **Gadarenes**, from Gadara, a town about five miles southeast of Lake Galilee. Although the town is five miles distant from Lake Galilee, ancient coins bearing the name Gadara often have a ship on them. Moreover, the Jewish historian Josephus indicates that Gadara possessed territory bordering on Lake Galilee.

The text refers to the area as **the country of the Gadarenes**, that is, the country of the people of Gadara. Whether to retain "people" or refer to the area by the name of the town, as in "the region of Gadara," will depend on what the receptor language normally does.

Two demoniacs met him, coming out of the tombs may sound to the reader, especially to the hearer, as though Jesus was the one coming out of the tombs. TEV does considerable restructuring to avoid this ambiguity: "**he was met by two men who came out of the burial caves there. These men had demons in them . . . .**" Another way this can be restructured is "He was met by two men who had evil spirits in them. The men were coming out of the burial caves."

The tombs were more specifically "**burial caves**," as TEV indicates. The dead were customarily placed in the rear of burial caves, leaving a small antechamber toward the front of the cave. It was there, in the front part of the cave, that these men would probably have lived. According to Jewish teaching, tombs were ritually unclean, but they would have been considered suitable homes for demons and demon-possessed people.

The idea of burying people in caves seems most odd in many parts of the world. For this reason some translators have preferred to say "the area of the tombs" or "places where they bury people." However, this does not give as complete a picture as TEV's "**burial caves**," and a slightly better rendering may be "the caves where the Jews used to bury people."

Fierce (so also TEV) may also mean "violent" (NEB) or even "savage" (NAB). At least one commentator suggests the meaning "difficult to subdue." Other words that can translate the word are "dangerous" or "uncontrollable."

Could is the preference of most translations. TEV and NEB have "**dared**." The verb literally means "be strong" or "able" (Brc).

GECL translates the entire verse: "On the other side of the lake Jesus came to the territory of Gadara. There two men from the burial caves ran out to meet him. They were possessed by demons and were so fierce that no one dared use that road."

8.29	RSV	TEV
	And behold, they cried out, "What have you to do with us, O Son of God? Have you come here to torment us before the time?"	At once they screamed, "What do you want with us, you Son of God? Have you come to punish us before the right time?"

And behold: see comments at 1.20 and 8.2. Here, phrases such as "At once" or "As soon as they saw Jesus" will be good, too.

Cried out (TEV "**screamed**") indicates a loud shout (NEB "shouted"). JB has "They stood there shouting . . . ." Notice that in this verse it is the men, not the spirits, shouting at Jesus.

What have you to do with us, O Son of God? is literally "What to us and to you, Son of God?" The construction "What to us and to you" is a Semitic idiom; in the Marcan (5.7) and Lukan (8.28) parallels it appears in the singular ("What to me and to you"). The same expression occurs in the Septuagint, with at least two different meanings. In Judges 11.12 Jephthah's reply to the Ammonite king means "What is your quarrel with us?" In 2 Samuel 16.10 David's reply to Abishai and Joab may be rendered "This is none of your business." In John 2.4, where these same words comprise Jesus' response to his mother during the wedding feast at Cana, the meaning is "You must not tell me what to do." Here the meaning is best explained by the question that follows, "**Have you come to punish us before the right time?**" (TEV).

The question is certainly a hostile one, and the translation should reflect this: "What's your business with us?" "What are you going to do with (or, to) us?" or "Why are you bothering us?" It can even be translated as something of a warning, as in "Don't interfere with us."

In 3.17 God speaks of Jesus as his **Son**, and in 4.3,6 the devil identifies Jesus as God's Son. According to the New Testament, demons also have supernatural insight, and it is on this basis that the demon-possessed men recognize who Jesus really is.

The vocative formula with **O** as in **O Son of God** is archaic and unnatural in English as well as in many other languages. Better will be "You who are Son of God" or simply "Son of God." Whether to put this before or after the question depends on the receptor language.

Have you come here to torment us before the time? reflects Jewish and Christian thought, according to which demons have power to trouble people until the day of God's final judgment upon them.

Torment may be **"punish"** (TEV), "make suffer," or "torture."

The time is specifically a reference to the final judgment, and so it may be rendered "before the Day of Judgment." NAB renders "before the appointed time"; NJB renders "before the time," with a note indicating that the Day of Judgment is meant. A common translation is "the time of judgment" or "the proper time for that."

8.30   RSV   TEV

| Now a herd of many swine was feed-ing at some distance from them. | Not far away there was a large herd of pigs feeding. |

Now indicates a transition in the narrative. TEV introduces a new paragraph. Here it can be translated as "It happened that . . ." or "There was a herd of swine . . . ."

The presence of a **herd of . . . swine** indicates that Jesus is in Gentile territory. **Swine** is a word for **"pigs."** The text indicates there were many of them. In English, "a large herd of pigs" is more natural than "a herd of many pigs," but languages will vary on this.

At some distance (so FRCL) or "In the distance" (NEB) is representative of most translations. Both NJB and NAB have "some distance away," while TEV and GECL 1st edition have **"Not far."**

It seems that **at some distance** does not indicate a great distance, since the pigs can be seen. Translations can either follow TEV or have a phrase like "Nearby" or "A little ways away." Notice that in most languages it is more natural to put the expression near the beginning of the sentence, not at the end.

8.31   RSV   TEV

| And the demons begged him, "If you cast us out, send us away into the herd of swine." | So the demons begged Jesus, "If you are going to drive us out, send us into that herd of pigs." |

In verse 29 the demon-possessed people address Jesus; here the demons themselves speak to him. This is the only place in the New Testament where this particular word for demon is used. Earlier Matthew used the more common word for demon (7.22), and in the following chapter he does so again (9.33-34). Elsewhere in the Gospel demons are mentioned in 10.8; 11.18; 12.24,27,28; and 17.18. Despite this fact, translators will normally use the same word they did in verse 28.

Begged, if not readily translated, can be "plead with" or "asked him fervently."

If you cast us out is stated in such a way in Greek as to indicate that the demons were certain that Jesus was going to drive them out. It may therefore be rendered "Since you are going to cast us out" or "We know you're going to cast us out." For **cast out** see comments on verse 16 and on 7.22.

No reason is given why the demons requested that Jesus allow them to enter the herd of pigs. It may be that they needed some physical bodies from which to carry out their activities. However, the request of the demons was self-destructive, because the pigs rushed down the cliff into the lake and were drowned. The implication is that the demons were destroyed at the same time.

8.32	RSV	TEV
	And he said to them, "Go." So they came out and went into the swine; and behold, the whole herd rushed down the steep bank into the sea, and perished in the waters.	"Go," Jesus told them; so they left and went off into the pigs. The whole herd rushed down the side of the cliff into the lake and was drowned.

And he said to them, "Go": in order to place greater emphasis on the command of Jesus, TEV inverts the order: " **'Go,' Jesus told them**." However, this will not be possible in all languages, and translators should use whatever order is most natural. Some will have to use indirect speech, as in "He told them they should go," but effort should be made to place the emphasis on the command.

Them, of course, refers to the demons who spoke to him in verse 31, not to the men.

The demons **came out**, that is, they "left the men" or "went out of the men." They then **went into** the pigs, or "entered the pigs," or "took possession of the pigs." Translators should use the normal expression for spirit possession in their language.

And behold: see comments on 1.20; 8.2. The expression is here used to focus attention on what happened when the demons went into the pigs. Perhaps this can be brought out by a phrase such as "At once" or "And then."

The exact relation between the verbs **rushed** and **perished** is not clear. In Greek **rushed** is singular whereas **perished** is plural. It is possible that the herd is the subject of each verb, and most translations imply that this is the case. But is also quite possible that the function of the plural is to indicate that both the pigs and the demons were drowned. This would then affirm that at the command of Jesus the demons met their destruction before the day of the final judgment.

This can possibly be emphasized with a rendering such as "The whole herd of pigs rushed down the steep bank into the sea, and the pigs and demons were drowned." But even without this being explicit, the implication is that the demons were destroyed. It is therefore probably enough to say that the herd was drowned.

As before, **sea** can be "**lake**."

Bank is often translated as "**cliff**," since it is rivers that have banks, not lakes. "Hillside" is also acceptable.

TEV translates **perished in the waters** as "**were drowned**."

The herdsmen fled, and going into the city they told everything, and what had happened to the demoniacs.	The men who had been taking care of the pigs ran away and went into the town, where they told the whole story and what had happened to the men with the demons.

Herdsmen (one word in Greek) is translated by a descriptive clause in TEV: "**men who had been taking care of the pigs.**" The difficulty is that of finding a technical term of the proper level for "men who take care of pigs." Both JB and NAB render "swineherds," but this can possibly be taken to mean "herds of swine" at first reading. NEB renders "men in charge of them." Most translations will do something similar to TEV.

Fled (TEV "**ran away**") is rendered idiomatically as "took to their heels" by NEB, NAB. Brc effectively translates this part of the verse as one concise sentence, "The herdsmen fled."

Few languages will use a participle like **going**, but will say instead "they went."

Instead of **city,** "**town**" is a more accurate reflection of the size of Gadara, for those languages that do distinguish between the two words.

Everything, and what had happened to the demoniacs is a rather odd structure in Greek; literally "everything and the things of the demon-possessed men." GECL renders "what they had experienced, and how the two demon-possessed men had been healed." **Everything** can also be "everything that had taken place."

The **demoniacs** are "the men who had been possessed by the evil spirits." Note that they no longer were possessed, since these spirits had been expelled.

8.34   RSV   TEV

And behold, all the city came out to meet Jesus; and when they saw him, they begged him to leave their neighborhood.	So everyone from the town went out to meet Jesus; and when they saw him, they begged him to leave their territory.

And behold (TEV "**So**"): see comments on 1.20; 8.2,32.

All the city is a Semitic way of referring to the people of a city: "everyone in the city" or "almost everyone in the city," since in this construction "all" frequently means "many" or "almost all."

Everyone **came out**, which may more naturally be "went out of [the city]" or "left [the city]."

Meet probably does not have the idea of "become acquainted with." More likely is the idea of "encounter."

And when . . . their neighborhood: in some languages it may be necessary to shift to direct discourse; for example, "they begged him, 'Please go away and leave our territory!' " **Neighborhood** can be "**territory**," "region," or "area."

For comments on **begged** see verse 31.

Chapter 9

9.1-8

RSV

TEV

Jesus Heals a Paralyzed Man

1 And getting into a boat he crossed over and came to his own city. 2 And behold, they brought to him a paralytic, lying on his bed; and when Jesus saw their faith he said to the paralytic, "Take heart, my son; your sins are forgiven." 3 And behold, some of the scribes said to themselves, "This man is blaspheming." 4 But Jesus, knowing[u] their thoughts, said, "Why do you think evil in your hearts? 5 For which is easier, to say, 'Your sins are forgiven,' or to say, 'Rise and walk'? 6 But that you may know that the Son of man has authority on earth to forgive sins"—he then said to the paralytic—"Rise, take up your bed and go home." 7 And he rose and went home. 8 When the crowds saw it, they were afraid, and they glorified God, who had given such authority to men.

1 Jesus got into the boat and went back across the lake to his own town.[f] 2 where some people brought to him a paralyzed man, lying on a bed. When Jesus saw how much faith they had, he said to the paralyzed man, "Courage, my son! Your sins are forgiven."

3 Then some teachers of the Law said to themselves, "This man is speaking blasphemy!"

4 Jesus perceived what they were thinking, and so he said, "Why are you thinking such evil things? 5 Is it easier to say, 'Your sins are forgiven,' or to say, 'Get up and walk'? 6 I will prove to you, then, that the Son of Man has authority on earth to forgive sins." So he said to the paralyzed man, "Get up, pick up your bed, and go home!"

7 The man got up and went home. 8 When the people saw it, they were afraid, and praised God for giving such authority to men.

[u] Other ancient authorities read *seeing*

[f] HIS OWN TOWN: *Capernaum* (see 4.13)

SECTION HEADING: "**Jesus Heals a Paralyzed Man**." For comments on "**Paralyzed**" see the comments on "paralytic" below in verse 2 and at 8.6. This title can be "Jesus heals a man who couldn't move (or, was paralyzed)."

In the structure of Matthew's Gospel, this story reveals another aspect of Jesus' authority, that of forgiving sins. This observation is based upon two factors: (1) the location of the narrative in this particular place, and (2) the manner in which Matthew omits details of the setting and focuses sharply on the words of Jesus in verse 6. Matthew is also concerned to remind his readers that Jesus has given to his followers this same authority to forgive sins.

Exclusive of verse 1, which serves as an introduction, the narrative may be divided into three parts on the basis of the participants involved: (1) Jesus and the paralyzed man (verse 2); (2) Jesus and the teachers of the Law (verses 3-6); (3) the healed man and the crowds (verses 7-8).

9.1   RSV   TEV

> And getting into a boat he crossed over and came to his own city.

> Jesus got into the boat and went back across the lake to his own town,[f]

[f]HIS OWN TOWN: *Capernaum (see 4.13).*

The words **And getting** show that a new episode is beginning but that it follows directly from the previous one. Some translators have found it necessary to say "Then" or "After that."

A boat, as in the Greek, is translated "**the boat**" by TEV in order to maintain continuity within the immediate unit (see 8.23 where the boat is previously mentioned).

He is represented by a pronominal suffix of the verb in Greek and is identified as "**Jesus**" by TEV because a new section is begun.

Crossed over (one verb in Greek) is translated "**went back across the lake**" by TEV and GECL.

To his own city, as the TEV footnote indicates, is Capernaum. NJB also supplies this information by way of a footnote, and NAB does so by a section heading: "A Paralytic at Capernaum." In 4.13 Matthew informs his readers that Jesus moved to the town of Capernaum after the death of John the Baptist.

The information about the town being Capernaum can be in a footnote, but should not be made specific in the text. **To his own city** may be rendered "to the town where he lived." It is important to avoid an expression that would mean the town where Jesus was born (Bethlehem) or where he grew up (Nazareth).

9.2   RSV   TEV

> And behold, they brought to him a paralytic, lying on his bed; and when Jesus saw their faith he said to the paralytic, "Take heart, my son; your sins are forgiven."

> where some people brought to him a paralyzed man, lying on a bed. When Jesus saw how much faith they had, he said to the paralyzed man, "Courage, my son! Your sins are forgiven."

And behold: see comments on 1.20 and 8.2.

They brought is translated "**some people brought**" by TEV. NJB has "some people"; NAB "the people"; NEB "some men." The meaning is doubtless "some people from the town."

In Greek **a paralytic** is a masculine form of an adjective meaning "a paralyzed person." The Greek text itself gives no hint of the person's age, whether he was a man or a boy. Most translations indicate that he was a man and consistently refer to him as a man throughout the narrative. LB, perhaps on the basis of the manner in which Jesus addresses him (**my son**), refers to him as a "boy" in this verse and again in verse 7. However, in verses 5 and 6 he is twice referred to as a "man." For the sake of consistency within the narrative, it is best to refer to him either as a man or a boy throughout, rather than to shift back and forth in this way. Moreover, though the person may be a boy, it is not legitimate to base it upon the noun of address used by Jesus. Technically, the term used here does mean "child," but it may even be used in an extended sense of "descendant." For example, the rich man is addressed by his ancestor Abraham with this same word in Luke 16.25. In the present context the best solution is to assume that this is merely a polite form of address from a superior to an inferior. Therefore **paralytic** may be rendered "a man who could not move" or "a man whose sickness made him so he couldn't move." See comments on 8.6.

The **bed** referred to was probably either a pallet or a rug. Therefore it is important to avoid using a word that would make it seem he was lying on a large bed with legs, springs, mattress, and so forth. "Cot" or "mat" are quite common translations.

It may not be best in some languages to say Jesus **saw** their faith, but rather that he "observed," **"perceived,"** or "realized how much faith they had."

Their faith, a noun phrase in Greek, is translated **"how much faith they had"** by TEV. GECL 1st edition renders "how much faith they had in him." The text may also be expressed, "that they believed he could heal the man" or "how strongly they believed he could heal the man."

Note that the text says **their faith**, which refers to the faith of those who brought the paralyzed man, but it can also include the faith of the sick man himself.

Take heart, my son is difficult to render naturally in English. NAB translates "Have courage, son" and JB "Courage, my child." **Take heart** (TEV **"Courage"**) may also mean "Don't worry" or "Have no fear" (GECL). Some translations have had the equivalent of "Cheer up" or "Don't be discouraged." In many languages it will be more natural to have Jesus address the man first before he encourages him: "My son, cheer up."

My son can be a problem. Here Jesus uses it as a term of endearment, as a friendly way to address the man. But in very many languages, to say "My son" or "My child" can only mean that Jesus was the man's father. Then it may be better to say "Young man" or "My friend." In some languages it may be more appropriate to omit the noun of address, as GECL does.

Your sins are forgiven is normally understood to mean "God has forgiven your sins," since in Jewish thought only God could declare a person's sins forgiven. The problem of understanding the meaning of the text is further complicated by the accusation of blasphemy made against Jesus. A person would not usually have been accused of blasphemy unless he had used the divine name. These problems have serious implications for translation, especially in those languages where passive verbs are not used or are used only rarely. Furthermore, any decision regarding the translation of "your sins are forgiven" will immediately affect the translation of the accusation made against Jesus in the next verse ("This man is blaspheming"). If a passive structure cannot be maintained, there are several possible alternatives: (1) "I say to you, 'God has forgiven your sins.'" (2) "I forgive your sins" or "In the name of God I forgive your sins."

For **forgiven**, see comments on 6.12.

9.3 RSV	TEV
And behold, some of the scribes said to themselves, "This man is blaspheming."	Then some teachers of the Law said to themselves, "This man is speaking blasphemy!"

And behold: see comments on 1.20. TEV has "**Then**"; NEB "At this"; JB "And at this."

Scribes (TEV "**teachers of the Law**") are first mentioned in 2.4, then in 5.20; 7.29; 8.19.

Said to themselves may mean they were muttering, or speaking to each other in low voices that others would not be able to hear, or it may mean they were only thinking these things. In any case, "knowing their thoughts" in verse 4 indicates that Jesus knew what thoughts they had.

Blaspheming (so also JB) is here equated with the claim to do something that is solely a divine prerogative, that is, acting in the name and with the authority of God. It is difficult to find an English term that conveys the idea the word has in this context. Here it means something like "This man is presuming on (or encroaching on, or usurping, or arrogating to himself) a divine privilege." In this context there is no direct insult to God, nor does it mean that someone has spoken against God, but rather that someone has somehow invaded the rights and privileges God reserves for himself. The verb is translated "insulting God" by Brc and "slandering God" by GECL, but these are not good models to follow. The problem with using such constructions as "**speaking blasphemy**" (TEV), "blasphemous talk" (NEB), and **blaspheming** is that they all contain a technical term which is fairly much limited to church vocabulary. The verb is used in this same sense in 26.65; but in 27.39 it is used in the context of the insults spoken against Jesus by the people who passed by as he was being crucified. Here the translation can be "He thinks he's God! This is an insult to God!"

9.4 RSV	TEV
But Jesus, knowing[u] their thoughts, said, "Why do you think evil in your hearts?	Jesus perceived what they were thinking, and so he said, "Why are you thinking such evil things?

[u] Other ancient authorities read *seeing*

As the RSV footnote points out, some Greek manuscripts have "seeing" in place of **knowing**. The UBS Greek New Testament prefers the manuscript text which RSV has placed in the margin. The reasons are explained by TC-GNT: (1) it is easy to understand how "seeing" was changed to **knowing**, though a change in the other direction is difficult to explain; and (2) the change may have been influenced by a recollection of Mark 2.8 and Luke 5.22, where a verb related to **knowing** occurs. Actually the difference is slight, and most translations represent the meaning "know"; NAB has "was aware of," and TEV "**perceived**." NJB renders "what was in their minds." Brc is more idiomatic: "knew what was going on in their minds."

The noun **thoughts** is found only four times in the New Testament (Matt 12.25; Acts 17.29; Heb 4.12); the related verb is used only twice (Matt 1.20; 9.4). Some languages will not have a noun like **thoughts** but will normally express the idea with a verb, as in "what they were thinking."

The construction with a participle **knowing**, (or, "seeing"), indicates that Jesus spoke to the teachers of the law as a result of what he knew about what they were thinking. TEV shows this with **"and so he said,"** but other renderings can be "therefore he said" or "as a result he said."

Evil is plural in Greek ("evil things"). TEV attempts to relate this to the context by **"such evil things,"** as does NJB ("such wicked thoughts"). **Evil** in this verse means simply "bad" or "wicked."

In Greek "evil things" is followed by **in your hearts**. TEV, NEB, and NAB delete the phrase, since it is implicit in English. As we pointed out in 5.28, for the Jews the heart was the seat of intellectual activity, thinking. If translators retain **in your hearts**, they should be sure that the translation is not talking about emotions, as could well be the case with "heart" in English. Brc translates Jesus' response as follows: "What put such mistaken ideas into your heads?" Other expressions that can be used include "Why do you have such evil thoughts (in your minds")?" and "Why do you let what you think be evil like that?"

This question can be understood as a rhetorical question and can be rendered "You are thinking such evil thoughts" or "You have no reason to think evil thoughts."

9.5	RSV	TEV
	For which is easier, to say, 'Your sins are forgiven,' or to say, 'Rise and walk'?	Is it easier to say, 'Your sins are forgiven,' or to say, 'Get up and walk'?

For which is easier . . . ? The Jews of the New Testament period believed that the healing of a person's body was evidence that God had forgiven him, and so Jesus bases his remarks on that presupposition. He is not in any way intimating that the forgiveness of sin was less difficult for him than the healing of the man's body.

Languages will demonstrate quite a variety in the way they handle this question. Some translations will have "Is it easier to say 'Your sins are forgiven' or to say 'Get up and walk'?" Others will structure the verse like this: "I can say 'Your sins are forgiven' and I can also say 'Get up and walk.' Which is easier?" Since the question can imply that Jesus was suggesting the one was easier than the other, another way to render the verse is "Isn't it just as easy (or, It's just as easy) to say 'Your sins are forgiven' as it is to say 'Get up and walk'?" Some translators will have to use indirect speech, as in "Isn't it just as easy to tell this man his sins are forgiven as it is to tell him to get up and walk?"

Your sins are forgiven is discussed in verse 2. See comments there.

Rise (TEV **"Get up"**) **and walk** is a fairly literal rendering of the Greek text. The translation should not imply that Jesus told the man to "walk away" or "walk off." Translators can perhaps say "Get up and walk about."

RSV　　　　　　　　　　　　　　TEV

| But that you may know that the Son of man has authority on earth to forgive sins"—he then said to the paralytic—"Rise, take up your bed and go home." | I will prove to you, then, that the Son of Man has authority on earth to forgive sins." So he said to the paralyzed man, "Get up, pick up your bed, and go home!" |

But that you may know is a literal translation of the Greek text; it is "**I will prove to you**" in TEV. NAB translates "To help you realize"; NEB "But to convince you"; and Brc "But just to show you." Another possible rendering is "But because I want you to know."

Son of man: see comments on 8.20.

Has authority on earth to forgive sins is a literal rendering of the Greek text. **On earth** is ambiguous. It may mean either "of the people here on earth" or "while he (that is, the Son of Man) is here on earth." If the former meaning is intended, then one may translate ". . . has authority to forgive people's sins." Otherwise one may translate ". . . has the authority to forgive people's sins while he is here on earth." The translation should not imply that the Son of Man's authority to forgive is limited in that the earth is the only place where he may forgive sins.

His **authority** comes from God, and there are languages which must show that, as in "So you will know God has given the Son of Man the authority." **Authority** can also be translated "power."

In the text, what Jesus says to the teachers of the law before turning to speak to the paralyzed man is an incomplete sentence. TEV has made it easier to follow by using a complete sentence: "**I will prove, then . . . .**" Another way to handle this is " 'Because I want you to know that the Son of Man has authority to forgive people's sins (while he is here on earth), I will do this.' Then Jesus said to the paralyzed man . . . ."

Rise again means "Get up" or "Stand up."

Take up, as seen in TEV, means "**pick up**."

Go home (most all translations) translates a Greek idiom with this precise meaning. The translation should not sound as if Jesus is getting rid of the man by sending him home, but that the man now is capable of returning home in good health.

RSV　　　　　　　　　　　　　　TEV

| And he rose and went home. | The man got up and went home. |

And he rose and went home is literally "and getting up he went home." NJB renders: "And the man got up and went home."

9.8   RSV   TEV

When the crowds saw it, they were   **When the people saw it, they were**
afraid, and they glorified God, who   **afraid, and praised God for giving**
had given such authority to men.   **such authority to men.**

The crowds (plural in Greek) is translated collectively in NJB and NAB as "the crowd"; TEV and NEB have "**the people.**"

The people saw **it**, that is, "what happened" or "what the man did."

In place of **they were afraid**, some Greek manuscripts have "they were amazed." However, the manuscript evidence for the verb "amazed" is weak; the change was probably made by scribes who failed to understand the real meaning of **were afraid** and wanted to substitute what they felt to be more appropriate. Part of the sense of **were afraid** can be seen by what the people did: they praised God. Thus the fear here refers to awe, to the kind of fear and respect felt in the presence of such a demonstration of power and authority. So translators may have "they were filled with awe."

Glorified God is here equivalent to "**praised God**" (TEV). The verb is used with this same sense in 5.16; 6.2; 15.31. As in those verses, some languages will most naturally use a short phrase such as "They began to say how great God was" or "They said, 'God is truly great.' "

Matthew uses the plural form **men**. To shift to the singular ("for giving such authority to a man!"), as in LB, is an intentional distortion of the meaning of the Greek. It is possible that the phrase **to men** means "for the sake of men," but such exegesis is extremely doubtful. Elsewhere in the Gospel, Matthew clearly indicates that Jesus' followers have been given the authority to forgive sins (Matt 16.19; 18.18). This story is an excellent example of an event from the life of Jesus that is narrated in such a way as to reflect its relevance for the life of the community represented by the author of the Gospel.

Men should be translated by a word or phrase that means "human beings." A word which refers only to males or to one man will not be correct.

9.9-13

RSV   TEV

Jesus Calls Matthew

9 As Jesus passed on from there, he saw a man called Matthew sitting at the tax office; and he said to him, "Follow me." And he rose and followed him.

10 And as he sat at table[v] in the house, behold, many tax collectors and sinners came and sat down with Jesus and his disciples. 11 And when the Pharisees saw this, they said to his disciples, "Why does your teacher eat with tax collectors and sinners?" 12 But when he heard it, he said, "Those who are well have no need of a physician, but those who are sick. 13 Go and learn what this means, 'I desire mercy, and not sacrifice.' For I

9 Jesus left that place, and as he walked along, he saw a tax collector, named Matthew, sitting in his office. He said to him, "Follow me."

Matthew got up and followed him.

10 While Jesus was having a meal in Matthew's house,[g] many tax collectors and other outcasts came and joined Jesus and his disciples at the table. 11 Some Pharisees saw this and asked his disciples, "Why does your teacher eat with such people?"

12 Jesus heard them and answered, "People who are well do not need a doctor, but only those who are sick. 13 Go and find out what is meant by

came not to call the righteous, but sinners."

v Greek *reclined*

the scripture that says: 'It is kindness that I want, not animal sacrifices.' I have not come to call respectable people, but outcasts."

g in Matthew's house; *or* in his (*that is,* Jesus') house.

SECTION HEADING: "**Jesus Calls Matthew.**" Translators should avoid a word that would mean that Jesus called out to Matthew. Better would be "Jesus calls (or, tells) Matthew to follow him" or ". . . to serve him."

It is difficult to trace Jesus' movements with precision. In all probability the office of the tax collector would have been outside the city, where goods from the territory of Philip (northeast of Lake Galilee) could have been taxed as they were brought into the territory of Herod Antipas (Galilee). With this in mind, two possibilities of interpretation present themselves: (1) If 9.1 is taken to mean that Jesus actually went into his home town of Capernaum, then he is now moving from inside the city in the direction of its outskirts. (2) If, on the other hand, 9.1 means "he went in the direction of his own town," then the events described here took place somewhere after Jesus had left Lake Galilee and before he entered Capernaum. In this case Jesus is heading toward the town rather than away from it.

9.9　　　　RSV　　　　　　　　　　　　　　　　TEV

As Jesus passed on from there, he saw a man called Matthew sitting at the tax office; and he said to him, "Follow me." And he rose and followed him.

Jesus left that place, and as he walked along, he saw a tax collector, named Matthew, sitting in his office. He said to him, "Follow me."

Matthew got up and followed him.

Passed on: see comment in the introduction to this section. Unfortunately, the verb does not indicate the direction in which Jesus was moving. In verse 27 the verb is used in essentially this same construction, and there it appears to mean "depart from" or "go away from." More frequently it is used with the meaning of "pass by" (Matt 20.30; Mark 2.14; 15.21; John 9.1).

Most translators will take **passed on** to mean here "he went away from." They may even have "Jesus left there. As he went . . . ," "As Jesus went along from that place," or "As Jesus left there."

The tax office: both NEB and JB specify that the taxes involved were customs. **The tax office** can be translated as "the place where they collect taxes for transporting goods." If the word "customs" is known by readers, the translation can be "where they collect customs." However, since Matthew was sitting there because he was one of those people who received the customs, it is also possible to say "he saw a man called Matthew who was collecting customs." Another model is seen in TEV. The translation can be "a customs (or, tax) collector in his place."

The **office** was probably a very simple structure or building. Translators can also say "his place."

Matthew: in the Gospel of Luke he is named Levi (5.27), while in Mark he is called Levi the son of Alphaeus (2.14). It seems probable that **Matthew** and Levi are the same persons, but there is no indication why the names differ in the various accounts. There is no textual or exegetical basis for the footnote in LB: "The Matthew who wrote this book."

And he said to him: in many languages it will be necessary to use names, as in "and Jesus said to Matthew (or, to him)."

Follow me must be taken in the sense of "come and be my disciple." The translator should take care not to suggest that Jesus is merely inviting Matthew to come and follow him in a physical and geographical sense, though this certainly is involved. For these reasons, then, a possible translation of **Follow me** is "Come be my disciple." "Come with me" may also be possible. Of course, some languages require indirect speech: "Jesus said to Matthew to come with him (or, come be his disciple)."

And he rose: in order to avoid the possibility of pronominal ambiguity, TEV introduces the noun "**Matthew**" where the Greek text has **he**. **Rose** can be "stood up" or "got up."

9.10   RSV   TEV

And as he sat at table[v] in the house, behold, many tax collectors and sinners came and sat down with Jesus and his disciples.

[v] Greek *reclined*

While Jesus was having a meal in Matthew's house,[g] many tax collectors and other outcasts came and joined Jesus and his disciples at the table.

[g]in Matthew's house; *or* in his *(that is, Jesus')* house.

It may be necessary to indicate in general terms the shift in temporal setting. For example, GECL begins "Later Jesus was the guest of Matthew." Another rendering would be "Later, Jesus went to Matthew's house."

It should be clear that **he** refers to Jesus, not Matthew.

The RSV footnote indicates that **sat at table** may also be translated "reclined at table." What the footnote is referring to is the manner in which people positioned themselves with one elbow on the floor while eating from a low table. They would not have been sitting in chairs.

One very natural way to translate **sat** (or, reclined) **at table** is "and as he was sitting at the table to eat." Another way is "while he was eating."

In the house . . . sat down with Jesus: this ambiguous construction is translated by TEV to indicate specifically that the meal was "**in Matthew's house**." However, the alternative rendering of TEV provides the other possible meaning: "in his (that is, Jesus') home." Most translations retain the ambiguity: "When Jesus was at table in the house" (NEB) and "While he was at dinner in the house" (JB). NAB is explicit: "while Jesus was at table in Matthew's home." Some scholars think that **with Jesus and his disciples** implies that Jesus was the host and that the meal must have been in his home.

Translators who can retain the ambiguity may want to do so, translating **in the house** literally. In cases where this is not possible, translators usually specify "in Matthew's house," but obviously they can also follow the alternative rendering of TEV, as in "in his house" or "at his home."

For **behold**, see comments on 1.20 and 8.2.

Tax collectors were regarded as sinful because their business brought them into constant contact with non-Jews (see comments on 5.46).

And sinners: in order to indicate that tax collectors were also regarded as sinners by the Jews, one may need to translate "and other sinful people" (TEV "**and other outcasts**"). The term **sinners** would have included not only persons of immoral character, but also Jews who ignored the stricter requirements of the Law as interpreted by the Pharisees in particular. AB has "non-observant (Jews)," and GECL "others who had just as bad a profession."

To retain **sinners** in the context of the Gospels is often misleading, since modern readers tend to understand it in the narrower sense of immoral people. But as we pointed out, the Jews used the term to cover a much wider group than that. "Outcasts" of TEV is sometimes a good model, but many translators have followed Brc, "people with whom no respectable Jew would have had anything to do."

The tax collectors and other sinners **sat down with Jesus and his disciples**. It is clear from the context that they sat down to eat also, but in some languages this will have to be stated explicitly.

9.11	RSV	TEV
	And when the Pharisees saw this, they said to his disciples, "Why does your teacher eat with tax collectors and sinners?"	Some Pharisees saw this and asked his disciples, "Why does your teacher eat with such people?"

Most modern translations do not slavishly follow the form of the Semitic Greek and do not retain the **And** at the beginning of this structure.

For **Pharisees**, see comments on 3.7. Note that the text says **the Pharisees**, as if they had already been mentioned or were assumed to be present wherever Jesus went. Since they have not been mentioned, "**some Pharisees**" as in TEV may be better.

For stylistic reasons, **with tax collectors and sinners** is translated "**with such people**" by TEV.

The question of the Pharisees is a rhetorical one. They are not so much asking for information as they are criticizing what Jesus is doing. The teachers of the Jewish religion had many regulations regarding eating. Anyone who willingly sat with outcasts indicated his acceptance of them and in a sense identified himself with them. To convey the tone of criticism, some translators have said "Your teacher eats with tax collectors and other sinners. Is that proper?"

Many languages must have an object with **eat**, possibly "eat food" or "eat a meal."

But when he heard it, he said, "Those who are well have no need of a physician, but those who are sick.	Jesus heard them and answered, "People who are well do not need a doctor, but only those who are sick.

The pronoun **he** refers to Jesus. Some translators use the proper noun, "Jesus."

Heard it: the Greek text does not indicate the object of the verb **heard**, but English structure requires one. NEB and GECL follow RSV in supplying **it** (NJB "this"), with the question of the Pharisees as the antecedent. NAB has "Overhearing the remark." TEV provides "**them**," which is actually an abbreviated form for ". . . them say this" or ". . . them ask this question." For some languages it may be necessary to be even more specific: "heard the question of the Pharisees" or "heard the Pharisees ask his disciples this question."

Jesus' reply takes the form of a parable in which tax collectors and other sinners (verse 10) are described as **those who are sick**.

Those may need to be rendered "those people" or "people." The sentence can be translated "People who aren't sick (or, People who are healthy) don't need a doctor, only sick people do." The order can also be reversed, as in "It is sick people who need a doctor, not those who are healthy."

Go and learn what this means, 'I desire mercy, and not sacrifice.' For I came not to call the righteous, but sinners."	Go and find out what is meant by the scripture that says: 'It is kindness that I want, not animal sacrifices.' I have not come to call respectable people, but outcasts."

Go and learn what this means is a formula frequently used by Jewish teachers when referring someone to a passage of scripture. TEV has ". . . **what is meant by the scripture that says**," thereby making a bridge to the scripture quotation which follows. In such a context it is obvious that **Go** is not to be taken literally, and in some languages it may be advisable to drop it from translation so as not to convey the wrong meaning.

The **I** in the citation refers to God, but if translators are not careful, it could seem to refer to Jesus. To avoid this, some translations have ". . . what is meant in God's Scriptures" or ". . . what is meant where God says in his Scriptures." Another way is "Go and learn what it means when God says in his book 'I want . . . ' " or ". . . that he wants." Without some kind of bridge, modern readers may not recognize that Jesus is quoting the Scriptures here.

I desire mercy, and not sacrifice is a quotation from Hosea 6.6. The same question is used again in 12.7, and in each instance it correctly follows both the Hebrew and the Greek Old Testament. The word **mercy** (TEV "**kindness**") is placed in the position of emphasis in the Greek text, "Mercy I want." **Sacrifice** is to be understood as "**animal sacrifices**" (TEV).

It may not be possible to desire something like **mercy** or "**kindness**." In such cases translators can say "I want people to be merciful (or, kind), not to make sacrifices (to me)" or "What I want from people is that they have mercy (on others), not that they offer me sacrifices."

Mercy can also be translated "**kindness**" or "compassion."

The Greek word meaning **For** shows that there is a logical relationship with what precedes, and it suggests that the meal that Jesus is sharing with the tax collectors and other outcasts is a fulfillment of the Hosea passage. The English **For** wrongly suggests that what follows is the reason or cause of what precedes, and so TEV omits it and allows the logical relationship to be clearly implicit.

For also shows that at this point the Hosea citation is finished, and Jesus is speaking of himself again. To make this clear, sometimes translators render **For** as "That's why I came . . ." or "It's because of that I came." It can also be "So I say to you that I came . . . ."

Call clearly means "call to be my followers." Brc has "bring an invitation to."

The righteous (TEV "**respectable people**") is one of Matthew's favorite expressions. See comments on 1.19 and 5.45. NEB has "virtuous people" (JB "the virtuous"), NAB "the self-righteous," and Brc "those who are good." **The righteous** means persons accepted within the Jewish religious structure. They are here contrasted with **sinners**, that is, persons not accepted within that structure. As in verse 10, so here also TEV uses "**outcasts**" in place of **sinners**.

Quite often translators try to show what Matthew means by **the righteous** by saying "those people who obey the Law of Moses."

The sentence may need to be restructured slightly, as in "The people I came to invite to follow me are the sinners, not the good people" or "I didn't come to call the good people to be my followers, but the sinners."

9.14-17

RSV   TEV

The Question about Fasting

14 Then the disciples of John came to him, saying, "Why do we and the Pharisees fast,ʷ but your disciples do not fast?" 15 And Jesus said to them, "Can the wedding guests mourn as long as the bridegroom is with them? The days will come, when the bridegroom is taken away from them, and then they will fast. 16 And no one puts a piece of unshrunk cloth on an old garment, for the patch tears away from the garment, and a worse tear is made. 17 Neither is new wine put into old wineskins; if it is, the skins burst, and the wine is spilled, and the skins are destroyed; but new wine is put into fresh wineskins, and so both are preserved."

14 Then the followers of John the Baptist came to Jesus, asking, "Why is it that we and the Pharisees fast often, but your disciples don't fast at all?"

15 Jesus answered, "Do you expect the guests at a wedding party to be sad as long as the bridegroom is with them? Of course not! But the day will come when the bridegroom will be taken away from them, and then they will fast.

16 "No one patches up an old coat with a piece of new cloth, for the new patch will shrink and make an even bigger hole in the coat. 17 Nor does anyone pour new wine into used wineskins, for the skins will burst, the wine will pour out, and the skins will be ruined. Instead, new wine is

^w Other ancient authorities add *much* or *often*

poured into fresh wineskins, and both will keep in good condition."

SECTION HEADING: "**The Question about Fasting**." The heading may have to be rendered "They ask Jesus about fasting," "Jesus teaches about fasting," or "Jesus teaches about when people should fast." See section heading and comments at 6.16.

9.14	RSV	TEV

Then the disciples of John came to him, saying, "Why do we and the Pharisees fast,^w but your disciples do not fast?"

^w Other ancient authorities add *much* or *often*

Then the followers of John the Baptist came to Jesus, asking, "Why is it that we and the Pharisees fast often, but your disciples don't fast at all?"

This section is bound closely to the previous one by the use of the adverb **Then**. Whereas the earlier passage dealt with the theme of eating, this passage is concerned with that of fasting. Evidently Jesus is still at the meal mentioned in the previous section, since he and his disciples do not get up and leave until verse 19.

The disciples of John are "the followers of John the Baptist," as the commentators point out. Most translations do not specify which John is meant, but GECL and TEV do so, and NJB gives a footnote indicating who is meant. The parallels in both Mark (2.18) and Luke (5.33) mention "the disciples of John," though in neither Mark nor Luke are they the ones who present Jesus with the question. Many translators will find it helpful to follow GECL and TEV and specify John the Baptist. For a discussion of "John the Baptist," see 3.1.

The text says **the disciples**, which would indicate it was all of John's disciples who came, but many translators do say "some of the disciples."

Of course, when it says they **came to him**, the text means "to Jesus."

Why do we . . . fast: the translation should not indicate that the disciples of John and the Pharisees were fasting right then, or that they fasted all the time. Rather, they made a habit of fasting. The text can read "fast regularly" or ". . . on a regular basis."

For comments on **Pharisees**, see 3.7.

For comments on **fast**, see 6.16.

As the RSV footnote indicates, there is a textual problem regarding the inclusion of the adverb which may mean either "much" or "often." The UBS Greek text placed it in square brackets, indicating that its presence in the text is disputed.

But your disciples do not fast: TEV has "**fast at all**" (so GECL 1st edition), representing one possible interpretation of the Greek present tense ("Why do we and the Pharisees make a rule of fasting, but your disciples do not do so?").

9.15 RSV	TEV
And Jesus said to them, "Can the wedding guests mourn as long as the bridegroom is with them? The days will come, when the bridegroom is taken away from them, and then they will fast.	Jesus answered, "Do you expect the guests at a wedding party to be sad as long as the bridegroom is with them? Of course not! But the day will come when the bridegroom will be taken away from them, and then they will fast.

And Jesus said to them: this is the first mention of **Jesus** by name in this narrative.

The wedding guests (NEB "the bridegroom's friends") translates a Semitic idiom, "sons of the bridechamber." A common rendering is "the people invited to a wedding." Another is to say "the friends of the bridegroom at a wedding."

Mourn can be expressed as "be sad" or "sorrowful."

Can . . . with them?: in Greek the form of Jesus' rhetorical question is such as to expect a negative answer, and so the basis for TEV "**Of course not!**" In some languages a statement may be better, "You (certainly) do not expect . . . ."

The days will come is translated somewhat more idiomatically by TEV ("**But the day will come**"), NEB ("The time will come"), and NJB ("But the time will come").

The verb **is taken away** occurs only here and in the parallels in Mark (2.20) and Luke (5.35). Some commentators understand the passive form of the verb to be a veiled allusion to Jesus' coming death. This may be so, but to make explicit reference to his death in the present context would destroy the parabolic content of the saying. GECL 1st edition translates by an active, which also satisfies the demands of the context: "must leave them." For some languages a shift to the future tense may be required (TEV "**will be taken away**").

Using an active sentence such as "must leave them" loses some of the idea of violent removal that the passive **is taken away** conveys. However, since the imagery here is important, it would certainly be wrong to supply "God" as the agent. Perhaps "won't be there (with them) any longer" or "won't be able to be there" will fit well.

9.16 RSV TEV

And no one puts a piece of unshrunk cloth on an old garment, for the patch tears away from the garment, and a worse tear is made.	"No one patches up an old coat with a piece of new cloth, for the new patch will shrink and make an even bigger hole in the coat.

The two sayings contained in verses 16-17 are in the form of proverbial sayings. In fact, Luke (5.36) specifically identifies them as parables (many languages will identify them as proverbs). Verse 16 describes a scene which is almost universally familiar. If a piece of **unshrunk** (that is, new) **cloth** is sewn on an old garment, the new patch will shrink when it is washed and make the hole even bigger than it was before. **Old garment** (TEV "**old coat**") may be translated "old piece of clothing."

It may be necessary to make explicit that putting a piece of cloth on an old garment is to repair it. **Puts** may therefore be translated as "sews on," "uses to repair," or "uses to patch."

Further, it is when the patched garment is washed that the patch shrinks and the tearing becomes worse. Some translations specify this: "For when the clothing is washed, the patch shrinks and it tears away from the cloth, making the tear worse."

9.17	RSV	TEV

Neither is new wine put into old wineskins; if it is, the skins burst, and the wine is spilled, and the skins are destroyed; but new wine is put into fresh wineskins, and so both are preserved."	**Nor does anyone pour new wine into used wineskins, for the skins will burst, the wine will pour out, and the skins will be ruined. Instead, new wine is poured into fresh wineskins, and both will keep in good condition."**

Neither is (TEV "**Nor does anyone**") translates a Greek impersonal construction ("Neither do they") which NEB represents as "Neither do you." All three translations are here aiming toward a natural equivalent. The parallels in Mark (2.22) and Luke (5.37) use the singular ("no one . . .").

No matter how this impersonal construction is translated at the beginning of this verse, whether "they," "you," or "anyone," the rest of the verse should use a similar form to be grammatical and cohesive.

Whereas the situation described in verse 16 is fairly well universal, the situation described in this verse has a somewhat limited cultural setting. **Wineskins** were usually made from whole goat hides with the neck and feet tied. Wine would then be stored in these skins. As the wine fermented, gases would be produced, causing the skin to expand. An old skin would burst under this pressure, because it had become dry and brittle and would already have expanded to its maximum. A new skin, on the other hand, would expand without bursting as the wine fermented.

There are two key pieces of cultural information that must be clear if this proverb is to be understood. First is the fact that the process of fermentation is clearly being referred to. **New wine** is unfermented wine or wine that is not fully fermented yet. It can be translated as "wine that is becoming fermented" or "fruit juice that hasn't fermented yet." Fermenting is almost universally known in one form or another. Some cultures say the wine "boils" or "cooks," for example.

In addition to calling the new wine "unfermented wine," it may be necessary to show it is the fermenting process that causes wine in the old wineskins to expand. One can say, for example, "No one puts unfermented wine into old wineskins. If he does, when the wine ferments, the skins burst."

A second relevant fact in this proverb is that new leather is slightly elastic. It has the power to expand. Old wineskins are already stretched to capacity and can only burst when put under pressure. This is a good reason not to use "bottles" or "calabashes" to translate **wineskins**. It would be better to say "container made from skins" or "container made from leather." Even if these are not known, the phrase is descriptive enough to make sense to readers.

The wine and the wineskins are **preserved**. This can be rendered "will not be destroyed" or "will not be lost."

RSV	TEV
	The Official's Daughter and the Woman Who Touched Jesus' Cloak
18 While he was thus speaking to them, behold, a ruler came in and knelt before him, saying, "My daughter has just died; but come and lay your hand on her, and she will live." 19 And Jesus rose and followed him, with his disciples. 20 And behold, a woman who had suffered from a hemorrhage for twelve years came up behind him and touched the fringe of his garment; 21 for she said to herself, "If I only touch his garment, I shall be made well." 22 Jesus turned, and seeing her he said, "Take heart, daughter; your faith has made you well." And instantly the woman was made well. 23 And when Jesus came to the ruler's house, and saw the flute players, and the crowd making a tumult, 24 he said, "Depart; for the girl is not dead but sleeping." And they laughed at him. 25 But when the crowd had been put outside, he went in and took her by the hand, and the girl arose. 26 And the report of this went through all that district.	18 While Jesus was saying this, a Jewish official came to him, knelt down before him, and said, "My daughter has just died; but come and place your hands on her, and she will live." 19 So Jesus got up and followed him, and his disciples went along with him. 20 A woman who had suffered from severe bleeding for twelve years came up behind Jesus and touched the edge of his cloak. 21 She said to herself, "If only I touch his cloak, I will get well." 22 Jesus turned around and saw her, and said, "Courage, my daughter! Your faith has made you well." At that very moment the woman became well. 23 Then Jesus went into the official's house. When he saw the musicians for the funeral and the people all stirred up, 24 he said, "Get out, everybody! The little girl is not dead—she is only sleeping!" Then they all started making fun of him. 25 But as soon as the people had been put out, Jesus went into the girl's room and took hold of her hand, and she got up. 26 The news about this spread all over that part of the country.

SECTION HEADING: **"The Official's Daughter and the Woman Who Touched Jesus' Cloak."** Since the passage contains these two incidents, most translators put both in the section heading. The first one can also be "Jesus brings to life a little girl" or "Jesus raises up an official's daughter." The second can be "Jesus heals a woman who touches his coat." The two can also be combined: "Jesus raises up an official's daughter and heals a woman when she touches his coat."

This is the first in a series of three miracle stories by which Matthew again emphasizes the authority of Jesus to heal. The miracles are probably introduced here in anticipation of Jesus' answer to John the Baptist in 11.5.

RSV	TEV
While he was thus speaking to them, behold, a ruler came in and knelt before him, saying, "My daughter has just died; but come and lay your hand on her, and she will live."	**While Jesus was saying this, a Jewish official came to him, knelt down before him, and said, "My daughter has just died; but come and place your hands on her, and she will live."**

While he was thus speaking to them is literally "While he was saying these things to them." TEV identifies **he** as "**Jesus.**"

Behold here serves to draw attention to the new participant in the narrative (see comments on 1.20). Perhaps here it can be "at that time" or "all at once."

Ruler (TEV "**Jewish official**") is rendered "synagogue leader" by NAB and "president of the synagogue" by NEB. NJB translates "one of the officials," with a footnote indicating that this person was the head of the synagogue. Both Mark (5.22) and Luke (8.41) explicitly identify the person as Jairus, a synagogue official. The term used by Matthew, however, is a much broader term, denoting an official or leader of any kind. It seems unwise to adapt Matthew's text to that of Mark and Luke, especially when there are so many obvious differences between the accounts, and it would have been simple enough for Matthew to have identified this person explicitly as a synagogue official had he so desired. In fact, the term may refer to either a Jew or a Gentile, but the presence of flute players (verse 23) would point to a Jewish household. Perhaps the best way to translate this **ruler** in Matthew is to say "a leader" or "one of the leaders of that place." One can also say "one of the important men there."

The leader **came in**. This can be "came into where Jesus was" or simply "came to Jesus." "Went" will be better in some languages.

He **knelt before him** to show honor. See 8.2 for a discussion of this.

My daughter has just died is in agreement with Luke (8.42) but in contrast with Mark (5.23), which speaks of the girl as "very sick" though not dead.

We are not given the age of the **daughter**, although she was a young girl, as we see in verse 24.

Hand is translated by the plural "**hands**" in TEV. Evidently the plural was chosen because of the Jewish custom of placing hands upon people for various reasons, including that of healing. It is impossible to say precisely where the hands would have been placed upon the girl, but if it is necessary to be specific in translation, then it seems quite probable that they would have been laid upon the girl's forehead or head.

To **lay** a hand can be "put" or "place." No term should be used that would be understood in a negative sense of doing harm to the girl.

And she will live may need to be translated "and she will come back to life." GECL renders "then she will live again!" The verb **live** does occasionally mean "live again" (see Rev 2.8; possibly also Rev 13.14).

9.19	RSV	TEV

And Jesus rose and followed him, with his disciples.	So Jesus got up and followed him, and his disciples went along with him.

And Jesus rose (TEV "**So Jesus got up**") presupposes that he was still sitting down for the meal (verse 10). According to Mark (5.21) the incident happened as Jesus was walking beside Lake Galilee. Another possibility would be as Brc has rendered it, "Jesus started out to go with him."

Followed him, with his disciples translates a typical Semitic Greek structure, literally "followed him and his disciples," in which Jesus is the subject of the singular verb "followed," and the disciples are understood as participating in the action of following. In some languages either a verb must be supplied (TEV "**and his disciples went along with him**"), or else a plural form of the verb must be introduced ("Jesus and his disciples followed him"). NEB ("and so did his disciples") and NAB ("and his disciples did the same") are similar to TEV.

9.20	RSV	TEV

And behold, a woman who had suffered from a hemorrhage for twelve years came up behind him and touched the fringe of his garment;	A woman who had suffered from severe bleeding for twelve years came up behind Jesus and touched the edge of his cloak.

And behold here also serves to draw attention to a new participant in the narrative (see verse 18).

A hemorrhage may be spoken of in less technical language as a "**severe bleeding**" (TEV). NEB is good because it suggests habitual but not constant bleeding: "had suffered from haemorrhages." If her hemorrhaging was from her womb, as seems quite likely to many scholars, then according to Leviticus 15.25-30 she was ritually unclean during those twelve years.

One way to translate this sentence is to say "during twelve years she had a frequent problem because of bleeding" or "very often she would suffer from bleeding. This had been going on for twelve years."

Touched is the meaning given the Greek verb by most translations. However, in other contexts the verb may mean "take hold of." It would not be correct to use a word that meant she accidentally brushed past Jesus. Her action was deliberate.

Fringe (so NJB) or "**edge**" (TEV, NEB) may be understood as a specific reference to the "tassel" (NAB, Brc) which Jewish men were obligated to wear on the four corners of their outer garments (see Num 15.37-41; Deut 22.12). The problem of interpretation is complicated by two factors. First, we do not know how precisely Jesus followed the ceremonial rules of his religion. And second, we cannot determine with any degree of certainty the way that the writer of the Gospel and the original readers may have understood the term. In light of these complications, it appears best not to give the term too specific a meaning, and it is probably best translated as "edge."

Garment is the same word used in verse 16; it may refer to a piece of clothing in general, or more specifically to an outer garment. Many translations use "cloak," and in verse 16 TEV had "coat." One should not follow the example of AB ("the hem of his himation"), which is a transliteration of the Greek. If in a culture men wear some type of outer cloak as part of their clothing, that can certainly be used for **garment** here. But many translators will use a very general term like "clothing."

for she said to herself, "If I only touch his garment, I shall be made well."	She said to herself, "If only I touch his cloak, I will get well."

For may need to be expanded, as in "she did that because."

She said to herself is a way of referring to what she was thinking. She believed that even touching the edge of Jesus' clothing would heal her. Thus some translators say "for she believed (or, thought) that even if she only touched his garment, she would be healed." One can also say "for she was thinking 'If I only . . . .' "

I shall be made well (JB "I shall be well again") translates the verb which normally means "to be saved." However, the meaning here is obvious. **I shall be made well** is a passive sentence where God is the understood agent. Translators can say "God will heal me." But "I will get well" is also possible.

In some languages it may be necessary to invert the order of verses 20b and 21. For example, ". . . came up behind Jesus. She said to herself, 'If only I touch his cloak, I will get well.' So she touched the edge of his cloak."

Jesus turned, and seeing her he said, "Take heart, daughter; your faith has made you well." And instantly the woman was made well.	Jesus turned around and saw her, and said, "Courage, my daughter! Your faith has made you well." At that very moment the woman became well.

Turned (TEV **"turned around"**) suggests that Jesus turned in the opposite direction from where he was headed, since in verse 20 it is stated that the woman came up from behind him.

The participle **seeing her** will often be rendered "when he saw her" or "he saw her and said."

Take heart was used in verse 2. Elsewhere it is found in the Gospel only in 14.27.

Daughter, as "son" in verse 2, represents a polite form of address and signifies nothing about the woman's age. **Daughter**, as with "son," may be difficult to translate naturally, as it, too, may give the impression that Jesus was the woman's father. "Young woman" or "My friend" may be possible, although in some cultures this latter may have romantic connotations and will have to be avoided.

As in verse 2, the vocative **Daughter** may have to precede **Take heart**.

Your faith has made you well rules out the possibility of interpreting the miracle as a magic act. It is the word of Jesus in response to the woman's faith that effects the healing. The sentence can be expressed as "Because you believe, you are cured" or "You are cured because you believed." Some languages will require an object for "believe," that is, something or someone she believed in. "Believed that I could cure you" is then possible.

Instantly is literally "from that hour" (see "in that hour" of 8.13), an expression indicating an immediate cure (TEV **"at that very moment"**; NEB "and from that moment"). Elsewhere Matthew uses this expression in 15.28; 17.18; a related construction ("from the sixth hour") occurs in 27.45. Neither Mark nor Luke uses either of these expressions. Translators can say "right away" or "right then."

The text uses a passive sentence, **was made well**. This can also be "was healed," but often an active sentence is better, as in **"became well"** (TEV) or "became better."

9.23 RSV	TEV
And when Jesus came to the ruler's house, and saw the flute players, and the crowd making a tumult,	Then Jesus went into the official's house. When he saw the musicians for the funeral and the people all stirred up,

Came to (NAB "arrived at") is more naturally taken to mean "went into" (NIV "entered"). RSV probably translates **came to** so as to avoid the erroneous conclusion that the healing of the woman took place immediately in front of the official's home. The context implies other activity by Jesus, which may need to be made explicit in translation: "Then Jesus went to the official's house. When he arrived there he went in and saw . . . ." In place of **came to** some languages will prefer "went to."

Flute players (TEV **"musicians"**): according to Jewish tradition, even the poorest people were expected to have two flute players and a wailing woman for a funeral. In order to clarify the role of the flute players, TEV adds **"for the funeral."** This information was immediately evident to a Jewish reader who was familiar with the funeral customs, but it will not be clear to other readers.

Many cultures are familiar with the **flute** or other instruments that are played by blowing through a wooden tube. If no such instrument exists, then translators can say "musical instruments for a funeral" or, as in TEV, **"musicians for the funeral."**

The crowd making a tumult is rendered "the crowd making a commotion" by NJB and "the general commotion" by NEB. The reference is to the mourners, who would have been wailing loudly in typical oriental fashion. Some translators will have "the crowd was making a big noise" or "he saw the way the crowd was generally in an uproar."

9.24 RSV	TEV
he said, "Depart; for the girl is not dead but sleeping." And they laughed at him.	he said, "Get out, everybody! The little girl is not dead—she is only sleeping!" Then they all started making fun of him.

Depart (TEV **"Get out"**) translates a second person plural imperative form in Greek. Since English does not differentiate between the singular and plural imperative forms, TEV has included **"everybody"** to help the reader understand that

Jesus' command included the crowd of mourners as well as the flute players. **Depart** can also be "All of you, leave" or "Everyone, leave now." Brc uses strong language, "Get out of here."

Girl (so also NEB) translates a Greek noun form which suggests the meaning "**little girl**" (TEV, NJB, NAB). Elsewhere the noun is used only in 9.25; 14.11; Mark 5.41,42; 6.22,28.

Before the verb **sleeping** TEV adds the adverb "**only**" to strengthen the contrast between **dead** and **sleeping**. The imagery of death as sleep has its background in the Old Testament (Dan 12.2). Translators may make this two sentences, as in "The girl is not dead. She is only asleep."

And they laughed at him (so also JB) is translated similarly by NEB ("and they only laughed at him"). But the verb may also mean "ridicule" (NAB "At this they began to ridicule him") or "**make fun of**" (TEV).

9.25	RSV	TEV
	But when the crowd had been put outside, he went in and took her by the hand, and the girl arose.	But as soon as the people had been put out, Jesus went into the girl's room and took hold of her hand, and she got up.

It may be necessary in some languages to change **But when the crowd had been put outside** into an active construction. For example, ". . . the family had made the crowd of people go outside the house" or ". . . had sent the people outside the house."

Went in may require further definition in some languages. TEV and GECL 1st edition have ". . . **into the girl's room**" and NEB has ". . . into the room."

Took her by the hand is translated "took the girl by the hand" by NEB. In the restructuring of TEV it is not necessary to state that it was the girl's hand he took, since in the clause immediately preceding, TEV indicates it was the girl's room.

Arose (TEV "**got up**"; NJB "stood up") translates the same verb form frequently used of Jesus' resurrection from death (see 28.6,7); it is also used of Peter's mother-in-law in 8.15.

9.26	RSV	TEV
	And the report of this went through all that district.	The news about this spread all over that part of the country.

And the report of this went (JB "And the news spread . . .") may need to be restructured so as to indicate who spread the news, "People began to spread the news about this . . ." or "People began to tell (each other) about this."

All that district (TEV "**that part of the country**") hints that the author did not live there at the time of his writing. **District** can be "region" or "that area."

RSV

TEV

Jesus Heals Two Blind Men

27 And as Jesus passed on from there, two blind men followed him, crying aloud, "Have mercy on us, Son of David." 28 When he entered the house, the blind men came to him; and Jesus said to them, "Do you believe that I am able to do this?" They said to him, "Yes, Lord." 29 Then he touched their eyes, saying, "According to your faith be it done to you." 30 And their eyes were opened. And Jesus sternly charged them, "See that no one knows it." 31 But they went away and spread his fame through all that district.

27 Jesus left that place, and as he walked along, two blind men started following him. "Have mercy on us, Son of David!" they shouted.

28 When Jesus had gone indoors, the two blind men came to him, and he asked them, "Do you believe that I can heal you?"

"Yes, sir!" they answered.

29 Then Jesus touched their eyes and said, "Let it happen, then, just as you believe!"—30 and their sight was restored. Jesus spoke sternly to them, "Don't tell this to anyone!"

31 But they left and spread the news about Jesus all over that part of the country.

SECTION HEADING: "**Jesus Heals Two Blind Men**." This heading can also be "Jesus restores sight to two blind men" or "Jesus heals two blind men so they can see."

This passage is without parallel in Mark or Luke, though it is similar to Matthew 20.29-34, which does have parallels (Mark 10.46-52; Luke 18.35-43).

9.27   RSV   TEV

And as Jesus passed on from there, two blind men followed him, crying aloud, "Have mercy on us, Son of David."

Jesus left that place, and as he walked along, two blind men started following him. "Have mercy on us, Son of David!" they shouted.

Passed on from there translates the same verb and adverb used in verse 9. Jesus' movements cannot be defined with exact precision. Translators should probably render **passed on from there** in a way similar to the phrase in verse 9, perhaps as "Jesus left there," "Jesus continued on from there," or "Jesus went on from there."

Followed (so also NJB) may have the force of "**started following**" (TEV). In this context **followed** will certainly mean "went behind him." It does not mean that they became disciples. TEV found it more natural to say "**started following**," and this will be true in many other languages as well.

The expression **crying aloud** means "shouting" or "calling loudly." It does not mean weeping. They were calling out repeatedly as they walked along. "They were shouting" will indicate this.

Have mercy on us is the cry of the blind men for help and healing from Jesus. They do not merely want his pity or sympathy; they want him to heal them. **Have mercy on us** should be translated by some phrase that is natural in the context. Examples may be "Take pity on us," "Be kind to us," or "Please be kind and help us."

Son of David is a Jewish Messianic title. It was first used in 1.1 (TEV "a descendant of David") and appears also in 15.22; 20.30; 21.9,15. Jesus is the Promised Savior, and so the time had arrived for the promised healing of the blind. See, for example, the prophecy in Isaiah 35.5.

The title **Son of David** could make some readers think that Jesus was David's son. Therefore "Descendant of David," "Descendant of King David," or "You who are of King David's family" have been used. However, the fact that **Son of David** was a Messianic title does get lost with such translations. This fact can be explained in a footnote, or the title itself can be in the text and the footnote can explain the meaning.

Many languages have formulas for titles, and they can be used here. A common way in West Africa, for example, is to say "You who are called Son of David."

In some languages the vocative cannot be at the end of a sentence but must be at the beginning, as in "Son of David, have mercy on us."

9.28	RSV	TEV
	When he entered the house, the blind men came to him; and Jesus said to them, "Do you believe that I am able to do this?" They said to him, "Yes, Lord."	When Jesus had gone indoors, the two blind men came to him, and he asked them, "Do you believe that I can heal you?" "Yes, sir!" they answered.

The house is most logically taken to be Jesus' own home in Capernaum, though according to the context it may refer back to the house mentioned in verse 10. Most translations are noncommittal, rendering either "**indoors**" (TEV, NEB) or "the house" (NJB, NAB). In Greek the phrase normally refers to one's own house; see comments at 9.10. Some translators will follow the normal meaning of the Greek phrase here and say "his house." Others will leave it unclear, saying "went inside" or "went in the house."

RSV says the blind men **came to him**. This can also be "went to him" or "approached him."

Do you believe places upon the blind men the necessity of faith in Jesus' power and willingness to heal them.

That I am able to do this is more precise in TEV ("**that I can heal you**"); NEB has "that I have the power to do what you want." Since the healing they wanted was to have their sight restored, the phrase can be rendered "that I can give you your sight" or "that I can make you see."

The noun of address rendered "**sir**" by TEV and most other translations may also mean **Lord** (RSV, NAB). The problem of interpretation relates to the perspective from which Matthew writes. That is, does he conceive of the men as acknowledging the lordship of Jesus at this point, or does he see them as merely addressing Jesus with a term of respect? Translators are referred to 8.2. Certainly support can be found for the Christian "Lord" here, but most translators have used the equivalent of "sir." Some languages may require a fuller response on the part of the men, as in "Yes, sir, we believe you can."

Then he touched their eyes, saying,
"According to your faith be it done
to you."

Then Jesus touched their eyes
and said, "Let it happen, then, just
as you believe!"—

Touched their eyes: the Greek text does not indicate whether Jesus reached out with both hands and touched the eyes of the two men at the same time, or whether he used only his right hand, touching their eyes in sequence. The combination of the aorist tense **touched** and the present tense **saying** may suggest simultaneous action. It also implies that Jesus was still touching their eyes as he spoke. Thus translators can say either "he touched their eyes and said" or "he touched their eyes, and as he did, he said."

According to your faith be it done is plural in Greek; TEV reverses the order: "**Let it happen, then, just as you believe.**" Some interpreters take **According to your faith** to mean "according to the degree of your faith" (Brc "in proportion to your faith"). However, the context suggests the meaning "Because of your faith" (NAB). **Be it done** is an affirmation, not a request or command. Jesus' response may then be translated ". . . and so I will give you your sight." GECL has "What you trusted me to do will happen." Another rendering is "You believed you would receive your sight, and so you will."

And their eyes were opened. And
Jesus sternly charged them, "See
that no one knows it."

and their sight was restored. Jesus
spoke sternly to them, "Don't tell this
to anyone!"

And their eyes were opened is a literal translation of a Semitic idiom; TEV and NEB have "**and their sight was restored.**" The Greek text does not indicate whether the men had previously been able to see, but a number of translations state that this was the case: "and they recovered their sight" (NAB) and "And their sight returned" (NJB). See also Brc, Phps, and AT. GECL, on the other hand, is noncommittal: "then they could see." The clause **their eyes were opened** is not to be understood literally, but rather in the sense of suddenly being able to see. "And they were able to see" or the rendering of GECL are good reflections of the meaning of the phrase.

Jesus sternly charged them (NEB "Jesus said to them sternly") is translated "Jesus warned them" by GECL 1st edition and "Then Jesus sternly warned them" by NJB. The verb **sternly charged** was originally used of the snorting of horses, and it may indicate either anger or displeasure. When used of persons it may carry the meaning "scold" or "reprimand." Elsewhere in the New Testament it is used only in Mark 1.43; 14.5; John 11.33,38. The context implies more of sternness than of anger.

The right tone of **sternly charged** may be conveyed with a phrase like "Jesus warned them very severely" or "Jesus gave them a sharp warning. He said . . . ."

See that no one knows it is more straightforward in TEV: "**Don't tell this to anyone**." Most English translations are fairly literal, but Phps renders "Don't let anyone know about this."

It may be necessary to use indirect speech, as in "Jesus warned them sharply not to tell anyone what had happened."

9.31	RSV	TEV
	But they went away and spread his fame through all that district.	**But they left and spread the news about Jesus all over that part of the country.**

But they went away translates a participial construction in Greek which may be understood in a temporal sense, "But when they had gone" (JB). It is possible to interpret the construction as having a cause-and-effect relation with the healing deed that Jesus had just performed, but this does not seem to be what the author intends. The problem with both RSV and TEV is that they leave open this possibility and even hint in that direction.

To keep the temporal sense as JB does, translators can also say "But after they had left" or "But later when they had gone away from there."

Spread . . . fame translates a Greek verb which appears in TEV and AT as "**spread the news about**." The verb comes from the same root as the noun rendered "report" by RSV in verse 26; it is found elsewhere in the New Testament only in 28.14 and Mark 1.45. Either "**spread the news about**" or "make known" may be considered the root meaning of the verb. Both NJB and NEB translate "they talked about him," while Phps and Brc each translate "they spread the story." It is logical to assume that the main topic of conversation was the healing of their eyes. Brc and Phps intimate that what they told was limited to what they had experienced, while other translations imply that they told other things as well. If this interpretation is followed, then one may translate "they spread the news of what Jesus had done for them" or ". . . of how he had restored their sight." If the broader interpretation is accepted, then one may translate ". . . of what Jesus had done for them and for others" or "how Jesus had restored their sight and had also healed other people of their diseases." Other expressions for **spread . . . fame** that translators can use include "they told many people about" or "they reported to everyone."

Through all that district once again assumes that the author is not living there at the time that the story is written (see verse 26). **District** (so also Phps, Brc) is too specialized in that it implies a governmental division, while "countryside" (NEB, NJB) would possibly exclude the villages and towns of that area. The rendering of AT (followed by TEV) and Mft ("all over that country") appears to be a better solution. GECL 1st edition renders "in the entire country."

RSV	TEV

Jesus Heals a Dumb Man

| 32 As they were going away, behold, a dumb demoniac was brought to him. 33 And when the demon had been cast out, the dumb man spoke; and the crowds marveled, saying, "Never was anything like this seen in Israel." 34 But the Pharisees said, "He casts out demons by the prince of demons."[a] | 32 As the men were leaving, some people brought to Jesus a man who could not talk because he had a demon. 33 But as soon as the demon was driven out, the man started talking, and everyone was amazed. "We have never seen anything like this in Israel!" they exclaimed. 34 But the Pharisees said, "It is the chief of the demons who gives him the power to drive out demons." |

[a] Other ancient authorities omit this verse

SECTION HEADING: "**Jesus Heals a Dumb Man**." This heading can be expressed "Jesus heals a man who could not talk" or "Jesus heals a man so he could talk again."

This story, the last in a series of four miracle stories, immediately precedes 9.35, a verse that summarizes the activity of the one who is the Messiah in both word and deed.

9.32 RSV TEV

As they were going away, behold, a dumb demoniac was brought to him. | As the men were leaving, some people brought to Jesus a man who could not talk because he had a demon.

As they (TEV "**the men**") **were going away** serves to link this story with the one immediately before it. Since verses 32-34 comprise a unit within themselves, it may be useful to replace **they** with "the two men whom Jesus had healed of their blindness" or "the two men whose sight had been restored."

Here again **behold** functions to introduce new participants into the narrative; see 1.20; 9.18,20.

Dumb translates an adjective which may mean either "unable to speak" or "unable to hear" (11.5); only the context will clarify the meaning. Here, of course, it means "**could not talk**" (TEV). TEV avoids the use of **dumb**, because English speakers often understand it to mean "stupid" or "ignorant."

Demoniac translates a participle which TEV represents by "**because he had a demon**." NAB has "who was possessed by a demon," and NEB "possessed by a devil." GECL 1st edition has "because an evil spirit ruled him."

Sometimes this sentence is easier to translate if the order is changed, as in "A man who had an evil spirit in him that made him unable to talk."

As we pointed out before, generally the notions of being possessed by a demon, an evil spirit, or a devil are translated the same way. See comments on 4.1 and 4.24.

Was brought (so also NEB) translates an active verb "they brought"; TEV retains the impersonal active form "**some people brought**."

RSV   TEV

And when the demon had been cast out, the dumb man spoke; and the crowds marveled, saying, "Never was anything like this seen in Israel."

But as soon as the demon was driven out, the man started talking, and everyone was amazed. "We have never seen anything like this in Israel!" they exclaimed.

And when the demon had been cast out translates a construction which indicates a temporal relation between this event and the response which follows. JB has "And when the devil was cast out," and NAB "Once the demon was expelled." **"As soon as"** of TEV and AT emphasizes the immediacy of the response, as does the restructuring of GECL, "Hardly had the evil spirit been driven out . . . ."

This sentence presupposes that Jesus threw out the demon. In many languages it will be necessary to state that specifically, as in "Jesus threw out the demon. When he had done that, the dumb man spoke," or "Jesus told the demon to leave. As soon as the demon was thrown out" or ". . . as soon as the demon left the man."

The dumb man spoke: most English readers would probably expect either "began to talk (or, speak)" (Phps, NAB) or "**started talking**" (TEV), and the Greek may also convey this meaning. Brc translates "the dumb man regained the power of speech"; NEB is rather high level: "and the patient recovered his speech." One can also say "the man was able to speak."

And the crowds marveled describes the people's reaction to the miracle; **marveled** was first used in 8.10 (see also 8.27). **Crowds** can be "all the people there" or "everyone."

Saying can be expressed as "and said" or "as they said."

Never was there anything like this seen in Israel may mean either "**We have never seen anything like this in Israel**" (TEV) or "Nothing like this has ever happened in Israel." The verb **was . . . seen** is sometimes used of a divine manifestation or revelation, and so there is also a third possibility, that of translating "God has never before revealed himself like this to the people of Israel." The second option seems most probable, and the response is to the total effect of Jesus' miracles recorded in chapters 8–9. The people are saying that nothing had ever happened like this, either in the history of their nation or in their own experience.

Thus the best rendering is "Nothing like this has ever happened in Israel," "There has never been anything like this known to happen in Israel," or "This is the first time something like this has happened in Israel."

RSV   TEV

But the Pharisees said, "He casts out demons by the prince of demons."[a]

But the Pharisees said, "It is the chief of the demons who gives him the power to drive out demons."

[a] Other ancient authorities omit this verse

As indicated in the UBS Greek text, there is a considerable degree of doubt regarding the inclusion of this verse. Since the accusation of the Pharisees plays no part in the continuation of the narrative, some scholars believe that the words have been brought in either from 12.24 or from Luke 11.15. On the other hand, the textual evidence itself is rather overwhelmingly in favor of the inclusion of this verse. It may be that Matthew places this statement here in order to prepare the reader for the controversy in 10.25.

Rather than attribute the source of Jesus' power to God, the Pharisees claim that it comes from **the prince** (TEV "**chief**") **of demons**, that is, the Devil himself. Most scholars interpret **by** to mean "with the power of" (the chief of demons), though the Greek construction may also mean "he has the power to cast out demons because he himself is their chief." GECL translates "He can drive out evil spirits because the chief of all the evil spirits gives him the power to do it." For many readers it will be helpful to identify the Devil as the chief of all the demons: ". . . the Devil, who is the chief of all evil spirits, gives him the power . . . ." If this identification is not made in the text, it should at least be done in a footnote.

It is important that **prince** is understood to mean "chief" or "leader," not "son of a king."

The translation of **Pharisees** was discussed at 3.7.

For **demons** and "Devil," see comments on 4.1.

9.35-38

RSV	TEV
	Jesus Has Pity for the People
35 And Jesus went about all the cities and villages, teaching in their synagogues and preaching the gospel of the kingdom, and healing every disease and every infirmity. 36 When he saw the crowds, he had compassion for them, because they were harassed and helpless, like sheep without a shepherd. 37 Then he said to his disciples, "The harvest is plentiful, but the laborers are few; 38 pray therefore the Lord of the harvest to send out laborers into his harvest."	35 Jesus went around visiting all the towns and villages. He taught in the synagogues, preached the Good News about the Kingdom, and healed people with every kind of disease and sickness. 36 As he saw the crowds, his heart was filled with pity for them, because they were worried and helpless, like sheep without a shepherd. 37 So he said to his disciples, "The harvest is large, but there are few workers to gather it in. 38 Pray to the owner of the harvest that he will send out workers to gather in his harvest."

SECTION HEADING: "**Jesus Has Pity for the People.**" This can also be "Jesus feels sorry for the people," or "Jesus has great love for the people."

This brief passage is an editorial comment in which Matthew summarizes the work of Jesus up to this point and prepares the way for the sending out of the twelve in the following chapter. In this regard the passage functions similarly to 4.23-25.

9.35

RSV	TEV
And Jesus went about all the cities and villages, teaching in their synagogues and preaching the gos-	**Jesus went around visiting all the towns and villages. He taught in the synagogues, preached the Good**

| pel of the kingdom, and healing every disease and every infirmity. | News about the Kingdom, and healed people with every kind of disease and sickness. |

As may be gathered from a reading of RSV, all of verse 35 is one sentence in Greek.

All: this may not indicate that Jesus went to every city and village, since in Hebrew the word frequently refers to a large number. Matthew does not define what **cities and villages** are intended. The district of Galilee is specifically mentioned in 4.23, and in 11.21,23 the three towns of Chorazin, Bethsaida, and Capernaum are mentioned. Chorazin and Capernaum were actually in Galilee, while Bethsaida was across the Jordan River from Capernaum, in the district of Galanitis. But in any case it would appear that the **cities and villages** may loosely be identified as those of Galilee. If the translation must be specific, one may render "all the towns and villages of Galilee" or "all the towns and villages near Lake Galilee."

Languages that do not have separate words for **cities** and **villages** can say "big towns" and "little towns," or even "all the towns." Some translators will find it difficult to keep the exaggerated style of Matthew, **all**, and will say "many of the towns."

This first sentence will be handled in different ways. Some examples are "Jesus went to all the towns and villages (in the area)" and "Jesus visited the towns and villages of that area."

Teaching . . . every infirmity: see comments on 4.23. The two verses are essentially identical at this point.

9.36   RSV   TEV

| When he saw the crowds, he had compassion for them, because they were harassed and helpless, like sheep without a shepherd. | As he saw the crowds, his heart was filled with pity for them, because they were worried and helpless, like sheep without a shepherd. |

Saw may be "looked at" or "observed."

Crowds may need to be "crowds of people."

Had compassion translates a Greek verb which is used quite frequently in the Gospels. In Matthew it is found in 14.14; 15.32; 18.27; 20.34. The root meaning is "to be stirred up with feeling." NJB renders "he felt sorry," and NEB "the sight of the people moved him to pity." NAB is similar to TEV, "his heart was moved with pity." Other suggestions are "he was filled with compassion for them" or "pity for them filled him." Many languages will have an idiom that describes this feeling of pity and love.

Harassed translates a participle derived from a verb stem which originally meant "flayed" or "skinned." In the New Testament, however, it always has a figurative meaning: "troubled," "harassed," "worried," or "bewildered," or possibly "confused" or "upset."

Helpless also translates a Greek participle. It derives from a verb which originally means "throw away (or, down)," but Matthew quite obviously uses it in a figurative sense. NEB translates as TEV does; several others have "dejected" (AT, NJB, Brc), while Phps translates "miserable." The two participles are represented in NAB as "They were lying prostrate from exhaustion," which seems to squeeze too much from the etymology of the verb, for it is hardly conceivable that the people were actually lying on the ground, physically exhausted! In addition to a literal translation of **helpless**, other possible words are "defeated" or "vulnerable."

The closest parallel to the expression **like sheep without a shepherd** is Numbers 27.17. But see also 1 Kings 22.17; 2 Chronicles 18.16; Isaiah 53.6; Ezekiel 34.5. This verse indicates that the call for laborers to go to the harvest (verses 37-38) is based upon the compassion of Jesus.

The simile **like sheep without a shepherd** can pose something of a problem in areas where sheep are not well known. It may be necessary to say "like animals that need to be watched, but have no one to take care of them." However, since sheep occur so often in the Bible, most translators have tried to retain "sheep" where possible, perhaps calling them "domestic animals called sheep." If possible, however, the sentence should not be too long or awkward.

9.37	RSV	TEV

Then he said to his disciples, "The harvest is plentiful, but the laborers are few;	So he said to his disciples, "The harvest is large, but there are few workers to gather it in.

Then translates a particle which may mean either "at that time" or "next in sequence." Matthew employs it rather frequently (90 times).

The harvest is plentiful, but the laborers are few is probably a proverbial saying. The **plentiful** harvest can be "rich" or "huge." In some languages one cannot speak of the harvest being big, but rather one must say "the crops that are ready to be harvested are abundant."

Laborers can be "workers" or "people who work in the fields." TEV uses an infinitive phrase to specify the work of the laborers: "**workers to gather it in**." The basis for the inclusion of this information is found in the Greek text of verse 38 ("laborers into his harvest"). GECL provides the same information, though in a different way: "Here is a rich harvest to gather in, but there are not enough workers." Instead of saying they are **few**, it is possible to say "but there are only a few people to gather it in" or "but there are not enough people to bring it in."

The **harvest** is a figure for people who are ready to be persuaded to trust in God, and there are translators who have said "These people are like crops in the field that are abundant and ready to be harvested. But there are only a few workers who can lead them to trust in God."

9.38	RSV	TEV

pray therefore the Lord of the harvest to send out laborers into his harvest."	Pray to the owner of the harvest that he will send out workers to gather in his harvest."

For comments on **pray**, see 5.44. It can be "you should pray" or left as an imperative **pray**. See TEV, for example. Of course in many languages one has to say "pray to the Lord of the harvest to ask him."

Therefore or "so" should appear in the sentence wherever it will be most natural. Some languages do not need such a transition at all in this context.

Lord of the harvest (TEV "**owner of the harvest**"; see NEB) is translated "harvest master" by NAB. The person referred to is God. The TEV and NEB renderings have been the most useful models for translators.

The noun phrase **into his harvest** is translated as a verb phrase in GECL 1st edition and TEV: "**to gather in his harvest**." Elsewhere Matthew uses the **harvest** as a symbol of the final judgment (13.30,39), but here the symbolism is slightly different. The harvest represents the masses of people who stand ready to respond to the message of salvation, and Jesus calls upon his followers to pray to God to send messengers who will proclaim the good news.

For those translators who choose to make the whole image into a simile (see verse 37), the **Lord** may be "God, who is like the owner of the harvest." To **send out laborers into his harvest** will then be "to send out his servants (or, his people) to lead them to trust in God" or ". . . to proclaim the good news."

Chapter 10

10.1-4

10.1-4

RSV	TEV
	The Twelve Apostles
1 And he called to him his twelve disciples and gave them authority over unclean spirits, to cast them out, and to heal every disease and every infirmity. 2 The names of the twelve apostles are these: first, Simon, who is called Peter, and Andrew his brother; James the son of Zebedee, and John his brother; 3 Philip and Bartholomew; Thomas and Matthew the tax collector; James the son of Alphaeus, and Thaddaeus;*ˣ* 4 Simon the Cananaean, and Judas Iscariot, who betrayed him.	1 Jesus called his twelve disciples together and gave them authority to drive out evil spirits and to heal every disease and every sickness. 2 These are the names of the twelve apostles: first, Simon (called Peter) and his brother Andrew; James and his brother John, the sons of Zebedee; 3 Philip and Bartholomew; Thomas and Matthew, the tax collector; James son of Alphaeus, and Thaddaeus; 4 Simon the Patriot, and Judas Iscariot, who betrayed Jesus.

ˣOther ancient authorities read Lebbaeus or Lebbaeus called Thaddaeus

SECTION HEADING: "**The Twelve Apostles**." This title can be "The twelve apostles of Jesus," "The twelve men Jesus chose to be apostles," or "Jesus chooses twelve men to be his apostles." For "**Apostles**" see comments on verse 2.

Jesus' instructions to a group of his disciples is given in two contexts: one is associated with the sending out of the twelve (Matt 10.15-42; Mark 6.7-13; Luke 9.1-6), while the other is addressed to the seventy-two (Luke 10.1-12). As with the Sermon on the Mount, so here also sayings of Jesus that are scattered in other contexts in Mark and Luke appear as a unified discourse in Matthew. This is especially noticeable in the placement of 9.37, which in Luke's Gospel forms the introduction to the sending out of the seventy-two (10.2)

Mark (3.13-19) narrates the selection of the twelve at a much earlier stage in Jesus' ministry, before he sends them out (6.7-13), but Matthew combines the selection and the sending into one episode.

10.1

RSV	TEV
And he called to him his twelve disciples and gave them authority over unclean spirits, to cast them out, and to heal every disease and every infirmity.	**Jesus called his twelve disciples together and gave them authority to drive out evil spirits and to heal every disease and every sickness.**

The word **And** again indicates the beginning of a new unit. For this reason many translators will use "Jesus" instead of **he**. TEV is an example. Further, in few languages is "and" a natural way to open a discourse unit, so it is usually either dropped or replaced by a phrase such as "Later" or "One day after that."

Called to him (so also AT, NEB) is translated "**called . . . together**" by TEV. NJB, Brc, NAB use the rather high level "summoned." Another way to render it is "told his twelve disciples to come to him." Direct speech can also be used: "said to his twelve disciples 'Come here.' "

In Matthew the group of disciples is frequently spoken of as "the twelve disciples" (11.1; 20.17; 26.14,20,47). According to 19.28 they will sit on twelve thrones to judge the twelve tribes of Israel, which suggests that they are somehow symbolic of the "new Israel."

For comments on **disciples**, see 5.1.

In 7.29 Matthew indicates that Jesus himself taught with authority; here it is said that Jesus **gave them authority**. **Authority** can be translated "power" as long as readers do not understand it to mean physical power. In this context the Greek word means primarily that he gave them the "right" to exercise "power" over unclean spirits. Words like "ability" or "skill" should be avoided. In this context "authority to command" has been used by some translators.

RSV indicates what the authority involves by adding **to cast them out** after the **unclean spirits**. TEV has rendered this more naturally in English, "**gave them authority to drive out evil spirits**." For **cast . . . out**, see comments on 7.22 and 8.16. This phrase can also be rendered "Jesus gave them the authority so that when they told evil spirits to leave people, the spirits had to obey them."

Unclean spirits are mentioned again in 12.43 but nowhere else in the Gospel. The terminology reflects the cultural viewpoint of the Jewish people; anyone possessed by evil spirits was considered unclean and was then excluded from the social and religious life of the community. In many cultures, especially where religious concepts of "clean" and "unclean" do not play a major role, the nearest equivalent is "**evil spirits**" (TEV, GECL, FRCL). Translators can also say "evil spirits that made people ceremonially unclean," but only if this does not result in a very awkward sentence. For **unclean** see the discussion of ritual cleanliness in 8.2, "clean." Perhaps the phrase can be "spirits that make people unfit for worshiping God."

Disease and **infirmity** are the same terms used in 4.23 and 9.35.

And to heal: note that the authority Jesus gives his disciples was also for healing. Some languages will have to repeat "authority," as in "and (he gave them) power to heal people of all kinds of diseases and sicknesses." Again, the idea of "skill" should be avoided.

10.2	RSV	TEV
	The names of the twelve apostles are these: first, Simon, who is called Peter, and Andrew his brother; James the son of Zebedee, and John his brother;	These are the names of the twelve apostles: first, Simon (called Peter) and his brother Andrew; James and his brother John, the sons of Zebedee;

The names . . . are these: translators should render this sentence naturally. "Here are the names of the twelve apostles" or "The twelve people who were Jesus' apostles were first Simon . . ." are possible translations.

Only here in Matthew are the twelve disciples referred to as **apostles**. The title is also found in the Lukan parallel (6.13); Luke uses it elsewhere as well to refer to the twelve (9.10; 11.49; 17.5; 22.14; 24.10). The reason for its more frequent occurrence in Luke is perhaps due to his desire to relate it to the continuation of his narrative in Acts. The word **apostle** literally means "one who is sent"; it is assumed that the person has the authority to act in behalf of the one who sent him, as is seen in verse 1.

Apostles can often be translated fairly literally as "Sent Ones." In some languages the sender has to be identified, and in Acts and in the Epistles translators have used "Sent Ones of God." Here in Matthew, however, "His twelve Sent Ones" or "the Sent Ones of Jesus" will be more appropriate. In other languages there is a word which has the semantic component of someone sent with the authority of another. In such a case that word can be used, possibly with the addition of "of Jesus."

The term is very close semantically to "messenger," "angel" (literally "messenger"), and "prophet," which means "spokesman" (see comments on 1.22). Care has to be taken to distinguish "apostle" from these. If the suggestions above do not do this, then it may be necessary to add the element of authority to **apostles**, as in "men sent with Jesus' authority."

Some languages have trouble with "Sent Ones," since they must specify some goal of the sending, as in "Ones sent to the world." But "Ones who carry Jesus' authority" is another possible solution.

There are several other lists of the twelve in the New Testament (Mark 3.16-19; Luke 6.13-16; Acts 1.13), and the lists are not entirely in agreement one with the other. However, they do have two things in common: they each begin with Peter and end with Judas.

The word **first** before the name of **Simon, who is called Peter** is best taken merely as a reference to his position in the list, not to some special position of authority which he may have held. Peter does have an outstanding role in the Gospel of Matthew, but there is no intimation that he holds a position of higher rank than any of the others.

From this discussion it follows that possible renderings of **first** can be "the first one is Simon . . . ," or simply "**first, Simon . . . ,**" as TEV has done.

Simon is a Jewish name, while **Peter** is Greek. For **Simon, who is called Peter**, see comments on 4.18.

The group is listed two by two. Together with Peter is his brother **Andrew**, which is also a Greek name.

The two brothers **James** and **John** are listed next. Both names are Jewish.

Translators should find ways to list these pairs of brothers in a way that is natural. See 4.18 and 4.21 for related discussions. Here a possible rendering is "first is Simon whose other name is Peter, and his brother Andrew; (then) James and his brother John. They were the sons of Zebedee (or, Zebedee was their father)."

10.3   RSV   TEV

Philip and Bartholomew; Thomas and   Philip and Bartholomew; Thomas and
Matthew the tax collector; James the   Matthew, the tax collector; James
son of Alphaeus, and Thaddaeus;[x]   son of Alphaeus, and Thaddaeus;

[x]Other ancient authorities read *Leb-*
baeus or *Lebbaeus called Thaddaeus*

    Philip is a Greek name. Traditionally **Bartholomew** is identified with
Nathanael (John 1.46).
    Thomas (the word means "twin") is here joined with **Matthew**, identified as
the **tax collector**. This identification links Matthew with the one mentioned in 9.9.
    Since **Matthew** was presumably no longer a **tax collector**, some translators say
"Matthew who used to be a tax collector" or "Matthew who had collected taxes
before."
    A second **James** (**the son of Alphaeus**) is mentioned. As we have seen
elsewhere (1.1 and 4.21), **the son of Alphaeus** will be "Alphaeus was his father"
in many languages.
    James is joined with **Thaddaeus**. There is textual evidence that the name
Thaddaeus should be replaced by the name Lebbaeus, and some Greek manuscripts
even combine the two forms of the text ("Thaddaeus who was called Lebbaeus" or
"Lebbaeus who was called Thaddaeus"). TC-GNT, however, believes the strongest
evidence supports the text that has **Thaddaeus**, which is also followed by most all
modern English translations; one exception is NEB, which has "Lebbaeus" in the text
and "Thaddaeus" in the margin.

10.4   RSV   TEV

Simon the Cananaean, and Judas   Simon the Patriot, and Judas Iscari-
Iscariot, who betrayed him.   ot, who betrayed Jesus.

    A second **Simon** is listed; he is further identified as **the Cananaean**. There is
some discussion regarding the meaning of the word transliterated **Cananaean** by
RSV and translated "**Patriot**" by TEV. Most modern commentators understand the
word to be an Aramaic equivalent of "zealot," referring to the zealous group of
Jewish revolutionaries who were anti-Rome. NAB renders "the Zealot Party
member"; NEB "a member of the Zealot party"; Brc "the Nationalist." The
presupposition of an Aramaic or a Hebrew background for the word "Cananaean"
is supported by Luke, who specifically refers to him as "the Zealot" (6.15).
    The concept conveyed by **Cananaean**, "zealot," or "nationalist" is very difficult
to translate in many cultures. In some cases "who was strong for his country (or,
people)" works well enough. In some parts of Africa "freedom fighter" has been the
closest natural equivalent, or "who worked to free his people."
    There is disagreement regarding the meaning of the name **Iscariot**, and so no
less than four solutions have been proposed: (1) it has been held to mean "man of
Kariot," a wording found in some manuscripts of John 6.71. (2) Others believe

"Kariot" to be a corruption of the Greek word for Jericho, according to which his name would mean "man of Jericho." (3) Still others have traced his name back to the Latin word *sicarius* ("murderous"), which derives from the noun *sicar* ("curved dagger"), thereby making a connection with the Zealot movement. (4) Finally, some see here a reflection of the Aramaic word meaning "false one" or "deceiver," in which case the title would reflect the name given Judas by the first Christians. If this solution is accepted, then the name would be equivalent to **"who betrayed Jesus"** (TEV). If this latter suggestion is accepted, then a possible translation is "Judas called Iscariot, which means he betrayed Jesus." However, it is best in translation to treat **Iscariot** as a name without attempting to give it meaning.

The text has **who betrayed him**, but since he had not yet done that, some render it "who later betrayed Jesus." Note that **him** refers to Jesus, as TEV has made clear.

It seems likely that most cultures understand betrayal and so will have a good way to translate **betrayed**. However, some will have to say "gave him over to his enemies" or "helped his enemies to catch (or, arrest) him." In some cases it is necessary to add "even though he was his friend" or "even though Jesus trusted him."

10.5-15

RSV

TEV

The Mission of the Twelve

5 These twelve Jesus sent out, charging them, "Go nowhere among the Gentiles, and enter no town of the Samaritans, 6 but go rather to the lost sheep of the house of Israel. 7 And preach as you go, saying, 'The kingdom of heaven is at hand.' 8 Heal the sick, raise the dead, cleanse lepers, cast out demons. You received without paying, give without pay. 9 Take no gold, nor silver, nor copper in your belts, 10 no bag for your journey, nor two tunics, nor sandals, nor a staff; for the laborer deserves his food. 11 And whatever town or village you enter, find out who is worthy in it, and stay with him until you depart. 12 As you enter the house, salute it. 13 And if the house is worthy, let your peace come upon it; but if it is not worthy, let your peace return to you. 14 And if any one will not receive you or listen to your words, shake off the dust from your feet as you leave that house or town. 15 Truly, I say to you, it shall be more tolerable on the day of judgment for the land of Sodom and Gomorrah than for that town.

5 These twelve men were sent out by Jesus with the following instructions: "Do not go to any Gentile territory or any Samaritan towns. 6 Instead, you are to go to the lost sheep of the people of Israel. 7 Go and preach, 'The Kingdom of heaven is near!' 8 Heal the sick, bring the dead back to life, heal those who suffer from dreaded skin diseases, and drive out demons. You have received without paying, so give without being paid. 9 Do not carry any gold, silver, or copper money in your pockets; 10 do not carry a beggar's bag for the trip or an extra shirt or shoes or a walking stick. A worker should be given what he needs.

11 "When you come to a town or village, go in and look for someone who is willing to welcome you, and stay with him until you leave that place. 12 When you go into a house, say, 'Peace be with you.' 13 If the people in that house welcome you, let your greeting of peace remain; but if they do not welcome you, then take back your greeting. 14 And if some home or town will not welcome you or listen to you, then leave that place and shake the dust off your feet. 15 I assure you that on the Judgment Day God will show more mercy to the people of Sodom and Gomorrah than to the people of that town!

SECTION HEADING: "**The Mission of the Twelve.**" "**Mission**" involves some task that people are sent to do, so the heading can be "What the twelve (apostles) were sent to do," "Jesus tells the twelve (men) what they should do," or "Jesus sends out his twelve apostles to do his work."

Matthew 10.5-42 constitutes the second of the five collections of Jesus' sayings in the Gospel. The discourse itself falls into three major divisions: (1) verses 5-15, which are concerned with the immediate missionary activity of the twelve; (2) verses 16-25, which deal with persecution; and (3) verses 26-42, which states in general terms the conditions of discipleship.

Most everything that Matthew includes in verses 5-42 has a parallel in either Mark or Luke or both. Only verses 5-6,8,16b are unique to Matthew. What is significant, however, is the manner in which Matthew places these teachings together into a unified discourse.

10.5	RSV	TEV

These twelve Jesus sent out, charging them, "Go nowhere among the Gentiles, and enter no town of the Samaritans,

These twelve men were sent out by Jesus with the following instructions: "Do not go to any Gentile territory or any Samaritan towns.

These twelve is emphatic in the Greek text. Thus, if possible, translators should use "these twelve men" and not simply "the twelve men." It may, however, be necessary to reverse the order of the verse, as in "Jesus sent out these twelve" or "Jesus told these twelve to go."

The verb **sent out** is made from the same stem as the noun "apostle," which was used of the twelve in verse 2.

Charging them is translated "**with the following instructions**" by TEV and NEB (NJB "instructing them as follows"). GECL translates this entire part of the verse, "Jesus sent out these twelve with the command: . . . ." It can also be expressed as "this is what he told them to do."

Go nowhere among the Gentiles (TEV "**Do not go to any Gentile territory**") is translated "Avoid the places where non-Jews live" by GECL. Matthew incorporates this command of Jesus in order to show that God has not abandoned the Jews, and that the message of salvation was to go to them first. As is seen in the GECL example cited, **Gentiles** can be rendered "non-Jews" or "people who are not Jews." The command can be "Don't go to the places where the non-Jews live."

And enter no town of the Samaritans: the use of the plural "**towns**" (TEV) or a structure such as "any Samaritan town" (NEB) represents more idiomatic English than does **no town of the Samaritans**. It is possible that the Greek word "town" translates an Aramaic word which may mean either "town" or "province," but no translation appears to follow this latter interpretation. This command can be translated "don't go into any town of the Samaritans."

10.6	RSV	TEV

but go rather to the lost sheep of the house of Israel.

Instead, you are to go to the lost sheep of the people of Israel.

But . . . rather is translated "**Instead**" by TEV. As both translations clearly indicate, a contrast is intended between where the disciples are not to go and where they are to go.

Go may need to be expressed as "You should go."

The lost sheep of the house of Israel is deceptive, since it sounds as though **the lost sheep** are a group within the larger group **of the house of Israel**. Actually, this is a Semitic way of referring to those same people. TEV avoids the figure of a house: "**the lost sheep of the people of Israel.**" GECL clearly identifies the two: "go to the lost flock, the people Israel." Many translators will want to retain the images of the metaphor, **the lost sheep of the house of Israel. The house of Israel** is a reference to the people of Israel, and they are being compared to **lost sheep**. Thus the phrase can be rendered "the people of Israel who are like lost sheep" or ". . . who are lost like sheep (with no shepherd)." It probably is not necessary to specify here in what way they are lost.

10.7	RSV	TEV

And preach as you go, saying, 'The kingdom of heaven is at hand.'

Go and preach, 'The Kingdom of heaven is near!'

The authority to heal was first granted (verse 1), which was followed by the command to go (verse 6); now the disciples are informed that their mission is to **preach**. For comments on **preach**, see 3.1. Note how TEV has reordered the two commands **preach** and **go**.

The kingdom of heaven is at hand is exactly the same as the message of John the Baptist (3.2) and Jesus (4.17). GECL 1st edition translates "God is now accomplishing his work and establishing his rule," and INCL has "God has already begun to reign as King."

10.8	RSV	TEV

Heal the sick, raise the dead, cleanse lepers, cast out demons. You received without paying, give without pay.

Heal the sick, bring the dead back to life, heal those who suffer from dreaded skin diseases, and drive out demons. You have received without paying, so give without being paid.

Sick is a participle made from the same stem as the noun **sickness** in 8.17; the root meaning is "be weak." Here **sick** may have to be "sick people."

Verse 1 mentioned the authority for healing the sick and casting out demons. Two related directions are now added: **raise the dead** (TEV "**bring the dead back** to life") and **cleanse lepers** (TEV **"heal those who suffer from dreaded skin diseases"**). On the cleansing of lepers, see comments on 8.2.

Raise the dead can be "raise to life those who are dead" or "bring back to life people who have died."

As we point out in 8.2, **cleanse** may have to be rendered as "heal." Similarly, **lepers** should probably be translated as in 8.2.

The verb translated **cast out** may be used in other contexts (it occurs, for example, in 7.4,5; 8.12; 9.25), but it is the word most generally used of the expulsion of demons (see 7.22; 8.16,31; 9.33,34).

For comments on **demons**, see 8.16, and see comments on "demoniacs" in 4.24.

Without paying and **without pay** translate the same word in its two occurrences. NEB translates "without cost . . . without charge"; NJB has "without charge" in both places.

It may be necessary in some languages to provide objects for the verbs **received** and **give**. And it may even be obligatory to indicate from whom it is they have received and to whom it is they are to give. One may then translate "I gave to you the authority to do these things and you did not have to pay me for it. So now you go and do these same things for others, and do not ask them to pay you."

10.9	RSV	TEV

Take no gold, nor silver, nor copper in your belts,		**Do not carry any gold, silver, or copper money in your pockets;**

The verb translated **take** normally has the meaning "acquire," "get," or "possess." **Take no gold** . . . may therefore be interpreted as either (1) a command not to take money for their journey or (2) a command not to accept money for their ministry. The present context, however, demands the meaning of **take** or "carry" (TEV), and so most scholars believe the first interpretation is intended here. **Take no gold** . . . can be expressed as "Don't carry with you (in your money belt) any gold . . . ."

Gold . . . silver . . . copper refer to coins made of these substances, which is the basis for TEV **"money."** One may need to render "gold coins, silver coins, or copper coins." Sometimes even this makes for a complicated sentence, and so translators may wish to drop the metals altogether and say simply "money of any kind."

Belts represents the place where a man would have usually carried his money. TEV **"pockets"** provides a cultural equivalent, as is "purse" of NEB and "purses" of NJB. NAB retains **belts**, while Brc translates "money-belts." Some translators will use a general term, as in "money carriers" or "things where you carry your money," but more often it is dropped altogether, as in "carry no money with you."

10.10 RSV	TEV
no bag for your journey, nor two tunics, nor sandals, nor a staff; for the laborer deserves his food.	do not carry a beggar's bag for the trip or an extra shirt or shoes or a walking stick. A worker should be given what he needs.

Bag (TEV "**beggar's bag**"; Brc "beggar's knapsack") is translated many different ways: "haversack" (NJB), "pack" (NEB), "traveling bag" (NAB), "knapsack" (Phps), "bag" (AT), and "wallet" (Mft). The problem is that the word may refer in general to any sort of bag that a traveler may put his things in or it may have the specialized sense of a bag carried by a beggar. As the survey of translations suggests, there is no agreement among scholars. Therefore translators can say either something like "bag for travelers" or "bag carried by beggars." Obviously the apostles were to carry nothing with them when they went out.

Two tunics (NJB "spare tunic") is translated "**an extra shirt**" by TEV, "no change of shirt" by NAB, and "second coat" by NEB. The noun **tunics** is the same one used in 5.40, though the singular form appears there. The meaning is that the disciple is not to wear one garment and carry another for a change of clothing. To do so would signal either affluence or a settled existence from which the disciple would not be free to travel. **Tunics**, as in 5.40, can be rendered "shirts" or by some similar garment, or perhaps by a general word like "garment" or "clothing."

The prohibition against **sandals** and **staff** (TEV "**walking stick**") is strange, especially in a land where snakes are ever present. Some scholars believe that it reflects an ancient cultic prohibition against entering the temple court area with dirty feet or with such attire as sandals, a bag, or a walking stick. Or it may be, as other scholars suggest, that the disciples are supposed to stand before the people they serve much as a man who is fasting and praying stands before God, without shoes on his feet or a stick in his hand. In cultures where **sandals** are not known, "**shoes**" (TEV) is an acceptable translation.

In some languages, instead of having the verb once and then a long list of things the disciples were not to take on their trip, it is better to repeat the verb, as in "Nor should you take a bag or extra shirt . . ." or "Also you should not carry with you a bag . . . ."

The word **for** shows the relationship between what preceded and the statement about the worker deserving to receive his keep. Jesus says that the apostles should take nothing with them when they travel because workers deserve to be supported, and thus the apostles are to depend on the goodwill of the people to whom they were ministering. Some languages make the relationship clear with a phrase such as "For it is true" or "I tell you this because." Others simply say "Because" or "For." TEV has conveyed the relationship in English by starting a new sentence.

Laborer means the same as "worker" in this context.

Deserves means "deserves to receive from his employer" or "earns from the person for whom he works"; TEV shifts to a passive "**should be given**."

His food (so also AT) is translated "his keep" by Phps, NJB, Brc; "his rations" by Mft; and "**what he needs**" by TEV. The root meaning of the word is "nourishment" or "food," and its specific rendering must be determined by the context in which it is used. See comments on 3.4; 6.25.

Deserves his food, in addition to the models cited above, can also be rendered in sentences such as "it is right for a worker to receive his keep" or "a worker should receive (or, deserves to receive) what he needs to live on."

10.11 RSV	TEV
And whatever town or village you enter, find out who is worthy in it, and stay with him until you depart.	"When you come to a town or village, go in and look for someone who is willing to welcome you, and stay with him until you leave that place.

Whatever town or village you enter can be "Whenever you enter a town or village" or "When you arrive in some town or village." If a language makes no distinction between **town** and **village**, then the translation can simply be "a town." See comments on 9.35.

Who is worthy is difficult to interpret, and a number of translations merely retain the word **worthy** without further qualification (RSV, NEB, NAB). Other translations suggest that worthiness means either "a deserving inhabitant" (Mft; Brc "someone who deserves the presence of my messengers") or "some suitable person" (AT). JB interprets the meaning to be "someone trustworthy," and Phps "someone who is respected." The exegesis of TEV (**"someone who is willing to welcome you"**) is followed by GECL 1st edition ("someone who is ready to receive you"); this meaning finds support in the mention of "a worthy house" (verse 13), which is contrasted with the person who "will not receive you" (verse 14).

And stay with him until you depart indicates that the disciples are not to search for better accommodations once they have found a home that will receive them. NEB translates "and make your home there until you leave."

Stay with him may be rendered as "live in his house" or "stay with him in his house."

Instead of simply **depart**, in some languages it may be necessary to say "depart from that town."

10.12 RSV	TEV
As you enter the house, salute it.	When you go into a house, say, 'Peace be with you.'

The house (so also NEB) refers specifically to the house mentioned in verse 11; one may then render "his house" (NJB, AT, Phps) or "his home" (NAB). "**A house**" of TEV suggests that a general rule is being laid down apart from a specific reference to the house of verse 11, but the alternative interpretation seems more appropriate. Thus a possible translation is "When you go into that house" or "When you enter that man's house."

Salute it (so also NJB) means "greet it" or better "greet the people who live there." NJB does provide a note indicating that the greeting is a wish of peace, and that the particular content of the wish is brought out in verse 13. A number of translations have attempted a dynamic equivalent: "give it your blessing" (Phps), "wish it well" (AT), "wish the house peace" (NEB). When verses 12 and 13 are taken together, Brc has the best restructuring: "Greet it" (verse 12) is rendered "give your greeting to it," which is made explicit in verse 13, where "let your peace remain on it" is translated "let your prayer for God's blessing rest upon it." INCL uses direct discourse and has the one entering say "May God bless you." See further at verse 13.

For languages in which it would sound strange to greet a house, as in **salute it**, it is better to say "give your greeting to the people in it." Of course it is also possible to use direct speech, as in "say to the people in it 'I greet you' " or ". . . 'May all be well with you.' "

10.13   RSV   TEV

And if the house is worthy, let your peace come upon it; but if it is not worthy, let your peace return to you. | **If the people in that house welcome you, let your greeting of peace remain; but if they do not welcome you, then take back your greeting.**

The house is used of the people of the house, and that is the basis for TEV, GECL, FRCL.

Worthy: see comments on verse 11. Here most translators render it as "if the people of that house receive you well" or ". . . treat you well." Similarly, **not worthy** would be rendered in a sentence such as "if those people do not receive you well."

Your peace means "the peace which you ask God to bring upon the house." In such a context "peace" covers a much wider area than the absence of strife, and it is best represented among the modern translations by Brc: "let your prayer for God's blessing rest upon it." This idea can also be expressed as "pray that God's peace be with those people" or "pray to God to put his blessing on them."

Let your peace return to you is translated "let your prayer for God's blessing return to you" by Brc. Among the Israelites the spoken blessing was thought to exist by itself and have a power of its own, so that the pronouncement of a blessing actually caused the blessing to take effect. On the other hand, if the blessing were recalled, the benefits would not take effect.

This concept of calling back a blessing is not always easy to express. Some possibilities are "take back the prayer of blessing" or "ask God not to honor your prayer to bless those people."

10.14   RSV   TEV

And if any one will not receive you or listen to your words, shake off the dust from your feet as you leave that house or town. | **And if some home or town will not welcome you or listen to you, then leave that place and shake the dust off your feet.**

Any one refers to the people of **that house or town** mentioned later in the verse. A literal rendering of **if any one will not receive you** is misleading, for it may imply that if any one person in the entire house or town does not receive Jesus' disciples, then they must leave. Therefore **if any one will not** is better phrased in English as "and if no one will" (Phps; AT "and where no one will"). One may then reorder the verse and translate "If no one in that house or town will welcome you . . . then leave it . . . ."

For comments on the verb **receive**, see verse 40.

Listen to your words is translated **"listen to you"** by TEV and AT; NEB renders "listen to what you say," while a number of other translations render "listen to what you have to say" (Phps, NAB, NJB).

Shake off the dust from your feet indicates an action of absolute rejection. Both Mark (6.11) and Luke (9.5) interpret the gesture for their readers: "as a testimony against them" (TEV "That will be a warning to them!"). In Acts 13.51 Barnabas and Paul shake the dust off their feet against the people of the city of Antioch. There the Greek has "against them," which TEV interprets "in protest against them." It may be helpful in the present passage also to interpret the significance of the action: "and shake the dust off your feet in protest against them" or ". . . as a sign that you have rejected them."

There have been translators who have not kept the form **shake off the dust from your feet** but only the meaning, as in "show (or, tell) those people that you have rejected them." Other translations have substituted an action from their own culture which has the same symbolic value. However, there does seem to be some value in keeping the biblical form if possible, if necessary adding a phrase that interprets it as we suggested above. The verse can then say "If no one in that house or town will welcome you or listen to what you have to say, then leave there and shake the dust off your feet as you leave, to show that you have rejected them."

10.15	RSV	TEV

Truly, I say to you, it shall be more tolerable on the day of judgment for the land of Sodom and Gomorrah than for that town.	I assure you that on the Judgment Day God will show more mercy to the people of Sodom and Gomorrah than to the people of that town!

Truly, I say to you: see comments on 5.18.

The use of the passive **it shall be more tolerable** is a typical Jewish way of referring to the action of God without mentioning his sacred name, and so GECL makes the same restructuring as TEV. The phrase **be more tolerable** can be translated "God will be less harsh in his punishment" or, similar to TEV, "God will be more merciful towards."

The use of **land** as a marker for the towns of **Sodom and Gomorrah** is confusing for the modern reader. It may be necessary to translate "the people of the towns of Sodom and Gomorrah." (Similarly, **that town** may be "the people of that town.") In the Old Testament (Gen 19; see also Isa 1.9), and frequently in the New Testament (Matt 11.22,24; Luke 17.29; Rom 9.29; 2 Peter 2.6; Jude 7), the towns of Sodom and Gomorrah are depicted as examples of the most sinful towns. But here the rejection of Jesus' message is described as even more terrible than the sins committed by the people of those towns.

Matthew's readers were completely familiar with the reputation of **Sodom and Gomorrah,** but many modern readers will not be, particularly in languages where there is no Old Testament. For this reason some translators say "the wicked people of Sodom and Gomorrah" or "those wicked towns of Sodom and Gomorrah." Some have said "towns of Sodom and Gomorrah that God destroyed because the people were so wicked."

The day of judgment is clearly a reference to the final judgment; INCL employs a technical term, originally from Islam, but now in everyday usage, which means the final judgment. **The day of judgment** is usually translated as "the Day when God will judge the world (or, the people of the world") or "the Day of God's final judgment of all people."

10.16-25

RSV

TEV

Coming Persecutions

16 "Behold, I send you out as sheep in the midst of wolves; so be wise as serpents and innocent as doves. 17 Beware of men; for they will deliver you up to councils, and flog you in their synagogues, 18 and you will be dragged before governors and kings for my sake, to bear testimony before them and the Gentiles. 19 When they deliver you up, do not be anxious how you are to speak or what you are to say; for what you are to say will be given to you in that hour; 20 for it is not you who speak, but the Spirit of your Father speaking through you. 21 Brother will deliver up brother to death, and the father his child, and children will rise against parents and have them put to death; 22 and you will be hated by all for my name's sake. But he who endures to the end will be saved. 23 When they persecute you in one town, flee to the next; for truly, I say to you, you will not have gone through all the towns of Israel, before the Son of man comes.

24 "A disciple is not above his teacher, nor a servant[y] above his master; 25 it is enough for the disciple to be like his teacher, and the servant[y] like his master. If they have called the master of the house Beelzebul, how much more will they malign those of his household.

[y] Or slave

16 "Listen! I am sending you out just like sheep to a pack of wolves. You must be as cautious as snakes and as gentle as doves. 17 Watch out, for there will be men who will arrest you and take you to court, and they will whip you in the synagogues. 18 For my sake you will be brought to trial before rulers and kings, to tell the Good News to them and to the Gentiles. 19 When they bring you to trial, do not worry about what you are going to say or how you will say it; when the time comes, you will be given what you will say. 20 For the words you will speak will not be yours; they will come from the Spirit of your Father speaking through you.

21 "Men will hand over their own brothers to be put to death, and fathers will do the same to their children; children will turn against their parents and have them put to death. 22 Everyone will hate you because of me. But whoever holds out to the end will be saved. 23 When they persecute you in one town, run away to another one. I assure you that you will not finish your work in all the towns of Israel before the Son of Man comes.

24 "No pupil is greater than his teacher; no slave is greater than his master. 25 So a pupil should be satisfied to become like his teacher, and a slave like his master. If the head of the family is called Beelzebul, the members of the family will be called even worse names!

SECTION HEADING: "**Coming Persecutions.**" This may need to be a short sentence such as "The apostles are going to suffer persecution" or "Jesus tells the apostles of how they are going to suffer."

This entire section deals with persecutions and sufferings that will be endured by the disciples for their Lord. The order of the sayings reflects a definite thematic arrangement. For example, those that concern suffering are found in almost precisely the same wording in the apocalyptic discourses in Mark (13.9-13) and Luke (21.12-17). Moreover, verse 16, which Matthew uses transitionally, appears in Luke at the beginning of Jesus' instructions to the seventy (Luke 10.3). The conclusion to the section (verses 24-25) then summarizes the theme of the entire passage: Jesus suffered unjustly, and his followers can expect no less.

10.16   RSV   TEV

"Behold, I send you out as sheep in the midst of wolves; so be wise as serpents and innocent as doves. | "Listen! I am sending you out just like sheep to a pack of wolves. You must be as cautious as snakes and as gentle as doves.

Behold: see comments on 1.20; most recently this particle of emphasis and transition was used in 9.20,32. Here it may be "Look" or "**Listen**" (TEV), or some similar word that Jesus might use to emphasize what he is about to say.

Send . . . out translates the same verb used in verse 5, and it derives from the same stem as the word "apostle" (see verse 2).

As sheep in the midst of wolves: TEV uses the marker "**pack**" before **wolves** since it is the proper designation in English for a group of wolves that run together. Some languages may require such a marker. The metaphor **sheep** . . . **wolves** is a common one in both Jewish and Greek sources. Sheep are used as a symbol of defenseless animals, while wolves are ravenous and wild, attacking the sheep.

Many translators will have to make clear to readers the basis of the comparisons in the phrase **as sheep in the midst of wolves**. An example is "When I send you out into the world, it is like sending defenseless sheep out among ravenous wolves." If **wolves** are not known, then translators may have to substitute "jackals" or "attacking dogs," or some similar animals.

The adjectives **wise** and **innocent** are translated in numerous ways: "**cautious**" and "**gentle**" (TEV), "wise" and "guileless" (AT, Mft), "wise" and "harmless" (Phps), "wise" and "pure" (Brc), "cunning" and "harmless" (JB), "wary" and "innocent" (NEB), "clever" and "innocent" (NAB). Depending upon the context the first of these adjectives may mean "wise," "sensible," or "thoughtful." If the analogy is to the characteristic of the snake as portrayed in Genesis, for example, then "shrewd" or "cunning" may be intended. This does not, however, seem to be the meaning which Matthew intends. The disciple is not encouraged to play the role of a clever diplomat, but rather to be aware of and alert to the ever present danger that he faces because of his calling. If this analysis of the text is correct, then both NEB ("wary") and TEV ("**cautious**") are on target. Other words translators can use are then "prudent" and "careful."

The meaning intended for the next adjective is even more difficult. Either Jesus is instructing his disciples to be "innocent" or "pure" (that is, to live lives that are genuine and that do not try to deceive) or else he is telling them to be "harmless" or "gentle" (that is, not to strike back at the people who come like wolves to destroy them). No final decision can be made. But if the meaning "cautious, wary, careful" is chosen for the meaning of the first adjective, then "harmless" or "gentle" provides a better balance. Care must be taken that the significance of **serpents** and **doves** in the receptor culture does not destroy or distort their emotional image in the Jewish setting. If this danger is felt to exist, then it is better to translate without using the comparison between the two animals: "I am sending you out among people who will attack you like wild animals. So be on your guard against them, but be gentle (or, pure) in the way that you live."

10.17	RSV	TEV
	Beware of men; for they will deliver you up to councils, and flog you in their synagogues,	Watch out, for there will be men who will arrest you and take you to court, and they will whip you in the synagogues.

Men is here used of people in general, not of males specifically, though in the Jewish culture men would have been the persons who did these things that the disciples are warned against. NAB translates the first sentence "Be on your guard with respect to others," while NEB has "And be on your guard, for men will . . . ." Brc make the reference impersonal. "You must be constantly on your guard. They will . . . ." **Beware** may be translated as "Watch out" or "Be very careful of."

Though **deliver . . . up** is used in other contexts, it is the verb consistently used of Judas' betrayal of Jesus. Matthew may have chosen it for this passage in order to affirm that what happened to the Lord will inevitably happen to his followers. There are several different ways translators have handled **deliver . . . up**. Some have found TEV a useful model: "**arrest you and take you to court**." Others have said "accuse you before the councils so they will arrest you." Perhaps a simpler rendering is "turn you over to the authorities of the councils (so they can put you on trial)."

Councils ("sanhedrins") is always used in its singular form elsewhere in the New Testament, where it has reference to the supreme religious court of the Jews. That court consisted of seventy leaders of the Jewish people and was presided over by the High Priest. In TEV this noun is generally translated "**Council**." Here, however, the reference is to the councils from local synagogues; these councils consisted of twenty-three influential members, and their responsibility was to keep peace among the members of the local Jewish community. **Councils** is often translated as "court." However, in cultures where there exist councils of elders in villages, then "elders" may be acceptable. This is especially true if these elders try cases relating to religious matters. Other translators have said "the leaders in the House of Prayer."

Their synagogues. The noun "synagogue" was first used in 4.23, then again in 6.2,5 and 9.35. Acts 22.19 shows that whippings could take place in the synagogue. Normally the whip used by the Jews was made of calf skin and donkey hide woven together. The minister of the synagogue or the synagogue attendant administered the punishment, and it was limited to a maximum of thirty-nine lashes. According to 2 Corinthians 11.24, Paul suffered this punishment five times. By the possessive **their**,

Matthew intends to separate between the Jewish community and the Christian Church. See other comments on "synagogue" at 4.23.

Flog, as indicated above, means "whipped," that is, "beaten with a whip."

and you will be dragged before governors and kings for my sake, to bear testimony before them and the Gentiles.	**For my sake you will be brought to trial before rulers and kings, to tell the Good News to them and to the Gentiles.**

Dragged (so also JB, GECL 1st edition) is translated "be brought" by many. In everyday speech the verb does mean "bring," but it may also acquire the technical sense of "arrest," "take into custody," "bring to trial." Since the context suggests the use of force, one may even translate "drag (you) to trial." In many languages it will be necessary to make the sentence active, as in "and those people will drag you to trial."

Governors was first used in 2.6, where it appears in a quotation from Micah 5.2. Elsewhere in the New Testament it is used only of Roman governors: Pontius Pilate (27.2,11,14,15,21,27; 28.14; Luke 20.20), Felix (Acts 23.24,26,33; 24.1,10), and Festus (Acts 26.30). **Governors** is sometimes rendered as "rulers (or, chiefs) sent from Rome" or ". . . sent by the Roman Emperor." A similar way is "men who ruled on behalf of the Roman Emperor." However, in this context "leaders" may suffice, or "rulers."

Kings (so all translations) includes persons such as Herod Agrippa I (Acts 12.1) and other members of the Herod family (for example, Herod Antipas), who ruled in various capacities under the Roman authority. If there is no word for **kings** in a culture, then "chiefs" is acceptable. If **governors** was translated as "leaders sent from Rome," then **kings** can be "the people's own chiefs (or, rulers)."

For my sake (so most translations) is placed initially by TEV for emphasis. Most translations retain the word order of the Greek text, but NAB translates "on my account" and places the phrase at the end of the sentence. Phps departs from the traditional rendering with "because of me," though still keeping to the Greek word order. Here it is best taken to mean "because you are my disciples (or, followers)" or "because you follow me."

To bear testimony translates a noun phrase in Greek ("for testimony [or, witness]"). This phrase does indicate some purpose. Jesus tells the disciples they will be brought to trial "so that you can tell about me." In many languages an object is required, and a least two possibilities present themselves: "concerning the Good News" (TEV, GECL 1st edition) or "concerning me" (Brc "but you must regard that as an opportunity to demonstrate . . . your loyalty to me"). No other translations are explicit, and the commentators do not offer much help, but either of these solutions is in keeping with the context. One may even need to supply a double object: "to tell the Good News about me" or "to tell the Good News about (or, from) God."

The persons referred to by **them and the Gentiles** are not evident. **Them** may be the governors and kings previously mentioned in the verse, in which case **Gentiles** probably were the non-Jewish populace in general. An alternative possibility is to take **them** as Jewish accusers and authorities in contrast to **Gentile** authorities.

If the first interpretation of **them** is chosen, then a possible translation is "to those rulers (or, to them) and to non-Jews." If the second is preferred, it can be expressed as "to those who accused you and to those non-Jewish rulers."

10.19   RSV   TEV

When they deliver you up, do not be anxious how you are to speak or what you are to say; for what you are to say will be given to you in that hour;	When they bring you to trial, do not worry about what you are going to say or how you will say it; when the time comes, you will be given what you will say.

They may need to be "those people" or "those men."

Deliver . . . up: see comments on verse 17.

Anxious: see 6.25. Here it may be "don't worry about" or "don't be upset thinking about . . . ."

How you are to speak or what you are to say is retained in this form by most translations. But NEB condenses the two clauses into one ("what you are to say"), on the assumption that the two clauses linked by **or** are in reality expressing the same thought. This sort of construction is used rather frequently in the Scriptures, and it is technically called a hendiadys. Support for this interpretation is found in the last part of the verse, which repeats only the second half of the construction: **what you are to say**. If translators try to retain the two clauses, they may possibly do something very similar to TEV. Otherwise they can say simply "what you are going to say" or "what you should say."

For here is a transitional of cause: "because" or "the reason I tell you that is."

Will be given to you, on the basis of what is said in verse 20, may be transformed into an active expression: "Your Father in heaven will give you" or "the Spirit of your Father in heaven will give you."

Sometimes **given** does not fit easily in the passage. "You will know" may be acceptable, although better is "your Father in heaven will cause you to know what you should say." Also possible is "you will be told" or "God will tell you (or, will show you)."

Notice that in the text, the object of **given** comes before the verb, a feature of a passive sentence. In the examples in the preceding paragraph, **what you are to say** comes after the verb. Even if the passive is retained, this order may be better, as in TEV "**you will be given what you will say.**"

In that hour: see 8.13 for essentially the same construction. TEV, NJB, and NEB all have "when the time comes." Phps and Brc have "at that time," and AT has "at that very moment." In many languages it will be better to put this phrase at the beginning of the clause: "for at that time, God will tell you what to say."

10.20   RSV   TEV

for it is not you who speak, but the Spirit of your Father speaking through you.	For the words you will speak will not be yours; they will come from the Spirit of your Father speaking through you.

For it is not you who speak is usually translated literally, but a literal translation may be misleading, since it could imply that the disciples themselves were not actually speaking. That is, the implication could be that something magical was happening, which would do injustice to the text. But the meaning is that, though the disciples themselves will perform the physical act of speaking, the inspiration for their words will in reality come from God and not from themselves. Among the modern English translations, only Phps is helpful in this regard: "For it will not be really you who are speaking . . . ."

The Spirit of your Father is an extremely difficult phrase. This is the only place in the New Testament where it occurs, and in every translation consulted it is reproduced literally. If the noun **Spirit** is problematic in the receptor language, then the phrase may be rendered "your Father himself" or "your heavenly Father himself." It is also common for translators to identify **the Spirit of your Father** as the Holy Spirit, as in "the Spirit of God your Father in heaven" or "the Holy Spirit sent by God your Father (in heaven)."

The entire verse may be translated as follows: "You will speak, but the words you speak will come from your Father in heaven. He will give you the words to say, and when you speak, it will be as though he were speaking through you."

10.21   RSV   TEV

Brother will deliver up brother to death, and the father his child, and children will rise against parents and have them put to death;	"Men will hand over their own brothers to be put to death, and fathers will do the same to their children; children will turn against their parents and have them put to death.

Deliver up: see verses 17,19; the verb is discussed in 4.12. Here the brothers are to be delivered up **to death**, so it can be rendered "will hand over their brothers to the authorities to be killed."

Instead of **brother . . . brother**, many translations will have "men (or, some men) . . . their brothers," as TEV has. Other languages will render the sentence "It will happen that men will hand over their own brothers to the authorities to be killed."

The father his child is problematic for at least two reasons: (1) the inclusion of the definite article **the** in a context that is unnatural in English and (2) the omission of the understood verb. Mft resolves the second of these problems by translating "the father will betray his child"; TEV deals with both difficulties: "**and fathers will do the same to their children**." However, in some languages to mention both "fathers" and "children" would be unnecessarily redundant, so that "men . . . their own children" would be better. Again, there are languages where it will be necessary to say "some men" or "some fathers."

It may be necessary to repeat the verb "deliver up to death" or use a form such as "will do the same thing."

Children will rise against their parents and have them put to death represents a fairly literal rendering of the Greek text. In place of **rise against** (RSV, Mft, JB) a number of translators prefer "**turn against**" (TEV, AT, NEB, NAB, Phps); Brc has "attack (and murder)." Elsewhere in the New Testament the verb is used only in Mark 13.12; the root meaning is "rise in rebellion" (see its usage in the Septuagint of Deut 33.11). For this reason, **rise against** can also be rendered as "rebel against."

Have them put to death means the children will have the authorities kill the parents, or that they will turn them over to the authorities who will kill them, very much as men will do with their brothers at the beginning of the verse. As with brothers and fathers, "some children . . . their parents" or "some people . . . their parents" will be clearer than a translation that can be understood to mean all children.

10.22	RSV	TEV

and you will be hated by all for my name's sake. But he who endures to the end will be saved.	Everyone will hate you because of me. But whoever holds out to the end will be saved.

You will be hated by all is altered to an active construction by TEV: "**Everyone will hate you**." Similarly NEB: "All will hate you." Phps avoids the use of "all" by translating "You yourselves will be universally hated" (Brc "You will be universally hated"). Both Phps and Brc are rather sophisticated, and the adverb "universally" may imply more than is intended in the original.

For my name's sake is translated "**because of me**" by TEV, since in Jewish thought a person's name stands for the person himself. The meaning is probably identical with "for my sake" of verse 18. NEB translates "for your allegiance to me"; AT has "on my account" (NAB "on account of me"); Brc translates "because of your connection with me." GECL shifts to a verb structure: "because you acknowledge me." As in verse 18, it may also be "because you are my followers."

But he who endures to the end will be saved occurs two other times in the New Testament; in Matthew 24.13 and Mark 13.13 the Greek wording is the same as here. To say the least, the saying is difficult to interpret, although the meaning of the verb itself is obvious. It is consistently rendered either **endures** or "**holds out**" (TEV, Mft, AT, NEB, NAB) by most translations, and elsewhere in the New Testament it occurs in contexts of suffering, persecution, and temptation (for example, Rom 12.12; 1 Cor 13.7; Heb 10.32; 12.3; James 1.12; 1 Peter 2.20).

He may be "the person" or "those people," whichever is more natural.

Some common ways to translate **endures** in this context are "remains faithful (to me)," "continues to trust in me," "stays strong in his faith (in me)," "doesn't stop serving me."

In Greek **to the end** lacks the definite article **the** and so may be understood adverbially: "finally," "fully," "altogether." In the context the meaning could then be expressed "without giving up" or "without denying one's faith," but this interpretation does not find favorable support among the scholars. Most scholars prefer the meaning **to the end** ("to the very end," AT, Mft, Phps), with the time reference being the end of persecution. One can then translate "whoever holds out until the persecution comes to an end . . ." or, in order to relate this to the previous sentence, "whoever remains faithful to me until the persecution comes to an end . . . ." So as not to refer to any one incident of persecution, this may need to be "until this period of persecution comes to an end."

Will be saved is also possible to interpret in more than one way. Some scholars take this as a reference to physical safety with the sense "will be brought safely through the period of persecution" (see NAB "will escape death" and Phps "will be safe and sound"). But most scholars seem to prefer to interpret **will be saved** of the believer's salvation. If the passive construction is impossible, then the clause may require considerable restructuring: "But if you remain faithful to me through all the persecution, then God will save you" or ". . . will save your soul." This shift to a second person subject may be required in some languages, especially since verse 22a and verse 23 are both in the second person. Such a shift is normal in Hebrew as well as in the Greek of the New Testament, which often follows Hebrew patterns. But for most languages it is jarring to shift between a second and a third person subject when referring to the same individual.

The agent, God, in the expression **will be saved** can also be placed first in the sentence, as in "but God will save those of you who remain faithful to me until the persecution comes to an end."

10.23	RSV	TEV
	When they persecute you in one town, flee to the next; for truly, I say to you, you will not have gone through all the towns of Israel, before the Son of Man comes.	When they persecute you in one town, run away to another one. I assure you that you will not finish your work in all the towns of Israel before the Son of Man comes.

When they persecute you in one town may be translated "When the people of one town persecute you."

Flee to the next represents the wording of the UBS Greek text. Some Greek manuscripts have an additional clause, "and if they persecute you in the other, then run away to the next." According to TC-GNT, the committee for the UBS Greek text believes that the additional clause was added in order to explain the following statement, though they acknowledge the possibility that it may have accidentally been omitted from the text, and so they judge their choice of text as "C," indicating a considerable degree of doubt. Most modern translations also prefer the shorter text, though both NJB and BJ include the additional clause.

Flee can be rendered as "run away" or "leave there quickly and go to the next town."

Truly, I say to you: for comments, see 5.18. The most recent occurrence of the phrase is in 10.15.

You will not have gone through is more literally "you will not have completed." The meaning is not merely that the disciples will not have had the opportunity to travel through all the towns of Israel, as TOB, BJ seem to imply, but that they will not have had the opportunity to perform their work of preaching and healing in all these towns (see verses 7-8). Therefore TEV has "**you will not finish your work in all the towns**." It may be necessary in some languages to say "you will not have had time to work" or "there won't be time to carry your message to."

Before the Son of man comes is extremely difficult to interpret. This is the third reference in the Gospel to the **Son of man**. The first two (8.20; 9.6) are evident allusions to the life and suffering of the Son of Man on earth, but here the emphasis is different, and the time reference is unclear. Some scholars believe this saying was fulfilled in the destruction of Jerusalem in A.D. 70 (see NJB footnote, which alludes to 24.1 and following). But there is little or no support for this in the context. A second group of scholars believe that the event in mind is the glorification of the Son of Man in his passion and resurrection. But there is no indication either that this is meant. The interpretation that enjoys widest acceptance among scholars is that the saying refers to the final coming of the glorified Son of Man, and this is also supported by other passages within Matthew's Gospel (see in particular 13.41; 16.27,28; 19.28; 24.27,30,37,39,44; 25.31; 26.64).

Comes will be translated literally by translators who prefer not to interpret it otherwise, but this ignores the fact that Jesus did mean it in a particular way that his disciples probably understood. Thus "comes with (or, into) the glory of God" is probably better.

That Jesus should refer to the Son of Man in the third person is difficult both exegetically and translationally. From an exegetical perspective at least two questions are paramount: (1) Is Jesus speaking of himself or of someone else? (2) Is this the proper context for the saying, or has Matthew placed here a saying which originated at another time and in another setting? On these issues scholarly opinion is sharply divided, and no answer will remain undebated. But in terms of translation the following observations and comments should be useful. First, it cannot be denied that from Matthew's own perspective the Son of Man is always identified with Jesus. Moreover, whatever the original setting of the saying, Matthew has chosen to place it in the mouth of Jesus at this particular moment in his Gospel. Therefore the real question that arises for the translator relates to the use of the third-person reference. See 8.20 for a discussion of that problem and of **Son of man**. As we point out there, third person must be changed in some languages to a first person reference. And this shift immediately involves the problem of the verb **comes**, since Jesus is standing there at the moment he makes this promise. One solution is to translate **comes** as "comes back" or "returns"; one may then translate "before I, the Son of Man, come back." But the shift to "come back" is not as satisfactory as is an alternative solution: ". . . until I, the Son of Man, come in glory" or ". . . come into my glory." This latter interpretation finds support in the other passages in the Gospel, where Jesus announces the coming of the Son of Man in glory.

In many languages a more natural order for this sentence is "For I assure you the Son of Man will come with the glory of God before you have carried out my message to all the towns of Israel."

10.24

RSV	TEV
"A disciple is not above his teacher, nor a servant[y] above his master;	"No pupil is greater than his teacher; no slave is greater than his master.

[y] Or *slave*

The function of verses 24-25 is to indicate that the followers of Jesus need not expect to be treated better than Jesus himself was treated.

Disciple (TEV "**pupil**"): see comments on 5.1.

Above (TEV "**greater than**") may be expressed in a number of ways: "better than" (AT), "superior to" (Phps, NJB), and "rank above" (NEB; NAB "outranks"). Brc renders so as to make explicit the persecution setting: "A scholar cannot hope to escape what his teacher has to suffer . . . ."

It may be necessary to reverse the order, as in "A teacher is always superior to his students." Note that, as the examples show, **above** means "more important than."

Servant (so also NEB) may also mean "**slave**" (so most translations), as the RSV footnote indicates. **Master**, on the other hand, probably should carry the meaning "owner" (Brc).

The second part of the verse should be treated more or less as the first part; for example, "and no slave is more important than his owner" or "and a slave owner is always more important than his slave."

10.25

RSV	TEV
it is enough for the disciple to be like his teacher, and the servant[y] like his master. If they have called the master of the house Beelzebul, how much more will they malign those of his household.	So a pupil should be satisfied to become like his teacher, and a slave like his master. If the head of the family is called Beelzebul, the members of the family will be called even worse names!

[y] Or *slave*

It is enough . . . like his teacher. TEV shifts away from the impersonal structure of the Greek to "**So a pupil should be satisfied to become like his teacher**."

Some translators may feel they have to say in what way the pupil should be **like his teacher**. If so, they may say "learn as much as his teacher knows" or "be as wise as his teacher." Similarly, a slave should be satisfied "to be as important (or, as powerful) as his owner."

If they have called the master of the house Beelzebul . . . is a saying unique to the Gospel of Matthew. The name occurs in this Gospel twice again in the controversy of 12.22-32, and in each instance **Beelzebul** functions as Satan. Most modern translations follow the spelling of the Greek manuscripts (TEV "**Beelze-**

bul"), though NEB adopts that contained in the Latin Vulgate ("Beelzebub"). The origin of the Greek word is uncertain, though the spelling "Beelzebub" appears to have originated from an attempt to identify this name with the god of the Philistine city of Ekron (2 Kgs 1.2). The readers should understand from the translation that **Beelzebul** is Satan: "If they call the head of the family Satan" (GECL). Translators can then add a footnote stating that the original text used another of Satan's names, Beelzebul. See also comments on 4.1. Some translators prefer to put **Beelzebul** in the text and have a note, either in parenthesis, "(that is, Satan)," or in a footnote that says "this is another name for Satan."

The impersonal **they have called** is equivalent to "**is called**" (TEV) or "people have called." It can also be "People have said about the head of the family, 'He is Beelzebul' " or "People have said that the head of the family is Beelzebul."

Master of the house, as seen in the examples above, is "the head of the family" or "head of the household."

How much more will they malign is "**will be called even worse names**" in TEV. **Malign** means to speak harmful lies about, or to slander. Jesus is saying, therefore, that people who have called the head of the family Satan will say even worse lies about the members of the family, or call them even more terrible names.

Those of his household (TEV "**the members of the family**") includes everyone living in the household, including slaves. The second clause may be rendered "They will say even worse things about the members of his family" or "they will call the members of the family even worse names."

Note that the construction with **if** does not ask whether the head of the family has been called Beelzebul, but rather carries the meaning seen in "Since people have called . . . then they will" or "In light of the fact that they have called . . . how much more."

10.26-31

RSV	TEV
	Whom to Fear
26 "So have no fear of them; for nothing is covered that will not be revealed, or hidden that will not be known. 27 What I tell you in the dark, utter in the light; and what you hear whispered, proclaim upon the housetops. 28 And do not fear those who kill the body but cannot kill the soul; rather fear him who can destroy both soul and body in hell.^{z} 29 Are not two sparrows sold for a penny? And not one of them will fall to the ground without your Father's will. 30 But even the hairs of your head are all numbered. 31 Fear not, therefore; you are of more value than many sparrows.	26 "So do not be afraid of people. Whatever is now covered up will be uncovered, and every secret will be made known. 27 What I am telling you in the dark you must repeat in broad daylight, and what you have heard in private you must announce from the housetops. 28 Do not be afraid of those who kill the body but cannot destroy the soul; rather be afraid of God, who can destroy both body and soul in hell. 29 For only a penny you can buy two sparrows, yet not one sparrow falls to the ground without your Father's consent. 30 As for you, even the hairs of your head have all been counted. 31 So do not be afraid; you are worth much more than many sparrows!

^{z} Greek *Gehenna*

SECTION HEADING: "**Whom to Fear**." There are several ways this section heading may be rendered. It can be "This is whom you should fear" or "Jesus tells whom we should fear," or the object can be made specific, as in "You should fear God." Another possibility is "Don't fear people; fear only God."

Verses 26-33 have a parallel in Luke 12.2-9. But in the two Gospels the sayings occur in entirely different contexts, and both the wording and the arrangement differ. The first part of this section (verses 26-31) opens and closes with similar words of encouragement ("So have no fear . . . Fear not, therefore . . ."), forming what is known as an "inclusion" or envelope construction.

10.26   RSV   TEV

"So have no fear of them; for nothing is covered that will not be revealed, or hidden that will not be known.

"So do not be afraid of people. Whatever is now covered up will be uncovered, and every secret will be made known.

So have no fear of them. The pronoun **them** may be interpreted either as a reference to people in general or more specifically to those who oppose the Christian message. "You must not fear any man" is the choice of GECL. Some translators understand **them** to refer to those in verse 25 who say bad things about the members of the family, that is, Jesus' followers. Thus they render **them** as "those people."

The negative construction of the Greek (**for there is nothing covered that will not be revealed . . . not to be known**) is reconstituted as a positive statement in TEV: "**Whatever is now covered up will be uncovered, and every secret will be made known.**" JB does similarly ("For everything that is now covered will be uncovered, and everything now hidden will be made clear"), as does Brc ("What is veiled must be unveiled, and what is hidden must be made known"). This shift to a positive form does not make the saying more easily understood, but it does resolve all the problems of communication. There still exists the difficulty of the impersonal form, which tends to make this sound like a proverbial saying. The proverbial form would certainly be satisfactory for the translation of the saying in its other contexts (Mark 4.22; Luke 8.17) but not here, where it functions as a command. That this is the case is clearly shown by what is said in verse 27, and so the text may be rendered "Whatever I now tell you in secret, you must tell in the open. Everything must be made known." Or ". . . in private, you must tell to everyone. You must make everything known." Translators who want to keep the sentence less specific can render this slightly differently: "For what people haven't known, you will tell about these things; you will make people know everything" or "You must tell people about all the things that are now secret; leave nothing hidden."

10.27   RSV   TEV

What I tell you in the dark, utter in the light; and what you hear whispered, proclaim upon the housetops.

What I am telling you in the dark you must repeat in broad daylight, and what you have heard in private you must announce from the housetops.

This verse forms a parallel to verse 26.

What I tell you may be "the things I am telling you."

Dark may be "in secret" or "in private." To say "in the night" would probably not reflect the meaning of Jesus here.

Light is translated "**broad daylight**" by TEV and NEB, while NJB has "daylight." **Light** can also be understood to mean "publicly," "where everyone can hear you."

The order of the sentence may have to be reversed, as in "You must repeat in daylight (or, in public) the things I am telling you privately."

What you hear whispered is literally "what you hear in the ears"; TEV has "**what you have heard in private**." To avoid a passive sentence, this sentence can also be rendered "what I have told you in private" or "what things we have talked about just among us."

The (flat) **housetops** were frequently used as a place from which public announcements were made, and so the contrast in this part of the verse is also evident. What Jesus tells his disciples in private is to be made known in the most public way possible. GECL 1st edition translates "and what is whispered in your ears, you must make known to all the world" or "you must announce to all the world."

10.28	RSV	TEV

And do not fear those who kill the body but cannot kill the soul; rather fear him who can destroy both soul and body in hell.[z]	**Do not be afraid of those who kill the body but cannot destroy the soul; rather be afraid of God, who can destroy both body and soul in hell.**

[z] Greek *Gehenna*

Do not fear . . . kill the soul may be translated "Do not be afraid of people. They can only kill the body, but not the soul."

The word **soul** must be interpreted in light of its Jewish background, where it has a wide range of meaning. For example, it can refer both to the vital life principle that animated all living creatures (humans and animals alike) and to an individual's real self that did not cease to exist at death. The second of these meanings is obviously in focus here. Jesus warns his followers not to be afraid of people; they may have the power to kill one's body, but they cannot kill one's soul.

This verse can pose several problems to translators. **Kill** the body may sound strange, in which case it will have to be "kill you (physically)" or "cause you to die."

Some languages will know of some force that men have that is their real self and that continues to exist after their death. If so, translators can use that here for **soul**. Others may be able to say "your spirit that does not die" or, if "spirit" poses a problem, "your true nature that lives on always."

Him who can destroy both soul and body in hell is correctly identified as "God" by TEV, GECL, and FRCL. Brc attempts to achieve the same goal by capitalizing "One," but this is of no help to the persons who must depend upon hearing the scripture read.

Hell is literally "Gehenna" (Mft, NAB, RSV footnote). Most translations have **hell**, though AT has "the pit," and Phps "the fires of destruction." See comments on 5.22 (also 5.29). **Hell** can also be here "the fires that destroy the wicked."

This relative clause may be easier to express as a separate sentence: "But instead you should fear God. He is the one who can kill you and destroy your soul in hell."

10.29 RSV	TEV
Are not two sparrows sold for a penny? And not one of them will fall to the ground without your Father's will.	For only a penny you can buy two sparrows, yet not one sparrow falls to the ground without your Father's consent.

Are not two sparrows sold for a penny? translates a negative rhetorical question. Since the particular form of the question expects the answer "yes," TEV shifts to a statement and translates "**For only a penny you can buy two sparrows.**" Brc renders "Everyone knows that two sparrows can be bought for one farthing . . . ." The question form can sometimes be retained with questions such as "It's true, isn't it, that two sparrows only cost a penny?" or "It only takes a penny to buy two sparrows, doesn't it?"

Sparrows may not be known, in which case translators can say "two common birds" or "two small birds."

The Greek word **penny** refers to a Roman copper coin worth about one sixteenth of the coin that was the workman's average daily wage. Translators may have a small unit of currency like **penny** that they can use. Sometimes "a small coin" is possible, and "very little money" is another common translation.

Will fall to the ground may need to be present tense, as in "falls to the ground." Other translations render it as "dies."

Without your Father's will (TEV "**without your Father's consent**") is literally "without your Father." Scholarly opinion supports this interpretation, which is followed in TEV, RSV, NEB, AT, Mft, NAB. But other scholars interpret the phrase to mean "without your Father knowing" (NJB; similarly Phps and Brc). The context seems to favor the first of these possibilities, and hellenistic Greek literature uses the phrase "without the gods" to mean "without the will of the gods." **Without your Father's will** may be rendered "unless God your Father has agreed" or ". . . without your Father willing it."

The sentence may be more natural if the order is different, as in "And yet, unless your Father agrees to it, not one of them will even fall to the ground."

10.30 RSV	TEV
But even the hairs of your head are all numbered.	As for you, even the hairs of your head have all been counted.

But even . . . of your head. In Greek the possessive pronoun **your** is given the position of emphasis: **"As for you"** (TEV, NAB, NEB) and "And so it is with you" (GECL 1st edition). BJ translates the verse "And you also! Your hairs themselves are all counted!"

Even the hairs of your head are all numbered (TEV ". . . **have all been counted**") may be altered to an active form: "Your Father even knows how many hairs are on your head." The point of the saying is to express God's intimate concern for his people, and to refer to him as "Father" would link the saying closely with the previous verse.

10.31   RSV   TEV

Fear not, therefore; you are of more   So do not be afraid; you are worth
value than many sparrows.   much more than many sparrows!

Fear not (TEV **"So do not be afraid"**) is without an object in Greek. NAB supplies an object ("So do not be afraid of anything"); it may even be better to translate "So do not be afraid of people" or "So do not be afraid of what people may do to you." The text stresses that one need fear only God, for in the final analysis it is he alone who determines the destiny of all people.

You are of more value than many sparrows is translated by GECL as "You are worth more to God than an entire flock of sparrows." Similar renderings are "God considers you much more valuable than many sparrows" and "As far as God is concerned, you are worth much more than even many sparrows."

Since the expression with **many sparrows** could be misunderstood to mean you are more important than many but not all sparrows, renderings such as "an entire flock" are often better.

10.32-33

              RSV   TEV

                                        Confessing and Rejecting Christ

32 So every one who acknowledges me before   32 "If anyone declares publicly that he
men, I also will acknowledge before my Father   belongs to me, I will do the same for him before
who is in heaven; 33 but whoever denies me   my Father in heaven. 33 But if anyone rejects me
before men, I also will deny before my Father who publicly, I will reject him before my Father in
is in heaven.   heaven.

SECTION HEADING: **"Confessing and Rejecting Christ." "Confessing . . . Christ"** here can be taken to mean "Declaring that one belongs to Christ" or ". . . that one believes in Christ." **"Rejecting Christ"** is the opposite, that is, "Declaring that one does not belong to Christ" or ". . . does not believe in Christ." So that the section heading will not be too long, it is possible to render it "Those who are for and those who are against Christ" or "To be for or against Christ."

Verses 32-33, by their affirmation of the unique relation between Jesus and the Father, add extra weight to the importance of enduring persecution for Jesus' sake.

RSV   TEV

So every one who acknowledges me | "If anyone declares publicly
before men, I also will acknowledge | that he belongs to me, I will do the
before my Father who is in heaven; | same for him before my Father in
| heaven.

So everyone who acknowledges me before men: Brc translates "If anyone publicly acknowledges his loyalty to me in front of his fellow men," and JB "So if anyone declares himself for me in the presence of men . . . ." Since one's acknowledgment of Jesus involves not only words but a direction of life, GECL 1st edition translates, "Whoever holds to me in front of people." The meaning may also be expressed "Whoever is willing to live his life for me in this world." Other common renderings are "Whoever declares publicly that he is my follower" or ". . . that he belongs to me."

I will also acknowledge (him) **before my Father who is in heaven** is in a balanced arrangement with the first half of the verse. Since this refers to the final judgment, when God sits on his throne to judge all people, the clause may be rendered "I will intercede for him on the day of final judgment, when my heavenly Father judges all people."

Often translators try to make this second part of the verse use a similar form to that of the first: "I will also declare to my Father in heaven (on the Day of Judgment) that that person is my follower" or ". . . belongs to me."

It may be better in some languages to use direct speech, as in ". . . declares 'I follow Jesus' " and ". . . I will say to my Father 'That person follows me.' "

RSV   TEV

but whoever denies me before men, | But if anyone rejects me publicly, I
I also will deny before my Father who | will reject him before my Father in
is in heaven. | heaven.

As in verse 32, the two halves of this verse form a balanced arrangement; and verses 32 and 33 balance with one another.

Denies me (TEV **"rejects me"**) means "denies that he is my follower" or "refuses to follow me as his Lord." A number of modern English translations render "disown" (NJB, NEB, Phps, Brc).

As in verse 32, translators should try to use similar forms in the two parts of the verse. Thus it can be rendered "But if anyone declares he is not my follower (or, does not belong to me), then on the Day of Judgment I will also declare to my Father that that person is not my follower (or, does not belong to me)."

Again, direct speech may be necessary, as in ". . . declares 'I do not follow Jesus' " and ". . . I will say to my Father 'That person does not follow me.' "

10.34-39

RSV   TEV

Not Peace, but a Sword

34 "Do not think that I have come to bring peace on earth; I have not come to bring peace, but a sword. 35 For I have come to set a man against his father, and a daughter against her mother, and a daughter-in-law against her mother-in-law; 36 and a man's foes will be those of his own household. 37 He who loves father or mother more than me is not worthy of me; and he who loves son or daughter more than me is not worthy of me; 38 and he who does not take his cross and follow me is not worthy of me. 39 He who finds his life will lose it, and he who loses his life for my sake will find it.

34 "Do not think that I have come to bring peace to the world. No, I did not come to bring peace, but a sword. 35 I came to set sons against their fathers, daughters against their mothers, daughters-in-law against their mothers-in-law; 36 a man's worst enemies will be the members of his own family.

37 "Whoever loves his father or mother more than me is not fit to be my disciple; whoever loves his son or daughter more than me is not fit to be my disciple. 38 Whoever does not take up his cross and follow in my steps is not fit to be my disciple. 39 Whoever tries to gain his own life will lose it; but whoever loses his life for my sake will gain it.

SECTION HEADING: "**Not Peace, But a Sword**." This may be "Jesus brings disagreement to people, not peace" or "What Jesus brings is not peace, but war."

These sayings appear with considerable variation and in a different context in Luke (12.51-53; 14.26-27). In essence the content of 10.16-25,28 is repeated.

10.34   RSV   TEV

"Do not think that I have come to bring peace on earth; I have not come to bring peace, but a sword.

"Do not think that I have come to bring peace to the world. No, I did not come to bring peace, but a sword.

Do not think that I have come to bring peace on earth (TEV ". . . **to the world**") is the interpretation of the text that is accepted by most all translators. The one exception appears to be AB, which renders "Do not think that I have come to impose peace on earth by force." However, this rendering requires a significant amount of linguistic gymnastics and is not supported by other commentators and translators. One pillar upon which this interpretation rests is the assumption that the Greek text represents a misunderstanding of the original Aramaic words of Jesus. But even if this were true, it still remains the duty of the translator to render the text according to the meaning that Matthew has given it. Moreover, this interpretation does not satisfy the needs of the context, which emphasizes the inevitable divisions the Christian message causes among people.

Do not think may be expressed as "You should not think that" or "You would be wrong if you thought that."

Many languages will require a destination for **have come** and will say "**to the world**," as TEV has done. This is based on the phrase **on earth** at the end of the sentence.

To bring peace may need some amplification, as in "to cause there to be peace among men" or "to cause people to live in peace."

I have not come to bring peace, but a sword is a negative parallel to the first half of the verse. **But a sword** may need to be produced in its full form: "but I came to bring a sword." Among the Jews the word **sword** was often used figuratively of war, murder, or strife. GECL has "No, I did not come to bring peace, but strife." NAB is also legitimate in rendering **sword** as "division," since both the Lukan parallel (12.51) and verses 35-36 speak of a division between family members. Some scholars believe that the symbolism here intended is that of persecution and martyrdom, but no translation seems to reflect this interpretation.

Most translators find that **sword** itself is not readily understood, so they instead say something like "I came to bring fighting" or "I came to cause men to fight each other (or, disagree with each other)." But see notes on verse 35, where a possible translation is offered that depends on using **sword** literally here.

10.35-36   RSV   TEV

35 For I have come to set a man against his father, and a daughter against her mother, and a daughter-in-law against her mother-in-law; 36 and a man's foes will be those of his own household.

35 I came to set sons against their fathers, daughters against their mothers, daughters-in-law against their mothers-in-law; 36 a man's worst enemies will be the members of his own family.

To set . . . against (so also TEV, NJB, NEB) is the wording of many translations; NAB has "to set . . . at odds with" and AT "to turn . . . against," and it can also be "to make sons their fathers' enemies."

This is the only passage to which the lexicons assign this meaning for the verb, which has "divide in two" as its primary meaning. But the primary meaning also suits the context well, especially the figure of the sword in verse 34. If this symbolism is carried into verse 35, then one can translate "I have come like a sword that separates sons from their fathers . . . ." And if the separation is understood in the sense of "setting against," then it is possible to arrive at ". . . that separates sons from their fathers and makes them enemies." Unless something of this nature is done, then there is not a clear relation between verses 34 and 35.

A man against his father may require slight rewording: "a son against his father." On the other hand, **a daughter against her mother** may need to be "a woman against her mother," and **a daughter-in-law against her mother-in-law** may be here "a woman against her mother-in-law." In the Jewish culture sons and daughters were to be obedient to their parents, and a **daughter-in-law** was expected to obey her **mother-in-law.**

A man's foes (TEV "worst enemies") **will be those of his own household** (TEV "the members of his own family"). GECL widens the application: "The closest relatives will become enemies." The purpose of the saying is to underline the division that comes in families when some of its members accept the Christian message and others do not. Since Jesus is addressing his disciples, it may be necessary to shift to the second person: "The members of your own family will become your worst enemies."

Most of verses 35-36 are taken from Micah 7.6, a quotation also found in Luke 12.53; but neither Gospel follows precisely either the Hebrew or the Septuagint. Some translators have indicated that Jesus is quoting (or referring to) an Old Testament passage. They have said "For, as it is written in the Scriptures, I have come . . . ."

10.37 RSV TEV

He who loves father or mother more than me is not worthy of me; and he who loves son or daughter more than me is not worthy of me.

"Whoever loves his father or mother more than me is not fit to be my disciple; whoever loves his son or daughter more than me is not fit to be my disciple.

Although Jesus calls upon his followers to love their families and to honor their parents, he makes it abundantly clear that no family loyalties must stand in the way of loyalty to God. Several commentators draw attention to Deuteronomy 33.8-11, where Levi is praised because he left his parents for the sake of God's covenant.

Since Jesus is still addressing his disciples, it may be necessary to render **he who loves** in the second person, "if any of you" or "if you."

Love . . . **more than** means "cares more for" (NEB). The parallel in Luke (14.26) takes advantage of a Semitic idiom in which "hate" means "love (one) less than (the other)." **Love** . . . **more than** or "cares more for" poses occasional problems. For example, in West Africa, where the comparative is generally expressed with a verb, the expression may have to be "If the love someone has for his father or mother does not surpass the love he has for me." Another way is "The caring someone has for his father and mother should not surpass the caring he has for me."

Is not worthy of me (so also NJB, NAB) is translated "does not deserve to be mine" by Phps. In such a context **worthy** means "show oneself fit to be," which is the basis of TEV, "**is not fit to be**."

Of me is translated "to be mine" by Phps and "to belong to me" by Brc; TEV has "**to be my disciple**." GECL 1st edition has done significant restructuring, but an idiomatic translation into English requires reversing the order of the two clauses: "I cannot use anyone who loves his father or mother more than me."

Quite often translators have as a translation of **is not worthy of me** "does not deserve to be one of my disciples." Another way is "I can't make anyone my disciple who does not love me more than (he loves) his father or mother."

The expression in the second part, with **son or daughter**, should be handled in the same way.

10.38   RSV   TEV

and he who does not take his cross   Whoever does not take up his cross
and follow me is not worthy of me.   and follow in my steps is not fit to be
                                           my disciple.

Take may have to be "carry."

He who may be "Anyone who," "Whoever," "Any person who," or whatever phrase is most natural.

The **cross** was an instrument of execution used by the Romans. It was looked upon as a particularly painful form of death, and the Romans reserved it for slaves and foreigners. The condemned man was required to carry his cross, or the crossbeam, to the place of execution. Crucifixion was a familiar sight in Jesus' day, and it easily became a symbol of discipleship.

Very often translators rendered **cross** as "crossed sticks" or "crossed boards." Readers then miss the whole idea of crucifixion. Sometimes the only crosses people know are crucifixes that are worn around the neck or that might hang on a wall. Again, the element of crucifixion or death is not obvious. But readers of Matthew's day would have thought instantly of death by crucifixion when they saw or heard the word "cross." To convey this information to modern readers, then, translators sometimes say "cross on which he can die" or ". . . on which they can kill him."

Follow me is translated "follow in my steps" by TEV, "follow in my footsteps" by NJB and Brc, "walk in my footsteps" by NEB. Here **follow** surely has the extended meaning of "follow as a disciple" (see comment on 4.20). GECL 1st edition has "come with me."

For comments on **is not worthy of me**, see verse 37.

10.39   RSV   TEV

He who finds his life will lose it, and   Whoever tries to gain his own life will
he who loses his life for my sake will   lose it; but whoever loses his life for
find it.   my sake will gain it.

A parallel to this verse occurs in Luke 17.33, with the exception that Luke does not include **for my sake**. On the meaning of **for my sake**, see comments on verse 18.

Finds, a literal rendering of the Greek verb, may also have the meaning indicated by TEV: **"tries to gain . . . find."** Certainly to translate **finds** literally can result in a wrong understanding. Nothing has been lost. "Tries to keep" or "tries to save" is better.

Life (so most modern translations) may also have the meaning of "soul" or "person"; in Luke 12.19-20,22-23 there are four occurrences of the word which parallel its usage here. NEB has "by gaining his life a man will lose it"; Brc "to find your life is to lose it"; NAB "he who seeks only himself brings himself to ruin." GECL translates "Whoever tries to hold on to his life will lose it," and MACL has "Whoever places supreme importance on his own life will never experience true life."

This rendering in MACL of **lose it** as "will never experience true life" is a very helpful model. **Lose it** does not mean "he will die" but rather "will not have true life."

And he who loses his life for my sake will find it states the opposite of the first clause. As one commentator notes: ". . . to 'lose one's life' could mean 'to die a violent death' because of one's faithfulness in following Christ; but it seem more likely that it vividly denotes self-denial . . . ." MACL translates "but whoever denies himself because of me will experience true life" and for the first part of the sentence INCL has "whoever loses his life because of faithfulness to me." The idea of self-denial seen in **loses his life** sometimes has to be rendered as "does not consider himself important" or "does not consider his life of great value."

Will find it may be translated "will gain eternal life" or ". . . true life."

10.40-42

RSV	TEV
	Rewards
40 "He who receives you receives me, and he who receives me receives him who sent me. 41 He who receives a prophet because he is a prophet shall receive a prophet's reward, and he who receives a righteous man because he is a righteous man shall receive a righteous man's reward. 42 And whoever gives to one of these little ones even a cup of cold water because he is a disciple, truly, I say to you, he shall not lose his reward."	40 "Whoever welcomes you welcomes me; and whoever welcomes me welcomes the one who sent me. 41 Whoever welcomes God's messenger because he is God's messenger, will share in his reward. And whoever welcomes a good man because he is good, will share in his reward. 42 You can be sure that whoever gives even a drink of cold water to one of the least of these my followers because he is my follower, will certainly receive a reward."

SECTION HEADING: "**Rewards**." This can also be "God will give rewards" or "God will reward those who welcome his servants."

As the paragraphing of the UBS Greek text indicates, this section is best continued through 11.1, which parallels 7.28 (see comments there). Verses 40-42 emphasize that the disciples must carry out in the present the same mission that Jesus had in his day; it also reminds the reader that one's response toward the disciple is in reality an expression of that same attitude toward the one whom he represents.

10.40 RSV	TEV
"He who receives you receives me, and he who receives me receives him who sent me.	"Whoever welcomes you welcomes me; and whoever welcomes me welcomes the one who sent me.

He who can be "The person who" or "Anyone who," "Whoever," or similar.

Receives (so also NEB) may be better translated "**welcomes**" (TEV, NJB, NAB, Phps, Brc); the verb was previously used in verse 14. Elsewhere in the New Testament it also has the meaning "receive in a hospitable manner" or "welcome as a guest." See Mark 6.11; Luke 9.5,53; 10.8,10; John 4.45; Colossians 4.10; Hebrews 11.31.

Him who sent me is a reference to God, and so it may be translated "God who sent me" or "the Father who sent me."

He who receives a prophet because he is a prophet shall receive a prophet's reward, and he who receives a righteous man because he is a righteous man shall receive a righteous man's reward.	Whoever welcomes God's messenger because he is God's messenger, will share in his reward. And whoever welcomes a good man because he is good, will share in his reward.

For comments on **receives**, see verse 40.

Prophet: TEV, GECL 1st edition, and DUCL have "God's messenger," since the primary work of New Testament prophets was that of speaking God's message. Matthew has earlier used this word of the Old Testament prophets (1.22; 2.5,15,17,23; 3.3; 4.14; 5.12; 8.17).

Because he is a prophet (so also NJB, Phps) is literally "in the name of a prophet." NEB has "whoever receives a prophet as a prophet," and Brc "the man who recognizes a prophet and welcomes him as such . . . ." One may even translate ". . . because he proclaims God's message." This can also be "Whoever receives hospitably one of God's spokesmen because he recognizes that is what the person is."

Shall receive a prophet's reward may be translated "he shall also be rewarded as a messenger of God" (GECL 1st edition) or "he will receive the same reward that a messenger of God receives." It is possible also to shift to an active construction and reverse the order of the two clauses: "God will reward anyone who welcomes his messengers. He will give them the same reward that he gives his messengers."

A **reward** is a recompense, what a person receives for having done some good thing. It is not "money" here. "The gift that God gives to someone who does well" is a possibility if a language has no word for **reward**.

Righteous man (see 1.19) is translated "**good man**" by TEV, NEB, Phps, Brc, and Mft. Both NJB and NAB have "a holy man," while AT translates "an upright man." GECL 1st edition has "a religious (or, devout) man." Here the reference may be either to a category of especially faithful Christians, or else to a special group of teachers within the church. Note that in 13.17 and 23.29 "righteous men" and "prophets" are also linked. One may translate "If you welcome a man because he is good, God will give you the same reward that he will give the good man."

As in 1.19 **a righteous man** can also be rendered as "a man who does God's will" or "a man who does what God requires."

And whoever gives to one of these little ones even a cup of cold water because he is a disciple, truly, I say to you, he shall not lose his reward."

You can be sure that whoever gives even a drink of cold water to one of the least of these my followers because he is my follower, will certainly receive a reward."

One of these little ones is described by the phrase **because he is a disciple** (literally "in the name of a disciple"). TEV combines these two phrases and renders **"one of the least of these my followers."** GECL 1st edition is similar to TEV; NAB has "one of these lowly ones because he is a disciple"; NEB "one of these little ones, because he is a disciple of mine." It is important in translation that **little ones** be understood of status rather than of age. Therefore it may be translated as "least important ones." The phrase can then be "one of these least important of my followers because he is my follower."

A cup of cold water reflects the show of hospitality in first-century Palestine. It may be necessary to add "to drink" or to say **"a drink of cold water,"** as in TEV.

For comments on **Truly, I say to you**, see 5.18.

The translation of this verse may be complicated, because Jesus is addressing his disciples (see verse 40), yet he is referring to them in the third person as **one of these little ones . . . because he is a disciple**. This results from the double orientation of Matthew's Gospel, by which Matthew relates Jesus' words to the actual church situation of his own day. So then Matthew will freely shift from the second person to the third person, if this better suits the needs of his congregation.

TEV has rendered the negative **shall not lose his reward** as a positive sentence, **"will certainly receive . . . ."** It may be necessary to make this passive an active, as in "God will certainly reward him" or "God will not fail to reward him."

See verse 41 for comments on **reward**.

Chapter 11

11.1-6

RSV	TEV
	The Messengers from John the Baptist
1 And when Jesus had finished instructing his twelve disciples, he went on from there to teach and preach in their cities.	1 When Jesus finished giving these instructions to his twelve disciples, he left that place and went off to teach and preach in the towns near there.
2 Now when John heard in prison about the deeds of the Christ, he sent word by his disciples 3 and said to him, "Are you he who is to come, or shall we look for another?" 4 And Jesus answered them, "Go and tell John what you hear and see: 5 the blind receive their sight and the lame walk, lepers are cleansed and the deaf hear, and the dead are raised up, and the poor have good news preached to them. 6 And blessed is he who takes no offense at me."	2 When John the Baptist heard in prison about the things that Christ was doing, he sent some of his disciples to him. 3 "Tell us," they asked Jesus, "are you the one John said was going to come, or should we expect someone else?"
	4 Jesus answered, "Go back and tell John what you are hearing and seeing: 5 the blind can see, the lame can walk, those who suffer from dreaded skin diseases are made clean,[h] the deaf hear, the dead are brought back to life, and the Good News is preached to the poor. 6 How happy are those who have no doubts about me!"

[h] MADE CLEAN: *See 8.2*

SECTION HEADING: "**The Messengers from John the Baptist**." This may be expressed as "John the Baptist sends some messengers to Jesus" or "John the Baptist sends some of his disciples to Jesus," possibly with the addition "to ask him questions" or "to ask him about who he was."

For "**John the Baptist**," see comments on 3.1.

TOB notes that 11.1 functions as both the conclusion to 9.3–10.42 and the introduction to the section which describes the response of John (11.2-19), the Galileans (11.20-24, and the Pharisees (12.1-45) to Jesus, who is present as the Messiah in word (5–7.29) and deed (8–9.34).

11.1 RSV	TEV
And when Jesus had finished instructing his twelve disciples, he went on from there to teach and preach in their cities.	**When Jesus finished giving these instructions to his twelve disciples, he left that place and went off to teach and preach in the towns near there.**

And when Jesus had finished instructing refers back to chapter 10. The verb **instructing** occurs only here in the Gospel of Matthew; it is found with more frequency in Luke–Acts (nine times), four times in 1 Corinthians, and once each in Galatians and Titus.

In some languages, to make it clear that **And when Jesus had finished instructing** refers to the previous section, translators say "When Jesus finished teaching these things," "After Jesus finished . . . ," or "Jesus finished giving instructions to his disciples. Then he left . . . ."

Instructing, as seen in the above examples, is often rendered "teaching." Some languages require a direct object for "teaching," so translators say "teaching all these things."

His twelve disciples may need to be "the twelve disciples who followed him."

He went on from there to teach and preach is translated "he left that place and went to teach and preach" by NEB. Some languages may require two verbs of motion such as are found in TEV: "**left . . . went off.**" Another way is "he left there to go . . . ."

In place of **to teach and preach**, GECL substitutes one verb and an object: "to proclaim the Good News." This is evidently done on the assumption that the two verbs in the Greek text are essentially equivalent in meaning. Translators who do wish to keep the two verbs should see the discussion at 3.1 for **preach**, and note that as elsewhere (for example, 5.2), **teach** may require either an object ("teach about the Good News") or an indirect object ("teach the people there").

In their cities (NEB "in the neighbouring towns") is most likely an allusion to Jewish towns, as the NJB footnote explains. Some scholars further restrict the reference to the Jewish towns of Galilee.

Their cities can appear to refer to towns or cities of the twelve disciples. This is probably not correct. "Towns of that area" is better, or "other towns of the Jews."

11.2   RSV   TEV

> Now when John heard in prison about the deeds of the Christ, he sent word by his disciples

> When John the Baptist heard in prison about the things that Christ was doing, he sent some of his disciples to him.

The question which John the Baptist raises about Jesus is appropriately placed at this position in Matthew's Gospel. Jesus himself has already performed a number of healing miracles, and he has commissioned his disciples both to continue this healing ministry and to preach the Good News. The question raised by John the Baptist thereby allows Matthew the opportunity of making explicit the meaning of Jesus' words and deeds: they affirm that Jesus is the Promised Messiah.

Now indicates a new topic is starting. It must not be misunderstood to mean "At this moment." Translators can say "It happened then" or "At that time," or it may be more natural to drop it.

John is identified by TEV, FRCL, and GECL as "John the Baptist." Most translators do this, in fact, because otherwise many readers who are not very familiar with the Bible would not guess which **John** was being referred to. For comments on "**John the Baptist**," see 3.1.

Matthew has much earlier informed his readers of John's imprisonment, but it is not until 14.3-4 that he states the reason why it was done. Here Matthew is not concerned with the why of John's imprisonment, but rather with using his question as a means of having Jesus clarify that his actions are Messianic deeds, and that he is therefore the Promised One.

The phrase **in prison** may need to be rendered by a relative clause such as ". . . John, who was in prison at that time."

It may be natural to say simply **John heard**. Some languages require an agent, as in "heard people tell about" or "heard from people about." Another way is "People told John about the things that Christ was doing. When John heard these things . . . ."

Deeds may need to be altered to a verb structure; see TEV ("**the things that . . . was doing**"), NJB and NEB ("what . . . was doing"), and NAB ("the works . . . was performing").

The Christ (so also Mft, FRCL, BJ, AT), the Greek equivalent of "the Messiah," is translated by many as a proper name, "Christ" (NEB, NJB, Phps, NAB, Lu, Zür). Both GECL 1st edition ("Jesus Christ") and DUCL ("Jesus") add their support to the interpretation of the phrase as a proper name, and some Greek manuscripts read "Jesus" in place of "the Christ." Either interpretation ("the Christ" or "Christ") may be arrived at from the best Greek manuscripts, which do possess the definite article. The fundamental question concerns Matthew's intention in mentioning the name, and it is more natural to assume that he is here demanding the same decision from his readers as Jesus is demanding from John. To read **the deeds of the Christ** would prejudice the decision; each reader must decide whether these "deeds of Christ" are indeed those of the Messiah. Thus "Christ" or "Jesus Christ" would probably fit the passage better.

His disciples: Matthew does not specify the number of John's disciples who were sent to Jesus; the parallel in Luke 7.18 specifies a small contingent of two disciples. There is no reason to translate John's **disciples** any differently from those of Jesus. See comments on 9.14. Many translations will say "some of his disciples," since **his disciples** may seem to mean all of them.

Sent word can be rendered in several ways; for example, "sent some of his disciples to ask," or "sent some of his disciples to Jesus. They asked him . . . ," or "He asked some of his disciples to go to Jesus to find out about him."

11.3	RSV	TEV
	and said to him, "Are you he who is to come, or shall we look for another?"	"Tell us," they asked Jesus, "are you the one John said was going to come, or should we expect someone else?"

In the text, the subject of **said** is singular, referring to John, but in most languages it will be more natural to make "his disciples" of verse 2 the subject.

In all probability **he who is to come** is a technical term for the expected Messiah (see 3.11; also note Dan 7.13; Heb 10.37; Rev 1.4). GECL makes this identification explicit, "Are you the Savior, the one who is to come . . . ?" TOB's footnote also indicates that this is a Messianic title.

The phrase **he who is to come** is a little awkward in many languages. Some have rendered it "Are you the one who we were told would come (to save us)?" or "Are you the one we know God is going to send (to save us)?" Since John the Baptist had proclaimed such a person (see 3.11-12), some translations have followed TEV and said **"the one John said was going to come."**

Or shall we look for another? may be rendered "or have we got to wait for someone else?" (JB, GECL). In Acts 3.5 TEV renders the same verb with the meaning "expect (something)," and in Acts 10.24 with the meaning "wait (for someone)." Elsewhere in Matthew the verb is found in 24.50.

Note that **we** does not refer only to John's disciples but means the Jewish people in general. To avoid misunderstanding, some translators have said "we all" or "we Jews."

11.4   RSV   TEV

And Jesus answered them, "Go and tell John what you hear and see:

Jesus answered, "Go back and tell John what you are hearing and seeing:

And Jesus answered them represents a Semitic Greek construction, literally "and answering Jesus said to them." As elsewhere, **And** is simply a device to show the story is continuing. Some languages use a word like "So" or "Then," and others do not need any word.

Go is a participle in Greek, while **tell** is an imperative. But the use of a participle for an imperative is not uncommon in Greek, especially when accompanied by an imperative.

Jesus does not answer John's question directly, but rather he orders the messengers to report what they **hear and see**. Quite possibly the reference is to the miracles of Jesus mentioned in chapters 8–9 and to the work of the disciples whom Jesus had earlier sent out to continue his work of preaching and healing. Upon the testimony of these events, the disciples of John are then to decide whether Jesus is the Coming One.

Some languages will require some kind of object for both **hear** and **see**. It will probably not be good to indicate specifically at this point in the passage what they are. Rather, some general phrase will suffice: "what you are hearing people say and what you are seeing yourselves." Some have wanted to make the object of **hear** "what I am saying to people," but "what people are saying" fits the context a little better.

The scriptural support for Jesus' appeal comes from Isaiah 35.5-6; 42.18; 61.1. Significant is the observation that in the Isaiah passage the coming salvation event is accompanied by the punishment of God's enemies (Isa 34.1-17; 61.5-7), while here Jesus speaks only of deliverance. Moreover, the Isaiah passages do not mention either the cleansing of lepers or the resurrection of the dead (verse 5). Finally, the proclamation of good news to the poor, here placed in the position of emphasis, is introduced as an entirely new element of the coming salvation. And it receives even further emphasis by the arrangement of hearing before that of seeing.

11.5	RSV	TEV
	the blind receive their sight and the lame walk, lepers are cleansed and the deaf hear, and the dead are raised up, and the poor have good news preached to them.	the blind can see, the lame can walk, those who suffer from dreaded skin diseases are made clean,[h] the deaf hear, the dead are brought back to life, and the Good News is preached to the poor.

[h] MADE CLEAN: *See 8.2.*

Both TEV and RSV end verse 4 with a colon to indicate that the list in verse 5 is what John's disciples are seeing and hearing. In many languages the normal way to show this relation is to begin the verse with a phrase such as "These things are" or "The things you see and hear are that the blind people are made to see . . . ."

TOB indicates that Jesus is quoting Isaiah here by putting the verse in italics. However, because the list is only partially from Isaiah, and from different places in Isaiah (as we point out above), then it is probably not necessary to do this. A footnote will be helpful, however.

The phrase **the blind receive their sight** may be rendered "people who are blind can see" or ". . . are made to see." However, some languages prefer to indicate the agent, as in "I make blind people see."

Actually it may be necessary to indicate the agent throughout this verse, as in "I make lame people walk, I make lepers clean, I make deaf people hear, I raise people to life, and I am preaching the Good News to the poor." However, the focus as it stands in the text is on these unfortunate people who are having something good done to them, and the rendering as above will result in some loss of this. So a translation such as "the blind people can see, crippled people can now walk . . . and poor people can now listen to the proclamation of the Good News" will be better.

Note that **the blind** does not mean all the blind people, but rather those who came to Jesus for help. "People who are blind" or "blind people" will be good translations. This is also the case with **the deaf**, **the dead**, and **the poor**.

It may also be necessary to put the blindness in the past tense, as "people who were blind can now see." This will be equally true for **the lame walk**. "People who were crippled can now walk" will be a good rendering. Similarly, **lepers** can be "those who were lepers," **the deaf** can be "those who were deaf," and **the dead** is translated "people who had died." Presumably, however, **the poor** remain poor.

Lepers are cleansed: see comments on 8.2.

Poor translates the same word discussed in 5.3. In this context it should be translated simply as "poor people," that is, people who are destitute. It is not referring to spiritual poverty here.

Have good news preached (literally "are evangelized") translates a verb which occurs more than twenty-five times in Luke–Acts, but only here in Matthew.

And blessed is he who takes no offense at me.''	**How happy are those who have no doubts about me!''**

Blessed: see comments on 5.3. As we suggest there, a common way to render this is "the man who does not lose faith in me is blessed" or ". . . is in a good position."

He who takes no offense at me: JB has "the man who does not lose faith in me," and NEB "the man who does not find me a stumbling block." TEV, on the other hand, employs a plural: **"those who have no doubts about me!"** The choice of a singular or plural form for the saying will depend entirely on what is felt natural in the receptor language. The Greek verb form is the same for middle and passive, and so it may mean either "take offense at someone" or "be led into sin (by refusing to believe in someone)."

Following the first meaning of **offense** may result in a rendering such as "the person who is not offended by me," ". . . by who I am," or ". . . by what I do." Following the second meaning would result in translations such as "the person who does not lose faith in me," "whose faith in me is not destroyed," or "who doesn't do wrong by refusing to believe in me." For occurrences of this verb with similar meanings see 13.57; 26.31,33; Mark 6.3; Luke 7.23.

11.7-15

RSV

TEV

7 As they went away, Jesus began to speak to the crowds concerning John: "What did you go out into the wilderness to behold? A reed shaken by the wind? 8 Why then did you go out? To see a man[a] clothed in soft raiment? Behold, those who wear soft raiment are in kings' houses. 9 Why then did you go out? To see a prophet?[b] Yes, I tell you, and more than a prophet. 10 This is he of whom it is written,

'Behold, I send my messenger before thy face,

who shall prepare thy way before thee.'
11 Truly, I say to you, among those born of woman there has risen no one greater than John the Baptist; yet he who is least in the kingdom of heaven is greater than he. 12 From the days of John the Baptist until now the kingdom of heaven has suffered violence,[c] and men of violence take it by force. 13 For all the prophets and the law prophesied until John; 14 and if you are willing to accept it, he is Elijah who is to come. 15 He who has ears to hear,[d] let him hear.

7 While John's disciples were leaving, Jesus spoke about him to the crowds: "When you went out to John in the desert, what did you expect to see? A blade of grass bending in the wind? 8 What did you go out to see? A man dressed up in fancy clothes? People who dress like that live in palaces! 9 Tell me, what did you go out to see? A prophet? Yes indeed, but you saw much more than a prophet. 10 For John is the one of whom the scripture says: 'God said, I will send my messenger ahead of you to open the way for you.' 11 I assure you that John the Baptist is greater than any man who has ever lived. But he who is least in the Kingdom of heaven is greater than John. 12 From the time John preached his message until this very day the Kingdom of heaven has suffered violent attacks,[i] and violent men try to seize it. 13 Until the time of John all the prophets and the Law of Moses spoke about the Kingdom; 14 and if you are willing to believe their message, John is Elijah, whose coming was predicted. 15 Listen, then, if you have ears!

[a] Or *What then did you go out to see? A man . . .*

[b] Other ancient authorities read *What*

[i] has suffered violent attacks; *or* has been coming violently.

then did you go out to see? A prophet?
c Or *has been coming violently*
d Other ancient authorities omit *to hear*

The first half of verse 7 forms a transitional statement, which is followed by three parallel questions and their answers (verses 7b-9). Verse 10 contains a scriptural testimony to John the Baptist, which is climaxed by Jesus' own high appraisal of John (verse 11). Verses 12-15 are difficult to interpret individually, and the relationship between the verses is not immediately clear. Verse 12 is particularly obscure, and it is omitted from the Lukan parallel. However, it does appear in Luke 16.16 (with the clauses inverted) in a section dealing with the Jewish Law.

11.7 RSV	TEV
As they went away, Jesus began to speak to the crowds concerning John: "What did you go out into the wilderness to behold? A reed shaken by the wind?	While John's disciples were leaving, Jesus spoke about him to the crowds: "When you went out to John in the desert, what did you expect to see? A blade of grass bending in the wind?

As in this context is a transition of time that means "While," as in "At the time they were leaving."

As they went away: TEV, FRCL, GECL, and Brc identify **they** as "**John's disciples.**" JB translates "As the messengers were leaving," which is similar to NEB and NAB.

The crowds, as in 8.1, may be better singular, "the crowd."

After **began to speak . . . concerning John**, in many languages it is necessary to say "He said."

What did you go out into the wilderness to behold? since the allusion is specifically to John the Baptist, TEV translates "**When you went out to John in the desert, what did you expect to see?**" In some cases, instead of simply "**went out**" it may be necessary to specify "went out to see" or "went out to listen to." Another way to render this question is "What did you expect to see when you went out into the wilderness (to hear John)?" Or the order may better be reversed: "When you went out to the desert to hear John, what did you expect to see?"

For **wilderness** or "desert," see comments on 3.1.

A reed shaken by the wind? presupposes the fuller form: "Did you go out into the wilderness to see a reed shaken by the wind?" TEV retains the singular form ("**a blade of grass**"), though a collective form may be more appropriate: "a reed-bed" (NEB) and "the long grass" (Brc). Jesus has in mind the tall canegrass which was found along the banks of the Jordan River.

Shaken by the wind (TEV "**bending in the wind**") is capable of being translated in a number of different ways: "swept by the wind" (NEB), "swaying in the wind" (NAB), and "waving in the breeze" (Phps).

It may be advisable to shift from a rhetorical question to a statement: "You did not go out into the desert merely to see a blade of grass bending in the wind." Or,

"When John was preaching in the desert, you went out to see him. You did not go there to see a blade of grass bending in the wind."

Some translators have retained the rhetorical question but supplied the answer: "When you went out into the desert, what did you expect to see? Was it long grass swaying in the wind? Of course not." Verse 8 would follow easily from this.

11.8	RSV	TEV

Why then did you go out? To see a man*ᵃ* clothed in soft raiment? Behold, those who wear soft raiment are in kings' houses.

What did you go out to see? A man dressed up in fancy clothes? People who dress like that live in palaces!

ᵃ Or *What then did you go out to see? A man . . .*

Why then did you go out? may be rendered "So why then did you go there?" Interestingly, one of the best ways to render this is to actually follow the textual variant, "So what did you go out to see?"

Soft raiment (TEV "**fancy clothes**") also has the possibility of many different translations: "fine clothes" (Phps, NJB), "dainty and delicate clothes" (Brc), "luxuriously dressed" (NAB), and "in silks and satins" (NEB). This is best understood as a contrast between the luxurious clothes of the rich and the rough garments worn by John the Baptist.

To see . . . soft raiment? may need a full expression: "Did you come out to see . . . soft raiment?" It may be even more advisable to drop the rhetorical question: "You did not go out to see . . . ." As in the previous verse, another way to handle the rhetorical question is to follow it with a reply, as in "(Did you go to see) a man dressed in luxurious clothes? Of course not."

Behold: see comments on 1.20. NAB has "Remember," and JB "Oh no."

Those who wear . . . kings' houses may be expressed as "people who wear fine clothes like that live in kings' houses" or ". . . live with kings," or "it is people who live in kings' houses who wear fine clothes like that." This does not necessarily mean kings themselves.

Kings' houses are palaces. Translators whose languages have such a word can certainly use it.

11.9	RSV	TEV

Why then did you go out? To see a prophet?*ᵇ* Yes, I tell you, and more than a prophet.

Tell me, what did you go out to see? A prophet? Yes indeed, but you saw much more than a prophet.

ᵇ Other ancient authorities read *What then did you go out to see? A prophet?*

Then is represented in TEV by "**Tell me.**" In Greek this conjunction serves to make a transition and to draw a contrast. It can also be rendered "So, then," or "So I ask you, what . . . ," or "If not (for these reasons), then why did . . . ?"

To see a prophet? may need the full question form: "Did you come out to see a prophet?" In Greek the form of this question differs from the questions in verses 7 and 8, which expect a negative reply. Here Jesus expects the people to reply "Yes, we came out to see a prophet." To the questions of verses 7-8 he would expect the reply "No, we did not come out to see a blade of grass . . . a man dressed in expensive clothes." As with the earlier questions, so here also a shift may be made to a statement: "You came out to see a prophet" or "Instead you came out . . . ."

There are several ways the meaning of these questions can be expressed. For example, one can say "You went out to see a prophet, didn't you?" or "So I ask you, why did you go out? It was to see a prophet, wasn't it?"

For comments on **prophet**, see 1.22.

Yes, I tell you is similar in form to the expression used in 5.18 and 26, except that here **Yes** substitutes for "truly." Once again, translation may necessitate a fuller expression: "I will tell you what you went out to see. You went out to see a prophet. Yes, you went out to see someone who is more than a prophet."

As can be seen from these examples, how this last sentence is rendered depends on how the rhetorical questions of this and the previous verse were handled. It should always flow well from those questions. Another rendering is "So, I ask you, why did you go out into the desert? It was to see a prophet. But I tell you that you saw much more than just a prophet."

More than a prophet, in addition to the ways it is expressed in the examples above, can also be "someone much greater than a prophet" or "someone who is more than an ordinary prophet."

11.10 RSV	TEV
This is he of whom it is written, 'Behold, I send my messenger before thy face, who shall prepare thy way before thee.'	For John is the one of whom the scripture says: 'God said, I will send my messenger ahead of you to open the way for you.'

Jesus now appeals to scripture in support of his affirmation that John is more than a prophet.

Of whom it is written is similar to the earlier quotation formulas (see 2.5). Both TEV and GECL 1st edition introduce God as the speaker of the words quoted from scripture, and GECL 1st edition translates: "John is the one of whom it speaks in the holy Scriptures: 'Here is my messenger, says God . . . .' "

Translators will need to find a natural way to introduce this quotation. Here are some other suggestions: "The man you saw is the one that God was speaking about in the Scriptures when he said . . ." and "God's Scriptures were speaking about this man in the place it says . . . ." TEV is also a useful model.

Translators who use "Scriptures" should refer to comments on 4.4.

For comments on **Behold**, see 1.20. It is a word that can be dropped or rendered by "I tell you" or "Look," or some other expression which will catch the attention of the audience.

Note that **my messenger** means "God's messenger." Hence the introduction of "God" in these examples. Readers must not think it is Jesus' messenger being referred to.

The scripture quotation derives from the Greek text of Malachi 3.1, but Matthew's wording differs in at least two respects from that of the Septuagint. (1) **Before thy face** (TEV "**ahead of you**") is not found in the Malachi passage, though it does appear in the Septuagint of Exodus 23.20. (2) In place of "before me" (a reference to God), Matthew substitutes **before thee** (TEV "**for you**"), that is, "before Jesus, the Messiah." In the original Malachi text (and also in Exo 23.20) the messenger was to go ahead of God and prepare the way for him. Matthew, however, reinterprets the text to mean that God now sends his messenger (John the Baptist) to prepare the way for the Messiah (Jesus). This is what gives John his unique position. He is a prophet, but his role supersedes that of other prophets in that he is the one who introduces the Messianic Age.

Before thy face is usually translated as in TEV. It does not mean literally "in front of your face" but rather refers to going ahead.

To **prepare thy way before thee** means "to get your road ready for you (to travel on)" or "to open the road so you can travel on it." If "road" would be understood only as a paved road, then translators should retain **way**, of course.

Even though "you" does refer to the Messiah, Jesus, most translators prefer not to say "Jesus" specifically. At most, if the sentence can not be understood otherwise, translators may say "before you, the Messiah."

11.11   RSV   TEV

Truly, I say to you, among those born of woman there has risen no one greater than John the Baptist; yet he who is least in the kingdom of heaven is greater than he.	I assure you that John the Baptist is greater than any man who has ever lived. But he who is least in the Kingdom of heaven is greater than John.

In some languages there needs to be an indication that the Malachi citation of verse 10 is finished. This can be done by beginning verse 11 with "Jesus continued by saying" or something similar.

Truly, I say to you: see comments on 5.18.

Among those born of woman: scholars agree that this expression is merely a way of contrasting human beings with supernatural beings, which is the basis for GECL: "John is more important than any man who has ever lived." Brc is accurate, though somewhat flowery: ". . . among mortal men no greater figure than John the Baptizer has ever emerged in history." Other ways to express it are "of all the people who have ever lived, not one of them is more important" and "no one who has ever lived has been more important than John the Baptist." Note that **greater** here means "more important."

Has risen, meaning "has appeared on the scene" or "has come into existence," is generally rendered as "has lived," as in the examples above.

Yet marks a contrast. It can also be "nevertheless" or "but." Quite often translators begin a new sentence at this point.

He who is least in the kingdom of heaven refers to the disciples of Jesus. See comments on 10.42. The phrase can be here "even the person who is the least important among those under God's rule" or "anyone under God's rule, even the least important person."

Greater than he (TEV "**John**") contrasts Jesus' disciples with John the Baptist. Their greatness is that of privilege to participate in the rule of God rather than greatness of achievement or character. GECL has "The least one in God's New World is greater than he"; MACL "The least one under God's rule enjoys blessings greater that those of John"; INCL "The least one among God's people is greater than John."

As in the first part of the verse, **greater** does not refer to physical size but to importance and privilege.

11.12	RSV	TEV

From the days of John the Baptist until now the kingdom of heaven has suffered violence,^{c} and men of violence take it by force.	**From the time John preached his message until this very day the Kingdom of heaven has suffered violent attacks,^{i} and violent men try to seize it.**
^{c} Or *has been coming violently*	
	^{i}has suffered violent attacks; *or* has been coming violently.

Needless to say, the interpretation and translation of this verse is extremely difficult. In Luke 16.16 the same saying is found in a context that concerns the role of the Law and the Prophets, but there the two clauses are inverted.

From the days of John the Baptist until now: a literal translation is ambiguous because it allows for the meaning "ever since John the Baptist has lived." Actually, the ministry of John is in focus, and so GECL translates "When John the Baptist appeared . . . ." Other translations follow TEV with an expression such as "from the time of John's ministry" or "from the time when John was preaching his message."

The Greek verb rendered **has suffered violence** is understood by RSV to be passive ("be taken by force, or violence"). It is possible, however, as RSV's alternative rendering indicates, to understand the verb as middle voice, with the meaning "has been coming violently" ("exercise force, or violence"). Also problematic is the nature of the force that is exercised, whether conceived of as good or evil.

Scholars evaluate the evidence differently. Consequently at least four possible interpretations result from the two translational possibilities mentioned above. Before these alternative possibilities are presented, it will be useful to make two further observations. (a) The noun **men of violence** comes from the same stem as the verb **has suffered violence**. The noun appears in the New Testament only here, while the verb itself is found in the Lukan parallel (16.16). In its few known occurrences outside the New Testament, the noun seems always to be used in a bad sense. (b) The verb translated **take by force** (TEV **"try to seize"**) appears elsewhere in the New Testament only in Matthew 13.19, where it is used of the devil; there TEV translates "snatches away."

(1) If the initial verb is interpreted as middle (as in the RSV alternative rendering), the Kingdom becomes the subject, and the exercise of force is automatically qualified as good ("makes its way with triumphant force"). NIV, one of the few translations representing this interpretation, renders "The kingdom of heaven has been forcefully advancing, and forceful men lay hold on it." Zür is similar.

(2) If the verb is interpreted as passive, then at least three possible interpretations exist. (a) The passive verb may be understood in a positive sense, descriptive of the eagerness, self-sacrifice, and devotion by which some urgently seek to enter the Kingdom. For example, "they are pressing into the Realm of heaven—these eager souls are storming it!" (Mft); "men have been taking the Kingdom of Heaven by storm and impetuously crowding into it" (AT); and "a situation . . . in which the Kingdom of Heaven is stormed, and in which those who are eager to storm their way into it clutch at it" (Brc). The problem with this interpretation is the necessity of assigning a good sense to both the noun "violent men" and the verb "seize," which contradicts what is known about the usage of the noun and verb elsewhere. Admittedly, however, the evidence is limited, and a positive sense may be intended.

(b) The renderings of RSV and TEV are representative of the majority of modern translations and allow for two interpretations. The reference may be to earthly powers which personify the demonic forces of evil that attempt to restrain the advance of the Kingdom.

(c) The second interpretation allowed for by RSV and TEV is that the reference is to Zealots or others like them who attempted to bring in the Kingdom by force and violence. This interpretation enjoys the widest support among scholars, though the resultant translation of (b) and (c) would be essentially the same.

Obviously translators can never be really sure of the best way to render this sentence. Further, finding a way to say the kingdom **has suffered violence** depends on how **kingdom of heaven** itself has been handled. Nevertheless, here are some possible renderings for translators to consider: "There have been attacks made against God's rule (or, the establishment of God's rule), and violent men have tried to seize it by force"; "violent men (and other forces) have used force to try to seize control of God's rule"; "there have been men who have tried by violent force to establish God's rule."

11.13   RSV   TEV

For all the prophets and the law prophesied until John;

Until the time of John all the prophets and the Law of Moses spoke about the Kingdom;

For comments on **prophets**, see 5.17 and 1.22. The normal order of "the law and the prophets" is reversed here.

The law is "**the Law of Moses**" (TEV), the first division of the Jewish Bible.
Prophesied: see comments on 7.22. TEV has "**spoke about the Kingdom**,"

and GECL "have announced God's New World." Although the Greek verb does not necessarily mean "predict," a number of translations do see that meaning here: "foretold the things that must happen" (INCL), "foretold things to come" (NEB), "foretold" (Phps), and "told of the things which were destined to happen" (Brc). NJB translates the entire first half of the verse "Because it was towards John that all the prophesies of the prophets and of the Law were leading . . . ." One may also translate "spoke about the time when God would establish his rule."

Until John raises exegetical problems. "From the days of John" (verse 12) apparently places John among the prophets, which would mean that the Kingdom is inaugurated after the time of John. However, Matthew elsewhere uses "from . . ." with the meaning "beginning with" (see 1.17; 2.16; 23.35; 27.45), and that would seem to be his intention here. In verse 9 Jesus has already stated that John is "more than a prophet," and in verses 18-19 he will closely identify himself with John in a manner such as to suggest that John is included within the Messianic era. The verse may then be translated "The Law of Moses and all the prophets spoke about (the coming of) the Kingdom before John began to proclaim his message."

With this understanding of **until John**, depending on the structure of the sentence, translators can also say "up to John" or "up to the time of John," or, as above, "before." Note, too, the order of the sentence can be reversed if necessary, as in "for before John began his ministry, the Law of Moses and the prophets had spoken about God's rule."

11.14   RSV   TEV

and if you are willing to accept it, he is Elijah who is to come.   **and if you are willing to believe their message, John is Elijah, whose coming was predicted.**

The word **willing** can also be translated as "prepared." Another way is to say "if you will accept it."

Accept it (TEV **"believe their message"**): in Greek the verb **accept** is without an object, but most languages will require one: "if you will believe me" (NJB), "if you are prepared to accept it" (NAB), "if you care to believe it" (Mft), "if you are ready to accept the idea" (AT), and "if you will accept it" (Zür).

Many translators tie the "it" of **accept it** to the following phrase, as in "accept that John is Elijah, whose coming was promised." This link can also be made by those who give "me" as the object, as in "believe me when I say John is Elijah." It is equally possible to refer to "prophesied" in verse 13, as in "if you are willing to believe what they said, then John is Elijah." However one renders **it** in the sentence, the point remains that Jesus was asserting that John was Elijah, and he was asking people if they were prepared to accept that.

He is Elijah is an allusion to John the Baptist, and he is mentioned by name in a number of modern translations. Many readers will take **he is Elijah** literally, as if John were a reincarnation of Elijah, or as if somehow Elijah had returned to earth. This would be wrong, of course. To avoid this, translators might say "John is the man the prophet was talking about when he said Elijah would return" or "when the Scriptures said Elijah would return, they were speaking of John."

Who is to come: Brc translates "who was destined to come," and NAB "the one who was certain to come." However, the focus seems not to be so much upon the certainty of his coming as upon the fact of his coming, because it had been promised through the Law and the prophets. In Malachi 4.5 it is stated that Elijah would return prior to the day of final judgment, and the present verse confirms that John fulfills the role of Elijah. GECL translates the verse "And if you believe it or not: John is actually Elijah, whose coming was predicted."

Note from some of the examples we have given for **who is to come** that it may be necessary to say who predicted or promised Elijah would return: "the man the prophets were talking about" or "when the scriptures said Elijah would return."

11.15	RSV	TEV

He who has ears to hear,[d] let him hear.

Listen, then, if you have ears!

[d] Other ancient authorities omit *to hear*

Most translations of this verse are fairly literal, as are RSV and TEV. The same saying is used twice again by Matthew (13.9,43); similar exhortations are found in Mark 4.9,23; Luke 8.8; 14.35; and Revelation 2.7,11,17,29; 3.6,13,22; 13.9. GECL has "Whoever can hear, should listen well!" and NAB, "Heed carefully what you hear!"

This sentence is not questioning whether or not the people have ears. No translation should give that impression. Rather its purpose is to make people pay attention to what was said. The NAB model cited above does that well. Other examples are "You have ears, don't you? Then pay attention to what I am saying" or "You can hear, can't you? Then listen to these things."

11.16-19

RSV	TEV
16 "But to what shall I compare this generation? It is like children sitting in the market places and calling to their playmates, 17 'We piped to you, and you did not dance; we wailed, and you did not mourn.' 18 For John came neither eating nor drinking, and they say, 'He has a demon'; 19 the Son of man came eating and drinking, and they say, 'Behold, a glutton and a drunkard, a friend of tax collectors and sinners!' Yet wisdom is justified by her deeds."[e]	16 "Now, to what can I compare the people of this day? They are like children sitting in the marketplace. One group shouts to the other, 17 'We played wedding music for you, but you wouldn't dance! We sang funeral songs, but you wouldn't cry!' 18 When John came, he fasted and drank no wine, and everyone said, 'He has a demon in him!' 19 When the Son of Man came, he ate and drank, and everyone said, 'Look at this man! He is a glutton and wine-drinker, a friend of tax collectors and other outcasts!' God's wisdom, however, is shown to be true by its results."

[e] Other ancient authorities read *children* (Luke 7.35)

Verses 16-19 include a parable (verses 16-17) and its application (verses 18-19). The parable itself speaks of children who want to play by pretending they are at a wedding or a funeral, but their friends will not dance when they want to play wedding or mourn when they want to play funeral. The application in verses 18-19 is clear: the Jewish people refused to respond either to John's message of judgment or to Jesus' message of joy.

"But to what shall I compare this generation? It is like children sitting in the market places and calling to their playmates,

"Now, to what can I compare the people of this day? They are like children sitting in the marketplace. One group shouts to the other,

Jesus now focuses on the people of his day and contrasts their response to John's message with the injunction of verse 15 to pay attention. The text has **But**, and TEV has "**Now**." Other possibilities include "As for the people of this day" and "But the people of this day, what can I say about them?"

Compare is frequently used to introduce parables. See comments on 13.24. It may be necessary to make a shift away from the question form: "I know what the people of this day are like. They are like children . . . ." If a question is retained, the sentence can be "What are the people of this day like? They are like . . ." or "What can I say about the people of today? I tell you, they are like . . . ."

This generation is translated "**people of this day**" by TEV and Brc. In mind are the contemporaries of John and Jesus who had the opportunity to hear their messages, but had rejected them both. AT has "this present age"; NAB's "this breed" lends a negative coloring to the address. "People today" and "people these days" are better renderings.

The precise situation described in the parable (verses 16b-17) is not clear. It may be that the children are quarreling with one another because some of them want to play wedding (a happy game) while others want to play funeral (a sad game). **Their playmates** would then be children within the same group. This interpretation is the one followed in Luke 7.32, where the children call "to one another." However, Matthew here uses a different construction (literally "to the others"), which intimates a second group of children. The situation in Matthew seems then to be that of one group of children trying to get another group to play games with them. First, they play happy wedding songs on their small flutes, but they cannot get the other group of children to dance while they play. Then they sing funeral songs, but they cannot get the other children to respond by crying. So the disagreement does not concern what game is to be played, but rather that one group refuses to play either game.

Some scholars who accept this interpretation find a key to its application in the participle **sitting**. For them, the children sitting in the market place represent the Pharisees and the other religious leaders who sit and give orders. Then they criticize everyone who refuses to obey their orders: John is criticized because he fasts when they want to play wedding games, and Jesus is criticized because he joyfully associates with outcasts, while they want to play funeral games. But this application of the parable is not as attractive as that which sees in John the one who calls people to play funeral, while Jesus is the one who calls people to play wedding. The Pharisees and the other religious leaders refuse to respond to either call.

It is like introduces the parable, **It** referring to the singular form **this generation**. Translators who have used "people" will put this in the plural: "They are like."

Like children should not imply that the people are immature or childish. The real comparison is between one group who wants to do something and another group who refuses to do it. The first group says, "Let's play . . ."; the response is always "We don't want to."

In many cultures **market places** are a feature of daily life and can be retained in the translation. In others "the streets," "the parks," or in some countries the area of the market called "the playgrounds" would be more likely as places where children would go to play.

To their playmates (so also Mft, NAB), as indicated in a previous paragraph, is literally "to the others." Phps has "to their friends," and TEV "**One group shouts to the other.**" The advantage of TEV is that it clearly distinguishes between the two groups.

However, in some languages, to make two sentences as TEV does can also leave the first sentence sounding as if the people are like children, that is, childish. In such cases translators can add "certain," as in "they are like certain children sitting in the market place. One group . . . ," or they can say "They are like a group of children sitting in the market place who call out to another group . . . ."

11.17	RSV	TEV

'We piped to you, and you did not dance; we wailed, and you did not mourn.'	'We played wedding music for you, but you wouldn't dance! We sang funeral songs, but you wouldn't cry!'

We piped to you (TEV "**We played wedding music for you**"): the "pipe" was in all likelihood a type of primitive clarinet, though it is impossible to define with precision what instrument is meant. Therefore it may be best to follow the example of those translations which generalize with a verb construction: "We played you a happy tune" (Brc) and "we played at weddings for you" (Phps). In those languages that cannot say "**played**" without indicating the instrument, translators can say "played on our flutes" or "played our instruments for weddings."

Dance would be the round dance, performed by men on the occasion of the wedding.

We wailed (NEB "wept and wailed") is translated "We sang dirges" by NJB, "We sang you a dirge" by NAB, and "We played at funerals" by Phps. The Greek verb may mean either "sing a funeral song" or "mourn." This activity was the responsibility of the women at the funeral. To say "we sang funeral songs" for **we wailed** will probably be a good solution in many languages. The custom is widely enough practiced that even cultures that do not do it will often understand the meaning of the expression.

And you did not mourn is translated "**But you wouldn't cry**" by TEV and Phps. NJB attempts to reproduce the funeral scene: "and you wouldn't be mourners."

Whatever is appropriate behavior at a funeral can be used here, as in "and you wouldn't cry like you should at funerals" or ". . . wouldn't cry like mourners."

This verse will probably be in direct speech, although there will be languages where the most natural way is to say "one group shouts to the other that they played wedding music for them but the others didn't dance, and they sang funeral songs but the others wouldn't cry like mourners."

11.18   RSV   TEV

| For John came neither eating nor drinking, and they say, 'He has a demon'; | When John came, he fasted and drank no wine, and everyone said, 'He has a demon in him!' |

Jesus is no longer reporting what the children said. It is sometimes necessary to make this clear, as in "People today are like them (or, that) because . . . ."

Verses 18-19 contain the application of the parable. **For John came neither eating nor drinking** is made shorter by GECL ("John fasted"); Brc restructures for clarification ("living the life of an ascetic"). To say **John came neither eating nor drinking** does not mean he was some supernatural being who did not eat or drink anything at all. It means firstly that he fasted regularly, that is, went without food in order to worship God. (See comments at 6.16.) Secondly, it states he drank no alcoholic drinks. Therefore the translation can be "For when John came he often went without food to worship God, and he drank nothing alcoholic (or, no wine)."

And can be "but," "and yet," or "and as a result."

They can be "people."

The sentence can be either direct speech, "and people say, 'He has an evil spirit,' " or indirect, as in "people say about him that he is possessed by an evil spirit."

He has a demon (TEV "**he has a demon in him**") means "he is possessed by an evil spirit" (GECL). Brc has "The man is demon-possessed!"; both NJB and NEB, "He is possessed." Neither Phps ("He's crazy!") nor NAB ("He is mad!") should be followed, since they fail to convey the idea of demon possession, which is integral to the biblical culture. For a discussion of spirit possession, see 4.24. "He has an evil spirit in him" or "an evil spirit has filled him" are just two examples of how it can be translated here.

11.19   RSV   TEV

| the Son of man came eating and drinking, and they say, 'Behold, a glutton and a drunkard, a friend of tax collectors and sinners!' Yet wisdom is justified by her deeds.''*e* | When the Son of Man came, he ate and drank, and everyone said, 'Look at this man! He is a glutton and wine-drinker, a friend of tax collectors and other outcasts!' God's wisdom, however, is shown to be true by its results." |

e Other ancient authorities read *children* (Luke 7.35)

The Son of man came eating and drinking: see 8.20 for a discussion of **Son of man**. GECL handles this part of the verse similarly to what it did with the first part of verse 18: "The Son of man eats and drinks . . . ."

Eating and drinking, as the context makes clear, means something beyond the ordinary meals required for existence. The allusion is perhaps to Jesus' participation in joyous events such as wedding celebrations, where food and drink were consumed in larger amounts than at a regular mealtime. But Brc has "enjoying life like a normal person," which is also possible. Since the expression **eating and drinking** here can refer to more than just sustenance, translators have tried "When the Son of man came, he enjoyed eating and drinking (wine)," "ate and drank with great enjoyment," or "ate and drank well."

Again, **they** can be "people."

Behold: see comments at 1.20. TEV has "**Look at this man**"; Phps "Look"; AT and NEB "Look at him!"

A **glutton** is someone who overindulges in eating; a **drunkard** is someone who overindulges in wine (TEV "**wine-drinker**"). This may well be how the phrase will be rendered: "Just look at him. He eats too much and drinks too much wine," or "He is always eating too much food and drinking too much wine."

Tax collectors and sinners (TEV "**other outcasts**") are mentioned together in 9.10; **tax collectors** are first discussed in 5.46. NAB renders **sinners** by "those outside the Law"; and Brc, "people with whom no respectable Jew would have anything to do!" Translators are referred to 9.10 and 5.46 for possible translations.

Quite often translators will have to repeat the subject, as in "and he is a friend of tax collectors and other outcasts."

As in the previous verse, the accusations may have to be in indirect speech: "People look at him and remark that he eats too much and drinks wine too much, and also that he is a friend of tax collectors and other outcasts."

Yet wisdom is justified by her deeds: this statement is obscure, and it is not aided by the alternative reading (see RSV footnote), which substitutes "children" (as in the Lukan parallel, 7.35) for **deeds**. Scholars agree that the **wisdom** is "God's wisdom," and so the basis for TEV. Both **deeds** and "children" would have a similar impact to the Jewish reader, since either would convey the idea of what wisdom had produced (TEV, NEB, Brc "**by its results**"; Mft "by all that she does"; AT, JB "by her actions").

Justified translates the same verb used in 12.37, the only other occurrence of this verb in Matthew. A noun made from this stem is discussed in 1.19. The verb itself is quite frequently employed by Paul with the meaning "be put right with God," which is obviously not what Matthew intends. Here the meaning is rather "be proved right" (see JB, NEB) or "be vindicated" (AT, Mft; Phps: "stands or fails").

Some languages will be able to use a passive or impersonal form, as in "God's wisdom can be proved to be true by its results" or "The wisdom of God will produce results that show it is right." Other languages will have an agent, as in "People will see God's wisdom is right by the results" or "People will see that God's wisdom is right by the way people act when they have it."

The word **Yet** does show a contrast with what people are saying about the Son of Man. "But," or "However," or some other contrastive marker should be used here.

11.20-24

RSV

TEV

The Unbelieving Towns

20 Then he began to upbraid the cities where most of his mighty works had been done, because they did not repent. 21 "Woe to you, Chorazin! woe to you, Bethsaida! for if the mighty works done in you had been done in Tyre and Sidon, they would have repented long ago in sackcloth and ashes. 22 But I tell you, it shall be more tolerable on the day of judgment for Tyre and Sidon than for you. 23 And you, Capernaum, will you be exalted to heaven? You shall be brought down to Hades. For if the mighty works done in you had been done in Sodom, it would have remained until this day. 24 But I tell you that it shall be more tolerable on the day of judgment for the land of Sodom than for you."

20 The people in the towns where Jesus had performed most of his miracles did not turn from their sins, so he reproached those towns. 21 "How terrible it will be for you, Chorazin! How terrible for you too, Bethsaida! If the miracles which were performed in you had been performed in Tyre and Sidon, the people there would have long ago put on sackcloth and sprinkled ashes on themselves, to show that they had turned from their sins! 22 I assure you that on the Judgment Day God will show more mercy to the people of Tyre and Sidon than to you! 23 And as for you, Capernaum! Did you want to lift yourself up to heaven? You will be thrown down to hell! If the miracles which were performed in you had been performed in Sodom, it would still be in existence today! 24 You can be sure that on the Judgment Day God will show more mercy to Sodom than to you!"

SECTION HEADING: "**The Unbelieving Towns**." This heading may be expressed as "Some towns where people would not believe Jesus" or "Some places where people did not repent (of their sins)."

Verse 20, found only in Matthew, serves as a transition to this section. Verses 21-24 do have a parallel in Luke 10.13-15, though in a significantly different setting, where they serve as part of the instructions which Jesus gives to the seventy-two before sending them out.

11.20　　　RSV

TEV

Then he began to upbraid the cities where most of his mighty works had been done, because they did not repent.

The people in the towns where Jesus had performed most of his miracles did not turn from their sins, so he reproached those towns.

Notice that, since this does begin a new paragraph, the pronoun **he** is usually replaced by "Jesus."

Upbraid (TEV "**reproached**") translates the verb rendered "revile" by RSV and "insult" by TEV in 5.11. Here it can be expressed as "say they were wrong," "condemn," or "accuse of being wrong." In some languages it is possible to say Jesus is condemning **the cities**, but often "people of the cities" will be better.

Cities, as in the other places we have seen, is more naturally "towns," to contrast them with the really large places like Jerusalem.

Where most of his mighty works had been done is altered to an active by TEV: "**where Jesus had performed most of his miracles**." For comments on **mighty works**, see 7.22.

The cities . . . because they did not repent: in many languages it will not be possible to speak of cities repenting; instead one must say "the people of the cities." **Repent** here means "turn from their sins" or "turn to God" (see comments on 3.2). GECL translates this part of the verse "Then Jesus began to say harsh things about the places . . . and still the people there had not changed."

Then marks a transition and may be rendered "At that time" or "After that." However, since there is a clause introduced by **because** at the end of the verse, translators must find a good way to handle **then** and **because** naturally in the same sentence. One way is "At that time, Jesus began to condemn the people in the cities where he had performed most of his miracles. He did that because those people refused to turn from their sins." However, many languages find it more natural to reverse the order of the verse in a manner similar to TEV. For example, "In the towns where Jesus had performed most of his mighty actions, people did not change their lives. So Jesus began at that time to accuse those people of being wrong."

11.21	RSV	TEV

RSV	TEV
"Woe to you, Chorazin! woe to you, Bethsaida! for if the mighty works done in you had been done in Tyre and Sidon, they would have repented long ago in sackcloth and ashes.	"How terrible it will be for you, Chorazin! How terrible for you too, Bethsaida! If the miracles which were performed in you had been performed in Tyre and Sidon, the people there would have long ago put on sackcloth and sprinkled ashes on themselves, to show that they had turned from their sins!

Many languages will begin the sentence with a marker of direct speech or the phrase "He said."

Woe or "Alas" is the rendering of most translations. A few attempt something dynamic: "**How terrible it will be**" (TEV), "Tragic will be your fate" (Brc), and "It will go ill with you" (NAB). Elsewhere Matthew utilizes this interjection in 18.7 (twice); 23.13,15,16,23,25,27,29; 24.19; 26.24. **Woe** is almost the opposite of "blessed" or "happy" in 5.3 and following. It means things are going to be bad for those towns, that they will receive God's punishment. Thus possible translations are "Terrible things are in store for you" or "How awful are the things that will happen to you."

Often it will be more natural to put **Chorazin** and **Bethsaida** at the beginning of the sentence, as in "Chorazin, terrible things will happen to you. Bethsaida, terrible things will happen to you." It may be more natural to address them together, as in "Chorazin and Bethsaida, how awful is the fate that awaits you."

In those languages where it is not natural to address a town, then translators will say "You people of Chorazin, you people of Bethsaida, the troubles coming to you are terrible."

The town of **Chorazin** is mentioned in the Bible only here and in Luke 10.13; it is located about two miles northwest of Capernaum.

Bethsaida (literally "house of fish") is probably a reference to the town of Bethsaida Julias, on the east bank of the Jordan, north of Lake Galilee. There is no mention in Matthew's Gospel of Jesus' having performed any miracles there. Mark alone mentions the healing of a blind man in Bethsaida (Mark 8.22-26).

Mighty works is the same expression used in verse 20; see comments on 7.22. If the passives **done in you** and **had been done** are not natural, then translators can say "if I had done the miracles in Tyre and Sidon that I did in your towns, these people . . ." or "if it had been in Tyre and Sidon that I performed the mighty works instead of your town, those people . . . ."

Tyre and **Sidon** were towns along the Phoenician coastline. Especially during Old Testament times these two towns were notorious for their evil, and Israel's prophets spoke against them (see Isa 23; Ezek 26–28; Amos 1.9,10; Joel 3.4; Zech 9.2-4). Some translators feel this implicit information is important, and say "those evil towns of Tyre and Sidon."

Sackcloth and **ashes** were signs of repentance and sorrow (see Isa 58.5; Jonah 3.6; Dan 9.3). **Sackcloth** was a coarse cloth that can be translated simply as "rough cloth." The significance of the act can then be indicated, too, as in "the rough cloth that shows they have turned from their sins." The **sackcloth** was worn, but the **ashes** were sprinkled on the head. Sentences that will convey the meaning of the actions clearly are "they would have repented long ago and worn the coarse cloth and sprinkled ashes on their heads to show it" and "long ago they would have worn the coarse cloth and put ashes on their heads to show they were turning from their sins." Some translations have dropped the actual actions and said simply "long ago they would have shown to all that they were turning from their sins." However, translators should try to retain these cultural actions in the text, since they were a common aspect of biblical culture.

11.22	RSV	TEV
	But I tell you, it shall be more tolerable on the day of judgment for Tyre and Sidon than for you.	I assure you that on the Judgment Day God will show more mercy to the people of Tyre and Sidon than to you!

But I tell you (TEV "**I assure you**") functions to make emphatic the statement which follows. NEB has the same rendering as RSV; Phps "Yet I tell you this"; AT "But I tell you." Elsewhere in the Gospel this formula is used only in verse 24 and in 26.64; it is equivalent in emphasis to "Truly, I say to you" (see comments at 5.18). Translators are referred to 10.15, where the language is almost exactly the same. **But I tell you** in this verse can be rendered the same as "truly, I say to you" in 10.15, with the sole difference being the **But**. This marks a slight contrast, and most translators do retain it, either with a word or with some construction.

TEV restructures the impersonal passive construction of the Greek (**it shall be more tolerable**) as an active formation with God as the subject: "**God will show more mercy to.**" FRCL has "the punishment will be less for . . . than for you"; and GECL, "the people of . . . will fare better than you." **It shall be more tolerable on the day of judgment** is the same as in 10.15. Here it is **Tyre and Sidon**, there "the land of Sodom and Gomorrah." A good rendering is "the people of (the towns of) Tyre and Sidon."

The contrast in 10.15 is "than for that town"; here the punishment will be easier **than for you**. Keeping these differences in mind, translators will be able to render this verse very much as they did in 10.15.

11.23	RSV	TEV

And you, Capernaum, will you be exalted to heaven? You shall be brought down to Hades. For if the mighty works done in you had been done in Sodom, it would have remained until this day.

And as for you, Capernaum! Did you want to lift yourself up to heaven? You will be thrown down to hell! If the miracles which were performed in you had been performed in Sodom, it would still be in existence today!

And you (TEV "**And as for you**") has the same function as "But I tell you" of verse 22. As in the previous verses there will be cases where it will not be possible to address a town. Then the translation will be "As for you, people of Capernaum."

Jesus made his home in **Capernaum** (4.13), and it can be referred to as his home town (9.1). The denunciation of Capernaum echoes Isaiah's words of judgment against the pride of Babylon (Isa 14.12-15).

Will you be exalted to heaven? (TEV "**Did you want to lift yourself up to heaven?**") is a judgment against the pride of the people of Capernaum. The cause of their pride is not stated, nor is it necessary to express in translation. It may well have been their prideful rejection of Jesus and his message. For translation it may be helpful to alter the rhetorical question form to a strong statement: "Even though you exalt yourself to heaven . . ." or "You may exalt yourself to heaven, but . . . ."

Exalted to heaven is not always easy to express. Some renderings translators may consider are these: "Did you think you were going to be raised right up to heaven?" "Did you think you could raise yourself up to heaven?" "Did you think you would be praised all the way up to heaven?" "Did you think you would become the most important town?" Any of these questions can be transformed into statements if translators those would be clearer: "You think you will be raised . . . ."

You shall be brought down may be better expressed in an active form with God as subject: "God will bring you down . . . ." It may be good to start this sentence with a word or expression that clearly marks the contrast with the previous sentence. "Instead, God will . . ." is an example.

Hades (so also Mft) is translated "hell" by many (TEV, NJB, BJ, Lu; Brc "the depths of hell"). FRCL renders "world of the dead" (AT, Phps "among the dead"; NAB "the realm of death"; Zür "Kingdom of the dead"; TOB "abode of the dead"). NEB has "the depths," and GECL "the abyss." **Hades** is merely a transliteration of the Greek word, and as such it is probably a meaningless term for many readers. For other readers who are familiar with the word, it may even convey overtones that are contradictory to the New Testament concept. The basic meaning of the term is "place of the dead," though it may be used in a more restricted sense; for example, "place where the wicked dead are punished." Many translators, for example TEV, have rendered **hades** as "**hell**." Keeping in mind that God is the agent, a translator can render it "God will throw you down to hell." Others have said ". . . down to the place of the dead." In line with this theme, another translation can be "God will destroy you" or "throw you down to the place of punishment."

For if the mighty works . . . : see verse 21 for a suggested restructuring.

Sodom was a city noted for its wickedness (see comments at 10.15). For an account of the destruction of Sodom, see Genesis 19.24-29. Here some translators will have "in the wicked city of Sodom."

It would have remained until this day means "it would still exist now." Brc has "it would still be standing today." Some will add in a footnote "God destroyed this town because of its wickedness."

11.24

RSV	TEV
But I tell you that it shall be more tolerable on the day of judgment for the land of Sodom than for you."	You can be sure that on the Judgment Day God will show more mercy to Sodom than to you!"

But I tell you are the words that introduced verse 22. See verse 22 also for proposals regarding the translation of this verse.

11.25-30

RSV	TEV
	Come to Me and Rest
25 At that time Jesus declared, "I thank thee, Father, Lord of heaven and earth, that thou hast hidden these things from the wise and understanding and revealed them to babes; 26 yea, Father, for such was thy gracious will.*f* 27 All things have been delivered to me by my Father; and no one knows the Son except the Father, and no one knows the Father except the Son and any one to whom the Son chooses to reveal him. 28 Come to me, all who labor and are heavy laden, and I will give you rest. 29 Take my yoke upon you, and learn from me; for I am gentle and lowly in heart, and you will find rest for your souls. 30 For my yoke is easy, and my burden is light."	25 At that time Jesus said, "Father, Lord of heaven and earth! I thank you because you have shown to the unlearned what you have hidden from the wise and learned. 26 Yes, Father, this was how you were pleased to have it happen. 27 "My Father has given me all things. No one knows the Son except the Father, and no one knows the Father except the Son and those to whom the Son chooses to reveal him. 28 "Come to me, all of you who are tired from carrying heavy loads, and I will give you rest. 29 Take my yoke and put it on you, and learn from me, because I am gentle and humble in spirit; and you will find rest. 30 For the yoke I will give you is easy, and the load I will put on you is light."

f Or *so it was well-pleasing before thee*

SECTION HEADING: "**Come to Me and Rest**." This heading can be rendered "Jesus invites people to come to him for rest" or "People will find rest by going to Jesus."

In this brief paragraph Matthew brings together three sayings. The first two (verses 25-26; verse 27) are present in almost exactly the same words in Luke 10.21-22. The third saying (verses 28-30) is not in any of the other Gospels, though it has a parallel in the apocryphal Gospel of Thomas. For at least three reasons the passage has caused New Testament scholars some degree of concern: (1) It seems to be totally out of context. **These things** of verse 25 has no antecedent in the immediate context, and **all things** of verse 27 cannot refer back to **these things**. Some few scholars do attempt to find in **these things** a reference to the miracles of Jesus mentioned in verses 21-23, but this is a doubtful interpretation. (2) The content of these verses, frequently called "a Johannine thunderbolt," more nearly reflects what is found in the Gospel of John than what is contained elsewhere in Matthew. (3) There is the problem of the unity between the three parts of the paragraph. Why, for example, would Luke have omitted verses 28-30, had they originally have been connected in his source with verses 25-27? Moreover, in verses 25-26 God is addressed in the second person, while in verse 27 he is referred to in the third person.

11.25   RSV   TEV

At that time Jesus declared, "I thank thee, Father, Lord of heaven and earth, that thou hast hidden these things from the wise and understanding and revealed them to babes;

At that time Jesus said, "Father, Lord of heaven and earth! I thank you because you have shown to the unlearned what you have hidden from the wise and learned.

At that time (so also TEV) is a temporal marker which loosely relates this passage to the context; this same formula occurs again in 12.1; 14.1. NAB separates this entire passage from the context by introducing it: "On one occasion Jesus spoke thus: . . . ." Other translations have had "Then" or "It was then that Jesus . . . ."

In place of the Greek word order (**I thank thee, Father, Lord of heaven and earth**), TEV attempts a more natural order for the opening of prayers in English: "**Father, Lord of heaven and earth! I thank you.**"

In the Greek **thank** very frequently has the meaning "confess," but it may also mean "admit," "agree," or even "thank" or "praise" (Mft, NAB). Here "thank" or "praise" are most appropriate.

In the Lord's Prayer Jesus teaches his disciples to address God as "Our Father" (Matt 6.9), and in his own prayer in Gethsemane he addresses God as "My Father" (26.39,42). In languages where **Father** used as a term of address must have a possessive, translators should say "my Father." There will also be a few situations where "God my Father" is necessary, lest readers think Jesus is praying to Joseph, his earthly father.

Lord of heaven and earth, a literal rendering of the Greek text, means "the Lord who rules heaven and earth" or "the ruler of heaven and earth."

Lord can be "ruler," "owner," or "master," or whatever title in a language is used for the one who controls the universe and to whom the whole universe owes allegiance.

Heaven and earth can be translated literally or as "the whole universe."

We pointed out above that TEV has put this phrase in a more natural word order. Many translators will do something similar. Both **Father** and **Lord of heaven and earth** refer to the same person, but in many languages to put these two phrases together as they appear here would seem to refer to two different people. In such cases translators will say something like "My Father, you who are Lord of heaven and earth, I thank you . . ." or "My Father, you are the Lord of the whole universe. I thank you . . . ."

Hidden is the same verb used in 5.14; it is found again in 13.35,44; 25.18,25. Here it may be "made so they can't be seen" or "kept them where the wise people can't see them."

The wise and understanding is rendered in a variety of ways by the major English translations:

> **"the wise and the learned"** (Mft, TEV)
> "the learned and the clever" (NJB, NAB)
> "the learned and wise" (NEB)
> "the learned and intelligent" (AT)
> "the wise and clever" (Brc)
> "the clever and intelligent" (Phps)

The same two adjectives appear in the Greek text of Isaiah 29.14, which is quoted by Paul in 1 Corinthians 1.19. It is doubtful that there is intended to be any real contrast between these two terms, since both are widely used to describe people of great wisdom and insight. In some languages the best solution may be to use only one term, while other languages may have an idiomatic expression sufficient to incorporate the meaning of both Greek words. It is possible also to use an adjective plus an intensifier; for example, "very wise" or "very clever." **The wise and understanding** refers to people, and many languages will require that this be explicit, as in "the wise and clever people."

Revealed is the same verb used in 10.26 and contrasts here with **hidden**; it is found twice again in Matthew: verse 27; 16.17. Here it may be rendered "shown," "let them see," "made them to know about," or "let them understand."

Babes: the primary meaning of this word is "infant" or "child." It may also mean "immature," "underage" (see Lu, Zür), or "innocent." When contrasted with adjectives such as "wise" and "learned," it may mean "unspoiled by learning" or "unspoiled by human instruction." TEV (**"unlearned"**) and GECL ("ignorant") are closer to this category, while a number of other translations retain essentially the root meaning: "mere children" (Phps, JB), "children" (AT), and "merest children" (NAB). For American readers neither NEB ("the simple") nor Mft ("simple-minded") are adequate, for they each imply feeblemindedness. The context suggests a contrast between persons who claim a sophisticated knowledge of God and those who, without making this claim, are able to recognize the presence of God in Jesus Christ.

From this discussion of **babes** it should be clear that "young people" or "children" would really give the wrong idea. "Uneducated" or even "those who don't yet know much" are better translations.

As we point out above, it is not at all clear what **these things** refer to. It would probably be wrong to make it refer back to verses 20-24, or ahead to verses 27-30. For this reason the reference should not be specified. TEV presents a helpful model. These sentences are similar: "I thank you that you have not allowed the wise and educated people to understand what you have shown clearly to those who do not know much," "I praise you for what you have done. You have revealed to ignorant people the very truths you have not permitted the wise and clever to see at all."

11.26 RSV TEV

yea, Father, for such was thy gra- **Yes, Father, this was how you were**
cious will.[f] **pleased to have it happen.**

[f] Or *so it was well-pleasing before thee*

Yea is an old form of "yes." Brc has "yes, indeed, Father." Of course "my
Father" will be better in some languages.

For such was thy gracious will represents the formal transfer of a Semitic
expression, as does the alternate translation in the RSV footnote, "so it was well-
pleasing before thee." Several modern translations attempt a natural equivalent: "for
that is what it pleased you to do" (NJB); "You have graciously willed it so" (NAB);
and "So you willed it to happen" (GECL). Other possibilities include "Yes, Father,
because that was what you chose to do," ". . . what you wanted," and ". . . what you
had decided to do." **Gracious** is not specifically rendered in these languages, for
probably it does not need to be, since here it is really just a marker of the polite
formality needed to address God. There have been translators who have used
sentences such as "For as God, this was what it pleased you to have happen."

11.27 RSV TEV

All things have been delivered to me **"My Father has given me all**
by my Father; and no one knows the **things. No one knows the Son except**
Son except the Father, and no one **the Father, and no one knows the**
knows the Father except the Son **Father except the Son and those to**
and any one to whom the Son **whom the Son chooses to reveal**
chooses to reveal him. **him.**

All things have been delivered to my by my Father is shifted to an active
formation by TEV: **"My Father has given me all things."** Few commentators offer
any real help regarding the interpretation and translation of **All things**. For many
languages a clear antecedent will be obligatory; otherwise **All things** will be
understood as "all material goods," which is erroneous. Two routes of interpretation
are possible: (1) The meaning may be the full authority (see 28.18) which the Father
has given Jesus: "My Father has given me all power" (GECL 1st edition). (2) Or **All
things** may mean "full knowledge (of God)," an interpretation which is supported
by two observations: (a) The Greek verb **delivered** most naturally suits the contexts
where a revelation is involved, and (b) the entire second half of the verse implies
that a revelation is what is intended. TOB's footnote also argues for the communication of a revelation, specifically of a revelation concerning the Kingdom and its
secrets. However, the context would suggest that the content of the revelation is God
himself. Accordingly one may translate "God the Father has given me full knowledge
of himself," in which "full" is the equivalent of "all."

With this interpretation, other ways to render the sentence are "God the Father
has made me know everything about him," "I know now everything about God my
Father. He himself gave me that," or ". . . He himself made me to understand."

It is significant that Jesus affirms **no one knows the Son except the Father** before stating **no one knows the Father except the Son**. This fits in well with the situation where the truth of who Jesus is remains hidden even to John the Baptist (verses 2-3) and to the people of his home town (verse 20-24). A similar thought is expressed in 16.17.

Knows: in biblical thought the idea of knowing supersedes mere knowledge, for it includes thorough, intimate knowledge that puts people in a special relationship to each other. In Amos 3.2, for example, the verb "know" is used of God's election of Israel as his people: "You only have I known of all the families of the earth." Jesus is here affirming that he and the Father stand in a unique and intimate relationship with one another: only the Father knows who Jesus really is, and only Jesus possesses true understanding of the Father.

Thus **knows** in this context means "knows who he really is." A possible rendering can then be "No one knows who the Son really is except God the Father, and no one knows God's true nature except the Son and whomever he chooses to reveal God to." The sentence can be expressed with a positive construction instead of a negative: "Only God the Father knows who the Son really is, and only the Son and those he chooses to reveal it to, know the true nature of God."

There will be languages where **the Son** will pose a problem, since the question will be raised "the son of whom?" Then translators must use "the Son of God." But if possible the title **the Son** should be retained.

Similarly **the Father** should be retained, but it may be necessary to say "God the Father."

Any one to whom may be better expressed as a plural in many languages: "**those to whom**" (TEV).

In Greek **chooses to reveal** is without an object, but most languages will require either **him** or "the Father."

Reveal is the rendering of most English translations; in this context it refers to revelation of the kind of knowledge the Father and the Son have of each other. Brc translates "make . . . known." The same verb appears in 10.26, where it is translated "be uncovered" by TEV. Both in the Septuagint and in the New Testament, this is the normal verb for the revelation of divine secrets. **Reveal** can often be something like "make known." However, quite often languages require that the knowledge being revealed be more specific, so translators have to say "show the true nature of God" or "reveal what God is really like."

The idea of **chooses** should not be left out. The verse says there are people "to whom the Son chooses to reveal God's nature." Some even make the last phrase a separate sentence: ". . . and only the Son knows God's true nature. Also there are people the Son chooses that he reveals God to."

11.28	RSV	TEV
	Come to me, all who labor and are heavy laden, and I will give you rest.	"Come to me, all of you who are tired from carrying heavy loads, and I will give you rest.

Verses 28-30 form the third and final part of this difficult section. At least one thing is evident: these verses must be understood in light of the immediate context (verses 25-27) and in terms of their place within the overall structure of the Gospel. In the immediate context they affirm Jesus' willingness to reveal the Father to whoever will accept his invitation. And in the flow of the Gospel they are spoken at a time when the people of Galilee and the nation's religious leaders have rejected Jesus.

Come to me is a literal rendering of the Greek text and is the reading reflected in most all translations. It comes as an invitation of Jesus, and its meaning is straightforward and clear enough.

Who labor and are heavy laden is interpreted by TEV as a construction in which the conjunction **and** links two verbs that say the same thing: "**who are tired from carrying heavy loads.**" Most other translations retain a form similar to that of the Greek text: "all you who labour and are overburdened" (NJB) and "all whose work is hard, whose load is heavy." Even more problematic than the form is the nature of the burden, which is easily misunderstood. It is the "yoke of the Jewish Law," as is clearly brought out in the following verses through the use of the term "yoke" (see verses 29-30). GECL completely restructures the verse in order to make the meaning unambiguous for its readers: "You are troubled by the commands which the teachers of the Law have placed upon you. Come to me; I will remove your burden."

There are languages where the vocative **all who labor and are heavy laden** must come first, very much as in the GECL example cited. Translators can say "All of you who are tired from your work and the heavy loads you carry, come to me and I will give you rest." But this retains the form and not the meaning, unlike GECL.

I will give you rest is quite clear and can usually be translated with a form similar to that of the text. Some translations will have "I will relieve you of your burdens" or "You will find rest with me."

11.29   RSV   TEV

Take my yoke upon you, and learn   Take my yoke and put it on you, and
from me; for I am gentle and lowly in   learn from me, because I am gentle
heart, and you will find rest for your   and humble in spirit; and you will
souls.   find rest.

Take . . . upon you: in place of the one verb of the Greek text, some languages will require a double verb: "**Take . . . put it on**" (TEV).

Jesus here uses **yoke** as a symbol of submission, and the most appropriate commentary is perhaps to be found in Jeremiah, chapters 27–28; there the prophet wears an ox yoke as a symbol of the nation's submission to the king of Babylonia. In cultures where the yoke does not convey this significance, it may be dropped: "Submit yourself to me," or "Be obedient to me," or "Accept the task that I give you."

A **yoke** is a heavy wooden bar that fits over the neck of an ox so that it can pull a cart or a plow. Some translators have misunderstood **take my yoke upon you** to refer to the yoke Jesus is carrying. But as we have pointed out above, Jesus is inviting people to submit themselves to him. Some translators keep the form and meaning by saying "Submit yourselves to me as an ox might take a yoke" or "Take the yoke of my leadership (or, Lordship) on you." However, if yokes are not known, trying to introduce them by saying "take the wooden bars on your shoulders so you can pull a cart" will result in an awkward sentence that will detract from the meaning. As we said, the form may be dropped, as in "Accept me as the one who directs you."

Learn from me indicates the nature of the obedience which Jesus demands. It is that of discipleship, for the verb **learn** is made from the same root as "disciple." The invitation of Jesus is, then, "Obey me (Take my yoke on you, or Take my task) and be my disciple." In fact **take my yoke . . . and learn from me** may be understood as the same kind of construction discussed in verse 28, in which "and" connects two thoughts that are equivalent. One can then translate the two commands as one: "Learn what it means to be my disciple." GECL effectively retains the two verbs, though doing away with the symbol of the yoke: "Place yourself under my direction and learn from me." **Learn from me** can also be rendered "accept my teachings," "learn the truths I teach," or "become my disciple."

Jesus invites people to accept him as their Lord because they will find him humble and gentle. Thus the relationship shown by **for** in the text should be shown clearly.

Lowly is used only here in the Gospel; a related verb is used in 18.4; 23.12 (twice). Most English translations are fairly consistent in retaining the form **in heart** or "**in spirit**" (TEV), though AT has "humble-minded." One may combine the two adjectives and translate "I am gentle and humble"; GECL has "I will not trouble you, and I despise no one." If "gentle" and "lowly" are believed to have the same meaning, they may be combined so that one strengthens the other: "I am very humble" or "I am very gentle."

In heart is actually not needed in English. If someone is described as humble and gentle, one can perhaps add "by nature," or one can say "my heart is humble," but otherwise "I am humble and gentle" will suffice.

And you will find rest for your souls may be misleading, implying that eternal rest is intended. **For your souls** is merely a Semitic way of saying "for yourselves," a phrase which may be unnecessary to carry over into translation. TEV telescopes: "**and you will find rest**." The rest to which Jesus refers is that of a proper fellowship with God; GECL has ". . . then your life will find fulfillment."

You will find rest is tied to the invitations to come to Jesus: "Submit to me," Jesus says, "and you will find rest in me," or ". . . then you will experience relief." Both "in me" and "then" make this relationship clear. Such explicit markers may not be necessary in all languages, depending on the structure of the passage.

11.30 RSV   TEV

For my yoke is easy, and my burden is light."

For the yoke I will give you is easy, and the load I will put on you is light."

My yoke and **my burden** are correctly interpreted by TEV to mean **"the yoke I will give you"** and **"the load I will put on you."** This shift is important in order to avoid a misunderstanding of the ambiguous phrases, as for example, "the yoke that I wear" or "the load that I bear." GECL shifts away from a noun structure: "What I command is good for you, and what I give you to bear is no load."

The noun **burden** is used also in 23.4; outside of Matthew's Gospel it occurs in Luke 11.46; Acts 27.10; Galatians 6.5.

To say **my yoke is easy** means it is "easy to wear." Translators who have retained the form in verse 29 may say "for the yoke I put on you is easy to wear" or ". . . does not cause you hardship." Similarly, **my burden is light** can be "the load I give you to carry is not heavy" or ". . . is easy to carry."

Translators who dropped the symbol **yoke** in verse 29 may say here "for the way I will lead you will be easy to follow (or travel, or will cause you no harm), and what I give you to carry will be easy (to bear)."

Chapter 12

12.1-8

RSV

TEV

The Questions about the Sabbath

1 At that time Jesus went through the grainfields on the sabbath; his disciples were hungry, and they began to pluck heads of grain and to eat. 2 But when the Pharisees saw it, they said to him, "Look, your disciples are doing what is not lawful to do on the sabbath." 3 He said to them, "Have you not read what David did, when he was hungry, and those who were with him: 4 how he entered the house of God and ate the bread of the Presence, which it was not lawful for him to eat nor for those who were with him, but only for the priests? 5 Or have you not read in the law how on the sabbath the priests in the temple profane the sabbath, and are guiltless? 6 I tell you, something greater than the temple is here. 7 And if you had known what this means, 'I desire mercy, and not sacrifice,' you would not have condemned the guiltless. 8 For the Son of man is lord of the sabbath."

1 Not long afterward Jesus was walking through some wheat fields on a Sabbath. His disciples were hungry, so they began to pick heads of wheat and eat the grain. 2 When the Pharisees saw this, they said to Jesus, "Look, it is against our Law for your disciples to do this on the Sabbath!"

3 Jesus answered, "Have you never read what David did that time when he and his men were hungry? 4 He went into the house of God, and he and his men ate the bread offered to God, even though it was against the Law for them to eat it—only the priests were allowed to eat that bread. 5 Or have you not read in the Law of Moses that every Sabbath the priests in the Temple actually break the Sabbath law, yet they are not guilty? 6 I tell you that there is something here greater than the Temple. 7 The scripture says, 'It is kindness that I want, not animal sacrifices.' If you really knew what this means, you would not condemn people who are not guilty; 8 for the Son of Man is Lord of the Sabbath."

SECTION HEADING: "**The Question about the Sabbath**." "**Sabbath**" is discussed below in verse 1. This section heading can be rendered "Some Pharisees (or, Some) ask Jesus about the day of rest." However, the question the Pharisees ask is sufficiently accusatory in nature that a better rendering may be "Some Pharisees accuse Jesus of breaking (or, violating) the day of rest." Other ways are "Jesus and the Pharisees argue about the Sabbath" or "The argument about (breaking) the Sabbath."

Matthew 12.1–16.12 pictures Jesus in direct confrontation with his opponents. He has already been misunderstood by John the Baptist and rejected by those people in whose cities he had worked miracles (11.16-24). Now open hostility erupts between Jesus and his opponents; it is initiated by the attacks made against him by the Pharisees (12.2,24,38), and climaxed by Jesus' warning against the teaching of the Pharisees and Sadducees (16.6-12). Chapter 12 even contains the observation that the Pharisees began seeking a way to take Jesus' life (verse 14).

Both the narrative of the question about the Sabbath (verses 1-8) and that of the man with the paralyzed hand (verses 9-14) are told in the form of pronouncement stories. A pronouncement story is one in which the emphasis in the story is upon the pronouncement or saying which comes from Jesus toward the end of the account. In the first of these two stories the pronouncement is found in verse 8 (TEV "For the Son of Man is Lord of the Sabbath"), while in the second it appears in verse 12 (TEV "So then, our Law does allow us to help someone on the Sabbath"). Although this second story also narrates a healing miracle (verse 13), the real focus is upon Jesus' remark to the Pharisees; it is this, more than the actual miracle, which leads them to make plans to kill Jesus (verse 14).

When Jesus heard of the plot against him, he left there and went to another place where he healed a number of sick people (verse 15). Matthew interprets these acts of healing as the fulfillment of what God had promised through the prophet (verses 22-24). The second half of the chapter opens with further healings by Jesus (verse 22), which cause the crowds to question whether he may possibly be the promised Son of David (verse 23). But the Pharisees already know of his true origin, and so they accuse him of being in league with Satan (verses 22-24). Jesus responds by demonstrating the error in the Pharisees' reasoning (verses 25-32) and by pointing out how evil they really are (verses 33-37). Finally the Pharisees demand of Jesus a miracle (verse 38). Jesus refuses, affirming that his very presence is sufficient testimony to who he is (verses 39-42). Then he traces the destructive route of evil, revealing how it goes from bad to worse (verses 43-45). Matthew concludes the chapter with another pronouncement story, by which Jesus tells that his disciples are his true relatives (verses 46-50).

12.1

RSV	TEV
At that time Jesus went through the grainfields on the sabbath; his disciples were hungry, and they began to pluck heads of grain and to eat.	Not long afterward Jesus was walking through some wheat fields on a Sabbath. His disciples were hungry, so they began to pick heads of wheat and eat the grain.

At that time is the same temporal marker used in 11.25; TEV translates "**Not long afterward**." Evidently Matthew intends that it be understood very loosely; a literal translation may in fact result in nonsense ("At that time Jesus took a walk one sabbath day through the cornfields" [JB]). NAB resolves the oddity by combining the two temporal markers: "Once on a sabbath." This latter rendering is often followed by translators. They use expressions such as "One time on a sabbath" or "At one time, on a sabbath." Others follow TEV, using phrases such as "A little later" or "A short time after that." A third option is actually quite close to the text: "About that time."

Jesus went through: since the journey was on foot, TEV renders "**Jesus was walking though**." In many languages it will be necessary to translate "Jesus and his disciples. . . ." Otherwise the reader will be shaken by the sudden appearance of the disciples in the last half of this verse. The text has **went through**, but in many languages it will be better to say "was (or, were) going through," as TEV has done. They were not going through the field and crops as such, but were probably following a path. "Were walking past" or "were going on a path through" are good ways to avoid misunderstanding.

Grainfields is translated "the standing grain" by NAB. NEB, Mft, NJB render "cornfields," which is the British English equivalent of the American English **"wheat fields"** (TEV). The Greek term means grain in general, but in Palestine the grain was either wheat or barley. Wheat was the more highly valued of the two grains, and if a choice must be made, it is more likely that the fields were wheat fields.

There are languages which have no word for **grain** and in which it is usual to name each type of crop, such as rice or wheat. As we said above, "wheat" will probably be acceptable. But a large number of cultures do not know wheat, and translators have wanted to substitute "rice" or "millet." This is not too bad, really, in this context, especially if that one grain can also be used generically for all grains or crops; but it does remove the translation from the context of the biblical culture. A very general word such as "fields of crops" or "fields of food" is one way to handle this problem. Another is "fields with the seeds they make bread from." The translation can have "the fields" or "some fields," whichever is more natural.

The **sabbath** is mentioned seven times in this one chapter (verses 1,2,5,8, 10,11,12), each mention having to do with the problem of what a person was permitted to do on this holy day of the Jews. According the Jewish calculation, their days began at sunset. This was the seventh day of the week, and it extended from sundown on Friday to sundown on Saturday. The day was set apart as a time of worship and rest, and much discussion went on among the Jews regarding the specifics of what could or could not be done on this particular day. The first fourteen verses of this chapter teach that the needs of humans have priority over the legalistic regulations connected with the Sabbath.

There have been translators who have wanted to render **sabbath** as "Sunday," the day Christians now observe as Sabbath, but others have preferred "Saturday," the day the Jews observed. Both are rather poor translations, since they put the emphasis on which day is observed, but not on the function or purpose of the Sabbath. A better translation is "day of rest." Some cultures have a day of rest of their own—y often it is the weekly market day—and in those cases translators say "day of rest of the Jews," particularly if their own day of rest is neither Saturday nor Sunday. Other possibilities are "the Jews' holy day" or "the Jewish day of honoring (or, worshiping) God."

Translators should order this sentence in a natural way. In some cases, for example, the natural word order will be "About that time, on a day of rest, Jesus and his disciples were walking through some wheat fields."

To pluck heads of grain is the basis for the accusation made by the Pharisees against the disciples of Jesus in the following verse. The Jewish teachers of religion had designated thirty-nine "main classes of work" which could not be performed on the Sabbath. The first three are listed as "sewing, plowing, reaping," and according to the Pharisaic interpretation of the Law, Jesus' disciples would have been guilty of reaping on the Sabbath. There was no law against eating on the Sabbath, and if a person's life were in immediate danger from starvation, he would have been permitted to reap and eat on the Sabbath. But since Jesus' disciples were not in danger of death by starvation, they were guilty of breaking one of the Sabbath regulations.

The meaning of the verb **to pluck** is seen in TEV "to pick." This is better than "harvest" or "reap," which would distort what the disciples were actually doing (just as the Pharisaic interpretation did).

Heads of grain translates one word in Greek. The translation of the term will be related to **grainfields**. If translators have said "wheat fields," for example, then they can say here "grains (or, seeds) of wheat" or "some of the wheat." If they have used "grain," then here they can say "some of the grain" or "some of the seeds of grain." In other words, whatever the translation says the fields contained, it is some of that which the disciples are now said to be picking and eating.

Heads of grain is also the understood object of the verb **to eat**. RSV follows the form of the Greek and does not insert an object. TEV has **"pick heads of wheat,"** followed here by **"eat the grain"** to avoid repetition. Both NJB and NEB supply the pronoun "them." In many languages **eat** will require an object such as "it" or them. "They began to pick some of the grain and eat it" or "They began picking and eating some of the grain" are possible renderings.

<table>
<tr><td>**12.2**</td><td>RSV</td><td>TEV</td></tr>
</table>

RSV	TEV
But when the Pharisees saw it, they said to him, "Look, your disciples are doing what is not lawful to do on the sabbath."	When the Pharisees saw this, they said to Jesus, "Look, it is against our Law for your disciples to do this on the Sabbath!"

Even though the text says **the Pharisees**, it does not mean all of them. "Some Pharisees" would be better. For comments on **Pharisees**, see 3.7.

Saw it: in Greek there is no expressed object of the verb **saw**; NJB and RSV supply **it**, while TEV and NEB have **"this."** Most languages will probably require an object. In some languages it will be even necessary to say "saw them doing this" or "saw the disciples picking and eating the grain."

Customarily the owner of a grain field allowed a path to run through his field, and it was expected that persons traveling through the field would pull and eat grain that grew along the pathway. However, persons were not allowed to go off into the field and pick grain to take away with them. Evidently the disciples were simply doing what was customary; they were picking and eating grain as they walked through the field. Had they done this on any other day of the week, there would have been no controversy. But the Pharisaic interpretation did not allow for such actions to be done on the Sabbath. The exact positions where the Pharisees, Jesus, and his disciples were standing is not clear. However, it is fairly logical to conclude that the Pharisees were watching Jesus and his disciples walk through the grain field, and when they had come out of the grain field, the Pharisees were standing there, waiting to accuse them.

They said to him: Jesus is not mentioned by name in the Greek text, but in a number of languages it is better to use the personal noun here rather than a pronoun. The choice should be determined by the demands of the receptor language.

Look (so also TEV, NJB, NEB) renders a Greek particle that was first used in 1.20. Here its function is to draw attention to what Jesus' disciples were doing. **Look**

may not be natural in some languages, but there will surely be some word or phrase with an equivalent function: "Take note of this," or "Are you seeing this?"

Your disciples . . . on the Sabbath: NJB renders "your disciples are doing something that is forbidden on the sabbath"; NEB is similar. In the context **what is not lawful** means "what our Jewish religious law forbids." No such prohibition is found in the Old Testament, but the Pharisees pressed the laws that governed the Sabbath to include this regulation. And the Pharisees gave the same authority to the laws which were derived from the Old Testament as the authority they gave to the Old Testament itself. **What is not lawful** may be "what the law forbids," "what our law says is not allowed," or "something we Jews are not allowed to do." There will be languages where, to get the full accusing tone of the Pharisees' statement, two sentences will be used, as in "Our law says people should not pick grain on the day of rest. But look, your disciples are doing that."

12.3	RSV	TEV
	He said to them, "Have you not read what David did, when he was hungry, and those who were with him:	Jesus answered, "Have you never read what David did that time when he and his men were hungry?

He said to them is translated **"Jesus answered"** by TEV. The use of the pronoun (**he**) or of the proper noun ("**Jesus**") will depend entirely upon the expectations of the receptor language. Further, it should be clear that **them** refers to the Pharisees, not to the disciples.

Have you not read . . . ? is a rhetorical question which assumes the answer "Yes." In languages where this literary device for showing emphasis is not common, one may translate "You have surely read" or "I know you have read." In some languages it may even be necessary to indicate where they read this: ". . . in our Law," or ". . . in our Bible," or ". . . in our holy Scriptures."

The question (or, affirmation) can also be reordered, as in "You know what David did, I am sure, because you have read in God's book . . . ."

It may be necessary to qualify **David** as "King David." The reference is to 1 Samuel 21.1-6.

When is translated **"at that time when"** by TEV; this restructuring is helpful in calling attention to a specific time in the past.

He was hungry, and those who were with him (TEV "**he and his men were hungry**"): in Hebrew and in languages influenced by Hebrew, such as the Greek of the New Testament, this sort of structure is common. One frequently finds a singular verb and subject followed by other subjects who join the main subject in the action indicated by the verb. In many languages, including English, the most natural restructuring is to link the subjects by the conjunction "and" and then to use a plural verb form, as in TEV.

Those who were with him refers to "his companions" or "his followers." "**His men**" of TEV is also good.

12.4 RSV	TEV
how he entered the house of God and ate the bread of the Presence, which it was not lawful for him to eat nor for those who were with him, but only for the priests?	He went into the house of God, and he and his men ate the bread offered to God, even though it was against the Law for them to eat it—only the priests were allowed to eat that bread.

How he entered . . . indicates this is a continuation of what one can read that David did. TEV starts a new sentence and drops the **how**. Other translations can also start a new sentence but begin it with "It says . . . ," "God's book says . . . ," or "You read there . . . ." It should follow naturally from the previous verse.

This incident took place before David's son Solomon built the Temple in Jerusalem, so it would be incorrect to translate **house of God** the same as "Temple." If "house of God" is used elsewhere for "Temple," here "place where God stayed" or "the tent of God's presence" will be better.

The account in 1 Samuel 21.1-6 does not indicate that David went into the house of God. It in fact suggests that the priest went in and brought the bread out to David. Moreover, David's men were not with him at the time. According to the account in 1 Samuel, David received the bread from Ahimelech the priest, after which he took it to his men, and then they (David and his men) ate it. Therefore considerable restructuring may be necessary in this verse in order to avoid a misunderstanding of the sequence of events. Most all translations of this verse seem to imply either that David went into the house of God and then brought the bread out to his men, who ate it outside the Temple together with him, or that David and his men went into the house of God, and then all of them ate the bread there.

It is not the role of the translator to attempt to harmonize two conflicting statements of the same event. On the other hand, some languages may require a more explicit outline of events than is included in the Greek text. For example, the Greek text states explicitly that David did go into the house of God, even though this information is apparently contrary to the account in the Old Testament. Moreover, purely on the basis of the Greek text alone, it is possible to assume that we have a structure similar to that discussed in verse 3, which can mean that the men accompanied David as he went into the house of God. However, whereas that conclusion was required for verse 3, it is not necessary to conclude here that the men accompanied David into the Temple. The Greek text is also ambiguous about the place where David ate the bread with the men.

As we said, translators should not harmonize. But it can be assumed that the account in these verses is based on 1 Samuel itself. Therefore in cases where Matthew's wording leaves more than one interpretation open, it is probably safe to assume he intended the alternative that agrees with 1 Samuel rather than the one that contradicts it.

If we follow the information given in 1 Samuel 21.1-6, then the following sequence of events results: (1) David went into the house of God; (2) he got the bread (from Ahimelech the priest); (3) he left the house of God; (4) he took the bread back to where his men were; and (5) he and his men ate the bread there. Of the modern English translations, only Mft explicitly defines the place where the men ate: "how he went into the house of God, and there they ate . . . ." If one assumes that the eating took place in the house of God, as Mft does, many languages will require "how he and his men went into the house of God, and there they ate . . . ." However, the sequence of events outlined above is preferable.

How he entered . . . and ate assumes that only David ate, which agrees with the parallels in Mark 2.26 and Luke 6.4. But some Greek manuscripts have "they ate"; the UBS Greek text supports this plural reading, since it is more logical that the reading would have been altered in the direction of the parallels in Mark and Luke than the other way around.

TEV provides a helpful model here: **"He** (or, David) **went into . . . and he and his men ate . . . ."** In most languages a sentence like this will leave it clear that David must have come out before he and his men ate the bread. Others, however, will require that more of the sequence of events be made explicit, as in "David went into God's house and got the bread offered to God. He brought it (out) and he and his men ate it."

The bread of the Presence (TEV **"the bread offered to God"**) is translated "the loaves of the offering" by NJB. NEB has "the sacred bread," Brc "the sacred loaves," and NAB "the holy bread." The bread referred to was in the form of twelve loaves which were laid on a table in the house of God each Sabbath. The bread was offered there to the Lord, and then on the following Sabbath it became the possession of the priests, who were required to eat it in a holy place. For regulations governing this bread, see Leviticus 24.5-9. Many translators have rendered **the bread of the Presence** as TEV has. A variation on this is "the bread that is for God." **Bread** is becoming more commonly known, but if it is not known, "food offered to God" is possible.

Which it was not lawful for him to eat nor for those who were with him is shortened by GECL: "although this was forbidden." The Law referred to is the Jewish Law (TEV **"even though it was against the Law for them to eat it"**).

Some translators will begin a new sentence: "They ate that bread even though the Law did not permit that" or ". . . even though that was against our Law."

Note that **nor for those who were with him** has been dealt with above. Practically all translators will find it more natural to mention David's followers early in the verse in conjunction with **ate**, not toward the end as the text has it.

But only for the priests? TEV makes two significant adjustments: (1) the shift from a question form to a statement and (2) the inclusion of a verb which is implicit in the Greek. This simplifies the reading, as may be seen from comparing NEB ("though neither he nor his men had a right to eat it, but only the priests") with Brc ("although he and his friends had no right to eat them, because only the priests are permitted to eat them"). Most translators will want to follow the lead of TEV and Brc, in some cases beginning new sentences: "Only the priests were allowed . . ." or "The Law allowed only the priests to eat that bread."

12.5	RSV	TEV

Or have you not read in the law how on the sabbath the priests in the temple profane the sabbath, and are

Or have you not read in the Law of Moses that every Sabbath the priests in the Temple actually break

guiltless?   **the Sabbath law, yet they are not
                                                   guilty?**

The argument in the previous verse was based on biblical history; the argument presented by Jesus in this verse is based upon the teaching of the Jewish Law, which recognized the differences between "light" and "heavy" commands. Jesus notes that the command for the priests to perform certain duties on the Sabbath outweighs the command not to work on the Sabbath. The form of Jesus' argument represents a typical argument used by Jewish teachers, and they would have accepted his conclusion as valid.

Or have you not read . . . ? is a difficult structure for many readers. In Greek the rhetorical question assumes a "Yes" answer, and it may be translated as an emphatic statement: "You have surely read in the Law of Moses that . . ." or "You surely know that the Law of Moses teaches . . . ."

Or links the previous argument of Jesus with this one. A word like "Further" or "To continue" may be more natural than **Or**. Another possibility is "I am sure that you have also read in the Law of Moses . . . ."

The law (TEV "**The Law of Moses**") is a reference to the first division of the Jewish Scriptures. Among other Sabbath day responsibilities, the priests had a special offering to present on that day (Num 28.9-10), and they had the responsibility of changing the bread offered to God (Lev 24.8).

For **priests**, see comments on 8.4. The same term should be used throughout the Bible, as much as it is possible.

Profane (Mft "desecrate") is translated "break" by NJB, NEB, AT, NAB, and "**actually break**" by TEV. The root meaning is conveyed by RSV; elsewhere in the New Testament the verb is used only in Acts 24.6 (TEV "defile the Temple"). Brc combines both concepts, "to break the Sabbath law, and thus to profane the Sabbath . . . ." In the context, either "defile the Sabbath day" or "break the Sabbath law" is satisfactory. This can also be "break the law about the day of rest." GECL restructures completely: "Or have you not read . . . that the priests also work in the Temple on the Sabbath? Thereby they break the law . . . ."

Are guiltless ("**are not guilty**" TEV, Mft, AT) is translated "without being blamed for it" by NJB and "and it is not held against them" by NEB. The level of language in NAB is somewhat higher: "without incurring guilt." The adjective **guiltless** occurs in the New Testament only here and in verse 7. As the translations indicate, the meaning is "innocent" or "not guilty." Some will render **are guiltless** as "not held to be guilty," "God won't judge them to be guilty for it," or "God won't judge them to have sinned."

Many translators will need to restructure the verse in a manner similar to GECL to help readers understand in what way the priests **profane the sabbath**. An example is "You know that when the priests do their work in the temple on the day of rest they actually break the law about the Sabbath. But you have surely read in the Law of Moses that they are not considered guilty for it."

| 12.6 | RSV | TEV |

I tell you, something greater than the temple is here.

I tell you that there is something here greater than the Temple.

I tell you is similar to the construction discussed in 5.20. Its function is to tie this verse with the preceding and to make emphatic the words that follow. "I assure you" or "Believe me" are other possible translations.

In the statement **something greater than the temple is here**, **the temple** stands in the emphatic position. Apparently no translations attempt to make explicit what or who was intended by **something greater than**. Moreover, none of the modern translations, including TOB, supply a note to explain the meaning. Some commentators suggest that the reference is to Jesus himself, whose authority supersedes both that of the Temple and the Sabbath (see verse 8). Others interpret it to refer to the Kingdom of God, which is ushered in by Jesus' presence. Since there is no scholarly consensus, one should not attempt to be explicit in translation.

In many languages it is difficult to use a completely neutral word like **something**, since they require more specific terms such as "someone" or "some teaching." However, translators should try "a new thing" or "a new truth" before resorting to either of these solutions. The more neutral, the better.

Greater can be rendered as "more important." The sentence should be restructured if the receptor language requires it, as in "There is something here that is more important than the Temple."

| 12.7 | RSV | TEV |

And if you had known what this means, 'I desire mercy, and not sacrifice,' you would not have condemned the guiltless.

The scripture says, 'It is kindness that I want, not animal sacrifices.' If you really knew what this means, you would not condemn people who are not guilty;

And if you had known what this means of RSV contrasts rather sharply with the restructuring of TEV, which begins the verse with "**The scripture says . . . .**" This restructuring is helpful for at least two reasons: it simplifies the sentence structure, and it identifies Jesus' words as a scripture quotation. The quotation comes from Hosea 6.6, a passage previously quoted in Matthew 9.13. See comments there.

The word **this** refers to this quotation from Hosea, but in many languages it is not usual to refer ahead to something that is not yet specified. So a third advantage of the restructuring of TEV is that this problem also is resolved.

Known what this means here means more than simply being aware of something. The Pharisees probably thought they understood the verse, but Jesus is saying "If you knew what this really means" or "If you understood the real meaning."

Note that the **I** in the quotation is God. The translation should not give the impression it is Jesus. Some can begin the verse by saying "God says in the Scriptures." Another way is to use indirect speech, as in "The Scriptures say that God wants people to be merciful . . . ."

Condemned is used again in verse 37; elsewhere in the New Testament it is found in Luke 6.37; James 5.6. In this context it means "declared people guilty," "judged people to be guilty," or "said that people have sinned."

Guiltless is the same adjective used in verse 5. In this sentence **guiltless** may be translated slightly differently because of the overall structure of the sentence, although the meaning is the same as in verse 5. The last part of the verse can be "You would not have said that innocent people were guilty of sin" or "You would not have called people sinners who are not guilty."

12.8 RSV TEV

For the Son of man is lord of the sabbath."

for the Son of Man is Lord of the Sabbath."

All three of the synoptic Gospels contain this verse in practically the same form. The Greek particle translated **For** by RSV (so also TEV) is essential to the argument. Jesus' claim is that he (**the Son of man**) is the one who has the authority to tell what may or may not be done on the Sabbath. See 8.20 for a discussion of the translation of **Son of man**. As there, our recommendation is to use third person in the translation, as in "the one who is Son of Man," but first person may be used if readers will otherwise fail to see at all that Jesus is referring to himself: "I, the one who is Son of Man."

To say the Son of man is **lord of the sabbath** means he "makes the rules over what may be done on the day of rest" or "controls (the laws about) the day of rest."

12.9-14

RSV TEV

The Man with a Paralyzed Hand

9 And he went on from there, and entered their synagogue. 10 And behold, there was a man with a withered hand. And they asked him, "Is it lawful to heal on the sabbath?" so that they might accuse him. 11 He said to them, "What man of you, if he has one sheep and it falls into a pit on the sabbath, will not lay hold of it and lift it out? 12 Of how much more value is a man than a sheep! So it is lawful to do good on the sabbath." 13 Then he said to the man, "Stretch out your hand." And the man stretched it out, and it was restored, whole like the other. 14 But the Pharisees went out and took counsel against him, how to destroy him.

9 Jesus left that place and went to a synagogue, 10 where there was a man who had a paralyzed hand. Some people were there who wanted to accuse Jesus of doing wrong, so they asked him, "Is it against our Law to heal on the Sabbath?"

11 Jesus answered, "What if one of you has a sheep and it falls into a deep hole on the Sabbath? Will he not take hold of it and lift it out? 12 And a man is worth much more than a sheep! So then, our Law does allow us to help someone on the Sabbath." 13 Then he said to the man with the paralyzed hand, "Stretch out your hand."

He stretched it out, and it became well again, just like the other one. 14 Then the Pharisees left and made plans to kill Jesus.

SECTION HEADING: "**The Man with the Paralyzed Hand.**" This section heading may have to be rendered by a short sentence: "Jesus heals a man with a paralyzed hand" or ". . . whose hand was paralyzed."

The actions of Jesus in this section serve as an illustration of the scripture which he quotes in 12.7: "It is kindness that I want, not animal sacrifices" (TEV). Matthew states explicitly that this event took place on the same day as that mentioned in the previous section, thus closely linking the two episodes.

12.9   RSV   TEV

And he went on from there, and   Jesus left that place and went
entered their synagogue.   to a synagogue,

And marks the transition to a new episode but does link it temporally. "Next" or "After that" will indicate this, too.

He: since this verse opens a new section, TEV introduces Jesus by name.

Went on from there is translated "**left that place**" by TEV and NAB. NJB and Brc have "moved on from there." Since **there** is not identified, it can easily be dropped, as in "After that he went to their synagogue." It depends on the demands of the receptor language.

The text has **went . . . and entered**. TEV does not specify that Jesus went into the synagogue, although that is probably understood. Again, translators should do whatever is natural.

Their synagogue has the wording "the synagogue" in Mark 6.2 and Luke 6.6. Most translations retain **their**, which may be Matthew's way of disassociating both Jesus and the Christian community of his own day from the Jewish community. If readers will not know who **their** refers to, then translators can put "the synagogue of the Jews at that place."

For comments on **synagogue**, see 4.23.

12.10   RSV   TEV

And behold, there was a man with a   where there was a man who had a
withered hand. And they asked him,   paralyzed hand. Some people were
"Is it lawful to heal on the sabbath?"   there who wanted to accuse Jesus
so that they might accuse him.   of doing wrong, so they asked him,
                                       "Is it against our Law to heal on the
                                       Sabbath?"

And behold: see comments on 1.20. The formula here functions to call attention to the man who had a paralyzed hand. Some translators will use a phrase like "And it happened that there . . ." or "There was a man there" (Brc). Others will make verse 10 a continuation of the sentence begun in verse 9. TEV is an example, and another possibility is ". . . he went into their synagogue, and there he saw a man . . . ."

Withered (so also NJB, NEB, Brc) is a literal meaning of the word, as is "dried up." However, when used of diseased body parts, the meaning is more naturally expressed in English as "paralyzed" or "crippled." It is possible to say either "a man with a paralyzed hand" or "a man whose hand was paralyzed."

The word translated **hand** generally has that meaning, though it may also mean "arm" (NEB).

Since the text does not specify who **they** refers to, instead of "Pharisees" (as in GECL), some translators use a general term like "**some people**" (TEV) or "the people there."

Is it lawful (TEV "**Is it against our Law**") has reference to the Jewish Law. **Is it lawful** has been rendered as "Is it allowed by our Law" or "Does the Law of Moses permit."

Heal may require an object, as in "heal people" or "cure people of their diseases."

And they asked him . . . so that they might accuse him: TEV both changes the order of the two clauses and alters the dependent clause to an independent clause: "**Some people were there who wanted to accuse Jesus of doing wrong.**" NEB, though retaining the order of the two clauses, does transform the dependent clause to an independent one: "They wanted to frame a charge against him."

Might accuse (TEV "**wanted to accuse . . . of doing wrong**") translates a legal technical term meaning "bring charges (against someone in court)." As TEV and NEB have restructured the verb in English, it requires an object, which will probably be necessary also for other languages. Brc does noteworthy restructuring: "In an attempt to find something which they could use as a charge against him, they asked him: . . . ." GECL identifies the unidentified **they** and translates "The Pharisees had watched Jesus closely and so they questioned him . . . ."

These people, or Pharisees, asked Jesus a question that they hoped would produce an answer from him that would contradict the teachings of the Law. Then they could accuse him of doing or saying something wrong. This is why the purpose clause is used in the text, **so that they might accuse him**. TEV, NEB, and Brc cited above have all attempted to convey this meaning. Other ways are "Some people were there who wanted to be able to accuse Jesus of breaking the Law (of Moses), so they asked him . . ." or "Some people there asked Jesus, 'Is it lawful to heal on the Sabbath?' They asked him that because they wanted to have reason to accuse him of doing wrong."

12.11   RSV   TEV

He said to them, "What man of you,   Jesus answered, "What if one
if he has one sheep and it falls into   of you has a sheep and it falls into a
a pit on the sabbath, will not lay hold   deep hole on the Sabbath? Will he
of it and lift it out?   not take hold of it and lift it out?

He said to them: TEV identifies the subject: "**Jesus answered**."

What man of you is the beginning of a long hypothetical question; that is, it pictures an event that may or may not happen to any one of his hearers. NJB translates "If any one of you," and TEV "**What if one of you.**"

Pit can be "a big hole" or "a deep hole."

Will not lay hold of it and lift it out? translates a rhetorical question in Greek which implies an emphatic positive response: "Any of us would take hold of it and lift it out."

TEV attempts to ease the difficulty of the lengthy negative question by dividing it into two questions, the second of which is an answer to the first. However, it may be better still to reply to the first question with a statement: "What if one of you . . . on the Sabbath? You would certainly take hold of it and lift it out." Or a complete shift away from the question form will perhaps be even clearer: "If any one of you has a sheep and it falls . . . you would surely take hold of it and lift it out."

There are actually many ways to handle long, hypothetical questions like this, and translators should consider carefully the demands of the receptor languages. Here are some more examples: "Suppose one of you has a sheep, and it falls into a hole on a day of rest. What would you do? You would take hold of it and lift it out (wouldn't you?)," "If any of you had one sheep and it fell into a big hole on the day of rest, wouldn't you take hold of it and lift it out?" and "Any one of you, if you had a sheep and it fell into a deep hole on a Sabbath, you would surely take hold of it and lift it out."

Note that the text seems to indicate that this hypothetical person has only one sheep. A sentence like "If you had a sheep that fell" may indicate that it was one of many he had.

12.12	RSV	TEV
	Of how much more value is a man than a sheep! So it is lawful to do good on the sabbath."	And a man is worth much more than a sheep! So then, our Law does allow us to help someone on the Sabbath."

This verse represents a style of argument which was widely employed by Jewish teachers. It is known as "the argument from the lesser to the greater"; in the present context the sheep is the "lesser" and the man is the "greater." Jesus' argument is based on the following logic: "Since it is allowable to give help to a sheep (the lesser) on the Sabbath, it is also allowable to give help to a man (the greater) on the Sabbath." As noted in verse 1, the Jewish teachers did allow for help to be given to a person on the Sabbath (for example, food to a starving person), if life were in danger. But the man's life is not here in jeopardy, and so the laws regarding the Sabbath are still in effect. Jesus' argument in this case is that the total well-being of a person has priority over the laws which define what may be done on the Sabbath.

Of how much more value . . . ! is formulated in Greek in such a way as to lay stress upon the words **Of how much more**, and most modern translations attempt to carry through this emphasis. For some language situations it may be obligatory to shift to a statement: "**And a man is worth much more than a sheep**" (TEV).

If the question form, **Of how much more value**, is retained, it is important that readers do not think Jesus wants his hearers to somehow put a price marker on the difference in value between sheep and people. A statement as in TEV or an imperative will help: "Think how much more valuable . . . ."

To be of **more value** means to be **"worth more"** (TEV) or "more important." A phrase like "costs more" would be wrong here.

So indicates that this statement of Jesus is the logical conclusion to his argument. "So then" or "Obviously, therefore" will be appropriate translations, as will "Since this is so."

So it is lawful refers once again to the Jewish Law (TEV **"Our Law does allow us"**); see comments on verse 10. As indicated in the introduction to this chapter, the real purpose of this entire narrative (verses 9-14) is to emphasize Jesus' pronouncement contained in this verse: **So it is lawful to do good on the sabbath**.

It is lawful can be "it is not against our Law," or "the Law does allow," or "it is permitted by the Law."

To do good can be rendered "to do good to someone" or "to do something good for someone." GECL has "to help a man."

Brc reformulates the reply of Jesus: "Obviously, there is no law to stop a man doing good on the Sabbath Day." Evidently "no law" of Brc means "not one of our laws relating to the Sabbath." The sentence can be reversed: "So to do good for someone on the Sabbath does not break the Law" or ". . . is permitted by the Law."

12.13	RSV	TEV

Then he said to the man, "Stretch out your hand." And the man stretched it out, and it was restored, whole like the other.	Then he said to the man with the paralyzed hand, "Stretch out your hand." He stretched it out, and it became well again, just like the other one.

Then he said to the man is significantly shorter than the parallel in Mark 3.5, which begins "Jesus was angry as he looked around at them, but at the same time he felt sorry for them, because they were so stubborn and wrong."

The man is identified by TEV as "the man with the paralyzed hand" because he has not been mentioned since verse 10.

Stretch out your hand is the rendering of most translations; NEB has "Stretch out your arm." **Stretch out** can also be "reach out" or "extend." As indicated in verse 10, the Greek word may mean either **hand** or "arm."

This can also be put in indirect speech, as in "Then he ordered the man to stretch out his hand (that was paralyzed)."

And the man stretched it out translates one word in Greek, a participle which mentions neither the subject (**the man**) nor the object (**it**). Many languages will demand that the object be specified as either "it" or "the hand," though they will allow for the identification of **the man** by a pronoun ("he").

And it was restored represents the root meaning of the Greek verb. However, the verb may also be used as a medical term meaning "cure," which is much more satisfactory in the context; see NEB ("and it was made sound again") and TEV ("**and it became well again**").

Matthew uses **and** twice in this verse as a marker of continuity. It relates events that are happening one after the other. In many languages the first occurrence here will be best rendered by "so" or perhaps will be dropped, but the second will in all likelihood be retained.

Whole like the other is made into a complete statement by GECL: "and it became as sound as the other."

Whole does not mean "complete," as if it were not all there before. Rather, in this context it means "healthy" or "well," or even "strong."

12.14	RSV	TEV
	But the Pharisees went out and took counsel against him, how to destroy him.	Then the Pharisees left and made plans to kill Jesus.

The story of the healing of the man's paralyzed hand is brought to a climax in the expression of the Pharisee's hostility against Jesus. **But** introduces the actions contrasted with what one might expect after Jesus first gave a good argument and then performed a miracle that helped someone. Instead of being impressed or won over to him, they decided he had to be killed. Thus translators should try to retain **But** or possibly say "But at this."

But the Pharisees went out translates a dependent participial clause in Greek, but most translations make it a coordinate clause, as RSV and TEV have done. For example, "At this the Pharisees went out" (NJB) and "So the Pharisees withdrew" (Mft). However, NAB ("When the Pharisees were outside") and NEB ("But the Pharisees, on leaving the synagogue . . .") retain a form similar to that of the Greek. Any of these restructurings represents a valid interpretation of the Greek text; it is the translator's responsibility to select a form that is accurate in terms of the Greek and natural for the intended audience.

The Pharisees have not yet been mentioned in this episode, so a phrase like "the Pharisees who were there" or "some Pharisees who were there" is perhaps in order. For **Pharisees**, see comments on 3.7.

They **went out**, probably "out of the synagogue," but it is also reasonable to say "left" or "went away."

Took counsel against him, how to destroy him is translated "laid a plot to do away with him" by NEB and "concocted a scheme to kill him" by Brc. Mark 3.6 indicates that the Herodians (supporters of Herod Antipas) joined the Pharisees in this plot against Jesus, but Matthew does not include this information. This same verb (**took**) plus noun (**counsel**) construction is also found in 22.15; 27.1,7; 28.12, but nowhere else in the New Testament. Only in 26.4 does Matthew use the verb form which in itself means "take counsel" or "make plans."

Took counsel gives the idea of meeting to discuss a matter. Since it is followed by **against**, the idea of "plot against" or "plan to do harm to" becomes clear. **Destroy** clearly means here "to kill" or "to have killed."

361

It is probably not necessary to have **him** twice, being the object of both **counsel against** and **destroy**. "Planned together how they could kill him" or "made plans of a way to have him killed" may be more natural.

So that readers do not think **him** refers to the man who was healed, many translators say "Jesus."

12.15-21

RSV | TEV

God's Chosen Servant

15 Jesus, aware of this, withdrew from there. And many followed him, and he healed them all, 16 and ordered them not to make him known. 17 This was to fulfil what was spoken by the prophet Isaiah:
18 "Behold, my servant whom I have chosen,
my beloved with whom my soul is well pleased.
I will put my Spirit upon him,
and he shall proclaim justice to the Gentiles.
19 He will not wrangle or cry aloud,
nor will any one hear his voice in the streets;
20 he will not break a bruised reed
or quench a smoldering wick,
till he brings justice to victory;
21 and in his name will the Gentiles hope."

15 When Jesus heard about the plot against him, he went away from that place; and large crowds followed him. He healed all the sick 16 and gave them orders not to tell others about him. 17 He did this so as to make come true what God had said through the prophet Isaiah:
18 "Here is my servant, whom I have chosen,
the one I love, and with whom I am pleased.
I will send my Spirit upon him,
and he will announce my judgment to the nations.
19 He will not argue or shout,
or make loud speeches in the streets.
20 He will not break off a bent reed,
nor put out a flickering lamp.
He will persist until he causes justice to triumph,
21 and on him all peoples will put their hope."

SECTION HEADING: **"God's Chosen Servant."** This title will depend somewhat on how verse 18 is eventually translated. It may be "The one God has chosen to serve him" or "The servant God has chosen." If a short sentence is needed, then it can be "Jesus is God's chosen servant" or "God chooses Jesus as his servant."

Although this passage is brief, it reveals significant insights into Matthew's understanding of Jesus' Messiahship. Jesus is indeed the one whom God has chosen, but his own people refuse to acknowledge who he is. As God's Chosen One, he does not shout against his enemies, and he deals gently with those who need his help. He will suffer and die, but he will triumph over death, and through him the Gentiles will put their hope in God.

12.15 RSV | TEV

Jesus, aware of this, withdrew from there. And many followed him, and he healed them all,

When Jesus heard about the plot against him, he went away from that place; and large crowds followed him. He healed all the sick

362

Jesus, aware of this (TEV **"When Jesus heard about the plot against him"**) translates a Greek construction which does not have an object expressed. But most languages will expect an object. GECL has "When Jesus heard of it," and Brc renders "Jesus was well aware of what they were doing . . . ." Since the text says **aware of this** and does not actually indicate whether Jesus heard of the plotting or simply knew of it on his own, many translators use "Jesus knew about this." **This** is often rendered "their plot" or "what they were planning (to do)."

Withdrew (TEV **"went away"**) is used quite frequently in Matthew's Gospel: 2.12,13,14,22; 4.12; 9.24; 12.15; 14.13; 15.21; 27.5. Outside of this Gospel it occurs in the New Testament only four times (Mark 3.7; John 6.15; Acts 23.19; 26.31).

To make the sentence natural, translators may need to restructure slightly, as in "Jesus knew about their plots and therefore went away from there" or "Jesus left that place, however, because he knew about their plotting against him."

The text uses yet again the word **And** to show continuity in the narrative. However, some translators have found it more natural to use "But."

Many (so also NJB, NEB); TEV has **"large crowds,"** while NAB has "many people." A textual problem does exist in the Greek text: some manuscripts have "many crowds," while others simply have **many**. TC-GNT favors the shorter wording, on the assumption that scribes may have sought to have strengthened **many** by the addition of the noun "crowds," especially since "many crowds" is a familiar phrase in the Gospel (4.25; 8.1; 13.2; 15.30; 19.2). It is quite obvious that RSV, NJB, and NEB adopt this shorter text, though it may appear that TEV does not. However, it is quite possible that TEV represents a translational adjustment for naturalness rather than an acceptance of the longer text. In English it is more natural to follow the adjective "many" with a noun, and this is what TEV has done. Brc, probably for the same reason, has "large numbers of people"; NAB and GECL have "many people."

Followed him: see comments on 4.20. It is difficult to determine whether Matthew intends the extended meaning of "follow as a disciple." Thus a translation such as "followed" or "went where he was" is possible, but so is "became his followers" or "followed him as disciples."

Them all has **many** as its antecedent, intimating that everyone who followed Jesus was sick and that Jesus healed them all. However, it is possible to understand the text to signify that within the crowds who followed Jesus were a large number of sick people, and that Jesus healed all of them (TEV **"all the sick"**). Most modern English translations seem not to recognize this problem; NEB ("he cured all who were ill") and GECL ("he healed all the sick") are sensitive to the difficulty. "He healed all of them who were sick" will be a clear rendering. This can be a separate sentence, as in TEV, or can be introduced by **and**, as in the text, whichever makes the passage read more smoothly.

12.16	RSV	TEV

and ordered them not to make him known.		**and gave them orders not to tell others about him.**

Some will continue the sentence begun in verse 15, linking the two verses by **and**, as in the text. Others will find it more natural to begin a new sentence here.

Ordered is the same verb translated "rebuked" in 8.26 (TEV "ordered . . . to stop"). See comments there.

The subject of **ordered** is Jesus, perhaps rendered by a pronoun, but the antecedent of **them** is not as clear. It could be those whom he had healed or all the people in the crowds. Most translations make it refer to the former group.

To make him known is translated **"to tell others about him"** by TEV. GECL 1st edition has "to speak openly of him," and NAB "to make public what he had done" (note Brc "to surround him with publicity"). The command not to make Jesus known is a frequent theme in the Gospel of Mark, but not in Matthew. A number of suggestions have been offered as to why Jesus gave this command, but the scholars remain of divided opinion. Fortunately this information is not necessary for the translator to know.

Some have understood **to make him known** to mean "to tell people who he was," but "to tell other people about him" will be better, or "to spread the word everywhere about him." It can be direct speech: "Jesus spoke to them very sternly and said 'Don't go talking about me everywhere.' "

12.17   RSV   TEV

This was to fulfil what was spoken   He did this so as to make come true
by the prophet Isaiah: what God had said through the
                                                    prophet Isaiah:

The quotation in verses 18-21 is taken from Isaiah 42.1-4. In verses 18-20 Matthew uses a text that agrees with neither the Hebrew Old Testament nor the Septuagint. In verse 21, however, he follows precisely the text of the Septuagint. This is the most lengthy selection that Matthew quotes from the Old Testament, and it is quite likely that the form of the text which he uses reflects a translation already familiar to his readers. The text is significant, not only because of its length but because of what it says about Jesus. He is addressed in terms similar to the words used at his baptism, but here is also included much more about the nature of his ministry.

This was to fulfil what was spoken by the prophet Isaiah: see comments on 1.22. **This** has been rendered by TEV as **"He did this."** "He told them this" is also possible.

For the rest of the verse, see comments on 1.22 and 2.17. "He said this to make come true what God had said through the prophet Isaiah" is a possible rendering.

As with other citations, the translation must make it clear that it is God's word that is being given. This can be done either by beginning verse 18 with "God says" or by stating in verse 17 "what God said through the prophet Isaiah," as in the example above.

12.18   RSV   TEV

"Behold, my servant whom I   "Here is my servant, whom I
    have chosen,   have chosen,

| my beloved with whom my soul is well pleased. | the one I love, and with whom I am pleased. |
| I will put my Spirit upon him, and he shall proclaim justice to the Gentiles. | I will send my Spirit upon him, and he will announce my judgment to the nations. |

Behold (TEV, JB, NEB "**Here is**") translates a particle frequently used as an attention getter; see comments on 1.20. "Look" or "Listen now" are other possible ways to translate it. However, TEV's "**Here is my servant**" is also a good model.

My servant may also be translated "my son." It is the same word used in 8.6; see comments there. Generally languages have at least one word for **servant**, that is, for someone who is employed to work for another, and who works willingly, not as a slave. If there is not a good word, then "the one (or, person) who works for me" is acceptable.

Whom I have chosen (so most all English translations) differs from the Hebrew, which has "whom I uphold" (so RSV and most other English translations). A construction like **whom I have chosen** is not possible in a large number of languages. One asks "chosen for what purpose?" This is solved when the phrase is restructured: "Here is the one I have chosen to be my servant" or ". . . to serve me."

Beloved is the same word used in 3.17; here there is no doubt regarding the presence of the possessive pronoun **my**, which stands firm in the Greek text. The Hebrew has "my chosen" (so RSV and most other English translations). TEV expresses **beloved** as "**the one I love**," which is a model many other translations will follow.

With whom my soul is well pleased agrees with the Hebrew and is a literal rendering of the text. Since in Hebrew one's **soul** may represent the person himself, TEV has "**with whom I am well pleased**." Note also NEB ("on whom my favour rests") and NAB ("in whom I delight"). To retain the idiomatic form of the Hebrew (as represented in the Greek) will certainly lead to a misunderstanding in many languages. GECL 1st edition translates the line "I love him and I rejoice over him." There is actually quite a variety of ways that translators have rendered **with whom my soul is well pleased**. Some have renderings like "I am very pleased with him" or "he is very pleasing to me." Many languages seem to have idiomatic expressions such as "he cools (or, sweets) my heart," common in West Africa, or "my heart rests on him."

The statements in the first two lines are in apposition. That is, they refer to the same person, but they are linked only by a comma. In many languages this construction will make readers think there were two different people being referred to. In such cases translators must do something like this: "Here is the one I have chosen to be my servant. He is the one I love and who pleases me so much."

I will put my Spirit upon him: here Matthew agrees with the Hebrew text, except for the verb tense in Hebrew, which is "I have put." TEV's use of the verb "**send**" in place of **put** cannot really be considered a dynamic improvement of the text. GECL 1st edition is helpful: "I will give him my Spirit." Both JB and NAB are good, though at a somewhat higher level of language: "I will endow him with my spirit." Translators should find a way to express **I will put my Spirit upon him** that is natural in the receptor language. Possibilities include "I will fill him with my

Spirit," "I will put my Spirit behind his back" (a common way in West Africa), "I will give him the power of my Spirit," and "I will give him my Spirit."

He shall proclaim justice differs from the Hebrew, which reads "He will bring forth justice." In context the noun **justice** (TEV **"my judgment"**) refers to the judgment which God will bring upon the people: "that I will judge them" (GECL 1st edition). Brc translates "that the time of judgment has come." With the exception of Mft ("religion") and JB ("the true faith"), most English translations have either "judgment" or "justice" as the representation of the Greek noun. In support of its rendering, JB provides a rather extensive footnote, indicating that this interpretation is derived from the meaning of the noun in both the Hebrew Old Testament and the Septuagint. One could accept this interpretation without reservation had Matthew here employed the word "righteousness," which appears so often in the Gospel. But even then, on the basis of verse 21 it still seems quite probable that the judgment is primarily conceived of as a favorable one. For English speakers the noun "judgment" most generally conveys the negative meaning of "punishment," which is not the emphasis in the context. As in the Old Testament, so with Matthew, the real emphasis is upon the saving work of the one whom God will send. Therefore either the more neutral term "justice" or the more specific term "salvation" will come nearer to expressing the intent of the passage.

To **proclaim justice**, then, means to announce the justice or salvation of God. This will be clear in a sentence like "He will announce to the Gentiles that the time of justice has come," "He will tell the Gentiles how they will receive justice from me," or "He will tell the Gentiles that they will receive salvation (or, justice) from my hand."

Gentiles (TEV **"nations"**) is a reference to the non-Jewish peoples of the world. See comments on 4.15. It can be translated as "people everywhere" or "all nations."

12.19	RSV	TEV
	He will not wrangle or cry aloud, nor will any one hear his voice in the streets;	He will not argue or shout, or make loud speeches in the streets.

He will not wrangle or cry aloud (TEV **"He will not argue or shout"**) is slightly different from the Hebrew text, which is "He will not shout or raise his voice." This statement about the Messiah fits well in Matthew's context. Jesus has been verbally attacked by the Pharisees, and they have even decided to kill him, but he withdraws and refuses to argue with them or shout about what he is doing.

Wrangle (also Mft and AT) occurs only here in the New Testament. It is possible, as some commentators suggest, that the word may be intended as a legal technical term. The meaning would then be "defend one's self" or "present one's own case." Translations, however, do not seem to reflect this interpretation. NJB has "brawl," NEB "strive," TEV **argue.** Brc combines the two verbs, "He will not be a loud-mouthed man of strife." Translators who understand **wrangle** as TEV has will use words like "dispute," or "quarrel," or "disagree violently with people." Note that in many languages one must argue with someone, "with people" in a context like this.

The word translated **cry aloud** may mean either "cry out for help" or "cry out with excitement." Or it may assume a more neutral function, as with "**shout**" in English (so TEV, JB, Mft, NEB). GECL 1st edition is similar to TEV, but the translators evidently intend a play on words: *streiten oder schreien*. **Cry aloud** does not refer to just one event but rather to habitual action, as in "He won't go about making a lot of noise," "He won't always be shouting loudly," or "He won't be a person who shouts a lot."

Nor will any one hear his voice appears in a quite different form in TEV, though both structures have the same two kernel sentences: "he speaks" and "someone hears." Most English translations maintain the form of the Greek text, though NEB and NAB shift to the passive "nor will his voice be heard . . . ." GECL renders "he will not make loud speeches."

Translators can follow either model for **hear his voice**, the one with the emphasis on other people hearing, or the other with the emphasis on him speaking. The former will result in translations such as "people won't be hearing him on every street corner" or "the public won't be hearing him out in the streets." The latter will result in "he won't be out in the streets making speeches" or "he won't be speaking loudly and publicly out in the towns all the time."

In the streets identifies the place of speaking as being public rather than private. Many languages can express this idiomatically. Note that **in the streets** has been rendered in these examples as "on every street corner" and "in the towns," as well as literally.

12.20	RSV	TEV
	he will not break a bruised reed or quench a smoldering wick, till he brings justice to victory;	He will not break off a bent reed, nor put out a flickering lamp. He will persist until he causes justice to triumph,

He will not break a bruised reed or quench a smoldering wick affirms that the Messiah will be gentle and kind to those who are helpless and weak. If it is not possible to retain either of the metaphors, **He will not break a bruised reed** may be translated as "he will be gentle to those who are weak." **A bruised reed** is a metaphor that makes use of a weak and frail object, and the meaning is that the Messiah will not deal harshly with those who are weak. Most scholars interpret the metaphor in this way, and it accords with the figure of speech which follows.

Or quench a smoldering wick is a second metaphor. If it is not possible to retain the metaphor, it may be rendered as "and kind to those who are helpless." Here the **smoldering wick** is acknowledged by all to reflect the symbolism of a flickering lamp; in fact, the flame is out and the glowing wick merely gives off smoke. The Messiah is so gentle and kind that he will not even put out a helpless, flickering lamp. Therefore in cultures where these aspects of the language may be misunderstood or noneffective, the figures may be removed and the parallelism done away with, since the two figures of speech each convey essentially the same meaning.

There are essentially three main ways translators can deal with **he will not break a bruised reed or quench a smoldering wick**. The first is to retain the form, that is, to more or less translate literally. **Break** may be "break off," **bruised** may be "bent," and **quench** may be "put out" or "extinguish." But otherwise the meaning of the metaphors is not given.

A second way is to retain both the form and meaning by using a simile. Examples include "He would no sooner break a bent reed or put out a flickering candle than he would harm people who are weak" and "Just as he wouldn't break a bent reed or snuff a flickering wick, he would not deal harshly with those who are frail and weak."

The third manner is to drop the figurative language altogether, just as TEV has done. Examples are "He will not treat harshly those who are weak, nor do any harm to those who are not strong" and "He will always treat in a gentle way the weak and frail so as not to harm them."

Till he brings forth justice to victory differs considerably from the Hebrew text of Isaiah, which RSV translates as "he will faithfully bring forth justice." JB has for the Matthew passage "till he has led the truth to victory," but it is difficult to see how the translators arrive at this. Mft is consistent with what he did in verse 18: "till he carries religion to victory." Taking this rendering of Mft as a model for **brings justice to victory**, translators can say "until he causes justice to triumph" or "until he causes my salvation to be victorious." However, this does not make clear enough what it means for justice to have **victory**. Therefore some have said "until he causes people to accept my justice" or "to acknowledge the salvation I offer."

Till gives the meaning that the servant will persist in being gentle with people until justice is victorious. In may be enough to say "until," but some have said "That's how he will be until . . . ."

12.21   RSV   TEV

> **and in his name will the Gen-**   **and on him all peoples will**
> **tiles hope."**   **put their hope."**

And in his name will the Gentiles hope has no kinship whatsoever to the Hebrew text of Isaiah 42.4b: "and the coastlands wait for his law." Except for the omission of a preposition, Matthew agrees word for word with the Septuagint.

In his name here means either "**on him**" (TEV) or "in him" (NEB), since in such a context **name** clearly stands for the person.

Gentiles is best taken in the sense of "the nations" (NJB, NEB) or "**all peoples**" (TEV). GECL translates the entire verse: "All people will place their hope in him."

In modern English, **hope** means to wait for and want something, but to not completely sure that it will happen. But in the Bible the idea is usually that of placing one's trust in and of having confidence in. Thus a good translation of this verse is "and all people (or, all nations) will put their trust in him" or ". . . will place their confidence in him." If the question "confidence to do what?" must be answered, translators can say "trust in him for their salvation," "all nations will look for their salvation to come from him," or "and it will be in him that all people will trust for their salvation."

12.22-32

RSV	TEV
	Jesus and Beelzebul

22 Then a blind and dumb demoniac was brought to him, and he healed him, so that the dumb man spoke and saw. 23 And all the people were amazed, and said, "Can this be the Son of David?" 24 But when the Pharisees heard it they said, "It is only by Beelzebul, the prince of demons, that this man casts out demons." 25 Knowing their thoughts, he said to them, "Every kingdom divided against itself is laid waste, and no city or house divided against itself will stand; 26 and if Satan casts out Satan, he is divided against himself; how then will his kingdom stand? 27 And if I cast out demons by Beelzebul, by whom do your sons cast them out? Therefore they shall be your judges. 28 But if it is by the Spirit of God that I cast out demons, then the kingdom of God has come upon you. 29 Or how can one enter a strong man's house and plunder his goods, unless he first binds the strong man? Then indeed he may plunder his house. 30 He who is not with me is against me, and he who does not gather with me scatters. 31 Therefore I tell you, every sin and blasphemy will be forgiven men, but the blasphemy against the Spirit will not be forgiven. 32 And whoever says a word against the Son of man will be forgiven; but whoever speaks against the Holy Spirit will not be forgiven, either in this age or in the age to come.

22 Then some people brought to Jesus a man who was blind and could not talk because he had a demon. Jesus healed the man, so that he was able to talk and see. 23 The crowds were all amazed at what Jesus had done. "Could he be the Son of David?" they asked.

24 When the Pharisees heard this, they replied, "He drives out demons only because their ruler Beelzebul gives him power to do so."

25 Jesus knew what they were thinking, and so he said to them, "Any country that divides itself into groups which fight each other will not last very long. And any town or family which divides itself into groups which fight each other will fall apart. 26 So if one group is fighting another in Satan's kingdom, this means that it is already divided into groups and will soon fall apart! 27 You say that I drive out demons because Beelzebul gives me the power to do so. Well, then, who gives your followers the power to drive them out? What your own followers do proves that you are wrong! 28 No, it is not Beelzebul, but God's Spirit, who gives me the power to drive out demons, which proves that the Kingdom of God has already come upon you.

29 "No one can break into a strong man's house and take away his belongings unless he first ties up the strong man; then he can plunder his house.

30 "Anyone who is not for me is really against me; anyone who does not help me gather is really scattering. 31 For this reason I tell you: people can be forgiven any sin and any evil thing they say;[j] but whoever says evil things against the Holy Spirit will not be forgiven. 32 Anyone who says something against the Son of Man can be forgiven; but whoever says something against the Holy Spirit will not be forgiven—now or ever.

j evil thing they say; *or* evil thing they say against God.

SECTION HEADING: "**Jesus and Beelzebul**." "**Beelzebul**" is discussed at 10.25. If the heading needs to be expressed as a short sentence, then one such as

"People say Jesus is Beelzebul" or "People say Jesus receives power from Beelzebul" will serve.

In Matthew and Luke 11.14-16, Jesus' healing of a man who could not talk is the basis for the Pharisees' accusation against Jesus: "It is only by Beelzebul, the prince of demons, that this man casts out demons" (verse 24). Mark places the accusation in a different context, and it is made by "the scribes who came down from Jerusalem" (Mark 3.22). The first part of the narrative (verses 22-24) is similar to 9.32-34, except that the man of this chapter is not only unable to talk, but he is blind as well.

12.22   RSV   TEV

Then a blind and dumb demoni-   Then some people brought to
ac was brought to him, and he   Jesus a man who was blind and
healed him, so that the dumb man   could not talk because he had a
spoke and saw.   demon. Jesus healed the man, so
                                       that he was able to talk and see.

Then points back to verse 15. Translators can also say "After that."

A blind and dumb demoniac is translated "**a man who was blind and could not talk because he had a demon**" by TEV. The causal relation is clearly indicated in the Greek sentence structure, and it should be made equally clear in translation. Demon possession is not a third illness, to be distinguished from the other two; it is in fact the cause of the man's blindness and of his inability to speak. As in 9.32, TEV avoids the use of **dumb**, because in American English it often means "stupid."

The Greek participle translated **demoniac** was first used in 4.24; see also 8.16,28,33; 9.32; 15.22. The idea may be expressed in a number of ways. NEB has "a man who was possessed," and NAB renders "A possessed man." GECL translates "an evil spirit ruled him."

TEV provides an excellent model for **a blind and dumb demoniac**: "**a man who was blind and dumb because he had a demon**." The phrase can also be restructured, as in "a man who had an evil spirit (in him) that made him so he was blind and could not speak."

Was brought to him, a passive formation in Greek, is translated "**some people brought**" by TEV. Several other translations also shift to the active: "they brought to him" (NJB) and "they brought him" (NEB). **Him**, of course, is Jesus.

And he healed him: the healing of the man is narrated briefly and without detail. TEV "**Jesus healed the man**." Matthew's primary concern is not with the miracle but with the accusation which the Pharisees level against Jesus (verse 24).

So that the dumb man spoke and saw sounds inconsistent to English speakers. If the man is **dumb** (unable to talk), how could he speak? "**So that he was able to talk and see**" of TEV resolves the difficulty. GECL is even better ("Jesus healed him, and he was able to speak and hear again"). NEB resolves the problem in yet another way: "Jesus cured him, restoring both speech and sight." A slightly different way avoids "again": "Jesus healed him, and he was thus able to speak and see."

12.23   RSV   TEV

And all the people were amazed, and   The crowds were all amazed at what
said, "Can this be the Son of Da-   Jesus had done. "Could he be the
vid?"   Son of David?" they asked.

All the people (so also NJB) is literally "all the crowds." Both TEV ("**The crowds**") and NEB ("The bystanders") introduce the component of "all" in conjunction with the verb phrase "were all amazed."

This is the only place where the verb **amazed** is found in Matthew's Gospel (literally "were beside themselves"). It occurs quite frequently in Luke's writings: three times in the Gospel and eight times in Acts. Elsewhere in the New Testament it is used once in 2 Corinthians and four times in Mark. Some languages may require the express mention of an object following the verb **amazed**: "**at what Jesus had done**" (TEV). GECL accomplishes the same goal through a German idiomatic expression: "Therefore the crowds fell into amazement." It is possible to combine what was done in TEV and GECL: "As a result of what Jesus had done, the crowds became amazed . . . ."

The text says that people **said**. "Asked themselves" or even "asked each other" may be better here.

Can this be the Son of David? translates a question form which normally would expect a negative reply. But it may also be used on occasion to indicate no more than an expression of uncertainty: "Is he perhaps . . . ?" (GECL). "Can it be that . . . ?" or "Is it possible he is . . . ?" are other ways to render this.

Son of David was a popular title for the promised Savior King (see comments on 1.1; 9.27); his appearance would be a sign that the long-awaited salvation had at last arrived. As in 1.1, this may be translated "the descendant of (King) David." However, if possible it is good to indicate it is a title: "The one who is called Descendant of David." Another way to express it is "The Descendant of David we look for."

12.24   RSV   TEV

But when the Pharisees heard it they   When the Pharisees heard this,
said, "It is only by Beelzebul, the   they replied, "He drives out demons
prince of demons, that this man   only because their ruler Beelzebul
casts out demons."   gives him power to do so."

The Pharisees are frequently mentioned as the arch opponents of Jesus. According to this verse they continue in that role, and their accusation made here is similar to that of 9.34. In fact, the charge which they now make against Jesus is practically identical with that of 9.34, with the exception that here **the prince of demons** is mentioned by name. For further comments on **Pharisees**, see 3.7.

There can be uncertainty as to what the **it** that the Pharisees heard refers to. Most translators have it refer back to the healing of the man in verse 22. A sentence like "But when the Pharisees heard about Jesus healing the man who had the evil spirit" would make this very explicit. On the other hand, translators who thought **it** refers to people wondering whether perhaps Jesus was the promised Son of David could have ". . . heard what the people were saying." There is no reason why the translation could not refer to either or both.

For **prince of demons** see comments on 9.34; **Beelzebul** is discussed at 10.25. GECL deletes the proper name: "He can drive out evil spirits only because the chief of all evil spirits gives him the power to do it!"

For **casts out demons**, see comments on 7.22 and 8.16, and for **demons**, see comments on 4.1.

As GECL shows, **by Beelzebul** means that Beelzebul gives him power to throw out evil spirits. A slightly different rendering of the sentence is "It is only because Beelzebul, who is the chief of evil spirits, gives him power that this man can throw evil spirits out of people."

12.25   RSV   TEV

Knowing their thoughts, he said to them, "Every kingdom divided against itself is laid waste, and no city or house divided against itself will stand;	Jesus knew what they were thinking, and so he said to them, "Any country that divides itself into groups which fight each other will not last very long. And any town or family which divides itself into groups which fight each other will fall apart.

Knowing (TEV "**Jesus knew**") translates a participle in which Jesus is not mentioned by name. A number of other translations also shift to a finite verb; both Mft and Brc mention Jesus by name as well.

The Greek noun phrase **their thoughts** is translated "**what they were thinking**" by AT, TEV, and Brc. NJB and NEB render "what was in their minds." The Greek noun used for **thoughts** appears in the New Testament only four times; see comments at 9.4.

Every kingdom (so also NJB, NEB, Brc) is phrased more idiomatically by the use of "any" in several translations (so Mft, AT, Phps); NAB has the indefinite article "a." Another indefinite structure is "If a kingdom . . . ." TEV shifts away from he use of **kingdom** to "**any country**." Translators can certainly do the same if that is more meaningful for their readers.

Divided against itself gives the image of anarchy or civil war. Therefore GECL has "whose leaders are against one another," and NAB has "torn by strife." TEV is considerably longer than the Greek text: "**that divides itself into groups that fight against each other**."

Is laid waste (TEV "**will not last very long**") translates a verb which means "become like a desert." Elsewhere in the New Testament it occurs only in Luke 11.17; Revelation 17.16; 18.17,19. Brc retains the original imagery, "is on the way to being laid waste," and a number of translations are similar to NJB, "is heading for ruin" (see NEB, Mft). NAB translates "is headed for its downfall," and Phps has "is bound to collapse." Another way is "will be destroyed."

Translations will vary between **city** (so also Brc) and **"town"** (NJB, TEV, NAB); it is not likely that either the geographical spread or the number of inhabitants would in any way compare with the modern concept of a city.

House (TEV **"family"**) would include not only the members of the immediate or extended family, but servants and slaves of the family as well. For this reason a number of translations prefer "household" (NJB, NAB, NEB, Brc). For most American speakers the first meaning of **house** is a physical structure in which people live.

No city . . . will stand may also be stated in English as "a city (or, town) . . . will not stand" (GECL 1st edition), which in turn is equivalent to TEV's **"any town . . . will fall apart."** Brc translates "No city . . . can survive." The idea of **will stand** is seen in Brc, but other ways to render it are "will remain" or "will continue to exist." If the sentence begins with a positive "any town and family," then the conclusion will be negative, as in "will not survive," "will be ruined," or "will be destroyed."

12.26	RSV	TEV
	and if Satan casts out Satan, he is divided against himself; how then will his kingdom stand?	So if one group is fighting another in Satan's kingdom, this means that it is already divided into groups and will soon fall apart!

In this verse Jesus makes explicit application of the parables of the divided country and the divided family of verse 25. This can be made explicit in the translation by beginning the verse "In the same way" or "Thus it is that if Satan . . . ."

In the clause **if Satan casts out Satan**, it is clear that the name of the leader of the group, **Satan**, is used to represent either one of Satan's demons or a group of Satan's demons. This is the basis for TEV ("**So if one group is fighting another in Satan's kingdom**") and GECL 1st edition ("If one demon is casting out the other, then Satan would be fighting against himself"). It is absolutely necessary that the readers be made to understand that Satan of this verse is the same person as Beelzebul of verses 24 and 27. It may be good to have a footnote saying that Satan and Beelzebul are two names for the same person. Another way to help readers make the identification is to expand the GECL 1st edition model: "If one evil spirit of Satan's kingdom is casting out another, then Satan would be fighting against himself." For further comments on **Satan**, see 4.1,10.

How then will his kingdom stand? is a rhetorical question in Greek and is translated by TEV **"this means that it is already divided into groups and will soon fall apart!"** An adequate and accurate translation of this verse may require much restructuring: "If what you say about me is true, then this shows that Satan's kingdom is already divided into groups. One group is fighting against another, and so his kingdom will soon fall apart." Or, patterned after GECL 1st edition, "You say that I am using Satan's power to cast out demons. This means that Satan is fighting against himself, and so his kingdom will not last much longer." A variation is "If one member of Satan's kingdom is casting out another, which is what you say is happening when I cast out evil spirits, then Satan is fighting against himself, so his kingdom will soon be destroyed."

12.27	RSV	TEV

RSV	TEV
And if I cast out demons by Beelzebul, by whom do your sons cast them out? Therefore they shall be your judges.	You say that I drive out demons because Beelzebul gives me the power to do so. Well, then, who gives your followers the power to drive them out? What your own followers do proves that you are wrong!

Verses 27-28, in which Jesus turns the Pharisees' argument against themselves, do not have a parallel in Mark, though one is present in Luke 11.19-20. The Pharisees claim that Jesus' work of casting out demons is done in the power of Satan. But the Pharisees' own followers also cast out demons, and so Jesus asks where their power to do this comes from. This is a question which they cannot answer without condemning themselves, and it simultaneously proves that they are wrong in their conclusions about the source of Jesus' power.

And if introduces a clause in Greek which assumes that the untrue statement, **I cast out demons by Beelzebul**, is a true statement. But the clause also includes in its scope the accusation made by the Pharisees in verse 24. One can then appropriately translate "If it is true, as you say, that I cast out demons by Beelzebul." Or, placed in statement form, "**You say that I drive out demons because Beelzebul gives me the power to do so**" (TEV).

By Beelzebul (TEV "**because Beelzebul gives me the power to do so**") is phrased in a dynamic way in a number of translations: "by Beelzebub's aid" (AT), "with Beelzebul's help" (NAB), and "by the help of Beelzebul" (Brc). Phps ("I am an ally of Beelzebub") and GECL ("because I am in league with Satan") are also good examples of what may be done.

By whom is preceded by a transitional in TEV ("**Well, then**") and GECL ("Then"), though many other translations into major modern languages do not employ such a device. This is a stylistic matter which will have to be evaluated in each language situation. TEV restructures the question beginning **by whom** to "**who gives your followers the power?**" This will be easier to follow in most languages.

Your sons (so also Mft, AT) is a Semitism (NJB footnote) which one commentator defines as here having the meaning of "membership in a group." TOB has "your disciples," Brc "your own disciples," and TEV "**your followers**." Certainly to translate **sons** literally would give the wrong meaning to Jesus' words.

Therefore (literally "Because of this") **they shall be your judges** is represented in TEV as "**What your own followers do proves that you are wrong!**" and in GECL as "Your own followers prove that you are in the wrong." The time reference is the present and immediate future, not the final judgment. Accordingly **they shall be your judges** is translated "Let them be the ones to judge you" (NAB), "If this is your argument, they themselves will refute you" (NEB), and "Ask them what they think of this argument of yours" (Brc). The text does not necessarily imply verbal refutation; the implication is rather that the miraculous deeds performed by the followers of the Pharisees are sufficient evidence in themselves to prove that the Pharisees' argument is erroneous. In most languages a simple sentence such as the one in TEV will be best here; for example, "Their actions demonstrate how wrong your argument is" or "What they are doing proves that your accusations cannot be right."

12.28	RSV	TEV
	But if it is by the Spirit of God that I cast out demons, then the kingdom of God has come upon you.	No, it is not Beelzebul, but God's Spirit, who gives me the power to drive out demons, which proves that the Kingdom of God has already come upon you.

In the Lukan parallel to this verse (11.20), the wording is the same except for his use of "God's finger" in place of Matthew's "God's Spirit." However, the two phrases mean the same thing; in the words of one scholar, "they refer to the mighty power of God which inspires Jesus in his exorcisms." One commentator classifies this verse as one of the most amazing in the Gospel, since it attests to Jesus as "the Kingdom of God in person."

As a quick reading of RSV and TEV will immediately reveal, TEV has done much restructuring in this verse. For example, TEV opens the verse with a strong negative "**No**," to make explicit from the outset that the words of Jesus which follow are a denial of the claims made by the Pharisees in verse 27. Moreover, since **But if it is** . . . introduces a statement in Greek which is assumed by the speaker to be true, TEV represents the entire first clause of the Greek text by "**No, it is not Beelzebul, but God's Spirit, who gives me the power to drive out demons.**"

Since this sentence is making an assertion, then another way to begin it is "But in fact it is God's Spirit who gives me the power to drive out demons." But this phrase is followed by one of result or conclusion, and so another way to restructure it is "Since in fact it is God's Spirit . . . then (it is clear) the kingdom . . . ."

It is by the Spirit of God that I is reformulated in TEV so that **the Spirit of God** becomes the subject and **I** takes on the role of an indirect object: "**God's Spirit, who gives me the power.**" This is legitimate, since **by the Spirit of God** means "by the help of the Spirit of God" (Brc, GECL) or "by the aid of God's Spirit (AT). However, in many languages it will be difficult to employ two agents for the same action, as in this instance: "I do this. But God's Spirit gives me the power to do it." Therefore one may translate "God's Spirit is doing this. But he is doing it through me."

Then translates a Greek particle which appears in TEV as "**which proves that.**" The force of the particle is to draw a conclusion on the basis of something previously stated. JB translates "then know that," NEB has "then be sure," and GECL renders "so you ought to be able to see that." Following this interpretation of **then**, and depending on how the whole sentence is being structured, it may be expressed as "then it is clear" or "then we can see that." Translators can also begin a new sentence with "Thus we can see that . . . ."

For a discussion of the **kingdom of God**, see 3.2.

The verb translated **has come** is used seven times in the New Testament (see Luke 11.20; Rom 9.31; 2 Cor 10.14; Phil 3.16; 1 Thes 2.16; 4.15). Depending upon the context, the meaning may be either "precede, arrive before" (see 1 Thes 2.16) or "attain, achieve." For the present passage a number of translations have "overtaken" (JB, NAB); TEV and NEB have **"has already come."** Brc translates "has reached you here and now." GECL 1st edition takes seriously the meaning of **kingdom of God** and so translates "that God has established his rule among you." Many translators have done something similar to GECL: "that God's rule has been established here among you" or "that God has begun his rule here among you."

12.29   RSV   TEV

Or how can one enter a strong   "No one can break into a
man's house and plunder his goods,   strong man's house and take away
unless he first binds the strong   his belongings unless he first ties up
man? Then indeed he may plunder   the strong man; then he can plunder
his house.   his house.

The theme of verse 28 is continued, though with a different figure of speech. Since it is foolish to suggest that Satan could have broken into his own house and tied himself up, the only logical conclusion is that someone stronger than Satan is present.

Or serves as a transitional between this and the preceding verse. NJB and NEB have "Or again," and Brc "To put it another way." TEV drops the transitional from explicit mention, depending upon the context to do the job.

Or how can . . . ? translates a rhetorical question which assumes the answer "He cannot" or "It is impossible." TEV moves away from the form of a rhetorical question to a statement: **"No one can break into . . . ."** GECL also chooses a statement, though in a form different from that of TEV: "Whoever would break in . . . must first . . . ." This sentence can also begin "It is impossible for anyone . . . ." Other translators have retained the rhetorical question, **Or how can . . . ?** but supplied an answer, "He can't" or "It can't be done, of course."

Enter (so also Mft) may be more dynamically rendered as **"break into"** (TEV, GECL, NEB), since the context demands either force or secrecy as the means of entry. NJB translates "make his way into"; both AT and Phps have "get into."

Strong man should probably be translated literally. It does not mean "important" or anything of that sort here, but refers to physical strength.

Plunder (TEV **"take away"**) does specifically imply the use of force. For example, in Matthew 13.19 it may be rendered either "snatch away" or "carry off," and in John 6.15 it may be translated "seize." Compare also its use in Acts 23.10 (RSV "take . . . by force"). It is rendered as "steal" in many languages.

Goods (so also NEB) is translated **"belongings"** by TEV and "property" by several others (NJB, NAB, AT). The Greek noun may be used in the most general sense, indicating "thing" or "object," though the context clearly indicates objects that belong to a person and that may be removed.

· **Binds** has been rendered "**ties up**" by TEV, which is exactly what the word means. Some languages need to specify an instrument such as "with a rope."

Then indeed may be "Only after he did that could he . . . ."

Plunder is an intensive form of the verb translated "plunder" earlier in the verse; "thoroughly plunder." Most English translations evidently prefer **plunder**, but NEB has "ransacking," and JB "burgle." One may also translate "then he can take away everything the (strong) man owns."

It is always important to note that **he** refers to the burglar, and **his house** is the house of the strong man.

12.30	RSV	TEV

He who is not with me is against me, and he who does not gather with me scatters.	"Anyone who is not for me is really against me; anyone who does not help me gather is really scattering.

It is not easy to determine the meaning of this verse in the context in which it appears, though the most likely meaning is that one cannot be neutral with regard to Jesus. This saying is found in the Lukan parallel (11.23) but not in Mark. On the other hand, a counterpart to this saying is found in Mark 9.40: "For whoever is not against us is for us."

He who is a masculine form in Greek; for many languages an indefinite form such as "**Anyone who**" (TEV, AT) will function more naturally.

With me (so also NEB) is translated "**for me**" by TEV; this avoids the possibility of misunderstanding the phrase to mean "in company with me." The meaning is "on my side" (Phps); Brc translates "If a man is not my ally." **With me** has also been translated "supports me" or "is in favor of what I am doing."

Is against me (TEV "**is really against me**") explains that there are two sides and only two sides: those who are for Jesus and those who are opposed to him. TEV introduces the intensifier "**really**" for the purpose of drawing out the full force of Jesus' affirmation. In place of **against me** Brc translates "my enemy." this is a satisfactory solution, assuming that "enemy" is understood to mean "one who opposes Jesus" without further implying "one whom Jesus opposes." In many cultures the word for "enemy" may imply mutual hostility; here, however, the hostility is limited to that of the person who opposes Jesus, and it is not reciprocal. To avoid these possible problems with "enemy" as a translation of **is against me**, many translators have "is opposed to me" or "opposes me."

Gather with me: TEV and GECL have "**help me gather**," transforming the noun phrase **with me** into a verb structure. **Gather with me** has sometimes been misunderstood to mean to meet with Jesus. The idea is more to gather people to Jesus or to God, much as one gathers in crops at harvest time. Thus it can be rendered "help me gather people (to me)" or "working with me to bring people to God." Brc makes it more general with "if a man is not helping my work."

Scatter: other than at the parallel in Luke 11.23, the verb occurs only three other times in the New Testament. It is used twice in the Gospel of John: in 10.12 (with "sheep" as the object) and in 16.32 (with "disciples" the subject of the passive verb). On the other hand, in 2 Corinthians 9.9 (with God as the subject and no expressed object) the force of the verb is positive, and TEV renders "gives generously." In the present context the focus is definitely negative, in contrast to the verb "gather." If the receptor language necessitates an object for the two verbs, one may render ". . . gather people (for God) . . . scatter (or, drive) people (away from God)."

Brc also uses a general expression to translate **scatters**: "is undoing it (my work)." But if translators have retained **gather** in some form, then "drive away" or "causes people to go away from God" will be better.

12.31   RSV   TEV

Therefore I tell you, every sin and   For this reason I tell you: people can
blasphemy will be forgiven men, but   be forgiven any sin and any evil
the blasphemy against the Spirit will   thing they say;^j but whoever says
not be forgiven.   evil things against the Holy Spirit will
                                           not be forgiven.

                                           ^jevil thing they say *or* evil thing they say
                                           against God.

Therefore (literally "Because of this," see verse 27) **I tell you** is translated "And so I tell you this" by NEB and "And so I tell you" by NJB. Normally the phrase implies a conclusion based upon something previously said. However, the context is less than clear regarding what Jesus refers to by "this." One of the problems is the presence of verse 30, which apparently disrupts the connection between verse 31 and the Beelzebul controversy of verses 24-29. NEB gives some help to the reader by making verse 30 a separate paragraph. Some have changed the meaning slightly with a phrase such as "In conclusion I tell you."

Every sin and blasphemy: some languages will expect the nouns **sin** and **blasphemy** to be reformulated as verbs or verb phrases. TEV renders **blasphemy** as a noun phrase ("any evil thing they say"), though retaining the noun **sin**. In the Septuagint the noun **blasphemy** is used primarily of the evil things that are said against God, and so TEV gives the alternative restructuring: "evil things they say against God." Even here, this is perhaps the more satisfactory interpretation; Brc and GECL 1st edition, for example, have "insult to God" as a rendering of the noun. The only other major English translations that avoid the technical term **blasphemy** are NEB ("slander") and AT ("abusive speech"). The word occurs also in 15.19; 26.65.

For more on **blasphemy**, see 9.3. Here it can be "insulting God," "spoiling God's name," "saying evil about God," or "speaking against God."

Sin can be "evil" or "evil things," or, since it contrasts with **blasphemy**, "wrong things against others." The text says **every sin and blasphemy**. Depending on the type of sentence constructed, it may be rendered "all the evil things and every insult of God" or "any of the evil things and any of the things they say against God."

Will be forgiven men: two observations are important: **men** is here equivalent to people in general, and the assumed agent of the passive **will be forgiven** is God. The following translation may then result: "God will forgive the evil things that people do to one another, and he will even forgive the evil things that they say against him . . . ." **Will be forgiven** is often rendered "**can be forgiven**" (so TEV) because the forgiveness is not automatic. It means God will forgive if the conditions are met.

But the blasphemy against the Spirit is literally "but the blasphemy of the Spirit." However, it is evident that "of" here means **against**. As the use of the capitalized **Spirit** indicates, RSV understands the reference to be to the "**Holy Spirit**" (TEV) or "Spirit of God."

Blasphemy in this second occurrence in the verse should be translated as the first time, except it now refers to speaking evil about or insulting God's Spirit.

For **Spirit** see 1.18, where "Holy Spirit" is discussed. Here "God's Spirit" will probably be best.

Will not be forgiven may need to be transformed into an active construction: "God will not forgive." The second half of this verse may then be translated "but God will not forgive those people who say evil things about the Holy Spirit" or "but God will not forgive you when you say evil things against the Holy Spirit."

What Jesus meant by **the blasphemy against the Spirit** must be decided upon the basis of the context alone. Immediately before making this pronouncement Jesus had healed a man who was born blind and who could not talk. He had not done this on his own power. The healing was the work of God's Spirit, a conclusion which should have been obvious (and probably was obvious) to the Pharisees. However, they refused to believe and willfully ascribed this work of God's Spirit to Satan. The reason that they could not be forgiven was because they were unwilling to open their eyes to the truth and acknowledge the presence of God active in the ministry of Jesus.

12.32

RSV	TEV
And whoever says a word against the Son of man will be forgiven; but whoever speaks against the Holy Spirit will not be forgiven, either in this age or in the age to come.	Anyone who says something against the Son of Man can be forgiven; but whoever says something against the Holy Spirit will not be forgiven—now or ever.

Verse 32 expands and intensifies the saying of Jesus in verse 31.

Word is used in the sense of something said: "**Anyone who says something against**" (TEV).

For a discussion of **Son of man**, see 8.20. Some translators will have felt that in 8.20 they had to use the first person, but that would not be true here.

For **will be forgiven**, see comments at verse 31. **Will be forgiven**, as in verse 31, could give the impression that forgiveness in this situation is automatic. Therefore TEV and GECL employ "**can be forgiven**," which implies possibility but not necessity. The verse may need to be translated "God will forgive people who say evil things against the Son of Man, but he will not forgive those people who say evil things against the Holy Spirit. He will not forgive them now or ever." Here again God's unwillingness to forgive has its basis in the refusal of repentance on the part of the people who speak evil things against God's Spirit. The true nature and person of the Son of Man was "hidden," but the work of God's Spirit was "open" and therefore evident to all. It was genuinely possible, therefore, for the Pharisees to misunderstand who Jesus (**the Son of man**) was, but there were no legitimate grounds for them to deny the work of God's Spirit manifest in his healing ministry.

For comments on **Holy Spirit**, see verse 31 and also 1.18.

Speaks against is clear enough, but it can easily be rendered by the term used for "blasphemy" in verse 31.

Either in this age or in the age to come: the Jewish teachers of Jesus' day often spoke of the two ages: the first age is the present, evil age, while the second age is the future, glorious age of salvation. Thus **in this age or in the age to come** is an inclusive statement, and so the basis for TEV's **"now or ever."** NJB has "either in this world or in the next," while both Brc and Phps have "in this world or in the world to come." Some translators have attempted to reflect the Jewish understanding of **either in this age or in the age to come** by saying "either in this time we live in or in the time to come when God will reign gloriously," or "not now nor in the future when God's reign is established." This may be unnecessarily long and awkward, however. "Not now or ever" conveys the finality of Jesus' words just as well.

12.33-37

RSV	TEV
	A Tree and Its Fruit
33 "Either make the tree good, and its fruit good; or make the tree bad, and its fruit bad; for the tree is known by its fruit. 34 You brood of vipers! how can you speak good, when you are evil? For out of the abundance of the heart the mouth speaks. 35 The good man out of his good treasure brings forth good, and the evil man out of his evil treasure brings forth evil. 36 I tell you, on the day of judgment men will render account for every careless word they utter; 37 for by your words you will be justified, and by your words you will be condemned."	33 "To have good fruit you must have a healthy tree; if you have a poor tree, you will have bad fruit. A tree is known by the kind of fruit it bears. 34 You snakes—how can you say good things when you are evil? For the mouth speaks what the heart is full of. 35 A good person brings good things out of his treasure of good things; a bad person brings bad things out of his treasure of bad things. 36 "You can be sure that on the Judgment Day everyone will have to give account of every useless word he has ever spoken. 37 Your words will be used to judge you—to declare you either innocent or guilty."

SECTION HEADING: **"A Tree and Its Fruit."** This section heading is the same as the one at 7.15 and can be translated the same way except by those translators who mentioned "false prophets" there. This passage does not speak of these, so one of the other renderings will be more appropriate.

This section illustrates that the Pharisees' attack on Jesus reveals their true nature. Just as the fruit that grows on a tree reveals what kind of tree it is, so the Pharisees' remarks about Jesus reveal what they are really like. A parallel to verses 33-37 is found in Luke 6.43-45 (see also Matt 7.16-20), but both the context and the application differ from that of the present passage.

12.33   RSV   TEV

"Either make the tree good, and   "To have good fruit you must
its fruit good; or make the tree bad,   have a healthy tree; if you have a
and its fruit bad; for the tree is   poor tree, you will have bad fruit. A
known by its fruit.   tree is known by the kind of fruit it
                                         bears.

Either make . . . and . . . or make . . . and: NJB omits **Either**; some versions
use a hypothetical statement, "If . . ."; one commentator suggests "Suppose the tree
is good . . ."; TEV restructures as "**To have . . . you must have . . . if you have . . .
you will have.**"

Brc links verse 33 with the previous section, where Jesus accused the Pharisees
of not acknowledging that God's Spirit is in work in him. Thus he tells the Pharisees
that they cannot have it both ways; either the tree and the fruit are bad or they are
both good, because the fruits from a tree reveal what kind of a tree it is. By
implication, therefore, if he, Jesus, is doing good, then his source of power, God's
Spirit, must be good, too. To convey this, Brc inserts "You must make up your
minds" at the end of verse 32, and goes on with a hypothetical statement of the type
"If . . . then . . . ."

Many translators will not feel comfortable with this type of addition, but they
can begin this verse by saying "Either you must decide that the tree is good, and then
so will the fruit be good, or that the tree is bad, and then so will its fruit be bad.
Because you can only know how the tree is by the fruit it bears."

Tree . . . fruit . . . tree . . . fruit: in the first part of the verse TEV inverts the
order to "**fruit . . . tree**," thus destroying the parallelism and making a more
complicated structure. It is possible to retain the order of TEV's initial statement and
to make the second parallel to it, which will result in a less complex construction:
"To have good fruit you must have a healthy tree; you will have bad fruit if you have
a poor tree."

The adjective **good** is the same one used to modify "fruit" in 7.17; a different
one is used there to modify "trees," though it is obvious that there is no difference
in meaning in the two passages. The adjective **bad** is the same one used of the
"tree" in 7.17 but not of the "fruit"; but here again it has the same meaning as in
7.17, namely, "decayed, rotten," or simply "bad."

To speak of a tree as **good** and **bad**, translators may have to say "healthy" and
"diseased" or "strong" and "weak." But in most languages "good" and "bad" will be
satisfactory.

As for **good** and **bad** fruit, this can be "fruits that can (or, cannot) be eaten"
or "fruit that is tasty (or, sweet)" and "fruit that tastes bad."

12.34   RSV   TEV

You brood of vipers! how can you   You snakes—how can you say good
speak good, when you are evil? For   things when you are evil? For the
out of the abundance of the heart   mouth speaks what the heart is full
the mouth speaks.   of.

<u>**You brood of vipers**</u>: see comments on 3.7.

<u>**How can you speak good . . . ?**</u> may be better expressed as a statement: "That is the way it is with you. You are evil, and so you cannot say good things." Of course, the original order can be retained, too, with a sentence like "how can you possibly say good things when you are evil?" If the rhetorical question is not natural in the receptor language, then the idea can be expressed as "it is not possible for you to say good, since you are yourselves evil."

<u>**For out of the abundance of the heart the mouth speaks**</u>: the noun <u>**abundance**</u> appears also in the Lukan parallel (6.45) and in Mark 8.8; 2 Corinthians 8.14 (twice). The picture is that of a substance which fills a container to overflowing. Jesus speaks of the heart as though it were a container, which may be filled with either good or evil. And whatever fills it, whether good or evil, overflows through a person's mouth in the form of the words which he speaks. It should be noted that in Jewish thought the **heart** does not represent the seat of emotions (as in English), but rather the entire person conceived of as a total being who thinks and wills. NAB translates <u>**heart**</u> as "mind." It is possible to translate without the metaphor of the mouth, as Brc indicates: "A man's words are nothing other than the overflow of what is in his heart." It may be advisable in other circumstances to do away with the metaphor entirely: "For what a person says reveals what he is really like." Or "You can tell what a person is really like by what he says." Other languages may require the use of other body parts; for example, "Your tongue speaks what is in your liver."

Many translators have tried to retain the image of the metaphor. One way has been to use a sentence such as "For whatever fills a person's heart (or, mind), that is what flows out when he speaks" or "For whatever a person is really like, when he speaks, that is the thing that comes out just like a bowl overflowing."

12.35	RSV	TEV
	The good man out of his good treasure brings forth good, and the evil man out of his evil treasure brings forth evil.	A good person brings good things out of his treasure of good things; a bad person brings bad things out of his treasure of bad things.

Verse 35 uses a different imagery to repeat the thought of verse 34. **The good man** is to be understood in the sense of "**A good person**" (TEV).

<u>**Good treasure**</u>: "**treasure of good things**" (TEV), "the store of good" (NEB), and "his store of goodness" (JB, NAB). The Greek word <u>**treasure**</u> may refer to the treasure itself, or to the box, room, or house in which the treasure is stored. Both the context (verse 34) and the parallel in Luke 6.45 ("good treasure of his heart") indicate that the place where the treasure is stored is compared to the heart. GECL removes the figure entirely and translates the verse "A good man brings forth good because he is good in his innermost being. An evil man can only bring forth evil because he is evil from the ground up."

Of course, there are ways to retain the figure and still convey the meaning. Examples are "A good man is able to bring out good things (or, actions) from the great good that is in him like a treasure" and "A good man has good stored up in him like a treasure, and so he does good things."

Some can use the same type of sentence for the **evil man**, but it may not seem natural to speak of a treasure of evil. Then possible renderings may be "An evil man can bring out only evil things (or, action) from the great evil that is in him like in a store room" or "An evil man has evil stored up in him like in a store house, and so he does evil things."

12.36　　　RSV　　　　　　　　　　　　　TEV

I tell you, on the day of judgment men will render account for every careless word they utter;

"You can be sure that on the Judgment Day everyone will have to give account of every useless word he has ever spoken.

This verse, which introduces the judgment in typical Matthean style, is found only in his Gospel.

I tell you is equivalent to the similar structure in 5.20.

On the day of judgment comes last in the Greek sentence structure; but it is emphatic, and its positioning in RSV and TEV at the first of the sentence is more natural for English speakers. AT has a fairly literal representation of the Greek word order: "But I tell you, for every careless word that men utter they will have to answer on the Day of Judgment." NEB also retains the phrase at the last of the sentence, though doing other restructuring: ". . . there is not a thoughtless word that comes from men's lips but they will have to account for it on the day of judgment."

The day of judgment is "the day when God will judge all people (of the world)."

Men is used of all people; TEV has "**everyone**."

To **render account** means to explain why things were said. The explanation will be before God, so the sentence can be "People are going to have to tell God why they said every useless word they did."

Careless (so also Phps, Brc) is translated "**useless**" by TEV and GECL. NAB has "unguarded" and NJB "unfounded." This same adjective is used in James 2.20, where the meaning is clearly "useless." JB has a footnote: "Not a merely 'idle' word but a malicious and baseless assertion, a calumny." To convey the meaning of **careless**, translators may say "every word that did harm" or "every word that they should not have said." But it must be clear that it was because they were harmful that these words should not have been said. One natural way in some languages to restructure this sentence is this: "But I assure you, when God comes to judge all people, at that time everyone will have to explain to him why they said every word they spoke which did harm."

12.37　　　RSV　　　　　　　　　　　　　TEV

for by your words you will be justi-fied, and by your words you will be condemned."

Your words will be used to judge you—to declare you either innocent or guilty."

In Greek there is a shift from a third person reference ("men . . . they") to a second person form of address: **Your . . . you**. Upon the basis of this observation, a number of commentators have concluded that Jesus is quoting a current proverbial statement. But it is also possible that the shift to the second person may indicate that Jesus is now addressing the Pharisees directly. This would seem to satisfy better the demands of the context, in which Jesus is in a controversy with the Pharisees over the healing of the blind and dumb man. In any case there are indications from Jewish sources that the Jewish teachers also believed that a person was judged not only by what he did but by what he said. So for this reason, too, it seems reasonable to retain the second person form of address.

Note that **for** indicates that this verse follows on logically from verse 36. Jesus says that people will have to give account of their harmful words because it is on the basis of what you say that God will judge.

The two parallel structures **For by your words** . . . **and by your words** are combined in TEV: "**Your words will be used to . . . .**" NEB reveals the awkwardness of a literal reproduction of the Greek: "For out of your mouth you will be acquitted; out of your mouth you will be condemned." GECL restructures: "Based on your own words you will be declared either innocent or guilty." In some languages it may be necessary to render **your words** by a verb structure and at the same time to indicate who will do the judging: "God will judge you by what you have said. If you have said the right things, he will declare you innocent. But if you have said the wrong things, he will declare you guilty." A similar model for translators is "For God will judge you and declare you innocent or guilty, based on the things you said (depending on whether they were right or wrong)."

Will be justified (TEV "**declare . . . innocent**") is also used in 11.19 but nowhere else in Matthew. It is a favorite term of the apostle Paul, and its traditional rendering is reflected in RSV.

Will be condemned (TEV "**declare . . . guilty**") is the same verb used in 12.7. Elsewhere in the New Testament it is used only in Luke 6.37 and James 5.6.

The translation of **will be justified** and **will be condemned** is related to "judging," since they are the possible actions of a judge. It may be sufficient to say "God will declare you innocent" and "God will declare you guilty," but in many languages the judging must be made explicit, as in "God will judge you and declare you innocent or guilty" or "God will declare you innocent or guilty when he judges you." We discussed the translation of "judging" in 7.1, and translators should refer to that discussion.

12.38-42

RSV   TEV

The Demand for a Miracle

38 Then some of the scribes and Pharisees said to him, "Teacher, we wish to see a sign from you." 39 But he answered them, "An evil and adulterous generation seeks for a sign; but no sign shall be given to it except the sign of the prophet Jonah. 40 For as Jonah was three days and three nights in the belly of the whale, so will the Son of

38 Then some teachers of the Law and some Pharisees spoke up. "Teacher," they said, "we want to see you perform a miracle."

39 "How evil and godless are the people of this day!" Jesus exclaimed. "You ask me for a miracle? No! The only miracle you will be given is the miracle of the prophet Jonah. 40 In the same

man be three days and three nights in the heart of the earth. 41 The men of Nineveh will arise at the judgment with this generation and condemn it; for they repented at the preaching of Jonah, and behold, something greater than Jonah is here. 42 The queen of the South will arise at the judgment with this generation and condemn it; for she came from the ends of the earth to hear the wisdom of Solomon, and behold, something greater than Solomon is here.

way that Jonah spent three days and nights in the big fish, so will the Son of Man spend three days and nights in the depths of the earth. 41 On the Judgment Day the people of Nineveh will stand up and accuse you, because they turned from their sins when they heard Jonah preach; and I tell you that there is something here greater than Jonah! 42 On the Judgment Day the Queen of Sheba will stand up and accuse you, because she traveled all the way from her country to listen to King Solomon's wise teaching; and I assure you that there is something here greater than Solomon!

SECTION HEADING: "**The Demand for a Miracle**." Often it is necessary to indicate who is asking for a miracle, and possibly whom they are asking. Thus the heading may be "Some teachers of the Law and Pharisees (or, Some leaders) ask Jesus to perform a miracle." Another possibility is "Jesus refuses to perform a miracle."

Luke 11.29-32 forms a parallel to verses 38-42; a partial doublet is also found in Matthew 16.1-4 (parallel Mark 8.11-12), which follows the feeding of the four thousand. In the present context the narrative continues the Beelzebul controversy.

12.38	RSV	TEV

Then some of the scribes and Pharisees said to him, "Teacher, we wish to see a sign from you."

Then some teachers of the Law and some Pharisees spoke up. "Teacher," they said, "we want to see you perform a miracle."

Since the narrative continues the controversy begun in verse 22, **Then** is appropriate, or "After that."

The scribes were first mentioned in 2.4; see comments there. For comments on **Pharisees**, see 3.7.

Jesus is first addressed as **Teacher** in 8.19; see comments there. As in the previous occurrence, so here also GECL drops the noun of address.

We wish to see a sign from you is translated "**we want to see you perform a miracle**" by TEV. Commentators are in unanimous agreement that **sign** here means more than the English word "**miracle**" implies. The word is in fact never used of healings or of miraculous deeds in any Gospel except the Gospel of John. Jesus' opponents are not merely asking for another miracle; they have seen him perform many miracles, and they still refuse to believe. What they are seeking is an unambiguous demonstration that it is God himself who is at work in and through the miracles of Jesus. In other words, they are looking for "a sign from heaven" (see Matt 16.1), a "super miracle" that will serve to validate the divine origin of all Jesus' other miracles. Only a few translations take seriously the need for radical restructuring: "some visible action of God which will prove your claims" (Brc) and "a definitive miracle that you actually are commissioned by God" (GECL 1st edition). Besides its usage here and in verse 39, the word is found elsewhere in the Gospel in 16.1,3,4; 24.3,24,30; 26.48.

Translators will do well to restructure **sign** in a manner similar to Brc and GECL 1st edition above. Examples include "some mighty act that would show that God is with you," "some great deed that would show us that your power comes from God," and "some act that only God could do."

12.39	RSV	TEV

But he answered them, "An evil and adulterous generation seeks for a sign; but no sign shall be given to it except the sign of the prophet Jonah.	"How evil and godless are the people of this day!" Jesus exclaimed. "You ask me for a miracle? No! The only miracle you will be given is the miracle of the prophet Jonah.

An evil and adulterous generation is translated in the form of an exclamation by TEV: "**How evil and godless are the people of this day!**" But the problem is that for English speakers "**How . . .**" is normally heard to introduce a question. It will be more natural to translate "You people are evil and godless!" or "Only evil and godless people (like you) would look for a sign."

Adulterous is here used of unfaithfulness to God, thus the reason for "**godless**" of TEV and NEB; NAB has "unfaithful," and Brc "apostate." Other ways to render it include "not faithful to God" and "disobedient to God." A literal translation may make readers think of people who were guilty of physical adultery.

An **evil . . . generation** means "evil people" or "people who are doing evil (things)." **Generation** refers to the people of a certain era. Here Jesus obviously is referring to "the people of this time" or "people today." Hence common translations are "the evil people of today who are unfaithful to God" or "these evil and disobedient people of today."

Generation seeks for a sign is altered to a second person reference by TEV and translated "**You ask me for a miracle.**" It may be more accurate to translate "You ask God to show you a special miracle." GECL retains the third person reference and translates "They don't want to know anything about God, but they want to see a miracle."

Some translators understand Jesus' words to contain a certain amount of irony or even bitterness, as in "So, the evil and unfaithful want a sign from God, do they?" or "These evil and unfaithful people of our day think God should give them a sign." Another rendering is "You want some visible action of God? You, who are evil and unfaithful to God?"

Notice that in some of these examples it is explicit that the real source of the sign is God. The use of the passive **shall be given** suggests that God is the intended agent, and so supports the interpretation proposed for "seeks a sign." One may then translate "The only miracle God will give you is . . . ."

The sign of the prophet Jonah is ambiguous. The most natural conclusion is that the sign receives its interpretation from the following verse, which speaks of what happened to Jonah. GECL makes this connection explicit: "The only proof they will receive is that which corresponds to what the prophet Jonah experienced." **The sign of the prophet Jonah** does not refer to a miracle Jonah performed but to the sign God gave him. Thus another rendering can be "the only visible action God will do for you is the same one he did for the prophet Jonah."

For comments on **prophet**, see 1.22.

12.40	RSV	TEV

RSV	TEV
For as Jonah was three days and three nights in the belly of the whale, so will the Son of man be three days and three nights in the heart of the earth.	In the same way that Jonah spent three days and nights in the big fish, so will the Son of Man spend three days and nights in the depths of the earth.

For as (TEV "**In the same way that**") is the signal by which verse 40 is made the key to the interpretation of "the sign of the prophet Jonah" of verse 39.

Was three days and three nights in the belly of the whale is taken directly from the Septuagint of Jonah 1.17 (Septuagint, 2.1). For people who have never been introduced to the story of Jonah, it may be necessary to provide a footnote.

TEV renders **was** as "**spent**." Other words are "stayed" or "passed."

Three days and three nights is not always natural. Some languages say simply "three days" or "three full days."

So will (TEV "**In the same way . . . so will**") translates a Greek structure which draws an analogy between the three days and nights spent by Jonah in the big fish and the period of time spent by the Son of Man **in the heart of the earth**. For a discussion of **the Son of man**, see 8.20. In this chapter he is mentioned in verses 8, 32, and 40; as elsewhere in the New Testament, the reference is to Jesus, and this should be clear in translation.

TEV has conveyed very clearly the meaning of the construction of **for as . . . so will**. In other languages the form may be slightly different, as in "For Jonah was . . . It will be just like that with . . . ." It may even be helpful to repeat the "sign" of verse 39, as in "For the sign to Jonah was that he spent three full days inside the big fish. In the same way, the sign to you will be when the Son of Man spends three days deep in the earth."

Whale (so also NAB) is the traditional rendering of the Greek word used here. TEV has "**big fish**"; the most accurate term is perhaps "sea monster" (Brc, NJB, NEB, GECL). The major problem with "sea monster" is that some readers may assume that this represents an attempt to make the Jonah story into a fairy tale. For this reason it is probably best to use a more neutral term such as "big fish" or "very big fish."

As for **belly**, some translators will say "stomach," but others will find it sufficient to say "inside."

Heart of the earth represents a literal translation of the Hebrew idiom used by Matthew. It is perpetuated by most translations, but NEB has "bowels of the earth," and TEV "**depths of the earth**." The place referred to is the grave rather than the world of the dead. Accordingly one may render "deep in the earth," "deep in the ground," or possibly "buried in the ground."

The men of Nineveh will arise at the judgment with this generation and condemn it; for they repented at the preaching of Jonah, and behold, something greater than Jonah is here.	**On the Judgment Day the people of Nineveh will stand up and accuse you, because they turned from their sins when they heard Jonah preach; and I tell you that there is something here greater than Jonah!**

The men of Nineveh means "**the people of Nineveh**" (TEV). NAB has "the citizens of Nineveh," and GECL "the inhabitants of Nineveh."

It may be necessary to specify that **Nineveh** was a city, as in "the city of Nineveh."

We suggested under verse 40 the possible need for a footnote about the story of Jonah. That note should include the fact he was sent to Nineveh, so that verse 41 follows naturally from 40.

Arise (TEV "**stand up**") may also mean "rise from the dead" (Brc). The verb is in fact frequently used in the New Testament of Jesus' own resurrection (Mark 8.31; 9.9,10,31; 10.34; 16.9; Luke 18.33; 24.7,46; John 20.9; Acts 17.3; 1 Thes 4.14), which is likely the reason that a number of translations prefer "rise" (Mft, JB, NAB, AT). NEB does not follow this interpretation in the text, but gives an alternative rendering, "rise again." Scholarly opinion is divided, and Aramaic scholars note that the phrase "will arise . . . with" represents an Aramaic idiom meaning "stand or rise up in judgment with." If this is the meaning, then **at the judgment** denotes the time when the people of Nineveh will make their accusation rather than the time of their rising from the dead. In either case, the context suggests that the idea of rising from the dead is probably not the one to be emphasized. This means that the best way to render **arise** may be simply "**stand up**," as in TEV, or perhaps "stand up to accuse" or "stand up as witnesses against."

At the judgment (TEV "**On the Judgment Day**") is a slightly different phrase from the one used in verse 36, but the meaning is the same. NEB renders "at the Judgment," and NJB renders "On Judgement day," as it did in verse 36. As there, it can also be "on the day God judges the earth" or "at the time when God judges people."

With this generation and condemn it is transferred to a second person by TEV and shortened: "**accuse you**." As in verse 39, **this generation** can also be "the people of today" or "you people of this day."

Since it will be God actually passing judgment on people and condemning them, when the text says that the people of Nineveh will **condemn**, a better rendering is "accuse" or "testify against." If an object of this action is required, it can be "accuse you of wrong doing" or "tell how you have sinned."

Repented (TEV "**turned from their sins**"): this is the final occurrence of this verb in the Gospel; it was first used in 3.2 (see comments there), then in 4.17; 11.20,21.

The Greek noun phrase **at the preaching of Jonah** is reformulated as a temporal clause by TEV: "**when they heard Jonah preach**." GECL translates "when Jonah warned them." The Greek noun **preaching** actually focuses more upon the content than it does upon the form of the proclamation and so may be rendered "message." One way to say it is "when they heard the message of Jonah" or "because of the message Jonah proclaimed to them."

And behold: see comments on 1.20. In this context it may be rendered "and now" or "but I tell you."

Something greater than is similar to the structure in 12.6. The Greek text does have a different word for **greater**, but no distinction in meaning is intended, and all translations appear to use the same adjective. As in 12.6, Mft makes explicit that the reference is to Jesus: "and here is One greater than Jonah." NAB also implies a personal reference, "but you have a greater than Jonah here." Brc, on the other hand, apparently applies this to the Kingdom of God, "and there is a greater event than Jonah here." The same exegetical and translational questions exist here as at 12.6; see comments there.

12.42 RSV	TEV
The queen of the South will arise at the judgment with this generation and condemn it; for she came from the ends of the earth to hear the wisdom of Solomon, and behold, something greater than Solomon is here.	On the Judgment Day the Queen of Sheba will stand up and accuse you, because she traveled all the way from her country to listen to King Solomon's wise teaching; and I assure you that there is something here greater than Solomon!

Of the South points to South Arabia, that is, Sheba. For the scripture references see 1 Kings 10.1-13; 2 Chronicles 9.1-12. The Jews would have considered both the queen of Sheba and the people of Nineveh (Jonah 3.5) to be heathens.

If translators render **queen of the South** literally, it can mislead readers into thinking she was the ruler of all that is south, perhaps even a supernatural ruler of all forces from that direction. "Queen of a land to the south" will avoid that. However, since it is clear that this in fact refers to the queen of Sheba, there is no reason not to say that in the translation.

Will arise at the judgment with this generation and condemn it is exactly the same as in verse 41.

In many languages, **came** will be rendered as "went."

From the ends of the earth represents the perpetuation of a Semitic idiom meaning "a very long distance." Most English translations favor retaining the idiom, or at least a fraction of it; NAB translates "from the farthest corner of the earth." TEV restructures: "**all the way from her country**." Translators can also say "a long distance" or "from a distant part of the earth."

Hear may better be "listen to" in some languages.

The wisdom of Solomon would have been immediately understood by any Jew, for he was a Jewish king noted for his wisdom. TEV both marks Solomon as a king and eliminates the abstract phrase **the wisdom of Solomon** by restructuring as "**King Solomon's wise teaching**." Many readers will require a footnote which further identifies Solomon. For many languages it will be impossible to speak of listening to a person's wisdom; what one listens to is a person's expression of his wisdom through words. Therefore "the wise things that Solomon taught."

The last phrase **and behold something greater than Solomon is here** has the same pattern as verse 41.

12.43-45

RSV   TEV

The Return of the Evil Spirit

43 "When the unclean spirit has gone out of a man, he passes through waterless places seeking rest, but he finds none. 44 Then he says, 'I will return to my house from which I came.' And when he comes he finds it empty, swept, and put in order. 45 Then he goes and brings with him seven other spirits more evil than himself, and they enter and dwell there; and the last state of that man becomes worse than the first. So shall it be also with this evil generation."

43 "When an evil spirit goes out of a person, it travels over dry country looking for a place to rest. If it can't find one, 44 it says to itself, 'I will go back to my house.' So it goes back and finds the house empty, clean, and all fixed up. 45 Then it goes out and brings along seven other spirits even worse than itself, and they come and live there. So when it is all over, that person is in worse shape than he was at the beginning. This is what will happen to the evil people of this day."

SECTION HEADING: "**The Return of the Evil Spirit.**" This may be rendered "An evil spirit returns to people," "How an evil spirit always comes back," or "Bad things will get worse."

The Lukan parallel to this section, 11.24-26, also occurs in the context of a conflict between Jesus and the Pharisees, and the two accounts are almost word-for-word the same. However, Luke does not indicate that the house was empty. Most significant, however, is the application that Matthew makes of this parable. Whereas Luke applies it to an individual (11.26), Matthew underscores its relevance for the entire generation of his day (12.45).

12.43   RSV   TEV

"When the unclean spirit has gone out of a man, he passes through waterless places seeking rest, but he finds none.

"When an evil spirit goes out of a person, it travels over dry country looking for a place to rest. If it can't find one,

The sentence begins with **When**, but it is really a hypothetical sentence. The present tense in this short narrative indicates that this kind of happening is what commonly takes place. Translators will have to determine how to express this in their own languages. It can be rendered "If an unclean spirit leaves" or "On those occasions when," or even "Suppose an evil spirit leaves a person, what happens? It travels through . . . ."

The unclean spirit: since no unclean spirit has yet been mentioned in the context, it will be better to use the indefinite article "**an**" (NEB, NJB) than to retain **the** of the Greek text. **Unclean spirit** (TEV "**evil spirit**") is the same expression used in 10.1, except for the plural form in the earlier passage.

The text does not say whether this evil spirit was thrown out of a person or left voluntarily. Most translators do follow the text, **has gone out**, with something like "leaves" or "goes out." However, since one supposes that such departures are usually the result of some exorcism, other translators have said "is driven out" or "is forced to leave."

A man is literally "the man"; one wonders why RSV would have retained the definite article before **spirit** while dropping it here. **Man** is the equivalent of "**person**" (TEV).

Translators should make sure that it is clear in their translation that **he** refers to the spirit, not to the person.

Passes through has been translated as "travels through" or "goes about in."

Waterless places were thought to be favorite dwelling places of demons (see Isa 13.21-22; 34.14). NEB has "deserts," and TEV "**dry country**."

The abstract noun **rest** is given the meaning "resting-place" by NEB; NAB has "a place of rest." It is best understood in the broad sense of "shelter" or "place to stay" (GECL); in Ruth 3.1 the Septuagint uses this Greek noun to refer to a home. The translation should not lead to the implication that the spirit is tired out and looking for a place to rest; rather he is looking for a permanent place of residence. Following this interpretation, translators can have "looking for a place to stay" or "trying to find a place to live."

But he finds none can also be "but it can't find one (or, any)" (so TEV) or "but there is no place for it (to stay)."

12.44	RSV	TEV
	Then he says, 'I will return to my house from which I came.' And when he comes he finds it empty, swept, and put in order.	It says to itself, 'I will go back to my house.' So it goes back and finds the house empty, clean, and all fixed up.

Says must be given the meaning "**says to itself**" (TEV, GECL) or "thinks." This sentence can also be in indirect speech; for example, "Then it decides to return to the house it came from."

My house from which I came can be "my former home" or "the place that I left."

Comes in this context can also be "arrives there" or "returns."

Finds should not be translated with the sense of finding something that was lost. It means here that the spirit discovers or sees that now this home is empty.

Empty, swept, and put in order is translated "vacant, clean, and all in order" by Mft and "unoccupied, cleaned, and all in order" by AT.

Empty translates a participle derived from a verb which, when used of a place or a house, means "empty," "vacant," "unoccupied." As stated earlier, this information is not found in the Lukan parallel.

Swept (TEV "**clean**"; NEB "swept clean") translates a participle made from a verb meaning "sweep." Elsewhere in the New Testament the verb occurs only in Luke 15.8.

Put in order (TEV "**all fixed up**") translates a participle made from a verb which may mean either "put in order" or "decorate." Evidently most translations prefer the meaning adopted by RSV and TEV.

Swept and **put in order** are both passives, and this may be a problem in some languages where agents are required. **Swept** could possibly be "clean." Another way is to supply an agent and use an active sentence, as in "(He saw that) someone had swept it out and put everything in the proper place."

12.45 RSV	TEV
Then he goes and brings with him seven other spirits more evil than himself, and they enter and dwell there; and the last state of that man becomes worse than the first. So shall it be also with this evil generation."	Then it goes out and brings along seven other spirits even worse than itself, and they come and live there. So when it is all over, that person is in worse shape than he was at the beginning. This is what will happen to the evil people of this day."

Goes (so also AT) is translated "**goes out**" by TEV, intimating that the spirit had entered the house before returning to the dry places to look for other evil spirits. Other translations use an idiom indicating departure from the house rather than from within it; for example, "off it goes" (Mft, NEB, NAB); "it . . . goes off" (NJB). Since the verb in itself is neutral, the specific rendering will need to be determined by the way the receptor language talks about movement from one space to another. One may even translate "it leaves the house." Some readers may feel that **he goes and brings with him** is too abbreviated. It may be necessary, for example, to indicate that the one evil spirit first looked for and found other evil spirits before bringing them along with him. GECL translates "Then he goes and finds seven other evil spirits, who are worse than he himself, and they come and live there."

Just as languages use "come" and "go" differently, so with "bring" and "take." Here **brings** may have to be "takes" or "leads back."

RSV has **him** and **himself** throughout this section, but in modern English "it" and "itself" are more natural. Translators should do whatever the receptor language demands for referring to an evil spirit.

Enter and dwell there is represented in TEV by "**come and live there**." Although "live there" implies entering the house, some languages will require specific mention of this event, as with **enter** of RSV and "come in" of NEB.

The last state of that man becomes is rendered more idiomatically by TEV: "**So when it is all over, that person is**." The function of the Greek is merely to contrast the previous situation of the man possessed by one evil spirit with what finally happens to him when he is possessed by eight evil spirits. JB translates "so that the man ends up by being worse than he was before," and GECL "so the man is worse off at the end than he was at the beginning."

As can be seen in the above examples, the man's **state** refers to the situation he finds himself in. "Things are worse for the man" and "the situation that man is in is worse" are two other possible renderings.

Discourse structure in some languages requires that **that man** be very clearly described, as in "that man with the spirit" or "the man whom the spirit left once."

So shall it be also with this evil generation is an application which Matthew alone makes of this parable. As noted in the introduction to the parable, Luke makes individual application of it, whereas Matthew has Jesus addressing the people collectively as an evil group. This may be a difficult concept to convey clearly, and a second-person construction may be preferable: "This is how it is with all of you people. You are worse off now than you were before." For Matthew the meaning is that the entire generation of people had refused Jesus and his message. Their refusal had in turn left a vacancy which was then filled by a whole flock of evil spirits, leaving the people in a worse condition than they were before encountering Jesus.

The translation should not make readers think that seven or eight evil spirits will come into the people of that day. Rather, it means that those people, too, are going to be worse off than ever. It is possible to say, however, "you will be filled with even more evil than before."

For a discussion of **this evil generation**, translators should see verses 39 and 41. "The evil people of this time" or "you evil people of today" are just two possibilities.

12.46-50

RSV   TEV

Jesus' Mother and Brothers

46 While he was still speaking to the people, behold, his mother and his brothers stood outside, asking to speak to him.*g* 48 But he replied to the man who told him, "Who is my mother, and who are my brothers?" 49 And stretching out his hand toward his disciples, he said, "Here are my mother and my brothers! 50 For whoever does the will of my Father in heaven is my brother, and sister, and mother."

g Other ancient authorities insert verse 47, *Some one told him, "Your mother and your brothers are standing outside, asking to speak to you"*

46 Jesus was still talking to the people when his mother and brothers arrived. They stood outside, asking to speak with him. 47 So one of the people there said to him, "Look, your mother and brothers are standing outside, and they want to speak with you."*k*

48 Jesus answered, "Who is my mother? Who are my brothers?" 49 Then he pointed to his disciples and said, "Look! Here are my mother and my brothers! 50 Whoever does what my Father in heaven wants him to do is my brother, my sister, and my mother."

k Some manuscripts do not have verse 47.

SECTION HEADING: "**Jesus' Mother and Brothers**." If a sentence is required, the heading can be "Jesus' mother and brothers come to see him" or "Jesus talks about who his real family is." It can also be "The real family of Jesus."

This passage has a parallel in both Mark 3.31-35 and Luke 8.19-21. Whereas in Mark it forms the climax to a series of conflicts between Jesus and the Pharisees, its function in the present context is not so easy to determine. However, it is logical to conclude that Matthew somehow intends it to be interpreted in light of what has immediately transpired, and he does provide a connecting link ("While he was still speaking to the people"), which is not introduced by either Mark or Luke. One may then fairly safely assume that the passage somehow forms a conclusion to the Beelzebul controversy. At the same time it adds a fresh note of warning: participation in the Messianic Kingdom cannot be guaranteed by accident of birth, whether it is birth into the family of Israel or even into Jesus' own family. Membership in the redeemed community of God's true people is achieved only by obedience to God's will.

12.46 RSV TEV

While he was still speaking to the people, behold, his mother and his brothers stood outside, asking to speak to him.^g

Jesus was still talking to the people when his mother and brothers arrived. They stood outside, asking to speak with him.

^g Other ancient authorities insert verse 47, *Some one told him, "Your mother and your brothers are standing outside, asking to speak to you"*

While he was still speaking: both TEV and GECL identify **he** as Jesus, since a new section begins with this verse.

The verb phrase **was still speaking** connects this narrative closely to that which precedes it (compare "While he was thus speaking to them" of 9.18); as noted above, this linking formula does not occur in the Marcan parallel (3.31).

Some translations, for example Brc, render **people** with "crowds" or "the crowd."

Behold (see comments on 1.20) is not represented by any specific word in TEV, JB, or NEB. Other translations have "at that time" or "it happened that."

Roman Catholic scholars generally interpret Jesus' **brothers** to be either "cousins" or "half-brothers" (that is, sons of Joseph by a previous marriage). NAB does not provide a note, but JB does: "Not Mary's children but near relations, cousins perhaps . . . ." JB bases its exegesis upon the influence of Hebrew or Aramaic on Matthew's Greek, since in these two languages "brother" has a wider meaning than in Greek. But, as other scholars observe, the word "brother" is used in John, Acts, and Paul's letters to refer to Jesus' relatives, and in each case these writings are addressed to non-Jews who would not understand the word to mean "cousin." Thus **brothers** should be retained in the translation, but possibly with an accompanying note if translators want it. Some languages have a word "sibling" that covers males and females. That will perhaps be acceptable, although the Greek word means male sibling. There are a number of languages where the normal way to say **brothers** is "sons of my (or, his) mother" or "sons of my (or, his) father." Either is acceptable here.

Stood outside is translated "**arrived. They stood outside**" by TEV. In English the inclusion of this additional verb is helpful; in other languages it may be obligatory. NEB, JB, and NAB each have "appeared," which somewhat relieves the difficulty. But unless something is done translationally, the reader will conclude either that Jesus' mother and brothers had been with him during the conflict with the Pharisees, or that they had suddenly made a miraculous appearance out of nowhere. Matthew himself has altered the first part of the verse to make a smoother transition, but he has not resolved the problem of the unannounced appearance of Jesus' family. "Arrived and were standing outside" is thus a common rendering.

The adverb **outside** is as ambiguous in Greek as it is in English. One is forced to ask "Outside of what?" GECL assumes that Jesus is in a house, and translates "in front of the house," while AT renders "outside the crowd." The basis for AT is the mention of the crowds in the earlier part of the verse. On the other hand GECL finds support in 13.1, "That same day Jesus left the house . . . ." The translator must assume either that Jesus is now in the house, and that in 13.1 he first leaves it, or that he is now outside the house but later enters the house, and then later (13.1) leaves it. This is in all probability a question that did not concern Matthew, but if one must be explicit, the simplest solution is that of GECL.

Asking translates a verb which does not necessarily imply verbal action, though it may be used in this sense. The basic meaning of the verb is "seek, look for"; it is translated "wanting" by NEB and "anxious" by NJB. NAB leaves the meaning implicit: "appeared outside to speak with him."

To make the translation of **asking** smooth and natural, translators can say "they wanted to speak to Jesus," "they were looking for Jesus so they could speak to him," or "they were asking to speak to Jesus." This latter can be in direct speech also: "They asked 'We would like to speak with Jesus.' "

12.47	RSV	TEV

[Some one told him, "Your mother and your brothers are standing outside, asking to speak to you."]

So one of the people there said to him, "Look, your mother and brothers are standing outside, and they want to speak with you."[k]

[k]*Some manuscripts do not have verse 47.*

Verse 47 is omitted by RSV, Mft, and NJB, with a footnote indicating that it was a later addition; AT drops the verse without a note. TC-GNT accounts for its absence from some Greek manuscripts on the assumption that it was accidentally omitted because both it and verse 46 begin in Greek with the same verb. The scribe's eyes may have unintentionally caught the ending of verse 47 in place of verse 46 and then went on to verse 48. But the UBS Greek New Testament does rate its decision in the "C" category because of "considerable degree of doubt" regarding what may have been in the original text. TEV includes the verse with a footnote that it is not found in some Greek manuscripts, thus following the decision of the UBS Greek text.

Some one (literally "A certain one") translates a Semitic Greek idiom; TEV has "**one of the people there**," and GECL 1st edition "one of the people."

Him is a reference to Jesus.

"**Look**": see comments on "Behold" in 1.20; this attention getter was most recently used in verse 46. Note: there is no "behold" in this verse in RSV.

The last part of the verse can follow verse 46 quite closely: "Your mother and your brothers have arrived and are outside. They want to speak with you." The whole thing can be indirect speech: "One of the people there told Jesus that his mother and brothers had come and were waiting outside because they wanted to talk to him."

12.48　　　RSV　　　　　　　　　　　　　　　　TEV

But he replied to the man who told　　　　Jesus answered, "Who is my
him, "Who is my mother, and who　　mother? Who are my brothers?"
are my brothers?"

　　But he replied to the man who told him is translated "**Jesus answered**" by
TEV and "Jesus answered him" by GECL. NEB renders "Jesus turned to the man who
brought the message and said . . . ." If verse 47 is omitted from the translation, then
there is no antecedent to **the man who told him**. The person to whom Jesus gave
his answer is not explicitly mentioned in this verse by TEV, since the antecedent is
clearly marked by TEV's rendering of verse 47.

　　Who is my mother, and who are my brothers? is divided into two separate
sentences by TEV, NEB, and NJB. The form, whether one question or two, must be
determined by the requirements of the receptor language. In some languages a
question may even imply that Jesus does not know who his mother and brothers are,
and that he is asking for the sake of information. Therefore it may be necessary to
render the questions "Who is really my mother? Who are really my brothers?" or
"Do you know who my mother is, and who my brothers are?" Or it may be better
to replace the question form with a statement: "She is not really my mother, and
these are not really my brothers." But such a reply may suggest that Jesus is denying
any physical ties to these people who literally are his immediate family. To avoid this
false assumption, verses 48-50 may be translated as a unit: "My true brothers and
sisters and mother are the people who do what my Father in heaven wants them to
do. My disciples are my true mother and brothers!"

12.49-50　　　RSV　　　　　　　　　　　　　　　　TEV

49 And stretching out his hand to-　　49 Then he pointed to his disciples
ward his disciples, he said, "Here　　and said, "Look! Here are my mother
are my mother and my brothers!　　and my brothers! 50 Whoever does
50 For whoever does the will of my　　what my Father in heaven wants him
Father in heaven is my brother, and　　to do is my brother, my sister, and
sister, and mother."　　　　　　　　my mother."

　　And marks the continuity of the discourse. "Then he . . ." will be necessary in
some cases.

　　Stretching . . . said is a common Greek construction that is most often
rendered by two independent verb clauses: "He stretched out . . . and said."
Stretching can be "he reached out his hand" or, as in TEV, "**he pointed toward.**"
This latter shows the meaning clearly.

　　For a proposed restructuring of these two verses, see comments on verse 48.
Another proposal is "Jesus pointed to his disciples and then asked the man, "Do you
want to know who my true mother and brothers are? Look, my disciples are the
ones, because the people who do the will of God my Father in heaven, they are my
true brother, and sister, and mother." Jesus' **disciples** were last mentioned in verse
2 (see 5.1 for a discussion of "disciple").

The will of my Father in heaven is translated as a clause by TEV, GECL, and FRCL: "**what my Father in heaven wants him to do.**" To make sure readers understand **Father in heaven** to be God, it may be necessary to say "God my Father in heaven."

Chapter 13

13.1-9

RSV

1 That same day Jesus went out of the house and sat beside the sea. 2 And great crowds gathered about him, so that he got into a boat and sat there; and the whole crowd stood on the beach. 3 And he told them many things in parables, saying: "A sower went out to sow. 4 And as he sowed, some seeds fell along the path, and the birds came and devoured them. 5 Other seeds fell on rocky ground, where they had not much soil, and immediately they sprang up, since they had no depth of soil, 6 but when the sun rose they were scorched; and since they had no root they withered away. 7 Other seeds fell upon thorns, and the thorns grew up and choked them. 8 Other seeds fell on good soil and brought forth grain, some a hundredfold, some sixty, some thirty. 9 He who has ears,[h] let him hear."

[h] Other ancient authorities add here and in verse 43 *to hear*

TEV

The Parable of the Sower

1 That same day Jesus left the house and went to the lakeside, where he sat down to teach. 2 The crowd that gathered around him was so large that he got into a boat and sat in it, while the crowd stood on the shore. 3 He used parables to tell them many things.

"Once there was a man who went out to sow grain. 4 As he scattered the seed in the field, some of it fell along the path, and the birds came and ate it up. 5 Some of it fell on rocky ground, where there was little soil. The seeds soon sprouted, because the soil wasn't deep. 6 But when the sun came up, it burned the young plants; and because the roots had not grown deep enough, the plants soon dried up. 7 Some of the seed fell among thorn bushes, which grew up and choked the plants. 8 But some seeds fell in good soil, and the plants bore grain: some had one hundred grains, other sixty, and others thirty."

9 And Jesus concluded, "Listen, then, if you have ears!"

SECTION HEADING: "**The Parable of the Sower**." For "**Parable**" see the discussion under verse 3 below. If using the same word here happens to result in a rather complex phrase, then "The story of the sower" is a possible rendering. Some translators will have a short sentence, such as "Jesus tells the parable of the sower." For a discussion of "**Sower**," see verse 3 also. Sometimes "farmer" is used.

Chapter 13, which contains a series of seven parables, begins a new section in the Gospel of Matthew. As we attempt to interpret and translate these parables, we must keep in mind their intention and function in the Gospel itself. Matthew intentionally places this chapter immediately following the breach between Jesus and the Pharisees. They represent official Judaism, and their rejection of him is an indication that the nation and its leaders as a whole are blind and cannot recognize the presence and reality of the Kingdom of God in the person of Jesus. By their actions the Pharisees have shown "that they look, but do not see, and they listen, but do not hear or understand" (13.13).

The structure of the chapter is complicated and difficult to analyze. However, it is generally divided into two parts: (1) parables addressed to the Jewish crowds

398

beside the sea (verses 1-35) and (2) parables spoken to the disciples in private (verses 36-52). These parables constitute the third of the five sections of discourse in the Gospel. As with the Sermon on the Mount, Matthew has collected teachings of Jesus that were given on different occasions and has placed them together. For example, the Parable of the Sower and its interpretation are found in Mark 4.1-9, 13-20; and Luke 8.5-15, as is the Parable of the Mustard Seed (Mark 4.30-32; Luke 13.18-19). The Parable of the Yeast finds its parallel in Luke 13.20-21. The remaining four parables (the Parable of the Weeds and its explanation; the Hidden Treasure; the Pearl; the Net) are all unique to Matthew's Gospel.

The final section of the chapter (verses 53-58) tells of Jesus' rejection at Nazareth.

13.1	RSV	TEV
	That same day Jesus went out of the house and sat beside the sea.	That same day Jesus left the house and went to the lakeside, where he sat down to teach.

That same day (so most translations) is introduced by Matthew in order to link the time of the preceding events with that of what follows. This particular information is lacking from both Mark and Luke. Matthew uses almost this same construction in 22.23. Some translators have made the link very explicit between the events at the end of chapter 12 and those in chapter 13 by saying "The same day that happened."

Went out of the house and sat beside the sea: some languages will require two verbs of motion in place of the one verb **went** (compare TEV "**left the house and went to the lakeside**"). Otherwise it may sound as though the house was immediately adjacent to the lake.

The house calls to mind Mark 3.19 ("Then he went home"), which is the beginning of the Marcan parallel to Matthew 12.22-32. In that section Matthew makes no mention of a house, but here it is assumed that Jesus has been indoors. Matthew 12.46 also apparently presupposes that Jesus is indoors; see comment there. The problem here is that the house is now introduced as though the readers already knew of it (old information), whereas it actually comes as something new to the reader (new information). It is impossible to reconcile the problem, unless one follows the exegesis of GECL in 12.46, where "outside" is interpreted to mean "outside the house."

The sea is Lake Galilee. Translators will render it as they have elsewhere. See comments at 4.18, for example.

TEV (followed by FRCL, but not by DUCL or GECL) specifies that Jesus sat down "**to teach**." The parallel in Mark 4.1 uses the verb "teach," but it is not used by either Matthew or Luke 8.4. Jewish teachers generally sat down when teaching, and that is probably the basis for the adjustment made by TEV (see comments at 5.1). The evidence is sufficient to conclude that Matthew intends to portray Jesus as going out beside the lake to deliver some sort of an inspired discourse. And in many languages one must choose between "preach" or "teach." "Teach" seems to represent best what Jesus does when he tells and explains the parables. Moreover, in many language situations a literal translation of 13.1 ("Jesus went out of the house and sat beside the lake") will be misunderstood, for it would imply that Jesus had gone there merely to sit down and meditate beside the lake. Matthew certainly intends for his readers to see something other than that when Jesus goes to the lake. But he indicates it, not by the inclusion of a specific verb such as "teach," but rather by the movement of Jesus from the shore of the lake to the boat from which he delivers his discourse to the crowd. Once again, it must be repeated that the argument is not conclusive. However, the inclusion of the verb **"to teach"** as a supplement to **"sat down"** is much more preferable than to leave the purpose for Jesus' sitting down to the imagination of the unskilled reader. Another possibility, while not including this information in verse 1, is to include it in verse 3: "he began to teach . . . ." Thus translators have two basic models they should consider here. If they do not include "teach" in this verse, they should make the idea explicit in verse 3.

Those who follow the TEV model may have a further complication if their language requires either a direct or an indirect object for "teach." They may have to say "to teach the people" or "to teach (the people) about God (or, God's kingdom)."

13.2

RSV	TEV
And great crowds gathered about him, so that he got into a boat and sat there; and the whole crowd stood on the beach.	The crowd that gathered around him was so large that he got into a boat and sat in it, while the crowd stood on the shore.

Evidently the **great crowds** understood that Jesus is prepared to address them. So they gather around him in a way that reminds one of the setting of the Sermon on the Mount (see 4.25–5.1). It may be necessary to say "the great crowd" or "many people." It is important to avoid using a word for **gathered** that might indicate the crowds were hostile.

Evidently Jesus feels that he can address them better from the boat, so he **got into a boat and sat there**. Notice how TEV says ". . . **was so large that he got into a boat.**" This relationship between the size of the crowd and Jesus getting into a boat is shown better in a few languages when the order to the sentence is reversed, as in "He got into a boat and sat there when (or, because) great crowds of people gathered round him."

According to verse 10 "the disciples came and said to him," which implies either that they entered the boat with Jesus at this time or that they later approached him in another boat. The least complicated conclusion is that the disciples entered the boat with Jesus, then later came up closer to him for the sake of making inquiry about the parables.

And is just a word used to indicate the narrative is continuing. **"While"** of TEV also does this.

The beach can be "the shore," "beside the lake," or "near the water."

And he told them many things in parables, saying: "A sower went out to sow.

He used parables to tell them many things.

"Once there was a man who went out to sow grain.

As above in verse 2, **And** shows continuity. "Then" or "At that time" will serve just as well. Some languages do not need any word at all.

He told them many things in parables (GECL 1st edition "He explained to them his message with the help of parables"): the Greek word translated **parable** literally means "comparison," but its meaning is best derived from the Hebrew word which it translates in the Septuagint. Except in five instances, it always translates the same Hebrew word, which has a wide range of meanings: proverb, by-word, allegory, fable, comparison, riddle, and parable. In recent years much scholarly research has been done on parables, and it is now the consensus that each parable is intended to convey only one point which concerns some aspect of the Kingdom of God. Jesus was not alone in the use of parables. Jewish teachers often used them, but as a rule they place parable and interpretation side by side. But Jesus did not provide the explanation along with the parable; instead he demanded of his hearers that they discern the truth of what he was saying, and that they respond accordingly.

A major problem in the interpretation of the parables is the realization that they reflect both the context in which Jesus lived and the contexts in which the authors of the Gospels wrote. Jesus' parables were so powerful, and the forms made them so easily remembered, that they were readily taken over by the authors of the Gospels and applied to their own life situations in much the same way that happens in pulpits today. This makes it extremely difficult to uncover the "original" meaning that a parable may have had before the time that it was placed in a particular Gospel. Moreover, since the circumstances that gave rise to one Gospel differ from those which produced another Gospel, the meaning of a parable will vary according to the context in which it is placed by the author of the Gospel. Therefore a significant clue to the interpretation of the parables of this chapter is the arrangement which they have in relation to one another and to the total Gospel of Matthew.

Many languages have stories that teach, and translators should note how their language refers to these when rendering **parables**. Sometimes one word covers both "parables" and "proverbs." In other cases a short phrase such as "stories that teach" or "stories with lessons" convey the meaning.

This sentence can be restructured if necessary. "He told them many parables to teach them things" and "He used parables to teach them his message" are examples. Instead of **saying**, most languages will more naturally have "he said."

A sower went out to sow begins in Greek with "Behold" (see comments on 1.20), which reflects a natural way to introduce a story in Semitic Greek. TEV shifts to a more acceptable introductory formula in English: **"Once there was a man . . . ."** In other cases "There was a man" or "It happened once that a man" will serve to introduce the man. GECL, NAB, NIV correctly define the **sower** as a "farmer." This is helpful, too, in areas of the world where farmers plant seeds rather than sow them by scattering them. The sentence can begin "There was a farmer who . . . ."

Went out can be rendered "went out to his fields" or ". . . to his farm."

The matter of sowing has to be dealt with, since the farmer did **sow**. This is a way of planting seeds by scattering them over soil that has been hoed or otherwise turned and made ready for growing crops. A common rendering is "to plant crops by scattering (or, throwing) seeds on the field." After the first occurrence in a narrative, this can be shortened to "scatter seed" or "throw seed."

The Greek text does not explicitly define what it was the man went out to sow, but on the basis of the following verses it was obviously some sort of grain, and TEV has made this information explicit: **"to sow grain."** It is possible that a language which has no term for "grain" in general may also require an object for the verb **sow**. In the Palestinian situation the grain would have been either wheat or barley. Wheat was the favorite of the two grains, but barley was also grown, especially for animals, and it was quite frequently the grain of the poor. If wheat or barley are not known, then "seed" or "food crops" are common general words that languages use.

13.4   RSV   TEV

And as he sowed, some seeds fell along the path, and the birds came and devoured them.

As he scattered the seed in the field, some of it fell along the path, and the birds came and ate it up.

The parables reflect everyday life in first-century Palestine. For example, the typical way of sowing grain before plowing the field is accurately described in this parable. Moreover, a grain field would often have a path going alongside it or even through it (see Deut 23.25; Matt 12.1).

As we pointed out above, **sowed** can be "scattered the seed (on the fields)."

Along the path (so also TEV) translates a Greek construction which may mean either "beside the path but not on it" (see NJB "on the edge of the path") or "on the path" (NEB "on a footpath"; Mft "on the road"). The present context also demands the meaning "path" or "footpath" (NEB) rather than "road" (Brc, Mft). To translate "road" would imply that a passageway large enough for vehicles is involved, whereas the reference is to a narrow pathway through a field. This may have to be made explicit, as in "along the path through the field."

The birds (so most translations) represents a literal rendering of the Greek text which has the definite article "the." However, in many languages, including perhaps English, it is more natural to drop the article (NAB "where birds came").

Devoured translates an intensive form of the verb "eat." It is used, for example, of the dragon in Revelation 12.4. Note also its usage in Mark 12.40 and Luke 15.30. It means to eat greedily, or hungrily, or completely, or like an animal. To convey the intensity of **devoured**, TEV has "**ate it up**," and Brc has "snapped them up." Similarly many translators will look for some expression that conveys more than "ate," perhaps "ate them all up."

13.5 RSV TEV

Other seeds fell on rocky ground, where they had not much soil, and immediately they sprang up, since they had no depth of soil,

Some of it fell on rocky ground, where there was little soil. The seeds soon sprouted, because the soil wasn't deep.

The reference to **rocky ground** can mean either ground full of rocks or a thin layer of soil on top of a rock ledge. The second of these two interpretations is more probable (Brc "on ground where there was only a thin skin of earth over the rock"). The sun would have heated the rocks immediately beneath the rocky ground, causing the seed on it to sprout more quickly than the seed on the remaining ground.

The text uses **they** referring to the seeds three times in this verse. For the phrase **they had not much soil**, it may be better to say "there was not much soil (for the seeds to grow in)" or "they did not have enough soil to grow in." Similarly **they had no depth of soil** can be "the soil wasn't deep enough for them" or "they didn't have soil there that was deep enough."

Immediately can be "quickly" or "**soon**" (TEV).

Whatever is the usual word for "sprouted" in a language can be used for **sprang up**.

13.6 RSV TEV

but when the sun rose they were scorched; and since they had no root they withered away.

But when the sun came up, it burned the young plants; and because the roots had not grown deep enough, the plants soon dried up.

They were scorched indicates a brief time lapse between verses 5 and 6, for in this verse **they** no longer refers to the seeds of verse 5, but rather to "**the young plants**" (TEV). Evidently the seeds sprout after the heat of the day, but the next day, when the sun comes out in full force again, the newly sprouted plants are scorched by the same heat that initially made the seeds sprout so quickly. In many languages it will be necessary to transform the Greek passive **were scorched** to an active with the agent expressed, as in TEV; for example, "the sun scorched the young plants."

As RSV indicates, **root** is singular in Greek; however, a number of translations prefer the plural "**roots**" (TEV, NAB, NJB, Phps). In many languages it will be necessary to render "because they did not have enough roots" or ". . . long enough roots," or ". . . the roots did not go deep enough," since plants require some degree of root before they will sprout. GECL restructures considerably but with the same impact: "because they did not have enough soil."

They withered away is translated "**the plants soon dried up**" by TEV.

13.7	RSV	TEV

Other seeds fell upon thorns, and the thorns grew up and choked them.

Some of the seed fell among thorn bushes, which grew up and choked the plants.

Other seeds fell upon thorns may leave the impression that the seeds were thrown into a patch of full-grown thorn bushes. It is only toward the end of the verse that the reader realizes that the thorn bushes were not already there at the time of the sowing. The reference is either to ground that contains the roots of old thorn bushes which will sprout in the coming season, or to ground in which thorn seeds have also fallen. This information may be necessary to provide in translation. For example, "Some of the seed fell among places where thorn bushes were going to grow up" or ". . . where the seeds (or, roots) of thorn bushes were already in the ground."

For **thorns**, translators should use some plant or weed that grows quickly and is covered by thorns.

Grew up translates a verb which means "shoot up" or "spring up" when used of plants. Jesus is here referring to thorn plants which grow simultaneously with the newly sprouted grain plants. They grow more quickly and have more durability than the grain plants, and so they choke out the grain.

Notice that despite the fact that **seeds** is repeated at the beginning of the verse, **them** really refers again to the newly sprouted grain. Thus "choked the young crops" or "choked the seeds that had sprouted" are possible translations.

Languages will generally have a way of referring to one plant being **choked** by another, although a short phrase such as "made it impossible for them to grow" may be required.

13.8	RSV	TEV

Other seeds fell on good soil and brought forth grain, some a hundred-fold, some sixty, some thirty.

But some seeds fell in good soil, and the plants bore grain: some had one hundred grains, other sixty, and others thirty."

Other seeds (TEV **"Some seeds"**) is literally "Others" (NJB). NEB renders "some of the seed." The reference is obviously to another group of seeds, and the wording is purely a stylistic matter.

Good soil or "good ground" (Brc) is a literal rendering of the Greek text and is followed by most translations. NJB has "rich soil." The reference is to soil that is fertile, sufficiently deep, and not plagued by thorn bushes.

And brought forth grain is literally "and they are giving fruit." In this context "fruit" is used generically of "grain," and "to give fruit" is a Semitic idiom equivalent in the present context to the meaning given by RSV and TEV.

How **brought forth grain** will be rendered depends to some extent on what the farmer was said to be sowing in verse 3. "Produced a harvest," "there was a good crop (from the seeds)," or "bore a lot of grain (or seeds, or food)" are possible ways.

The real purpose of the parable is to draw attention to the miracle of harvest: **some a hundredfold, some sixty, some thirty**. God brings about a miracle, and the seed that falls into the good soil bears tremendously. The last phrases, **some a hundredfold, some sixty, some thirty**, also depend on what was sown in verse 3 for their translation. If crops that have heads of grain are known, then translators can say "some plants had heads of one hundred seeds (or, grains), some had heads of sixty, and some had thirty." Other translators will say "Some plants produced one hundred seeds (or, fruits) . . . ." For those who have had to use "food" or "crop" for **grain**, the translation can be "The seeds produced a crop, some of them one hundred times more than had been planted, some sixty times more, and others thirty times more."

13.9

RSV	TEV
He who has ears,[h] let him hear."	And Jesus concluded, "Listen, then, if you have ears!"

[h] Other ancient authorities add here and in verse 43 *to hear*

This verse repeats 11.15 word for word.

13.10-17

RSV	TEV
	The Purpose of the Parables
10 Then the disciples came and said to him, "Why do you speak to them in parables?" 11 And he answered them, "To you it has been given to know the secrets of the kingdom of heaven, but to them it has not been given. 12 For to him who has will more be given, and he will have abundance; but from him who has not, even what he has will be taken away. 13 This is why I speak to them in parables, because seeing they do not see, and hearing they do not hear, nor do they understand. 14 With them indeed is fulfilled the prophecy of Isaiah which says:	10 Then the disciples came to Jesus and asked him, "Why do you use parables when you talk to the people?" 11 Jesus answered, "The knowledge about the secrets of the Kingdom of heaven has been given to you, but not to them. 12 For the person who has something will be given more, so that he will have more than enough; but the person who has nothing will have taken away from him even the little he has. 13 The reason I use parables in talking to them is that they look, but do not see, and they listen, but do not hear or understand. 14 So the prophecy of Isaiah applies to them:

'You shall indeed hear but never understand,
  and you shall indeed see but never perceive.
	'This people will listen and listen, but not understand;
	  they will look and look, but not see,

15 For this people's heart has grown dull,
  and their ears are heavy of hearing,
  and their eyes they have closed,
  lest they should perceive with their eyes,
  and hear with their ears,
  and understand with their heart,
  and turn for me to heal them.'
	15 because their minds are dull,
	  and they have stopped up their ears
	  and have closed their eyes.
	  Otherwise, their eyes would see,
	  their ears would hear,
	  their minds would understand,
	  and they would turn to me, says God,
	  and I would heal them.'

16 But blessed are your eyes, for they see, and your ears, for they hear. 17 Truly, I say to you,	16 "As for you, how fortunate you are!

405

many prophets and righteous men longed to see what you see, and did not see it, and to hear what you hear, and did not hear it.

Your eyes see and your ears hear. 17 I assure you that many prophets and many of God's people wanted very much to see what you see, but they could not, and to hear what you hear, but they did not.

SECTION HEADING: "**The Purpose of the Parables**." This can be rendered "Why Jesus told (people) the parables" or "What the parables mean." If a short sentence is required, then "Jesus tells why he told parables" will be acceptable.

Matthew now introduces a proportionately long section in which Jesus elaborates the purpose of his parables (13.10-17). Mark 4.10-12 and Luke 8.9-10 are parallel to verses 10-15, and Luke 10.23-24 is parallel to verses 16-17. The structure of this section is relatively simple: verse 10 provides the question of the disciples as the occasion for Jesus' explanation of the purpose of parables, which is then given in verses 11-17. But the exegesis of the individual verses and the understanding of the flow of the argument is extremely difficult.

13.10   RSV   TEV

Then the disciples came and said to him, "Why do you speak to them in parables?"

Then the disciples came to Jesus and asked him, "Why do you use parables when you talk to the people?"

Came apparently indicates movement within the boat itself, rather than arrival in a separate boat. See comment at verse 2. Thus "approached him" or "went nearer to him" will be good. Whether "came" or "went" is better will depend on the receptor language.

Both Matthew and Luke 8.9 state that it was **the disciples** who approached Jesus with the question. Mark 4.10 has "those who were about him with the twelve." For a discussion on **disciples**, see 5.1. In this context it refers either to the twelve or to a few close followers, since not too many could approach him while he was in a boat, and he only revealed the secrets of the parables to a few chosen followers. Further, the use of **the** makes many think of the twelve. Therefore "his disciples" is possible.

Why do you speak to them in parables? varies in both Mark 4.10 and Luke 8.9. Mark employs indirect discourse and has "Those who were about him with the twelve asked him concerning the parables," and Luke, who also prefers indirect discourse, has "his disciples asked him what this parable meant."

Matthew distinguishes between the way in which Jesus addresses his disciples and the way he addresses the outsiders (**them**), implying a difference in understanding between the two groups. **Them** may have to be "these people" or "the people."

The question can be "Why do you use parables to teach these people?" or "Why do you teach the people with parables?" It can also be in indirect discourse, as in Luke and Mark. For an explanation of **parables**, see verse 3.

RSV   TEV

And he answered them, "To you it   Jesus answered, "The knowl-
has been given to know the secrets   edge about the secrets of the King-
of the kingdom of heaven, but to   dom of heaven has been given to
them it has not been given.   you, but not to them.

And he answered them: in Greek Jesus' answer is introduced by a conjunction which may be used either as the equivalent of marking direct discourse or with
the meaning "because." RSV, TEV, NEB, NIV, and GECL follow the first alternative,
while JB, Mft, Phps, TOB follow the other choice. The context supports either
interpretation, and no final argument may be offered for one as opposed to the
other. Some translators who follow this second interpretation will be working in
languages that introduce a causative reply like this: "I use parables because the
knowledge about the secrets . . . ."

Note that **them** in this verse refers in the first occurrence to the disciples and
in the second to the crowds.

To you it has been given to know translates a passive construction in which
God is the assumed actor. That is, "God has given you the knowledge . . . ." GECL
1st edition makes this explicit, "God has let you understand his intentions with the
world."

Both Matthew and Luke 8.10 have the plural **secrets**, while Mark 4.11 has the
singular. Elsewhere Matthew reflects a preference for the plural (see 8.26), though
his use of the plural here may be determined by the numerous themes which he sees
in the parables. The noun "secret" (or "mystery") is frequently used in Jewish
apocalyptic literature, where it refers to "secrets" made known to God's elect people
but hidden from others. Most often these "secrets" relate to events connected with
the end of time (for example, resurrection, final judgment, Messianic kingdom, and
the immortality of the soul). The noun is used similarly in the Greek translation of
the book of Daniel (2.18,19,27,28,29,30,47 [twice]). Daniel is the only nonapocryphal
book of the Septuagint where this word is used, though it is also found in Tobit
12.7,11; Judith 2.2; Wisdom of Solomon 2.22; 6.22; 14.15,23; Sirach 22.22;
27.16,17,21; and 2 Maccabees 13.21. In Wisdom of Solomon 2.22 the reference is to
"God's wisdom." **Secrets** may be rendered as "secret (or, hidden) truths,"
"knowledge hidden from people," "knowledge (or truths, or things) that other people
do not know," or "the knowledge people can't find out (or, learn)." It can be either
singular or plural, depending on the receptor language.

Kingdom of heaven: see comments on 3.2. MACL translates "the manner in
which God establishes his rule on this earth," and INCL has "the secret concerning
God and his rule."

But to them it has not been given: the implied agent is God, "but God has
not given this understanding to others." None of the translations consulted mentions
God explicitly, but GECL 1st edition comes close by the manner in which it connects
this clause with the previous: "God has allowed you to understand his purpose for
the world, but to others it remains hidden." JB, through the use of "revealed,"
implies an act of God: "but they are not revealed to them." There will be many
languages, however, where translators will find it helpful to mention God, as in our
example above.

13.11

Them may be "these people" or "other people."

RSV	TEV
For to him who has will more be given, and he will have abundance; but from him who has not, even what he has will be taken away.	For the person who has something will be given more, so that he will have more than enough; but the person who has nothing will have taken away from him even the little he has.

This saying, repeated in 25.29 (see Mark 4.25; Luke 8.18), is difficult; some scholars even speak of it as "obscure." It is in the form of a proverb, and commentators note the similarity between it and the proverbial sayings of certain Jewish teachers. For example, some of them taught that God gave wisdom to the wise, but not to the foolish, thereby filling vessels that were already full, while leaving others empty. Here the application is to Jesus' disciples; they have received an understanding of the way that God works, and to them he will grant a deeper understanding. But others have refused this wisdom, and so in the final judgment God will take from them what they have.

For is not used as a preposition; it serves to indicate a logical connection between verses 11 and 12. Obviously many languages have a simple word that corresponds to **For**. Others have to strengthen it with a phrase like "(For) you see, to him . . ." or "This is true because."

Him who has (TEV "**person who has something**"): as may be observed from RSV, the Greek text does not have an expressed object of the verb **has**, and for many languages an object will be required. To supply "**something**" (TEV) may imply material possessions and possibly even money. And the restructuring of NAB will definitely cause the majority of readers to think in material terms: "To the man who has, more will be given until he grows rich." Many languages will require an object after **has**, and some decision must be made. In the context the implied object is "understanding," especially as it relates to the activity of God in establishing his Kingdom in the world. Therefore one may translate "who has understanding," or "who understands the secrets of God's Kingdom," or "who understands the secret ways that God goes about establishing his Kingdom in the world."

Will more be given may need to be transformed into an active construction with God as subject: "God will give more understanding." Actually the whole first part of the sentence may need to be restructured, as in "For the person who has understanding, God will give that person more of it" or "For it is the person who has understanding to whom God will give more of it."

Note that **him** means "person" and does not refer to males only.

And he will have abundance is translated "**so that he will have more than enough**" by TEV and ". . . will be plentifully supplied" by AT. The meaning is that the person will receive more than is sufficient, but the wording of TEV may imply that he receives more than he actually wants. One may translate "until he has all the understanding that he needs, and even more."

Him who has not (TEV "**the person who has nothing**"): as with "**something**" in the first half of this verse, so "**nothing**" may also be understood of material possessions. Therefore one may need to translate similarly, "who does not have any understanding."

It is not logical to state that **even what he has** will be taken from the person who has nothing. But the statement is one of exaggeration for emphasis, as is typical in parables. In order to stress the smallness of **what he has**, TEV translates "**even the little he has**" (NAB "what little he has").

Will be taken away may be translated "God will take away from him."

The second part of the verse may be restructured also, as was the first part: "but the person who has no understanding, God will take from him even the little he has" or "but God will take away from the person who has no understanding even the little he has."

13.13	RSV	TEV

This is why I speak to them in parables, because seeing they do not see, and hearing they do not hear, nor do they understand.	The reason I use parables in talking to them is that they look, but do not see, and they listen, but do not hear or understand.

This is why I speak to them in parables: verse 13 is best interpreted as the continuation of Jesus' response to the question raised by the disciples in verse 10. In verses 11-12 he contrasts those who have understanding with those who do not, and now he focuses upon those who are without understanding. As the quotation from Isaiah indicates (verses 13-15), the people do not understand because they refuse to understand.

In many languages the pronoun **This** is confusing, since it most naturally refers back to verses 11 and 12. To avoid this, translators can follow TEV, "**The reason I use parables in talking to them is . . . ,**" or say "Therefore I speak to them in parables, because . . . ."

Again, **them** refers to "these people" or just "people."

Speak to them can be "talk to them" or "teach them."

Because is the same conjunction with which Matthew introduces the words of Jesus in verse 11 (not expressly translated there in RSV). This Greek word may either mean **because** or may be used to introduce a quotation, serving as the equivalent of opening quotation marks. Matthew uses it twice in this passage, but it does not appear at all in the parallels in Mark and Luke. This suggests that Matthew here intends a causative force rather than merely a marker of direct discourse. Two observations strengthen this conclusion: (1) Matthew opens this verse with a formula which specifically indicates cause (**This is why**), and (2) he alone of the Gospel writers quotes directly Isaiah 6.9-10. The parables thus confirm the people's refusal to respond to Jesus' message.

Seeing they do not see: the combination of a finite verb form (**see**) and a participle of the same (or equivalent) verb stem (**seeing**) is a way of stating something with great emphasis in the biblical languages. GECL restructures, using different verb forms: "Because they see, but understand nothing; they hear, but comprehend nothing." The text uses the same verb twice, howbeit in different forms: **seeing they do not see**. In some languages the meaning can best be conveyed by adding some modifier, as in "They can see, but yet they don't (see)" or "They can see, but they don't really see." Some translations such as TEV and GECL use two different verbs. An example is "They can see, but don't perceive."

In some languages people will ask "they don't see (or, perceive) what?" Possible objects can be "what is there (to see)" or "the truth," or even "they perceive nothing."

These same problems arise with **hearing . . . hear**. "They can hear, but yet they don't" or ". . . but don't really hear" are possible translations. The text adds **nor do they understand**, which TEV and NIV reduce to "or understand." The problem is that it doesn't really add meaning to the sense of **do not see** or **do not hear**, but translators can make it a separate sentence, "They don't understand at all (or, anything)."

13.14-15   RSV   TEV

RSV	TEV
14 With them indeed is fulfilled the prophecy of Isaiah which says:	14 So the prophecy of Isaiah applies to them:
'You shall indeed hear but never understand, and you shall indeed see but never perceive.	'This people will listen and listen, but not understand; they will look and look, but not see,
15 For this people's heart has grown dull, and their ears are heavy of hearing, and their eyes they have closed, lest they should perceive with their eyes, and hear with their ears, and understand with their heart, and turn for me to heal them.'	15 because their minds are dull, and they have stopped up their ears and have closed their eyes. Otherwise, their eyes would see, their ears would hear, their minds would understand, and they would turn to me, says God, and I would heal them.'

With them indeed is fulfilled the prophecy of Isaiah which says: this fulfillment formula (see 1.22) is slightly different from that used elsewhere in Matthew's Gospel, where purpose is stated ("in order that it might be fulfilled"). In addition the verb has a prepositional prefix which may serve to make it more emphatic. However, most interpreters see no distinction in meaning between the two forms, apart from these formal differences. A very simple way to render this phrase is to say "So they make come true what the prophet Isaiah predicted (or, said would happen). He said . . . ." Another way is "The prophet Isaiah said certain things would happen, and now with these people those things are happening. He said . . . ."

For comments on "prophet," see 1.22. **Prophecy** is the spoken or written message of a prophet.

The quotation is taken word for word from the Septuagint of Isaiah 6.9-10, as is the same quotation in Acts 28.26-27. Of all the fulfillment quotations used by Matthew, this is the only one attributed directly to Jesus. It is also the only one where the quotation agrees in all details with the Septuagint, though 1.23 may also agree word for word with Isaiah 7.14, if one follows the Septuagint manuscripts which have the words "they shall call." Of significance also is the observation that this quotation is found only in Matthew's Gospel, though the Marcan parallel (4.12) apparently refers to this passage without quoting it. These observations combine to suggest that for Matthew the quotation is of vital importance.

You of the Greek text is translated "**This people**" by TEV. The problem is that the Greek text shifts from the second-person subject (**you**) of verse 14 to a third-person subject (**this people's heart**) in verse 15, although referring to the same people. In order to avoid an unnatural shift in grammatical subjects, TEV uses "**This people**" and third-person references throughout. There are languages where the plural "these people" will be better, but another possible singular form is "this generation of people."

The repetition of the verb (**shall indeed hear**, **shall indeed see**) represents an emphatic formula similar to that discussed in verse 13. In some languages the repetition of the verb will lessen the impact rather than intensify it, so the translator must be alert to the expectations of the receptor language. GECL, for example, does not repeat the verb. One may translate "No matter how much these people listen . . . look." This part of the quotation from Isaiah is similar to the words of Jesus in the previous verse and can be rendered in a similar fashion. **Hear** may need to be "listen," but **understand** will probably be retained.

The emphasis conveyed by **indeed** can be translated by repetition, as seen in TEV, or by "really" or "certainly." For example, "These people will certainly hear (the truth), but they will never understand (it)." Similarly, **see** may be translated "look at," and **perceive** may be "comprehend." Thus the line can be "and they will certainly look (at the truth), but will never see (or, comprehend) it."

Heart has grown dull: in Hebrew thought the **heart** represents a person's thinking and willing capacity. Brc translates "The mind of this people . . . ," and TEV has "**their minds . . . .**" **Dull** may also be rendered "slow to learn" or "unable to learn." GECL translates "For this people is inwardly dull." Since the text says their heart or thinking **has grown dull**, one rendering will be "These people are no longer able to learn (anything)." The form and meaning can both be retained in a sentence like "Their minds have become too dull to learn anything."

Their ears are heavy of hearing: most modern English translations are not very dynamic, though NAB renders "they have scarcely heard with their ears." The translation should avoid the implication that the person's ears are physically malfunctioning. The meaning is that they cannot hear because they do not want to hear. One way to translate, then, is to say "they have stopped listening" or "they refuse to listen anymore." To retain the form can result in a rather awkward sentence or one that is hard to understand, but one possibility is "As if their ears were a burden too heavy to carry, they have stopped listening."

And their eyes they have closed (TEV "**and have closed their eyes**"): in the TEV restructuring the subject of the verb **have closed** is left implicit in this clause, since it is stated explicitly ("they") in the preceding clause. RSV reflects the order of the Greek sentence (object-subject-verb), which is unnatural for English readers and is restructured by most translations. To say "and they have closed their eyes" will probably be understood in most languages. If not, "They refuse to use their eyes" or "They refuse to look" will convey the meaning.

Lest (TEV "**Otherwise**"; JB "for fear"): a Greek particle is here used as a conjunction, marking an emphatic contrast between the preceding clause and the clause which follows. A literal translation of **lest** is "so that not," as in "so that they won't be able to see with their eyes." Translators who prefer to start a new sentence, as TEV has with "**Otherwise**," can use a construction like "If they had not done this, then they would be able to see."

The three lines following **lest** follow the reverse order of the first three in verse 15. A possible model is "So that they won't be able to see with their eyes, or hear with their ears, or understand anything with their minds." The people know that if they hear or see or learn, they will turn to God to heal them. But they don't want to turn to God, and that is why they refuse to hear, see, or learn! This needs to be made clear in the translation. The last line of the verse, **and turn to me to heal them**, can follow on from the previous line: ". . . understand anything with their minds and as a result turn to me . . . ."

And turn to me to heal them is followed in TEV by "**says God**" (so also DUCL, FRCL, GECL) to indicate that in verses 14b-15 God is the speaker in the quotation taken from Isaiah. Otherwise the reader is certain to assume that Isaiah is the one addressing the people.

The trouble with "**says God**" of TEV is that in many languages it has to precede the quotation. One way is to begin the last line "If they did, God says, 'They would turn to me . . . .'" Another way is to use indirect speech: "As a result, as God says, they would turn to him . . . ." Or God can be kept in the third person, as in "then they would turn to God for him . . . ." Some translators have preferred to indicate at the beginning of verse 14 that Isaiah was speaking for God, as in ". . . what Isaiah predicted when he spoke God's word . . . ."

Turn is often used for "repent," and that can be used here. Other translators have "turn to me" or "return to me."

For me to heal them gives the purpose of the people's turning to God. "So I can heal them" or "And then I would heal them" are translations that show this.

Heal here refers to spiritual rather than physical healing, but most translations retain the words "cure" or "healing," finding it unnecessary to specify further the kind of healing God gives.

13.16	RSV	TEV

RSV	TEV
But blessed are your eyes, for they see, and your ears, for they hear.	"As for you, how fortunate you are! Your eyes see and your ears hear.

The Isaiah citation ends with verse 15, and some languages have to indicate this. One way is to begin verse 16 with "Jesus continued by saying."

A parallel to verses 16-17 is found in Luke 10.23-24, where Jesus congratulates his disciples because of their good fortune in living in the promised Messianic age. The wording in the two passages is slightly different.

Blessed in this context can be "fortunate" or expressed as a sentence such as "God has been very good to you" or "God has blessed you." These examples show that the one who blessed them was God himself.

Your eyes: in Greek the pronoun **your** is placed in an emphatic position in the sentence, to show contrast. TEV attempts to transfer this same emphasis by restructuring "**As for you**." GECL translates the entire verse "But you should rejoice, since your eyes can see and your ears can hear."

To say that the **eyes** and **ears** are **blessed** is certainly possible, as "Your eyes are indeed fortunate" or "God has blessed your eyes." However, it is not so much the **eyes** and **ears** that are blessed as the disciples themselves. TEV shows this clearly with "**how fortunate you are!**" GECL, cited above, makes this clear, too.

Note that in this verse **see** and **hear** really mean "can see" and "can hear."

13.17   RSV   TEV

RSV	TEV
Truly, I say to you, many prophets and righteous men longed to see what you see, and did not see it, and to hear what you hear, and did not hear it.	I assure you that many prophets and many of God's people wanted very much to see what you see, but they could not, and to hear what you hear, but they did not.

Truly, I say to you (TEV "**I assure you**"): see comment at 5.18.

For **prophets**, see comments on 1.22.

Righteous men is the plural masculine form of the adjective first used in 1.19, where it was translated "just" (see also 5.45). TEV translates "**God's people**"; JB "holy men"; NEB "saints"; GECL "devout people"; and Brc "many a good man." Other common renderings are "men who did God's will" and "men who obeyed God."

Longed is the rendering of several translations (NJB, NAB, Brc); NEB has "desired," and TEV "**wanted very much.**"

To see . . . and did not hear it may be restructured and shortened: ". . . to see and hear what you have seen and heard, but they did not" or ". . . but they did not see or hear it."

There will be cases where what the disciples are seeing and hearing will have to be made more explicit. Brc has "to see the events which you are seeing" and "to hear the words which you are hearing."

13.18-23

RSV   TEV

Jesus Explains the Parable of the Sower

18 "Hear then the parable of the sower. 19 When any one hears the word of the kingdom and does not understand it, the evil one comes and snatches away what is sown in his heart; this is what was sown along the path. 20 As for what was

18 "Listen, then, and learn what the parable of the sower means. 19 Those who hear the message about the Kingdom but do not understand it are like the seeds that fell along the path. The Evil One comes and snatches away what was

sown on rocky ground, this is he who hears the word and immediately receives it with joy; 21 yet he has no root in himself, but endures for a while, and when tribulation or persecution arises on account of the word, immediately he falls away.[i] 22 As for what was sown among thorns, this is he who hears the word, but the cares of the world and the delight in riches choke the word, and it proves unfruitful. 23 As for what was sown on good soil, this is he who hears the word and understands it; he indeed bears fruit, and yields, in one case a hundredfold, in another sixty, and in another thirty."

sown in them. 20 The seeds that fell on rocky ground stand for those who receive the message gladly as soon as they hear it. 21 But it does not sink deep into them, and they don't last long. So when trouble or persecution comes because of the message, they give up at once. 22 The seeds that fell among thorn bushes stand for those who hear the message; but the worries about this life and the love for riches choke the message, and they don't bear fruit. 23 And the seeds sown in the good soil stand for those who hear the message and understand it: they bear fruit, some as much as one hundred, others sixty, and others thirty."

[i] Or *stumbles*

SECTION HEADING: "**Jesus Explains the Parable of the Sower.**" It may be necessary to indicate to whom Jesus explained the parable: "Jesus explains to his disciples what the parable of the sower means."

This allegorical interpretation of the Parable of the Sower (13.1-9) has a parallel in Mark 4.13-20 and Luke 8.11-15. Of all the parables in the synoptic Gospels, this is the only one that is specifically interpreted in this manner.

13.18	RSV	TEV

"**Hear then the parable of the sower.**

"**Listen, then, and learn what the parable of the sower means.**

Hear then is literally "You therefore hear," in which "You" is placed in the position of emphasis, as is "your" in verse 16. Both NEB ("You, then, may hear . . .") and JB ("You, therefore, are to hear . . .") reflect very closely the Greek sentence structure. The "You" refers to the disciples as opposed to the crowds of people who were thronging around Jesus.

A literal translation of the remainder of this verse is confusing, for it gives the impression to the reader that Jesus is about to tell the parable: **Hear then the parable of the sower**. Jesus is not calling upon his disciples to hear the parable again, but to understand its meaning. TEV tries to bring this out by translating "**Listen, then, and learn what the parable of the sower means.**" GECL translates "I will tell you what the parable of the sower means."

It is interesting to note that there are languages, for example many in West Africa, where **hear** commonly is used to mean "understand." Readers will have little difficulty with a literal rendering. However, in most other cases something like TEV or GECL will be better. Other possibilities are "Now, therefore, listen to the meaning" or "Therefore you should listen now to the meaning."

For comments on **parable** and **sower**, see verse 3.

RSV	TEV
When any one hears the word of the kingdom and does not understand it, the evil one comes and snatches away what is sown in his heart; this is what was sown along the path.	**Those who hear the message about the Kingdom but do not understand it are like the seeds that fell along the path. The Evil One comes and snatches away what was sown in them.**

RSV offers a literal rendering of this verse, while TEV makes a few noteworthy translational adjustments. For stylistic reasons **any one** is changed to the plural "**Those who.**" Then the last sentence in Greek (**this is what was sown along the path**) has been altered to a simile ("**those . . . are like . . .**") and joined to the first sentence in TEV. Finally, **the word of the kingdom** has been made explicit: "**the message about the Kingdom.**" It may even be necessary to qualify **the word of the kingdom** more precisely: "there are people who have heard the Good News that God will establish his reign" (GECL 1st edition). INCL has ". . . the news concerning God and his reign." Translators should study these adjustments carefully, since in some cases they will be useful models to follow.

Whether to retain **any one** or use a plural will certainly depend on the receptor language style.

As for **the word of the kingdom**, translators can follow the examples cited above from GECL and INCL, or they may say "the news I give about God's rule."

Understand is the meaning followed by most all translators. But GECL 1st edition renders "(do not) take (the message) seriously," which is supported by both the immediate context and other contexts in which the verb is found. Another attempt that has been made to render **understand** is "make it part of his understanding." Since this is a fairly high level of language, others have said instead "understand it completely" or "try sincerely to understand it." Note that all these examples are attempting to include in the translation an element of willingness on the part of the hearer.

The evil one appears as "Satan" in the Marcan parallel (4.15). For some readers it may be necessary to make the identity explicit: "the Evil One, that is, Satan" or ". . . , that is, the Devil." GECL has "God's enemy comes . . . ." Readers should see also comments at 4.1 and 5.37.

Snatches away can be "takes away" or "grabs and carries off."

In his heart: in Hebrew thought the **heart** was the instrument used for thinking and willing, and so both NAB and AT render "mind." In the present context the meaning is sufficiently expressed by "**in them**" or "within them," since the analogy is that of the word placed in the heart in the same way that seed is placed in the soil.

The expression **what is sown in his heart** may or may not be readily comprehensible. If the image simply is not clear, then translators can say "the message that he heard" or "the true word that was put in his heart (or, mind)." To avoid a passive construction, translators can also say "that God put in him." However, it is obviously better to retain the imagery of the parable, so that "the word God sowed in his heart" or "the message planted in them" and similar sentences are better solutions. Note that **sown** can be "planted."

As noted above, **this is what was sown along the path** is translated as a simile in TEV. This shift from a metaphor to a simile by the inclusion of **"are like"** simplifies the understanding of the text. In fact, in some languages the shift to a simile will be obligatory. But even this adjustment does not resolve one major contradiction which causes difficulty for numerous readers. That is, the seed is identified with the hearers, whereas the true equation is that the seed is the message. The parable makes sense only if the soil is identified with the hearers. And this problem may be resolved if **this is what was sown along the path** is taken to mean "This kind of person is represented by the picture of the seed sown on the side of the road" (Brc) or "This is like the seed sown by the road-side" (Phps). GECL resolves the problem by translating "With them it is like the seed which fell on the road." Another way many translators have used is "When that happens, it is just like when some of the seed fell along the path."

13.20	RSV	TEV

As for what was sown on rocky ground, this is he who hears the word and immediately receives it with joy;

The seeds that fell on rocky ground stand for those who receive the message gladly as soon as they hear it.

As for what was sown on rocky ground: for the meaning of **rocky ground** see verse 5. The same translational problems exist here as in the previous verse, and JB translates "The one who received it on patches of rock is the man who hears the word and welcomes it at once with joy." GECL renders "With others it is as with the seed which fell on rocky ground. They hear the Good News and receive it at once with joy."

In many cases it is easier to translate this verse if the order is reversed: "And when a person hears the word and accepts it joyfully, that is just like when some of the seed fell on rocky ground." Even with this order, it is usually possible to continue with the next verse naturally, as in "That person has no root . . . ." However, there are also translators who treat verses 20 and 21 together, moving this first phrase of verse 20 to the end of verse 21: "And there are other people who hear the word and immediately accept it gladly. But the message does not really take root in them, and when trouble or persecution comes because of this message, they abandon it quickly. When that happens, it is just like when some of the seed fell on rocky ground."

The text says **what was sown**, but most of the examples we have given say "the seed that was sown."

Again, the singular **he who hears** can just as easily be plural, "people who hear," depending on the receptor language.

This verse says simply **hears the word**, which differs from the "word of the kingdom" of verse 19. "Hears the message," ". . . message I bring," or ". . . message from God" are all possibilities.

Receives it can be rendered "accepts it," "welcomes it," or even "believes it."

Immediately . . . with joy is given emphasis in the Greek sentence structure. Translators should therefore find a way of doing the same in the receptor language texts. Examples are "Right then with enthusiasm" and "Immediately and with much joy."

13.21	RSV	TEV
	yet he has no root in himself, but endures for a while, and when tribulation or persecution arises on account of the word, immediately he falls away.[i]	But it does not sink deep into them, and they don't last long. So when trouble or persecution comes because of the message, they give up at once.

[i] Or *stumbles*

Yet he has no root in himself: in such a context **root** is used symbolically of "stability" or "steadfastness." RSV retains the root imagery, but this is not necessary and perhaps not even the best procedure to follow, since the comparison shifts from a plant to a person. INCL maintains the figure with some effectiveness ("but the message does not take root in them"), while TEV drops the imagery ("**But it does not sink deep in them**"). Other possibilities include "but it does not make a deep impression on them," "they don't really make it part of them," "but the word does not really establish itself in their lives."

Endures for a while translates an adjective in Greek which means "temporary" or "lasting only for a while." Other than the Marcan parallel (4.17), the word occurs elsewhere in the New Testament only twice (2 Cor 4.18; Heb 11.25). NEB has "no staying-power"; GECL "unstable" or "unsteady." The phrase **endures for a while** can be handled in either of two ways. The subject can be the person who received the word, as in "he believes only for a short time" or "he accepts the message only for a little while." A second way is for the word to be the subject, as in "the word stays in him only for a short time" or "this word does not remain a part of his life very long." Of course, this phrase should flow naturally from the previous one.

Tribulation (TEV "**trouble**") is found elsewhere in Matthew in 24.9,21,29. **Persecution** occurs only here in the Gospel. The word refers to a campaign to oppress or punish people because of their belief or their race. The combination of the two words is found elsewhere only in Mark 4.17 and 2 Thessalonians 1.4, though Romans 8.35 is similar with the addition of "hardship" (TEV). The first of these two nouns (**tribulation**; TEV "**trouble**") is used of difficulties in general; the second does refer to **persecution** in particular. Depending on the receptor language, translators have used words like "troubles," "suffering," and "hard times" for **tribulation** and **persecution**. However, some translators have employed verbal phrases to render these terms, as in "when people (start to) persecute him and cause him to suffer" or ". . . make trouble for him and give him suffering."

These things happen **on account of the word**, that is, "because he has believed (or, accepted) the message." As in verse 19 **word** is used in the sense of "**message**" (TEV).

Fall away (TEV "**give up**") occurs with similar meaning in 24.10; Mark 4.17; 14.27,29; John 16.1. It can be rendered as "he stops believing the word" or "he abandons his faith."

As for what was sown among thorns, this is he who hears the word, but the cares of the world and the delight in riches choke the word, and it proves unfruitful.	The seeds that fell among thorn bushes stand for those who hear the message; but the worries about this life and the love for riches choke the message, and they don't bear fruit.

What was sown among thorns: see verse 7.

Translators can continue to treat in the same way the comparisons Jesus is making. An example is "As for the seed that fell in the place where there were thorn bushes, that is like the case of the person who hears the word . . ." or ". . . that is like what happens when someone hears the word . . . ."

Note that the words **As for** indicate that the focus here changes from the seed that fell on rocky ground to the seed scattered among the thorns. In English, to begin the sentence with **he who hears the word** would mean that this focus would be lost, so we have not given that as a suggestion. If translators do need to restructure that way, they should be sure to find a way in their language to insure that the focus is retained on **what was sown among thorns**.

The phrase **hears the word** can also be "listens to the message."

The cares of the world is translated "the worries of this life" by Phps (TEV ". . . **about this life**"). The reference is to the ordinary concerns of daily life which are a part of everyone's existence. These are not evil in themselves, as NAB suggests ("worldly anxiety"), though they may become evil when they dominate a person's life. One may translate "the concerns of daily life."

The noun translated **delight** by RSV and "**love**" by TEV has as its basic meaning "deception" or "deceitfulness." However, the word may also mean either "pleasure in" or "love for," which is the generally acknowledged meaning that it has in 2 Peter 2.13. One may translate ". . . but they worry about this life so much and love riches so much that they choke the message . . . ." GECL 1st edition reverses the order of the last two clauses, "but they produce nothing, because they are completely filled with concerns about daily needs and allow themselves to be lead astray by riches."

Note that **cares** and **delight** are both nouns which are expressed by verbs in these examples we have given. Many translators will find that this renders the verse easier to read. Another example is "but he is so concerned about matters of daily life and he loves riches so much that he doesn't give the message a chance to grow." An example using nouns is "but he lets the concerns of daily life and his love for riches take so much of his life that the message cannot survive" or ". . . that the message has no place."

It proves unfruitful means that the word or message cannot bear fruit. Fruit is often used as a symbol to represent actions, or it can represent results. In this context, then, the meaning is "and it (the word) does not produce good results (in that person)" or "and the word does not affect the deeds (or, life) of that person."

13.23   RSV   TEV

As for what was sown on good soil, this is he who hears the word and understands it; he indeed bears fruit, and yields, in one case a hundredfold, in another sixty, and in another thirty."

And the seeds sown in the good soil stand for those who hear the message and understand it: they bear fruit, some as much as one hundred, others sixty, and others thirty."

Note that as in verse 22, **As for** puts the focus on the seed. Therefore another way the sentence can be rendered is "As for the seed that was scattered on the good soil, that is like what happens when a person hears the word and understands it . . . ."

What was sown on good soil pertains to the seeds of verse 8 (TEV "**the seeds sown in the good soil**"). For **good soil**, see verse 8.

This is, an equational marker indicating a metaphor, is altered to a simile by TEV through the rendering "**stand for**" (see also verse 19). GECL translates "with others it eventually ends up like the seed which was sown on good ground." Brc translates "The picture of the seed which was sown on the good ground represents the man who hears the word and understands it." Brc also structures the last sentence of this verse in such a manner as to retain "the man" as the subject and at the same time to indicate clearly that **a hundredfold ... sixty ... thirty** are references to the original amount of seed placed on the soil: "He indeed bears a crop which produces sometimes a hundred times, sometimes sixty times, sometimes thirty times as much as he received."

The idea of a person bearing fruit can be difficult for many readers. Translators generally find that using similes is very helpful, as in "he will do many good things, just like the seeds that produced plants with one hundred or sixty or thirty grains"—verse 8 for the appropriate plant language—or "his life will become like the seeds that produced plants that had one hundred or sixty or thirty seeds each." But see also the Brc example cited above.

13.24-30

RSV   TEV

The Parable of the Weeds

24 Another parable he put before them, saying, "The kingdom of heaven may be compared to a man who sowed good seed in his field; 25 but while men were sleeping, his enemy came and sowed weeds among the wheat, and went away. 26 So when the plants came up and bore grain, then the weeds appeared also. 27 And the servants^j of the householder came and said to him, 'Sir, did you not sow good seed in your field? How then has it weeds?' 28 He said to them, 'An enemy has done this.' The servants^j said to him, 'Then do you want us to go and gather them?' 29 But he said, 'No; lest in gathering the weeds you

24 Jesus told them another parable: "The Kingdom of heaven is like this. A man sowed good seed in his field. 25 One night, when everyone was asleep, an enemy came and sowed weeds among the wheat and went away. 26 When the plants grew and the heads of grain began to form, then the weeds showed up. 27 The man's servants came to him and said, 'Sir, it was good seed you sowed in your field; where did the weeds come from?' 28 'It was some enemy who did this,' he answered. 'Do you want us to go and pull up the weeds?' they asked him. 29 'No,' he answered, 'because as you gather the weeds you might pull up some of

root up the wheat along with them. 30 Let both grow together until the harvest; and at harvest time I will tell the reapers, Gather the weeds first and bind them in bundles to be burned, but gather the wheat into my barn.' "

the wheat along with them. 30 Let the wheat and the weeds both grow together until harvest. Then I will tell the harvest workers to pull up the weeds first, tie them in bundles and burn them, and then to gather in the wheat and put it in my barn.' "

_j_ Or _slaves_

SECTION HEADING: **"The Parable of the Weeds."** See verse 1; translators can use the same type of structure here. For **Weeds**, see comments on verse 25.

This parable (verses 24-30), together with its interpretation (verses 36-43), is found only in the Gospel of Matthew. In its place Mark has the Parable of the Seed Growing Secretly (4.26-29), which does not satisfy the needs of Matthew's context. The Marcan parable stresses continued and automatic progress, whereas Matthew emphasizes the inevitability of a harvest despite the terrible opposition.

13.24   RSV   TEV

Another parable he put before them, saying, "The kingdom of heaven may be compared to a man who sowed good seed in his field;

Jesus told them another parable: "The Kingdom of heaven is like this. A man sowed good seed in his field.

Another parable he put before them, saying appears also in verse 31 but nowhere else. Commentators note that the formula resembles that used by Moses when giving the Law to the people (Exo 19.7) and by Christian teachers in presenting their teaching to the Christian community (1 Tim 1.18; 2 Tim 2.2). Since a new section begins here, TEV explicitly identifies **he** as Jesus; in TEV the sentence is also restructured in a more natural order for English speakers, and **saying** has been dropped because it is redundant.

In the preceding verses Jesus has been explaining to his disciples the meaning of the parable of the sower. Thus some translators have interpreted **them** to refer to the disciples. However, as we see in verse 36, this parable was addressed to the crowds. Thus a possible rendering is "Jesus told the people (or, crowds) another parable. (He said . . .)." Note that this makes "Jesus" the subject, not **another parable**.

As elsewhere in Matthew, **the kingdom of heaven** refers to the rule of God. GECL has, "with God's new world, it is like . . . ." InCl translates, "When God rules . . . ."

May be compared to translates a Semitic formula used to introduce a comparison. The full meaning is "As it is with the kingdom of God, so it is with (the situation described in the following story)." In translation it is important to realize that Jesus is not comparing the rule of God to a man, but to the total situation that takes place when the man does such and such. Accordingly MACL translates "When God establishes his rule, the situation will be the same as . . ."; Brc has "What happens in the Kingdom of Heaven . . . is like what happened when a man sowed good seed in his field." Another common way to translate is to say "God's rule is like this: a man sowed . . . ."

For **sowed** and **seed**, see verses 3 and 4. **Good seed** can be rendered "seed that is good for planting."

13.25   RSV   TEV

but while men were sleeping, his enemy came and sowed weeds among the wheat, and went away.	One night, when everyone was asleep, an enemy came and sowed weeds among the wheat and went away.

But while men were sleeping is reproduced in a somewhat natural story-telling style by TEV: "**One night, when everyone was asleep.**" **Men** are best interpreted as people in general (TEV, NEB, NJB, NAB) rather than as a specific reference to the men who were responsible for the care and cultivation of the field, as with Phps ("But while his men were asleep").

His enemy (so also NJB, NEB) is literally "the enemy," but in such constructions "the" has the force of the possessive **his**; TEV has "**an enemy,**" which is also acceptable. One may translate "someone who did not like the man" or "someone who wanted to do harm to the man." When the parable is allegorized, "the enemy" becomes "the devil" (verse 39).

Came may have to be "went." Further, some languages will require a destination, as in "went to the fields."

Weeds is more specifically "darnel" (Brc, NJB, NEB), a poisonous plant which frequently grows in wheat fields. In the early stages of growth this weed is difficult to distinguish from wheat.

In some languages **sowed weeds** will have to be "sowed the seeds of weeds" or "sowed the seeds of a poisonous plant."

13.26   RSV   TEV

So when the plants came up and bore grain, then the weeds appeared also.	When the plants grew and the heads of grain began to form, then the weeds showed up.

Then the weeds appeared also must not be taken to imply that the weeds suddenly shot up after the wheat had matured. The meaning is that the distinction between the weeds and the wheat was not evident until heads of grain began to form on the wheat. A sentence that would make this point clear is "When the plant began to bear grain (or, fruits), at that time people were able to see the weeds, too."

13.27   RSV   TEV

And the servants^j of the householder came and said to him, 'Sir, did you	The man's servants came to him and said, 'Sir, it was good seed you

not sow good seed in your field? How then has it weeds?'	sowed in your field; where did the weeds come from?'

j Or *slaves*

The servants of the householder (TEV "**The man's servants**") are the servants or slaves (RSV footnote) of the owner of the house, the man who sowed good seed in his field (verse 24). (See comments on **householder** at verse 52.) TEV attempts to translate so as to make clear that verses 24 and 27 refer to the same person, "**the man.**" NAB renders "The owner's slaves." It may be helpful in translation to identify the man in verse 24 as the owner of the field; for example, "24 . . . a man who owned a field and sowed good seed in it." Then verse 27 can be translated either "The owner's slaves . . ." or "The man's slaves . . . ." In many languages the identity will be clear if translators use a demonstrative pronoun such as "the servants of that farmer," or ". . . of that man," or ". . . of that man who owned the field."

Came will be "went" in some languages.

Sir, did you not sow good seed in your field? translates a question which expects the answer "Yes, I did sow good seed in my field." TEV shifts to a statement, to ease understanding of the difficult negative question: "**Sir, it was good seed you sowed in your field.**" Phps (see also Brc) retains the question form, but in a conversational style which makes comprehension less difficult than RSV's more complicated style: "Sir, didn't you sow good seed in your field?" For **Sir**, see comments on 8.2.

How then has it weeds? (TEV "**Where did the weeds come from?**") may also be rendered as a statement: "But now there are many weeds in the field." In fact, since the men are giving a report to their master, it may be better to restructure entirely: "Sir, many weeds are now growing in the field where you planted the wheat." Some would add to this statement "How can this be?" or "How did this come about?"

13.28 RSV	TEV
He said to them, 'An enemy has done this.' The servants*j* said to him, 'Then do you want us to go and gather them?'	'It was some enemy who did this,' he answered. 'Do you want us to go and pull up the weeds?' they asked him.

j Or *slaves*

An enemy (TEV "**some enemy**") is redundant in Greek; literally "an enemy, a man." GECL translates "This must have been done by someone who wants to hurt me."

Gather them is translated "**pull up the weeds**" by TEV, since for English speakers **gather** is more appropriately used of wheat and other edible plants. Moreover, on the basis of verse 29, uprooting is obviously intended.

The text uses two verbs in the question, **go** and **gather**. To retain the two is necessary in many languages, but some translations will have simply "Do you want us to pull up the weeds?"

13.29 RSV	TEV
But he said, 'No; lest in gathering the weeds you root up the wheat along with them.	'No,' he answered, 'because as you gather the weeds you might pull up some of the wheat along with them.

Gathering . . . root up: in some languages it may be that **gathering** will not include pulling up the roots. One may then translate "because as you pull up the weeds you might pull up some of the wheat along with them." As in other occurrences of **wheat**, in cases where it is not known, "grain" or "crops" may be used.

13.30 RSV	TEV
Let both grow together until the harvest; and at harvest time I will tell the reapers, Gather the weeds first and bind them in bundles to be burned, but gather the wheat into my barn.' "	Let the wheat and the weeds both grow together until harvest. Then I will tell the harvest workers to pull up the weeds first, tie them in bundles and burn them, and then to gather in the wheat and put it in my barn.' "

Both is clearly a reference to "**the wheat and the weeds**" (TEV).

Until the harvest; and at harvest may be unnecessary repetition in some languages. Note TEV ("**until harvest. Then . . .**"), which drops **at harvest** of the second clause.

Harvest is generally known in languages, but "time of gathering the crops" is sometimes the way people speak of it.

TEV has translated **reapers** as "**harvest workers.**" This can also be "people who work in the fields to gather the crops" or "workers who bring in the harvest."

Gather the weeds . . . into my barn is direct discourse in the Greek text. Some languages, for stylistic reasons, may prefer indirect discourse as in TEV.

Weeds . . . to be burned may reflect the custom of using dried weeds for fuel whenever there was a shortage of wood. However, in the context of the parable, the implication is that the weeds are burned immediately. This is probably because the parable has now become an allegory of the final judgment.

Gather the wheat into my barn: in many languages it will be necessary to specify both the action of gathering and that of storing with separate verbs, as TEV has done ("**gather in the wheat and put it in my barn**").

A **barn** is a "storage house" or "building for storing grain." Some translators use "granary" here.

13.31-32

| RSV | TEV |

The Parable of the Mustard Seed

RSV	TEV
31 Another parable he put before them, saying, "The kingdom of heaven is like a grain of mustard seed which a man took and sowed in his field; 32 it is the smallest of all seeds, but when it has grown it is the greatest of shrubs and becomes a tree, so that the birds of the air come and make nests in its branches."	31 Jesus told them another parable: "The Kingdom of heaven is like this. A man takes a mustard seed and sows it in his field. 32 It is the smallest of all seeds, but when it grows up, it is the biggest of all plants. It becomes a tree, so that birds come and make their nests in its branches."

SECTION HEADING: "**The Parable of the Mustard Seed**." See similar heading at verse 1. For "**Mustard Seed**," see comments on verse 31.

Mark also includes the parable of the Mustard Seed at this point in his narrative (4.30-32), though Luke places it in a different context (13.18-21). The purpose of both this parable and that of the Yeast, which follows at verse 33, is to contrast an insignificant beginning with significant results. The tree and the huge batch of dough stand in sharp contrast to the tiny seed and the small amount of yeast.

13.31

RSV	TEV
Another parable he put before them, saying, "The kingdom of heaven is like a grain of mustard seed which a man took and sowed in his field;	Jesus told them another parable: "The Kingdom of heaven is like this. A man takes a mustard seed and sows it in his field.

Another parable he put before them, saying is a word-for-word repetition of the introduction to the preceding parable (see verse 24).

The kingdom of heaven is like is the Greek translation of an Aramaic formula which means "It is the case with the kingdom of heaven as with a mustard seed" (see verse 24). As in verse 24, one way to begin the verse is to say "God's rule is like this: a man took a mustard seed . . . ." GECL 1st edition renders "When God accomplishes his work, it will be as with a mustard seed which someone planted in a field." INCL ("When God rules, the situation will be as in this parable: . . .") and MACL ("When God establishes his rule, the situation will be the same as with a mustard seed which the man took and planted in his garden") are similar to their restructurings of verse 24.

A grain of mustard seed perpetuates a Semitic idiom; most modern English translations have "**a mustard seed**," as does TEV.

Since the verb **sows** implies more than one seed as an object, one may need to translate "A man takes some mustard seeds and sows them in his field."

Mustard may not be known, so translators may say "a seed of a tree called mustard," borrowing the term from the text they are following. The exact product of a mustard tree is not relevant here, but there is some value in retaining **mustard** since the tree is referred to in several places in the New Testament.

13.32 RSV	TEV
it is the smallest of all seeds, but when it has grown it is the greatest of shrubs and becomes a tree, so that the birds of the air come and make nests in its branches."	It is the smallest of all seeds, but when it grows up, it is the biggest of all plants. It becomes a tree, so that birds come and make their nests in its branches."

It is the smallest of all seeds is translated "There is no smaller seed" by GECL. Although the mustard seed is not actually the smallest of all seeds, some commentators note that the mustard seed was used in a proverb common among Jewish teachers to denote the smallest thing or the smallest amount possible. In Jesus' time mustard was cultivated both for its seed and as a vegetable. Translators need to be sure it is clear that the text is referring to mustard seeds in general, not to the specific seed the man sows in the parable. Hence some translations will say "the seed of a mustard plant is the smallest of any kind of seed."

But when it has grown draws the contrast between the small seed and the large plant which it produces upon maturity. No concern is given to the process or growth. In languages where it is not seeds that grow, it may be necessary to say "But when the plant has grown." **Shrubs** (TEV "**plants**"; NEB "garden-plant") refers to edible garden plants, that is, vegetables.

If a language has a general word for "plants" that can be used for **shrubs**, that is best. However, "bushes" or "plants people grow (for food)" are other possibilities. Each language divides the various sizes and types of plants into categories differently, rarely corresponding to English categories of "bush," "shrub," and "tree." Translators will have to use whatever term from their language seems to be most appropriate.

When fully grown, the mustard plant **becomes a tree** of eight to twelve feet in height. **Birds of the air** (better "**birds**" ; see comment at 6.26) are attracted to the mustard tree because of it shade and its fruit, though they do not normally nest in it. Commentators note that the reference to a huge tree in which birds come to roost is used symbolically in the scriptures of a powerful kingdom which protects its dependent states (see Ezek 17.23; 31.6; Dan 4.20-22). In apocalyptic literature and in the writings of Jewish teachers, birds sometimes represent Gentiles who come to seek refuge with Israel.

There are languages that have no word for **tree** in general, naming instead each particular species. In that case translators should pick some local tree that is about the same height and say "grows to be like _____," using the name of the local tree.

13.33

RSV	TEV
	The Parable of the Yeast
33 He told them another parable. "The kingdom of heaven is like leaven which a woman took and hid in three measures of flour, till it was all leavened."	33 Jesus told them still another parable: "The Kingdom of heaven is like this. A woman takes some yeast and mixes it with a bushel of flour until the whole batch of dough rises."

SECTION HEADING: "**The Parable of the Yeast**." See comments on section heading at verse 1 for a method to treat this heading. For "**Yeast**," see comments on verse 33 below.

In Luke 13.20-21 the Parable of the Yeast also follows that of the Mustard Seed. Needless to say, the two parables are frequently referred to as twin parables because they each convey the same message. This parable is not found in Mark.

13.33 RSV	TEV
He told them another parable. "The kingdom of heaven is like leaven which a woman took and hid in three measures of flour, till it was all leavened."	Jesus told them still another parable: "The Kingdom of heaven is like this. A woman takes some yeast and mixes it with a bushel of flour until the whole batch of dough rises."

He told them another parable is a slightly different introduction from that of verses 24 and 31, but the meaning and function is the same. Again, many translators will render **he** as "Jesus." Also, as with the others, the parable may have to be introduced by "He said."

The kingdom of heaven is like translates the same form found in verse 31; see comments there. GECL, tying this verse closely with the preceding, translates "Or it is just like what happens with yeast." INCL renders "When God reigns, the situation will be as yeast which a woman took . . . ." Another way to show this link with the previous parable is to start the parable by saying "God's rule is also like this: a woman took . . ." or "God's rule can also be said to be like this: a woman . . . ." Notice that in these examples, **a woman** is the subject.

In Jewish thought **leaven** (TEV "**yeast**") symbolizes what is unclean or sinful; all traces of yeast had to be removed from the Jewish household before Passover. In the parable, however, no negative implications are intended. In fact, as with the symbol of the tree and the birds, the figure of yeast may have been chosen as an indirect allusion to the inclusion of the Gentiles. But it is obvious that this sort of information is not allowable in translation.

Leaven poses some difficulty in areas where it is not well known. Some translators have looked for other fermenting agents in their own cultures and modified that for this verse. For example, some African translations say "(the substance like) beer froth that makes the bread dough to expand." A more general word such as "condiment" or "medicine" can sometimes be used. Such words can be modified by the function of yeast, as in "the medicine (or, condiment) that makes the bread dough ferment (or, expand)." As bread is becoming more and more prevalent in the world, the word **leaven** is often borrowed at the same time. Translations will then either have the borrowed form alone or in a phrase such as "leaven that ferments bread dough."

Hid is translated as "**mixes**" by TEV, which seems more appropriate in this context.

Three measures (TEV "**a bushel**") represents an enormous amount of flour, amounting to approximately 39.4 liters or 50 pounds. It is estimated that the bread baked from this amount of dough would be sufficient for more than one hundred persons. The use of exaggerated numbers and amounts is characteristic of parables and of proverbial sayings. Translators sometimes translate **three measures** as "three containers" or as three of some well known local equivalent measure such as "three pans." The other choice would be to use whatever the local way would be of speaking of approximately 50 pounds or 39.4 liters of flour, much as TEV does with **"a bushel."**

Till it was all leavened (TEV **"until the whole batch of dough rises"**) is translated "till it was leavened all though" by NJB. In NAB the sentence is as follows: "Eventually the whole mass of dough began to rise."

13.34-35

RSV	TEV
	Jesus' Use of Parables
34 All this Jesus said to the crowds in parables; indeed he said nothing to them without a parable. 35 This was to fulfill what was spoken by the prophet:[k]	34 Jesus used parables to tell all these things to the crowds; he would not say a thing to them without using a parable. 35 He did this to make come true what the prophet had said,
"I will open my mouth in parables, I will utter what has been hidden since the foundation of the world."	"I will use parables when I speak to them; I will tell them things unknown since the creation of the world."

[k] Other ancient authorities read *the prophet Isaiah*

SECTION HEADING: **"Jesus' Use of Parables."** This can be "Why Jesus told (the people) parables" or "Why Jesus used parables."

In Mark's chapter on parables these two verses form the conclusion (4.33-34). But Matthew adds (1) his explanation of the Parable of the Weeds (verses 36-43), (2) three brief parables (verses 44-50), and (3) a second conclusion (verses 51-52).

13.34 RSV	TEV
All this Jesus said to the crowds in parables; indeed he said nothing to them without a parable.	**Jesus used parables to tell all these things to the crowds; he would not say a thing to them without using a parable.**

In the Greek text **said . . . parables . . . said . . . parables** is actually in the order "said . . . parables . . . parables . . . said," which forms what is known as a chiastic structure (see 5.45; 6.24; 7.6):

But this arrangement is somewhat difficult for many speakers of English, so both RSV and TEV switch to a more natural order. In other languages the usage of any type of parallelism would destroy the intended impact, and one may therefore have to restructure and combine the two parts: "Jesus used nothing but parables to tell these things to the people."

All this refers to the previous passages, the preceding parables.

As elsewhere **the crowds** may be "the people," "the crowd," or "all the people."

The expression **said nothing** could make it seem he did not speak at all except when he told the parables. More likely is that he "taught nothing" or "didn't teach anything" except by using a parable.

13.35   RSV   TEV

This was to fulfill what was spoken   He did this to make come true what
by the prophet:^k   the prophet had said,
    "I will open my mouth in para-   "I will use parables when I
      bles,   speak to them;
    I will utter what has been hid-   I will tell them things un-
      den since the foundation of   known since the creation of
      the world."   the world."

^k Other ancient authorities read *the prophet Isaiah*

This was to fulfill what was spoken by the prophet: see comments on 1.22. Here the phrase may be "He did this to make come true what the prophet said would happen." The form used here is exactly the same as in 8.17, except there **the prophet** is identified as Isaiah. In fact some Greek manuscripts even include "by Isaiah the prophet" here. As TC-GNT indicates, its inclusion is obviously the more difficult wording, since the passage actually comes from Psalm 78.2 rather than from Isaiah. On the other hand, it is also possible that Isaiah's name was inserted because he is the most famous of the Old Testament prophets. In light of the conflicting and difficult evidence, the UBS Greek text committee decided in favor of omitting the prophet's name. But they rate this a "C" decision, indicating a considerable degree of doubt regarding the wording of the text.

It may be good in some languages to introduce the citation with "he said" or some similar marker of direct discourse.

I will open my mouth in parables makes use of the Semitic idiom "to open one's mouth," which means "to speak." Thus it can be rendered as "I will speak in parables" or "I will use parables when I speak (to them)."

Utter (so also NEB) originally meant "belch" but later developed the meaning "proclaim" or "**tell**" (TEV). Most modern English translations evidently prefer **utter**; JB has "expound" and NAB "announce." In the present context the verb is obviously used as a parallel to the verb "speak" of the first sentence. Other possible renderings of **utter** are "explain to them" or "teach them about." GECL translates the entire quotation as "I will speak in parables, only in parables will I uncover what has been hidden since the creation of the world."

What has been hidden since the creation of the world may be translated "things which God has not let people know since he created the world" or "things which people have never known before."

13.36-43

RSV   TEV

Jesus Explains the Parable
of the Weeds

36 Then he left the crowds and went into the house. And his disciples came to him, saying, "Explain to us the parable of the weeds of the field." 37 He answered, "He who sows the good seed is the Son of man; 38 the field is the world, and the good seed means the sons of the kingdom; the weeds are the sons of the evil one, 39 and the enemy who sowed them is the devil; the harvest is the close of the age, and the reapers are angels. 40 Just as the weeds are gathered and burned with fire, so will it be at the close of the age. 41 The Son of man will send his angels, and they will gather out of his kingdom all causes of sins and all evildoers, 42 and throw them into the furnace of fire; there men will weep and gnash their teeth. 43 Then the righteous will shine like the sun in the kingdom of their Father. He who has ears, let him hear.

36 When Jesus had left the crowd and gone indoors, his disciples came to him and said, "Tell us what the parable about the weeds in the field means."

37 Jesus answered, "The man who sowed the good seed is the Son of Man; 38 the field is the world; the good seed is the people who belong to the Kingdom; the weeds are the people who belong to the Evil One; 39 and the enemy who sowed the weeds is the Devil. The harvest is the end of the age, and the harvest workers are angels. 40 Just as the weeds are gathered up and burned in the fire, so the same thing will happen at the end of the age: 41 the Son of Man will send out his angels to gather up out of his Kingdom all those who cause people to sin and all others who do evil things, 42 and they will throw them into the fiery furnace, where they will cry and gnash their teeth. 43 Then God's people will shine like the sun in their Father's Kingdom. Listen, then, if you have ears!

SECTION HEADING: "**Jesus Explains the Parable of the Weeds.**" "**Explains**" can be "tells the meaning of." For "**Weeds**," see comments on verse 25.

The Parable of the Weeds is found in the apocryphal Gospel of Thomas (57), but no interpretation accompanies it. The interpretation of the parable indicates that only God himself may distinguish the good from the evil; it is God's business alone to decide who belongs to the Kingdom.

13.36   RSV   TEV

Then he left the crowds and went into the house. And his disciples came to him, saying, "Explain to us the parable of the weeds of the field."

When Jesus had left the crowd and gone indoors, his disciples came to him and said, "Tell us what the parable about the weeds in the field means."

He left: TEV and GECL identify **he** as Jesus, since this verse opens a new section in the Gospel.

Left the crowds may be "went away from where the crowd was" or "left that place where the crowds were."

Into the house (TEV "**Indoors**") translates a Greek construction which may mean "in his house" (NAB "he went home"). The house referred to is the one in Capernaum (see 8.14; 9.10).

It may not be possible to say he **went into the house** without indicating first where he went, as in "He left the crowds and went to his house. He went in, and . . . ."

It will be difficult to say **the house** in many languages unless it is clear which house is being referred to. Thus "his house" or "the house where he was staying" may be necessary.

And is simply a word to show the continuity of the story.

His disciples came to him implies that they had gone into the house with Jesus, and it may be necessary to indicate this explicitly in translation. For example, "When Jesus and his disciples had left the crowd and had gone indoors, his disciples came to him . . . ." Or "Jesus left the crowd and went indoors. His disciples went with him, and when they were inside alone they came to him and said . . . ."

Came may have to be "went."

Explain (so also GECL, NJB, NEB) is translated "**Tell . . . what . . . means**" by TEV. Elsewhere in the New Testament this verb is found only in 18.31.

13.37 RSV   TEV

He answered, "He who sows the good seed is the Son of man;

        Jesus answered, "The man who sowed the good seed is the Son of Man;

In place of saying **He who sows . . . is the Son of man**, it may be better to shift to a simile: "The sower . . . stands for the Son of Man" (Brc) or ". . . is like (or, represents) the Son of Man."

For **the Son of man**, see comments on 8.20.

13.38 RSV   TEV

the field is the world, and the good seed means the sons of the kingdom; the weeds are the sons of the evil one,

the field is the world; the good seed is the people who belong to the Kingdom; the weeds are the people who belong to the Evil One;

The field is the world may also be changed to a simile ("The field stands for [or, represents] the world"), as may the other figures in the parable. RSV in fact does this in one place: **the good seed means the sons of the kingdom**.

Sons of the kingdom (TEV "**people who belong to the Kingdom**") is also used in 8.12. In the earlier passage it refers to the Jews, who by right should have belonged to God's Kingdom but had disqualified themselves because of their rejection of Jesus. Here it refers to the people who in truth do belong to God's Kingdom. The idea of "belonging to the Kingdom" may be difficult and unclear, and so one may translate "the people who have submitted themselves to the rule of God" (GECL). INCL translates "those who have become the people of God." Another expression is "the people who are under the rule of God."

Sons of the evil one is translated "**people who belong to the Evil One**" by TEV. Here also **sons** is a Semitic idiom used to describe people who either belong to or are characterized by the "of" phrase that follows it. In other contexts it may be possible to interpret **the evil one** to mean "evil" in an impersonal sense (see 6.13), but in verse 39 he is explicitly identified as both "the enemy" and "the devil." Therefore GECL translates **the evil one** as "the enemy of God" and then in verse 39 says of him "the enemy who planted the weeds is Satan." In translation it should be made clear that Jesus is referring to the same being, not to three separate beings ("the evil one," "the enemy," "the devil"). It may then be helpful to translate "The weeds represent the people who belong to God's enemy, the devil. He is the evil one who sowed the weeds . . . ." Instead of "belong to," translators may have "are ruled over by" or "who serve."

For "the Devil," see comments on 4.1 and verse 39 below.

13.39	RSV	TEV

and the enemy who sowed them is the devil; the harvest is the close of the age, and the reapers are angels.	and the enemy who sowed the weeds is the Devil. The harvest is the end of the age, and the harvest workers are angels.

The enemy: see comments on verses 25, 28.

Devil is first used in 4.1; then in 4.5,8,11; and once again in 25.41. It is the term used in the Septuagint to translate Satan, which is a Hebrew word.

Harvest must be understood as the gathering in of the crops rather than of the gathered crop itself. One may translate "the gathering of the crop stands for . . ." or "the time of the harvest stands for . . . ."

The close of the age represents a Jewish and early Christian thought that time is divided into two ages: the present evil age and the future glorious age. Therefore "**the end of the age**" (TEV) is equivalent to "the end of the world" (NJB, Brc, NAB) or "the end of time." Closely allied to this thought is the belief that the world is proceeding in a direction determined by God, and the real understanding of the present may be known only as one understands the future. Matthew is the only New Testament writer to use this expression (13.39-40,49; 24.3; 28.20).

Reapers (TEV "**harvest workers**"): many languages, especially where life is based upon an agricultural economy, will have specialized terms that will be immediately understood. NAB renders "harvesters," which itself is not widely used in American English. Most translators of modern English Bibles have subconsciously limited themselves to a single-word translation. "The workers who do the harvesting" or ". . . who gather in the crops when they're ready" may in fact be the simplest renderings.

It may be advisable to translate **angels** as "God's angels" (GECL 1st edition); this should not cause confusion when in verse 41 the Son of Man sends out "his angels." **Angels** itself was discussed at 1.20. "God's messengers," "God's heavenly messengers," or "God's servants from heaven" may be appropriate here.

13.40	RSV	TEV

Just as the weeds are gathered and burned with fire, so will it be at the close of the age.	**Just as the weeds are gathered up and burned in the fire, so the same thing will happen at the end of the age:**

Note that "burned in the fire" is generally more natural than **burned with fire**. But some will have simply "burned."

It is quite possible that the reader will miss the comparison intended in **so will it be at the close of the age**. That is, it may sound as though **weeds** will be gathered up and burned in the fire at the end of the age in the same way that they are gathered and burned at harvest time. One may then translate ". . . so the people who belong to the Evil One will be gathered and burned in the fire at the end of the age." Then verses 41-42 will immediately be understood as an explanation of the manner in which this is accomplished.

The close of the age will be as in verse 39.

13.41	RSV	TEV

The Son of man will send his angels, and they will gather out of his kingdom all causes of sins and all evildoers,	**the Son of Man will send out his angels to gather up out of his Kingdom all those who cause people to sin and all others who do evil things,**

For **Son of man**, see comments on 8.20.

The translation of **his angels** will depend somewhat on how **angels** has been dealt with elsewhere (see 1.20), but "his servants" or "his messengers (or, servants) from heaven" are possible renderings in this verse.

There is a good deal of controversy which surrounds the meaning of the phrase **his kingdom**. For example, some scholars attempt to distinguish between "the Kingdom of God" and "the Kingdom of the Son of Man." For them the Kingdom of the Son of Man is the equivalent of the church in the present, while the Kingdom of God is the Kingdom in its final consummation. They then speak of the Kingdom of the Son of Man as belonging to the present world (verse 41), while the Kingdom of the Father (God) is to come in the future (verse 43). But these two terms are best taken to be synonyms, a judgment supported by 16.28 and 20.21, where the Kingdom of the Son of Man definitely refers to the Kingdom in its final consummation. If these two terms are synonyms, then one may translate "The Son of Man will send out his angels, and they will separate from the presence of God all who have led others to be unfaithful to God and who themselves have done evil" (GECL 1st edition).

INCL translates "The Son of Man will send his angels to gather from among his people . . . ." In this verse it is obvious that "Kingdom" is used both of those people who actually obey the Son of Man (or, of God) and of those people who only profess to obey the Son of Man (or, of God).

Some translators have retained **kingdom** here by saying "gather from among the people of God's Kingdom," but "from among the people under God's rule" is also reasonable.

Gather out has been translated "weed out" by Brc to retain as much as possible the imagery of the parable. Translations very similar to GECL above are "separate from the other people under God's rule" or "take out from . . . ."

All causes of sin translates a neuter form in Greek, literally "all stumbling blocks" (NEB "whatever makes men stumble"; JB "all things that provoke offences"). One scholar describes this phrase as "a strange reference" which is "only comprehensible on the basis of Zephaniah 1.3." But although the form is neuter, in the present context of judgment, the phrase makes no sense at all unless people are the cause of stumbling (**sin**) to others. Matthew's language may be influenced by the form of the text in Zephaniah, but he evidently has people in mind: "all those who are a cause of sin to others" (Brc) and "all who draw others to apostasy" (NAB).

Evildoers may be rendered as "all people who do evil." The term can be rendered the same way as the phrase in 7.23.

13.42   RSV   TEV

and throw them into the furnace of   and they will throw them into the
fire; there men will weep and gnash   fiery furnace, where they will cry and
their teeth.   gnash their teeth.

The subject of **throw** is still "the angels" of verse 41, and the object, **them**, is the people who cause others to sin or who do evil. Translators should translate verses 41 and 42 together to make the sentence natural in their language.

The furnace of fire originates from Daniel 3.6. But in the apocryphal book of 2 Esdras 7.36, "the furnace of hell" is mentioned as the final place of the wicked as opposed to "the paradise of delight" where the righteous will live. **Furnace of fire** may be a problem if readers are not familiar with furnaces. Since, as we point out, this expression can well refer to hell, then "the fires of hell" or "into hell, which is like a great fire" are possible translations. Otherwise "the great fire" can be used.

Weep and gnash their teeth: see comments on 8.12.

13.43   RSV   TEV

Then the righteous will shine like the   Then God's people will shine like the
sun in the kingdom of their Father.   sun in their Father's Kingdom. Lis-
He who has ears, let him hear.   ten, then, if you have ears!

The righteous (TEV **"God's people"**) is translated "those who have done God's will" by GECL 1st edition. See comments on 1.19.

Will shine like the sun may have its roots in Daniel 12.3 (TEV "The wise leaders will shine with all the brightness of the sky. And those who have taught many people to do what is right will shine like the stars forever"). For the most part a literal rendering of **will shine like the sun** will be possible. For those languages where readers will have difficulty, however, translators can say "Then the people who do what God requires will be clearly visible, like the sun shining brilliantly."

In the kingdom of their Father is translated "in the new world of their Father" by GECL 1st edition. MACL has "After the Father establishes his reign"; INCL is close to GECL ("In the new world of God their Father"). "In the rule that God their Father will establish" is another possibility.

He who has ears, let him hear: see comments on 11.15.

13.44

RSV   TEV

The Parable of the Hidden Treasure

44 "The kingdom of heaven is like treasure hidden in a field, which a man found and covered up; then in his joy he goes and sells all that he has and buys that field. | 44 "The Kingdom of heaven is like this. A man happens to find a treasure hidden in a field. He covers it up again, and is so happy that he goes and sells everything he has, and then goes back and buys that field.

SECTION HEADING: **"The Parable of the Hidden Treasure."** See section heading at verse 1 for possible ways to render the heading. As for **"Hidden Treasure,"** see comments on verse 44 below.

Both this parable and the Parable of the Pearl (verses 45-46) illustrate the absolute worth of God's Kingdom, together with the need for urgency and sacrifice for the sake of entering it. Some interpreters believe that the Parable of the Pearl describes God seeking after people, but the context does not seem to support this interpretation.

13.44   RSV   TEV

"The kingdom of heaven is like a treasure hidden in a field, which a man found and covered up; then in his joy he goes and sells all that he has and buys that field. | **"The Kingdom of heaven is like this. A man happens to find a treasure hidden in a field. He covers it up again, and is so happy that he goes and sells everything he has, and then goes back and buys that field.**

The kingdom . . . is like is the same introductory formula used in verses 31 and 33. MACL renders "The situation with the Kingdom of God is the same as . . . ." INCL translates "When God rules, the situation is like this parable: . . . ." GECL 1st edition ties the two parables closely together: "The new world into which God calls you is like a treasure which was hidden in a field . . . 45 Whoever understands God's invitation acts like a merchant looking for beautiful pearls . . . ."

Treasure refers to something very valuable, although exactly what it may be is not specified. "Something very valuable" or "a very expensive object" are possible renderings.

To say it was **hidden** may mean it was "buried." Some languages will not be able to use a passive and will require instead "that someone had hidden (or, buried) in a field."

The parable can be structured in various ways: "There was something very expensive that had been hidden in a field. A man found it and . . ." or "A man found in a field a very expensive object that had been hidden there. He covered it up . . . ."

The **man** is most likely to be understood as a day laborer who himself owns no property. While working in someone else's field, he accidentally uncovers a treasure hidden there.

Covered up translates a verb which may have the more general meaning of "hides it" (NJB), but here the meaning is clearly "buried it" (NEB). Although the verb is an aorist indicative, TEV and a number of other English translations use the present tense, because this is a more natural way in English to tell a story in a vivid fashion. Translators should use the tense that is most natural in their languages.

The adjective "**again**" (TEV, NJB, NEB, NAB) is necessary in the English restructuring, though it is not present in the Greek text.

In Jesus' day it was quite common for people either to bury their valuables or to hide them at a distance from the premises on which they lived, to keep them from being stolen by thieves and robbers. So the situation described there is something that would be immediately understood by Jesus' hearers. In telling this parable Jesus is neither excusing nor condemning the man's actions. Rather he is calling attention to the man's wisdom and shrewdness in sacrificing everything he owns in order to secure this one valuable treasure. How a day laborer could get enough money to buy the field is unimportant. Exaggeration is common in parables, and such features are designed to contribute toward the overall impact and meaning.

In his joy is placed in emphatic position in the Greek text, and many translations put it first in the clause in order to underline its importance in the verse (NEB "and for sheer joy went . . ."). **In his joy** can be rendered as "He became very, very happy and went . . ." or "Because he was so happy, he went and sold . . . ."

"**Then goes back**" of TEV describes an action not recorded in the Greek text. However, in many languages it will be necessary to indicate this action specifically. In fact, some languages will require even more. For example, "then he takes the money, goes back, and buys that field."

He goes and sells all that he has and buys that field can also be rendered "he sold everything he owned so he could then go and buy that field" or "he sold all he owned, then bought that field."

13.45-46

RSV	TEV
	The Parable of the Pearl
45 "Again, the kingdom of heaven is like a merchant in search of fine pearls, 46 who, on finding one pearl of great value, went and sold all that he had and bought it.	45 "Also, the Kingdom of heaven is like this. A man is looking for fine pearls, 46 and when he finds one that is unusually fine, he goes and sells everything he has, and buys that pearl.

SECTION HEADING: **"The Parable of the Pearl."** See section heading at verse 1 for ways of translating this heading. For **"Pearl,"** see comments on verse 45 below.

13.45 RSV	TEV
"Again, the kingdom of heaven is like a merchant in search of fine pearls,	**"Also, the Kingdom of heaven is like this. A man is looking for fine pearls,**

Again (used also in verse 47) serves to join this parable closely to the one which comes before it; TEV translates **"also."** The use of this particle supports the conclusion that the two parables are intended to convey the same point, and most commentators interpret them in this light. INCL translates this verse "When God rules, the situation will be as it is in this parable: . . . ." MACL begins "The situation with the rule of God is the same as that of a merchant who . . . ." The link with the previous parable shown by **Again** can also be conveyed by a phrase like this: "Here is another parable about God's rule. It is like this. A merchant . . . ," "The rule of God can also be said to be like this: a merchant . . . ," or "Another parable that shows how it is when God rules is this: a merchant . . . ."

The noun **merchant** occurs only here and in Revelation 18.3,11,15,23, and it apparently means "wholesale dealer." But some scholars question that meaning in the present context, since it is uncertain whether the man is looking for pearls that he can sell at a profit or for pearls to place in his own personal collection. The parable is much more effective if one assumes that the man intends to keep the valuable pearl for himself. This is the reason TEV uses **"man."** But there are translators who still prefer "a business man" or "a trader."

In search of (TEV **"looking for"**) can be "looking for pearls he could buy." He was not looking on the ground for pearls, or doing any searching like that.

Pearls were highly valued by the people of Jesus' day, and in Revelation 18.21 they were listed together with gold, silver, and precious stones as articles of commerce. **Pearls** may not be known. "Stones of great cost" or "beautiful stones people can use for jewelry" can be used, possibly with the addition of "called pearls." To say they are **fine** can be conveyed by a phrase such as "that were very beautiful," but "that were worth a great deal of money" or "that cost a lot" is probably better.

13.46   RSV   TEV

who, on finding one pearl of great value, went and sold all that he had and bought it.	and when he finds one that is unusually fine, he goes and sells everything he has, and buys that pearl.

Finding obviously does not indicate the man found it lying about somewhere, but rather "he found a very valuable one for sale."

One pearl of great value is translated "**one that is unusually fine**" by TEV. NEB has "one of very special value"; NJB "one of great value"; NAB "one really valuable pearl."

Sold translates a Greek perfect tense, but there is some suspicion among grammarians that the form is here equivalent to the aorist, since it is used in parallel with an aorist tense and is itself not known to possess an aorist form. For effect TEV utilizes the present "**sells**."

Went and sold all that he had and bought it may be rendered "went and sold everything he owned so he could buy that pearl."

For stylistic reasons TEV translates **it** of the Greek text as "**that pearl**."

13.47-50

RSV   TEV

The Parable of the Net

47 "Again, the kingdom of heaven is like a net which was thrown into the sea and gathered fish of every kind; 48 when it was full, men drew it ashore and sat down and sorted the good into vessels but threw away the bad. 49 So it will be at the close of the age. The angels will come out and separate the evil from the righteous, 50 and throw them into the furnace of fire; there men will weep and gnash their teeth.

47 "Also, the Kingdom of heaven is like this. Some fishermen throw their net out in the lake and catch all kinds of fish. 48 When the net is full, they pull it to shore and sit down to divide the fish: the good ones go into the buckets, the worthless ones are thrown away. 49 It will be like this at the end of the age: the angels will go out and gather up the evil people from among the good 50 and will throw them into the fiery furnace, where they will cry and gnash their teeth.

SECTION HEADING: "**The Parable of the Net**." See similar heading at verse 1. For "**Net**," see comments below in verse 47.

This parable is similar in structure to the Parable of the Weeds (verses 24-30), and it apparently conveys the same message. Moreover, there is a remarkable similarity between the interpretation of the earlier parable (especially verses 40-42) and verses 49-50. In fact the closing application of this parable is even more suitable to that of the weeds, because weeds (not fish!) are thrown into a furnace to be burned. Both parables are unique to Matthew.

13.47 RSV TEV

"Again, the kingdom of heaven is like a net which was thrown into the sea and gathered fish of every kind; | "Also, the Kingdom of heaven is like this. Some fishermen throw their net out in the lake and catch all kinds of fish.

Again, the kingdom of heaven is like repeats the formula used at the first of verse 45. GECL 1st edition renders "When God's new world comes, it will be like a net . . ."; and Brc "To take another illustration, what happens in the Kingdom of Heaven is like what happened when a net was cast into the sea." MACL translates "When God establishes his reign, the situation will be the same as that of a net . . . ."

As in the previous parable, there are different ways the transition from the preceding paragraph, **Again,** can be rendered. In addition to the examples above, translators can also have "Here is another parable about God's rule," "When God rules, it can also be seen to be like this," or "God's rule is also like this."

The **net** was a large draw net with floats at the top to keep it from sinking, and weights at the bottom. It was often dragged ashore in a large semicircle by several men.

The Greek passive **a net which was thrown into** is altered to an active in TEV ("**Some fishermen throw their net out**"). For many languages an active restructuring will be the only satisfactory solution.

In some languages **net** has to be further specified as "a net for catching fish."

Sea here can be "the water," "the lake," or "the sea."

Net . . . gathered fish of every kind is made into a passive by NEB: "where fish of every kind were caught in it." Some languages may require an active structure with the fishermen as subject: "The fishermen caught all kinds of fish in their net."

Fish of every kind means "fish that were good to eat and fish that were not good to eat," as the next verse makes clear; the fish are not to be interpreted symbolically.

13.48 RSV TEV

when it was full, men drew it ashore and sat down and sorted the good into vessels but threw away the bad. | When the net is full, they pull it to shore and sit down to divide the fish: the good ones go into the buckets, the worthless ones are thrown away.

When it was full (so also NEB) has reference to the net: "**When the net is full**" (TEV).

In Greek both **drew** and **sat down** are participles dependent upon the main verb **sorted**, literally "drawing it upon the shore and sitting down they sorted . . . ." Here again the structure in translation depends upon the demands of the receptor language. GECL, for example, translates "If the net is full, then the fishermen drag it to land, sit down and sort out the fish."

The expression **sorted . . . into vessels** may have to be expanded, somewhat as TEV has done. For example, one can say "separated (or, divided) the good fish from the bad. Then they put the good fish into buckets . . . ."

The good (GECL "the good fish") refers to fish that are edible, while **the bad** (TEV **"the worthless ones"**) refers to fish that cannot be eaten. In a Jewish context **bad** fish would be those which they were specifically forbidden by their Law to eat. The root meaning of the word **bad** is "decayed" or "rotten," but that is certainly not the meaning here. Elsewhere the word is also known to mean "unusable" or "unfit (to be eaten)." Translators can therefore either retain "good fish" and "bad fish" or use something like "fish good for eating" and "fish that can't be eaten."

Vessels (TEV **"buckets"**) is rendered "pails" by NEB, "basket" by JB, and "containers" by NAB. The Greek word covers a wide range of meaning, and the translation should reflect what is natural in the receptor language. Either a general term or a specific term may be chosen, as the samplings from modern English translations illustrate.

13.49	RSV	TEV

So it will be at the close of the age. The angels will come out and separate the evil from the righteous,	It will be like this at the end of the age: the angels will go out and gather up the evil people from among the good

So it will be at the close of the age: for comments on **close of the age**, see verse 39. This statement points forward to what follows, and it may be prudent to make evident the tie between the parable and its application; for example, "This story about the fish tells us (or, gives us a picture of) what it will be like at the end of time." If such an analogy is not made explicit, the reader may not immediately see the connection between the story of the fish and what follows.

The angels will come out is translated "the angels of God will come" by GECL. It may even be useful to render "God will send his angels . . . ."

For **angels**, see comments on 1.20.

Whether to say **come out** or "go out" will depend on the receptor language. The angels will presumably be leaving heaven to separate the evil people from the righteous here on earth. Some languages will need to make that clear. Others can say simply "will come and separate people."

Separate can also be "take out from" or "gather (together) away from."

The evil from the righteous: the preposition **from** (TEV **"from among"**) indicates that Matthew is here describing God's judgment on the Christian community rather than on the world. There both **the evil** and **the righteous** live side by side, professing to be God's chosen people, but in the judgment a separation will be made.

Righteous is translated "just" by RSV in 1.19 (see comments there); Matthew consistently uses this term to characterize people who obey God in whatever way they are called upon to do so. **Righteous** can be translated as "the people who obey God's commands," "people who live as God requires," or "**good** (people)" (TEV). **Evil** can be "evil people" or "people who do evil."

439

13.50   RSV   TEV

and throw them into the furnace of   **and will throw them into the fiery**
fire; there men will weep and gnash   **furnace, where they will cry and**
their teeth.   **gnash their teeth.**

This verse is a repetition of verse 42 and 8.12 (see comments at 8.12).

13.51-52

RSV   TEV

New Truths and Old

51 "Have you understood all this?" They   51 "Do you understand these things?" Jesus
said to him, "Yes." 52 And he said to them,   asked them.
"Therefore every scribe who has been trained for   "Yes," they answered.
the kingdom of heaven is like a householder who   52 So he replied, "This means, then, that
brings out of his treasure what is new and what is   every teacher of the Law who becomes a disciple
old."   in the Kingdom of heaven is like a homeowner
                                                 who takes new and old things out of his storage
                                                 room."

SECTION HEADING: **"New Truths and Old."** This can also be rendered
"New teachings and old teachings." If a short sentence is required, the heading can
say "Jesus talks about old and new teachings."

Verses 51-52, without parallel in any of the other Gospels, constitute Matthew's
conclusion to the parables. In particular, the emphasis upon understanding and the
contrast between the old and the new are frequently-met concepts throughout this
Gospel.

13.51   RSV   TEV

"Have you understood all this?"   **"Do you understand these**
They said to him, "Yes."   **things?" Jesus asked them.**
                                             "Yes," they answered.

<u>All this</u> (TEV **"these things"**) refers back to the teaching in parables contained
in this chapter.

<u>They</u> are the disciples and perhaps should be made explicit, since they are last
identified in verse 36. GECL translates with considerable restructuring: " 'Have you
understood all this?' Jesus asked his disciples, and they answered, 'Yes!' "

In fact, many translators will need to restructure somewhat as GECL has done,
to make clear who is asking the question of whom. An example is "Jesus asked his
disciples, 'Do you understand all these things?' and they answered, 'Yes.' " It may be
better to use indirect speech, as in "Jesus asked his disciples if they had understood
all these things, and they said they had."

RSV   TEV

And he said to them, "Therefore every scribe who has been trained for the kingdom of heaven is like a householder who brings out of his treasure what is new and what is old."

So he replied, "This means, then, that every teacher of the Law who becomes a disciple in the Kingdom of heaven is like a homeowner who takes new and old things out of his storage room."

Therefore usually introduces a result or a conclusion, but here the logical link between the previous verse and this is not obvious. The verse is a more general conclusion to the passage, and a transition such as "So then," "Well then," or even "It follows, therefore" may be more appropriate.

Scribe (see comments at 2.4) is translated "**teacher of the Law**" by TEV (NEB "teacher of the law"). Brc has "an expert in the Law" and GECL 1st edition "every expert of the sacred Scriptures." Although **scribe** is frequently used in this Gospel (23 times), this is the only place where it is used of a believer. Most scholars see here a reference to believers in general, though some few see a veiled reference to Matthew, himself since the word translated **who has been trained** sounds something like Matthew in Greek.

Has been trained for (a participle in Greek) is variously translated: "**becomes a disciple in**" (TEV), "has become a learner in" (NEB), and "has been instructed in the meaning of" (Brc). Matthew also uses this verb in 27.57; 28.19, though elsewhere in the New Testament it is found only in Acts 14.21. A major question concerns how the participle is to be related to the phrase **the kingdom of heaven**; and there are at least two possibilities: (1) one may follow MACL ("Every teacher of the Scriptures who has learned how God establishes his rule in the world . . .") or (2) one may go the route of GECL 1st edition ("Every expert in the sacred Scriptures who has submitted himself to God's rule . . ."). Translators who follow the first interpretation can also say "Every teacher of the Law who has learned about God's rule (or, reign)," ". . . learned the truth about God's rule," or ". . . the meaning of God's rule." Those who follow the second may have "Every teacher of the law who has learned what it means for God to rule over him" or ". . . learned to put himself under God's rule."

It is worth noting that most of these examples use active sentences with the verb "learn" instead of the passive one, **has been trained**. Translators thus avoid the question of who trained these teachers of the Law for the Kingdom of heaven.

Householder (so also NEB) is "**homeowner**" in TEV. The problem is that for American speakers of English **householder** is not in current usage; NAB has "the head of a household," which is satisfactory. Elsewhere Matthew uses this noun in 10.25; 13.27; 20.11; 21.33; 24.43. The noun itself can mean either one who owns the house or one who is the head of a household, and quite often the two are not closely distinguished.

There is also a question regarding the meaning of **what is new and what is old**. Some scholars believe that Matthew here intends a contrast between the new (Jesus' interpretation of the Law) and what is old (Judaism's interpretation of the Law). But both **what is new** and **what is old** are here spoken of favorably, which leads to the conclusion that an alternative interpretation must be sought. At least two options present themselves: (1) Matthew may be thinking of the Old Testament together with Jesus' interpretation and application of it, or (2) he may have in mind the Church's application of the Law (**what is new**) in light of Jesus' interpretation of it (**what is old**). Fortunately this is not the sort of information that should or may be placed in a translation. Translators should leave it quite general, as in "old things" and "new things."

Brings out may need to be "takes out" in some languages. The text does not specify to where the householder takes these things or why, and the translation should be suitably general also. It is assumed that these are things to be used in the household.

Treasure (see 2.11; 6.19,20,21; 12.35) is translated **"storage room"** in TEV and "storeroom" in NJB and NAB. As the translations indicate, the noun may refer either to the treasure or to the place where the treasure is stored, which seems to be the meaning here. "Place where he stores his things" is thus an acceptable rendering.

13.53-58

RSV

TEV

Jesus Is Rejected at Nazareth

53 And when Jesus had finished these parables, he went away from there, 54 and coming to his own country he taught them in their synagogue, so that they were astonished, and said, "Where did this man get this wisdom and these mighty works? 55 Is not this the carpenter's son? Is not his mother called Mary? And are not his brothers James and Joseph and Simon and Judas? 56 And are not all his sisters with us? Where then did this man get all this?" 57 And they took offense at him. But Jesus said to them, "A prophet is not without honor except in his own country and in his own house." 58 And he did not do many mighty works there, because of their unbelief.

53 When Jesus finished telling these parables, he left that place 54 and went back to his home town. He taught in the synagogue, and those who heard him were amazed. "Where did he get such wisdom?" they asked. "And what about his miracles? 55 Isn't he the carpenter's son? Isn't Mary his mother, and aren't James, Joseph, Simon, and Judas his brothers? 56 Aren't all his sisters living here? Where did he get all this?" 57 And so they rejected him.

Jesus said to them, "A prophet is respected everywhere except in his home town and by his own family." 58 Because they did not have faith, he did not perform many miracles there.

SECTION HEADING: "Jesus Is Rejected at Nazareth." This may need to be turned into an active sentence such as "The people of Nazareth reject Jesus," ". . . do not accept Jesus," or ". . . are unwilling to believe in Jesus." But see the discussion below. Another possible heading is "Jesus goes to Galilee" or "Jesus teaches in Galilee."

A number of scholars see here the beginning of a new division in the Gospel, which extends through 20.34. But, as one may surmise, other scholars analyze the text quite differently. Some, for example, do introduce a new section here, but they close it at either 18.35 or 20.28, while still others do not begin a new section until 16.13. Nevertheless, 13.53 clearly signals the closing of the discourse on parables and simultaneously marks a transition to Jesus' journey to Jerusalem. Therefore one may give to 13.53–20.34 the heading "Jesus in Galilee and on his Way to Jerusalem."

Various teachings and deeds of Jesus are contained within this unit, but they are without an evident outline. On three occasions (16.21-28; 17.22-23; 20.17-19) Jesus' forthcoming suffering and death are proclaimed, and 19.1 finds him no longer in Galilee but in the vicinity of Jerusalem. When Jesus announces his death for the third and final time, Jerusalem is specifically mentioned as the ultimate goal of his journey (20.18).

Jesus' rejection at Nazareth has parallels both in Mark 6.1-6 and Luke 4.16-30, though for thematic reasons Luke places it much earlier. Matthew follows Mark in narrating it at this juncture, though he omits Mark 4.35–5.34, which he records earlier (8.23-34; 9.18-26).

13.53	RSV	TEV

> **And when Jesus had finished these parables, he went away from there,**

> **When Jesus finished telling these parables, he left that place**

And when Jesus had finished these parables: see comment at 7.28 (see also 11.1; 19.1; 26.1). Note that it may be necessary to say "finished teaching by means of these parables."

13.54	RSV	TEV

> **and coming to his own country he taught them in their synagogue, so that they were astonished, and said, "Where did this man get this wisdom and these mighty works?**

> **and went back to his home town. He taught in the synagogue, and those who heard him were amazed. "Where did he get such wisdom?" they asked. "And what about his miracles?**

And coming is often rendered "When he came to" or ". . . arrived in." The noun translated **own country**, except for its occurrence in Hebrews 11.14, is found only in the Gospels, where it is limited to those passages which relate of Jesus' rejection by his own people (Matt 13.54; Mark 6.1,4; Luke 4.23; John 4.44). If the RSV interpretation is correct, then the territory under consideration was the area in the vicinity of Nazareth. But the noun may also mean "**home town**" (TEV, NJB, NEB), in which case the reference is to Nazareth (see the NJB footnote).

Translators should be careful not to say "Nazareth," of course, since the text does not specify it. Either "home town" or "the area he was from" are acceptable.

In Greek the verb **taught** is an imperfect, which may imply an extended teaching ministry in that area.

Them can be rendered as "the people there" or "the people of that place."

For **synagogue**, see comments on 4.23. Since the text says **their synagogue**, it can be translated as "the synagogue of those people" or "the synagogue there."

The **so that** indicates that his teaching was such as to cause amazement. Possible renderings are "and they were amazed at his teaching" or "his teaching amazed the people."

Were astonished (TEV "**were amazed**"): see comments on 7.28.

Said is quite general, but they were not talking to Jesus. "Said to each other" may be better.

Where did this man get this wisdom and these mighty works? is literally "From where to this one such wisdom and miracles?" But a literal translation would be absolute nonsense, and most translations attempt something more dynamic. The first part of the question can follow RSV and TEV quite closely or possibly be rendered as "Where did he learn all these things?" or "How come he is so wise?" The second part may better be rendered "How can he do these miracles?" "How is it he is able to do these miracles?" or "Where does he get the power (or, authority) to perform these great miracles?" Note that this will mean using two separate questions instead of one as in RSV.

Wisdom was previously mentioned in 11.19 and 12.42. **Mighty works** is the same word used in 7.22. As one commentator notes, these two terms "refer to the two main aspects of Jesus' ministry: his teaching and his miracles . . . ."

13.55	RSV	TEV

Is not this the carpenter's son? Is not his mother called Mary? And are not his brothers James and Joseph and Simon and Judas?	Isn't he the carpenter's son? Isn't Mary his mother, and aren't James, Joseph, Simon, and Judas his brothers?

Is not this the carpenter's son? is phrased differently in Mark 6.3: "Is not this the carpenter?" The assumed reply is "Yes," as is reflected in NJB ("This is the carpenter's son, surely?") and Phps ("He's only the carpenter's son"). The noun "carpenter" may refer to one who builds with wood or stone. Wood is a somewhat rare commodity in Palestine, and houses are most frequently constructed with stone. It is quite possible, therefore, to argue for the meaning "stone mason," though the majority of the translators evidently prefer "carpenter."

In 12.46-47 Jesus' mother and brothers are mentioned, though not by name. The observation that Joseph is not mentioned may be due to the fact that he is no longer living at the time this incident occurs. In the Marcan parallel (6.3) the names of Jesus' brothers and the order in which they are mentioned differs slightly from Matthew. In place of **Joseph**, Mark has Joses, but it is possible to take Joses as an alternative form of **Joseph**, as TEV and NEB have done. But the order in which the brothers are mentioned is also slightly different: Matthew has the order **Simon and Judas**, while Mark has "Judas and Simon." There seems to be no particular significance in this shift of order, but it is problematic in cultures where readers expect the older children to be listed first.

The questions in verses 55 and 56 are all rhetorical. They are not asking for information but are ways of showing surprise that someone who is only a son of a carpenter can have such wisdom and do such wonderful acts. In addition to the models cited above, other renderings have been "He's only the son of the carpenter, isn't he?" or "Surely this man is only the son of the carpenter?" The verse will then continue "His mother is Mary, isn't she? And James, Joseph, Simon, and Judas are his brothers. And his sisters live right here. So how does he come to have this wisdom and power?"

It may be necessary to change all of verse 55 and the first part of verse 56 to a series of statements: "55 We know who he is. He is the son of the carpenter, and Mary is his mother. We also know his brothers James, Joseph, Simon, and Judas. 56 And all his sisters are living here in our village (or, district)."

13.56	RSV	TEV

And are not all his sisters with us? Where then did this man get all this?"	Aren't all his sisters living here? Where did he get all this?"

As with the three rhetorical questions of verse 55, **And are not all his sisters with us?** also expects an affirmative reply. As in the various examples above, **are . . . with us** means "live here with us" or ". . . in our town (or, area)."

All this (so also TEV, NEB, NAB) is literally "all these things." NJB translates "it all." In many languages to translate literally "all these things" would automatically signify material possessions. The reference is best taken to the wisdom and power referred to in verse 54. One may then translate "Where did he get such wisdom and power?" or "Where did he get such wisdom? And where did he get the power to work these miracles?"

13.57	RSV	TEV

And they took offense at him. But Jesus said to them, "A prophet is not without honor except in his own country and in his own house."	And so they rejected him. Jesus said to them, "A prophet is respected everywhere except in his home town and by his own family."

And they took offense at him translates a Semitic idiom which TEV represents as "**And so they rejected him.**" The same verb occurs earlier in the chapter (verse 21) as well as in 11.6, with similar meaning. GECL translates "And they would have nothing to do with him"; NJB "And they would not accept him." Some will have "And they would not believe in him" or "They refused to have anything to do with him."

Jesus' response to the people who reject him (**A prophet is not . . . except . . . own home**) is considered a proverbial statement by a number of scholars. TEV alters the difficulty of the compound negative (**not without . . . except**) to a more simplified positive expression: "**A prophet is respected everywhere except . . . .**" Another way to express this is "Everyone respects (or, people everywhere respect) a prophet except those in his own town and his own family."

Some translators who have understood this statement to be proverbial have wanted to substitute a local proverb with the same meaning, but this is probably not necessary, since the meaning here is quite clear.

For comments on **prophet**, see 1.22.

Own country: see comments on verse 54.

13.57

House obviously refers to people rather than to a physical structure; both TEV and NEB have **"family."**

13.58   RSV   TEV

And he did not do many mighty works there, because of their unbelief.   **Because they did not have faith, he did not perform many miracles there.**

Did not do is slightly different from the Marcan parallel (6.5), "could not do."

Mighty works: the same word is used in verse 54; in both instances the meaning is "miracles."

The noun phrase **because of their unbelief** may be translated "because they did not believe in him" (GECL 1st edition "because they rejected him").

In some languages it will be necessary to reverse the order of the sentence: "They did not believe in him, and for this reason Jesus did not do many miracles there" or "Since they did not believe in him, Jesus did not perform many mighty acts there."

Chapter 14

14.1-12

RSV

TEV

The Death of John the Baptist

1 At that time Herod the tetrarch heard about the fame of Jesus; 2 and he said to his servants, "This is John the Baptist, he has been raised from the dead; that is why these powers are at work in him." 3 For Herod had seized John and bound him and put him in prison, for the sake of Herodias, his brother Philip's wife;[1] 4 because John said to him, "It is not lawful for you to have her." 5 And though he wanted to put him to death, he feared the people, because they held him to be a prophet. 6 But when Herod's birthday came, the daughter of Herodias danced before the company, and pleased Herod, 7 so that he promised with an oath to give her whatever she might ask. 8 Prompted by her mother, she said, "Give me the head of John the Baptist here on a platter." 9 And the king was sorry; but because of his oaths and his guests he commanded it to be given; 10 he sent and had John beheaded in the prison, 11 and his head was brought on a platter and given to the girl, and she brought it to her mother. 12 And his disciples came and took the body and buried it; and they went and told Jesus.

[1] Other ancient authorities read *his brother's wife*

1 At that time Herod, the ruler of Galilee, heard about Jesus. 2 "He is really John the Baptist, who has come back to life," he told his officials. "That is why he has this power to perform miracles."

3 For Herod had earlier ordered John's arrest, and he had him tied up and put in prison. He had done this because of Herodias, his brother Philip's wife. 4 For some time John the Baptist had told Herod, "It isn't right for you to be married to Herodias!" 5 Herod wanted to kill him, but he was afraid of the Jewish people, because they considered John to be a prophet.

6 On Herod's birthday the daughter of Herodias danced in front of the whole group. Herod was so pleased 7 that he promised her, "I swear that I will give you anything you ask for!"

8 At her mother's suggestion she asked him, "Give me here and now the head of John the Baptist on a plate!"

9 The king was sad, but because of the promise he had made in front of all his guests he gave orders that her wish be granted. 10 So he had John beheaded in prison. 11 The head was brought in on a plate and given to the girl, who took it to her mother. 12 John's disciples came, carried away his body, and buried it; then they went and told Jesus.

SECTION HEADING: "**The Death of John the Baptist**" may be better rendered in some languages by a short sentence such as "John the Baptist is put to death" or "How John the Baptist was killed (or, executed)."

Matthew's account of the death of John the Baptist is similar to Mark's (6.14-29), though there are some significant differences as well. By means of a temporal marker ("At that time"), Matthew ties the death of John closely to the rejection of Jesus at Nazareth. Mark, on the other hand, utilizes the account to provide an interim between the sending out of the twelve (6.6-13) and their return (6.30). Moreover, in Mark the story is told as if it were an event in the moderately distant past, while Matthew tells the story as if no flashback had occurred with the story of John. But Matthew apparently intends the account to be a further indication of the manner in which the fates of the two prophets, John and Jesus, were interwoven. He has already informed his readers that Jesus was first openly acknowledged as Son of God at the time that John baptized him (3.16-17). Then, at the beginning of Jesus' wanderings through Galilee, messengers come to him from John (11.2), as they now do at the close of this narrative (verse 12).

In this passage we see the literary technique of flashback, whereby events are referred to that occurred prior to the story currently being narrated. Thus the account about the death of John is interrupted by the information which tells why Herod had arrested John.

Not all languages use flashbacks, but most do, although not always in the same way. Often (as here) it is a technique to bring in needed information without losing the story line of the principal story. In some languages it is used to bring about some rhetorical effect such as surprise. Translators need to study the narrative techniques of their language before deciding to maintain, modify, or eliminate the flashback in this passage. Would it be natural? Would it sound strange? Would it have the wrong effect?

14.1　　　　RSV　　　　　　　　　　　　　　　　TEV

At that time Herod the tetrarch heard about the fame of Jesus;　　　**At that time Herod, the ruler of Galilee, heard about Jesus.**

As we point out above, **At that time** ties this account of John's execution to the events in the previous chapter, but it does not indicate an exact time. Translators can say "In those days" or "Some time soon after that."

Herod was Herod Antipas, one of the sons of Herod the Great.

Tetrarch (TEV "**ruler of Galilee**") transliterates a title which means "ruler of a fourth part." **Herod** ruled only in Galilee (4 B.C.–A.D. 39), and so the basis for TEV's rendering. Some translators who have followed TEV in this have found it necessary to indicate that "**Galilee**" here refers to a province or region, not the lake. "The ruler of the region on the west side of Lake Galilee" will do this. Others have tried to keep more of the literal meaning of **tetrarch** and said "ruler of a part of the kingdom (of the Jewish people)." But this often results in an awkward sentence and gives too much prominence to the word. Another solution is to say "king over the region of Galilee."

Heard about the fame of Jesus: NJB has "heard about the reputation of Jesus" and GECL 1st edition "heard about the deeds of Jesus." NEB restructures: ". . . reports about Jesus reached the ears of Prince Herod." In the Greek text the verb **heard** has an object which comes from the same stem as the verb, and in such a context the noun would generally mean "account" or "report." In context it is legitimate to translate "about the things that Jesus had done and taught."

There are some languages where it is necessary to indicate who was passing on reports to Herod. "Herod heard people tell about the things Jesus was doing" or "people told Herod about the things Jesus was doing" are possible.

and he said to his servants, "This is John the Baptist, he has been raised from the dead; that is why these powers are at work in him."

"He is really John the Baptist, who has come back to life," he told his officials. "That is why he has this power to perform miracles."

And continues the narration. "Then" is also possible. Other translators have found it more natural to restructure the two verses slightly: "People were talking about the things that Jesus was doing. When Herod the ruler of Galilee heard these reports, he said to his officials . . . ."

The **he** of **he said** is Herod, not Jesus.

Servants translates the noun first used in 2.16; most recently it occurred in 12.18. Here the persons referred to are Herod's court officials, and NJB uses the collective term "his court." NEB renders "attendants," and Phps translates "his men."

This is John the Baptist (so also NEB) is emphatic in the Greek sentence structure, which explains the restructuring of TEV ("**He is really John the Baptist**") and NJB ("This is John the Baptist himself"). It may be necessary to render **this** as "Jesus" or "this man Jesus."

For **John the Baptist**, see comments on 3.1.

Has been raised from the dead (NEB "has been raised to life") may also be translated as an intransitive verb, "has risen from the dead" (NJB, Mft, AT) and "**has come back to life**" (TEV).

Has been raised is a passive construction, and many languages more naturally use an active sentence such as "God has raised him back to life." However, in order to avoid having Herod refer to God directly, a sentence such as "is alive again" or "**has come back to life**" (TEV) may be better.

That is why these powers are at work in him reflects a popular belief among the Jews and others that a person who has come back from the dead possesses unusual powers which enable him to perform miracles. GECL 1st edition translates "That is why he can perform such miracles"; TEV has "**That is why he has this power to perform miracles**." For comments on "**miracles**," see 7.22. "That is why he can do such mighty acts" or "That is why he has this power to do such acts" are also renderings that may be natural here.

For Herod had seized John and bound him and put him in prison, for the sake of Herodias, his brother Philip's wife;[l]

For Herod had earlier ordered John's arrest, and he had him tied up and put in prison. He had done this because of Herodias, his brother Philip's wife.

[l] Other ancient authorities read *his brother's wife*

For explains why Herod thought of John the Baptist when he heard about what Jesus was doing. In many languages it will be necessary to say something like "Herod thought this because he had seized . . . ."

Had seized, a participle in Greek, narrates an action which took place prior to the events of verses 1-2. In order to clear up all doubt regarding the sequence of events, some Greek manuscripts insert the adverb "earlier." This translational device is pursued as well by several modern translations (for example, TEV and GECL); Phps has "For previously Herod had arrested John," and NAB renders "Recall that Herod had had John arrested."

Had seized may invite a misunderstanding (many translations say "had arrested"). Herod did not actually perform this action himself; he ordered, or caused, others to do it in his behalf. Thus "had ordered John to be arrested" represents a more accurate representation of the actual events. It may be better to shift to direct discourse: "had ordered his men, 'Go and arrest John the Baptist.' " Another way to express this is "had ordered his men to arrest John."

Bound him and put him in prison: here again it is necessary to substitute a causative verb (either "had caused" or "had ordered"), to avoid the possible misunderstanding that Herod himself physically tied up John and put him in prison. Brc translates the sequence of events: "had arrested John . . . and had imprisoned him in chains."

The mention of **Herodias, his brother Philip's wife** occasions much difficulty, and in place of **his brother Philip's wife** some Greek manuscripts have a shorter text: "his brother's wife" (RSV footnote). The difficulty is further complicated by information provided by Josephus, the Jewish historian. He identifies Herodias' first husband as a son of Herod the Great, who himself was named Herod; and he further records that it was Herod the Great's son "(Herod) Philip" (Luke 3.1) who married Herodias' daughter Salome. In light of these observations TC-GNT concludes "It appears, therefore, that either Josephus failed to give the full name of Herodias' first husband (Herod Philip), or Mark confused Herodias' husband and son-in-law." Matthew has in all probability followed Mark (6.17), where he found the name **Philip**. Later, certain scribes adopted the shorter reading in Luke (3.19), where the name was omitted, thus harmonizing Matthew's account with that of Josephus. Most modern translations include **Philip** in the text. RSV gives a footnote which includes the other manuscript tradition; NJB has a footnote explaining the basis for the shorter text.

The phrase **his brother Philip's wife** could make it seem that Philip and Herodias were still married to each other at the time of John's arrest. As is clear in the following verses, this was not the case. "He did this because of Herodias, who had been the wife of his brother Philip" or "He did this because of Herodias. She had been married before to his brother Philip" are possible ways to express this. However, there are many languages where even this will be unnatural, because the normal way to tell a story is to narrate things in chronological order. Some of these will use occasional flashbacks, but not two or three in a row as here. In such cases it is often better to restructure verses 3 and 4 something like this: "Previously, Herod had married Herodias, but before that, she had been the wife of Herod's brother Philip. John told Herod that this was not lawful, and so for the sake of Herodias, Herod ordered his men to arrest John and put him in prison." Or "At one time Herodias had been married to Herod's brother Philip. But then she married Herod, and John told Herod . . . ." But see also the comments on flashbacks at the beginning of this section.

14.4	RSV	TEV

because John said to him, "It is not lawful for you to have her."

For some time John the Baptist had told Herod, "It isn't right for you to be married to Herodias!"

Many translators will begin a new sentence here, as we suggest in the above paragraph.

Said translates a Greek imperfect tense which draws attention to the continuation of the event in past time. Thus TEV renders "**For some time . . . had told**" and GECL 1st edition "had repeatedly reproached (him)." To translate **said** may wrongly imply that this was a one-time event, done only on this occasion. "John had been saying" or ". . . had been telling Herod" will also indicate this action was repeated.

It is not lawful appeals to the teaching of Jewish religious law, which would not have permitted a man to marry his brother's wife while the brother was still alive (see Lev 18.16; 20.21). Herod Antipas claimed to be a loyal Jew, and so it could be expected that the prophet John would speak out against what he had done. Since John's argument is based upon the commands of the Jewish Law, one may translate "Our (Jewish) Law does not permit . . ." or "Our Jewish religion does not allow us to . . . ."

For you to have her means "for you to marry her" (GECL) or "**for you to be married to Herodias**" (TEV). Some languages will prefer that a shift be made to indirect discourse: "because John had told him that he had no right to marry her" (Brc). Translators should be careful not to use an expression which may mean simply to commit adultery or sleep with her.

Note our discussion in the previous verse of possible ways to restructure this passage.

14.5	RSV	TEV

And though he wanted to put him to death, he feared the people, because they held him to be a prophet.

Herod wanted to kill him, but he was afraid of the Jewish people, because they considered John to be a prophet.

And though he wanted to put him to death (TEV "**Herod wanted to kill him**"): in contexts where numerous participants are involved, it is wise to identify them by name as frequently as good style will allow. According to Mark (6.19) it was Herodias, not Herod, who wanted to do away with John. Mark further indicates that it was Herod's fear of John as a "righteous and holy man" (6.20), rather than his fear of the people, that kept him from killing John before this time. However, the translator is obligated to translate each Gospel for its own sake without attempting an unjustified harmonization.

Sometimes translators have some difficulty with the relationship shown in this sentence by the word **though**. The implication is that Herod could not kill John as he wanted because of his concern about the way people felt about John. "Herod wanted to have John killed, but he feared popular reaction" is one way to render this.

TEV has rendered **put . . . to death** as "kill." Many translators will do something similar, but others will keep the form, with phrases such as "have killed" or "order his soldiers (or, people) to kill."

The people are "the Jewish people" (TEV), as the last clause of the verse clearly implies: **because they held him to be a prophet**. Only the Jewish people would have been concerned with the question of whether John was a prophet or not; to identify **the people** as "the Jewish people" reflects the historical setting and is not to be considered anti-Semitism.

Held here means "believed." "The Jews believed John was a prophet" or ". . . considered him to be a prophet" are possibilities.

For **prophet** see comments on 1.22.

14.6   RSV   TEV

But when Herod's birthday came, the daughter of Herodias danced before the company, and pleased Herod,   On Herod's birthday the daughter of Herodias danced in front of the whole group. Herod was so pleased

With verse 6 a shift in time and setting is indicated, and at least one new character is introduced into the narrative. For these reasons it may be helpful for the reader if a new paragraph is begun.

But indicates a contrast, but because of the way the sentence is constructed, it may seem that **when Herod's birthday came** contrasts with the previous verse. The real contrast is between the fact that Herod did not feel he could put John to death (previous verse), and the fact that he eventually did just that on the occasion of the girl's dancing at his birthday. Some translators have said something like "But finally he was able to do so" or "But at the time of his birthday, he did. The daughter of Herodias danced . . . ."

Herod's birthday may more explicitly be described as "Herod's birthday celebrations" (Brc, Phps). Some translators have said "When Herod had a feast to celebrate his birthday."

The daughter of Herodias is presumably Salome, her daughter by her first husband, Herod Philip. As far as is known, Salome was the only daughter of Herodias. In translation, however, she should not be identified by name, since her name appears nowhere in the Gospel.

In some cases, to say simply **danced** will not be as well understood as "entertained the people there by dancing."

The company are "all the guests" (GECL). **Before the company** may be translated "before all the people who had come for Herod's birthday celebration."

And pleased Herod is translated as a passive by TEV: "**Herod was so pleased.**"

It may be more natural to restructure the whole sentence: "But at the time of his birthday, Herod did put John to death. The daughter of Herodias entertained the company with her dancing, and she pleased Herod very much."

14.7	RSV	TEV

so that he promised with an oath to give her whatever she might ask.	that he promised her, "I swear that I will give you anything you ask for!"

This verse follows on directly from the previous one. **So that** is the link, and it may be translated as "... and her dancing pleased Herod so much that he promised ..." or "He was so pleased that he promised ...."

He promised with an oath to give her is in part transformed into direct discourse in TEV: "**he promised her, 'I swear that I will give ....'**" **Promised with an oath** translates a structure which is the strongest possible way of making a promise; NJB has "that he promised on oath to give." Another possible restructuring, utilizing partial direct discourse, is "he made an oath and promised her, 'I will give you ....'"

See 5.33 for a discussion of **oath** and other forms of swearing.

Whatever she might ask is too brief for some languages. "Anything she might ask for" or "anything that she asked him to give her" are other renderings.

14.8	RSV	TEV

Prompted by her mother, she said, "Give me the head of John the Baptist here on a platter."	At her mother's suggestion she asked him, "Give me here and now the head of John the Baptist on a plate!"

Prompted by her mother (so also NJB, NEB) is made into a noun construction by TEV ("**At her mother's suggestion**"). The verb **prompted** occurs only here in the New Testament, though it is used in the Septuagint in the positive sense of "give instructions" (Exo 35.34; Deut 6.7). On the basis of this usage, one may then translate "being instructed by her mother" or "following her mother's instructions." Mark states explicitly that the girl went out to ask her mother what to do (6.24), but Matthew does not indicate whether or not her mother was present in the room at the time that Herod made the vow. However, in an Oriental setting it is quite likely that she would not have been present, because the entertainment would have been designed primarily for men. If explicit movements of going and coming are demanded by the receptor language, it is possible to translate "She went out and asked her mother what she should do. Her mother told her what to ask for, then she went back into the room and asked him ...." A shorter rendering is "Her mother told her what to do, and so she said (to Herod) "Give me ...." Of course, some languages

453

will use indirect speech, as in ". . . so she asked Herod to give her . . . ." See comment at verse 11.

Give me is a command which the girl expects to be fulfilled at that very moment, thus the reason for **"Give me here and now"** of TEV and GECL 1st edition.

The head of John the Baptist here on a platter is stated in Greek in such a manner as to retain the surprise element until the last: "Give me here, on a platter, the head of John the Baptist." The order in RSV and TEV is more natural, though the effect may not be as dramatic. GECL 1st edition maintains the more dramatic order of the Greek. The noun translated **platter** (TEV "plate") may refer to any kind of flat dish; the word originally meant "board" or "plank." In cultures where plates are not normally used, translators will use "bowls" or whatever is the normal object on which someone would carry food.

14.9　　　　　RSV　　　　　　　　　　　　　TEV

And the king was sorry; but because of his oaths and his guests he commanded it to be given;

　　　The king was sad, but because of the promise he had made in front of all his guests he gave orders that her wish be granted.

Herod Antipas is here referred to in Greek as **the king**, though his title in verse 1 is "ruler of the fourth part of a kingdom." If translators used "ruler" in verse 1, they may wish to use the same here. Or they can simply switch to "king," as the Greek text does.

Was sorry (so also Mft, AT) represents a participle which is generally translated as a finite verb, **"was sad"** (TEV), "was distressed" (NJB, NEB, Brc), "had his misgivings" (NAB), and "was appalled" (Phps). The root meaning of the word is "be sad" (see comments at 17.23). It may be necessary to add "because of what he had promised" or "because of her request."

But because of his oaths and his guests means "but because of the oaths he had made in the presence of his guests." Brc has "because he had given his sworn promise in front of his guests."

For **oaths**, see comments on 5.33. Translators should use the same term they did in verse 7.

In the clause **he commanded it to be given**, the full meaning is "he commanded (the head of John the Baptist) to be given (to the girl)." Brc has "he ordered her request to be granted," and Phps "he gave orders that she should be given what she had asked." Other translators will use a fuller form, possibly with an active verb; for example, "he commanded his men (or, soldiers) to give her John's head" or ". . . what she had asked for."

14.10　　　　　RSV　　　　　　　　　　　　　TEV

he sent and had John beheaded in the prison,

　　So he had John beheaded in prison.

Although **sent** (a participle in Greek) has no expressed object, many languages will require one: "sent his men to the prison to behead John the Baptist" or "sent the executioner . . . ."

Beheaded can be "kill him by cutting off his head."

The last part of verse 9 and verse 10 are sometimes put into direct speech, as in ". . . he commanded his soldiers, 'Give her what she has asked for. Go to the prison and cut off John's head.' "

14.11 RSV TEV

and his head was brought on a platter and given to the girl, and she brought it to her mother.	The head was brought in on a plate and given to the girl, who took it to her mother.

His head was brought will be an impossible structure in many languages. GECL indicates the agent of the passive verb by making the last half of verse 10 and the first half of verse 11 into one sentence: *"10* He sent the executioner to the prison; he beheaded John *11* and brought the head on a plate and gave it to the young girl." It is not necessary to assume that the executioner is the one who brought the head in, though this is a valid assumption. One may also translate *"10* He sent his executioner to behead John the Baptist in prison. *11* Then a servant brought . . . ."

Girl literally means "little girl," though it is known that Salome was born in A.D. 10, which would mean that she was eighteen to twenty years old at this time. Matthew has previously used the word to describe the ruler's daughter (9.24,25), who was twelve years old, according to Mark (5.42).

And she brought it to her mother assumes that the mother was not in the same room with the guests; see verse 8. In some languages **brought** will have to be rendered "took." The phrase may be followed by "and gave it to her."

14.12 RSV TEV

And his disciples came and took the body and buried it; and they went and told Jesus.	John's disciples came, carried away his body, and buried it; then they went and told Jesus.

And indicates that the discourse is continuing. In some languages it can be dropped, and in others it can be rendered "After that."

His disciples are obviously "John's disciples," and a number of modern translations are explicit. Here again, the many pronouns of the Greek text will prove confusing if sufficient caution is not taken.

Came may have to be "went" or even "went to the prison."

The body may be translated "John's body" or "his body."

Both Mark and Matthew mention that John's disciples carried away his body and buried it, but only Matthew indicates that they went and told Jesus. In some languages it may be necessary to indicate what they told Jesus, as in GECL: "then they went to Jesus and told him what had happened." It is also possible to translate ". . . what had happened to John" or ". . . that Herod had had John beheaded."

14.13-21

RSV   TEV

Jesus Feeds Five Thousand Men

13 Now when Jesus heard this, he withdrew from there in a boat to a lonely place apart. But when the crowds heard it, they followed him on foot from the towns. 14 As he went ashore he saw a great throng; and he had compassion on them, and healed their sick. 15 When it was evening, the disciples came to him and said, "This is a lonely place, and the day is now over; send the crowds away to go into the villages and buy food for themselves." 16 Jesus said, "They need not go away; you give them something to eat." 17 They said to him, "We have only five loaves here and two fish." 18 And he said, "Bring them here to me." 19 Then he ordered the crowds to sit down on the grass; and taking the five loaves and the two fish he looked up to heaven, and blessed, and broke and gave the loaves to the disciples, and the disciples gave them to the crowds. 20 And they all ate and were satisfied. And they took up twelve baskets full of the broken pieces left over. 21 And those who ate were about five thousand men, besides women and children.

13 When Jesus heard the news about John, he left there in a boat and went to a lonely place by himself. The people heard about it, and so they left their towns and followed him by land. 14 Jesus got out of the boat, and when he saw the large crowd, his heart was filled with pity for them, and he healed their sick.

15 That evening his disciples came to him and said, "It is already very late, and this is a lonely place. Send the people away and let them go to the villages to buy food for themselves."

16 "They don't have to leave," answered Jesus. "You yourselves give them something to eat!"

17 "All we have here are five loaves and two fish," they replied.

18 "Then bring them here to me," Jesus said. 19 He ordered the people to sit down on the grass; then he took the five loaves and the two fish, looked up to heaven, and gave thanks to God. He broke the loaves and gave them to the disciples, and the disciples gave them to the people. 20 Everyone ate and had enough. Then the disciples took up twelve baskets full of what was left over. 21 The number of men who ate was about five thousand, not counting the women and children.

SECTION HEADING: TEV has "**Jesus Feeds Five Thousand Men,**" but as is clear from verse 21, Jesus fed women and children as well. For this reason it may be better to say here "Jesus feeds a large crowd of people" or "Jesus feeds five thousand men as well as many other people."

The four Gospels contain six accounts of miraculous feedings of multitudes, which suggests the importance they attached to these events. Matthew himself includes two accounts, that of the feeding of the five thousand (14.13-21) and that of the four thousand (15.32-39). In Mark (6.30-44) and Luke (9.10-17) the feeding of the five thousand is placed immediately after the return of the disciples whom Jesus had sent out. But Matthew prefers to record it after the news of John's death.

14.13   RSV   TEV

Now when Jesus heard this, he withdrew from there in a boat to a lonely place apart. But when the

When Jesus heard the news about John, he left there in a boat and went to a lonely place by him-

crowds heard it, they followed him on foot from the towns.	self. The people heard about it, and so they left their towns and followed him by land.

Now is a transition as the narrative shifts to another episode. In many languages, for example English, no formal marker is needed (see TEV).

Heard this: in Greek no object is expressed after the verb **heard**, but English requires one; TEV has "**the news about John.**" Even if it is possible to translate without the express mention of an object, it is wise to supply one because this verse opens a new section. INCL and MACL translate "When Jesus had heard this news"; NJB has "When Jesus received this news"; and NEB "When he heard what had happened Jesus . . . ."

He withdrew from there in a boat to a lonely place apart assumes that Jesus first got into the boat, and some languages will expect this fact to be stated explicitly. Moreover, **apart** translates a construction which actually means "privately, by himself," thus raising a question concerning the whereabouts of Jesus' disciples at this time. Were they in the boat with Jesus during his journey to a lonely place, or did they show up later, either with the crowds or on their own? "The disciples came to him and said" of verse 15 provides no answer; this statement does not mean that the disciples had just at that moment arrived, but rather that "they came up to him." Finally, the preposition **to**, signifying "in the direction of," may require translation as a verb. On the assumption that the disciples accompanied Jesus on his journey in the boat, it is valid to translate "He and his disciples got into a boat. Then they left there and headed for a lonely place where Jesus could be alone."

It is probably not necessary to specify where **there** refers to. The text does not actually tell us where Jesus was when he got the word, so the translation can be "went away" or "went away from that place."

There are languages where it will not sound natural to speak of getting into a boat unless it is also specified on which body of water the boat was. For example, translators may have to say ". . . got into a boat on the lake and went from there . . . ." However, translators should be careful not to make things like this specific unless their language really does require it.

A lonely place apart can be rendered "a place where there were no other people" or "a deserted area."

The crowds (a favorite term in the Gospel) is rendered "**the people**" by NJB and TEV; NEB has "people."

Heard it: this is the second time in this verse when the verb **heard** is used in Greek without an expressed object; NJB has "heard of this," and NEB "heard of it." One may feel compelled to express the object more precisely: "heard that Jesus had left in a boat."

Followed him on foot from the towns implies two actions on the part of the people, though only one is specifically marked by a verb: (1) the people left their towns, and (2) they followed Jesus. TEV mentions both actions and places the events in chronological order: "left . . . followed."

Although elsewhere in the Gospel **followed** may be used of discipleship, the literal meaning alone is intended here.

By foot (TEV "**by land**") contrasts travel by land with travel on water. Matthew does not state why the people decided to go by land instead of by boat, though the implication is that other boats were not available.

Followed him on foot could be "walked after him" or "walked to where he was."

The towns has been translated by TEV as "**their towns**," but this can also be "the towns where they lived" or "the towns of that area."

14.14　　　RSV　　　　　　　　　　　　　TEV

As he went ashore he saw a great throng; and he had compassion on them, and healed their sick.	Jesus got out of the boat, and when he saw the large crowd, his heart was filled with pity for them, and he healed their sick.

He may require identification as "**Jesus**," and **went ashore** may necessitate an indication of prior action, "**got out of the boat**." In fact the verb **went ashore** literally means "got out"; the problem is that the text does not state what it was that Jesus got out of. Phps ("When Jesus emerged from his retreat") is unlikely. More likely is the meaning "**out of the boat**" (AT, GECL, TEV) or "disembarked" (Mft, Brc, NAB); **went ashore**, "stepped ashore" (NJB), and "came ashore" (NEB) assume departure from a boat.

Throng is the singular form of the word "crowds" of verse 13; TEV translates **great throng** as "**large crowd**."

He had compassion (TEV "**his heart was filled with pity**") literally means "his insides were stirred up." This can also be rendered as "he felt very sorry for them" or by a figurative expression from the receptor language. Some West African languages use an expression such as "his stomach (or heart, or liver) was hot (or, sad) because of them."

The noun translated **sick** occurs only here in Matthew; elsewhere in the New Testament it is found in Mark 6.5,13; 1 Corinthians 11.30. The literal meaning of the noun is "powerless," though it may also mean "sick, ill." Of course **their sick** refers to "people (among them) who were sick" or "the sick people there."

The relations between the verbs in this verse are slightly different in the RSV text (**As he went . . . he saw . . . ; and he had compassion . . . and healed**) and in TEV ("**Jesus got out . . . and when he saw . . . his heart was filled . . . and he healed**"). Translators should be careful to structure the sentence in the way that will be most natural in their language.

14.15　　　RSV　　　　　　　　　　　　　TEV

When it was evening, the disciples came to him and said, "This is a lonely place, and the day is now over; send the crowds away to go	That evening his disciples came to him and said, "It is already very late, and this is a lonely place. Send the people away and let them go to

into the villages and buy food for
themselves."

the villages to buy food for themselves."

Evening may mean either the time immediately before or immediately after
sunset; the context suggests before sunset, or else it would have been too late for the
people to go to the villages to buy food. **When it was evening** can be expressed
"That evening" or "When it began to get dark."

Here, as in many similar places, it may be necessary to render **the disciples**
by "his disciples."

Came to translates a verb which means "approach" or "come up to." The verb
does not suggest that the disciples were at a distance; to the contrary, the implication
is that the disciples were already present, but approached Jesus to say something to
him.

The root meaning of the word rendered **lonely** (so most translations) is
"abandoned" or "deserted," though the word may also mean "a desert region."

The day is now over (NEB "the day has gone") is given a less specific time
reference by TEV ("**It is already very late**"), Phps ("it is very late"), and JB ("the
time has slipped by"). Some commentators propose that the meaning is more exactly
"it is too late to teach people any more," and Brc is also specific: "it is now past the
time for the evening meal."

Send . . . away may sound harsh in some languages; but the sound of
harshness can be removed by shifting to a question: "Why don't you send the people
away . . . ?" or "Shouldn't you send the people away . . . ?"

In some translations **the villages** is rendered so that readers think it means the
villages where the people in the crowds lived. To avoid this, "villages in the area" or
"villages around here" may be better.

The word translated **food** is the normal Greek word for food; Mark (6.36) has
"something to eat." Either structure will satisfy the needs of the context.

14.16	RSV	TEV

Jesus said, "They need not go away;
you give them something to eat."

　"They don't have to leave,"
answered Jesus. "You yourselves
give them something to eat!"

They need not go away is rendered in more natural English in TEV: "**They
don't have to leave.**" Other possibilities include "It is not necessary for them to
leave" and "They can stay here."

In Greek the pronoun **you** is emphatic. Some translators try to show this by
saying "It is for you to give them something to eat" or "You yourselves give them
some food."

Something to eat is not the same form which Mark uses in 6.36 (see verse
15); it is literally "to eat" (an infinitive which is not accompanied by an object), but
an object will be required in most translations. "Some food" or "some food to eat"
are common renderings.

14.17   RSV   TEV

They said to him, "We have only five loaves here and two fish."	"All we have here are five loaves and two fish," they replied.

We have only may better be rendered as "All we have" or "The only food that we have."

Bread (particularly barley bread instead of wheat bread) and fish comprised the basic diet of the poor in Galilee. The mention of **five loaves** may be deceptive, since people of the western world are accustomed to thinking of a loaf of bread as sufficient for several people for several meals. The Palestinian bread loaves were much smaller, and three loaves were generally considered sufficient for one person during a meal. Five loaves then would have been approximately enough bread for two people.

The **two fish** would have been either smoked or pickled; these were considered a delicacy when eaten as a relish for the bread.

Some translators will put the information about the size and nature of bread in Galilee into footnotes. But others will render **five loaves** as "five small loaves of bread." In 4.3 and later we suggested "bread" is often a figure for food in general. That is not the case here with **loaves**, where it is actually bread being referred to.

14.18   RSV   TEV

And he said, "Bring them here to me."	"Then bring them here to me," Jesus said.

And he said: TEV identifies the pronoun *he* as Jesus ("Jesus said").

It may be necessary in some languages to substitute a descriptive phrase for **them**: "the loaves of bread and the fish."

In many languages indirect speech will be preferable, as in "Jesus told them to take (or, bring) the bread and fish to him."

14.19   RSV   TEV

Then he ordered the crowds to sit down on the grass; and taking the five loaves and the two fish he looked up to heaven, and blessed, and broke and gave the loaves to the disciples, and the disciples gave them to the crowds.	He ordered the people to sit down on the grass; then he took the five loaves and the two fish, looked up to heaven, and gave thanks to God. He broke the loaves and gave them to the disciples, and the disciples gave them to the people.

Ordered should not be translated in such a manner as to indicate that Jesus is giving a harsh command. It may be better to translate "told" or "said to the people, 'Sit down . . . .' " Note that this can be either direct speech or indirect, as in the RSV text and in TEV.

Sit down literally means "lie down" or "recline" (at a meal), which was the normal position assumed for a meal in the Palestinian setting. In 8.11 the same verb is used of the Messianic banquet.

Taking the five loaves may be misleading to many readers. The meaning is not that Jesus took the bread from his disciples, but rather that he took (better "held") the bread in his hand (while giving thanks to God). In fact, it may be assumed upon the basis of verse 18 that the disciples had already given the loaves and the fish to Jesus. The sequence of events may then be spelled out as follows: "After the disciples had brought the bread to Jesus, he ordered the people to sit on the grass. Then he held the five loaves and the two fish in his hands . . . ."

The Greek noun rendered **heaven** may also mean "sky." Here the meaning is heaven, the place of God's abode. Thus the translation may be "looked up at the sky" or simply "looked up."

Blessed may be understood to mean either "thanked God for them" (GECL 1st edition) or "asked God's blessing upon them." Since "them" has reference to the bread and fish, one may also translate ". . . the bread and fish" or ". . . the food." Translators do need to be careful with **blessed**, since in many societies only people can be blessed, and then only by God; all a person can do is ask God to bless someone. In other cases the word means that Jesus was asking God to make the food holy. In situations like these, "thanked" is the only appropriate translation.

The Greek verb rendered **broke** is used in the New Testament and in the Septuagint only of the breaking of bread. In a Jewish household this was done by the father as the signal to begin the meal. It may be better to render "broke . . . in pieces" (AT, GECL).

Many translators will begin a new sentence here at the verb **broke**, as TEV has done.

Note that Jesus broke the bread. The text does not indicate that he broke the fish into pieces, and in fact he probably did not, since it was the breaking of bread that was symbolic of the beginning of a meal, as we indicated above.

The text does not specify into how many pieces he broke the bread, nor what size they were. Translators can say "little pieces" but should be sure that readers won't think of crumbs. They would have to be pieces of a size that could be distributed.

In some languages, once the loaves were broken into pieces, one would have to say that Jesus distributed the pieces, not the loaves.

And the disciples gave them to the crowds is literally "And the disciples to the crowd," in which the verb **gave** is carried over in Greek from the previous clause. But most languages, as English, will require the inclusion of the verb in both clauses. Jesus gave the pieces of bread to the disciples who in turn gave them to the crowds. Instead of repeating the verb **gave**, some translators will have something like ". . . gave them to the disciples for them to distribute to the crowd."

Nothing is said of the distribution of the fish, though some languages may require that this action be specified. But if this is done, it should be handled in such a manner as to keep the bread in focus. This is extremely important, for Matthew intends his readers to see reflections of the Lord's Supper in this feeding miracle. If specific mention of the fish is required, one may add at the end of the verse "He also gave his disciples the fish, and they gave them to the people."

14.20   RSV   TEV

And they all ate and were satisfied. And they took up twelve baskets full of the broken pieces left over.	Everyone ate and had enough. Then the disciples took up twelve baskets full of what was left over.

They all refers to the people in the crowd, not to the disciples.

Were satisfied (TEV **"had enough"**) means "eat one's fill" and may even be used of birds which gorge themselves on the flesh of slain men and animals (Rev 19.21). Elsewhere in the Gospel the verb is found in 5.6; 15.33. Here it can be rendered as "had enough to eat" or by a phrase such as "each person had as much to eat as he wanted."

When the text says **they took up**, it is the disciples who did the gathering up, not the crowds. Two "they"s in the sentence can be confusing to readers. **Took up** can be "gathered up" or "collected."

That the disciples took up twelve baskets full of leftovers is a further indication of the sufficiency of the meal. One scholar notes that the word translated **baskets** is used by an ancient writer of "the little food baskets which Jews carried so that they might eat only food prepared according to the food laws." However, in the New Testament it probably refers to "a large, heavy basket for carrying things." Translators in languages that have a number of different words for **baskets** according to the size or material should choose a basket that the disciples might reasonably have found there that people would have used for carrying produce or food. If baskets are simply unknown, then some generic word for a container can be used.

They took up twelve baskets full may be intended to suggest that each of the disciples took up one basket full.

The broken pieces left over (TEV **"what was left over"**) is translated "the scraps remaining" by JB and "the scraps left over" by NEB. Brc has "of pieces of bread that were left over."

Note that the words **left over** indicate that the bread the disciples gathered was not just pieces and crumbs on the ground, but bread that the people had left when they had eaten their fill.

As with the distribution, there was probably some fish picked up, too, although the text does not mention it explicitly. If translators do mention the fish, however, the focus should still be on the bread.

14.21   RSV   TEV

And those who ate were about five thousand men, besides women and children.	The number of men who ate was about five thousand, not counting the women and children.

Those who ate may require an object: "those who ate the bread and fish." It is interesting to note that some Greek manuscripts do include "the loaves" as object of the verb, and one Latin manuscript even has "bread and fish."

Both Matthew and Mark (6.44) note that **five thousand** took part in the meal, though only Matthew emphasizes the number by the additional comment **besides women and children**. GECL translates the verse "About five thousand men had taken part in the meal, in addition to the women and children." **Besides women and children** may necessitate restructuring as a complete statement: "In addition some women and children had also eaten all the bread and fish that they wanted."

The separate mention of the women and children makes it very clear that **five thousand** refers specifically to the **men**. It would not be correct, therefore, to say "five thousand people."

Translators will find many ways to restructure this verse to make it more natural. Examples are "There were about five thousand men who ate (the bread and fish), not counting the women and children who were there, too" and "Altogether, about five thousand men as well as women and children were given food (or, bread and fish) to eat."

14.22-33

RSV

TEV

Jesus Walks on the Water

RSV	TEV
22 Then he made the disciples get into the boat and go before him to the other side, while he dismissed the crowds. 23 And after he had dismissed the crowds, he went up on the mountain by himself to pray. When evening came, he was there alone, 24 but the boat by this time was many furlongs distant from the land,*m* beaten by the waves; for the wind was against them. 25 And in the fourth watch of the night he came to them, walking on the sea. 26 But when the disciples saw him walking on the sea, they were terrified, saying, "It is a ghost!" And they cried out for fear. 27 But immediately he spoke to them, saying, "Take heart, it is I; have no fear."	22 Then Jesus made the disciples get into the boat and go on ahead to the other side of the lake, while he sent the people away. 23 After sending the people away, he went up a hill by himself to pray. When evening came, Jesus was there alone; 24 and by this time the boat was far out in the lake, tossed about by the waves, because the wind was blowing against it.
	25 Between three and six o'clock in the morning Jesus came to the disciples, walking on the water. 26 When they saw him walking on the water, they were terrified. "It's a ghost!" they said, and screamed with fear.
	27 Jesus spoke to them at once. "Courage!" he said. "It is I. Don't be afraid!"
28 And Peter answered him, "Lord, if it is you, bid me come to you on the water." 29 He said, "Come." So Peter got out of the boat and walked on the water and came to Jesus; 30 but when he saw the wind,*n* he was afraid, and beginning to sink he cried out, "Lord, save me." 31 Jesus immediately reached out his hand and caught him, saying to him, "O man of little faith, why did you doubt?" 32 And when they got into the boat, the wind ceased. 33 And those in the boat worshiped him, saying, "Truly you are the Son of God."	28 Then Peter spoke up. "Lord, if it is really you, order me to come out on the water to you."
	29 "Come!" answered Jesus. So Peter got out of the boat and started walking on the water to Jesus. 30 But when he noticed the strong wind, he was afraid and started to sink down in the water. "Save me, Lord!" he cried.
	31 At once Jesus reached out and grabbed hold of him and said, "What little faith you have! Why did you doubt?"
	32 They both got into the boat, and the wind died down. 33 Then the disciples in the boat worshiped Jesus. "Truly you are the Son of God!" they exclaimed.

m Other ancient authorities read *was out on the sea*
n Other ancient authorities read *strong wind*

SECTION HEADING: with the title **"Jesus Walks on the Water,"** it may be necessary to replace **"Water"** with the specific name of the water involved, as in ". . . on Lake Galilee." In some languages it is even necessary to indicate that he was walking on the surface, not just wading: ". . . on top of the lake."

Matthew follows Mark (6.45-52) in placing this narrative immediately after the feeding of the five thousand; it is not included in Luke, though there is a parallel in John (6.16-21). Only Matthew records Peter's unsuccessful attempt to walk on the water (verses 28-31), and he alone climaxes the narrative with the confession "Truly you are the Son of God!" (verse 33). This confession then becomes the clue to the understanding of the account in Matthew's Gospel. By means of it Matthew reminds his readers who Jesus truly is, and so strengthens their faith.

14.22   RSV   TEV

> Then he made the disciples get   Then Jesus made the disciples
> into the boat and go before him to   get into the boat and go on ahead to
> the other side, while he dismissed   the other side of the lake, while he
> the crowds.   sent the people away.

By the use of **Then** to introduce this paragraph, it is impossible to determine if RSV, TEV, and NEB are following the longer wording of the Greek text (literally "and immediately") or the shorter wording (literally "and"). The longer wording is apparently preferred by JB and Phps ("Directly after this") as well as by NAB ("Immediately afterward") and Brc ("Immediately"). While some scholars feel that "immediately" was later introduced into the text by some scribe who was influenced by the Marcan form (6.45), the conclusion of TC-GNT is "that its absence from a few witnesses is due to accidental omission." The adverbial construction translated **Then** may be represented in a variety of ways; its primary function is to tie this narrative closely to that of the feeding of the five thousand. Expressions such as "After that," "Soon after," or "Later" will do this.

Note that TEV has made the **he** of the text clearly **"Jesus."** As we always advise in cases such as this, translators must do what is most natural.

Made (so also TEV, NJB, NEB) translates a verb which means "compelled" or "forced," though in some contexts it may be softened to mean "urged strongly" or "urged." In Matthew it occurs only here. In the remainder of the New Testament the verb is found in Mark 6.45 (parallel to this verse); Luke 14.23; Acts 26.11; 28.19; 2 Corinthians 12.11; Galatians 2.3,14; 6.12. It would certainly give an incorrect impression if **made** were translated by a phrase that indicated Jesus used physical force. "Commanded," "told," or "had (his disciples) get into" will be better.

The definite article in **the boat** assumes that the boat is known information previously mentioned. A boat was mentioned in verse 13, and this is undoubtedly the boat referred to here. All the standard translations, with the exception of NEB, include the definite article; NEB renders "made the disciples embark," without mention of a boat. Phps, on the other hand, clarifies the force of the definite article by translating "their boat." Evidently the definite article **the** was in the source that Matthew used, and he retained it. However, that information about a boat was introduced much earlier in this narrative, and some languages may employ their own forms for referring to old information that has not been mentioned for some time. In some cases it may be "that boat they had traveled in before," although this is an awkward rendering and may give undue prominence to **the**. "The boat there," or in some cases even "a boat," may be better.

Go before him can be rendered "go ahead of him" or "go before he did." It means before or ahead of him in time, not necessarily in space.

The other side (TEV "**the other side of the lake**") is the traditional way of mentioning the eastern shore of Lake Galilee (see 8.18). Mark (6.45) states that the town of Bethsaida, also on the eastern shore, was the intended destination, though Matthew is not so specific. That the movement of the boat was from west to east is further confirmed by verse 34, which has them landing near Gennesaret (a town on the western shore) on their return. This further suggests that the feeding of the five thousand took place on the western shore, perhaps near the plain of Gennesaret.

The other side should probably not be rendered as "the eastern shore," despite the fact that it is probably the side being referred to. Such a translation would place emphasis on something that wasn't really in focus. "Across the lake" or "the other side from where they were" will be more general.

While he dismissed the crowds is repeated in a slightly different form at the beginning of verse 23 ("And after he had dismissed the crowds"). GECL restructures and shortens by joining the two verses: "Immediately after this Jesus sent his disciples to the other side in a boat. He then sent the people home and went up a mountain by himself to pray. When it became dark, he was still there." This kind of restructuring will be natural in many languages, but in others the repetition in the text will be better. In such cases translators may have "After that, Jesus had his disciples get into the boat and go ahead of him across the lake. While they were going, he dismissed the crowds. After he had done that . . . ."

Dismissed may be "told to go home" or "sent away."

Crowds, as in other places, may be rendered "the people" or "all the people who were there."

14.23	RSV	TEV
	And after he had dismissed the crowds, he went up on the mountain by himself to pray. When evening came, he was there alone,	After sending the people away, he went up a hill by himself to pray. When evening came, Jesus was there alone;

The mountain (TEV "a hill"): translations differ in their choice of **mountain** or "hill" (see comments on 5.1), but most all of them retain the definite article **the** of the Greek text. NJB retains the definite article but in a nonspecific construction: "the hills." In English "the hills" means "a hilly place" or "a place where there are many hills"; it does not denote a particular hill or hilly area. Here translators usually say "the hill there" or use an indefinite form like that in TEV.

By himself belongs with **to pray** (NEB "to pray alone"), though it may be necessary to repeat the phrase with the verb **went up** as well: "went up the mountain by himself in order to pray alone."

The verb **pray** is used of prayer in general and is the most frequent term found in the New Testament for prayer. For those languages that do not have a specific word for **pray**, a frequent equivalent is "speak with God," "ask things of God," or, in some cases, "worship God."

When evening came (so also NJB, TEV, Brc, Mft) is a literal rendering of the Greek text; NEB has "It grew late." Other possibilities include "When night fell," "When it became late," "After dusk," or "When it became dark."

He was there alone may need to be rendered "He was still there alone," so as not to imply that in the interim Jesus had not been alone. GECL translates "When it became dark he was still there." The restructuring of NEB is also helpful: "It grew late, and he was there by himself."

14.24　　　　　　RSV　　　　　　　　　　　　　　　　　TEV

RSV	TEV
but the boat by this time was many furlongs distant from the land,*m* beaten by the waves; for the wind was against them.	and by this time the boat was far out in the lake, tossed about by the waves, because the wind was blowing against it.

m Other ancient authorities read *was out on the sea*

By this time (so also TEV, Brc) is literally "but . . . already" (NIV). However, the function of the temporal phrase is to indicate that the boat had been moving to its present position, so that this event was taking place precisely at the moment that Jesus was alone on the mountain in prayer. NAB has "Meanwhile"; both Phps and NJB have "while . . . by now."

There are languages where it is not normal to speak of **the boat** alone, but as "the boat with the disciples" or "the boat the disciples were in."

Many furlongs distant from the land is expressed in more contemporary language by TEV: "**far out in the lake**." The Greek word rendered **furlong** by RSV was about two hundred yards; consequently **many furlongs** would intimate that the disciples had gone some distance into the lake, which measures about four and a half miles across. JB is similar to TEV: "far out on the lake." But, as RSV's footnote indicates, there is an alternative textual choice. Some manuscripts have "in the middle of the lake" in place of **many furlongs distant from the land**. TC-GNT believes that this alternative reading was made by some scribe who attempted to make Matthew's text read similar to Mark (6.47). In either case, neither reading gives a specific measurement; both merely state that the boat was now some distance from the shore, and therefore any phrase that conveys this information will be faithful to the intent of the text. Brc translates "a good distance from land."

Beaten (TEV "**tossed about**") is also a participle, made from the same verb as the one translated "in . . . distress" in 8.6 (see comments there). Scholars are in almost unanimous agreement that in Matthew it is the boat, rather than the disciples (as in Mark 6.48), which is in danger from the waves. This alteration is in keeping with Matthew's theology, in which the boat has become an image of the church.

Consequently **beaten by the waves** may have to be made into an active sentence such as "the waves were beating against the boat."

For the wind was against them is translated "**because the wind was blowing against it**" by TEV. The Greek text has no expressed object of the adjective represented by **against** in RSV, but if an object must be expressed, then "it" (the boat) is preferable to **them** (the disciples), since the boat is the expressly mentioned subject of the sentence. NJB skirts the problem ("for there was a head-wind"), while NEB translates **beaten by the waves; for the wind was against them** by the abbreviated form "battling with a head-wind and a rough sea." For **the wind was against them,** translators can choose the perspective of the wind, as in "for the wind was blowing against them," or that of the boat, as in "for they were going straight into the wind."

Some translators will find it more natural to restructure the sentence somewhat: "By this time, the boat (with the disciples) was far from the shore. It was going into the wind, and the waves were beating against it."

14.25	RSV	TEV

And in the fourth watch of the night he came to them, walking on the sea.	**Between three and six o'clock in the morning Jesus came to the disciples, walking on the water.**

The **And** at the beginning of the verse simply indicates the narrative is continuing. Translators can drop it or render it with whatever word or phrase in their language is natural in the paragraph, possibly "Then."

In the fourth watch of the night reflects the Roman custom of dividing the time between 6 P.M. and 6 A.M. into four equal periods of three hours each. Each one of these time periods was called a **watch**. The Jews and the Greeks, on the other hand, divided the night into three watches. Brc translates "About three o'clock in the morning," and GECL is less specific still: "Toward morning." There are many ways that languages refer to the time indicated by **in the fourth watch of the night**. Besides an expression like that of TEV, translators can have "just before dawn" or "very early in the morning (before dawn)."

In place of **he came to them**, it may be advisable to substitute nouns ("Jesus came to his disciples"), since in the Greek text Jesus was last mentioned by name in verse 16.

Came may better be rendered "went."

Walking on the sea (so most translations) is rendered "walking on the lake" by JB, NAB, Brc. **Walking** represents the normal Greek word for "walk," and **on the sea** means specifically "on the surface of the water," thus indicating a miraculous event; for example, "walking over the lake" (NEB). The phrase in English, **walking on the sea** in both RSV and TEV, is open to being interpreted that the disciples were walking on the sea, not Jesus. This is clearly wrong. Translators can make clear who is walking by using two sentences, as in "Jesus went (or, came) to his disciples. He was walking on the water." Another possibility is "Jesus walked over the water (and went) to his disciples."

As we discussed in connection with the section heading above, the translation must not give the impression Jesus was wading in the water. The passage says clearly that he was walking "on top of the water" or "on the surface of the sea."

14.26   RSV   TEV

But when the disciples saw him walking on the sea, they were terrified, saying, "It is a ghost!" And they cried out for fear.	When they saw him walking on the water, they were terrified. "It's a ghost!" they said, and screamed with fear.

Were terrified translates a much stronger verb than the one used in the Marcan parallel (6.49). In its active form the verb may mean "disturb" or "throw into confusion" (for example, Acts 15.24; Gal 1.7; 5.10). When used in the passive the verb may mean "be frightened" or "be terrified" (for example, Matt 2.3; 14.26; Mark 6.50; Luke 1.12; 24.38). In the present passage the majority of translations are identical with RSV and TEV; NEB has "they were so shaken that." Many translators will find the NEB cited above a useful model, as in "They were so frightened that they thought it was a ghost, and they began to scream with fear," or "They were so terrified that they said 'It's a ghost.' And they began to scream in fear."

Ghost (so most translations) translates a noun that occurs only here and in Mark 6.49 in the New Testament. It may be used of any apparition, particularly that of a spirit. Most cultures will have a word for a spirit people might see. It is not necessary to look for a word that specifically refers to the spirit of someone who died, although, as with the English **ghost**, that is the word often used.

Cried out for fear is translated **"screamed with fear"** by TEV and "cried out in fear" by NJB. NEB, which does not use the verb "terrified" in the previous clause, translates "that they cried out in terror."

14.27   RSV   TEV

But immediately he spoke to them, saying, "Take heart, it is I; have no fear."	Jesus spoke to them at once. "Courage!" he said. "It is I. Don't be afraid!"

But immediately (TEV **"at once"**) translates an adverbial construction which indicates action in immediate sequence; the phrase is emphatic in Greek. For stylistic reasons TEV has moved the phrase to the end of the sentence. Translators should do whatever is most natural.

The sentence with **spoke . . . saying**, two similar verbs, may be more naturally rendered "But immediately Jesus said to them, 'Don't be afraid.' " TEV uses two separate sentences, another possibility. Other translators will use indirect speech, as in "spoke to them and told them not to be afraid."

Take heart (so also NEB) is translated **"Courage"** by TEV, NJB, Brc, and Mft; AT and NIV have "Take courage." It is almost impossible to find a satisfactory expression at the proper English level; even "Get hold of yourselves" (NAB) falls somewhat short of a dynamic equivalent for English speakers. The function of the expression is to offer encouragement; the same verb is used here as in 9.2,22. If there is a good, idiomatic expression in the receptor language, translators can certainly use it. "Be calm" or "Don't be afraid" are common renderings.

It is I (so most all English translations) is rather high level, and it also sounds rather stiff and formal. In the Gospel of John this affirmation is frequently used of a divine revelation (6.35; 8.12,58; 9.5; 10.9,11; 11.25; 15.1), which may be the intention here as well. However, the high level rendering does not in any way aid the reader in determining if this is indeed the meaning, and it may tend to draw more attention to the form than to the content. GECL effectively utilizes a more colloquial expression; in English a similar colloquial expression is "It's me."

Have no fear is translated "**Don't be afraid**" by TEV; JB and NEB choose "Do not be afraid." Here again one should seek for a colloquial expression which conveys the meaning. In translation it may be necessary to rearrange the statements in an order which more naturally reflects the expectations of the receptor language. For example, "It's me, Jesus! Don't be afraid! There is nothing to worry about."

In many languages it is not natural to use two such similar phrases so close together, **take heart** and **have no fear**. Then translators can say simply "Don't be afraid; it's me."

14.28	RSV	TEV

And Peter answered him, "Lord, if it is you, bid me come to you on the water."	Then Peter spoke up. "Lord, if it is really you, order me to come out on the water to you."

And Peter answered him, a literal rendering of the Greek text, is translated "Then Peter got up his courage and said" by GECL 1st edition. Notice that both TEV and GECL have rendered the **And**, the word that shows the story is continuing, as "**Then.**"

Answered may not be the most appropriate word since Jesus has not asked a question. TEV has used "**spoke up.**"

For English speakers **Lord** suggests that Peter is making a full confession of the lordship of Jesus Christ. The same problem of interpretation exists here as in 8.25 (see comments there), where the Greek noun of address may mean either **Lord** or "sir" (INCL: "Sir, if you really are Jesus . . ."). The perspective from which Matthew writes is of supreme importance: how much does he intend to reflect the actual historical situation at the time that this happened, and to what degree has he modified the account for the encouragement of his readers? It does not appear that Peter and the other disciples recognized who Jesus really was until after he had caused the storm to stop (see verse 33). So then, if the translation is made from the perspective of the time in which this event is placed in the ministry of Jesus, the word may well be understood as an honorific. On the other hand, Matthew may intend the meaning **Lord**, because he addresses his message to a church for whom this has become the proper confession. Probably more translators use this Christian sense of **Lord** than use "Sir."

If it is you (so also NJB, NEB) is translated "**if it is really you**" by TEV and NAB. One commentator notes that this is an expression of certainty rather than doubt.

Bid (TEV "**order**"; NJB, NEB "tell me") is one of Matthew's favorite words; it is used of Jesus in 8.18 and 14.19, of Herod in 14.9, and of Pilate in 27.58. The basic meaning of the word is "order" or "command"; Brc translates "give . . . an order."

On the water (so also most translations) is literally "on the waters." The use of the plural may be influenced by the Old Testament, since the Hebrew word for "water" always takes a plural form.

As with the similar phrase in verse 25, the readers should understand that Peter is asking to walk on top of the water. "Walk to you on top of the water" or "walk across the top of the sea to you" will show this.

14.29	RSV	TEV

He said, "Come." So Peter got out of the boat and walked on the water and came to Jesus;	"Come!" answered Jesus. So Peter got out of the boat and started walking on the water to Jesus.

Either by pronoun or proper name, it must be clear that **he** refers to Jesus.

Some languages will require an indirect object, as in ". . . said to Peter." Other languages will use indirect speech, as in "He told Peter to come to him."

Got out (so also TEV) translates a participle in Greek; the main verb is actually a double verb (**walked . . . and came**), which TEV and NJB represent as "**started walking.**" This form reflects Semitic Greek usage, in which two verbs may be used of a single action; both NEB and NIV use only one verb ("walked"). Since the verb **walked** is used in the aorist indicative tense, it may focus upon the beginning of the action, as TEV and NJB suggest (note also "began to walk" of NAB). There are languages where **walked . . . and came** would indicate that Peter actually reached Jesus, whereas it seems more likely the meaning is he began walking toward Jesus.

14.30	RSV	TEV

but when he saw the wind,ⁿ he was afraid, and beginning to sink he cried out, "Lord, save me."	But when he noticed the strong wind, he was afraid and started to sink down in the water. "Save me, Lord!" he cried.

ⁿ Other ancient authorities read *strong wind*

When he saw is translated "**when he noticed**" by TEV, since in English people do not normally "see" wind. "Became aware of" is another possible rendering, or even "When he realized how the wind was blowing."

He refers to Peter, not to Jesus, and some translations have to specify this.

As RSV's footnote indicates, some Greek manuscripts read "strong wind" in place of **wind**. In fact, other manuscripts even have "very strong wind," which is generally regarded as a scribe's attempt to heighten the dramatic effect. But a firm decision concerning the inclusion or exclusion of the adjective "strong" is more complicated. In light of the impossibility of a dogmatic decision, the UBS Greek Text retains the adjective in the text, though placing it in square brackets to indicate that its presence there is disputed. "Strong" is retained in most English translations, with the exception of RSV, Brc, and NIV, though renderings vary considerably: "the strength of the wind" (Mft), "how strong the wind was" (NAB), "the fury of the wind" (Phps), "the strength of the gale" (NEB), and "the force of the wind" (JB). GECL renders "the high waves," on the logic that what he saw was not the wind but the waves which were the result of the strong wind.

The text states that **he was afraid**. More natural, however, is "he became afraid (or, frightened)."

Sink translates a verb used in the New Testament only by Matthew; it occurs again in 18.6. It may be necessary to locate the sinking, as in "into the water."

There are several ways to link the events of this verse. TEV is one useful model. Another is "But when he noticed the strong wind, he became afraid. He started to sink into the water, and cried out."

Peter calls Jesus **Lord**. Here the Christian sense is clearly called for rather than "Sir."

Save translates the same verb used in 8.25. Here the phrase may be rendered "Rescue me" or "Don't let me drown."

14.31 RSV	TEV
Jesus immediately reached out his hand and caught him, saying to him, "O man of little faith, why did you doubt?"	At once Jesus reached out and grabbed hold of him and said, "What little faith you have! Why did you doubt?"

Immediately (TEV "**At once**") stands in the position of emphasis in the Greek text.

Reached out his hand and caught him is somewhat abbreviated in TEV: "**reached out and grabbed hold of him.**" In NJB this part of the verse is translated "Jesus put out his hand at once and held him"; GECL has "Jesus at once stuck out his hand, took hold of him (and said)."

O man of little faith translates one word in Greek. TEV has "**What little faith you have!**" and NEB "How little faith you have!" GECL translates "You have too little faith." It may be necessary to indicate the object of the faith, as Mft: "How little you trust me!" One may also translate "Why don't you trust me more than that?" or "You ought to trust me more than that!"

Doubt (in the New Testament only here and in 28.17) is the primary meaning of the verb, though it may also mean "hesitate" (NEB) or "waver" (AT). The tense is perhaps best represented by Brc ("begin to doubt"), since Peter's initial steps on the water would suggest that he did initially have faith that he could go to Jesus.

It is quite common for languages to require the translator to specify what Peter failed to trust. Translators can say "Why didn't you believe you could walk on the water?" or "Didn't you believe I could make you walk on the water?"

14.32   RSV   TEV

And when they got into the boat, the   **They both got into the boat, and**
wind ceased.   **the wind died down.**

    Got (into) translates a Greek participle which indicates an action which took place before that of the main verb **ceased** (TEV "**died down**").
    They refers to Peter and Jesus, as TEV makes clear, "**they both.**"
    The text can be rendered either to indicate that the wind stopped because they got into the boat, or simply that it was after they got into the boat that the wind stopped.
    The wind **ceased** or "stopped blowing (hard)."

14.33   RSV   TEV

And those in the boat worshiped   Then the disciples in the boat wor-
him, saying, "Truly you are the Son   shiped Jesus. "Truly you are the Son
of God."   of God!" they exclaimed.

    Those are "**the disciples**" (TEV); see verse 22, which makes this identification positive.
    The phrase **in the boat** seems to contrast with Peter and Jesus, who had been outside the boat. It should not imply the presence of other disciples who were not in the boat. One may translate "Then the disciples (who were) in the boat worshiped him."
    Worshiped is the same verb first used in 2.2, but see comments also at 2.11. NJB has "bowed down before," and NEB "fell at his feet." Certainly in this verse, with the following affirmation by the disciples about Jesus, **worshiped** means more than just honored.
    Truly can be rendered "Indeed" or "In fact," or in a phrase such as "You really are the Son of God."
    Truly you are the Son of God is stated in the Greek text in the most emphatic way possible. Even though the definite article **the** is not present in Greek, the meaning is definitely **the Son of God** and not "a son of God." This is the first confession in the Gospel of Jesus' divine sonship, and as such it anticipates the confession of 16.16.
    The Son of God has sometimes been a problem. As we point out, to say "a Son" is not correct, since that phrase can be used with any believer. Consequently "the One who is God's Son" is necessary in some languages. There are many languages which use one general term for male or female children, and only add "male" when it is necessary to distinguish between sons and daughters. The general term can certainly be used here.
    Another problem comes in cultures which reject the notion of God having a child. To say "the one for whom God was like a father to him" simply does not have the strong statement of divine origin. "The one who comes from God as a Son" or "the one God sends as a Son" may be better. However, even in cultures with this problem, translators have often felt that the claim of the Scriptures is such that it

must be translated as "the Son of God" and an explanation be given in accompanying notes.

Saying (TEV "**exclaimed**") translates a participle. A number of translations retain this form, though they shift to a more descriptive verb: "exclaiming" (NEB), "declaring" (NAB), and "crying" (Phps). The participle does indicate that the way the disciples worshiped Jesus was by declaring their belief that he was God's Son. "Worshiped him as they said" or "worshiped him by saying" are possible renderings.

<h2 style="text-align:center">14.34-36</h2>

RSV	TEV
	Jesus Heals the Sick in Gennesaret
34 And when they had crossed over, they came to land at Gennesaret. 35 And when the men of that place recognized him, they sent round to all that region and brought to him all that were sick, 36 and besought him that they might only touch the fringe of his garment; and as many as touched it were made well.	34 They crossed the lake and came to land at Gennesaret, 35 where the people recognized Jesus. So they sent for the sick people in all the surrounding country and brought them to Jesus. 36 They begged him to let the sick at least touch the edge of his cloak; and all who touched it were made well.

SECTION HEADING: "**Jesus Heals the Sick in Gennesaret**." "**Sick**" may have to be specified as "sick people." See verse 34 for a discussion of "**Gennesaret**." A possible rendering is "Jesus heals the people who are sick in Gennesaret."

Matthew continues to follow the Marcan outline (6.53-56) in the recording of the landing at Gennesaret and of the healings which took place there. He considerably abbreviates the account, though he does retain the essential feature of the healings: the touching of Jesus' garment (verse 36; Mark 6.56).

14.34 RSV TEV

And when they had crossed over, they came to land at Gennesaret.

They crossed the lake and came to land at Gennesaret,

And when they had crossed over: see comments on "the other side" in verse 22.

Often it will be important to repeat what body of water **they had crossed over**, as in "crossed over the lake." Note that this is a continuation of the trip they had already begun. Therefore it may be necessary to say "When they had reached the other side" or "When they finished (their) crossing and came to the other side."

Came to land may be "landed (or, got out) at the land of Gennesaret."

Gennesaret was a village located on the northwest shore of Lake Galilee. But the name also applied to the fertile and densely populated plain west of Lake Galilee and south of Capernaum. By the use of the word "place" to describe Gennesaret in the following verse, the intimation is made that reference is to the plain rather than to the village. Some languages will have "the region (or, the territory) of Gennesaret."

14.35   RSV   TEV

And when the men of that place | where the people recognized Jesus.
recognized him, they sent round to | So they sent for the sick people in all
all that region and brought to him all | the surrounding country and brought
that were sick, | them to Jesus.

When . . . recognized him represents a Greek participle, which most translations prefer to transform into a temporal clause, as does RSV. However, TEV chooses "**where . . . recognized Jesus,**" and NEB "There Jesus was recognized by the people of that place." GECL has a different style yet: "The people of that place recognized Jesus and spread the news of his arrival in the entire region." Of course, restructuring may be done in an unlimited number of ways, provided that the logical connection is not interrupted.

Notice that these models we have cited use an expression such as "**people**" rather than **men**. The text is not referring only to adult males.

Recognized him can be "knew that it was Jesus," "knew he was Jesus," or "saw that it was Jesus."

Sent is without an object in the Greek text. TEV supplies "**for the sick people**"; NEB has "sent out word"; NAB drops **sent** and substitutes "spread the word." **They sent . . . and brought to him all that were sick** may be translated "They sent people to tell everyone in that region that Jesus was there. Then those people brought everyone who was sick . . ." or "They sent people to bring to Jesus all the sick people in that region."

All is intentionally introduced by Matthew; it is lacking in the Marcan parallel (6.55). When Matthew refers to the healing activity of Jesus, he likes to use "all" or "every" (see 4.24; 9.35).

14.36   RSV   TEV

and besought him that they might | They begged him to let the sick at
only touch the fringe of his garment; | least touch the edge of his cloak;
and as many as touched it were | and all who touched it were made
made well. | well.

In Greek the subject of **besought** is an unmarked "they" (masculine plural), which may refer either to sick people or to the people who brought the sick people to Jesus. NEB shifts to a passive in order to avoid the difficulty: "and he was begged to allow them . . . ." Both TEV and GECL 1st edition specify that "they" are those who brought the sick people to Jesus. It is possible to translate "Then the people who brought the sick people to Jesus begged him to let their sick . . . ." Translators who choose the other interpretation will have something like "Then the sick people begged Jesus to let them touch . . . ."

That they might only touch reflects the ancient belief that a person might be healed through physical contact with someone of unusual powers. As a rule, the person with the power to heal would have reached out to touch those who were sick, but these people have such great faith in Jesus that they believe his healing power overflows into **the fringe of his garment**. There is no hint in the text that Jesus encouraged this belief, though what they did was evidently interpreted as a genuine act of faith, because Matthew states **as many as touched it were made well**.

Fringe refers specifically to the part of the long garment that reached down to the feet. In 23.5 the word is used in the specific sense of "tassel," referring to the tassels each Israelite man was obligated to wear on the four corners of his outer garment. See Numbers 15.38-39 and Deuteronomy 22.12. According to 9.20, a woman with a flow of blood was made well when she touched the fringe of Jesus' garment. **Fringe** can be "the bottom" or "the foot," or, as in TEV, **"edge."**

The phrase **as many as** means "whoever," "every person who," or **"all who"** (TEV).

Were made well is rendered "were completely cured" by JB, NEB, Brc. Mft translates "got perfectly well," and NAB "were fully restored to health." Although Matthew abbreviates Marks' account, he heightens the miraculous element by introducing "all" in verse 35 and by introducing the intensive form of the verb where Mark uses the ordinary form. **Were made well** can also be rendered "were healed," "were cured," or by phrases such as "their illnesses (or, diseases) left them" and "were cured (of their illness)." It may also be translated as an active verb: "And Jesus' power made everyone well who touched the edge of his garment."

Chapter 15

RSV

TEV

The Teaching of the Ancestors

1 Then Pharisees and scribes came to Jesus from Jerusalem and said, 2 "Why do your disciples transgress the tradition of the elders? For they do not wash their hands when they eat." 3 He answered them, "And why do you transgress the commandment of God for the sake of your tradition? 4 For God commanded, 'Honor your father and your mother,' and, 'He who speaks evil of father or mother, let him surely die.' 5 But you say, 'If any one tells his father or his mother, What you would have gained from me is given to God,^{o} he need not honor his father.' 6 So, for the sake of your tradition, you have made void the word^p of God. 7 You hypocrites! Well did Isaiah prophesy of you, when he said:

8 'This people honors me with their lips,
  but their heart is far from me;
9 in vain do they worship me,
  teaching as doctrines the precepts of men.' "

^{o} Or *an offering*
^{p} Other ancient authorities read *law*

1 Then some Pharisees and teachers of the Law came from Jerusalem to Jesus and asked him, 2 "Why is it that your disciples disobey the teaching handed down by our ancestors? They don't wash their hands in the proper way before they eat!"

3 Jesus answered, "And why do you disobey God's command and follow your own teaching? 4 For God said, 'Respect your father and your mother,' and 'Whoever curses his father or his mother is to be put to death.' 5 But you teach that if a person has something he could use to help his father or mother, but says, 'This belongs to God,' 6 he does not need to honor his father.^{l} In this way you disregard God's command, in order to follow your own teaching. 7 You hypocrites! How right Isaiah was when he prophesied about you!

8 'These people, says God, honor me with their words,
   but their heart is really far away from me.
9 It is no use for them to worship me,
   because they teach man-made rules as though they were my laws!' "

^{l} his father; *some manuscripts have* his father or mother.

SECTION HEADING: "**The Teaching of the Ancestors**" may be "The lessons the ancestors handed down" or "What the people of long ago taught." It can also be rendered by a short sentence such as "Jesus talks about what the ancestors taught."

In recording the arrival of the scribes and Pharisees from Jerusalem at this time, Matthew remains within the Marcan framework of events (7.1-13). The scene takes place in the vicinity of Gennesaret, where these men have been sent as an official delegation to check on the activities of Jesus. They open their investigation by attempting to entrap him with a question (verses 1-2). But Jesus counters with a question of his own (verse 3), which leads into an attack on his opponents' hypocrisy (verses 4-6). In support of his accusation Jesus appeals to the prophet Isaiah (verses 7-9), whose words he applies to the existing situation (verses 10-11). Jesus' disciples are quick to inform him that he has offended the Pharisees by his remarks (verse 12), to which he responds with a parable (verse 13) and a direct attack on the Pharisees (verse 14). As spokesman for the band of disciples, Peter requests Jesus to explain to them the meaning of the parable (verse 15). Jesus expresses his surprise at the disciples' lack of understanding (verse 16), but he nevertheless interprets for them the meaning of what he said (verses 17-20).

15.1   RSV   TEV

Then Pharisees and scribes came to Jesus from Jerusalem and said,

Then some Pharisees and teachers of the Law came from Jerusalem to Jesus and asked him,

Then indicates that the narrative is continuing. It can mean that the Pharisees and scribes came to Jesus shortly after he began healing in the Gennesaret region (chapter 14), but translators should use some general word or phrase such as "After that" or "Some time later."

For **Pharisees**, see comments at 3.7. **Scribes** or "**teachers of the Law**" was discussed at 2.4.

It is significant that these **Pharisees and scribes** originated **from Jerusalem**, since they could have as easily come from any other Palestinian town. The implication is that they were an official delegation from Jerusalem, the acknowledged headquarters of Judaism. **Pharisees and scribes** were last mentioned together in 12.38 ("Then some of the scribes and Pharisees said to him"). Except for the present verse, **scribes** are always listed first when the two groups are mentioned together (5.20; 12.38; 23.3,13,14,15). However, there seems to be no particular emphasis intended by the reversal of the usual order.

As we have shown previously, **came** in many languages can only be used for approaching the place where the readers of this translation are or, in other languages, where the writer of the narrative is, so that in any case "went" would be better.

15.2   RSV   TEV

"Why do your disciples transgress the tradition of the elders? For they do not wash their hands when they eat."

"Why is it that your disciples disobey the teaching handed down by our ancestors? They don't wash their hands in the proper way before they eat!"

Transgress (so also Mft) is translated "**disobey**" by TEV. A number of English translations prefer "break" (NEB, Brc, NIV, Phps, AT). NAB selects "act contrary to," and NJB "break away from." The verb literally means "go aside" or "turn aside"; however, when used of rules or regulations the meaning is "break" or "disobey." In Matthew the question is phrased somewhat stronger than in Mark, which has "Why do your disciples not live according . . . ?" (Mark 7.5). GECL translates the two parallel passages in the same way, following the wording found in Mark.

The tradition of the elders (so also NJB, NIV) is translated "**the teaching handed down by our ancestors**" in TEV. These traditions refer to the oral (and later, written) interpretation of the Old Testament laws, which developed over centuries in order to make these laws applicable in current situations. Finally, in New Testament times, these traditions became as authoritative as the Old Testament laws themselves. NEB translates the phrase as "the ancient tradition," Phps "our ancient tradition," and AT "the rules handed down by our ancestors." It is important to render **the tradition of the elders** differently than "the Law." "**Teaching**" (as in TEV) or "the things our ancestors taught us" will be better.

Some translators have understood **Why . . . ?** as a genuine request for information. Others have seen it to be a rhetorical question which really functions as an accusation. As a result they have rendered it with a statement such as "Your disciples are violating the teachings of our ancestors" or "It is wrong for your disciples not to follow our forefathers' teaching." In some languages an effective translation will be "Your disciples are not following what our ancestors taught us. Is that proper?" Probably either interpretation is acceptable.

For can easily be mistranslated. The Pharisees are indicating in what way the disciples are violating the tradition of the elders. This can be indicated with a phrase such as "Look, they don't even wash their hands properly before they eat." Another way will be to reverse the order of the verse, as in "Your disciples don't wash their hands properly before they eat, and that is against the teaching of our ancestors. Why do they act this way?" Other translators will find it more natural to simply drop **For**, as TEV has done.

"**In the proper way**" (Phps "properly") is included by TEV to make explicit the meaning of **wash their hands**. Otherwise, readers may understand that the reference is to the washing of hands before a meal for hygienic purposes. The reference is to the special way of washing one's hands as defined by the Pharisees for the sake of ritual cleanliness. Brc translates "give their hands the prescribed washings." GECL translates "Why do they not purify their hands . . . ," and they follow this with a glossary note concerning the meaning of the verb "purify." Translators can also try "wash their hands the way our religion teaches" or, if there is no word for "religion," "the way we should if we are to honor God properly."

When they eat is literally "whenever they eat bread." NEB renders "before meals," and NAB "before eating a meal." It is important that the sequence of events be maintained in the proper order. That is, the washing of the hands took place before the eating of the meal, not during the course of the meal, as **when** or "whenever" might imply. Both NEB and NAB supply "a meal" as the object of the verb **eat**. The Greek text has "bread," since this was the basic element in a Jewish meal. JB translates "eat food," with the footnote "Lit[erally]. 'eat bread.' " In many languages an object will be necessary after the verb "eat," and whatever word is used must suggest a regular meal.

15.3   RSV   TEV

He answered them, "And why do you transgress the commandment of God for the sake of your tradition?

Jesus answered, "And why do you disobey God's command and follow your own teaching?

According to Mark (7.6) Jesus initiates his response with a quotation from Isaiah. Matthew handles the confrontation differently, by introducing first Jesus' fierce denunciation of the Pharisees, and later he introduces the quotation (verses 8-9). To answer a question with a question (verse 3) was a typical method of debate among the Jewish teachers, and Jesus employs this mode of argument to show how the Pharisees had disobeyed God's commands in order to follow their own teaching.

This question is intended to imitate the form of the question which they asked of Jesus, and so translators should treat **why** in the same way they did in the previous verse, either as a request for information or as an accusation.

Transgress is the same verb here as in verse 2.

The commandment of God may be more clearly phrased as "what God commanded us to do" or "what our Scriptures tell us that God commanded us to do."

For the sake of your tradition (TEV **"and follow your own teaching"**) may be translated "in order to do what you teach" or ". . . to do what you say God wants his people to do."

15.4   RSV   TEV

For God commanded, 'Honor your father and your mother,' and, 'He who speaks evil of father or mother, let him surely die.'

For God said, 'Respect your father and your mother,' and 'Whoever curses his father or his mother is to be put to death.'

For God commanded represents the Greek manuscripts which have literally "For God commanded, saying." TEV follows a different manuscript tradition which has "**For God said.**" According to TC-GNT, it is the opinion of the committee for the UBS Greek text that the presence of the verb **commanded** may be accounted for on the basis of "the commandment of God" in verse 3. However, they acknowledge that there is a considerable degree of doubt regarding which of the two readings is preferable. Some languages will automatically require a shift to "commanded," even if the accepted reading is assumed to be "said"; other languages may use "said" with the extended meaning of "commanded."

Honor your father and your mother comes from Exodus 20.12. Most English translations have **honor**; TEV translates "**Respect.**" JB translates "Do your duty to," with a footnote indicating that the verb is literally "honor," but "implying a reverence shown in practical ways." Certainly it would be wrong to translate with something that simply means "to praise," since it is repeated behavior that is involved.

He who speaks evil of father or mother, let him surely die is a quotation from Exodus 21.17. Both this and the previous quotation are apparently from the Septuagint, though minor differences exist. In place of **speaks evil of**, a number of translations have "**curses**" (TEV, NJB, Mft, NEB, Brc). AT has "abuses." Elsewhere in the New Testament the verb occurs only in the Marcan parallel (7.10) and in Acts 19.9, where TEV translates "said evil things about." Considered in light of the Old Testament, the verb may cover a wider area of meaning than that of verbal abuse. "Mistreat," or "fail to show proper respect to," or "fail to do one's duty to" are also possible meanings.

The text has simply **father or mother**, but most translators find it necessary to show that the commandment is specifically against speaking evil of one's own parents, as in "his father or mother."

Let him surely die can be a little awkward. As the TEV model indicates, it is execution that is meant. "That person should be put to death" is a possible translation.

There are two commandments cited in this verse. In some languages translators will need to use a phrase such as "God also commanded" before the second one, to make clear that it is not just a continuation of the first commandment.

In some languages indirect speech is the more natural way to speak of God's commandments, as in "For God commanded (us) to respect our fathers and mothers" or "For God commanded that every person should show respect for his father and mother."

15.5　　　　RSV　　　　　　　　　　　　TEV

But you say, 'If any one tells his father or his mother, What you would have gained from me is given to God,[o] . . .

But you teach that if a person has something he could use to help his father or mother, but says, 'This belongs to God,'

[o] Or *an offering*

Verses 5 and 6 contain an illustration of the manner in which the Pharisees and the teachers of the Law allowed people to avoid doing their duty to their parents. Note that some editions of the Greek text end verse 5 as shown in RSV, while others end it earlier, as in TEV. TEV follows the preference of the UBS Greek New Testament.

In Greek **you** is emphatic and is in contrast to "God" of verse 4. The meaning is "on the one hand God said . . . but on the other hand you teach . . . ." To make this emphasis on **you** clear, some translators have said "But you for your part."

Say, as with "said" of verse 4, may also have an extended meaning; TEV renders "**teach**." GECL translates **But you say** as "But you affirm."

In this verse there is a quote inside a quote (Jesus says to the Pharisees and teachers of the Law that they say that if a man says to his parents). TEV simplifies the structure by using indirect speech: "**But you teach that if a person** . . . ." This may be a useful model for translators in other languages as well. In fact there are languages for which the best rendering will be indirect speech for the whole verse, as in "But you teach that if a person has something he could use to help his father and mother, but tells them that he has promised to give that to God, then he does not have to do his duty to his parents."

What you would have gained from me refers to something a person has that could be of help to his parents. It may be food or money, for example, but the text does not specify, nor should the translation. "What I have that could help you," "This that I have that normally I would have given you," or "My things I could give to you (to help you)" are possible translations.

Given to God (RSV footnote "an offering") translates one word in Greek which is literally "gift." NIV represents it by "a gift devoted to God," NEB has "set apart for God," and NJB "dedicated to God." It is interesting that so many translations are sensitive of the need to be dynamic in order to aid the reader to understand the verse. Jesus is speaking about a situation where a person possesses something that can be used to help his parents. However, by "dedicating" it to God, it is removed from the use of his parents, though he himself may continue to benefit from it. This custom is not known outside the New Testament. In fact, Jewish teachers explicitly affirm that one's duty to father or mother has priority over a number of other commandments, including that of the Sabbath. Evidently the persons to whom Jesus was speaking had a very rigorous attitude toward vows.

Most translators will restructure **given to God** very much like the models cited above. "Something I have promised to give to God" or "something set aside for an offering to God" are similar possibilities.

<u>15.6</u> RSV	TEV
he need not honor his father.' 6 So, for the sake of your tradition, you have made void the word*ᵖ* of God. *ᵖ* Other ancient authorities read *law*	he does not need to honor his father.*ˡ* In this way you disregard God's command, in order to follow your own teaching. *ˡ*his father; *some manuscripts have* his father or mother.

Most translators will render **honor** here the same as they did in verse 4, although "do your duty to" fits most easily in this context. "Do the thing that would honor" is another good rendering.

As the TEV footnote indicates, some manuscripts have "his father or mother" in place of **his father**. But the UBS Greek New Testament has a very high degree of doubt concerning which is the better manuscript. And in either case there is no real difference in meaning. GECL translates "his parents."

So is literally "and"; TEV has "**In this way**." The meaning may be expressed more fully as "By allowing a person to do this."

For the sake of your tradition is slightly reformulated in TEV: "**in order to follow your own teaching**." **Tradition** is the same noun used in verse 3. GECL has "through your own regulations."

Made void is translated "**disregard**" by TEV. Both JB and NEB render "made . . . null and void." NAB and AT render "nullified" (NIV "nullify"). Elsewhere in the New Testament the verb is found in the Marcan parallel (7.13) and in Galatians 3.17, where it is used as a technical legal term (RSV "annul a covenant"). "Count for nothing" or "make have no value" are other phrases that convey the meaning well, but sometimes "disobey" or "pay no attention to" have been used by translators.

The word of God (TEV "**God's command**") appears as "the law of God" in some manuscripts (see the RSV footnote). However, in the present context both "word" and "law" are synonymous with "command." Restructuring may be necessary: "what God commanded you to do."

Notice that TEV has reordered the verse. As we have advised throughout this Handbook, the important thing is for translators to decide what form or order is the most natural in their language.

15.7	RSV	TEV

You hypocrites! Well did Isaiah prophesy of you, when he said:	You hypocrites! How right Isaiah was when he prophesied about you!

In verses 7-8 Jesus characterizes the hypocrisy of the Pharisees by means of a quotation from Isaiah 29.13. The quotation agrees quite closely with the Septuagint, which is significantly different from the wording of the Hebrew.

Hypocrites was first used in 6.2. The important thing here is to use a word or expression that is terse and forcible, something that can be said to someone to accuse them. "You people who pretend to be one thing but are really another" simply would be too awkward in this context. "You pretenders!" or "You fakers!" is better, although if necessary translators can use two phrases such as "You people! You pretend one thing and do the opposite!"

Well did Isaiah prophesy of you, when he said is translated in JB as "It was you Isaiah meant when he so rightly prophesied"; NEB has "Isaiah was right when he prophesied about you."

Prophesy is the verb related to "prophet," which we discussed at 1.22. "To speak God's message" or "speak for God" are common ways of translating it. In this verse translators can say "Isaiah was right when he gave God's word about you" or "When Isaiah gave this message from God, he was certainly talking about you. He said . . . ."

15.8	RSV	TEV

'This people honors me with their lips, but their heart is far from me;	'These people, says God, honor me with their words, but their heart is really far away from me.

This people (singular in Greek) is altered to a plural form ("**These people**") in TEV and GECL 1st edition in order to achieve a more natural usage.

"**Says God**" is introduced by TEV and a number of other CLTs in order to indicate the speaker. Otherwise it is possible to conclude that Isaiah is the one speaking. In many languages the phrase "says God" will have to be at the beginning of the sentence, as in "God says." Of course, translators who have rendered "prophesy" in verse 7 with an expression such as "speak God's word" (see above) will probably not need to repeat "God" in this verse.

With their lips is a common Hebrew expression meaning **"with their words"** (TEV) or "with words" (GECL). Both NJB and NEB use the English idiom "lip-service." **Honors me with their lips** may be translated "say great things about me," "praise me," "say how wonderful I am," or "these people say things that honor me." Direct discourse is possible: "say, 'God is wonderful.' "

Far from: TEV adds the intensifier **"really"** to help draw the contrast between this and the previous clause. One may translate "but they do not really care about me," or "but they do not honor me with their thoughts," or "but they do not mean what they say." **Their heart** can refer to the thinking of the people or to their innermost feelings. "They don't really hold me dear" or "In their hearts they don't think of me very much" are other ways this phrase can be expressed.

<u>15.9</u> RSV	TEV
in vain do they worship me, teaching as doctrines the precepts of men.' "	It is no use for them to worship me, because they teach man-made rules as though they were my laws!' "

In vain do they worship me is quite clearly expressed in TEV, "**It is no use for them to worship me.**" "The worship they do has no value," "Their worship does not accomplish anything," or "They may as well give up their worship" also express the meaning.

Teaching may need an indirect object such as "other people."

Teaching as doctrines translates a Hebrew idiom in which both nouns originate from the same root. In Isaiah, from which the quotation is taken, **doctrines** describe the laws and teachings which God had given his people, thus the basis for TEV: **"they teach . . . as though they were my laws."**

Precepts of men (TEV **"man-made rules"**) are the rules and regulations that originated from human sources. The sentence may then be "They teach other people to follow man-made rules as though they were God's laws." GECL 1st edition attains a somewhat dramatic effect in its rendering of the clause: "for they teach laws which they themselves have thought up."

Since verse 7 ends with ". . . prophesy of you, when he said," it may be more natural to shift to a second person in verses 8-9: "You people . . . because you teach laws that you yourselves have created."

15.10-20

RSV   TEV

**The Things That Make
a Person Unclean**

10 And he called the people to him and said to them, "Hear and understand: 11 not what goes into the mouth defiles a man, but what comes out of the mouth, this defiles a man." 12 Then the disciples came and said to him, "Do you know that the Pharisees were offended when they heard this saying?" 13 He answered, "Every plant which my heavenly Father has not planted will be rooted up. 14 Let them alone; they are blind guides. And if a blind man leads a blind man, both will fall into a pit." 15 But Peter said to him, "Explain the parable to us." 16 And he said, "Are you also still without understanding? 17 Do you not see that whatever goes into the mouth passes into the stomach, and so passes on?*q* 18 But what comes out of the mouth proceeds from the heart, and this defiles a man. 19 For out of the heart come evil thoughts, murder, adultery, fornication, theft, false witness, slander. 20 These are what defile a man; but to eat with unwashed hands does not defile a man."

q Or *is evacuated*

10 Then Jesus called the crowd to him and said to them, "Listen and understand! 11 It is not what goes into a person's mouth that makes him ritually unclean; rather, what comes out of it makes him unclean."

12 Then the disciples came to him and said, "Do you know that the Pharisees had their feelings hurt by what you said?"

13 "Every plant which my Father in heaven did not plant will be pulled up," answered Jesus. 14 "Don't worry about them! They are blind leaders of the blind; and when one blind man leads another, both fall into a ditch."

15 Peter spoke up, "Explain this saying to us."

16 Jesus said to them, "You are still no more intelligent than the others. 17 Don't you understand? Anything that goes into a person's mouth goes into his stomach and then on out of his body. 18 But the things that come out of the mouth come from the heart, and these are the things that make a person ritually unclean. 19 For from his heart come the evil ideas which lead him to kill, commit adultery, and do other immoral things; to rob, lie, and slander others. 20 These are the things that make a person unclean. But to eat without washing your hands as they say you should—this doesn't make a person unclean."

SECTION HEADING: **"The Things That Make a Person Unclean"** may need to be expressed by a short sentence such as "Jesus says (or, teaches about) what makes a person unclean." For **"Unclean,"** see comments on verse 11 below.

See the introduction to this chapter for a statement of the role which verses 10-20 play in its development.

15.10   RSV   TEV

And he called the people to him and said to them, "Hear and understand:

Then Jesus called the crowd to him and said to them, "Listen and understand!

And he called is translated **"Then Jesus called"** by TEV because this begins a new section.

If translators render **called** with a word that means "called out" or "shouted," the emphasis will probably be wrong. "Summoned" or "invited to come to him" is more appropriate.

The people (TEV "**the crowd**") are the people of 14.34-36.

Hear and understand is translated "**Listen and understand**" by TEV and NJB; NEB has "Listen to me, and understand this." The function of the two imperatives is to lead the crowd to listen carefully and to try to understand what Jesus is going to say to them. "Listen to me so you can understand" is also good.

15.11 RSV	TEV
not what goes into the mouth defiles a man, but what comes out of the mouth, this defiles a man."	It is not what goes into a person's mouth that makes him ritually unclean; rather, what comes out of it makes him unclean."

This verse is in the form of what is technically known as an antithetic parallelism, in which the two halves of the verse each convey essentially the same message but in contrasting ways: **what goes into** contrasts with **what comes out of**.

What goes into the mouth obviously refers to food and drink, and some translators have felt it necessary to say that: "the food and drink a person puts in his mouth." However, it is usually sufficient to say "what a person puts in his mouth."

Defiles (so also Mft, Brc) is rendered "makes . . . unclean" by NJB and NIV: TEV has "**makes . . . ritually unclean**." According to Jewish teaching a person must be "clean" when he approaches God in worship, and "cleanliness" was defined both in terms of moral deeds and ritual actions. Any one who had committed a sinful deed or had failed to comply with ritual regulations was considered "unclean" or "defiled" and was therefore not permitted to worship God. One may translate "that makes a person unfit to worship God," or ". . . a person unacceptable to God," or ". . . a person's worship unacceptable to God." Translators who want to keep the image of "unclean" can say "that makes a person unclean in God's sight" or "unclean before God." In the last half of the verse, TEV replaces "**makes . . . ritually unclean**" with "**makes . . . unclean**" because the nature of the uncleanliness is clearly defined by TEV in the first part of the verse.

A man means "a person," although it is true that in the Jewish setting men were the only ones who actively participated in the worship services. Most translations will have "a person" or "someone," however.

What comes out of the mouth clearly does not refer to food, and translators who used "food" in the first part of the verse will have to make sure the readers don't think this phrase refers to food, too. It is best not to be specific about what comes out of the mouth, but "the words a person speaks" is sometimes necessary.

TEV has followed the structure of the text, the antithetic parallelism discussed above. There are languages where a better structure will be "It is not what a person puts in his mouth that make him unfit to worship God; the things that make him unclean like that are the things that come out of his mouth," or even "A man does not become unclean in God's sight because of something he puts in his mouth. Rather, the things that make him unclean are what come out of his mouth."

15.12 RSV TEV

Then the disciples came and said to him, "Do you know that the Pharisees were offended when they heard this saying?"

Then the disciples came to him and said, "Do you know that the Pharisees had their feelings hurt by what you said?"

Then the disciples came and said to him implies the beginning of a private session between Jesus and his disciples, as do the similar statements in 13.10 and 14.15 (see also 5.1), which suggest a movement of Jesus and his disciples away from the crowds. This conversation breaks off in verse 20, following which Jesus departs to the territory near the towns of Tyre and Sidon.

In this context **came** may better be "approached Jesus" or "went near him." **Pharisees** was discussed in 3.7.

Were offended translates the passive form of the verb first used in 5.29. TEV has "**had their feelings hurt**"; NJB and Brc "were shocked"; NEB "have taken great offence." "Were upset" is also good.

This saying is literally "this word"; the phrase may refer either to verse 11 (which may be taken as a proverbial saying), as RSV might imply, or more generally to all that Jesus has just said: "**what you said**" (TEV, Brc, NJB) and "what you have been saying" (NEB).

There are various ways this question can be restructured, including "Do you know that the Pharisees were shocked by what you said?" "Do you know that what you said upset the Pharisees (when they heard it)?" and "Do you know that the Pharisees were really upset when you said that?"

15.13 RSV TEV

He answered, "Every plant which my heavenly Father has not planted will be rooted up.

"Every plant which my Father in heaven did not plant will be pulled up," answered Jesus.

Every plant . . . will be rooted up is a literal translation of the Greek text. NJB makes a slight alteration: "Any plant . . . will be pulled up by the roots." The figure of a plant as a symbol for God's true people has its background in Isaiah 60.21 and was used widely among the Jews, including the sect at Qumran. Jesus could not have made a stronger attack on the Pharisees than to accuse them of not being the true vine which God had planted. It may be necessary to shift to an active: "My Father in heaven will pull up every plant which he did not plant." It may even be necessary to specify who these plants are: "Those Pharisees are like plants which my Father in heaven did not plant, and he will pull up every one of them."

Notice from these examples that in some languages **every plant** will be rendered "any plant," and that **rooted up** can be translated "pulled up by the roots."

Heavenly Father may have to be "God, my Father in heaven."

15.14 RSV TEV

Let them alone; they are blind guides. And if a blind man leads a blind man, both will fall into a pit."

"Don't worry about them! They are blind leaders of the blind; and when one blind man leads another, both fall into a ditch."

Let them alone (so also Brc) is translated "Leave them alone" by NJB and NEB. The problem with these renderings is that they may imply the meaning "Don't bother with them" or "Don't disturb them." The true meaning is "Don't be concerned about them" or "**Don't worry about them**" (TEV); it may also be stated without the use of a negative: "Forget about them."

It is imperative to make clear that **them** refers to the Pharisees, not to the plants! The problem may be resolved if a comparison is used in verse 13, such as "The Pharisees are like plants"; otherwise **Let them alone** may be translated "Don't worry about those Pharisees!"

Blind guides is followed in some Greek manuscripts by the qualifying phrase "of the blind" (see footnotes in NEB and NIV). In the UBS Greek New Testament the phrase is found in brackets, indicating its uncertainty in the text. Some languages will require that **blind guides** be expressed in the form "blind people who guide" with the object stated, as in "blind people who try to guide others.

On the basis of **If a blind man leads a blind man**, one may then translate either "blind people who guide other blind people" or "**blind leaders of the blind**" (TEV).

In this context **leads** should not be translated by a word that means simply "goes in front of." It obviously refers to directing someone such as a blind person so that he knows where to go.

Commentators note that "leader of the blind" was a title enjoyed by Jewish teachers (see Rom 2.19). Jesus' accusation is that the Pharisees cannot lay claim to this title, because they themselves are blind and in need of someone to lead them. GECL 1st edition translates in dynamic fashion: "They would lead the blind, and they themselves are blind."

Pit (also NJB) translates the same noun used in 12.11; it also is used in Luke 6.39, though nowhere else in the New Testament. The word basically means any sort of deep hole, and so may also be rendered "ditch" (NEB "the ditch"). Brc has "a hole in the road."

15.15 RSV TEV

But Peter said to him, "Explain the parable to us."

Peter spoke up, "Explain this saying to us."

But Peter said to him is more literally "But answering, Peter said to him"; NEB has "Then Peter said," and NJB "At this, Peter said to him."

Explain (so TEV, NJB, Mft) is translated "Tell . . . what . . . means" by NEB and Brc. The Greek verb is used only here in the New Testament, though it is found in the Septuagint of Job 6.24, where it has the same meaning.

Parable: the reference is to the content of verse 11 rather than to that of verses 12-14. TEV prefers **"this saying,"** and Brc "this difficult saying," because for English readers **parable** does not include the wide range of meanings that the Greek word does. Most translations do not make it clear that **the parable** refers to the saying in verse 11; in fact, in most cases readers get the impression it is what Jesus just said in verse 14 that is being referred to. For this reason some translators have said "Tell us the meaning of that saying you quoted to the Pharisees" or "Explain for us the meaning of what you said to the Pharisees." Of course, if there is in a language some word or other form that clearly relates **the parable** to the saying in verse 11, that should be used.

15.16	RSV	TEV

And he said, "Are you also still without understanding?	Jesus said to them, "You are still no more intelligent than the others.

He is identified as Jesus by TEV, NJB, NEB, GECL. The choice between a pronoun and a proper name will depend upon the expectations of the receptor language.

Are you also still without understanding? is in the form of a rhetorical question with the adverb **still** in emphatic position. TEV shifts to a statement: **"You are still no more intelligent than the others."** The contrast is between Jesus' disciples and the rest of the people, not between Peter and the remaining disciples, as RSV and TEV might be interpreted to suggest. In the Greek sentence the pronoun **you** (plural) is explicitly employed, thus intimating that it also is emphatic. It is possible to translate "You, my own disciples, are still . . . ."

Without understanding (an adjective in Greek) is translated **"no more intelligent** (than)" by TEV. In some translations there is a very effective shift to a verb construction: "unable to understand" (Brc), "not . . . yet understand" (JB), and "incapable of understanding" (NAB). Elsewhere in the New Testament this adjective is used only in Mark 7.18; Romans 1.21,31; 10.19.

The rhetorical question and the use of **without understanding** make Jesus' response quite harsh. Translators may say "You are my disciples, and you are still so unintelligent," "How can you, my own disciples, be so stupid?" or "You are my disciples, but you still have as little understanding as they."

15.17	RSV	TEV

Do you not see that whatever goes into the mouth passes into the stomach, and so passes on?[q]	Don't you understand? Anything that goes into a person's mouth goes into his stomach and then on out of his body.

[q] Or *is evacuated*

Do you not see . . . and passes on? is in the form of a lengthy rhetorical question which many readers will find difficult to decipher. In order to make it less difficult, TEV divides the question into a brief question ("**Don't you understand?**") followed by a statement. As a careful reading of RSV implies, the question intimates that the disciples do not yet understand, and so the anticipated reply would be a negative one.

The mouth may strike some readers as somewhat odd; TEV has "**a person's mouth**," and Brc "a man's mouth." NEB handles the problem in a slightly different fashion: "whatever goes in by the mouth."

And so passes on (RSV footnote "is evacuated") is a reference to the evacuation of body waste through the bowels. In translation care should be taken that the way of stating this is natural, but yet not offensive. NEB renders "and so is discharged into the drain"; NJB has "and is discharged into the sewer."

The entire verse may be reformulated as two or more statements, thus avoiding any rhetorical questions: "You still don't understand what I am talking about. I mean that whatever a person eats, first goes into his mouth, then into his stomach, and finally it goes out of his body."

15.18 RSV	TEV
But what comes out of the mouth proceeds from the heart, and this defiles a man.	But the things that come out of the mouth come from the heart, and these are the things that make a person ritually unclean.

What comes out of the mouth has specific reference to the things that a person says. Most translations retain the parallelism between "goes into the mouth" and **comes out of the mouth**, which is good if the meaning comes across clearly to the readers. But it is quite possible that **what comes out of the mouth** will at first reading be understood of something other than words. It may then be advisable to translate as "But the words that a person speaks (from his mouth)."

In Jewish thought **the heart** represented the total person, an individual's "true self." **Proceeds from the heart** may be translated "comes from within the person himself," or else an equivalent idiom in the receptor language can be used. It may not be natural to speak of words coming from the heart or inner self. "The words that come out of a person's mouth reflect (or, represent) that person's thinking" or ". . . represent that person himself" might be better in some languages. It is important to note that many languages will use some part of the body other than **heart** as the center of the inner self, possibly the liver or stomach.

Defiles a man: see comments at verse 11.

15.19 RSV	TEV
For out of the heart come evil thoughts, murder, adultery, fornication, theft, false witness, slander.	For from his heart come the evil ideas which lead him to kill, commit adultery, and do other immoral

things; to rob, lie, and slander others.

Out of the heart is emphasized in Greek, as may be concluded from the position which it occupies in the sentence order of RSV and TEV.

Translators normally render **heart** very much as they did in verse 18.

Out of . . . come sometimes has to be restructured. Examples include "For it is in the heart that evil thoughts, murder . . . have their origin," "For it is the heart that evil thoughts . . . come from," and "For evil thoughts, murder . . . all come from the heart." But it is important to retain the emphasis on **out of the heart**.

These sins which come from a person's heart are listed as nouns in the text. However, in many languages it will be more natural to list them as verbs. An example is "For it is what is in a person's heart that makes him think evil, murder . . . and speak evil about others." Other languages will find it natural to reverse the order of the verse, as with "For when a person thinks evil, murders . . . and speaks evil of other people, he does those things because of what is in his heart."

The list of sins that defile a person is shorter in Matthew than in Mark (7.21-23). After the first one (**evil thoughts**) the rest of the sins mentioned follow the order in which they are forbidden according to the Ten Commandments (Exo 20.13-16).

TEV has interpreted **evil thoughts** to be the thing which leads to the other sins, and other translators may find this restructuring useful also. Most, however, simply list it as one of the sins that defile a person.

Murder is not the same as "killing" but refers specifically to killing that is not condoned by society. Thus, killing in warfare or executions ordered by a court are not included.

Fornication is the same word translated "unchastity" in 5.32; see comment there. The noun may be used of any sort of illicit sexual intercourse; TEV has "**other immoral things.**"

In many cultures the distinction between **adultery** and **fornication** is not the same as in the Bible, where the latter refers to sexual misconduct in general, and the former to cases where a married woman is involved. Quite often there is one term in a language which covers general sexual misconduct. It is also common for there to be a general word for such illicit behavior between people who are married to someone else. For translators in languages where either of these situations prevails, one solution is to use that general word or expression for rendering **fornication**, and the same word for **adultery** but with the added phrase "with a married woman." However, in a listing of sins like this one here, it is not necessary to make the distinction so rigidly, and many translators will simply use the general term that covers both words of the text, or do something similar to TEV.

False witness (so also NAB) is translated as a verb in TEV ("**lie**"), as are the other sins in the list; NJB and NEB have "perjury"; Brc has "lies about other people." The only other occurrence of the noun in the New Testament is in 26.59, where it is used as a technical legal term; however, the related verb, used also in a technical sense in 26.60, is employed with a nontechnical meaning in 1 Corinthians 15.15.

Slander (so also NJB, NEB; TEV "**slander others**") is transliterated "blasphemy" by NAB. Although in other contexts the word may more naturally mean "slander against God" or "blasphemy," the present context is strongly in favor of the meaning "slander against others," as is suggested both by the place which it occupies in the overall list and by the observation that it immediately follows "false witness." Elsewhere in Matthew (12.31; 26.65) it is used of slander against God.

The usual translation of **slander** is "say bad things about other people." In some languages a phrase such as "ruin the name of other people" is the closest equivalent.

15.20

RSV	TEV
These are what defile a man; but to eat with unwashed hands does not defile a man."	These are the things that make a person unclean. But to eat without washing your hands as they say you should—this doesn't make a person unclean."

Verse 20 is essentially a repetition of verse 11, only in negative form. See comments there. See also verse 2 for a discussion of **unwashed hands**.

15.21-28

RSV	TEV
	A Woman's Faith
21 And Jesus went away from there and withdrew to the district of Tyre and Sidon. 22 And behold, a Canaanite woman from that region came out and cried, "Have mercy on me, O Lord, Son of David; my daughter is severely possessed by a demon." 23 But he did not answer her a word. And his disciples came and begged him, saying, "Send her away, for she is crying after us." 24 He answered, "I was sent only to the lost sheep of the house of Israel." 25 But she came and knelt before him, saying, "Lord, help me." 26 And he answered, "It is not fair to take the children's bread and throw it to the dogs." 27 She said, "Yes, Lord, yet even the dogs eat the crumbs that fall from their masters' table." 28 Then Jesus answered her, "O woman, great is your faith! Be it done for you as you desire." And her daughter was healed instantly.	21 Jesus left that place and went off to the territory near the cities of Tyre and Sidon. 22 A Canaanite woman who lived in that region came to him. "Son of David!" she cried out. "Have mercy on me, sir! My daughter has a demon and is in a terrible condition." 23 But Jesus did not say a word to her. His disciples came to him and begged him, "Send her away! She is following us and making all this noise!" 24 Then Jesus replied, "I have been sent only to the lost sheep of the people of Israel." 25 At this the woman came and fell at his feet. "Help me, sir!" she said. 26 Jesus answered, "It isn't right to take the children's food and throw it to the dogs." 27 "That's true, sir," she answered, "but even the dogs eat the leftovers that fall from their masters' table." 28 So Jesus answered her, "You are a woman of great faith! What you want will be done for you." And at that very moment her daughter was healed.

SECTION HEADING: "**A Woman's Faith**" may be rendered "A woman who believed (or, trusted) in Jesus (very much)," but if that is awkward, translators can make the heading refer instead to what Jesus did, as in "Jesus heals the daughter of a Canaanite woman."

It is significant that this narrative immediately follows the discussion of "clean" and "unclean" in both Matthew and Mark (7.24-30), because the woman is Canaanite and therefore "unclean" from the Jewish perspective. The story solemnly declares that though she is a Gentile, her faith is sufficient to confirm her as "clean" and therefore acceptable in God's sight.

15.21   RSV   TEV

    And Jesus went away from there and withdrew to the district of Tyre and Sidon. | **Jesus left that place and went off to the territory near the cities of Tyre and Sidon.**

This verse begins a new episode, and in many languages it is more natural not to have the **And**. Some translations will have "After that" or "Later," however.

Jesus is definitely the central character in the narrative, but verse 23 makes clear that he did not leave by himself. One may need to translate "Jesus and his disciples."

Went away from there and withdrew to may be reduced in some languages to one verb; for example, "went from there to."

There (TEV **"that place"**) refers to Gennesaret on the northwest shore of Lake Galilee, where Jesus landed (14.34).

Tyre and Sidon were towns about thirty to fifty miles northwest of Gennesaret on the Mediterranean coast. Sidon was about 25 miles north of Tyre. Matthew does not indicate that Jesus went to either of these towns, but only to their **district** (TEV **"to the territory near"**). He could have merely crossed the border and remained on the edge of the region, or he could have gone much farther into the region. Translators can say "the region around" or "the area where the towns of Tyre and Sidon were." To translate "Jesus . . . walked the fifty miles to Tyre and Sidon" (LB) is inaccurate and without support in the text.

15.22   RSV   TEV

And behold, a Canaanite woman from that region came out and cried, "Have mercy on me, O Lord, Son of David; my daughter is severely possessed by a demon." | A Canaanite woman who lived in that region came to him. "Son of David!" she cried out. "Have mercy on me, sir! My daughter has a demon and is in a terrible condition."

And behold translates a frequently used attention getter; see comments on 3.16, where it is first used in the Gospel. As there, a phrase such as "And it happened that" can be used, or the phrase can be dropped if it is not natural in the receptor language.

Canaanite is found numerous times in the Old Testament, though it is used only here in the New Testament. The problem is that there was no longer a political country called "Canaan" in New Testament times. Some scholars are of the opinion that this was the Semitic manner of referring to the people of Phoenicia at the time that Matthew's Gospel was written.

Canaanite woman is frequently rendered as "a woman from Canaan," but here this results in the awkward phrase "a woman from that area who was from Canaan." And it is not proper to say that she came from a country that no longer existed. "A woman who lived in that area who was of the people from Canaan" or "a woman from the area who was of the group called Canaanites" may be better.

From that region is best taken to mean that the woman lived in that region: "living in that locality" (NAB) and "from those parts" (NEB; Brc "these parts").

Came out translates the same verb rendered "went away" in verse 21, and it raises a question regarding the exact location of Jesus at the moment that the Canaanite woman came to him with her request. The problem is that the Greek of verse 21 may imply that Jesus only headed in the direction of Tyre and Sidon, but did not in fact get beyond the borders of northern Galilee. If this is accepted as the meaning, then **came out** states that the woman left her territory and went down to northern Galilee where Jesus was at the time. Without hesitation JB's footnote says "Since the woman has left pagan territory it is in Israel that Jesus grants his favour." Both Zür and Lu support this interpretation, as does Mft ("came out of these parts"). But **came out** may describe no more than the woman's departure from her home or village; or it may be used loosely in the sense of "came" (NEB), which seems to be the intent of "presented herself" (NAB) and "**came to**" (TEV, GECL, NIV, Brc, Phps). RSV is ambiguous, with **woman from that region came out** (similarly AT).

Cried is not used here to mean "weep." Rather the woman "cried out" (TEV) or "shouted."

The noun of address by which the woman appeals to Jesus may mean either **Lord** (so also NAB, Phps) or "**sir**" (TEV, JB, NEB, Brc). If the meaning is "sir," then it is equivalent to an honorific and so may be omitted from explicit mention in English translation. On the other hand, if the meaning is **Lord**, then this will have to be stated explicitly in the text. See comment at 8.25.

Son of David is a Jewish messianic title (see comments at 12.23). It is especially noteworthy that a Canaanite woman would speak to Jesus in this way.

In many languages, **O Lord, Son of David** will have to be the first thing the woman says. **O** is no longer common in English as a means of addressing people, which is why TEV has dropped it. There are also translators who will find that the two terms of address together is not natural, and they may find it better to separate them somewhat, as TEV has.

In some languages the title **Son of David** does not lend itself naturally as a term of address. This is true, for example, in languages where the formula for a title would result in "the One people call Son of David." A woman calling out in a desperate attempt to get someone's attention would certainly not take time to say all that. **Son of David** with a footnote to explain that it is a messianic title will be much more appropriate.

For **have mercy on me**, see comments at 9.27.

Severely possessed by a demon (TEV "**has a demon and is in a terrible condition**") translates two words in Greek, a verb modified by an adverb, which mean literally "terribly possessed." Both NJB and NEB render "is tormented by a devil"; Brc translates "is possessed by a demon and is very ill." Phps is fairly dramatic: "is in a terrible state—a devil has got into her!" Another possible rendering is "is suffering very much because she is possessed by an evil spirit."

For **possessed by a demon**, see comments at 4.24.

15.23 RSV	TEV
But he did not answer her a word. And his disciples came and begged him, saying, "Send her away, for she is crying after us."	But Jesus did not say a word to her. His disciples came to him and begged him, "Send her away! She is following us and making all this noise!"

Neither the silence of Jesus nor the request of the disciples are included in the Marcan parallel (7.26-27), which suggests that both details may be of particular significance for Matthew. The use of a question by the disciples to express their misunderstanding, thereby clearing the way for Jesus to give further instruction to them, is also typical of Matthew's style.

He, of course, is Jesus, not the demon.

Came is used as it was in 13.10; the disciples are already present on the scene, but they "come up to him" or "gather around him." Perhaps they were walking behind Jesus in a somewhat loosely knit group, followed by the woman; but now they move up to where Jesus was walking ahead of the group. Translators can say "approached" or "went up to."

Begged translates an imperfect verb tense which may imply the continuation of action: "Kept asking" (New American Standard Bible [NASB]). For many English readers **begged** and "pleaded with" (NJB) would suggest action in progress.

Send her away of RSV, TEV, NEB, Brc (NAB "Get rid of her") represents the interpretation pursued in most translations. But as NJB points out with allusion to 18.27 and 27.15, the text may be translated "Give her what she wants." This meaning is also given as an alternative possibility in TOB, but it finds very little support elsewhere. For this reason most translations will have a phrase such as "Tell her to go away."

For she is crying after us is made into a complete sentence with two verbs by TEV: "**She is following us and making all this noise!**" The Greek verb represented by **crying** is first used in 8.29, where it is translated **cried out**. The difficulty with RSV is that the reader may assume literal crying on the part of the woman, when the verb actually means "cry out," "scream," "shout," as in verse 22. TNT lends itself to ambiguity, especially should the reader pause in the wrong place: "She is crying out behind us." **Crying** may be rendered "shouting out so loudly." "She is following us making a lot of noise" or "She keeps on shouting and following us" are other possibilities.

15.24   RSV   TEV

He answered, "I was sent only to the lost sheep of the house of Israel."   Then Jesus replied, "I have been sent only to the lost sheep of the people of Israel."

This verse, unique to Matthew's Gospel, recalls Jesus' instructions to the twelve (10.6). The Greek text does not indicate to whom Jesus is speaking, whether to the disciples, the woman, or both. But in light of what follows in the narrative, and especially in view of verse 26, it is most natural to conclude that Jesus is here addressing the woman. This is also the exegesis which recommends itself, if "send her away (without granting her request)" is what the disciples advised immediately before, in verse 23. Most translations try to leave it open whom Jesus was specifically addressing, by saying simply "answered" or "replied."

I was sent may be transformed into an active: "God sent me." Some translators think that **sent** is too general and want to specify what Jesus' mission was, as in "sent to save." However, this states more than the text does, and should be avoided if possible.

The lost sheep of the house of Israel offers at least two possible interpretations: (1) **Of the house of Israel** may be understood as a qualifier of certain **sheep** (meaning people) within the **house** (meaning nation) of Israel. The literal interpretation of RSV and others (NEB, NJB, Mft) seems to imply this interpretation, as do AT ("the lost sheep of Israel's house") and NIV ("the lost sheep of Israel"). (2) **Of the house of Israel** may be understood as describing the same people referred to figuratively by **the lost sheep**, which is the basis for TEV: "**the lost sheep, the people of Israel.**"

There are two separate metaphors that translators have to handle, **lost sheep** and **house of Israel**. **Sheep**, as we suggest above, stands for people, and **lost sheep** are people who don't know where they are, who are vulnerable, perhaps because they have wandered from the shepherd's care (the shepherd would be God). **House of Israel** refers to the nation or people of Israel. One common way to translate these metaphors is to use similes. Translators who follow the second interpretation of this phrase (see above) can have "the people of Israel who are like lost sheep," ". . . who have strayed from God like lost sheep," or ". . . who are like sheep that have lost their shepherd." Those who prefer the first interpretation can have "those of the people of Israel who are like lost sheep."

15.25   RSV   TEV

But she came and knelt before him, saying, "Lord, help me."   At this the woman came and fell at his feet. "Help me, sir!" she said.

Came causes certain complications in analyzing the precise sequence of events, as do the other verbs of motion in the narrative ("went away" in verse 21; "came out" in verse 22; "came" in verse 23). For example, by itself verse 22 does not clearly show whether Jesus and his disciples were walking along or were stationary, whether sitting or standing, at the time the woman initially approached them. But the introduction of "after us" in verse 23 definitely pictures the group in movement, with the woman trailing along behind them. Then in verse 24 it seems that Jesus addresses the woman directly (While they are still walking along? Or has the group now stopped?), and verse 25 now states that the woman **came** to Jesus and **knelt before him**, begging him to help her.

Most translations represent a rather formal rendering of the Greek, without seriously dealing with these difficulties. However, GECL apparently takes **came** as the equivalent of a helping verb for **knelt** (similar to the Hebrew use of "rise," as in "rise and go," Luke 15.18) and so translates without this verb: "Then the woman threw herself down before Jesus and said . . . ." Another common rendering of **came** is "approached" or "went up to," assuming that her kneeling involved her approaching him more closely than she had before. Translators are free to represent these actions and motions in ways that are normal in their own languages.

Knelt (similarly JB, Mft, Brc) is translated "**fell at his feet**" by NEB and TEV; AT and Lu "fell down before him"; Zür "threw herself down in front of him"; NAB "did him homage." This is the verb most frequently used in the New Testament of worship in general, and it is found first in this Gospel in 2.2. The root meaning is "approach in dog-like fashion," and it describes the manner in which a subject might approach a king or some other holy person or object. Consequently the meaning may be either "fall down and worship" or "worship." The present context suggests that the woman is either kneeling or, more likely, prostrating herself on the ground, pleading with Jesus to heal her child. Brc conveys the idea of **knelt** with "knelt in front of him in entreaty." A similar translation would be "knelt in front of him to beg him." It is better to use this example than something else that means "worship."

Lord, help me: here again one is compelled to decide between the meaning "sir" (an honorific) and "Lord." In the original setting the meaning was most probably "sir," but when Matthew uses it in his Gospel, he is doubtless conscious of the meaning that it has for the Christian community at the time he writes.

15.26   RSV   TEV

And he answered, "It is not fair to   Jesus answered, "It isn't right
take the children's bread and throw   to take the children's food and throw
it to the dogs."   it to the dogs."

It is not fair (so also NJB, Mft) is translated "It is not right" by NEB, AT, and NAB (TEV "**It isn't right**"). Brc has "It is not proper." The Greek adjective which appears as "fair," "right," and "proper" in these translations literally means "good," and it may be used in a wide variety of contexts. Some Greek manuscripts have a wording which means "lawful" or "permitted," but TC-GNT believes that this was an attempt by a later scribe to strengthen the reply of Jesus to the woman. Translations evidently do not reflect this alternative possibility. Since the context suggests the meaning "appropriate," one may even translate "people do not . . . ."

The children's bread may be rendered "the food for the children" or "the food the children eat." **Bread** (TEV "**food**") was the basic element in the Jewish meal and can refer to the meal itself or to food in general.

The intention of **throw** is not to frighten the dogs away but to give them something to eat. "Throw it (the food) to the dogs for them to eat" will eliminate this misunderstanding in those cases where it exists.

Commentators generally note the sayings of certain Jewish teachers who referred to Gentiles as **dogs**, but this does not support the argument that all Jews felt this way toward them. And there is no evidence from other New Testament sources that Jesus himself ever spoke of Gentiles in this manner. In fact, it is most probable that the saying is not intended to make a derogatory remark about Gentiles, but rather to differentiate order of priority: **children** (symbolizing the Jews) are fed before the household pets (**dogs** symbolizing the Gentiles). In a Palestinian household, which had children and household dogs, the children would be fed first, after which the dogs would be given the scraps from the table. The woman must have understood Jesus' remark in this way, as her response in verse 27 intimates. Consequently JB translates "house-dogs," with a footnote indicating the root meaning of the word is "little or pet dogs." TOB, apparently accepting the same exegesis, but without a footnote, has "little dogs." There are languages which make a distinction between wild and domestic **dogs**, and in such cases "pet dogs" is a good rendering. In other cultures, however, "dogs" will suffice.

15.27	RSV	TEV
	She said, "Yes, Lord, yet even the dogs eat the crumbs that fall from their masters' table."	"That's true, sir," she answered, "but even the dogs eat the leftovers that fall from their masters' table."

Yes (so also Phps; AT "O yes"; NJB "Ah yes") translates a Greek particle which indicates affirmation or emphasis. Both GECL and Zür have "Certainly"; TEV "**That's true**"; NEB and Brc "True." "Please" (NAB) is also a possible meaning, as TOB's footnote indicates with reference to Philippians 4.3 and Philemon 20. This would mean a slight modification of the woman's reply.

This verse makes it clear that the **dogs** in this passage are indeed pets.

Crumbs are often translated as "scraps that are left over" or "pieces of food that are left." This is especially true when "bread" in verse 26 is expressed as "food."

Crumbs that fall is translated "**leftovers that fall**" by TEV, but an alternative translation of the verb **fall** is possible, as one authority on the parables notes. Both here and in Luke 16.21 the verb may be given the meaning "to be thrown," thus resulting in an entirely different scene: Jesus would not be speaking of the **crumbs that fall** from the table during the course of the meal, but rather of table scraps that are taken after the meal and thrown to the dogs. If this interpretation is accepted, then the present passage may be translated "the leftovers (that are thrown) from their master's table" or ". . . that their master gives them."

15.28 RSV TEV

Then Jesus answered her, "O woman, great is your faith! Be it done for you as you desire." And her daughter was healed instantly.

So Jesus answered her, "You are a woman of great faith! What you want will be done for you." And at that very moment her daughter was healed.

Then has been expressed as "**So**" by TEV. Perhaps the most natural rendering in English is that of Brc: "At that."

O woman, great is your faith is translated "**You are a woman of great faith**" by TEV (NJB, NAB "Woman, you have great faith"; Mft "O woman, you have great faith"). The shift from **great is your faith** to "you have great faith" is more natural for English speakers, as is the omission of the noun of address, **woman**, which explains the shift in TEV. Other translations have also recognized these two factors, and a few of them have even dropped the noun of address: both AT and Brc translate "You have great faith," and Phps renders "You certainly don't lack faith." It may be necessary to express **faith** as a verb, which will simultaneously require an object. Examples are "You certainly believe that I will do what you request (or, are begging me to do)" and "You believe in me a great deal." Some translators have tried to convey that this is really an exclamation by Jesus. One way is to say "Woman, I can see you really have a lot of faith (in me)."

Be it done for you as you desire translates a third person imperative in Greek, which is represented in JB as "Let your wish be granted." However, the problem for English speakers is that English does not have a third person imperative, and so many will understand JB to have the meaning "You yourself permit that it be granted." One may translate "Your wish will be granted" or "God will grant your wish."

Instantly (TEV "**at that very moment**") is literally "from that hour" (the same form used in 9.22).

In a Greek sentence it is natural for the subject to precede the verb, but here **was healed** is placed before **her daughter** for the sake of emphasizing the healing. If it is necessary to shift to an active form of the verb, one may translate "At that very moment God healed her daughter."

15.29-31

RSV TEV

Jesus Heals Many People

29 And Jesus went on from there and passed along the Sea of Galilee. And he went up on the mountain, and sat down there. 30 And great crowds came to him, bringing with them the lame, the maimed, the blind, the dumb, and many others, and they put them at his feet, and he healed them, 31 so that the throng wondered, when they saw the dumb speaking, the maimed whole, the lame walking, and the blind seeing; and they glorified the God of Israel.

29 Jesus left there and went along by Lake Galilee. He climbed a hill and sat down. 30 Large crowds came to him, bringing with them the lame, the blind, the crippled, the dumb, and many other sick people, whom they placed at Jesus' feet; and he healed them. 31 The people were amazed as they saw the dumb speaking, the crippled made whole, the lame walking, and the blind seeing; and they praised the God of Israel.

SECTION HEADING: "**Jesus Heals Many People**" may need to be "Jesus heals many people of their diseases."

In place of Matthew's summary account of these multiple healings, Mark includes at this point in his Gospel the story of the healing of the deaf mute (7.31-37). Since Gentile settlements were located all around Lake Galilee, especially on its eastern banks, it is quite likely that Matthew wishes to describe here an active healing ministry of Jesus among the Gentiles. The closing remark of verse 31, "they glorified the God of Israel," supports the supposition that these healings took place among Gentiles.

15.29	RSV	TEV
	And Jesus went on from there and passed along the Sea of Galilee. And he went up on the mountain, and sat down there.	Jesus left there and went along by Lake Galilee. He climbed a hill and sat down.

Jesus went on . . . passed along the Sea of Galilee: according to verse 21 Jesus is somewhere in northern Galilee, in the vicinity of the towns of Tyre and Sidon. In order to get from there to Lake Galilee, he would have moved in a southeasterly direction, which Matthew describes by the brief phrase **went on from there**, without indicating any of the territories through which Jesus would have passed en route. Some languages will require more verbs of motion than the two of the Greek text, **went on . . . passed along**, though GECL 1st edition is even more succinct: "Then Jesus walked along Lake Galilee again."

Most translations will render **went on** very much as TEV has, "**left there**." However, for **passed along the Sea of Galilee** they often say that Jesus went "along the coast" (so Brc) or "by the shore." As we discussed elsewhere, **Sea** is usually "Lake" (see also 4.18).

Just as Matthew does not state where Jesus **passed along the Sea of Galilee**, whether on the eastern or western shore, neither does he identify **the mountain** which Jesus **went up**. However, the mention of a mountain (or "hill") does hint at activity in the area north of Lake Galilee, which would satisfy the demands of either interpretation.

For these reasons, then, most translators do not try to specify which mountain **the mountain** refers to, and say instead "a mountain" or "a hill." See also comments at 5.1.

Matthew does not indicate why Jesus **sat down**, though sitting was the usual position that a Jewish teacher took when offering instruction (5.1; 13.1). However, there is no indication in the context that teaching is in any way intended, and it is quite obvious from the verses which follow that Matthew's primary concern here is with Jesus' healing ministry.

15.30 RSV	TEV
And great crowds came to him, bringing with them the lame, the maimed, the blind, the dumb, and many others, and they put them at his feet, and he healed them,	Large crowds came to him, bringing with them the lame, the blind, the crippled, the dumb, and many other sick people, whom they placed at Jesus' feet; and he healed them.

Great crowds is somewhat picturesque in NEB and Brc: "crowds flocked to him." **Crowds** can be expressed as "many people."

The lame, the maimed, the blind, the dumb: in place of using adjectives as nouns as in RSV, it may be preferable in many languages to do as Phps has done: "people who were lame, blind, crippled, dumb." Both Matthew and his readers would have understood the healing of so many people as a sign that the promised age of salvation had finally arrived (see Isa 35.5-6).

Lame is the same word used in 11.5 (see also 18.8; 21.14). **Maimed** (so also in verse 31; 18.8) is **"crippled"** in TEV; the word may be used of anyone who has an arm or leg that is in any way abnormal and not capable of being used. **Dumb** (a word which may mean either "unable to speak" or "deaf") was used previously in 9.32, 33; 11.5; 12.22.

And many others obviously means **"and many other sick people"** (TEV). It can also be translated as "people with many other kinds of diseases."

Put (TEV **"placed"**) translates a verb which originally meant "throw," signifying violence, a meaning which is obviously not intended in the context. To **put them at his feet** means to "place them in front of Jesus" or to "put them down by Jesus."

It is important in the translation to keep clear who is being referred to by **they** and **them**. It was the great crowds of people who brought the sick people to Jesus and placed them at his feet.

Healed represents a different Greek verb than the verb in verse 28; however, there is no difference in meaning between them.

15.31 RSV	TEV
so that the throng wondered, when they saw the dumb speaking, the maimed whole, the lame walking, and the blind seeing; and they glorified the God of Israel.	The people were amazed as they saw the dumb speaking, the crippled made whole, the lame walking, and the blind seeing; and they praised the God of Israel.

In Greek this verse is a continuation of the sentence from verse 30, which RSV renders rather literally: **so that the throng wondered, when they saw . . . .** Many English translations prefer to begin a new sentence: "The crowds were astonished to see" (NJB); "Great was the amazement of the people when they saw" (NEB); "His power to heal left the people amazed, when they saw" (Brc); "The result was great astonishment in the crowds as they beheld" (NAB).

In some languages it does not seem natural to speak of the **dumb speaking** since they are no longer dumb. Translators can say "formerly dumb" or "people who had been dumb before." The same is true with the afflictions mentioned in the rest of the verse.

For the **maimed** to be made **whole** means they were "made fit again," or were "made well," or "recovered the use of their limbs."

The formerly **lame** were now **walking** or, possibly better, were now "able to walk."

Greek manuscripts differ considerably concerning the order and inclusion of the four groups of people who were healed. However, as NJB's footnote indicates, the major textual problem relates to the phrase **the maimed whole**. According to TC-GNT, the committee for the UBS Greek text acknowledges that the phrase may have been added in order to complete the series of four mentioned in verse 30. But they are of the opinion that it was originally a part of the Greek text, which was later omitted by scribes who felt it was unnecessary to say both that **the maimed** were made **whole** and **the lame** were **walking**.

They glorified is more naturally expressed by **"they praised"** of TEV and NJB. GECL has "Aloud they praised the God of Israel." Of course, the text indicates it was the crowds who were praising God, not just the healed people. There are languages where the verse will need to be restructured: "The crowds saw people who had been dumb now speaking . . . and formerly blind people now able to see. When they saw this, they were amazed, and they praised the God of Israel."

The meaning of **God of Israel** is "God whom the people of Israel worship." Not all translations will need to make that explicit, but if a literal translation left readers thinking the reference was to a local god that had power in that place, then the fuller form may be needed.

15.32-39

RSV	TEV
	Jesus Feeds Four Thousand Men
32 Then Jesus called his disciples to him and said, "I have compassion on the crowd, because they have been with me now three days, and have nothing to eat; and I am unwilling to send them away hungry, lest they faint on the way." 33 And the disciples said to him, "Where are we to get bread enough in the desert to feed so great a crowd?" 34 And Jesus said to them, "How many loaves have you?" They said, "Seven, and a few small fish." 35 And commanding the crowd to sit down on the ground, 36 he took the seven loaves and the fish, and having given thanks he broke them and gave them to the disciples, and the disciples gave them to the crowds. 37 And they all ate and were satisfied; and they took up seven baskets full of the broken pieces left over. 38 Those who ate were four thousand men, besides women and children. 39 And sending away the crowds, he got into the boat and went to the region of Magadan.	32 Jesus called his disciples to him and said, "I feel sorry for these people, because they have been with me for three days and now have nothing to eat. I don't want to send them away without feeding them, for they might faint on their way home." 33 The disciples asked him, "Where will we find enough food in this desert to feed this crowd?" 34 "How much bread do you have?" Jesus asked. "Seven loaves," they answered, "and a few small fish." 35 So Jesus ordered the crowd to sit down on the ground. 36 Then he took the seven loaves and the fish, gave thanks to God, broke them, and gave them to the disciples; and the disciples gave them to the people. 37 They all ate and had enough. Then the disciples took up seven baskets full of pieces left over. 38 The number of men who

ate was four thousand, not counting the women and children.

39 Then Jesus sent the people away, got into a boat, and went to the territory of Magadan.

SECTION HEADING: "**Jesus Feeds Four Thousand Men**" is essentially the same section heading as at 14.13, except for the number of people.

Matthew (14.13-21; 15.32-39) and Mark (6.30-44; 8.1-10) each narrate two miraculous feedings of multitudes, though Luke (9.10-17) tells only of the feeding of the five thousand. Many scholars are of the opinion that the group of four thousand consisted of Gentiles, since the miracle took place in Galilee and follows immediately upon the narrative of the Canaanite woman and the summary account of Jesus' healing ministry among the Gentiles. Those scholars who accept this interpretation generally assume that the message in the account is that Gentile Christians may now live in anticipation of sharing in the coming Messianic banquet.

15.32	RSV	TEV

Then Jesus called his disciples to him and said, "I have compassion on the crowd, because they have been with me now three days, and have nothing to eat; and I am unwilling to send them away hungry, lest they faint on the way."	Jesus called his disciples to him and said, "I feel sorry for these people, because they have been with me for three days and now have nothing to eat. I don't want to send them away without feeding them, for they might faint on their way home."

In place of **Then Jesus called his disciples to him and said**, Mark has a more detailed introduction: "Not long afterward another large crowd came together. When the people had nothing left to eat, Jesus called the disciples to him and said . . ." (8.1, TEV).

Then (so also AT) translates a Greek particle generally rendered "But" (so NJB, Phps). TEV, together with several other translations (NAB, Mft, Brc), does not represent this particle by any particular word in translation. To render "But" in English assumes a contrast with what precedes, which is not the intention of the Greek text. In Greek the particle is frequently used, as here, merely to mark a transition.

Called (so also TEV, NJB, NEB) is a participle that is dependent upon the main verb **said**. The verb **called** was first used in 10.1; in this chapter it appears first in verse 10, then here; elsewhere in Matthew it is used in 18.2,32; 20.25. Here "asked him to come near him" will convey the meaning.

Have compassion on represents a verb that signals the deepest possible feelings of compassion (TEV, NEB, NJB "**feel sorry for**"); it was previously used in 9.36.

They have been with me now three days, and have nothing to eat is ambiguous, both in Greek and in English. It is possible to interpret the words to mean that the people had been with Jesus for three days, during which time they had gone without food. This interpretation receives at least indirect support from the observation that the adjective **hungry** may also mean "without eating" or "without food," and it derives from a verb which means "to fast." Matthew may then be describing a scene in which the people spontaneously followed Jesus, without preparing food to take along with them, and as a result they had gone without food for three days. On the other hand, Matthew may be depicting a situation in which the people had originally taken along some food with them, but now had run out of anything to eat, as is indicated by TEV ("**and now have nothing to eat**"), AT ("and they have nothing left to eat"), and Phps ("and have no more food"). Most translations remain ambiguous, and as a rule the issue is left undiscussed in the commentaries.

I am unwilling to send them away hungry can be expressed "I don't want to have them leave here while they are hungry" or "I don't want to ask them to leave until they have had something to eat."

Lest means "so that not." Some translations use a positive phrase beginning with "for" or "because otherwise." Others keep the negative by saying "so that they don't." Another method is to use a new sentence starting with "I am afraid some of them would faint otherwise" or "I don't want any of them to faint."

In contexts such as this, the verb **faint** may mean "become weary," or "be worn out," or "collapse" (so NJB, NAB, Brc, Phps). AT translates "give out." In other contexts it is possible for the verb to mean "give up" (Gal 6.9). "Pass out" is another possibility.

Although in itself the phrase **on the way** may signify travel of any sort, the present context clearly signals that the meaning is "**on their way home**," as TEV, GECL, FRCL make clear.

15.33	RSV	TEV

And the disciples said to him, "Where are we to get bread enough in the desert to feed so great a crowd?"

The disciples asked him, "Where will we find enough food in this desert to feed this crowd?"

Said is translated "**asked**" by TEV and "offered for consideration" by GECL 1st edition; NEB translates "replied."

Although most translators understand **bread** to mean "food" here, as it often does, the Greek text actually has "loaves of bread," which is why Brc and some others translate "loaves."

Feed translates a verb which means "feed so as to satisfy one's appetite" (see 5.6; 14.20; 15.37); NAB, Mft, Brc have "satisfy."

So great a crowd is literally "such a crowd" (JB, NEB), implying a large crowd (Brc "a crowd like this"). The disciples' question, **Where . . . to feed so great a crowd**, emphasizes two factors: the total absence of food and the immensity of the crowd.

The question the disciples ask can be "Where are we going to find enough food out here in the desert for all these people?" "Where in this desert will we get enough food (or, bread) to feed a crowd this big?" or "Where in this wilderness are we supposed to get food that will satisfy this many people?"

It is quite likely that the disciples didn't really think there was any place where they could get bread in that quantity, so their question is not really asking for information. For that reason, some translations have used a statement here such as "There is nowhere out here in the desert where we can get enough bread to feed a crowd like this."

Note that **desert** really refers to a remote, uninhabited area. See 3.1.

15.34   RSV   TEV

And Jesus said to them, "How many   "How much bread do you
loaves have you?" They said, "Sev-   have?" Jesus asked.
en, and a few small fish."   "Seven loaves," they answered,
                                                                   "and a few small fish."

Said may cover a broader area of meaning in Greek than it does in certain other languages, which may require "**asked**" (TEV).

Loaves: see comment at 14.17. Rather than have Jesus ask how many loaves are available, TEV renders the question "**How much bread**?" This model is especially helpful for translators in languages where translating "loaves of bread" will be something of a problem. Of course, in the context of the reply of the disciples, **seven**, it is impossible not to speak of loaves of bread.

And a few small fish is found in the Marcan parallel, not in the disciples' reply (8.5) but in the narrative (8.7). Matthew obviously does include it as a part of the disciples' reply. **Small fish** translates a single word in Greek; in the New Testament the word occurs only here and in Mark 8.7. Outside the New Testament there are indications that the word has lost the sense of "little" or "small" and means simply "fish." But Matthew would appear to have selected the diminutive form **small fish** in order to underline further the miraculous aspect of Jesus' deed. See the discussion at 14.17.

15.35   RSV   TEV

And commanding the crowd to sit   So Jesus ordered the crowd to
down on the ground,   sit down on the ground.

As RSV indicates, the Greek of this verse opens a sentence which is continued in verse 36. But a number of translations make verse 35 into either a complete sentence (TEV, Brc) or an independent clause (NAB, NJB, AT). Moreover, since TEV begins a new paragraph with verse 35, the name Jesus is introduced as subject of the participle **commanding** ("**So Jesus ordered**"). Many translations prefer "ordered," though "instructed" (NJB) is also accurate.

Sit down (so most all translations) translates a Greek verb normally used of reclining at a meal. This is the only occurrence of this verb in the Gospel of Matthew. In some languages it may be helpful to render Jesus' command in direct discourse: "So Jesus told the crowd, 'Sit down on the ground.' "

15.36   RSV   TEV

he took the seven loaves and the fish, and having given thanks he broke them and gave them to the disciples, and the disciples gave them to the crowds.	Then he took the seven loaves and the fish, gave thanks to God, broke them, and gave them to the disciples; and the disciples gave them to the people.

In Greek **took** is the main verb of the sentence begun in verse 35. Moreover, it translates the same verb used in 14.19. The remaining three verbs, **having given thanks**, **broke**, and **gave**, are also found in 14.19. **Took** may be rendered as "picked up" or "held (in his hand)." See 14.19 for further discussion.

Fish translates the normal Greek word for fish, as opposed to the word which technically means "little fish" in verse 34. In both verses GECL renders "fish," assuming that the author intended no distinction between the two words.

Having given thanks: the Greek text does not specify to whom it was that Jesus gave thanks, but TEV, GECL 1st edition, FRCL indicate it was "**to God.**" Some languages will also require that translators indicate that he thanked God "for the food."

In 14.19 it seemed Jesus broke only the loaves of bread, but in this verse he breaks the fish, too.

As previously noted, **gave** is the same verb used in 14.19; however, the tense used here is imperfect, perhaps laying stress upon the action of distributing the bread and fish.

And the disciples gave them to the crowds is literally "and the disciples to the crowds." The same construction is found in 14.19, and in both instances it is necessary to supply a verb in the English restructuring. Some Greek manuscripts read "his disciples" in place of **the disciples**, but the meaning is the same, and many languages will require "his disciples" in any case.

15.37   RSV   TEV

And they all ate and were satisfied; and they took up seven baskets full of the broken pieces left over.	They all ate and had enough. Then the disciples took up seven baskets full of pieces left over.

And they all ate and were satisfied is translated "They all ate as much as they wanted" by NJB. The verb clause **and were satisfied** is translated "to their hearts' content" by NEB. The Greek verb was previously used in 5.6; 14.20; 15.33. It implies both sufficiency and complete satisfaction in eating.

And they took: according to English usage, the pronoun **they** would most naturally refer back to "they" (or the crowds) of the clause "and they all ate." This is also true even according to Greek grammar, but most scholars assume that **they** are "**the disciples**" (TEV, GECL, FRCL), since the disciples are the ones who distributed the food. Consequently translators may have to say "The people in the crowd all ate until they were full. Then the disciples gathered up . . . ."

Not only does the number of baskets differ from the account of the feeding of the five thousand, but the word used for **baskets** is also different in the two accounts (14.20). Here the word specifically refers to a fisherman's basket woven from marsh grass. It is the same word used of the basket by which Paul was let down from the city wall (Acts 9.25). Elsewhere in the New Testament the word is used at Matthew 16.10; Mark 8.8,20. A standard dictionary of classical Greek defines the word as a "large basket," without specifying any particular dimensions. For this reason most translators say simply "large basket." See also comments at 14.20.

In many languages one wouldn't gather up baskets. **Took up seven baskets full** will more naturally be expressed "gathered up enough left over broken pieces to fill seven large baskets."

15.38   RSV   TEV

Those who ate were four thousand men, besides women and children.

The number of men who ate was four thousand, not counting the women and children.

Whereas in 14.21 the number of men are said to have been "about five thousand," the Greek text here says specifically **four thousand**. GECL, on the assumption that the number was intended to be a round number instead of a precise number, translates "about four thousand men."

Those who ate were four thousand men can be expressed in different ways: **"The number of men who ate was four thousand"** (TEV), "There were four thousand men who ate," or "Four thousand men had eaten."

Besides women and children may be translated as a separate sentence: "Many women and children also ate" or "This does not count the women and children who ate."

15.39   RSV   TEV

And sending away the crowds, he got into the boat and went to the region of Magadan.

Then Jesus sent the people away, got into a boat, and went to the territory of Magadan.

And sending away the crowds: TEV identifies the subject of the participle **sending** and simultaneously shifts to a finite verb: **"Then Jesus sent the people away."** For TEV this is important, since it makes verse 39 into a separate paragraph. In place of TEV's **"sent . . . away,"** GECL translates "sent home," which is certainly the contextual meaning. In many languages it will not only be helpful but necessary to translate as GECL has done, for the sake of avoiding a rendering which sounds harsh. For example, translators can say "Then Jesus told the crowds to go home (or, return to their homes)." It can also be in direct speech: "Then Jesus said to the crowds, 'You should go home.' "

Got into the boat can begin a new sentence, as in "Then he got into the boat." However, in many languages it can just as naturally be connected to the previous phrase: "After Jesus told the crowds to return to their homes, he got into the boat."

He got into the boat and went: in other contexts this may mean that Jesus and his disciples got into the boat and left, since Matthew occasionally will use such a construction in this manner. However, as 16.5 attests, Jesus gets into the boat this time without his disciples.

Neither RSV nor TEV indicate the textual problem regarding the name **Magadan**. Although TC-GNT favors this name, it acknowledges that "not only the site, but even the existence of such a place-name is uncertain." The parallel in Mark (8.10) has "the district of Dalmanutha," which TC-GNT further points out is "an equally unknown site and name." Some Greek manuscripts have substituted the well-known "Magdala," a Semitic word meaning "tower," for **Magadan**; most translations prefer **Magadan**.

Chapter 16

RSV   TEV

The Demand for a Miracle

1 And the Pharisees and Sadducees came, and to test him they asked him to show them a sign from heaven. 2 He answered them,*^r* "When it is evening, you say, 'It will be fair weather; for the sky is red.' 3 And in the morning, 'It will be stormy today, for the sky is red and threatening.' You know how to interpret the appearance of the sky, but you cannot interpret the signs of the times. 4 An evil and adulterous generation seeks for a sign, but no sign shall be given to it except the sign of Jonah." So he left them and departed.

^r Other ancient authorities omit the following words to the end of verse 3

1 Some Pharisees and Sadducees who came to Jesus wanted to trap him, so they asked him to perform a miracle for them, to show that God approved of him. 2 But Jesus answered, "When the sun is setting, you say, 'We are going to have fine weather, because the sky is red.' 3 And early in the morning you say, 'It is going to rain, because the sky is red and dark.' You can predict the weather by looking at the sky, but you cannot interpret the signs concerning these times!*^m* 4 How evil and godless are the people of this day! You ask me for a miracle? No! The only miracle you will be given is the miracle of Jonah."

So he left them and went away.

^m Some manuscripts do not have the words of Jesus in verses 2-3.

SECTION HEADING: "**The Demand for a Miracle**" is often rendered by a short sentence such as "The Pharisees ask for a miracle" or "The Pharisees ask Jesus to perform a miracle." For "**Miracle**," see comments on 12.38.

Matthew follows Mark (8.11-13) in stating that the miraculous feeding led the Pharisees to request that Jesus perform a "sign from heaven" to verify his authority.

As TEV's footnote indicates, "Some manuscripts do not have the words of Jesus in verses 2-3." The evidence against the inclusion of these words is impressive, but scholars disagree as to how the evidence ought to be interpreted. The majority of scholars apparently consider the passage a later inclusion, perhaps, from Luke 12.54-56. But there are others who argue that the words were deleted by scribes who lived in climates such as Egypt, where rain is not signified by a red sky in the morning. In light of these considerations the UBS Greek New Testament retains the passage within square brackets.

16.1   RSV   TEV

And the Pharisees and Sadducees came, and to test him they

Some Pharisees and Sadducees who came to Jesus wanted to

asked him to show them a sign from heaven.	**trap him, so they asked him to perform a miracle for them, to show that God approved of him.**

As a comparison between RSV and TEV will immediately reveal, TEV has rather radically restructured this verse.

As in many other places, **And** indicates the narrative is continuing. Some translators will have "Later" or "Some time later."

Pharisees and Sadducees were traditional enemies, but they are here pictured as joining in a united front against Jesus. In 3.7 Matthew narrates that Pharisees and Sadducees were rebuked by John the Baptist, but they are not otherwise linked in the Gospel of Matthew except in this chapter. In fact, apart from these two passages, they seem not to be joined together elsewhere in any of the Gospels. For **Pharisees** and **Sadducees**, see comments at 3.7. Here the text has **the**, as if all of the Pharisees and Sadducees came, or possibly some particular ones already mentioned in the text. "**Some**" as in TEV is probably better, or perhaps "a deputation of."

In Greek both **came** and **to test** are participles dependent upon the main verb **asked**, and they are without specified objects. However, **him** follows **asked**, so that it may be assumed that these two groups came "**to Jesus**" (so TEV, GECL, FRCL, Brc) in order **to test him**.

Came will probably more naturally be "went" in many languages.

Since **to test** is definitely negative, it is permissible to see here the meaning "**to trap**" (TEV) or "to catch." At a more sophisticated level it can be translated "to discredit him."

Note the purpose shown by **to**. Sometimes translators mark this with sentences such as "They wanted to discredit Jesus, so they asked him" (similar to TEV), "In order to trap him, they asked him," and "They asked him a question that would lead him into a trap. They said . . . ."

Sign (TEV "**miracle**") is the same word used in 12.38 (see comments there).

A sign from heaven is translated "**miracle . . . to show that God approved of him**" by TEV. As elsewhere in Matthew **heaven** is a way of speaking of God's abode, and indirectly of God himself. A **sign from heaven** would then be a miracle that God himself allowed or did in order to reveal some truth about himself. In the present context, its function would be to show that Jesus had the approval of God. GECL 1st edition translates the sentence "They wanted proof from him that God had really commissioned him." In fact, translators have found a variety of ways to render **sign from heaven**. "A mighty act that showed God's power" and "a mighty act that showed he had power from God" are quite common. Brc has retained **heaven** and shown that it indirectly refers to God by saying "visible divine action from heaven." Most translators will replace **heaven** with "God," however, as in the examples above.

There will be languages where the request from the Pharisees and Sadducees will more naturally be in direct speech: "They asked him, 'Do some great act to show you have God's power.' "

16.2   RSV   TEV

He answered them,[r] **"When it is eve-ning, you say, 'It will be fair weather; for the sky is red.'**

But Jesus answered, "When the sun is setting, you say, 'We are going to have fine weather, because the sky is red.'

[r] Other ancient authorities omit the following words to the end of verse 3

As indicated in the introduction to this section, there is some doubt whether the words of Jesus in this and the following verse were actually a part of the original text. Most modern translations include the words, but they are relegated to a footnote in NEB and Mft, while AT deletes them without comment. NJB, on the other hand, includes them in the text, with a footnote indicating that they should be omitted. Perhaps the solution represented in RSV and TEV is to be recommended: include them in the text with an accompanying footnote.

When it is evening (TEV "**When the sun is setting**") is linked in GECL with **for the sky is red** and translated "When the evening sky is red." The weather indicators of verses 2-3 differ from those of the Lukan parallel (12.54-56), according to which a west wind from the Mediterranean Sea brought rain, while a southeast wind from the desert ushered in the dreaded sirocco, a very hot and dry wind. Matthew, on the other hand, indicates that a red sky in the evening signals **fair weather**, while a **red and threatening** sky in the morning warns of **stormy** weather.

Translators should use the normal way in their language for speaking of **evening**. "When night is coming" and "When the sun goes down" are examples.

The phrase **it will be fair weather** refers to the weather on the next day, as in "the weather tomorrow will be good."

Not all languages use the same terminology to say **the sky is red**. In this context one of the important aspects is that this is not a threatening sky, which is the case in the next verse.

Jesus does not mean that the Pharisees and Sadducees say this about the weather every evening, which the text may lead some to understand. Rather, he is saying that as a general rule, if the sky is red in the evening, people will predict good weather for the next day. "Sometimes in the evening . . . ," "When the sky is red in the evening . . . ," or "If you see the sky is red in the evening" are often better ways to render this. In many languages translators have found it better to reverse the order: "Sometimes in the evening you may say, 'The sky is red, so tomorrow the weather will be good.' " Another restructuring is "When the sky is red in the evening, you say that tomorrow the weather will be good." This example uses indirect speech, which many translators will find more natural.

16.3   RSV   TEV

And in the morning, 'It will be stormy today, for the sky is red and threat-ening.' You know how to interpret the appearance of the sky, but you

And early in the morning you say, 'It is going to rain, because the sky is red and dark.' You can predict the weather by looking at the sky, but

cannot interpret the signs of the times.	you cannot interpret the signs concerning these times!*ᵐ*

ᵐSome manuscripts do not have the words of Jesus in verses 2-3.

As with "When it is evening" in verse 2, **in the morning** is a general statement. "When the sky is red and threatening in the morning" or "Sometimes in the morning" are possible translations.

Not all languages use **morning** in the same way. For some it is the term used until noon, and for others it refers to a shorter period. However, in this context it is used for the early morning, when the sun is coming up and causes the sky sometimes to be red. "At dawn," "When the sun is coming up," or "Early in the morning" are expressions that can be used.

It will be stormy (TEV "**It is going to rain**") translates one word in Greek; its primary meaning is "rainy and stormy weather" (Acts 27.20) or "season of bad weather," from which is derived the meaning "winter" (Matt 24.20; Mark 13.18; 2 Tim 4.21). **It will be stormy** has many equivalents in most languages; for example, "There will be storms today," "The weather will be stormy today," and "The weather will be very bad today."

The words **red and threatening** describes a sky that is overcast and indicates that there will be a storm. However, it is the sun that turns these clouds red as it comes up.

As in verse 2, the order may need to be changed in many languages: "When it is red and threatening in the morning, you say there is going to be a storm" or "Some mornings you see that the sky is red and overcast, and you say it is going to be stormy that day."

Interpret the appearance of the sky is more literally rendered in NJB: "read the face of the sky." The meaning is clearly "**predict the weather by looking at the sky**" (TEV), which GECL arranges in a more natural order: "You can tell from the appearance of the sky what the weather will be like." One can also translate "You can look at the sky and know what the weather will be like."

But you cannot interpret the signs of the times represents a clause in which the verb **interpret** must be supplied in translation: "But the signs of the times you cannot." **The signs of the times** appears in TEV as "**the signs concerning these times**" and in GECL as "the events of this time." Jesus is referring to his own deeds, especially his miracles, which attest to the presence of the Kingdom.

Interpret is often rendered "explain" or "understand." "Say what (they) mean" is good in some contexts. There is an element of future in the word **signs**, so that "predict on the basis of these events what will happen" will express all the meaning clearly.

As we indicate above, **signs of the times** is generally translated in a way that refers to the things going at that time. Possible ways to render this sentence may include "you don't know how to explain the things happening now," "you don't know what these things happening now indicate for the future," or "there are things happening now, but you don't know what they mean."

16.4   RSV   TEV

RSV	TEV
An evil and adulterous generation seeks for a sign, but no sign shall be given to it except the sign of Jonah." So he left them and departed.	**How evil and godless are the people of this day! You ask me for a miracle? No! The only miracle you will be given is the miracle of Jonah." So he left them and went away.**

An evil and adulterous generation: the word **adulterous** is used here, as frequently in the Old Testament, in the religious sense of "unfaithful to God." NJB translates "unfaithful" and NAB renders "faithless." GECL 1st edition translates this adjective as a separate clause, connecting it with the sentence that follows: "They do not want to know about God, but they want to see a miracle."

The sign of Jonah: see comment at 12.38-39. The only difference in 12.39 and the first part of this verse is that 12.39 says "the prophet Jonah" instead of **Jonah**. However, many translators use "the prophet Jonah" here, too, since their readers are unlikely to know who **Jonah** was.

Since the two verbs **left** and **departed** refer essentially to the same event, it is possible to use only one verb: "So he turned and went away." GECL has "So he left them standing and went away," which is similar to JB's "And leaving them standing there, he went away." Brc reverses the order: "He went away and left them."

16.5-12

     RSV   TEV

The Yeast of the Pharisees and Sadducees

RSV	TEV
5 When the disciples reached the other side, they had forgotten to bring any bread. 6 Jesus said to them, "Take heed and beware of the leaven of the Pharisees and Sadducees." 7 And they discussed it among themselves, saying, "We brought no bread." 8 But Jesus, aware of this, said, "O men of little faith, why do you discuss among yourselves the fact that you have no bread? 9 Do you not yet perceive? Do you not remember the five loaves of the five thousand, and how many baskets you gathered? 10 Or the seven loaves of the four thousand, and how many baskets you gathered? 11 How is it that you fail to perceive that I did not speak about bread? Beware of the leaven of the Pharisees and Sadducees." 12 Then they understood that he did not tell them to beware of the leaven of bread, but of the teaching of the Pharisees and Sadducees.	5 When the disciples crossed over to the other side of the lake, they forgot to take any bread. 6 Jesus said to them, "Take care; be on your guard against the yeast of the Pharisees and Sadducees." 7 They started discussing among themselves, "He says this because we didn't bring any bread." 8 Jesus knew what they were saying, so he asked them, "Why are you discussing among yourselves about not having any bread? What little faith you have! 9 Don't you understand yet? Don't you remember when I broke the five loaves for the five thousand men? How many baskets did you fill? 10 And what about the seven loaves for the four thousand men? How many baskets did you fill? 11 How is it that you don't understand that I was not talking to you about bread? Guard yourselves from the yeast of the Pharisees and Sadducees!" 12 Then the disciples understood that he was not warning them to guard themselves from the yeast used in bread but from the teaching of the Pharisees and Sadducees.

SECTION HEADING: **"The Yeast of the Pharisees and Sadducees"** is sometimes rendered as a short sentence: "Jesus warns his disciples about the yeast of the Pharisees and Sadducees." As the disciples find out eventually, the **"Yeast"** Jesus is referring to is "teaching," but since it is clear in the passage that the disciples didn't understand this immediately, it is best not to use "teaching" in the section heading. For **"Yeast,"** see comments on verse 6 below.

This short narrative has a double function: (1) to remind the disciples that Jesus takes care of their physical needs, and (2) to warn them against the "yeast" of the Pharisees and Sadducees.

16.5	RSV	TEV

When the disciples reached the other side, they had forgotten to bring any bread.

When the disciples crossed over to the other side of the lake, they forgot to take any bread.

When the disciples reached the other side: for **the other side** see comment at 8.18; TEV has **"the other side of the lake,"** and JB "the other shore." GECL 1st edition translates the clause "When the disciples crossed over by boat to the other shore."

Had forgotten (so also NJB, NEB, GECL) expresses more accurately the time sequence than does the simple past (**"forgot"**) of TEV. Obviously the disciples forgot to take bread along with them before they left in the boat, though they only realized it after they had crossed the lake; TEV would imply that the two actions of forgetting the bread and of crossing the lake happened simultaneously. One may then translate "The disciples forgot to take bread along with them when they crossed over to the other side of the lake (where Jesus was)." Or "The disciples crossed over to the other side of the lake where Jesus was, but they had forgotten to take any bread with them."

Note in the above examples that **bring** has been rendered **"take,"** which is the more natural form in English. Translators should use whichever is better in their language.

There are many cases where **bread** represents "food," but that choice would not be the best translation here. In verse 6 the disciples think Jesus speaks of yeast because they had forgotten bread, a food made with yeast, so **bread** should be retained.

16.6	RSV	TEV

Jesus said to them, "Take heed and beware of the leaven of the Pharisees and Sadducees."

Jesus said to them, "Take care; be on your guard against the yeast of the Pharisees and Sadducees."

The two verbs of warning, **Take heed . . . beware**, each have their distinct original meaning and history of usage, but in this context they mean essentially the same thing. GECL places the two verbs together in the construction "Be on your guard against . . . ." "Watch out for" and "Be careful" are other appropriate warnings.

In place of **the leaven of the Pharisees and Sadducees**, Mark has "the leaven of the Pharisees and the leaven of Herod" (8.15), while in another context Luke has "the leaven of the Pharisees, which is hypocrisy" (12.1). Moreover, where Matthew explains the meaning of leaven (verse 12), Mark leaves his readers to draw their own conclusions. Although Jesus here uses **leaven** (TEV "**yeast**") figuratively, its significance must not be explained in translation until verse 12, the place in the narrative where the explanation is given. Otherwise the astonishment of the disciples will make absolutely no sense.

Leaven or "**yeast**" is not known in many parts of the world, but there are sometimes other types of fermenting agents that can serve as an equivalent. Translators can then say "fermenting agent for bread (or, dough)." For example, in parts of Africa where beer is commonly brewed from grain, the froth on top contains the fermenting agent, and some of it can be preserved as a starter for the next batch. Translators in those areas have sometimes said "substance like beer froth that makes bread dough rise." In other cases, where the fermentation process is even less well understood, translators have used a functional description such as "substance that spoils (or raises, or causes to rise) the dough so you can make bread from it." To simply borrow the word **leaven** or "**yeast**" would not help here, since it is the fermenting or spoiling process that is in focus. See also comments at 13.33.

The leaven is **of the Pharisees and Sadducees**, that is, "the yeast they use." It is extending the image too far to believe that the reference is to something spoiled inside them.

16.7 RSV TEV

And they discussed it among themselves, saying, "We brought no bread."

They started discussing among themselves, "He says this because we didn't bring any bread."

And they: it may be useful to identify **they** as "The disciples" (GECL), since the last group of persons mentioned were "the Pharisees and Sadducees" of verse 6.

Discussed (TEV "**started discussing**") translates a verb which may mean "consider" or "reason (out something)," while the phrase **among themselves** may also mean "inwardly."

What the disciples began discussing, represented by the pronoun **it**, may need to be made more definite. Translators can say "discussing what Jesus had said" or ". . . these words."

We brought no bread will strike many readers as completely senseless, unless there is further qualification, and some translations indicate an awareness of the difficulty: "**He says this because we didn't bring any bread**" (TEV); "It is because we have not brought any bread" (NJB); and "It is because we have brought no bread" (NEB). GECL overcomes the problem by shifting to indirect discourse: "The disciples took this to refer to their forgetfulness." Brc also effectively utilizes indirect discourse: "They kept on talking among themselves about bringing no loaves." In Mft the whole of verse 7 is translated "They argued among themselves, 'But we have not brought any bread!' "

16.8 RSV	TEV
But Jesus, aware of this, said, "O men of little faith, why do you discuss among yourselves the fact that you have no bread?	Jesus knew what they were saying, so he asked them, "Why are you discussing among yourselves about not having any bread? What little faith you have!

Aware does not have an expressed object in Greek, and one must be supplied in translation; RSV has **of this**, and NJB "it." On the assumption that the verb rendered "discussed" in verse 7 implies conversation, TEV supplies the object, "**what they were saying**," and Brc, "what they were arguing about." NEB, assuming that the thoughts of the disciples were the unexpressed object, has "what was in their minds."

O men of little faith: outside of Luke 12.28, this form of address appears only in Matthew's Gospel (see 6.30; 8.26; 14.31). GECL translates "Have you so little faith?"

As we indicate in the discussion at 14.31, some languages will need an object for **faith**, as in "You believe in me so little" or "How can you not believe I will provide for your need?" TEV has put this exclamation at the end of the verse; many other languages will also find this more natural.

Discuss and **among yourselves** represent the same Greek verb and phrase used in verse 7.

The fact that you have no bread: except for the shift from the first person plural ("we have") to the second person plural (**you have**), this is the same construction found in verse 7. In place of **have** some Greek manuscripts have "bring"; however, the UBS Greek text prefers **have**, though with "a considerable degree of doubt." Fortunately the meaning is essentially the same, regardless of which reading is accepted.

16.9-10 RSV	TEV
9 Do you not yet perceive? Do you not remember the five loaves of the five thousand, and how many baskets you gathered? 10 Or the seven loaves of the four thousand, and how many baskets you gathered?	9 Don't you understand yet? Don't you remember when I broke the five loaves for the five thousand men? How many baskets did you fill? 10 And what about the seven loaves for the four thousand men? How many baskets did you fill?

These questions are not asking whether or not the disciples really do remember, but they are rhetorical questions which are meant to rebuke the disciples for not perceiving or remembering. For this reason it may be advisable to restructure the questions of these verses as statements. For example, "You still don't understand! You have already forgotten about the time that I fed five thousand men with five loaves of bread. After that meal you took up enough leftovers to fill twelve baskets. You have even forgotten about the four thousand men that I fed with seven loaves. After that meal you took up enough leftovers to fill seven baskets."

Baskets in verse 9 is the same word used in the account of the feeding of the five thousand (14.20), while **baskets** in verse 10 is the same word used in the account of the feeding of the four thousand (15.37).

The five loaves of the five thousand refers specifically to the five loaves he used to feed the five thousand men, as has been made explicit in the example above. "How I fed five thousand men with five loaves" is also possible. **The seven loaves of the four thousand** can be treated in a similar fashion.

In the above example, too, we rendered **how many baskets you gathered** with the phrase "leftovers to fill twelve (or, seven) baskets." Another possibility is "filled up twelve (or, seven) baskets with the bread left over."

16.11   RSV   TEV

How is it that you fail to perceive that I did not speak about bread? Beware of the leaven of the Pharisees and Sadducees."	**How is it that you don't understand that I was not talking to you about bread? Guard yourselves from the yeast of the Pharisees and Sadducees!"**

Both the question form and the negative relative clause (**that I did not . . .**) within another negative relative clause (**that you fail . . .**) may cause some difficulty for some readers. But these potential problems can be resolved. For example, "By now you should have realized that I was not talking to you about bread." In some West African languages the most natural way to render this will be "I wasn't talking about bread. Can't you see that?"

Beware of translates the same verb used in verse 6; it was first used in 6.1 (see comments there).

In translation it may be beneficial for the reader if a clear tie is made between the two statements of this verse; for example, "Don't you understand that when I told you to watch out for the leaven of the Pharisees and Sadducees I wasn't talking about bread?" or "I told you to beware of the leaven of the Pharisees and Sadducees. I wasn't talking about bread. Can't you understand that?"

The leaven ("**yeast**") **of the Pharisees and Sadducees** may wrongly be interpreted to mean either "the yeast which the Pharisees and Sadducees own" or ". . . which the Pharisees and Sadducees are selling (or, distributing)." However, the difficulty is not too severe, since an explanation is given in the next verse. Nevertheless, it is possible to be more specific, even here: ". . . from the teaching of the Pharisees and Sadducees, which is like yeast (that spreads throughout a lump of dough)."

16.12 RSV TEV

Then they understood that he did not tell them to beware of the leaven of bread, but of the teaching of the Pharisees and Sadducees.

Then the disciples understood that he was not warning them to guard themselves from the yeast used in bread but from the teaching of the Pharisees and Sadducees.

"**The disciples**" of TEV translates **they** of the Greek text. It is important that the subject be specified here, for the same reason discussed in verse 7 (see comments there).

The leaven of bread is translated "**the yeast used in bread**" by TEV. The expression may also be rendered "the yeast that one puts in bread" or, if there is a firm distinction between "bread" (cooked dough) and "dough" (uncooked bread), then a further adjustment may be made: "the yeast which one places in dough (to make it rise)."

For some languages a reversal of sentence order, placing the negative sentence last, may be more natural: "Then the disciples understood that he was referring to the teaching of the Pharisees and Sadducees. He was not warning them to guard themselves from the yeast used in bread." Other possibilities are "Then the disciples understood that when Jesus told them to watch out for the leaven of the Pharisees and Sadducees, he didn't mean the leaven used in making bread (or, leaven that makes bread dough rise). He meant the teaching of the Pharisees and Sadducees," and "Then the disciples realized that he was warning them about the teaching of the Pharisees and Sadducees, which was like (or, which had a spoiling effect like) yeast in bread dough."

There will be readers who will find even these sentences difficult, particularly if in the translation the fermenting or spoiling effect of yeast has not been made clear enough. If translators are not able to convey this notion of "spoiling" in the word or phrase used for **leaven**, then it may be necessary here to have a very explicit simile such as "teaching that spoils (others) like leaven causes bread dough to ferment."

The **teaching** of the Pharisees and Sadducees is what they taught, not what was taught to them, and some translators will have to make that explicit.

16.13-20

RSV TEV

Peter's Declaration about Jesus

13 Now when Jesus came into the district of Caesarea Philippi, he asked his disciples, "Who do men say that the Son of man is?" 14 And they said, "Some say John the Baptist, others say Elijah, and others Jeremiah or one of the prophets." 15 He said to them, "But who do you say that I am?" 16 Simon Peter replied, "You are the Christ, the Son of the living God." 17 And Jesus answered him, "Blessed are you, Simon Bar-Jona! For flesh and blood has not revealed this to you, but my Father who is in heaven. 18 And I tell you,

13 Jesus went to the territory near the town of Caesarea Philippi, where he asked his disciples, "Who do people say the Son of Man is?"

14 "Some say John the Baptist," they answered. "Others say Elijah, while others say Jeremiah or some other prophet."

15 "What about you?" he asked them. "Who do you say I am?"

16 Simon Peter answered, "You are the Messiah, the Son of the living God."

17 "Good for you, Simon son of John!"

you are Peter,[s] and on this rock[t] I will build my church, and the powers of death[u] shall not prevail against it. 19 I will give you the keys of the kingdom of heaven, and whatever you bind on earth shall be bound in heaven, and whatever you loose on earth shall be loosed in heaven." 20 Then he strictly charged the disciples to tell no one that he was the Christ.

[s] Greek *Petros*
[t] Greek *petra*
[u] Greek *the gates of Hades*

answered Jesus. "For this truth did not come to you from any human being, but it was given to you directly by my Father in heaven. 18 And so I tell you, Peter: you are a rock, and on this rock foundation I will build my church, and not even death will ever be able to overcome it. 19 I will give you the keys of the Kingdom of heaven; what you prohibit on earth will be prohibited in heaven, and what you permit on earth will be permitted in heaven."

20 Then Jesus ordered his disciples not to tell anyone that he was the Messiah.

SECTION HEADING: "**Peter's Declaration about Jesus**." It is often necessary to indicate what Peter declared, as in "Peter declares Jesus is the Messiah." For "Messiah" or "Christ," see comments on 1.1,16,17.

"Jesus walks the road to suffering and death" is a suitable title of 16.13–20.34. Throughout this section Matthew follows closely the Marcan framework, but he freely reworks the account of Peter's confession and formulates 17.24–18.35 into guidelines for the Christian community. Moreover, he incorporates two parables which are unique to his own Gospel: "The Parable of the Unforgiving Servant" (18.21-35) and "The Workers in the Vineyard" (20.1-16).

16.13   RSV   TEV

Now when Jesus came into the district of Caesarea Philippi, he asked his disciples, "Who do men say that the Son of man is?"

Jesus went to the territory near the town of Caesarea Philippi, where he asked his disciples, "Who do people say the Son of Man is?"

Now is not to be translated literally. It marks the beginning of a new episode in the narrative. Further, in many languages it is not normal to use **when** unless somehow the passage had already indicated that Jesus was heading toward Caesarea Philippi. For this reason translators often begin the verse simply with "Jesus went to (or, arrived in) the district of Caesarea Philippi." Another common way is "Jesus went to the area of Caesarea Philippi. When he arrived there . . . ."

Came translates a participle which a number of translations render as a dependent clause: **when . . . came** (RSV, NEB, NJB). But it is also possible to represent this construction as an independent clause, as in TEV: "**Jesus went**." The choice between **came** and "**went**" will depend upon the expectations of the receptor language.

The district of Caesarea Philippi: TEV qualifies the **of** phrase and identifies Caesarea Philippi as a town, since this is the first time that the name is mentioned in the Gospel: "**the territory near the town of Caesarea Philippi**." The town is located on the southeastern slope of Mount Hermon.

Men is definitely to be understood in the sense of "**people**" (TEV).

<u>Say</u> in this sentence does not simply mean to say something one time. The meaning is more like "are saying." That is, Jesus was asking what people were saying about him in the course of their discussions.

The first occurrence of the title **Son of man** is found in 8.20; see comments there. It should be noted that the Marcan parallel (8.27) has "Who do men say that I am?" In addition some early Greek manuscripts of Matthew 16.13 also have "say that I am," which indicates that there was some attempt in the early church to make explicit who was meant by this term. Moreover, when the question is repeated in verse 15, a shift is made to the first person ("I"). Nevertheless, as we point out at 8.20, it is generally advisable to retain the ambiguity of Matthew with "Son of Man" or "the One called Son of Man." Only if retaining the third person in this verse would make the question addressed to the disciples in verse 15 seem odd, should translators say "I, who am the Son of Man."

Further, it is important that readers not think that Jesus was asking which person was the Son of Man. It is not as if people were asking "Is Barabbas the Son of Man?" or "Is Herod the Son of Man?" or anything like that. Rather, Jesus is asking who people think the one who is called the Son of Man (namely, himself) really is.

16.14	RSV	TEV

And they said, "Some say John the Baptist, others say Elijah, and others Jeremiah or one of the prophets."	"Some say John the Baptist," they answered. "Others say Elijah, while others say Jeremiah or some other prophet."

If the Son of Man is specifically identified with Jesus in verse 13, then the reply in verse 14 may require a second-person reference: "Some say that you are . . . ." Many languages will require a short sentence as a response, as in "Some people say the Son of Man is (really) (or, you are) John the Baptist."

In the Greek sentence only the verb **said** appears, but English requires the introduction of **say . . . say**, as in RSV and TEV.

According to 14.2, Herod Antipas thought that Jesus was John the Baptist come back to life. Evidently there were others who shared this belief along with him. For **John the Baptist**, see comments on 3.1.

Elijah may not be well known to many readers, especially in languages where the Old Testament has not yet been translated or widely distributed. It may be helpful in such cases to say "the prophet (of long ago) Elijah." On the belief that **Elijah** would return prior to the day of final judgment, see comment at 11.14.

Jeremiah or one of the prophets: in order not to convey the false impression that Jeremiah was not one of the prophets, TEV translates "**Jeremiah or some other prophet**." Since Jeremiah was definitely considered a prophet by the Jewish community, it is quite obvious that Matthew has no intention of excluding him from among the prophets. In fact, this is in all probability Matthew's way of placing Jeremiah at the forefront of the prophets.

For some translators, the fact that the people named here are all dead needs to be indicated. This is especially the case when there are many readers who do not have great familiarity with the Bible. Sometimes a footnote is necessary. Other times, to say something like "prophet of long ago" or "John the Baptist reappeared" is sufficient.

16.15   RSV   TEV

**He said to them, "But who do you   "What about you?" he asked
say that I am?"   them. "Who do you say I am?"**

In Greek the pronoun **you** (plural) appears in emphatic position, which is the basis for TEV's restructuring: "**What about you . . . Who do you say . . . ?**" The intention of the question is to contrast the opinion of persons outside the circle of disciples with the opinion that the disciples themselves held of Jesus. This seems also to be the intention of both NJB (" 'But you,' he said, 'who do you say I am?' ") and NEB (" 'And you,' he asked, 'who do you say I am?' "), and similarly GECL. It may be that the translators of these two versions intended Jesus' question to be understood in light of "he asked his disciples" (verse 13), but it is also possible that the average reader will have forgotten this information, especially since it is Simon Peter who immediately responds to Jesus' question. In translation it is thus best to retain the indirect object **them** and, if there is a plural form of **you** in the receptor language, to use it also.

The emphasis can be kept on **you** with an expression such as "But for your part, who do you say (or, think) that I am?" or "But what is your opinion? Who am I really?"

16.16   RSV   TEV

**Simon Peter replied, "You are the   Simon Peter answered, "You
Christ, the Son of the living God."   are the Messiah, the Son of the living
                                             God."**

The Christ (so also NJB, NIV) is no more than a transliteration of the Greek, concerning which one commentator observes: "The transliteration of the Gr. *Christos* by Christ in various English versions is inexcusable . . . In its original context the question posed by Jesus and answered by Peter as spokesman demanded commitment to Jesus as *Messiah*." Together with TEV, both NEB and NAB have "**Messiah.**" On the meaning of the title "**the Messiah**" see comments at 1.17 and 1.1. In the present passage the title occurs both here and again in verse 20, where it appears in the words of Jesus. GECL translates the first occurrence as "you are Christ," with a reference to the word list, where "Christ" is defined as "the Promised Savior." Then the command of Jesus to his disciples in verse 20 is rendered "Tell no one that I am the Promised Savior." It seems better to render the term as "the Promised Savior" in each of these occurrences (or to use whatever translation has been used elsewhere; see comments at 1.1). Then the ordinary reader will understand that when Jesus uses "the Promised Savior" (verse 20), his point of reference is Peter's confession of him as "the Promised Savior" (verse 16). TEV maintains this continuity by rendering **"the Messiah"** in both places, but the term is probably not understood by a majority of English readers.

The Son of the living God is a title that occurs only here in the New Testament. In 3.17 "a voice from heaven" refers to Jesus as "my beloved Son," and in 14.33 the disciples confess "Truly you are the Son of God." But the full formula as it occurs here is found nowhere else in the New Testament. In the Old Testament and in Judaism, "Son of God" is rather frequently used of persons whom God has chosen to act in his behalf and for the benefit of his people. However, as the confession occurs in the New Testament, it speaks of Jesus' divine origin and of his deity. See also 14.33 where "Son of God" is discussed.

Living affirms that God possesses life himself and is the source of all life. The confession that Jesus is **the Son of the living God** means that in a unique way Jesus shares in that life, and that he himself has power to impart life to others. Translators have generally followed one of two ways to render **living God**. Some make the term contrast with other gods who are not living: "that God (or, our God) who is alive (or, who lives forever)." Others have made **living** more an attribute of God: "God, who is alive" or "God, who lives forever."

16.17　　　　RSV　　　　　　　　　　　　　TEV

And Jesus answered him, "Blessed are you, Simon Bar-Jona! For flesh and blood has not revealed this to you, but my Father who is in heaven.

　　　　"Good for you, Simon son of John!" answered Jesus. "For this truth did not come to you from any human being, but it was given to you directly by my Father in heaven.

Many translations drop **And** or render it with "Then."

In some languages **answered** will only be used in a context where a question has been asked. "Said" is then more natural.

Blessed translates the same expression used in the Beatitudes; see comment in the introduction to 5.3-12. However, it may not be natural to render **Blessed** in the same way here. "You are indeed fortunate" may be possible, as long as it does not mean that Peter was lucky. A common translation is "Things are well with you, Simon son of John, because . . . it was revealed to you by my heavenly Father."

Bar-Jona (so also Brc) is a transliteration of the Greek, which is in turn a transliteration of the Aramaic meaning "son of Jonah" (NJB, NEB, Phps, TOB, GECL 1st edition). The name is unexpected, since in John 1.42 Simon's father is identified as John. One scholar notes that "despite the prophet of this name, there is no trace of 'Jonah' as a proper name in the centuries before and after Jesus," and so he concludes, together with other scholars, that **Jona** is best understood as an abbreviation of "Johanan" (the equivalent of "John"); TEV and FRCL have "**John.**"

There will be languages where the vocative, **Simon Bar-Jona**, will more likely be at the beginning of Jesus' words: "Simon son of John, things are well with you."

For flesh and blood has not revealed this to you: since **flesh and blood** is a Jewish way of referring to a human being in his totality, Brc translates "for it was no human being who revealed this to you," and NAB has "No mere man has revealed this to you." It is quite possible that the expression intends to emphasize man as being subject to sickness and death, always limited in strength and knowledge, and so the basis for NEB: "You did not learn that from mortal man." Moreover, it is quite possible that **flesh and blood**, as used here, refer specifically to Peter himself, in which case one may translate "You did not learn this on your own." "You did not learn this by any human means" will actually allow for either of these interpretations.

Notice from these examples that **revealed** can be rendered by a passive ("has been revealed" or "has been taught") or active ("no human revealed this to you" or "no one taught you"). Peter can even be the subject, as in "You did not learn."

In the Greek sentence the verb **revealed** is not followed by an object, but English requires one, and translations have traditionally supplied **this** as object. In place of **this** TEV uses **"this truth"** and simultaneously adopts a structure in which the noun phrase becomes subject of the verb: **"this truth did not come from."** In place of **this** one may also use "this information," or "this insight," or "this understanding."

But my Father who is in heaven: this is a literal rendering of the Greek text and assumes "has revealed it to you" of the previous clause. Thus NEB has "it was revealed to you by my heavenly Father"; and TEV translates **"but it was given to you directly by my Father in heaven."** See discussion of the phrase at 5.16.

In heaven draws the contrast between God, whose realm and power are unlimited, with people, who are creatures of flesh and blood.

16.18

RSV	TEV
And I tell you, you are Peter,[s] and on this rock[t] I will build my church, and the powers of death[u] shall not prevail against it.	And so I tell you, Peter: you are a rock, and on this rock foundation I will build my church, and not even death will ever be able to overcome it.

[s] Greek *Petros*
[t] Greek *petra*
[u] Greek *the gates of Hades*

And I tell you translates a strongly emphatic transitional formula; NJB renders "So I now say to you"; NEB "And I say this to you"; GECL "Therefore I say to you."

You are Peter, and on this rock is translated in TEV as **"Peter: you are a rock, and on this rock foundation . . . ."** As RSV's footnotes indicate, there is a word play in Greek between **Peter** (Greek *Petros*) and **rock** (Greek *petra*). Although the word play is clear enough in Greek, it would have been even more obvious in Aramaic, the language which Jesus spoke. As can be seen from the transliteration of the Greek words, the masculine derivative form *Petros* (**Peter**) has a different ending from the root word *petra*, which is feminine and means **rock**. Aramaic, however, would not distinguish between masculine and feminine forms, so that the result would be "You are *kefa*, and on this *kefa* I will build . . . ." Some translations attempt to make this equation explicit: ". . . You are Peter, the Rock; and on this rock . . ." (NEB); ". . . you are Peter—the man whose name means a rock— on this rock . . ." (Brc); and ". . . you are Peter the rock, and it is on this rock . . ." (Phps). Some interpreters have attempted to avoid the evident meaning of the text by assuming that **rock** refers either to Peter's confession or to his faith, since both "confession" and "faith" are feminine nouns in Greek, as is the word **rock**. Different interpretations will inevitably arise regarding the implications of Jesus' statement, but the text is clear in what it says, and it must be translated in this light.

A good translation of **I tell you, you are Peter, and on this rock** depends on this play on words. **I tell you, you are Peter** will sound strange indeed if the wordplay that follows is not made clear. Putting the information in a footnote will not be sufficient except for quite skilled readers. As a result, most translators do something similar to Phps (cited above) or TEV.

Although the verb **build** may be used in a literal sense of constructing a physical structure (7.24), it is not used in that sense here, for **church** means "congregation," "people," "assembly," or, more specifically, "community of believers," without reference to a physical building. Except for the appearance of **church** in 18.17, the noun is not used elsewhere in any of the Gospels.

Church, "community," and "group" are all singular forms. Jesus is referring to the institution he will found. To say "I will create believers around you," for example, will not convey this.

There are therefore three problems the translator has to solve in **on this rock I will build my church**: 1) **church** means the community of believers; 2) **build** is used figuratively; 3) **rock** must be retained because of the play on words. Some translators have rendered the whole verse as a simile: "in the same way that a building can be built on a rock (foundation), so I will make you the support for the community of those who believe in me" or "I will develop around you the group of those who follow me, just like a building is constructed on a rock foundation." A less cumbersome rendering would be "when I create my community of believers, you are the rock that will be the foundation."

And the powers of death shall not prevail against it (NEB "and the powers of death shall never conquer it") is translated "**and not even death will ever be able to overcome it**" by TEV. A more literal rendering is given by NIV: "and the gates of Hades will not overcome it." Actually "Hades" of NIV is not a translation but rather a transliteration of a Greek word which has "place of the dead" as its primary meaning (see 11.23 for the only other occurrence of the word in Matthew). Here the picture is that of a "gate" through which one enters the "world of the dead," from which there is no return. Therefore "world of the dead" becomes equivalent to "death," while "gate" symbolizes the power that death has over its victims. An excellent Old Testament example which parallels the usage here is found in Isaiah 38.10, where Hezekiah complains that the little time he has to live will be dominated by the fact of his impending death: "I am consigned to the gates of Sheol [meaning 'world of the dead'] for the rest of my years." The **powers of death** (TEV "**death**") represent humanity's last and most feared enemy, but Jesus affirms that his community of faith need not fear its awesome power: "no enemy shall be able to destroy it, not even death" (GECL). Also good is "not even death is powerful enough to destroy (or, defeat) it."

It, of course, refers to **church**. The text must not seem to say that death is not strong enough to defeat believers; the idea is that death is not strong enough to defeat the community of believers that Jesus is going to create.

16.19 RSV	TEV
I will give you the keys of the kingdom of heaven, and whatever you bind on earth shall be bound in heaven, and whatever you loose on earth shall be loosed in heaven."	I will give you the keys of the Kingdom of heaven; what you prohibit on earth will be prohibited in heaven, and what you permit on earth will be permitted in heaven."

The keys of the kingdom of heaven: there is general agreement that **keys** symbolize authority, but there is wide disagreement among scholars regarding the nature and extent of this authority given to Peter. Some scholars see here the picture of **the kingdom of heaven** as a large palace with doors to which Peter has been given the keys. Peter would then be the "gate keeper of heaven," having the authority to decide who could or could not enter its gates. In support of this exegesis is the analogy between "gates" (verse 18) and "keys" (verse 19) on the one hand, and "the world of the dead (verse 18) and "the kingdom of heaven" (verse 19) on the other hand.

There is, however, an alternative interpretation according to which Peter is not the gate keeper of heaven, but the steward of the Kingdom of heaven upon earth. In this regard his primary function is that of "binding and loosing," which would mean the authority to render the correct interpretation to the Law of Christ. Peter would then stand in contrast to the teachers of the Law of 23.13, who are the self-appointed interpreters of God's Law.

Fortunately, satisfactory translations of this verse may be made without giving explicit support to these or any other doctrinal positions, and it is important that this procedure be followed. For many Christians this is an extremely sensitive passage, and translations should allow for openness of interpretation. GECL produces a text that is both dynamic and nonsectarian: "I will give you the keys to God's New World." In some languages **keys** will have to occur with "doors," as in "keys of the doors to God's New World."

Keys are not always well known, so translators have to use a descriptive phrase such as "an object that controls whether a door or container can be opened." Since this can possibly lead to a rather cumbersome translation ("I will give you the things that control whether God's rule can be opened or closed"), some translators have used a phrase such as "I will have you control whether God's rule is open or closed" or "I will give you control concerning the people that are ruled over by God." Note that this last example does not say "control over." In any case the term used for **keys** should relate to the terms used for binding and loosing in the following clauses.

For more comments on **kingdom of heaven**, see the discussions at 3.2 and 5.3.

Bound in heaven . . . loosed in heaven: "to bind" and "to loose" translate technical terms used by Jewish teachers in the sense of "to forbid" and "to permit." **Heaven** here represents a typical Jewish way of referring to God without mentioning his sacred name. Therefore one scholar states: "Everything decided by the 'lower court' is confirmed by the 'superior court,' i.e., God himself." One may then translate "What you forbid (here on earth), God (in heaven) will also forbid . . . ."

Some translators have rendered this in a way that makes it seem that whatever Peter prohibits or permits on earth will apply to those beings that are in heaven, too.

Rather, "God in heaven will give his approval to the things you prohibit or permit on earth" will be better.

In many languages translators will have to indicate what Peter prohibits or permits. "What you prohibit (or, permit) people to do on earth, God in heaven will give his approval to" is possible.

16.20 RSV TEV

Then he strictly charged the disciples to tell no one that he was the Christ.

Then Jesus ordered his disciples not to tell anyone that he was the Messiah.

He strictly charged: in the Greek text Jesus is not specifically given as the subject of the verb **strictly charged**, but it may be helpful to mark him as such, since he was last mentioned by name in verse 17.

Strictly charged is translated "**ordered**" by TEV and "gave . . . strict orders . . . to" by NEB and NJB. This is the only occurrence of this verb in Matthew, though it occurs elsewhere in the New Testament in Mark 5.43; 7.36; 8.15; 9.9; Acts 15.24; Hebrews 12.20).

As indicated in verse 16, **the Christ** (TEV "**the Messiah**") is rendered "the Promised Savior" by GECL. Moreover, GECL shifts to direct discourse: "Then Jesus urged his disciples: 'Tell no one that I am the Promised Savior.' "

16.21-28

RSV TEV

Jesus Speaks about His Suffering and Death

21 From that time Jesus began to show his disciples that he must go to Jerusalem and suffer many things from the elders and chief priests and scribes, and be killed, and on the third day be raised. 22 And Peter took him and began to rebuke him, saying, "God forbid, Lord! This shall never happen to you." 23 But he turned and said to Peter, "Get behind me, Satan! You are a hindrance[v] to me; for you are not on the side of God, but of men."

24 Then Jesus told his disciples, "If any man would come after me, let him deny himself and take up his cross and follow me. 25 For whoever would save his life will lose it, and whoever loses his life for my sake will find it. 26 For what will it profit a man, if he gains the whole world and forfeits his life? Or what shall a man give in return for his life? 27 For the Son of man is to come with his angels in the glory of his Father, and then he will repay every man for what he has done. 28 Truly, I say to you, there are

21 From that time on Jesus began to say plainly to his disciples, "I must go to Jerusalem and suffer much from the elders, the chief priests, and the teachers of the Law. I will be put to death, but three days later I will be raised to life."

22 Peter took him aside and began to rebuke him. "God forbid it, Lord!" he said. "That must never happen to you!"

23 Jesus turned around and said to Peter, "Get away from me, Satan! You are an obstacle in my way, because these thoughts of yours don't come from God, but from man."

24 Then Jesus said to his disciples, "If anyone wants to come with me, he must forget himself, carry his cross, and follow me. 25 For whoever wants to save his own life will lose it; but whoever loses his life for my sake will find it. 26 Will a person gain anything if he wins the whole world but loses his life? Of course not! There is nothing he can give to regain his life. 27 For the Son of Man is about to come in the glory of his

some standing here who will not taste death before they see the Son of man coming in his kingdom."

^v Greek *stumbling block*

Father with his angels, and then he will reward each one according to his deeds. 28 I assure you that there are some here who will not die until they have seen the Son of Man come as King."

SECTION HEADING: "**Jesus Speaks about His Suffering and Death**" may not be clear in all languages, particularly those where this type of sentence will normally be interpreted to mean he was talking about the past, not the future. Further, it may be necessary to say to whom Jesus was speaking. "Jesus tells his disciples that he will suffer and be killed" or "Jesus tells his disciples that people will arrest him and kill him" are sometimes better.

Commentators note that the adverbial phrase **From that time** (verse 21) definitely indicates a new phase in the Gospel. Jesus is indeed the Messiah, the Promised Savior King, as Peter has acknowledged. However, even Peter fails to recognize the full implication of this confession, and so Jesus now begins to teach his disciples the true meaning of his Messiahship. The main emphasis in the rest of the Gospel is upon a proper understanding of what Jesus must do in order to be Messiah, and of what his disciples are required to do in order to be true followers of the Messiah.

16.21   RSV   TEV

From that time Jesus began to show his disciples that he must go to Jerusalem and suffer many things from the elders and chief priests and scribes, and be killed, and on the third day be raised.

From that time on Jesus began to say plainly to his disciples, "I must go to Jerusalem and suffer much from the elders, the chief priests, and the teachers of the Law. I will be put to death, but three days later I will be raised to life."

In at least five significant respects the first part of this verse differs from the parallel in Mark (8.31—9.1): (1) Mark uses the simple conjunction "and" to join this episode with the previous one, whereas Matthew uses the adverbial phrase **From that time**. Thus in translation this adverbial marker should be made prominent. (2) In place of the verb "teach" Matthew uses a stronger verb (**show**), which TEV renders "**say plainly to**"; both NEB and NJB have "make it clear to," while Phps translates "explain to." The helping verb is correctly rendered **began** by most all English translations, except that NAB has "started to indicate." The problem with "started to" for English speakers is that it could imply that this is something that Jesus intended to do but did not accomplish. (3) Mark uses the pronoun "them" as an indirect object, which Matthew replaces with the more explicit **his disciples**, thus laying greater stress upon their role in this learning process. (4) By the construction **Jesus . . . he**, Matthew unambiguously identifies Jesus as the one who must experience these sufferings, whereas Mark returns to the phrase "the Son of Man." It is interesting that this is a reversal of what the two writers did earlier (Matt 16.13; Mark 8.27). (5) Matthew makes specific mention of Jerusalem as the place where Jesus must suffer; neither Mark (8.31) nor Luke (9.22) mention the city by name.

As we indicate above, **From that time** requires a clear adverbial marker like "From then on" or "That was the time when Jesus began."

Quite frequently, as here, **must** is used in the Gospels of a necessity imposed upon a person in the fulfillment of the divine will (see 17.10; 24.6; 26.54). Some translators have even used a phrase like "that God required that" or "that it was God's will that" to convey the full force of **must**.

The elders and chief priests and scribes constituted the highest Jewish council in Jerusalem, known as the Sanhedrin. They had supreme authority in matters of the Jewish faith, and the Roman government even allowed them to exercise some power in the regulation of Jewish life. **The elders** were first mentioned in 15.2 (see comments there); **chief priests and scribes** were first mentioned in 2.4 (see comments there).

That he must go . . . and be killed, and on the third day be raised is shifted into direct discourse in GECL, FRCL, and TEV: "**I must go . . . I will be put to death, but three days later I will be raised to life.**" In addition to the shift to direct discourse, one may also employ an active construction for the passives **be killed** and **be raised**: "They will put me to death . . . God will raise me back to life."

This sentence often gets a little long and awkward, and some translators break it up into two or more sentences; for example, "Jesus began to explain to his disciples that it was God's will he go to Jerusalem. There the elders, the chief priests, and the teachers of the Law would cause him to suffer greatly and then would have him killed." Those who use direct discourse may have "Jesus began to explain to his disciples, 'I must go to Jerusalem. There the elders, chief priests, and the teachers of the Law will make me suffer many things, and they will have me put to death.' "

It is probably better to say "have put to death," as above, than to render the verse as if the elders and others will actually be the ones killing Jesus.

The verb **be raised** (TEV "**be raised to life**") may also be used with the meaning "rise" (meaning "I will come back to life"; see 14.2 where the same verb is used), but it is better understood as God's action in raising Jesus back to life. Therefore "But God will raise me back to life" or "But I will be raised back to life" are possible translations.

On the third day (so also NEB, NJB) may be translated "**three days later,**" as in TEV. Of course, each translator will use whatever expression is natural. For the Jews, the day of the event spoken of was the first day, the day after that was the second day, and the day after that was **the third day**. Languages which count the day after the event as the first day may have "two days later." (Note that English is such a language, and therefore TEV is actually translated incorrectly.) But because "third day" or "in three days" are phrases that are frequently used in the Bible with some symbolic value, many translators prefer an expression like that in RSV.

16.22 RSV	TEV
And Peter took him and began to rebuke him, saying, "God forbid, Lord! This shall never happen to you."	Peter took him aside and began to rebuke him. "God forbid it, Lord!" he said. "That must never happen to you!"

And indicates that the narrative is continuing. "Then" will be good in some languages, or it may be more natural to drop the transition (so TEV).

Took (so also Mft) may have the more specific meaning "**took . . . aside**" (TEV, NAB, NIV) or "led him away from the others." NEB translates "took him by the arm," and Brc "caught hold of him."

Rebuke (so also NEB, NIV) is difficult to render in English at a common language level. Both AT and Mft translate "reprove," while Phps, JB, NAB have "remonstrate with." Brc attempts to go in the direction of a more dynamic equivalent: "sternly forbade him to talk like that." Other possibilities are "scold him for talking like that" and "tell him he shouldn't talk like that." Elsewhere in the Gospel the verb is used six times: 8.26; 12.16; 16.20; 17.18; 19.13; 20.31.

God forbid (so also Mft, Brc) is supplied with an object in TEV: "**God forbid it.**" More literally the expression is "Mercy to you," but in such a context the "mercy" would be interpreted as originating from God. NEB translates "Heaven forbid!" and NJB "Heaven preserve you . . . ." Both AT and Phps have "God bless you . . . !" while NIV renders by the one word "Never . . . !" Similar expressions are "May God never permit that this happen" and "May God stop this from happening." NAB joins this with the next sentence, **This shall never happen to you**, and translates "May you be spared, Master! God forbid that any such thing ever happen to you!"

This shall never happen to you is best interpreted as a negative expression equivalent to "God forbid" of the previous sentence. It is possible to unite the two sentences into one, especially in languages where repetition tends to diminish the effect: "May God never let this happen to you."

16.23	RSV	TEV

RSV	TEV
But he turned and said to Peter, "Get behind me, Satan! You are a hindrance[v] to me; for you are not on the side of God, but of men."	**Jesus turned around and said to Peter, "Get away from me, Satan! You are an obstacle in my way, because these thoughts of yours don't come from God, but from man."**

[v] Greek *stumbling block*

Turned translates a participle which is dependent upon the main verb **said** in the Greek sentence structure. But most English translations represent them both as finite verbs, as do GECL and FRCL. Other languages may require quite different ways of dealing with the two forms. Brc renders **turned** dramatically with "swung round." Similar expressions would include "turned toward Peter" or "turned and faced Peter."

Get behind me (so NJB, Mft), a literal rendering of the Greek, is translated "**Get away from me**" by TEV; NEB ("Away with you") and Phps ("Out of my way") are similar to TEV. As some commentators note, the meaning may well be "Get out of my sight" (AT, Brc, NAB) or "Out of my sight" (NIV).

Satan (see comments on 4.10) is here used of Peter, and some translations attempt to make the identification clear for the reader: "you Satan" (AT) and "you satan" (NAB). But other languages may necessitate a totally different restructuring:

"You are acting like Satan," or "You are playing the role of Satan," or "You are speaking the words of Satan."

These latter examples show clearly what Jesus means when he calls Peter **Satan**, but they may lose some of the sharp sting that "Satan" by itself has. Since in the following sentence Jesus shows what he means when he calls Peter this, translators often try to keep the rebuke **Satan** in this sentence and then start the next one with "I call you that because you are an obstacle . . . ."

The noun rendered **hindrance** (so also Mft) or "**obstacle**" (TEV, NJB) is generally given the literal meaning "stumbling block" (NEB, NIV, RSV footnote). Several translations shift to a verb phrase: ". . . you stand right in my path" (Phps); "You hinder me" (AT); "You're doing your best to trip me up!" (Brc); and "You are trying to make me trip and fall" (NAB).

Often translators have to show in what way Peter is being a **hindrance**, as in "You are hindering me from doing God's will" or ". . . from doing what I must do."

For you are not on the side of God contrasts with **but of men**; literally the two clauses read "for you are not thinking the things of God, but the things of men." NEB retains the verb "think" but inverts the order: "You think as men think, not as God thinks" (so also Phps "you think the thoughts of man and not those of God"). On the other hand, NIV follows the order of the Greek as much as English allows: "you do not have in mind the things of God, but the things of men." For many translators, an easier way to express this is "You are thinking like a man, not the way God does" or "The way you are thinking is like a man, not like God."

16.24	RSV	TEV
	Then Jesus told his disciples, "If any man would come after me, let him deny himself and take up his cross and follow me.	Then Jesus said to his disciples, "If anyone wants to come with me, he must forget himself, carry his cross, and follow me.

Several commentators put section headings before verses 24-28 which read something like "The way of suffering that the disciples must follow." The impact of these verses is to remind the followers of Jesus that they must walk the same route that he went.

In the previous verse, the exchange was between Peter and Jesus. What Jesus says now is to all the disciples, so that even if translators do not have a section heading here, most of them will begin a new paragraph. Brc makes the transition quite clear with "Jesus went on to say to his disciples."

Any man is obviously inclusive, with the meaning "**anyone**" (TEV, Mft, NIV).

If . . . would come after me is in reality a call to discipleship; therefore NJB has "If anyone wants to be a follower of mine," and NEB "If anyone wishes to be a follower of mine." Although **come after** does assume a nonliteral meaning for later Christians, it was required of the first disciples that they accompany Jesus on his journey to Jerusalem. Thus one may wish to retain the literal form as much as clarity will allow: "**If anyone wants to come with me**" (TEV; AT and GECL are similar). It will be important, however, to make sure the readers don't think Jesus is only talking about his trip to Jerusalem. "Be my follower," "follow after me," or "go with me" are frequent translations.

Deny himself (so also NAB, NIV, Mft) represents the traditional rendering of most English translations, though some modern translations are more dynamic: "renounce himself" (NJB), "leave self behind" (NEB), "disregard himself" (AT), "give up all right to himself" (Phps), and "once and for all say No to himself" (Brc). GECL 1st edition translates "no longer thinks of himself." In the only other occurrences of the verb in this Gospel, it is used of Peter's denial that he knows Jesus (26.34,35,75).

The phrase beginning with **let him** has often been expressed as "he should" or "he must" (TEV). It may be easier in some languages to restructure the sentence as "The person who wants to follow me should no longer think of himself" or "Before a person can follow me, he has to stop thinking of himself."

Take up (so also NEB, NJB) is the root meaning of the verb translated "**carry**" in TEV. Depending on the context, however, the verb may mean "take up" or "carry," or even "take up and carry." Many languages will require the use of two verbs: "take up and carry."

For a discussion of **take up his cross**, see 10.38.

16.25	RSV	TEV

RSV	TEV
For whoever would save his life will lose it, and whoever loses his life for my sake will find it.	For whoever wants to save his own life will lose it; but whoever loses his life for my sake will find it.

This verse is very similar to 10.39, and translators are referred to that discussion.

Would save his life is translated "wants to save his life" by Mft, Phps, NJB. NEB translates "cares for his own safety," and Brc "keep his life safe." AT renders "preserve his own life." The word which appears as **life** in so many translations actually has "soul" as its first meaning. But all scholars agree that here it is used of the total person, without an assumed distinction between "life" and "soul." TOB, which translates "life," has a footnote stating that both Hebrew and biblical Greek frequently use this noun as an equivalent of the pronouns "I," "you," and "he" or "she." Moreover, in the Lukan parallel (9.25) to this verse, the pronoun "himself" is used in place of **life**.

Some translations of **would save his life** have the idea "wants to keep on living (forever)." This is probably not the best rendering. "Wants to keep his life safe" or "considers his life of greatest importance" are better.

Similarly, it is probably better not to render **loses his life** to mean "if someone dies" or, worse, "commits suicide," although it can be understood as a reference to martyrdom. Expressions of self-denial such as "is prepared to lose his life" (Brc) or "considers his own life as unimportant in order to become my disciple" are better.

Will lose it and **will find it** are normally expressed as "will not (or, will) have true life" or "will not (or, will) have (the) life that doesn't end."

For my sake may be clear in the context, but if not, "to become my follower" or "because he is my disciple" are possible.

The combination of the verbs **would save . . . will lose . . . loses . . . will find** raises some questions regarding the time perspective of this saying. That is, should it be taken in relation to the disciple's life in the world here and now, or does it point toward life after death? In all probability the saying includes both perspectives; a footnote in NJB describes the saying as a "paradox" because it oscillates "between two senses of human 'life': its present stage and its future. . . ." The verse may then be translated "Whoever considers his own life to be of supreme importance will never experience true life. But whoever denies the importance of his own life in order to become my follower will experience true life." In place of "true life" it is possible to use "eternal life."

16.26	RSV	TEV
	For what will it profit a man, if he gains the whole world and forfeits his life? Or what shall a man give in return for his life?	Will a person gain anything if he wins the whole world but loses his life? Of course not! There is nothing he can give to regain his life.

For what will it profit . . . and forfeits his life? is a rhetorical question which expects the answer "Nothing." Therefore TEV restructures the question, "**Will a person gain anything if he wins the whole world but loses his life?**" and follows it with the answer "**Of course not!**" In other languages it may be necessary to say "For a person certainly won't gain anything at all if he wins the whole world but loses his life," or "For it is certainly of no value if, in winning the whole world, a person loses his life." In some languages "obtain" may be better than "win."

Man, as with "any man" in verse 24, refers to people in general, and so is equivalent to "**person**" (TEV).

Or what shall a man give in return for his life? is also a rhetorical question which expects the answer "Nothing." This time TEV restructures it as a statement: "**There is nothing he can give to regain his life.**" Both RSV and TEV seem to interpret **life** of this sentence as a person's physical life here on earth, an interpretation which is apparently supported by NAB: "What profit would a man show if he were to gain the whole world and destroy himself in the process? What can a man offer in exchange for his very self?" NEB seems to have a more psychological understanding: "What will a man gain by winning the whole world, at the cost of his true self? Or what can he give that will buy that self back?" However, it is more probable that the reference is to eternal life, which would be the basis for Mft's shift from "life" in verse 25 to "soul" in this verse: "What profit will it be if a man gains the whole world and forfeits his own soul?" NIV makes this same shift.

Many translators will use the same expression for **life** as they did in the previous verse, such as "true life" or "life that does not end."

For a person to gain **the whole world** does not mean to rule the world. It means to have "everything in the world," or possibly "everything he wants."

16.27 RSV TEV

For the Son of man is to come with his angels in the glory of his Father, and then he will repay every man for what he has done.	**For the Son of Man is about to come in the glory of his Father with his angels, and then he will reward each one according to his deeds.**

At least two aspects of this verse call for general comment: (1) Matthew omits the warning that the Son of Man will deny at his coming those who have denied him on earth, though it is placed in emphatic position in the Marcan parallel (8.38); and (2) Matthew includes an allusion to Psalm 62.12, which indicates that the Son of Man "will reward each one according to his deeds." The omission is best accounted for by the fact that the saying is found earlier in Matthew's Gospel (10.33), while the psalm allusion represents a major theme of the Gospel.

For does not just link verse 27 to the previous question but to what Jesus has been speaking about since verse 24. To make this clear, some translations will have "In fact" or "I tell you all this because."

Is to come (so also NEB; TEV **"about to come"**; NJB "is going to come") translates the Greek text literally. Although this form of the verb may signify no more than the simple future, the context does intimate that the event is conceived of as about to take place in the immediate future, within the lifetime of the people to whom Jesus is speaking. The same Greek verb formation is used in 17.12,22, where the immediate future is definitely in view. Some translations have had "will come soon." In many languages **come** will require some direction or location, so that "come among men," "appear," or "come back" are more natural.

For **Son of man**, see discussion at 8.20. Even though it is generally preferable to retain third-person reference, here Matthew clearly intends that his readers will understand that Jesus is the exalted Lord, the **Son of man**. If the third-person reference in effect denies this intention in a language, one may then translate "For I will return as the Son of man . . . ."

His angels most naturally is taken to mean "his Father's angels." or "God's angels." For **angels**, see comments at 1.20.

In the glory of his Father may be rendered either "in the same glory that his Father has" or "with the glory that his Father gives him." **Glory** is used to refer to the power, brilliance, splendor, presence, authority, and majesty of God, and in various contexts one or another of these aspects can be emphasized in the translation. Here almost any one can fit, but because the verse goes on to speak of judgment, "power that comes from God" or "authority that God gives" are the more common translations.

Note that TEV has restructured slightly, putting **"with his angels"** after **"come in the glory."** Some translators will even make two separate sentences, as in ". . . will come with God's great authority. God's messengers will come with him."

As in many other contexts, **his Father** can be "his Father in heaven" or "God his father."

And then he will repay every man for what he has done comes from Psalm 62.12. NJB translates "he will reward each one according to his behaviour," and Brc "he will settle accounts with each man on the basis of how each man has lived."

GECL 1st edition translates "Then he shall give to each one what he deserves on the basis of his deeds."

Repay is expressed as "**reward**" in TEV. For many readers this is misleading, since for them it will refer only to good things given. But in this verse people are to be punished or blessed depending on whether their actions were bad or good. Therefore ways to translate the sentence include "He will give blessings or punishment to people according to whether they have done good or evil" and "He will punish or reward people according to the things they did."

Note that **he** refers to the Son of Man.

As in most cases, **every man** refers to all people, not just men, and translators can use "all people" or "each person."

16.28	RSV	TEV
	Truly, I say to you, there are some standing here who will not taste death before they see the Son of man coming in his kingdom."	I assure you that there are some here who will not die until they have seen the Son of Man come as King."

Truly, I say to you: see discussion at 5.18; 6.2, where similar constructions are used.

There are some standing here: the use of the verb **standing** is not to imply that some people were standing and others sitting. Rather, in the present context it means "those of you who are here with me now." It can be rendered "some of you standing here with me now." The reference is to the disciples (see verses 13, 21, 24).

Taste death is a Jewish way of saying "**die**" (TEV) without actually mentioning the word itself; the same expression is also used in John 8.52; Hebrews 2.9. In place of the negative form, **will not taste death**, GECL 1st edition has "will yet be alive."

Before they see the Son of man coming may be translated "until the Son of Man comes," which is similar to GECL. The omission of the verb **see** does not represent a shift in focus; the intention of the verse is to affirm the coming of the Son of Man within the lifetime of some of Jesus' disciples.

Coming in his kingdom (so also NEB, NIV) is a literal rendering of the Greek text as is "coming with his kingdom" of NJB, since the Greek preposition may mean either **in** or "with." However, neither of these translations really conveys the impact that the construction had for Jewish readers, for whom **in his kingdom** would have meant "to rule as king." Both TEV ("**come as King**") and Phps ("coming as king") retain a noun phrase to express the concept, while others more effectively shift to an infinitive phrase, showing activity via a verb form: "coming himself to reign" (Mft) and "come to reign" (AT). GECL 1st edition has "when the Son of Man comes with power and glory."

Coming presents some of the same problems here as in the previous verse. That is, "coming here to men (or, to earth)" may be more natural than the simple verb with no location.

Similarly, it may be helpful to indicate over whom or what the Son of Man will reign, as in "rule the world" or "establish his reign over all men."

Although 16.13-28 is divided into two sections by TEV (13-20; 21-28) by the insertion of a section heading before verse 21, it should be noted that the entire section reflects a unity within itself. Both at the beginning (verse 13) and at the end (verse 28), the Son of Man comes into focus, and this is the clue to the framework of the entire section.

Chapter 17

17.1-13

RSV

TEV

The Transfiguration

1 And after six days Jesus took with him Peter and James and John his brother, and led them up a high mountain apart. 2 And he was transfigured before them, and his face shone like the sun, and his garments became white as light. 3 And behold, there appeared to them Moses and Elijah, talking with him. 4 And Peter said to Jesus, "Lord, it is well that we are here; if you wish, I will make three booths here, one for you and one for Moses and one for Elijah." 5 He was still speaking, when lo, a bright cloud overshadowed them, and a voice from the cloud said, "This is my beloved Son,[w] with whom I am well pleased; listen to him." 6 When the disciples heard this, they fell on their faces, and were filled with awe. 7 But Jesus came and touched them, saying, "Rise, and have no fear." 8 And when they lifted up their eyes, they saw no one but Jesus only.

9 And as they were coming down the mountain, Jesus commanded them, "Tell no one the vision, until the Son of man is raised from the dead." 10 And the disciples asked him, "Then why do the scribes say that first Elijah must come?" 11 He replied, "Elijah does come, and he is to restore all things; 12 but I tell you that Elijah has already come, and they did not know him, but did to him whatever they pleased. So also the Son of man will suffer at their hands." 13 Then the disciples understood that he was speaking to them of John the Baptist.

[w] Or *my Son, my* (or *the*) *Beloved*

1 Six days later Jesus took with him Peter and the brothers James and John and led them up a high mountain where they were alone. 2 As they looked on, a change came over Jesus: his face was shining like the sun, and his clothes were dazzling white. 3 Then the three disciples saw Moses and Elijah talking with Jesus. 4 So Peter spoke up and said to Jesus, "Lord, how good it is that we are here! If you wish, I will make three tents here, one for you, one for Moses, and one for Elijah."

5 While he was talking, a shining cloud came over them, and a voice from the cloud said, "This is my own dear Son, with whom I am pleased—listen to him!"

6 When the disciples heard the voice, they were so terrified that they threw themselves face downward on the ground. 7 Jesus came to them and touched them. "Get up," he said. "Don't be afraid!" 8 So they looked up and saw no one there but Jesus.

9 As they came down the mountain, Jesus ordered them, "Don't tell anyone about this vision you have seen until the Son of Man has been raised from death."

10 Then the disciples asked Jesus, "Why do the teachers of the Law say that Elijah has to come first?"

11 "Elijah is indeed coming first," answered Jesus, "and he will get everything ready. 12 But I tell you that Elijah has already come and people did not recognize him, but treated him just as they pleased. In the same way they will also mistreat the Son of Man."

13 Then the disciples understood that he was talking to them about John the Baptist.

SECTION HEADING: TEV has simply "**The Transfiguration**," which is rather a high-level word. "Jesus' appearance is changed" or "The appearance of Jesus changes (or, is changed)" will be easier for many readers to understand. If this proves too complex, then translators can consider "Jesus appears (or, talks) with Moses and Elijah."

The significance of this event in the ministry of Jesus is underscored by the observation that all three of the Synoptic Gospels place it at this point. In the words of one commentator, it is "God's answer to the announcement of the passion." Both Matthew (17.1-13) and Luke (9.28.36) significantly modify Mark's account (9.2-13). Some of these differences, especially as they pertain to the interpretation and translation of Matthew's Gospel, will be noted as they occur.

17.1

RSV	TEV
And after six days Jesus took with him Peter and James and John his brother, and led them up a high mountain apart.	Six days later Jesus took with him Peter and the brothers James and John and led them up a high mountain where they were alone.

And after six days: this formal representation of the Greek text is replaced by the more natural English expression "**Six days later**" in TEV, NEB, and NJB. Brc has "About a week later."

Took translates a present tense in Greek, a form often used in Greek narrative for the sake of vividness. In oral narration English speakers will also occasionally use the present tense for the same purpose, but it is generally not done in formal writing.

In some languages, instead of saying **Jesus took with him Peter and James and John**, it may be better to say "had Peter, James and John go with him" or "asked Peter, James and John to go with him."

In place of the awkward **Peter and James and John his brother**, Mark has "Peter and James and John" (9.2), and Luke has "Peter and John and James" (9.28). It is thought that **John** may have been identified as the brother of James because he was not as well known to the readers of Matthew's Gospel as was James, who was later put to death for his faith (Acts 12.2). **And John his brother** may prove difficult for contemporary readers, who may assume from the wording of RSV that **Peter and James** compose one group, to be distinguished from James, the brother of Jesus. To avoid this confusion TEV translates ". . . **the brothers James and John**," and GECL ". . . the two brothers James and John."

Led can be understood in a general sense of "took," but most translators use a phrase such as "went ahead of" or "had them follow him."

In Jewish thought **a high mountain** was a suitable place for a divine revelation; see 4.8; 5.1; 28.16. Christian tradition tends to identify the mountain with Mount Tabor (588 meters), though Mount Hermon (2,774 meters) is closer to Caesarea Philippi.

For some translators **up a high mountain** is quite natural, but for others "to the top of a high mountain" is better.

Apart translates the adverbial phrase first used in 14.13; it also occurs in verse 19 of this chapter and in 20.17; 24.3. TEV and NEB have "**where they were alone**," and NAB, Mft, NIV each have "by themselves."

17.2	RSV	TEV

And he was transfigured before them, and his face shone like the sun, and his garments became white as light.

As they looked on, a change came over Jesus: his face was shining like the sun, and his clothes were dazzling white.

And he was transfigured before them: the phrase **before them** means "in their presence" (NEB, NJB). TEV inverts the order of the Greek text and avoids the traditional **was transfigured**: "**As they looked on, a change came over Jesus.**" Elsewhere in the New Testament the verb "transfigured" occurs only in the Marcan parallel (9.2), and in Romans 12.2 ("transformed") and 2 Corinthians 3.18 ("changed"). The basic meaning is "undergo a change in form." In the transfiguration accounts it refers to a change that is outwardly visible; in the other two passages the change is internal and cannot be seen by the physical eye. Some English translations provide a dynamic equivalent: "his whole appearance was changed" (Phps) and "his appearance underwent a change" (AT). Another expression is "the way he looked to them changed." Some have found it natural to say "And as they were watching, they saw him change."

His face shone like the sun, and his garments became white as light explains the nature of the change that came over Jesus. In the Gospel of Mark the nature of the change is not explained; there "he was transfigured" is simply followed by the additional statement "and his clothes became shining white—whiter than anyone in the world could wash them" (9.3, TEV). Luke does explain the change, though in different terms from that of Matthew: "his face changed its appearance, and his clothes became dazzling white" (9.29, TEV). A comparison of the three accounts reveals that in Matthew the transformed Jesus is more nearly described in terms which identify him with God, who covers himself with light (Psa 104.2).

His face shone like the sun can also be expressed as "his face shone as brightly as the sun." Similarly **his garments became white as light** means his clothes were shining brightly, so that "his garments shone (or, shone white) like light" can be used. But translators may find that a fairly literal rendering of the text is natural, too. **Garments** refers to "**clothes**" (TEV), or "clothing."

17.3	RSV	TEV

And behold, there appeared to them Moses and Elijah, talking with him.

Then the three disciples saw Moses and Elijah talking with Jesus.

And behold (TEV "**Then**"): see comment at 1.20.

There appeared to them: the Greek verb **appeared** may also be interpreted "was seen," and the phrase **to them** may mean "by them." TEV follows the first of these two alternatives and also makes explicit the persons referred to by the pronoun **them**; thus the translation "**Then the three disciples saw . . . .**" If translators keep the word **appeared**, they may find it natural to say "Moses and Elijah appeared there, and the three disciples saw them talking with Jesus." But the TEV model usually proves quite useful here.

Both Matthew and Luke (9.30) read **Moses and Elijah** in place of "Elijah with Moses" of Mark (9.4). Although Elijah was regarded by the Jews as the forerunner of the Messiah, the linking together of Moses and Elijah is to affirm that both the Law (symbolized by Moses) and the prophets (represented by Elijah) bear witness to Jesus. But naturally the translator can only translate the text, without alluding to this symbolism.

Many readers will not be familiar with **Moses** or **Elijah**. Certainly it is important to convey that these were great Jewish leaders of times past. Some translators have "Moses and Elijah of long ago." It is also possible to have a footnote indicating that Moses was the great leader who led them out of captivity, and that Elijah was a great prophet.

Talking with him: for stylistic reasons TEV explicitly identifies **him** as Jesus. Some translators start a new sentence here: "All of a sudden the disciples saw Moses and Elijah appear. They were talking with Jesus."

17.4   RSV   TEV

And Peter said to Jesus, "Lord, it is well that we are here; if you wish, I will make three booths here, one for you and one for Moses and one for Elijah."

So Peter spoke up and said to Jesus, "Lord, how good it is that we are here! If you wish, I will make three tents here, one for you, one for Moses, and one for Elijah."

And Peter said to Jesus (TEV "**So Peter spoke up and said to Jesus**") is more literally "But answering Peter said to Jesus." Here again stylistic considerations will determine what should be done in the receptor language.

See 8.2 for a discussion of **Lord**. Most translators understand it in the Christian sense here, although Brc has "Master."

It is well that we are here (TEV, AT "**how good it is that we are here**"): this statement may be taken to indicate either that the disciples were overjoyed at being there with Jesus (NJB, Phps "it is wonderful for us to be here"; Brc "it is a wonderful thing for us to be here"), or that the disciples felt the need to serve Jesus together with his two visitors (Mft "it is a good thing we are here"). RSV seems to accept this second interpretation, though its rendering is somewhat ambiguous.

In many languages it is not possible to be ambiguous, however, since there are different ways of saying **we**, depending on whether Peter was speaking of himself and the other two disciples only, or of the three plus Jesus, or of all six who were there. Most translators seem to have felt that in this context Peter was probably referring to all of them, and they have rendered the phrase as "It is really wonderful that we (all) are here." However, a translation like Mft (cited above), which is narrower, or RSV, is certainly acceptable.

If you wish can be "If you want me to" or even "Would you like me to?"

Three booths (Phps, Brc "three shelters") refer to temporary shelters in which Jesus and his companions could spend the night. For Matthew these words were doubtless intended to recall the Festival of Shelters, during which time the Jewish people constructed rough shelters to live in as a commemoration of the years when their ancestors wandered through the wilderness. On the festival see Leviticus 23.33-44.

Most cultures are familiar with some type of temporary shelter that can be used to translate **booths**. "Tents," "field huts," or even "temporary shelters" have all been used by translators.

17.5

RSV	TEV
He was still speaking, when lo, a bright cloud overshadowed them, and a voice from the cloud said, "This is my beloved Son,^{w} with whom I am well pleased; listen to him."	While he was talking, a shining cloud came over them, and a voice from the cloud said, "This is my own dear Son, with whom I am pleased— listen to him!"

^{w} Or *my Son, my* (or *the*) *Beloved*

There are two problems with pronouns in this verse. Translators have to be sure that the **he** who is still speaking is Peter, and they also have to decide who **them** refers to. It seems clear here that all six people were enveloped in the cloud, not just Jesus, Moses, and Elijah. Some translators start the verse with "While Peter was still speaking, a bright cloud came over (all) of them."

Bright translates the same Greek word used in 6.22 ("full of light"). The **bright cloud** is a symbol of God's presence (Exo 13.21-22; 16.10; 19.9). According to 2 Maccabees 2.8, it was expected to reappear in the messianic age. Although to speak of a **bright cloud** may not be normal for some people, the expression can usually be translated easily. "Brilliant cloud," "very white cloud," or "white and dazzling cloud" are phrases translators can consider.

Overshadowed: most English translations retain this literal meaning, though Brc and NIV have "enveloped," and TEV has "**came over**." Since the cloud is full of light, it seems quite possible that the contextual meaning of the verb should be "covered them with its brightness" rather than "covered them with its shadow." Elsewhere in the New Testament the verb appears in the parallels of Mark (9.7) and Luke (9.34), and in Luke 1.35; Acts 5.15. Only in the Acts passage does it seem to have its original meaning of "overshadow." Commentators note that the experience recalls that of Exodus 40.34: "Then the cloud covered the Tent and the dazzling light of the Lord's presence filled it" (TEV).

The last half of this verse is word-for-word the same as 3.17, except that here **from the cloud** replaces "from heaven." See comment at 3.17.

17.6

RSV	TEV
When the disciples heard this, they fell on their faces, and were filled with awe.	When the disciples heard the voice, they were so terrified that they threw themselves face downward on the ground.

The effect of this experience on the disciples (verses 6-7) is without parallel in either Mark or Luke.

Some translators have found that **the disciples** needs to be rendered as "the three disciples," although the context makes this clear enough for most readers.

In the Greek text the verb **heard** is a participle in Greek and does not have an expressed object. But in English an object is obligatory, and most translations supply **this** (RSV, NJB, NAB, NIV); AT has "it." On the other hand Mft ("the voice"), Phps ("this voice"), and NEB ("At the sound of the voice"), together with TEV, provide "**voice**" as the object. GECL translates "When the disciples heard these words." One may even need to translate "When the disciples heard the voice from heaven say these words."

They fell on their faces and were filled with awe: TEV both reverses the order of the two clauses and shifts from a coordinate connection (**and**) to a causative one: "**they were so terrified that they threw themselves downward on the ground.**" It is typical of the biblical languages that they will utilize coordinate structures for what would be more naturally expressed by a different construction in other languages. Here it is obvious that **they fell on their faces** as a result of being **filled with awe**, and TEV has merely made the relation explicit. NEB retains the original sequence but shifts from a coordinate structure: "the disciples fell on their faces in terror." The same is true of Phps and NJB: "the disciples fell on their faces, overcome with fear." Brc has "they flung themselves face down on the ground, for they were terrified."

Fell on their faces is normally not translated literally. **Fell** does not mean they fell accidentally (after stumbling, perhaps), and to fall literally **on their faces** would be quite painful. Most languages will have an idiomatic way of expressing the idea that they deliberately lay down on the ground, possibly with their faces touching the ground, as an act of reverence or great respect.

As can be seen from the examples in the paragraphs above, **filled with awe** does not really reflect the idea of the text. "**Terrified**" is much more accurate.

17.7   RSV   TEV

But Jesus came and touched them, saying, "Rise, and have no fear."

Jesus came to them and touched them. "Get up," he said. "Don't be afraid!"

Came . . . **touched** . . . **saying** translates three verb forms in Greek; **came** and **saying** are actually third person singular forms, while **touched** is a participle. TEV restructures somewhat differently, using three third-person verb forms: "**came . . . touched . . . said.**" Both RSV and TEV, as other standard English translations, merely reflect stylistic variations, and either one is valid. GECL and Lu have "But Jesus came to them, touched them and said . . . ." The touching of the disciples, as with the command **Rise** (TEV "**Get up**"), is reminiscent of the manner in which Jesus touched the sick and dead (8.13,15; 9.25,29) and commanded the daughter of Jairus to get up from her sickbed (9.25).

Came is often more naturally "went to them" or "approached them."

The text does not specify how Jesus **touched** the disciples, nor will most translations. However, if the language does require more detail, then "touched them with his hand" can be used.

Some translators have rendered **have no fear** as "You don't have to be afraid" or "Don't be afraid anymore," but "**Don't be afraid**" of TEV is usually natural.

17.8	RSV	TEV
	And when they lifted up their eyes, they saw no one but Jesus only.	So they looked up and saw no one there but Jesus.

Lifted up their eyes translates a Hebrew idiom which means "**looked up**" (TEV, AT, NAB, NIV, Brc). A literal rendering may sound ridiculous, implying that the disciples may have dropped their eyes on the ground when they fell face downward!

No one but Jesus only: the inclusion of the modifier "only" in the Greek text is for the sake of emphasizing that Jesus was the only one present. TEV has "**no one there but Jesus**." "They didn't see anyone but Jesus" or "the only person they saw was Jesus" will also convey the meaning.

17.9	RSV	TEV
	And as they were coming down the mountain, Jesus commanded them, "Tell no one the vision, until the Son of man is raised from the dead."	As they came down the mountain, Jesus ordered them, "Don't tell anyone about this vision you have seen until the Son of Man has been raised from death."

As they were coming down the mountain may need to be rendered "As Jesus and his disciples were coming down the mountain."

Jesus commanded them: for other commands to silence see 8.4; 9.30; 12.16; 16.20. This is the last time that Jesus issues such a command in this Gospel.

The vision (TEV "**this vision you have seen**"): this is the only place in the Gospels where the word **vision** occurs; in the Marcan parallel (9.9) the text reads "what they had seen." GECL and NIV render **vision** as "what you have seen." The same thing is done also by Phps and Brc, though they both shift to indirect discourse: "Jesus warned them not to tell anyone about what they had seen" (Phps) and "Jesus gave them strict orders not to tell anyone what they had seen (Brc). Visions and dreams were acceptable means of divine revelation (see 1.20; 2.12,13,19). The distinguishing factor is the time element: visions may take place at any moment; dreams are reserved for the time when a person is sleeping. There will be many languages where **vision** is a word known well enough that translators will more likely follow the TEV model than Phps or Brc (cited above).

For **Son of man**, see the discussion at 8.20.

Is raised from the dead: see comments at 16.21 and 14.2. TEV and NEB follow the same interpretation as RSV, since the Greek verb for **raised** is passive in form. The understanding that the verb has an active meaning, "has risen from death," is the exegesis adopted by GECL 1st edition, Lu, NJB, NAB, based on the opinion of some scholars that Matthew intentionally and regularly used the same passive form for resurrection as the verb for "awaken" (as in 1.24; 25.7).

Translators may have to restructure this command: "Don't tell anyone about this vision you have seen before the time when God raises the Son of Man from death" or "You must not tell anyone about what you saw here until after the Son of Man has been raised from death."

17.10

RSV	TEV
And the disciples asked him, "Then why do the scribes say that first Elijah must come?"	Then the disciples asked Jesus, "Why do the teachers of the Law say that Elijah has to come first?"

And the disciples asked him is followed in the Greek text by the participle "saying," which functions to introduce direct discourse. There is strong textual evidence for "his disciples" in place of **the disciples**, but the meaning is the same, and translators will have to restructure according to what is most natural in their own language. For example, "Then Jesus' disciples asked him . . . ."

The scribes were last mentioned in 16.21; the first mention of them is in 2.4.

The question concerning **Elijah** may have been prompted either by the appearance of Elijah on the mountain or else by the standard belief of the Jews that Elijah would prepare the way for the coming Messiah.

Then why do the scribes say that first Elijah must come? is open to misunderstanding, especially if read in light of Jesus' mention of the raising of the Son of Man from death (verse 9). The question then means "Why do the scribes say that Elijah must come before the Son of Man is raised from death?" This is, of course, not what the disciples meant by the question, though the rules of English grammar demand such a meaning. The problem arises because Matthew has left out information which was well known to him and to his readers. Such information is known as "shared information," and it is generally omitted by a writer when he is certain that his readers will understand the background of his remarks. For readers who do not share this same background the question may more accurately be translated "Why do the scribes say that Elijah must come before the Messiah comes?"

Come has sometimes been rendered "return." The disciples were referring to Elijah coming back to be among the living on earth, and "come back to life," "come back to be among us" or even "come back to earth" may be necessary.

For comment on **Elijah**, see 16.14.

17.11

RSV	TEV
He replied, "Elijah does come, and he is to restore all things;	"Elijah is indeed coming first," answered Jesus, "and he will get everything ready.

The statement **Elijah does come** has been rendered by Brc as "It is quite true . . . that Elijah is to come." The implication is that he will precede the coming of the Messiah, so some have said "Elijah will come back first." **Come** may be rendered as in verse 10.

Restore all things (NAB "restore everything") is translated "set everything in order" by Brc, "**get everything ready**" by TEV, and "restore the whole people of God" by GECL. Elsewhere Matthew uses the verb **restore** only in 12.13 in connection with the healing of a man's crippled hand: "and it was restored, whole like the other." The reference to Elijah is perhaps best understood as that of Malachi 4.5-6, where it is promised that Elijah will come before the day of the Lord to reconcile parents and children with one another.

17.12	RSV	TEV

but I tell you that Elijah has already come, and they did not know him, but did to him whatever they pleased. So also the Son of man will suffer at their hands."	But I tell you that Elijah has already come and people did not recognize him, but treated him just as they pleased. In the same way they will also mistreat the Son of Man."

But I tell you translates the same formula used in 8.11; see also 12.6,36.

Translators should use the same verb for **come** here as in the two previous verses.

They did not know him translates a clause in which **they** is used of the Jewish people in general; TEV has "**people**." **They did not know him, but did to him whatever they pleased** may be translated "No one recognized who he was, and everyone treated him just as they pleased." The translation of **did to him whatever they pleased** should convey the idea that people mistreated him in a shameful or disgraceful fashion.

The Son of man will suffer at their hands translates a type of passive structure in which **their hands** represents the agent who brings suffering upon **the Son of man**. TEV restructures as "**they will also mistreat the Son of Man**."

The word **so** relates the way the people mistreated Elijah and the way they will treat the Son of man. Brc has "In exactly the same way." "Similarly, they are also going to make the Son of Man suffer" will also express the correct idea.

17.13	RSV	TEV

Then the disciples understood that he was speaking to them of John the Baptist.	Then the disciples understood that he was talking to them about John the Baptist.

This verse, as the last sentence of the previous verse, is not found in the Marcan parallel. Both RSV and TEV represent a fairly literal rendering of the Greek text.

Some translators will find that they need to make the connection between John and Elijah quite explicit: "Then the disciples understood that in speaking to them about Elijah, Jesus was really speaking about John the Baptist."

17.14-21

RSV	TEV
	Jesus Heals a Boy with a Demon

RSV

14 And when they came to the crowd, a man came up to him and kneeling before him said, 15 "Lord, have mercy on my son, for he is an epileptic and he suffers terribly; for often he falls into the fire, and often into the water. 16 And I brought him to your disciples, and they could not heal him." 17 And Jesus answered, "O faithless and perverse generation, how long am I to be with you? How long am I to bear with you? Bring him here to me." 18 And Jesus rebuked him, and the demon came out of him, and the boy was cured instantly. 19 Then the disciples came to Jesus privately and said, "Why could we not cast it out?" 20 He said to them, "Because of your little faith. For truly, I say to you, if you have faith as a grain of mustard seed, you will say to this mountain, 'Move from here to there,' and it will move; and nothing will be impossible to you."[x]

[x] Other ancient authorities insert verse 21, *"But this kind never comes out except by prayer and fasting"*

TEV

14 When they returned to the crowd, a man came to Jesus, knelt before him, 15 and said, "Sir, have mercy on my son! He is an epileptic and has such terrible fits that he often falls in the fire or into water. 16 I brought him to your disciples, but they could not heal him."

17 Jesus answered, "How unbelieving and wrong you people are! How long must I stay with you? How long do I have to put up with you? Bring the boy here to me!" 18 Jesus gave a command to the demon, and it went out of the boy, and at that very moment he was healed.

19 Then the disciples came to Jesus in private and asked him, "Why couldn't we drive the demon out?"

20 "It was because you do not have enough faith," answered Jesus. "I assure you that if you have faith as big as a mustard seed, you can say to this hill, 'Go from here to there!' and it will go. You could do anything!"[n]

[n] *Some manuscripts add verse 21*: But only prayer and fasting can drive this kind out; nothing else can *(see Mk 9.29)*.

SECTION HEADING: **"Jesus Heals a Boy with a Demon."** Whether translators can follow the TEV section heading or not depends on how they translate verse 18. As will be discussed below, in verse 15 the boy is said to be an epileptic, but in verse 18 the text indicates that he has an evil spirit in him. Consequently translators can have either "Jesus heals an epileptic boy" or "Jesus heals a boy who has an evil spirit in him." For "epileptic," see comments at verse 15.

All three of the Synoptic Gospels place this healing miracle immediately following the descent of Jesus and his disciples from the mountain (Mark 9.14-29; Luke 9.37-43a). Both Matthew and Luke abbreviate significantly the Marcan account, and they do so fairly much at the same places. For Matthew the main focus is upon the saying of Jesus concerning faith (verse 20), which is not found in either of the other two accounts.

And when they came to the   When they returned to the
crowd, a man came up to him and   crowd, a man came to Jesus, knelt
kneeling before him said,   before him,

Mark's introduction to the narrative (9.14-16) is considerably longer than that
of Matthew (17.14) or Luke (9.37).

And when they came to the crowd: since a new section begins here, it may
be advisable to identify by name the persons involved: "When Jesus and his disciples
returned to the crowd" or "When Jesus and his disciples came back down the
mountain to where the crowd was."

A man came up to him: TEV identifies **him** as Jesus, though it seems better
to introduce him in verse 14; however, if that is not done, then Jesus should
definitely be marked by name at this point in the narrative. In some languages **came
up to him** will more naturally be "went up to him" or "approached Jesus."

Kneeling translates a participle dependent upon the main verb **came**. The
receptor language will determine the particular form of these two verb forms; TEV
has "... **came to Jesus, knelt before him.**" Some translators will start a new
sentence: "... approached Jesus. He knelt before Jesus and said."

17.15   RSV   TEV

"Lord, have mercy on my son, for he   and said, "Sir, have mercy on my
is an epileptic and he suffers terri- son! He is an epileptic and has such
bly; for often he falls into the fire, terrible fits that he often falls in the
and often into the water.   fire or into water.

Lord (so also NJB, NAB) is translated "**Sir**" by TEV, Mft, NEB, and Brc. See
comment at 8.2.

TEV and RSV both have **have mercy on**. Translators can use this or "take pity
on," or any expression that will be natural in the receptor language.

As we discussed in 4.24, the word rendered **epileptic** means literally
"moonstruck." This is the origin of the English word "lunatic," a word for someone
who is mentally deranged, and it is for this reason some translations have "lunatic"
(Phps, JB). NAB has "demented." **Epileptic** is the preference of TEV, NEB, NIV and
others. Although **epileptic** may be more accurate as far as modern medical
terminology is concerned, it does not convey the emotional impact as well as
"lunatic." It may be best to translate: "He sometimes goes out of his mind."

Suffers terribly (so also Phps; Mft "suffers cruelly"; NIV "suffering greatly")
represents the wording of some Greek manuscripts. Other manuscripts have "is in
a terrible condition." The UBS Greek New Testament prefers the first of these two
choices, though it indicates there is a "considerable degree of doubt" regarding which
may be the superior wording. Actually, the only significant difference in meaning is
the emphasis: the first wording emphasizes the actual pain involved, while the second
choice stresses more the intensity of the illness. But in translation it is quite possible
that the restructuring will be essentially the same. For example, it is difficult to

determine the textual base of NAB ("in a serious condition"), TEV ("**has such terrible fits**"), and NEB ("has bad fits"), though it is assumed that TEV follows the UBS Greek text.

Often he falls into the fire, and often into the water describes some of the effects of the boy's illness. In translation it may be necessary to repeat the subject and verb in the second clause: ". . . and often he falls into the water." It is also possible to place the two clauses together, as in TEV: "**he often falls in the fire or into the water**."

TEV has linked **suffers terribly** and **falls** ("**has such terrible fits that he often falls . . .**"). In fact this is done quite often by translators. Some possibilities include "For he is an epileptic, and when he falls, often it is into a fire or into water, so that he suffers greatly" and "For he is an epileptic, and he suffers so much when he falls into the water or a fire (because of a fit)."

It is usually not necessary to specify what **fire** or **water** the boy falls into, but in some languages translators have used "a river or lake" for **water**.

17.16   RSV   TEV

And I brought him to your disciples,   I brought him to your disciples, but
and they could not heal him."   they could not heal him."

Brought raises questions concerning the sequence of events: some languages must indicate specifically whether the time reference is the immediate past or the remote past. Did the man bring the boy to Jesus' disciples before their ascent up the mountain, or did he bring him to them after their descent? Moreover, a further question arises concerning what persons are included in the group designated **your disciples**. Were Peter, James, and John included (verse 19 may possibly imply that this was the situation), or were they with Jesus on the mountain at the time that the boy was brought for healing to the other disciples? The impression that one receives is that the boy was brought to Jesus immediately upon his descent from the mountain, which assumes that the boy had previously been brought to Jesus' disciples (with Peter, James, and John absent) during the time that Jesus was on the mountain. However, the function of this event in Matthew's Gospel must be taken into consideration. For him the real focus is upon the saying of Jesus in verse 20, a saying which Matthew addresses to the disciples of his own day. Thus **your disciples** must be inclusive of all, including the three who were with Jesus on the mount of transfiguration; but translators will probably still find it most natural to use a normal past-tense for of **brought**. Note that in some languages **brought** will more naturally be "took."

17.17   RSV   TEV

And Jesus answered, "O faithless   Jesus answered, "How unbe-
and perverse generation, how long   lieving and wrong you people are!
am I to be with you? How long am I How long must I stay with you? How

to bear with you? Bring him here to me."

long do I have to put up with you? Bring the boy here to me!"

Jesus answered: presumably it was the man he was answering, yet his words seem to be addressed either to the disciples or, more likely, after experiencing the lack of faith of the disciples, he is making a general statement about the people of that day. For this reason, in some languages **answered** will more naturally be "Jesus responded by saying (to the disciples)."

To address someone with **O** is not natural in current English, and TEV does not use it.

A **faithless . . . generation** means that the people of that day had no faith. Translators could say "You people have no faith" or "You people don't believe in God at all." As we suggested above, Jesus probably included the disciples as well as the crowds as being people with no faith.

Perverse, representing a participle used as an adjective, is the choice of many English translations. Phps prefers "difficult," TEV has "**wrong**," and AT selects "obstinate" as the meaning. The same form of the participle is also used in Philippians 2.15, where TEV translates "sinful." The basic meaning of the form is "misled" or "led astray," which explains the rendering **perverse**. However, for English readers **perverse** may not be the best choice because it comes too close in sound to "pervert," which implies unnatural sexual behavior. Other expressions such as "misguided" or "confused" are closer to the meaning. One possibility for translating **perverse** will be to use a verb instead of an adjective. The sentence can be "You people! You have no faith and you don't know what is right or wrong."

Both RSV (**How long am I to be with you?**) and TEV ("**How long do I have to put up with you?**") represent fairly literal renderings of the Greek text, which is in the form of a rhetorical question that does not anticipate an answer. It may be altered to a statement: "I hope I don't have to put up with you much longer."

Bring him here: it may be advisable at this point to identify **him** as "**the boy**" (TEV).

17.18   RSV   TEV

And Jesus rebuked him, and the demon came out of him, and the boy was cured instantly.

Jesus gave a command to the demon, and it went out of the boy, and at that very moment he was healed.

And Jesus rebuked him is translated "**Jesus gave a command to the demon**" by TEV, and "Jesus then spoke sternly to the boy" by NEB. The problem is that **him** of the Greek text is not specified. However, there are at least two strong arguments in favor of identifying **him** with the boy: (1) The grammatical relation between verses 17 and 18 demands that the reference is to the boy, and (2) except for the rebuke of the storm in 8.26, every other occurrence of the verb in the Gospel is addressed to people; never is it used of demons (see 12.16; 16.22; 19.13). Nevertheless, the excellent scholarship behind Mft, NIV, AT, Phps, and GECL identifies the demon as the one to whom Jesus directed the rebuke, and this meaning is implied in NJB: "And when Jesus rebuked it the devil came out of the boy." If this exegesis is believed to be valid, then direct discourse may be employed: "Jesus gave a stern command to the demon. He said, 'Come out of the boy' " Whether translators say "And Jesus spoke sharply to the boy" or ". . . to the demon," it is the demon that understands and responds. Translators should therefore let **him** refer to the boy or the demon according to whichever seems the more natural to their readers.

For comments on **rebuked**, see 8.26. Normally this word means to give a command not to do something. But to say "Jesus told him to quit what he was doing" is probably a little awkward. "Spoke sternly to" or "ordered harshly" will fit better in this context.

For **demon**, see the comments at 4.24 and 4.1.

The demon **came out of him**: "went out of him" or "left him" may be better for some languages, but of course translators should use whatever expression would be most commonly used for freeing someone of spirits.

Although both RSV and TEV follow the form of the Greek in retaining verse 18 as one sentence, it will be more effective in some languages to divide it into several smaller units. For example, a new sentence can begin either with the statement that the demon came out of the boy, or with the observation **and the boy was cured instantly**. GECL makes the last clause of this sentence into a separate statement, thus emphasizing the fact of the healing.

Instantly (literally "from that hour") is translated "**at that very moment**" by TEV; Brc has "there and then," and NJB "from that moment." See comments at 8.13 and 9.22.

17.19   RSV   TEV

Then the disciples came to Jesus privately and said, "Why could we not cast it out?"   **Then the disciples came to Jesus in private and asked him, "Why couldn't we drive the demon out?"**

Then (so also TEV, NJB, NIV) translates a Greek particle indicating an indefinite moment of time. A number of translations render "Afterwards" (NEB, Brc, Phps); AT translates "Afterward, when he was alone . . . ." GECL renders "Later."

Came to may be "approached" or "went up to."

The adverb **privately** may be taken with either the verb **came to** (a participle in Greek) or the verb **said**. The end result is practically the same. Brc renders **privately** by "when they were alone."

Cast . . . **out** is the same verb used in 7.22. Many languages will have an indigenous term for the casting out of demons.

It clearly is "**the demon**" (TEV). Other translations, such as GECL ("the evil spirit"), also make the pronominal reference explicit.

He said to them, "Because of your little faith. For truly, I say to you, if you have faith as a grain of mustard seed, you will say to this mountain, 'Move from here to there,' and it will move; and nothing will be impossible to you."*x*

"It was because you do not have enough faith," answered Jesus. "I assure you that if you have faith as big as a mustard seed, you can say to this hill, 'Go from here to there!' and it will go. You could do anything!"*n*

x Other ancient authorities insert verse 21, *"But this kind never comes out except by prayer and fasting"*

nSome manuscripts add verse 21: But only prayer and fasting can drive this kind out; nothing else can (see Mk 9.29)

For stylistic reasons TEV translates **He said to them** as "**answered Jesus**" and places the clause after the quotation. Many languages will find the order "speaker–speaker's words" simpler than "speaker's words–speaker," while other languages find it necessary to mark the speaker before and after the quotation.

The noun phrase **your little faith** is transformed into a clause with subject and verb in TEV: "**you do not have enough faith.**" In place of the noun **little faith**, some Greek manuscripts have the noun "without faith," which scholars believe was introduced by a later scribe because it is a better known word. In fact the support for **little faith** is so much superior to that of the alternative, that none of the modern translations even note the other reading. GECL translates "your faith was not great enough." In instances where **faith** must be rendered as a verb, one may translate "you did not really believe that God would do it" or ". . . would heal the boy."

The purpose of the entire narrative is to focus upon the saying of Jesus regarding faith in the last part of this verse. **For truly I say to you** translates the same formula used in 5.18.

If you have faith as a grain of mustard seed is problematic from at least two perspectives: (1) the average reader will not realize that in the biblical culture the mustard seed was considered one of the smallest seeds; and (2) it is not clear than the comparison is between the size of the seed and the size of the disciples' faith. GECL is somewhat more explicit ("If your faith is only as large as a mustard seed"), as is NEB ("if you have faith no bigger even than a mustard-seed").

Another problem arises in languages where **faith** is normally expressed as a verb. Translators may say "If the way you believe in God is small, just like a mustard seed," but it may be better to drop the comparison and say simply "If you believe in God even a little bit." Note from these examples that if it is necessary to have an object of **faith** it should be "God."

A grain of mustard seed really means "a mustard seed." See comment at 13.32. "The small seed of the mustard plant" is a good way to render it when readers are not familiar with mustard. It is not essential to the story to try to use some plant that readers know.

The word translated **mountain** may also mean "**hill**" (TEV). However, for cultures familiar with mountains and hills, the better choice will doubtless be **mountain**, since the intention is to contrast the small size of the mustard seed with the enormous size of the largest physical object known. Although the words are reminiscent of certain verses from Isaiah (40.4; 49.11), they probably had assumed the form of a proverbial saying for the overcoming of seemingly insurmountable difficulties. In the context, **this mountain** can refer to the one Jesus had descended a short time previously. The translation should not make it seem Jesus was referring to a mountain he was standing on.

You will say (so also NEB) is a simple future in Greek, but the force of the verb is obviously conditional (either "you can say" or "you could say") as a number of translations indicate (for example, JB, Mft, NIV, AT, Phps, GECL).

Both RSV (**Move from here to there**) and TEV ("**Go from here to there**") represent formal translations of the Greek.

If it is more natural to use indirect discourse, translators can have "You could order this mountain to move from this place to that place (or, from one place to another)."

Will move is also a future verb form, but "and it would move" will probably fit the sentence better.

And nothing will be impossible to you represents an unusual and awkward word order for native speakers of English, which TEV simplifies to "**You could do anything**" To accomplish this restructuring, two steps were taken: (1) The two negative forms (**nothing . . . impossible**) were reduced to one simplified positive form, and (2) the unnatural word order (**nothing will be . . . to you**) was changed into a word order that is common among speakers of the language. One way some translations have retained the negatives and still been fairly natural is "There is nothing you couldn't do."

[17.21] RSV TEV

["But this kind never comes out except by prayer and fasting"] [But only prayer and fasting can drive this kind out; nothing else can.]

As footnotes in RSV and TEV both indicate, some manuscripts add verse 21. It is the consensus of scholars that this verse was added to the Gospel at a later date, perhaps under the influence of the parallel in Mark 9.29. There are no apparent reasons why a scribe would have removed the verse, if it had been an original part of the text.

This kind . . . comes out . . . by prayer and fasting is semantically equivalent to "**only prayer and fasting can drive this kind out**" (TEV). For some languages it may be necessary to translate the two nouns **prayer** and **fasting** as verbs: "Only if you pray and fast will you be able to drive this kind out" or "You can drive this kind out only as you pray and fast." Since **this kind** is a reference to demons, GECL translates ". . . can such spirits be driven out."

For a discussion of **fasting**, see comments at 6.16. The sentence can be "You can only drive out this kind of evil spirit by praying and worshiping God by not eating" or "This kind of evil spirit can only be driven out of a person when people have prayed and worshiped God by going without food."

17.22-23

RSV   TEV

**Jesus Speaks Again
about His Death**

22 As they were gathering[y] in Galilee, Jesus said to them, "The Son of man is to be delivered into the hands of men, 23 and they will kill him, and he will be raised on the third day." And they were greatly distressed.

22 When the disciples all came together in Galilee, Jesus said to them, "The Son of Man is about to be handed over to men 23 who will kill him; but three days later he will be raised to life." The disciples became very sad.

[y] Other ancient authorities read *abode*

SECTION HEADING: "**Jesus Speaks Again About His Death**" is similar to the heading at 16.21. Translators can say "Jesus tells his disciples again about his death" or "Jesus talks again about how people will kill him."

17.22   RSV   TEV

As they were gathering[y] in Galilee, Jesus said to them, "The Son of man is to be delivered into the hands of men,

When the disciples all came together in Galilee, Jesus said to them, "The Son of Man is about to be handed over to men

[y] Other ancient authorities read *abode*

As they were gathering: two reasons favor identifying **they** as "**the disciples**" (TEV): (1) the disciples are the last group previously mentioned in the context (verse 19); and (2) in the other two accounts of the prediction of the passion, Matthew specifies the disciples as the ones to whom Jesus made the announcement (16.21; 20.17). Thus the clause may be translated either "**When the disciples all came together**" (TEV) or "When Jesus and all his disciples came together." As RSV's footnote indicates, some Greek manuscripts have the equivalent of "were living" in place of **were gathering**, but most translations prefer the wording which RSV and TEV have in the text. Three exceptions are AT ("were going about"), Phps ("went about together"), and Brc ("were moving about"), all of which give an alternative interpretation of the verb "were living."

The phrase **were gathering** can make it sound in some languages as if the disciples were scattered before they gathered together again. In cases like these, translators may have to say "The disciples met together." "Were together" will not be correct, since the verb does carry some sense of "coming" or "gathering."

For comments on **Son of man**, see 8.20.

Is to be (TEV "**is about to be**") translates the same verb used in 16.27; 17.12. It may designate either an indefinite future or an immediate future, as in GECL ("Soon the Son of Man will be handed over to men"). It may be preferable to shift to an active construction: "Soon the enemies (or, some people) of the Son of Man will hand him over to men 23 who will kill him . . . ."

Delivered: see 4.12, where it also means "had been arrested." The verb is the same, but "arrested" does not fit this context as well as "handed over to" or "taken and put under the authority of."

Into the hands of men is a Hebraic idiom meaning "to the power of men." A similar expression, "into the hands of sinners," is used in 26.45.

The text does not say who the men are to whom Jesus will be **delivered**; it says simply **men**. Some translators have thought this meant men in general, that is human beings, and so have rendered the verse "The Son of Man will be delivered (by God) over to the power of men, and they will kill him." More common (and more likely in our opinion) is the interpretation that **men** simply means "certain people," so that a possible translation is "The Son of Man will be handed over to be under the power of some people (or, certain people) who will kill him."

17.23   RSV   TEV

and they will kill him, and he will be raised on the third day." And they were greatly distressed.

who will kill him; but three days later he will be raised to life." The disciples became very sad.

And he will be raised on the third day, except for the shift to a third person form, translates the same words found in 16.21.

Were . . . distressed is the same verb translated "was sorry" in 14.9; elsewhere in Matthew's Gospel it is used in 18.31; 19.22; 26.22,37. It is sometimes necessary to say "they were very sorry to hear this" or "they were sad because of what he said."

They refers to the disciples, as TEV indicates.

17.24-27

RSV   TEV

Payment of the Temple Tax

24 When they came to Capernaum, the collectors of the half-shekel tax went up to Peter and said, "Does not your teacher pay the tax?" 25 He said, "Yes." And when he came home, Jesus spoke to him first, saying, "What do you think, Simon? From whom do kings of the earth take toll or tribute? From their sons or from others?" 26 And when he said, "From others," Jesus said to him, "Then the sons are free. 27 However, not to give offense to them, go to the sea and cast a hook, and take the first fish that comes up, and when you open its mouth you will find a shekel; take that and give it to them for me and for yourself."

24 When Jesus and his disciples came to Capernaum, the collectors of the Temple tax came to Peter and asked, "Does your teacher pay the Temple tax?"

25 "Of course," Peter answered.

When Peter went into the house, Jesus spoke up first, "Simon, what is your opinion? Who pays duties or taxes to the kings of this world? The citizens of the country or the foreigners?"

26 "The foreigners," answered Peter.

"Well, then," replied Jesus, "that means that the citizens don't have to pay. 27 But we don't want to offend these people. So go to the lake and drop in a line. Pull up the first fish you hook, and in its mouth you will find a coin worth enough for my Temple tax and yours. Take it and pay them our taxes."

552

SECTION HEADING: as is often the case with headings, "**Payment of the Temple Tax**" may better be rendered by a short sentence such as "Jesus talks about the temple tax." See verse 24 below for a discussion of this "**tax**."

Only Matthew includes this narrative in his Gospel, and he must have done so because of the particular needs of the community he addressed. Every male Jew twenty years and over was required to pay an annual Temple tax; only priests, and occasionally teachers of the Law, were exempt. And so the earliest Jewish converts to Christianity must have raised the question whether they should continue to make this payment. The narrative provides a two-fold reply: (1) although the "sons" (that is, the Christian converts) were free, they were still called upon to acknowledge the holiness of the Temple; and (2) God will provide for the needs of his people, even if it demands a miracle.

17.24	RSV	TEV
	When they came to Capernaum, the collectors of the half-shekel tax went up to Peter and said, "Does not your teacher pay the tax?"	When Jesus and his disciples came to Capernaum, the collectors of the Temple tax came to Peter and asked, "Does your teacher pay the Temple tax?"

When they came to Capernaum introduces a new section where public reading is frequently begun. Therefore it is important to identify **they** as "**Jesus and his disciples**" (TEV, NIV, GECL, FRCL).

Capernaum has already been identified as a town in this gospel, but some translators have nevertheless said here "the town of Capernaum."

The collectors of the half-shekel tax went up to Peter and said: there is apparently a time lapse between the arrival of the group in Capernaum and this event, since Jesus is evidently in the house (verse 25) at the time that the tax collectors approach Peter. The verse may then be opened as follows: "Jesus and his disciples came to Capernaum. While they were there, the collectors of the Temple tax came to Peter and asked . . . ."

The half-shekel tax (literally "the two-drachma coin") indicates the amount, while TEV defines the nature of the tax ("**the Temple tax**"). NJB translates "the half-shekel," with a footnote "a yearly tax levied on individuals for the upkeep of the Temple." Reference is to the tax which, according to Exodus 30.13, was required of every male Jew from the age of twenty onward. After the destruction of the Temple in A.D. 70, the Romans continued to collect this annual tax, but applied it to the support of the Temple of Jupiter Capitolinus.

It is not the amount of **the half-shekel tax** that is really important in this verse, but rather the nature of it, as seen in TEV. Translators can say "the tax all the men (or, all Jewish men) paid for the Temple expenses" or "the tax paid to support the Temple."

The collectors of the half-shekel tax can then be "the men who collected the money everyone (or, all Jewish men) paid for the Temple."

Some translators have wanted to give some indication of the amount of money and have said "the tax of money of half a shekel" or even "the money called a half-shekel that people had to pay to the Temple." It is also possible to indicate in a footnote that this was about half the wages a laborer would earn in a day. But this is marginal information and does not need to be specified in the text. Another rendering some have used is "the small amount of money people had to pay to support the Temple." But translators should be careful not to make the expression too cumbersome nor such that it gives more emphasis to the amount of money than to its function.

For "**Temple**," see comments on 4.5.

Does not your teacher pay the tax? is a difficult question form in English, which is simplified in TEV: "**Does your teacher pay the Temple tax?**" The question does seem to expect "Yes" as an answer, so "Your teacher does pay his Temple tax, doesn't he?" will also be a good rendering. **Tax** is the same Greek word translated **half-shekel tax** by RSV in the first half of the verse; both TEV and NEB have "**Temple tax**" for each of the two occurrences.

17.25 RSV	TEV
He said, "Yes." And when he came home, Jesus spoke to him first, saying, "What do you think, Simon? From whom do kings of the earth take toll or tribute? From their sons or from others?"	"Of course," Peter answered. When Peter went into the house, Jesus spoke up first, "Simon, what is your opinion? Who pays duties or taxes to the kings of this world? The citizens of the country or the foreigners?"

Yes appears in TEV as "**Of course**." NEB translates "He does," NIV has "Yes, he does," and NAB has "Of course he does." Any translation is satisfactory which indicates a strong affirmative. Languages that normally use indirect discourse can have "Peter assured him that Jesus did pay the tax."

When he came home translates another participial clause in which the subject is not explicitly mentioned, though in the main clause **Jesus** is stated as subject. NIV ("When Peter came into the house") is similar to TEV's "**When Peter went into the house**." JB makes the identification explicit, though in an entirely different way: " 'Oh yes' he replied, and went into the house."

The use of **home** indicates that the house Peter entered was the one where Jesus lived, and some translators have said "When Peter returned to Jesus' house" or ". . . the house where Jesus lived." This is acceptable, but this fact is not in focus here, and if translators find that the expression they would have to use to include this information makes the sentence long or awkward, then "**the house**" (TEV) is certainly better.

Jesus spoke to him first, saying is somewhat abbreviated in TEV: "**Jesus spoke up first**." NJB restructures slightly: "But before he could speak." Brc is similar: "before he could even mention the matter."

What do you think? is translated "**what is your opinion?**" by TEV. NEB renders "What do you think about this." The reference is to the questions which follow. Translators may say "Here is a question, Simon. What do you think about it?"

"Simon, what is your answer to this question (I have)?" or "I have a question for you, Simon."

Simon is used as a noun of address in place of Peter, the name used in the narration. Elsewhere in Matthew's Gospel **Simon** occurs in 4.18; 10.2; 16.16,17.

From whom do the kings of the earth take toll or tribute? is a form in which the **kings** are the subject of a verb for collecting taxes; this may be altered to have the taxpayers as subject: "Who pays . . . to the kings of the earth." The focus on who pays can be made explicit with "Who are the people who have to pay taxes and fees to the kings of the earth?" The question may also be restructured slightly: "When kings collect fees and taxes, whom do they take them from?" or "Who are the people that kings make pay taxes and fees?"

The **kings of the earth** may be rendered more simply as "rulers" or "kings."

It is probably impossible to draw a firm distinction between **toll** and **tribute**; one standard Greek dictionary defines **toll** as "(indirect) tax, customs, duties" and **tribute** as "tax, poll tax." The English translations are quite diverse in the terms which they choose: "tax or toll" (NEB), "duty and taxes" (NIV), "duties and taxes" (AT), "customs or taxes" (Mft), and "**duties or taxes**" (TEV). Translators should feel free to use whatever words are used in their languages for fees and taxes that people often have to pay. It is not necessary to keep the exact distinction between **toll** and **tribute**, nor even to use two different words if two different kinds of taxes are not known.

From their sons or from others? is difficult for at least the following reasons: (1) it presupposes the existence of a subject, verb, and object which are not explicitly mentioned here but are implied from the previous question and are understood in the Greek to be carried over to this question ("Do the kings collect these taxes from . . . ?"); and (2) **their sons** is a Hebrew idiom which will not be understood by many readers with the meaning that it has in the present context. The reference is to citizens of a king's own country who would normally not have been taxed, whereas **others** (citizens of conquered countries) would have been taxed. TEV translates **their sons . . . others** as "**The citizens of the country . . . the foreigners.**" This can also be "from their own people or from foreigners?" The two questions may be restructured into one: "When kings take taxes and fees, do they take them from their own people or from foreigners?"

Today many governments collect taxes and fees from their own people, and some translators may need a footnote indicating that in those days, kings normally taxed the people they had conquered, not their own citizens.

17.26	RSV	TEV

And when he said, "From others," Jesus said to him, "Then the sons are free.

"The foreigners," answered Peter.

"Well, then," replied Jesus, "that means that the citizens don't have to pay.

Then the sons are free means they are exempt from taxes. Mft translates "So their own people are exempt," and NEB is similar; TEV has ". . . **that means that**

555

the citizens don't have to pay." To retain **free** some translators have said "Then the citizens are free from having to pay tax."

17.27 RSV	TEV
However, not to give offense to them, go to the sea and cast a hook, and take the first fish that comes up, and when you open its mouth you will find a shekel; take that and give it to them for me and for yourself."	But we don't want to offend these people. So go to the lake and drop in a line. Pull up the first fish you hook, and in its mouth you will find a coin worth enough for my Temple tax and yours. Take it and pay them our taxes."

However, not to give offense to them is represented much more clearly in TEV: "**But we don't want to offend these people.**" Another rendering is "But we don't want these people to be upset with us (or, because of us)." One may need to identify **them** (TEV "**these people**") as "these men who have come to collect the taxes," or "these people who are here with us," or "these people who are not my disciples."

Go to the sea and cast a hook is translated "go and cast a line in the lake" by NEB. NIV has "go to the lake and throw out your line." The Greek noun does have **sea** as its first meaning, but the body of water referred to here is Lake Galilee. To translate **sea** would imply for many readers the Mediterranean Sea, especially if they were not well acquainted with the geography of Palestine. "**A line**" (or "your line") is much more idiomatic English than is the literal **a hook**. Of course, whether **hook** or "**line**" is used, some translators will have to add "for catching fish." The instructions can be "Go down to the lake and throw out your fishing line" or "Go down to the lake with your line and catch a fish."

A literal translation such as is found in RSV and Brc, **take the first fish that comes up**, may suggest voluntary action on the part of the fish. "Take the first fish that bites" (JB), "Pull up the first fish you hook," and "Take the first fish you catch" are more natural English expressions to describe catching fish.

When you open its mouth you will find a shekel will not be understood by the average English readers, who will not be familiar with a coin called **shekel**. Moreover, even if the reader should be familiar with **shekel** as the name of a coin, it is not likely that he would readily identify it as equal in value to two of the coins mentioned in verse 24. NEB has "silver coin," which is indicated in the context to be of sufficient amount for the payment of the Temple tax for Jesus and Peter. GECL is able to use one word which means "assessment" or "tax amount"; TEV qualifies **shekel** as "**a coin worth enough for my Temple tax and yours.**"

Take that and give it to them for me and for yourself is somewhat shortened in TEV: "**Take it and pay them our taxes**"; GECL has "Take it and pay the assessment for both of us!"

Chapter 18

18.1-5

RSV	TEV
	Who Is the Greatest?
1 At that time the disciples came to Jesus, saying, "Who is the greatest in the kingdom of heaven?" 2 And calling to him a child, he put him in the midst of them, 3 and said, "Truly, I say to you, unless you turn and become like children, you will never enter the kingdom of heaven. 4 Whoever humbles himself like this child, he is the greatest in the kingdom of heaven.	1 At that time the disciples came to Jesus, asking, "Who is the greatest in the Kingdom of heaven?"
	2 So Jesus called a child, had him stand in front of them, 3 and said, "I assure you that unless you change and become like children, you will never enter the Kingdom of heaven. 4 The greatest in the Kingdom of heaven is the one who humbles himself and becomes like this child. 5 And whoever welcomes in my name one such child as this, welcomes me.
5 "Whoever receives one such child in my name receives me;	

SECTION HEADING: "**Who Is the Greatest?**" For some translators, changing from a question to statement will be easier to express: "The disciples ask Jesus who is the most important." Another option is "Jesus tells who is the most important (or, greatest) in God's kingdom."

Matthew 18.1–19.2 is generally recognized by New Testament scholars as a document of guidelines for conduct within the Christian community. Although "child" (verses 2,4,5), "children" (verse 3), and "these little ones" (verse 6) serve as the point of departure for Jesus' instructions, the real application of the chapter is to the believers of Matthew's day who are referred to by these terms. In the first part of the chapter there are parallels to both Mark and Luke (Matt 18.1-5 has Mark 9.33-37 and Luke 9.46-48 as parallels, and Matt 18.6-9 has Mark 9.42-48 and Luke 17.1-2 as parallels), and later there are other parallels to Luke (Matt 18.10-14 is parallel to Luke 16.3-7, and Matt 21–22 is parallel to Luke 17.3-4). But the place that the chapter occupies within the framework of the Gospel and the arrangement of the material within the chapter indicate that it is best understood as a "handbook for Christian discipleship."

18.1

RSV	TEV
At that time the disciples came to Jesus, saying, "Who is the greatest in the kingdom of heaven?"	**At that time the disciples came to Jesus, asking, "Who is the greatest in the Kingdom of heaven?"**

557

Matthew departs from Mark by the inclusion of the discussion about the Temple tax (17.24-27). Now in this brief narrative he again adopts the Marcan scheme of events, though the differences in presentation are such as to suggest that Matthew has concentrated on the question of rank in the Kingdom rather than on the actual rivalry of the Twelve.

At that time (so also TEV, NEB) is literally "In that hour" (see comment at 8.13). GECL translates "About this time." The function of the phrase is to indicate that the following event took place in immediate sequence to the discussion of the Temple tax. Translators can also say "Shortly after that" or "A short time later."

The disciples came to Jesus is a fairly literal rendering of the Greek text. For many languages it will be better to translate "Jesus' disciples came to him." In some, translators will find "went" more natural than **came**.

The question of the disciples, **Who is the greatest in the kingdom of heaven?** is not easy to restructure meaningfully. GECL translates "Who will be the greatest in God's new world?" and INCL has "Who will be considered the greatest among God's people?" **Greatest** here means "most important" or "of highest rank," so translators must avoid a translation that will refer to size.

Kingdom of heaven was discussed at 3.2. This question of the disciples can be rendered "When God's rule is established, who will be the most important in it?" or "Of the people who are part of God's reign, who is the most important?" or "Who is the most important person in God's kingdom?"

18.2	RSV	TEV
	And calling to him a child, he put him in the midst of them,	**So Jesus called a child, had him stand in front of them,**

And calling to him a child is unusual word order for English speakers; TEV introduces Jesus by name and restructures: "**So Jesus called a child.**" The question put to Jesus by the disciples in verse 1 is answered both by deed (verse 2) and word (verses 3-5). Matthew implies that the child was present in the house at the time, so that Jesus was not required to get up and go outside to call for a child. As was customary for Jewish teachers who were engaged in giving instruction, Jesus probably had been sitting, and there is no hint in the text that he moved from this position when calling the child.

The phrase **calling to him** does not mean that Jesus called out loud to the child, as if he or she were far away, but means simply "summoned" or "asked to come to him." There are languages where direct discourse will be natural, as in "Jesus said to a child there, 'Come here.' "

Child is the same word used in 2.8 (see there).

He put him in the midst of them (TEV "**had him stand in front of them**") may be transformed into direct discourse: "And said to the child, 'Stand here in front of these people' " or ". . . 'Stand here where all of these people can see you.' " A causative form may be employed: "and caused him . . . ." One may also translate "and placed him in front of his disciples" or ". . . where all of his disciples could see him."

RSV	TEV
and said, "Truly, I say to you, unless you turn and become like children, you will never enter the kingdom of heaven.	and said, "I assure you that unless you change and become like children, you will never enter the Kingdom of heaven.

As both RSV and TEV indicate, this verse is a continuation of the sentence begun in verse 2. For many languages it will be advisable to begin a new sentence with verse 3.

Truly, I say to you translates the same expression used in 5.26, except that **you** is plural here. Its function is to place heavy emphasis upon the saying which follows.

Unless you turn and become like children does not refer to a return to the state of childhood in all its respects. As TOB's footnote correctly indicates, the contrast is between the pretentious attitude of the disciples and the lack of pretention on the part of a child. Children are humble and unconcerned about status, whereas the disciples are each hoping for the highest position within the kingdom. Phps translates "unless you change your whole outlook and become like little children"; Brc is similar: "unless you change the whole direction of your lives . . . ." In place of the negative form, a positive statement may be substituted: "You must completely change your attitude and . . . ."

There are translators who have felt that they should make the basis of the simile **like children** explicit by using an expression such as "become humble like children are" or "become unpretentious the way children are." However, if as we suggest above, **turn** is translated with an expression such as "change your lives," then it is not necessary to fill out the comparison like this. "Unless you change and take the attitude a child has" can be sufficient.

Translators can use "a child" or **children**, whichever fits the context better.

You will never enter the kingdom of heaven may also require considerable restructuring. GECL has "then you will never enter into God's new world." Other translations have said "then you will never become a part of God's kingdom" or "then you will never be one of the people under the rule of God." By changing "unless" to "only if," InCl is able to use a positive statement: "only if you change and become as children, can you become a part of God's people."

RSV	TEV
Whoever humbles himself like this child, he is the greatest in the kingdom of heaven.	The greatest in the Kingdom of heaven is the one who humbles himself and becomes like this child.

Whoever humbles himself like this child: as a comparison of RSV and TEV will immediately indicate, TEV reverses the order of the two clauses in this verse. **Like this child** may prove difficult because it lacks an explicit comparison. Brc ("It is the man who thinks as little of his importance as this little child") and Phps ("It is the man who can be as humble as this little child") both attempt to spell out the meaning clearly, as does NAB ("Whoever makes himself lowly, becoming like this child"). One may also translate: "Who becomes as humble as this child" or ". . . as a child."

The person who **humbles himself** accepts a position of low status, considers himself insignificant, or is meek. The examples of Brc and NAB above are good renderings.

For **greatest in the kingdom of heaven**, see comments at verse 1.

18.5   RSV   TEV

"Whoever receives one such   And whoever welcomes in my name
child in my name receives me;   one such child as this, welcomes me.

In several translations (RSV, NJB, NAB) a new paragraph is introduced with verse 5. This is apparently done on the basis of the assumption that (1) **child** serves as the connecting link between the two paragraphs, and that (2) the application of Jesus' teaching begins with verse 5. On the other hand, it is just as logical to propose that the verse forms a natural conclusion to the discussion of who is the greatest, and that "one of these little ones" of verse 6 is actually the connecting link between the two paragraphs.

Whoever may be "any person who," or it can be restructured slightly in a phrase like "If someone welcomes a child like this one in my name, that person welcomes me."

Receives was discussed in 10.40. "**Welcomes**" (TEV) or "accepts" are the most common ways of expressing the word here.

One such child (TEV "**one such child as this**") is fairly representative of what appears in most all translations. "A child like this one" is also common. **Child** may refer either to an actual child or, more probably, to "the one who humbles himself and becomes like this child" of verse 4. By means of a footnote NJB indicates that the second of these two alternatives is intended here.

In my name is a literal rendering of the Greek text; Mft and Phps, who are among the very few who avoid a literal translation, have "for my sake." One may also translate "because of me" or "because he is one of my disciples."

Receives me is translated "**welcomes me**" by TEV, NJB, NAB, NIV (similarly Phps). The picture is that of welcoming or accepting a person into one's group or home. Translators normally render **receives me** with the same verb they used at the beginning of the verse for **receives one such child**.

18.6-9

RSV   TEV

Temptations to Sin

6 but whoever causes one of these little ones who believe in me to sin,^{z} it would be better for him to have a great millstone fastened round his neck and to be drowned in the depth of the sea.

7 "Woe to the world for temptations to sin!^{a} For it is necessary that temptations come, but

6 "If anyone should cause one of these little ones to lose his faith in me, it would be better for that person to have a large millstone tied around his neck and be drowned in the deep sea. 7 How terrible for the world that there are things that make people lose their faith! Such things will

woe to the man by whom the temptation comes! 8 And if your hand or your foot causes you to sin,[z] cut it off and throw it away; it is better for you to enter life maimed or lame than with two hands or two feet to be thrown into the eternal fire. 9 And if your eye causes you to sin,[z] pluck it out and throw it away; it is better for you to enter life with one eye than with two eyes to be thrown into the hell[b] of fire.

[z] Greek *causes . . . to stumble*
[a] Greek *stumbling blocks*
[b] Greek *Gehenna*

always happen—but how terrible for the one who causes them!

8 "If your hand or your foot makes you lose your faith, cut it off and throw it away! It is better for you to enter life without a hand or a foot than to keep both hands and both feet and be thrown into the eternal fire. 9 And if your eye makes you lose your faith, take it out and throw it away! It is better for you to enter life with only one eye than to keep both eyes and be thrown into the fire of hell.

SECTION HEADING: "**Temptations to Sin**" is drawn from verse 7 of RSV. One possible rendering is similar to the TEV translation of that verse; for example, "Things that make people sin" or "Things which lead people to sin." Another way of handling it is to say "Jesus warns about causing others to sin." As we point out below, not all translators will begin a new paragraph and have a section heading here.

18.6 RSV	TEV
but whoever causes one of these little ones who believe in me to sin,[z] it would be better for him to have a great millstone fastened round his neck and to be drowned in the depth of the sea.	"If anyone should cause one of these little ones to lose his faith in me, it would be better for that person to have a large millstone tied around his neck and be drowned in the deep sea.

[z] Greek *causes . . . to stumble*

In the text, verse 6 is a continuation of the sentence begun in verse 5, but TEV has begun a new paragraph here and even has a section heading. Some translators will begin new paragraphs at the beginning of verse 7 or verse 8. The key factor in determining where to begin the paragraph is the translation of **one of these little ones**, discussed below. If translators interpret the phrase to refer to children, then they will not begin a new paragraph here. However, our opinion (see below) is that the expression is figurative and refers to believers. Beginning a new paragraph is a natural result of this interpretation.

The verb **causes . . . to sin** (see comment on 5.29), used three times in verses 6-9, together with the related noun "temptations to sin" (see comments on 13.41), used three times in verse 7, reveal the theme that unites this series of sayings which represent a major thrust of the Gospel (5.29-30; 11.6; 15.12; 16.23; 17.27; 24.10; 26.31-35). TEV combines **who believe in me** with the literal "causes . . . to stumble" and translates "**should cause one of these little ones to lose his faith in me.**" GECL 1st edition is similar: "whoever destroys the childlike faith which someone has in me." The broader interpretation of RSV (**causes . . . to sin**) is certainly possible, but the context strongly suggests that the specific nature of the sin has to do with causing a fellow believer to lose faith in Jesus. Mft seems to walk a line midway between these two interpretations: "But whoever is a hindrance to one of these little ones who believe in me."

Most translations have dropped the literal "stumble" noted in the RSV footnote because of the strong possibility it will be understood literally. It is possible, however, in at least a few languages to retain the form with an expression such as "stumble into sin" or "stumble in their belief (in me)."

For those who prefer the interpretation of **causes . . . to sin** followed by GECL 1st edition and TEV, "**cause . . . to lose his faith in me**," it may be necessary to use a verb to express "faith," as in "causes one of these little ones to stop believing in me."

One of these little ones (see comment at 10.42) renews the theme which was inaugurated by the mention of "child" in verses 4-5, though the meaning of **these little ones** is clearly figurative and refers to Jesus' disciples. Therefore it would be inaccurate to translate "one of these little children." However, "one of these little ones" in a translation will probably still seem to be referring to children. "One of these people, like children to me" will perhaps convey the meaning, but translators may be more comfortable with a translation similar to that in GECL (cited above), possibly "Those people who do trust in me like children, if someone causes them to lose their faith, it would be better for that person to have a huge millstone tied around his neck and be thrown into the deep part of the sea."

Although there are numerous places where Matthew associates faith with Jesus, this is the only place in the entire Gospel where he uses the phrase **in me** (meaning "in Jesus") for the object of faith. This observation underscores the significance that Matthew attaches to the message of the chapter: there can be no greater sin than to cause one of these "little ones" to lose faith in Jesus. The illustration in the second half of the verse describes precisely how enormous that sin really is.

A great millstone (TEV "**a large millstone**") is literally "a donkey millstone," referring to the large stone that was turned by a donkey, rather than to the small stone used at a handmill. Needless to say, even the best swimmer would drown with such a stone tied around his neck. In areas where readers will not know what **a great millstone** is, translators can say "a large stone" or "a large stone for grinding grain." But translators will need to be sure readers don't think of a small stone for grinding grain by hand.

To have . . . fastened . . . and be drowned may be translated impersonally as "to have someone tie . . . and drown him" or ". . . and cause him to drown." Another way to express it is "It would be better for that person if someone tied a large millstone around his neck and threw him into the deepest part of the sea."

In the depth of the sea (TEV "**in the deep sea**") may also be phrased "in the deepest part of the sea." **Depth** is used only here in Matthew, and outside the Gospel it is used just once (Acts 27.5). The noun refers to the open sea, the deepest part of the sea.

18.7	RSV	TEV

"Woe to the world for temptations to sin!*a* For it is necessary that

How terrible for the world that there are things that make people lose

temptations come, but woe to the man by whom the temptation comes!	their faith! Such things will always happen—but how terrible for the one who causes them!

^a Greek *stumbling blocks*

Woe (TEV "**How terrible**"): see comment at 11.21.

The world here speaks of "the people of the world" as opposed to "God's people."

The noun translated **temptations to sin** (literally "stumbling blocks," or better, "traps") in its initial occurrence, and **temptations** in its other two occurrences in this verse, is discussed in 13.41, and the corresponding verb in 5.29 and 18.6.

Sin often needs a subject, in this case, the people of the world. Brc has restructured in a helpful way: "The tragedy of the world is the existence of the things which make men sin." Similar translations are "How terrible it is that there are things in the world that make people sin" and "The terrible thing about the world is that there are things that lead people to sin."

For it is necessary that temptations come can be rendered as "It is inevitable that there will be things that cause people to sin," "Things that make people give up their faith are always going to happen," "We cannot avoid having things happen that could cause us to sin," or "Things that can cause us to sin must happen."

By whom temptation comes is translated "**for the one who causes them**" by TEV and "for the one who is guilty of it" by GECL 1st edition. Brc translates the last part of the verse "but tragic is the fate of the man who is responsible for the coming of such a thing!"

The phrase **the man by whom** is not referring to one specific individual, but means "any person who causes someone else to do wrong." "But how terrible it will be for someone who is the cause of another sinning" will be one way to render the idea of this sentence. The verse can be "There are bound to be things that make people sin, but the person who is responsible for those things has a terrible fate in store."

18.8-9 RSV	TEV

| 8 And if your hand or your foot causes you to sin,^z cut it off and throw it away; it is better for you to enter life maimed or lame than with two hands or two feet to be thrown into the eternal fire. 9 And if your eye causes you to sin,^z pluck it out and throw it away; it is better for you to enter life with one eye than with two eyes to be thrown into the hell^b of fire. | 8 "If your hand or your foot makes you lose your faith, cut it off and throw it away! It is better for you to enter life without a hand or a foot than to keep both hands and both feet and be thrown into the eternal fire. 9 And if your eye makes you lose your faith, take it out and throw it away! It is better for you to enter life with only one eye than to keep both eyes and be thrown into the fire of hell. |

^z Greek *causes . . . to stumble*
^b Greek *Gehenna*

These two verses are similar to 5.29-30; therefore, only a few additional comments need be made: (1) The body parts differ. In 5.29-30 the arrangement is "right eye . . . right hand"; here it is **your hand or your foot . . . eye**. (2) The place of final punishment is described in slightly different terms. In 5.29-30 it is "hell" as opposed to **eternal fire . . . fire of hell** of the present passage. (3) The expression **enter life**, absent from the earlier passage, is used twice here.

The expression **enter life** is difficult, because for many readers it will mean simply "enter into this life," that is, "be born." The reference is to eternal life, and GECL translates "to live with God" (verse 8) and "to live eternally" (verse 9). INCL translates both times as "to live with God." "To receive real life" or "to have the life that doesn't end" are also good. TOB provides a footnote, indicating that the meaning is eternal life, and at the same time noting that the word "life" is used in the same sense as in 7.14; 19.16,29; 25.46.

The majority of translators and commentators understand both **eternal fire** and **hell of fire** as reference to the place of final destruction. Phps, however, wrongly distinguishes between the two: "the everlasting fire . . . the fire of the rubbish-heap." One way to avoid a false distinction is to render **eternal fire** by "hell, where the fire doesn't go out (or, burns forever)" and **hell of fire** as "the fire of hell" or "hell, where the fire is." For more comments on the terms **hell** and "Gehenna," see also 5.22,29.

<hr/>

18.10-14

RSV

TEV

The Parable of the Lost Sheep

10 "See that you do not despise one of these little ones; for I tell you that in heaven their angels always behold the face of my Father who is in heaven.^{c} 12 What do you think? If a man has a hundred sheep, and one of them has gone astray, does he not leave the ninety-nine on the mountains and go in search of the one that went astray? 13 And if he finds it, truly, I say to you, he rejoices over it more than over the ninety-nine that never went astray. 14 So it is not the will of my^d Father who is in heaven that one of these little ones should perish.

10 "See that you don't despise any of these little ones. Their angels in heaven, I tell you, are always in the presence of my Father in heaven.^{o} 12 "What do you think a man does who has one hundred sheep and one of them gets lost? He will leave the other ninety-nine grazing on the hillside and go and look for the lost sheep. 13 When he finds it, I tell you, he feels far happier over this one sheep than over the ninety-nine that did not get lost. 14 In just the same way your^p Father in heaven does not want any of these little ones to be lost.

^{c} Other ancient authorities add verse 11, *For the Son of man came to save the lost*
^{d} Other ancient authorities read *your*

^{o} *Some manuscripts add verse 11*: For the Son of Man came to save the lost *(see Lk 19.10).*
^{p} your; *some manuscripts have* my.

SECTION HEADING: "**The Parable of the Lost Sheep**." For a discussion of "**Parable**," see 13.3. Here "The story of the lost sheep" or "Jesus tells a story about a lost sheep" are possible headings. "**Lost Sheep**" is sometimes a problem if it indicates to readers that the sheep had somehow been misplaced. "Jesus tells the story of the sheep that became lost" or ". . . that the owner could not find" may be necessary.

This parable also occurs in the Gospel of Luke (15.3-7), but there the application is totally different. Here it is addressed to the disciples, with the intention of encouraging them to seek those who have gone astray within their own fellowship. In Luke, on the other hand, it is a condemnation of the self-righteous attitude of the scribes and Pharisees.

The expression **these little ones**, which is found in verses 10 and 14, serves as the link between this and the preceding section.

18.10 RSV	TEV
"See that you do not despise one of these little ones; for I tell you that in heaven their angels always behold the face of my Father who is in heaven.^{c}	"See that you don't despise any of these little ones. Their angels in heaven, I tell you, are always in the presence of my Father in heaven.^{o}
^{c} Other ancient authorities add verse 11, *For the Son of man came to save the lost*	^{o}*Some manuscripts add verse 11*: For the Son of Man came to save the lost *(see Lk. 19.10).*

See that you do not despise may be translated "Be careful not to look down on" or "Make sure you never consider one of these little ones as unimportant."

Despise is also used in 6.24; see comments there. Although some translators have wanted to render it as "hate," most translators have something similar to Brc: "think of one of these little ones as of no importance."

For comments on **one of these little ones**, see verse 6 and 10.42.

In heaven their angels always behold the face of my Father who is in heaven emphasizes the importance that God attaches to those who believe in him. The Jews believed in guardian angels (see Dan 10.10-14; Acts 12.15; Rev 1.20; 12.7), but Jewish teachers taught that only the highest category of angels had access to the presence of God. Jesus is thereby affirming that **these little ones** are of such significance to God that the most powerful angels represent them in his presence.

In heaven . . . in heaven will be unnecessarily repetitious in many languages. Moreover, the meaning of **behold the face of my Father** is not very clear. The meaning is well expressed by GECL: "Their angels always have access to my Father in heaven." Except for the repetition of "in heaven," Brc is excellent: "I tell you that in heaven their guardian angels always have the right of access to the presence of my Father who is in heaven."

For **angels**, see comment on 1.20. The use of **their** sometimes is a problem for translators, since the expression they might use in the receptor languages may give the idea that these little ones owned the angels. "Guardian angels" of Brc is a helpful model, and some translators have said "the angels assigned to take care of them" or "the angels who look after them."

Again, as we suggest above, "right of access" of Brc is a helpful model for translating **behold the face of my father**. This can also be expressed as "always can approach" or "always have the right to speak with God." In some West African languages "can always take the case of these little ones to God" is natural.

[18.11] RSV   TEV

[For the Son of man came to save   **[For the Son of Man came to save**
the lost.]   **the lost.]**

As RSV's footnote indicates (see also TEV), this verse is not found in the earliest and best Greek manuscripts. TC-GNT concludes that it was obviously borrowed from Luke 19.10, most likely with the intention of providing a connection between verse 10 and verses 12-14.

The phrase **Son of man** is first used in 8.20; see comments there.

To save the lost may need to be rendered "to save lost people."

Some translators have found they have to make the relation indicated by **For** quite explicit, as in "For the reason the Son of Man came" or "For the work of the Son of Man is to save."

18.12 RSV   TEV

What do you think? If a man has a   "What do you think a man does
hundred sheep, and one of them has   who has one hundred sheep and
gone astray, does he not leave the   one of them gets lost? He will leave
ninety-nine on the mountains and go   the other ninety-nine grazing on the
in search of the one that went   hillside and go and look for the lost
astray?   sheep.

As RSV indicates, in Greek this verse consists of two questions, the second of which is difficult because of its length and form: **If a man . . . , does he not . . . ?"** To make comprehension easier TEV adopts the form of a question followed by a statement. The verse may be simplified even more if introduced as "What do you think a man will do in the following circumstances?" or "What would a man do in the following circumstances?" The man in the parable may more appropriately be referred to in the second person: "What would you do if you had a hundred sheep and one of them got lost?" In some languages a first person plural inclusive form will be more natural: "What would we (inclusive) do . . . ?"

There will be languages where using questions like Jesus does here will not be natural at all. There translators can say "Think about what a man would do in a case like this" or "Let me give you an example. Suppose a man . . . ."

The second question is often restructured: "Suppose someone has a hundred sheep and one of them wanders away. What does he do? He leaves the ninety-nine on the hillside and goes to look for the one that is lost, doesn't he?" or "Suppose someone has a hundred sheep but one of them gets lost. Don't you think he would leave the ninety-nine where they were and go look for that one sheep? Of course he would."

Has gone astray . . . went astray: the verb "go astray" (TEV **gets lost**) is used here for the first time in the Gospel. In 24.4,5,11,24 it is used of persons who give up their faith; elsewhere it is found in 22.29. It can be rendered here as "wandered away" (Brc) or "got separated from the flock."

Note that **on the mountains** is often rendered as **"on the hillside"** (TEV). This was where the sheep were grazing.

18.13 RSV	TEV
And if he finds it, truly, I say to you, he rejoices over it more than over the ninety-nine that never went astray.	When he finds it, I tell you, he feels far happier over this one sheep than over the ninety-nine that did not get lost.

If he finds it can also be translated here as "When he finds it," if that is better in the receptor language.

Truly, I say to you (first introduced in 6.2) translates the same formula used in verse 3. Here it serves to emphasize the words of Jesus which follow.

He rejoices over it more than over the ninety-nine that never went astray: for readers who already understand the intention of the parable, this statement will make sense, but for others this will not be the case, for it will not seem logical. Ninety-nine sheep are certainly worth more than any one sheep, and no sensible shepherd would leave a large number of sheep at the mercy of predators in order to look for one lost sheep. In the interpretation and translation of these words, two things should be kept in mind: (1) the parable represents an intended exaggeration, introduced for the sake of emphasis; and (2) the emphasis in the parable is upon a specific event, the recovery of a lost sheep, in contrast to the usual circumstances in which all the sheep remain safely within the fold. The meaning may then be stated: "A shepherd who has a hundred sheep is happy when ninety-nine of them do not get lost. But what really makes him happy is when he finds the one sheep that did get lost." Or "A shepherd is happy when ninety-nine of his sheep do not wander away and get lost. But what really makes him happy is when he finds the one that did get lost." Another possibility is "The joy that man has because he found that one sheep is much more than the joy he had because of the other ninety-nine who didn't get lost."

18.14 RSV	TEV
So it is not the will of my[d] Father who is in heaven that one of these little ones should perish.	In just the same way your[p] Father in heaven does not want any of these little ones to be lost.

[d] Other ancient authorities read *your*

[p]your; *some manuscripts have* my.

So (NAB, Brc "Just so") translates a single word in Greek; TEV has **"In just the same way"**; AT "In just that way"; NEB and NIV "In the same way." Since the function of the word is to draw a conclusion by way of analogy from the previous verse, NJB translates "Similarly."

My Father (so also AT) is written **"your Father"** (TEV, NEB, NJB, GECL, TOB) in other Greek manuscripts. TC-GNT notes that **my Father** occurs nineteen times in

Matthew, while "your Father," in either the singular or plural form, occurs eighteen times. Therefore either of these terms can be spoken of as Matthean. Although the textual support for **my father** is strong, TC-GNT believes that it probably was brought in under the influence of verse 10 (see also verse 35). Of the more than a dozen translations checked, only RSV and TEV give the alternative wording. In light of the considerable degree of doubt concerning which text may be original, some translators will give the alternative text in a footnote. But this variance does not change the meaning of the passage significantly.

It is not the will of my Father who is in heaven contains a noun phrase, **the will of my Father**, which is transformed into a clause by TEV (**"your Father in heaven does not want"**) and NIV ("your Father in heaven is not willing"). For many languages this shift will be more natural than the form of the Greek. Some commentators note that the noun **will** translates an Aramaic word which may also mean "good pleasure," thus giving the basis for "there is joy in heaven" of Luke 15.7. This may be true, but Matthew obviously prefers the meaning "the will of God" (see 6.10; 7.21; 12.50; 18.14; 21.31; 26.42), though on one occasion he does use "the good pleasure of God" (so 11.26). Here, as always, the text must be rendered according to the meaning given by the individual author.

For a fuller discussion of **my Father who is in heaven**, see 5.16. As there, "God, my (or, your) Father in heaven" may be necessary.

TEV has rendered **perish** as "get lost," which is the same image as was used with the sheep. Of course, this refers to being lost spiritually and to being far from the love of the heavenly shepherd, God. Translators can use "die," "become lost eternally," or "lost from him." But readers must not in any way get the impression this refers somehow to people physically wandering about not knowing where they are.

Before proceeding to the next section, it should be noted that both here and in verse 10 GECL translates **these little ones** as "the simple people." In verse 10 they are specifically identified as members of the Christian fellowship by the rendering "the simple people in the (Christian) community." Verse 14 is then translated "That is the way it is with your Father in heaven. He does not want any of these simple people to get lost."

18.15-17

RSV	TEV
	A Brother Who Sins
15 "If your brother sins against you, go and tell him his fault, between you and him alone. If he listens to you, you have gained your brother. 16 But if he does not listen, take one or two others along with you, that every word may be confirmed by the evidence of two or three witnesses. 17 If he refuses to listen to them, tell it to the church; and if he refuses to listen even to the church, let him be to you as a Gentile and a tax collector.	15 "If your brother sins against you,*q* go to him and show him his fault. But do it privately, just between yourselves. If he listens to you, you have won your brother back. 16 But if he will not listen to you, take one or two other persons with you, so that 'every accusation may be upheld by the testimony of two or more witnesses,' as the scripture says. 17 And if he will not listen to them, then tell the whole thing to the church. Finally, if he will not listen to the church, treat him as though he were a pagan or a tax collector.

ᑫ Some manuscripts do not have against you.

SECTION HEADING: this section outlines what to do to help a brother who has erred. Thus **"A Brother Who Sins"** may better be expressed as "What to do (to help) a brother who has sinned" or "How to help an erring brother." For a discussion of **"Brother,"** see 5.22 and comments on 18.15.

Verses 15-20 make a specific application of the parable of the lost sheep by providing guidelines for winning back a disciple who has gone astray through sinning. TEV separates between verses 15-17 and 18-20, but this is not advisable, since all six verses deal with the same theme of reclaiming the "one lost sheep."

18.15 RSV	TEV
"If your brother sins against you, go and tell him his fault, between you and him alone. If he listens to you, you have gained your brother.	"If your brother sins against you,ᑫ go to him and show him his fault. But do it privately, just between yourselves. If he listens to you, you have won your brother back.

ᑫSome manuscripts do not have against you.

As one commentator notes, Judaism distinguishes between "neighbor" (a person of shared nationality) and "brother" (a person of shared religion). Here "your fellow believer" may be appropriate for **brother**. See comments at 5.22.

Against you may not have been an original part of the text. TC-GNT notes the possibility that the phrase was brought in by a later scribe under the influence of "against me" of verse 21. On the other hand, it points out that the omission could have been either intentional (so as to apply the passage to sin in general) or accidental (because of the similarity of sound between the last part of the Greek word "sin" and the Greek phrase "against you"). Therefore in the UBS Greek text the words are enclosed in square brackets to indicate that their presence in the text is disputed. The words are dealt with in a variety of ways in the translations, as the following sampling will illustrate: (1) they are included in TEV, with a footnote indicating the possibility that they should be omitted; (2) they are omitted by NEB, with a footnote indicating the possibility that they should be included; (3) RSV includes the words without a footnote; and (4) GECL 1st edition omits the words without a footnote.

In some languages **sins** is normally translated by a word or phrase that means to do wrong against God or disobey God. In such cases translators will have to render **sins against you** as "does wrong to you" or "does something evil against you." Of course, if they choose to not include **against you** in the text, as discussed above, then translators will simply use the normal expression for **sins**.

The first step in winning back a disciple who has sinned is to go to him and show him his fault privately. The Greek verb translated **tell . . . his fault** is used only here in the Gospel of Matthew. In a more general sense it may mean "convince (someone) of something" or "point out something (to someone)." Both RSV and TEV ("**show him his fault**") may be too harsh, while NJB ("have it out with him") implies heated argument. The tone of the passage is better reflected in NEB ("take the matter up with him") and GECL 1st edition ("speak with him about it"). The verb is used in the Septuagint translation of Leviticus 19.17; RSV, there translating the Hebrew text, has "but you shall reason with your neighbor." Other expressions that translators can use include "explain to him how he has sinned" and "talk with him about the matter."

Between you and him alone is translated as a clause in TEV: "**But do it privately.**" The German translations (Lu, Zür, GECL) utilize the idiom "under four eyes," which means "privately" or "confidentially." NEB translates "strictly between yourselves," and NJB "alone, between your two selves."

This phrase **between you and him alone** may be restructured with the previous one, **go and tell him his fault**. For example, "Go and talk with him privately about his sin" or "Go to him, and when you are alone with him, you can discuss the matter."

Listens to (so most all translations) means "pay attention to." Although the verb itself may mean nothing beyond mere hearing, the context implies responsive and effectual listening. Thus "If he sees that you are right" or "If he admits that he has done wrong" are good translations.

You have gained your brother may be more effectively rendered "you have won him back as a brother" (GECL). TEV has "**you have won your brother back.**" In some languages one does not speak of gaining or winning a brother. "Then he will have become your brother again" or "Then you and he will once more be able to call each other brothers" are better expressions in these languages.

18.16   RSV   TEV

But if he does not listen, take one or two others along with you, that every word may be confirmed by the evidence of two or three witnesses.

But if he will not listen to you, take one or two other persons with you, so that 'every accusation may be upheld by the testimony of two or more witnesses,' as the scripture says.

If he does not listen is the negative of the phrase in verse 15. "If he does not admit he has done wrong" or "If he does not pay attention to what you say" are ways to translate it.

To say next **take one or two others along with you** implies a second visit to the person. For some, this will need to be made explicit, as in "Go see him again, but take one or two other people with you."

One or two others (so most translations) is literally "one or two." TEV has "**one or two other persons,**" and the full meaning will be "one or two other Christian brothers." This is the second step in winning back a lost brother, and it has its basis in Deuteronomy 19.15: "Every accusation may be upheld by the testimony of two or more witnesses."

Word (TEV "**accusation**") may here refer to either (1) the charge brought against the brother (JB "the evidence of two or three witness is required to sustain any charge," and TEV "**every accusation may be upheld by the testimony of two or more witnesses**") or (2) the discussion which results between the brother who has sinned and the one who discusses the matter with him (Phps "so that everything that is said may have the support of two or three witnesses"). The latter interpretation is probably correct, as one commentator remarks: "The presence of one or two of the brethren is meant to protect the sinner; the admonisher may well be wrong, or someone else may find the right words when he cannot." Translators who follow this interpretation will say something like "so that the things you point out to him can be confirmed by two or three other witnesses (or, people)" or "so that two or three others can confirm the things you accuse him of."

"**As the scripture says**," though not in the Greek text, is included by TEV to indicate the nature of the quotation. This is especially important for hearers of the scripture, for whom the quotation marks (or the inclusion of the words in italics, as with NJB) will mean nothing. There are actually several ways to indicate this is a citation, should translators wish to do so: "Do this in order to follow the scripture that says that two or three witnesses are needed to make an accusation against someone" or "The Scriptures say that you need to do this before you can accuse someone of doing wrong."

18.17	RSV	TEV
	If he refuses to listen to them, tell it to the church; and if he refuses to listen even to the church, let him be to you as a Gentile and a tax collector.	And if he will not listen to them, then tell the whole thing to the church. Finally, if he will not listen to the church, treat him as though he were a pagan or a tax collector.

Refuses to listen (TEV "**will not listen**") translates a different Greek verb from the one used in verse 16. The verb used here appears elsewhere in the New Testament only in Mark 5.36, and it may mean either "overhear" (intentionally or accidentally) or "refuse to listen to." Most English translations do not distinguish between the two verbs, though Mft has "will not listen . . . refuses to listen," and NAB has "ignores . . . ignores." Phps has "will not listen . . . won't pay attention."

Tell it to the church is the third and final step in attempting to reconcile a brother who has gone astray. In Greek the verb **tell** is not accompanied by a direct object, and so AT translates "tell the congregation," and Mft "tell the church." Most languages, however, will require the express mention of an object, which is represented by **it** in a number of English translations (RSV, NJB, NIV, NAB). Some translations are more specific: "report the matter" (NEB); "tell the matter" (Phps); and "report the whole trouble" (Brc). GECL has "bring the matter before the church."

For a discussion of **church**, see 16.18.

And if . . . even (so also NEB, NIV) is translated "**Finally, if**" by TEV in order to indicate that the last and most drastic step is now to be taken with regard to the brother.

Let him be to you as is translated **"treat him as though he were"** by TEV. GECL renders "then deal with him as"; NEB is similar to TEV: "you must then treat him as you would."

Gentile (TEV **"pagan"**) is found twice elsewhere in this Gospel (5.47; 6.7) and once elsewhere in the New Testament (3 John 7). See comments at 5.47. GECL has "unbeliever."

For **tax collector**, see comment at 5.46.

We offered several ways to express these two terms in the discussions at 5.46 and 47. Since they occur together here, "Tax collectors and other unbelievers" may be natural.

18.18-20

RSV	TEV
	Prohibiting and Permitting
18 Truly, I say to you, whatever you bind on earth shall be bound in heaven, and whatever you loose on earth shall be loosed in heaven. 19 Again I say to you, if two of you agree on earth about anything they ask, it will be done for them by my Father in heaven. 20 For where two or three are gathered in my name, there am I in the midst of them."	18 "And so I tell all of you: what you prohibit on earth will be prohibited in heaven, and what you permit on earth will be permitted in heaven. 19 "And I tell you more: whenever two of you on earth agree about anything you pray for, it will be done for you by my Father in heaven. 20 For where two or three come together in my name, I am there with them."

SECTION HEADING: as stated earlier, verses 18-20 should be considered part of the section dealing with the one lost sheep, verses 15-20, and therefore it is better not to follow TEV and not to use a section heading here. However, if the decision is made to begin a new section here, the TEV heading **"Prohibiting and Permitting"** may need to be expressed as a sentence, as in "Jesus talks about authority to prohibit and permit (things)," "Jesus tells the disciples they have authority to allow or stop things on earth," or, possibly better because it is less cumbersome, "The disciples will have much authority."

18.18 RSV	TEV
Truly, I say to you, whatever you bind on earth shall be bound in heaven, and whatever you loose on earth shall be loosed in heaven.	**"And so I tell all of you: what you prohibit on earth will be prohibited in heaven, and what you permit on earth will be permitted in heaven.**

Truly, I say to you is the same emphatic formula used in verses 3 and 13. **You** is plural in each passage, and TEV translates **"all of you"** to indicate the plural form here, though not in verse 3 or 13.

Except for minor variations, the remainder of this verse is essentially the same as 16.19 (see discussion there). The differences may be listed: (1) **you** is plural here, though singular in the earlier passage; (2) the phrase translated **in heaven** is literally "in the heavens" in 16.19; (3) **whatever** is a slightly different form of the pronoun than that used in the 16.19 parallel; and (4) the pronoun **whatever** is plural here, as compared with the singular form used earlier.

But the real distinction between the two passages is not revealed in their minor variations, but rather in their applications: what was earlier promised to Peter (16.19) is now promised to the entire Christian community, thus making the present passage parallel to John 20.23.

The use of the plural **you** in this verse instead of the singular in 16.19 must be reflected in the translation, and possibly it will also be good to use some plural form for **whatever**; for example, "whatever things." But the use of **in heaven** instead of a plural form is not significant. In other respects translators should render this verse as they did 16.19.

18.19	RSV	TEV

Again I say to you, if two of you agree on earth about anything they ask, it will be done for them by my Father in heaven.		"And I tell you more: whenever two of you on earth agree about anything you pray for, it will be done for you by my Father in heaven."

Again (TEV "**And . . . more**") translates a Greek adverb which may indicate either repetition (as in RSV) or continuation (Mft "another thing"; Brc "Still further"). The context suggests the second of these two possibilities. Translators may say, for example, "Another thing I will tell you," "In addition to that," or "I will tell you something else."

In some Greek manuscripts "truly" is present, thereby making **I say to you** the same form as that used in verses 3, 13, and 18. Most modern translations do not include it in the text, though Brc has "I tell you truly," and Lu has "Truly, I say to you"; JB has "I tell you solemnly."

Two of you . . . they ask . . . for them is unnatural for English readers, since **you**, **they**, and **them** refer to the same persons. TEV avoids this awkwardness by rendering "**two of you . . . you pray for . . . for you.**" NEB and NJB also make similar shifts to second person pronominal usage throughout. Grammatically it will be equally possible to use third person throughout: "two people . . . they pray for . . . for them." However, Jesus is addressing his disciples and means two of them. Consequently "you" should be retained, as in TEV.

The contrasting phrases **on earth . . . in heaven** link this verse with verse 18. In this respect a pleasing balance is achieved, but for many readers **two of you . . . on earth** will sound awkward. One may therefore prefer to translate "whenever any two of you." A relative clause may allow translators to retain **on earth**; for example, "two of you who are here on earth." But this should only be done if the resulting sentence in the receptor language is natural.

If is sometimes more naturally expressed as "When," "Whenever," or "Any time that."

Agree . . . about anything they ask refers specifically to prayer, as the person asked (**my Father in heaven**) signifies. TEV therefore translates "**agree about anything you pray for.**" GECL renders "if two of you on earth pray together about something." If the verb **ask** is maintained in translation, then it may be obligatory in some languages to indicate the person of whom the request is made: ". . . ask my Father in heaven for something, he will do it for you." Even where the verb **ask** is translated specifically as "pray," some languages may still require specific mention of the Father in heaven as the one to whom the prayers are directed.

In the present context **anything** refers to the settlement of disputes within the Christian community and should not be translated in such a way as to imply the provision of material goods as an answer to prayer. Moreover, as "in my name" of verse 20 indicates, the prayer must be in keeping with God's will.

With these things in mind, translators may render the passage as "If two of you here on earth agree about something you ask God to do," "Whenever two of you here on earth agree to ask God to do something," or "If here on earth two of you agree on something and ask God to do it."

It will be done for them by my Father in heaven may require restatement in an active form: "my Father in heaven will do it for you."

For comments on **my Father in heaven**, see 5.16.

18.20   RSV   TEV

For where two or three are gathered   For where two or three come togeth-
in my name, there am I in the midst   er in my name, I am there with
of them."   them."

Two or three does not mean only two or three people (no more and no less!) but means "two or more people." Of course, if the literal translation is natural and correctly understood, then it can be retained.

The Greek verb translated **are gathered** (TEV "**come together**") may be used with a number of different meanings. However, the context suggests that the meaning is either "come together to pray" or "come together as reconciled brothers" (see verse 16 in particular).

For the most part translators are consistent in rendering literally the phrase **in my name**. One exception is AT, which translates "my followers," reflecting well the contextual setting. **Are gathered in my name** may then be translated "come together as my followers." It is possible also to translate either "come together to pray as my followers" or "are reconciled because they are my followers."

There I am in the midst of them addresses the disciples from the perspective of the risen Lord rather than from that of the earthly Jesus. This frequent and unmarked shift in perspective is a unique feature of the Gospels, and it tends to make translation difficult. TEV ("**I am there with them**") is a useful model. Other examples are "I am there with them also" and "I am present with them, too."

18.21-35

RSV

TEV

**The Parable of
the Unforgiving Servant**

21 Then Peter came up and said to him, "Lord, how often shall my brother sin against me, and I forgive him? As many as seven times?" 22 Jesus said to him, "I do not say to you seven times, but seventy times seven.*e* 23 "Therefore the kingdom of heaven may be compared to a king who wished to settle accounts with his servants. 24 When he began the reckoning, one was brought to him who owed him ten thousand talents;*f* 25 and as he could not pay, his lord ordered him to be sold, with his wife and children and all that he had, and payment to be made. 26 So the servant fell on his knees, imploring him, 'Lord, have patience with me, and I will pay you everything.' 27 And out of pity for him the lord of that servant released him and forgave him the debt. 28 But that same servant, as he went out, came upon one of his fellow servants who owed him a hundred denarii;*g* and seizing him by the throat he said, 'Pay what you owe.' 29 So his fellow servant fell down and besought him, 'Have patience with me, and I will pay you.' 30 He refused and went and put him in prison till he should pay the debt. 31 When his fellow servants saw what had taken place, they were greatly distressed, and they went and reported to their lord all that had taken place. 32 Then his lord summoned him and said to him, 'You wicked servant! I forgave you all that debt because you besought me; 33 and should not you have had mercy on your fellow servant, as I had mercy on you?' 34 And in anger his lord delivered him to the jailers,*h* till he should pay all his debt. 35 So also my heavenly Father will do to every one of you, if you do not forgive your brother from your heart."

21 Then Peter came to Jesus and asked, "Lord, if my brother keeps on sinning against me, how many times do I have to forgive him? Seven times?"

22 "No, not seven times," answered Jesus, "but seventy times seven,*r* 23 because the Kingdom of heaven is like this. Once there was a king who decided to check on his servants' accounts. 24 He had just begun to do so when one of them was brought in who owed him millions of dollars. 25 The servant did not have enough to pay his debt, so the king ordered him to be sold as a slave, with his wife and his children and all that he had, in order to pay the debt. 26 The servant fell on his knees before the king. 'Be patient with me,' he begged, 'and I will pay you everything!' 27 The king felt sorry for him, so he forgave him the debt and let him go.

28 "Then the man went out and met one of his fellow servants who owed him a few dollars. He grabbed him and started choking him. 'Pay back what you owe me!' he said. 29 His fellow servant fell down and begged him, 'Be patient with me, and I will pay you back!' 30 But he refused; instead, he had him thrown into jail until he should pay the debt. 31 When the other servants saw what had happened, they were very upset and went to the king and told him everything. 32 So he called the servant in. 'You worthless slave!' he said. 'I forgave you the whole amount you owed me, just because you asked me to. 33 You should have had mercy on your fellow servant, just as I had mercy on you.' 34 The king was very angry, and he sent the servant to jail to be punished until he should pay back the whole amount."

35 And Jesus concluded, "That is how my Father in heaven will treat every one of you unless you forgive your brother from your heart."

e Or *seventy-seven times*
f This talent was more than fifteen years' wages of a laborer
g The denarius was a day's wage for a laborer
h Greek *torturers*

r seventy times seven; *or* seventy-seven times.

SECTION HEADING: "**The Parable of the Unforgiving Servant**" may need to be expressed by a short sentence such as "Jesus tells a parable about a servant who did not forgive (others)" or "Jesus teaches about how people must forgive others."

Matthew 18.21-35 actually contains two parables, both of which are related to the theme of verse 15 ("If your brother sins against you"). The first of the two parables (verses 21-22), which has a parallel in Luke 17.4, focuses upon the need for repeated forgiveness within the Christian fellowship. It also forms an introduction to the second parable (verses 23-35), which is unique to Matthew's Gospel. This parable does not deal with the theme of repeated forgiveness, but rather with the magnitude of divine forgiveness and how it must be applied within the believing community. The similarity of verse 26 to verse 29 and of verse 30 to verse 34, as the contrast between the debts mentioned in verses 24 and 28, affirms the absolute necessity of human forgiveness in light of divine forgiveness. The magnitude of God's forgiveness can be compared only to the enormity of the punishment which he will inflict upon those who profess to share in his forgiveness but who themselves are unforgiving of their brothers.

18.21   RSV   TEV

Then Peter came up and said to him, "Lord, how often shall my brother sin against me, and I forgive him? As many as seven times?"

Then Peter came to Jesus and asked, "Lord, if my brother keeps on sinning against me, how many times do I have to forgive him? Seven times?"

Came up can be "approached" or "went up."

Him is identified by name in TEV (**"Jesus"**), since a new section opens here.

Lord, how often . . . and I forgive him represents the form of the Greek sentence. Both NEB ("Lord, how often am I to forgive my brother if he goes on wronging me?") and NJB ("Lord, how often must I forgive my brother if he wrongs me?") invert the order of the two clauses. Some languages will prefer the order of the Greek sentence, because the clauses are in a logical and chronological arrangement. Some translators have said "Lord, how many times do I have to forgive my brother for the sins he does against me?" and others have followed the text a little more closely with "Lord, how many times can my brother sin against me and I still forgive him?" or "Lord, for how many of my brother's sins against me should I forgive him?" Another rendering is "Lord, if my brother keeps on sinning against me, for how many of these sins should I continue forgiving him?"

Lord was discussed at 8.2. Here the Christian sense of "Lord" will be most appropriate.

By **brother** Peter does not mean his sibling but either "fellow man," as in Brc, or "fellow believer." The latter seems to fit better in this passage, as we explained above.

Sin against me will not be correct in those languages where the term **sin** is used exclusively in the context of doing something against God. "Do wrong to me" or "do evil against me" will be better.

Forgive was discussed at 6.12. In some languages people can forgive another person's actions, and in other languages they can forgive the people. Still others even require the full form, that is, forgiving other people their actions. Thus **forgive him** can also be "forgive him his sins" or "forgive his bad deeds."

As many as seven times? is literally "until seven?" Many languages will require the explicit mention of a subject and predicate: "Must I forgive him as many as seven times?"

18.22 RSV	TEV
Jesus said to him, "I do not say to you seven times, but seventy times seven.*e*	"No, not seven times," answered Jesus, "but seventy times seven,*r*
e Or *seventy-seven times*	*r* seventy times seven; *or* seventy-seven times.

I do not say to you seven times may be too confusing for some readers, and translators will need "You should not forgive him just seven times," "I don't tell you to forgive him only seven times," or "I tell you not just seven times, but you should forgive him seventy times seven."

Seventy times seven, as the footnotes in RSV and TEV state, may mean seventy-seven times (see also AT). But the point is that there is no limit to the number of times that forgiveness must be offered to an individual. Moreover, the one who forgives is not to keep record of the number of times he forgives his brother.

There are some languages, for example many in Africa, where the numbering system is so complicated that **seventy times seven** is a very awkward phrase, so much so that the point Jesus is making is obscured. Some translators have solved the problem by saying "seven times, and then seven again, and then seven again for ten times" or "seven times and then again and again until you can't count." The latter probably catches Jesus' intent perfectly.

18.23 RSV	TEV
"Therefore the kingdom of heaven may be compared to a king who wished to settle accounts with his servants.	because the Kingdom of heaven is like this. Once there was a king who decided to check on his servants' accounts.

The English word **Therefore** is not a good translation of the Greek phrase here. Jesus has just said that there should be no limit to forgiveness, and now he goes on to give the reason for that statement, which has to do with the magnitude of divine forgiveness as seen in this next parable. So a better translation than **Therefore** is "I tell you this because God's rule is like this story" or "The reason you must forgive like that can be seen in this parable about God's rule. It is like this." Note that a phrase like "God's kingdom is like a king" is not really the correct comparison. Jesus is comparing God's rule to the situation in the whole parable.

For **the kingdom of heaven**, see comment at 3.2; for **may be compared to**, see comment at 13.24. GECL translates "When God establishes his Kingdom, he will act like a king who wanted to check up on those who were in charge of his possessions"; INCL "When God establishes his rule, the situation will be like that described in this parable"; and Brc "That is why what happens in the Kingdom of Heaven can be compared with the situation which arose when a king wished to settle accounts with his servants."

Settle accounts is often used in a very negative sense in English. It can be understood as taking revenge, or possibly as dismissing the servants. In fact, in this verse the correct idea is better seen in a phrase such as "examine the accounts" or "check on what each of his servants owed him."

In this parable, and in the total biblical context, a king's **servants** were his higher officials. In this case this is evident from the large amount of money entrusted to them (see verse 24). Translators should therefore try to use a word that will refer to officials or high-ranking servants rather than inferior ones.

18.24	RSV	TEV

When he began the reckoning, one was brought to him who owed him ten thousand talents;^{f}	He had just begun to do so when one of them was brought in who owed him millions of dollars.

^{f} This talent was more than fifteen years' wages of a laborer

When he began (TEV "**He had just begun to do so**") translates a participial construction in Greek, which GECL makes into an adverbial phrase ("At the very first").

Reckoning can be rendered by "checking the accounts" or, as in TEV, with a phrase like "began to do this."

The passive **was brought** probably suggests that the man was in prison. In those languages which will not naturally use a passive, translators should say "his people (or, his other servants) brought to him." "Took" or "led" will be better than **brought** in many languages.

One refers, of course, to "one of his servants" or "one of his people."

Ten thousand talents is transformed into contemporary U.S. currency by TEV ("**millions of dollars**"). Both the sum (ten thousand) and the monetary unit (talent) are significant, for in the ancient Near East ten thousand was the highest number used in calculating, and the talent was the largest currency unit of that time. In other words, the amount is intended to stagger the imagination; it is the highest sum imaginable, to be contrasted with the trifling amount of the debt in verse 28. NEB indicates that the debt "ran into millions," while the footnote of NJB states "the amount is deliberately fantastic." RSV's footnote points out that a single talent was "more than fifteen years' wages of a laborer."

Some translators have maintained the biblical form, **ten thousand talents**, but tried to give it some meaning by using an expression such as "ten thousand huge units of money called talents" or "ten thousand talents, each one the money of fifteen years' wages." Others have followed the RSV with a literal translation in the text and a footnote suggesting the value. Another common method translators have used is to employ a very general term such as "a huge sum of money." There can be problems in using a modern local currency, as TEV ("**millions of dollars**") and Brc ("two and a half million pounds") have done. For one thing, currencies can change value radically so that a few years after publication the meaning may be quite different. Then, too, to use modern money removes the passage from its historical context. Any expression that will indicate that the sum of money is almost beyond imagination can be considered by translators.

18.25 RSV	TEV
and as he could not pay, his lord ordered him to be sold, with his wife and children and all that he had, and payment to be made.	The servant did not have enough to pay his debt, so the king ordered him to be sold as a slave, with his wife and his children and all that he had, in order to pay the debt.

He could not pay can be expressed as "he did not have the money to pay the debt" or "he was unable to repay." It may be necessary to add an indirect object, as "repay his master" or "pay the king the money he owed him."

His lord in this context means "his master" or "the king."

Ordered him to be sold is represented in TEV as "**ordered him to be sold as a slave**," which makes the meaning immediately obvious for the reader. The man and everything he owned were to be sold as compensation for the debt. This action is purely for the sake of revenge on the part of the king, since even at the highest value of slaves the total amount would have still been insignificant as compared with the monstrous debt of verse 24.

This last part of the verse may need to be restructured, as in "his master ordered that the man and his wife and children be sold as slaves and that everything he owned also be sold in order to pay the debt" or "the king ordered his people to take the man and his wife and children and sell them as slaves, and also to sell the man's possessions. This money would be used to pay off the debt."

The severity of the punishment is thereby in keeping with the enormity of the debt. According to the Jewish Law, a man could not be sold except in the case of theft. And the sale of a man's wife was strictly forbidden. So Jesus draws upon an illustration from a non-Jewish setting to underscore the severity of the punishment. Both the magnitude of the debt and the enormity of the punishment are intended to stagger the imagination.

18.26 RSV	TEV
So the servant fell on his knees, imploring him, 'Lord, have patience with me, and I will pay you everything.'	The servant fell on his knees before the king. 'Be patient with me,' he begged, 'and I will pay you everything!'

So may also be rendered "Then" or "At this." TEV finds it more natural in English to drop this transitional.

Fell on his knees (so also TEV) translates a participle which is literally "falling" or "having fallen," and the action is best understood as falling face down rather than upon the knees. Moreover, the meaning of the verb **imploring** (TEV "begged") is "approach in dog-like fashion," descriptive of the manner in which a dog approaches its master on all fours in hopes of escaping punishment. Though root meanings may be deceptive, the root meaning seems best to suit the needs of the context. NAB, though at a high language level, is accurate: "prostrated himself in homage and said." NJB translates "the servant threw himself down at his master's feet," and AT has "threw himself down before him and implored him." The man is about to lose everything, and so he approaches his king in the most humble way possible. Translators should use whatever expression makes this clear; for example, "knelt down" or "lay down on the ground in front of."

Have patience translates a verb made from the same stem as the adjective used in the Septuagint, with the meaning "patient" or "long-suffering." Sometimes an expression such as "be patient" does not fit well, and translators say instead "give me some time."

I will pay you everything may be expressed as "I will pay you back everything I have taken," "I will give you everything I owe you," or "I will pay back the entire debt." **I will pay you everything** is, of course, an exaggeration. It is inconceivable that the man could have repaid the enormous amount. For example, the annual income of King Herod was only nine hundred talents, and for this man to have repaid ten thousand talents would have been an impossible feat.

18.27   RSV   TEV

And out of pity for him the lord of that servant released him and forgave him the debt.	The king felt sorry for him, so he forgave him the debt and let him go.

Out of pity (TEV **"felt sorry"**) translates a Greek verb which focuses upon the intestines as the place where the emotions of sorrow and pity are experienced. **Out of** means "because of" in this context. "Because he felt sorry for him" will express this, for example. The sentence can also be restructured slightly, as in "The king took pity on the official, and so set him free and canceled the debt."

The lord of that servant is translated **"the king"** by TEV in order to maintain continuity throughout the story; otherwise there is the possibility that the reader may wrongly distinguish between "the king" and "the lord of that servant." See also verses 31 and 34 and the discussion there.

Released him may refer to the man's release from prison; Brc has "let him go free," and Phps "set him free."

Forgave has the specific sense of "canceled" (AT, NJB). Using language that their readers will understand, translators have sometimes said something like "told him he would not have to pay what he owed."

Debt translates a Greek noun which is used only here in the New Testament. It technically means a "loan," but most translations prefer to use the broader term of "debt."

RSV   TEV

But that same servant, as he went out, came upon one of his fellow servants who owed him a hundred denarii; *g* **and seizing him by the throat he said, 'Pay what you owe.'**	**"Then the man went out and met one of his fellow servants who owed him a few dollars. He grabbed him and started choking him. 'Pay back what you owe me!' he said.**

g The denarius was a day's wage for a laborer

The RSV text continues with **But**, which TEV has rendered as "**Then.**" Translators should use whatever fits naturally in the context. Some have had "But as that official was going out."

Presumably the official **went out** from the king's palace or house, and in some translations it will be necessary to indicate that.

Came upon is best taken to indicate a chance meeting.

A hundred denarii (a denarius was the daily wage paid a laborer) is transformed into contemporary U.S. currency (TEV "**a few dollars**"). When a comparison is made between the value of the talent and the denarius, one discovers that the debt which the first servant owed the king is 500,000 times more than the debt owed him by his fellow servant. NAB does an excellent job at contrasting the two debts without indicating any specific monetary unit: "who owed him a huge amount" (verse 24) and "who owed him a mere fraction of what he himself owed" (verse 28).

Before translating **a hundred denarii**, translators should read again what was said at verse 24 about money. Again, some translators will keep the biblical word and have "a small amount of money, one hundred denarii," or simply do the same thing that RSV has done and use a footnote. NAB, cited above, is an excellent model, and many translators have had "a small portion of the money he had owed the king" or "a hundred denarii, money that was almost nothing when compared to what the king had forgiven him." Again, there are problems if translators try to use a local modern currency.

Seizing . . . by the throat translates two verbs in Greek (TEV "**grabbed . . . started choking**") which may be understood as depicting either a single action or two separate actions. AT ("he caught him by the throat") indicates a single action, as do Mft, Brc. On the other hand, NEB suggests two actions in sequence: "and catching hold of him he gripped him by the throat"; similarly NJB "he seized him by the throat and began to throttle him." Since either interpretation is possible on the basis of the Greek text, it is advisable in translation to do whatever seems the most dramatic.

Pay what you owe will require an indirect object in some languages (TEV "**Pay back what you owe me**"). One may also translate "Pay me the money that you owe me" or ". . . that you borrowed from me."

18.29 RSV TEV

So his fellow servant fell down and besought him, 'Have patience with me, and I will pay you.'

His fellow servant fell down and begged him, 'Be patient with me, and I will pay you back!'

Fell down means to fall face downward to the ground (see verse 26). It is obvious that the falling is intentional, and so one must guard against a verb which implies tripping or unintentional falling. Although the word is not the same as that used in verse 26, the meaning is close enough that translators can use a similar expression; for example, "knelt down to beg him." The urgency of the fellow servant's plea is conveyed by Brc with "threw himself at his feet."

Have patience translates the same verb used in verse 26. JB translates "Give me time."

18.30 RSV TEV

He refused and went and put him in prison till he should pay the debt.

But he refused; instead, he had him thrown into jail until he should pay the debt.

In the translation of this verse, care should be taken that there is no confusion in the use of the pronouns **He** (in its two occurrences) and **him**.

He refused may be better as direct discourse: "He said, 'I will not' " or ". . . 'I refuse to do that.' "

And went and put him in prison is more literally "but going away he threw him into jail." The verb "threw" is definitely causative and is so rendered by many translations: "had him jailed" (NEB). But the function of the participle "going away" is questionable. Some translations represent it as a separate action from that of having the man jailed (RSV, NIV, Mft). Others translate it with the force of an auxiliary to the main verb; see for example GECL ("so he immediately had him put in jail") and NAB ("Instead, he had him put in jail"). Still others have said "he ordered the authorities to put the man in jail until he paid the debt in full."

Debt translates a different noun from that used in verse 27, though the reference is clearly the same. GECL 1st edition renders this last clause "until he should pay everything." One may need to be even more specific: "until the man should pay him everything that he owed him."

18.31 RSV TEV

When his fellow servants saw what had taken place, they were greatly distressed, and they went and reported to their lord all that had taken place.

When the other servants saw what had happened, they were very upset and went to the king and told him everything.

Fellow servants is the same noun used in verses 28 and 29. For many translators, "the king's other servants (or, officials)" is a natural expression.

Distressed, a verb signifying shock and amazement, is used in the Septuagint of Nehemiah 5.6; Jonah 4.4,9. The story would have been shocking to Jesus' disciples also, since it was not customary to imprison a person for debt in Palestine.

Their lord is translated "**the king**" by TEV (see comment at verse 27, where "the lord of that servant" is also translated "the king" by TEV). In addition see verse 34.

Reported translates a verb that may be used when a man reports to his superior. Elsewhere in the New Testament it is found only in 13.36. Here "told the king" is probably acceptable.

18.32 RSV	TEV
Then his lord summoned him and said to him, 'You wicked servant! I forgave you all that debt because you besought me;	So he called the servant in. 'You worthless slave!' he said. 'I forgave you the whole amount you owed me, just because you asked me to.

Summoned is translated "**called . . . in**" by TEV (NJB, NEB "sent for") and **him** is identified as "**the servant.**" It may be necessary to render "called in the servant who had owed him so much money" or ". . . whose debt he had canceled."

In the context **wicked** probably means something like "**worthless**" (TEV) or "good for nothing." NEB renders "You scoundrel!" and Brc has "You utter scoundrel!" In translation it is suggested that a strong, though not vulgar, expression be used.

In Greek **all that debt** (TEV "**the whole amount you owed me**") is given a position of emphasis. In some languages it may be more logical to invert the order of the two clauses: "You begged me to forgive you, and so I canceled your entire debt." Some translators have made the expression even stronger by saying "all that huge debt."

18.33 RSV	TEV
and should not you have had mercy on your fellow servant, as I had mercy on you?'	You should have had mercy on your fellow servant, just as I had mercy on you.'

This verse is in a real sense the key to the entire parable: those persons whose debt of sin God has forgiven are obligated in return to forgive the sins that others commit against them.

And should not you have . . . ? is more literally "and was it not necessary for you to have . . . ?" Since this type of structure is extremely difficult for English speakers, TEV has made three adjustments in hopes of relieving the difficulty: (1) the rhetorical question is changed to a statement; (2) the negative form is altered to a positive; and (3) the impersonal structure ("it was necessary for you") is made into

a second person form ("**You should have had mercy**"). The verb translated **should
. . . have** (literally "it was necessary") normally indicates a binding compulsion or
obligation; see, for example, its usage in Luke 2.49; 15.32; 18.1; Acts 5.29; 1
Thessalonians 4.1; Titus 1.11.

In other languages it has still been possible to retain a question in rendering
the sentence, as for example in "And so what should you have done? You should
have had mercy on your fellow servant just as I had mercy on you." Another example
is "You should have had mercy on your fellow servant as I did on you, shouldn't
you?"

That the verb **had mercy on** is used twice in this verse emphasizes the
importance attached to it. For some languages the two clauses may more naturally
be reversed: "I had mercy on you, and that is why you should have had mercy on
your fellow servant."

18.34   RSV   TEV

And in anger his lord delivered him   The king was very angry, and he
to the jailers,^h till he should pay all   sent the servant to jail to be pun-
his debt.   ished until he should pay back the
                                             whole amount."

^h Greek *torturers*

And in anger (TEV "**was very angry**") translates a participle which is given
a position of emphasis in the Greek sentence. NEB renders "And so angry was the
master," and Brc "The master was furious."

Once again TEV substitutes "**the king**" for **his lord** in order to maintain
continuity throughout the parable. See verses 27 and 31.

The king **delivered him**, or possibly better, "handed him over" (Brc) or
"ordered his servants to take the man to the torturers."

To the jailers (TEV "**to jail to be punished**") is more literally "to the
torturers" (NJB), as RSV's footnote points out. NEB has "he condemned the man to
torture." Torture was not allowed among the Jews, though it is known to have been
used by Herod the Great. But in other countries of the ancient Near East torture was
regularly used, especially in cases of a disloyal governor or one who was late in the
payment of taxes. The mention of "torture" is to intensify the degree of punishment
which the man would receive. For this reason many translate the phrase as "to the
people who would punish him" or "to the people (in jail) who would make him
suffer."

Till he should pay all his debt is almost word-for-word the same as the last
part of verse 30, except for the inclusion of the modifier **all**. That is, the man's own
punishment is described in terms of the punishment which he inflicted on his fellow
servant. Moreover, the man's situation is helpless and his punishment is endless,
because there is no opportunity for him to make restoration.

RSV   TEV

So also my heavenly Father will do to every one of you, if you do not forgive your brother from your heart."

And Jesus concluded, "That is how my Father in heaven will treat every one of you unless you forgive your brother from your heart."

"**And Jesus concluded**" is introduced by TEV as a means of indicating the end of the parable and a transition to its application. In Greek this is accomplished by two words which RSV translates **So also** (TEV "**That is how**"; NEB, NJB "And that is how"). Translators can also say "That's the way God will deal with you" or "That's the way it will be with God my heavenly Father. If you do not forgive your brother from your heart, God will deal with you as the king did with that man."

Will do to every one of you: translations vary considerably, since the verb **do** has a wide variety of meanings, dependent upon the context in which it is used. Both NEB and NJB have "will deal with you"; Mft and Brc have "will do the same to you."

From your heart (so also TEV) or "from your hearts" (NEB, AT) represents a literal rendering of the Greek text and is followed by most English translations. An exception is Brc, who translates "genuinely." In the same vein are "sincerely" or "completely." A similar expression is used in the command to love God (22.37), and it is here used to underscore the absolute nature of forgiveness. One scholar concludes his remarks on this section with the comment, "God's forgiveness is not for decoration but for use."

Chapter 19

19.1-12

Jesus Teaches about Divorce

1 Now when Jesus had finished these sayings, he went away from Galilee and entered the region of Judea beyond the Jordan; 2 and large crowds followed him, and he healed them there.

3 And Pharisees came up to him and tested him by asking, "Is it lawful to divorce one's wife for any cause?" 4 He answered, "Have you not read that he who made them from the beginning made them male and female, 5 and said, 'For this reason a man shall leave his father and mother and be joined to his wife, and the two shall become one flesh'? 6 So they are no longer two but one flesh. What therefore God has joined together, let not man put asunder." 7 They said to him, "Why then did Moses command one to give a certificate of divorce, and to put her away?" 8 He said to them, "For your hardness of heart Moses allowed you to divorce your wives, but from the beginning it was not so. 9 And I say to you: whoever divorces his wife, except for unchastity,^{j} and marries another, commits adultery."^{k}

10 The disciples said to him, "If such is the case of a man with his wife, it is not expedient to marry." 11 But he said to them, "Not all men can receive this saying, but only those to whom it is given. 12 For there are eunuchs who have been so from birth, and there are eunuchs who have been made eunuchs by men, and there are eunuchs who have made themselves eunuchs for the sake of the kingdom of heaven. He who is able to receive this, let him receive it."

^{j} Other ancient authorities, after *unchastity*, read *makes her commit adultery*
^{k} Other ancient authorities insert *and he who marries a divorced woman commits adultery*

1 When Jesus finished saying these things, he left Galilee and went to the territory of Judea on the other side of the Jordan River. 2 Large crowds followed him, and he healed them there.

3 Some Pharisees came to him and tried to trap him by asking, "Does our Law allow a man to divorce his wife for whatever reason he wishes?"

4 Jesus answered, "Haven't you read the scripture that says that in the beginning the Creator made people male and female? 5 And God said, 'For this reason a man will leave his father and mother and unite with his wife, and the two will become one.' 6 So they are no longer two, but one. Man must not separate, then, what God has joined together."

7 The Pharisees asked him, "Why, then, did Moses give the law for a man to hand his wife a divorce notice and send her away?"

8 Jesus answered, "Moses gave you permission to divorce your wives because you are so hard to teach. But it was not like that at the time of creation. 9 I tell you, then, that any man who divorces his wife for any cause other than her unfaithfulness, commits adultery if he marries some other woman."

10 His disciples said to him, "If this is how it is between a man and his wife, it is better not to marry."

11 Jesus answered, "This teaching does not apply to everyone, but only to those to whom God has given it. 12 For there are different reasons why men cannot marry: some, because they were born that way; others, because men made them that way; and others do not marry for the sake of the Kingdom of heaven. Let him who can accept this teaching do so."

SECTION HEADING: **"Jesus Teaches about Divorce"** is similar to the section heading at 5.31. In some languages **"Divorce"** is translated by a phrase that includes the participants, as in "Jesus teaches about when a man divorces his wife." On the other hand, since the passage is really dealing with marriage, "Jesus teaches about marriage" will also be good.

19.1 RSV	TEV
Now when Jesus had finished these sayings, he went away from Galilee and entered the region of Judea beyond the Jordan;	When Jesus finished saying these things, he left Galilee and went to the territory of Judea on the other side of the Jordan River.

Now when Jesus had finished these sayings is the fourth in a series of five summary statements which signify the conclusion of major divisions within the Gospel (7.28; 11.1; 13.53; 26.1). The phrase is almost exactly the same as the one in 7.28, and translators should refer to the comment there. Beginning in chapter 19 Matthew returns to the Marcan order of events, which he follows in broad outline throughout the remainder of the Gospel. Chapter 19 deals with three topics: (1) marriage (verses 1-12); (2) children (verses 13-15); and (3) possessions (verses 16-30).

He went away from Galilee signifies that Jesus has now concluded his Galilean ministry. The verb translated **went away** is found in the New Testament only here and in 13.53, which is also one of Matthew's summary statements.

As elsewhere, **Galilee** will often be "the region of Galilee."

The region of Judea beyond the Jordan is a strange statement, inasmuch as there was no Judea east of the Jordan River. It is possible (though highly improbable on the basis of the Greek text) to assume that Matthew is describing a journey to Judea by way of a trans-Jordan route as opposed to a journey through Samaria. If this is the case, then Jesus would have followed the east side of the Jordan River through a portion of Decapolis (the territory of the ten Greek cities) and then through Perea, where he would have crossed the Jordan River at a place near Jericho. From there he would have gone to Jerusalem. Even if this is what happened, this is not what Matthew says, and one is limited by the information provided by Matthew. All translations are faithful to the meaning of the text except LB, which renders "he left Galilee and circled back to Judea from across the Jordan River." This is not acceptable, of course, and translators should instead do something similar to TEV (**"territory of Judea on the other side of the Jordan River"**) or Brc ("that part of Judaea which lies on the far side of the Jordan").

19.2 RSV	TEV
and large crowds followed him, and he healed them there.	Large crowds followed him, and he healed them there.

Large crowds followed him (see also 4.25; 8.1; 12.15; 14.13; 20.29; 21.9) differs from Mark, which states "crowds gathered to him" (10.1). In the Gospel of

Matthew the masses are always receptive to Jesus and his message until 27.25, where they reject him under the influence of their leaders.

And he healed them there differs from Mark, which has "he taught them." For Matthew healing is a significant part of Jesus' ministry. **He healed them there** can give the impression that everyone in the crowd was sick. "He healed the sick people (among them)" will then be necessary. **There** in some languages may occur at the beginning of the sentence: "There he healed the sick people (among them)."

19.3	RSV	TEV
	And Pharisees came up to him and tested him by asking, "Is it lawful to divorce one's wife for any cause?"	Some Pharisees came to him and tried to trap him by asking, "Does our Law allow a man to divorce his wife for whatever reason he wishes?"

Pharisees or "**Some Pharisees**" (TEV, NJB, NEB, NIV) may be said to represent the Greek text. Other Greek manuscripts have "The Pharisees" (see KJV), but TC-GNT believes that the definite article "the" was supplied by later scribes, as was also done in some manuscripts in the parallel at Mark 10.2. If translators have translated **Pharisees** in a way that indicates they were a sect or some kind of group, then it will be natural here to say "some members of the Pharisees group." See discussion at 3.7.

Came up to him may be "approached him" or "went up to him." The text does not indicate whether the Pharisees had traveled far to talk to Jesus or were already there in the area.

Tested (TEV "**tried to trap**") translates a verb which is used in the same sense in 16.1 (see also 22.18,35); it is also used in the temptation narrative (4.1,3). As we indicated at 16.1, the use of **tested** in this kind of context shows that the Pharisees were trying to discredit Jesus. "**Tried to trap**" of TEV indicates that, as does "came to him with what they intended to be a test question" of Brc. "Tried to catch Jesus out" or "asked Jesus a trick question" may also convey the meaning, if these expressions are not too colloquial or considered slang in the receptor language.

Tested him by asking is more literally "tested him and saying." But this is a typical Semitic expression in which "and" is deceptive. Here "and" is not used to link equal parts; rather it is used as a means of indicating that the first part of the construction ("tested") is explained by the second part ("saying"). Fortunately the majority of modern translations are consistent in making this meaning evident.

Is it lawful (so also NEB) has the Mosaic Law as the point of reference; TEV translates "**Does our Law allow**," and NJB is similar ("Is it against the Law").

Divorce was previously discussed in the Sermon on the Mount (5.31-32); it is now brought up in the context of debate. Among the Jewish teachers of religion, this was a frequent matter of debate, and the focal point of discussion was always the phrase "something unbecoming" of Deuteronomy 24.1.

The formulation of the question, **to divorce one's wife**, reflects accurately the historical situation, since among the Jews a woman could not divorce her husband.

Many translators will find it more natural to use **"a man . . . his wife"** as TEV does instead of **one's** of the RSV text.

For any cause (so also AT) is translated **"for whatever reason he wishes"** by TEV, an interpretation which is accepted by most other translations (Brc "for any reason he likes"; NJB "on any pretext whatever"; NEB "on any and every ground"). According to this interpretation, the legitimacy of divorce is assumed, and so the question deals with the grounds on which it may be carried out. However, the phrase may be understood as a question regarding the legitimacy of divorce, an interpretation represented by Phps ("on any grounds whatever") and by NEB's alternative wording ("Is there any ground on which it is lawful for a man to divorce his wife?"). If this second interpretation is accepted, then Matthew is not considerably different from Mark.

19.4	RSV	TEV

He answered, "Have you not read that he who made them from the beginning made them male and female,

Jesus answered, "Haven't you read the scripture that says that in the beginning the Creator made people male and female?

Have you not read is transformed into the more natural question form "Haven't you read" by TEV, and **"the scripture"** is introduced as the object of the verb **"read."** The question may also take the form of a statement: "Surely you have read" or "Surely you know" (GECL 1st edition).

He who made them is translated "the one who created them" by Phps, and "the Creator" by TEV, NEB, AT, and NIV. **He who made them from the beginning made them male and female** appears in GECL 1st edition as "In the beginning God created man and woman." Translators can also consider "Surely you have read (in God's scriptures) that in the beginning when God created people he made both men and women" and "Haven't you read God's word that teaches that in the beginning the Creator made people male and female?"

19.5	RSV	TEV

and said, 'For this reason a man shall leave his father and mother and be joined to his wife, and the two shall become one flesh'?

And God said, 'For this reason a man will leave his father and mother and unite with his wife, and the two will become one.'

In place of **and said**, TEV has **"And God said."** Most readers will immediately recognize that the same being is referred to in both verses 3 and 4; for others it may be necessary to have either "the Creator . . . He" or "God . . . He." It is important for verses 4 and 5 to flow together smoothly and naturally. If translators use a phrase such as "God's word" in verse 4, for example, then here they may wish to say "God also said" or "And he said" (Brc). Note that no matter how this is structured, it must not seem that Jesus is the subject of **said**.

For this reason . . . shall become one flesh is a quotation from Genesis 2.24. In the Genesis narrative the phrase **For this reason** is important, because it serves to connect verse 24 of Genesis 2 with verse 23 and to explain it. However, in the present context it serves no obvious function. Nevertheless most translators retain the phrase, since it was part of the quotation Jesus gave (see, for example, TEV). The problem for some is that the phrase does not refer to anything in the immediate context and consequently poses problems to the readers. Many translators will have a footnote showing the reference to the Genesis passage, or even a note such as "In God's word, that was what the first man said when God created woman as his companion." Other translators have provided sufficient context by structuring verses 4 and 5 together, as for example "Surely you have read in God's word about how God created mankind? He made both male and female, and that is why it also says, 'For this reason a man . . . one flesh.' "

Be joined to translates a verb which may be used of sexual union (see 1 Cor 6.16) but may also be used of any type of close association. Brc translates "joined inseparably to"; NEB has "be made one with"; GECL translates "live with."

And the two shall become one flesh, a formal rendering of the Greek text, is representative of what most other translations have done. Slightly different are JB ("and the two become one body") and GECL 1st edition ("The two are then one body"), while TEV (**"and the two will become one"**) and NAB ("and the two shall become as one") make significant departures from a formal transfer. Brc combines **be joined to . . . shall become one flesh** into a single statement: "and will be joined inseparably to his wife." The restructuring of TEV and NAB, though perhaps satisfactory for some levels of English readers, will be entirely unsatisfactory in a number of other languages. Readers will ask "Become one what?" All in all, it may be best to translate "will be like one body" or ". . . like one person."

19.6   RSV   TEV

So they are no longer two but one   So they are no longer two, but one.
flesh. What therefore God has joined   Man must not separate, then, what
together, let not man put asunder."   God has joined together."

In this verse it is once more Jesus speaking his own words; the Genesis citation ends at the end of verse 5. (It is not clear why Brc keeps the first part of verse 6 as part of that quote.) Some translators have had to indicate this shift with a phrase such as, "So I tell you that they . . . ."

So they are no longer two but one flesh (TEV "So they are no longer two, but one"): here again most translations are fairly literal. Two exceptions are Phps ("So they are no longer two separate people but one") and Brc ("and they two shall become so completely one that they shall be no longer two persons but one"). As in verse 5 it will probably be best to use a simile in most languages: "So from then on the two of them are like one person."

God has joined together: marriage is viewed as within the divine will and purpose. The verb literally means "yoke together (equally)," as of two oxen.

In the second sentence of this verse, TEV inverts the order of the two clauses (compare RSV). **Man** is here used generically of "people," though most translations maintain the literal form. In addition, **let not man** (TEV "**Man must not**") is equivalent to "no one must." Finally, **What** means "those whom" or "the man and woman whom." The second part of the verse may then be translated "no one must separate a man and woman whom God has joined together as husband and wife." Or, on the assumption that the verb means "try to separate" (AT), one may translate "no one must try to separate . . ." or "no one must even try to separate . . . ."

19.7	RSV	TEV

They said to him, "Why then did Moses command one to give a certificate of divorce, and to put her away?"	The Pharisees asked him, "Why, then, did Moses give the law for a man to hand his wife a divorce notice and send her away?"

They said to him: TEV, together with GECL and FRCL, identifies the speakers as "**The Pharisees**" on the basis of verse 3. The Greek verb "say" covers a wide area of meaning in English, and the translations vary; for example, "they objected" (NEB), "they asked" (NIV), and "they retorted" (Phps).

Why then did Moses command one . . . and to put her away is once again a literal representation of the Greek text, except for the inclusion of the pronouns **one** and **her**. Both of these pronominal forms are necessary in English, though **one** is entirely absent from the Greek text, and **her** is found only is some Greek manuscripts. In the UBS Greek text, the pronoun **her** is placed in brackets in order to indicate that its position in the text is doubtful. Since the Greek text is very concise, it is quite possible that **her** was introduced by some later scribe for the sake of clarification (other Greek manuscripts have "his wife," which is surely a scribal clarification). On the other hand, **her** may have been dropped from the text so as to make the passage read like its parallel in Mark 10.4. In either case most languages will require not only the specification of the object but of the subject. NEB (similarly TEV) indicates both subject and object of the divorce procedure: "Why then . . . did Moses lay it down that a man might divorce his wife by note of dismissal?" GECL is slightly different in its restructuring: "Why is it then, that according to the Law of Moses a man may send his wife away by means of a written notice of divorce?" On the other hand, NJB translates without indicating either subject or object of the transaction: "Then why did Moses command that a writ of dismissal should be given in cases of divorce?"

The RSV text is a little awkward and may give the impression that Moses commanded people to get a divorce. The correct meaning is that Moses allowed a man to get a divorce if he wished to, and he provided a way to do it. So the sentence can be translated "But Moses provided (or, gave) a law that says a man may divorce his wife by giving her a divorce notice and sending her away. Why did he do that?" or "Why, then, did Moses give a commandment about how a man can divorce his wife by giving her a divorce notice and sending her away?"

The phrase **put her away** is better rendered as "**send her away**" (TEV) or "have her leave his house."

19.8 RSV	TEV

He said to them, "For your hardness of heart Moses allowed you to divorce your wives, but from the beginning it was not so.	Jesus answered, "Moses gave you permission to divorce your wives because you are so hard to teach. But it was not like that at the time of creation.

Jesus does agree that Moses permitted divorce. But he makes two significant observations regarding the ruling that Moses made: (1) divorce was a concession which resulted from the rebellious attitude of the Jewish people, and (2) it is contrary to God's original intention in creation. This second observation would have carried much weight, since Jewish teachers affirmed that when two passages of scripture were in conflict, the earlier passage was to be regarded as superior. This would mean that the law of divorce which Moses introduced was made invalid by the prior law of creation.

He said to them: both TEV and GECL specifically identify **He** as Jesus.

Your hardness of heart, a noun phrase in Greek, is transformed into a full clause in TEV ("**because you are so hard to teach**") and JB ("It was because you were so unteachable"). NIV, though retaining the figure of speech, also shifts away from a noun phrase: "because your hearts were hard." In English the **heart** is considered to be the organ which controls the emotions, while in Jewish thought it was related to the rational side of the human being. Therefore NEB translates "because your minds were closed," and NAB "Because of your stubbornness."

There are many languages where the phrase **Moses allowed you to divorce** will more naturally come at the beginning of Jesus' response to the Pharisees, as it is in TEV: "**Moses gave you permission to divorce your wives because you are so hard to teach**." Another way to structure the sentence is "You refused to pay attention to God's teaching, so Moses let you get divorces from your wives."

Your and **you** are plural forms. Jesus is speaking to the Pharisees who were there, of course, but the context indicates that he was referring to the Jewish people in general when he said "you." Some translators have said "you people."

But from the beginning it was not so is translated by TEV as "**But it was not like that at the time of creation**." GECL has "But it was originally not so." One may also translate "But it was not that way at the time that God first created man and woman" or "But that was not the way things were at the beginning."

19.9 RSV	TEV

And I say to you: whoever divorces his wife, except for unchastity,[j] and marries another, commits adultery."[k]	I tell you, then, that any man who divorces his wife for any cause other than her unfaithfulness, commits adultery if he marries some other woman."

[j] Other ancient authorities, after *unchastity*, read *makes her commit adultery*
[k] Other ancient authorities insert *and he*

who marries a divorced woman commits
adultery

And I say to you (TEV "**I tell you, then**") may be more effectively translated "For that reason I tell you" (GECL). The form of the saying is similar to that of 5.22, except that here the pronoun "I" is not placed emphatically in the Greek text.

Whoever divorces his wife, except for unchastity is almost word-for-word identical with the equivalent part of 5.32. The only difference is that **whoever divorces** translates a subjunctive, while "if a man divorces" of 5.32 translates a participle. For important comments concerning the exegesis and translation of this part of the verse see 5.32.

There are several ways translators have found to render this verse; for example, "If a man divorces his wife, unless she had been unfaithful to him (or, unless the marriage was unlawful), if he gets married again (to someone else) he is committing adultery," "Anyone who divorces his wife and then marries someone else commits adultery, unless the reason for the divorce was that his wife had been unfaithful (or, unless the reason for the divorce was that the marriage was illegal)," or "If someone gets a divorce from his wife for some reason other than that she had committed adultery (or, other than that the marriage was illegal), if he then marries someone else, he is committing adultery."

Unchastity or "unfaithful," if that is the interpretation chosen, will be expressed in some languages as "slept with another man."

There are two textual problems in this verse which need some attention: (1) After the word **unchastity** (TEV "**unfaithfulness**") some manuscripts add "makes her commit adultery" (see the RSV footnote). If this is an original part of the text, it means "makes her commit adultery when she marries again." However, it is the opinion of TC-GNT that this is a later addition, introduced on the basis of 5.32. Apparently none of the modern translations include this wording. (2) At the end of the verse, some manuscripts add "and he who marries a divorced woman commits adultery" (see the RSV footnote). Although it is possible that this statement was accidentally omitted by copyists, TC-GNT believes it more probable that the wording represents a later attempt to make the text similar to 5.32. Of the modern translations this clause is found only in Mft and NAB.

19.10	RSV	TEV

The disciples said to him, "If such is the case of a man with his wife, it is not expedient to marry."

His disciples said to him, "If this is how it is between a man and his wife, it is better not to marry."

There is now a shift in the participants. Jesus has been speaking to the Pharisees, but it is now **the disciples** who ask him a question. "**His disciples**" of TEV is probably better, since it avoids all possibility that the Pharisees might be called disciples.

If such is the case of a man with his wife is a judgment made solely from the perspective of the husband, not of both husband and wife, which is what may be concluded from TEV ("**If this is how it is between a man and his wife**").

When the disciples use the word **such**, they mean the fact that a man can only get a divorce if his wife has been unfaithful to him (or, if the marriage is illegal). Some translators make this explicit; for example, Brc "If that is the only ground on which a man may divorce his wife."

It is not expedient to marry (TEV "**it is better not to marry**") also reflects the viewpoint of the man, since in a Jewish situation wives were not allowed to divorce their husbands. The two clauses may then be rendered: "If this is the situation, then a man is better off not to marry."

19.11   RSV   TEV

But he said to them, "Not all men   Jesus answered, "This teaching
can receive this saying, but only   does not apply to everyone, but only
those to whom it is given.   to those to whom God has given it.

But he said to them appears in TEV with the pronominal subject **he** identified as Jesus ("**Jesus answered**").

Not all men can receive this saying is transformed in TEV to read "**This teaching does not apply to everyone.**" The precise meaning of Jesus' words is disputed, and both the verb **receive** and the noun **saying** have multiple possibilities of interpretation. NAB and NIV each translate "Not everyone can accept this teaching." This would seem also to be the interpretation adopted by Phps: "It is not everybody who can accept this principle." Brc ("This principle . . . is not practical for everyone") follows Mft ("but this truth is not practicable for everyone"), which is similar in meaning to TEV.

An alternative interpretation of Jesus' words is represented in TOB and GECL, where the verb **receive** is used of mental activity, a usage it has in some passages outside the New Testament. GECL translates the verse "Not everyone can understand what I have just said, but only those to whom God has given this understanding."

The antecedent of **this saying** may be either the remark of the disciples in verse 10 or Jesus' teaching on marriage in verses 3-9 (especially verse 6). "**This teaching**" of TEV, NAB, and NIV, as well as "what I have (just) said" of NJB and GECL specifically link the remark to Jesus' teaching on marriage, as seems also to be the case with "this truth" of Mft and "This principle" of Brc and Phps. Some translators have thought **this saying** was referring ahead to what Jesus was about to say, and so have had "what I will tell you now." However, this does not seem as probable, and translators will do better to do something similar to TEV or GECL, cited above.

Those to whom it is given is transformed into an active statement, with subject identified by TEV ("**to whom God has given it**") and Brc ("for those whom God has enabled to accept it"). GECL makes a similar restructuring.

In some languages it will be better to restructure the verse: "Only the people to whom God has given the understanding will be able to grasp the meaning of this saying" or "People to whom God has given the ability will be able to accept this principle—no one else."

RSV	TEV
For there are eunuchs who have been so from birth, and there are eunuchs who have been made eunuchs by men, and there are eunuchs who have made themselves eunuchs for the sake of the kingdom of heaven. He who is able to receive this, let him receive it."	For there are different reasons why men cannot marry: some, because they were born that way; others, because men made them that way; and others do not marry for the sake of the Kingdom of heaven. Let him who can accept this teaching do so."

RSV gives a literal rendering of this verse. The first part of the verse employs a literary device known as ellipsis, where words may be omitted if they are not necessary for the understanding of the text. In English this is most frequently done in commands where the subject is not mentioned. For example, "Stop!" is a command which assumes both a definite subject and a specific action, neither of which are indicated. When the verse is read through to the end, it becomes clear that the verse contains an explanation of some reasons why men do not marry, which TEV makes explicit: "**For there are different reasons why men cannot marry**" (see also GECL and FRCL).

For indicates that Jesus is explaining his statement. Some translators have said "I tell you this because" or "What I said is true because." In other cases it is more natural in the paragraph to have no transition word, starting simply with "There are some men."

For there are eunuchs who have been so from birth (TEV "**some, because they were born that way**") provides the first explanation of why some men do not marry. Phps translates "For some are incapable of marriage from birth," and Brc "There are some who have been born incapable of marriage." NAB ("Some men are incapable of sexual activity from birth") and GECL 1st edition ("Some men are impotent from birth on") are even more specific.

There are eunuchs who have been made eunuchs by men (TEV "**others, because men made them that way**") provides the second explanation. GECL translates "others—such as eunuchs—are made impotent by something that happens later on." NAB translates "some have been deliberately made so," referring back to "incapable of sexual activity" of the previous clause. Another rendering some have used is "Other men can't get married because men did something to them so they couldn't." In other languages sentences like the ones above will be too vague to be understood, and translators will have to be quite specific, as in "Other men have been castrated."

And there are eunuchs who have made themselves eunuchs for the sake of the kingdom of heaven (TEV "**and others do not marry for the sake of the Kingdom of heaven**") is the third explanation. Both NAB ("some there are who have freely renounced sex for the sake of God's reign") and Brc ("There are some who have voluntarily made marriage impossible for themselves for the sake of the Kingdom of Heaven") represents a step in the right direction, though neither of them deals adequately with **the kingdom of heaven**, as does GECL 1st edition ("Still others deny themselves marriage so that they can serve God better").

Some have taken **made themselves eunuchs** to refer to self-mutilation, and others understand it to mean simply that these men renounced sexual activity. The latter is probably better, but a translation like Brc (above) does leave open both interpretations. "Have voluntarily treated their bodies as if they were unable to engage in sexual activity" is another possibility.

For the sake of the kingdom of heaven can be "so they can accept God's rule fully," "so that as people ruled over by God they can do his will," or "so they can do only the things that serve God's kingdom." For **kingdom of heaven**, see comments on 3.2.

He who is able to receive this, let him receive it: the verb **receive** is the same verb used in verse 11, and, as one would expect, the translations deal with it here in a manner similar to what they did in its earlier occurrence. Most translators will use the same word in the two verses. For example, TOB has, "Let those who are capable of understanding, understand"; GECL is succinct: "Understand it, if you can!"

19.13-15

RSV	TEV
	Jesus Blesses Little Children
13 Then children were brought to him that he might lay his hands on them and pray. The disciples rebuked the people; 14 but Jesus said, "Let the children come to me, and do not hinder them; for to such belongs the kingdom of heaven." 15 And he laid his hands on them and went away.	13 Some people brought children to Jesus for him to place his hands on them and to pray for them, but the disciples scolded the people. 14 Jesus said, "Let the children come to me and do not stop them, because the Kingdom of heaven belongs to such as these." 15 He placed his hands on them and then went away.

SECTION HEADING: **"Jesus Blesses Little Children"** can be misunderstood to mean Jesus blessed all children, so the heading may have to be "Jesus blesses some small children." In languages where all blessings are seen to come from God, the title can be "Jesus asks God to bless some children" or "Jesus prays for some small children."

Matthew follows Mark (10.13-16) in narrating this brief episode at this place in the framework of his Gospel. There are, however, slight differences in the two accounts. According to Matthew, the children are brought to Jesus so that he might place his hands upon them and pray for them (verse 13), whereas Mark states that they were brought to Jesus so that he might "touch" them (10.13). In the words of one scholar, this shows that "Matthew thus understands blessing as intercession based on authority." A second difference is Matthew's omission of Jesus' teaching that a person must become childlike in order to enter the kingdom of heaven (Mark 10.15). But since this declaration was previously recorded in 18.3, Matthew evidently felt that it was not necessary to repeat it. Mark (10.13) and Matthew (verse 13) alike indicate the indignation of the disciples at the bringing of the child to Jesus, but only Mark (10.14) records that Jesus became angry with the disciples for behaving this way.

RSV   TEV

Then children were brought to him that he might lay his hands on them and pray. The disciples rebuked the people;	Some people brought children to Jesus for him to place his hands on them and to pray for them, but the disciples scolded the people.

As RSV indicates, this brief narrative is introduced in Greek by a transitional, **Then**. Not all languages will require the retention of this form, though other languages may require more. It is omitted by JB and NEB.

Children were brought represents a Greek passive structure which is transformed into an active structure by several translations: "**Some people brought children**" (TEV), "people brought little children" (NJB), and "Several people brought their children" (GECL). NEB employs an impersonal active form: "They brought children."

Were brought will have to be "were taken" in many languages, or if the active verb form is used, "some people took." In cases where translators have had to supply an agent for **were brought**, the sentence may have to be restructured slightly to avoid confusion about who Jesus is being asked to bless. For example, "Some people brought their children to Jesus because they wanted him to lay his hands on the children and pray for them."

To him is translated "**to Jesus**" by TEV, which normally follows the policy of introducing participants by name in each new section, especially in passages likely to be used separately in public reading.

Lay his hands on them may be inadequate in some languages; that is, one may have to specify on what part of their body Jesus placed his hands. If so, "on their head" will probably be the best choice.

And pray is stated more explicitly in TEV ("**to pray for them**"). But some languages may require even more; for example, "to pray to God to bless them." Direct discourse is also a possibility: ". . . and pray, 'May God bless you.' "

Rebuked translates the same verb used in 8.26; 12.16; 16.22; 17.18; 20.31. In this verse "told them not to do that" or "scolded them" will be appropriate.

The people is literally "them" (NAB). But a literal translation of the text, especially if the passive form of the Greek is maintained, identifies "the children" as the referent of the pronoun "them." NIV translates "those who brought them"; TEV and Mft follow the pattern of RSV. JB ("The disciples turned them away") and Brc ("but the disciples warned them off") seems to suggest that the rebuke is directed toward the children, but this is surely not Matthew's intention. Consequently translators should follow RSV and TEV (**the people**) at this point.

19.14   RSV   TEV

but Jesus said, "Let the children come to me, and do not hinder them; for to such belongs the kingdom of heaven."	Jesus said, "Let the children come to me and do not stop them, because the Kingdom of heaven belongs to such as these."

Let here has the sense of "allow" or "permit."

If translators are using direct discourse, as in RSV, then **come** may be the most natural word to use. However, if indirect discourse is used, then either "come" or "go" is possible, depending on the receptor language. For example, "Then Jesus told his disciples to let the children come (or, go) to him." "Approach" is also possible.

Hinder may also mean either "forbid" or "stop" (TEV, NJB); NEB prefers "try to stop."

To such belongs the kingdom of heaven, apart from a slight variation in the word order, is almost identical with "theirs is the kingdom of heaven" of 5.10. The major difference is the substitution of **such** for "theirs" in the Greek text. **Such** can be reflected in the translation by "people like these children." See comment at 5.10.

19.15   RSV   TEV

**And he laid his hands on them and   He placed his hands on them
went away.   and then went away.**

In the context the act of laying hands on the children may be meaningful, but in some languages **laid his hands on them** will more naturally be "laid his hands on in blessing" or "laid his hands on as he blessed them."

Both RSV and TEV, as most other translations, provide a fairly literal rendering of this verse. Attention should be given to the need for care in rendering **them**, which GECL represents by "the children." As in verse 13, it may need to be specified where Jesus placed his hands; for example, "on the heads of the children" or "on the head of each of the children."

And went away is part of the same sentence in the text, but many translations will begin a new sentence such as "Then he went away" or "After that Jesus left that place."

19.16-22

            RSV   TEV

The Rich Young Man

16 And behold, one came up to him, saying, "Teacher, what good deed must I do, to have eternal life?" 17 And he said to him, "Why do you ask me about what is good? One there is who is good. If you would enter life, keep the commandments." 18 He said to him, "Which?" And Jesus said, "You shall not kill, You shall not commit adultery, You shall not steal, You shall not bear false witness, 19 Honor your father and mother, and, You shall love your neighbor as yourself." 20 The young man said to him, "All these I have observed; what do I still lack?" 21 Jesus said to him, "If you would be perfect, go, sell what you possess and give to the poor, and you will have treasure in heaven; and come, follow me." 22

16 Once a man came to Jesus. "Teacher," he asked, "what good thing must I do to receive eternal life?"

17 "Why do you ask me concerning what is good?" answered Jesus. "There is only One who is good. Keep the commandments if you want to enter life."

18 "What commandments?" he asked.

Jesus answered, "Do not commit murder; do not commit adultery; do not steal; do not accuse anyone falsely; 19 respect your father and your mother; and love your neighbor as you love yourself."

20 "I have obeyed all these commandments," the young man replied. "What else do I

When the young man heard this he went away sorrowful; for he had great possessions.	need to do?"
	21 Jesus said to him, "If you want to be perfect, go and sell all you have and give the money to the poor, and you will have riches in heaven; then come and follow me."
	22 When the young man heard this, he went away sad, because he was very rich.

SECTION HEADING: "**The Rich Young Man**" is perhaps not an appropriate heading here, for reasons stated below. "Jesus teaches about the danger of riches" or "(Jesus teaches about) rich people and God's rule" is better.

This narrative, verses 16-30, is also included in both Mark (10.17-31) and Luke (18.18-30). It is developed in essentially the same way by all three writers, though there are some significant variations in detail. One must keep in mind that both the narrative itself (verses 16-22) and the teaching that grows out of it (verse 23-30) are viewed by Matthew as instructions to the church of his day regarding the matter of possessions. In this respect the section heading of TEV, "**The Rich Young Man**," probably places the emphasis in the wrong place. A more accurate statement would be something like "The danger of riches" (see GECL, NAB). NJB has "The rich young man" here, but "The danger of riches" at verse 23.

19.16	RSV	TEV
	And behold, one came up to him, saying, "Teacher, what good deed must I do, to have eternal life?"	Once a man came to Jesus. "Teacher," he asked, "what good thing must I do to receive eternal life?"

And behold translates a Semitism which may be used either to indicate emphasis or to mark a transition. Here it seems to function solely as a transitional, and so TEV renders it as "**Once**." Some translations have had something like "It happened one time that." Other translations do not even represent it in the text (Mft, AT, Brc).

One is a masculine form in Greek, and so several translations utilize "**man**" (TEV, NJB, NEB). Mark describes the individual in the same way, though Luke (18.18, TEV) speaks of him as "a Jewish leader" (RSV "a ruler").

As elsewhere **came up to** may more naturally be "went up to" or "approached."

TEV identifies **him** as Jesus, because this sentence begins a new section and paragraph.

Teacher is the wording of most translations. In some Greek manuscripts the adjective "good" is also found (KJV "Good master"), but TC-GNT concludes that this modifier was brought in by later copyists from the parallel accounts in Mark (10.17) and Luke (18.18). For comments on **teacher**, see 8.19.

What good deed (so also Mft, AT, NJB) is translated "**what good thing**" by TEV, NIV. In Greek the neuter adjective **good** appears alone, without specific mention of the noun which it modifies. Therefore NEB and NAB render "what good." However, for many languages it will be impossible to leave the modifier **good**

without specific mention of the noun it modifies. Since the reference is obviously to some meritorious deed or action, the proposals represented by RSV and Mft are perhaps the best solutions. Brc restructures "what must I do to make myself good enough . . . ?"

Eternal life is mentioned three times in the Gospel, twice in this chapter (verses 16,29) and once in 25.46. Originally it was primarily a qualitative term, descriptive of life in the "age" in which God would rule (**eternal** derives from the noun "age"). But it later developed the meaning **eternal** or "everlasting," since it was believed that the coming age of God's rule would be endless. Elsewhere Matthew uses the adjective in the combination of "eternal fire" (18.8) and "eternal punishment" (25.46). So it is quite likely that the meaning is best expressed as "everlasting" or **eternal**.

Have eternal life has sometimes been translated as "receive eternal life." In either case there is an implied giver of this life, God, and some languages require that this be made explicit, as in "for God to give me life that doesn't end."

Sometimes it is necessary to restructure the sentence, as for example, "Teacher, if I am to have eternal life, what good deed must I do?" or "For God to give me eternal life, what good thing do I have to do?"

19.17 RSV	TEV
And he said to him, "Why do you ask me about what is good? One there is who is good. If you would enter life, keep the commandments."	"Why do you ask me concerning what is good?" answered Jesus. "There is only One who is good. Keep the commandments if you want to enter life."

For purely stylistic reasons TEV translates **And he said to him** as "**answered Jesus**" (so also GECL) and places it after the quotation.

Matthew's account of Jesus' response to the young man, **Why do you ask me about what is good? One there is who is good**, differs considerably from that recorded in Mark (10.18) and Luke (18.19). But in a few ancient Greek manuscripts the reply has been changed so as to harmonize with the other two Gospels ("Why do you call me good? No one is good but God alone"), and it was these harmonized manuscripts that were available to the translators of the KJV.

Why do you ask me about what is good (so also NJB, AT, Mft) is translated "Why do you ask me what is good?" by GECL. The question is straightforward and raises no real problems, though there is an inconsistency between the question raised by the young man and the reply given him by Jesus. However, there is nothing that can legitimately be done to resolve that difficulty, though NEB does make an attempt in that direction: " 'Master, what good must I do to gain eternal life?' 'Good?' said Jesus. 'Why do you ask me about that?' "

Most translators see this question, **Why do you ask me about what is good?** to be a mild rebuke. Consequently they have expressed the question in a way that makes that clear in the receptor language; for example, "You should not be asking me about what is good" or "You ask me about what is good. Is that proper?"

One there is who is good is given a more natural word order in TEV: "**There is only One who is good.**" Since God is the **One** referred to, it is possible to translate "God is the only one who is good."

The two clauses of the Greek sentence, **If you would enter life, keep the commandments**, are inverted by TEV in order to achieve a more natural arrangement for English speakers: "**Keep the commandments if you want to live.**" However, the order of the two clauses may be maintained in a way that is logical: "There is only One who is good! If you want to live with him, then obey his commands."

The phrase **enter life** is not particularly meaningful in many languages. It is actually equivalent in meaning to "have eternal life" of the previous verse, and translators can say here "receive eternal life" or use a sentence such as "if you want God to give you eternal life."

Keep the commandments is a uniquely Matthean emphasis (see, for example, 23.3; 28.20). Mark (10.19) and Luke (18.20) each have "You know the commandments." The commandments referred to are actually those given by God through Moses. "Keep God's commandments" is possible, as is "Follow the commandments Moses gave us."

19.18	RSV	TEV
	He said to him, "Which?" And Jesus said, "You shall not kill, You shall not commit adultery, You shall not steal, You shall not bear false witness,	"What commandments?" he asked. Jesus answered, "Do not commit murder; do not commit adultery; do not steal; do not accuse anyone falsely;

Notice that this verse and verse 17 both begin with **He said to him**. Of course, in the context the participants are clear, but it may be necessary to have here "And the man said to Jesus." **He said to him** appears in TEV as "**he asked**" and in GECL as "asked the man."

Which? (so also JB) of the Greek text is translated "Which commandments?" by NEB and "**What commandments?**" by TEV; AT, NIV, NAB have "Which ones?"

A comparison of the commandments as given in Matthew and Mark (10.19) yields interesting results: (1) Matthew does not follow the Marcan sequence of commandments; (2) "Do not cheat" (not one of the Ten Commandments) is omitted from Matthew's list; and (3) Matthew adds the command to **love your neighbor as yourself** (taken from Lev 19.18), which he repeats in 22.39, where it does have parallels in Mark (12.31) and Luke (10.27). The other four commandments originate from either Exodus 20.13-16 or the parallel in Deuteronomy 5.17-20. In Greek the series of five commands is introduced by the definite article "the" (impossible to produce in English translation), which suggests that by the time Matthew wrote his Gospel, these five commandments had been placed together as a recognized unit.

Rather than simply have Jesus list the commandments, some translators have tried to indicate that he is quoting from the Law of Moses. They have said "Jesus answered by stating these commandments from God's Law" or "Jesus said to the man, 'The laws are that you shall not . . . .' "

Traditionally in the Old Testament the commandments were listed in second person, "You shall" or "You shall not." In other languages, however, it may be more natural to say "A person shall (or shall not)" or "Everyone (or, no one) should." In English "should" or "must" are better as commands than "shall."

You shall not kill was discussed at 5.21. For discussion of **You shall not commit adultery**, see 5.27.

You shall not steal: translators may have to make other participants explicit, as in "You shall (or, must) not take anything that belongs to someone else." Whatever is the usual way to speak of stealing should be used.

You shall not bear false witness, this traditional rendering of English translations (see also AT, NAB) refers specifically to a courtroom setting. NEB has "do not give false evidence," and NIV "do not give false testimony"; in TEV the command is rendered "**do not accuse anyone falsely**." Another possibility is "Don't lie about someone in court."

19.19 RSV	TEV
Honor your father and mother, and, You shall love your neighbor as yourself."	respect your father and your mother; and love your neighbor as you love yourself."

The commandment **Honor your father and mother** was discussed at 15.4.

Surprisingly (at least to many English speakers) **love** often proves to be very difficult to translate. Translators should avoid a word that would mean "lust" and should look instead for a word or phrase that means "to have concern for" or "to care about very strongly."

Neighbor is translated "fellow man" by GECL. In the Leviticus context the reference is to fellow Jews, but in the setting of the Gospel the word is inclusive of all persons with whom an individual has any contact.

As has been taken by some in the sense of "in the same manner as," but probably "just as much as" is better. Thus the sentence can be "You should be concerned for your fellow men as much as you are concerned for yourself." Notice that although **neighbor** is singular, it is often natural to render it with a plural, "fellow men."

19.20 RSV	TEV
The young man said to him, "All these I have observed; what do I still lack?"	"I have obeyed all these commandments," the young man replied. "What else do I need to do?"

For stylistic reasons TEV translates **The young man said to him** as "the young man replied" and places it after the quotation of the man's words. For many languages it will be more natural to retain the order of the Greek and introduce the speaker before giving his words. **Young man** is used in Matthew's Gospel only here and in verse 22. There is no way to determine with precision the age limitations indicated by the word.

All these, a reference to the commandments quoted by Jesus in verse 19 (TEV "**all these commandments**"), is placed in an emphatic position in the Greek text. There is poor textual support for the phrase "from my youth up" (KJV), which was obviously brought into the text on the basis of the parallels in Mark (10.20) and Luke (18.21). At the risk of shifting **All these** to a less emphatic position, TEV restructures the clause to reflect a more natural word order for English speakers: "**I have obeyed all these commandments.**" A way to retain the emphasis on **all these** is to say "All of these commandments are ones I have obeyed."

What do I still lack? is translated "What more do I need to do?" by NJB and "Where do I still fall short?" by NEB. According to Mark, the young man does not ask the question; instead, Jesus says to him "You lack one thing" (10.21).

19.21 RSV	TEV
Jesus said to him, "If you would be perfect, go, sell what you possess and give to the poor, and you will have treasure in heaven; and come, follow me."	Jesus said to him, "If you want to be perfect, go and sell all you have and give the money to the poor, and you will have riches in heaven; then come and follow me."

The conditional clause **If you would be** is more naturally "**If you want to be**" or "The way for you to be."

In the translation of this verse it is important to realize that Jesus is not here distinguishing between two categories of Christians, as though some were perfect and others were not. The word **perfect** is found elsewhere in Matthew's Gospel only in 5.48, where it is used in the context of showing love to one's enemies. Here it is also used in connection with the command to love, as verse 19 clearly indicates. According to Matthew then, to be **perfect** is to love as God does, which is expressed through radical forgiveness and unselfish giving.

Perfect has posed a problem for many translators. Some have had "without any fault" or "completely as you should be." Others have connected the idea to God's perfection and said "completely the way God wants you." Another common translation has been to tie it to the original question the man asked about eternal life and say "completely qualified for (God's) eternal life."

It is also important to realize that the command **go, sell what you possess and give to the poor** does not describe a universal route by which all of Jesus' disciples may become "perfect." Rather it represents a unique command given to a particular individual in a specific situation. Although radical forgiveness and absolute obedience are demanded of all disciples, this does not require that in each instance a disciple must sell all his possessions and give the money to the poor.

What you possess (NEB "your possessions") is translated "everything you have" by Brc, and "your property" by Mft and AT. There are only three occurrences of the noun in Matthew's Gospel: in 24.47 RSV translates it as "possessions," and as "property" in 25.14.

In Greek **give** is not accompanied by a direct object, though it is followed by an indirect object, indicating the persons to whom the gift is to be made: **to the poor**. But here the command is absolute, requiring that the man convert everything that he owns into cash and then give that money to the poor. The radical nature of the command is reflected in the choice of an aorist imperative of the verb **give**, which would imply immediate and absolute giving. Thus several translations have "**give the money to the poor**" (TEV, Mft, AT, NJB). A translation like this avoids the problem of readers thinking the man was to give the possessions rather than the money to the poor.

Treasure in heaven (so also NJB, NAB) is rendered "**riches in heaven**" by TEV and NEB. **Heaven** here stands for "God," while **treasure** represents the "reward" which God will bestow upon those who are obedient to him. GECL translates the phrase as "riches with God that cannot be lost." Translators should also see 6.20 where a similar expression is discussed. Under no circumstance should readers get the impression that somehow up in the sky there are some valuable objects that a person will have, possibly after he dies.

And come, follow me (TEV "**come and follow me**") is a fairly literal rendering of the Greek, and it is representative of what most other translations have done. Although an actual following of Jesus is involved in this situation, the verb has its extended meaning of "follow as a disciple," which is why many translators have said "be my disciple" or "follow as my disciple."

19.22   RSV   TEV

When the young man heard this he went away sorrowful; for he had great possessions.

When the young man heard this, he went away sad, because he was very rich.

This refers to what Jesus has just said, and can be rendered if necessary as "these words."

The Greek participle translated **sorrowful** (TEV "**sad**") comes from the same verb as that used of the disciples in 26.22. It also is used of Jesus during his experience in Gethsemane (26.37). It may have to be expressed by a separate verb, as in "he went away and was very sad," or better, "he became very sad and went away." Brc has "he went sadly away."

For he had great possessions (TEV "**because he was very rich**") is the sole reason given for the man's rejection of Jesus. **Possessions** is not the same noun used in verse 21. Although it may be used of possessions of any type, it later came to have the more restricted meaning of "piece of ground" (see Acts 5.1). Here it is best taken in the broadest sense possible, though it is quite possible that the man's possessions consisted primarily of land. Translators can say, "because he owned many things" or "because he owned a lot of property."

19.23-30

RSV   TEV

23 And Jesus said to his disciples, "Truly, I say to you, it will be hard for a rich man to enter the kingdom of heaven. 24 Again I tell you, it is easier for a camel to go through the eye of a needle than for a rich man to enter the kingdom of God." 25 When the disciples heard this they were greatly astonished, saying, "Who then can be saved?" 26 But Jesus looked at them and said to them, "With men this is impossible, but with God all things are possible." 27 Then Peter said in reply, "Lo, we have left everything and followed you. What then shall we have?" 28 Jesus said to them, "Truly, I say to you, in the new world, when the Son of man shall sit on his glorious throne, you who have followed me will also sit on twelve thrones, judging the twelve tribes of Israel. 29 And every one who has left houses or brothers or sisters or father or mother or children or lands, for my name's sake, will receive a hundredfold,[l] and inherit eternal life. 30 But many that are first will be last, and the last first.

[l] Other ancient authorities read *manifold*

23 Jesus then said to his disciples, "I assure you: it will be very hard for rich people to enter the Kingdom of heaven. 24 I repeat: it is much harder for a rich person to enter the Kingdom of God than for a camel to go through the eye of a needle."

25 When the disciples heard this, they were completely amazed. "Who, then, can be saved?" they asked.

26 Jesus looked straight at them and answered, "This is impossible for man, but for God everything is possible."

27 Then Peter spoke up. "Look," he said, "we have left everything and followed you. What will we have?"

28 Jesus said to them, "You can be sure that when the Son of Man sits on his glorious throne in the New Age, then you twelve followers of mine will also sit on thrones, to rule the twelve tribes of Israel. 29 And everyone who has left houses or brothers or sisters or father or mother or children or fields for my sake will receive a hundred times more and will be given eternal life. 30 But many who now are first will be last, and many who now are last will be first.

At the conclusion of his dialogue with the rich young man, Jesus commented to his disciples that it is difficult for a rich man to enter the Kingdom of heaven (verses 23-24). His remark astonished the disciples (verse 25), who were of the opinion that riches were a sign of God's approval, thus assuring the rich of an entry into his kingdom. Verse 26 contains Jesus' response to the disciples astonishment, after which Peter affirmed that he and the other disciples had given up everything to follow Jesus (verse 27). Jesus' reply to Peter is in three parts: (1) the "Twelve" will be rewarded with a unique place in the coming age (verse 28); (2) everyone who has made sacrifices for the sake of Jesus will be abundantly repaid (verse 29); and (3) in the coming age there will be a reversal of roles (verse 30), implying that the poor would be made rich and the rich would become poor.

19.23   RSV   TEV

And Jesus said to his disciples, "Truly, I say to you, it will be hard for a rich man to enter the kingdom of heaven.

Jesus then said to his disciples, "I assure you: it will be very hard for rich people to enter the Kingdom of heaven.

Jesus now turns to his disciples to comment on the young man. **And** may be expressed as "Then."

Truly, I say to you translates the same expression used in 6.5. It was last used in 18.3,13,18.

It will be hard for a rich man to enter the kingdom of heaven is a fairly formal representation of the Greek text. A few translations, however, have attempted a dynamic equivalent: GECL translates "A rich man finds it difficult to get into God's new world"; MACL "It is very difficult for a rich man to surrender himself to God's rule"; and INCL "It is very difficult for a rich man to become one of God's people." Another good solution is "It is very difficult for a rich man to become a subject of God (or, a subject in God's kingdom)."

19.24　　　　RSV　　　　　　　　　　　　TEV

RSV	TEV
Again I tell you, it is easier for a camel to go through the eye of a needle than for a rich man to enter the kingdom of God."	I repeat: it is much harder for a rich person to enter the Kingdom of God than for a camel to go through the eye of a needle."

Again I tell you is almost the identical transitional formula used in 18.19; here it serves the same emphatic function as "Truly I say to you" of verse 23. In fact **I tell you** translates the same Greek words as does "I say to you" of verse 23.

The order of the two Greek clauses, **it is easier for a camel to go through the eye of a needle** and **than for a rich man to enter the kingdom of God**, is inverted by TEV. This requires that a shift be made from **it is easier for** to "it is much harder for," thus forming an excellent balance with "will be hard for" of the previous verse: "**it is much harder for a rich person to enter . . . than for a camel to go through.**" For some languages it will be more effective to mention the comparison first, as do the Greek text and RSV. In yet other languages, the normal way to make the comparison is to say something like "It would be difficult for a camel to go through the eye of a needle, but it would be even more difficult for a rich man to become one of God's subjects."

Since it is impossible for a camel to go through **the eye of a needle**, some interpreters have sought alternative meanings for **eye** and **camel**. However, Jesus is probably using a proverbial expression known to his hearers, which is intended to be an exaggeration. And, as has previously been noted, it is the nature of parables to exaggerate for the sake of emphasis and interest.

In areas where a **camel** is unknown, translators can use a descriptive phrase such as "a large animal with a humped back," "a large beast of burden called a camel," or "a domestic animal bigger than a cow." Jesus is illustrating his point by comparing the biggest domestic animal the people there knew with something very small, and there is therefore no real reason to substitute some other animal for **camel**. However, if retaining **camel** results in an unduly awkward sentence or one where too much focus is on what a camel actually is, then translators can consider using some other large animal such as a horse or a cow.

Most societies are familiar with needles but may call **the eye of a needle** different things; for example, "the mouth of a needle."

This is one of the rare passages where **kingdom of God** is used by Matthew in place of the more common "kingdom of heaven" (see 12.28; 21.31,43). That the two expressions are synonymous is supported by the observation that **kingdom of God** is here used parallel with "kingdom of heaven" of verse 23. NJB employs "kingdom of Heaven" in both places, while NAB prefers "kingdom of God." It is suggested that whatever form is chosen for verse 23 be maintained in verse 24. The problem is that for Jesus' audience (as for Matthew's readers) the two terms were immediately recognized as synonyms, whereas for contemporary readers this may not be evident.

See also the discussion on "kingdom of heaven" at 3.2.

19.25 RSV	TEV
When the disciples heard this they were greatly astonished, saying, "Who then can be saved?"	When the disciples heard this, they were completely amazed. "Who, then, can be saved?" they asked.

In some Greek manuscripts **the disciples** is replaced by "his disciples." But the difference is minor, since in such a construction **the** is equivalent to "his." Moreover, some languages will require the form "his disciples."

Were greatly astonished (NJB "were astonished") translates a verb plus adverb construction. NEB has "were amazed," and TEV **"were completely amazed."** The adverb is literally "very" or "exceedingly"; here it is used to intensify the force of the verb, which is translated "were astonished" by RSV in 7.28. Elsewhere the verb appears in 13.54; 22.33. As we described at the beginning of this section, the disciples believed that having riches was a sign of God's approval, so that entry into God's Kingdom was assured for the wealthy. Thus Jesus' words came as a surprise, for if the rich couldn't get in, how much more difficult would it be for them, poor men all! Translators may have "were completely taken aback," "were disconcerted," or "were surprised and confused."

Who then can be saved? or something very similar, is found in most all translations. For languages which do not allow a passive construction, one may translate "Who then are the people whom God will save?" or "Who then are the people who will become God's people?" or "How then is it possible for anyone to become one of God's subjects?" or even "Is it possible, then, for God to save anyone?"

Saved sometimes causes readers to ask themselves "Saved from what?" To which the reply must be "Saved from destruction to having eternal life instead." For this reason it is sometimes translated here as "receive eternal life" or "become one of God's subjects" (see above). However, because the concept of being saved is used repeatedly in the Scriptures, many translators prefer to retain the word.

19.26 RSV	TEV
But Jesus looked at them and said to them, "With men this is impossible, but with God all things are possible."	Jesus looked straight at them and answered, "This is impossible for man, but for God everything is possible."

Looked at (the same verb used in 6.26, but nowhere else in the Gospel) is the choice of most English translations, though TEV prefers "**looked straight at.**" The verb is actually an intensive form of the verb which means "look (at)," and it is difficult to know how much impact the intensified form is intended to carry. If a stronger force is intended than the unintensified form will represent, then 6.26 may be translated "take a close look at" or "consider carefully," and the present text translated in a way similar to TEV.

With men . . . are possible is restructured considerably in GECL 1st edition: "Men cannot do it, but God can do anything." It is obvious that **men** is here used of "people" in general.

It is also clear that in this context **this** means being saved. The translation can therefore be "People cannot achieve salvation, but God can do anything," or possibly "It is impossible for people to save themselves, but God is able to do all things."

19.27   RSV   TEV

Then Peter said in reply, "Lo, we   Then Peter spoke up. "Look,"
have left everything and followed   he said, "we have left everything and
you. What then shall we have?"   followed you. What will we have?"

Lo (TEV "**Look**") translates a Greek particle traditionally rendered "Behold." Its function is to serve as an attention getter. Since the pronoun **we** is emphatic in the Greek text, JB translates particle plus pronoun as "What about us?" Other translations (NEB, Brc) do not render the particle by a specific word, assuming that the context itself will convey the intended impact. In GECL the word is represented by "You know."

Have left everything and followed you is also the translation of a number of other English versions (TEV, NJB, Phps). NEB and Brc translate "have left everything to become your followers," thereby specifically indicating that the verb "follow" is here used of discipleship. See further comment at 4.20.

What then shall we have? means "What will we get for this?" (GECL). This question in not found in either Mark (10.28) or Luke (18.28), but for Matthew it serves as a transition to Jesus' answer of verse 28 (also absent from Mark and Luke). Peter is asking what reward they will receive for their sacrifice, and the question can be rendered "What will God give us?" or "What reward will we receive?"

19.28   RSV   TEV

Jesus said to them, "Truly, I say to   Jesus said to them, "You can
you, in the new world, when the Son   be sure that when the Son of Man
of man shall sit on his glorious   sits on his glorious throne in the
throne, you who have followed me   New Age, then you twelve followers
will also sit on twelve thrones, judg-   of mine will also sit on thrones, to
ing the twelve tribes of Israel.   rule the twelve tribes of Israel.

Truly I say to you is repeated word for word from verse 23; see also the related form "Again I tell you" of verse 24.

New world (so also Mft, AT, Phps) translates a Greek noun which appears as **"New Age"** in TEV and NAB. This noun literally means "rebirth" or "regeneration," and elsewhere in the New Testament it is used only in Titus 3.5. The Jewish historian Josephus employs it of the renewal of the land of Israel after a period of hardship, while the Jewish philosopher Philo uses it to describe the renewal of the earth following the flood. JB translates "when all is made new"; TOB "at the time of the renewal of all things"; NIV "the renewal of all things." Brc and Lu have "at the rebirth of the world." However, as one scholar notes, in the context of Matthew's Gospel it is "hardly likely that it includes a conscious reference to a new creation." Many translators have wanted to show that **new world** refers somehow to a coming messianic age, and have said "the new world that is to come" or "the new world God will establish."

Son of man: see comment at 8.20.

Glorious throne (so also TEV, NIV, AT) is more literally "throne of his glory" (Mft; NJB "his throne of glory"). But this is a Hebrew idiom in which "of glory" is the equivalent of an adjective used to modify "throne," thus providing the basis for **glorious throne**. Legitimate also is "his throne in heavenly splendour" (NEB), which does not necessarily locate the throne in heaven but rather qualifies it as possessing splendor (or "glory") of a heavenly origin or nature. In fact, if "judging" is here equated with "rule," then Matthew definitely conceives of the place of judgment as being on earth (JB's footnote explains it to have "the biblical sense of 'govern' ").

Not all cultures will be familiar with **throne**. Some translators have said "king seat" or an equivalent, but another possibility is to recognize that the term is being used here as a symbol of reigning or ruling. An expression such as "sit on his glorious seat to rule," or simply "establish his glorious rule," will show this.

Notice how TEV has restructured this verse slightly. A similar rendering is "When the Son of Man establishes his glorious reign in the future new world."

You who have followed me: TEV alters the verb construction to a noun construction, simultaneously shifting the numeral "twelve" from a position before "thrones" ("on twelve thrones") to become a modifier of "followers" (**"you twelve followers of mine"**).

Will . . . sit on twelve thrones means that each of the twelve followers will sit on a separate throne. As suggested above, **judging** may best be taken in the sense of "govern" (JB footnote) or **"rule"** (TEV), similar to the manner in which the noun "judge" is used in the Old Testament of one who was "ruler" of a tribe or a group of tribes.

Translators can treat **thrones** as they did **throne** above. For example, "You twelve men who are my followers will become rulers also and rule the twelve tribes of Israel."

The fact that the twelve tribes had been dispersed and integrated into other nations over the centuries, and that the Jews hoped for their reestablishment, cannot be rendered in the text. Therefore **the twelve tribes of Israel** is usually translated literally, and the historical information about them may be placed in a footnote. But translators can also say "the twelve tribes founded by our ancestor Israel."

It is possible that **the twelve tribes of Israel** is here used of the New Israel (that is, the church), but this is an identity which cannot be made in the translation itself. In any case the literal meaning is the more natural one, and there is no reason to depart from this interpretation.

19.29	RSV	TEV

RSV	TEV
And every one who has left houses or brothers or sisters or father or mother or children or lands, for my name's sake, will receive a hundred-fold,^{*l*} and inherit eternal life.	**And everyone who has left houses or brothers or sisters or father or mother or children or fields for my sake will receive a hundred times more and will be given eternal life.**

^l Other ancient authorities read *manifold*

In this verse Jesus' promise of reward is extended beyond the circle of the twelve to encompass all who will ever be called upon to make a sacrifice for him.

Left (so most translations) here means "left behind" or even "given up."

NEB very effectively combines **houses . . . or lands** as "land or houses" and places the phrase following the listing of relatives: "And anyone who has left brothers or sisters, father, mother, or children, land or houses." **Land** translates the same word used in 13.44. In the plural it can mean either "farm (or, farms)" or "village (or, villages)." It can be translated as "property" or "**fields**" (so TEV).

For my name's sake appears as "**for my sake**" in a number of translations (TEV, AT, Phps, NAB, NIV, Brc). It will be similar in meaning to the formulas used in 18.5,20; see also comment at 10.22. One may translate "for the sake of following me" or "for the sake of being my disciple."

A hundred-fold or "a hundred times more" (see Mft, Brc, NJB, Lu, NIV) represents the wording of some Greek manuscripts; others have the equivalent of "many times as much" (NAB, NEB, AT, Phps, GECL 1st edition, TOB). The UBS Greek New Testament prefers the wording followed by RSV and TEV (see Mark 10.30), though the other wording obviously has strong support (see Luke 18.30).

When translating **a hundred-fold** as "a hundred times more," it may be necessary to indicate what it is a hundred times more than. "A hundred times more than they gave up" will do this.

Translators may also have to specify from whom people **will receive**, as in "will receive from God" or "God will give those people."

Inherit eternal life differs slightly from the phrase "have eternal life" of verse 16. **Inherit** is the traditional verb used in the Scriptures of God's bestowal of blessings on his people. But to translate literally may imply to some readers that God has died. Therefore TEV translates "**will be given eternal life.**" GECL 1st edition expresses **will receive . . . and inherit . . .** by one verb: "will receive it all back many times over and in addition eternal life." It is also possible to identify the "hidden agent" of the verb "will receive" as God: "God will give him eternal life as well." For **eternal life**, see the discussion at verse 16.

But many that are first will be last, and the last first.	**But many who now are first will be last, and many who now are last will be first.**

This verse is repeated, only in reverse order, at the conclusion of the parable of the workers in the vineyard (20.16), and so it is probably intended to serve as a transition to the parable. The function of the words is to contrast a person's status in this present age with his status in the coming age. One may then translate "But many people who are first now will be last in the age to come, and many who are last now will be first in the age to come."

Some may get the wrong impression with **first** and **last** and understand these words in the sense of time. "Greatest" and "least" or "most important" and "least important" will then be better.

Chapter 20

20.1-16

RSV

TEV

1 "For the kingdom of heaven is like a householder who went out early in the morning to hire laborers for his vineyard. 2 After agreeing with the laborers for a denarius*m* a day, he sent them into his vineyard. 3 And going out about the third hour he saw others standing idle in the market place; 4 and to them he said, 'You go into the vineyard too, and whatever is right I will give you.' So they went. 5 Going out again about the sixth hour and the ninth hour, he did the same. 6 And about the eleventh hour he went out and found others standing; and he said to them, 'Why do you stand here idle all day?' 7 They said to him, 'Because no one has hired us.' He said to them, 'You go into the vineyard too.' 8 And when evening came, the owner of the vineyard said to his steward, 'Call the laborers and pay them their wages, beginning with the last, up to the first.' 9 And when those hired about the eleventh hour came, each of them received a denarius. 10 Now when the first came, they thought they would receive more; but each of them also received a denarius. 11 And on receiving it they grumbled at the householder, 12 saying, 'These last worked only one hour, and you have made them equal to us who have borne the burden of the day and the scorching heat.' 13 But he replied to one of them, 'Friend, I am doing you no wrong; did you not agree with me for a denarius? 14 Take what belongs to you, and go; I choose to give to this last as I give to you. 15 Am I not allowed to do what I choose with what belongs to me? Or do you begrudge my generosity?'*n* 16 So the last will be first, and the first last."

m The denarius was a day's wage for a laborer

n Or *is your eye evil because I am good?*

1 "The Kingdom of heaven is like this. Once there was a man who went out early in the morning to hire some men to work in his vineyard. 2 He agreed to pay them the regular wage, a silver coin a day, and sent them to work in his vineyard. 3 He went out again to the marketplace at nine o'clock and saw some men standing there doing nothing, 4 so he told them, 'You also go and work in the vineyard, and I will pay you a fair wage.' 5 So they went. Then at twelve o'clock and again at three o'clock he did the same thing. 6 It was nearly five o'clock when he went to the marketplace and saw some other men still standing there. 'Why are you wasting the whole day here doing nothing?' he asked them. 7 'No one hired us,' they answered. 'Well, then, you go and work in the vineyard,' he told them.

8 "When evening came, the owner told his foreman, 'Call the workers and pay them their wages, starting with those who were hired last and ending with those who were hired first.' 9 The men who had begun to work at five o'clock were paid a silver coin each. 10 So when the men who were the first to be hired came to be paid, they thought they would get more; but they too were given a silver coin each. 11 They took their money and started grumbling against the employer. 12 'These men who were hired last worked only one hour,' they said, 'while we put up with a whole day's work in the hot sun—yet you paid them the same as you paid us!' 13 'Listen, friend,' the owner answered one of them, 'I have not cheated you. After all, you agreed to do a day's work for one silver coin. 14 Now take your pay and go home. I want to give this man who was hired last as much as I gave you. 15 Don't I have the right to do as I wish with my own money? Or are you jealous because I am generous?' "

16 And Jesus concluded, "So those who are last will be first, and those who are first will be last."

SECTION HEADING: **"The Workers in the Vineyard"** may be too elliptical in some languages. Translators can have "The story (or, parable) about the workers in the vineyard" or "Jesus tells a parable about some workers in a vineyard." As we discuss in verse 1 below, **"Vineyard"** is a problem for many translators in areas where grapes do not grow, and it may therefore be necessary to use a short phrase to translate this word. But that can make the section heading very cumbersome, so another heading to use is "Jesus tells a parable about rewards for serving God (or, serving in God's kingdom)."

In this parable God is symbolized by the owner of the vineyard, and its teaching is summarized in his concluding statement, "I am generous." The theme of the reversal of one's situation in the world to come is also in Matthew's mind, as may be observed by his placement of the parable between 19.30 ("But many that are first will be last, and the last first") and 20.16 ("So the last will be first, and the first last").

20.1	RSV	TEV

"For the kingdom of heaven is like a householder who went out early in the morning to hire laborers for his vineyard.	"The Kingdom of heaven is like this. Once there was a man who went out early in the morning to hire some men to work in his vineyard.

For at the beginning of this chapter demonstrates rather clearly that sometimes the chapter breaks interrupt the natural discourse units. In fact the parable Jesus tells here is meant to explain further his statement in 19.30 that "many that are first will be last, and the last first." Some translators have tried to make this clear by starting the verse with "The reason I said that" or "What I said can be understood in this way. The Kingdom of heaven is like . . . ." Another way is to begin "Jesus continued by saying, 'The Kingdom of heaven . . . .' " However, most translators feel that solutions like these are not very natural, and simply drop the **For**.

Except for the inclusion of **For**, the introductory formula to this parable, **the kingdom of heaven is like**, is the same as in 13.31 (see also 13.24). Brc translates "The situation in the Kingdom of Heaven is like the situation in the following story"; MACL "When God establishes his reign, the situation will be like that of a man who owns a vineyard"; and INCL "When God reigns the situation will be as it is in this parable . . . ."

Householder is the same noun rendered "master of the house" by RSV in 10.25. See comment at verse 11. In this context it may be sufficient to say simply "**a man**" (TEV), "a farmer," or "a property owner."

In some languages it will be necessary to say where the man **went out** to. From verse 3 it seems that he "went to the marketplace."

Early in the morning (so also TEV) translates an expression which probably means "at dawn"; NJB has "at daybreak." This reflects the daily circumstances of Palestine, and several commentators note a saying of the Jewish rabbis: "The working day lasts from the time that the sun appears in the sky until the time that stars appear in the sky."

Laborers were not the regular employees of the man, but were people who hired out by the day. Translators can say "workers" or use a phrase like "to hire men to work."

A **vineyard** is a field of grapevines, but grapes and vineyards are not known in many parts of the world. Quite often translators use an expression like "a farm for grapes" or "the fields for the fruit wine comes from." However, the fact that this is a vineyard as opposed to some other kind of farm is not really important in this parable, and if the translation of **vineyard** results in an awkward phrase that detracts from the flow of the story, then it will be sufficient to use a general word such as "fields" or "farm."

20.2

RSV	TEV
After agreeing with the laborers for a denarius*m* a day, he sent them into his vineyard.	He agreed to pay them the regular wage, a silver coin a day, and sent them to work in his vineyard.

m The denarius was a day's wage for a laborer

A **denarius** (TEV "**the regular wage, a silver coin**") was the wage generally paid a laborer for a day's work (see RSV footnote). The word was first used in 18.28. Some translators have retained both the form and function with a phrase such as "a denarius, the wages for a day." Others have followed Brc with "a normal day's wage." It is best not to use a local currency term. For one thing, that would remove the story from its biblical context, and for another, modern currencies change value far too quickly.

After agreeing with the laborers is rather elliptical. In many languages translators will have to state what they agreed to: "He agreed to pay them the regular wage" (TEV) or "He came to an agreement with the workmen to work for a normal day's wage" (Brc).

He sent them into his vineyard, that is, he sent them to work in his vineyard. Translators should not specify the kind of work, such as pruning or harvesting, but use as general a term as possible.

20.3

RSV	TEV
And going out about the third hour he saw others standing idle in the market place;	He went out again to the market-place at nine o'clock and saw some men standing there doing nothing,

About the third hour (TEV "**at nine o'clock**"; GECL "about nine o'clock"). Although the Jewish day began at sunset, the hours of the day are calculated from sunrise, so that "the third hour" would be between eight and nine o'clock in the morning. NEB translates "three hours later," and NAB "about midmorning."

Others can either be "other men" or "other workers."

Standing (so most translations) may mean no more than "present," implying that the men were sitting around in the marketplace passing their time away with idle gossip.

Idle (so also NJB, NEB) is rendered "**doing nothing**" by TEV, Mft, NIV ("with nothing to do" by AT). NAB has "without work," and "unemployed" is the choice of Brc.

TEV has taken the phrase **in the market place** and made it specifically the place the man went to ("**went out again to the marketplace**"). Whether to say the man went to the marketplace or that the men were already there (RSV) should depend on the receptor language.

20.4	RSV	TEV

and to them he said, 'You go into the vineyard too, and whatever is right I will give you.' So they went.	so he told them, 'You also go and work in the vineyard, and I will pay you a fair wage.'

GECL, Brc, NEB, Phps begin a new sentence with this verse, though most translations rather slavishly follow the form of the Greek by letting the sentence that begins in verse 3 continue over into this verse.

Brc has rendered **too** here as "along with the other men," something which many other translators may find natural, too. Of course it is implied that these people are expected to work in the vineyard.

Whatever is right (TEV "**a fair wage**") is given the place of emphasis in the Greek construction (**and whatever is right I will give you**). However, most translators put the verb before the object, as TEV has ("I will pay you a fair wage"). The workers automatically would have assumed that they would be given less than the full daily wage of a denarius. One commentator correctly refers to this parable as illustrative of "the surprising righteousness of God," since what the workers receive at the end of the day far exceeds their expectations.

20.5	RSV	TEV

Going out again about the sixth hour and the ninth hour, he did the same.	So they went. Then at twelve o'clock and again at three o'clock he did the same thing.

About the sixth hour (see verse 3) is translated "**at twelve o'clock**" by TEV, and **the ninth hour** is rendered "**at three o'clock**." Most translations follow the same pattern for expressing time in this verse that they do in verse 3.

It may be more natural to state the times at the end of the sentence, as in "He did the same thing at twelve o'clock and at three o'clock."

20.6 RSV TEV

And about the eleventh hour he went out and found others standing; and he said to them, 'Why do you stand here idle all day?'

It was nearly five o'clock when he went to the marketplace and saw some other men still standing there. 'Why are you wasting the whole day here doing nothing?' he asked them.

And about the eleventh hour is translated "**It was nearly five o'clock**" by TEV. GECL specifies that this was the last time that the man went to the market to secure workers: "But about five o'clock when he went to the market for the last time . . . ."

Standing: see verse 3.

Why do you stand here idle all day?: the question expresses rebuke rather than surprise. TEV indicates this with the phrase "**wasting the whole day**." In other languages the rebuke can be conveyed with a statement and a question: "You have been idle all day. Is that good? (or, Why have you done that?)"

Idle: see comments on verse 3.

20.7 RSV TEV

They said to him, 'Because no one has hired us.' He said to them, 'You go into the vineyard too.'

'No one hired us,' they answered. 'Well, then, you go and work in the vineyard,' he told them.

For stylistic reasons **They said to him** is translated "**they answered**" by TEV and placed after the quotation. Languages will vary regarding what arrangement is more effective. Also for stylistic reasons TEV and FRCL introduce "**Well, then**" into the speaker's remarks as a transitional.

Hired us may need to be expanded to "hired us to work."

Go is translated "**go and work**" by TEV (also GECL and FRCL). Many languages may even require an explicit indication of the nature of the work that the men were sent to do in the vineyard. But see comments at verse 2.

Too here is used as in verse 4. TEV has not translated it explicitly here in verse 7.

20.8 RSV TEV

And when evening came, the owner of the vineyard said to his steward, 'Call the laborers and pay them their wages, beginning with the last, up to the first.'

"When evening came, the owner told his foreman, 'Call the workers and pay them their wages, starting with those who were hired last and ending with those who were hired first.'

The owner of the vineyard is shortened to **"the owner"** by TEV, since this information is clearly implicit.

Steward (TEV, Phps, Brc, NAB **"foreman"**) is used elsewhere in the New Testament only in Luke 8.3 and Galatians 4.2, where the meaning differs considerably. Here the person is someone whom the owner of the vineyard has appointed to be in charge of the workmen. It may be translated as "supervisor of the workers" or as "the man in charge of the workers."

Call the laborers and pay them their wages: according to Leviticus 19.13 and Deuteronomy 24.15, day laborers were to be paid each day before sunset for that day's work, so the scene described is obviously very typical.

Beginning with the last, up to the first is somewhat expanded by TEV for the sake of clarity: **"starting with those who were hired last and ending with those who were hired first."** Although **beginning with** may have the meaning "including," the interpretation of the text represented by RSV and TEV is the meaning preferred by most other modern translations as well. This may need to be a separate sentence; for example, "First pay the people we hired last and then others, so the ones we hired first are the last ones you pay."

20.9	RSV	TEV

And when those hired about the eleventh hour came, each of them received a denarius.	The men who had begun to work at five o'clock were paid a silver coin each.

Eleventh hour should be translated the same as it was in verse 6, although if translators used "about" in the translation, as in "about five o'clock," then that word will probably be inappropriate in this verse.

Many translators will follow TEV and expand **came** to "came to be paid" or "came to receive their wages."

For **denarius** see comment at verse 2. Brc has "a normal full day's wage."

Received is formulated as a passive in TEV: **"were paid."** Some languages will require a complete restructuring of the sentence. For example, "So the foreman paid a silver coin to each of the men who had begun to work at five o'clock in the afternoon" or ". . . paid the full day's wages to each of the men . . . ."

20.10	RSV	TEV

Now when the first came, they thought they would receive more; but each of them also received a denarius.	So when the men who were the first to be hired came to be paid, they thought they would get more; but they too were given a silver coin each.

The first are further identified by TEV as **"the men who were the first to be hired."** In other languages an adequate translation of **the first** may be quite different. GECL has "the men who had begun work the earliest," and NEB has "the men who had come first."

They thought they would receive more may be translated as direct discourse: "they thought, 'He will pay us more money.' "

20.11   RSV   TEV

And on receiving it they grumbled at   **They took their money and started**
the householder,   **grumbling against the employer.**

And on receiving is more naturally "When they received" or "When the owner gave them their money." In Greek **receiving** has no expressed object, but most English translations supply **it** (so NJB, NEB); TEV has "**took their money.**"

Grumbled may legitimately be translated "**started grumbling**" (TEV) or "began to grumble" (Brc). "Complained" or "criticized" are other words for **grumbled**.

Householder refers to the owner of the vineyard who has hired the men to work for him (see verse 1); TEV, NEB, and AT have "**employer**," NAB prefers "owner," and in NJB and NIV "landowner" is used.

20.12   RSV   TEV

saying, 'These last worked only one   'These men who were hired last
hour, and you have made them equal   worked only one hour,' they said,
to us who have borne the burden of   'while we put up with a whole day's
the day and the scorching heat.'   work in the hot sun—yet you paid
                                          them the same as you paid us!'

The text has **saying**. Whether translators have "grumbled by saying," or start a new sentence with "They said," or retain **saying** will depend on the receptor language.

These last worked only one hour: commentators note that the laborers are so indignant that they omit any form of polite address when making accusations against their employer. This is in contrast to the polite form of address used by their employer in verse 13. **These last** is translated "**These men who were hired last**" by TEV; NJB and Brc have "The men who came last"; GECL "The others who came last"; and NEB "These latecomers."

Only one hour (so also TEV) is literally "one hour," but English requires the use of **only** or of some equivalent form in order to make the comparison.

And you have made them equal to us: the equalization is that of wages: "**yet you paid them the same as you paid us!**" (TEV) and "and you have treated them the same as us" (NJB, Brc).

Who have borne the burden of the day and the scorching heat is placed prior to the previous clause by TEV in order to make the contrast more effective, though most translations retain the sentence order of the Greek. NEB, maintaining the original clause order, translates "who have sweated the whole day long in the blazing sun." Some translators start a new sentence here, as in "And yet we are the ones who worked all day in the heat of the sun."

20.13 RSV	TEV
But he replied to one of them, 'Friend, I am doing you no wrong; did you not agree with me for a denarius?	'Listen, friend,' the owner answered one of them, 'I have not cheated you. After all, you agreed to do a day's work for one silver coin.

One of them is understood by some scholars to mean "a certain one of them," referring to the one who was objecting the most. But no translation renders in this way, which is probably the wisest choice.

Friend is a polite way of addressing someone whose name is unknown (though it may also be used of one's close companions); it indicates that the person who uses it is both friendly and approachable. The word occurs only two other times in the New Testament (Matt 22.12; 26.50), and in each of these three occurrences the person addressed is in the wrong. "My friend" will be better in some languages.

I am doing you no wrong is somewhat awkward for English speakers. TEV has "**I have not cheated you**"; NEB "I am not being unfair to you"; and GECL "I do you no injustice."

Did you not agree with me for a denarius? translates a rhetorical question which expects the answer "Yes." For speakers of English the question form and the word order (**did you not**) are somewhat difficult; but it is possible to do away with both the question and the unusual negative construction: "**you agreed to do a day's work for one silver coin**" (TEV). Other restructurings are also possible. For example, "you agreed" may be made to read either "you agreed with me" or "we agreed." One may also translate "We agreed that you would work a full day, and I would pay you a full day's wages." Perhaps the most natural way in English is to add a negative question at the end of the statement, as in "You agreed to work for a denarius (or, a normal day's pay), didn't you? (or, isn't that so?)"

20.14 RSV	TEV
Take what belongs to you, and go; I choose to give to this last as I give to you.	Now take your pay and go home. I want to give this man who was hired last as much as I gave you.

Take what belongs to you, and go may be more explicitly rendered as in TEV: "**Now take your pay and go home**" (NEB "Take your pay and go home"). With reference to the coin mentioned in the previous verse, GECL translates "You have received it, now go." One scholar, who has done much research on the parables, suggests that **go** carries the meaning "you have no more business here." He also indicates that **I choose** means "it is my firm intention."

<u>**I choose**</u> can be rendered impersonally in English, as in "It is my choice" or "It is my wish" (Brc). However, sentences like "I have decided" or "I want" may be better.

<u>**This last**</u> translates a masculine singular form in Greek (TEV **"this man who was hired last"**), but for some languages a plural form may be more natural, especially in light of verses 6-7,9.

<u>**As I give to you**</u> is literally "as to you." When translating at a common language level, it will be expected in some languages that the verb be repeated as in RSV and TEV (**"as much as I gave you"**).

20.15	RSV	TEV

Am I not allowed to do what I choose with what belongs to me? Or do you begrudge my generosity?"ⁿ

Don't I have the right to do as I wish with my own money? Or are you jealous because I am generous?' "

ⁿ Or *is your eye evil because I am good?*

<u>**With what belongs to me**</u> is translated **"with my own money"** by TEV, NEB, NIV. Since the preposition <u>**with**</u> may also mean "in" or "on," the phrase may also mean "on my own land" or "on my own estate." Nevertheless, this alternative possibility is not represented in any of the standard translations. It is possible to change the question form to a strong affirmation: "I have the right to do what I wish with my own money!" NEB does away with the question form: "Surely I am free to do what I like with my own money."

<u>**Do you begrudge**</u> (so also AT) translates an idiomatic expression (literally "is your eye evil") which TEV and NEB take to mean **"are you jealous."** NJB, NIV, and NAB each use the term "envious." The same idiom is found in the list of sins in Mark 7.22. "Are you annoyed" is also acceptable.

<u>**Generosity**</u> (so also AT; TEV, Mft, NJB **"generous"**) translates the adjective "good," which here has the specific connotation of generosity. The question <u>**Or do you begrudge my generosity?**</u> may take the form of a statement: "You should not be jealous just because I am generous." It may be necessary to indicate some recipient of <u>**generosity**</u>, as in "Are you jealous because I am generous toward someone else?" or "Does it make you jealous when I am generous to these people?"

20.16	RSV	TEV

So the last will be first, and the first last."

And Jesus concluded, "So those who are last will be first, and those who are first will be last."

<u>**So**</u> is translated **"And Jesus concluded"** by TEV. All translations indicate a shift in speaker by closing the quotation at the end of verse 15, and some translations try to help further by introducing a new paragraph with verse 15. However, this solution is of no assistance to persons who must depend upon hearing the scripture

read, and its value is questionable even for those who read the scripture for themselves. A number of CLTs follow TEV in introducing Jesus as the speaker.

The last translates a masculine plural form in Greek. It may be necessary, not only to mark this as a specific reference to people, but to indicate the time periods: "So those people who are last now will someday be first . . . ." As in 19.30, to which this verse refers, **last** and **first** do not refer to time but to rank. Translators can use the same expressions here as they did there, possibly "least important" and "most important."

20.17-19

RSV	TEV
	Jesus Speaks a Third Time about His Death
17 And as Jesus was going up to Jerusalem, he took the twelve disciples aside, and on the way he said to them, 18 "Behold, we are going up to Jerusalem; and the Son of man will be delivered to the chief priests and scribes, and they will condemn him to death, 19 and deliver him to the Gentiles to be mocked and scourged and crucified, and he will be raised on the third day."	17 As Jesus was going up to Jerusalem, he took the twelve disciples aside and spoke to them privately, as they walked along. 18 "Listen," he told them, "we are going up to Jerusalem, where the Son of Man will be handed over to the chief priests and the teachers of the Law. They will condemn him to death 19 and then hand him over to the Gentiles, who will make fun of him, whip him, and crucify him; but three days later he will be raised to life."

SECTION HEADING: "**Jesus Speaks a Third Time about His Death**." This heading is almost the same as the one at 17.22. (But see also 16.21.)

Matthew follows the outline of Mark's Gospel in the inclusion of the third prediction of Jesus' death at this time. The event will take place in Jerusalem, and for the first time it is described as a death by crucifixion (verse 19). In fact the only other place in the Gospels where Jesus' forthcoming death is spoken of in these terms is in Matthew 26.2. In the introduction to the narrative, Matthew considerably abbreviates the Marcan account (compare verse 17 with Mark 10.32).

20.17 RSV	TEV
And as Jesus was going up to Jerusalem, he took the twelve disciples aside, and on the way he said to them,	**As Jesus was going up to Jerusalem, he took the twelve disciples aside and spoke to them privately, as they walked along.**

This section begins with a construction which makes it seem the readers already know Jesus was on his way to Jerusalem: **And as Jesus was going**. For this reason many translators restructure the first part of the verse: "Jesus was going (or, Jesus and his disciples were going) up to Jerusalem. As he was on the way, he took the twelve disciples aside and spoke to them."

In place of **And as Jesus was going up to Jerusalem** (so most translations), some Greek manuscripts have "As Jesus was about to go up to Jerusalem" (Mft; see also AT, NAB). TC-GNT concludes that the verb "about to" was included by later scribes in order to clear up a point of geography. It is only from the city of Jericho onward that one actually goes "up" to Jerusalem, and Jericho is not mentioned until verse 29. Therefore at this point Jesus is only "about to" get to the place (Jericho) where he will "go up" to Jerusalem. For most languages it will probably be necessary to indicate from the outset of this verse that Jesus' disciples were accompanying him: "As Jesus and his twelve disciples were going up to Jerusalem, he took them aside . . . ."

Took . . . aside (TEV "**took . . . aside . . . privately**") translates a verb plus adverb construction. Brc and Mft have "he took the Twelve aside by themselves" (AT "he took the Twelve off by themselves"), while GECL has "he called them to himself privately." The Greek verb itself may mean either "take" or "take aside," while the adverbial construction is literally "to himself." RSV seems to translate the verb as **took** and the adverbial construction as **aside**, because in Mark 10.32 (where the adverbial construction does not follow the verb) RSV translates this same verb as "taking." However, even in Mark, and without the adverb, the verb must surely mean "take aside," or else the Marcan passage makes no sense. For example, JB here translates "took . . . to one side" and has "taking . . . aside" at Mark 10.32, while NEB and NIV have "took . . . aside" for both passages (NAB has "took . . . aside" and "taking . . . aside"). By way of summary one may conclude: (1) In both Matthew 20.17 and Mark 10.32 the verb must mean "take aside." (2) The Matthean addition "by himself" must somehow show up in translation so as to distinguish the Matthean text from that of Mark. The best solution is to handle this in a manner similar to that of TEV, GECL, Brc, AT, and Mft.

On the way (so also NEB, JB), a noun construction in Greek, is translated "**as they walked along**" by TEV, Phps, Brc. GECL 1st edition uses an adverb which means "along the way." The phrase does not necessarily imply movement, and for some languages the force of the phrase is contained in the verb "was going up."

20.18   RSV   TEV

"Behold, we are going up to Jerusa-   "Listen," he told them, "we are go-
lem; and the Son of man will be de-   ing up to Jerusalem, where the Son
livered to the chief priests and   of Man will be handed over to the
scribes, and they will condemn him   chief priests and the teachers of the
to death,   Law. They will condemn him to death

Behold (TEV, Phps, GECL "**Listen**") here functions as an attention getter, and a number of translations render the text effectively without a specific word to represent it (Mft, AT, Brc, NIV). On the other hand, it is represented in JB, NEB, and NAB as "Now." For stylistic reasons TEV introduces "**he told them**" following "**Listen**."

And the Son of man will be delivered to: for **Son of man** see comment at 8.20. This expression may need to be translated as an impersonal construction: "where some people will hand the Son of Man over to." The verb **delivered** was first used in 4.12 (see comment there) and at 17.22); it is the verb commonly used of the handing over of Jesus to his enemies, including the betrayal by Judas.

Chief priests and scribes first appear together in 2.4 (see comments there). TEV prefers to use **"the teachers of the Law"** in place of **scribes**.

Condemn is used elsewhere in Matthew only in 12.41,42; 27.3. Here it is used of a legal decision. There will be some languages where **condemn him to death** will be expressed by two verbs, as in "They will declare that he is guilty and must be killed." Many translators will make this last statement a new sentence, as TEV has.

20.19	RSV	TEV

and deliver him to the Gentiles to be mocked and scourged and crucified, and he will be raised on the third day."		and then hand him over to the Gentiles, who will make fun of him, whip him, and crucify him; but three days later he will be raised to life."

In TEV this verse is a continuation of the last sentence begun in verse 18. In the Greek text verses 17-19 comprise only one sentence (see RSV), but the places at which new sentences are begun will depend entirely upon the demands of the receptor language. In any case the subject of **deliver** is still the chief priests and the teachers of the Law.

Deliver is the same word as in the previous verse.

Gentiles (the word used by most English translations) translates the Greek word most frequently used of non-Jews. "Non-Jews" is certainly the most common rendering, but NEB translates "the foreign power," and Phps has "the heathen." GECL translates "the foreigners who do not know God."

Mocked (TEV **"make fun of"**) translates the same verb used in 27.29,31,41; elsewhere it is used only in 2.16.

Scourged: prisoners condemned to death were beaten with a whip before being executed. This punishment was severe, and it was illegal to beat a Roman citizen with a whip (see Acts 22.25, where a different word is used of the same kind of beating). Some translations have had simply "beat," but the word here means "beat with a whip," so "flog" or "whip" will be better.

Crucified indicates execution by Roman authorities. Jewish execution was of four kinds: stoning, burning (pouring a heated substance down a person's throat), beheading, and strangling. Crucifixion involved attaching someone to crossed wooden beams or boards (usually by nailing) and leaving him hanging there until he died. If the translation does not indicate clearly to readers that **crucified** includes the semantic feature of execution or death (for example, "nailed to boards" may not clearly imply death), then the thrust of what Jesus is saying is lost. So this feature needs to be made explicit in the translation. For example, translators can say "executed (or, killed) on a cross" or "executed by being nailed to crossed boards."

On the third day (so also NJB, NEB), the same expression used in 16.21 and 17.23, is translated **"three days later"** by TEV. The form of the expression is slightly different from the parallel in Mark 10.34 (literally "after three days").

Will be raised (NEB "will be raised to life again") translates the same verb form used in 17.23 (see comment there and at 16.21). As there, if the passive form cannot be used, then the agent, God, can be made explicit: "God will raise him to life again."

20.20-28

RSV   TEV

A Mother's Request

20 Then the mother of the sons of Zebedee came up to him, with her sons, and kneeling before him she asked him for something. 21 And he said to her, "What do you want?" She said to him, "Command that these two sons of mine may sit, one at your right hand and one at your left, in your kingdom." 22 But Jesus answered, "You do not know what you are asking. Are you able to drink the cup that I am to drink?" They said to him, "We are able." 23 He said to them, "You will drink my cup, but to sit at my right hand and at my left is not mine to grant, but it is for those for whom it has been prepared by my Father." 24 And when the ten heard it, they were indignant at the two brothers. 25 But Jesus called them to him and said, "You know that the rulers of the Gentiles lord it over them, and their great men exercise authority over them. 26 It shall not be so among you; but whoever would be great among you must be your servant, 27 and whoever would be first among you must be your slave; 28 even as the Son of man came not to be served but to serve, and to give his life as a ransom for many."

20 Then the wife of Zebedee came to Jesus with her two sons, bowed before him, and asked him for a favor.

21 "What do you want?" Jesus asked her.

She answered, "Promise me that these two sons of mine will sit at your right and your left when you are King."

22 "You don't know what you are asking for," Jesus answered the sons. "Can you drink the cup of suffering that I am about to drink?"

"We can," they answered.

23 "You will indeed drink from my cup," Jesus told them, "but I do not have the right to choose who will sit at my right and my left. These places belong to those for whom my Father has prepared them."

24 When the other ten disciples heard about this, they became angry with the two brothers. 25 So Jesus called them all together and said, "You know that the rulers of the heathen have power over them, and the leaders have complete authority. 26 This, however, is not the way it shall be among you. If one of you wants to be great, he must be the servant of the rest; 27 and if one of you wants to be first, he must be your slave—like the Son of Man, who did not come to be served, but to serve and to give his life to redeem many people."

SECTION HEADING: **"A Mother's Request."** This may need to be expressed as a short sentence such as "A mother asks Jesus for something (or, for a favor)." It may even be helpful to identify the mother, as in "The mother of two disciples requests something from Jesus."

For Matthew this narrative concludes the series of instructions that Jesus gives his community for life in this world (17.24–20.28). Jesus himself sets the example as he gives these teachings on his way to Jerusalem and the cross. The community of Jesus' followers is not to be concerned with greatness (18.1-5; 20.20-25) but with service (20.26-27), as Jesus' own example indicates (20.28).

20.20   RSV   TEV

Then the mother of the sons of Zebedee came up to him, with her sons, and kneeling before him she asked him for something.

Then the wife of Zebedee came to Jesus with her two sons, bowed before him, and asked him for a favor.

Then translates the particle with which Matthew begins this section. By the use of this particle he makes a closer association between the question of greatness and the third prediction of Jesus' suffering and death than does Mark, who uses the conjunction "And" (10.35). Brc has "It was then," and others have said "After that."

For whatever reason, Matthew indicates that it was **the mother of the sons of Zebedee** (TEV **"the wife of Zebedee"**) who approached Jesus and made the request in behalf of her two sons. Mark (10.35) specifically states that it was "James and John, the sons of Zebedee" who came to Jesus with the request. It is also significant that Matthew further protects these two disciples by designating them as **the sons of Zebedee** without mentioning their names. By this alteration of the Marcan narrative, Matthew reveals that he is more interested in the teaching to be gained from the story by his readers than he is in specifically identifying the two disciples. To mention the disciples by name, as does LB, immediately shifts the intended focus of Matthew's account. It is possible to render **her sons** as "her two sons," however, since the number is specified in verse 21.

Some translators retain the form, **the mother of the sons of Zebedee**. This is acceptable as long as it does not give readers the impression that she was the mother of Zebedee's children but not his wife. If that is the case, then translators should do something similar to TEV: **"the wife of Zebedee."**

Him is Jesus, and it may be necessary to identify him by name (so TEV).

Kneeling before him translates the same verb used in 18.26 (see comments there); NEB and NJB have "bowed low."

Asked him for something (TEV **"asked him for a favor"**) is more literally "asked something from him." NAB has "begged a favor," while NJB inverts the order of the two verb constructions: "to make a request of him, and bowed low."

20.21 RSV TEV

And he said to her, "What do you want?" She said to him, "Command that these two sons of mine may sit, one at your right hand and one at your left, in your kingdom."

"What do you want?" Jesus asked her.

She answered, "Promise me that these two sons of mine will sit at your right and your left when you are King."

And he said to her: TEV translates "**Jesus asked her**" and places these words after the speaker's words. But this is purely a stylistic maneuver, and each language will have its own preference of form.

You is singular; Jesus is addressing only the mother.

Command that (AT, Mft "Give orders that") is literally "Say that." TEV and NAB each have "**Promise me that,**" which is similar to "Promise that" of NJB; NEB has "I want you . . . to give orders that." On the basis of the Greek text, any of these solutions are valid. However, if either **Command that** or "Give orders that" is used, then some languages may require explicit mention of the person or persons to whom the order is given. Since the woman is actually making a request of Jesus, it is possible to translate either as Brc ("I want my two sons . . . to sit") or NIV ("Grant that").

One at your right hand and one at your left may be clear enough for some readers, but others may require a footnote (as in TOB) indicating that these two places represented positions of authority and power. Some translators have made this information explicit in the text, with a phrase such as "at the important (or, honored) positions to your right and to your left."

At your right hand may more naturally be "at your right side" or even "at your right." **At your left** is similar.

In your kingdom will be clearer if translated in the fashion of Phps and TEV: "**when you are King.**" For the meaning of **kingdom** see comments at 3.2. GECL has "when you assume your rulership"; and other languages may be more natural if the clause order is reversed: "Promise me that when you are king, you will let one of my two sons sit at your right and one sit at your left."

20.22	RSV	TEV

But Jesus answered, "You do not know what you are asking. Are you able to drink the cup that I am to drink?" They said to him, "We are able."	"You don't know what you are asking for," Jesus answered the sons. "Can you drink the cup of suffering that I am about to drink?" "We can," they answered.

But Jesus answered is translated "**Jesus answered the sons**" by TEV. It is important to mention specifically that Jesus is now addressing the sons (in Greek the plural form of the pronoun **you** is used); otherwise the readers will automatically assume that the words are addressed to the mother of the two men, since she is the one who made the request. At this point Matthew begins to follow more closely the Marcan form of the text.

You do not know what you are asking is a fairly literal rendering of the Greek text, and it is found in a number of English translations.

Are you able has sometimes been rendered "Are you willing" or "Are you prepared."

Cup is qualified by TEV and GECL as "**cup of suffering,**" to show that the term is used figuratively. If translators retain the image of **cup**, they must be sure that readers do not think Jesus is referring literally to something he will drink. Rather he is referring to the bitter suffering he must experience. Brc completely does away with the figure: "Can you pass through the bitter experience through which I must pass?" Others have had "Are you willing (or, able) to suffer as I am going to suffer?" In some languages it will be impossible to speak of "drinking a cup," since one actually drinks from a cup. NAB resolves this dilemma by translating the question raised here as "Can you drink of the cup I am to drink of?" Then in verse 23 the response of Jesus is phrased as ". . . from the cup I drink of . . . ." Phps overcomes the difficulty by dropping the cup imagery altogether: "Can you two drink what I have to drink?"

We are able (TEV "**We can**") is the answer of the two sons of Zebedee. It is obvious that a first person exclusive form of the pronoun **We** should be used; moreover it should be a form which will refer only to two persons (the two sons) and not to three (the two sons plus their mother), if the receptor language requires such a distinction.

He said to them, "You will drink my cup, but to sit at my right hand and at my left is not mine to grant, but it is for those for whom it has been prepared by my Father."	"You will indeed drink from my cup," Jesus told them, "but I do not have the right to choose who will sit at my right and my left. These places belong to those for whom my Father has prepared them."

Them translates a masculine plural form of the pronoun, thereby directing Jesus' remarks to the two brothers. It is better to make this specific, however, in verse 22, where the plural form of the verb ("[We] are able") is introduced.

Translators can render **drink my cup** very much as they did in verse 22.

To sit at my right hand and at my left occurs initially in the Greek clause, thus making it emphatic. But this is not the natural position for an object in English, and so TEV and a number of other modern English translations place this phrase following the verb **to grant** (TEV "**to choose who will sit at my right and at my left**"). For comments on **at my right hand and at my left**, see verse 21.

The impersonal construction, **is not mine to grant**, is transformed by TEV to "**I do not have the right to choose**." GECL ("But I cannot decree who will sit on my right and on my left") is similar in form to TEV, while Brc has "is not in my power to give you."

But it is for those for whom it has been prepared by my Father: TEV clarifies the referent of **it . . . it** and simultaneously shifts from a passive to an active construction: "**These places belong to those for whom my Father has prepared them**." NJB also makes explicit the meaning of the pronouns: "but as for seats at my right hand and at my left, these are not mine to grant . . . ."

Prepared (so most translations) is best not given so specific a theological sense as "destined" (Mft, AT); the primary meaning of the verb is "get ready" or "keep ready," and Matthew uses it elsewhere of a road (3.3), of a meal (22.4; 26.17,19), of eternal fire (25.41), and in a context much like the present one, of "the kingdom" (25.34). NEB has "assigned" and NJB has "allotted." Overall, however, it seems best to use the most neutral term possible, such as "get ready" or "prepare."

The latter part of this verse, **but it is for those for whom it has been prepared by my Father**, proves awkward in many languages because of the combinations of impersonal constructions and the passive voice. It may be necessary to restructure, for example, as "But my Father has reserved those places for those people he has chosen to be there," "The people who will sit there are the ones whom my Father prepared the places for," or even "My father chose the people he wants to sit there, and he prepared the places for them."

My Father, of course, refers to God. It may be necessary to say "God my Father" or "my Father in heaven."

**And when the ten heard it, they were
indignant at the two brothers.**

**When the other ten disciples
heard about this, they became angry
with the two brothers.**

The ten: some languages will require that **ten** be followed by the noun which
it modifies, which is "disciples." Moreover, since James and John are also disciples,
the full construction should be "**the other ten disciples**" (TEV). Several translations
have "the other ten" (AT, Phps, NJB, NEB), leaving "disciples" without specific
mention.

TEV has rendered **heard it** as "**heard about this**." Sometimes translators have
to say "heard what those two had done" or "heard about the mother's request."

Indignant is the preference of many English translations (NEB, NJB, NIV, NAB),
though for some speakers it may appear somewhat high level. Both TEV and Mft
prefer "**angry**." Elsewhere in the Gospel this verb is found in 21.15; 26.8.

The two brothers are specifically mentioned in the Greek text, but "the ten
. . . the two brothers" is restructured by GECL as "the other ten . . . the two." Each
language must, of course, do what seems most natural in the context. Once again
(see verse 20) LB introduces the names "James and John" (see Mark 10.41), thereby
violating the integrity of the Matthean text, which intentionally avoids mention of the
two names throughout the narrative. Mentioning the disciples by name draws
immediate attention to these two men and their own prideful ambition, rather than
to the teaching of humility and self-denial that Matthew is trying to convey to his
readers through the inclusion of the narrative.

**But Jesus called them to him and
said, "You know that the rulers of
the Gentiles lord it over them, and
their great men exercise authority
over them.**

**So Jesus called them all together
and said, "You know that the rulers
of the heathen have power over
them, and the leaders have complete
authority.**

Them is translated "**them all**" by TEV in order to avoid the possible misunderstanding that the reference is to "the two brothers" mentioned toward the end of
verse 24.

The rulers of the Gentiles lord it over them may be better translated
"foreign kings rule over their subjects" or even "rulers oppress their people" (GECL),
without specific reference to their being foreign rulers. This seems also to be the
understanding of NEB: "in the world, rulers lord it over their subjects." At the very
least **them** should be identified as either "their subjects" or "their people."

The expression **lord it over them** probably can best be translated by an
expression that means to have complete authority over them. An example is "rule
over them in everything."

Their great men exercise authority over them, which forms a parallel to the
previous statement, is rendered by GECL 1st edition as "and a man who has power

makes it felt by others." Brc is similar: "in their society the mark of greatness is the exercise of authority." If the form of RSV is maintained, then it may be necessary to indicate the persons over whom this **authority** (TEV "**complete authority**") is exercised: ". . . complete authority over their subjects."

Although for English readers **great men** may suggest heroes or the like, the context implies negative, or at the very best, neutral overtones. TEV's "**leaders**" would then seem more satisfactory. GECL 1st edition translates the two clauses as follows: "Rulers tyrannize their people, and those who have power make it felt by others."

20.26	RSV	TEV

It shall not be so among you; but whoever would be great among you must be your servant,

This, however, is not the way it shall be among you. If one of you wants to be great, he must be the servant of the rest;

It shall not be so among you: although the Greek text does use the future tense (**shall . . . be**), more than simple futurity is intended. The meaning is better expressed as "It is not to be so among you" (AT) or "It cannot be like that with you" (NAB). Since the idea of "oughtness" is really what is intended, GECL is best: "But it should not be that way with you." One may also translate "But that is not the way that you should act toward one another."

Great represents a literal rendering of the Greek text and is followed by most all translations; GECL translates "something special." Other possible phrases are "be considered great" and "be important."

Your servant is translated "**the servant of the rest**" by TEV. GECL shifts to a verb construction: "must serve the others."

20.27	RSV	TEV

and whoever would be first among you must be your slave;

and if one of you wants to be first, he must be your slave—

Attention should be given to the need of introducing a new sentence here, although RSV and TEV, as well as most other English translations, follow the pattern of the Greek sentence structure by continuing the same sentence through verse 27. This verse forms a parallel to what was said in the previous verse; here **first** substitutes for "great," and **slave** substitutes for "servant." Thus **first** can be translated as "most important" or "highest rank."

Your slave (as opposed to "slave of all" in Mark 10.44) refers to lowly service within the Christian community and represents a uniquely Matthean concern. Once again GECL very effectively shifts to a verb construction: "must subordinate himself to all." It can also be expressed as "take the very lowest position" or "be the one who serves all."

20.28   RSV   TEV

even as the Son of man came not to   **like the Son of Man, who did not**
be served but to serve, and to give   **come to be served, but to serve and**
his life as a ransom for many."   **to give his life to redeem many peo-**
                                            ple."

Even as indicates that Matthew introduces the saying about the Son of Man
as a pattern for Christian discipleship, as distinguished from Mark (10.45), where the
saying serves to indicate the reason for the coming of the Son of Man ("For the Son
of Man also came not to be served but to serve . . ."). This distinction between the
two accounts is completely obliterated by LB, which translates "For I, the Messiah,
did not come to be served . . . ."

Even as the Son of man may better be formulated as a complete statement:
"He must be like the Son of Man," "He must do as the Son of Man did," or "It is
just the same with the Son of Man. He did not come to . . . ." For **Son of man**, see
comments at 8.20.

Came not to be served may be translated as an active construction: "did not
come so that others would serve him."

To serve may require an object: "others" or "other people." Care must be
taken that the verb chosen to translate **serve** does not imply service at the table.

To give his life means simply "to die voluntarily." Of course a literal
translation is often understood perfectly.

The Greek noun construction, **as a ransom for many**, has become a verb
construction in TEV ("**to redeem many people**"). It is extremely important that the
word chosen to translate **ransom** not imply a payment of some sort. The Hebrew
background of the term focuses upon the act of setting free, not upon the payment
of a ransom. Moreover, if the idea of a ransom (as for hostages) is maintained, then
some languages will require mention of the person or persons to whom the payment
is made. This question cannot be answered on the basis of the Greek text, since there
is no assumption here of a payment. One may best translate "to set many people
free," or even "to set many people free from their sins."

20.29-34
          RSV   TEV

Jesus Heals Two Blind Men

29 And as they went out of Jericho, a great   29 As Jesus and his disciples were leaving
crowd followed him. 30 And behold, two blind   Jericho, a large crowd was following. 30 Two blind
men sitting by the roadside, when they heard that   men who were sitting by the road heard that Jesus
Jesus was passing by, cried out,*ᵒ* "Have mercy on   was passing by, so they began to shout, "Son of
us, Son of David!" 31 The crowd rebuked them,   David! Have mercy on us, sir!"
telling them to be silent; but they cried out the   31 The crowd scolded them and told them
more, "Lord, have mercy on us, Son of David!"   to be quiet. But they shouted even more loudly,
32 And Jesus stopped and called them, saying,   "Son of David! Have mercy on us, sir!"
"What do you want me to do for you?" 33 They   32 Jesus stopped and called them. "What
said to him, "Lord, let our eyes be opened."   do you want me to do for you?" he asked them.
34 And Jesus in pity touched their eyes, and   33 "Sir," they answered, "we want you to
immediately they received their sight and followed   give us our sight!"

him.

^{o} Other ancient authorities insert *Lord*

34 Jesus had pity on them and touched their eyes; at once they were able to see, and they followed him.

SECTION HEADING: "**Jesus Heals Two Blind Men**." This section heading is the same as the one at 9.27. See comments there.

Matthew continues to follow the Marcan sequence of events in the placing of this healing miracle at some point outside Jericho. Both Matthew (verse 29) and Mark (10.46) observe that the miracle happened as Jesus and his disciples were leaving the city, while Luke (18.35) notes that it took place as the group was entering the city. This is the final event recorded of Jesus before he enters the city of Jerusalem, and Matthew assigns it special significance, as may be observed by a comparison of his account with the Marcan parallel (10.46-52). Matthew tells of two blind men (compare 9.27-31) as compared with Mark, who mentions only one, a beggar named Bartimaeus. Thus the two men serve as two witnesses to strengthen the affirmation that Jesus is Lord (verses 30,31,33), a confession which is made in Matthew's Gospel only by believers. Furthermore, these men become permanent disciples of Jesus, as is intimated by Matthew's omission of Mark's "on the way" (10.52) after the statement that "they followed him." Finally, in keeping with an emphasis that emerges elsewhere throughout the Gospel, Matthew observes that the healing of the men reveals Jesus' compassion (verse 34; compare 9.36; 14.14; 15.32; 18.27).

20.29	RSV	TEV

And as they went out of Jericho, a great crowd followed him.	**As Jesus and his disciples were leaving Jericho, a large crowd was following.**

And again marks a continuation of the narrative. It can be omitted if that is more natural.

And as they went out of Jericho: though brief, this narrative is often read in isolation from the one which comes before it, and so it is good policy to identify the participants intended by **they**: "**As Jesus and his disciples were leaving Jericho**" (TEV).

In some languages the fact that the text has not said Jesus and his disciples had entered Jericho will make this verse seem odd. However, adding a sentence such as "They went to Jericho" may be seen as adding too much to the text. Rather they should say something like "Later, as they were going out of the city of Jericho" or ". . . having passed through the city of Jericho."

A great crowd followed him places Jesus in focus, but in some languages it will be more natural to substitute "them" (meaning Jesus and his disciples) for **him**, which is what GECL 1st edition does. TEV, on the other hand, leaves this information implicit by translating "**a large crowd was following**," assuming that the reader will conclude from the first clause that Jesus and his disciples are indicated.

20.30   RSV   TEV

And behold, two blind men sitting by
the roadside, when they heard that
Jesus was passing by, cried out,*
"Have mercy on us, Son of David!"

Two blind men who were sitting by
the road heard that Jesus was passing by, so they began to shout, "Son
of David! Have mercy on us, sir!"

*Other ancient authorities insert *Lord*

In Greek this verse is introduced by two words which RSV translates **And
behold** (see comment at 1.20). The formula here functions as a means of introducing
the two blind men into the narrative, and most modern English translations do not
use a specific word to render the Greek expression. NAB, however, translates "and
suddenly." JB very effectively uses the transitional "Now" and isolates the statement
about the presence of the blind men: "Now there were two blind men sitting at the
side of the road." Another possibility is "It happened that two blind men . . ." or "It
happened there were two blind men . . . ." Brc and many others make this statement
about the blind men a separate sentence, as for example, "(It happened) there were
two blind men sitting beside the road. When they heard that Jesus was passing, they
cried out."

When they heard that Jesus was passing by may be restructured as direct
discourse: "when they heard people say, 'Jesus is about to pass by.' "

Have mercy on us is the same plea uttered by the blind men in 9.27. As RSV's
footnote indicates, some Greek manuscripts include the noun of address, which may
be translated either "Lord" (RSV footnote) or "**sir**" (TEV). Both the position and
presence of the noun is in question, and the committee on the UBS Greek text
decided that the "least unsatisfactory resolution of all the diverse problems" of the
text was to place the word within square brackets (see TC-GNT). A number of
translations have "Lord" and place the noun in emphatic position immediately before
the phrase "Son of David." On the other hand, NEB deletes it entirely. The same
translational problem exits here as in earlier passages (see 8.2).

Son of David, first appearing in 1.1, is also the title by which the two other
blind men previously addressed Jesus (9.27). This was a popular name for the
expected Messiah, and it reflected nationalistic hopes. Commentators draw attention
to Isaiah 29.18 and 35.5, where restoration of sight was one characteristic of the
Messianic Age.

It may be more natural to have the men address Jesus before asking for his
mercy: "Son of David, have mercy on us." See comments at 9.27.

20.31   RSV   TEV

The crowd rebuked them, telling
them to be silent; but they cried out
the more, "Lord, have mercy on us,
Son of David!"

The crowd scolded them and
told them to be quiet. But they shouted even more loudly, "Son of David!
Have mercy on us, sir!"

Rebuked translates the verb first used in 8.26. NJB and TEV each have "scolded," while NEB, Brc, Phps have either "sharply told" or "told sharply." Clearest of all may be "told them sharply not to do that" or "told them sharply that they should be quiet."

Telling them to be silent may be expressed as direct discourse: "told them, 'Be quiet.'"

Lord, have mercy on us, Son of David! is often translated by two sentences (TEV), since this makes handling two vocatives easier, but "Lord, Son of David, have mercy on us" is another way translators have tried.

20.32 RSV	TEV
And Jesus stopped and called them, saying, "What do you want me to do for you?"	Jesus stopped and called them. "What do you want me to do for you?" he asked them.

Called them may need to be translated "called the two blind men," since both the blind men and the crowd are mentioned in the previous verse.

What do you want me to do for you? is more naturally rendered by an indirect form in some languages: "Jesus asked them what they wanted him to do for them."

20.33 RSV	TEV
They said to him, "Lord, let our eyes be opened."	"Sir," they answered, "we want you to give us our sight!"

Lord is translated "**Sir**" by TEV (see 8.2).

Let our eyes be opened is a Semitic way of saying "**we want you to give us our sight**" (TEV). GECL translates "we should like to be able to see," and Brc has "the only thing we want is to be able to see." Phps ("let us see again") and NJB ("let us have our sight back") are based upon the meaning which they find in the Greek verb translated "received their sight" in verse 34 (see comments there).

20.34 RSV	TEV
And Jesus in pity touched their eyes, and immediately they received their sight and followed him.	Jesus had pity on them and touched their eyes; at once they were able to see, and they followed him.

In pity translates the same Greek verb used in 9.36. As noted in the introduction to this section, this information is not included by either Mark or Luke. TEV expresses this as a verb, "**had pity on them**."

Touched their eyes is another unique feature of Matthew's account; both Mark and Luke contain only Jesus' statement that their faith had saved them, followed by the notation that they gained their sight.

Received their sight (TEV "**were able to see**") translates a verb which may also mean "able to see again." It is impossible to be dogmatic, and translations are fairly well divided in their interpretation of the verb.

If it is at all possible to do so, the verb **followed** should be translated in such a way as to leave open the possible meaning "followed as disciples."

Chapter 21

21.1-11

RSV	TEV
	The Triumphant Entry into Jerusalem

RSV

1 And when they drew near to Jerusalem and came to Bethphage, to the Mount of Olives, then Jesus sent two disciples, 2 saying to them, "Go into the village opposite you, and immediately you will find an ass tied, and a colt with her; untie them and bring them to me. 3 If any one says anything to you, you shall say, 'The Lord has need of them,' and he will send them immediately." 4 This took place to fulfil what was spoken by the prophet, saying,

5   "Tell the daughter of Zion,
     Behold, your king is coming to you,
     humble, and mounted on an ass,
     and on a colt, the foal of an ass."

6 The disciples went and did as Jesus had directed them; 7 they brought the ass and the colt, and put their garments on them, and he sat thereon. 8 Most of the crowd spread their garments on the road, and others cut branches from the trees and spread them on the road. 9 And the crowds that went before him and that followed him shouted, "Hosanna to the Son of David! Blessed is he who comes in the name of the Lord! Hosanna in the highest!" 10 And when he entered Jerusalem, all the city was stirred, saying, "Who is this?" 11 And the crowds said, "This is the prophet Jesus from Nazareth of Galilee."

TEV

1 As Jesus and his disciples approached Jerusalem, they came to Bethphage at the Mount of Olives. There Jesus sent two of the disciples on ahead 2 with these instructions: "Go to the village there ahead of you, and at once you will find a donkey tied up with her colt beside her. Untie them and bring them to me. 3 And if anyone says anything, tell him, 'The Master[s] needs them'; and then he will let them go at once."

4 This happened in order to make come true what the prophet had said:

5   "Tell the city of Zion,
     Look, your king is coming to you!
     He is humble and rides on a donkey
     and on a colt, the foal of a donkey."

6 So the disciples went and did what Jesus had told them to do: 7 they brought the donkey and the colt, threw their cloaks over them, and Jesus got on. 8 A large crowd of people spread their cloaks on the road while others cut branches from the trees and spread them on the road. 9 The crowds walking in front of Jesus and those walking behind began to shout, "Praise to David's Son! God bless him who comes in the name of the Lord! Praise be to God!"

10 When Jesus entered Jerusalem, the whole city was thrown into an uproar. "Who is he?" the people asked.

11 "This is the prophet Jesus, from Nazareth in Galilee," the crowds answered.

[s] The Master; *or* Their owner.

SECTION HEADING: "**The Triumphant Entry into Jerusalem**" may better be rendered as a short sentence such as "Jesus enters Jerusalem triumphantly (or, victoriously)," "Jesus goes into Jerusalem in triumph," or even "Jesus enters Jerusalem."

Chapters 21–25 narrate events which took place in Jerusalem immediately prior to Jesus' passion and crucifixion. Throughout this section of his Gospel, Matthew continues to follow Mark in broad outline, but he exercises freedom both in the use of his Marcan source and in the inclusion of materials from other sources, so that what results is a distinctively Matthean composition. These five chapters divide easily into two major sections: (1) conflicts during the last days in Jerusalem (21.1–22.46) and (2) final teachings in Jerusalem (23.1–25.46).

Jesus' triumphant entry into Jerusalem (21.1-11), followed immediately by the cleansing of the Temple (21.12-17) and the placing of a curse on a fig tree (21.18-22), leads the chief priests and the elders to question the origin of Jesus' authority (21.23). One scholar observes that Jesus' reply to their question is structured similarly to a trial scene (21.23–22.14), which culminates in a warning for the readers for whom Matthew addresses his Gospel (22.11-14). A second trial-like scene (22.15–25.31), which also includes warnings to the believing community of Matthew's day (24.11-12; 24.37–25.46), serves to intensify the seriousness of Jesus' instructions. In brief outline these twin trial schemes may be represented as follows:

(1) Israel's Leaders are Placed on Trial (21.23-27)	(1) Israel is Placed on Trial (22.15-46)
(2) Verdict (21.28-32)	(2) Verdict (23.1-32)
(3) Sentence (21.33-43)	(3) Sentence (23.33-36)
(4) Execution of the Sentence (22.1-7)	(4) Execution of the Sentence (23.37–24.2)
(5) Application: Warning to the Church (22.11-14)	(5) Application: Warning to the Church (24.11-12; 24.37–25.46), dominated by the theme of the coming of the Son of Man (24.27–25.31)

21.1   RSV   TEV

And when they drew near to Jerusalem and came to Bethphage, to the Mount of Olives, then Jesus sent two disciples,

As Jesus and his disciples approached Jerusalem, they came to Bethphage at the Mount of Olives. There Jesus sent two of the disciples on ahead

All four of the Gospels tell of Jesus' triumphant entry into Jerusalem (Mark 11.1-11; Luke 19.28-38; John 12.12-19), but they each do it in a way that differs from that of the other three. In the comments to follow, attention will be given to some of the unique features that appear in Matthew.

When they drew near is translated "**As Jesus and his disciples approached**" by TEV. Since this part of the Gospel is frequently used in public reading separately from the previous narrative, it is important that the reader and hearer understand from the outset who is meant by **they** of the Greek text. In many languages **when they drew near** will have to be preceded by some statement indicating that they were going toward Jerusalem; for example, "Jesus and his disciples went toward Jerusalem. As they were getting close . . . ."

Jesus' approach to the city of Jerusalem was made from the direction of Jericho, that is from the east. The exact location of the village of **Bethphage** is unknown, though it is probably east of Bethany. The name means "house of figs," with reference to a particular kind of fig that ripens late in the season. **Bethphage** is mentioned only in conjunction with Jesus' final entry into Jerusalem; both Mark (11.1) and Luke (19.29) have "to Bethphage and Bethany," whereas Matthew does not mention Bethany until 26.6. Since **Bethphage** will not be known to most readers, it may be helpful to say "the village of Bethphage."

The Mount of Olives is a part of the main mountain range which runs north and south through central and southern Palestine. It overlooks Jerusalem from the east and is separated from the city by the deep crevice of the Kidron Valley.

The structure of the text, **to Bethphage, to the Mount of Olives**, with **to** occurring twice, is odd in English and may be misunderstood if translated literally. "**Bethphage at the Mount of Olives**" of TEV is better. Translators can also say "to Bethphage, a village at the Mount of Olives."

Mount is a little misleading, since it refers here to a hill, not to a mountain. "Hill" (Brc) is therefore better. Also, readers must not get the impression that what is involved is a large heap of olives. "Hill (or, Mount) of Olive Trees" is sometimes a better translation.

Sent is perhaps better expressed by "**sent . . . on ahead**" (TEV, AT), "sent . . . ahead" (Phps), or "sent on" (Brc). Notice that TEV starts a new sentence here. Translators will need to look at verses 1, 2, and 3 together to decide on the most natural way to structure the whole passage. **Sent** may have to be rendered "told two of his disciples to go on ahead of them."

21.2	RSV	TEV

RSV	TEV
saying to them, "Go into the village opposite you, and immediately you will find an ass tied, and a colt with her; untie them and bring them to me.	with these instructions: "Go to the village there ahead of you, and at once you will find a donkey tied up with her colt beside her. Untie them and bring them to me.

The meaning of **saying to them** is "**with these instructions**" (TEV, NEB, NAB). GECL uses a verb construction: "and instructed them."

The village opposite is a reference to Bethphage. Many translators will find that TEV's "**the village there ahead of you**" will be a more natural expression than the RSV text.

Immediately (TEV "**at once**") represents a slightly different adverbial form than the one employed in the Marcan parallel (11.2), though there is no difference in meaning. Here it may better be expressed as "as soon as you enter the village."

An ass tied, and a colt with her is translated "**a donkey tied up with her colt beside her**" by TEV, and "a donkey tethered with her foal beside her" in NEB. Only in Matthew's Gospel are the two animals mentioned, and the care with which

Matthew mentions these two animals is to verify that Zechariah 9.9 is fulfilled in the actions of Jesus. Although the quotation from Zechariah does mention two animals, only one was actually intended by the author of the Zechariah text, who was writing in the parallel form of Hebrew poetry, where two terms are used to mention a single animal. But Matthew felt it important to adhere strictly to a literal interpretation of the Zechariah text, and so he introduces two animals into Jesus' instructions to his disciples. See comments at verse 5. Of course, here translators must refer to two animals, as Matthew did.

Note that the context indicates that the **ass** is a female. In some languages this will need to be stated explicitly as "a female donkey."

The text seems to indicate that only the adult donkey was tied up, and the **colt**, a young donkey, was simply there beside its mother. In some cases translators have said "a donkey tied up, and her colt will be there beside her. "Even though the text goes on to say **untie them**, it will be better to say "untie it." Of course, **tied** gives the idea that the donkey was tied to a post or tree, not that it was tied up so it could not move at all.

Untie translates a participle dependent upon the imperative **bring**. However, in such a construction the participle itself is equivalent to an imperative. In translating, one must take care that the verb **"bring"** does not imply "carry"; the meaning is obviously "lead."

21.3

RSV	TEV
If any one says anything to you, you shall say, 'The Lord has need of them,' and he will send them immediately."	And if anyone says anything, tell him, 'The Master[s] needs them'; and then he will let them go at once."

[s]The Master; *or* Their owner.

If any one says anything to you: TEV omits **to you**, since this information is clearly implicit. On the other hand, it is important that **anything** be understood as indicating more than a casual remark made to the disciples. The meaning is "If anyone objects," or "If anyone says, 'Why are you doing that?' " or ". . . 'Don't do that!' " Some have said "If anyone says anything to you about what you are doing."

Lord or "Master" (used of Jesus) is the preference of the vast majority of translations, though the meaning may also be "Their owner" (TEV's footnote). TOB is so strongly convinced that **Lord** is the correct interpretation that the translators provide a footnote which states that this is the only place in the Gospel of Matthew where Jesus specifically refers to himself by this title.

The text states **he will send them**, but if translators are not careful, it may not be clear that **he** refers to the person who raised objections about the disciples taking the donkeys. "Then that person will let them go at once" is clearer.

The text uses the word **send**, which TEV has rendered as **"let . . . go."** This latter expression does not imply quite as much willingness on the part of the owner of the donkeys, but since the idea is that he is giving permission to the disciples to take them, whichever expression is more natural can be used.

Immediately, though not the same form of the adverb used in verse 2, is its equivalent; that Matthew would use this adverb twice in such swift sequence suggests that he intends to emphasize the absolute authority with which Jesus gives the command.

21.4	RSV	TEV

This took place to fulfil what was spoken by the prophet, saying,

This happened in order to make come true what the prophet had said:

This verse repeats 1.22 word for word, except that here **This** substitutes for "All this" of the earlier introductory formula, and "the Lord" is not explicit here. It is implicit, however, and translators can use the same expression here as they did there.

21.5	RSV	TEV

"Tell the daughter of Zion,
Behold, your king is coming to you,
humble, and mounted on an ass,
and on a colt, the foal of an ass."

"Tell the city of Zion,
Look, your king is coming to you!
He is humble and rides on a donkey
and on a colt, the foal of a donkey."

Tell the daughter of Zion is a Hebrew idiom, which is rendered literally by most English translations, ancient and modern. The source for **Tell the daughter of Zion** is Isaiah 62.11, while the remainder of the quotation is found in Zechariah 9.9. In this construction the noun **daughter** is equivalent to either "**city**" (TEV) or "the people of the city." GECL goes one step beyond TEV and identifies the lesser known **Zion** as Jerusalem: "Say to the city of Jerusalem."

Behold (see comment at 1.20) has as its primary function that of drawing attention to the event which is to follow. It may be best to leave it implicit (so GECL, NAB). Mft, AT, NEB capture the effect by translating "Here is your king . . . ."

It is significant that Matthew omits a line from Zechariah 9.9, where **your king is coming to you** is followed by "He comes triumphant and victorious." Obviously Matthew's primary concern was to focus upon the king's humility.

In areas where the people do not have kings, **your king** may be translated "your ruler."

The adjective **humble** is used elsewhere in Matthew's Gospel in 5.5 ("meek") and 11.29 ("gentle"); see comment at 5.5, where GECL translates "who renounces the use of force." Note that TEV starts a new sentence here, something many other translators have found to be helpful for readers, too.

Mounted is generally rendered "seated (or, sitting)" or "riding."

On an ass, and on a colt, the foal of an ass: Matthew definitely intends to refer to two separate animals, as all translations indicate except LB, which cheats by translating "on a donkey's colt." The same sort of manipulation takes place in verse 7, where LB translates "threw their garments over the colt," with a footnote "Implied." But the Greek text does not in any way imply this, and LB has basically rewritten the text in an attempt to harmonize Matthew with the other Gospels, and to resolve the difficult image of Jesus riding on two animals. In doing this, LB has obscured the uniquely Matthean presentation.

Some who translate too literally have made it seem that the king is riding on three animals (a donkey, a colt, and the foal of a donkey), but obviously **a colt** and **the foal of an ass** refer to the same animal. To say "a colt, which is the young of a donkey" will sound very condescending, so that if the two expressions are not understood to refer to the same animal, then translators can drop one of the phrases and say simply "he rides on a donkey, and on a donkey's young." If translators want to retain some poetic form, they may need to look for some other device which in their language will have the effect of the parallelism in the text.

21.6	RSV	TEV

The disciples went and did as Jesus had directed them;	So the disciples went and did what Jesus had told them to do:

The disciples may better be translated "The two disciples" (GECL), since reference was last made to them in verse 1.

Went may require a direction, as in "went to the village" or "went ahead."

And did as Jesus had directed them is rendered by Phps with a noun to replace the second verb ("and followed Jesus' instructions"); similarly Brc ("and carried out Jesus' instructions").

21.7	RSV	TEV

they brought the ass and the colt, and put their garments on them, and he sat thereon.	they brought the donkey and the colt, threw their cloaks over them, and Jesus got on.

Rather than make this verse a continuation of the sentence begun in verse 6, it may be best to introduce a new sentence here, as do NJB, NIV, Brc, Phps. One may want to translate "They brought the donkey and the colt to Jesus. Then they threw their cloaks over them, and Jesus got on." In Greek the last clause of this verse is literally "and Jesus sat on them," a reference to either the cloaks or the animals. The meaning is probably that Jesus sat on the cloaks which had been placed on the animals. As verse 5 clearly indicates, Matthew understood that Jesus rode upon both animals, though he does not indicate how this was done, whether simultaneously or on one after the other. If one must specify the object upon which Jesus sat by some form other than a pronoun, it may be best to translate "They threw their cloaks over the donkey and the colt, and Jesus sat on the cloaks." This is a valid translation, inasmuch as the obvious intent of throwing the cloaks upon the animals was for Jesus to sit on the cloaks, and it leaves open the question of just how Jesus rode on the two donkeys, something that Matthew does not answer.

Garments is a general word for clothing, but in this verse, to say the disciples threw their clothes over the donkeys may indicate they (the disciples) were then partially or wholly naked. As indicated by TEV's "**cloaks**," the reference is probably to their outer garments. See 5.40 for suggestions on translating "**cloaks**."

21.8	RSV	TEV

Most of the crowd spread their gar- ments on the road, and others cut branches from the trees and spread them on the road.	A large crowd of people spread their cloaks on the road while others cut branches from the trees and spread them on the road.

Most of the crowd . . . and others may need to be restructured slightly." Most of the people in the crowd . . . and some of them (or, some of the rest of them)" is an example.

After **spread their garments on the road**, GECL adds "as a carpet." In many places of the modern world it is customary to roll out a carpet for a visiting dignitary, but there is the possibility that the action of the people (especially that of spreading tree branches in the road) may be understood in a negative sense. The addition of GECL immediately avoids this potential misunderstanding. Another quite common solution is to add "for him to ride on." Another is to add "to honor him," either after **on the road** or at the end of the verse.

As with the garments the disciples spread over the donkeys, **garments** here probably refers to the outer coats. See verse 7 above.

Regarding the **branches**, it seems unlikely that the crowd cut large branches. As with the coats, the idea is to have something for the donkeys to walk on. It was a way of showing honor to Jesus.

21.9	RSV	TEV

And the crowds that went before him and that followed him shouted, "Ho- sanna to the Son of David! Blessed is he who comes in the name of the Lord!Hosanna in the highest!"	The crowds walking in front of Jesus and those walking behind began to shout, "Praise to David's Son! God bless him who comes in the name of the Lord! Praise be to God!"

The crowds that went before him and that followed him refers to the people who were joining him as he made his way into the city. It does not necessarily mean the disciples or the believers. Translators can say "The people walking in front of and behind Jesus."

As a comparison of TEV and RSV will indicate, "**Jesus**" of TEV translates the pronoun **him** of the Greek text. Both GECL and FRCL also use the proper name.

For English readers the verb **shouted** may imply a loud cry, without specific content. In translation one should take care that the reader (and especially the hearer) understands that the content of the shout is given immediately following the verb.

Hosanna (TEV **"Praise"**) represents a transliteration of the Hebrew expression meaning "Save us now!" or "Please save us!" But as the NIV footnote indicates, it had become "an exclamation of praise" used by the Israelites as a liturgical formula. A number of translations use an expression that will be suitable to shout to royalty as they pass by in procession. See, for example, "God save the Son of David!" (Phps; similarly Brc).

Son of David is a messianic title that we discussed at 9.27.

Blessed is he who (so also NAB, NIV) may be translated **"God bless him who"** (TEV, Brc), since **blessed** is here used as a prayer invoking God's blessings upon the person whose name is used immediately after it. **In the name of the Lord** is translated literally by all English translations; GECL has "as the Lord's representative," and MACL has "with the Lord's authority." The entire exclamation, **Blessed is he who comes in the name of the Lord!** is taken from Psalm 118.26, which was used in the liturgy for the Festivals of Shelters, Dedication, and Passover.

Translators who follow the interpretation that **in the name of the Lord** means "with the Lord's authority" may say "Blessings on (or, May God bless) the one who comes with the Lord's authority (or, with the Lord's power)." Those who understand this expression to refer to a representative from the Lord may say "Blessings on (or, May God bless) the one who comes as his messenger (or, the one he sends to serve us)."

Hosanna in the highest!: the phrase **in the highest** represents a way of speaking of God without mentioning the sacred name; GECL has the literal equivalent of "praise be to God in the height," and TEV has **"Praise be to God."**

21.10   RSV   TEV

And when he entered Jerusalem, all the city was stirred, saying, "Who is this?"

When Jesus entered Jerusalem, the whole city was thrown into an uproar. "Who is he?" the people asked.

In place of **he**, TEV has **"Jesus"** because the mention of "God" and "the Lord" in the previous verse may be confusing if the proper name is not used here.

Was stirred (so also AT, NIV) is translated **"was thrown into an uproar"** by TEV. NEB is probably best: "went wild with excitement" (compare Mft "was in excitement over him"). For some a simple phrase like "everyone in the city became excited" may be most natural. The same verb is used of the earthquake which took place following the crucifixion (27.51), and of the guards who witnessed the angel of the Lord roll away the stone from the tomb (28.4). The related noun is used in 8.24; 24.7; 27.54; 28.2, translated "earthquake" or "great storm."

All the city . . . saying is clearly a reference to the people of the city, and so both NEB and NJB translate "people asked." TEV is similar except for the definite article: **"the people asked."**

21.11

RSV

And the crowds said, "This Is the prophet Jesus from Nazareth of Galilee."

TEV

"This Is the prophet Jesus, from Nazareth in Galilee," the crowds answered.

If **the crowds** are to be distinguished from "all the city" of verse 10, then one may follow GECL and translate "the crowds who accompanied Jesus."

This Is the prophet Jesus from Nazareth of Galilee may be understood in two different ways: (1) Jesus is a prophet: "This is Jesus. He is a prophet from the city of Nazareth in Galilee." (2) Or, if the reference is to the prophet promised in Deuteronomy 18.18: "This is Jesus from the town of Nazareth in Galilee. He is the (promised) prophet." The Greek text lends itself to either interpretation, though the second possibility seems more likely.

For a discussion of **prophet**, see 1.22.

21.12-17

RSV

TEV

Jesus Goes to the Temple

12 And Jesus entered the temple of God[p] and drove out all who sold and bought in the temple, and he overturned the tables of the money-changers and the seats of those who sold pigeons. 13 He said to them, "It is written, 'My house shall be called a house of prayer'; but you make it a den of robbers."

14 And the blind and the lame came to him in the temple, and he healed them. 15 But when the chief priests and the scribes saw the wonderful things that he did, and the children crying out in the temple, "Hosanna to the Son of David!" they were indignant; 16 and they said to him, "Do you hear what these are saying?" And Jesus said to them, "Yes; have you never read,

'Out of the mouth of babes and sucklings
   thou hast brought perfect praise'?"
17 And leaving them, he went out of the city to Bethany and lodged there.

12 Jesus went into the Temple and drove out all those who were buying and selling there. He overturned the tables of the moneychangers and the stools of those who sold pigeons, 13 and said to them, "It is written in the Scriptures that God said, 'My Temple will be called a house of prayer.' But you are making it a hideout for thieves!"

14 The blind and the crippled came to him in the Temple, and he healed them. 15 The chief priests and the teachers of the Law became angry when they saw the wonderful things he was doing and the children shouting in the Temple, "Praise to David's Son!" 16 So they asked Jesus, "Do you hear what they are saying?"

"Indeed I do," answered Jesus. "Haven't you ever read this scripture? 'You have trained children and babies to offer perfect praise.' "

17 Jesus left them and went out of the city to Bethany, where he spent the night.

[p] Other ancient authorities omit *of God*

SECTION HEADING: some translators have found that the TEV section heading, "**Jesus Goes to the Temple**," does not reflect what the passage is really about, that is, the expulsion of the merchants and moneychangers. Consequently they have preferred something like "Jesus drives (or chases) the merchants from the Temple."

The cleansing of the Temple is recorded in all four Gospels (Mark 11.15-19; Luke 19.45-48; John 2.13-22), but with significant differences. John places it in the early days of Jesus' ministry, in sharp contrast to the Synoptic Gospels, which record it as an event of the last week. According to Mark, it happened on the second day of this final week; on the first day Jesus merely went into the Temple and looked around before returning to Bethany to spend the night (11.11). Matthew and Luke (19.45) date it on the first day of Jesus' entry into Jerusalem, immediately following the triumphant entry. Within Matthew's account there are several unique emphases which will be noted in the comments.

21.12

RSV	TEV
And Jesus entered the temple of God[p] and drove out all who sold and bought in the temple, and he overturned the tables of the money-changers and the seats of those who sold pigeons.	Jesus went into the Temple and drove out all those who were buying and selling there. He overturned the tables of the moneychangers and the stools of those who sold pigeons,

[p] Other ancient authorities omit *of God*

In Greek this verse and the next consist of a series of clauses connected by the conjunction **And** (see RSV), reflecting the form of Semitic Greek. Translators should use whatever devices are natural in their language to show the progression of the text. For example, most drop the **And** at the beginning of the verse or say something like "Later." Or the **And** can be rendered more naturally as "Then" or "When Jesus entered the city."

Temple translates a Greek word which refers to the entire complex, rather than specifically to the Temple building itself. The events described probably took place in the Court of the Gentiles, where moneychangers were allowed to set up their tables prior to the Festival of Passover. To distinguish between this word and the word which refers to the Temple proper, several translations have "Temple precincts" (Brc, Phps, NAB), while NIV has "temple area." In some areas, for example in West Africa, "Temple compound" will capture the idea exactly.

Temple of God (so also Mft) is "Temple" in most translations. The phrase **of God** is believed by TC-GNT to be "a natural expression, made in order to emphasize the profanation of the holy place." Although it is not found in the parallel passages (Mark 11.15; Luke 19.45; see John 2.14), it is not something that a scribe would have deleted in order to make Matthew agree with the other Gospels, since it would not really have been objectionable to anyone. Moreover, the manuscript evidence in favor of "**Temple**" as opposed to **temple of God** is very strong.

Temple was discussed at 4.5. If translators have regularly been using an expression that uses "God"—for example, "House of God"—then it may be difficult to render **Temple of God** any differently. Translators would not, of course, retain a repetition of **of God**.

Drove out (so most translations) translates a verb which suggests the exercise of force (literally "threw out"). It is in fact the same verb which Matthew uses of the exorcism of demons (9.34; 10.1,8; 12.26; 17.19). The text does not say whether Jesus used force or simply commanded the people to leave (much as he drove out demons!). "Made them leave," "forced them out," "told them to get out," or "told them 'Get out' " will all be acceptable renderings.

In the Greek text of Matthew, **all who sold and bought** (literally "all those selling and buying") are placed together as a single group, assuming they are all merchants, whereas Mark (11.15) specifically speaks of two groups as "those selling and those buying," assuming that the merchants are selling and the pilgrims are buying; Luke (19.45), on the other hand, is concerned to mention only "those who were selling" (merchants). The phrase is referring to the sale and purchase of animals, wine, oil, and other commodities necessary for sacrifice.

Sold and bought may require direct objects, as in "selling and buying what they needed for sacrifice." Notice that "were selling and buying" in English reflects the fact that this was something in process. **Sold and bought** translated literally could mean it had happened once only.

The text says Jesus **overturned the tables of the money-changers**, that is, he turned over the tables where the moneychangers were conducting their business.

Money-changers were provided as a convenience to the Jewish pilgrims who exchanged their Roman and Greek coins for the proper coin with which the Temple tax had to be paid (see 17.24-27). With so many currencies in the world, most people are familiar with the process of changing money. However, some translators have had to say "people who exchanged money from one country for the money they used in the Temple."

Seats can be "chairs" or "stools."

Pigeons were the poor man's sacrifice (see Luke 2.24). In many areas translators say "pigeons for sacrifice," to ensure that their function here is understood. Matthew does not include Mark's additional comment, "and he would not let anyone carry anything through the Temple courtyards" (11.16), a practice which was looked upon as desecrating the holy place by using it as a short cut.

<u>**21.13**</u>   RSV   TEV

He said to them, "It is written, 'My house shall be called a house of prayer'; but you make it a den of robbers."

and said to them, "It is written in the Scriptures that God said, 'My Temple will be called a house of prayer.' But you are making it a hideout for thieves!"

Them refers to the people who were buying and selling and to the moneychangers, not just these latter. "He said to all those people" will make this clear.

It is written translates the same formula used at 4.4 (see comment there). **"That God said"** (GECL "that God explained") is included by TEV in order to indicate the speaker referred to by the pronoun **My** of the quotation.

My house refers to the Temple, the place where God was said to dwell and where people worshiped him. Some translators have said "My house of worship" or "The house where people worship me."

Shall be called a house of prayer is more adequately rendered by GECL 1st edition as "should be a house for prayer." One may translate "should be a house where people come to pray to me." Or, if **prayer** is understood in the wider sense of worship, "a house where people come to worship me." Some translators have wanted to retain an element of **called** by saying "People will call my house a place for prayer" or "Regarding my Temple, people will know (or, say) that it is for worship." But the passive **shall be called** does serve to keep **my house** in focus, and therefore examples like these should only be used if they maintain that focus. The quotation is taken from Isaiah 56.7, but Matthew omits "for the people of all nations," which is important to Mark (11.17).

When Jesus says **but you**, he is addressing the moneychangers and merchants directly. He is no longer quoting from God's word.

A den of robbers (NAB "a den of thieves") is a fairly traditional rendering. **Den** is literally "cave"; it was customary in those days for thieves and robbers to use caves as a place for their hideout and as a place for storing their stolen goods. Some translators have understood **den** to mean a gathering place for robbers, but in fact it was a place where they could hide (possibly after committing a crime) and be safe, so that "hiding place" is a better translation. Jesus is here alluding to Jeremiah 7.11: "Do you think that my Temple is a hiding place for robbers?" (TEV).

21.14 RSV TEV

And the blind and the lame came to him in the temple, and he healed them.

The blind and the crippled came to him in the Temple, and he healed them.

This verse begins with **And** in Greek, a word that indicates that the narrative is continuing, but it will probably not be right to make it seem that the blind and the lame came to Jesus immediately after he chastised the merchants and moneychangers. Most translations begin a new paragraph here.

The healing of **the blind and the lame** is mentioned only by Matthew, and it is of significance in his account. This is, in fact, the only mention in the first three Gospels of a healing in Jerusalem, which doubly underlines its significance. Earlier Matthew also linked the healing of the blind and the lame to each other (15.30-31), but here the combination takes on a deeper meaning in light of 2 Samuel 5.8, where it is stated "The blind and the crippled cannot enter the Lord's house" (TEV). The healing therefore reveals glimmers of the Messianic Age (see Isa 35.5-6) and affirms that the blind and the crippled, together with "the children" (verse 15), are now legitimately in God's Temple, whereas the chief priests and the teachers of the Law (verse 15) have disqualified themselves by their rejection of Jesus.

The use of "the" in **the blind and the lame** can make it seem as if all blind people and all crippled people went to Jesus to be healed. Translators may have to say "the blind and crippled people from there" or "many blind or crippled people."

Came may more naturally be "went" in many languages.

Lame was discussed at 15.30.

The text does not say explicitly the blind and lame came to Jesus to be healed, but that seems to be understood, and some translations have said "came (or, went) to Jesus so he would heal them." However, in most languages this will not be necessary, since the context makes it so clear.

It may be argued that **in the temple** is redundant and should be left implicit in translation, since the Temple has already been twice referred to in this account and will be mentioned again in the following verse. However, the real focus of the verse is to indicate that the Temple is the place where the healing occurred, thus qualifying the blind and the crippled to be there. Sometimes it is helpful to say "where he was in the Temple."

21.15   RSV   TEV

But when the chief priests and the scribes saw the wonderful things that he did, and the children crying out in the temple, "Hosanna to the Son of David!" they were indignant;

The chief priests and the teachers of the Law became angry when they saw the wonderful things he was doing and the children shouting in the Temple, "Praise to David's Son!"

Chief priests and **scribes** were discussed at 2.4.

The wonderful things (so also TEV, NJB, NEB) is the rendering of most English translations; AT and GECL have "the wonders." The reference is to the miracles of healing, and the word used to describe these healings focuses upon the aspect of wonder. It is used only here in the New Testament, though it occurs quite frequently in the Old Testament, where it is used of the wonders that God performed in Egypt (Exo 3.20). Brc has "astonishing things," and some have said "miracles."

The children crying out in the temple also introduces information not included in the Marcan parallel. Matthew has previously shown Jesus' concern for children (19.13-15), and he has recorded Jesus' teaching that a person must become like a child before he can enter the Kingdom (18.1-5; see also 18.25). So it is not surprising that he mentions this event which is not included in any of the other Gospels. It may sound odd to say that the chief priests and teachers of the law **saw** children crying out or shouting, so some translators have said "and when they heard the children shouting out."

Hosanna to the Son of David translates the same expression used in verse 9.

Were indignant translates the same verb used in 20.24; it will appear again in 26.8.

In the translation of this verse, it will probably be necessary to reorder some of the events: "The chief priests and the teachers of the Law saw the wonderful miracles that Jesus was doing. They also heard the children shouting in the Temple, 'Praise to David's Son!' So they became angry at Jesus, 16 and said to him . . . ."

21.16   RSV   TEV

and they said to him, "Do you hear what these are saying?" And Jesus said to them, "Yes; have you never read,
   'Out of the mouth of babes and
      sucklings

So they asked Jesus, "Do you hear what they are saying?"
   "Indeed I do," answered Jesus. "Haven't you ever read this scripture? 'You have trained children and babies to offer perfect praise.' "

> **thou hast brought perfect praise'?"**

Do you hear what these are saying? is not a question asked merely for the sake of information. But since Jesus replies **Yes**, it may not be possible to transform the question into an exclamation or affirmation. One way to convey the tone of the question is to say "Can't you hear what they are saying?" or possibly "Are you listening to what they are saying?"

Have you never read points directly to the scripture text which follows. Therefore GECL has "Have you never read in the Holy Scriptures . . . ?" and NEB, with specific reference to the following quotation, has "have you never read that text . . . ?" In cases where translators feel that the intent of this rhetorical question will be misunderstood, they may use an affirmation such as "Surely you have read in God's word."

Before translators can address the problems of this quotation, they have to be sure that the phrase **out of the mouth** will be understood as speech of some kind. Some make this clear with a rendering like "You have caused infants and children to speak words of perfect praise." Others even keep the image of the text with a rendering such as "You have made the mouths of infants and children speak words of perfect praise." Both of these examples begin with the second part of the quotation, because that order is generally easier for readers to comprehend. But there are languages where the order of the text is quite acceptable, as in "With the words of children and infants you have made perfect praise (for yourself)." In quite a few languages translators will have to indicate who is the recipient of the praise, by using phrases such as "praise to you" or "to praise you perfectly."

The noun translated **babes** (TEV **"children"**) is first used in 11.25 (see comment there). It appears here in a parallel structure with **sucklings** (literally "nursing babies"). NAB has "infants and children," while NIV has "children and infants."

The scripture passage referred to is Psalm 8.3 of the Septuagint (8.1-2a in English), where the Greek translators used **praise** to represent a Hebrew word which meant "strength" or "power." The modifier **perfect** (so also TEV, Brc), results from the Greek "perfective" prefix of the verb translated **hast brought** by RSV (TEV **"trained . . . to offer"**). The verb itself means "bring to perfection," and so Mft translates "brought praise to perfection." Lu accomplishes the same effect by translating the verb as "prepared," which is then followed by two synonyms which mean "praise."

Hast brought is in the middle voice, and when taken with the subject **you** means "You brought (something) to perfection for yourself." NEB reflects this middle voice: "Thou hast made . . . sound aloud thy praise." By this appeal to scripture Jesus affirms that his actions are approved and authenticated by God himself. Children, together with the blind and the crippled, are now the recipients of God's grace through Jesus the Messiah.

RSV   TEV

And leaving them, he went out of the city to Bethany and lodged there.   **Jesus left them and went out of the city to Bethany, where he spent the night.**

And leaving them (TEV "**Jesus left them**") translates a participial construction in Greek which is dependent upon the main verb **went out**. TEV's restructuring is purely stylistic.

If the pronoun **them** must be translated more explicitly, one can say "the people in the Temple." At least one commentator notes that the action of Jesus is both solemn and symbolic; when he leaves the Temple, God himself departs from the Jewish system of worship.

21.18-22

RSV   TEV

Jesus Curses the Fig Tree

18 In the morning, as he was returning to the city, he was hungry. 19 And seeing a fig tree by the wayside he went to it, and found nothing on it but leaves only. And he said to it, "May no fruit ever come from you again!" And the fig tree withered at once. 20 When the disciples saw it they marveled, saying, "How did the fig tree wither at once?" 21 And Jesus answered them, "Truly, I say to you, if you have faith and never doubt, you will not only do what has been done to the fig tree, but even if you say to this mountain, 'Be taken up and cast into the sea,' it will be done. 22 And whatever you ask in prayer, you will receive, if you have faith."

18 On his way back to the city early next morning, Jesus was hungry. 19 He saw a fig tree by the side of the road and went to it, but found nothing on it except leaves. So he said to the tree, "You will never again bear fruit!" At once the fig tree dried up.

20 The disciples saw this and were astounded. "How did the fig tree dry up so quickly?" they asked.

21 Jesus answered, "I assure you that if you believe and do not doubt, you will be able to do what I have done to this fig tree. And not only this, but you will even be able to say to this hill, 'Get up and throw yourself in the sea,' and it will. 22 If you believe, you will receive whatever you ask for in prayer."

SECTION HEADING: "**Jesus Curses the Fig Tree.**" In languages where "**Curses**" will suggest that Jesus swore at the tree, rather than that he actually called a curse down on it, translators may say "Jesus and the fig tree" or "The story of the fig tree without fruit." For "**Fig Tree,**" see verse 19 below.

Matthew's account of this event is shorter than that of Mark, who divides his account into two parts (11.12-14 and 20-25), separated by the cleansing of the temple (11.15-19). But the fact that both evangelists connect the story closely with the cleansing of the temple indicates that for them it is symbolic of God's judgment upon the Jewish religion, which has failed to produce the fruit that God expected of it. For Matthew the event assumes a second meaning as well. It illustrates the absolute faith that God expects of his people (verses 21-22). But it must not be forgotten that for Jesus, faith means a total submission to and dependence upon God's will.

21.18   RSV   TEV

In the morning, as he was returning to the city, he was hungry.	On his way back to the city early next morning, Jesus was hungry.

RSV is a literal rendering of the Greek. TEV introduces the proper name **"Jesus"** in the second clause, though it may be best to follow the restructuring of GECL: "Early the next morning Jesus started back to Jerusalem. On the way he became hungry." It may even be necessary to begin with "Early the next morning Jesus got up and started back to . . . ."

21.19   RSV   TEV

And seeing a fig tree by the wayside he went to it, and found nothing on it but leaves only. And he said to it, "May no fruit ever come from you again!" And the fig tree withered at once.	He saw a fig tree by the side of the road and went to it, but found nothing on it except leaves. So he said to the tree, "You will never again bear fruit!" At once the fig tree dried up.

And seeing a fig tree may require a transitional: "As he was walking along, he saw a fig tree . . . ."

Many people are not familiar with the **fig tree**. There is sometimes a temptation for translators to substitute a local fruit tree in the translation, but it may be better to use either a general term such as "fruit tree" or "tree of fruit called fig," or possibly to compare it to a local fruit that is somewhat similar, as in "tree of a fruit like . . . ."

By the wayside means "next to the road" (TEV **"by the side of the road"**).

In Greek **nothing** is emphatic in the text of both Matthew and Mark (11.13). Sometimes it is more natural to say "no fruit" or "no figs."

May no fruit ever come from you again! is more emphatic than Mark's "May no one ever eat fruit from you again!" (11.14). Mark expresses a strong wish, whereas Matthew has the equivalent of a command or even of a curse. Some possible ways to render this include "I command that you never have any figs (or, fruit) again" or "I declare that you will never again bear fruit." It should be noted, however, that the form of the text, **may no fruit . . .**, is natural in many languages. Sometimes indirect speech is necessary, as in "Jesus commanded that the tree never again bear any fruit."

And the fig tree withered at once contrasts with Mark (11.20), which states that the disciples did not notice the withering of the fig tree until the next morning. The dramatic effect of the event is reflected by Brc: "And there and then the fig tree withered." It is significant that the adverb **at once** is found only twice in the Gospel, here and in verse 20.

Withered here can be rendered as "dried up" or "died."

21.20   RSV   TEV

When the disciples saw it they marveled, saying, "How did the fig tree
wither at once?"

The disciples saw this and were
astounded. "How did the fig tree dry
up so quickly?" they asked.

When the disciples saw it, that is, when they saw what happened to the tree.

Marveled (TEV "**were astonished**") translates a verb made from the same stem as the noun translated "wonderful things" in verse 15. The verb is first used in 8.10 (see comment there).

The disciples ask the question **How**, but "What caused" or "Why" may be more natural for some translators.

In the question of the disciples, **at once** (TEV "**so quickly**") is in the emphatic position. It is the way the curse was fulfilled immediately which astounded the disciples.

21.21   RSV   TEV

And Jesus answered them, "Truly, I
say to you, if you have faith and
never doubt, you will not only do
what has been done to the fig tree,
but even if you say to this mountain,
'Be taken up and cast into the sea,'
it will be done.

Jesus answered, "I assure you
that if you believe and do not doubt,
you will be able to do what I have
done to this fig tree. And not only
this, but you will even be able to say
to this hill, 'Get up and throw yourself in the sea,' and it will.

Jesus' response to the disciples' question is reminiscent of what he said in 17.20. In the earlier passage, however, the emphasis was upon the effective power of even a minimum faith, whereas here the emphasis is on the contrast between faith and doubt.

Truly, I say to you translates the same expression used in 6.2; most recently it was used in 18.13,18,19; 19.23,28.

If you have faith is expressed by TEV by a verb without an object: "**if you believe . . . .**" In some languages it will be necessary to indicate the object of belief: "if you believe in God" or ". . . really believe in God."

Doubt translates a verb used only one other time in Matthew. In 16.3 it appears in the active form with the meaning "interpret" or "discern." Here the form is that of the aorist passive, which may mean "doubt," "waiver," "hesitate" (see Mark 11.23; Acts 10.20; Rom 4.20; 14.23; James 1.6; and Jude 22). In translation it may be necessary to indicate whom or what one doubts: "if you believe God and do not doubt what he can do" or ". . . and do not doubt his power."

The expression **what has been done to the fig tree** is a passive form that may have to be translated with an active one. This will require a subject, so that translators may say "what I did to the fig tree."

This mountain has been translated as "**this hill**" by many translations, for example TEV and Brc. The use of **this** probably indicates that Jesus was pointing to some hill they were passing at the time. If it is natural in the receptor language to retain **this**, that should be done. Otherwise translators can say "this hill we see" or "this hill here."

Be taken up and cast into the sea translates an aorist passive imperative. But a middle or reflexive form is more effective for English readers: "Get up and throw yourself" (JB) and "Go, throw yourself." (NIV). No particular **sea** is specified. It is best to be as general as possible in the translation, too.

It will be done is translated "it will happen" by Phps, Brc, GECL. For some languages it may even be necessary to translate either "it will do what you said" or "it will throw itself into the sea."

The rather long sentence of RSV has been translated by two sentences in TEV. Many translators find this model helpful.

21.22	RSV	TEV

	RSV	TEV
	And whatever you ask in prayer, you will receive, if you have faith."	If you believe, you will receive whatever you ask for in prayer."

RSV represents a fairly literal rendering of this verse, which has been rearranged rather significantly by TEV, where the last clause, **if you have faith**, has been placed first ("**If you believe**"). In translation attention should be given to at least the following considerations: (1) **In prayer** may be redundant, especially if the petition is identified as directed toward God. (2) God may need to be explicitly indicated as the one toward whom the disciples are to direct their requests and in whom they are to **have faith**. (3) **You will receive** may be clearer if the implied giver is made explicit ("God will give you"). (4) A more logical arrangement may be sought; for example, "If you believe that God can do what you ask, then ask him (or, pray to him), and he will do it," or "If you pray to God and believe that he will do what you ask, then he will do it."

It is important to note from these examples that, despite the use of **receive**, the emphasis is not on receiving some material thing from God, but rather on him doing what you ask him to do. Thus "he will do what you ask" reflects more accurately the meaning than "he will give you the thing you ask for."

21.23-27

RSV	TEV
	The Question about Jesus' Authority

RSV	TEV
23 And when he entered the temple, the chief priests and the elders of the people came up to him as he was teaching, and said, "By what authority are you doing these things, and who gave you this authority?" 24 Jesus answered them, "I also will ask you a question; and if you tell me the answer, then I also will tell you by what authority I do these things. 25 The baptism of John, whence was it? From heaven or from men?" And they argued with one another, "If we say, 'From heav-	23 Jesus came back to the Temple; and as he taught, the chief priests and the elders came to him and asked, "What right do you have to do these things? Who gave you such right?" 24 Jesus answered them, "I will ask you just one question, and if you give me an answer, I will tell you what right I have to do these things. 25 Where did John's right to baptize come from: was it from God or from man?" They started to argue among themselves,

en,' he will say to us, 'Why then did you not believe him?' 26 But if we say, 'From men,' we are afraid of the multitude; for all hold that John was a prophet." 27 So they answered Jesus, "We do not know." And he said to them, "Neither will I tell you by what authority I do these things.

"What shall we say? If we answer, 'From God,' he will say to us, 'Why, then, did you not believe John?' 26 But if we say, 'From man,' we are afraid of what the people might do, because they are all convinced that John was a prophet." 27 So they answered Jesus, "We don't know."

And he said to them, "Neither will I tell you, then, by what right I do these things.

SECTION HEADING: "**The Question About Jesus' Authority**" may need to be expressed as a short sentence; for example, "The priests ask Jesus about his authority," "Some people ask Jesus who gives him authority (to do things)," or "Some priests challenge Jesus' authority." If this is too long, "The authority of Jesus" may be a good rendering.

The question about Jesus' authority (21.23-27) is the first in a series of five controversies which develop between Jesus and the representatives of the Jewish religion (21.23–22.46). Each of these individual controversies follows a question-and-answer format, which was a traditional procedure for the discussion of religious questions. The function of a counterquestion was not necessarily to avoid answering the question which prompted it, but rather to serve as a way either of leading to the proper answer or of forcing one's opponent to concede the point.

This first question concerns the authority by which Jesus does "these things" (Matt 21.23; Mark 11.28; Luke 20.2), which probably refers back to the arrangements for his triumphant entry, the entry itself, and the cleansing of the temple. But since Matthew sets it in a context in which Jesus is teaching, it is quite likely that he intends for the question to cover the source of Jesus' authority to teach as well.

21.23	RSV	TEV

And when he entered the temple, the chief priests and the elders of the people came up to him as he was teaching, and said, "By what authority are you doing these things, and who gave you this authority?"

Jesus came back to the Temple; and as he taught, the chief priests and the elders came to him and asked, "What right do you have to do these things? Who gave you such right?"

And when he entered the temple is translated "**Jesus came back to the Temple**" in TEV, which continues to follow the pattern of beginning each new section by identifying the pronominal referents of the Greek text by their proper names. Both GECL and FRCL have done the same thing. In some languages it will be important to specify the sequence of events: "Jesus went back to the Temple. When he went in . . . ."

Here again the Greek word for **temple** refers, not to the building proper, but to the large complex which was built around it. Jesus was probably on one of the porches that surrounded the court of the Gentiles at this time.

The chief priests and the elders confront Jesus again in 26.3,47; the terminology is slightly different from "the chief priests and the scribes" (verse 15), who confront him during the cleansing of the temple. The word **elders** is used first in 15.2. Here it is followed by the construction **of the people**, which TEV leaves

653

implicit, assuming that it is equivalent to "Jewish." **Elders** can often be translated literally and be understood, especially in societies where the men (generally not the women) of a certain age and status are leaders of the community. But otherwise "leaders" can be used.

Came up to may better be "went up to" or "approached."

As has sometimes been misunderstood by translators to mean "since" or "because," but in this verse it is used to mean "while."

As he was teaching: Matthew emphasizes the teaching ministry of Jesus here (see Mark "as he was walking"), although the following question relates specifically to the things that Jesus was doing. In languages where **teaching** requires an object, Jesus can be said to be teaching "about God." It may also be necessary to say whom he was teaching. Some general phrase such as "the people" will serve well here.

By what authority are you doing these things, and who gave you this authority? though stated as two questions, actually are asking the same question: "Who gave you the right to do these things?" The men who raised the issue assumed that the answer was either God, Satan, Jesus himself, or some other human authority (TOB footnote). GECL 1st edition renders the two questions thus: "Who has given you the right to come in here like this? Who authorized you?"

These things may well refer to what Jesus had done the day before, when he chased the merchants and moneychangers from the Temple, but translators should probably not specify this in their translations. Brc has "What right have you to act as you are doing?"

21.24	RSV	TEV

Jesus answered them, "I also will ask you a question; and if you tell me the answer, then I also will tell you by what authority I do these things.	Jesus answered them, "I will ask you just one question, and if you give me an answer, I will tell you what right I have to do these things.

In the two statements, **I also will ask you . . . I also will tell you**, the pronoun I is stated emphatically. This indicates that Jesus is placing himself on equal status with the Jewish leaders who have come to question him.

When Jesus says **tell me the answer**, he really means "tell me the correct answer."

21.25	RSV	TEV

The baptism of John, whence was it? From heaven or from men?" And they argued with one another, "If we say, 'From heaven,' he will say to us, 'Why then did you not believe him?'	Where did John's right to baptize come from: was it from God or from man?" They started to argue among themselves, "What shall we say? If

we answer, 'From God,' he will say to us, 'Why, then, did you not believe John?'

It is occasionally necessary to preface this verse with a phrase such as "Here is the question: the baptism of John . . ." or "So I ask you, the baptism of John . . . ."

The baptism of John, whence was it? In such a context **baptism** refers to the authority to baptize, and so the basis for TEV: **"Where did John's right to baptize come from . . . ?"** GECL translates "From where did John the Baptist receive the authority to baptize?" A shift to the active voice may be better: "Who gave John the Baptist his authority to baptize?" or ". . . the right to baptize?" It can also be "When John baptized (people), who gave him the right to do it?"

From heaven or from men? The noun **heaven** is a typical Jewish way of speaking of God without mentioning his name, and so Brc translates "Was it divine or human?" (NAB "Was it divine or merely human?") NEB is similar to TEV: "was it from God, or from men?" Here also a shift to an active structure is possible: "Did God give him this authority or did some man give it to him?" or ". . . or did some human being give it to him?"

And they argued with one another: the imperfect tense of the verb **argued** can focus upon the beginning of the action, as in TEV: **"They started to argue among themselves . . . ."** This is also the interpretation of NEB ("This set them arguing among themselves"), Phps ("At this they began arguing among themselves"), and Brc ("They began to argue with each other"). The verb may also mean "think" or "reason," which is the basis for NAB ("They thought to themselves"). However, the context definitely suggests an actual conversation carried on among the Jewish leaders.

The translation of **from heaven** in the argument the chief priests and elders had amongst themselves should be phrased as it was in Jesus' question to them earlier in the verse. Of course, it may have to be expressed as a short sentence such as "If we say 'John's authority came from God' " or "If we say that John's authority came from God."

Why then did you not believe him? may need to be restructured to say "Why, then, did you not believe John's message?" or ". . . believe what John said?"

21.26	RSV	TEV

But if we say, 'From men,' we are afraid of the multitude; for all hold that John was a prophet."		But if we say, 'From man,' we are afraid of what the people might do, because they are all convinced that John was a prophet."

From men should be expressed in the same way it was translated in verse 25. Again, as with "from heaven" in verse 25, a short sentence may be required: "But if we say 'Some person gave it to him' " or "But if we say that his authority came from a person."

In the Gospel of Mark (11.32), **we are afraid of the multitude; for all hold that John was a prophet** appears as a parenthetical statement by the author and not as a direct statement of the Jewish leaders. By transferring this to a direct statement of Jesus' opponents, Matthew lays greater stress both upon the fear which the Jewish leaders had of the masses and upon their alienation from the ordinary folk.

In RSV the English of this verse is rather awkward, and the TEV restructuring is somewhat confusing. One may then want to follow the pattern of GECL: "But if we say, 'From man,' then we will have the people against us, because they are all convinced that John was a prophet." Or "We cannot say, 'John acted on his own authority.' The people are convinced that John was a prophet, and the people might do something bad to us if we say that." Or "The people are convinced that John was a prophet, and they might harm us if we say, 'Some human being gave John his authority.' "

For comment on **prophet** see 1.22.

21.27	RSV	TEV

So they answered Jesus, "We do not know." And he said to them, "Neither will I tell you by what authority I do these things.

So they answered Jesus, "We don't know."

And he said to them, "Neither will I tell you, then, by what right I do these things.

We do not know is rendered in conversational style by TEV: "**We don't know**." The response may require more complete expression: "We do not know who gave John his authority."

Neither will . . . these things may also be restructured: "So then I will not tell you who gave me the right to do these things." GECL has "Then I will not tell you who authorized me."

21.28-32		
	RSV	TEV

The Parable of the Two Sons

28 "What do you think? A man had two sons; and he went to the first and said, 'Son, go and work in the vineyard today.' 29 And he answered, 'I will not'; but afterward he repented and went. 30 And he went to the second and said the same; and he answered, 'I go, sir,' but did not go. 31 Which of the two did the will of his father?" They said, "The first." Jesus said to them, "Truly, I say to you, the tax collectors and the harlots go into the kingdom of God before you. 32 For John came to you in the way of righteousness, and you did not believe him, but the tax collectors and the harlots believed him; and even when you saw it,

28 "Now, what do you think? There was once a man who had two sons. He went to the older one and said, 'Son, go and work in the vineyard today.' 29 'I don't want to,' he answered, but later he changed his mind and went. 30 Then the father went to the other son and said the same thing. 'Yes, sir,' he answered, but he did not go. 31 Which one of the two did what his father wanted?"

"The older one," they answered.

So Jesus said to them, "I tell you: the tax collectors and the prostitutes are going into the Kingdom of God ahead of you. 32 For John the

you did not afterward repent and believe him.	Baptist came to you showing you the right path to take, and you would not believe him; but the tax collectors and the prostitutes believed him. Even when you saw this, you did not later change your minds and believe him.

SECTION HEADING: **"The Parable of the Two Sons"** may have to be expressed as a short sentence such as "Jesus tells a parable (or, story) of two sons" or ". . . of a father and his two sons."

The parable of the two sons is the first in a series of three parables (21.28-32, 33-45; 22.1-14) which deal with the theme of Jesus' rejection by the Jewish authorities, who should have been the first to have received him and his message. This parable is found only in the Gospel of Matthew, though it does have affinities with the better known parable of the lost son (Luke 15.11-32).

TC-GNT comments that the "textual transmission of the parable of the two sons is much confused," and it evaluates the three principal forms in which the text has been transmitted:

(1) According to some manuscripts, the first son says "No" but afterwards repents and goes to work in the field. The second son says "Yes" but does not go. The question "Which of the two did the will of his father?" is answered with "The last" (meaning the second one). Some scholars argue for the priority of this text on the basis that it is the most difficult of the three possibilities. But TC-GNT replies that it is "not only difficult, it is nonsensical," and it rejects this as a valid option.

(2) According to other manuscripts the first son says "Yes" but does nothing. The reply of the second son is "No," but he later repents and goes to work in the field. "Which of the two did the will of his father?" The answers contained in this manuscript tradition vary between "The latter," "The last," "The second," and "The first." However, the translations which adopt this form of the text (NEB, NAB, AT, Mft, Zür) have either "The second (one)" or its equivalent, "The last." TOB follows (3) but does provide a footnote saying that some manuscripts reverse the order of the responses in verse 29 and 30. No other translations provide a textual note.

(3) According to still other manuscripts, the first son says "No" but then repents and goes into the field to work. The second son says "Yes" but does not go to work. "Which of the two did the will of his father?" The answer is "the first." This is the preference of most modern translations, as well as the choice of the UBS Greek text for three reasons: (a) If the first son had obeyed, there would have been no need to ask the second one to do the work. (b) The form of the text represented by (2) probably reflects an attempt on the part of scribes to make the parable conform to a chronological scheme by means of identifying the disobedient son with either the Jews in general or with the chief priests and elders (verse 23), and the obedient son with either the Gentiles or with the tax collectors and prostitutes (verse 31). (c) The wide variety of answers which (2) gives to the question "Which of the two did the will of his father?" attests to the instability of that textual tradition. Therefore the decision of the UBS Greek text favors (3), although it is rated "C," indicating "a considerable degree of doubt."

In light of the highly complex nature of this particular textual problem, it may be best to follow either (2) or (3), depending upon the tradition with which the readers are most familiar or which has the support of the major translations in the region.

"What do you think? A man had two sons; and he went to the first and said, 'Son, go and work in the vineyard today.'

"Now, what do you think? There was once a man who had two sons. He went to the older one and said, 'Son, go and work in the vineyard today.'

"**Now**" of TEV represents either a translational equivalent of the Greek participle, translated "But" by NEB, or a transitional marker introduced for the sake of English readers, which is more probable. Brc translates "What do you think?" but adds "Jesus went on," which serves both as a transitional marker and as an indicator that Jesus is still speaking.

What do you think? translates the same question form used in 17.25 and 18.12, with the exception that in 17.25 "you" is singular (addressed to Simon Peter) as opposed to the plural "you" of 18.12 and this verse. The problem with a literal rendering of the question, as in most translations, is that it has no point of reference for the reader. One's initial response to the question can well be "What do I think about what?" GECL resolves this difficulty by rendering "What do you say to the following story?"

A man had two sons is literally "A man had two children." TEV uses "**There was once . . .**" (AT, Phps, Brc, NIV, NAB "There was"), which is a normal pattern for introducing a story in English. This introductory formula leaves open the possibility that the story is true, whereas a formula such as "Once upon a time . . ." would indicate immediately that the story to follow is not true. In all probability this is a parable, but in translation one should not intentionally imply that the story has no basis in reality. On the other hand, in the telling of the story one should use an opening formula that is neutral.

As indicated above, the word **sons** actually means "children" (the same word used in the quotation in 2.18). However, when used in a context which specifically identifies the sex of the children as males (as the Greek does in verse 31), it is permissible to translate "sons." There is no indication of the age of the sons, but the fact they were old enough to be asked to work in the fields indicates they were not small children.

"**The older one**" of TEV (NAB "the elder") is literally **the first** (so most translations). There is no way to decide whether "the first (verse 28) . . . the second (verse 30)" means "first one . . . then the other" or "the older . . . then the younger." TEV bases its interpretation on the assumption that in the Jewish culture a man would apparently have approached the older son first.

The noun **Son** is the singular form of the word translated **sons** in the first part of the verse. When used to address someone it was considered a term of endearment. For example, Jesus uses it when addressing the paralyzed man in 9.2. GECL here translates "my son," whereas in 9.2 the translators chose to leave it implicit.

Vineyard was discussed at 20.1. As there, the fact that the field in question is a vineyard is not essential to the story, and if the normal translation for the term results in an awkward sentence here, then a general form such as "farm" or "fields" is possible.

The command may need to be expressed with an indirect form such as "asked the son to go and work in the vineyard that day."

21.29   RSV   TEV

And he answered, 'I will not'; but   'I don't want to,' he answered, but
afterward he repented and went.   later he changed his mind and went.

I will not implies an absolute refusal. NJB has "I will not go," and Lu "No, I will not go." Other languages may require a fuller statement: "No, I will not go to work in the vineyard." An indirect form may also be natural, as in "but he told his father he would not go" or "but he refused to go."

Repented is repeated again in verse 32. Elsewhere in the Gospel it is used only of Judas (27.3); otherwise in the New Testament it appears only twice (2 Cor 7.8; Heb 7.21). It may also mean "regret" (Lu, NAB); GECL "regretted his answer." A number of translations have "**changed his mind**" (TEV, Mft, AT, NEB, Phps, Brc).

21.30   RSV   TEV

And he went to the second and said   Then the father went to the other son
the same; and he answered, 'I go,   and said the same thing. 'Yes, sir,'
sir,' but did not go.   he answered, but he did not go.

And he went to the second and said the same is the third in a series of three events: (1) the father went to the first son and told him to work in the vineyard; (2) the first son went to work in the vineyard; and (3) the father went to the second son and told him to work in the vineyard. But the actual sequence of events would appear to be (1), (3), and then (2). That is, the father would apparently not have gone to the second son if he had known that the first son had already gone to work in the vineyard. If the father in the story somehow represents God, as one feels he does, then it must be concluded that both the narrator and the hearers would have assumed that the father would have known that the first son already went to work in the vineyard at the time that he went to the second son.

There have been translations which have tried to reflect this sequence of events by saying at the beginning of the verse "In the meantime" or "When the first son refused to go." This is not necessary, however, since the context makes this point clear.

It may be necessary to replace **he** with "**the father,**" as in TEV and Brc.

And said the same thing may need to be spelled out in more detail, as in "and said the same thing he had to the first son" or even "and said, 'Son, go and work in my vineyard today.' "

I go, sir (TEV, Lu "**Yes, sir**") translates what is a very polite affirmative answer in Greek (literally "I, sir"). A number of translations render "I will, sir" (NEB, NIV, AT), while Brc and NJB have "Certainly, sir." GECL reflects the politeness in the answer "Yes, father." It may be necessary to give the answer in more complete form: "I am on my way, sir" (NAB).

21.30

But did not go means "but he did not go to work in the vineyard" or ". . . vineyard, as he said he would."

21.31   RSV   TEV

Which of the two did the will of his father?" They said, "The first." Jesus said to them, "Truly, I say to you, the tax collectors and the harlots go into the kingdom of God before you.	Which one of the two did what his father wanted?" "The older one," they answered. So Jesus said to them, "I tell you: the tax collectors and the prostitutes are going into the Kingdom of God ahead of you.

The beginning of this verse may require that the person speaking and the persons addressed be specifically identified: "Then Jesus asked the chief priests and the elders, 'Which one of the two did what his father wanted?' " Moreover, **the two** may better be rendered "the two sons."

The first is translated **"The older one"** by TEV (see comments at verse 28).

They said . . . said to them: both pronouns refer to "the chief priests and the elders" of verse 23. If they are identified specifically at the beginning of the verse, the pronominal references will be clear; otherwise the reader may totally forget the persons to whom Jesus is speaking at this time.

Truly, I say to you translates the same emphatic formula used in 5.26; see comments there and at 5.18.

The tax collectors and the harlots is a combination used in the New Testament only here and in verse 32. According to Jewish opinion these two groups would have no part in the coming world. But Jesus declares that they will **go into the kingdom of God before** the chief priests and elders. The expression **kingdom of God** is used also in verse 43; it has occurred previously in 12.28 and 19.24. Elsewhere in this Gospel Matthew always uses "the kingdom of heaven," but the two terms are synonymous (see comment at 3.2). In this regard it is interesting that Brc translates "Kingdom of Heaven," thus retaining the more familiar Matthean term. Some scholars believe that the reason for the change here is due to Matthew's source, and this is quite likely the best conclusion. For the most part, translations do not do drastic restructuring. GECL has "enter God's new world." MACL translates "God will permit tax collectors and prostitutes to enjoy the blessings of his rule"; INCL has, "Tax collectors and prostitutes will become members of God's community." For other suggestions, see 19.23.

Tax collectors was discussed at 5.46.

Harlots is a somewhat archaic word for **"prostitutes."** Most languages do have such a word, but some use a phrase such as "women who sleep with men for money." Often a euphemism is required, such as "women of bad reputation."

Both **before you** and **"ahead of you"** (TEV) are ambiguous; the phrase may mean either "before you go in" or "in place of you." The use of the present tense of the verb **go** tends to suggest that the latter sense is intended. In the actual context of Jesus' ministry these outcasts were the ones who responded to him, whereas the religious leaders failed to do so, thus excluding themselves from the Kingdom of God. It seems legitimate to translate "will have a better chance to enter . . . than you do" or "they will enter . . . but you will not."

21.32	RSV	TEV

For John came to you in the way of righteousness, and you did not believe him, but the tax collectors and the harlots believed him; and even when you saw it, you did not afterward repent and believe him.	**For John the Baptist came to you showing you the right path to take, and you would not believe him; but the tax collectors and the prostitutes believed him. Even when you saw this, you did not later change your minds and believe him.**

The transition word **For** is important here. Jesus explains why the tax collectors and prostitutes are more likely to enter God's rule than the chief priests and elders. In some languages it is even necessary to translate it as "I say this because John . . . ."

Note that TEV makes clear that **John** refers to "**John the Baptist.**"

Came to you can give the impression that John the Baptist went directly to the chief priests and elders, but "came to you people" or "came to you all, the people of Israel" reflects the meaning more accurately.

In the way of righteousness is translated "**showing you the right path to take**" by TEV; GECL is similar. For a detailed discussion of **righteousness**, see comments at 3.15. It is possible to understand the phrase as a qualifier of John the Baptist himself, as do JB ("For John came to you, a pattern of true righteousness") and Phps ("For John came to you as a truly good man"). However, most scholars take this as a reference to his message: "to show you the right way to live" (NEB), "to show you the right way" (Lu), and "and showed you how to live as God wants you to live" (Brc; similarly INCL).

And you did not believe him may also be translated "and you would not believe his message" or ". . . what he said."

Believed him contrasts the response of the tax collectors and prostitutes to that of the chief priests and the elders.

Even when you saw it refers to the belief of the tax collectors and prostitutes. It may then be translated "that the tax collectors and prostitutes had accepted his message" (GECL).

Afterward repent repeats the adverb and verb of verse 29. As there, "change your minds" is a possible translation. Thereby a dramatic contrast is drawn between the repentant attitude of the first son and the refusal of this group to change their minds.

And believe him may be translated "and believe his message"; GECL focuses upon the effect of accepting his message: "Not once . . . did you hearken to him and change your lives."

RSV

TEV

The Parable of the Tenants in the Vineyard

33 "Hear another parable. There was a householder who planted a vineyard, and set a hedge around it, and dug a wine press in it, and built a tower, and let it out to tenants, and went into another country. 34 When the season of fruit drew near, he sent his servants to the tenants, to get his fruit; 35 and the tenants took his servants and beat one, killed another, and stoned another. 36 Again he sent other servants, more than the first; and they did the same to them. 37 Afterward he sent his son to them, saying, 'They will respect my son.' 38 But when the tenants saw the son, they said to themselves, 'This is the heir; come, let us kill him and have his inheritance.' 39 And they took him and cast him out of the vineyard, and killed him. 40 When therefore the owner of the vineyard comes, what will he do to those tenants?" 41 They said to him, "He will put those wretches to a miserable death, and let out the vineyard to other tenants who will give him the fruits in their seasons."

42 Jesus said to them, "Have you never read in the scriptures:

'The very stone which the builders rejected
has become the head of the corner;
this was the Lord's doing,
and it is marvelous in our eyes'?

43 Therefore I tell you, the kingdom of God will be taken away from you and given to a nation producing the fruits of it."[q]

45 When the chief priests and the Pharisees heard his parables, they perceived that he was speaking about them. 46 But when they tried to arrest him, they feared the multitudes, because they held him to be a prophet.

[q] Other ancient authorities add verse 44, *"And he who falls on this stone will be broken to pieces; but when it falls on any one, it will crush him"*

33 "Listen to another parable," Jesus said. "There was once a landowner who planted a vineyard, put a fence around it, dug a hole for the wine press, and built a watchtower. Then he rented the vineyard to tenants and left home on a trip. 34 When the time came to gather the grapes, he sent his slaves to the tenants to receive his share of the harvest. 35 The tenants grabbed his slaves, beat one, killed another, and stoned another. 36 Again the man sent other slaves, more than the first time, and the tenants treated them the same way. 37 Last of all he sent his son to them. 'Surely they will respect my son,' he said. 38 But when the tenants saw the son, they said to themselves, 'This is the owner's son. Come on, let's kill him, and we will get his property!' 39 So they grabbed him, threw him out of the vineyard, and killed him.

40 "Now, when the owner of the vineyard comes, what will he do to those tenants?" Jesus asked.

41 "He will certainly kill those evil men," they answered, "and rent the vineyard out to other tenants, who will give him his share of the harvest at the right time."

42 Jesus said to them, "Haven't you ever read what the Scriptures say?

'The stone which the builders rejected as worthless
turned out to be the most important of all.
This was done by the Lord;
what a wonderful sight it is!'

43 "And so I tell you," added Jesus, "the Kingdom of God will be taken away from you and given to a people who will produce the proper fruits."[t]

45 The chief priests and the Pharisees heard Jesus' parables and knew that he was talking about them, 46 so they tried to arrest him. But they were afraid of the crowds, who considered Jesus to be a prophet.

[t] *Some manuscripts add verse 44:* Whoever falls on this stone will be cut to pieces; and if the stone falls on someone, it will crush him to dust *(see Lk 20.18).*

SECTION HEADING: "**The Parable of the Tenants in the Vineyard**" may need to be expressed by a short sentence such as "Jesus tells the parable of the tenants in the vineyard" or "Jesus tells a parable about some wicked tenants." "**Vineyard**" was discussed at 20.1. "**Tenants**" will be discussed below at verse 33.

The theme of conflict between Jesus and the Jewish leaders is continued in this second parable about a vineyard, which also has parallels in Mark (12.1-12) and Luke (20.9-19). The introduction to the parable (verse 33) has close affinities with "The Song of the Vineyard" of Isaiah 5.1-7, especially as it occurs in the Greek Old Testament, the Septuagint. As Matthew tells the story, it reveals definite allegorical characteristics: the landowner is God; the vineyard is Israel; the tenants are Israel's rulers and leaders; the slaves (or messengers) are the prophets (the two groups probably representing the preexilic and postexilic prophets); the son is Jesus himself; the punishment (verse 43) is God's rejection of Israel; and the people to whom the vineyard will be given are the Gentiles. Although these allegorical elements are obviously intended in the way that Matthew frames the story, these identifications should not be made explicit in the translation itself. Translators may consider pointing them out in footnotes, however.

21.33	RSV	TEV
	"Hear another parable. There was a householder who planted a vineyard, and set a hedge around it, and dug a wine press in it, and built a tower, and let it out to tenants, and went into another country.	"Listen to another parable," Jesus said. "There was once a landowner who planted a vineyard, put a fence around it, dug a hole for the wine press, and built a watchtower. Then he rented the vineyard to tenants and left home on a trip.

Although the previous section (verses 28-30) is not specifically identified as a parable, this parable is introduced with the words **Hear another parable**. Jesus is still talking to the chief priests and elders. However, the section heading makes a break in the text, and some translators have begun the verse with "Jesus went on to say." On the meaning of the word **parable**, see comment at 13.3.

There was is translated "**There was once**" by TEV (see verse 28).

Householder (TEV, NEB, NJB "landowner") is a favorite Matthean word (see 10.25); it is also used in 13.27,52; 20.1,11; 24.43. In this context "property owner" or "a man who owned a farm" may be natural. Some translators have used "farmer" if that term clearly meant that the person owned the farm.

Translators in languages where a **vineyard** will be unknown should see the comments at 20.1.

Hedge (so also NAB, Brc) is translated "wall" by NEB and NIV, and "**fence**" by TEV and Mft. Several translations prefer a verb phrase: "fenced it in" (AT) and "fenced it round" (NJB, Phps). This statement represents the clearest indication that Matthew has in mind the Greek Old Testament text of Isaiah 5.2, which replaces "he dug it up" of the Hebrew with "I fenced it in."

Dug a wine press in it is translated "**dug a hole for the wine press**" by TEV, which intends to help the reader who may not be familiar with the custom of digging a hole to use as a place to press grapes. Brc is even more explicit: "and dug out a pit in which the juice could be extracted from the grapes." The words **in it** do not mean the wine press was dug in the fence or hedge; it was in the vineyard, inside the area surrounded by the fence.

Tower is more specifically "**watchtower**" (TEV, NEB, GECL, NIV). Reference is to the custom of erecting a tower from which one can be on the lookout against thieves and animals which may break into the vineyard to steal the grapes when they are either ripe or almost ripe.

Let it out to tenants probably means on a sharecropping basis, according to which the rent was a certain percentage of the harvest (see verse 34: "**to receive his share of the harvest**" [TEV]). This kind of arrangement is known in many parts of the world. Where it is not, translators can say "had some men do the work on the farm in exchange for receiving some of the crop" or "found some people who agreed to take care of the vineyard for him."

Went into another country is translated "went abroad" by a number of modern translations (Mft, NJB, NEB, Phps, Brc). The intimation is that the owner is a foreigner, and that he is returning to his home abroad. At least this interpretation makes more sense of the other details in the story. Translators can say "traveled to another country" or "left on a trip to a distant place."

21.34   RSV   TEV

When the season of fruit drew near,   **When the time came to gather the**
he sent his servants to the tenants,   **grapes, he sent his slaves to the**
to get his fruit;   **tenants to receive his share of the**
                                            harvest.

The season of fruit obviously means "the time of harvest" (Lu); GECL has "at the time of grape gathering," while NEB has "vintage season" (NAB, NJB "vintage time"). Translators can also say "When it came time to harvest the grapes (or, fruit)" or "When the grapes (or, fruit) were ready for harvesting."

Drew near (TEV "**came**") is the same verb used in 3.2, though here the aorist tense is substituted for the perfect tense of the previous passage. See comments there.

Servants (so most translations) is rendered "**slaves**" by TEV, AT, and NAB. GECL has "messengers."

Tenants was discussed in the previous verse. In those languages where the word was rendered by a short descriptive phrase, then here either "the people in charge of the vineyard" or "those people taking care of the vineyard" is good.

To get his fruit (TEV "**to receive his share of the harvest**") may refer to the totality of the harvest rather than to a portion of it, as Mark (12.2) and Luke (20.10) specifically indicate. However, it is quite possible, and indeed probable, that Matthew's text may also be understood in this sense. For example, NEB ("the produce due to him"), NAB ("to obtain his share of the grapes"), AT ("to receive his share"), and Phps ("to receive his share of the crop"; Brc "his due share . . .").

21.35	RSV	TEV

and the tenants took his servants and beat one, killed another, and stoned another.	The tenants grabbed his slaves, beat one, killed another, and stoned another.

One obvious difference between Matthew and the texts of Mark and Luke is that Matthew uses the plural of **servants**, while Mark and Luke both retain the singular. This is in keeping with the allegorical intention of Matthew, who sees in the group of servants the representation of the prophets.

Beat one, killed another, and stoned another also differs markedly from Mark and Luke, according to which the mistreatment of the owner's representatives is done to one of them at a time, in an ascending degree of injury and insult.

Stoned can mean the tenants threw stones at the servant, but the word was generally used to mean they killed someone in this way. If it is possible to remain neutral on this point, as English is, that may be best. "Attacked with stones" is a way to do this.

21.36	RSV	TEV

Again he sent other servants, more than the first; and they did the same to them.	Again the man sent other slaves, more than the first time, and the tenants treated them the same way.

The commentators point out that the **servants** mentioned in this verse are intended to represent the postexilic prophets. Even the bitter experience of the exile did not cause Israel to alter its attitude toward God.

Again . . . other servants may be problematic for some readers to whom it may suggest that these **other servants** were now being sent a second time (**again**). To remove this difficulty, one may translate "After this, the man sent other servants."

More than the first may require translation as a separate sentence: "He sent more slaves this time than he did the first time."

Did the same to them (TEV "**treated them the same way**") may be translated "did the same thing to them that they did to the other slaves." The text has simply **they** and **them**. Translators will have to make sure it is clear that it was the tenants who did the same thing to these servants.

21.37	RSV	TEV

Afterward he sent his son to them, saying, 'They will respect my son.'	Last of all he sent his son to them. 'Surely they will respect my son,' he said.

His son differs significantly from the text of Mark, which has "a beloved son" (12.6). GECL translates "his own son."

Saying, though an accurate rendering of the Greek, here it must mean "said to himself," a meaning which the Greek verb has in certain contexts. GECL translates "he thought," and NAB has "thinking." In translation it may be necessary to invert the order of the two sentences: "Then the man thought, 'They will surely respect my son.' So he sent his son to them."

Will respect (used only here in Matthew) is the rendering preferred by most. TEV introduces **"Surely"** to intensify the contrast between the treatment of the servants and what the owner believes will be the treatment accorded his son. GECL accomplishes the same goal by translating "They will at least have respect for my son." **Will respect** can be expressed as "act respectfully toward," "treat with respect," or "have regard for."

21.38   RSV   TEV

But when the tenants saw the son,   But when the tenants saw the son,
they said to themselves, 'This is the   they said to themselves, 'This is the
heir; come, let us kill him and have   owner's son. Come on, let's kill him,
his inheritance.'   and we will get his property!'

But when the tenants saw the son may need to be translated ". . . saw the son coming" (GECL). **Said to themselves** may wrongly imply silent thought rather than oral conversation. "Said one to another" (NAB, NEB) will be better.

The heir is translated **"the owner's son"** by TEV. That he is the heir is brought out indirectly by TEV in what follows: ". . . **let's kill him, and we will get his property!**" Some scholars argue that the reasoning of the tenants reflects a law which was in effect in Galilee during the time of Jesus. According to this law, there were certain circumstances under which an inheritance could be considered ownerless property, and thus could be claimed by the persons who secured immediate possession of it. If this interpretation is allowed, then the tenants would have assumed that the owner of the property was dead, and that his son was now coming to take possession of the land. Therefore if they kill the son, the property would belong to them. Other scholars argue, however, that the murder of the son is a purely literary feature of the story and does not reflect this law. But regardless of which interpretation is adopted, the impact is basically the same, and the translation will not differ.

Many languages have a word they can use for **heir**. Occasionally translators have to say something like "the one who will inherit (everything) when the owner dies" or "the one who will have these things when the owner dies."

The **inheritance** is what the heir will receive. "All the property he will get from his father" or "everything the father will leave him when he dies" are possible translations.

21.39   RSV   TEV

And they took him and cast him out   So they grabbed him, threw him out
of the vineyard, and killed him.   of the vineyard, and killed him.

666

Took in this verse may be "grabbed," "seized," or "caught."

Cast him out of the vineyard, and killed him represents the reverse order of events from that found in Mark: "killed him, and cast his body out of the vineyard" (12.8). As the commentators note, Matthew seems to be adjusting the order to conform with Jesus' death, which took place outside the city of Jerusalem.

Cast is a somewhat archaic word that most modern English translations render as "threw."

21.40 RSV	TEV
When therefore the owner of the vineyard comes, what will he do to those tenants?"	"Now, when the owner of the vineyard comes, what will he do to those tenants?" Jesus asked.

"**Now**" (TEV, NJB, Phps) translates a Greek particle generally rendered **therefore** (RSV, NIV). It is the kind of word which does not require explicit mention in translation, and some prefer to leave it implicit (NAB, NEB). TEV begins a new paragraph here, and this may prove helpful in other languages as well. However, it may then be necessary to preface Jesus' question with "So Jesus asked them."

When therefore the owner of the vineyard comes is included only by Matthew; Mark has "What will the owner of the vineyard do?" (12.9), and Luke, "What then will the owner of the vineyard do to them?" (20.15). Some languages may require this mention of movement by the owner, but for Matthew it is really more than that. For him it emphasizes the coming judgment, perhaps with specific reference to the return of the Lord. However, it must be emphasized that in translation one cannot be explicit on the basis of Matthew's assumed intention. GECL lays stress upon this phrase without going beyond the limits of translation: "when he himself comes."

Sometimes the order of the question needs to be changed to be natural in the receptor language, as for example in "Now what will the owner of the vineyard do to those tenants when he himself comes?"

Matthew does not indicate the persons of whom Jesus asked this question, but some translations will require "them" at the least. Other translations may require a more specific indirect object: "the chief priests and the elders" (see verse 23).

21.41 RSV	TEV
They said to him, "He will put those wretches to a miserable death, and let out the vineyard to other tenants who will give him the fruits in their seasons."	"He will certainly kill those evil men," they answered, "and rent the vineyard out to other tenants, who will give him his share of the harvest at the right time."

They said to him is unique in Matthew, who allows the hearers to pronounce their own judgment. Note the similar manner in which Matthew includes "we are afraid of the multitude" (verse 26) as a remark of the chief priests and the elders rather than as an observation by the narrator (as in Mark 11.32).

Will put those wretches to a miserable death represents a play on words in Greek: "He will bring those bad men to a bad end" (NEB) and "He will bring those wretches to a wretched end" (NJB). However, as attested by NEB and NJB, when the play on words is transferred into English, the effect is less than desirable. A more literal rendering is "He will kill those bad people badly," in which the adverb "badly" may qualify either the merciless character of the death (Phps "without mercy") or else its horrible nature (AT "a miserable death").

Let out translates the same verb used in verse 33 (so also Mark 12.1; Luke 20.9). Here Mark (12.9) and Luke (20.16) shift to a verb which means "give" or "turn over to."

Who will give him the fruits in their seasons is a statement found only in Matthew. Its structure and meaning are similar to "the season of fruit" of verse 34 (see comment there). GECL is dynamic: "who promptly turn over to him his share at harvest time."

21.42 RSV	TEV
Jesus said to them, "Have you never read in the scriptures: 'The very stone which the builders rejected has become the head of the corner; this was the Lord's doing, and it is marvelous in our eyes'?	Jesus said to them, "Haven't you ever read what the Scriptures say? 'The stone which the builders rejected as worthless turned out to be the most important of all. This was done by the Lord; what a wonderful sight it is!'

In the scriptures: GECL translates "what stands written in the Holy Scriptures." This is a rhetorical question, and for many languages it will require shifting to a statement: "You have surely read the passage of scripture which says . . . ." There were similar questions at 12.3 and 19.4, and translators should see there for further suggestions. The scripture referred to is Psalm 118.22-23, and the quotation derives from the Septuagint. Matthew apparently intends an analogy: "The landowner's son is rejected and put to death, while here a stone is rejected as worthless, but it turns out to be the most important stone of all."

Rejected may require further definition, as in TEV ("**rejected as worthless**") or GECL 1st edition ("thrown away as useless").

Head of the corner ("cornerstone," NEB, AT), that is, the main foundation stone set at the corner of the building to align it accurately, is one possible interpretation. But the meaning may also be "keystone" (JB, NAB) or "capstone" (NIV), the last stone placed in the arch so as to lock the other stones together. TEV and GECL 1st edition assume a more neutral position ("**the most important of all**"), since scholarship is sharply divided on this issue.

The word **builders** is generally enough, in context, to make it clear that the **stone** in question is rejected or accepted for use in a building. However, on occasion

rejected is translated as "thrown away as of no use in building," and **head of the corner** is rendered as "the most important of all in the building."

Has become may be expressed as "has turned out to be" or "is in fact."

This was the Lord's doing (TEV "**This was done by the Lord**") may require the shift to an active construction, as in GECL: "The Lord has performed this wonder, and we have seen it." Another possibility is "It was the Lord who did this."

It is marvelous in our eyes is a Semitism which may have to be expressed as "how wonderful it is to see it," "what a great thing this is to see," or "we have seen what a wonderful thing that is." It is not that the stone is wonderful; the text says that for the Lord to make the rejected stone become the most important is what causes the wonder.

21.43	RSV	TEV

RSV	TEV
Therefore I tell you, the kingdom of God will be taken away from you and given to a nation producing the fruits of it."*q*	"And so I tell you," added Jesus, "the Kingdom of God will be taken away from you and given to a people who will produce the proper fruits."*t*
q Other ancient authorities add verse 44, "And he who falls on this stone will be broken to pieces; but when it falls on any one, it will crush him"	*t Some manuscripts add verse 44: Whoever falls on this stone will be cut to pieces; and if the stone falls on someone, it will crush him to dust (see Lk. 20.18).*

Therefore I tell you indicates an emphatic transition; NAB "For this reason, I tell you."

The kingdom of God will be taken away from you will need radical restructuring in most languages in order to make sense. The rendering of RSV and TEV makes the kingdom sound as though it is some kind of physical object, perhaps a trophy of some sort, which may be taken from one person and handed to another. Attention will also have to be given to the need to alter the passive to an active, with God as subject. For example, "God will take his community away from you and give it to those who obey him" (GECL 1st edition); "Every privilege that you have as God's people will be taken away from you and given to a nation who will obey God's commands" (INCL); "the blessings of God's rule will be taken from you and given to people who . . ." (MACL); "God will take away from you the privilege of being part of his rule." For further discussion of **kingdom of God**, see verse 31 and 19.24.

Given to a nation is another passive construction that may require an active form instead; for example, "he will give the privilege to another nation instead."

TEV has translated **nation** as "**a people.**" In either case the reference is to a nation or state, a specific group, and not just to people in general.

Producing the fruits of it means "will obey God" or ". . . God's commands," as GECL 1st edition's and INCL's restructurings indicate. The imagery is similar to that of 3.8 and 7.16, and so one may translate "who will do the right things."

[21.44] RSV TEV

[And he who falls on this stone will be broken to pieces; but when it falls on any one, it will crush him.]

[Whoever falls on this stone will be cut to pieces; and if the stone falls on someone, it will crush him to dust.]

There is considerable degree of doubt concerning the presence of this verse in the text. A number of scholars believe it to have been introduced early into Matthew's text on the basis of Luke 20.18. However, as TC-GNT indicates, the wording is not the same, and a scribe would more appropriately have introduced it after verse 42. On the other hand it is easy to see how a scribe's eye could have glanced over the verse, since in Greek the last word of verse 43 is similar to the last word of verse 44. It is included in NIV, Mft, AT, TOB, though NIV and TOB provide footnotes concerning the textual problem. NAB and GECL 1st edition place it in brackets, without a footnote; in Lu it is placed in brackets followed by a footnote indicating its absence from some ancient manuscripts. RSV, TEV, NEB, and NJB place it in the margin with a footnote. At least one scholar suggests that the background for the reference is Daniel 2.44-45 and Isaiah 8.14, and he concludes that the verse was not brought in from Luke but represents an original part of the Matthean text. If it is not included as part of the text, it should be listed in a footnote.

If the verse is included as a part of the translation, it should be clear that **this stone** refers back to the stone mentioned in verse 42. Moreover, **will be broken to pieces** should not be interpreted as punishment for falling on the stone, but as a description of what happens when one falls on the stone: "Whoever falls on this stone will be cut to pieces by the stone." The verb **broken to pieces** is found elsewhere in the New Testament only in Luke 20.18; the root meaning is "crush (together)" or "dash to pieces." NAB renders "smashed to bits" and TEV has "**cut to pieces.**"

Crush translates a verb which means "winnow" or "crush"; elsewhere in the New Testament it is found only in Luke 20.18. If **crush** does not give the idea of death, then "crush to death" or "kill" can be used.

21.45 RSV TEV

When the chief priests and the Pharisees heard his parables, they perceived that he was speaking about them.

The chief priests and the Pharisees heard Jesus' parables and knew that he was talking about them,

The chief priests and the Pharisees is a slight shift from verse 23, which has "the chief priests and the elders." In the Marcan parallel (12.12) the pronoun "they" is used (with reference to "the chief priests and the scribes and the elders" of 11.27). The parallel in Luke (20.19) has "The scribes and the chief priests." By placing the chief priests and the Pharisees together, Matthew reflects the historical opposition which Jesus shared from both of these groups during his earthly ministry, though they would not generally have been united in a single group as pictured here.

For **Pharisees**, see comments on 3.7.

Heard his parables, they perceived that he was speaking about them is somewhat stronger than what is found in the parallels of Mark (12.12) and Luke (20.19): "because they knew that he had told this parable against them." Throughout this chapter Matthew constantly emphasizes that Jesus' opponents are their own judges (see verses 16,26,41).

Note that TEV has translated **perceived** as "**knew**." "Recognized" can also be used.

21.46 RSV TEV

RSV	TEV
But when they tried to arrest him, they feared the multitudes, because they held him to be a prophet.	so they tried to arrest him. But they were afraid of the crowds, who considered Jesus to be a prophet.

They tried to arrest him may be more accurately expressed as either "they wanted to arrest him" (NEB) or "they would have liked to arrest him" (NJB). GECL is similar to NJB. **Arrest** may have to be expressed as "seize" or "take away to jail."

Multitudes (TEV "**crowds**") is singular in Mark (12.12); Luke has "the people" (20.19), a term which normally refers to the Jewish people.

Because they held him to be a prophet is found only in Matthew. GECL restructures the last part of the verse: ". . . but they did not risk it, because the crowd considered him a prophet." Another rendering is ". . . but they were afraid to try it since they knew that the crowds considered Jesus to be a prophet."

Chapter 22

RSV

TEV

The Parable of the Wedding Feast

1 And again Jesus spoke to them in parables, saying, 2 "The kingdom of heaven may be compared to a king who gave a marriage feast for his son, 3 and sent his servants to call those who were invited to the marriage feast; but they would not come. 4 Again he sent other servants, saying, 'Tell those who are invited, Behold, I have made ready my dinner, my oxen and my fat calves are killed, and everything is ready; come to the marriage feast.' 5 But they made light of it and went off, one to his farm, another to his business, 6 while the rest seized his servants, treated them shamefully, and killed them. 7 The king was angry, and he sent his troops and destroyed those murderers and burned their city. 8 Then he said to his servants, 'The wedding is ready, but those invited were not worthy. 9 Go therefore to the thoroughfares, and invite to the marriage feast as many as you find.' 10 And those servants went out into the streets and gathered all whom they found, both bad and good; so the wedding hall was filled with guests.

11 "But when the king came in to look at the guests, he saw there a man who had no wedding garment; 12 and he said to him, 'Friend, how did you get in here without a wedding garment?' And he was speechless. 13 Then the king said to the attendants, 'Bind him hand and foot, and cast him into the outer darkness; there men will weep and gnash their teeth.' 14 For many are called, but few are chosen."

1 Jesus again used parables in talking to the people. 2 "The Kingdom of heaven is like this. Once there was a king who prepared a wedding feast for his son. 3 He sent his servants to tell the invited guests to come to the feast, but they did not want to come. 4 So he sent other servants with this message for the guests: 'My feast is ready now; my steers and prize calves have been butchered, and everything is ready. Come to the wedding feast!' 5 But the invited guests paid no attention and went about their business: one went to his farm, another to his store, 6 while others grabbed the servants, beat them, and killed them. 7 The king was very angry; so he sent his soldiers, who killed those murderers and burned down their city. 8 Then he called his servants and said to them, 'My wedding feast is ready, but the people I invited did not deserve it. 9 Now go to the main streets and invite to the feast as many people as you find.' 10 So the servants went out into the streets and gathered all the people they could find, good and bad alike; and the wedding hall was filled with people.

11 "The king went in to look at the guests and saw a man who was not wearing wedding clothes. 12 'Friend, how did you get in here without wedding clothes?' the king asked him. But the man said nothing. 13 Then the king told the servants, 'Tie him up hand and foot, and throw him outside in the dark. There he will cry and gnash his teeth.' "

14 And Jesus concluded, "Many are invited, but few are chosen."

SECTION HEADING: "**The Parable of the Wedding Feast**." Translators may have to express this as a short sentence such as "Jesus tells a parable about a wedding feast." "**Parable**" was discussed at 13.3.

A parallel to this parable is found in Luke (14.15-24), though there are significant differences in structure and detail. Many scholars believe that verses 11-14 (not contained in the Lukan parallel) originally comprised a separate parable which

Matthew joined to the parable of verses 1-9. Moreover, some scholars believe that verses 6-7 reflect the events of A.D. 70, when the Roman army destroyed Jerusalem, thus revealing an early adaptation of Jesus' parable to the then-existing situation.

Scholars also note the parallels contained in the apocryphal Gospel of Thomas (64) and in the parable attributed to the Jewish teacher Jochanan, who died about A.D. 80. But the parable as it stands in the Gospel of Matthew has a unifying theme, which is Jesus' reply to the open hostility of his opponents. This is in fact the final in a series of three parables which address the challenge to Jesus' authority (see 21.28-32 and 21.33-44), and it warns of a twofold danger: (1) that of disregarding God's invitation to the Messianic feast (verses 1-10), and (2) that of presuming upon God's grace, failing to realize that participation in the kingdom demands an appropriate life-style (verses 11-14).

22.1

RSV	TEV
And again Jesus spoke to them in parables, saying,	Jesus again used parables in talking to the people.

As is often the case, **And** shows some continuity with the previous passage but at the same time marks a new episode. The **again** is more important for the translator, however, since Jesus has just been teaching with parables in the previous chapter. Brc begins the chapter "Once again." Another possibility is "Jesus continued teaching with parables."

Them is translated "**the people**" by TEV, but this is one instance where TEV seems to have misidentified the pronominal referent. The reference is surely to the Jewish religious leaders who are identified both as "the chief priests and the elders" (21.23) and "the chief priests and the Pharisees" (21.45). If it is necessary to be specific in translation, one will do better to translate "those people who had questioned his authority."

Parables is a typical Matthean expression; in context it refers back to the two immediately preceding parables. For **parables** see 13.3.

Saying translates a Greek structure which is literally "answering . . . he said" (the same formula used in 21.24), and so may indicate that Jesus is using this parable as a specific reply to the question regarding his authority (21.23). If they choose this interpretation, translators will have something like "Jesus continued to answer those people with parables. He said . . . ." On the other hand, the construction "answering . . . he said" may mean merely "he said" (as it does in 11.25), but the former alternative is probably better.

22.2

RSV	TEV
"The kingdom of heaven may be compared to a king who gave a marriage feast for his son,	"The Kingdom of heaven is like this. Once there was a king who prepared a wedding feast for his son.

The kingdom of heaven may be compared to translates the same formula used in 13.24. As there, the kingdom of heaven should be compared to the whole parable, not to a king, as the RSV may seem to mean. See TEV, but also note Brc: "The situation in the Kingdom of Heaven is like the situation which arose when a king gave a wedding banquet for his son."

Note that TEV has used the formula "Once there was . . . ." Translators should use the same formula here that they used in 20.1.

In contrast to the Lukan parallel (14.16), the "man" is here **a king**, and the "great feast" is now **a marriage feast for his son**. In translation it must not be implied, of course, that the king himself prepared the meal. One may translate either "who caused a wedding feast to be prepared for his son" or "who ordered his servants to prepare a wedding feast for his son." Direct discourse may be preferable: "who told his servants, 'Prepare a wedding feast for my son.' "

Wedding feast may require some explanation if there is no expression in the receptor language that means exactly the same thing. Translators may have to say "There was a king whose son was getting married, so the king prepared a feast for him (or, a feast to celebrate)."

22.3   RSV   TEV

and sent his servants to call those   He sent his servants to tell the invit-
who were invited to the marriage   ed guests to come to the feast, but
feast; but they would not come.   they did not want to come.

According to one scholar, **to call those who were invited to the marriage feast** represents "a special courtesy, practiced by upper circles in Jerusalem," in which the invitation was repeated immediately prior to the time of the banquet. If this exegesis is correct, then the first part of the verse may necessitate some restructuring in order to reflect a more precise chronological order: ". . . who prepared a wedding feast for his son, 3 and invited some guests to the feast. When it was time for the feast, he sent his servants to tell the guests to come." On the other hand, another scholar notes the possibility that Matthew may have in mind a Semitic idiom which means "the guests to be invited." This seems to be the interpretation of GECL 1st edition: "He had sent his servants to invite the guests." Other translations apparently prefer the traditional rendering.

But they would not come indicates a strong refusal on the part of the invited guests; NAB, Phps, Brc, NIV have "they refused to come."

22.4   RSV   TEV

Again he sent other servants, saying,   So he sent other servants with this
'Tell those who are invited, Behold, I   message for the guests: 'My feast is
have made ready my dinner, my   ready now; my steers and prize
oxen and my fat calves are killed,   calves have been butchered, and
and everything is ready; come to the   everything is ready. Come to the
marriage feast.'   wedding feast!'

The sending of **other servants** recalls 21.36 ("Again he sent other servants"). Brc has "He sent out a second lot of servants."

Saying of the Greek text is translated **"with this message for the guests"** by TEV. It is also possible to translate "So he sent other servants, and told them to say to the guests . . . ." Depending upon the interpretation of the previous verse, this will be either a second or third invitation offered the guests. Most commentators and translators believe it to be the third invitation, following immediately upon their previous rejection. In either case, through this use of multiple invitations, Matthew emphatically underscores the refusal of the guests to respond to the invitation.

Behold serves as an attention getter (see 1.20); NEB has "See now!"

Dinner translates a noun which originally meant "breakfast" but which later was used of other meals as well, including a **"feast"** (TEV, NEB) or "banquet" (NJB). Elsewhere in the New Testament the noun occurs only in the Lukan parallel (11.38) and in Luke 14.12; the corresponding verb is used in Luke 11.37. Since **dinner** is here placed in parallel with **marriage feast** (see below and verse 2), one will want to be sure in translation that the readers understand the reference is to the same meal. **Behold, I have made ready my dinner** is translated "All preparations for the feast are completed" by GECL; NEB identifies the persons for whom the preparations have been made: "I have prepared this feast for you."

Oxen and **fat calves** (Brc "oxen and specially fattened calves") is a way of speaking of the most choice animals. The word translated **oxen** (TEV "steers") is used in the New Testament elsewhere only in Hebrews 9.13 and 10.4, where it refers to a sacrificial animal. If **oxen** are unknown, the translators may say "young bulls" or, if even that posed some problem for readers, "best cattle." **Fat calves** (TEV "prize calves"), a word used only here in the New Testament, describes cattle that have been fattened for a special occasion. Often that is exactly what translators say: "the calves that have been fed specially to be fat and good for eating." But "best calves for eating" may be an easier expression.

TEV renders **are killed** by **"have been butchered."** If a passive construction like this is awkward, then "I have butchered" may be better.

And everything is ready may need to be translated "and everything else is ready," or else rendered as a separate statement, "Everything is ready!"

22.5	RSV	TEV
	But they made light of it and went off, cne to his farm, another to his business,	But the invited guests paid no attention and went about their business: one went to his farm, another to his store,

They refers back to "those who are invited" at the beginning of verse 4; TEV identifies **they** through the use of the phrase **"the invited guests."**

Made light of appears in TEV and Mft as **"paid no attention"**; NEB, AT, and Phps have "took no notice of"; NJB has "they were not interested"; NAB has the one word "ignored." Elsewhere in the New Testament the verb is used in 1 Timothy 4.14; Hebrews 2.3; 8.9. The phrase can also be rendered "they disregarded" or "they did not take seriously." **It** may need to be replaced by "the invitation."

Went off, one to his farm, another to his business is considerably restructured in TEV: **"went about their business: one went to his farm, another went to his store."** It will also be acceptable to say "went somewhere else. Some went to the farms, others to their businesses."

One . . . another is probably best taken in a collective sense: "some went to their farms, others went to their place of business." **Business** (TEV, GECL **"store"**) or "trade" is the primary meaning of the noun, which occurs nowhere else in the New Testament; a related noun occurs in John 2.16.

22.6	RSV	TEV

while the rest seized his servants, treated them shamefully, and killed them.	while others grabbed the servants, beat them, and killed them.

Seized, treated . . . scornfully, killed: these actions are without parallel in Luke. **Treated . . . shamefully** (Mft, AT "ill-treated"; NJB "maltreated") may also mean "insulted" (NAB; Phps "treated . . . with insults") or **"beat"** (TEV). NEB has "attacked . . . brutally." The Greek text seems to suggest that the rest of the invited guests did these actions to all the servants.

22.7	RSV	TEV

The king was angry, and he sent his troops and destroyed those murderers and burned their city.	The king was very angry; so he sent his soldiers, who killed those murderers and burned down their city.

Angry may be too weak to express adequately the feelings of the king in response to the mistreatment and murder of his servants. "Furious" is the preference of NJB, NEB, and Brc (NAB "grew furious"), while Mft and NIV have "enraged." In many languages, rather than saying the king **was angry**, "became angry" would be more natural.

As in TEV, **and** may better be translated "**so**."

He sent his troops and destroyed those murderers and burned their city: in place of **destroyed** TEV chooses "killed," which is more natural for English speakers when persons are used as the object. In such a context the verbs **destroyed** and **burned** assume a causative force, since it is obvious that the king himself did not perform these actions: ". . . sent his soldiers with orders to kill . . . and burn" or ". . . gave his soldiers orders, 'Go and kill all those people and burn their city to the ground.' " The sentence can also be "sent his soldiers to kill those murderers and to burn down their city."

22.8 RSV	TEV
Then he said to his servants, 'The wedding is ready, but those invited were not worthy.	Then he called his servants and said to them, 'My wedding feast is ready, but the people I invited did not deserve it.

This verse narrates another invitation sent out to invite guests to the wedding feast, but the guests who are now invited are not the ones who received the original invitation. Of the original guests the king says **those invited were not worthy** (see 10.10,11,13,37,38 for **worthy** in the sense used here). In the Lukan form of this parable, the servant goes out twice to invite new guests; he first is sent to the "streets and alleys of the town," and since there is still room in the house, he is sent afterwards to the "country roads and lanes" (14.21-23). Although some scholars propose that verse 8 originally followed verse 5, this is not the form of the parable which Matthew transmits, and translation must reflect accurately the text as it exists.

The text has **his servants**, but for some readers that poses a problem, since in verse 6 the servants he sent out were killed. Therefore "his other servants" is sometimes necessary.

As in TEV, **the wedding** may more naturally be translated as "the wedding feast," using the same expression as in verse 2.

Those invited may have to be expressed as "those people I invited."

Most translators will express **were not worthy** in a way similar to TEV, possibly "did not deserve the invitations" or "did not deserve to be invited."

22.9 RSV	TEV
Go therefore to the thoroughfares, and invite to the marriage feast as many as you find.'	Now go to the main streets and invite to the feast as many people as you find.'

Thoroughfares (TEV "**main streets**") is literally "the intersections of the roads." The reference is probably to the points at which the roads of the town intersect (JB "the crossroads in the town"); in effect this means "throughout the entire city" (GECL 1st edition). The point is that the servants should go out to where they will most likely find people, so that "the main intersections" or "the city streets" will probably convey the meaning correctly.

As many as you find means simply "whomever you meet" or "all the people you find there" (as long as "find" does not imply that somehow these people had been lost).

As many as you find is less specific than Luke, who identifies the new guests as "the poor and maimed and blind and lame" (14.21). It is quite obvious that Luke here reflects his own interest in the presentation of the Good News to the poor and blind (see Luke 4.18). The persons whom the servants did invite, when described by Matthew ("both bad and good" of verse 10), point toward the conclusion which Matthew gives to the parable (verses 11-13).

22.10   RSV   TEV

And those servants went out into the streets and gathered all whom they found, both bad and good; so the wedding hall was filled with guests.	So the servants went out into the streets and gathered all the people they could find, good and bad alike; and the wedding hall was filled with people.

Translators in areas where **streets** are not common can simply say "into the towns" or, better, "out on the public roads."

Gathered all whom they found (a fairly literal rendering of the Greek text) may also be rendered "invited everyone whom they found" (GECL 1st edition). The difficulty with a literal rendering is that the reader is left with the impression that the persons who were invited were first gathered together into a large group and then went as a group to the wedding. The text seems to mean rather that the people whom they invited came individually, but comprised a large crowd when they all arrived. "Brought to the wedding feast" may be a good translation.

Both bad and good: on the assumption that the order "bad . . . good" is purely a linguistic feature, having no theological significance, TEV places the two adjectives in an order that is more natural for English speakers: "**good and bad alike**." Note also GECL 1st edition: ". . . whether he was a good or bad man." The statement is reminiscent of 13.24-30, 36-43, 47-50.

This sentence may need to be restructured slightly to be more natural; for example, "invited everyone they met, both good people and bad, and brought them to the wedding feast."

The **wedding hall** is the room or place where the feast was to be held. If there is no direct equivalent in a language, translators may simply use a descriptive phrase: "the room for the wedding feast."

The wedding hall was filled with guests may need to be translated either "the people came in and filled the wedding hall" or "so many people came that the wedding hall was full of guests."

22.11   RSV   TEV

"But when the king came in to look at the guests, he saw there a man who had no wedding garment;	"The king went in to look at the guests and saw a man who was not wearing wedding clothes.

As noted in the introduction to this section, verses 11-14 comprise a separate parable with a message of its own apart from the context in which it appears. In fact it makes little sense, if any at all, in its present location. How could a guest be expected to have secured a **wedding garment** if he had been invited directly off the street to come to the wedding? But this is not Matthew's concern. For him the message of the parable is that a person who is invited to the Messianic banquet must not remain as he was when he was called. Participation in the banquet requires a transformation of life that is consistent with the profession of discipleship which one makes.

Look at reflects the situation in which, as a sign of courtesy, the host does not partake of the banquet but arrives later to see which guests have come and to talk with them. The translation may say "to see the guests who were there."

Wedding garment may be rendered as "wedding clothes," or the whole expression may be expressed as "was not wearing the proper clothes for a wedding."

Since verses 11-14 are set off from the rest of the parable, as we noted above, then it is quite common to start a new paragraph here, as RSV and TEV have done.

22.12 RSV	TEV
and he said to him, 'Friend, how did you get in here without a wedding garment?' And he was speechless.	'Friend, how did you get in here without wedding clothes?' the king asked him. But the man said nothing.

Friend is a polite form of address (see 20.13); it is the noun by which Jesus addresses Judas when he comes to betray him in the garden (26.50).

How did you get in here without a wedding garment? is divided into two sentences by GECL: "How did you get in here? You are not wearing festive clothes." Another possibility is "Friend, you are not wearing the proper clothes for a wedding. How come you are here?" When the king asks **how did you get in**, he is not asking about the method by which the man came. Rather it is a way of exclaiming about the inappropriate clothes the man is wearing. Since the question is rhetorical, one may also render "You are not wearing the proper clothes for a wedding feast, and so you have no right to be here."

And he was speechless is rendered "The man had no excuse" by GECL. More literally the text is "And the man was silent" (NJB). One may also translate "There was nothing that the man could say."

22.13 RSV	TEV
Then the king said to the attendants, 'Bind him hand and foot, and cast him into the outer darkness; there men will weep and gnash their teeth.'	Then the king told the servants, 'Tie him up hand and foot, and throw him outside in the dark. There he will cry and gnash his teeth.' "

Attendants (TEV "**servants**") is the noun frequently translated "deacon" in certain other contexts, though it may have the broader meaning of "servant" or "helper." Here it is apparently used as a synonym for "servant" of verses 1-10, though NJB, NEB, Brc join RSV in translating **attendants**, which seems to distinguish between the two groups. Translators who wish to keep this same distinction may also say "servants in the house" or "those serving the guests." Otherwise it is often impossible to render this term any differently than "servants."

Hand and foot (so also TEV) is literally "feet and hands." Both RSV and TEV are simply following a pattern which is more natural in English, and the same thing is done in German by GECL, Lu, and Zür. To **bind him hand and foot** means to tie up his hands and his feet or to tie him up so he can't even move his hands and feet.

The outer darkness is a Semitic expression which JB and NEB more appropriately render as "out into the dark." The same expression occurred at 8.12, and translators should see the discussion there.

There men will weep and gnash their teeth translates an impersonal construction: "There shall be weeping and gnashing of teeth." The same expression is used in 8.12 and is symbolic of the suffering that one endures in Hell. The question that the translator must face is whether it should apply to the individual in the parable, or whether the shift is made to everyone who will finally share this horrible fate. In other words, is this phrase part of the parable, something the king says to his servants, or a general point Jesus is making after completing the parable? The context seems to suggest that Matthew intends the more comprehensive application. As TOB comments at verse 11, "God's invitation is free, but it is also demanding." Thus translators should probably not add "So Jesus concluded" at this point. And further, it is better to say "There men will weep and gnash their teeth" than to say that it is the man who will (as TEV does). But the text itself allows for either interpretation.

22.14	RSV	TEV
	For many are called, but few are chosen."	And Jesus concluded, "Many are invited, but few are chosen."

"And Jesus concluded" of TEV represents **For** of the Greek text, which indicates a transition from the parable to its application.

Many are called, but few are chosen is difficult, both exegetically and translationally. The statement may refer primarily to verses 1-10, or else to verses 11-13; it is also possible that it is comprehensive, including the teaching of both parables, which is probably the best solution. As one scholar notes, **are called** and **are chosen** may be synonymous in other contexts, but here they are set in contrast to one another. In the context of the parable this may be either a statement that only a few among the Jews are "chosen" (verses 1-10), or a warning to Christians not to take their calling lightly (verses 11-14). But in either case **are called** and **are chosen** describe God's activity: "God invites many, though he chooses only a few." Fortunately it is not the translator's task to resolve the theological issues and questions, but rather to render faithfully the meaning of each specific passage. Notice that **called** is generally rendered in this verse as "invited." If either of these words requires a complement, then translators may have to say "called (or, invited) to be a part of his kingdom" or "invited to accept God's kingship (or, accept God's ruling over them)."

Despite the fact that it is God who also chooses, those who **are chosen** are those whose faithfulness endures to the end (see 24.22,31). Translators may have to say "but only a few are faithful enough to be chosen" or "but it is only a few people who are faithful enough for God to choose them." Again, if "choose" requires a complement it can be "chosen to enter his kingdom" or "chosen to receive his rule," or the sentence can even be "God invites many, but he chooses only those who accept his invitation."

22.15-22

RSV   TEV

The Question about Paying Taxes

15 Then the Pharisees went and took counsel how to entangle him in his talk. 16 And they sent their disciples to him, along with the Herodians, saying, "Teacher, we know that you are true, and teach the way of God truthfully, and care for no man; for you do not regard the position of men. 17 Tell us, then, what you think. Is it lawful to pay taxes to Caesar, or not?" 18 But Jesus, aware of their malice, said, "Why put me to the test, you hypocrites? 19 Show me the money for the tax." And they brought him a coin.[r] 20 And Jesus said to them, "Whose likeness and inscription is this?" 21 They said, "Caesar's." Then he said to them, "Render therefore to Caesar the things that are Caesar's, and to God the things that are God's." 22 When they heard it, they marveled; and they left him and went away.

[r] Greek *a denarius*

15 The Pharisees went off and made a plan to trap Jesus with questions. 16 Then they sent to him some of their disciples and some members of Herod's party. "Teacher," they said, "we know that you tell the truth. You teach the truth about God's will for man, without worrying about what people think, because you pay no attention to a man's status. 17 Tell us, then, what do you think? Is it against our Law to pay taxes to the Roman Emperor, or not?"

18 Jesus, however, was aware of their evil plan, and so he said, "You hypocrites! Why are you trying to trap me? 19 Show me the coin for paying the tax!"

They brought him the coin, 20 and he asked them, "Whose face and name are these?"

21 "The Emperor's," they answered.

So Jesus said to them, "Well, then, pay to the Emperor what belongs to the Emperor, and pay to God what belongs to God."

22 When they heard this, they were amazed; and they left him and went away.

SECTION HEADING: the TEV heading, "**The Question about Paying Taxes**," may be too abbreviated for some readers. Translators may have to say "Jesus answers questions about paying taxes" or "Jesus discusses paying taxes." Another possibility is "Some Pharisees ask Jesus about paying taxes." Since the issue is not merely taxes, some translators have had renderings such as "The Obligations People have to Rulers and to God."

By introducing the parable of the wedding feast (22.1-14), Matthew departed from the Marcan framework. He now returns to follow Mark, and in so doing continues the series of five controversies between Jesus and the religious leaders of the nation which began in 21.23; the remaining four are: the question about paying taxes (verses 15-22), the question about rising from death (verses 23-33), the question of the most important commandment (verses 34-40), and the question about the Messiah (verses 41-46). As one scholar comments: "For Matthew the four disputations constituted a single unit. Except for the question asked by the Sadducees, which could not possibly be placed in the mouth of the Pharisees, these disputations have become a single controversy between Jesus and Judaism in its Pharisaic form."

22.15   RSV   TEV

Then the Pharisees went and took counsel how to entangle him in his talk.

The Pharisees went off and made a plan to trap Jesus with questions.

Then represents the beginning of a new passage. Translators should probably not use a word that would make readers think this dispute with the Pharisees followed straight on from the discussion with the chief priests that ended at verse 14. In English many translations drop it, for example TEV and Brc. Others say "Some time after that."

The Pharisees contrasts with Mark, who has "Some Pharisees and some members of Herod's party" (12.13). Moreover, for Matthew the chief priests of verses 21.23,45 are now forgotten. Of course probably not all the Pharisees were involved as **the Pharisees** could indicate. Most translators have "some Pharisees." For **Pharisees** see 3.7.

Went has been translated as "**went off**" by TEV. The meaning is not that they went to some particular place, but rather that they got together for a meeting. Translators might say "met together" or "left to meet."

Took counsel how to entangle him: in keeping with its translation principles, TEV substitutes the proper name "**Jesus**" for the pronoun **him** when a new section is introduced. In the Greek text he is last mentioned by name in verse 1.

Took counsel translates a Greek expression which implies mutual participation in the making of a plan (see NJB "to work out between them"), which is most simply expressed in English as "**made a plan**" (TEV; NEB "agreed on a plan," and NIV "laid plans"). Since the plans are against someone, it may be more appropriate to translate "made a plot" (AT) or "plotted" (Mft). NAB focuses upon the initiation of the action: "began to plot."

Entangle (TEV "**trap**") translates a verb which literally means "lay a snare"; in the New Testament it is used only here, and obviously in a figurative sense. Mark narrates the same event by the use of a different verb. It can be rendered also as "catch him out" or "trick him into saying something that would be bad for him."

In his talk is more literally "by a word." The reference may be either to the verbal attacks (that is, questions) which will be directed against Jesus, or to the answers which Jesus will give to these questions. TEV, NEB, NJB, and NIV suggest that the trap relates to Jesus' answers to their questions. Others choose to be ambiguous: "in argument" (AT, Phps), "in talk" (Mft), and "a verbal trap" (Brc). On the other hand, GECL is in agreement with the exegesis of TEV: "how they could entice Jesus into a trap with a leading (or, a catching) question." Those translators who follow the exegesis of TEV and the GECL can use an expression such as "how they could use questions to catch Jesus out" or "how they could ask questions that would trap Jesus." On the other hand, those who understand **in his talk** to refer to Jesus' reply may have "trap him so he would say something wrong" or "trick him into saying something wrong." An ambiguous rendering is "trap him in an argument."

22.16 RSV TEV

RSV	TEV
And they sent their disciples to him, along with the Herodians, saying, "Teacher, we know that you are true, and teach the way of God truthfully, and care for no man; for you do not regard the position of men.	Then they sent to him some of their disciples and some members of Herod's party. "Teacher," they said, "we know that you tell the truth. You teach the truth about God's will for man, without worrying about what

people think, because you pay no attention to a man's status.

Their disciples (that is, the disciples of the Pharisees) and **the Herodians** represent two extremes in the controversy that follows. The Herodians were supporters of the descendants of Herod as the ruling party, and as such would have been in favor of Roman rule. On the other hand, the Pharisees were the conservative religious element, and they would have found it distasteful to be compelled to support the Roman government by their contributions. This then depicts the dilemma in which the Pharisees hope to snare Jesus. To say that one should not pay taxes to the Romans would put him at odds with the civil authorities, while he would have lost favor with the people if he had advocated the payment of taxes to the Roman authorities.

The **disciples** of the Pharisees can certainly be translated by the same word or expression used for the disciples of Jesus.

As for **Herodians**, a good translation is "Herod's supporters" or "supporters of Herod as ruler." "Members of the group that supported Herod (to be ruler)" is also possible, but the shorter examples are better.

Teacher is first used of Jesus in 8.19; see comments there.

"You tell the truth" (TEV, AT; Brc "you speak the truth") translates **you are true**. A number of translations render "you are an honest man" (Phps, NEB, NJB). In context the focus is not upon Jesus' overall honesty or integrity (NIV "a man of integrity"), but upon his role as a teacher who speaks what is true (NAB, "you are a truthful man"), which is the basis for TEV.

And teach the way of God truthfully: GECL has "you tell each person clearly and plainly how he must live according to God's will." Brc translates "you really do teach the life that God wishes us to live." The TEV translation probably reflects the meaning most closely, however, in saying that Jesus is properly teaching God's laws ("You teach the truth about God's will for man"). "What you teach about God's laws (or, will) is the truth (or, correct)" is another good expression.

And care for no man, a literal representation of the Greek text, may easily be misunderstood. GECL expresses the meaning clearly: "you do not allow yourself to be influenced by people." Close to GECL, though with a slightly different focus, is Phps: "you are not swayed by men's opinion of you." "You don't care what people think" is also good. In some languages translators will need an object for "think," however, as in "you don't care what people think about your teaching."

You do not regard the position of men translates the Semitic idiom: "you do not look into the face of men." A literal translation may imply guilt or shame on Jesus' part, whereas the real emphasis is upon the impartiality with which Jesus treats people, regardless of their status (AT "you are impartial"). GECL connects this clause with the previous one: ". . . influenced by people, no matter how important they are." Some translators will make this a new sentence: "You don't care whether someone is important or not" or "It does not matter to you whether someone is an important person or not."

22.17 RSV	TEV
Tell us, then, what you think. Is it lawful to pay taxes to Caesar, or not?"	Tell us, then, what do you think? Is it against our Law to pay taxes to the Roman Emperor, or not?"

The sentence **Tell us, then, what you think** is similar to the one by which Jesus addressed Peter in 17.25.

Is it lawful may be taken either in a general sense (Mft, AT, Brc "is it right"), or else with specific reference to the Jewish Law (GECL 1st edition "According to the Law of God, are we allowed"). Translators who follow this latter interpretation can also have "Does the Law of Moses permit us" or simply "Is it lawful."

Pay taxes to Caesar may have to be restructured slightly, particularly if otherwise readers thought that the money had to be paid directly to Caesar rather than to one of the tax collectors who worked for the Roman Empire. "Pay the taxes that Caesar requires" is good.

Originally **Caesar** was a proper name, but it later became used as a title meaning "Emperor," which is the way that it is used here: **"the Roman Emperor"** (TEV, GECL).

22.18 RSV	TEV
But Jesus, aware of their malice, said, "Why put me to the test, you hypocrites?	Jesus, however, was aware of their evil plan, and so he said, "You hypocrites! Why are you trying to trap me?

Some languages generally render the word **aware** with a phrase that means to make someone conscious of something. But there is no indication here that anyone told Jesus what the plan was. "Knew" would be a better translation, as for example in "But Jesus knew what their evil intention was."

Malice (so also NJB, AT, Mft) may be more accurately phrased as **"evil plan"** (TEV), "evil intent" (NIV), or "evil intention" (Phps). Brc is rather high level: "Jesus was well aware of their malicious motives." The noun was first used in 5.11, where RSV translates it as "evil."

Put . . . to the test (TEV **"trap"**) is not the same verb used in verse 15. Except for the problematic verse 35 (see below), in Matthew's Gospel the word is used only of Satan (4.1,3) or of the Pharisees (16.1; 19.3; 22.18). Once again Brc uses a rather sophisticated level of English, but he does dynamic restructuring of the noun of address (**you hypocrites**) plus the question: "You are not out for information . . . you are out to make trouble in your two-faced maliciousness." GECL shifts to an exclamatory statement: "You hypocrites, you are only laying a trap for me!" "You are just trying to test me!" is also good.

Hypocrites was first used in 6.2 (see comment there). As with most terms of address, it will in many languages have to appear first in the sentence. But another solution is to retain it at the end of the verse, but as a separate sentence: "What hypocrites you are!"

22.19 RSV TEV

Show me the money for the tax."
And they brought him a coin.^r

Show me the coin for paying the
tax!"
They brought him the coin,

^r Greek *a denarius*

The money for the tax is more literally "the coin of the tax." **Tax** translates
the same noun rendered "tribute" in the phrase "toll or tribute" in 17.25. Most
translators will do something quite similar to what TEV has done; for example, "Show
me the coin (or, money) people use to pay the tax with."

Coin translates "denarius" (see the RSV footnote), the Roman coin required
for the payment of the taxes. This was a silver coin, and on it was inscribed not only
the face of the Roman Emperor but the religious claims made by the Emperor. For
example, Emperor Tiberius (see Luke 3.1) had on his coins the inscription "God and
high priest." Some languages do not have a general word **coin** but only names for
the specific coins that exist in their currencies. If a phrase such as "silver money" or
"metal money" is not possible, then translators should try a comparison such as
"money like a . . . ," using some local coin.

22.20 RSV TEV

And Jesus said to them, "Whose
likeness and inscription is this?"

and he asked them, "Whose face
and name are these?"

This verse is restructured much better by GECL 1st edition: "He held out the
coin where they could see it and asked them, 'Whose picture and name are inscribed
on this?' " Translators may also consider a rendering like "Then Jesus said to them,
'Whose picture and name are written (or, do you see) on this coin (or, money)?' "
Notice that in these examples **likeness** is translated as "picture." "Image" is also
possible. Translators should not use a word that would mean "photograph," however.
The **inscription** is the writing of the name of the Emperor, which is why it is
translated as "name." This question as well as the reply of verse 21 and Jesus'
counterquestion to his opponents are the same in Mark (12.16-17) and Luke
(20.24-25).

22.21 RSV TEV

They said, "Caesar's." Then he said
to them, "Render therefore to Caesar
the things that are Caesar's, and to
God the things that are God's."

"The Emperor's," they an-
swered.
So Jesus said to them, "Well,
then, pay to the Emperor what belongs to the Emperor, and pay to
God what belongs to God."

This verse is quite straightforward, and RSV represents a fairly literal rendering of the Greek text. Jesus' answer is precise yet not specific. The hearers are still called upon to make their own decision regarding what belongs to the Emperor and what belongs to God.

As in verse 17, **Caesar's** is normally translated as "**The Emperor's**" (TEV) or "The Roman Emperor's." In some languages a complete sentence will be more natural, as in "They are of the Emperor," or even "They are the picture and name of the Emperor."

TEV expresses the **therefore** with "**Well, then,**" which is more natural in English.

Render means "**pay**" (TEV), "give back to," or "return to." Some translators have used an imperative here, but a structure like "You should give back" is better.

It is sometimes more natural to put the emphasis on the object of the returning, as in "Whatever belongs to the Emperor you should give back to the Emperor, and whatever belongs to God you should give back to God."

22.22

RSV	TEV
When they heard it, they marveled; and they left him and went away.	When they heard this, they were amazed; and they left him and went away.

Both Mark (12.17) and Luke (20.26) indicate that Jesus' opponents **marveled** (see 8.10) at his response. The concluding statement (**and they left him and went away**) is recorded earlier in Mark (12.12), where it immediately precedes this section about the payment of taxes. Luke lays even stronger emphasis upon what resulted from Jesus' reply: "And they were not able in the presence of the people to catch him by what he said; but marveling at his answer they were silent." GECL translates the verse: "They had not expected this answer. They left Jesus in peace and went away." Another rendering that may be natural is "When they heard Jesus' answer, they were astonished. So they left him and went away." In some languages "They went away from him" will be more natural.

22.23-33

RSV	TEV
	The Question about Rising from Death
23 The same day Sadducees came to him, who say that there is no resurrection; and they asked him a question, 24 saying, "Teacher, Moses said, 'If a man dies, having no children, his brother must marry the widow, and raise up children for his brother.' 25 Now there were seven brothers among us; the first married, and died, and having no children left his wife to his brother. 26 So too the second and third, down to the seventh. 27 After them all, the woman died. 28 In the resur-	23 That same day some Sadducees came to Jesus and claimed that people will not rise from death. 24 "Teacher," they said, "Moses said that if a man who has no children dies, his brother must marry the widow so that they can have children who will be considered the dead man's children. 25 Now, there were seven brothers who used to live here. The oldest got married and died without having children, so he left his widow to his brother. 26 The same thing happened to the

rection, therefore, to which of the seven will she be wife? For they all had her."

29 But Jesus answered them, "You are wrong, because you know neither the scriptures nor the power of God. 30 For in the resurrection they neither marry nor are given in marriage, but are like angels[s] in heaven. 31 And as for the resurrection of the dead, have you not read what was said to you by God, 32 'I am the God of Abraham, and the God of Isaac, and the God of Jacob'? He is not God of the dead, but of the living." 33 And when the crowd heard it, they were astonished at his teaching.

[s] Other ancient authorities add *of God*

second brother, to the third, and finally to all seven. 27 Last of all, the woman died. 28 Now, on the day when the dead rise to life, whose wife will she be? All of them had married her."

29 Jesus answered them, "How wrong you are! It is because you don't know the Scriptures or God's power. 30 For when the dead rise to life, they will be like the angels in heaven and will not marry. 31 Now, as for the dead rising to life: haven't you ever read what God has told you? He said, 32 'I am the God of Abraham, the God of Isaac, and the God of Jacob.' He is the God of the living, not of the dead."

33 When the crowds heard this, they were amazed at his teaching.

SECTION HEADING: **"The Question about Rising from Death"** is similar in form to the one at verse 15, and translators can handle it in a similar manner; for example, "Jesus answers questions about rising from death," "Jesus discusses (or, teaches about) rising from death," or "Some Sadducees ask about rising from death." If a subject is needed for "rising," then the heading can be "Jesus teaches about people rising from the dead."

The Sadducees were arch opponents of the Pharisees, who considered them to be politically and theologically liberal. Their political views were unacceptable to the Pharisees, because the Sadducees supported the Roman government, and so would have had no problem with the question of paying taxes to the Emperor. On the other hand, the Sadducees denied the possibility of a resurrection and were thereby opposed to the Pharisees, for whom this was one of their basic beliefs. The question raised by the Sadducees is designed to discredit Jesus among the populace, most of whom would have ascribed to the belief in the resurrection of the dead. They had doubtless raised this same issue on occasion with the Pharisees. It is presented in a logical manner, with the intention of making their opponents appear ridiculous. Nevertheless, the way in which they raise the question with Jesus is described in less hostile terms than was the question of the Pharisees. This may be due to the fact that at the time of the writing of the Gospel, the Sadducees as a group had died out.

22.23   RSV   TEV

The same day Sadducees came to him, who say that there is no resurrection; and they asked him a question,

That same day some Sadducees came to Jesus and claimed that people will not rise from death.

For a discussion of **Sadducees**, see 3.7. There is no article in the text, but most translators use "some," as in TEV.

As discussed elsewhere, **came** will have to be "went" in many receptor languages.

The text says simply that the Sadducees **say** there is no resurrection, but "did not believe" or "claimed that there was no" may be more natural.

Who say that there is no resurrection is in the present tense in the Greek, reflecting the viewpoint of the writer. Normally a translation attempts to reflect the writer's position, but some readers today will need to have this in the past tense, otherwise they may be confused. Translators will have to decide which tense to use, basing the decision on local language requirements.

We have given several examples of translations of **resurrection** in the examples above. One further example is seen in a sentence like "The Sadducees claimed that people do not rise again (to life) after they die."

RSV represents a fairly literal rendering of this verse, but it may be helpful to follow a somewhat more chronological order. For example, "The Sadducees were a Jewish group who did not believe that people would rise from death. And on the same day that the Pharisees tried to trick Jesus with a question, they came to him and said . . . ." GECL has "On the same day the Sadducees came to Jesus. The Sadducees did not believe that the dead would rise. 24 'Teacher,' they asked him . . . ." Another possibility is "On that same day, some Sadducees came to Jesus to ask him a question. They were a group that did not believe that the dead would rise. 24 They asked him, 'Teacher . . . .' "

22.24 RSV	TEV
saying, "Teacher, Moses said, 'If a man dies, having no children, his brother must marry the widow, and raise up children for his brother.'	"Teacher," they said, "Moses said that if a man who has no children dies, his brother must marry the widow so that they can have children who will be considered the dead man's children.

The Sadducees follow the pattern of the Pharisees in addressing Jesus as **Teacher** (see verse 16). Their question reflects the Jewish law according to which the brother of a dead man would marry his brother's widow, if the man had died without having any children. This law was instituted in Israel to provide the dead man with offspring, so that his name would continue after him.

Moses said may also be translated "The Law of Moses teaches." What follows can be either direct discourse, as in the RSV text, or indirect, as in TEV. Translators should do what is more natural in their own language.

If a man dies . . . for his brother represents a somewhat free adaptation of the Septuagint rendering of Deuteronomy 25.5-6, and it differs slightly from each of the two other forms of the quotation (Mark 12.19; Luke 20.28). Because of the similarity in sound between the Greek noun for "resurrection" (*anastasin*) and the Greek verb for **raise up** (*anastēsei*) in this verse, some scholars conclude that Matthew even intends a play on words. But the evidence is rather meager, since the two words are at a distance from one another in the Greek text. Moreover, it is extremely doubtful if such a wordplay could be effectively transferred in translation.

TEV has significantly restructured **raise up children for his brother** so as to convey clearly the meaning: "so that they can have children who will be considered the dead man's children." Brc has a somewhat simpler rendering: "raise a family for his brother." In any case it will be necessary in some languages to have a footnote briefly explaining the Jewish custom.

22.25	RSV	TEV
	Now there were seven brothers among us; the first married, and died, and having no children left his wife to his brother.	Now, there were seven brothers who used to live here. The oldest got married and died without having children, so he left his widow to his brother.

Now serves as a transitional from the quotation to the story of the seven brothers who, one after the other, married the same woman. It is not a temporal marker, therefore, but a way of starting a story.

Among us may better be represented as "**who used to live here**" (TEV). Phps has "Now, we had a case of seven brothers," and GECL "Now, at one time there were seven brothers here." The story is told as though it narrates a genuine life situation, though the use of the number **seven** suggests they added something to make the story more interesting and simultaneously to emphasize the absurdity of belief in the resurrection.

The first . . . died . . . left his wife to his brother may give the impression that the man had at death willed his widow to his brother. GECL 1st edition relieves the difficulty by translating "The oldest brother married and died without children. 26 So the second married his widow . . . ."

22.26	RSV	TEV
	So too the second and third, down to the seventh.	The same thing happened to the second brother, to the third, and finally to all seven.

As may be gathered from a reading of RSV, the Greek text of this verse leaves the verb implicit. But some readers may find themselves confused with such an abbreviated presentation. In this respect GECL is helpful: "Therefore the second married the widow, but he also died childless; and with the third one there was no difference. So it happened with all seven." NEB is clear and to the point: "The same thing happened with the second, and the third, and so on with all seven."

22.27	RSV	TEV
	After them all, the woman died.	Last of all, the woman died.

The verse may be translated "Finally the woman also died."

22.28   RSV   TEV

In the resurrection, therefore, to which of the seven will she be wife? For they all had her."	Now, on the day when the dead rise to life, whose wife will she be? All of them had married her."

The Greek noun phrase **In the resurrection** is restructured by TEV as a dependent clause: "**on the day when the dead rise to life.**"

To which of the seven will she be wife? is a Semitic form of Greek, which is better represented in English by TEV: "**whose wife will she be?**" It may be more effective if the order of the elements is reversed: "Whose wife will she be when God raises the dead to life?"

For they all had her is less than adequate for readers of American English, for in such a context **had** may imply no more than "had sexual relations with." The meaning is clearly "had her as a wife" (Brc), and so the basis for TEV: "**All of them had married her.**" A more dramatic ending may be achieved for the story if the pattern of GECL is followed: "She had married all seven!"

22.29   RSV   TEV

But Jesus answered them, "You are wrong, because you know neither the scriptures nor the power of God.	Jesus answered them, "How wrong you are! It is because you don't know the Scriptures or God's power.

You are wrong (so also NJB, AT) translates a verb which literally means "be misled" (NAB "You are badly misled"; Brc "You are on the wrong track altogether"), but it may be used to mean either "deceive oneself" or "be mistaken" (NEB "You are mistaken").

It may be necessary to specify in what way they are misled or mistaken, as in "You are wrong in saying the dead will not rise." Jesus is not saying they are wrong in their fabricated story, but rather in not believing in the resurrection.

Translators need to be careful in translating **because**. The Sadducees are mistaken or misled because they don't know the Scriptures, not because they told the story about the seven brothers. "The reason you are mistaken is that you don't know . . ." would show the relationship correctly.

The scriptures are translated "the Holy Scriptures" by GECL, and **the power of God** is rendered "what God can do." **You neither know the scriptures** (TEV "**you don't know the Scriptures**") may be translated as either "you don't know what the Scriptures teach" or ". . . what is in the Scriptures." Brc has "you do not know . . . the meaning of the scriptures."

It is sometimes not natural to use **know** with words like "Scriptures" or "God's power," and "know about" may be better.

22.30 RSV   TEV

For in the resurrection they neither
marry nor are given in marriage, but
are like angels^s in heaven.

For when the dead rise to life, they
will be like the angels in heaven and
will not marry.

^s Other ancient authorities add *of God*

In the resurrection: see comment at verse 28.

They neither marry nor are given in marriage: the impersonal use of **they**
is a way of speaking of people in general, while **marry** and **are given in marriage**
reflect the Jewish marriage custom of the time, according to which men "married"
and women were "given in marriage." Brc has "men and women neither marry nor
are married," but NEB is better: "men and women do not marry." GECL translates the
entire verse as follows: "When the dead rise, they will no longer marry, but they will
live as the angels in heaven." But if GECL is followed as a translation model at this
point, then care must be taken to ensure that "live as the angels" is not misunderstood. In context the reference is to the fact that angels do not marry. TEV achieves
a fuller measure of clarity through reversing the order of the clauses: "they will be
like angels in heaven and will not marry."

In place of **angels** some manuscripts have "angels of God" (see RSV margin).
TC-GNT favors the shorter reading on the grounds that "of God" is a "natural
expansion, which, if present in the text originally, would not have been likely to be
omitted." But see 1.20 for a discussion of **angels**. Some translators will have been
using an expression for this word that contains the idea "of God" in any case. If they
have not, then it should not be added here.

22.31 RSV   TEV

And as for the resurrection of the
dead, have you not read what was
said to you by God,

Now, as for the dead rising to life:
haven't you ever read what God has
told you? He said,

And as for the resurrection of the dead may be dealt with in a manner
similar to what was done with "in the resurrection" of verses 28 and 30: "**as for the
dead rising to life**" (TEV) or "as for the matter of the dead rising to life." GECL 1st
edition is effective: "But if you doubt that the dead will rise . . . ."

Have you not read what was said to you by God expects an affirmative
reply: "Yes, we have read . . . ." It may be advisable to shift to a strong statement:
"You have surely read what God has said" or "If you doubt . . . then evidently you
have never read what God has said" (GECL 1st edition). One may want to indicate
the source which the Jews are expected to have read: "You have surely read what
God said in our Scriptures."

22.32

RSV	TEV
'I am the God of Abraham, and the God of Isaac, and the God of Jacob'? He is not the God of the dead, but of the living."	'I am the God of Abraham, the God of Isaac, and the God of Jacob.' He is the God of the living, not of the dead."

Although the Sadducees did not acknowledge all the books of the Jewish Bible, they did accept the authority of the "Books of Moses" (Genesis through Deuteronomy). Therefore Jesus appeals to Exodus 3.6 as the basis for his response to their question. The verse does not deal specifically with the matter of the resurrection, but it does address the issue of life after death and so carries the same weight. Jesus' argument is as follows: When God spoke to Moses, he identified himself as the God of Abraham, Isaac, and Jacob. But since he is the God of the living and not of the dead, this signifies that Abraham, Isaac, and Jacob must still have been alive at the time that God spoke to Moses.

There are languages which do not normally use the direct discourse **I am**. Indirect discourse may have to be used, as in "God said he was the God of Abraham, Isaac, and Jacob."

The God of will be unsatisfactory in a number of languages, since it may imply ownership of God. One may then wish to translate "the God worshiped by . . . ." The fact that this verse leaves certain basic assumptions unexpressed makes it difficult to restructure satisfactorily. But one solution is as follows: " 'I am the God whom Abraham, Isaac, and Jacob worship.' God is not worshiped by dead people, but by people who are alive." In this way the reader will understand the logic of the argument: Abraham, Isaac, and Jacob worship God. But since only living people worship God, this means that Abraham, Isaac, and Jacob were still alive at the time that God spoke to Moses. Or it is possible to reverse the clause order: "Only living people worship God, and the Scriptures say, 'I am the God whom Abraham, Isaac, and Jacob worship.' "

For some readers **Abraham**, **Isaac**, and **Jacob** may need further identification such as "our ancestors (or, fathers) Abraham, Isaac, and Jacob."

In the text the expression **the God of** is repeated for each of the three ancestors. However, it is often more natural to use it only once, as in the examples above.

22.33

RSV	TEV
And when the crowd heard it, they were astonished at his teaching.	When the crowds heard this, they were amazed at his teaching.

The crowd . . . were astonished at his teaching is almost a word-for-word repetition of Matthew's comment at the conclusion of the Sermon on the Mount (7.28). Mark does not make this observation here, though he does do so at 11.18. Luke summarizes the reaction toward Jesus' teaching even more emphatically than Matthew (20.39-40).

22.34-40

<table>
<tr><td align="center">RSV</td><td align="center">TEV</td></tr>
</table>

The Great Commandment

34 But when the Pharisees heard that he had silenced the Sadducees, they came together. 35 And one of them, a lawyer, asked him a question, to test him. 36 "Teacher, which is the great commandment in the law?" 37 And he said to him, "You shall love the Lord your God with all your heart, and with all your soul, and with all your mind. 38 This is the great and first commandment. 39 And a second is like it, You shall love your neighbor as yourself. 40 On these two commandments depend all the law and the prophets."

34 When the Pharisees heard that Jesus had silenced the Sadducees, they came together, 35 and one of them, a teacher of the Law, tried to trap him with a question. 36 "Teacher," he asked, "which is the greatest commandment in the Law?"
37 Jesus answered, " 'Love the Lord your God with all your heart, with all your soul, and with all your mind.' 38 This is the greatest and the most important commandment. 39 The second most important commandment is like it: 'Love your neighbor as you love yourself.' 40 The whole Law of Moses and the teachings of the prophets depend on these two commandments."

SECTION HEADING: sometimes the TEV heading, "**The Great Commandment**," is expressed as "The greatest commandment." There are also cases where it will need to be expressed as a short sentence such as "Jesus teaches about the greatest commandment" or "Jesus tells what the great commandment is."

Matthew places the discussion of the most important commandment at the same place in his Gospel that it is found in Mark (12.28-34), but there are significant differences in the details of the two accounts. Luke also includes the incident, though much earlier (10.25-28), and in his account the questioner himself provides the answer. In contrast with Mark (see 12.28), Matthew sees in this narrative a further attempt of the Pharisees to trap Jesus.

22.34 RSV TEV

But when the Pharisees heard that he had silenced the Sadducees, they came together.

When the Pharisees heard that Jesus had silenced the Sadducees, they came together,

Matthew once again identifies **the Pharisees** as the most hostile of Jesus' opponents. According to Mark, it was "one of the scribes" who approached Jesus, and it is not necessary to assume that he was a member of the Pharisaic party. Moreover, in Mark the man presents his question to Jesus because he is impressed with Jesus' reply to the Sadducees (12.28). Matthew specifically states that the purpose of the question is "to test" Jesus (verse 35).

The **But** at the beginning of this verse can be seen to contrast the reaction of the Pharisees to how Jesus had dealt with the Sadducees with the reaction of the crowd in verse 33. However, since most translators do have the section heading at the beginning of the verse, it is often more natural to drop **But** and start with "**When**" (TEV).

Pharisees and **Sadducees** were discussed at 3.7.

Had silenced translates the same verb used in verse 12; it occurs nowhere else in Matthew's Gospel. In this verse it may best be rendered as "had answered the

Sadducees in such a way they could not say anything" or "had made the Sadducees stop asking him questions."

Together translates a construction used several times in Luke's writings (Luke 17.35; Acts 1.15; 2.1,44; 4.26); it also occurs in 1 Corinthians 11.20; 14.23. It may mean either "at the same place" (Acts 2.1) or "together" (so most translations), a usage well attested by the papyri. Some translators have said "they met together," but the idea is really more that they went to Jesus in a group. Thus "met and went together to Jesus" or "went to Jesus in a group" is better. Of course, translators will use either "came" or "went," depending on the receptor language.

22.35

RSV	TEV
And one of them, a lawyer, asked him a question, to test him.	and one of them, a teacher of the Law, tried to trap him with a question.

For many languages it will be advisable to begin a new sentence with this verse.

Lawyer (so also NAB) represents the traditional rendering of English translations; both TEV and GECL prefer **"a teacher of the Law,"** in which **"Law"** is used of the Jewish Scriptures. "An expert in the Law" is the wording of AT and Phps (NIV with lower case "l"), while Lu has "a teacher of scripture." The word is found nowhere else in Matthew's Gospel, and it is absent from some major witnesses to the Greek text. Both NEB and NJB assume that it was introduced here from the parallel passage in Luke 10.25, and so they omit it from the body of their translations and place it in the margin. In the UBS Greek text the word is placed in square brackets, signifying a "considerable degree of doubt" concerning the original reading.

Most of the translations in English set **a lawyer** off from the first part of the sentence with commas. However, in some languages a short sentence will be better, as in "One of them was a teacher of the Law. He asked . . . ."

Test was first used in 4.1 (see there), where it was given the meaning "tempt"; more recently it was translated "put to the test" in 22.18. Since it is used here in a negative sense, TEV renders **"tried to trap,"** and NAB has "one of them . . . in an attempt to trip him up, asked him." GECL's restructuring is similar to that of TEV. Many translators will be able to translate this in a way similar to 22.15.

22.36

RSV	TEV
"Teacher, which is the great commandment in the law?"	"Teacher," he asked, "which is the greatest commandment in the Law?"

Teacher is the same noun of address used of Jesus in verses 16 and 24.

Which is the great commandment in the law? is a literal rendering of the Greek text, except that in Greek the verb **is** is unexpressed because it is not required by the rules of Greek grammar. In place of **great**, many languages will prefer the superlative form **"greatest"** (TEV). Mark frames the question somewhat differently: "Which commandment is the first of all?" (12.28). But Matthew is concerned with the role of the Jewish Law for the Christian community, and this is what has determined the manner in which he introduces the question. Note also verse 38.

Great commandment can be rendered fairly literally in many languages, but in others "most important commandment" is more natural.

For comments on **the law**, see 5.17.

22.37	RSV	TEV

And he said to him, "You shall love the Lord your God with all your heart, and with all your soul, and with all your mind.	Jesus answered, " 'Love the Lord your God with all your heart, with all your soul, and with all your mind.'

Many translators will identify **he** as "Jesus" and **him** as "the Pharisee." Another option is to do what TEV has done: "Jesus answered."

You shall love can be three very difficult words to translate. In the first place, the sentence is a command, but translators sometimes have to decide between the singular and plural forms. It is singular in the Greek text, and some translators will use that form also, but it seems clear that the command is being given to the people of Israel, so that the plural form may in fact be better. The normal form for a command should be used, possibly "You must love" or simply "Love."

As a second problem, **love** is often difficult since it contains the elements of affection or liking as well as devotion and commitment to. Translators should find a word or expression that contains both of these ideas.

In the Old Testament **the Lord** was a term that replaced the name of God. However, it would not be appropriate to use that name here, since the Greek text did follow the custom of using "the Lord." **Your God**, as in verse 32, can be translated as "the God you worship." Thus **the Lord your God** can be translated "The Lord, who is the God you worship."

The scripture which Jesus quotes is Deuteronomy 6.5. Matthew employs three terms (**heart . . . soul . . . mind**), while four appear in Mark 12.30 ("heart . . . soul . . . mind . . . strength"). The difference may be accounted for on the assumption that Mark combined the readings of two manuscripts of the Septuagint, while Matthew had a preference for the three-membered form of the Hebrew text. In either case no distinction may be drawn between the meanings of the individual terms. In Hebrew thought a person is not divided into various compartments, as is traditionally done in Greek philosophy, and together these terms summarize the totality of what a person really is. As one scholar notes: "Any one of them would have been sufficient (in terms of Hebrew anthropology) to denote the entirety of a man." The words of Jesus may be effectively translated "You must love the Lord your God in all that you think or feel or do." However, if translators do have some means of using two or three different words, as in the text, this may give the sentence some of the emphasis of the original. An example is "Love the Lord your God with all your strength and all your thinking." Another possibility is "Love the Lord your God completely."

22.38   RSV   TEV

This is the great and first command-   **This is the greatest and the most**
ment.   **important commandment.**

Jesus' response combines **great** (see verse 36) with **first** (see Mark 12.28). In
such a context **first** is the equivalent of **"most important"** (TEV).
Sometimes the emphasis can be conveyed with a sentence such as "This commandment is the most important of all."

22.39   RSV   TEV

And a second is like it, You shall   **The second most important com-**
love your neighbor as yourself.   **mandment is like it: 'Love your**
                                          neighbor as you love yourself.'

And a second is like it is more explicit in TEV: **"The second most important**
commandment is like it." The Greek phrase **is like it** may mean either "similar but
not of equal value" or "similar and of equal value." The context suggests the second
of these interpretations, which is well represented by GECL: "The second is equally
important." Brc has "And there is a second one like it."
     You shall love your neighbor as yourself comes from the Septuagint of
Leviticus 19.18, where **neighbor** is limited to fellow Israelites and foreigners who live
among the Israelites. Here, however, the reference is enlarged to include anyone
with whom one's life comes into contact. The verse does not contain two commands
("love yourself" and "love your neighbor as much as you love yourself"). Rather it
contains an assumption ("you do love yourself") followed by a command ("love your
neighbor as much as you love yourself"). See also the comments at 19.19, where the
command is first mentioned.

22.40   RSV   TEV

On these two commandments de-   **The whole Law of Moses and the**
pend all the law and the prophets."   **teachings of the prophets depend on**
                                           these two commandments."

Depend (on) translates a verb which literally means "hang on" (see NEB, NJB,
Mft, NIV). Translators who follow this interpretation can say "All the Law of Moses
and the teachings of the Prophets are based on these two commandments." But it
may also mean either "sum up" (AT) or "contain" (GECL 1st edition "In these two
commands is contained everything that the Law of Moses and the teaching of the
prophets have said concerning God's will").
     Matthew here inserts the modifier **all** (TEV **"whole"**) before the set phrase **the**
law and the prophets (see comment at 5.17; 7.12).
     For English speakers it is more natural to make a slight shift in the word order
of the sentence (see TEV), which may be the case for certain other languages as well.

22.41-46

RSV

TEV

The Question about the Messiah

41 Now while the Pharisees were gathered together, Jesus asked them a question, 42 saying, "What do you think of the Christ? Whose son is he?" They said to him, "The son of David." 43 He said to them, "How is it then that David, inspired by the Spirit,ᶠ calls him Lord, saying,

44　'The Lord said to my Lord,
　　Sit at my right hand,
　　till I put thy enemies under thy feet'?

45 If David thus calls him Lord, how is he his son?" 46 And no one was able to answer him a word, nor from that day did any one dare to ask him any more questions.

41 When some Pharisees gathered together, Jesus asked them, 42 "What do you think about the Messiah? Whose descendant is he?"

"He is David's descendant," they answered.

43 "Why, then," Jesus asked, "did the Spirit inspire David to call him 'Lord'? David said,

44　'The Lord said to my Lord:
　　Sit here at my right side
　　until I put your enemies under your feet.'

45 If, then, David called him 'Lord,' how can the Messiah be David's descendant?"

46 No one was able to give Jesus any answer, and from that day on no one dared to ask him any more questions.

ᶠ Or *David in the Spirit*

SECTION HEADING: "**The Question about the Messiah**" follows the pattern of those at verses 15 and 23, but here it is Jesus who asks the questions. Translators may have "Jesus asks the Pharisees who the Messiah is" or "Jesus discusses who the Messiah is."

Matthew continues to reproduce the Marcan outline of events as he records the question about the Messiah immediately following the discussion of the most important commandment (Mark 12.35-37). But Matthew does make at least one significant alteration: he has Jesus speak directly to the Pharisees (verse 41) rather than to the people who have gathered in the temple area to hear him teach (Mark 12.35). This shift of audience accomplishes two things for Matthew: (1) it brings Jesus' series of confrontations with his opponents to a victorious climax, and (2) it serves as a transition to his condemnation of the Pharisees (chapter 23).

22.41　　　RSV

TEV

Now while the Pharisees were gathered together, Jesus asked them a question,

When some Pharisees gathered together, Jesus asked them,

Were gathered together translates a different form of the Greek verb "came together" in verse 34 and suggests a continuation of the scene begun in verse 34. Evidently the Pharisees have gathered about Jesus in the hopes that one of their experts in the Jewish Scriptures would be able to trap him with a question (verse 35), but now Jesus makes a counterattack with a question of his own. GECL draws the connection between verses 34 and 41 in the following way: "34 When the Pharisees heard . . . they all came together . . . 41 Jesus turned to the Pharisees who had gathered . . . ." NJB and NEB show the relation between the two verses in similar fashion. Another good rendering is "Now while the Pharisees were still gathered there together."

22.42	RSV	TEV

saying, "What do you think of the Christ? Whose son is he?" They said to him, "The son of David."

"What do you think about the Messiah? Whose descendant is he?"

"He is David's descendant," they answered.

The Christ (TEV "**the Messiah**"): see comments at 1.1,17; 2.4.

What do you think is a familiar question form in Matthew's Gospel (see 17.25; 18.12; 21.28; 22.17; and 26.66). In each case the question is asked either by Jesus himself or about Jesus at very crucial points in the Gospel.
Here it may be expressed "What is your opinion about the Messiah?" or "What is your opinion about who the Messiah is descended from?"

Whose son is he? Obviously **son** is here used in the extended sense of "**descendant**" (TEV), a meaning which it frequently has in the Old Testament. The two questions (**What do you think of the Christ? Whose son is he?**) are actually one, which means "Whose descendant will the Messiah be?" Both Mark (12.35) and Luke (20.41) have only one question.

The son of David is shorter in Greek than the translation implies; the Greek text simply has "the of David," a construction in which "son" is left implicit. Other languages will require even more detail than RSV; for example, "The Messiah will be a descendant of King David."

22.43	RSV	TEV

He said to them, "How is it then that David, inspired by the Spirit,*ᵗ* calls him Lord, saying,

"Why, then," Jesus asked, "did the Spirit inspire David to call him 'Lord'? David said,

ᵗ Or David in the Spirit

How is it then (NJB "Then how is it") represents a Greek construction which means "By what right?" or "On what grounds?"

Inspired by the Spirit, as the RSV footnote indicates, is literally "in the Spirit" or "by means of the Spirit." The reference is clearly to the "Spirit of God" (GECL). Both AT and NAB have "under the Spirit's influence." Mft ("How is it then that David is inspired . . . ?") and NEB ("by inspiration") also arrive at a proper interpretation of the text, since "inspired" and "by inspiration" are equivalent in meaning to "inspired by God's Spirit."

David . . . calls him Lord. The quotation from Psalm 110 (to be given in the following verse) is offered as proof that David himself addressed the promised Messiah as **Lord**. The problem of the authorship of the psalm, raised by modern biblical scholarship, would not have been an issue for the Jews of the first century, who assigned all the psalms to David.

The verse may need to be restructured. TEV offers a good example, but another is "How do you explain the fact then that David, at a time when he was inspired by God's Spirit, called him Lord? David said . . . ."

22.44   RSV   TEV

'The Lord said to my Lord,   'The Lord said to my Lord:
Sit at my right hand   Sit here at my right side
till I put thy enemies under thy   until I put your enemies un-
    feet'?   der your feet.'

The Lord of Psalm 110.1 is understood absolutely of God, while **my Lord** is used of the Promised Messiah. If David then refers to the Messiah (who is also his "son") as **my Lord**, this automatically reveals that the Messiah is superior to David. Matthew is not so much concerned to prove the Davidic origin of Jesus (this is assumed in the structure of his Gospel), but rather to demonstrate that Jesus, who is both descendant of David and Messiah, is superior to David.

If at all possible, translators should retain the expressions of the text, **the Lord** and **my Lord**. However, if the resulting translation is extremely confusing, they may say "The Lord God said to my Lord" or "God, who is the Lord, said to my Lord." A footnote could indicate that **my Lord** referred to the Messiah, although occasionally translators have felt they had to say "my Lord, the Messiah."

Sit at my right hand is an affirmation of authority and power. One may translate "Sit here beside me, at the place of authority" or even "Sit here to my right, the place of authority."

Till I put thy enemies under thy feet is a Hebrew expression meaning "until I make your enemies bow down before you" or "until I defeat your enemies for you." Translators may either use an expression like that or retain the form of the text if they think readers will understand it.

22.45   RSV   TEV

If David thus calls him Lord, how is   If, then, David called him 'Lord,' how
he his son?"   can the Messiah be David's descen-
        dant?"

How is he his son? is a literal representation of the Greek and is translated **"how can the Messiah be David's descendant?"** by TEV. This requires no more than identifying **he** as **"the Messiah,"** and **his son** as **"David's descendant."** This may have to be restructured, however, as for example in "If David calls him Lord, how can the Messiah be his descendant?" or "If David calls the Messiah Lord, how can the Messiah then be his son?"

This question, which puts the Pharisees to absolute silence (see verse 46), reveals Jesus' complete conquest of his opponents, and it leads directly into his condemnation of the Pharisees in chapter 23.

22.46   RSV   TEV

And no one was able to answer him   No one was able to give Jesus
a word, nor from that day did any   any answer, and from that day on no

one dare to ask him any more questions.	**one dared to ask him any more questions.**

It may be more effective to render these two clauses as separate sentences: "No one could give him an answer. From then on no one dared question him" (GECL 1st edition). Or "No one was able to answer the questions that Jesus asked the Pharisees. And from that moment on, everyone was afraid to try to trap Jesus with any more questions."

Chapter 23

23.1-12

**Jesus Warns against the Teachers
of the Law and the Pharisees**

1 Then said Jesus to the crowds and to his disciples, 2 "The scribes and the Pharisees sit on Moses' seat; 3 so practice and observe whatever they tell you, but not what they do; for they preach, but do not practice. 4 They bind heavy burdens, hard to bear,*u* and lay them on men's shoulders; but they themselves will not move them with their finger. 5 They do all their deeds to be seen by men; for they make their phylacteries broad and their fringes long, 6 and they love the place of honor at feasts and the best seats in the synagogues, 7 and salutations in the market places, and being called rabbi by men. 8 But you are not to be called rabbi, for you have one teacher, and you are all brethren. 9 And call no man your father on earth, for you have one Father, who is in heaven. 10 Neither be called masters, for you have one master, the Christ. 11 He who is greatest among you shall be your servant; 12 whoever exalts himself will be humbled, and whoever humbles himself will be exalted.

u Other ancient authorities omit *hard to bear*

1 Then Jesus spoke to the crowds and to his disciples. 2 "The teachers of the Law and the Pharisees are the authorized interpreters of Moses' Law. 3 So you must obey and follow everything they tell you to do; do not, however, imitate their actions, because they don't practice what they preach. 4 They tie onto people's backs loads that are heavy and hard to carry, yet they aren't willing even to lift a finger to help them carry those loads. 5 They do everything so that people will see them. Look at the straps with scripture verses on them which they wear on their foreheads and arms, and notice how large they are! Notice also how long are the tassels on their cloaks!*u* 6 They love the best places at feasts and the reserved seats in the synagogues; 7 they love to be greeted with respect in the market places and to have people call them 'Teacher.' 8 You must not be called 'Teacher,' because you are all brothers of one another and have only one Teacher. 9 And you must not call anyone here on earth 'Father,' because you have only the one Father in heaven. 10 Nor should you be called 'Leader,' because your one and only leader is the Messiah. 11 The greatest one among you must be your servant. 12 Whoever makes himself great will be humbled, and whoever humbles himself will be made great.

u TASSELS ON THEIR CLOAKS: *These tassels were worn as a sign of devotion to God (see Num 15.37-41).*

SECTION HEADING: "**Jesus Warns Against the Teachers of the Law and the Pharisees**" is quite long, and some translators shorten it to "Jesus warns against the religious leaders" or "Jesus condemns the Jewish leaders." If "**Warns**" is retained, it may be necessary to say whom Jesus warns, as in "Jesus tells his followers to be careful of the teachers of the Law and the Pharisees."

Chapters 23-25 constitute the final in a series of five discourse sections which Matthew has incorporated into his Gospel (see comment at introduction to chapter 5). Chapter 23 itself divides easily into three parts: (1) a warning against hypocrisy and an encouragement to humility (verses 1-12); (2) condemnation of the Pharisees because of their hypocrisy (verses 13-36); and (3) Jesus' love for Jerusalem (verses 37-39).

23.1   RSV   TEV

Then said Jesus to the crowds and to his disciples,   Then Jesus spoke to the crowds and to his disciples.

Then is a transitional marker frequently used in this Gospel; here it signals a shift in both audience (**to the crowds and to his disciples**) and subject matter. Translators can either drop it, retain it, or use a transition like "After that."

23.2   RSV   TEV

"The scribes and the Pharisees sit on Moses' seat;   "The teachers of the Law and the Pharisees are the authorized interpreters of Moses' Law.

Scribes and **Pharisees** were discussed at 2.4 and 3.7 respectively.

Those who **sit on Moses' seat** are those who have "official authority" (TOB footnote), and so TEV defines them as **"the authorized interpreters of Moses' Law."** As one commentator points out, the metaphor may have been derived from the existence of "an actual stone seat in front of the synagogue where the authoritative teacher (usually a scribe) sat." But in any case the words of Jesus reflect the claim of the Pharisees that Moses, the ultimate authority, "can be understood only as interpreted by the Pharisees and teachers of the Law." In the Mishnah, which preserves much of the Jewish oral teaching, the chain of command is stated in the following way: "Moses received the Law from Sinai and committed it to Joshua, and Joshua to the elders, and the elders to the Prophets; and the Prophets committed it to the men of the Great Synagogue." Most English translations prefer a literal representation of the text, but at least two are dynamic: "have inherited the authority of Moses" (Brc) and "speak with the authority of Moses" (Phps). Translators should also consider "have the right (or, authority) to interpret the Law of Moses (for others)."

23.3   RSV   TEV

so practice and observe whatever they tell you, but not what they do; for they preach, but do not practice.   So you must obey and follow everything they tell you to do; do not, however, imitate their actions, because they don't practice what they preach.

So practice and observe whatever they tell you indicates that Jesus respects the authority of the scribes and the Pharisees, even though he opposes their hypocrisy. **Practice and observe** (TEV "**obey and follow**") are used synonymously and so may be translated as one verb such as "obey."

But not what they do is elliptical and may have to be expanded to "but don't do what they do" or "but don't follow their actions."

Observe whatever they tell you refers to the hypocrisy of the Pharisees, which is defined more precisely as **for they preach, but do not practice**. In most languages **preach** and **practice** will require the explicit mention of an object. For example, "for they teach you to do certain things, but they do not do these things themselves." Or "for they tell you what Moses' Law requires a person to do, but they themselves do not obey the Law."

23.4	RSV	TEV

They bind heavy burdens, hard to bear,^u and lay them on men's shoulders; but they themselves will not move them with their finger.	They tie onto people's backs loads that are heavy and hard to carry, yet they aren't willing even to lift a finger to help them carry those loads.

u Other ancient authorities omit *hard to bear*

They bind heavy burdens is a figure that suggests that the way the Teachers of the Law and the Pharisees required people to do many difficult things to fulfill the law was like giving them heavy loads to carry. For some the biblical form will be relatively well understood, as in TEV: "**They tie onto people's backs loads that are heavy and hard to carry.**" Other translators will use comparisons of some sort; for example, "They force people to obey difficult rules that are like burdens on their backs." Another possibility is to drop the image altogether, as in "They oblige people to do very difficult things" or "They give people many obligations that are difficult to carry out."

The phrase **hard to bear** (two words in the Greek text) is not present in some Greek manuscripts. TC-GNT indicates that its absence is "perhaps due to stylistic refinement or to accidental oversight"; however, on the other side it notes that "it is possible that the words may be an interpolation from Luke 11.46." For this reason the words are included in square brackets in the UBS Greek text, indicating that the committee feels there is "a considerable degree of doubt" regarding which wording may be superior. The phrase is best included as part of **bind heavy burdens**, perhaps as "(things) hard to support" or "(things) difficult to carry out."

Men's is a reference to people in general, while **shoulders** is replaced in TEV by "**backs,**" a more suitable English term for the place where burdensome loads are carried. But whereas backs and shoulders are in the same area of the body, to say "on their heads" in societies where that is the way of carrying things would be very different from the biblical culture and would not be acceptable.

Move them is more accurately expressed as either "help them carry them" (GECL 1st edition) or "**help them carry those loads**" (TEV).

With their finger: TEV shifts to a more appropriate expression, though with considerable restructuring ("**to lift a finger to help them**"); NJB, NAB, NIV, and Brc also use "lift a finger," while NEB has "raise a finger." If this figure of speech is not clear, translators may say "But they don't do one little thing to help them carry these loads (or, fulfill these obligations)."

23.5	RSV	TEV
	They do all their deeds to be seen by men; for they make their phylacteries broad and their fringes long,	They do everything so that people will see them. Look at the straps with scripture verses on them which they wear on their foreheads and arms, and notice how large they are! Notice also how long are the tassels on their cloaks!*u*

u TASSELS ON THEIR CLOAKS: *These tassels were worn as a sign of devotion to God (see Num 15.37-41).*

They do all their deeds is expressed as "**They do everything**" by TEV. It can also be "Everything they do is done" or "All of their acts are done."

To be seen by men is rendered by GECL 1st edition as "it is only to be seen by people." TEV removes the passive in favor of an active construction: "**so that people will see them.**"

Phylacteries (so most translations) represents a technical religious term which will not be understood by most readers. TEV handles the specialized term with the explanatory phrase "**straps with scripture verses on them which they wear on their foreheads and arms.**" Several translations retain the traditional rendering and provide a footnote to help the reader (so NIV, Phps, NAB), while Brc ("prayer-boxes") attempts a one word equivalent; GECL follows its dynamic equivalent translation ("prayer-straps") with an explanatory note, thus being doubly helpful. **Phylacteries** were the small leather boxes in which were placed a piece of material on which had been written Exodus 13.1-6 and Deuteronomy 6.4-9; 11.13-21. In obedience to the Lord's command, these small containers were tied to the forehead and upper left arm near the heart (see Exo 13.9,16; Deut 6.8; 11.18). **Make . . . broad** means that the Pharisees attempted to emphasize the degree of their devotion to God by enlarging their phylacteries beyond the size of those ordinarily worn by other Jewish men.

There is no good reason to retain the word **phylacteries**, and most translators will use an explanatory phrase like that in TEV. However, this is a rather long expression, and sometimes to find a good way to combine this with **make . . . broad** requires some restructuring; for example, "the leather boxes with scripture verses in them that these people wear (on their foreheads and arms) are very big," "they make sure that the boxes with scripture verses that they wear are really big," or "see how big they make those little boxes with scripture verses in them, the ones they wear on their foreheads and arms."

Fringes were "**tassels**" which were worn by Jews on the corners of their outer garments "as a sign of devotion to God" (TEV footnote). This was in obedience to the command of Numbers 15.37-41 (see also Deut 22.12). Jesus himself wore them (see 9.20; 14.36), but his criticism of the Pharisees was that they made theirs unnecessarily **long** in order to draw attention to their piety. TEV has put the information about "**tassels**" in a footnote. How-

MAN WEARING A PHYLACTERY

ever, some translators have included this in their translations with sentences such as "and the tassels on their coats that show their devotion to God, see how long they make these" or "and they make very long the tassels on their coats that people wear to show they are devoted to God."

One possible restructuring of the whole verse that shows the meaning of Jesus' words clearly is "Those things people wear to show their devotion to God such as the pouches with scripture verses on the forehead and arms or the tassels on the coats, these people make sure theirs are very large and long."

23.6	RSV	TEV

and they love the place of honor at feasts and the best seats in the synagogues,

They love the best places at feasts and the reserved seats in the synagogues;

The place of honor at feasts would be the position immediately to the right of the host; in addition to sitting beside the host, the person there would be served first with the choice portions. This can be translated as "**the best places**" (TEV) or "the places for the most honored people."

The best seats in the synagogues (TEV "**the reserved seats in the synagogues**") were the seats on the elevated podium, while the remainder of the people sat on the floor. GECL renders the entire verse "During feasts they sit at the places of honor, and during worship they sit in the most prominent places."

For **synagogues** see comment at 4.23.

23.7	RSV	TEV

and salutations in the market places, and being called rabbi by men.	they love to be greeted with respect in the market places and to have people call them 'Teacher.'

It may be advisable to begin this verse with a new sentence, as does GECL. TEV retains the single sentence structure but transforms **salutations** into a verb construction and repeats the subject and verb ("they love") from the previous verse: **"they love to be greeted with respect."** It may be preferable to use an active formation: "they love other people to greet them with respect."

Market places were earlier mentioned in 11.16; 20.3.

Rabbi is a transliteration of a Hebrew word which means "my great one"; in Jesus' day it was used exclusively as an honorific for teachers. In verse 8 the identification is made of **rabbi** and "teacher," which is the basis for TEV's **"to have people call them, 'Teacher.'"** Elsewhere in Matthew's Gospel the word is employed only by Judas when he addresses Jesus during the last meal (26.25) and at the time of betrayal (26.49).

In many societies "Teacher" is a term of respect and can be used to translate **rabbi**. Sometimes "My teacher" is better. However, if readers will fail to understand by this that a term of respect was involved, and if they will think that these people were actually the teachers of the people addressing them, then some other respectful title that can be used for a teacher should be used.

Men in this context refers to people in general.

23.8	RSV	TEV

But you are not to be called rabbi, for you have one teacher, and you are all brethren.	You must not be called 'Teacher,' because you are all brothers of one another and have only one Teacher.

Verses 8-11 affirm that the Christian community is essentially a fellowship in which God is the "one Father" (verse 9) and Jesus alone is the **teacher** in an absolute sense. This means then that within this community there must be no striving for positions of authority. On the contrary, the "greatest" of believers is the one who humbles himself and becomes "servant" of all other believers (verse 11).

But you are not to be called may be better understood as an active statement: "But you must not let others call." The command may be understood to mean being called teacher by anyone, and it can be translated "You must not let anyone call you." Or the verse may be somewhat rearranged and "others" identified as "brothers" or "fellow believers." For example, "But all of you are brothers (fellow believers), and so none of you should call the other 'Teacher.' You have only one teacher." See also 5.22 for further discussion of **brethren** or "brothers."

You have one teacher may be translated "there is only one person who is your teacher" or "you only have one teacher."

RSV   TEV

And call no man your father on   And you must not call anyone here
earth, for you have one Father, who   on earth 'Father,' because you have
is in heaven.   only the one Father in heaven.

And call no man your father is not a prohibition against using the noun of address of one's biological father; rather the injunction is against using it as an honorific in addressing someone of superior rank. See the NJB footnote, which points out that in this context **father** is "another title of honour." One may then translate "Do not give anyone on earth the honorary title of 'Father.' The only one worthy of this title is your Father in heaven."

23.10   RSV   TEV

Neither be called masters, for you   Nor should you be called 'Leader,'
have one master, the Christ.   because your one and only leader is
                                        the Messiah.

Some scholars maintain that this verse is either a second form of the saying contained in verse 8 or else a commentary which developed on that saying. If this judgment is correct, then verse 10 is parallel to verse 8 and therefore anticlimactic. But the verse may be understood as a logical development in the total argument of verses 8-12: just as there is only one heavenly Father (verse 9), so there is only one who has the authority to represent him absolutely, and that one is the Messiah.

Master translates a noun which is found only here in the New Testament. Its root meaning is "interpreter," which explains the renderings "teacher" (NJB, NEB, NAB) and "**Leader**" (TEV). **Neither be called masters** may have a similar structure to verse 8, possibly "Don't let anyone call you 'Leader' " or "Don't call each other 'Teacher.' "

For the problem of translating **the Christ** (TEV "**the Messiah**") see comment at 1.17. GECL translates the last clause of this verse as "because there is only one who leads you, and he is Christ, the promised Savior."

23.11   RSV   TEV

He who is greatest among you shall   The greatest one among you must
be your servant;   be your servant.

This and the following verse make it absolutely clear that Christian discipleship involves more than the renunciation of honorific titles. Above all else it demands self-denial and service to one's brothers (see 20.26-27).

The exegetical and translational problems of this verse are similar to those of 20.26; see comments there. The verse can be rendered "The person who is the most important among you shall be the one to serve the others" or "The person who is your leader will be the one to serve you."

23.12　　　RSV　　　　　　　　　　　TEV

whoever exalts himself will be humbled, and whoever humbles himself will be exalted.

Whoever makes himself great will be humbled, and whoever humbles himself will be made great.

In many languages **will be humbled** and **will be exalted** are better translated as active forms with God as the expressed subject (so GECL). In English a shift from the indefinite relative pronoun **whoever** to the second person pronoun "you" will probably sound more natural. "If (any of) you make yourself great, God will humble you. If (any of) you humble yourself, God will make you great." For some languages a first person plural inclusive form will be more natural: "If we . . . God will . . . us."

Will be humbled and **humbles himself** are two forms of the same verb, but by virtue of their grammatical role, they do in fact mean slightly different things. **Humbles himself** can be expressed as "puts himself in a low position" but also "keeps a humble attitude." **Will be humbled**, on the other hand, does not involve an attitude of humility so much as it means to be made unimportant or brought to a low position, in this case by God, as seen in the example in the previous paragraph.

23.13-28

RSV

TEV

Jesus Condemns Their Hypocrisy

13 "But woe to you, scribes and Pharisees, hypocrites! because you shut the kingdom of heaven against men; for you neither enter yourselves, nor allow those who would enter to go in.ᵛ 15 Woe to you, scribes and Pharisees, hypocrites! for you traverse sea and land to make a single proselyte, and when he becomes a proselyte, you make him twice as much a child of hellʷ as yourselves.

16 "Woe to you, blind guides, who say, 'If any one swears by the temple, it is nothing; but if any one swears by the gold of the temple, he is bound by his oath.' 17 You blind fools! For which is greater, the gold or the temple that has made the gold sacred? 18 And you say, 'If any one swears by the altar, it is nothing; but if any one swears by the gift that is on the altar, he is bound by his oath.' 19 You blind men! For which is greater, the gift or the altar that makes the gift sacred? 20 So he who swears by the altar, swears by it and by everything on it; 21 and he who swears by the temple, swears by it and by him who dwells in it; 22 and he who swears by heaven, swears by the throne of God and by him who sits upon it.

23 "Woe to you, scribes and Pharisees, hypocrites! for you tithe mint and dill and cummin, and have neglected the weightier matters of the

13 "How terrible for you, teachers of the Law and Pharisees! You hypocrites! You lock the door to the Kingdom of heaven in people's faces, but you yourselves don't go in, nor do you allow in those who are trying to enter!ᵛ

15 "How terrible for you, teachers of the Law and Pharisees! You hypocrites! You sail the seas and cross whole countries to win one convert; and when you succeed, you make him twice as deserving of going to hell as you yourselves are!

16 "How terrible for you, blind guides! You teach, 'If someone swears by the Temple, he isn't bound by his vow; but if he swears by the gold in the Temple, he is bound.' 17 Blind fools! Which is more important, the gold or the Temple which makes the gold holy? 18 You also teach, 'If someone swears by the altar, he isn't bound by his vow; but if he swears by the gift on the altar, he is bound.' 19 How blind you are! Which is the more important, the gift or the altar which makes the gift holy? 20 So then, when a person swears by the altar, he is swearing by it and by all the gifts on it; 21 and when he swears by the Temple, he is swearing by it and by God, who lives there; 22 when someone swears by heaven, he is swearing by God's throne and by him who sits on it.

23 "How terrible for you, teachers of the Law and Pharisees! You hypocrites! You give to

law, justice and mercy and faith; these you ought to have done, without neglecting the others. 24 You blind guides, straining out a gnat and swallowing a camel!

25 "Woe to you, scribes and Pharisees, hypocrites! for you cleanse the outside of the cup and of the plate, but inside they are full of extortion and rapacity. 26 You blind Pharisee! first cleanse the inside of the cup and of the plate, that the outside also may be clean.

27 "Woe to you, scribes and Pharisees, hypocrites! for you are like whitewashed tombs, which outwardly appear beautiful, but within they are full of dead men's bones and all uncleanness. 28 So you also outwardly appear righteous to men, but within you are full of hypocrisy and iniquity.

v Other authorities add here (or after verse 12) verse 14, *Woe to you, scribes and Pharisees, hypocrites! for you devour widows' houses and for a pretense you make long prayers; therefore you will receive the greater condemnation*
w Greek *Gehenna*

God one tenth even of the seasoning herbs, such as mint, dill, and cumin, but you neglect to obey the really important teachings of the Law, such as justice and mercy and honesty. These you should practice, without neglecting the others. 24 Blind guides! You strain a fly out of your drink, but swallow a camel!

25 "How terrible for you, teachers of the Law and Pharisees! You hypocrites! You clean the outside of your cup and plate, while the inside is full of what you have gotten by violence and selfishness. 26 Blind Pharisee! Clean what is inside the cup first, and then the outside will be clean too!

27 "How terrible for you, teachers of the Law and Pharisees! You hypocrites! You are like whitewashed tombs, which look fine on the outside but are full of bones and decaying corpses on the inside. 28 In the same way, on the outside you appear good to everybody, but inside you are full of hypocrisy and sins.

v *Some manuscripts add verse 14:* How terrible for you, teachers of the Law and Pharisees! You hypocrites! You take advantage of widows and rob them of their homes, and then make a show of saying long prayers! Because of this your punishment will be all the worse! *(see Mk 12.40).*

SECTION HEADING: "**Jesus Condemns Their Hypocrisy.**" It may not be clear who "Their" refers to, so "Jesus condemns the hypocrisy of the teachers of the Law and the Pharisees" may be better. This is a little long, however, so some translators have had "The hypocrisy of the religious leaders."

This thunderous series of judgments against Pharisaic hypocrisy is without parallel elsewhere in any of the other Gospels. In fact the only other place in the Scriptures where a similar series is encountered is in Isaiah 5.8-23. But the shout of "woe" is frequently met in the prophetic and apocalyptic writings of the Old Testament, where it is usually directed against either the enemies of God's people or the unfaithful among God's people.

23.13	RSV	TEV

"But woe to you, scribes and Pharisees, hypocrites! because you shut the kingdom of heaven against men; for you neither enter yourselves, nor allow those who would enter to go in."

"How terrible for you, teachers of the Law and Pharisees! You hypocrites! You lock the door to the Kingdom of heaven in people's faces, but you yourselves don't go in, nor do you allow in those who are trying to enter!"

ᵛ Other ancient authorities add here (or after verse 12) verse 14, *Woe to you, scribes and Pharisees, hypocrites! for you devour widows' houses and for a pretense you make long prayers; therefore you will receive the greater condemnation*

ᵛ *Some manuscripts add verse 14:* How terrible for you, teachers of the Law and Pharisees! You hypocrites! You take advantage of widows and rob them of their homes, and then make a show of saying long prayers! Because of this your punishment will be all the worse! *(see Mk 12.40).*

Because the passage is interrupted by the section heading, and because Jesus now addresses the scribes and Pharisees (he was previously addressing the crowds and his disciples), many translators find it necessary to begin the verse with "Jesus went on to say" or "Jesus then said to the teachers of the Law and the Pharisees." But since he does address them directly, this addition is not always essential.

Woe: see comment at 11.21.

Scribes and Pharisees now become the persons to whom Jesus speaks, and this represents a shift from the audience indicated in verse 1 ("to the crowds and to his disciples").

Hypocrites: see comment at 6.2. This is sometimes rendered by a separate sentence: "You are hypocrites!" TEV is good in English: **"You hypocrites!"**

Jesus does not say **because** to relate what follows to **hypocrites** but rather to relate what follows to the **woe to you**. In other words, the relating is not "You are hypocrites because you lock the door" but is instead "Woe to you because you lock the door."

You shut the kingdom . . . against men is employed by Luke as the climax in Jesus' judgment against the scribes (11.52). But here it functions as the first in the series of seven woes directed against the scribes and the Pharisees. The figure of "shutting" probably means that these men hold in their hands the "key" (that is, scripture and its interpretation) by which may be opened the door of the Kingdom. But instead of using scripture as a means of opening the door for people, they use it as a means of "shutting" or "locking" the door and thereby keeping people out. The figure of locking the Kingdom of heaven in people's faces (see TEV) is translated "You block the entrance to God's new world" by GECL and "You hinder people from becoming members of God's community" by INCL. Translators should use the same expression for **kingdom of heaven** here as they have throughout the Gospel. See 3.2.

The hypocrisy of the Pharisees is to be condemned because of its two terrible effects: (1) **you neither enter yourselves**, (2) **nor allow those who would enter to go in**. It may be appropriate to introduce a new sentence at this place: "As a result, you yourselves do not enter into God's Kingdom, and you keep others from entering, even though they want to." Or ". . . you block the way for yourselves and for all others who want to enter."

[23.14]   RSV   TEV

[Woe to you, scribes and Pharisees, hypocrites! for you devour widows'

[How terrible for you, teachers of the Law and Pharisees! You hypocrites!

| houses and for a pretense you make long prayers; therefore you will receive the greater condemnation.] | You take advantage of widows and rob them of their homes, and then make a show of saying long prayers! Because of this your punishment will be all the worse!] |

This verse is not included in RSV or in most other modern translations (NJB, NEB, TEV, Lu, NAB, NIV), and TC-GNT believes that the evidence is positive that it was brought in from the parallels in Mark 12.40 and Luke 20.47. It does not appear in the best Greek manuscripts, and in the manuscripts in which it does appear its position varies (some place it before verse 13 and some after verse 13).

The first part of this verse is identical to verse 13. Even **for** can be handled exactly the same way as **because** was there. **You devour widows' houses** is translated with the figure of speech removed by TEV: "**You take advantage of widows and rob them of their homes.**" The reference is to the unethical way in which these leaders sometimes took advantage of the situation of widows and would take from them their homes and property. Translators in West Africa often do not have to remove the figurative language, because the word "eat" is frequently used to refer to stealing or misusing money or property. They can thus say "For you eat the houses (or, property) of widows." But where such imagery would mean nothing, translators should do something similar to TEV or have a phrase like "you take from widows everything they have."

The noun construction **for a pretense** is translated as a verb phrase by TEV: "**make a show.**" One may also translate "try to impress others" or "try to show off before others." In GECL the two clauses of this sentence are inverted and translated "You say long prayers in order to make a good impression, but in reality you are cheats, who deprive helpless widows of their possessions." Some translators have structured the sentence like this: "For you take from widows everything they have and yet say long prayers in order to impress other people." Or like this: "Although you take from widows all their property, you try to impress other people by saying long prayers."

Therefore you will receive the greater condemnation translates a construction in which God is the implied agent of the verb phrase **will receive . . . condemnation.** Accordingly it is permissible to translate "because of this God will punish you all the more!" **Greater condemnation** is in comparison to the **condemnation** (TEV "**punishment**") that God will inflict upon others. In some languages the persons involved in the comparison must be expressed: "God will punish you more severely than he will punish others."

23.15 RSV	TEV
Woe to you, scribes and Pharisees, hypocrites! for you traverse sea and land to make a single proselyte, and when he becomes a proselyte, you	"How terrible for you, teachers of the Law and Pharisees! You hypocrites! You sail the seas and cross whole countries to win one convert;

make him twice as much a child of hell[w] as yourselves.	and when you succeed, you make him twice as deserving of going to hell as you yourselves are!

[w] Greek *Gehenna*

Jesus condemns the Scribes and Pharisees exactly as in verse 13: **Woe to you, scribes and Pharisees, hypocrites!** Translators should use the same expression they did there.

You traverse sea and land gives an indication of the intense missionary activity conducted by the Jews. Jesus does not criticize them for their missionary enthusiasm, but rather because conversion leaves their converts worse off than they were before.

Translators should find some expression in their language to express naturally **traverse sea and land**; for example, "travel by land and by sea," "travel great distances," "travel everywhere," or "travel over ocean and land."

Proselyte (TEV "**convert**") is the technical term used of a non-Jew who had fully embraced Judaism, even to the point of accepting circumcision. Often Christians know the term "**convert**" (TEV) or **proselyte** primarily in the context of someone becoming Christian. Of course here the Pharisees were trying to have people convert to Judaism, so it may be necessary to make that clear. **Make a single proselyte** may then be "to persuade one person to accept your religion" or "to persuade one person to worship God in your way." **When he becomes a proselyte** can then be "when he believes your way" or "when he accepts your religion." Or translators may take the approach of TEV: "**when you succeed.**"

Twice as much a child of hell as yourselves: the phrase **a child of** (literally "a son of") translates a Hebrew idiom which means "one characterized by," or "one who belongs to," or "one deserving of." Therefore TEV translates "**twice as deserving of going to hell**"; GECL 1st edition has "so that he doubly deserves punishment in hell." Both NEB and NJB prefer "twice as fit for hell." The **twice as much** means twice as much as the Pharisees and teachers of the Law are. "He deserves punishment in hell twice as much as you yourselves" will express this. The background of this remark is perhaps the observation that converts tend to become more zealous (or more fanatical) than those who converted them. As RSV's footnote indicates, **hell** is literally "Gehenna" (see comment at 5.22).

23.16 RSV	TEV
"Woe to you, blind guides, who say, 'If any one swears by the temple, it is nothing; but if any one swears by the gold of the temple, he is bound by his oath.'	"How terrible for you, blind guides! You teach, 'If someone swears by the Temple, he isn't bound by his vow; but if he swears by the gold in the Temple, he is bound.'

Among the Jewish religious teachers of Jesus' day there was a rule of scripture interpretation known as "the lesser and the greater" or "the light and the heavy" (see "the weightier matters of the law" in verse 23), and the Pharisees were evidently applying it to the matter of vows. Their argument would have been that vows made by "lesser" holy objects (the temple, the altar, and heaven) were not binding, whereas vows made by "greater" holy objects (the gold, the gift, and the throne of God) were binding.

But Jesus employs this same method of scripture interpretation to condemn them for the narrow and erroneous applications which they drew from it. Not only had the Pharisees in two instances drawn inaccurate distinctions between what is "lesser" (the gold and the gift) and "greater" (the temple and the altar), but they had failed to recognize that vows made by the lesser sacred objects were just as binding as those made by the more sacred objects. Therefore, if vows made by the gold in the temple, the gift (on the altar), and the throne of God are binding, so are vows made by the temple, the altar, and heaven. In fact, vows made by any sacred object are binding, since they are ultimately vows made in the presence of God.

Woe to you may be expressed here the same as in the preceding verses. However, Jesus now addresses the Scribes and Pharisees as **blind guides**, an expression used also in 15.14. See comments there. Some translators find it better to express this warning with a short sentence. Brc is an example: "Tragic will be your fate, for you are blind guides."

TEV has translated **who say** as "**You teach**," which more accurately reflects the situation. Both TEV and RSV retain the direct discourse, but in a number of languages it will be more natural to use indirect discourse, as in "You teach people that if someone swears."

For **swears**, see the discussion at 5.33. Here the reference is obviously to promising to do something and calling upon something holy to be a witness, in this case the Temple or the gold of the Temple to serve as a witness. If there is no word in the receptor language that expresses this idea exactly, translators may say "promises (God) to do something and uses the Temple to confirm (or, witness) the promise" or "promises he will do something and calls on the Temple to confirm it."

The gold of the temple may be the gold with which the temple is decorated, or the gold vessels used in the Temple's service, or even the gold stored in the Temple treasury. No final decision is possible. Translators may say "the gold things that belong to the Temple" or ". . . are in the Temple."

In the context **it is nothing** (NAB "it means nothing"; NJB "it has no force") contrasts with **he is bound by his oath**, and so means "**he isn't bound by his vow**" (TEV). Some translators put "he doesn't have to do what he promised." **He is bound by his oath** can be "he has to do what he promised." Both expressions represent the technical terminology used by Jewish teachers of religion.

23.17	RSV	TEV
	You blind fools! For which is greater, the gold or the temple that has made the gold sacred?	Blind fools! Which is more important, the gold or the Temple which makes the gold holy?

Blind fools (so also TEV) translates a Semitic construction, "fools and blind people." **Fools** was discussed at 5.22. Many translations can retain the structure of an adjective and a noun (**blind fools**), but sometimes this has to be restructured as "You are blind and foolish."

In this verse **greater** means "more important" or "of more value."

Which is . . . ? may be restructured as an emphatic statement: "Surely you know that the Temple is more important than the gold that is in it. It is the Temple that makes the gold sacred." Sometimes the force of Jesus' question can be conveyed by a question that follows the statement, as with "The Temple is more important than the gold in it because it is the Temple that gives the gold its importance. Don't you know that?"

Made the gold sacred may be translated "set the gold apart for God" or "set the gold apart for the service of God." In some cases an even fuller translation is helpful: "it is because it is in the Temple that the gold becomes dedicated to God's service."

23.18 RSV	TEV
And you say, 'If any one swears by the altar, it is nothing; but if any one swears by the gift that is on the altar, he is bound by his oath.'	You also teach, 'If someone swears by the altar, he isn't bound by his vow; but if he swears by the gift on the altar, he is bound.'

The exegetical and translational problems of this verse are similar to those of verse 16; see comments there. See also 5.23 for a discussion of **altar**. As for the **gift**, some translators find it necessary to indicate who is offering the gift and, in some cases, to whom it is being offered: "the offering someone has given to God."

23.19 RSV	TEV
You blind men! For which is greater, the gift or the altar that makes the gift sacred?	How blind you are! Which is the more important, the gift or the altar which makes the gift holy?

The exegetical and translational comments of this verse are similar to those of verse 17; see comments there. Here an example can be "You people are blind. Surely the altar is more important that the gift itself. It is because it is there on the altar as an offering to God that the gift becomes something for him. Can't you see that?"

23.20 RSV	TEV
So he who swears by the altar, swears by it and by everything on it;	So then, when a person swears by the altar, he is swearing by it and by all the gifts on it;

He who swears can be expressed as "the person who swears" or "anyone who swears."

In light of Jewish teaching regarding "the lesser and the greater," Jesus' conclusion is easily understood. Since the altar is greater than the gifts that are on it, then whoever swears by the altar is swearing by those gifts as well. **And by everything on it** may also be translated "and by all the gifts which people have placed on it."

23.21

RSV	TEV
and he who swears by the temple, swears by it and by him who dwells in it;	and when he swears by the Temple, he is swearing by it and by God, who lives there;

The exegetical and translational problems of this verse are similar to those of verse 20; see the translation there.

Him who dwells in it is God, and so both TEV and GECL render "**God, who lives there.**"

23.22

RSV	TEV
and he who swears by heaven, swears by the throne of God and by him who sits upon it.	and when someone swears by heaven, he is swearing by God's throne and by him who sits on it.

Throne was discussed at 5.34. As there, it may be translated simply as "the place from where God rules." But, since the idea of sitting is explicit in the verse, a better sentence may be "the seat from where God rules."

Him who sits upon it is also a reference to God, and in some languages this may need to be made explicit: "God, who sits on it" (GECL).

23.23

RSV	TEV
"Woe to you, scribes and Pharisees, hypocrites! for you tithe mint and dill and cummin, and have neglected the weightier matters of the law, justice and mercy and faith; these you ought to have done, without neglecting the others.	"How terrible for you, teachers of the Law and Pharisees! You hypocrites! You give to God one tenth even of the seasoning herbs, such as mint, dill, and cumin, but you neglect to obey the really important teachings of the Law, such as justice and mercy and honesty. These you should practice, without neglecting the others.

According to Deuteronomy 14.23, grain, wine, and olive oil were required to be tithed, though there is no mention of the requirement to tithe seasoning herbs such as **mint and dill and cummin**. It is possible though that this regulation was imposed by the Pharisaic interpretation of the Law.

To **tithe** means to give a tenth of one's earnings to God, and so **you tithe** is rendered "**You give to God one tenth**" by TEV and GECL. Other languages may require similar restructuring, especially where "church talk" is unfamiliar to the majority of readers.

Mint is a plant whose leaves and stem contain a pleasant smelling oil (the Greek word means "sweet smelling"). Among the Jews the plant was used to season food, and on occasion it was put in medicine. It was found in ditches, on river banks and even in the mountains, and so it was plentiful and inexpensive. (See *Fauna and Flora*, pages 143-144.)

Dill is a plant which contains aromatic seeds which the Jews used for seasoning. The plant was cultivated by the Jews, but it also grew wild, and like mint it was plentiful. At least one rabbinic source indicates that not only the seeds, but also the stem and leaves of the dill plant were to be tithed. (See *Fauna and Flora*, page 117.)

Cummin is a plant of the carrot family. It was cultivated by the Jews for its spicy seeds, which were used in bread as well as in other foods. For a description of the way in which cumin was harvested, see Isaiah 28.25,27. (See *Fauna and Flora*, pages 114-118.)

Most translators treat **mint, dill**, and **cumin** together with a generic word such as "seasoning" and the transliterated form of the major known metropolitan language such as English, French, or Spanish; for example "the herbs (or, plants) for seasoning food called 'mint, dill, and cumin.' " The idea of "seasoning" may be expressed with some idiomatic expression such as "plants that make the food sweet."

It may not be clear that tithing these seasonings meant giving one tenth of what one grew of them. In such a case a sentence like "You even give to God one tenth of the seasonings called 'mint, dill, and cumin' that you have grown" will be helpful.

Neglected translates a Greek verb which covers a wide range of meaning. For its usage here, compare Mark 7.8 (RSV "leave"), Romans 1.27 (RSV "gave up"), and Revelation 2.4 (RSV "abandoned"). Other possibilities include "fail to obey" and "you do not obey."

The weightier matters of the law reflects the distinction made by the Jewish teachers between "weighty" commands (the more important commands) and "light" commands (the lesser important commands). Jesus declares that their evaluation is in error; what they consider to be **the weightier matters of the law** (compliance with its small details) are insignificant when compared with what are the truly "weighty" commands (**justice, mercy**, and **faith**).

According to the teaching of the Old Testament, **justice** and **mercy** are closely related concepts. Whereas Roman law favored the rich and powerful, the laws of the Old Testament were designed to protect the poor and helpless. These concepts were not abstract but required action, and often translations make this explicit by saying "you have failed to follow the more important commandments of the Law, those which require you to treat other people fairly and with mercy."

Faith is a comprehensive term which is used to define the proper relation that should exist between God and his people, and among God's people. It is best represented by "faithfulness" (NIV) or "good faith" (Phps, NJB, NEB, NAB). It can also be "to be faithful to God" or "to be faithful in doing all that is required of you." A verb construction is possible for the three terms: "to treat others with fairness and mercy and to be faithful to God."

In the expression **these you ought to have done**, the pronoun **these** refers back to **justice**, **mercy**, and **faith**: "It is these commands that you should follow" or "those are the commands that you should have been obeying."

Without neglecting the others signifies the importance that the Jewish Law (the Old Testament laws) held for the author of the Gospel. Good possibilities include "but you must not forget to do the others as well," "but at the same time you cannot fail to do those lesser important laws," and "but this does not mean you don't have to do those smaller laws."

23.24	RSV	TEV

You blind guides, straining out a gnat and swallowing a camel!	Blind guides! You strain a fly out of your drink, but swallow a camel!

Blind guides translates the same expression used in verse 16.

Straining out a gnat describes the custom of the strictest sect of Pharisees who strained everything they drank for fear of swallowing an insect that was considered unclean. **Gnat** represents the traditional rendering; TEV has "fly," and "midge" (a small gnat-like fly) is the choice of NEB and Brc. The word may also mean "mosquito" (Phps), and there is even the possibility that it may refer to a certain worm which was sometimes found in wine. GECL effectively renders "smallest gnat." **Straining out a gnat** sometimes requires restructuring for the sense to be clear, as in "you strain what you drink through a cloth so you won't swallow even a gnat (or, small fly)."

Swallowing a camel intentionally introduces an exaggerated figure of speech in order to demonstrate the absolute inconsistency of the Pharisaic application of the Law. Jesus may have intended a play on words, since in the Aramaic translation the word **gnat** is similar to the word "camel." Moreover, according to Leviticus 11.4, the camel is an unclean animal which Jews were not allowed to eat. GECL translates this phrase as "but you swallow a camel without seeing it." It is possible to introduce a simile: "You take care to strain the smallest insect out of your drink, but you are like people who swallow a camel without even knowing it." Or the imagery may be dropped completely if it is believed that the readers will not grasp its significance: "you exert yourselves to obey all the insignificant details of the Law, but you neglect the most important part of the Law, without even knowing it."

Obviously it will not be too serious a problem if readers are not very familiar with **camel**, which is not used literally here. What translators in such languages may do if they do want to keep the image is say "a huge animal called 'camel.' "

23.25	RSV	TEV

"Woe to you, scribes and Pharisees, hypocrites! for you cleanse the	"How terrible for you, teachers of the Law and Pharisees! You hypo-

outside of the cup and of the plate, but inside they are full of extortion and rapacity.	crites! You clean the outside of your cup and plate, while the inside is full of what you have gotten by violence and selfishness.

The custom of cleaning the cups and plates was for religious as well as for sanitary reasons. But that can't really be included in the translation. **Cleanse** should be translated as simply "wash" or "clean." Something of the irony of Jesus' accusation may be captured with a phrase like "for you are so careful to wash (or, clean) the outside of your cups and plates" or "for you clean so carefully."

Full of extortion and rapacity (NIV "full of greed and self-indulgence") may leave the wrong impression with the reader. In Greek the preposition **of** is literally "from," which here has the meaning "resulting from" or "gotten from." The meaning is accurately expressed by GECL: "But what you eat and drink out of it you have acquired by your greed." TEV has "**full of what you have gotten by violence and selfishness**." Even clearer renderings are "but the food and drink that are in them you got by means of violence and selfishness" and "but you fill them with food and drink that you got through force and greed."

23.26	RSV	TEV

You blind Pharisee! first cleanse the inside of the cup and of the plate, that the outside also may be clean.	Blind Pharisee! Clean what is inside the cup first, and then the outside will be clean too!

Jesus uses a singular form of address here, **You blind Pharisee!** but he is surely addressing all of them as a group, not just one individual. Most translators will retain the singular form, unless readers will then only understand the sentence to be addressed to one person. Then they can use "You blind people, you Pharisees" or "You are so blind, you Pharisees."

The **cup** and **plate** may be understood figuratively of the Pharisees, in which case **first cleanse the inside of the cup and of the plate** may be translated "Give attention first of all to inner purity, then everything outside will also be pure" (GECL). On the other hand, if the cup and plate are understood in a nonfigurative sense, then there is no need to remove the imagery from the translation. Translators can say "First be sure that what is inside the cup and plate is clean."

23.27	RSV	TEV

"Woe to you, scribes and Pharisees, hypocrites! for you are like whitewashed tombs, which outwardly appear beautiful, but within they are full of dead men's bones and all uncleanness.	"How terrible for you, teachers of the Law and Pharisees! You hypocrites! You are like whitewashed tombs, which look fine on the outside but are full of bones and decaying corpses on the inside.

Although it is quite possible that Jesus uses the cup and plate (verse 26) to speak figuratively of the Pharisees themselves, it is only in this verse that the application is made explicit.

The **whitewashed tombs** of which Jesus speaks reflect the annual practice of whitewashing the tombs in the city of Jerusalem so that none of the visitors coming there would accidentally touch one and become ceremonially unclean. Jesus' accusation against the Pharisees is that they, like the tombs, may appear clean and beautiful on the outside, but inwardly they are filthy and defiled. A Palestinian tomb could have been located in a variety of places: in a pit, a cave, an unused cistern, or, in the case of the wealthy, a chamber carved out of the rock. "Whitewash" is quite widely known, but if it is not, then **whitewashed tombs** may be "tombs that are painted white."

These tombs that appear beautiful on the outside are on the inside **full of dead men's bones and all uncleanness**, a concept that can be expressed by "full of the bones of the dead and all kinds of rottenness (or, rotting matter)."

23.28 RSV	TEV
So you also outwardly appear righteous to men, but within you are full of hypocrisy and iniquity.	In the same way, on the outside you appear good to everybody, but inside you are full of hypocrisy and sins.

This verse continues the analogy begun in verse 27 and makes explicit its application. **So** marks this comparison and may be rendered as "**In the same way**" (TEV) or "You are just like that."

Righteous is a key word in the Gospel (see comment under "just" in 1.19). Possibly here translators can say "appear to others as if you were good" or "look like people who do what God requires."

Iniquity (literally "lawlessness") is also a key term in the Gospel; see comment under "evildoers" at 7.23.

It may be unnatural to speak of being **full of hypocrisy and iniquity**. "You are completely hypocritical and sinful" or "you are really hypocrites and completely sinful" are alternatives to consider.

23.29-36

RSV	TEV
	Jesus Predicts Their Punishment
29 "Woe to you, scribes and Pharisees, hypocrites! for you build the tombs of the prophets and adorn the monuments of the righteous, 30 saying, 'If we had lived in the days of our fathers, we would not have taken part with them in shedding the blood of the prophets.' 31 Thus you witness against yourselves, that you are sons of those who murdered the prophets. 32 Fill up,	29 "How terrible for you, teachers of the Law and Pharisees! You hypocrites! You make fine tombs for the prophets and decorate the monuments of those who lived good lives; 30 and you claim that if you had lived during the time of your ancestors, you would not have done what they did and killed the prophets. 31 So you actually admit that you are the descendants of those who

then, the measure of your fathers. 33 You serpents, you brood of vipers, how are you to escape being sentenced to hell?*ʷ* 34 Therefore I send you prophets and wise men and scribes, some of whom you will kill and crucify, and some you will scourge in your synagogues and persecute from town to town, 35 that upon you may come all the righteous blood shed on earth, from the blood of innocent Abel to the blood of Zechariah the son of Barachiah, whom you murdered between the sanctuary and the altar. 36 Truly, I say to you, all this will come upon this generation.

ʷ Greek *Gehenna*

murdered the prophets! 32 Go on, then, and finish up what your ancestors started! 33 You snakes and sons of snakes! How do you expect to escape from being condemned to hell? 34 And so I tell you that I will send you prophets and wise men and teachers; you will kill some of them, crucify others, and whip others in the synagogues and chase them from town to town. 35 As a result, the punishment for the murder of all innocent men will fall on you, from the murder of innocent Abel to the murder of Zechariah son of Berechiah, whom you murdered between the Temple and the altar. 36 I tell you indeed: the punishment for all these murders will fall on the people of this day!

SECTION HEADING: for those who do insert a heading, the TEV '**Jesus Predicts Their Punishment**" may need some restructuring. In the first place, it may have to be specified who "**Their**" refers to. Secondly, "**Punishment**" may need to be expanded to include who will do the punishing. The heading may be, then, "Jesus predicts God will punish the scribes and Pharisees" or "Jesus tells how God will punish the teachers of the Law and the Pharisees."

It is somewhat unfortunate that TEV introduces a new section with verse 29, because it introduces the last in the series of pronouncements against the Pharisees. Apparently the logic for such a decision is that from here on (or from verse 33 on) the focus in the passage shifts to God's judgment on the Pharisees because of their hypocrisy. Translators should decide whether to retain the section heading or not on the basis of the structure and flow of discourse in their own languages.

23.29 RSV	TEV
"Woe to you, scribes and Pharisees, hypocrites! for you build the tombs of the prophets and adorn the monuments of the righteous,	"How terrible for you, teachers of the Law and Pharisees! You hypocrites! You make fine tombs for the prophets and decorate the monuments of those who lived good lives;

A link is drawn between verse 29 and verses 27-28 through the repetition of the word **tombs**. Since the **tombs of the prophets** implies tombs out of the ordinary, TEV translates "**fine tombs**," and GECL "wonderful tombs." It was customary in that day to build outstanding **monuments** to mark the graves of heroes and other famous men (see Acts 2.29, which mentions David's tomb).

Prophets was discussed at 1.22. Here it may have to be "the prophets of old" to be sure readers do not think the reference is to building tombs and grave markers in anticipation of the death of the prophets.

The **righteous** are defined by TEV as "**those who lived good lives**" (see comment under "just" at 1.19, and note the use of the word in verse 28).

The prophets and **the righteous** represent two categories of people who were known for their faithful devotion to God. The honor attributed to them by the

Pharisees was an attempt to deny that they would have rejected the prophets, had the Pharisees lived during the days of their ancestors (see verse 30).

It appears that **tombs** and **monuments** are used synonymously, with **tombs of the prophets** and **monuments of the righteous** forming a parallel construction. One may then translate "you build fine tombs for the prophets and other faithful servants of God, and you keep their tombs decorated." Or "you build . . . and you decorate the tombs that others have built for them."

23.30   RSV   TEV

saying, 'If we had lived in the days of   and you claim that if you had lived
our fathers, we would not have taken   during the time of your ancestors,
part with them in shedding the blood   you would not have done what they
of the prophets.'   did and killed the prophets.

Saying may have the more specific connotation of "claiming" (see TEV). Note that TEV has used indirect discourse and the second person "**you**" instead of the direct discourse and **we** of the RSV text. This will be more natural in many other languages as well.

Had lived sometimes is rendered "had been alive."

Fathers has the extended meaning of "**ancestors**" (TEV).

Shedding the blood is a Hebrew idiom meaning "kill" or "murder" (TEV, GECL, NEB). The sentence may be expressed then as "We (or, you) would not have joined them in killing the prophets" or "We (or, you) would not have helped them to murder the prophets."

23.31   RSV   TEV

Thus you witness against your-   So you actually admit that you are
selves, that you are sons of those   the descendants of those who mur-
who murdered the prophets.   dered the prophets!

Thus may be expressed "In this way" or "**So**" (TEV). Brc has "By your very statement."

Witness against yourselves: the meaning seems to be that through their rejection of Jesus the Pharisees give evidence that they are indeed descendants of those people **who murdered the prophets** in earlier generations. Brc translates this as "you provide evidence." This expression can also be used in a sentence such as "you provide evidence against yourselves by acknowledging you are the descendants of those who murdered the prophets."

Sons of (see "fathers" in verse 30) has the extended meaning of "**descendants**" (TEV). The Hebrew expression also conveys the notion of persons of like character and disposition.

23.32	RSV	TEV

Fill up, then, the measure of your fathers.

Go on, then, and finish up what your ancestors started!

Fill up (TEV "**Go on . . . and finish up**") has the meaning of "bring to completion" or "finish off" (NEB, NJB).

The measure of your fathers is more clearly translated "what your fathers began" (NEB), assuming that **fathers** is correctly understood to mean "ancestors."

TOB believes the reference to be to the murder of Jesus, though this information may not be allowed in the text.

23.33	RSV	TEV

You serpents, you brood of vipers, how are you to escape being sentenced to hell?[w]

You snakes and sons of snakes! How do you expect to escape from being condemned to hell?

[w] Greek *Gehenna*

Brood of vipers is the same expression used by John the Baptist in 3.7. Matthew evidently intends to make a close correlation between the message and fate of John the Baptist and that of Jesus. **Serpents** is a different word in Greek than **vipers**, but there is no distinction in meaning; the use of two parallel expressions represents a stylistic feature of Hebraic Greek. Translators do not necessarily have to use the name of a member of the viper family if this snake is not known. And if to call someone a snake is not such a terrible thing, translators may have to modify the words slightly to something like "You treacherous and dangerous snakes!" or "How treacherous and dangerous you are, just like a family of snakes!"

How are you to escape being sentenced to hell? As more than one commentator notes, this is in the style of a saying derived from Jewish apocalyptic literature. **Hell** is the same word discussed at 5.22. It may be more effective to shift the rhetorical question to an affirmation: "You cannot expect to escape from being sentenced to hell!" Moreover, effective translation may require the explicit mention of who it is that will condemn them to hell: "God is certain to condemn you to hell! You cannot hope to escape!"

23.34	RSV	TEV

Therefore I send you prophets and wise men and scribes, some of whom you will kill and crucify, and some you will scourge in your synagogues and persecute from town to town,

And so I tell you that I will send you prophets and wise men and teachers; you will kill some of them, crucify others, and whip others in the synagogues and chase them from town to town.

Therefore represents three words of the Greek text: a prepositional phrase ("because of this") followed by "behold" (see at 1.20). GECL translates the construction as a separate sentence: "Listen well!" **Therefore I** is translated "**And so I tell you**" by TEV.

The use of the present tense **I send** quite probably reflects the situation of Matthew's day in which prophets and wise men and teachers are actively working in the church. However, the verse is written from the time reference of Jesus' own day, and the present tense may be used in Greek of a future event which is certain to take place. TEV employs the future tense: "**I will send.**" One may render "I will surely send," to stress the certainty.

Prophets, as elsewhere, may be translated "people who will speak God's message."

Wise men translates the same noun used in 11.25; it occurs nowhere else in Matthew's Gospel. They are probably to be understood as men whose wisdom enables them to make practical application of the Christian message to varied circumstances and situations.

Scribes: this is the only place in the Gospel (with the possible exception of 13.52) where the word is used of Christians as opposed to Jews. Probably the best .way to translate it in this context is with "**teachers**" (TEV) or possibly "teachers of God's way." Some New Testament scholars believe that "prophets" and "wise men" and "teachers" represent three classifications of leaders in the church to which Matthew is writing this Gospel.

It is possible that **kill and crucify** means "kill by nailing to a cross." On the other hand, if more than one form of killing is thought to be in the mind of the author, then one may translate "you will kill some of them by nailing them to crosses, and you will kill some in other ways." Among Jews crucifixion was never used as a legal form of punishment, but the reference does not necessarily imply legal execution.

Scourge in your synagogues refers specifically to punishment by beating with a whip. It was done in the synagogues according to the instructions of Deuteronomy 25.2. In 20.19 the same verb is used of the beating given persons immediately preceding execution.

For **synagogues,** see comments on 4.23.

Persecute (TEV "**chase**") translates the verb used in 5.10,11,12. NEB renders "hound"; Phps, NJB, Brc have "hunt" (NAB "hunt down").

23.35 RSV	TEV
that upon you may come all the righteous blood shed on earth, from the blood of innocent Abel to the blood of Zechariah the son of Barachiah, whom you murdered between the sanctuary and the altar.	As a result, the punishment for the murder of all innocent men will fall on you, from the murder of innocent Abel to the murder of Zechariah son of Berechiah, whom you murdered between the Temple and the altar.

RSV continues in this verse with the sentence begun in verse 34, which leads to an accumulation of almost seventy words in some extremely difficult constructions.

Both TEV and GECL introduce a new sentence here, and consideration should be given to the need for doing something similar in other languages as well. The problem with the TEV **"As a result,"** however, is that the idea of purpose of the RSV **that . . . may come** is not obvious. It may be good to start the verse with "I will send them like that so that." Brc restructures the passage beginning verse 34 with "Let me tell you why I send," and then begins verse 35 with "The reason is that."

Righteous here has the specialized meaning of "innocent" (so Phps, NEB, AT, GECL), and **blood** means "murder" as in verse 30. Therefore **that upon you may come all the righteous blood shed on earth** may be rendered as in TEV: **"As a result, the punishment for the murder of all innocent men will fall on you."** One may even translate "And so God will punish you for the murder of all innocent people who have ever lived."

According to Genesis 4.8 **Abel** is the first person to have been murdered, but there is much uncertainty regarding the identification of **Zechariah the son of Barachiah**, and at least three solutions have been put forward: (1) The prophet Zechariah was the son of a man named Berechiah (Zech 1.1), but there is no intimation that he was ever murdered. (2) Josephus the Jewish historian records the murder of a certain Zechariah son of Baruch in the temple shortly before the fall of Jerusalem in A.D. 70. (3) More probable is the Zechariah mentioned in 2 Chronicles 24.20-22 (the last book in the Hebrew Bible). Although his name is given as Azariah in the Septuagint, he is called Zechariah in the Hebrew text, and he was a priest, which would have given him access to the area **between the sanctuary and the altar**. That Luke (11.51) refers to him merely as Zechariah, without mention of his father's name, suggests either (a) that the identification was problematic for Luke as well, or (b) that Luke thought in terms of the Hebrew Bible, according to which the murders of Abel and Zechariah would have been the first and last ones recorded in the Scriptures.

In some cases translators will have a short footnote saying "Abel and Zechariah were the first and last people listed as having been murdered in the Hebrew Bible, in which Chronicles, not Malachi, is the last book. Jesus means by this phrase all the innocent people murdered in the Old Testament." However, this information is not really essential to the understanding of the text, and certainly it would never be included in the translation itself.

The text says **whom you murdered**, but obviously it was not the people Jesus was speaking to here who murdered. He was speaking to them as a continuation of the people of the Old Testament. In many translations, retaining the **you** poses no problem, as readers will understand that these people did not themselves kill Zechariah. In other cases translators will say something like "you Jews." Another solution is to emphasize shared responsibility; for example, "whom your people murdered between the Temple building and the altar for sacrifices."

Between the sanctuary and the altar may need to be translated "between the Temple building and the place where sacrifices are offered."

23.36 RSV TEV

RSV	TEV
Truly, I say to you, all this will come upon this generation.	I tell you indeed: the punishment for all these murders will fall on the people of this day!

Truly, I say to you translates the same emphatic formula used in 5.26 (singular "you") and 6.2 (plural "you," as here); see comment at 5.18.

All this (literally "all these things") is translated "**the punishment for all these murders**" by TEV and "for all these shameful deeds" by GECL. In Greek the reference is unclear; it may be limited to the murders mentioned in verse 35 or expanded to incorporate all the evil deeds of verses 29-35, including the murders.

This generation (TEV "**the people of this day**") may have the wider meaning of "all Israel," who from this moment on reject Jesus (see 27.25).

All this will come upon this generation is a Hebrew way of saying "This generation will be punished for all this" or "God will punish all of you because of these evil things that you and your ancestors have done."

23.37-39

RSV TEV

Jesus' Love for Jerusalem

RSV	TEV
37 "O Jerusalem, Jerusalem, killing the prophets and stoning those who are sent to you! How often would I have gathered your children together as a hen gathers her brood under her wings, and you would not! 38 Behold, your house is forsaken and desolate.*x* 39 For I tell you, you will not see me again, until you say, 'Blessed is he who comes in the name of the Lord.' "	37 "Jerusalem, Jerusalem! You kill the prophets and stone the messengers God has sent you! How many times I wanted to put my arms around all your people, just as a hen gathers her chicks under her wings, but you would not let me! 38 And so your Temple will be abandoned and empty. 39 From now on, I tell you, you will never see me again until you say, 'God bless him who comes in the name of the Lord.' "

x Other ancient authorities omit *and desolate*

SECTION HEADING: "**Jesus' Love for Jerusalem**" uses a noun, "**Love**," for what is often more easily expressed in a verb phrase, as in "Jesus loves Jerusalem" or "Jesus has great love for Jerusalem." Sometimes translators have to expand "Jerusalem" to "the people of Jerusalem."

There is almost a word-for-word agreement between this brief passage and its parallel in Luke 13.34-35, though the contexts are quite dissimilar. The background for the imagery of a hen gathering her brood under her wings lies in the Old Testament, where God is compared to a bird which zealously protects its young (Deut 32.11; Psa 36.7; Isa 31.5), and where the "wings" of God are used as a symbol of protection from one's enemies (Psa 17.8; 57.1; 61.4; 63.7; 9.14). Moreover, the Jewish teachers spoke of their converts as coming "under the wings of God's Presence," which is akin to what Boaz said to Ruth: ". . . a full reward be given you by the LORD, the God of Israel, under whose wings you have come to take refuge!" (Ruth 2.12). Finally, it was believed among the Jews that at the end of time God would gather his people together in a great salvation event. So then, in the employment of this symbolism, Jesus is affirming that through their rejection of him the people of Israel have missed the long-awaited moment of salvation.

"O Jerusalem, Jerusalem, killing the prophets and stoning those who are sent to you! How often would I have gathered your children together as a hen gathers her brood under her wings, and you would not!	"Jerusalem, Jerusalem! You kill the prophets and stone the messengers God has sent you! How many times I wanted to put my arms around all your people, just as a hen gathers her chicks under her wings, but you would not let me!

It must be made clear in translation that **Jerusalem** is here used of the people of Jerusalem. "People of Jerusalem" or "O, you people of Jerusalem" may be necessary. But neither of these is as effective as the text, which should be retained if readers can understand it.

Killing . . . stoning is similar in construction to "kill and crucify" of verse 34. It may need to be a separate sentence: "You kill the prophets and you stone to death the messengers God sent to you." As in the earlier passage the order may need to be reversed here as well: "stoning to death (some) and killing (some) by other means."

Prophets . . . those . . . sent to you may be interpreted as parallel expressions, employed for the sake of emphasis: "God sent people to proclaim his message to you. But you stoned some of them to death, and you murdered some of them in other ways." Or ". . . But you murdered some of them by stoning them, and you murdered some by other means."

How often . . . would not: the difficulty with this exclamatory construction is that it may initially be read (or heard) as a question. One may find it advisable to transform the question into a strong affirmative statement: "Many times I wanted . . . but you would not let me."

Your children, when used of a city, represents a Hebrew idiom in which the noun **children** is the equivalent of "inhabitants" (TEV "**your people**").

How often . . . under her wings appears in GECL as a separate sentence: "How often would I have gathered your inhabitants around me, as a hen gathers her young under her wings!" As in this example, **gathered . . . together** is often translated as "gathered around me" or "bring you all around me."

In those few areas of the world where chickens are not common, translators should substitute some other bird or fowl, such as a partridge, that also gathers her young together in time of danger.

And you would not is expressed in TEV as "**but you would not let me.**" Some languages will require an even more comprehensive statement: "but you would not let me do it" or "but you would not allow me to gather you in that way."

23.38	RSV	TEV

Behold, your house is forsaken and desolate.*x*

And so your Temple will be abandoned and empty.

x Other ancient authorities omit *and desolate*

As previously, **Behold** seeks to capture the attention of the audience just prior to an important point. But many languages will not have a word or phrase that corresponds directly to this. TEV has "**And so**," and others, for example Brc, simply drop it. "Well then" is one possibility.

House may refer to the entire city of Jerusalem, or it may be limited to the Temple (12.4; 21.13), and chapter 24 opens with the remark that "Jesus left the temple." Accordingly, it seems that Matthew intends for his readers to understand that all events between 21.23 and 23.39 took place within the precincts of the Temple compound. One may then follow TEV's "**And so your Temple . . . .**"

To say that the Temple **is forsaken** often raises the question "By whom?" Since it is God's dwelling, translators may have to say "God has left your Temple." So Brc: "God no longer has his home among you." Another possible interpretation is that reference is to the Temple's impending destruction, when people will no longer be coming there to worship; "So there will be no one in your Temple." Note that TEV uses a future tense here, which may be more natural.

As the RSV footnote points out, **and desolate** (one word in the Greek text) is absent from some ancient manuscripts. Since Jesus is obviously alluding to Jeremiah 22.5 (where the word is present in the Septuagint, though in the form of a verb rather than of an adjective), it may be argued that it was later introduced into the Gospel in order to make Matthew's text conform more closely to that of the Septuagint. On the other hand, the textual evidence for its inclusion is favorable, and according to TC-GNT, the judgment of the committee for the UBS Greek text is that some scribes must have omitted it because of the feeling that after **forsaken** it is repetitious. Therefore the decision of the committee was to include it in the text, though with a "C" rating, indicating a considerable degree of doubt regarding what may have been the original text. JB includes the word in the text, though accompanied by a footnote; NEB omits it from the text, also accompanied by a footnote.

Desolate means "empty." The sentence can be rendered "God has left your Temple, and it is empty."

23.39	RSV	TEV

For I tell you, you will not see me again, until you say, 'Blessed is he who comes in the name of the Lord.' "

From now on, I tell you, you will never see me again until you say, 'God bless him who comes in the name of the Lord.' "

For I tell you repeats the emphatic formula of 5.20; see the translation there.

Again (TEV "**From now on**") is repeated in 26.29 (RSV "again") and 26.64 (RSV "hereafter"). The phrase is peculiar to Matthew's Gospel, and it is evidently significant in his understanding of the last things.

You will not see me again, until must be understood in the framework of Matthew's Gospel as looking forward to the final salvation event, though Luke (13.35) employs it of the triumphant entry of Jesus into Jerusalem. The quotation which follows is taken from Psalm 118.26, and it represents a portion of the shout by which the pilgrims welcomed Jesus upon his entry into Jerusalem (Matt 21.9; Mark 11.9; Luke 19.38). GECL has "you will see me next, only when . . . ," thereby eliminating the more difficult negative form in favor of a simpler positive one.

Blessed is he who comes in the name of the Lord: see comment at 21.9.

Chapter 24

24.1-2

RSV   TEV

**Jesus Speaks of the Destruction
of the Temple**

1 Jesus left the temple and was going away, when his disciples came to point out to him the buildings of the temple. 2 But he answered them, "You see all these, do you not? Truly, I say to you, there will not be left here one stone upon another, that will not be thrown down."

1 Jesus left and was going away from the Temple when his disciples came to him to call his attention to its buildings. 2 "Yes," he said, "you may well look at all these. I tell you this: not a single stone here will be left in its place; every one of them will be thrown down."

SECTION HEADING: "**Jesus Speaks of the Destruction of the Temple.**" "**Destruction**" may be expressed better as a verb, as in "Jesus says that the Temple will be destroyed" or "Jesus tells how enemies will destroy the Temple."

Chapters 24–25 form the fifth and final discourse unit within the Gospel. chapter 24, frequently referred to as the "apocalyptic discourse," is concerned with two matters: (1) the destruction of Jerusalem and (2) events scheduled to take place in relation to the end of the world. Chapter 25, which both begins (verses 1-13) and ends (verses 31-46) with material unique to Matthew's Gospel, consists of parables that focus upon the relation between the present life and the final judgment. In all three of the Synoptic Gospels, the apocalyptic discourse immediately precedes the passion narrative. Mark (12.41-44) and Luke (21.1-4) place the story of the widow's offering immediately before the discourse, whereas Matthew links it with the threat of God's final judgment on the Temple and the promise of the one who comes in the name of the Lord (23.38-39). Matthew follows Mark's outline, though he makes stylistic modifications of his own and intersperses the discourse with sayings from a source which he and Luke had in common (compare verses 26-28, 37-39, and 40-41 with Luke 17.22-37).

24.1   RSV   TEV

Jesus left the temple and was going away, when his disciples came to point out to him the buildings of the temple.

Jesus left and was going away from the Temple when his disciples came to him to call his attention to its buildings.

Jesus left the temple and was going away is similar to what is found in most other translations. Since **left** (a participle in Greek) and **was going away**

729

describe essentially the same action, one may compress the two verbs into one: "As Jesus was leaving the Temple" or "After Jesus had left the Temple."

Came translates a verb used more than fifty times in the Gospel, though only twice with Jesus as subject (17.7; 28.18). Neither Mark nor Luke include this information, perhaps because the disciples are thought of as already being with Jesus at this time. The contextual meaning seems to be "came up (closer)." In some languages "went up" is more natural.

Point out is a fairly literal representation of the Greek verb; TEV, AT, and NIV have **"to call his attention to,"** and Phps has "drew his attention to," as translations of **to point out to him**.

The buildings of the temple may more precisely be spoken of as "the buildings of the Temple area" (NAB) or "the entire Temple complex" (GECL).

24.2   RSV   TEV

But he answered them, "You see all   "Yes," he said, "you may well look at
these, do you not? Truly, I say to   all these. I tell you this: not a single
you, there will not be left here one   stone here will be left in its place;
stone upon another, that will not be   every one of them will be thrown
thrown down."   down."

Since the previous verse does not really report on what the disciples said to Jesus, **answered** may not be the most natural thing to say in the translation. TEV has "**said**," for example.

You see all these, do you not? is a difficult negative rhetorical question which expects a positive response. Both TEV ("**Yes . . . you may well look at these**") and NEB ("Yes, look at it all") simplify by shifting to a positive statement. Others retain the question form, though in a less complex construction: "Does all this astound you?" (GECL 1st edition) and "Do you see all these buildings?" (NAB).

Truly, I say to you translates the same formula discussed at 5.18.

There will not be left here one stone upon another may also be expressed "every stone here will be removed from its place" or ". . . from its proper place in the building." A shift may be made to an active: "The time will come when your enemies will remove (or, tear down) every stone from its proper place in the building."

That will not be thrown down may also be expressed by a positive statement: "all will be scattered on the ground" (GECL) and "everything will be destroyed" (JB). Brc rather effectively translates the clause as "There is not a building here which will not be utterly demolished."

24.3-14

                RSV   TEV

                                            Troubles and Persecutions

3 As he sat on the Mount of Olives, the   3 As Jesus sat on the Mount of Olives, the
disciples came to him privately, saying, "Tell us,   disciples came to him in private. "Tell us when all

when will this be, and what will be the sign of your coming and of the close of the age?" 4 And Jesus answered them, "Take heed that no one leads you astray. 5 For many will come in my name, saying, 'I am the Christ,' and they will lead many astray. 6 And you will hear of wars and rumors of wars; see that you are not alarmed; for this must take place, but the end is not yet. 7 For nation will rise against nation, and kingdom against kingdom, and there will be famines and earthquakes in various places: 8 all this is but the beginning of the birth-pangs.

9 "Then they will deliver you up to tribulation, and put you to death; and you will be hated by all nations for my name's sake. 10 And then many will fall away,[y] and betray one another, and hate one another. 11 And many false prophets will arise and lead many astray. 12 And because wickedness is multiplied, most men's love will grow cold. 13 But he who endures to the end will be saved. 14 And this gospel of the kingdom will be preached throughout the whole world, as a testimony to all nations; and then the end will come.

[y] Or *stumble*

this will be," they asked, "and what will happen to show that it is the time for your coming and the end of the age."

4 Jesus answered, "Watch out, and do not let anyone fool you. 5 Many men, claiming to speak for me, will come and say, 'I am the Messiah!' and they will fool many people. 6 You are going to hear the noise of battles close by and the news of battles far away; but do not be troubled. Such things must happen, but they do not mean that the end has come. 7 Countries will fight each other; kingdoms will attack one another. There will be famines and earthquakes everywhere. 8 All these things are like the first pains of childbirth.

9 "Then you will be arrested and handed over to be punished and be put to death. All mankind will hate you because of me. 10 Many will give up their faith at that time; they will betray one another and hate one another. 11 Then many false prophets will appear and fool many people. 12 Such will be the spread of evil that many people's love will grow cold. 13 But whoever holds out to the end will be saved. 14 And this Good News about the Kingdom will be preached through all the world for a witness to all mankind; and then the end will come.

SECTION HEADING: "**Troubles and Persecutions.**" If this needs to be expanded to a short sentence, translators can have "Jesus' followers will suffer greatly," "Jesus' followers will have troubles and be persecuted," or "Jesus tells how people will persecute his followers."

Neither Jesus nor Matthew is concerned to provide a detailed outline of the events which are to take place at the end of history. In fact their intention is very much the opposite, for they each warn against foolish speculation over such events which are within the knowledge and control of God alone. True discipleship means faithful endurance of persecution (verses 9-10, 12-13), the ability to recognize false prophets (verse 11), and steadfast proclamation of the Christian message (verse 14). The disciple has no time to waste in arguing over things that are beyond his ability to know.

24.3	RSV	TEV

As he sat on the Mount of Olives, the disciples came to him privately, saying, "Tell us, when will this be, and what will be the sign of your coming and of the close of the age?"

As Jesus sat on the Mount of Olives, the disciples came to him in private. "Tell us when all this will be," they asked, "and what will happen to show that it is the time for your coming and the end of the age."

As he sat: because a new section begins here, TEV and others (GECL, FRCL) identify **he** as "**Jesus**."

The Mount of Olives (see 21.1) will be mentioned once again in 26.30. Mark (13.3), but not Luke (21.6), also identifies the location as the Mount of Olives.

The disciples (Luke 21.7, "they") are mentioned by name in Mark: "Peter, James, John, and Andrew" (13.3). That Matthew omits the names in favor of **the disciples** intimates that Matthew's most vital concern is with those disciples of his own day.

As elsewhere, **came** will more naturally be "went" in many languages.

Privately (TEV "**in private**") is also found in Mark (13.3), though not in Luke (21.7). The meaning here is that there was no one else around. They were alone with him.

Matthew, even more emphatically than Mark (13.4), divides the response of the disciples into two distinct questions: (1) **when will this be**, and (2) **what will be the sign of your coming and of the close of the age?** The first of the two questions relates to the destruction of Jerusalem, which is a historical event that may be predicted with relative certainty by the observation of other events. It receives an answer in verses 15-28 and 32-35. But the second question concerns a happening that is not one in a series of cause-and-effect events. It speaks of an act of God, a divine intervention into history that comes suddenly and without warning. Therefore it cannot be predicted or determined by anything that takes place in the course of human events. Consequently the time of its occurrence is within the knowledge of God alone (verses 29-31, 36). Therefore the only answer to this question can be: cease all speculation, faithfully perform your tasks as disciples, and be ready at any moment (verses 37-44). Although the disciples may be interested in predicting the events that accompany the end of history, Jesus' sole concern is that his followers correctly fulfill their role as disciples. That is why he gives them a stern warning accompanied by an exhortation (verses 4-14) before proceeding to answer the two questions.

Since most translators will have put a section heading at the beginning of this verse, it may not be clear that **when will this be** refers to Jesus' statement about the destruction of the Temple. Brc has "these events," but some translators will have to be even more specific, with a question like "When will the Temple be destroyed?"

TEV has expressed **sign** with "**What will happen to show**."

Among the Gospel writers only Matthew uses the noun **coming** of Jesus' coming into power and glory, and in his Gospel it is confined to this chapter (verses 3,27,37,39). In the world of the New Testament, the Greek noun for **coming** was a technical term used of official visits by royalty, and it literally meant "presence" or "appearance." For Paul and writers of other New Testament letters, the noun is used specifically of Jesus' coming in glory (1 Cor 15.23; 1 Thes 2.19; 3.13; 4.15; 5.23; 2 Thes 2.1,8,9; James 5.7,8; 2 Peter 1.16; 3.4,12; 1 John 2.28). To translate **your coming** as "your return" (LB) is to transgress the boundaries of valid translation; whereas the Greek word connotes a glorious or victorious manifestation (not necessarily on earth!), the English word "return" conveys a totally different picture.

To retain **coming** does pose a problem for translators in languages where an event is not normally expressed as a noun. They can use a sentence such as "What things will happen to show that it is time for you to come" or "...that now you will come." In some languages "appear" is used.

Jesus' coming or appearance will mark the **close of the age**, or the end of history as we know it. It means much more, therefore, than the destruction of the world. If it means nothing to say "the end of this age" (the most common translation) or "the end of history," translators may say "the end of time" or "the end of the world" (but not "the destruction of the world").

<hr>

24.4   RSV   TEV

And Jesus answered them, "Take   **Jesus answered, "Watch out,**
heed that no one leads you astray.   **and do not let anyone fool you.**

A nearly word-for-word agreement exists between verses 4-8 and Mark 13.5-8. Matthew makes several stylistic improvements over his Marcan source, but the only significant difference is his alteration of "I am (he)" (Mark 13.6) to "I am the Christ" (verse 5).

Take heed that no one leads you astray (NIV "Watch out that no one deceives you"), though representing an imperative accompanied by a subjunctive in the Greek text, is in reality the equivalent of two imperatives: **"Watch out, and do not let anyone fool you"** (TEV). **Leads . . . astray** is a concept of primary importance in Matthew's understanding of the dangers of discipleship. Elsewhere in this same chapter he repeatedly warns that false Messianic claimants and false prophets will attempt to lead the disciples astray (verses 5,11,24), and in 18.12-13 he employs the verb three times of disciples who have already gone astray like sheep. Only in 22.29 is the verb used of Jesus' opponents, the Pharisees; there the middle voice of the verb is translated "you are wrong" by RSV.

Take heed is usually rendered with an expression such as "Watch out" or "Be on your guard," as in the examples above, but sometimes translators find it more natural to use a sentence such as "Make sure that no one deceives you" or "Be careful not to let anyone fool you." It is not necessary to specify further how they might be led astray, since Jesus tells exactly that in the next verse.

<hr>

24.5   RSV   TEV

For many will come in my name,   **Many men, claiming to speak for me,**
saying, 'I am the Christ,' and they   **will come and say, 'I am the Messi-**
will lead many astray.   **ah!' and they will fool many people.**

RSV **many** is rendered **"many men"** by TEV, but "many people" is equally possible, although in this context a man is more likely than a woman.

Will come translates a verb that is frequently used in the New Testament and ordinarily refers to a person's arrival. **Come** may, however, pose a problem in languages where it is only used to mean coming to where the listeners or readers are. In those cases "appear" will be better.

In my name is best understood in light of **saying, 'I am the Christ,'** which is the basis for the restructuring of several modern translations: "attempting to impersonate me" (NAB), "claiming to be me" (GECL 1st edition), **"claiming to**

speak for me" (TEV), and "claiming that they are my representatives" (Brc). Several Messianic pretenders did arise in the first century (see Acts 5.36-37; 21.38), but as far as is known, none of them pretended to be Jesus himself.

I am the Christ conforms to both the confession of Peter (16.16) and the expectation of the Jews (2.4). For **Christ**, see discussions at 1.1; 1.16; and 1.17. In many languages this claim will have to be in indirect speech: "For many people will come claiming that they speak for me, saying they are the Messiah."

The expression **lead . . . astray** can be rendered as in verse 4 above, but it does have the meaning of causing people to believe wrongly or even to do something that is not right. Thus "mislead" or "cause to follow the wrong thing" are close to the meaning of the text.

24.6   RSV   TEV

And you will hear of wars and ru-   You are going to hear the noise of
mors of wars; see that you are not   battles close by and the news of
alarmed; for this must take place,   battles far away; but do not be trou-
but the end is not yet.   bled. Such things must happen, but
                                          they do not mean that the end has
                                          come.

Wars and rumors of wars is the well-known and traditional rendering. But the noun translated **rumors** may also mean "noise" (of battle), which is the grounds for "**the noise of battles close by and the news of battles far away**" (TEV). Both GECL ("when wars break out near and far") and NEB ("the noise of battle near at hand the news of battles far away") reflect this same exegesis. The word **rumors** in English is usually used for news about things that may or may not have happened, but it is important to note that the sense here is that there will be wars everywhere. The TEV rendering is thus a good model to follow.

Are . . . alarmed translates a verb which also appears in the Marcan parallel (13.7); elsewhere in the New Testament it is used only in 2 Thessalonians 2.2. Translators may render the sentence as "Don't let yourself become frightened" or "Be sure that you don't panic."

This must take place states a basic assumption of apocalyptic literature: history is under the control of God, and so the course of human events is determined by divine decree (see Dan 2.28). This belief, which developed among the Jews during a period of extreme persecution, is now used to encourage Christian believers to remain calm, even when earth-shaking events are taking place. Nothing can take place that contradicts the divine will.

Note that **this** refers to the wars that will go on, not to the panic or fear the disciples might experience. In some languages the pronoun used will make this clear, but other translators will say "these things (or, events)" or even "these wars."

But the end is not yet receives fuller explanation in TEV: "**but they do not mean that the end has come.**" NEB prefers a positive reformulation: "but the end is still to come." Verse 8 repeats the affirmation that the end is not signaled by historical happenings.

The end refers to the end of the age, the same as "the close of the age" in verse 3, and translators can render it with a similar expression.

24.7	RSV	TEV

For nation will rise against nation, and kingdom against kingdom, and there will be famines and earthquakes in various places:	Countries will fight each other; kingdoms will attack one another. There will be famines and earthquakes everywhere.

Another traditional conviction of apocalyptic authors is that international wars and natural disasters (**famines and earthquakes**) will all take place immediately prior to the end of history. But Matthew corrects this belief by indicating that these are all part of the natural course of history and are in no way to be looked upon as indicators of the end of time (see verses 6b,8).

Nation will rise against nation is generally assumed to be a reference to international wars. However, **kingdom against kingdom** may refer to civil wars, or it may be taken as parallel to "nation will rise against nation." Matthew probably had no firm distinction in mind; the significance of the two clauses may well be "There will be wars and civil strife everywhere."

The expression **rise against** can be translated in a rather general sense of fighting or warfare, as in TEV, but can also be rendered with the somewhat more specific notion of "attack." One possible translation is "For nations will attack each other and kingdoms will go to war."

Famines are, alas, too well known. If, however, there is no specific word for them, translators can use an expression such as "in many places there will be no food for people to eat" or "people in some places will be starving."

24.8	RSV	TEV

all this is but the beginning of the birth-pangs.	All these things are like the first pains of childbirth.

All this refers to the natural disasters and wars that will be happening all over the world. Translators can say "all these things" or "all these events." The function of this verse is to turn the Christian community away from empty speculation regarding the end. At the most, the presence of wars, famines, and earthquakes may be compared to the first pains of childbirth and are not to inspire anxious predictions and details of coming events.

Rendering this verse as a simile, as TEV has, will be helpful for many readers: "All these events are like the first pains of childbirth of the new age."

24.9 RSV TEV

"Then they will deliver you up to tribulation, and put you to death; and you will be hated by all nations for my name's sake.

"Then you will be arrested and handed over to be punished and be put to death. All mankind will hate you because of me.

Then may be "At that time" or "When that happens."

Deliver . . . up (TEV "**arrested and handed over**") translates the same verb rendered "arrested" in 4.12; see comment there.

The **they** does not refer to anyone in particular, but this construction is simply a way of saying that this will all happen to the disciples but without specifying who will do it. TEV uses a passive construction ("**you will be arrested and handed over to be punished and be put to death**"), but in many languages this will not be natural at all, and translators will instead say something like "your enemies (or, people) will arrest you and hand you over to those who will punish you and kill you" or "the authorities will arrest you and make you suffer. They will put you to death."

To tribulation (NEB "for punishment") is restructured as a verb phrase by TEV ("**to be punished**") and NJB ("to be tortured").

You . . . you . . . you may be understood in a distributive sense: "they will torture some of you, they will put some of you to death, and others of you will be hated . . . ." But the meaning may also be "they will torture you and then put you to death. You will be hated . . . ."

You will be hated by all nations may be transformed into an active construction: "the entire world will hate you" (GECL) and "**All mankind will hate you**" (TEV).

For my name's sake is somewhat improved in TEV ("**because of me**"), though others come closer to expressing the meaning more clearly: "for your allegiance to me" (NEB), "because of your connection with me" (Brc), and "because you acknowledge me" (GECL). One may also translate "because you are my followers."

24.10 RSV TEV

And then many will fall away,^{y} and betray one another, and hate one another.

Many will give up their faith at that time; they will betray one another and hate one another.

^{y} Or *stumble*

Many has sometimes been translated as "many of you" or even "many of my followers." But "many people" is also acceptable.

Fall away, as the RSV footnote indicates, is literally "stumble"; this is one of Matthew's favorite terms, used fourteen times throughout the Gospel (see comment at 5.29). TEV translates it "**give up their faith.**" Similar translations are "will stop believing in me" or "give up being my followers."

Betray represents the same verb translated "deliver . . . up" in verse 9. Significantly, this is the verb that is consistently used of Jesus' own betrayal. Matthew is thereby saying that the disciples must share the same fate as their Lord. In this verse it may be translated literally as "betray," or it may be expressed as "turn each other over to the authorities."

Hate is used in a similar context in 10.22.

24.11	RSV	TEV

And many false prophets will arise and lead many astray.	Then many false prophets will appear and fool many people.

The appearance of **false prophets** (see comment at 7.15) indicates that the Christian community will face dangers of betrayal from within as well as persecution from the outside world. Note Paul's comment in Acts 20.29-30, which attests of the same experience to be faced by the church in Ephesus.

The false prophets **will arise**. Some translators say "will appear" or use a sentence such as "at that time there will be many people who say they speak God's word but in fact do not."

Lead . . . astray translates the same verb used in verses 4 and 5.

24.12	RSV	TEV

And because wickedness is multiplied, most men's love will grow cold.	Such will be the spread of evil that many people's love will grow cold.

Wickedness is first mentioned in 7.23 (RSV has "evildoers," which is literally "doers of evil/wickedness"). **Wickedness is multiplied** will be impossible to transfer directly into many languages; one may need to render "increasingly, wicked people will be everywhere" or "more and more people will be doing wicked things everywhere."

Most men's love will grow cold as a result of the spread of evil. The reference may be to either love for God or love for others; in Matthew the emphasis is generally upon the latter. One may then translate "many people's love for others will grow cold," or "many people will no longer love others as they should," or "many people will quit loving others." This is the only place in the New Testament where the verb **grow cold** is used of love.

The two parts of this verse are related by **because**, which TEV translates by "**Such will be . . . that . . . .**" Another version can be "More and more wicked . . . . As a consequence, many people will stop loving . . . ."

24.13	RSV	TEV

But he who endures to the end will be saved.	But whoever holds out to the end will be saved.

In Mark's Gospel (13.13) **he who endures to the end** is placed in the context of the need for faithfulness during a time of persecution. But for Matthew the emphasis is different; this saying signifies the need for standing firm against false prophets and for showing love in a world where evil is constantly spreading. In fact the "wickedness" of which Matthew speaks in verse 12 is probably no less than the opposite of love.

Will be saved: this verse is identical to 10.22b. Translators should see comments there. **Will be saved** here is definitely used in the full Christian sense of one's final salvation.

24.14

RSV	TEV
And this gospel of the kingdom will be preached throughout the whole world, as a testimony to all nations; and then the end will come.	And this Good News about the Kingdom will be preached through all the world for a witness to all mankind; and then the end will come.

This saying, in a somewhat abbreviated form, is found earlier in the Marcan discourse on the last things (13.10). Matthew seems to have transferred it here in order to focus upon the urgency of love (verse 12).

Gospel was discussed at 1.1. **Kingdom** was first discussed at 3.2. **This gospel of the kingdom** may best be interpreted with TEV to mean "**Good News about the Kingdom**," or ". . . about the coming rule of God," or ". . . about how God is coming to rule." In GECL 1st edition the first part of this verse is translated "The good news must first be proclaimed throughout the entire world. Everyone must hear the invitation to God's New World." In this context the **gospel of the kingdom** may also be expressed as "this Good News about God's reign" or "this Good News about being part of God's Kingdom."

Will be preached is a passive construction which must often be expressed as an active one, as in "People will preach everywhere in the world about the Good News of God's ruling" or "People must proclaim everywhere in the world the Good News about how God will reign." But it must be related if possible to **as a testimony to all nations**. Brc has "so that all nations may be confronted with the truth," but another possibility is "so that everyone will have the chance to hear (or, accept) it." The sentence can possibly be restructured, as for example "And it must happen that people proclaim the Good News about God's rule everywhere in the world, so that all countries have an opportunity to accept it."

And then the end will come may be translated "only then will the end of the world come" or "only then will God bring the world to an end."

24.15-28

RSV	TEV
	The Awful Horror
15 "So when you see the desolating sacrilege spoken of by the prophet Daniel, standing in	15 "You will see 'The Awful Horror' of which the prophet Daniel spoke. It will be standing

the holy place (let the reader understand), 16 then let those who are in Judea flee to the mountains; 17 let him who is on the housetop not go down to take what is in his house; 18 and let him who is in the field not turn back to take his mantle. 19 And alas for those who are with child and for those who give suck in those days! 20 Pray that your flight may not be in winter or on a sabbath. 21 For then there will be great tribulation, such as has not been from the beginning of the world until now, no, and never will be. 22 And if those days had not been shortened, no human being would be saved; but for the sake of the elect those days will be shortened. 23 Then if any one says to you, 'Lo, here is the Christ!' or 'There he is!' do not believe it. 24 For false Christs and false prophets will arise and show great signs and wonders, so as to lead astray, if possible, even the elect. 25 Lo, I have told you beforehand. 26 So, if they say to you, 'Lo, he is in the wilderness,' do not go out; if they say, 'Lo, he is in the inner rooms,' do not believe it. 27 For as the lightning comes from the east and shines as far as the west, so will be the coming of the Son of man. 28 Wherever the body is, there the eagles^z will be gathered together.

^{z} Or *vultures*

in the holy place." (Note to the reader: understand what this means!) 16 "Then those who are in Judea must run away to the hills. 17 A man who is on the roof of his house must not take the time to go down and get his belongings from the house. 18 A man who is in the field must not go back to get his cloak. 19 How terrible it will be in those days for women who are pregnant and for mothers with little babies! 20 Pray to God that you will not have to run away during the winter or on a Sabbath! 21 For the trouble at that time will be far more terrible than any there has ever been, from the beginning of the world to this very day. Nor will there ever be anything like it again. 22 But God has already reduced the number of days; had he not done so, nobody would survive. For the sake of his chosen people, however, God will reduce the days.

23 "Then, if anyone says to you, 'Look, here is the Messiah!' or 'There he is!'—do not believe him. 24 For false Messiahs and false prophets will appear; they will perform great miracles and wonders in order to deceive even God's chosen people, if possible. 25 Listen! I have told you this ahead of time.

26 "Or, if people should tell you, 'Look, he is out in the desert!'—don't go there; or if they say, 'Look, he is hiding here!'—don't believe it. 27 For the Son of Man will come like the lightning which flashes across the whole sky from the east to the west.

28 "Wherever there is a dead body, the vultures will gather.

SECTION HEADING: "**The Awful Horror**." Translators will need to decide how to translate this term in verse 15, which is **the desolating sacrilege** in RSV, before translating the heading. If translators feel that a clause is necessary, they can say "Jesus tells about the awful horror (that will come)" or "The awful horror will come."

Matthew 24.15-22 is in close agreement with Mark 13.14-20, except for two alterations each in verses 15 and 20: (1) In verse 15 Matthew places the "desolating sacrilege" in "the holy place," in contrast to Mark's observation that it will be "set up where it ought not be"; and Matthew adds that this was "spoken of by the prophet Daniel." (2) The parallel to verse 20 in Matthew is in Mark "Pray that it may not happen in winter." Matthew replaces "that it may not happen" with "that your flight may not be," and expands "in winter" to "in winter or on a sabbath."

By shifting to "in the holy place" (a reference to the Jewish Temple), Matthew immediately relates this prophecy to Jesus' condemnation of the failure of worship in the Temple (23.38-39). And the expansion of "in winter" to "in winter or on the sabbath" suggests that Matthew is addressing a Christian community which is still scrupulously obeying the laws of the Sabbath.

24.15 RSV	TEV
"So when you see the desolating sacrilege spoken of by the prophet Daniel, standing in the holy place (let the reader understand),	"You will see 'The Awful Horror' of which the prophet Daniel spoke. It will be standing in the holy place." (Note to the reader: understand what this means!)

The desolating sacrilege is terminology taken from the book of Daniel (9.27; 11.31; 12.11), where it refers to the heathen altar which Antiochus Epiphanes set up in the Jerusalem temple in 167 B.C. (1 Maccabees 1.54-58). It is here applied to any forbidden object that may be erected in the Temple in order to defile it. Mft translates "the appalling Horror"; AT has "the dreadful desecration"; TEV renders "**The Awful Horror.**" Other translators will want to convey more accurately the actual meaning of the form, even if it makes for a slightly longer expression. Examples include "the forbidden thing (or, idol) that defiles the Temple" or "the shameful thing that makes God's things (or, altar) impure." In some African languages the idea of defilement is expressed as "spoil God's Temple."

This shameful thing was **spoken of by the prophet Daniel**. In many languages an active construction will be better, as with "the shameful thing that defiles God's temple and which the prophet Daniel spoke about." For some, "wrote about" will be better. Note, too, that TEV begins a new sentence to translate **standing in the holy place**. Another way to structure this is "You will see (standing) in the holy place the awful thing that defiles God's Temple. The prophet Daniel wrote about it."

Holy place has sometimes been rendered "God's place" or simply "the Temple."

Both Matthew and Mark (13.14) include the editorial comment, **let the reader understand**. Together with RSV and TEV, a number of other modern translations place the comment within parentheses (so NEB and NJB). Sometimes readers are addressed in third person, as in "Readers should be careful to understand what this means," but in other languages second person is better; for example "You readers . . . ."

24.16 RSV	TEV
then let those who are in Judea flee to the mountains;	"Then those who are in Judea must run away to the hills.

This and the next several verses give specific instructions for what one must do to escape the catastrophe that is going to strike Judea and Jerusalem.

Then may be translated "When this happens" or "When you see this happen."

Those who are in Judea is best taken to mean "those who live in Judea." **Judea** was discussed in 2.1.

The expression of RSV, **let . . . flee to the mountains**, is more clearly expressed by TEV's "**must run away to the hills.**" "Run to the hills to escape" is also good. This is a command in the third person, not a granting of permission.

24.17 RSV   TEV

let him who is on the housetop not go down to take what is in his house;	A man who is on the roof of his house must not take the time to go down and get his belongings from the house.

This verse is very similar in form to the Marcan parallel (13.15), except that Matthew has smoothed out the grammar, as he frequently does. The situation reflected is that of the Palestinian house with its flat roof, which was generally accessible by a stairway from the outside of the house. One must not leave the impression that the man is up there repairing the roof of his house. Translators may say "a person who happens to be on the roof of his house should not take the time to go down and take his possessions from his house."

24.18 RSV   TEV

and let him who is in the field not turn back to take his mantle.	A man who is in the field must not go back to get his cloak.

This also reflects the Palestinian situation in which a person normally lived in a town or village from which he would walk the distance to his field. The reader is warned not to take time to go back to town to get his belongings, but rather to run for safety immediately. Brc expresses this quite well: "Anyone who is at work in the field must not turn back to pick up his coat."

Mantle is first used in 5.40, where RSV translates "cloak."

24.19 RSV   TEV

And alas for those who are with child and for those who give suck in those days!	How terrible it will be in those days for women who are pregnant and for mothers with little babies!

This verse can surely be understood in any culture. Pregnant women (**those who are with child**) and women with small children (**those who give suck**) cannot move quickly or easily. Moreover, these statements reflect the fact that invading armies took particular delight in ripping open pregnant women and dashing the heads of babies against rocks.

Translators should use whatever expression is natural and polite for speaking of pregnant women, **those who are with child**. As for **those who give suck**, in some societies such a reference to a mother nursing her baby will be perfectly acceptable, but for others, this expression or its equivalent is not polite, and translators have to do something similar to TEV, "**mothers with little babies**."

Notice that TEV has moved the expression "in those days" near to the beginning of the sentence. This is more natural in English.

24.20 RSV	TEV
Pray that your flight may not be in winter or on a sabbath.	**Pray to God that you will not have to run away during the winter or on a Sabbath!**

TEV and many other translations render **pray** as "pray to God."

The problem with the noun **flight** is that for many modern readers the first meaning will be the departure of a plane, especially in the combination **that your flight may not be**. Therefore TEV has "that you will not have to run away," which is similar to NEB ("when you have to make your escape") and JB ("that you will not have to escape"). AT and Mft are worse than the literal rendering of RSV: "that you may not have to fly in winter."

Winter (so most translations) represents a noun which may also mean "rainy and stormy weather" (see 16.3; Acts 27.20). A number of commentators point out that winter is the time of swollen rivers, which would make escape difficult. But at least one commentator believes that the reference is rather to the scarcity of provisions during the winter season. In either case, all scholars agree that the comment somehow reflects the Palestinian situation. In fact, in areas where the season of **winter** is completely unknown, many translators say "the cold and rainy season."

According to traditional Jewish interpretation, the law of human life held priority over the laws which governed the sabbath. Therefore in the interest of protecting human life, the sabbath could be broken. Only the strictest interpretation of the Law would not allow for a person to run **on the sabbath** in order to escape death. That Matthew would add this note, hints at the high esteem that the Law must have held among his intended audience. **Sabbath** was discussed first at 12.1.

24.21 RSV	TEV
For then there will be great tribulation, such as has not been from the beginning of the world until now, no, and never will be.	**For the trouble at that time will be far more terrible than any there has ever been, from the beginning of the world to this very day. Nor will there ever be anything like it again.**

Tribulation (see verse 9) belongs to the vocabulary of apocalyptic literature; the noun is first used in 13.21. "Troubles" (TEV) and "suffering" are the most common ways to translate it. In some languages, however, it is not possible to use these terms in the abstract, and translators have to say "people will suffer more than at any other time since the beginning of the world."

No, and never will be may be translated "and nothing as terrible as this will ever happen again."

RSV   TEV

And if those days had not been shortened, no human being would be saved; but for the sake of the elect those days will be shortened.	But God has already reduced the number of days; had he not done so, nobody would survive. For the sake of his chosen people, however, God will reduce the days.

And if those days had not been shortened appears as an active construction in the Marcan parallel: "And if the Lord had not shortened the days" (13.20). For Mark "the Lord" is clearly a reference to God the Father rather than to Jesus. But Matthew probably realized how easily Mark's account could be misunderstood, and so it was a simple matter for him to shift to the passive. For Matthew's readers with their Jewish heritage, the understood agent of the passive verb would have been God: "But God has already reduced the number of those days."

Days . . . shortened may imply for some readers the cutting short of the length of each day. TEV's "**reduced the number of days**" resolves the problem. By shifting from **days** to "time," NEB ("If that time of troubles were not cut short") and NJB ("And if that time had not been shortened") suggest alternative possibilities of resolving the ambiguity. GECL is effective: "If God had not cut short the time of terror."

The sequence of verb tenses in this verse is problematic: **if those days had not been shortened** (as past tense) is followed by **those days will be shortened** (a future tense). In other words, the first half of the verse presupposes that what is announced in the second half has already taken place. Mark (13.20) uses the past tense in both halves of the saying. Perhaps what Matthew intends may be stated "If God had not already decided to cut short the number of days, then no one would survive. But God will cut short . . . ."

The elect is translated "his chosen people" by TEV (NEB "God's chosen"; Brc "God's chosen ones"; Phps "God's people"). The terminology is once again drawn from Jewish apocalyptic sources but here applied to the Christian community. Terrible suffering will be experienced in those times, but God's grace will see his people safely through. Possible renderings of the verse are, then, "If God had not decided to reduce the number of days of the suffering, no one would be able to survive. But for the sake of his chosen people, he will cut this period short," and "That period of suffering will be so terrible that no one would be able to survive unless God decided to shorten it. But for the sake of his chosen people, God will reduce the number of days of the suffering."

RSV   TEV

Then if any one says to you, 'Lo, here is the Christ!' or 'There he is!' do not believe it.	"Then, if anyone says to you, 'Look, here is the Messiah!' or 'There he is!'—do not believe him.

The culmination in the hostility against God and God's people will come in the form of the appearance of false Messiahs and false prophets. Verses 23-28 warn against being deceived by such pretenders.

Lo is not current English, and most translations do the same as TEV: **"Look."**

In some languages indirect speech will be natural, as in "Then if anyone tells you that some person in this place or someone in that place is the Messiah, do not believe it." Other translators will find it natural to reverse the order of the sentence, as in "So you must not believe people when they tell you 'Look, here is the Messiah' or 'There he is.' "

The Christ (so NJB, NIV) is translated **"the Messiah"** by TEV, NEB, and NAB. Scholarly opinion is unanimous that the term is here used in the technical sense of the promised savior king, a meaning which should come through clearly in translation. The term was first discussed at 1.12.

24.24   RSV   TEV

For false Christs and false prophets will arise and show great signs and wonders, so as to lead astray, if possible, even the elect. | For false Messiahs and false prophets will appear; they will perform great miracles and wonders in order to deceive even God's chosen people, if possible.

False Christs refers to people who say they are the Messiah but are not, which is precisely the way many translators render the phrase. **False prophets** will be similar. See also verse 11.

That the pretenders should perform **great signs and wonders** recalls the language of Deuteronomy 13.2-4, especially as it is found in the Septuagint. **Signs** translates the same noun used in 12.38 (see there). **Wonders** appears only here in Matthew; in the New Testament the word always occurs in the plural and in combination with **miracles** (Mark 13.22; John 4.48; Acts 2.19,22, 43; 4.30; 5.12; 6.8; 7.36; 14.3; 15.12; Rom 15.19; 2 Cor 12.12; 2 Thes 2.9; Heb 2.4). It is doubtful that any distinction should be sought between the two terms, but if there is a difference, then **wonders** may carry overtones of an evil omen. However, the fact that **signs and wonders** is a set phrase hints strongly that no distinction is to be made between the two terms. Translators should simply find two different ways of speaking about miracles performed to demonstrate something; for example, "great acts that show great power and amaze people."

Lead astray (so also in verses 4,5,11) occurs for the final time in this chapter.

Translators may need to reorder the verse to be more natural in their language; for example, "they will perform great acts of power that amaze people in order, if at all possible, to lead astray even God's chosen people."

24.25   RSV   TEV

Lo, I have told you beforehand. | Listen! I have told you this ahead of time.

Lo is the attention getter generally translated "Behold" in RSV (see 1.20). Mft and Brc do not represent it by a word in the translation; TEV has "**Listen,**" and GECL "Remember."

I have told you beforehand (Mft "I am telling you this beforehand") may also be translated "I am warning you about these things before they happen" (NEB, JB "I have forewarned you").

24.26　　　　RSV　　　　　　　　　　　　　TEV

So, if they say to you, 'Lo, he is in the wilderness,' do not go out; if they say, 'Lo, he is in the inner rooms,' do not believe it.	"Or, if people should tell you, 'Look, he is out in the desert!'—don't go there; or if they say, 'Look, he is hiding here!'—don't believe it.

Verses 26-28 are without parallel in the Marcan discourse on the last things, nor do they appear elsewhere in his Gospel. Luke, on the other hand, does share this material in common with Matthew, though he includes it in an entirely different context (17.23-24,37). Matthew utilizes that passage to intensify his warning for the believers of his day not to be led astray by false Messianic pretenders. When the true Messiah makes his sudden and final appearance on the scene, there will be no doubt. It will be as evident as a flash of lightning that lights up the entire sky.

If they say to you may require a singular form in some languages ("if someone says to you"), or it may be necessary to adopt an entirely different construction (for example, "if you should hear").

Lo (TEV "**Look**"): see verse 25.

The pronoun **he** may have to be "the Messiah." However, in the following verse it is the Son of Man who is referred to (obviously equated here with the Messiah), and some have wanted to use that term in this verse. That is certainly acceptable.

It was believed among some of the Jewish people that the Messiah would make a sudden appearance **in the wilderness**, much as Moses did. For comments on **wilderness**, see 3.1.

He is in the inner rooms is translated rather differently by TEV (**"he is hiding here"**) and NJB ("he is in some hiding place"). **Inner rooms** is the plural form of the noun used in 6.6 (see comments there). The meaning is not altogether certain, though it may reflect the Jewish belief that the Messiah would remain in hiding until he made his sudden appearance (see John 7.27). Some translators will have "he is indoors here." Brc has "he is in the secret rooms."

Do not believe it may need to be translated either "don't believe them" or "don't believe what they say."

24.27　　　　RSV　　　　　　　　　　　　　TEV

For as the lightning comes from the east and shines as far as the west,	For the Son of Man will come like the lightning which flashes across the

so will be the coming of the Son of man. **whole sky from the east to the west.**

The Son of man is identified with "the Christ" (Messiah) of verse 23. Neither here nor in 16.20 does Jesus deny that he is the Messiah, but in both passages he specifically reinterprets the title in light of the Son of Man figure (see 16.21-28). This same reinterpretation is made during the course of the trial. To the question of the high priest, "Tell us if you are the Christ, the Son of God" (26.63), Jesus answers, "You will see the Son of man seated at the right hand of Power, and coming on the clouds of heaven" (26.64). For a discussion of **Son of man**, see 8.20.

For as lightning comes from the east and shines as far as the west appears in a slightly different form in Luke (see 17.24). Two emphases are made: the coming of the Son of Man will be a universal event to be witnessed by everyone, and it will take place suddenly.

The translation of **the coming of the Son of man** can be something of a problem. In some languages it is necessary to say from where he will come, and sometimes where he will come to as well. One way to solve this is to say "will come from heaven (or, from the skies)," and another is to say "come to the world." An alternative is to say "will appear."

Note how TEV has restructured the verse. Another possibility is "For when the Son of Man comes, it will be just like the lightning that flashes across the whole sky."

24.28   RSV   TEV

Wherever the body is, there the eagles^z will be gathered together.   **"Wherever there is a dead body, the vultures will gather.**

^{z} Or *vultures*

The saying of Jesus contained in this verse most probably reflects a proverbial saying familiar to the people of his day. Its purpose is to refute the arguments of persons who claimed that the Son of Man (or Messiah) had already arrived, and that he could be found in such and such a place.

The Greek word used here for **eagle** may also mean "vulture" or "buzzard" (RSV footnote), which is also true for the word used for **eagle** in the Hebrew Old Testament. But the meaning of "vulture" is better suited to the context.

The argument of the parable and its application is as follows: Just as surely as vultures flock about a corpse, so the coming of the Son of Man will be recognized by everyone. Therefore to ask when or where he will make his appearance is a senseless and useless question. When it happens, there will be no doubt.

TEV has rendered **body** as "dead body," and Brc has "carrion." Another way to render the sentence is "The dead body can be found because that is where the vultures are gathered" or "The location of the dead body is known because of the vultures there."

24.29-31

RSV	TEV
	The Coming of the Son of Man
29 "Immediately after the tribulation of those days the sun will be darkened, and the moon will not give its light, and the stars will fall from heaven, and the powers of the heavens will be shaken; 30 then will appear the sign of the Son of man in heaven, and then all the tribes of the earth will mourn, and they will see the Son of man coming on the clouds of heaven with power and great glory; 31 and he will send out his angels with a loud trumpet call, and they will gather his elect from the four winds, from one end of heaven to the other.	29 "Soon after the trouble of those days, the sun will grow dark, the moon will no longer shine, the stars will fall from heaven, and the powers in space will be driven from their courses. 30 Then the sign of the Son of Man will appear in the sky; and all the peoples of earth will weep as they see the Son of Man coming on the clouds of heaven with power and great glory. 31 The great trumpet will sound, and he will send out his angels to the four corners of the earth, and they will gather his chosen people from one end of the world to the other.

SECTION HEADING: **"The Coming of the Son of Man"** may need to be expressed as a short sentence; for example, "What will happen when the Son of Man comes" or "What will happen at the end of the age." See verse 3 for a discussion of both of these terms.

24.29 RSV	TEV
"Immediately after the tribulation of those days the sun will be darkened, and the moon will not give its light, and the stars will fall from heaven, and the powers of the heavens will be shaken;	**"Soon after the trouble of those days, the sun will grow dark, the moon will no longer shine, the stars will fall from heaven, and the powers in space will be driven from their courses.**

Matthew once again takes up the Marcan sequence of events. But the transitional marker **Immediately** differs from "In those days" of the Marcan parallel (13.24). This adverb is found thirteen times in Matthew's Gospel, though only once in Mark. However, an adverb of the same meaning but with a slightly different spelling is used forty-one times in Mark and only five times in Matthew. Therefore the use of "immediately" as a transitional marker is actually much more a feature of Mark's Gospel than it is of Matthew's Gospel, which adds importance to its usage here.

Tribulation (see 13.21) was earlier used in this chapter in verses 9 and 21. TEV translates **"trouble"**; one may also use a phrase such as "those terrible times" or "those terrible things have happened." Care should be taken that the reader does not interpret this as a reference to verse 28! It can be translated either as "Immediately after those times of suffering" or as "Immediately after that time when people will suffer so much."

The cosmic events depicted in this verse represent typical Jewish figures of speech frequently used to describe the universal and world-shaking significance of what God will do at the end of history. Note, for example, Isaiah 13.9-10; 34.4. This is not dissimilar to what Peter proclaimed at Pentecost (Acts 2.17-20, especially verses 19-20).

The sun will be darkened: the problem with the passive is that in many languages one must indicate the agent involved: "God will make the sun turn dark, and the moon will no longer shine." TEV avoids the direct use of a passive: **"the sun will grow dark."**

The powers of the heavens are identified by the TOB footnote as "the stars and the celestial powers." In the ancient world there was thought to be a correspondence between stars and the invisible celestial powers that they represented. And so what happened to the visible stars was also attacking the invisible powers that controlled them. NEB translates "the celestial powers will be shaken." One may also translate as a summary statement: "God will shake loose everything in the skies."

24.30   RSV   TEV

then will appear the sign of the Son of man in heaven, and then all the tribes of the earth will mourn, and they will see the Son of man coming on the clouds of heaven with power and great glory;	Then the sign of the Son of Man will appear in the sky; and all the peoples of earth will weep as they see the Son of Man coming on the clouds of heaven with power and great glory.

The sign of the Son of man may be interpreted in at least two different ways: (1) The phrase may mean "the sign which is the Son of man," thereby identifying **the Son of man** with **the sign**. In support of this interpretation are "the sign of the prophet Jonah" (12.39) and "the sign of Jonah" (16.4), where "the sign" is equated with Jonah himself. With regard to this interpretation, the TOB footnote states "The sign is probably the Son of Man himself."

(2) Other scholars argue that **the sign** and **the Son of man** are not to be identified. One commentator concedes that though this identification may fit with verse 3, it is practically impossible to accept on the basis of verse 30, where the Son of Man apparently appears after the sign is seen. Therefore a solution must be sought in another direction, and the clue is said to be the observation that Matthew alone mentions **the sign** and "the great trumpet" (verse 31). In Old Testament warfare trumpets and military standards (signs) are frequently mentioned together (Isa 18.3; Jer 4.21; 6.1; 51.27). Similarly when Old Testament writers mention the day of the Lord, they attribute to it a standard of its own and a trumpet blast (Isa 27.13). And among the Jews who settled in Qumran, both trumpets and standards played a significant role. Following this line of argument one may then conclude that the coming of the Son of Man to establish God's kingdom will be signaled by the raising of his standard and by the blast of a great trumpet.

Most translators will follow this second interpretation of **the sign of the Son of man** but will not make the sign explicit. Examples are "then people will see in the sky the thing which shows that the Son of Man is coming" and "then there will appear in the sky the thing that will make people know the Son of Man is coming."

Translators should continue to render **Son of man** as in 8.20.

In heaven will be misunderstood by many readers as the place of God's abode; "**in the sky**" (TEV) signifies the region where the sun, moon, and stars are located, and clarifies what is meant by the phrase.

All the tribes of the earth will mourn derives from Zechariah 12.10-14, where **tribes** is used of the Jewish people. But for Matthew the quotation is enlarged to mean "All the peoples of the world" (NEB).

Mourn translates a verb which in the active form means "cut" or "cut off" (as in 21.8); when used in the middle voice it means "beat" (one's breast as an act of mourning), the meaning it has here and in 11.17. NJB ("beat their breasts") and NAB ("will strike their breasts") both focus upon the action itself without interpreting its significance. Most translations do it the other way around; they translate as "mourn" or "lament" without reference to the act of beating one's breast. GECL 1st edition renders "will cry out in fear," which is probably the best way to render it. Matthew is obviously describing the response of people who have not looked with anticipation for the coming of the Son of Man.

On the clouds of heaven differs from both "in clouds" (Mark 13.26) and "in a cloud" (Luke 21.27).

With power and great glory (so Luke 21.27) also differs from Mark ("with great power and glory" [13.26]). To come **with power** does not refer to the speed of his approach or the manner of coming, but rather to the fact that he will be seen to have great power as he comes. **Glory** in this context can mean radiance or splendor, but it is more likely that it refers to majesty. In either case, **glory** is something associated with God. Thus **with power and great glory** can be rendered by a short sentence: "He will have power and the great majesty of God" or "As he comes, people will see his power and the great splendor he has from God."

24.31	RSV	TEV
	and he will send out his angels with a loud trumpet call, and they will gather his elect from the four winds, from one end of heaven to the other.	The great trumpet will sound, and he will send out his angels to the four corners of the earth, and they will gather his chosen people from one end of the world to the other.

Neither Mark nor Luke mention **with a loud trumpet call**. Both this literal rendering and TEV ("**the great trumpet will sound**") may be impossible for languages where trumpets cannot "sound" of themselves. One may then translate "When an angel blows a loud blast on a trumpet" or ". . . makes a blast on a great trumpet." TEV uses the definite article, "**the great trumpet**," but since it has not been referred to previously, perhaps the indefinite "a great trumpet" is better.

His angels: Mark 13.27 has "**the angels.**" **Angels** was discussed at 1.20.

His elect are "God's chosen people," though the context offers no further explanation.

Heaven is best understood as "sky." The people of the ancient world thought of the sky as a dome which was positioned over the flat earth, and this is the basis for TEV, "**from one end of the world to the other.**"

From the four winds, from one end of heaven to the other (Mark 13.27, "from the four winds, from the ends of the earth to the ends of heaven") may be compressed and translated "from all over the world." GECL translates the verse as "When the great trumpet sounds, he will send forth his angels in every direction in order to bring together from all over those people whom he has chosen."

According to Matthew the subject of the verb **gather** is **they** ("his angels"), whereas in Mark the subject is "he" ("the Son of man").

24.32-35

RSV	TEV
	The Lesson of the Fig Tree
32 "From the fig tree learn its lesson: as soon as its branch becomes tender and puts forth its leaves, you know that summer is near. 33 So also, when you see all these things, you know that he is near, at the very gates. 34 Truly, I say to you, this generation will not pass away till all these things take place. 35 Heaven and earth will pass away, but my words will not pass away.	32 "Let the fig tree teach you a lesson. When its branches become green and tender and it starts putting out leaves, you know that summer is near. 33 In the same way, when you see all these things, you will know that the time is near, ready to begin.ʷ 34 Remember that all these things will happen before the people now living have all died. 35 Heaven and earth will pass away, but my words will never pass away.

ʷ the time is near, ready to begin; *or* he is near, ready to come.

SECTION HEADING: **"The Lesson of the Fig Tree."** Sometimes this is rendered "What people can learn from the fig tree" or "Jesus tells what people should learn from a fig tree."

Matthew's wording of these few verses is in close agreement with that of Mark (13.28-31). The only substantial difference is to be found in verse 33, where Matthew alters Mark's "these things" (13.29) to "all these things." The parable itself has been given at least two contrasting interpretations: (1) If applied to the coming of the Son of Man, its function is to encourage both patience and certainty. (2) If applied to the destruction of Jerusalem, it has an entirely different message. It then serves to draw an analogy between the putting out of leaves by a fig tree and the events of the times. Just as new leaves on the fig tree signal the appearance of figs, so the approach of enemy armies signals the imminent destruction of Jerusalem. Therefore the destruction of Jerusalem (a historical event of cause and effect) may be predicted with relative certainty, but the coming of the Son of Man (a supernatural event within God's decision alone) cannot be predicted (verses 36-44).

24.32   RSV   TEV

"From the fig tree learn its lesson: as soon as its branch becomes   **"Let the fig tree teach you a lesson. When its branches become**

tender and puts forth its leaves, you know that summer is near.	green and tender and it starts putting out leaves, you know that summer is near.

Lesson is literally "parable" (see 13.3) and is represented as such in NJB: "Take the fig tree as a parable." However, the meaning is here extended to mean "something to be learned" or "lesson" (NEB, NIV). Both AT and TEV translate **From the fig tree learn a lesson** as **"Let the fig tree teach you a lesson."** But many languages will not allow for a tree to "teach"; thus the restructuring of NEB will be more natural: "Learn a lesson from the fig-tree." One may even translate "Look at the fig tree, and see what you can learn from it."

Fig tree was discussed at 21.19. Note that here the definite article **the** does not mean that Jesus is referring to one specific fig tree but rather to fig trees in general. In languages where the translation is "fig trees," plurals will be used in the rest of the verse, so that **its leaves** will be "their leaves," and so forth.

Becomes tender (TEV **"become green and tender"**) translates an adjective which is used of the young shoots that come out on the branches. Similarly **puts forth its leaves** means to put out foliage. The two expressions may be translated as a single expression; for example, NEB translates "When the tender shoots appear." Both Brc and GECL have "When the sap rises in its branches." One may also translate "When the tree begins to bud." Of course, in many languages it will be perfectly natural to render both expressions; as for example, "begin to bud and put out new leaves."

People have different ways of referring to seasons. The English **summer is near** may have to be "it will soon be summer" or "the summer season will soon start." Summer is the hot season, but the most important feature in this context is that it is the season when plants and trees renew their growth. Translators should use whatever term in their language refers to this season.

24.33 RSV	TEV
So also, when you see all these things, you know that he is near, at the very gates.	In the same way, when you see all these things, you will know that the time is near, ready to begin.^{w}
	^{w}the time is near, ready to begin *or* he is near, ready to come.

So also marks the comparison. In the same way people can tell from the first shoots of green on trees after the winter that summer is coming, so Jesus' followers will know from all the signs he has just talked about in the previous verses that the Son of Man is soon to come. TEV **"In the same way"** is a good model.

The pronoun **you** is emphatic in the Greek sentence construction: "And as for you, when you see . . . ."

All these things may refer to all the events of verses 15-31, or else the reference may be limited to either the events of verses 15-28 or those of verses 29-31. But the greening of the branches and the putting forth of leaves are both preliminary to the main event, which is the coming of the summer (verse 32). Thus it is hardly likely that **all these things** could possibly include or be limited to the coming of the Son of Man (verses 29-31), which is the main event in the series of end-time happenings. The reference is then best taken to include only the preliminary events of verses 15-28, and its goal is to warn the believers to act wisely when they realize that the fall of Jerusalem is very close. In the translation itself, however, it may be impossible to make the reference specific. "Those things I told you about" may be the best translation one can render.

He is near may also be translated **"the time is near"** (see TEV). The problem is that the Greek text is without expressed subject, thereby leaving open the possibility for either interpretation. As one may expect, the translations vary in the way in which they handle the text: NEB has "that the end is near, at the very door" with a marginal reading "that he is near," while JB has "that he is near, at the very gates," with a footnote "the Son of Man coming to establish his Kingdom."

Translators who accept the interpretation he is near may have either "that he is waiting nearby to come" or "he is nearby, like someone at the gate waiting to come in." Most translators, however, will follow the interpretation of TEV, **"the time is near,"** and translate either "the time when this age will end is very close" or "the time for the new age is near, ready to begin."

24.34 RSV   TEV

Truly, I say to you, this generation will not pass away till all these things take place.

Remember that all these things will happen before the people now living have all died.

Truly, I say to you (TEV **"Remember"**): see discussion at 5.18.

This generation will not pass away is transformed into a positive statement by several translations: "all these events will happen within the lifetime of this generation" (Brc), "the present generation will live to see it all" (NEB), and "this generation will experience all these things" (GECL). Differences of opinion exist with regard to the meaning of (1) **this generation** and (2) **all these things take place**. NIV translates **this generation** literally but follows with a footnote, "Or race." And one New Testament scholar believes that "Matthew means not just the first generation after Jesus but all the generations of Judaism that reject him." However, there is no linguistic evidence to substantiate either of these conclusions, and they must be brushed aside as attempts to avoid the obvious meaning. In its original setting the reference was solely to Jesus' own contemporaries, though in the context of Matthew's Gospel it seems to have been expanded to include as well the generation of his readers. TEV, **"the people now living,"** represents a widely accepted interpretation of **this generation. Will not pass away** then means "these people will not die."

All these things take place is accompanied by a footnote in NJB: "This statement refers to the destruction of Jerusalem and not to the end of the world." Other scholars believe that the reference is to the final events of history, including the coming of the Son of Man. No final decision is possible, though the weight of evidence supports the judgment expressed in NJB; if translations must be specific, this is the best alternative, but they should leave it general if at all possible.

Note that TEV has reversed the order of the verse, which does change the focus of the verse somewhat. However, translators should follow whichever order seems most natural in their language.

24.35

RSV

TEV

Heaven and earth will pass away, but my words will not pass away.

Heaven and earth will pass away, but my words will never pass away.

The interpretation of this verse should cause no difficulty. GECL very effectively omits the verb from the second clause ("Heaven and earth shall pass away, but not my words"), but many languages will require the repetition of the verb in the second clause.

Heaven and earth is sometimes rendered as "the earth and the sky" or as "all the universe." **Will pass away** may be translated literally in some languages, but in others will be "will no longer exist" or "will disappear."

As for **my words**, often translated as "my word," sometimes a positive expression is necessary, such as "will always exist," but most translators prefer to retain the negative form and say "my words will never cease to exist." **My words** may also be translated "what I say," "what I teach," or "my teachings."

24.36-44

RSV

TEV

No One Knows the Day and Hour

36 "But of that day and hour no one knows, not even the angels of heaven, nor the Son,*a* but the Father only. 37 As were the days of Noah, so will be the coming of the Son of man. 38 For as in those days before the flood they were eating and drinking, marrying and giving in marriage, until the day when Noah entered the ark, 39 and they did not know until the flood came and swept them all away, so will be the coming of the Son of man. 40 Then two men will be in the field; one is taken and one is left. 41 Two women will be grinding at the mill; one is taken and one is left. 42 Watch therefore, for you do not know on what day your Lord is coming. 43 But know this, that if the householder had known in what part of the night the thief was coming, he would have watched and would not have let his house be broken into. 44 Therefore you also must be ready; for the Son of man is coming at an hour you do not expect.

36 "No one knows, however, when that day and hour will come— neither the angels in heaven nor the Son;*x* the Father alone knows. 37 The coming of the Son of Man will be like what happened in the time of Noah. 38 In the days before the flood people ate and drank, men and women married, up to the very day Noah went into the boat; 39 yet they did not realize what was happening until the flood came and swept them all away. That is how it will be when the Son of Man comes. 40 At that time two men will be working in a field: one will be taken away, the other will be left behind. 41 Two women will be at a mill grinding meal: one will be taken away, the other will be left behind. 42 Watch out, then, because you do not know what day your Lord will come. 43 If the owner of a house knew the time when the thief would come, you can be sure that he would stay awake and not let the thief break into his house. 44 So then, you also must always be ready, because the Son of Man will come at an hour when you are not expecting him.

a Other ancient authorities omit *nor the Son*

> *x Some manuscripts do not have* nor the
> Son.

SECTION HEADING: **"No One Knows the Day and Hour"** may have to be expanded to "No one knows when the Son of Man will come" or "No one knows when these things will happen."

These verses, together with the parable that follows (verses 45-51), serve a double function: (1) to warn the readers that the Son of Man may come at any moment; and (2) to encourage them to live wisely in the light of that inevitable day of judgment. Matthew has considerably reshaped this final section of his discourse, drawing from both Mark and the source common to him and Luke.

24.36   RSV   TEV

"But of that day and hour no one knows, not even the angels of heaven, nor the Son,*a* but the Father only.

"No one knows, however, when that day and hour will come—neither the angels in heaven nor the Son;*x* the Father alone knows.

a Other ancient authorities omit *nor the Son*

xSome manuscripts do not have nor the Son.

In the text the object, **of that day and hour**, precedes the subject and verb, **no one knows**. But this may not be natural, and most translators have "But no one knows the day and hour when that will happen" or "But no one knows exactly when all this will take place." It may be helpful to then start a new sentence such as "Even the angels of heaven don't know, nor even the Son," or possibly "Even the angels of heaven and the Son do not know the time." Some repeat the verb: "Even the angels of heaven don't know; even the Son does not know."

As both RSV and TEV indicate, **nor the Son** is lacking in some Greek manuscripts, though the phrase is found in the best representatives of the standard text types. It is possible that the words were added on the basis of Mark 13.32, but TC-GNT believes it more probable that they were omitted "because of the doctrinal difficulty they present." In addition, the Greek sentence structure suggests that the phrase was originally there. Nevertheless, the UBS Greek New Testament rates its decision "C," indicating "a considerable degree of doubt" regarding what may have been the original reading. Almost all modern translations include the phrase, and some (NEB, NAB, Lu) do so without even indicating the alternative possibility.

Of course, in many languages **the Son** cannot stand alone, and a parent must be specified. In this case "the Son of God" is probably best.

But the Father only: in the Greek text the adjective **only** is made emphatic by Matthew, though not by Mark. However, the difference is difficult to represent in translation, and it does not come through in RSV, for example, which renders the Marcan parallel as "but only the Father" (13.32). Again, it may be helpful to add the verb: "but only the Father knows" or, to convey also the emphasis of the text, "but it is only the Father who knows" or "but the Father knows, and he alone." As elsewhere in the Gospel, **Father** is often rendered "God the Father."

Luke omits this verse and concludes his discourse on the last things with a passage (21.34,36) that has no parallel in either Mark or Matthew. Mark concludes his discourse by following this verse with sayings (13.33-37) that are found in Matthew 25.14-15b; 24.42; 25.13.

24.37-38   RSV   TEV

37 As were the days of Noah, so will be the coming of the Son of man. 38 For as in those days before the flood they were eating and drinking, marrying and giving in marriage, until the day when Noah entered the ark,

37 The coming of the Son of Man will be like what happened in the time of Noah. 38 In the days before the flood people ate and drank, men and women married, up to the very day Noah went into the boat;

Although verses 37-41 are without parallel in the discourses of either Mark or Luke, Luke includes this material earlier (17.26-27, 34-35), combining it with the illustration of Lot's experience in Sodom (17.28-29).

TEV's restructuring of verse 37 intimates that the contrast is between what happened to the people of Noah's day and what will happen to the people who are on earth when the Son of Man comes. Such an interpretation finds support in verse 39: "... **the flood came and swept them all away.**" However, it seems more likely that the intention of the saying is to indicate that the affairs of daily life (**eating and drinking, marrying and giving in marriage**) continued up to the moment that Noah entered the boat. The message is then that judgment falls, not because people are engaged in particularly evil activities, but rather because they conduct the normal affairs of life without consideration of the approaching divine judgment. Accordingly NEB translates "As things were in Noah's day, so will they be ..."; GECL has "When the Son of Man comes, it will be as it was during the time of Noah. 38 At that time before the great flood came they ate and drank and married as usual ...." Brc apparently allows for either or both interpretations: "What happened in the time of Noah will happen again at the coming of the Son of Man."

For **the coming of the Son of man**, see verse 27 and comments.

Complete understanding of this verse requires some knowledge of the Old Testament story of Noah, his ark, and the flood. But much of this information cannot be put into the translation itself and can only appear in a short footnote or the Glossary. What translators can do in the text is, if necessary, render the **flood** as "the time when God covered the whole world with water" or "the time when the whole world was flooded," and render **the ark** as "the boat Noah built" or "the boat that God told Noah to build so he could escape the flood." But this was a boat big enough to carry many animals as well as several people, so translators should use a term that is appropriate.

The pronoun **they** is usually translated as "**people**" (TEV).

Translators should be careful not to render the activities **eating and drinking, marrying and giving in marriage** so that readers think that was what people were doing at the actual moment of the flood, but rather that people continued with these kinds of activities as usual. See the GECL example in the second paragraph of this discussion.

For **marrying and giving in marriage**, see discussion at 22.30.

24.39   RSV   TEV

and they did not know until the flood came and swept them all away, so will be the coming of the Son of man.

yet they did not realize what was happening until the flood came and swept them all away. That is how it will be when the Son of Man comes.

They did not know (TEV "**they did not realize what was happening**"): most languages will doubtless require the explicit mention of an object after the verb know: "they knew nothing until the flood came" (NEB) or "they suspected nothing" (NJB).

Swept them all away can be rendered "carried them all away" or "destroyed them all."

The coming of the Son of man may necessitate restructuring similar to TEV: "when the Son of Man comes."

The comparison **so will be** of the text is translated "**That is how it will be**" by TEV. Some translators will find they need to reverse the order, as in "When the Son of Man comes, it will be just like that."

24.40   RSV   TEV

Then two men will be in the field; one is taken and one is left.

At that time two men will be working in a field: one will be taken away, the other will be left behind.

Verses 40-41 contain two illustrations which show that life will continue as usual until the time when the Son of man comes. In the words of one scholar, the emphasis is upon "the sharp cleavage caused by the coming of the Son of Man, rather than the unexpectedness of the event."

The expression **two men** does not refer to two specific men but is really just an example of how things will be. Translators may say "At that time, if there are two men working in the field, one will be taken and one will be left."

One is taken and one is left may require restructuring in the active: "The Son of man will take one of them away, but he will leave the other." Or ". . . one of them with him, but he will not take the other one."

The use of the present tense (**is taken** . . . **is left**) in verses 40-41 reflects narrative style and simultaneously emphasizes the absolute certainty of Jesus' words. Luke (17.34-35) prefers the future, as in fact do most translations. See the examples in the discussion of these verses.

24.41 RSV	TEV
Two women will be grinding at the mill; one is taken and one is left.	Two women will be at a mill grinding meal: one will be taken away, the other will be left behind.

In Palestine it was customary for two women to work together when grinding at the mill. The mill referred to here was the hand mill, not the large mill that was worked by donkey-power (see 18.6). Some languages will require an object: "grinding grain at the mill." If a choice of grain must be made, then in the Palestinian setting it would have been wheat or barley. In fact, in some languages where mills are not too well known and grinding is usually done on smooth stones, if it is done at all, it may be necessary to say simply "two women will be grinding their grain." As with verse 40, since this is an illustration, a translation can use a sentence such as "If two women are grinding grain together (at a mill)."

24.42 RSV	TEV
Watch therefore, for you do not know on what day your Lord is coming.	Watch out, then, because you do not know what day your Lord will come.

Verses 42-44 stress the need for watchfulness, since no one knows when the Son of Man will come. **Watch** is used here for the first time in the Gospel of Matthew; it is found also in verse 43 and in 25.13; 26.38,40,41. The basic meaning of the word is "keep awake," though it is frequently used in a figurative sense of "be on guard" or "be watchful." Whether translation should follow the order of the text, **Watch therefore**, or reverse it, as in "Therefore you should be on your guard," will depend on the receptor language.

What day is "what hour" in the Lukan tradition (12.39). However, the meaning is the same, and one may even render it as "when" or "at what time." In 25.13 Matthew combines the two: ". . . you know neither the day nor the hour."

Your Lord is an interesting shift from "the Son of man" (verses 39,44). It is quite possible that **your Lord** was introduced by Matthew under the influence of Mark 13.34-35, which gives a brief parable about "the lord of the house" who returns without warning to check up on his servants. Matthew makes specific application to the Christian community: "the lord of the house" has now become **your Lord** in the absolute sense.

Lord has been discussed elsewhere in this Handbook. See particularly 8.2. Here it occurs with the second person **your**. The fact that Jesus is referring to himself has led some translators to use first person, as in "I who am your Lord." But as is the case with Son of Man, discussed at 8.20, if at all possible translators should not use "I."

24.43   RSV   TEV

But know this, that if the household-   If the owner of a house knew the
er had known in what part of the   time when the thief would come, you
night the thief was coming, he would   can be sure that he would stay
have watched and would not have let   awake and not let the thief break into
his house be broken into.   his house.

But know this (TEV "**you can be sure that**") appears in an emphatic position in the Greek sentence structure. GECL adopts an idiomatic expression meaning "keep this clearly in mind"; NEB has "Remember," and NJB "You may be quite sure of this."

Householder is also used in the parable of the weeds, 13.24-30 (see also Mark 13.34-35). The noun was earlier translated "master of the house" in 10.25 (see also its usage in 13.27,52; 20.1,11; 21.33). Here "the head of the household" or "the owner of the house" may be appropriate.

What part of the night is literally "what watch" (see comment at 14.25). Some translators say "when during the night" or "what time of night."

Watched here means "kept watch" or "kept guard." It can also be "stayed awake."

Be broken into is literally "be dug through," describing the way that a thief would dig though the sun-dried brick wall of a Palestinian house. For some cultures this imagery may be retained, but for others it will not be understood. This passive construction may have to be active, as in the sentence "he would not have let anyone (or, that thief) break into his house." The expression does not necessarily mean that the thief actually breaks down the walls of the house, but it does refer to some kind of forced entry, as a thief would do.

24.44   RSV   TEV

Therefore you also must be ready;   So then, you also must always be
for the Son of man is coming at an   ready, because the Son of Man will
hour you do not expect.   come at an hour when you are not
                                          expecting him.

In Greek the pronoun **you** is expressed explicitly and placed in emphatic position. This is significant because Greek does not require the explicit use of the pronoun in instances when a form of the verb indicates the subject.

The context clearly implies that **be ready** has the more specific meaning of "**always be ready**" (TEV) or "be ready at any time." NJB has "stand ready," which conveys the same impact. In some languages it is necessary to say what the disciples must be ready for. A good sentence then is "Therefore you must be ready for the Son of Man's coming, because he will come when you do not expect him."

At an hour you do not expect (TEV "when you are not expecting him") is the real focus of interest in the last half of the verse.

24.45-51

RSV

TEV

The Faithful or
the Unfaithful Servant

45 "Who then is the faithful and wise servant, whom his master has set over his household, to give them their food at the proper time? 46 Blessed is that servant whom his master when he comes will find so doing. 47 Truly, I say to you, he will set him over all his possessions. 48 But if that wicked servant says to himself, 'My master is delayed,' 49 and begins to beat his fellow servants, and eats and drinks with the drunken, 50 the master of that servant will come on a day when he does not expect him and at an hour he does not know, 51 and will punish[b] him, and put him with the hypocrites; there men will weep and gnash their teeth.

45 "Who, then, is a faithful and wise servant? He is the one that his master has placed in charge of the other servants to give them their food at the proper time. 46 How happy that servant is if his master finds him doing this when he comes home! 47 Indeed, I tell you, the master will put that servant in charge of all his property. 48 But if he is a bad servant, he will tell himself that his master will not come back for a long time, 49 and he will begin to beat his fellow servants and to eat and drink with drunkards. 50 Then that servant's master will come back one day when the servant does not expect him and at a time he does not know. 51 The master will cut him in pieces[y] and make him share the fate of the hypocrites. There he will cry and gnash his teeth.

[b] Or *cut him in pieces*

[y] cut him in pieces; *or* throw him out.

SECTION HEADING: "**The Faithful or the Unfaithful Servant**" is not always easy to translate. Some translators replace "**or**" with "and." Others make a short sentence such as "Servants must be faithful (or, obedient)."

Similarly to what he did in 21.29–22.14, Matthew once again introduces a series of three parables (24.45–25.30) without the benefit even of a transitional marker. The message which unites the parables is the urgency for faithfulness and readiness. The first in the trio is also found in Luke, but in an entirely different context (12.35-40), where it explains the parable of the watchful servants (12.35-40). The parable of 25.14-30 is also utilized by Luke, but in a quite different context and with significant variations of detail (19.12-27).

24.45   RSV

TEV

"Who then is the faithful and wise servant, whom his master has set over his household, to give them their food at the proper time?

"Who, then, is a faithful and wise servant? He is the one that his master has placed in charge of the other servants to give them their food at the proper time.

For many readers this verse will prove an impossible construction because it asks a question which is never really answered. TEV attempts to remove the difficulty by transforming the difficult rhetorical question into a question followed by its answer: "**Who, then . . . servant? He is the one . . . at the proper time.**" GECL accomplishes the same effect by altering the question form to an exhortation: "Then be like the faithful and wise servant to whom his master gave the responsibility of supervising the entire household and of giving each one of them his daily rations at the proper time." Another good model is Brc: "Suppose there is a dependable and sensible servant."

For the first time in this Gospel, the adjective **faithful** is used; it will be used again in 25.21,23. Various translations render it "obedient" or "dependable."

Wise is previously used in 7.24 and 10.16; it will be used four more times in chapter 25 (verses 2,4,8,9). This adjective is not found in either Mark or John, and it is used only twice by Luke (12.42; 16.8). Thus it must be considered a unique emphasis of Matthew's Gospel. Common translations include "sensible" and "intelligent."

To be **set over** means to be in charge of.

Household is used only here in the New Testament. In Greek papyri of that era it may mean either "household" or "family." Luke uses another collective noun which means "servants" (12.42). One may translate "other servants in his household."

Food translates a noun which literally means "nourishment"; see comment at 3.4. The word that is used in the Lukan parallel (12.42) appears only once in the New Testament; it literally means "allowance of grain" or "allowance of food."

24.46   RSV   TEV

Blessed is that servant whom his master when he comes will find so doing.

How happy that servant is if his master finds him doing this when he comes home!

Blessed translates the same adjective used in the Beatitudes (see comment at 5.3).

So doing is translated "**doing this**" by TEV. The full meaning is "doing the work that his master has assigned him." NEB translates "at his task" (similarly GECL), and JB has "at this employment." Brc translates by a verb construction: "engaged on that very task."

The verse may have to be restructured slightly; for example, "Things will be very good for that servant if the master comes and finds him doing that work (he assigned him)."

24.47   RSV   TEV

Truly, I say to you, he will set him over all his possessions.

Indeed, I tell you, the master will put that servant in charge of all his property.

Truly, I say to you: see comment at 5.18.

Possessions (see 19.21 and 25.14) may be used of anything that a person owns; NJB has "everything he owns," while others have "**property**" (TEV, NEB, NAB, Phps).

Verses 45-47 need to be translated together if the passage is to be natural. One possibility is:

> Suppose there is a servant who is loyal and obedient so that his master puts him in charge of the rest of the household and tells him to give them all their food supplies at the proper time. If the master comes and finds him doing this work, then things will be well for that servant because the master will put him in charge of all his property.

24.48   RSV   TEV

But if that wicked servant says to himself, 'My master is delayed,'   **But if he is a bad servant, he will tell himself that his master will not come back for a long time,**

Wicked in the Greek is also used in 21.41 (see comments and translation there) and 27.23 ("evil"), but nowhere else in the Gospel. There is a slight translation problem here because the previous verses have been describing a good servant, and now the phrase **that wicked servant** seems to refer to the same person. TEV has "**If he is a bad servant,**" and Brc has "But, if a bad servant says to himself."

To himself is literally "in his heart." However, in biblical psychology the "heart" is primarily the place of thought rather than of emotion, though sometimes it may also denote the entire person. GECL translates "But if he is untrustworthy and tells himself . . . ."

My master is delayed, as RSV indicates, represents direct discourse of the Greek text. TEV shifts to indirect: "**that his master will not come back for a long time.**"

Delayed translates a verb which may mean either "stay away for a long time" or "take a long time in doing something." **Is delayed** implies that circumstances had come about which had caused the man to stay longer than he had originally intended, but this is not necessarily the meaning of the Greek text. Brc seems to be more accurate: "I need not expect my master for a long time yet."

24.49   RSV   TEV

and begins to beat his fellow servants, and eats and drinks with the drunken,   **and he will begin to beat his fellow servants and to eat and drink with drunkards.**

Attention should be given to the possible need of introducing a new sentence with this verse. If a shift was made to direct discourse in verse 48, then it is assumed that a new sentence would have begun there.

Fellow servants is used outside of Matthew's Gospel only in Colossians (1.7; 4.7) and Revelation (6.11; 19.10; 22.9). Besides here, Matthew uses the noun in the parable of chapter 18 (verses 28,29,31-33). In Colossians and Revelation these "fellow servants" are clearly believers, which is doubtless the same meaning that Matthew sees in the term. Luke refers to those persons as "the male servants and the female servants" (12.45). Many translators render this as "the other servants he works with" or "the other servants of the household."

To say that the servant **begins to beat** the other servants does not mean that he got into fights with them. But as the one left in charge, he could punish them severely, including beating them or having them beaten. Some translators use "abuse" or "mistreat." These solutions are certainly acceptable if the implication is that the treatment was severe, as beating would be.

A lack of love, resulting in the abuse of power (**begins to beat his fellow servants**) and in self-indulgence (**drinks with the drunken**), describes the sin of the "wicked servant." **Drinks with the drunken** does not necessarily imply that the man himself became a drunkard; the meaning may well be "to eat and drink with his drunken friends" (NEB) or "to carouse with drunkards" (GECL). But it is difficult to see how the man would have avoided the excesses of his drunken friends, and it is quite likely that Matthew intends to say that he did exactly the same thing that they did. There are languages which don't have a good word for **the drunken**, and translators may say something like "began to spend his time eating and drinking with people who drank too much (or, with people who were often intoxicated)."

24.50-51   RSV   TEV

RSV	TEV
50 the master of that servant will come on a day when he does not expect him and at an hour he does not know, 51 and will punish[b] him, and put him with the hypocrites; there men will weep and gnash their teeth.	50 Then that servant's master will come back one day when the servant does not expect him and at a time he does not know. 51 The master will cut him in pieces[y] and make him share the fate of the hypocrites. There he will cry and gnash his teeth.
[b] Or *cut him in pieces*	[y] cut him in pieces; *or* throw him out.

The master of that servant . . . 51 . . . and put him with agrees word for word with Luke 12.46. The difference comes at the end, where Matthew ⌐ **the hypocrites** and Luke has "the unfaithful." **There men will weep and gnash their teeth**, one of Matthew's favorite formulas (see 8.12), is not to be found in the Lukan parallel.

The connection between verse 50 and the previous one depends on the if-clause in verses 48-49: "if that wicked servant . . . begins to beat his fellow servants, and eats and drinks with the drunken, then his master will arrive at a time when the servant does not expect him."

When he does not expect him is potentially ambiguous, and so TEV identifies the pronominal subject: "**when the servant does not expect him.**" It is possible to translate all of verse 50 as "Then the servant's master will come back at the day and the time when the servant does not expect him." Or, with even fewer words, "Then one day his master will come back fully unexpected" (GECL).

As the RSV footnote indicates, **punish** may also be translated "cut in pieces." The root meaning of the verb is to dismember a person who has been condemned to death, though the only other place in the New Testament where the verb is used suggests the meaning "punish with absolute severity" (Luke 12.46).

Put him with is translated "**make him share the fate of**" by TEV; it is also possible to render "treat him the same way that hypocrites are treated" or "give him the same punishment that one gives hypocrites."

Hypocrites was discussed at 6.2. Despite the fact that in Matthew this is one of the worst things that Jesus says about certain people, it does seem a little strange in this context. Brc has rendered it "those whose religion is only a pretence." "Those who pretend to be faithful to God but aren't" may also be good.

Weep and gnash their teeth was discussed at 8.12.

Verses 48-51 also need to be translated together if they are to sound natural in the receptor language. An example is:

> But if that servant is wicked, he will think to himself that his master will be gone for some time, and therefore he can begin to beat the other servants of the household and spend his time eating and drinking with drunkards. But then the master will come home totally unexpectedly, and he will punish that servant and treat him the same way that people are treated who only pretend to obey God. And those people cry out and gnash their teeth in pain.

Chapter 25

RSV

TEV

The Parable of the Ten Girls

1 "Then the kingdom of heaven shall be compared to ten maidens who took their lamps and went to meet the bridegroom.[c] 2 Five of them were foolish, and five were wise. 3 For when the foolish took their lamps, they took no oil with them; 4 but the wise took flasks of oil with their lamps. 5 As the bridegroom was delayed, they all slumbered and slept. 6 But at midnight there was a cry, 'Behold, the bridegroom! Come out to meet him.' 7 Then all those maidens rose and trimmed their lamps. 8 And the foolish said to the wise, 'Give us some of your oil, for our lamps are going out.' 9 But the wise replied, 'Perhaps there will not be enough for us and for you; go rather to the dealers and buy for yourselves.' 10 And while they went to buy, the bridegroom came, and those who were ready went in with him to the marriage feast; and the door was shut. 11 Afterward the other maidens came also, saying, 'Lord, lord, open to us.' 12 But he replied, 'Truly, I say to you, I do not know you.' 13 Watch therefore, for you know neither the day nor the hour.

[c] Other ancient authorities add *and the bride*

1 "At that time the Kingdom of heaven will be like this. Once there were ten girls who took their oil lamps and went out to meet the bridegroom. 2 Five of them were foolish, and the other five were wise. 3 The foolish ones took their lamps but did not take any extra oil with them, 4 while the wise ones took containers full of oil for their lamps. 5 The bridegroom was late in coming, so the girls began to nod and fall asleep.

6 "It was already midnight when the cry rang out, 'Here is the bridegroom! Come and meet him!' 7 The ten girls woke up and trimmed their lamps. 8 Then the foolish ones said to the wise ones, 'Let us have some of your oil, because our lamps are going out.' 9 'No, indeed,' the wise ones answered, 'there is not enough for you and for us. Go to the store and buy some for yourselves.' 10 So the foolish girls went off to buy some oil; and while they were gone, the bridegroom arrived. The five girls who were ready went in with him to the wedding feast, and the door was closed.

11 "Later the other girls arrived. 'Sir, sir! Let us in!' they cried out. 12 'Certainly not! I don't know you,' the bridegroom answered."

13 And Jesus concluded, "Watch out, then, because you do not know the day or the hour.

SECTION HEADING: **"The Parable of the Ten Girls"** may need to be expressed as "Jesus tells a parable about ten girls." As discussed below in verse 1, **"Girls"** can also be "young women."

This parable, which is unique to Matthew, has as its basic theme the need for readiness. It is also related to the previous parable through the word "wise" (24.45; 25.2). The translator's primary concern is with the interpretation of the parable in light of its setting within the structure of the Gospel. And at this point the function of the parable is clear: the Christian community must exercise wisdom and be ready at any moment (even when sleeping!), because they do not know the day or the hour when the Lord will appear in his glory.

"Then the kingdom of heaven shall be compared to ten maidens who took their lamps and went to meet the bridegroom.*c*

"At that time the Kingdom of heaven will be like this. Once there were ten girls who took their oil lamps and went out to meet the bridegroom.

c Other ancient authorities add *and the bride*

Then (TEV "**At that time**") translates a particle used by Matthew about ninety times, but only six times by Mark and thirteen times by Luke. It has a wide range of meaning. Many translators relate it to the previous passage and say "When these things happen," making sure it is clear that the "things" are the already-mentioned events.

The kingdom of heaven shall be compared to, except for the use of the future tense, translates the same construction discussed at 13.24. The meaning here is that the kingdom is like the situation described in the story of the ten girls. GECL 1st edition connects this parable with the preceding chapter by translating "When the Son of Man comes as Lord, it will happen as in the following story." Support for this comes from the fact that in the parable only the bridegroom is mentioned (verses 5,6,10,11), never the bride. Although it may be a correct theological judgment that Matthew does identify the consummation of the kingdom with the coming of the Son of Man, it does not seem proper to make that identity at a place where it is not specifically introduced by Matthew himself. One may prefer to translate "On that day when God comes to establish his rule, the situation will be similar to what is described in the following story."

The story itself is thought to reflect what was a rather typical wedding scene of first-century Palestine. The wedding guests were entertained in the bride's home until late evening. There they waited for the bridegroom, whose coming was announced by messengers. Some time after nightfall (in this parable, about midnight) the groom came to claim his bride and to take her to his father's home, where the wedding ceremony and other festivities took place. Both the coming of the bridegroom to the bride's home and the procession to his father's home were accompanied by bright lights, especially by torches. One scholar on the parables notes that it is customary among the Arabs of Palestine for the groom to be late for the wedding. The delay results from the traditional haggling over the gifts due the bride's relatives, for if such haggling is neglected, this may indicate that the bride is not to be prized very highly.

Maidens (TEV, NEB "girls") translates a Greek noun, the root meaning of which is "virgin" (see NIV). However, the word may also be used in the broader sense of "unmarried girl," and a number of translations prefer "bridesmaids" (AT, Phps, Brc, JB) or "young women guests at a wedding." The advantage to a translation such as this is that the setting of the wedding is established, so that **bridegroom** is not unexpectedly introduced. Translations often have "young women," since "girls" may be misunderstood to refer only to very young girls.

Lamps, meaning "**oil lamps**" (TEV), is the interpretation of the text followed by most translations. See 5.15 for suggestions on translating this term. It is possible, however, that the noun may mean "torches" (that is, sticks wrapped with rags soaked in oil), as it does in John 18.3. These would each burn for only about fifteen minutes, after which fresh oil would need to be poured on them. If "torches" are meant, then verse 1 merely sets the stage, and the girls do not actually light their torches until verse 7. Accordingly the request of the foolish girls in verse 8 would be, "Let us have some of your oil, because our torches will soon be going out." Most commentators and translators apparently prefer the meaning expressed by RSV and TEV, as stated above.

As we discussed above, **went to meet the bridegroom** is a reference to going to the bride's house to wait for the groom. Translators may say "went to wait with the bride for the bridegroom to arrive." Further, it may be necessary to indicate it was at night, as in "went one night to wait."

In place of **the bridegroom** some early manuscripts (Greek, Latin, and Syriac) have "the bridegroom and the bride." TC-GNT concedes it is possible that the words "and the bride" were "omitted because they were felt to be incompatible with the widely held view that Christ, the bridegroom, would come to fetch his bride, the church." However, TC-GNT thinks it is doubtful that ancient scribes would have been "so sensitive to the logic of the allegory." Moreover, since it was generally customary for the wedding to take place in the home of the bridegroom, it seems more probable that the words "and the bride" were added in order to reflect this situation. The UBS Greek New Testament rates its decision "C," indicating a considerable degree of doubt regarding which wording may be the original one. Of the modern translations, only Mft includes "and the bride" in the text; NJB and RSV follow the shorter text, indicating the alternative possibility in their footnotes.

25.2	RSV	TEV
Five of them were foolish, and five were wise.		**Five of them were foolish, and the other five were wise.**

Foolish translates the same Greek noun used in 5.22.
Wise translates the same Greek word used in 24.45; it was first used in 7.24.

25.3	RSV	TEV
For when the foolish took their lamps, they took no oil with them;		**The foolish ones took their lamps but did not take any extra oil with them,**

In many languages it is not really very natural to have a transition like **For** here, and most translations omit it. However, **For** can be seen as necessary in explaining why Jesus called the young women foolish. In that case verses 2 and 3 can be restructured something like this: "Five of them were wise, but five were foolish because they didn't take with them any oil for their lamps." In fact, it is also possible to include verse 4 in the restructuring and say "Five of them were wise, and they took containers of oil, but five were foolish . . . ."

Oil is translated "**extra oil**" by TEV on the basis of "our lamps are going out" of verse 8. This intimates that the girls originally had oil in their lamps but failed to take an additional supply to refill them. But it also makes sense to say merely that they didn't take any oil with them, since in either case the point is that they did not have lamps that could be lit.

25.4	RSV	TEV

but the wise took flasks of oil with their lamps.

while the wise ones took containers full of oil for their lamps.

Flasks of oil (TEV "**containers full of oil for their lamps**") is translated "oil for refilling" by GECL; one may even translate "extra oil." The **flasks** were probably pottery containers. Sometimes "jar" is used, but other translations use general terms such as "container" or "container for oil."

25.5	RSV	TEV

As the bridegroom was delayed, they all slumbered and slept.

The bridegroom was late in coming, so the girls began to nod and fall asleep.

Translators have handled **As** in a variety of ways. Some, for example TEV, show the relationship between the two parts of the verse by stating that the bridegroom was delayed, and then having "**so**" or "as a result." Others will begin the verse with "when" or "since."

Was delayed translates the same verb discussed in 24.48. This then provides the second linguistic link with the preceding parable, which also employs the adjective "wise" in the mention of the "wise servant" (24.45). In this verse translators may have "was late in arriving," "did not come for a long time," or "did not come when they expected him."

They all includes only "**the girls**" (TEV) rather than all the guests at the wedding.

Slumbered and slept is more accurately "grew drowsy and fell asleep" (Mft, AT, NJB) or "dozed off to sleep" (NEB), with the first verb probably implying near sleep (though it may also mean sleep), and the second indicating actual sleep.

25.6	RSV	TEV

But at midnight there was a cry, 'Behold, the bridegroom! Come out to meet him.'

"It was already midnight when the cry rang out, 'Here is the bridegroom! Come and meet him!'

Midnight (so NEB, NJB, TEV, NIV, NAB) means twelve o'clock at night for most English readers. This is too specific for the Greek text, which is better phrased as "in the middle of the night" (GECL, AT, Phps, Brc). One may also translate "late at night" or "very late at night."

25.6

There was a cry is translated "a cry was heard" by NEB. TEV does away with the passive (**"when the cry rang out"**), and NAB alters it to an impersonal form ("someone shouted").

Behold: see comment at 1.20. The bridegroom is now near enough that his approach can be noticed, or else someone has run ahead to announce his arrival. In place of **Behold, the bridegroom**, several modern translations have **"Here is the bridegroom"** (TEV, NEB) or "The bridegroom is here" (JB). Of course, the bridegroom was not there yet, and "The bridegroom is coming" or "Here comes the bridegroom" may be better. For some translators the indirect form may be more natural, as in "someone shouted that the bridegroom was coming and they should go out to meet him."

To meet him translates a Greek prepositional phrase (literally "for meeting him"), which is found also in Acts 28.15 and 1 Thessalonians 4.17, as well as in some manuscripts of Matthew 27.32.

25.7	RSV	TEV

Then all those maidens rose and trimmed their lamps.	The ten girls woke up and trimmed their lamps.

All those maidens is translated **"The ten girls"** by TEV and GECL. The precise form used will be determined by the best way in the receptor language to refer to these girls again.

Rose is translated **"woke up"** by some (TEV, GECL, NJB, NAB) and "got up" by NEB. In many languages it will be necessary to indicate both actions: ". . . woke up. Then they got up and trimmed their lamps."

Trimmed is a technical term used in English to describe what one does to make a lamp burn most efficiently. The lamps are probably already lit, so what is needed is adjusting the wick, that is, adjusting how much of the wick is exposed for burning, and adding oil. Translators should use whatever expression in their language will describe this kind of activity, possibly "adjusted their lamps."

25.8	RSV	TEV

And the foolish said to the wise, 'Give us some of your oil, for our lamps are going out.'	Then the foolish ones said to the wise ones, 'Let us have some of your oil, because our lamps are going out.'

From the discussion about the lamps in verse 3, it is clear that the verb **going out** may mean either "will soon be going out" or "will go out too soon."

RSV   TEV

But the wise replied, 'Perhaps there   'No, indeed,' the wise ones an-
will not be enough for us and for   swered, 'there is not enough for you
you; go rather to the dealers and   and for us. Go to the store and buy
buy for yourselves.'   some for yourselves.'

"No, indeed" of TEV (NEB, NAB, NIV "No") represents an attempt to
underscore the emphatic nature of the reply.

Perhaps there will not be enough for us and for you may imply doubt on
the part of the five wise young ladies, but this is not the intention of their remark.
It is more clearly phrased in NEB: "No . . . there will never be enough for all of us."
GECL has a somewhat stern rebuke: "Impossible. Then there would not be enough
for us or for you." A better possibility, a less stern reply, is "If we did that, there
wouldn't be enough oil for all of us."

Go rather to the dealers (TEV "Go to the store") reflects accurately the
Palestinian situation. On a festive occasion such as this, everyone in the village would
have been awake, and it would have been possible to purchase oil even at midnight.
Dealers can also be expressed as "the people who sell oil."

25.10   RSV   TEV

And while they went to buy, the   So the foolish girls went off to buy
bridegroom came, and those who   some oil; and while they were gone,
were ready went in with him to the   the bridegroom arrived. The five girls
marriage feast; and the door was   who were ready went in with him to
shut.   the wedding feast, and the door was
                                     closed.

The story now reaches its climax. The bridegroom arrives, and the girls who had
their lamps ready accompany him into the wedding feast. Observe that the theme of
readiness ties this parable to the saying of 24.4: "Therefore you also must be ready."

The text has merely **while they went to buy**, but in many languages it will be
necessary to mention their departure explicitly before using **while**. See for example
TEV, "**So the foolish girls went off to buy some oil; and while they were gone
. . . .**"

Came may be "arrived" or "arrived for the wedding."

Those who were ready went into the wedding with the bridegroom. **Those**
could seem to refer to all the guests, but in the context of the parable, **those** clearly
refers to the five sensible young women who were ready with enough oil. TEV has
"**the five girls who were ready**," and others have "the five sensible girls."

To say **went in . . . to the marriage feast** may need to be expanded to "went
into the house where the wedding feast was to be held." Since the wedding was at
the bridegroom's house, far enough away to require lamps to see the way there, then
"went to the house" may be better.

The door was shut may be translated "the servants closed the door."

25.11	RSV	TEV

Afterward the other maidens came also, saying, 'Lord, lord, open to us.'	"Later the other girls arrived. 'Sir, sir! Let us in!' they cried out.

Within the setting of the parable, **Lord** must be interpreted as a polite form of address to a superior (TEV "**Sir**"), though Matthew may have also intended an indirect allusion to the Christian's Lord. The problem is that in English it is almost impossible to transfer the double meaning. This will doubtless be the case for many other languages as well, where an honorific directed toward a human superior will be a different form from that which one uses to address a deity.

Open to us will possibly require an object: "open the door for us" (NEB, NJB). Or one may translate as in TEV and GECL: "**Let us in**."

25.12	RSV	TEV

But he replied, 'Truly, I say to you, I do not know you.'	'Certainly not! I don't know you,' the bridegroom answered."

But he replied is more literally "but answering he said," which is merely a traditional formula in Semitic Greek. It may be important to identify the speaker: "**the bridegroom answered**" (TEV).

Truly, I say to you: see 5.18 and comments there.

The phrase **I do not know you** is similar to the one in 7.23, but here a rendering such as "I do not know who you are" (so Brc) is the most usual.

25.13	RSV	TEV

Watch therefore, for you know neither the day nor the hour.	And Jesus concluded, "Watch out, then, because you do not know the day or the hour.

"**And Jesus concluded**" is introduced as a transitional marker by TEV to show that the bridegroom is no longer speaking. The verse is similar in function to 24.44, and its purpose is to make clear the teaching of the parable.

You know neither the day nor the hour may require further amplification: "You do not know either the day or the hour when the Son of Man will come" or ". . . when God's rule will be established."

25.14-30	RSV	TEV

The Parable of the Three Servants

14 "For it will be as when a man going on a journey called his servants and entrusted to them	14 "At that time the Kingdom of heaven will be like this. Once there was a man who was

his property; 15 to one he gave five talents,[d] to another two, to another one, to each according to his ability. Then he went away. 16 He who had received the five talents went at once and traded with them; and he made five talents more. 17 So also, he who had the two talents made two talents more. 18 But he who had received the one talent went and dug in the ground and hid his master's money. 19 Now after a long time the master of those servants came and settled accounts with them. 20 And he who had received the five talents came forward, bringing five talents more, saying, 'Master, you delivered to me five talents; here I have made five talents more.' 21 His master said to him, 'Well done, good and faithful servant; you have been faithful over a little, I will set you over much; enter into the joy of your master.' 22 And he also who had the two talents came forward, saying, 'Master, you delivered to me two talents; here I have made two talents more.' 23 His master said to him, 'Well done, good and faithful servant; you have been faithful over a little, I will set you over much; enter into the joy of your master.' 24 He also who had received the one talent came forward, saying, 'Master, I knew you to be a hard man, reaping where you did not sow, and gathering where you did not winnow; 25 so I was afraid, and I went and hid your talent in the ground. Here you have what is yours.' 26 But his master answered him, 'You wicked and slothful servant! You knew that I reap where I have not sowed, and gather where I have not winnowed? 27 Then you ought to have invested my money with the bankers, and at my coming I should have received what was my own with interest. 28 So take the talent from him, and give it to him who has the ten talents. 29 For to every one who has will more be given, and he will have abundance; but from him who has not, even what he has will be taken away. 30 And cast the worthless servant into the outer darkness; there men will weep and gnash their teeth.'

[d] This talent was more than fifteen years' wages of a laborer

about to leave home on a trip; he called his servants and put them in charge of his property. 15 He gave to each one according to his ability: to one he gave five thousand gold coins, to another he gave two thousand, and to another he gave one thousand. Then he left on his trip. 16 The servant who had received five thousand coins went at once and invested his money and earned another five thousand. 17 In the same way the servant who had received two thousand coins earned another two thousand. 18 But the servant who had received one thousand coins went off, dug a hole in the ground, and hid his master's money.

19 "After a long time the master of those servants came back and settled accounts with them. 20 The servant who had received five thousand coins came in and handed over the other five thousand. 'You gave me five thousand coins, sir,' he said. 'Look! Here are another five thousand that I have earned.' 21 'Well done, you good and faithful servant!' said his master. 'You have been faithful in managing small amounts, so I will put you in charge of large amounts. Come on in and share my happiness!' 22 Then the servant who had been given two thousand coins came in and said, 'You gave me two thousand coins, sir. Look! Here are another two thousand that I have earned.' 23 'Well done, you good and faithful servant!' said his master. 'You have been faithful in managing small amounts, so I will put you in charge of large amounts. Come on in and share my happiness!' 24 Then the servant who had received one thousand coins came in and said, 'Sir, I know you are a hard man; you reap harvests where you did not plant, and you gather crops where you did not scatter seed. 25 I was afraid, so I went off and hid your money in the ground. Look! Here is what belongs to you.' 26 'You bad and lazy servant!' his master said. 'You knew, did you, that I reap harvests where I did not plant, and gather crops where I did not scatter seed? 27 Well, then, you should have deposited my money in the bank, and I would have received it all back with interest when I returned. 28 Now, take the money away from him and give it to the one who has ten thousand coins. 29 For to every person who has something, even more will be given, and he will have more than enough; but the person who has nothing, even the little that he has will be taken away from him. 30 As for this useless servant—throw him outside in the darkness; there he will cry and gnash his teeth.'

SECTION HEADING: "**The Parable of the Three Servants**" may be "Jesus tells a parable about three servants." Or the title may tell more about the servants, as in "Jesus tells a parable about faithful and unfaithful servants."

This is the third in the series of three parables by which Matthew illustrates certain aspects of the coming of the Son of Man. In the first (24.45-51) he warned against the danger of becoming so engrossed with the present that one fails to take into consideration the inevitability of the future. Then, in the second of the three parables (25.1-13), he warned against a future expectation that did not deal adequately with the present. Now, in this final one of the series (25.14-30), Matthew illustrates how the present must be lived in light of the future. The theme of a long lapse of time is common to all three parables (24.48; 25.5; 25.19).

25.14   RSV   TEV

"For it will be as when a man going on a journey called his servants and entrusted to them his property;

"At that time the Kingdom of heaven will be like this. Once there was a man who was about to leave home on a trip; he called his servants and put them in charge of his property.

Verse 13 is influenced by the ending of Mark's discourse on the last things (13.35), while verse 14 is evidently dependent upon Mark 13.34. One commentator observes that in both Gospels the sentence is incomplete, requiring "some sort of addition, such as 'The Kingdom of God is like . . . .' " In Greek the verse begins with the same two particles, "just as" and "for," which RSV renders **For it will be as**. TEV has "**At that time the Kingdom of heaven will be like this**," and Brc has "What will happen in the Kingdom of Heaven is like what happened when a man went on a journey abroad." Both TEV and Brc take seriously the need to restructure more radically.

Going on a journey translates the same verb represented as "went into another country" by RSV in 21.33. In the Lukan parallel the **man** is identified as "A nobleman . . . to receive a kingdom," and a different verb phrase ("went into a far country") is used (19.12).

The man **called** his servants, that is, "he summoned them" or "called them to meet with him."

Entrusted is the choice of several English translations (NIV, NJB, for example); TEV has "**put . . . in charge of**." The servants did not become owners of the property, but it was their responsibility to take good care of it.

Property translates the same noun used in 19.21 and again in 24.47. It occurs nowhere else in the Gospel. It is clear that the talents were his property, but it is not clear if other things were included, such as land and buildings.

25.15   RSV   TEV

to one he gave five talents,^d to another two, to another one, to each according to his ability. Then he went away.

He gave to each one according to his ability: to one he gave five thousand gold coins, to another he gave two thousand, and to another he

772

^d This talent was more than fifteen years' wages of a laborer .

gave one thousand. Then he left on his trip.

Even though the text uses the word **gave**, the meaning is not that he gave a gift to each servant, but that he entrusted the money to them to manage. Some translators have had to say "gave to take care of."

Five talents is stated in a more dynamic form in several translations: "five bags of gold" (NEB) and **"five thousand gold coins"** (TEV). The **talent** was worth between five and six thousand denarii (see 18.24,28). Sometimes it is tempting to express the value in modern currencies such as pounds or dollars or francs. But this should be avoided, since currencies may quickly change their market value. It is the relative value of five, two, and one that is important, not the actual value, and so it may be better to us something more general such as "five bags of gold," or "five bags of money," or "five thousand pieces of gold." If translators can use a term that refers to coins, it is better than one which refers to paper money, which may become rotten in the ground if it is buried.

According to his ability relates to the servants, not to the man who is giving out the money. Brc makes this clear by saying "He gave each man a sum proportionate to his ability." Another way to express this is "the amount he gave each man depended on how skillful that servant was." Whether to put this expression at the beginning of the sentence (TEV) or at the end (RSV, Brc) will depend on the receptor language.

25.16	RSV	TEV

He who had received the five talents went at once and traded with them; and he made five talents more.

The servant who had received five thousand coins went at once and invested his money and earned another five thousand.

At once is the same adverb translated "immediately" in 4.20. Here it emphasizes the immediacy with which the servant acted: "Immediately the man who had received the five thousand went . . ." (NAB).

Traded with them translates an idiomatic expression, literally "worked with them"; TEV has "**invested his money,**" NIV "put his money to work," and AT "went into business with the money." In societies where investing money is not commonly done, translators may have to say "did business with the money."

Made five talents more is more literally "gained another five"; GECL translates "was able to double the amount."

25.17	RSV	TEV

So also, he who had the two talents made two talents more.

In the same way the servant who had received two thousand coins earned another two thousand.

So also (TEV "**In the same way**") is placed first in the Greek sentence structure and is used to draw a parallel between the action of the two servants.

Both RSV (**made two talents more**) and TEV ("**earned another two thousand**") may be inadequate models for languages which will expect the explicit mention of what the servant did: "the servant . . . invested his money and earned another two thousand coins."

25.18 RSV	TEV
But he who had received the one talent went and dug in the ground and hid his master's money.	But the servant who had received one thousand coins went off, dug a hole in the ground, and hid his master's money.

Jewish teachers used to say that anyone who immediately buries money entrusted to him is no longer liable, because he has taken the safest course possible in protecting the money. On the other hand, if a man wraps the money in a cloth and it is lost, then he is responsible to replace the money (compare Luke 19.20).

But contrasts the action of the third servant with that of the first ("went at once and traded") and the second ("so also").

Dug in the ground is usually rendered "dug a hole in the ground."

The text states explicitly that this was **his master's money**, but this does not mean that the money of the other servants was not also their master's. Translators often have "the money his master had given him to take care of."

25.19 RSV	TEV
Now after a long time the master of those servants came and settled accounts with them.	"After a long time the master of those servants came back and settled accounts with them.

After a long time parallels "is delayed" (24.48) and "was delayed" (25.5) of the first and second parables in this series of three.

Settled accounts with them does not refer to a past event but rather to something yet to take place, and so one may need to translate "in order to settle accounts with them." NEB is sensitive to the problem: "and proceeded to settle accounts with them." The same expression was used in 18.23. In this verse translators may say "asked them to account for what they had done with the money" or "checked with them about the money."

25.20 RSV	TEV
And he who had received the five talents came forward, bringing five talents more, saying, 'Master, you	The servant who had received five thousand coins came in and handed over the other five thousand. 'You

delivered to me five talents; here I have made five talents more.'	gave me five thousand coins, sir,' he said. 'Look! Here are another five thousand that I have earned.'

Both RSV and TEV are potentially ambiguous; the servant did not give just the five thousand he had made, but the entire amount of ten thousand. Rather radical restructuring may be necessary in order to avoid possible confusion to the reader. For example, "The servant who had received five thousand coins came in and said, 'You entrusted me with five thousand coins, and with them I have earned five thousand more. Here they are!'" (GECL 1st edition).

25.21 RSV	TEV
His master said to him, 'Well done, good and faithful servant; you have been faithful over a little, I will set you over much; enter into the joy of your master.'	'Well done, you good and faithful servant!' said his master. 'You have been faithful in managing small amounts, so I will put you in charge of large amounts. Come on in and share my happiness!'

Well done, good and faithful servant may need to be stated more fully: "You have done the right thing. You are a good and faithful servant." Brc translates the second sentence "You have shown yourself to be a good and trustworthy servant." **Faithful** is also used in 24.45, thus making another link between the first and third in this series of three parables.

Over a little is transformed into a verb construction by TEV: "**in managing small amounts.**" NEB ("You have proved trustworthy in a small way") would imply for American readers that the man had not been very trustworthy. GECL retains a noun phrase but makes the meaning clear: "You have proved yourself trustworthy in small matters."

I will set you over much may be too elliptical. Better may be "I will give you a much larger responsibility" or "I will put you in charge of (managing) large amounts." It is good, however, if the translations of **little** and **much** can be parallel, as in "small matters . . . large matters" or "small amounts . . . large amounts."

"**Come on in and share my happiness!**" represents an attempt on the part of TEV to make sense out of the literal **enter into the joy of your master**. A number of scholars believe that the noun **joy** here is used with the meaning "feast" or "banquet." The footnote in NJB ("The happiness of the heavenly banquet") goes beyond the context of the parable itself. But GECL makes excellent sense within the setting of the parable: "Come to my banquet and celebrate with me!" In this case, **enter** seems to indicate physically coming in (to the house where the banquet was). But **enter** can equally well be an invitation to share in the happiness, as in "I am really happy about this, and I want you to be happy with me."

Note from these examples that the third person, **of your master**, is often rendered by first person "me" or "my."

25.22 RSV TEV

And he also who had the two talents came forward, saying, 'Master, you delivered to me two talents; here I have made two talents more.'

Then the servant who had been given two thousand coins came in and said, 'You gave me two thousand coins, sir. Look! Here are another two thousand that I have earned.'

The problems of interpreting and translating this verse are similar to those of verse 20. See discussion there.

25.23 RSV TEV

His master said to him, 'Well done, good and faithful servant; you have been faithful over a little, I will set you over much; enter into the joy of your master.'

'Well done, you good and faithful servant!' said his master. 'You have been faithful in managing small amounts, so I will put you in charge of large amounts. Come on in and share my happiness!'

The problems of interpreting and translating this verse are similar to those of verse 21. See comments there.

25.24 RSV TEV

He also who had received the one talent came forward, saying, 'Master, I knew you to be a hard man, reaping where you did not sow, and gathering where you did not winnow;

Then the servant who had received one thousand coins came in and said, 'Sir, I know you are a hard man; you reap harvests where you did not plant, and you gather crops where you did not scatter seed.

In the words of one commentator, this servant "shows as soon as he opens his mouth that he is not interested in his lord's advantage but in saving his own skin."

The adjective **hard** is used only here in the Gospel of Matthew; elsewhere in the New Testament it is found in John 6.60; Acts 26.14; James 3.4 ("strong" of wind); Jude 15 ("harsh"). The two illustrations (sowing and reaping; winnowing and gathering) probably reflect proverbial sayings (see Job 31.8; John 4.37); they are used to illustrate what the servant means by the accusation that his master is a **hard man**. Most translators describe the master here as "strict" or, as in Brc, "a shrewd and ruthless businessman."

The four verbs (**reaping** . . . **sow** . . . **gathering** . . . **winnow**) may require the explicit mention of objects, as for example, "reap harvests," "sow (or, plant) seeds," "gather crops," and "winnow chaff." But this is complicated by the observation that the final verb in this series is literally "scatter" and may mean either "scatter" (of seed) or "winnow" (of chaff). The TEV rendering as "**scatter seed**" probably is best in this context. In either case the idea of taking profits where someone else has done the work is clear.

It is possible to follow chronological order, shift to a comparison, and at the same time combine the two figures of speech into one: "You are a hard man. You are like someone who does not plant seeds but expects to gather a crop" or "You are like someone who expects to gather a crop from a garden (or, field) that someone else has planted."

25.25	RSV	TEV

so I was afraid, and I went and hid your talent in the ground. Here you have what is yours.'		I was afraid, so I went off and hid your money in the ground. Look! Here is what belongs to you.'

Was afraid . . . went translate participles dependent upon the main verb **hid**. But simplified English sentence structure almost requires that all three be translated as finite verbs, as in RSV and TEV. GECL, which uses a verb that may mean either "bury" or "hide in the ground," is brief and to the point: "I was afraid, so I buried your money." Some languages will require more detail: "I was afraid of what you might do to me if I lost the money. So I went to a certain place and dug a hole and hid the money in it." Or, "I was afraid that you might punish me if I lost your money . . . ."

Here (TEV "**Look**") is related to the particle usually translated "behold" or "lo" by RSV; it functions primarily as an attention getter. See comment at 1.20.

Here you have what is yours may not be altogether clear to some readers. GECL 1st edition has "Here you have your money back"; NJB "Here it is; it was yours, you have it back"; Brc "Here you are! Your money is safe!"

25.26	RSV	TEV

But his master answered him, 'You wicked and slothful servant! You knew that I reap where I have not sowed, and gather where I have not winnowed?		'You bad and lazy servant!' his master said. 'You knew, did you, that I reap harvests where I did not plant, and gather crops where I did not scatter seed?

Wicked translates an adjective used some twenty-six times in the Gospel (twice by Mark and thirteen times by Luke); its first occurrence is in 5.11, where it is translated "evil." This is not the same adjective rendered "wicked" in 24.48, though there seems to be no difference in the meaning which Matthew attributes to the two words.

Slothful (TEV "**lazy**") is used only here in Matthew's Gospel; it appears twice in the remainder of the New Testament (Rom 12.11; Phil 3.1). The basic meaning is "idle" or "lazy," though in the Philippians passage the meaning may be "troublesome." It is sometimes more natural to turn these accusations into short statements such as "You are a wicked and lazy servant."

You knew . . . winnowed? is a rhetorical question that is sometimes difficult to express. Some have followed TEV (**"You knew, did you, that . . . ?"**) or have "You knew that I . . . winnowed. Is that so?" But the question may better be restructured as a statement for many languages. See for example Brc: "You knew very well that . . . ." Also possible is "You are quite right to say that . . . ." In fact the Greek text itself may be interpreted as a statement rather than as a rhetorical question.

Reap . . . sowed . . . gather . . . winnowed: see comment at verse 24.

25.27	RSV	TEV

Then you ought to have invested my money with the bankers, and at my coming I should have received what was my own with interest.	Well, then, you should have deposited my money in the bank, and I would have received it all back with interest when I returned.

Then translates a particle which draws a conclusion from something previously said. TEV and NJB each have **"Well, then"**; NAB "All the more reason"; Brc "That is all the more reason why." "Therefore" or "So" are also possible.

You ought to have (TEV **"you should have"**) represents an impersonal construction in Greek ("it was necessary for you to have"), which will require a second-person form in many languages.

Invested my money with the bankers is "**deposited my money in the bank**" in TEV. Not all translators will feel that their readers are familiar enough with banks to translate in this way, nor even with the idea of investing to make more money. They can then say "loan the money to people who need it then, and who after some time will give you back more."

At my coming may require a shift such as one finds in TEV: "**when I returned.**" TEV also inverts the order of events ("**I would have received it all back . . . when I returned**"); but most languages will probably prefer the chronological order of the Greek text, which is retained in RSV (**at my coming I should have received**).

The translation of **interest** will depend also on the knowledge of banking. Where many readers are not familiar with it, translators can have "with some more (or, extra) money as well."

25.28	RSV	TEV

So take the talent from him, and give it to him who has the ten talents.	Now, take the money away from him and give it to the one who has ten thousand coins.

So (TEV **"Now"**) translates the same particle used in verse 27 ("Then").

The Greek text does not state to whom it was that the servant's master gave the command, but some languages may require that this information be made explicit:

"Then the master of that servant said to some (or, one) of his other servants, 'Take the money away . . . .' "

Apparently the first two servants showed the master what they had earned, but they had not (yet) turned it over to him, because here the text says the servant **has the ten talents**. Verse 29 confirms this.

25.29

RSV	TEV
For to every one who has will more be given, and he will have abundance; but from him who has not, even what he has will be taken away.	For to every person who has something, even more will be given, and he will have more than enough; but the person who has nothing, even the little that he has will be taken away from him.

The structure and content of this verse are similar to that of 13.12. See the discussion there. **Has** and **be given** often require a direct object, but it should be unspecified, as in **"has nothing"** (TEV) and "will be given more of it." Note also that TEV renders **abundance** with a general expression, **"more than enough,"** but this can also be "more than enough of it."

Taking **even what he has** from someone who has nothing may be a problem unless it is understood as in TEV, **"even the little that he has."**

Several commentators are of the opinion that the passive verbs **will . . . be given** and **will be taken away** must be understood as ways of speaking of God without mentioning the sacred name. If this judgment is followed, then one may translate "God will give" and "God will take away." Such a shift causes no problem in 13.12, but it is almost impossible here because of verse 30, where apparently the master of the servants is still speaking. Therefore if the actor in this verse needs to be mentioned, the best solution is to shift to a first person singular subject with the master of the servants speaking: "To every person who has something, I will give even more, and he will have more than enough. But for the person who has nothing, I will take away from him even the little that he has."

25.30

RSV	TEV
And cast the worthless servant into the outer darkness; there men will weep and gnash their teeth.'	As for this useless servant—throw him outside in the darkness; there he will cry and gnash his teeth.'

Elsewhere in the New Testament the adjective **worthless** is found only in Luke 17.10. TEV's **"As for this useless servant—throw him . . ."** represents an attempt to express the position of emphasis which **the worthless servant** occupies in the Greek sentence. It may be better to use a complete sentence: "But this servant is worthless! Take him and throw him . . . ."

Outer darkness was discussed at 8.12.

There men will weep and gnash their teeth has no subject in Greek. TEV supplies a different subject: **"there he will cry and gnash his teeth."** GECL retains the impersonal structure: "Throw this good-for-nothing out in the darkness, where there is nothing except crying and gnashing of teeth." Matthew employs this formula six times (see comment at 8.12); outside his Gospel it is used only in Luke 13.28.

25.31-46

RSV

TEV

The Final Judgment

31 "When the Son of man comes in his glory, and all the angels with him, then he will sit on his glorious throne. 32 Before him will be gathered all the nations, and he will separate them one from another as a shepherd separates the sheep from the goats, 33 and he will place the sheep at his right hand, but the goats at the left. 34 Then the King will say to those at his right hand, 'Come, O blessed of my Father, inherit the kingdom prepared for you from the foundation of the world; 35 for I was hungry and you gave me food, I was thirsty and you gave me drink, I was a stranger and you welcomed me, 36 I was naked and you clothed me, I was sick and you visited me, I was in prison and you came to me.' 37 Then the righteous will answer him, 'Lord, when did we see thee hungry and feed thee, or thirsty and give thee drink? 38 And when did we see thee a stranger and welcome thee, or naked and clothe thee? 39 And when did we see thee sick or in prison and visit thee?' 40 And the King will answer them, 'Truly, I say to you, as you did it to one of the least of these my brethren, you did it to me.' 41 Then he will say to those at his left hand, 'Depart from me, you cursed, into the eternal fire prepared for the devil and his angels; 42 for I was hungry and you gave me no food, I was thirsty and you gave me no drink, 43 I was a stranger and you did not welcome me, naked and you did not clothe me, sick and in prison and you did not visit me.' 44 Then they also will answer, 'Lord, when did we see thee hungry or thirsty or a stranger or naked or sick or in prison, and did not minister to thee?' 45 Then he will answer them, 'Truly, I say to you, as you did it not to one of the least of these, you did it not to me.' 46 And they will go away into eternal punishment, but the righteous into eternal life."

31 "When the Son of Man comes as King and all the angels with him, he will sit on his royal throne, 32 and the people of all the nations will be gathered before him. Then he will divide them into two groups, just as a shepherd separates the sheep from the goats. 33 He will put the righteous people at his right and the others at his left. 34 Then the King will say to the people on his right, 'Come, you that are blessed by my Father! Come and possess the kingdom which has been prepared for you ever since the creation of the world. 35 I was hungry and you fed me, thirsty and you gave me a drink; I was a stranger and you received me in your homes, 36 naked and you clothed me; I was sick and you took care of me, in prison and you visited me.' 37 The righteous will then answer him, 'When, Lord, did we ever see you hungry and feed you, or thirsty and give you a drink? 38 When did we ever see you a stranger and welcome you in our homes, or naked and clothe you? 39 When did we ever see you sick or in prison, and visit you?' 40 The King will reply, 'I tell you, whenever you did this for one of the least important of these brothers of mine, you did it for me!'

41 "Then he will say to those on his left, 'Away from me, you that are under God's curse! Away to the eternal fire which has been prepared for the Devil and his angels! 42 I was hungry but you would not feed me, thirsty but you would not give me a drink; 43 I was a stranger but you would not welcome me in your homes, naked but you would not clothe me; I was sick and in prison but you would not take care of me.' 44 Then they will answer him, 'When, Lord, did we ever see you hungry or thirsty or a stranger or naked or sick or in prison, and we would not help you?' 45 Then the King will reply, 'I tell you, whenever you refused to help one of these least important ones, you refused to help me.' 46 These, then, will be sent off to eternal punishment, but the righteous will go to eternal life."

SECTION HEADING: "**The Final Judgment**" poses two problems. In the first place "**Final**" is sometimes understood to mean "at the end of the world" and sometimes "the last." "The end of the age" is the best interpretation, however. Secondly "**Judgment**" may require a subject and possibly also an object. Consequently translators may have "The Son of Man will judge all people" or "The judging the Son of Man will do (of people) at the end of this age."

This scene of the last judgment brings to a conclusion the fifth and final discourse of the Gospel (chapters 23–25) and leads directly into the passion narrative (chapters 26–27). New Testament scholarship is sharply divided on the issue of just how much of the chapter goes back directly to Jesus, but there is unanimous agreement that in its final form there is evidence of Matthew's hand at work. The function of the chapter is not to argue for "justification by works" but rather to awaken the believing community to the imperative of putting its faith into action. The judgment scene is in fact closely related to the parable of the servant who is both lazy (25.26) and useless (25.30). And it calls to mind lessons taught in the parables of the unfaithful servant (24.45-51) and of the ten girls (25.1-13): the interval before the Lord's coming demands constant vigilance which must express itself through works of love.

25.31	RSV	TEV

"When the Son of man comes in his glory, and all the angels with him, then he will sit on his glorious throne.	"When the Son of Man comes as King and all the angels with him, he will sit on his royal throne,

In his glory is translated "**as King**" by TEV. Justification for this is to be found in verse 34, where **the Son of man** is suddenly referred to as "the King." If this identification of Son of Man (verse 31) and King (verse 34) is not somehow made explicit, then the reader will be tempted to assume that a new character is introduced into the narrative in verse 34. **Glory** refers to the splendor and majesty and power that is associated with God or with a king, so some translators have "in royal splendor" or "with the power he has as king."

In his glory, and all the angels with him is similar to the construction of 16.27: "with his angels in the glory of his Father."

For **throne**, see the discussion at 19.28 and also 5.34. As there, it may be helpful to indicate the function of sitting on the throne by stating that he will sit on the throne "to judge." By translating **his glorious throne** as "**his royal throne**," TEV makes the second half of the verse conform to the first half, in which **the Son of man** is identified as "**the King.**" In GECL 1st edition the entire verse appears as "When the Son of Man comes with power and glory in the company of all his angels, then he will sit on his royal throne."

25.32   RSV   TEV

Before him will be gathered all the nations, and he will separate them one from another as a shepherd separates the sheep from the goats,	**and the people of all the nations will be gathered before him. Then he will divide them into two groups, just as a shepherd separates the sheep from the goats.**

Before him means "in front of him" and does not refer to before him in time.

Will be gathered may imply an agent, as in "They will gather all the nations before him," but it may also have the meaning "will come together" or "will gather themselves together" (see, for example, 22.41; 26.3; 27.17). Several commentators believe that the verb refers primarily to the action of a shepherd gathering his sheep, and that is the symbolism intended here. But Matthew uses this verb twenty-four times in his Gospel, and in all of the New Testament it appears some fifty-nine times, but never with "sheep" as its object. Since it is unlikely, therefore, that sheep are implied, there is also little basis for assuming the shepherd as agent. So it is not very likely that Matthew intends that the verb be understood in a sense of someone actually gathering the people for this judgment scene. Thus "will gather together" will be the better rendering.

In place of **all the nations**, GECL has "all the people of the earth." NJB footnote indicates that the meaning is "Every human being of every period of history." This is important because the translation should not give the impression that the judge will separate righteous nations from others; it is the righteous people as individuals who will be separated from the others.

As a shepherd separates the sheep from the goats reflects Palestinian life. During the day the sheep and goats graze together, but at night they are separated, because goats must be kept warm at night, while sheep prefer to sleep in the open air. TEV and Brc have rendered **separate them one from another** as "**divide** (or, separate) **them into two groups.**" For a description of **sheep** and **goats**, see *Fauna and Flora of the Bible*, pages 75-76 and 36-38.

25.33   RSV   TEV

and he will place the sheep at his right hand, but the goats at the left.	**He will put the righteous people at his right and the others at his left.**

On the basis of verse 46, where it becomes obvious that **the sheep** of this verse are actually "the righteous," TEV translates **the sheep** as "**the righteous people**" and **the goats** as "**the others.**" The problem is that at some point in the narrative a shift must be made to signify that the King is not addressing actual "sheep" and "goats" (verse 34) but rather people who in some way are symbolized by these two groups of animals. Otherwise a ridiculous scene results: a king sits on his throne and passes judgment on a herd of sheep and goats! Some translators have retained **sheep** and **goats** by using a rather long comparison: "just as the shepherd puts the sheep at his right hand and the goats at his left, so the Son of Man (or, the King) will put the righteous people at his right and the others at his left."

At his right hand . . . at the left: in a Jewish setting both positions normally signify positions of authority, though the place of greatest honor is the one on the right. As **right** and **left** are used in this passage (verses 34, 41), the contrast is between the place of favor (on the right-hand side of the king) and that of disfavor (on the left-hand side of the king).

25.34	RSV	TEV
	Then the King will say to those at his right hand, 'Come, O blessed of my Father, inherit the kingdom prepared for you from the foundation of the world;	Then the King will say to the people on his right, 'Come, you that are blessed by my Father! Come and possess the kingdom which has been prepared for you ever since the creation of the world.

The King is translated "the Judge" by GECL 1st edition. This may not be the best model, since **the King** does no more than pronounce a judgment made by his Father (**O blessed of my Father**), who stands behind the scene as the real judge.

Come translates an adverb which is often used as a verb of exhortation. Here it has the force of an invitation to share in the benefits of God's kingdom.

The phrase **O blessed of my Father** often needs to be expressed with a verbal phrase; for example, "you people whom my Father has blessed," "you who have earned the blessing of my Father," or even as a separate sentence, "You are people my Father has blessed." Other expressions are "you people who have received so much good from my Father" and "you are people my Father has done so much good for." As elsewhere, **Father** may be "God my Father."

Inherit is a typical Semitic figure of speech for the way in which one freely receives something from God. It is translated "**Come and possess**" by TEV and "enter and possess" by NEB. See comment at 5.5.

In discussions of **the kingdom** we have suggested expressions such as "God's reign (or, rule)" and "God's New World." However, in conjunction with **inherit** or "**possess**," this same expression may prove awkward and unnatural. Translators may try "Come and receive the blessings (or, benefits) of God's rule," or they may use an active sentence with God as the agent: "Come and God will give you the blessings of his kingdom." See 3.2 and 5.3.

In the text, **come** and **inherit** are separated by the vocative **O blessed of my Father**. In most languages it is more natural to move the vocative to the beginning of the sentence and put the two invitations together: "come and possess."

Prepared for you from the foundation of the world presupposes God as subject of two actions: God has prepared (something) for you, and he created the world. Therefore one may translate "which God prepared for you before (or, at the time that) he created the world." GECL translates the King's pronouncement "Come here, you whom my Father has blessed! Receive God's New World, which he has had ready for you from the beginning."

25.35-36   RSV   TEV

35 for I was hungry and you gave me food, I was thirsty and you gave me drink, I was a stranger and you welcomed me, 36 I was naked and you clothed me, I was sick and you visited me, I was in prison and you came to me.'	35 I was hungry and you fed me, thirsty and you gave me a drink; I was a stranger and you received me in your homes, 36 naked and you clothed me; I was sick and you took care of me, in prison and you visited me.'

For marks the relation between the preceding invitation and these two verses. The King invites those blessed by his Father to receive their inheritance because of the way they treated him (the King). Translators may need to say "I invite you to come because . . ." or "You will receive this because . . . ." The righteous are rewarded on the basis of their works of love for persons in desperate need.

I was hungry . . . thirsty . . . a stranger . . . naked . . . sick . . . in prison: some have felt that this suggests a "mystical identification of Christ and the needy," but it is enough to make clear that it is through service to those who are in need that Christ himself chooses to be served. Thus the translation must use the first person, **I was hungry**.

In some languages **I was hungry** is more naturally "When I was hungry," in which case the **and** of the following phrase may not be needed. "When I was hungry, you gave me something to eat."

You gave me food (literally, "you gave me to eat") is better than TEV's "**you fed me**," which may imply the inability of the hungry person to feed himself.

Gave me drink may need to be slightly restructured: "you gave me water to drink." In the dry and hot climate of Palestine, the giving of water to a thirsty person was a special act of kindness.

Stranger most probably signifies anyone unknown to a person, though it may also carry the meaning "foreigner."

Welcomed (TEV "**received . . . in your homes**") translates the active form of the verb rendered "will be gathered" of verse 32. Here the meaning is "welcome as a guest"; GECL appropriately renders "accepted me as one of your own."

I was naked and you clothed me is not to suggest that the person who provided the clothes actually placed them on the naked person. One may translate "I did not have any clothes, and you gave me clothes to wear." Some translators understand **naked** as an exaggeration and translate it as "I didn't have enough to wear" or "had no clothes."

Visited can be "came (or, went) to see me," but in this context the idea of taking care of is probably better. See TEV "**took care of**." For the last verb, **came** does refer to going to see a person in prison, so "**visited**" of TEV is quite appropriate there.

25.37   RSV   TEV

Then the righteous will answer him, 'Lord, when did we see thee hungry	The righteous will then answer him, 'When, Lord, did we ever see you

and feed thee, or thirsty and give thee drink?	hungry and feed you, or thirsty and give you a drink?

Righteous is commented on at 1.19, where it is translated "just." GECL has "those who have done God's will," which clearly is the contextual meaning.

Lord (so most translations) is here best understood in the full Christian sense of the word; Brc has "Sir," which is satisfactory for other contexts but falls short here.

Or thirsty and give thee drink? may require the repetition of the first part of the sentence: "When did we ever see you thirsty and give you something to drink?" or ". . . and give you water to drink?"

25.38	RSV	TEV

And when did we see thee a stranger and welcome thee, or naked and clothe thee?	When did we ever see you a stranger and welcome you in our homes, or naked and clothe you?

Or naked and clothe thee? may also require a full statement: "When did we ever see you in need of clothes and give you something to wear?"

25.39	RSV	TEV

And when did we see thee sick or in prison and visit thee?'	When did we ever see you sick or in prison, and visit you?'

This verse may require restructuring as two separate questions: "When was it that you were sick and we took care of you? When did we visit you in prison?"

25.40	RSV	TEV

And the King will answer them, 'Truly, I say to you, as you did it to one of the least of these my brethren, you did it to me.'	The King will reply, 'I tell you, whenever you did this for one of the least important of these brothers of mine, you did it for me!'

Truly, I say to you is similar to "For truly, I say to you" of 5.18; see comment there.

Least is the same adjective used in 2.6; 5.19 (twice); 25.45. See comment at 5.19. For many languages **the least of these** will be insufficient, and one may be required to translate as TEV's **"the least important of these brothers of mine."** Another good way is "Whenever you did it for one of my brothers, even one of the least important ones." Of course, although **brethren** is masculine, the text includes all people, whatever their sex. "Brothers and sisters" is acceptable.

At this point Matthew clearly identifies Jesus with those persons who are suffering for whatever reason. In the words of one scholar, "For Matthew anyone is Jesus' brother [or sister] who obeys his word and does the will of the Father, but also anyone who suffers and is in need." Therefore it is important that readers don't think this means real blood brothers. It may be necessary to say "these people who are like brothers to me, even the least important ones."

TEV has rendered RSV **as** by "**whenever.**" This can be restructured, if necessary: "You have done these things for others, and I consider that you have done them for me."

You did it to me: this may be "it is as if you did it to me" or ". . . as valid as if . . . ," or "I consider that you did it to me."

25.41   RSV   TEV

Then he will say to those at his left hand, 'Depart from me, you cursed, into the eternal fire prepared for the devil and his angels;

    "Then he will say to those on his left, 'Away from me, you that are under God's curse! Away to the eternal fire which has been prepared for the Devil and his angels!

You cursed is more literally "you who have been cursed," in which God is the understood agent: "**you that are under God's curse**" (TEV). **Depart from me, you cursed, into the eternal fire** is translated in GECL as "Get out of my sight! God has cursed you! Go to the eternal fire . . . ." To curse is to call down evil on someone or something, so that **you cursed** can also be "God has called down evil on you" or "you are to receive the evil that God has sent for you."

Prepared for the devil also presupposes God as the agent, and so one may translate "which God has prepared for the devil . . . ."

Eternal fire is discussed at 18.8.

The devil was discussed at 4.1.

Since **angels** frequently has the connotation of good spiritual beings, it may be advisable to follow the pattern of GECL: "Satan and his helpers."

25.42-43   RSV   TEV

42 for I was hungry and you gave me no food, I was thirsty and you gave me no drink, 43 I was a stranger and you did not welcome me, naked and you did not clothe me, sick and in prison and you did not visit me.'

42 I was hungry but you would not feed me, thirsty but you would not give me a drink; 43 I was a stranger but you would not welcome me in your homes, naked but you would not clothe me; I was sick and in prison but you would not take care of me.'

The exegesis and restructuring of these verses, except for a shift to the negative form, will be similar to that of verses 35-36. See comments and translation there.

25.44 RSV TEV

Then they also will answer, 'Lord, when did we see thee hungry or thirsty or a stranger or naked or sick or in prison, and did not minister to thee?'	Then they will answer him, 'When, Lord, did we ever see you hungry or thirsty or a stranger or naked or sick or in prison, and we would not help you?'

See comments at verses 38-39. The major difference is that here, instead of listing the specific ways that these people failed to help ("feed thee," "give thee drink," etc.), the term **minister** is used to cover them all. It can be translated "**help**" (TEV) or "take care of."

25.45 RSV TEV

Then he will answer them, 'Truly, I say to you, as you did it not to one of the least of these, you did it not to me.'	Then the King will reply, 'I tell you, whenever you refused to help one of these least important ones, you refused to help me.'

See comments at verse 40. Here the text has simply **one of the least of these** and does not mention "brothers." Translators usually say "one of these least important people." Brc has "one of these, even for the least of them."

25.46 RSV TEV

And they will go away into eternal punishment, but the righteous into eternal life."	These, then, will be sent off to eternal punishment, but the righteous will go to eternal life."

Will go away (TEV "**will be sent off**") is perhaps best interpreted to mean "God will send them away."

Eternal punishment can be expressed by "where they will be punished forever" or "punishment that never stops."

The righteous: see verse 37 and 1.19.

Eternal life: see comment at 19.16.

In GECL this verse is translated "Eternal punishment awaits these people. But the others, who have done God's will, will receive eternal life."

Chapter 26

RSV

TEV

The Plot against Jesus

1 When Jesus had finished all these sayings, he said to his disciples, 2 "You know that after two days the Passover is coming, and the Son of man will be delivered up to be crucified." 3 Then the chief priests and the elders of the people gathered in the palace of the high priest, who was called Caiaphas, 4 and took counsel together in order to arrest Jesus by stealth and kill him. 5 But they said, "Not during the feast, lest there be a tumult among the people."

1 When Jesus had finished teaching all these things, he said to his disciples, 2 "In two days, as you know, it will be the Passover Festival, and the Son of Man will be handed over to be crucified." 3 Then the chief priests and the elders met together in the palace of Caiaphas, the High Priest, 4 and made plans to arrest Jesus secretly and put him to death. 5 "We must not do it during the festival," they said, "or the people will riot."

SECTION HEADING: **"The Plot against Jesus."** This may need to be expressed as a short sentence with a subject and verb; for example, "The religious leaders of the Jews (or, the chief priests) plot to kill Jesus."

Chapters 26–28 contain Matthew's account of the events surrounding the death and resurrection of Jesus. In recounting Jesus' suffering and death (chapters 26–27), Matthew followed closely the Marcan sequence of events (14.1–15.47), omitting only Mark 14.51-52 and a portion of Mark 15.21. For Matthew everything that happened— Jesus' suffering and death, as well as his resurrection—was in keeping with God's will and purpose. Jesus could have called down twelve armies of angels to protect himself (26.53), but he refused to resort to the use of force in order to avoid God's will. Instead he went the route of suffering and death, thus fulfilling the divine purpose (26.42, 53-54). His death was a necessary event in God's scheme of things, for only in this way was the forgiveness of sins made possible (26.28). But it is also within God's will that this crucified one should be raised from death and be given all authority in heaven and on earth (28.18).

Mark's brief introduction to the story of Jesus' suffering and death (14.1-2) is followed closely in Luke (22.1-2). But Matthew considerably expands the introduction (26.1-5) by dividing it into two distinct scenes (verses 1-2 and 3-5) and emphasizing from the outset the elements that he believes to be of uppermost importance.

26.1   RSV   TEV

When Jesus had finished all these sayings, he said to his disciples,	When Jesus had finished teaching all these things, he said to his disciples,

When Jesus had finished all these sayings is similar to the formula used at the close of the other four discourses in the Gospel (7.28; 11.1; 13.53; 19.1), except that **all** is here included, perhaps to suggest that Jesus' teaching ministry has now come to an end. Noticeable also is the omission of any statement indicating movement on the part of Jesus, such as accompanies the other summary statements (8.1; 11.1b; 13.53b; 19.1b).

He said to his disciples represents another alteration in the account. But it does provide the medium by which what is given as an editorial comment by Mark (14.1) and Luke (22.1) may be transformed by Matthew to a direct statement of Jesus to his disciples.

26.2   RSV   TEV

"You know that after two days the Passover is coming, and the Son of man will be delivered up to be crucified."	"In two days, as you know, it will be the Passover Festival, and the Son of Man will be handed over to be crucified."

Matthew's shift to direct discourse also serves as a literary device which enables Jesus to speak of his forthcoming crucifixion. Explicit mention of **the Passover** is not made in either Mark or Luke, though Matthew will mention it three other times in this chapter (verses 17, 18, 19).

The "**as you know**" of TEV is much more natural in this context than the **you know** of RSV. Whether to put this at the beginning of the sentence or after the phrase **after two days**, as TEV has, or in some other position, should depend on what sounds best in the receptor language.

After two days is more naturally expressed in English as "**In two days**" (TEV), or "two days from now," or "in two days' time" (NJB, NEB, Brc, NAB).

In the past many translators borrowed the English word **Passover**, but this then has no meaning for their readers. For French speaking areas this is even worse, since the modern word for Easter (*Paques*) sounds the same as the word for Passover (*Paque*), so that readers will think only of the modern Christian holiday, not the Jewish one. The situation in Spanish areas is similar, since *pascua* can be used for both holidays. So borrowing is not a good solution at all. **Passover** was an important festival in the Jewish calendar, the time when the Jews celebrated their delivery from slavery in Egypt. For translators, the first thing to consider is that this was a festival, and they should use that in the translation ("the festival of . . ."). Some translators have tried to give the literal meaning with something like "the festival of Passing Over" or "the festival of the Time When the Angel Passed Over." But better is to capture the symbolism with a phrase like "the festival of Redemption" or "festival of Deliverance."

It is easy to mistranslate this sentence so as to make it seem that the disciples knew not only that the Passover would be in two days, but also that at that time Jesus would be arrested and killed. This can be solved by having two sentences: "As you know, in two days it will be time for the festival of Deliverance. At that time, someone will hand over . . . ."

The Son of man was last mentioned in 25.31, in reference to his coming in glory.

Will be delivered up translates the verb traditionally used of Jesus' betrayal (see comment under "had been arrested" at 4.12). That the Son of Man would be crucified is also mentioned in Jesus' third prediction of his death and resurrection (20.19). Although it is not indicated who will hand Jesus over and crucify him, some languages may require the shift to an active construction. If this is the case, then it will be possible to translate "Someone will hand the Son of Man over to his enemies, and they will crucify him."

Crucified was discussed at 20.19.

26.3   RSV   TEV

    Then the chief priests and the elders of the people gathered in the palace of the high priest, who was called Caiaphas,

    Then the chief priests and the elders met together in the palace of Caiaphas, the High Priest,

The scene now shifts to **the palace of the high priest, who was called Caiaphas**, a detail not mentioned by Mark and Luke. John also notes that Caiaphas was high priest at this time (11.49), but elsewhere Luke (3.2; Acts 4.6) states that Annas was the high priest. The confusion is probably due to the fact that Annas was deposed as high priest in A.D. 15 and replaced by Caiaphas in A.D. 18. However, Annas did not die until A.D. 36, and until his death he is said to have retained a great deal of power and influence among the Jews.

It is important that readers see that verse 3 is a new episode. **Then** is not Jesus still talking, nor does it relate what he said in verse 2 to the fact that the chief priests and elders met to plot to kill him. Brc has "It was then," but "At that time" may be good, too.

The chief priests and the elders of the people differs slightly from Mark (14.1) and Luke (22.2), which have "the chief priests and the scribes." See comment at verse 47. **Chief priests** was discussed at 2.4. For **elders of the people** see 16.21, although there **of the people** does not appear. **High priest** can be translated as the "the leader of the priests."

Palace poses a problem for some translators, since this word is often used only for the house of a king or chief. In that case one can say simply "the house of (or, for) the leader of the priests."

The identification of the high priest, **who was called Caiaphas**, may need to be a separate sentence: "The high priest was (named) Caiaphas."

26.4

RSV	TEV

and took counsel together in order to arrest Jesus by stealth and kill him. | **and made plans to arrest Jesus secretly and put him to death.**

Took counsel (TEV "**made plans**") translates a verb which appears only here in the Gospel of Matthew, though a related noun form is used in 12.14; see comment there.

By stealth of RSV and AT is certainly not everyday English. The primary meaning of the noun **stealth** is "deceit" or "treachery," which is the basis for "by some trick" of NJB, NEB, NAB; "by some stratagem" (Brc). Both TEV and GECL prefer to use the adverb "**secretly.**"

Kill him is translated "**put him to death**" by TEV to indicate that the nature of the death is that of legal execution rather than of murder. NJB is even better: "have him put to death."

26.5

RSV	TEV

But they said, "Not during the feast, lest there be a tumult among the people" | **"We must not do it during the festival," they said, "or the people will riot."**

Not during the feast is made into a complete statement by TEV: "**We must not do it during the festival.**" **The feast** is obviously a reference to the Passover (see verse 2).

The impersonal construction of the Greek text, represented by RSV's **lest there be a tumult among the people**, is translated by TEV as "**the people will riot.**" The noun rendered **tumult** is also used in 27.24 but nowhere else in the Gospel.

For many translators indirect discourse is more natural; as for example, "But they did not feel they could arrest Jesus and have him put to death during the festival, because there was a possibility that the people would riot."

26.6-13

RSV	TEV
Jesus Is Anointed at Bethany
6 Now when Jesus was at Bethany in the house of Simon the leper, 7 a woman came up to him with an alabaster flask of very expensive ointment, and she poured it on his head, as he sat at table. 8 But when the disciples saw it, they were indignant, saying, "Why this waste? 9 For this ointment might have been sold for a large sum, and given to the poor." 10 But Jesus, aware of this, said to them, "Why do you trouble the woman? For she has done a beautiful thing to me.	6 Jesus was in Bethany at the house of Simon, a man who had suffered from a dreaded skin disease. 7 While Jesus was eating, a woman came to him with an alabaster jar filled with an expensive perfume, which she poured on his head. 8 The disciples saw this and became angry. "Why all this waste?" they asked. 9 "This perfume could have been sold for a large amount and the money given to the poor!"
10 Jesus knew what they were saying, and

11 For you always have the poor with you, but you will not always have me. 12 In pouring this ointment on my body she has done it to prepare me for burial. 13 Truly, I say to you, wherever this gospel is preached in the whole world, what she has done will be told in memory of her."

so he said to them, "Why are you bothering this woman? It is a fine and beautiful thing that she has done for me. 11 You will always have poor people with you, but you will not always have me. 12 What she did was to pour this perfume on my body to get me ready for burial. 13 Now, I assure you that wherever this gospel is preached all over the world, what she has done will be told in memory of her."

SECTION HEADING: "**Jesus is Anointed at Bethany**" is a passive construction, but many languages will require an active one; for example, "In Bethany a woman anoints Jesus." Of course, in verse 7 the word "**Anointed**" does not occur, and there and in this heading "pours oil on" may be best.

The account of the anointing at Bethany is found in all four Gospels, though in Luke it appears in a completely different setting (7.36-50), where it functions to teach a lesson on forgiveness. In John (12.1-8) it is recorded as having taken place immediately before Jesus' triumphant entry into Jerusalem (12.9-19), and there the central figure is Mary, the sister of Lazarus. In general Matthew follows Mark (14.3-9), though he does make one important alteration: "the disciples" (verse 8) are now the ones who raise the question ("Why this waste?"), in place of Mark's "some (of the people)" (14.4).

<table>
<tr><td>**26.6**</td><td>RSV</td><td>TEV</td></tr>
</table>

Now when Jesus was at Bethany in the house of Simon the leper,

Jesus was in Bethany at the house of Simon, a man who had suffered from a dreaded skin disease.

Jesus was at Bethany may be inadequate as a transitional for languages which expect a marker indicating movement from one place to another. Accordingly one may translate "In the meanwhile Jesus had gone to Bethany, and . . . ." The village of Bethany was previously mentioned in 21.17; it lies east of the Mount of Olives, on the other side of the mountain from Jerusalem.

This is the only mention in Matthew's Gospel of **Simon the leper**. TEV translates **the leper** as "**who had suffered from a dreaded skin disease**" (see comment at 8.2). We assume Simon had been cured by this time or he would not have been able to stay at home and entertain guests. Therefore many translators have "a man named Simon who had suffered from a dreaded skin disease."

<table>
<tr><td>**26.7**</td><td>RSV</td><td>TEV</td></tr>
</table>

a woman came up to him with an alabaster flask of very expensive ointment, and she poured it on his head, as he sat at table.

While Jesus was eating, a woman came to him with an alabaster jar filled with an expensive perfume, which she poured on his head.

The **him** refers to Jesus, not to Simon, although Simon was the last person referred to in the RSV text.

Came up to will have to be "went up to" in many languages.

Alabaster flask translates a Greek noun which has as its first meaning "alabaster" (a soft stone of creamy color), and as a secondary meaning "container made of alabaster." The stone itself was imported from Egypt, and thousands of small alabaster perfume flasks have been excavated by archaeologists in Palestine. Most translators render this as "a small container made of a stone called alabaster." They may even describe the container as "a container for oil (or, ointment)."

Very expensive translates a different adjective from that used by Mark (14.3), which there probably has the meaning "genuine" or "pure." Moreover, Mark identifies the perfume in more detail, indicating the substance from which it was made ("nard").

The Greek word translated **ointment** may also be rendered "**perfume**" (TEV); it is used again in verse 12, though nowhere else in the Gospel. If neither of these terms is well known, translators may have "oil that smells good (or, sweet)" or "oil to make the skin smell good." That which is called **ointment** today is more like a cream than oil, and it cannot be poured. TEV's "**expensive perfume**" means an expensive kind of perfume.

As he sat at table (TEV "**While Jesus was eating**") may need to be stated earlier in the narrative, as in TEV. If this suggestion is adopted, one may then translate verses 6 and 7 as "In the meanwhile Jesus had gone to the village of Bethany and was eating a meal in the house of Simon . . . ." Other translators will want to keep the verses separate and say "Jesus had gone to the village of Bethany and was at the house of Simon who had had a serious skin disease. While he was at the table eating . . . ."

For modern readers it may seem strange that the woman would apparently burst into Simon's home without any invitation. But as one commentator has suggested, the gesture of the woman would not be extraordinary in a Jewish home of that time; it could have been dictated by love, joy, or recognition, although neither Mark nor Matthew say anything about the sentiments which provoke the action. What the woman did was important, not why she did it.

26.8	RSV	TEV

But when the disciples saw it, they were indignant, saying, "Why this waste?

The disciples saw this and became angry. "Why all this waste?" they asked.

A previously indicated, **the disciples** are "some (of the people)" in the Marcan account (14.4). It is also significant that, as the narrative appears in the Gospel of John, it is Judas alone who makes the objection (12.4-5).

Were indignant (TEV "**became angry**"): see comment at 20.24.

Saying (TEV "**they asked**") may need to be more specific: "they said to one another." Evidently Jesus overheard their remark (see verse 10).

If **Why this waste?** needs to be expanded, it can be "Why did she waste this perfume?" "What was the point in wasting the oil like that?" or "Look at how she wasted that perfume." If **waste** is a problem, "poured it out for nothing" is possible. In some languages, to fully express the accusation the disciples are making, a statement followed by a question is effective: "She wasted that perfume. Was that good?"

26.9 RSV	TEV
For this ointment might have been sold for a large sum, and given to the poor."	**"This perfume could have been sold for a large amount and the money given to the poor!"**

Might have been sold is a passive construction that may better be "she could have sold."

A large sum may need to be stated in its full form: "a large sum of money" (Brc).

And given to the poor is translated **"and the money given to the poor"** by TEV (compare NJB, NEB, NIV, NAB) so that no one will think that the perfume could have been sold and yet at the same time be given to the poor. Phps restructures in a slightly different manner ("Couldn't this perfume have been sold for a lot of money which could be given to the poor?"), while Brc has ". . . a large sum of money, and the proceeds could have been used to help the poor."

26.10 RSV	TEV
But Jesus, aware of this, said to them, "Why do you trouble the woman? For she has done a beautiful thing to me.	**Jesus knew what they were saying, and so he said to them, "Why are you bothering this woman? It is a fine and beautiful thing that she has done for me.**

In the Greek text the verb **aware of** (TEV **"knew"**) is not followed by an object, but one must be supplied in translation: **aware of this**, "knew what they were saying" (TEV), and "knew that they were angry" (GECL 1st edition). Matthew places **aware of** in an emphatic position in the sentence.

Why do you trouble the woman? has been rendered as **"Why are you bothering this woman?"** by TEV. Others have "Why are you criticizing this woman?" Since Jesus does not really want an answer, some translators have "Stop bothering this woman."

A beautiful thing (so NIV, Phps, Mft; AT, NEB "a fine thing"; Brc "a lovely thing") is more literally "a good deed" (NAB) or "a good work." A footnote in NJB points out that the Jews classified "good works" as either "almsgiving" or "charitable deeds." The latter category was considered superior, and included in it was that of the burial of the dead. Therefore according to this interpretation the woman had performed "one of the good works" (JB) which was superior to that of giving to the poor (verse 9). Since the woman's deed was an expression of spontaneous love, it seems probable that Jesus was actually praising the motive behind what the woman did rather than the deed itself.

26.11	RSV	TEV

For you always have the poor with you, but you will not always have me.

You will always have poor people with you, but you will not always have me.

For you always have the poor with you gives the reason for what Jesus has just said in verse 9. GECL translates "There will always be poor people with you."

But you will not always have me may be stated in such a way that subject and object are inverted: "but I will not always be with you." One may even be more explicit; for example, "but you will not always have the opportunity to do something for me."

26.12	RSV	TEV

In pouring this ointment on my body she has done it to prepare me for burial.

What she did was to pour this perfume on my body to get me ready for burial.

In pouring . . . she is translated **"What she did was to pour"** by TEV. But both restructurings result in rather difficult sentence constructions for English speakers. GECL translates the verse as follows: "She poured this perfume on my body in order to prepare it for burial." Another possible translation is "When she poured this perfume on my body she was preparing it (or, me) for burial." Jesus is not saying the woman knew he was going to die and be buried. But he had already spoken of his death to his disciples in verse 2, and quite naturally he applies what the woman does to that concern.

26.13	RSV	TEV

Truly, I say to you, wherever this gospel is preached in the whole world, what she has done will be told in memory of her."

Now, I assure you that wherever this gospel is preached all over the world, what she has done will be told in memory of her."

Truly, I say to you is the same emphatic formula discussed at 5.18. TEV's "Now" in "Now, I assure you" is to indicate the relation between Jesus' words of verses 10-12 and his comment which follows in verse 13.

Wherever this gospel is preached . . . will be told in memory of her represents the exegesis accepted by most translations. A good rendering is "Whenever people preach this message of Good News (about God's ruling) anywhere in the world, they will tell about what this woman has done, too, so that people will remember her."

What she has done will be told in memory of her is restructured by GECL as "people will tell what she has done, and they will think about her."

26.14-16

RSV	TEV
	Judas Agrees to Betray Jesus
14 Then one of the twelve, who was called Judas Iscariot, went to the chief priests 15 and said, "What will you give me if I deliver him to you?" And they paid him thirty pieces of silver. 16 And from that moment he sought an opportunity to betray him.	14 Then one of the twelve disciples—the one named Judas Iscariot— went to the chief priests 15 and asked, "What will you give me if I betray Jesus to you?" They counted out thirty silver coins and gave them to him. 16 From then on Judas was looking for a good chance to hand Jesus over to them.

SECTION HEADING: most translators can render the TEV heading fairly literally, "**Judas Agrees to Betray Jesus.**" Some say "Judas is given money to betray Jesus."

The woman's act of devotion in pouring perfume on Jesus is now contrasted with Judas' deed of betrayal. Each of the four Gospels indicates that it was Judas who turned Jesus over to his enemies, but none of them explain precisely why he did it. Only Matthew (27.3-10) and Luke (Acts 1.18-19) narrate Judas' death, and they evidently follow separate traditions.

26.14   RSV   TEV

Then one of the twelve, who was called Judas Iscariot, went to the chief priests	**Then one of the twelve disciples—the one named Judas Iscariot— went to the chief priests**

Then translates a particle used ninety times by Matthew; it indicates a loose temporal connection. Some translations have "after that." Both the qualifier **who was called** and the Greek form of the verb **went** are also characteristic of Matthew's style.

The twelve (disciples) are listed in 10.1-4, immediately preceding their mission to the "lost sheep of the people of Israel" (10.6). Concerning the meaning of the name **Iscariot**, see comments at 10.4. But it is used as a name and should not be translated. For English readers it is perhaps simpler to translate "Then Judas Iscariot, one of the twelve disciples, went . . . ."

The chief priests are last mentioned in verses 3-5, where Matthew said that they "made plans to arrest Jesus secretly and put him to death."

26.15 RSV TEV

and said, "What will you give me if I deliver him to you?" And they paid him thirty pieces of silver.

and asked, "What will you give me if I betray Jesus to you?" They counted out thirty silver coins and gave them to him.

If I deliver him: the verb **deliver** (TEV "**betray**") is commented on at 4.12, where RSV translates the passive form as "had been arrested." Some translations have "help you arrest him" or "deliver him to you so you can arrest him." Sometimes it is more natural to reverse the order of the sentence: "If I help you arrest Jesus, what will you give me?"

Since this is the opening of a new section, TEV specifically identifies **him** as Jesus.

Paid (so also NJB, NAB) is translated by two verbs in TEV: "**counted . . . gave**" The Greek verb itself has a number of different meanings, and it may possibly be used in the sense of "offered" or "agreed to pay" (Lu; Phps, Brc "settled with . . . for"), as the NEB footnote indicates.

Only Matthew mentions **thirty pieces of silver** (TEV "**thirty silver coins**") as the price of betrayal. The amount is not significant, and it was probably determined by Zechariah 11.12 ("So they paid thirty pieces of silver as my wages"). According to Exodus 21.32 this is also the amount which the owner of a bull had to pay a person whose slave had been killed by the bull. One scholar notes that in New Testament times inflation was such that "the sum was worth only about a tenth as much."

The amount of money given to Judas, **thirty pieces of silver**, was not in itself important, as we pointed out above, but there is some value in retaining the form, since it does tie this amount in with the Zechariah reference. Translators should not try to convert this to modern currencies such as pounds or francs, but if a literal translation is unacceptable, they can say "thirty pieces of money made from silver."

26.16 RSV TEV

And from that moment he sought an opportunity to betray him.

From then on Judas was looking for a good chance to hand Jesus over to them.

On the basis of this verse some scholars conclude that "the prospect of payment is the actual motive behind Judas' treachery."

From that moment represents the same construction used in 16.21, where it is translated "From that time" by RSV. It is also used in 4.17.

Opportunity (so also NJB, NEB, NAB) is translated "**good chance**" by TEV, and GECL has "favorable opportunity." Elsewhere in the New Testament the word is used only in Luke 22.6. One good rendering of the sentence is "From then on Judas began looking for a good opportunity to betray Jesus."

26.17-25

RSV

TEV

**Jesus Eats the Passover Meal
with His Disciples**

17 Now on the first day of Unleavened Bread the disciples came to Jesus, saying, "Where will you have us prepare for you to eat the passover?" 18 He said, "Go into the city to a certain one, and say to him, 'The Teacher says, My time is at hand; I will keep the passover at your house with my disciples.' " 19 And the disciples did as Jesus had directed them, and they prepared the passover.

20 When it was evening, he sat at table with the twelve disciples;[e] 21 and as they were eating, he said, "Truly, I say to you, one of you will betray me." 22 And they were very sorrowful, and began to say to him one after another, "Is it I, Lord?" 23 He answered, "He who has dipped his hand in the dish with me, will betray me. 24 The Son of man goes as it is written of him, but woe to that man by whom the Son of man is betrayed! It would have been better for that man if he had not been born." 25 Judas, who betrayed him, said, "Is it I, Master?"[f] He said to him, "You have said so."

[e] Other authorities omit *disciples*
[f] Or *Rabbi*

17 On the first day of the Festival of Unleavened Bread the disciples came to Jesus and asked him, "Where do you want us to get the Passover meal ready for you?"

18 "Go to a certain man in the city," he said to them, "and tell him: 'The Teacher says, My hour has come; my disciples and I will celebrate the Passover at your house.' "

19 The disciples did as Jesus had told them and prepared the Passover meal.

20 When it was evening, Jesus and the twelve disciples sat down to eat. 21 During the meal Jesus said, "I tell you, one of you will betray me."

22 The disciples were very upset and began to ask him, one after the other, "Surely, Lord, you don't mean me?"

23 Jesus answered, "One who dips his bread in the dish with me will betray me. 24 The Son of Man will die as the Scriptures say he will, but how terrible for that man who will betray the Son of Man! It would have been better for that man if he had never been born!"

25 Judas, the traitor, spoke up. "Surely, Teacher, you don't mean me?" he asked.

Jesus answered, "So you say."

SECTION HEADING: **"Jesus Eats the Passover Meal with His Disciples."** In some situations "Celebrates the Passover" is better than **"Eats the Passover Meal,"** but it depends on how **"Passover"** has been translated. See comments on verse 2.

Verses 17-25 narrate two events: (1) preparation for the Passover (verses 17-19), and (2) identification of Jesus' betrayer (verses 20-25). Matthew considerably abbreviates the Marcan account of the Passover preparation (14.12-16) by the omission of at least three bits of information: (1) that the first day of Unleavened Bread was also the time "when they sacrificed the passover lamb" (14.12), (2) that the person whom the disciples are to meet would be "carrying a jar of water" (14.13), and (3) that the man would show them "a large upper room furnished and ready," where they were to prepare the meal (14.15). The emphasis is also different in the two Gospels: Mark underscores the miraculous power of Jesus (14.16: "and found it as he had told them"), while Matthew focuses upon the coming of Jesus' hour (26.18: "My time is at hand," without parallel in either Mark or Luke) and the obedience of the disciples in following Jesus' instructions (26.19).

By including next the narrative of the identification of the traitor (verses 20-25), Matthew continues to follow the Marcan outline of events (14.17-21). Luke, however, introduces the meal itself (22.15-20) before the announcement of the traitor (22.21-23). Matthew adds weight to the treachery of the betrayal by recording Judas' question, "Is it I, Master?" (verse 25). Noticeable also is Judas' usage of "Master" (literally "Rabbi") as a means of addressing Jesus, in contrast to "Lord" as the noun of address employed by the other disciples.

26.17 RSV TEV

Now on the first day of Unleavened Bread the disciples came to Jesus, saying, "Where will you have us prepare for you to eat the passover?"

On the first day of the Festival of Unleavened Bread the disciples came to Jesus and asked him, "Where do you want us to get the Passover meal ready for you?"

Some scholars believe that Passover and the festival of Unleavened Bread existed as separate festivals, perhaps even before the time of Moses. In Exodus the two are combined, with "Passover" usually referring to the first day of the festival, when the lamb was eaten, although both names have been used for the entire festival. In some contexts "Passover" refers to the sacrificial lamb that became the Passover meal.

Since the Jewish day was calculated from sunset, **the first day of Unleavened Bread** would strictly speaking mean the 15th of Nisan, which would have begun at sunset on the 14th. But it may well be that the morning of the 14th is meant, for that was the time when all leaven was removed from Jewish households. Preparation for the meal would have continued throughout the day. Then the meal itself would have begun toward evening on the 14th, and it would have continued into the night, thus ending on the 15th. The festival of **Unleavened Bread** lasted seven days (Nisan 15-22), and it also commemorated the safe rescue of the Jewish ancestors from Egypt. During these seven days the Jewish people ate unleavened bread (bread made without yeast), to recall the day on which they had departed from Egypt in haste.

The first day of Unleavened Bread has been rendered by TEV as "**the first day of the Festival of Unleavened Bread.**" It is not necessary in the translation to explain exactly what was involved in this festival, although the information can be put into a footnote or into the glossary. **Unleavened Bread** may not be known, and translators sometimes have "bread with no yeast." For "yeast" or "leaven" see comments on 13.33.

Came may have to be "went" or "went up to."

Where will you have us prepare for you to eat the passover? is practically word-for-word the same as Mark 14.12 ("Where will you have us go and prepare for you to eat the passover?"). Most translators expand **passover** to "the Passover meal" or "the meal that celebrates the deliverance," using, of course, whatever translation of **passover** they have been using elsewhere.

26.18 RSV TEV

He said, "Go into the city to a certain one, and say to him, 'The Teacher says, My time is at hand; I will keep

"Go to a certain man in the city," he said to them, "and tell him: 'The Teacher says, My hour has

the passover at your house with my disciples.' "   **come; my disciples and I will celebrate the Passover at your house.' "**

A certain one may imply that Jesus actually told the disciples the person's name, or that the person was known to the disciples, but that for some reason Matthew decided not to mention the name in his Gospel. Accordingly GECL renders "Go to a man in the city—he told them the man's name—and tell him . . . ." The use of "so-and-so" (Mft, JB, Brc) implies to the English reader that the name was known, as does "Go to this man in the city and tell him" (NAB).

The Teacher may more appropriately be rendered "our Teacher" as in GECL, because in a context of this sort the definite article **the** may carry this meaning. For **Teacher** as a title of Jesus in the Gospel of Matthew, see comment at 8.19.

Time (so Mft, AT, Lu, Zür) is the traditional rendering of the Greek noun found here. A few modern English translations prefer "appointed time" (NEB, NAB, NIV), while Brc has "hour of crisis" (TEV, GECL **"hour"**). The noun is used several other times in the Gospel (8.29; 11.25; 12.1; 13.30; 14.1; 16.3; 21.34,41; 24.45), but the general consensus of scholarship is that here it has the specialized meaning of a moment appointed by God. One possible translation, therefore, is "the time God has set for me." To state specifically that this refers to his death is probably not necessary.

Since **time** derives from the same stem as "opportunity" of verse 16, it may well be that Matthew intends for his readers to see a contrast between this saying of Jesus and the remark made in verse 16.

At hand translates an adjective made from the same stem as the verb discussed at 3.2 (see comments there). The meaning may be either "has come" or "is near."

I will keep . . . with my disciples is a Semitic Greek construction which is equivalent to "I and my disciples will keep" (TEV **"my disciples and I will celebrate"**).

At your house is literally "with you," but as may be gathered from the reading of most translations, the meaning is as RSV and TEV have expressed it.

All languages handle direct and indirect discourse differently, and this verse can be something of a problem. Jesus tells the disciples what they should tell the certain person what he (Jesus) says to him (the person). The **I** and **my** refer to Jesus. Translators should use direct or indirect discourse as required by the receptor language. For some, both are used, as in "Jesus told his disciples to go into the city to a certain person and tell him that the Teacher says this: 'My time has arrived. I and my disciples will celebrate the passover at your house.'"

26.19   RSV   TEV

And the disciples did as Jesus had directed them, and they prepared the passover.   **The disciples did as Jesus had told them and prepared the Passover meal.**

The disciples refers to the twelve (see verse 17), whereas both Mark (14.13) and Luke (22.8) indicate that only two disciples were sent, whom Luke identifies as Peter and John.

Did as Jesus had directed them parallels 21.6; only Matthew provides this information, which emphasizes the obedience of the disciples to Jesus' command.

26.20   RSV   TEV

When it was evening, he sat at   When it was evening, Jesus and
table with the twelve disciples;*e*   the twelve disciples sat down to eat.

e Other authorities omit *disciples*

When it was evening (so also Mark 14.17) suggests a time after sunset, when the Passover meal was eaten (see comment at verse 17). But this also would have been the time when the main meal of each day was generally eaten. Translators commonly have "that evening" or "that night."

He sat at table with the twelve disciples is a construction similar to that discussed in verse 17, and so may be translated as in TEV: "**Jesus and the twelve disciples sat down to eat.**" As the RSV footnote points out, **the twelve disciples** is "the twelve" in some Greek manuscripts. But the full meaning in either case is **the twelve disciples** (or even "his twelve disciples"), and some languages will require the complete form.

Whereas Mark opens the scene with the statement "Jesus came with the twelve disciples" (14.17, TEV), Matthew omits the statement and begins the scene with the eating of the meal itself (Luke 22.14 has "When the hour came, Jesus took his place at the table with the apostles," TEV).

26.21   RSV   TEV

and as they were eating, he said,   During the meal Jesus said, "I tell
"Truly, I say to you, one of you will   you, one of you will betray me."
betray me."

And as they were eating: TEV and GECL transform the verb **were eating** into a noun, in the phrase "**During the meal.**" In place of the pronominal subject **he**, TEV substitutes the proper name, "**Jesus said.**" Brc introduces an indirect object to indicate to whom Jesus addressed his remarks: "During the meal he said to them."

Truly, I say to you was most recently used in verse 13; see comment at 5.18.

Betray is the same verb translated "delivered up" in verse 2; see comment at 4.12.

26.22   RSV   TEV

And they were very sorrowful, and   The disciples were very upset
began to say to him one after anoth-   and began to ask him, one after the
er, "Is it I, Lord?"   other, "Surely, Lord, you don't mean
                                         me?"

And they were very sorrowful: TEV identifies the pronominal subject **they** as "**The disciples**" in order to avoid the erroneous conclusion that Jesus himself was included within the group that was upset.

Were very sorrowful (TEV "**were very upset**") translates the same verb plus adverb construction that is used in 14.9 and 17.23 (see discussion there) and 18.31.

Is it I, Lord? translates a question form which expects a negative response: "Of course not." Therefore both TEV ("**Surely . . . you don't mean me?**") and Brc (". . . surely it can't be me?") shift to a form in English which suggests the presupposed answer. In some languages the shift to a statement may be necessary: "Lord, I am sure that you don't mean me."

26.23 RSV	TEV
He answered, "He who has dipped his hand in the dish with me, will betray me.	Jesus answered, "One who dips his bread in the dish with me will betray me.

He who has dipped his hand in the dish with me, will betray me indicates that the betrayer will be a close friend, one who shares the common bowl with Jesus. This is a particularly treacherous act, since the meal signified a tie between those who participated in it. Commentators are agreed that the words of Jesus reflect Psalm 41.9.

This sentence sometimes has to be restructured to be natural; for example, "The person who will betray me is one who has dipped his bread in the dish with me." If at all possible, this image of dipping bread in the dish should be retained. If translators find the act so foreign that their readers will not understand it, they can say "The person who has dipped his bread in the dish with me as we ate together."

26.24 RSV	TEV
The Son of man goes as it is written of him, but woe to that man by whom the Son of man is betrayed! It would have been better for that man if he had not been born."	The Son of Man will die as the Scriptures say he will, but how terrible for that man who will betray the Son of Man! It would have been better for that man if he had never been born!"

"**The Son of Man will die**" of TEV and GECL translates **The Son of man goes**. But all commentators are agreed that the verb **goes** is used figuratively of Jesus' journey to his death: "is going to his fate" (NJB) and "is going the way appointed for him" (NEB).

As it is written of him is similar to the "quotation formula" first used in 2.5. GECL translates "as it is predicted in the Holy Scriptures." Note that these translations use the future tense ("**will die**") to render the present tense **goes**, since that is clearly the meaning of the form here. As elsewhere, there may be need of an active sentence such as "as people wrote in the Scriptures." Brc renders the sentence "the Son of Man goes out on the road the scripture says he must go."

Woe (TEV "**how terrible**") translates the same expression first used in 11.21; see also 23.13.

Betrayed, here used of **the Son of man**, has "me" as its object in verse 23. In this way Jesus is clearly identified as the Son of Man. The passive **by whom the Son of man is betrayed** may better be rendered by an active construction; for example, "who will betray the Son of Man" (TEV).

In place of the impersonal construction **it would have been better for that man**, it is possible to translate "That man would have been better off, if he had never been born!" The threat is similar to that of 18.6-7.

26.25	RSV	TEV

Judas, who betrayed him, said, "Is it I, Master?"[f] He said to him, "You have said so."

Judas, the traitor, spoke up. "Surely, Teacher, you don't mean me?" he asked.
Jesus answered, "So you say."

[f] Or *Rabbi*

Judas was last mentioned in verse 14; here he is identified as the one **who betrayed him**, which may be translated "the one who had agreed to turn Jesus over to his enemies."

Is it I, Master? is word-for-word the same question in Greek as that of the rest of the disciples (verse 22), except that Judas substitutes **Master** (TEV "**Teacher**") as a noun of address for "Lord." **Master** (RSV footnote: "Rabbi") is discussed at 23.7. In many languages this noun of address must precede the question.

You have said so (TEV "**So you say**") translates an expression which, dependent upon the context, may be understood as either a denial or an affirmation. The majority of scholars apparently interpret Jesus' reply to be in agreement with Judas' question: "You have said so, and what you say is true." Brc has "You have said it yourself!" The TEV question and response do not relate clearly to each other and do not make the best model.

26.26-30

RSV	TEV

The Lord's Supper

26 Now as they were eating, Jesus took bread, and blessed, and broke it, and gave it to the disciples and said, "Take, eat; this is my body." 27 And he took a cup, and when he had given thanks he gave it to them, saying, "Drink of it, all of you; 28 for this is my blood of the[g] covenant, which is poured out for many for the forgiveness of sins. 29 I tell you I shall not drink again of this fruit of the vine until that day when I drink it new with you in my Father's kingdom."

30 And when they had sung a hymn, they went out to the Mount of Olives.

26 While they were eating, Jesus took a piece of bread, gave a prayer of thanks, broke it, and gave it to his disciples. "Take and eat it," he said; "this is my body."

27 Then he took a cup, gave thanks to God, and gave it to them. "Drink it, all of you," he said; 28 "this is my blood, which seals God's covenant, my blood poured out for many for the forgiveness of sins. 29 I tell you, I will never again drink this wine until the day I drink the new wine with you in my Father's Kingdom."

g Other ancient authorities insert *new*

30 Then they sang a hymn and went out to the Mount of Olives.

SECTION HEADING: **"The Lord's Supper"** is a technical term used by many churches. Many translators have similarly used the usual term in their language. Others have a short sentence such as "Jesus eats his final meal (with his disciples)."

Matthew's account of the Lord's Supper closely parallels that of Mark (14.22-26), though it differs in at least two places: (1) the introduction of the command "eat" in verse 26, and (2) the shift from indirect discourse of Mark 14.23 ("and they all drank of it") to direct discourse ("Drink of it, all of you") of verse 27. The result is a more balanced text in which the command to eat follows immediately upon the distribution of the bread, and the command to drink accompanies the passing of the cup. The accounts of the Supper in Luke (22.14-20) and Paul (1 Cor 11.23-25) reflect further differences. Although it is not within the scope of this Handbook to discuss the Lukan and Pauline traditions, perhaps it should at least be noted that Luke 22.19b-20 is practically identical with 1 Corinthians 11.24b-25.

26.26   RSV   TEV

Now as they were eating, Jesus took bread, and blessed, and broke it, and gave it to the disciples and said, "Take, eat; this is my body."

While they were eating, Jesus took a piece of bread, gave a prayer of thanks, broke it, and gave it to his disciples. "Take and eat it," he said; "this is my body."

Now as they were eating is almost word-for-word the same as "and as they were eating" of verse 21.

In the Greek text **Jesus** is specified as the subject of the verb **took**, since both he and Judas participated in the dialogue of verse 25.

Took ... blessed ... broke ... gave translate the same series of four verbs used in 14.19 (see comment there) and 15.36.

Bread (so also NEB, NAB, NIV) is translated "a loaf" by several major English translations (Mft, AT, Phps, Brc); TEV has **"a piece of bread,"** and "some bread" is the reading of JB. See comment at 14.17. If TEV's **"a piece of bread"** implies that the bread was already broken, then TEV should not be used as a model.

The phrase **take, eat** does not have an explicit direct object, but translators often say "take this (bread) and eat it."

The equational formula of the Greek text (**this is my body**) is followed by most translations. Mft ("it means my body") and Brc ("This means my body") are the exception. Because of the ways that different churches have interpreted this phrase, however, these solutions are not advisable. It is better to retain the formula of the text, that is, to say "is" here and leave it to the readers to interpret.

And he took a cup, and when he had given thanks he gave it to them, saying, "Drink of it, all of you;	Then he took a cup, gave thanks to God, and gave it to them. "Drink it, all of you," he said;

The text says that he took **a cup**, but many translators find it helpful to say "a cup of wine." See 9.17 for a discussion of "wine."

Took . . . had given thanks . . . gave is similar to the series of verbs used in verse 26, with **had given thanks** replacing "blessed," and "broke" being omitted because of the shift from bread to a cup. TEV specifies that the **thanks** were given "**to God**," while GECL translates "spoke a prayer of thanks," thereby accomplishing the same goal.

Drink of it is preferable to "**Drink it**" of TEV, since in many languages persons do not drink a cup but rather drink from one (NAB, NIV "from it"). The text may appropriately be rendered "Then he took a cup that was full of wine . . . and said, 'Each of you, drink some of the wine from this cup.' "

for this is my blood of the^g covenant, which is poured out for many for the forgiveness of sins.	"this is my blood, which seals God's covenant, my blood poured out for many for the forgiveness of sins.

^{g} Other ancient authorities insert *new*

Commentators note the similarity of thought between this verse and both Exodus 24.8 ("the blood of the covenant which the LORD has made with you") and Zechariah 9.11 ("the blood of my covenant with you").

This is my blood, especially in the restructuring of TEV, may possibly be mistaken as a reference to the cup, but in reality it points to the wine, as one discovers in verse 29. One may then need to translate "This wine is my blood." Both Mft ("this means my blood") and Brc ("This means my life-blood") restructure similarly to what they did with the mention of the bread in verse 26, but for the same reason this is not a good solution to follow.

As the RSV footnote indicates, **the covenant** is expanded to "the new covenant" in some Greek manuscripts. However, as TC-GNT concludes, the adjective "new" was apparently brought into the text from the parallel in Luke 22.20. If it had originally been a part of the text, there is no reason why a scribe would later have dropped it.

Of the covenant is translated "**which seals God's covenant**" by TEV, since in the establishing of a covenant between God and his people, it was customary to use blood as a means of showing that the covenant was valid. Very often the idea of a **covenant**, particularly the notion of sealing or guaranteeing it, are not well known. Then translators need to express the phrase as "this is my blood that makes certain (or, establishes) the agreement God has made (with his people)."

Poured out has sometimes been rendered "shed" (for example, Brc). Whichever expression is used, the readers must understand that it refers to death.

In the phrase **for many** Matthew uses a different preposition than is found in the Marcan parallel (14.24). Commentators note that Matthew's shift is in the direction of what the Septuagint has in Isaiah 53.4, where the same preposition that Matthew employs is found in the construction "for us." The adjective **many** is not restrictive in the sense of excluding some; rather it is all-inclusive, as it frequently is in the Hebrew of the Old Testament, and many translations have "all people."

For the forgiveness of sins is not explicitly mentioned in any of the other accounts of the Lord's Supper. Significantly enough, this phrase is not found in Matthew's account of the preaching of John the Baptist (3.1-6), though it is included in the Marcan account (1.4). It may be necessary to provide a subject for the **forgiveness of sins**, as in "so that God may forgive their sins." GECL 1st edition accurately expresses the meaning of the verse as "This is my blood, which is poured out for all people for the forgiveness of their sin. God seals his covenant with it." Another possibility is "This is my blood, which is shed for all people so that God will forgive their sins. This blood establishes God's agreement with his people."

26.29	RSV	TEV

I tell you I shall not drink again of this fruit of the vine until that day when I drink it new with you in my Father's kingdom."	I tell you, I will never again drink this wine until the day I drink the new wine with you in my Father's Kingdom."

I tell you is translated "yet I tell you" in 6.29. This is one in a series of emphatic introductory formulas found throughout the Gospel.

Except for three minor alterations, verse 29 is the same as Mark 14.25: (1) Mark has a slightly different adverbial construction for **not . . . again**; (2) the prepositional phrase **with you** is not found in the Marcan parallel; and (3) in place of **my Father's kingdom**, Mark has "the kingdom of God."

One scholar comments that **not . . . again** "may mean that Jesus is already renouncing the festive cup, consciously taking the first step toward his death." However, the weight of scholarly opinion supports the conclusion that Jesus did at this time drink wine with his disciples. Thus, if translation requires that the text be explicit, it is best to state that Jesus did drink with his disciples on this Passover occasion, which was the last time he did so before his death. For example, some translations have had "never again after this."

"Never again drink this wine" of TEV translates **not drink again of this fruit of the vine**. Although TEV has effectively rendered the idiomatic expression **fruit of the vine** as "wine," it has created another problem. That is, the combination of "never again . . . this wine" may suggest that Jesus will drink the same wine again in the kingdom. Both GECL 1st edition and Phps have "I will drink no more wine," which resolves the problem.

Translations differ in their interpretation of **drink it new with you**. Some, for example TEV, make **new** modify the wine, as in "until I drink the new wine with you." Others, for example Brc, understand **new** to refer to a new way of drinking the wine, as in "until I drink it new with you" or "until I drink it with you in a new way." The text seems to support either interpretation.

In my Father's kingdom is rendered dynamically by several translations: "when my Father has completed his work" (GECL), "when my Father has established his rule" (MACL), and "in my Father's New World" (INCL).

26.30	RSV	TEV

And when they had sung a hymn, they went out to the Mount of Olives.

Then they sang a hymn and went out to the Mount of Olives.

It may be advisable to identify **they** as "Jesus and his disciples."

The **hymn** was in all probability the second half of the "Hallel," a song of praise to the Lord, which was sung at the end of the Passover. The "Hallel" consisted of two parts (Psa 113 or Psa 113–114 and Psa 115–118), the first part of which was recited at the beginning of the Passover meal. GECL 1st edition translates "the song of thanks." "A song of praise to God" is a common translation.

The Mount of Olives was last mentioned in 24.3. It lies to the east of the city of Jerusalem.

In some translations, for example TEV, this verse is a single paragraph which is followed by a new section and heading. Also it is common to find this verse as the first sentence of the next paragraph, so that the next section heading comes at the beginning of this verse rather than after it. Translators should decide according to the needs of the receptor language.

26.31-35

RSV	TEV

Jesus Predicts Peter's Denial

31 Then Jesus said to them, "You will all fall away because of me this night; for it is written, 'I will strike the shepherd, and the sheep of the flock will be scattered.' 32 But after I am raised up, I will go before you to Galilee." 33 Peter declared to him, "Though they all fall away because of you, I will never fall away." 34 Jesus said to him, "Truly, I say to you, this very night, before the cock crows, you will deny me three times." 35 Peter said to him, "Even if I must die with you, I will not deny you." And so said all the disciples.

31 Then Jesus said to them, "This very night all of you will run away and leave me, for the scripture says, 'God will kill the shepherd, and the sheep of the flock will be scattered.' 32 But after I am raised to life, I will go to Galilee ahead of you."

33 Peter spoke up and said to Jesus, "I will never leave you, even though all the rest do!"

34 Jesus said to Peter, "I tell you that before the rooster crows tonight, you will say three times that you do not know me."

35 Peter answered, "I will never say that, even if I have to die with you!"

And all the other disciples said the same thing.

SECTION HEADING: "**Jesus Predicts Peter's Denial.**" See the previous verse for a discussion of where this heading may occur. In those languages where

807

"**Denial**" will require an object, translators may have "Jesus predicts that Peter will deny him (or, deny he knows him)" or "Jesus says that Peter will say he doesn't know him."

Matthew continues to follow the Marcan outline (14.27-31) in the inclusion of the prediction of Peter's denial on the way to Gethsemane. Luke (22.31-34) and John (13.36-38) each give their own versions of the prediction, though in a different setting.

26.31 RSV	TEV
Then Jesus said to them, "You will all fall away because of me this night; for it is written, 'I will strike the shepherd, and the sheep of the flock will be scattered.'	Then Jesus said to them, "This very night all of you will run away and leave me, for the scripture says, 'God will kill the shepherd, and the sheep of the flock will be scattered.'

Then translates the same particle that Matthew uses ninety times throughout his Gospel.

Translators who have a section heading before this verse will sometimes feel they need to make the connection with the previous passage stronger than with **Then**. "When they reached the Mount of Olives" is one way to do this.

It may be useful to identify **them** as "the disciples," especially if this was not done in verse 30.

You will all (TEV "**all of you**") is emphatic in the Greek sentence structure even more so than in Mark, who does give some emphasis by including the pronoun **you** as a separate form apart from the verb itself.

Fall away (TEV "**run away and leave**") translates the verb rendered "causes . . . to sin" in 5.29; see comment there. In this verse many translators use expressions such as "abandon me" or "lose your faith in me."

Because of me, not found in the Marcan parallel (14.27), represents another unique Matthean emphasis. The meaning seems to be that what is going to happen to Jesus will cause all of the disciples to lose their faith. Therefore one good way to render the sentence is "because of what will happen to me, tonight every one of you will give up your faith in me."

This night is not found in the Marcan parallel, though it does occur in the parallel to verse 34 (Mark 14.30). Quite often "tonight" is the natural expression to use. It modifies **fall away**, not **because of me**.

For it is written (TEV "**for the scripture says**") translates the same formula used in 2.5 (see comments there); its last occurrence was in verse 24 of the present chapter. The scripture reference is to Zechariah 13.7, and the form of the quotation in Matthew differs slightly from that in Mark. Matthew has a different word order and adds the phrase **of the flock**, which is not found in Mark. But these differences are of no real substance, since **the sheep of the flock** is best understood as a stylistic variation of "the sheep" in Mark (14.27).

In the words of one commentator, the use of the first person future (**I will strike**) "suggests that it is God who will smite Jesus, with the result that 'the flock' (the band of disciples) will be dispersed." Accordingly **strike** must be given the extended meaning of "strike . . . down" (NEB) or "**kill**" (TEV, GECL, FRCL), and the subject identified as God: "God will kill." For translators who render **it is written** with a phrase such as "God's writing" or "God has written," then the fact that it is he who strikes may already be clear: "as it says in God's writings, 'I will strike.' "

Will be scattered may require transformation into an active form to balance with the first verb: "will kill the shepherd and scatter the sheep of the flock" or "and the sheep of his flock will scatter."

26.32	RSV	TEV

But after I am raised up, I will go before you to Galilee."

But after I am raised to life, I will go to Galilee ahead of you."

But after I am raised up is an obvious reference to Jesus' resurrection from death, and TEV makes this fact explicit: "**But after I am raised to life**." It may be necessary to alter this statement to an active construction: "after God raises me back to life" or ". . . from death."

I will go before you to Galilee may refer either to Jesus' resurrection or to his final appearance. On this issue scholarly opinion is sharply divided. The usual interpretation of this phrase is that of TEV, "**I will go to Galilee ahead of you**." That is, Jesus will go there before they do, and the presumption is that they will meet him there. Brc has "I will go on ahead of you into Galilee." There are some who have understood this to mean Jesus will lead the disciples to Galilee, as in "I will lead the way for you into Galilee." The first interpretation is probably better.

26.33	RSV	TEV

Peter declared to him, "Though they all fall away because of you, I will never fall away."

Peter spoke up and said to Jesus, "I will never leave you, even though all the rest do!"

Peter declared to him and "**Peter spoke up and said to Jesus**" (TEV) represent attempts to render in a dynamic fashion "but answering Peter said to him" of the Greek text.

Fall away (used twice by Peter in this verse) is the same verb used by Jesus in verse 31: "You will all fall away . . . ." Thus the verse may be "Even though all the others lose their faith because of what happens to you, I will never lose mine."

26.34	RSV	TEV

Jesus said to him, "Truly, I say to you, this very night, before the cock crows, you will deny me three times."

Jesus said to Peter, "I tell you that before the rooster crows tonight, you will say three times that you do not know me."

Truly, I say to you is the same emphatic formula used in 5.26; it is somewhat stronger than "I tell you" of verse 29.

This very night is not really very natural English, and TEV's **"tonight"** does not have the same emphasis. One good way to express this is "Before this night is over."

Before the cock crows differs from Mark, who has "before the cock crows twice" (14.30). In that part of the world roosters generally crowed about midnight and then again about three o'clock in the morning. So the Romans gave the designation "rooster crow" to the period of time in between these two crowings of the roosters. Matthew may have in mind the main crowing of the rooster (that is, the second one), but he does not in any way hint in that direction. LB attempts to overcome the contradiction between the accounts of Matthew and Mark by translating Matthew's account as "before the cock crows at dawn." But this is definitely not what Matthew says, and it contradicts the clear meaning of "this very night, before the cock crows."

Even though the text has **the cock**, no particular fowl is being spoken of. In some languages a more natural expression is "before a rooster crows," "before there is a rooster-crow," or "before you hear a rooster crow." (Note that **cock** and **"rooster"** are two different words for male chickens used in different dialects of English.)

Deny is the same verb used in 16.24. Elsewhere in the Gospel the verb is found only in verses 35 and 75 of this chapter. A number of English translations, following Mft, use the verb "disown" (NEB, NJB, Phps, AT, Brc, NIV). **Deny me** is translated **"say that you do not know me"** by TEV. Another option is "say that you are not my follower."

26.35	RSV	TEV

Peter said to him, "Even if I must die with you, I will not deny you." And so said all the disciples.

Peter answered, "I will never say that, even if I have to die with you!"

And all the other disciples said the same thing.

Even if I must die with you is worded slightly more emphatically by Matthew than by Mark ("If I must die with you"), though Mark does add the intensifier "vehemently" after the verb "said" (14.31). Peter uses the word **must** here. What he means is that even if it means that he will die with Jesus, he will not deny him. One way to convey this is to restructure the sentence somewhat, as TEV has, with a sentence such as "I will not deny I am your follower even if that means I have to die with you." Or the order of the text can be retained: "Even if it would mean I would die with you, I will not deny that I know you."

All the disciples may more accurately be translated **"all the other disciples"** (TEV), so as not to exclude Peter from the group of disciples.

RSV | TEV

Jesus Prays in Gethsemane

36 Then Jesus went with them to a place called Gethsemane, and he said to his disciples, "Sit here, while I go yonder and pray." 37 And taking with him Peter and the two sons of Zebedee, he began to be sorrowful and troubled. 38 Then he said to them, "My soul is very sorrowful, even to death; remain here, and watch[h] with me." 39 And going a little farther he fell on his face and prayed, "My Father, if it be possible, let this cup pass from me; nevertheless, not as I will, but as thou wilt." 40 And he came to the disciples and found them sleeping; and he said to Peter, "So, could you not watch[h] with me one hour? 41 Watch[h] and pray that you may not enter into temptation; the spirit indeed is willing, but the flesh is weak." 42 Again, for the second time, he went away and prayed, "My Father, if this cannot pass unless I drink it, thy will be done." 43 And again he came and found them sleeping, for their eyes were heavy. 44 So, leaving them again, he went away and prayed for the third time, saying the same words. 45 Then he came to the disciples and said to them, "Are you still sleeping and taking your rest? Behold, the hour is at hand, and the Son of man is betrayed into the hands of sinners. 46 Rise, let us be going; see, my betrayer is at hand."

[h] Or *keep awake*

36 Then Jesus went with his disciples to a place called Gethsemane, and he said to them, "Sit here while I go over there and pray." 37 He took with him Peter and the two sons of Zebedee. Grief and anguish came over him, 38 and he said to them, "The sorrow in my heart is so great that it almost crushes me. Stay here and keep watch with me."

39 He went a little farther on, threw himself face downward on the ground, and prayed, "My Father, if it is possible, take this cup of suffering from me! Yet not what I want, but what you want."

40 Then he returned to the three disciples and found them asleep; and he said to Peter, "How is it that you three were not able to keep watch with me for even one hour? 41 Keep watch and pray that you will not fall into temptation. The spirit is willing, but the flesh is weak."

42 Once more Jesus went away and prayed, "My Father, if this cup of suffering cannot be taken away unless I drink it, your will be done." 43 He returned once more and found the disciples asleep; they could not keep their eyes open.

44 Again Jesus left them, went away, and prayed the third time, saying the same words. 45 Then he returned to the disciples and said, "Are you still sleeping and resting? Look! The hour has come for the Son of Man to be handed over to the power of sinful men. 46 Get up, let us go. Look, here is the man who is betraying me!"

SECTION HEADING: as will be seen in verse 36, in Matthew "**Gethsemane**" is called a place, not a garden. So the TEV heading "**Jesus Prays in Gethsemane**" can either be translated literally or as "Jesus prays (to God) at a place called Gethsemane."

Even though Matthew is dependent upon Mark for the story of what happened at Gethsemane, he constructs his narrative in such a manner that it becomes a pattern of prayer for the Christian community to follow. The primary emphasis, as Matthew has structured the account, is upon absolute obedience to the Father's will ("thy will be done" repeats word-for-word the petition of 6.10b).

26.36 RSV | TEV

Then Jesus went with them to a place called Gethsemane, and he said to his disciples, "Sit here, while I go yonder and pray."

Then Jesus went with his disciples to a place called Gethsemane, and he said to them, "Sit here while I go over there and pray."

In the construction **Jesus went with them**, the pronoun **them** refers back to "all his disciples" of verse 35. Mark simply has "they went," without further specification of subject (14.32). For some languages it will be preferable to translate "Jesus and his disciples went."

Gethsemane, the name of an olive orchard on the Mount of Olives, is the transliteration of a Hebrew phrase meaning "(olive) oil-press." The name is used only twice in the New Testament, here and in the Marcan parallel (14.32). John describes the spot as a "garden" (18.1), while Luke speaks only of "the place" (22.40) with reference to the Mount of Olives (22.39). As suggested above for the heading, it can be translated "place called Gethsemane."

Go yonder and is not included in the Marcan parallel (14.32). **Pray** is the most general word for prayer in the New Testament; Matthew first uses it in 5.44.

The use of **here** and **yonder** (which means "over there") may be misunderstood by readers in some languages to refer to places where the readers are. In this case indirect discourse is better: "Jesus told his disciples to sit down where they were while he went to another place to pray."

26.37	RSV	TEV

RSV	TEV
And taking with him Peter and the two sons of Zebedee, he began to be sorrowful and troubled.	He took with him Peter and the two sons of Zebedee. Grief and anguish came over him,

The two sons of Zebedee are mentioned by name ("James and John") in the Marcan parallel (14.33). Since they were identified by name at 4.21 and 10.2, translators may safely follow the text of Matthew, as RSV and TEV have done. For Matthew this narrative serves as a model for prayer and discipleship.

To be sorrowful translates the same verb used in 14.9 and 17.23; in the Marcan parallel (14.33) a different verb is used ("to be greatly distressed"). But Matthew has probably made the alteration in order to make the verb parallel the adjective "very sorrowful" of verse 38.

Troubled translates a verb which is used only here and in Philippians 2.26. It denotes deep emotion and has as its root meaning "be away from one's home or people." JB translates "great distress"; AT has "distress of mind" (Phps "agony of mind"); and TEV chooses "**anguish**."

The word **began** is actually quite awkward in English when used with emotions like **sorrowful** and **troubled**. Translators can say "he became very sad and greatly upset" or follow TEV, "grief and anguish came over him."

26.38	RSV	TEV

RSV	TEV
Then he said to them, "My soul is very sorrowful, even to death; remain here, and watch[h] with me."	and he said to them, "The sorrow in my heart is so great that it almost crushes me. Stay here and keep watch with me."

[h] Or *keep awake*

My soul is a typical Semitic way of referring to oneself, especially when deep emotions are involved. As indicated in verse 37, the adjective **very sorrowful** is derived from the same stem as the verb "to be sorrowful," except that the adjective is a more intensive form. **My soul is very sorrowful** is translated "My heart is ready to break with grief" by NEB. GECL uses an idiomatic expression: "On me there lies a burden, which has almost crushed me." When the sorrow is **even to death**, the meaning is that it is so great it could even bring on the death of the person. Some translators then add the phrase "I could even die (from the sorrow)," but others use intense expressions like the "**crushed**" of TEV and GECL, or sentences like "the grief that I feel is so great it could overcome (or, destroy) me."

Remain translates a verb which is used frequently in the Gospel of John (forty times), and often with a figurative sense; Matthew uses the verb only three times (elsewhere 10.11; 11.23), and the meaning is always obvious.

Watch (RSV footnote "keep awake") is used twice again in the Gethsemane narrative (verses 40,41); elsewhere in the Gospel it is used in an appeal for alertness for the coming of the Son of Man (24.42,43; 25.13). TEV has "**keep watch with me**," and Brc has "share my vigil."

With me is not found in Mark (14.35). Throughout the Gethsemane account Matthew emphasizes the relationship between Jesus and his disciples in a way that Mark does not; note, for example the phrase "to the disciples" (verses 40,45), as well as "with them" of verse 36.

26.39	RSV	TEV
	And going a little farther he fell on his face and prayed, "My Father, if it be possible, let this cup pass from me; nevertheless, not as I will, but as thou wilt."	He went a little farther on, threw himself face downward on the ground, and prayed, "My Father, if it is possible, take this cup of suffering from me! Yet not what I want, but what you want."

"**Threw himself face downward on the ground**" of TEV is more literally **he fell on his face**. In place of **on his face**, Mark has "on the ground" (14.35). The problem with a literal translation in English is that it implies accidental falling, whereas the text indicates the intentional assumption of this position for fervent prayer (see Gen 17.3,17; Num 14.5; 16.4; Josh 7.6). Brc is similar to TEV: "flung himself face down on the ground in prayer."

Matthew presents Jesus' prayer in direct discourse, whereas Mark uses first indirect discourse (14.35b), which he follows with direct discourse (14.36). **My Father** recalls the address "Our Father" of the Lord's Prayer (6.9). Noticeably absent from Matthew is the Aramaic word for Father ("Abba, Father"), which is found in the Marcan parallel (14.36).

The impersonal form of **if it be possible** is natural in many languages, as in "if it can be done," but often it needs to be transformed to an active clause, in which case God is the agent: "if you can do it."

"**This cup of suffering**" (TEV) is literally **this cup** (see comment at 20.22). In the Old Testament a cup is sometimes used as a symbol of punishment and revenge

(Isa 51.17; Jer 49.12; Ezek 23.32), but here it is used of suffering, and several modern language translations make this clear (GECL, INCL, MACL, FRCL). Some translations have dropped the image altogether and said "this suffering." Brc, for example, has "this bitter ordeal."

Let this cup pass from me can be expressed somewhat literally as "allow it to happen that this cup of suffering will leave me" or "allow me to not have to take this cup of suffering." It may be more natural, however, to use an imperative or request form; for example, "please take this cup of suffering away from me," "don't make me take this cup of suffering," or "let me avoid having to go through this experience of suffering."

Sometimes the whole request needs to be restructured: "My Father, permit me, if you can, to escape this cup of suffering."

Not as I will is a short way of saying "things should happen not in the way I want" or "it is not what I want that should happen."

The clause **but as thou wilt** (TEV **"but what you want"**) is without a verb in Greek, and one must be supplied from the previous clause (**not as I will**). GECL inverts the order of the two clauses: "But what must happen is what you want, not what I want."

26.40   RSV   TEV

And he came to the disciples and found them sleeping; and he said to Peter, "So, could you not watch^h with me one hour?

^{h} Or *keep awake*

Then he returned to the three disciples and found them asleep; and he said to Peter, "How is it that you three were not able to keep watch with me for even one hour?

He came to the disciples can be expressed as "He went back to the disciples."

"The three disciples" of TEV, GECL, FRCL is literally **the disciples**; however, TEV's restructuring reminds the reader that only the three disciples (Peter and the two sons of Zebedee) are the ones meant.

And he said to Peter may need to be structured as a new sentence: "So he said to Peter . . ." (GECL, FRCL).

You is translated **"you three"** by TEV to show that the Greek text uses the second person plural pronoun, a form which is not distinguished in English from the second person singular pronoun "you." In languages such as French and German, where the distinction does exist, this translational adaptation is unnecessary; however, to translate with only "you" in English definitely suggests that Jesus' words are addressed only to Peter and not to the other two disciples.

With me repeats the phrase used in verse 38; see comment there.

The use of **So** with the rhetorical question **could you not watch with me one hour?** has the force of a somewhat bitter accusation or denunciation. In most languages such a question will be properly understood, but in some it will be more effective to have a statement: "So! You can't even keep watch with me for an hour!"

RSV   TEV

Watch[h] and pray that you may not   Keep watch and pray that you will
enter into temptation; the spirit in-   not fall into temptation. The spirit is
deed is willing, but the flesh is   willing, but the flesh is weak."
weak."

[h] Or *keep awake*

Watch should be translated here as in verse 38.

The **that** of **pray that you may not enter into temptation** can be interpreted to mean "Ask God to make sure you are not tempted (or, tested)," but it is also possible to understand "Pray to God, and then you won't be tempted."

Enter into temptation recalls the third petition of the Lord's Prayer: "And lead us not into temptation" (6.13). Different verbs are used in the two passages ("lead" versus "enter"), but **into temptation** occurs in both, and it seems a valid conclusion that they mean the same. Translations vary between (1) the more general meaning of enter or fall into temptation (RSV, NIV, Mft) and (2) the more specific meaning of being put to the test or of undergoing a trial (NJB, NEB, NAB, AT, GECL; Phps "face temptation"). See further at 6.13.

The spirit indeed is willing, but the flesh is weak (so also TEV, JB, NEB) is a literal and meaningless rendering of the Greek text. A literal translation may tend to suggest a contrast between "spirit" and "flesh" in the Pauline sense, which is not at all the meaning in the context. The distinction is rather "between man's physical weakness and the noble desires of his will," as one commentator states it. GECL translates "You have good intentions, but you are only weak human beings." Brc ("I know that you mean well and that you want to do the right thing, but human nature is frail") and Phps ("Your spirit is willing, but human nature is weak") are similar.

RSV   TEV

Again, for the second time, he went   Once more Jesus went away
away and prayed, "My Father, if this   and prayed, "My Father, if this cup
cannot pass unless I drink it, thy will of suffering cannot be taken away
be done."   unless I drink it, your will be done."

TEV has rendered **for the second time** by "Once more." Translators should use a natural expression.

There are minor differences between the prayers of verses 39 and 42, though here there is no essential shift in meaning: (1) **Unless I drink it** is added in verse 42; (2) "nevertheless, not as I will" of verse 39 is omitted in verse 42; and (3) "but as thou wilt" (verse 39) is worded slightly differently from **thy will be done** (verse 42). In GECL the petition is restructured to say "My Father, if there is no other way, and I must drink this cup of suffering, then what you want must be done." INCL does away with the imagery of the cup: "Father, if I must experience this suffering . . . ."

26.43 RSV	TEV

And again he came and found them sleeping, for their eyes were heavy.

He returned once more and found the disciples asleep; they could not keep their eyes open.

And again he came may sound rather abrupt in some languages; if a connection with the preceding verse is needed, one may translate "When he had finished praying, he returned once more . . . ."

Them (TEV "**the disciples**") is a reference to the three disciples, Peter and the two sons of Zebedee (see verses 37, 40).

Sleeping is the opposite of "watch" (verses 38, 40), the root meaning of which is "keep awake" (RSV footnote).

Their eyes were heavy is an idiomatic expression which TEV translates "**they could not keep their eyes open.**" Each language will have its own way of indicating the inability to stay awake.

26.44 RSV	TEV

So, leaving them again, he went away and prayed for the third time, saying the same words.

Again Jesus left them, went away, and prayed the third time, saying the same words.

Both here and in verse 42, TEV introduces the proper name "**Jesus,**" where the Greek text has the third person pronoun **he**. This same translational procedure is followed by GECL in both verses, and by FRCL here, though not in verse 42. The expectations of the receptor language determine the choice between retaining the pronominal form and introducing the proper name.

This time Matthew does not repeat the prayer; he states only that Jesus prayed the third time, saying the same words. The reference is clearly to the prayer of verse 42 and most probably to the last clause in particular, "thy will be done."

26.45 RSV	TEV

Then he came to the disciples and said to them, "Are you still sleeping and taking your rest? Behold, the hour is at hand, and the Son of man is betrayed into the hands of sinners.

Then he returned to the disciples and said, "Are you still sleeping and resting? Look! The hour has come for the Son of Man to be handed over to the power of sinful men.

Came may more naturally be "went." As in the previous verse, translators will either retain **he** or use "Jesus" according to the style of the receptor language.

Are you still sleeping and taking your rest? is taken as a question by most translations (NEB, TEV, Mft, AT, NIV, Lu, GECL), though some believe it to be a command (NJB, NAB, Zür, TOB). Since the Greek text originally had no punctuation, either alternative is possible. If the words are understood as a command, then the implication is that the disciples may as well continue to sleep, because they have missed their opportunity to stay awake and keep watch for Jesus. The translation will then be "Go ahead and sleep and continue taking your rest." But most translators see this sentence as a question that Jesus uses to rebuke the disciples. Examples are "How can you still be sleeping and taking your rest?" and "You are still sleeping and resting. Is that what you should be doing?"

Behold (TEV **"Look"**) translates the same particle first used in 1.20; see comment there.

In verse 40 the **hour** is used as a measurement of length of time, but here the phrase is used with the sense of a definite moment in time, as in 24.36,44,50; 25.13.

At hand (TEV **"has come"**) translates the same form of the Greek verb used in 3.2.

And the Son of man is betrayed may be problematic in that most languages expect the employment of a future tense in place of the present **is betrayed**. But Greek will occasionally substitute a present tense on occasions when the certainty of the event is to be emphasized. For English speakers the construction may also present a second difficulty: the coordinate conjunction **and** is not generally used to denote purpose. Therefore TEV translates the clause as **"for the Son of Man to be handed over,"** and NJB opts for "when the Son of Man is to be betrayed." See 17.22 where the same expression occurs.

As in 17.22 **hands** represents a Semitic idiomatic expression indicating power; TEV translates **into the hands of** as **"to the power of."**

In place of **sinners** (TEV **"sinful men"**) GECL has "God's enemies," thus structuring the wording to suit the specific context.

26.46	RSV	TEV

RSV	TEV
Rise, let us be going; see, my betrayer is at hand."	Get up, let us go. Look, here is the man who is betraying me!"

Rise, let us be going is clearly stated in modern English by TEV: **"Get up, let us go."** **See** is more naturally **"Look."** **My betrayer is at hand** can be "the man who has betrayed me is here."

26.47-56

RSV	TEV

The Arrest of Jesus

RSV	TEV
47 While he was still speaking, Judas came, one of the twelve, and with him a great crowd with swords and clubs, from the chief priests and the elders of the people. 48 Now the betrayer had given them a sign, saying, "The one I shall kiss is the man; seize him." 49 And he came up to Jesus at once and said, "Hail, Master!"[i] And he kissed him. 50 Jesus said to him, "Friend, why are you	47 Jesus was still speaking when Judas, one of the twelve disciples, arrived. With him was a large crowd armed with swords and clubs and sent by the chief priests and the elders. 48 The traitor had given the crowd a signal: "The man I kiss is the one you want. Arrest him!" 49 Judas went straight to Jesus and said, "Peace be with you, Teacher," and kissed him.

here?"[j] Then they came up and laid hands on Jesus and seized him. 51 And behold, one of those who were with Jesus stretched out his hand and drew his sword, and struck the slave of the high priest, and cut off his ear. 52 Then Jesus said to him, "Put your sword back into its place; for all who take the sword will perish by the sword. 53 Do you think that I cannot appeal to my Father, and he will at once send me more than twelve legions of angels? 54 But how then should the scriptures be fulfilled, that it must be so?" 55 At that hour Jesus said to the crowds, "Have you come out as against a robber, with swords and clubs to capture me? Day after day I sat in the temple teaching, and you did not seize me. 56 But all of this has taken place, that the scriptures of the prophets might be fulfilled." Then all the disciples forsook him and fled.

[i] Or Rabbi
[j] Or do that for which you have come

50 Jesus answered, "Be quick about it, friend!"[z]

Then they came up, arrested Jesus, and held him tight. 51 One of those who were with Jesus drew his sword and struck at the High Priest's slave, cutting off his ear. 52 "Put your sword back in its place," Jesus said to him. "All who take the sword will die by the sword. 53 Don't you know that I could call on my Father for help, and at once he would send me more than twelve armies of angels? 54 But in that case, how could the Scriptures come true which say that this is what must happen?"

55 Then Jesus spoke to the crowd, "Did you have to come with swords and clubs to capture me, as though I were an outlaw? Every day I sat down and taught in the Temple, and you did not arrest me. 56 But all this has happened in order to make come true what the prophets wrote in the Scriptures."

Then all the disciples left him and ran away.

[z] Be quick about it, friend!; or Why are you here, friend?

SECTION HEADING: "**The Arrest of Jesus**" may need to be expressed as a sentence; for example, "Jesus is arrested" or "The religious leaders arrest Jesus."

Except for a few typical stylistic alterations and the inclusion of a dialogue about the use of the sword (verses 52-54), Matthew follows the Marcan outline (14.43-50) in his account of the arrest of Jesus. At the beginning of the dialogue on the sword and following it, transitional markers are evident: "Then" (verse 52) and "At that hour" (verse 55). At least two major themes emerge in the course of this brief dialogue, and these same themes are common to the entire account of Jesus' arrest: (1) Jesus has the power to destroy his enemies, but he renounces the use of force and depends entirely upon the will of God; and (2) all of the events surrounding his arrest bring about the fulfillment of the Scriptures.

26.47   RSV   TEV

While he was still speaking, Judas came, one of the twelve, and with him a great crowd with swords and clubs, from the chief priests and the elders of the people.

Jesus was still speaking when Judas, one of the twelve disciples, arrived. With him was a large crowd armed with swords and clubs and sent by the chief priests and the elders.

Both Mark and Matthew note that Judas arrived as Jesus was still speaking to his disciples. But Mark emphasizes the suddenness of his arrival, while Matthew shifts the focus to Judas himself, as a literal rendering of the transitional statements in the two Gospels will demonstrate: "And immediately, while he was still speaking,

Judas came, one of the twelve" (Mark 14.43) and "While he was still speaking, Judas came, one of the twelve" (Matt 26.47).

Since most translators have a section heading at the beginning of this verse, they find it necessary to replace **he** with "**Jesus.**"

As was the case at verse 14, **the twelve** is perhaps better "the twelve disciples." It does seem odd to use this description here, since **Judas** has already been introduced into the story and his identity is known by the readers. Some translators have said "Judas, the one who was one of the twelve disciples."

Came is often more naturally "**arrived.**" Whether this should precede or follow **one of the twelve** depends on the style of the receptor language.

Matthew has **a great crowd** in place of Mark's "a crowd" (14.43).

Swords and clubs are mentioned again in verse 55. For the person who must depend upon hearing the Scriptures read, both RSV (**with swords and clubs, from the chief priests and the elders**) and NJB ("men armed with swords and clubs, sent by the chief priests and elders") may leave the wrong impression that the weapons, and not the men, were sent by the chief priests and the elders.

Whereas Matthew mentions only **the chief priests and the elders** (as in 26.3), Mark includes "the scribes" as well (14.43).

Finally, Matthew qualifies **the elders** by the phrase **of the people**, as he does in verse 3; Mark omits this detail in both places (14.1,43). TEV drops the phrase from explicit mention in the text on the grounds that it is unnecessarily repetitious. But one scholar suggests that it may well be Matthew's way of "laying the groundwork for the people's acceptance of responsibility for Jesus' death (27.25)." It may then be best to retain the phrase in translation.

The whole verse may need to be restructured, and there are different ways that will be good in different languages. Examples include "While Jesus was still speaking, Judas, one of the twelve disciples, arrived. With him was a large crowd of people who had swords and clubs. These people had been sent by the chief priests and the elders of the people," and "Jesus was still speaking when Judas arrived, the one who was one of the twelve disciples. With him was a large crowd that had been sent by the chief priests and the elders of the people. They had swords and clubs with them."

26.48	RSV	TEV
	Now the betrayer had given them a sign, saying, "The one I shall kiss is the man; seize him."	The traitor had given the crowd a signal: "The man I kiss is the one you want. Arrest him!"

Betrayer: see verse 15 for a discussion of "betray." As in verse 25, Judas in referred to as **the betrayer**, a fact which Matthew will not let his readers forget (see 27.3). Mark also keep this description before the eyes of his readers (Mark 14.42,44), though it is apparently absent from Luke and John.

"**The crowd**" of TEV translates **them** of the Greek text. However, the nearest antecedent is "the chief priests and the elders" and not the "great crowd" mentioned earlier in verse 47. Most translations do not specifically identify the antecedent, though FRCL follows TEV in doing so.

Sign (TEV "**signal**") is used elsewhere in the Gospel with the extended meaning of "miracle" (see its use at 12.38). The city of Jerusalem and the region around Jerusalem overflowed with pilgrims during the time of Passover. This may be why it was necessary for Judas to give a prearranged signal to identify Jesus to the people who were sent out to arrest him. But another reason may be that he did not want to make it obvious that he was betraying Jesus.

To greet someone with a **kiss**, whether on the hand or foot, was a show of respect, the equivalent of using an honorific. Of course, the text does not say where Judas kissed Jesus, and neither should the translation. GECL defines the kiss as "a kiss of greeting," which is perhaps the best example to follow.

Seize (so also NEB, Mft, AT) may also mean "**arrest**" (TEV, NIV). **Seize him** is rendered rather dynamically by Phps: "Get him!"

It is often better to use indirect discourse in this verse; for example, "The traitor had told them that he would signal to them which person they should arrest, by kissing him (in greeting)" or "The traitor had told them that when he gave a kiss of greeting to someone, that would be the person to arrest."

26.49	RSV	TEV

And he came up to Jesus at once and said, "Hail, Master!"[i] And he kissed him.

Judas went straight to Jesus and said, "Peace be with you, Teacher," and kissed him.

[i] Or *Rabbi*

And he came up to Jesus at once and said is translated by GECL so that **he** of the Greek text is clearly marked: "Judas went immediately to Jesus and said." Compare also TEV.

Hail (so also Mft, NEB) is definitely archaic for speakers of American English. Moreover, it has the disadvantage of sounding like "Hell!" which is frequently used as a swear word. More appropriate choices are "Greetings" (NJB, NIV, Brc, Phps), "Good evening" (AT), "Peace" (NAB), or "**Peace be with you**" (TEV). The word is used again in 27.29; 28.9.

Master (TEV "**Teacher**") is a translation of the Aramaic term transliterated "Rabbi" by NJB and NEB. It is also the term by which Judas addresses Jesus during the course of the last meal (verse 25). See comment on "rabbi" at 23.7.

Two pronouns are used in **And he kissed him**. Normally translators find it is clear who does the kissing, but in some cases it is helpful to say "And Judas kissed him."

26.50	RSV	TEV

Jesus said to him, "Friend, why are you here?"[j] Then they came up and laid hands on Jesus and seized him.

Jesus answered, "Be quick about it, friend!"[z]

Then they came up, arrested Jesus, and held him tight.

^j Or *do that for which you have come*   ^zBe quick about it, friend!; *or* Why are you here, friend?

Friend is the same noun of address used in 20.13 and 22.12, but nowhere else in the New Testament. See comment at 20.13.

The meaning of the Greek question translated **why are you here?** is in doubt, and so RSV provides the alternative possibility in the margin: "do that for which you have come." TEV follows the reverse arrangement, with "**Be quick about it**" in the text and "Why are you here . . . ?" in the margin. NEB, NJB, NIV follow the same procedure as TEV; AT and Phps adopt the question form without a footnote, while Mft and Brc have the equivalent of TEV in the text and also omit a footnote. Given the observation that throughout the passion narrative Jesus is pictured as being in total control of the situation, it seems quite possible that the choice of TEV is the better one. However, it is quite obvious that one cannot be dogmatic, and a footnote should definitely accompany whatever choice is given in the text. Even if translators do make this a question, it should be clear that Jesus is not asking for information but is using a question with some rhetorical effect. Both Mark and Luke omit this difficult comment from their accounts.

They are identified by GECL as "the armed men."

Laid hands on is translated "**arrested**" by TEV, and **seized** (previously used in verse 48) is rendered "**held . . . tight**" by TEV.

26.51	RSV	TEV

And behold, one of those who were with Jesus stretched out his hand and drew his sword, and struck the slave of the high priest, and cut off his ear.

One of those who were with Jesus drew his sword and struck at the High Priest's slave, cutting off his ear.

And behold (see 1.20; 8.2) is the means by which Matthew "makes a special point of the sword episode," as one scholar observes.

One of those who were with Jesus appears in Mark as "one of those who stood by" (14.47). Matthew certainly intends that this person be understood as "One of Jesus' friends" (Brc), or even more specifically as "one of Jesus' disciples" (Phps) or "one of the followers of Jesus" (NJB).

The text states that he **stretched out his hand and drew his sword**. This can be rendered as "reached out and drew his sword" or, more naturally in many languages as a single action, "**drew his sword**" (so TEV) or "pulled out his sword."

Sword can be translated as "long knife for war" or "weapon like a big knife (or, machete)."

Struck the slave of the high priest, and cut off his ear may erroneously suggest two separate actions: (1) striking the slave of the High Priest and (2) cutting off his ear. In the Greek text **struck** is actually a participle dependent upon the main verb **cut off**, indicating a single action: striking at the slave (perhaps in an attempt to kill him), but managing only to slice off his ear. Therefore TEV has "**struck at the High Priest's slave, cutting off his ear**" (NJB, NEB, NAB, Phps are similar).

821

Matthew does not say which ear, but for languages which normally specify which one, it is possible to say either "one of his ears" or, since Luke does supply the information, "his right ear."

The text says **the slave**, which can be understood to mean the High Priest had only one slave, although the more likely meaning is that only one of his slaves was there. "One of the slaves" will correct this problem.

26.52 RSV	TEV
Then Jesus said to him, "Put your sword back into its place; for all who take the sword will perish by the sword.	"Put your sword back in its place," Jesus said to him. "All who take the sword will die by the sword.

As previously indicated, verses 52-54 contain material which is unique to Matthew's Gospel. The account emphasizes the contrast between the nonviolent attitude of Jesus and that of his disciples. **Put your sword back into its place** (a fairly literal rendering of the Greek) is expanded by Phps ("... into its proper place") but abbreviated by both NJB ("Put your sword back") and NEB ("Put up your sword").

All who take the sword will perish by the sword is also a literal rendering of the Greek text, and this is representative of what is found in most translations. Jesus thereby affirms that it is better to suffer injustice than to use violence as a means of protection or retribution, and this affirmation is underscored by his willingness to walk the route of suffering and death.

To make the meaning of **take the sword** clear, translators can say "use the sword" or "fight with the sword." **Perish by the sword** can be "will die by means of a sword" or "will be killed by a sword." In cases where an active is required, it can be "it is with a sword also that someone will kill him."

Sometimes, in languages where swords are not known, translators have wanted to express the meaning of Jesus' words in general terms such as "people who are violent and go to war will themselves be killed by violence and war." But in light of this scene, where one disciple has actually used a sword, it is best to keep this term in the translation.

26.53 RSV	TEV
Do you think that I cannot appeal to my Father, and he will at once send me more than twelve legions of angels?	Don't you know that I could call on my Father for help, and at once he would send me more than twelve armies of angels?

"Don't you know that I could" of TEV (NAB "Do you not suppose I can") is a simplification of the Greek sentence construction, which places the negative in a position which is difficult for English speakers: **Do you think that I cannot**. It is possible to achieve still further simplification by transforming the rhetorical question into a statement: "I could call on my Father for help, and . . . ." Or even "Do not forget that I could . . . ."

Appeal to (so also NJB, NEB) sounds rather formal and is somewhat high-level English. TEV has **"call on . . . for help."** The same verb is used in 8.5, where RSV translates "beseeching" (see comment there).

In order to convey the notion of help, several translations supplement **send me**: "to my defence" (NJB), "to my aid" (NEB), and "to defend me" (Phps). In the TEV restructuring it is immediately clear that the function of the **angels** is to provide help ("**I could call on my Father for help**").

Legions (TEV **"armies"**) is the transliteration of the plural form of the Greek noun "legion," which referred to a unit of the Roman army. At the time of Caesar Augustus, a "legion" numbered about six thousand soldiers, not including the auxiliary troops, which were generally of approximately equal number. Most English speakers do not know what is meant by a "legion," though persons familiar with military terminology will understand "twelve regiments of angels" (Brc). The intention of the expression is to suggest a vast number of angels, sufficient to defend Jesus against all of his enemies. In fact, many translators have to say simply "twelve groups of angels to fight" or "twelve large fighting groups of angels."

For **angels** see discussion at 1.20.

26.54	RSV	TEV
	But how then should the scriptures be fulfilled, that it must be so?"	But in that case, how could the Scriptures come true which say that this is what must happen?"

Be fulfilled: see comment at 1.22.

That it must be so and **"which say that this is what must happen"** (TEV) are both unclear as regards the intended antecedent. Phps is better: "which say that all this must take place."

TEV expresses very well the intention of Jesus' question. **But how then** is a short way of saying "But if God did that" or "But if God sent angels to protect me." In some languages the meaning of the rhetorical question is expressed as a statement: "But if that happened, the Scriptures that say this must happen could not come true."

26.55	RSV	TEV
	At that hour Jesus said to the crowds, "Have you come out as against a robber, with swords and clubs to capture me? Day after day I sat in the temple teaching, and you did not seize me.	Then Jesus spoke to the crowd, "Did you have to come with swords and clubs to capture me, as though I were an outlaw? Every day I sat down and taught in the Temple, and you did not arrest me.

At that hour is one of Matthew's favorite transitional markers (see 8.13). Mark uses "and" (14.48), while Luke prefers "but" (22.53). "Then" is probably the most common translation.

The crowds is "them" in Mark (14.48) and "the chief priests and officers of the temple and the elders who had come out against him" in Luke (22.52).

The question which Jesus asked the crowd (**Have you . . . a robber?**) is word-for-word the same as that found in the Marcan parallel. Luke omits **to capture me**, but otherwise has the same wording. TEV somewhat rearranges the sentence order (compare RSV for a literal rendering), and GECL goes even further: "Did you have to carry swords and clubs in order to arrest me? Am I an outlaw?"

Robber of RSV could lead translators to use "thief," but in fact in this context a word for a simple thief is not as appropriate as "outlaw" or "bandit," words that describe criminals who may be dangerous.

The two phrases **Day after day** and **In the temple** are each placed in an emphatic position in the Greek sentence.

Whereas both Matthew and Mark (14.49) state that Jesus was **teaching** in the temple, Luke is more general: "was with you . . . in the temple" (22.53). But Matthew emphasizes Jesus' role as a teacher even further by the observation that he **sat**, since Jewish teachers sat down while giving instruction.

As elsewhere with **teaching**, some kind of object may be required; for example, "teaching people" or "teaching about God."

Seize (TEV "**arrest**") is the same verb used in verses 4 and 48.

26.56   RSV   TEV

But all of this has taken place, that   But all this has happened in order to
the scriptures of the prophets might   make come true what the prophets
be fulfilled." Then all the disciples   wrote in the Scriptures."
forsook him and fled.   Then all the disciples left him
                                                      and ran away.

All this includes all the events of verses 47-56.

That the scriptures of the prophets might be fulfilled is slightly different from the formula used in verse 54. This is further expression of the conviction that all of the events surrounding the arrest, trial, and death of Jesus were ultimately under the control of God. **Might be fulfilled** is discussed at 1.22. **The scriptures of the prophets** is represented in GECL by "the predictions of the prophets." TEV is an excellent model: "**All this has happened in order to make come true what the prophets wrote in the Scriptures.**"

All the disciples is the wording of Matthew; Mark has "all" (14.50), then adds the statement about the young man who fled away naked (14.51-52). Luke makes no mention of the disciples or anyone else leaving Jesus and running away.

Forsook translates a verb which carries the general notion of "leave" or "abandon," in whatever sense is appropriate to the context. It is often rendered "**left**" (TEV).

Fled translates a verb which means "ran away" or "escaped."

26.57-68

RSV

TEV

Jesus before the Council

57 Then those who had seized Jesus led him to Caiaphas the high priest, where the scribes and the elders had gathered. 58 But Peter followed him at a distance, as far as the courtyard of the high priest, and going inside he sat with the guards to see the end. 59 Now the chief priests and the whole council sought false testimony against Jesus that they might put him to death, 60 but they found none, though many false witnesses came forward. At last two came forward 61 and said, "This fellow said, 'I am able to destroy the temple of God, and to build it in three days.' " 62 And the high priest stood up and said, "Have you no answer to make? What is it that these men testify against you?" 63 But Jesus was silent. And the high priest said to him, "I adjure you by the living God, tell us if you are the Christ, the Son of God." 64 Jesus said to him, "You have said so. But I tell you, hereafter you will see the Son of man seated at the right hand of Power, and coming on the clouds of heaven." 65 Then the high priest tore his robes, and said, "He has uttered blasphemy. Why do we still need witnesses? You have now heard his blasphemy. 66 What is your judgment?" They answered, "He deserves death." 67 Then they spat in his face, and struck him; and some slapped him, 68 saying, "Prophesy to us, you Christ! Who is it that struck you?"

Jesus before the Council

57 Those who had arrested Jesus took him to the house of Caiaphas, the High Priest, where the teachers of the Law and the elders had gathered together. 58 Peter followed from a distance, as far as the courtyard of the High Priest's house. He went into the courtyard and sat down with the guards to see how it would all come out. 59 The chief priests and the whole Council tried to find some false evidence against Jesus to put him to death; 60 but they could not find any, even though many people came forward and told lies about him. Finally two men stepped up 61 and said, "This man said, 'I am able to tear down God's Temple and three days later build it back up.' "

62 The High Priest stood up and said to Jesus, "Have you no answer to give to this accusation against you?" 63 But Jesus kept quiet. Again the High Priest spoke to him, "In the name of the living God I now put you under oath: tell us if you are the Messiah, the Son of God."

64 Jesus answered him, "So you say. But I tell all of you: from this time on you will see the Son of Man sitting at the right side of the Almighty and coming on the clouds of heaven!"

65 At this the High Priest tore his clothes and said, "Blasphemy! We don't need any more witnesses! You have just heard his blasphemy! 66 What do you think?"

They answered, "He is guilty and must die."

67 Then they spat in his face and beat him; and those who slapped him 68 said, "Prophesy for us, Messiah! Guess who hit you!"

SECTION HEADING: "**Jesus Before the Council.**" A heading that is less brief may be "Jesus is tried by the council" or "Jesus is taken to the council for trial." "**Council**" was discussed at 5.22, but see also verse 59 below.

Matthew continues to follow Mark's overall outline of events, though he introduces a few alterations which reflect his own interpretation of what took place. The Jewish trial unfurls some strange contradictions: Jesus is innocent, but he is condemned by a High Priest who is guilty of abusing the judicial process. The Son of God is falsely accused of blasphemy, and the future judge of the world is unjustly condemned by a human court.

26.57

RSV

TEV

Then those who had seized Jesus led him to Caiaphas the high

Those who had arrested Jesus took him to the house of Caiaphas,

priest, where the scribes and the
elders had gathered.

the High Priest, where the teachers
of the Law and the elders had gathered together.

Matthew specifically identifies the subject of the verb **led** as **those who had seized Jesus**; Mark (14.53) and Luke (22.54) each have the pronoun "they" as subject of the verb. Translators need to be sure they don't render **led** with a word that means simply they went in front of Jesus or showed him the way. "**Took**" of TEV is better.

To Caiaphas the high priest is translated "**to the house of Caiaphas, the High Priest**" by TEV. Neither Mark (14.53, "to the high priest") nor Luke (22.54, "into the high priest's house") identify the high priest by name. Matthew previously mentioned **Caiaphas** in verse 3.

Matthew states that **the scribes and the elders** comprised the group who had gathered to place Jesus on trial; Mark (14.53) notes that "the chief priests" were also present. Luke (22.54) does not identify the persons present for the ordeal. Matthew probably omits mention of "the chief priests" on the assumption that they were already gathered there, waiting to bring Jesus to trial. **Scribes** was discussed at 2.4, and **elders** at 15.2. **Elders** can be "the senior leaders" or "the older men in leadership position," if **elders** alone is not clear.

26.58   RSV   TEV

But Peter followed him at a distance,
as far as the courtyard of the high
priest, and going inside he sat with
the guards to see the end.

Peter followed from a distance, as
far as the courtyard of the High
Priest's house. He went into the
courtyard and sat down with the
guards to see how it would all come
out.

The text says Peter followed **him**, a pronoun which TEV has dropped. In many languages, however, it is necessary to retain the object. Further, it can be said that Matthew is emphasizing that it was Jesus whom Peter was following, so this is yet another reason to retain **him**.

At a distance sometimes needs to be a separate phrase such as "but he stayed a little distance behind him."

He followed **as far as the courtyard**, that is, until they reached the courtyard. Although **courtyard** is the same word translated "palace" in verse 3, it becomes clear from verse 69 ("Peter was sitting outside in the courtyard") that the reference here is to the open area outside the palace buildings, perhaps partly surrounded by them.

Guards is the same word used in 5.25; these are the only two occurrences of this noun in the entire Gospel. Although the basic meaning of the word is "servants" or "attendants," here the **guards** were probably members of the Temple guard, Jewish soldiers under the command of the High Priest. Where there is not a common word for "guards," translators may say "soldiers from the Temple."

The end (NAB "the outcome") is rendered as a verb construction in TEV, "**how it would all come out.**" **To see the end** is found only in Matthew's Gospel; Mark has in its place "warming himself at the fire" (14.54).

26.59	RSV	TEV
	Now the chief priests and the whole council sought false testimony against Jesus that they might put him to death,	The chief priests and the whole Council tried to find some false evidence against Jesus to put him to death;

For **chief priests** see comments on 2.4. Among the priests, some of them held positions of high status, and these were known as **chief priests**, though their precise relation to the priests in general is not clear. Most prominent among the priests was the High Priest, who alone could make the sin offering on the Day of Atonement.

The whole council is the Sanhedrin, the highest Jewish court, which had final authority in matters governing the religion and life of the Jewish people. In Jesus' day it consisted of the elders, the chief priests (including former High Priests and the male members of their families), and the scribes (generally Pharisees). It had a total number of seventy-one members, though as few as twenty-three were allowed to meet and conduct the business of the council. See 5.22 for comments on **council**. Note that the chief priests were members of this group, but **the chief priests and the whole council** may give the wrong impression that they were not members. Some translators have "the chief priests and the rest of the council (or, and the other members of the group of elders)."

According to Jewish law a trial could not be held at night. Moreover, when charges were brought against a person which could result in his being condemned to death, the trial had to be conducted on two consecutive days, and the witnesses had to be interrogated privately.

That the **council sought false testimony against Jesus** is explicitly stated by Matthew; Mark (14.55) merely has "testimony against," though in the next verse he does indicate that "many bore false witness against him," thus signifying that the evidence was indeed false. However, Matthew evidently intends to underline from the very outset that the trial was prejudicial and illegal.

The council **sought false testimony against Jesus**. This may be expressed as "looked for people who would lie about what Jesus had done." They wanted this evidence so **that they might put him to death**. The **they** is not the lying witnesses but the council members. The translation can be "the chief priests and the rest of the council of elders looked for people who would lie about what Jesus had done so that there would be a reason to have Jesus killed" or ". . . looked for people who would say that Jesus had done things that would justify his being put to death, even though what they said were lies."

but they found none, though many false witnesses came forward. At last two came forward	but they could not find any, even though many people came forward and told lies about him. Finally two men stepped up

In Greek **they found none** is more literally "they did not find"; however, most languages will require the express inclusion of an object (NEB "they failed to find one"). The translation should not say "they couldn't find anyone." They did find plenty of people who would lie, but they couldn't find the kind of evidence they were looking for. "They couldn't find anything" is a common translation. GECL entirely restructures: "but this did not happen."

"**Even though many people came forward and told lies about him**" of TEV translates a Greek participial construction: **though many false witnesses came forward**. Since verse 59 specifically indicates that they were actually seeking testimony that was "false," that word need not be repeated: "even though a series of witnesses came forward" (GECL). It is often helpful to restructure this verse by saying "but even though many people appeared before the council and told lies about Jesus, they didn't say things that gave the council reasons to have Jesus put to death."

Came forward is used fifty-one times in Matthew's Gospel (first in 4.3), twice with Jesus as subject (at the Transfiguration, 17.7, and in the giving of the Great Commission, 28.18). In both occurrences in this verse, "appeared before the council" or "went to give testimony" will express the meaning.

Matthew specifically indicates the number of witnesses: **two**. This is important inasmuch as it was necessary to have two witnesses whose testimony agreed, in order to convict someone on serious charges.

26.61   RSV   TEV

and said, "This fellow said, 'I am able to destroy the temple of God, and to build it in three days.' "	and said, "This man said, 'I am able to tear down God's Temple and three days later build it back up.' "

This fellow of RSV is usually rendered "this man" and is probably used to convey the feeling of contempt.

I am able to destroy replaces Mark's "I will destroy" (14.58); through this slight alteration Matthew emphasizes the divine power and authority of Jesus.

That it is **the temple of God** further underscores Jesus' divine authority. Contrast Mark 14.58, "this temple that is made with hands."

Rather than **build**, most translations have "rebuild."

"**Three days later**" of TEV does not mean quite the same in English as RSV's **in three days**. The construction in the text is probably best understood as "time within which," as RSV has rendered it, but translators can also follow TEV if that would be more natural.

The witnesses use direct discourse when reporting on what Jesus said. Sometimes indirect discourse is better, as in "This man said that he could destroy God's Temple and then build it again in three days."

26.62   RSV   TEV

And the high priest stood up and   The High Priest stood up and
said, "Have you no answer to make?   said to Jesus, "Have you no answer
What is it that these men testify   to give to this accusation against
against you?"   you?"

And said is literally "and said to him"; TEV identifies "him" as Jesus in order to avoid the possibility of confusion with the person who is speaking in verse 61.

Have you no answer to make? is more literally "Do you answer nothing?" However, the form of the Greek sentence may be deceptive for English speakers, and the meaning is as RSV and TEV have expressed it ("**Have you no answer to give . . . ?**").

What is it that these men testify against you? is placed as part of the first question by TEV in the phrase "**to this accusation against you**" ("**Have you no answer to give to this accusation against you?**"). GECL is also economical in its restructuring: "Have you nothing to bring against these accusations?" Whether one question is used or two, the point remains that **What is it that these men testify against you?** is not asking for information about what the men had testified as much as it is asking Jesus to refute what they said or to explain himself. "What do you say to this accusation (or, to these things they have said about you)?"

26.63   RSV   TEV

But Jesus was silent. And the high   But Jesus kept quiet. Again the High
priest said to him, "I adjure you by   Priest spoke to him, "In the name of
the living God, tell us if you are the   the living God I now put you under
Christ, the Son of God."   oath: tell us if you are the Messiah,
          the Son of God."

To say that Jesus **was silent** means he "did not say anything" or "**kept quiet**" (TEV).

The order of **I adjure you by the living God** is inverted by TEV: "**In the name of the living God I now put you under oath.**" GECL prefers "I place you under oath and ask you in the name of the living God . . . ." See 5.33 and following verses for comments on oaths and swearing. In this verse Brc has provided a good model: "I call on you to tell us on oath, in the name of the living God." Another possibility is "I call on you to declare (or, to tell the truth) with the living God as your witness."

The Christ (so also Lu, Mft, AT, NJB) is translated "**the Messiah**" by TEV and several others (NEB, NAB, Brc). See comments at 1.1,17; 2.4. To translate **the Christ, the Son of God** may leave the reader with the impression that the two titles are equivalent and that one may be interchanged with the other. To shift to a double question form, as GECL, would at least leave open the possibility that the two titles are not identical: "Are you the promised Savior? Are you the Son of God?"

26.64   RSV   TEV

Jesus said to him, "You have said so. But I tell you, hereafter you will see the Son of man seated at the right hand of Power, and coming on the clouds of heaven."

Jesus answered him, "So you say. But I tell all of you: from this time on you will see the Son of Man sitting at the right side of the Almighty and coming on the clouds of heaven!"

Jesus' reply (**You have said so**) places the burden of decision upon the High Priest, in contrast to the openly affirmative "I am" of Mark (14.62). A number of translations retain Jesus' answer in a form similar to that of the Greek text: "You say it" (Lu), "It is you who say it" (NAB), and "The words are yours" (NEB; JB "The words are your own"). Renderings such as these have the effect of saying "That's your way of saying it, but I don't necessarily agree (or, I may or may not say it that way myself)." Others take Jesus' answer to be an absolute affirmative: "Yes" (GECL), "Yes, it is as you say" (NIV), "It is true" (AT), and "You have said so, Yes" (Phps). Although either interpretation can be supported, we tend the prefer the former.

But I tell you is the same expression used in 11.22,24; it is equivalent in emphasis to "For truly, I say to you" of 5.18 (see discussion there). The word translated **But** can mean "Moreover," which would go better with the second interpretation of **You have said so**. Because **you** here is plural, contrasting with the singular **You have said so** of the previous sentence, TEV translates "**But I tell all of you.**"

Hereafter of RSV is somewhat ambiguous. TEV's "**from this time on**" (NJB "from this time onward") or "from now on" (NEB, Brc, Lu, GECL) reflects more accurately the meaning of the Greek construction. Several translations depart from the obvious meaning and translate either "Soon" (NAB, AT) or "in the future" (NIV, Phps; Mft "in future") in order to make Jesus' statement chronologically precise. However, as one scholar expresses it, "Matthew's overall meaning is that 'from this time on' they will see only the triumphant Son of Man, to whom all power in heaven and earth is given (28.18), and who will return to judge the world (25.31)."

The Son of man . . . on the clouds of heaven, taken from Daniel 7.13, agrees very closely with the Marcan parallel. The one significant difference is the shift from "with the clouds of heaven" (Mark 14.62) to "on the clouds of heaven." Whereas both forms are represented in the two textual traditions of Daniel 7.13 in the Septuagint, the form chosen by Matthew probably lays greater stress upon the exalted position of the Son of Man.

The expression **at the right hand** is similar to the expression discussed at 22.44. TEV has rendered **Power** as "**the Almighty**," but for many translators "Almighty God" of Brc is even better.

The Son of Man will be **coming**, with the understood destination of earth. Some translations will in fact say "coming to earth." Since he will be coming **on the clouds of heaven**, translators may say "coming to earth, riding on the clouds of heaven" or even "riding to earth on the clouds of heaven." Many translations feel that **of heaven** does not add anything to the meaning of the clouds and can easily be dropped.

A problem for translators is the fact that the Son of Man is both **seated** and **coming**. One way to handle this is to say "you will see the Son of Man, the one who sits at the right side of Almighty God, coming to earth on the clouds."

Matthew clearly intends an identification of the speaker (Jesus) with the Son of Man, and the reply of the high priest in the following verse makes it obvious that he too took it in that way. But translators should not use the first person "I." See comments at 8.20.

26.65 RSV	TEV
Then the high priest tore his robes, and said, "He has uttered blasphemy. Why do we still need witnesses? You have now heard his blasphemy.	At this the High Priest tore his clothes and said, "Blasphemy! We don't need any more witnesses! You have just heard his blasphemy!

The high priest tore his robes: according to the Mishnah, when the charge of **blasphemy** (see 12.31) was made against someone, "the judges stand on their feet and rend their garments, and they may not mend them again" (Sanhedrin 7.5). However, this same source also states, "The blasphemer is not culpable unless he pronounces the Name itself," which suggests that "Power" was understood as a reference to God himself. Therefore TEV translates "Power" (verse 64) as "the Almighty" (so also GECL).

The **robes** were his outer garment, but "clothes" seems the easiest way to render it. Some translators have to name the garment, and they can say "coat" or "cloak." He did not tear the clothing to pieces but merely made a tear in the garment, so **tore his robes** can be "tore part of his clothing" or "ripped his outer garment." It may be helpful to have a footnote explaining the significance of this act, that is, it was done as a sign of grief or horror. Some translators put this in the text: "tore his robes to show his grief."

Sometimes it helps to indicate the High Priest is addressing the Council here, as in "and said to the Council."

He has uttered blasphemy has often been translated "He has spoken evil things about God" or "He has insulted God." However, see the discussion at 9.3. Perhaps here the High Priest can say "He thinks he's equal to God! This is an insult to God!"

Why do we still need witnesses? is a rhetorical question. In some languages the meaning can be expressed with a strong statement: "We don't need any more witnesses."

Witnesses: see verses 59-61; the meaning is "witnesses against him" or "people to tell what he did."

His blasphemy may need to be transformed into a verb construction: "heard him insult God" or "heard him say that he is equal with God."

26.66   RSV   TEV

What is your judgment?" They an-   What do you think?"
swered, "He deserves death."   They answered, "He is guilty
                                                              and must die."

What is your judgment? is to be understood as the request for a formal decision of the court. Compare, for example, "What is your verdict?" (NAB, Brc, GECL, Phps) and "What is your decision?" (AT). TEV's "**What do you think?**" is perhaps too informal.

They are the entire Jewish high court, including the "scribes and elders" of verse 57. The use of direct discourse in the pronouncement of the death penalty (**"He deserves death"**) contrasts with the indirect discourse of Mark 14.64 ("And they all condemned him as deserving death"). **Deserves death** means "deserves the death penalty," as the context makes abundantly evident. In place of the noun **death**, TEV employs the verb phrase "**must die.**" It is clear, of course, that the reason they say he deserves death is because they find him guilty. In some languages this will have to be made explicit, as in TEV: "**He is guilty and must die.**"

26.67   RSV   TEV

Then they spat in his face, and   Then they spat in his face and
struck him; and some slapped him,   beat him; and those who slapped
                                                              him

The persons indicated by **they** are not specifically identified. In the words of one scholar: "In Matthew's abbreviated account it looks as though the members of the Council themselves spat on Jesus and struck him; the various groups are not well defined." Matthew does seem to distinguish between those who spat in his face and beat him and those who slapped him, though no further distinction is possible on the basis of the Greek text. One may translate, "Then some of the men spat in his face and beat him. Others slapped him [68] and said . . . ."

In some societies spitting on someone is part of a blessing, but here it was definitely an insult. Translators in such cultures may have to say "spat in his face to insult him."

The text does not say where on his body Jesus was **struck** and **slapped**, nor should the translation, although slapping would normally be on the face.

26.68   RSV   TEV

saying, "Prophesy to us, you Christ!   said, "Prophesy for us, Messiah!
Who is it that struck you?"   Guess who hit you!"

Prophesy to us refers specifically to the second command: **Who is it that struck you?** Several translations restructure, though in different ways, so as to make this relationship evident: "Now, Messiah, if you are a prophet, tell us who hit you"

(NEB), "Show us you are a prophet, you Christ! Who was it that struck you?" (AT), and "You Savior, who just struck you? You are after all a prophet!" (GECL 1st edition).

Christ is to be understood as a Messianic title ("Messiah"), not as a proper name, as some translations imply (see comments at 1.1,17). One may wish to translate **you Christ** as "you who claim to be the chosen King" or ". . . chosen Savior."

26.69-75

RSV	TEV
	Peter Denies Jesus
69 Now Peter was sitting outside in the courtyard. And a maid came up to him, and said, "You also were with Jesus the Galilean." 70 But he denied it before them all, saying, "I do not know what you mean." 71 And when he went out to the porch, another maid saw him, and she said to the bystanders, "This man was with Jesus of Nazareth." 72 And again he denied it with an oath, "I do not know the man." 73 After a little while the bystanders came up and said to Peter, "Certainly you are also one of them, for your accent betrays you." 74 Then he began to invoke a curse upon himself and to swear, "I do not know the man." And immediately the cock crowed. 75 And Peter remembered the saying of Jesus, "Before the cock crows, you will deny me three times." And he went out and wept bitterly.	69 Peter was sitting outside in the courtyard when one of the High Priest's servant girls came to him and said, "You, too, were with Jesus of Galilee." 70 But he denied it in front of them all. "I don't know what you are talking about," he answered, 71 and went on out to the entrance of the courtyard. Another servant girl saw him and said to the men there, "He was with Jesus of Nazareth." 72 Again Peter denied it and answered, "I swear that I don't know that man!" 73 After a little while the men standing there came to Peter. "Of course you are one of them," they said. "After all, the way you speak gives you away!" 74 Then Peter said, "I swear that I am telling the truth! May God punish me if I am not! I do not know that man!" Just then a rooster crowed, 75 and Peter remembered what Jesus had told him: "Before the rooster crows, you will say three times that you do not know me." He went out and wept bitterly.

SECTION HEADING: "**Peter Denies Jesus**." Translators can use the same expression for "**Denies**" here that they used in verse 34.

The scene is set in sharp contrast to that of Jesus before the Jewish high court. There Jesus acknowledges who he is, though it cost him his life, while here Peter denies his Lord and strengthens his denial with an oath.

26.69 RSV	TEV
Now Peter was sitting outside in the courtyard. And a maid came up to him, and said, "You also were with Jesus the Galilean."	**Peter was sitting outside in the courtyard when one of the High Priest's servant girls came to him and said, "You, too, were with Jesus of Galilee."**

833

Now Peter was sitting outside in the courtyard draws the readers' attention back to verse 58: "But Peter followed him at a distance, as far as the courtyard of the high priest, and going inside he sat with the guards . . . ." Translators may drop the **Now** or render it "At that time" or "During these events."

The **outside** refers to outside the place where Jesus was on trial. "Out in the courtyard of that house" may be good.

A maid (compare "a maid" of Luke 22.56) appears in Mark as "one of the maids of the high priest" (14.66). The noun **maid** is the feminine noun related to the one translated "child" in 2.8; normally it means "servant girl" or "slave girl," which is what we recommend for the translation. Since there is no basis within Matthew's Gospel to make further identification possible, one should not follow the model of TEV, which identifies the servant girl as "**one of the High Priest's servant girls**," unless the language requires naming whose slave she was.

Came up to him can be "approached him" or "went up to him," if that is more natural.

In place of **Jesus the Galilean**, Mark has "the Nazarene, Jesus" (14.67), information which Matthew introduces as the comment of the second servant girl who approaches Peter. Moreover, Mark adds the two interesting details, that Peter was "warming himself" and that the servant girl "looked at him."

You is emphatically marked in the Greek text. To translate **You also** or "you, too" may imply for some readers that someone else has been previously mentioned in the conversation. The function of **also** is better understood as either a simple transitional marker or else as a further means of emphasizing the pronoun **you**. For example, translators may have "You! You were with Jesus from Galilee."

To have been **with Jesus** in this context means more than just having been where he was. It has the idea of "you were one of the people of Jesus of Galilee."

26.70	RSV	TEV

But he denied it before them all, saying, "I do not know what you mean."	But he denied it in front of them all. "I don't know what you are talking about," he answered,

But he denied it before them all is a fairly literal rendering of the Greek text, which is slightly restructured by GECL: "Peter denied it before all the people and said . . . ."

Denied means "claimed it was not true." But he made this denial by saying **"I do not know what you mean,"** which can also be rendered "I don't know what you're talking about."

26.71	RSV	TEV

And when he went out to the porch, another maid saw him, and she said to the bystanders, "This man was with Jesus of Nazareth."	and went on out to the entrance of the courtyard. Another servant girl saw him and said to the men there, "He was with Jesus of Nazareth."

For speakers of American English **porch** implies a floor, usually with a roof, attached to the outside of a building at a doorway; the meaning is more accurately "gateway" (NEB, NJB, NIV) or **"entrance of the courtyard"** (TEV). Mark (14.68) employs a slightly different word, which RSV there translates "gateway" (footnote "fore-court").

Whereas Matthew indicates that **another maid** (TEV "Another servant girl") asked him the second time, Mark indicates that it was the same servant girl who had asked the previous question.

The second servant girl does not address Peter as the first girl had done; instead she makes her remarks **to the bystanders** (TEV "to the men there"). "To the people there" may be better.

This man was with Jesus of Nazareth may need to be translated "He was with that man Jesus from the town of Nazareth."

26.72   RSV   TEV

And again he denied it with an oath,   Again Peter denied it and an-
"I do not know the man."   swered, "I swear that I don't know
                                                that man!"

Denied it may need to be expanded to read "denied that he was with Jesus of Nazareth." Only Matthew notes that Peter used an **oath** to strengthen his denial. **With an oath, "I do not know the man"** may be restructured as in TEV: **"I swear that I don't know that man!"** or as "I declare before God that I don't know the man." But for further ideas on **oath**, see the discussion at 5.33.

26.73   RSV   TEV

After a little while the bystanders   After a little while the men
came up and said to Peter, "Certain-   standing there came to Peter. "Of
ly you are also one of them, for your   course you are one of them," they
accent betrays you."   said. "After all, the way you speak
                                                gives you away!"

Came up (TEV **"came to Peter"**) may need to be translated "walked over to where Peter was" or "came closer to Peter." The translation should not imply that the men approached from a long distance.

One of them (so also TEV, NJB, Brc) is translated "belonged to them" by GECL. It is also possible to translate "are one of the ones who was with Jesus of Nazareth" or "are one of the ones who was with that man."

Your accent betrays you is translated "your accent gives you away" by NEB. "Your Galilean accent makes it obvious" (Brc) clarifies what is meant by **accent** or **"the way you speak"** (TEV). The phrase may need to be turned around: "We can tell from your accent."

26.74 RSV TEV

Then he began to invoke a curse upon himself and to swear, "I do not know the man." And immediately the cock crowed.

Then Peter said, "I swear that I am telling the truth! May God punish me if I am not! I do not know that man!"

Just then a rooster crowed,

Began to invoke a curse upon himself (JB, Brc, and NIV have the equivalent of "call down curses on himself"): this appears to have God as the assumed source of the curse, and so GECL renders the verse as "But Peter swore: 'May God punish me if I am lying! I do not know the man!' " (compare TEV). A different interpretation is pursued by Mft ("he broke out cursing and swearing"), as by Lu, NEB, NAB, Phps.

Immediately (TEV "**Just then**") may be translated "as soon as he said this."

As at verse 34, **the cock** is not a specific fowl previously mentioned. Hence "**a rooster**" of TEV.

26.75 RSV TEV

And Peter remembered the saying of Jesus, "Before the cock crows, you will deny me three times." And he went out and wept bitterly.

and Peter remembered what Jesus had told him: "Before the rooster crows, you will say three times that you do not know me." He went out and wept bitterly.

Peter remembered the saying of Jesus refers back to verse 34. Here **the saying of Jesus** can be "what Jesus had said."

Matthew and Luke (22.61) agree in their presentation of Jesus' prediction: **Before the cock crows, you will deny me three times**. In contrast Mark has "Before the cock crows twice, you will deny me three times" (14.72). Rather than use direct discourse, for some languages indirect will be better: "then Peter remembered that Jesus had told him that before the rooster crowed (that night) he would deny Jesus three times."

And he went out and wept bitterly is word-for-word the same in Matthew and Luke (22.62). **Went out** presumably means out of the courtyard of the High Priest.

For Peter to weep **bitterly** means to weep a great deal, of course, but more than that. Translators should think how they would feel if they had done what Peter did and find the appropriate expression in their language. Perhaps "wept in great anguish" or ". . . in great sorrow."

Chapter 27

RSV   TEV

Jesus Is Taken to Pilate

1 When morning came, all the chief priests and the elders of the people took counsel against Jesus to put him to death; 2 and they bound him and led him away and delivered him to Pilate the governor.

1 Early in the morning all the chief priests and the elders made their plans against Jesus to put him to death. 2 They put him in chains, led him off, and handed him over to Pilate, the Roman governor.

SECTION HEADING: "**Jesus Is Taken to Pilate**" uses a passive construction which may need to be transformed to an active one; for example, "The leaders of the people take Jesus to Pilate" or "Pilate judges Jesus."

Verse 1 of this chapter may be understood either as a continuation of the gathering mentioned in 26.57-68 or else as a second gathering of the council. Mark apparently conceives of two separate and distinct gatherings (14.53-65; 15.1a), and it is only in the second of these that the "whole council" comes together. Matthew may also be speaking of two gatherings, but it is more likely that he has in mind only one, since he already notes in 26.59 that the "whole council" had gathered. Inasmuch as scholarly opinion differs regarding the number of gatherings intended by Matthew, it is permissible to translate 27.1 as either a continuation of the earlier gathering or else as a separate one.

27.1   RSV   TEV

When morning came, all the chief priests and the elders of the people took counsel against Jesus to put him to death;

Early in the morning all the chief priests and the elders made their plans against Jesus to put him to death.

When morning came is translated "**Early in the morning**" by TEV; GECL is even more specific with "Early the next morning."

As in 21.23, so here also **the elders** is followed by the qualifying phrase **of the people**, which TEV omits on the grounds that it is redundant.

Took counsel is used earlier in 12.14; see comments there. **Took counsel against Jesus to put him to death** is a fairly literal rendering of the Greek text; Brc translates "laid their plans to make sure that Jesus would be put to death." NIV is even more precise: "came to the decision to put Jesus to death." But a better example is "made plans on how they would have Jesus put to death."

27.2	RSV	TEV

RSV	TEV
and they bound him and led him away and delivered him to Pilate the governor.	They put him in chains, led him off, and handed him over to Pilate, the Roman governor.

Bound him is interpreted by TEV to mean "**put him in chains**," though it is not necessary to assume that chains were in fact used. **Bound** is here used causatively: "had him bound" or "They commanded their servants, 'Tie him up' " or ". . . 'Put him in chains.' "

For some translators, **led him away** needs to be "led him away from there," or better yet, relating it to the next phrase, "led him from there to hand him to Pilate."

Delivered is better translated "handed over." It is the same verb frequently rendered "betray," and from it comes the form "the betrayer."

Pilate (Pontius Pilate) was the Roman governor of Judea during the period A.D. 26-36. The title **governor** describes Pilate's military authority and would not have been his official title. According to what is known from other sources, Pilate was an extremely corrupt person, given to violence and acts of cruelty. A **governor** does not rule so much as he administers on behalf of the rulers. But this distinction is not always possible to keep. "Ruler of that province (or, area) for the Roman Emperor" or "the one the Roman Emperor put in charge of that area" may express this idea.

27.3-10

RSV	TEV
	The Death of Judas

RSV	TEV
3 When Judas, his betrayer, saw that he was condemned, he repented and brought back the thirty pieces of silver to the chief priests and the elders, 4 saying, "I have sinned in betraying innocent blood." They said, "What is that to us? See to it yourself." 5 And throwing down the pieces of silver in the temple, he departed; and he went and hanged himself. 6 But the chief priests, taking the pieces of silver, said, "It is not lawful to put them into the treasury, since they are blood money." 7 So they took counsel, and bought with them the potter's field, to bury strangers in. 8 Therefore that field has been called the Field of Blood to this day. 9 Then was fulfilled what had been spoken by the prophet Jeremiah, saying, "And they took the thirty pieces of silver, the price of him on whom a price had been set by some of the sons of Israel, 10 and they gave them for the potter's field, as the	3 When Judas, the traitor, learned that Jesus had been condemned, he repented and took back the thirty silver coins to the chief priests and the elders. 4 "I have sinned by betraying an innocent man to death!" he said. "What do we care about that?" they answered. "That is your business!" 5 Judas threw the coins down in the Temple and left; then he went off and hanged himself. 6 The chief priests picked up the coins and said, "This is blood money, and it is against our Law to put it in the Temple treasury." 7 After reaching an agreement about it, they used the money to buy Potter's Field, as a cemetery for foreigners. 8 That is why that field is called "Field of Blood" to this very day. 9 Then what the prophet Jeremiah had said came true: "They took the thirty silver coins, the

Lord directed me."

amount the people of Israel had agreed to pay for him, 10 and used the money to buy the potter's field, as the Lord had commanded me."

SECTION HEADING: "**The Death of Judas**" can be "How Judas died" or "Judas killed himself."

The account of Judas' death appears only here in the Synoptic Gospels. A second account, with significant variations, is found in Acts 1.18-20.

27.3	RSV	TEV

When Judas, his betrayer, saw that he was condemned, he repented and brought back the thirty pieces of silver to the chief priests and the elders,	When Judas, the traitor, learned that Jesus had been condemned, he repented and took back the thirty silver coins to the chief priests and the elders.

Judas was last mentioned in the text in 26.47; he is once again characterized as **his betrayer** (see comment at 10.4). If **his** could be misunderstood to refer to Pilate or anyone other than Jesus, then translators should use "Jesus' betrayer."

Saw (so most translations) assumes that Judas was close enough to the trial scene to see the outcome for himself. On the other hand it is possible to assume with TEV and a few others that Judas receives this information later as a secondhand report: "**learned**" (so also GECL; NJB "found").

That he was condemned would in normal English grammar refer to Judas, which is obviously not the intention. Therefore TEV substitutes the proper noun "**Jesus**" for the pronoun **he** of the Greek text.

Condemned in this context means not only that Jesus was judged guilty, but that he was subsequently condemned to death. Some translators have had "found guilty and deserving of death." It is often necessary to transform this passive into an active sentence, as in "the council had found Jesus guilty and deserving of death" or ". . . and that he deserved to die."

Repented translates the same verb used in 21.29. Since this is not the normal verb used in the New Testament for repentance (see 3.2; 4.17; 11.20,21; 12.41), a number of translations prefer to employ another verb: NEB and NIV have "seized with remorse" (similarly NJB, Phps), NAB has "began to regret his action deeply," and Brc chooses "realized the horror of what he had done."

The thirty pieces of silver (TEV "**the thirty silver coins**"): the use of the definite article presupposes knowledge of the event described in 26.15. In some cases it is best to say "the thirty pieces of silver the chief priests and the elders had given him" or ". . . that he received for betraying Jesus." Whereas in the earlier narrative only "the chief priests" are mentioned in conjunction with the betrayal, here Matthew includes both **the chief priests and the elders**.

27.4 RSV	TEV
saying, "I have sinned in betraying innocent blood." They said, "What is that to us? See to it yourself."	"I have sinned by betraying an innocent man to death!" he said. "What do we care about that?" they answered. "That is your business!"

Innocent blood is a Hebrew idiom for the death of "**an innocent man**" (TEV). GECL inverts the order of the two clauses: "An innocent man will be killed, and I have betrayed him." In fact some translations find it natural to restructure even more radically, as they put **I have sinned** at the end of these clauses: "I have betrayed an innocent man who will now be put to death. This was a sin." Or "A man will die because I sinned and betrayed him."

The literal expression **What is that to us?** (so also NEB, NJB) is translated "**What do we care about that?**" by TEV. A statement may be substituted for the rhetorical question: "We don't care about that" or "That has nothing to do with us" (Brc).

See to it yourself is represented in TEV by a form familiar to speakers of American English: "**That is your business!**" However, this restructuring may prove difficult for persons without a thorough knowledge of the language. It may be better to render "That is your concern" (NJB) or "That's your problem!"

Verses 4-5 seem to suggest that Judas approached the chief priests within the Temple building itself, and that this happened while they were in session. But such a supposition encounters at least two difficulties: (1) according to verse 2 the chief priests had already gone to the residence of Pilate, and (2) it is impossible that the Temple building would have been accessible to the general public. It is difficult to know precisely what Matthew had in mind, but for languages which require that the translation be specific, it is best to state that Judas threw the coins into the Temple, though not actually entering himself. This much is supported by the Greek, which does not explicitly state that Judas actually went in.

27.5 RSV	TEV
And throwing down the pieces of silver in the temple, he departed; and he went and hanged himself.	Judas threw the coins down in the Temple and left; then he went off and hanged himself.

Throwing down translates a Greek participle which is masculine singular, though this information is not conveyed by a literal translation into English. Therefore, since it is possible for the readers to conclude that the chief priests and elders took the coins and then threw them down (see verse 3), TEV identifies Judas as subject. Both NEB ("So he threw") and Phps ("And Judas flung") also identify Judas as subject.

Temple is the same noun used in 23.16; it is the more inclusive noun, including the entire Temple area. In 4.5 the noun is used which refers more specifically to the sanctuary.

He departed; and he went may be translated with only one verb of motion: "then he went off" (GECL).

Hanged himself does not agree with the manner of Judas' death as recounted in Acts 1.18, but translators should be faithful to this text. Some languages will require an instrument, as in "hanged himself with a rope," and others will even need to make it explicit that the hanging brought about his death, as in "hanged himself and died."

27.6

RSV	TEV
But the chief priests, taking the pieces of silver, said, "It is not lawful to put them into the treasury, since they are blood money."	The chief priests picked up the coins and said, "This is blood money, and it is against our Law to put it in the Temple treasury."

Taking the pieces of silver may need to be expressed as "picked up (or, gathered) the pieces of silver."

The treasury the priests referred to was the Temple treasury, the financial resources of the Temple. If there is no good direct translation, translators may have to use a short description such as "put it with the money that belongs to the Temple."

The them refers to the pieces of silver, but it is sometimes more natural to say "this money."

TEV inverts the order of the two clauses contained in the dialogue of the chief priests, thereby allowing the causative clause since they are blood money to come first. This results in a more logical and more easily understood arrangement.

TEV retains the literal phrase blood money because of the anticipated play on words (see "Field of Blood" in verse 8). However, for many languages it will be impossible to speak meaningfully of blood money. One may then wish to translate the phrase otherwise (for example, "money received because a person was killed" or "the price of a man's life," as in Brc) and follow it with a footnote, indicating the play on words. The principle referred to by the priests probably derives from Deuteronomy 23.18, which forbids that money earned through prostitution be accepted in the Temple treasury. Here the law is expanded to include any "unclean" money.

27.7

RSV	TEV
So they took counsel, and bought with them the potter's field, to bury strangers in.	After reaching an agreement about it, they used the money to buy Potter's Field, as a cemetery for foreigners.

Took counsel: see verse 1 and 12.14. TEV expresses it well: "reaching an agreement."

Potter's field was the former name of the field purchased with the money received from Judas. A **potter** is someone who makes pots from clay. Whether it was the field of **the potter** or of a potter is not clear (verse 10 has "the potter"), and translators can use either: "the field of a (or, the) potter." They can also have "the field called Potter's Field."

The field would be used **to bury strangers in**. This may be expressed in a separate sentence such as "It can be used as a burial ground for foreigners." Concerning the purchase, one scholar comments: "The unclean money is used for an unclean purpose, the purchase of a cemetery for foreigners, presumably Gentiles."

27.8   RSV   TEV

Therefore that field has been called   That is why that field is called "Field
the Field of Blood to this day.   of Blood" to this very day.

That field has been called may have to be transformed into an active sentence: "People call that field."

Field of Blood was the name given to potter's field following its purchase with "blood money" received by Judas. For a different explanation of **Field of Blood**, see Acts 1.19, where the name is derived from the spilling of Judas' blood on that field.

To this day refers to the time when Matthew was writing, but translators cannot say something like "up to the time this book was written," since their task is to translate what Matthew said to his own audience.

27.9   RSV   TEV

Then was fulfilled what had been   Then what the prophet Jeremi-
spoken by the prophet Jeremiah,   ah had said came true: "They took
saying, "And they took the thirty   the thirty silver coins, the amount the
pieces of silver, the price of him on   people of Israel had agreed to pay
whom a price had been set by some   for him,
of the sons of Israel,

Then was fulfilled what had been spoken by the prophet Jeremiah translates the same words used in 2.17; it is the last in the series of quotation formulas found in the Gospel (see 1.22). One way to express it here is "When this happened it made come true what the prophet Jeremiah had said would happen. He said . . . ." The text is composite, and in this regard the NJB footnote is instructive:

> Actually this is a free quotation from Z[echariah] 11.12-13 combined with the idea of the purchase of a field, an idea suggested by J[eremiah] 32.6-15. This, plus the fact that Jeremiah speaks of potters (18.2f) who lived in the Hakeldama District (19.1f), explains how the whole text could by approximation be attributed to Jeremiah.

They took represents a form in Greek which may also be translated "I took" (NEB footnote), the meaning it has in the Septuagint of Zechariah 11.13. Except for the alternative wording of NEB, the third person plural form **They took** is preferred by all translations.

The price of him on whom a price had been set by some of the sons of Israel is a laboriously literal rendering. Many others also retain a form similar to that of the Greek text, but NAB ("a price set by the Israelites") and GECL ("what he was worth to the Israelites") effectively eliminate the unnecessary repetition. NIV has "the price set on him by the people of Israel," which is close to TEV: **"the amount the people of Israel agreed to pay for him."** Of course, the text says **some of the sons**, so that "some of the people" or "some of those people who were Israelites" may be better.

27.10	RSV	TEV

and they gave them for the potter's field, as the Lord directed me."	and used the money to buy the potter's field, as the Lord had commanded me."

The clause **gave them for the potter's field** may have to be "used them to pay for the potter's field" or "paid for the potter's field with them."

As the Lord directed me comes from Jeremiah; it is Matthew's way of indicating that all the events of the passion narrative are in keeping with God's will and purpose.

Some translators have found that this rather long sentence in verses 9 and 10 is easier to read if it is restructured somewhat as follows:

> The prophet Jeremiah had said "They took the thirty pieces of silver which was the amount the people of Israel had agreed to pay for him, and they used that money to buy the potter's field. This was what the Lord had instructed me to do." When the chief priests bought the field, these things came true.

27.11-14

RSV	TEV
	Pilate Questions Jesus
11 Now Jesus stood before the governor; and the governor asked him, "Are you the King of the Jews?" Jesus said, "You have said so." 12 But when he was accused by the chief priests and elders, he made no answer. 13 Then Pilate said to him, "Do you not hear how many things they testify against you?" 14 But he gave him no answer, not even to a single charge; so that the governor wondered greatly.	11 Jesus stood before the Roman governor, who questioned him. "Are you the king of the Jews?" he asked. "So you say," answered Jesus. 12 But he said nothing in response to the accusations of the chief priests and elders. 13 So Pilate said to him, "Don't you hear all these things they accuse you of?" 14 But Jesus refused to answer a single word, with the result that the Governor was greatly surprised.

SECTION HEADING: **"Pilate Questions Jesus"** can be expressed "Pilate asks Jesus questions" or "Jesus is taken to the Roman governor (for trial)."

As several commentators note, this is the first in a series of five brief scenes: (1) the interrogation (verses 11-14); (2) Jesus or Barabbas (verses 15-18); (3) the message from Pilate's wife (verses 19-20); (4) the demand made by the crowd (verses 21-23); and (5) the outcome (verses 24-26). In all five of these scenes, two factors stand out clearly: the innocence of Jesus, and the guilt of the crowd and their leaders. It is also obvious that Jesus is in absolute command throughout, although he says hardly a word.

The first of these five scenes is structured similarly to that of Mark (15.2-5). But Matthew lays greater stress upon Jesus' silence (see verses 12,14) and Pilate's amazement (compare "the governor wondered greatly" of verse 14 with "Pilate wondered" of Mark 15.5).

27.11   RSV   TEV

Now Jesus stood before the   Jesus stood before the Roman
governor; and the governor asked   governor, who questioned him. "Are
him, "Are you the King of the Jews?" you the king of the Jews?" he asked.
Jesus said, "You have said so."   "So you say," answered Jesus.

Now indicates that the narrative is moving along to the next episode. In English it is more natural to drop it, but some say "At that time."

The word **stood** does not mean that Jesus stood up at that time but rather that he "was standing."

The account of Jesus' trial before Pilate (verses 1-2) was interrupted by the narrative of Judas' death (verses 3-10) but now it is resumed. In order to aid in the transition, Matthew immediately identifies both of the main characters in the drama: **Jesus stood before the governor**. This is slightly different from Mark's opening observation, "And Pilate asked him" (15.2), which parallels Matthew's second remark, **and the governor asked him**. Mark prefers to identify Pilate by name, though Matthew consistently speaks of him by his military title of **governor** (verses 11,14,15,21,27), not reintroducing him by name (see verse 2) until verse 13 ("Then Pilate said to him"). Mark nowhere refers to Pilate by his official title.

For **governor** see discussion at verse 2.

Are you the King of the Jews? is framed in precisely the same way in both Mark (15.2) and Luke (23.3). The title **King of the Jews** is also used of Jesus by the wise men (2.2). It thereby becomes the title by which Jesus is known among the non-Jews.

Both Jesus' reply, **You have said so**, and Pilate's question are the same in all three of the Synoptic Gospels. See also 26.25,64 for the same response. Jesus' answer is intentionally evasive, probably because of the political overtones attached to the title in the thinking of Pilate. Jesus is indeed king of the Jews, but in a sense which would not be understood by the Roman governor.

27.12   RSV   TEV

But when he was accused by the chief priests and elders, he made no answer.	**But he said nothing in response to the accusations of the chief priests and elders.**

Both the passive verb construction of the Greek text (**was accused by**) and the noun construction of TEV ("**the accusations of**") are more difficult than a construction consisting of an active verb and a direct object: "the chief priests and the elders accused him." In many languages the form of GECL will be preferable to that of RSV or TEV: "But when the chief priests and elders made charges against him, he said nothing." Another good possibility is "The chief priests and elders then accused him of doing wrong, but Jesus did not say anything in reply."

27.13   RSV   TEV

Then Pilate said to him, "Do you not hear how many things they testify against you?"	**So Pilate said to him, "Don't you hear all these things they accuse you of?"**

Do you not hear how many things they testify against you? is a significantly different question than that of "Have you no answer to make?" (Mark 15.4). By reframing the question Matthew intentionally portrays Jesus as one who lives in a world where human accusations do not matter. TEV effectively eliminates the awkward and unusual **Do you not . . . ?** question form by replacing it with "**Don't you hear . . . ?**"

In translation it may be preferable to reverse the order of the two clauses: "They are accusing you of many evil things. Don't you hear what they are saying?"

27.14   RSV   TEV

But he gave him no answer, not even to a single charge; so that the governor wondered greatly.	**But Jesus refused to answer a single word, with the result that the Governor was greatly surprised.**

Gave . . . no answer implies refusal on the part of Jesus, and so TEV and NEB ("**refused to answer**") make this meaning explicit. The restructuring of NIV ("But Jesus made no reply, not even to a single charge") is similar to that of JB ("he offered no reply to any of the charges").

Both Matthew and Mark (15.5) indicate that the **governor** (Mark: "Pilate") **wondered** (TEV "**was . . . surprised**"), to which Matthew adds the adverb **greatly**.

Brc has expressed this sentence well: "But to Pilate's surprise Jesus did not answer even one single word."

27.15-26

<table>
<tr><td>RSV</td><td>TEV</td></tr>
</table>

Jesus Is Sentenced to Death

15 Now at the feast the governor was accustomed to release for the crowd any one prisoner whom they wanted. 16 And they had then a notorious prisoner, called Barabbas.[k] 17 So when they had gathered, Pilate said to them "Whom do you want me to release for you, Barabbas[k] or Jesus who is called Christ?" 18 For he knew that it was out of envy that they had delivered him up. 19 Besides, while he was sitting on the judgment seat, his wife sent word to him, "Have nothing to do with that righteous man, for I have suffered much over him today in a dream." 20 Now the chief priests and the elders persuaded the people to ask for Barabbas and destroy Jesus. 21 The governor again said to them, "Which of the two do you want me to release for you?" And they said, "Barabbas." 22 Pilate said to them, "Then what shall I do with Jesus who is called Christ?" They all said, "Let him be crucified." 23 And he said, "Why, what evil has he done?" But they shouted all the more, "Let him be crucified."

24 So when Pilate saw that he was gaining nothing, but rather that a riot was beginning, he took water and washed his hands before the crowd, saying, "I am innocent of this man's blood;[l] see to it yourselves." 25 And all the people answered, "His blood be on us and on our children!" 26 Then he released for them Barabbas, and having scourged Jesus, delivered him to be crucified.

[k] Other ancient authorities read *Jesus Barabbas*
[l] Other authorities read *this righteous blood or this righteous man's blood*

15 At every Passover Festival the Roman governor was in the habit of setting free any one prisoner the crowd asked for. 16 At that time there was a well-known prisoner named Jesus Barabbas. 17 So when the crowd gathered, Pilate asked them, "Which one do you want me to set free for you? Jesus Barabbas or Jesus called the Messiah?" 18 He knew very well that the Jewish authorities had handed Jesus over to him because they were jealous.

19 While Pilate was sitting in the judgment hall, his wife sent him a message: "Have nothing to do with that innocent man, because in a dream last night I suffered much on account of him."

20 The chief priests and the elders persuaded the crowd to ask Pilate to set Barabbas free and have Jesus put to death. 21 But Pilate asked the crowd, "Which one of these two do you want me to set free for you?"

"Barabbas!" they answered.

22 "What, then, shall I do with Jesus called the Messiah?" Pilate asked them.

"Crucify him!" they all answered.

23 But Pilate asked, "What crime has he committed?"

Then they started shouting at the top of their voices: "Crucify him!"

24 When Pilate saw that it was no use to go on, but that a riot might break out, he took some water, washed his hands in front of the crowd, and said, "I am not responsible for the death of this man! This is your doing!"

25 The whole crowd answered, "Let the responsibility for his death fall on us and on our children!"

26 Then Pilate set Barabbas free for them; and after he had Jesus whipped, he handed him over to be crucified.

SECTION HEADING: "**Jesus Is Sentenced to Death.**" An agent may have to be supplied, as in "Pilate sentences Jesus to death."

This section continues the series of five scenes begun with Pilate's questioning of Jesus (verses 11-14). The second scene, the choice between Jesus and Barabbas, is contained in verses 15-18.

27.15

<table>
<tr><td>RSV</td><td>TEV</td></tr>
</table>

Now at the feast the governor was accustomed to release for the

At every Passover Festival the Roman governor was in the habit of

| crowd any one prisoner whom they wanted. | setting free any one prisoner the crowd asked for. |

Many translators will render **the feast** with the more specific "the Festival of the Passover" (see TEV).

Was accustomed may be expressed as "**was in the habit of**" (TEV) or in a clause such as "it was the governor's custom."

| **27.16** | RSV | TEV |

| And they had then a notorious prisoner, called Barabbas.[k] | At that time there was a well-known prisoner named Jesus Barabbas. |

[k] Other ancient authorities read *Jesus Barabbas*

Matthew does not state the charge made against the prisoner; he merely states that he was a **notorious prisoner, called Barabbas**. The Greek adjective translated **notorious** (TEV "**well-known**") is used elsewhere in the New Testament only in Romans 16.7, where it has a positive value. But in the present context the meaning may well be **notorious** (Mft, AT, NJB, NAB, Phps), that is, widely but unfavorably known. Some translations say "a prisoner whom everyone knew about because of his bad deeds." **They had . . . a prisoner** can also be expressed as "there was a prisoner."

In this and the following verse, the UBS Greek text has placed the name "Jesus" in brackets (see the RSV footnote), indicating its questionable position in the text. On the one hand, as TC-GNT states, the textual evidence for its presence in the text is "relatively slender," but it is quite likely that the name was "deliberately suppressed in most witnesses for reverential considerations." As one may suppose, translations are far from unanimous: "**Jesus Barabbas**" is the wording of TEV, GECL, NEB, Mft, Lu, and Brc; only **Barabbas** is found in RSV, NJB, Phps, NAB, NIV, and AT. Translators are free to include or exclude "Jesus," but they may need to add an explanatory footnote.

| **27.17** | RSV | TEV |

| So when they had gathered, Pilate said to them, "Whom do you want me to release for you, Barabbas[k] or Jesus who is called Christ?" | So when the crowd gathered, Pilate asked them, "Which one do you want me to set free for you? Jesus Barabbas or Jesus called the Messiah?" |

[k] Other ancient authorities read *Jesus Barabbas*

The antecedent of **they** is "the crowd" of verse 15, and TEV has made this identification for its readers.

The text does not say where the crowd **gathered**, but it is most likely at Pilate's house, which translators may need to make explicit in the text.

Christ is translated "the Messiah" by TEV in order to show that the word is to be understood as a Messianic title rather than as a proper name (see 1.17). "The so-called Messiah" of NAB and AT is perhaps even closer to the full meaning in the context, since Pilate's question was no doubt sarcastic. In place of **Jesus who is called Christ** (so also verse 22), Mark has "the King of the Jews" (15.9).

27.18	RSV	TEV
	For he knew that it was out of envy that they had delivered him up.	He knew very well that the Jewish authorities had handed Jesus over to him because they were jealous.

In this concluding verse of the second scene, TEV has done considerable restructuring:

(1) **Knew** is given the English idiomatic equivalent **"knew very well"** (similarly GECL, FRCL).

(2) **They** are fully identified as **"the Jewish authorities,"** though on the basis of verse 12 it is also possible to render "the chief priests and the elders." (GECL retains the impersonal force of the Greek by translating **they** as "one.")

(3) **"To him,"** though not in the Greek text, is introduced for the sake of clarity; it will be required in some languages.

(4) The noun construction **out of envy** (NJB, NAB "out of jealousy") is altered to a verb construction, **"because they were jealous."** But even this may have to be expanded in some languages to "because they were jealous of Jesus."

27.19	RSV	TEV
	Besides, while he was sitting on the judgment seat, his wife sent word to him, "Have nothing to do with that righteous man, for I have suffered much over him today in a dream."	While Pilate was sitting in the judgment hall, his wife sent him a message: "Have nothing to do with that innocent man, because in a dream last night I suffered much on account of him."

The third scene (verses 19-20) opens with this verse, which contains an incident recorded only by Matthew. Both the use of the word **righteous** (used of Joseph in 1.19) and the dream motif (compare the birth and childhood narratives) reflect special concerns of Matthew's Gospel.

Not all translators retain the transition **Besides**. Some do by saying "In addition to that" or "He also said that because."

"Pilate" (TEV) is not identified by name in the Greek text, but since a new scene is introduced, it may be wise to do so in translation.

The judgment seat refers to the official seat on which a judge sat when making a decision (see Acts 18.12,16,17; 25.6,10,17). In Romans 14.10 and

2 Corinthians 5.10 it is used of the judgment seat of God. A number of translations refer specifically to the seat itself (NIV "on the judge's seat"; NAB "presiding on the bench"), while others depict a court scene without specifically mentioning the judge's seat (Brc "presiding over his court"; NEB "sitting in court"; TEV "**in the judgment hall**"). One other possibility is "while he was sitting to pass judgment."

His wife sent word to him is more literally "his wife sent to him saying." For most languages it will perhaps be obligatory to indicate what was sent; TEV, NJB, and NAB have "**his wife sent him a message**," which is close to the restructuring of NIV, Phps, and Brc. NEB shifts to a type of passive construction: "a message came to him from his wife."

Have nothing to do with is often better expressed "Don't have anything to do with."

Righteous (see 1.19) is rendered "**innocent**" by a number of translations (TEV, NEB, NIV, AT, Mft, Brc), because this is apparently the meaning it has in the context.

Today (so most translations) is rendered "**last night**" by TEV, GECL, NEB, and Phps. This adverb does not always refer specifically to daytime as opposed to nighttime; it may even be used of the entire twenty-four hour period which marks off one "day" from another. In fact, it is used as in conjunction with "night" in Mark 14.30, where the combination means either "this very night" or simply "tonight." Both GECL ("Because of him I had a terrible dream last night") and Phps ("I had terrible dreams about him last night!") are rather dramatic in their renderings, as is JB ("I have been upset all day by a dream I had about him").

Notice from these last examples that **suffered** is not translated to mean she was in pain, but rather that she had been bothered greatly by the dream she had about Jesus. "I had a dream about him today that upset me very much" will express this.

27.20   RSV   TEV

Now the chief priests and the elders persuaded the people to ask for Barabbas and destroy Jesus.	The chief priests and the elders persuaded the crowd to ask Pilate to set Barabbas free and have Jesus put to death.

Matthew now focuses in verses 20-23 upon the dialogue which took place between Pilate and the crowd who wanted to have Jesus put to death. It is significant that Matthew enlarges the leaders of the crowd to include **the chief priests and elders** in contrast with Mark's "the chief priests" only (15.11). By so doing he makes the leadership of the entire nation guilty of Jesus' execution. Moreover he strengthens the account in at least three other ways, all of which come to light in this verse: (1) "stirred up" of the Marcan account is replaced with **persuaded**; (2) the plural form of **people** is substituted for "crowd" of Mark; and (3) following **to ask for Barabbas** he includes **destroy Jesus**, which is not found in the Marcan parallel.

In the translation of this verse it may be advisable to begin with a transitional marker as in GECL: "In the meanwhile."

To ask for Barabbas clearly means "to ask . . . to set Barabbas free" (TEV). Moreover **to . . . destroy Jesus** is definitely causative, as TEV indicates: "have Jesus put to death."

27.21	RSV	TEV

The governor again said to them, "Which of the two do you want me to release for you?" And they said, "Barabbas."	But Pilate asked the crowd, "Which one of these two do you want me to set free for you?" "Barabbas!" they answered.

Verses 21-23, the fourth in the series of five scenes, narrates the demands by the crowd: "Free Barabbas and put Jesus to death!"

As previously noted, Matthew likes to emphasize the position which Pilate held, and so he frequently refers to him as **the governor** throughout this chapter.

Care should be taken that **them** and **they** are understood to be the crowd.

Which of the two do you want me to release for you? is found in Matthew but not in the Marcan parallel. The point of reference is the custom mentioned in verse 15.

The reply of the crowds (**"Barabbas"**) is also found only in Matthew. Here again Matthew utilizes direct discourse as a means of allowing Jesus' opponents to condemn themselves.

27.22	RSV	TEV

Pilate said to them, "Then what shall I do with Jesus who is called Christ?" They all said, "Let him be crucified."	"What, then, shall I do with Jesus called the Messiah?" Pilate asked them. "Crucify him!" they all answered.

Matthew now refers to the governor by name, **Pilate**. In the next verse the pronoun "he" will be employed.

Jesus who is called Christ translates the same construction used in verse 17; see discussion there. Mark has "the man whom you call the King of the Jews" (15.12).

In place of **They all** Mark has "they" (15.13). Here again Matthew strengthens the intensity of the Jewish accusation against Jesus—the chief priests and the elders have now persuaded the crowds, and all of them together demand that Jesus be put to death.

Let him be crucified (a third person passive imperative) is a shift from "Crucify him" (a second person active imperative) of the Marcan tradition (15.13). Scholars do not agree on the reason for the shift to the passive. Some believe that it is nothing more than a stylistic variation with no real significance. Others maintain that it does indeed convey a theological interest of the author, which may be either (1) an attempt to place less guilt upon Pilate as the one responsible for Jesus' death or (2) a way of making the form of the request conform with the use of the passive in the confession of Jesus as the one "who was crucified" (28.5). In verse 23 the same shift is made to the passive. However, in a great many languages this expression will have to be active, so translators will either follow TEV (**"Crucify him!"**) or use an expression like "Have the soldiers crucify him!" For discussion of **crucified** see 20.19.

27.23　　　RSV	TEV
And he said, "Why, what evil has he done?" But they shouted all the more, "Let him be crucified."	But Pilate asked, "What crime has he committed?" Then they started shouting at the top of their voices: "Crucify him!"

TEV renders **he** by "Pilate." Throughout this passage translators should use nouns or pronouns according to the needs of the receptor language.

The noun translated "**crime**" by TEV (so also Phps, NAB, NIV, GECL, Brc) need not refer specifically to a criminal act but may indicate **evil** in general (RSV, Lu). However, inasmuch as a trial scene is indicated, the context almost demands the specific meaning given by TEV. To translate "What harm has he done?" (JB, NEB) appears to be too weak, at least for American speakers of English.

All the more translates an adverb which may also mean "with more intensity" or "louder" (NEB, NJB "they shouted all the louder").

27.24　　　RSV	TEV
So when Pilate saw that he was gaining nothing, but rather that a riot was beginning, he took water and washed his hands before the crowd, saying, "I am innocent of this man's blood;_l_ see to it yourselves."	When Pilate saw that it was no use to go on, but that a riot might break out, he took some water, washed his hands in front of the crowd, and said, "I am not responsible for the death of this man! This is your doing!"

_l_ Other authorities read _this righteous blood_ or _this righteous man's blood_

This final in the series of five scenes (verses 24-26) is unique to Matthew's Gospel. Through it the author accomplishes at least two goals: (1) the acknowledgment on the part of the Roman governor that Jesus is innocent, and (2) the Jewish acceptance of the responsibility for the death of Jesus.

So when Pilate saw that he was gaining nothing is expressed very well in Phps: "When Pilate realized that nothing more could be done." **Gaining** can also be "accomplishing" or "achieving."

Riot represents the word rendered "tumult" in 26.5, where the chief priests and the elders are making their plans to capture Jesus at a time when the people would not riot. Matthew perhaps intends to show that a riot was now in the making, but one which was actually initiated by the chief priests and the elders, who have finally won the people over to their side.

That Pilate **washed his hands** in sight of the crowd is a claim that he is assuming no responsibility for what the Jews want to do to Jesus. Commentators note that the ritual of hand washing to show one's innocence of a crime is of Jewish origin, going back to Deuteronomy 21.6-7. But one commentator notes that the action was "almost proverbial," thereby intimating that it was not confined to the Jewish people.

In the Old Testament **blood** is used to refer to a violent death (for example, murder or execution), and then to refer to the responsibility for that death. Therefore **I am innocent of this man's blood** means "I am not responsible for this man's death." In verse 25 "His blood be upon us and on our children" assumes the second of these two meanings: "Let the responsibility for his death fall on us and on our children!" (TEV). In many languages, of course, the **blood** can be retained with complete understanding.

As the footnotes in RSV and NJB point out, some Greek manuscripts have "I am innocent of this man's righteous blood." However, the adjective "righteous" is not likely to have been omitted by a later scribe, had it been an original part of the Greek text. On the other hand, it is precisely the sort of information which pious scribes would have added to the text for the sake of underscoring Pilate's acknowledgment of Jesus' innocence.

"**This is your doing**" of TEV is more literally **see to it yourselves**. The meaning is "This is something for which you will have to answer" (GECL), as the response of the crowd (verse 25) clearly established. Other translators have "this is your responsibility."

27.25 RSV TEV

And all the people answered, "His blood be on us and on our children!"	The whole crowd answered, "Let the responsibility for his death fall on us and on our children!"

Matthew once again emphasizes that **all the people** were responsible for the death of Jesus (see comment at verse 22).

His blood be on us and on our children: see verse 24 for comments on "blood." **Children** is sometimes translated as "descendants." Brc renders Pilate's denial of his responsibility and the people's response as follows: " 'I am not responsible for this man's death,' he said. 'The responsibility is yours.' 25 The whole people answered: 'Let the responsibility for his death be on us and on our children.' "

27.26 RSV	TEV

Then he released for them Barabbas, and having scourged Jesus, delivered him to be crucified.

Then Pilate set Barabbas free for them; and after he had Jesus whipped, he handed him over to be crucified.

Then he released: in the Greek text Pilate is not mentioned by name, but TEV, followed by GECL and FRCL, does so in order to help the readers.

For them may be translated "for the crowd and their leaders" or "for the Jewish crowd and their leaders."

Scourged Jesus is not something Pilate would have done himself, and the verb obviously carries a causative force: "He ordered Jesus to be first scourged" (JB). It was common practice for the Romans to whip prisoners condemned to be crucified. **Scourged** can be translated very much as "flog" was at 10.17. The basic meaning is seen in TEV's "**whipped**."

Delivered is the verb commonly used of Jesus' betrayal, though in its initial occurrence in the Gospel it is used of John the Baptist ("had been arrested" of 4.12). Here it may be helpful to identify to whom Pilate **delivered** Jesus, and who would do the crucifying, as in "handed him over to the soldiers so they could crucify him." A shift to direct discourse may be preferable: "Then Pilate told his soldiers, 'Whip this man Jesus and then crucify him.' "

27.27-31

RSV	TEV

The Soldiers Make Fun of Jesus

27 Then the soldiers of the governor took Jesus into the praetorium, and they gathered the whole battalion before him. 28 And they stripped him and put a scarlet robe upon him, 29 and plaiting a crown of thorns they put it on his head, and put a reed in his right hand. And kneeling before him they mocked him, saying, "Hail, King of the Jews!" 30 And they spat upon him, and took the reed and struck him on the head. 31 And when they had mocked him, they stripped him of the robe, and put his own clothes on him, and led him away to crucify him.

27 Then Pilate's soldiers took Jesus into the governor's palace, and the whole company gathered around him. 28 They stripped off his clothes and put a scarlet robe on him. 29 Then they made a crown out of thorny branches and placed it on his head, and put a stick in his right hand; then they knelt before him and made fun of him. "Long live the King of the Jews!" they said. 30 They spat on him, and took the stick and hit him over the head. 31 When they had finished making fun of him, they took the robe off and put his own clothes back on him. Then they led him out to crucify him.

SECTION HEADING: "**The Soldiers Make Fun of Jesus**." In some dialects of English, "**Make Fun of**" does not give the same force as "mock." Translators can study verses 28 and 29 and decide what will be the most appropriate word in their language to describe how the soldiers treated Jesus.

Matthew follows Mark (15.16-20) closely in the account of the mockery by the Roman soldiers. Luke omits this scene altogether, though he does narrate a similar event which took place earlier in the palace of Herod (23.6-16). It was customary for

853

soldiers to make fun of condemned prisoners, and a part of their mockery would doubtless have related to the charge levied against the individual.

27.27   RSV   TEV

Then the soldiers of the gover-   Then Pilate's soldiers took Je-
nor took Jesus into the praetorium,   sus into the governor's palace, and
and they gathered the whole battal-   the whole company gathered around
ion before him.   him.

Although it is true that Matthew sticks closely to Mark throughout this narrative, the evidence of his editorial hand is seen in the first word, **Then**, which is found about ninety times in his Gospel.

Matthew alone identifies the men as **the soldiers of the governor**; Mark has "the soldiers" without further identification.

Praetorium is translated "**governor's palace**" by TEV. Scholars are of divided opinion whether this refers to the palace of Herod in the western part of the city, where they believe the trial before Pilate took place, beginning at verse 11, or whether it refers to the fortress Antonia northwest of the Temple area. Brc has given perhaps the most accurate translation with "their headquarters."

Battalion (so also AT) is a military term and is translated in a number of different ways: "cohort" (NJB, NAB), "**company**" (TEV, NEB, Brc, NIV), "regiment" (Mft), and "guard" (Phps). The official number of men in such a unit was six hundred, though the number could vary, and it is quite unlikely that such a large number were involved in the mockery of only one man. Nevertheless, a good way to translate **battalion** where military units are not known is to say "all their fellow soldiers" or "all the other soldiers in their group."

27.28   RSV   TEV

And they stripped him and put a   They stripped off his clothes and put
scarlet robe upon him,   a scarlet robe on him.

TEV correctly translates **stripped** as "**stripped off his clothes**."

A scarlet robe differs from the Marcan parallel, which has "a purple robe" (15.17). Matthew evidently has in mind the robe worn by a Roman soldier, whereas by the use of "purple" Mark is thinking of a royal robe. **Scarlet** is a brilliant form of "red," the color term used by many translators. The "purple" Mark refers to ranged from a maroon shade to what we call purple; the various possible dying processes yielded a variety of "purple" colors.

27.29   RSV   TEV

and plaiting a crown of thorns they   Then they made a crown out of
put it on his head, and put a reed in   thorny branches and placed it on his

his right hand. And kneeling before him they mocked him, saying, "Hail, King of the Jews!"	head, and put a stick in his right hand; then they knelt before him and made fun of him. "Long live the King of the Jews!" they said.

Plaiting or "weaving" is the technical meaning of the verb translated "**made**" by TEV. But the word is probably used very freely; NJB has "and having twisted some thorns into a crown."

"**Thorny branches**" (TEV, GECL) is probably more accurate than the traditional **thorns**, since it is most likely that the thorns would still have been attached to their branches.

Only Matthew indicates that the soldiers **put a reed in his right hand**. Although the root meaning of the word is **reed** (RSV, NJB) or "cane" (NEB, Brc), the word may also have a broader meaning, and "**stick**" is the rendering of Mft, Phps, and TEV. It represented a scepter, the symbol of a king's authority.

For a translation of **mocked**, see the discussion of "make fun of" at the section heading before verse 27.

The way in which the soldiers made fun of Jesus was by **kneeling before him** and saying, "**Hail, King of the Jews!**" These words are patterned after the manner in which the emperor's subjects would greet him: "Hail, Caesar!" The greeting **Hail** is translated "**Long live**" by TEV, AT, and GECL, because this is a more natural expression for greeting royalty. Moreover, for English speakers who are not familiar with the use of **Hail** as a greeting, it may be taken for "hell," which is frequently employed as a swear word. The word is used also in 26.49; 28.9. Many languages will have a fixed form of greeting which is used solely of royalty or of the ruling power. For example, Malay has a set expression which means "Yes, your highness" or "May your highness prosper." Others will have something such as "We salute you, King of the Jews" or "O King of the Jews, we honor you."

27.30	RSV	TEV

And they spat upon him, and took the reed and struck him on the head.	They spat on him, and took the stick and hit him over the head.

That the soldiers **spat upon him** signified contempt or hatred; for biblical examples see Numbers 12.14; Deuteronomy 25.9; Job 30.10; Isaiah 50.6. See also 26.67 and comments.

When the soldiers **took the reed and struck him on the head** they intended not only to hurt him physically, but to insult him. At least this is the significance that the action would have in a Jewish context (see 5.39).

27.31	RSV	TEV

And when they had mocked him, they stripped him of the robe, and	When they had finished making fun of him, they took the robe off and put

put his own clothes on him, and led him away to crucify him.	**his own clothes back on him. Then they led him out to crucify him.**

Led . . . away (so also NJB, NEB) differs slightly from Mark who has "led . . . out" (15.20).

Him occurs in the Greek only once, as the object of **led . . . away**, but it must be supplied as the object of **to crucify**, as RSV and most other translations have done. Mark has the pronoun as the object of each verb (15.20). For another example of Matthew's abbreviated style, see verse 58.

27.32-44

RSV	TEV
	Jesus Is Crucified
32 As they went out, they came upon a man of Cyrene, Simon by name; this man they compelled to carry his cross. 33 And when they came to a place called Golgotha (which means the place of a skull), 34 they offered him wine to drink, mingled with gall; but when he tasted it, he would not drink it. 35 And when they had crucified him, they divided his garments among them by casting lots; 36 then they sat down and kept watch over him there. 37 And over his head they put the charge against him, which read, "This is Jesus the King of the Jews." 38 Then two robbers were crucified with him, one on the right and one of the left. 39 And those who passed by derided him, wagging their heads 40 and saying, "You who would destroy the temple and build it in three days, save yourself! If you are the Son of God, come down from the cross." 41 So also the chief priests, with the scribes and elders, mocked him, saying, 42 "He saved others; he cannot save himself. He is the King of Israel; let him come down now from the cross, and we will believe in him. 43 He trusts in God; let God deliver him now, if he desires him; for he said, 'I am the Son of God.' " 44 And the robbers who were crucified with him also reviled him in the same way.	32 As they were going out, they met a man from Cyrene named Simon, and the soldiers forced him to carry Jesus' cross. 33 They came to a place called Golgotha, which means, "The Place of the Skull." 34 There they offered Jesus wine mixed with a bitter substance; but after tasting it, he would not drink it. 35 They crucified him and then divided his clothes among them by throwing dice. 36 After that they sat there and watched him. 37 Above his head they put the written notice of the accusation against him: "This is Jesus, the King of the Jews." 38 Then they crucified two bandits with Jesus, one on his right and the other on his left. 39 People passing by shook their heads and hurled insults at Jesus: 40 You were going to tear down the Temple and build it back up in three days! Save yourself if you are God's Son! Come on down from the cross!" 41 In the same way the chief priests and the teachers of the Law and the elders made fun of him: 42 "He saved others, but he cannot save himself! Isn't he the king of Israel? If he will come down off the cross now, we will believe in him! 43 He trusts in God and claims to be God's Son. Well, then, let us see if God wants to save him now!" 44 Even the bandits who had been crucified with him insulted him in the same way.

SECTION HEADING: "**Jesus Is Crucified**" may have to be transformed into an active sentence such as "The soldiers crucify Jesus" or "The soldiers kill Jesus on a cross."

In the Greek text the crucifixion proper is mentioned only by a participle in verse 35a. Matthew's primary concern is to draw attention to the insults hurled at Jesus (verses 39-44), though he is also interested in the charge against Jesus (verse 37) and in the dividing of Jesus' clothes among the soldiers (verse 35b).

RSV   TEV

As they went out, they came   As they were going out, they
upon a man of Cyrene, Simon by   met a man from Cyrene named Si-
name; this man they compelled to   mon, and the soldiers forced him to
carry his cross.   carry Jesus' cross.

The text says **they went out** without saying what they were going out of, but
"out of the city" seems most likely.

Came upon is best understood to mean "happened to find" or "happened to
meet."

Cyrene was a Greek city on the north coast of Africa. For some it is helpful
to say "the city of Cyrene." **Simon** is also mentioned by Mark (15.21) and Luke
(23.26). He may have been someone well known in the Christian community to
which Mark wrote, because there he is further identified as "the father of Alexander
and Rufus." For Matthew he seems to have been no more than a name.

That the soldiers forced Simon to carry Jesus' cross is not exceptional. The
rigors of the trial and of the beating which followed would have left Jesus physically
exhausted. It was customary for the condemned man to carry the cross beam (not the
entire cross) on his shoulder; the upright of the cross would have remained in a
stationary position at the site of execution. **Cross** was discussed previously at 10.38.
Here translators can say "board (or, beam) on which they would execute him (or, put
him to death)."

Compelled translates the same verb used in 5.41; see comment there.
They forced Simon to carry **his cross**. Some have to specify "Jesus' cross."

RSV   TEV

And when they came to a place   They came to a place called Golgo-
called Golgotha (which means the   tha, which means, "The Place of the
place of a skull),   Skull."

Golgotha is an Aramaic word meaning "skull." Matthew indicates that the
Greek equivalent is **the place of a skull** (GECL "Skull"). The exact location of this
site is disputed, though it is generally assumed that the name suggests that it
somewhat resembled a skull.

RSV   TEV

they offered him wine to drink, min- There they offered Jesus wine mixed
gled with gall; but when he tasted it, with a bitter substance; but after
he would not drink it.   tasting it, he would not drink it.

They are perhaps Pilate's soldiers (verse 27), the last identified subject. It is
certain that "they" of the following verse refers to the soldiers, and "they" of verse

32 seems also to refer to them. The **him**, on the other hand, is clearly Jesus, not Simon.

The **wine** (first discussed at 9.17) offered to Jesus may well have been "drugged wine" (Brc), since it was customary to offer a condemned man a wine containing some sort of narcotic to ease the pain. But this may not be what Matthew intended. For Mark the pain-relieving ingredient is the myrrh which had been mixed in the wine (15.23). But influenced by Psalm 69.21, Matthew substitutes a bitter substance, literally **gall**, and there is no indication that he had in mind the meaning "some bitter drug" (Phps). Translators should have either **"a bitter substance"** (TEV) or "a bitter substance called gall."

When he tasted it is mentioned only by Matthew; **would not drink** is slightly different from Mark, which has "did not take" (15.23).

27.35	RSV	TEV

And when they had crucified him, they divided his garments among them by casting lots;	They crucified him and then divided his clothes among them by throwing dice.

In some other contexts **crucified** has been translated as "nailed to crossed boards to kill" or "executed by being nailed to a cross." In this verse Jesus has been nailed to the cross, but he is not yet dead, so "nailed to the cross" is more appropriate.

Crucified represents a participle in the Greek text, and it is dependent upon the main verb **divided**, which introduces an allusion to Psalm 22.18. In translation it may be necessary to mention the **casting lots** before the dividing of his clothes among them, so as to reflect a chronological arrangement. An example is "they cast lots (or, threw dice) to see who would have different pieces (or, parts) of his garments (or, clothes)."

"Throwing dice" is an attempt by TEV in the direction of a cultural equivalent. Most translations have either **casting lots** (RSV, NJB, NEB) or "drawing lots" (Mft, AT, Brc).

27.36	RSV	TEV

then they sat down and kept watch over him there.	After that they sat there and watched him.

Only Matthew indicates that the men **sat down and kept watch over him** after gambling for his clothes. The meaning is not that they sat there simply to stare at Jesus (TEV **"watched him"**), but rather to "keep watch" (NEB, Mft, AT) so that they might prevent any rescue attempt on the part of Jesus' friends or followers.

27.37   RSV   TEV

And over his head they put the
charge against him, which read,
"This is Jesus the King of the Jews."

Above his head they put the written
notice of the accusation against him:
"This is Jesus, the King of the
Jews."

The charge against him (Brc "a written copy of the charge against him")
refers to the custom of displaying a statement of the criminal's crime on the cross.
It would either have been carried over his neck on the way to the cross, or else
someone would have gone in front of him carrying it in the procession. It can be
expressed as "a notice that told why he was being put to death."
The King of the Jews is the title used of Jesus in 2.2; see comments there.

27.38   RSV   TEV

Then two robbers were crucified with
him, one on the right and one on the
left.

Then they crucified two bandits with
Jesus, one on his right and the other
on his left.

"**Bandits**" (TEV, Phps, NEB) is rendered **robbers** by most English translations.
It is the same word used in 21.13; 26.55.

27.39   RSV   TEV

And those who passed by derided
him, wagging their heads

People passing by shook their
heads and hurled insults at Jesus:

Those who passed by were various spectators and part of the crowds of
people going to and coming from the city; they were not the soldiers. So "people
who went by there" may be good.
Derided is translated "**hurled insults**" by TEV and NIV, while NAB has "kept
insulting." The Greek verb is the one traditionally rendered "blaspheme" when God
is the one who is insulted (see 9.3; 26.65).
Wagging their heads indicates scorn or insult (see Psa 22.7; 44.14; 109.25; Job
16.4; Isa 37.22; Jer 18.16; 48.27). The significance of this gesture may not be
understood, so translators have either used a word that will show derision (Brc has
"tossed their heads at him"), or have combined the two ideas in the verse, as in
"wagged their heads to insult him."

27.40   RSV   TEV

and saying, "You who would destroy
the temple and build it in three days,

You were going to tear down the
Temple and build it back up in three

save yourself! If you are the Son of God, come down from the cross."	days! Save yourself if you are God's Son! Come on down from the cross!"

The charge that Jesus said he would **destroy the temple and build it in three days** was made against him at his trial (26.61). Many translators break this sentence into two: "You were going to destroy the Temple and then build it back in three days. Now save yourself!" Some also tie this latter clause to what follows: "Save yourself if you are the Son of God."

If you are the Son of God recalls the temptation in the wilderness (4.3,6).

The order may be more natural if rearranged: "If you are God's Son, then free yourself and come down from the cross!" (GECL).

27.41

RSV	TEV
So also the chief priests, with the scribes and elders, mocked him, saying,	In the same way the chief priests and the teachers of the Law and the elders made fun of him:

TEV makes **So also** clear with **"In the same way."**

By mentioning **the chief priests, with the scribes and elders**, Matthew intends to show that all the leaders of the Jews had rejected Jesus (see verses 22,25).

Mocked (TEV "made fun of") translates the same verb used in verses 29 and 31; elsewhere it is used in 2.16 and 20.19.

27.42

RSV	TEV
"He saved others; he cannot save himself. He is the King of Israel; let him come down now from the cross, and we will believe in him.	"He saved others, but he cannot save himself! Isn't he the king of Israel? If he will come down off the cross now, we will believe in him!

Saved translates a verb which covers a broad area of meaning; GECL translates "He helped others, but he cannot help himself!"

"Isn't he the king of Israel?" (TEV) translates a statement: **He is the King of Israel**. It may be more effectively translated if linked with what follows: "If he is really the king of Israel, he should come down from the cross! Then we would believe him" (GECL). Phps is similar: "If this is the king of Israel, why doesn't he come down from the cross now, and we will believe him!" During the course of Jesus' ministry, "some of the scribes and Pharisees" had demanded of Jesus a miracle (12.38-42), as had "the Pharisees and Sadducees" (16.1-4). It was probably expected of the Messiah that he would have the power to perform miracles, and now the supreme miracle is demanded of him.

Believe in him is best taken in the sense of "believe that he is the Messiah."

27.43 RSV TEV

He trusts in God; let God deliver him now, if he desires him; for he said, 'I am the Son of God.' " **He trusts in God and claims to be God's Son. Well, then, let us see if God wants to save him now!"**

He trusts in God can be rendered by "He believes God will be with him (or, take care of him)" or "He depends on God to be with him."

He trusts in God; let God deliver him now, if he desires him echoes Psalm 22.8, as the shaking of heads (verse 39) hints of Psalm 22.7. Commentators also note the similarity between the scene here and the philosophy expressed in the Wisdom of Solomon 2.6-20 (especially verses 17-20). **Let God deliver him now, if he desires him** is effectively restructured in TEV: "**let us see if God wants to save him now.**" The order may be reversed: "If God wants to save him, let him do that now."

27.44 RSV TEV

And the robbers who were crucified with him also reviled him in the same way. **Even the bandits who had been crucified with him insulted him in the same way.**

Apparently neither Matthew nor Mark (15.32) knew of the tradition concerning the bandit who repented (Luke 23.40-43).

27.45-56

RSV TEV

The Death of Jesus

45 Now from the sixth hour there was darkness over all the land*^{m}* until the ninth hour. 46 And about the ninth hour Jesus cried with a loud voice, "Eli, Eli, lama sabachthani?" that is, "My God, my God, why hast thou forsaken me?" 47 And some of the bystanders hearing it said, "This man is calling Elijah." 48 And one of them at once ran and took a sponge, filled it with vinegar, and put it on a reed, and gave it to him to drink. 49 But the others said, "Wait, let us see whether Elijah will come to save him."*^{n}* 50 And Jesus cried again with a loud voice and yielded up his spirit.

51 And behold, the curtain of the temple was torn in two, from top to bottom; and the earth shook, and the rocks were split; 52 the tombs also were opened, and many bodies of the saints who had fallen asleep were raised, 53 and coming out of the tombs after his resurrection they went into the holy city and appeared to many.

45 At noon the whole country was covered with darkness, which lasted for three hours. 46 At about three o'clock Jesus cried out with a loud shout, "*Eli, Eli, lema sabachthani?*" which means, "My God, my God, why did you abandon me?"

47 Some of the people standing there heard him and said, "He is calling for Elijah!" 48 One of them ran up at once, took a sponge, soaked it in cheap wine, put it on the end of a stick, and tried to make him drink it.

49 But the others said, "Wait, let us see if Elijah is coming to save him!"

50 Jesus again gave a loud cry and breathed his last.

51 Then the curtain hanging in the Temple was torn in two from top to bottom. The earth shook, the rocks split apart, 52 the graves broke open, and many of God's people who had died were raised to life. 53 They left the graves, and after Jesus rose from death, they went into the

861

54 When the centurion and those who were with him, keeping watch over Jesus, saw the earthquake and what took place, they were filled with awe, and said, "Truly this was the Son[x] of God!"

55 There were also many women there, looking on from afar, who had followed Jesus from Galilee, ministering to him; 56 among whom were Mary Magdalene, and Mary the mother of James and Joseph, and the mother of the sons of Zebedee.

Holy City, where many people saw them.

54 When the army officer and the soldiers with him who were watching Jesus saw the earthquake and everything else that happened, they were terrified and said, "He really was the Son of God!"

55 There were many women there, looking on from a distance, who had followed Jesus from Galilee and helped him. 56 Among them were Mary Magdalene, Mary the mother of James and Joseph, and the wife of Zebedee.

[m] Or *earth*
[n] Other ancient authorities insert *And another took a spear and pierced his side, and out came water and blood*
[x] Or *a son*

SECTION HEADING: "**The Death of Jesus**" may be also "Jesus dies."

This section may be divided into seven brief scenes, three of which precede and three of which follow the account of Jesus' death (verse 50), which is central in the series. The three scenes before the death balance out with those which follow: (1) Darkness over all the earth (verse 45) and the earthquake (verses 51-53); (2) Jesus' loud shout to God (verse 46) and the confession of the soldier (verse 54); (3) the crowd of those who mocked Jesus (verses 47-49) and the crowd of witnesses (verses 55-56).

27.45   RSV   TEV

Now from the sixth hour there was darkness over all the land[m] until the ninth hour.

At noon the whole country was covered with darkness, which lasted for three hours.

[m] Or *earth*

From the sixth hour . . . until the ninth hour (so also NJB, NIV) is transformed by TEV to read "**At noon . . . for three hours.**" Brc has "From twelve o'clock midday until three o'clock in the afternoon" and NEB has "From midday . . . until three in the afternoon." The calculation is according to the Roman day, which began at six in the morning.

There was darkness over all the land (so also NJB) is restructured as a passive construction in TEV: "**the whole country was covered with darkness.**" Matthew probably sees in these events the fulfillment of Amos 8.9: "The time is coming when I will make the sun go down at noon and the earth grow dark in daytime" (TEV).

All the land probably refers to the land of Israel (TEV "**the whole country**"), though it may also be interpreted to mean "all the earth" (RSV footnote). Although most translations reflect the first of these two possibilities, it is quite possible that Matthew intends his readers to understand the crucifixion as a cosmic event, affecting the entire created order.

27.46	RSV	TEV

And about the ninth hour Jesus cried with a loud voice, "Eli, Eli, lama sabachthani?" that is, "My God, my God, why hast thou forsaken me?"

At about three o'clock Jesus cried out with a loud shout, "Eli, Eli, lema sabachthani?" which means, "My God, my God, why did you abandon me?"

"**At about three o'clock**" of TEV translates **And about the ninth hour** of the Greek text. Most translations handle this similarly to the way that they express telling time in the previous verse.

Eli, Eli represents the Hebrew version of Psalm 22.1; "Eloi, Eloi" (Mark 15.34) comes from the Aramaic.

Since this cry, **Eli, Eli, lama sabachthani**, is actually translated by Matthew, translators only need write these Hebrew words in their own orthography.

Jesus' loud shout (**My God . . . forsaken me**) is taken by some to mean that Jesus believed God had abandoned him at this moment. Others take into consideration the entire Psalm, especially verses 24 and 26, and see here the prayer of one who still trusts in God to vindicate him. Fortunately the translator is not forced to make a choice between these two interpretations. TEV has rendered **forsaken** with the more contemporary "**abandoned**."

27.47	RSV	TEV

And some of the bystanders hearing it said, "This man is calling Elijah."

Some of the people standing there heard him and said, "He is calling for Elijah!"

Bystanders can be "onlookers" or "people who were near."

According to the Old Testament (2 Kgs 2.9-12) Elijah was taken up alive into heaven, and it was common belief among the Jews that he might come to help them in time of need. In Hebrew his name sounds very similar to the cry "Eli" (verse 46), though it is not similar in sound to "Eloi" (Mark 15.34).

Some translators render **calling Elijah** as "calling on Elijah for help." In addition it often helps readers who do not know who **Elijah** was, to say "the prophet Elijah."

27.48	RSV	TEV

And one of them at once ran and took a sponge, filled it with vinegar, and put it on a reed, and gave it to him to drink.

One of them ran up at once, took a sponge, soaked it in cheap wine, put it on the end of a stick, and tried to make him drink it.

One of them refers to one of the soldiers.

At once ran and took a sponge is probably better expressed by NJB ("quickly ran to get a sponge") and GECL ("ran quickly for a sponge"). If **sponge** is not known, translators may have to use a very general description like "something that soaks up water (or, liquids)."

Vinegar (so also Mft, Brc) is the traditional rendering. It is found also in NJB, but with a footnote: "Sour drink of the Roman soldier." The interpretation expressed in the footnote of NJB is perhaps correct, and a number of modern translations head in this direction: "**cheap wine**" (TEV, NAB), "sour wine" (AT, NEB), and "wine vinegar" (NIV). It is quite possible that the act was originally one of sympathy or mercy, which was later interpreted as an act of cruelty on the basis of Psalm 69.21: ". . . and for my thirst they gave me vinegar to drink."

As in verse 29, **reed** is probably better translated as "stick."

Gave it to him to drink (Brc, NIV "offered . . . to drink") may be intended in the Greek to convey the idea of force or coercion: "**tried to make . . . drink**" (TEV, NAB). The Greek is one word, "gave-to-drink," corresponding to the similar English word "fed."

27.49 RSV TEV

But the others said, "Wait, let us see whether Elijah will come to save him."[n]

But the others said, "Wait, let us see if Elijah is coming to save him!"

[n] Other ancient authorities insert *And another took a spear and pierced his side, and out came water and blood*

According to Mark's account (15.36) the same person who offered Jesus the wine is also the one who now mocks him. But Matthew distinguishes between this man and the others, who said **Wait, let us see whether Elijah will come to save him**. The verb **Wait** may be taken either as a command (equivalent to "don't do it!") or with the weakened meaning, "Now then we will see if Elijah comes to save him."

"Seizing a lance, another pricked his side, and out came water and blood" (Mft) is inserted here by some Greek manuscripts, though of the modern translations only Mft places it in the text. A few others (RSV, Brc) make reference to this alternative reading in a footnote. The UBS Greek New Testament reflects the opinion that the words were later brought into Matthew's Gospel on the basis of John 19.34 (see TC-GNT).

27.50 RSV TEV

And Jesus cried again with a loud voice and yielded up his spirit.

Jesus again gave a loud cry and breathed his last.

Jesus **cried . . . with a loud voice**, an expression that means to shout loudly. The text does not say what he said.

Yielded up his spirit (NAB, NIV, Mft, AT "gave up his spirit") is translated "**breathed his last**" by TEV. The meaning is he "died" (Brc, GECL, Lu). One must be careful in translation not to imply that the divine Spirit departed from Jesus before he died, as some heretical groups of the first century affirmed on the basis of this text. To "give up the spirit" is a Hebrew idiom for dying (see Gen 35.18), just as "to breath one's last" is an English idiom for the same experience.

27.51	RSV	TEV
	And behold, the curtain of the temple was torn in two, from top to bottom; and the earth shook, and the rocks were split;	Then the curtain hanging in the Temple was torn in two from top to bottom. The earth shook, the rocks split apart,

The phrase **And behold** was discussed at 1.20. Some translations drop it here, but many do translate it, using an expression such as "And then it happened" or simply "Then."

Mark also mentions that **the curtain of the temple was torn in two, from top to bottom**. The curtain referred to is the one which separated the Holy Place from the Most Holy Place (Exo 26.31-35; 40.21), which was thought to be the dwelling place of God on earth. Many translations have to do something similar to TEV, "**the curtain hanging in the Temple.**"

Both the observation that the split was **from top to bottom** and the employment of the passive **was torn in two** point to God as the one behind the drama, and so one may translate "God caused the curtain that was hanging in the temple to tear in two, from top to bottom." In addition it may be necessary to provide a footnote, describing what curtain is intended and what its significance was.

That **the earth shook, and the rocks were split** is recorded only by Matthew, as is the case with the events of verses 52-53. In Greek both **shook** (literally "were shaken") and **were split** are passive forms implying that God himself is the actor in these supernatural events. In some languages it may be necessary to translate "God caused the earth to shake, and he split the rocks apart."

27.52	RSV	TEV
	the tombs also were opened, and many bodies of the saints who had fallen asleep were raised,	the graves broke open, and many of God's people who had died were raised to life.

This verse continues the sequence of events from verse 51. If translators have made God the agent of the earth shaking and rocks splitting, then for **the tombs also were opened** they may have either "and God also opened the tombs" or "and the tombs opened."

Bodies is to be understood of the total person, viewed as a "body," a meaning the noun "body" frequently has in Jewish thought. The translation must not suggest that a group of unanimated **bodies** came floating up out of the ground! **Many bodies of the saints** are then "the saints."

Saints is literally "holy ones," and the term may refer either to God's people in general (TEV **"many of God's people"**) or else to a special category of devout Israelites who had died before Jesus' day. Both Brc and GECL have the equivalent of TEV, while several other translations specifically employ the other interpretation: "God's saints" (NEB), "holy men" (JB), and "holy people" (NIV).

Fallen asleep may be used figuratively of "the sleep of death," which is the basis for TEV's **"died."** In 28.13 the verb is used in its literal sense, though it is also used figuratively in other New Testament passages (for example, Acts 7.60; 1 Cor 7.39; 1 Thes 4.13,14,15).

Were raised also translates a Greek passive verb, which further suggests the activity of God himself. The full meaning is **"were raised to life"** (TEV) or "God raised to life many of his chosen people who had died and were in their graves."

27.53   RSV   TEV

and coming out of the tombs after   They left the graves, and after Jesus
his resurrection they went into the   rose from death, they went into the
holy city and appeared to many.   Holy City, where many people saw
                                                                    them.

It may be better to connect **coming out of the tombs** with the events of the previous verse, and then begin a new sentence with **after his resurrection**: "52 the graves broke open. Many of God's people who had died were raised to life 53 and left their graves. Later, after Jesus rose from death, they went into the city of Jerusalem, where many people saw them."

"After Jesus rose from death" of TEV translates a Greek noun phrase **after his resurrection**. GECL renders "when Jesus was resurrected"; one may also translate "after God had raised Jesus from death."

For many readers it may be advisable to translate **the holy city** as either "the city of Jerusalem" or "Jerusalem, the holy city of the Jews."

The Greek verb construction translated **appeared to many** may mean either "appeared to many people" or "were seen by many people." NJB follows one interpretation ("appeared to a number of people"), while NEB follows the other ("where many saw them").

27.54   RSV   TEV

When the centurion and those who   When the army officer and the
were with him, keeping watch over   soldiers with him who were watching
Jesus, saw the earthquake and what   Jesus saw the earthquake and ev-
took place, they were filled with awe,   erything else that happened, they

and said, "Truly this was the Son^x of God!"	were terrified and said, "He really was the Son of God!"

x Or *a son*

The centurion is discussed at 8.5. GECL has "the Roman officer," and Brc "the company commander."

Those who were with him has been correctly rendered by TEV as "the soldiers with him." The reference is not to the spectators.

Keeping watch translates the same verb used in verse 36.

Were filled with awe (so also NEB) translates a verb ("were afraid") plus adverb ("greatly"), which are rendered "**were terrified**" by TEV, NJB, NIV, Phps. Others, for example Brc, have more the idea "were tremendously amazed" or "were filled with great wonder."

Truly may be "in truth" or expressed as "this man really was the Son of God."

The Son of God (so TEV, NAB, NIV) translates a phrase which in Greek does not have the definite article, and so a number of translations render "a Son of God" (JB, NEB, Mft, AT, Phps, Brc). The real question concerns the perspective from which Matthew writes. On the lips of the Roman soldiers the phrase may mean no more than "a divine being" (that is, "a son of God"), but in light of Matthew's faith it must certainly be taken to mean "the Son of God." It may be advisable in translation to place one reading in the text and the other in the margin, as RSV has done.

Matthew again contrasts with Mark in having several soldiers make the confession, as opposed to the one soldier in Mark (15.39). But even more significant is the cause of the confession; in Matthew it is the sight of the miraculous events taking place, while in Mark it is nothing other than the death of Jesus itself which evokes this confession.

27.55	RSV	TEV

There were also many women there, looking on from afar, who had followed Jesus from Galilee, ministering to him;	There were many women there, looking on from a distance, who had followed Jesus from Galilee and helped him.

Matthew indicates that **many women** were present, while Mark initially refers only to "women" without any qualifying phrase (15.40), though later he adds that there were also "many other women who came up with him to Jerusalem" (15.41). Luke mentions the women together with the others who had known Jesus personally (23.49). Both Matthew and Luke identify the women as those **who had followed Jesus from Galilee**, to which Matthew adds **ministering to him**. Mark speaks of this first group of women as those "who, when he was in Galilee, followed him, and ministered to him" (15.41). In the context **followed** means "accompanied" or "went with," not to walk behind or to come later, as the verb might wrongly suggest in English.

The order of this verse is not the most natural in many languages. A possible restructuring can be "There were also many women there who had followed Jesus from Galilee and taken care of his needs. They were watching all this from some distance away."

RSV	TEV
among whom were Mary Magdalene, and Mary the mother of James and Joseph, and the mother of the sons of Zebedee.	Among them were Mary Magdalene, Mary the mother of James and Joseph, and the wife of Zebedee.

Matthew lists three of the women by name, as does Mark (15.40), though in place of **the mother of the sons of Zebedee** (see 20.20), Mark names "Salome." **Mary Magdalene** and **Mary the mother of James and Joseph** will each be mentioned twice again in the course of events to follow (verse 61; 28.1). Indeed their faithful following of Jesus adds continuity to the account.

Mary Magdalene is often treated as a name but is sometimes expressed as "Mary from Magdala."

To say **the mother of the sons of Zebedee** is quite strange in many languages, and translators often do the same as TEV: "**the wife of Zebedee.**"

There are three women listed, and translators have to be careful to structure their sentence so that it doesn't seem that **the mother of James and Joseph** is the same woman as **the mother of the sons of Zebedee**.

27.57-61

RSV	TEV
	The Burial of Jesus
57 When it was evening, there came a rich man from Arimathea, named Joseph, who also was a disciple of Jesus. 58 He went to Pilate and asked for the body of Jesus. Then Pilate ordered it to be given to him. 59 And Joseph took the body, and wrapped it in a clean linen shroud, 60 and laid it in his own new tomb, which he had hewn in the rock; and he rolled a great stone to the door of the tomb, and departed. 61 Mary Magdalene and the other Mary were there, sitting opposite the sepulchre.	57 When it was evening, a rich man from Arimathea arrived; his name was Joseph, and he also was a disciple of Jesus. 58 He went into the presence of Pilate and asked for the body of Jesus. Pilate gave orders for the body to be given to Joseph. 59 So Joseph took it, wrapped it in a new linen sheet, 60 and placed it in his own tomb, which he had just recently dug out of solid rock. Then he rolled a large stone across the entrance to the tomb and went away. 61 Mary Magdalene and the other Mary were sitting there, facing the tomb.

SECTION HEADING: "**The Burial of Jesus**" may also be "Jesus is buried" or "Joseph of Arimathea buries Jesus."

The account of Jesus' burial is somewhat briefer in Matthew than in Mark (15.42-47), and there are certain indications that he may be following an independent tradition. Attention will be drawn to some of the distinct features of Matthew's account in the detailed discussion.

   When it was evening, there came a rich man from Arimathea, named Joseph, who also was a disciple of Jesus.

   When it was evening, a rich man from Arimathea arrived; his name was Joseph, and he also was a disciple of Jesus.

When it was evening, except for the substitution of **evening** for "morning," is exactly the same construction used in 27.1. The temporal marker with which Mark (15.42) begins this section is somewhat longer. A new day begins in the evening; the day of Jesus' suffering is now at an end.

As elsewhere, **came** may have to be "went," in which case a destination may be necessary such as "went to Pilate." Also possible is "a rich man from Arimathea named Joseph arrived at Pilate's (house)."

Matthew identifies the person who requested Jesus' body as **a rich man**, even before he mentions the place from which he comes (**Arimathea**) or his name (**Joseph**). Neither Mark nor Luke indicate that he was rich; Mark says he was "a respected member of the council" (15.43), and Luke identifies him as "a member of the council, a good and righteous man" (23.50).

Luke identifies Arimathea as a "city of the Jews," and scholars tend to locate it in the hill country about ten miles east of Joppa, although the exact site is uncertain.

Was a disciple of Jesus is more literally "was discipled to Jesus," a verbal construction similar to that translated "has been trained for" in 13.52. See discussion there.

Some translators restructure the verse; for example, "When it was evening, a rich man from the town of Arimathea went to Pilate. This man's name was Joseph, and he also was a disciple of Jesus."

He went to Pilate and asked for the body of Jesus. Then Pilate ordered it to be given to him.

He went into the presence of Pilate and asked for the body of Jesus. Pilate gave orders for the body to be given to Joseph.

He went to Pilate and asked for the body of Jesus is word-for-word the same as the Lukan text (23.52). Mark is similar to this point, but he adds an incident not included in the other accounts (15.44-45a).

The response to Joseph's request is stated in a concise and straightforward manner: **Then Pilate ordered it to be given to him**. In the Greek text neither the direct object **it** nor the indirect object **to him** is expressed, though for English readers it is necessary to provide both. For some languages it may be obligatory to be even more precise and supply "the body of Jesus" where RSV has **it**, and "to Joseph" in place of **to him**. For another example of Matthew's conciseness of style, see verse 31. It was customary for the Romans to leave a crucified body on the cross until it rotted, but on occasion a corpse would be granted to relatives or friends upon request.

The construction **ordered it to be given to him** may better be "gave orders that they should give it to him."

27.59   RSV   TEV

And Joseph took the body, and   **So Joseph took it, wrapped it in a**
wrapped it in a clean linen shroud,   **new linen sheet,**

Whereas Mark indicates that Joseph "bought" a linen sheet in which to wrap the body of Jesus (15.46), Matthew says only that it was **clean**. Luke mentions neither the purchase of the sheet nor the cleanliness of it (23.53). TEV apparently derives the meaning of "**new**" from the context, assuming that the cleanliness of the cloth was due to its never having been used before. This is the obvious conclusion that one may gather from Mark's text, though this should not influence the translation of Matthew's Gospel. To render "fresh" (NAB) is a legitimate representation of **clean**.

A **shroud** is normally translated as "**sheet**," but in places where that word is not known, then "piece of cloth" is good. **Linen** is the fiber used to weave the cloth, and again, this may not be known. Some translators borrow the word from English ("a clean cloth of linen"), and others simply drop it altogether.

27.60   RSV   TEV

and laid it in his own new tomb,   **and placed it in his own tomb, which**
which he had hewn in the rock; and   **he had just recently dug out of solid**
he rolled a great stone to the door of   **rock. Then he rolled a large stone**
the tomb, and departed.   **across the entrance to the tomb and**
                                              went away.

His own new tomb, which he had hewn in the rock: sometimes the Jews used natural caves for tombs, and at other times they dug their tombs out of solid rock, as Joseph had done for his own tomb. Matthew is the only one who mentions that the tomb was **new**, and he probably has in mind that it was "unused" (NEB; GECL "and yet was unused"). If this is the meaning, then it agrees with what Luke says about the tomb (23.53). This is not an attempt to harmonize the Gospels. However, since it is known that several people could be buried in a single tomb, the meaning of "unused" or "where no one else had previously been buried" seems to be what Matthew means by **new**. Some translators say "the tomb he had just had dug out of the rock for himself and that had not been used" or "the tomb for himself that had never been used and which had been dug out of solid rock." Since Joseph was a rich man, it is almost certain that **which he had hewn** must be taken in a causative sense, which is the basis for shifting to a type of passive structure: "just recently dug out of solid rock."

Matthew tells that **a great stone** was rolled across the entrance to the tomb; Mark merely states that it was "a stone" (15.46); Luke does not indicate that a stone was rolled over the entrance way, though in the account of the resurrection he indicates that the women "found the stone rolled away" (24.2).

After rolling the large stone across the entrance of the tomb, Joseph "**went away.**" He disappears as quickly as he appeared; all that is known of him is contained in this brief account of Jesus' burial.

27.61	RSV	TEV

RSV	TEV
Mary Magdalene and the other Mary were there, sitting opposite the sepulchre.	Mary Magdalene and the other Mary were sitting there, facing the tomb.

Mary Magdalene and the other Mary were previously referred to in verse 56. They will be mentioned again in 28.1.

Were . . . sitting is an unusual combination of a singular verb (**were** is literally "was") followed by a feminine plural form of the participle **sitting**. This has resulted in a number of opinions concerning what may have originally been in the text. Some translations attempt to convey something of the form of the present text: "Mary of Magdala was there, and the other Mary, sitting . . ." (NEB), and "Mary of Magdala was there with the other Mary, sitting . . ." (Brc). The combination of verb plus participle may also be taken to mean "remained there, sitting" (AT; similarly NAB).

Sepulchre means the same as "tomb" in the previous verse and can be translated the same way.

27.62-66

RSV	TEV
	The Guard at the Tomb
62 Next day, that is, after the day of Preparation, the chief priests and the Pharisees gathered before Pilate 63 and said, "Sir, we remember how that imposter said, while he was still alive, 'After three days I will rise again.' 64 Therefore order the sepulchre to be made secure until the third day, lest his disciples go and steal him away, and tell the people, 'He has risen from the dead,' and the last fraud will be worse than the first." 65 Pilate said to them, "You have a guard*o* of soldiers; go, make it as secure as you can."*p* 66 So they went and made the sepulchre secure by sealing the stone and setting a guard.	62 The next day, which was a Sabbath, the chief priests and the Pharisees met with Pilate 63 and said, "Sir, we remember that while that liar was still alive he said, 'I will be raised to life three days later.' 64 Give orders, then, for his tomb to be carefully guarded until the third day, so that his disciples will not be able to go and steal the body, and then tell the people that he was raised from death. This last lie would be even worse than the first one." 65 "Take a guard," Pilate told them; "go and make the tomb as secure as you can." 66 So they left and made the tomb secure by putting a seal on the stone and leaving the guard on watch.

o Or *Take a guard*

p Greek *know*

SECTION HEADING: "**The Guard at the Tomb.**" This does not mean one person but is a collective noun that refers to a group of soldiers or guards. It may be necessary to have a short sentence such as "Guards are placed at the tomb," or "Soldiers guard the tomb," or "Pilate sends guards to the tomb."

Matthew's purpose for the inclusion of this narrative is evident: he writes it in response to the accusation that Jesus' disciples had stolen his body from the tomb and had falsely claimed that he had risen from death, as he had said he would. In this respect it is closely related to the narrative of 28.11-15. A secondary purpose of the account is also obvious: through raising Jesus from death, God revealed his supremacy over all earthly powers, Roman as well as Jewish. Of special interest is the observation that in none of the resurrection accounts is there any dispute about the matter of the empty tomb. It is rather the explanation of this fact that causes division and at the same time reveals the difference between belief and unbelief.

27.62 RSV	TEV
Next day, that is, after the day of Preparation, the chief priests and the Pharisees gathered before Pilate	**The next day, which was a Sabbath, the chief priests and the Pharisees met with Pilate**

The **day of Preparation** is the technical Jewish term for the day immediately preceding the Sabbath. Commentators generally agree that Matthew introduced the phrase there because he had dropped it earlier from verse 57, where it is included in the Marcan parallel (15.42). Most translations perpetuate a fairly literal rendering of the text, though GECL is similar to the restructuring of TEV ("**The next day, which was a Sabbath**"). FRCL renders "After the day of preparation for the sabbath," and NEB "the morning after that Friday."

The only other place in Matthew's Gospel where **the chief priests and the Pharisees** are grouped together is in 21.45, where they are representative of the leading opponents of Jesus. It is strange that on the day of the Sabbath they would have defiled themselves by gathering **before Pilate**, the Roman governor. According to John 18.28 the chief priests refused to enter the governor's residence so as not to defile themselves before Passover.

To say they **gathered before Pilate** may give the false impression that they formed a big crowd in front of him, but the meaning really is that they "met with Pilate" or "went together to see Pilate."

27.63 RSV	TEV
and said, "Sir, we remember how that imposter said, while he was still alive, 'After three days I will rise again.'	and said, "Sir, we remember that while that liar was still alive he said, 'I will be raised to life three days later.'

Sir represents the same Greek word rendered "Lord" when used of Jesus, though it may also be used in a purely honorific sense, as it is here. Matthew may have intentionally chosen this word in order to contrast Jesus, the true Lord (see 28.18), with Pilate.

Imposter (so most modern English translations) derives in Greek from the same stem as does the noun "fraud" in verse 64; TEV shows the relationship between the two words by translating "**liar . . . lie**" in the two passages. NIV here retains "deceiver" of the KJV tradition. The accusation that Jesus was an imposter is also reflected in another early Christian source: "a godless and lawless sect was begun by Jesus a Galilean imposter [the same Greek word used here]. We crucified him, but during the night his disciples stole his body from the grave . . . and so they are deceiving people" (Justin, *Dialogues Against Trypho*, 108).

I will rise again may also be translated "I will rise again to life," "I will be raised to life again," or "God will raise me to life again" (see comment at 16.21).

27.64 RSV	TEV
Therefore order the sepulchre to be made secure until the third day, lest his disciples go and steal him away, and tell the people, 'He has risen from the dead,' and the last fraud will be worse than the first."	Give orders, then, for his tomb to be carefully guarded until the third day, so that his disciples will not be able to go and steal the body, and then tell the people that he was raised from death. This last lie would be even worse than the first one."

Pilate had previously given instructions for Jesus' body to be given to Joseph for burial. Now the Jewish leaders request that he order the tomb **to be made secure** (so also NEB, NIV). The meaning seems to be that a security guard was requested to be placed at the tomb; "to have the grave closely guarded" (Phps), "for special security measures to be taken in regard to the tomb" (Brc), and "**to be carefully guarded**" (TEV).

Until the third day: elsewhere Matthew prefers "on the third day" (16.21; 17.23; 20.19). Brc has "for the next three days."

Lest means "so that not," as in the clause "so that his disciples won't go and steal him away" or "Then his disciples will not be able to go and steal him away."

The text has **go**, but translators may have to say "go to the tomb."

Steal him away is more often "steal him" or "steal his body."

Some late Greek manuscripts add "during the night" after **steal him away**. But, as TC-GNT indicates, this phrase was obviously added later by a scribe on the basis of 28.13.

Has risen (see verse 63) is here followed by the qualifying phrase **from the dead**. The picture is that of another "world" or place where the departed dead are gathered.

This last fraud (see the discussion of "imposter" in verse 63) evidently refers to the belief in Jesus' resurrection. The "first fraud" is then the Messianic claims which Jesus is accused of having made.

27.65 RSV TEV

Pilate said to them, "You have a guard° of soldiers; go, make it as secure as you can."^p

"Take a guard," Pilate told them; "go and make the tomb as secure as you can."

° Or *Take a guard*
^p Greek *know*

You have a guard (so also NAB) is translated "You may have your guard" by NJB and NEB. Accompanying the translation in JB is a footnote which states the meaning as "I now put one at your disposal" (GECL "I am giving you a guard"). But as the RSV footnote notes, the text may also be translated "Take a guard" (NIV, Mft, AT). One should avoid the faulty assumption that the words mean "You already have your own guard."

As discussed at the heading at verse 62, **guard** is a collective term referring to a group, not to just one person. "A group of soldiers to guard" may be necessary.

Make . . . secure is the same verb used in verse 64.

As you can, as the RSV footnote indicates, is literally "as you know"; the meaning may also be expressed "as you know how" (NIV).

27.66 RSV TEV

So they went and made the sepulchre secure by sealing the stone and setting a guard.

So they left and made the tomb secure by putting a seal on the stone and leaving the guard on watch.

Made . . . secure is the same verb used in verses 64 and 65; evidently Matthew employs it these three times in close sequence so as to remove any doubt concerning the reality of the resurrection event.

No one is quite certain what is meant by the act of **sealing the stone**. It may refer to the normal way of securing a tomb, or else to a special kind of sealing. One scholar has suggested that a rope was drawn over the stone and then a seal attached to it. Others believe that the sealing was done by means of filling the space between the face of the rock and the stone used for a door with soft clay, and then stamping on it the seal of the Jewish authorities. The apocryphal Gospel of Peter says that it was sealed with seven seals, though this judgment is without support elsewhere. Some scholars call attention to the parallel between the sealing of the tomb and of the lion's den (Dan 6.17), since these two themes sometimes occur together in early Christian art.

Since **sealing** is not known in all societies, then in this verse one possible translation is "put a mark on the stone to know if it was moved" or "put their mark on the stone so no one would move it."

Setting a guard points back to the guard given the Jewish leaders by Pilate (verse 65). TEV has **"leaving the guard on watch."** A more complete translation is "They left the soldiers there to guard the tomb."

Chapter 28

28.1-10

RSV | TEV

The Resurrection

1 Now after the sabbath, toward the dawn of the first day of the week, Mary Magdalene and the other Mary went to see the sepulchre. 2 And behold, there was a great earthquake; for an angel of the Lord descended from heaven and came and rolled back the stone, and sat upon it. 3 His appearance was like lightning, and his raiment white as snow. 4 And for fear of him the guards trembled and became like dead men. 5 But the angel said to the women, "Do not be afraid; for I know that you seek Jesus who was crucified. 6 He is not here; for he has risen, as he said. Come, see the place where he*q* lay. 7 Then go quickly and tell his disciples that he has risen from the dead, and behold, he is going before you to Galilee; there you will see him. Lo, I have told you." 8 So they departed quickly from the tomb with fear and great joy, and ran to tell his disciples. 9 And behold, Jesus met them and said, "Hail!" And they came up and took hold of his feet and worshiped him. 10 Then Jesus said to them, "Do not be afraid; go and tell my brethren to go to Galilee, and there they will see me."

q Other ancient authorities read *the Lord*

1 After the Sabbath, as Sunday morning was dawning, Mary Magdalene and the other Mary went to look at the tomb. 2 Suddenly there was a violent earthquake; an angel of the Lord came down from heaven, rolled the stone away, and sat on it. 3 His appearance was like lightning, and his clothes were white as snow. 4 The guards were so afraid that they trembled and became like dead men.

5 The angel spoke to the women. "You must not be afraid," he said. "I know you are looking for Jesus, who was crucified. 6 He is not here; he has been raised, just as he said. Come here and see the place where he was lying. 7 Go quickly, now, and tell his disciples, 'He has been raised from death, and now he is going to Galilee ahead of you; there you will see him!' Remember what I have told you."

8 So they left the tomb in a hurry, afraid and yet filled with joy, and ran to tell his disciples.

9 Suddenly Jesus met them and said, "Peace be with you." They came up to him, took hold of his feet, and worshiped him. 10 "Do not be afraid," Jesus said to them. "Go and tell my brothers to go to Galilee, and there they will see me."

SECTION HEADING: often the TEV heading, "**The Resurrection,**" is better expressed as a short sentence such as "Jesus rises from death" or "God raises Jesus from death."

In general Matthew's account of the resurrection follows that of Mark (16.1-8), though he includes two scenes not found in the Marcan source: (1) the appearance of the angel and the accompanying earthquake (verses 2-4), and (2) the appearance of the risen Lord (verses 9-10). The first of these two scenes narrates the miraculous removal of the stone and accounts for the appearance of the angel, whose presence is simply assumed in the Marcan text. In the second scene Jesus himself repeats the angel's command for the disciples to go to Galilee (see Mark 16.7 and Matt 28.7).

Now after the sabbath, toward the dawn of the first day of the week, Mary Magdalene and the other Mary went to see the sepulchre.

After the Sabbath, as Sunday morning was dawning, Mary Magdalene and the other Mary went to look at the tomb.

Matthew begins his account of the resurrection with two temporal markers, **after the sabbath** and **toward the dawn of the first day of the week**. The first of these temporal markers is sufficiently clear: the sabbath had come to an end. But the second marker is not altogether clear. The Jewish day actually began at sunset; it was the Roman day which began with sunrise. Nevertheless the vast majority of translations apparently accept the meaning as represented in RSV and TEV ("**as Sunday morning was dawning**"). But the same verb is used here as in Luke 23.54 ("and the sabbath was beginning"; RSV footnote ". . . was dawning"), and so Matthew may well mean "late on the sabbath, at the beginning of the first day of the week." If this interpretation is accepted, then the events took place in the evening following the sabbath day, and the scene is that of two women traveling in the darkness to visit the tomb. Thus Matthew's account would contrast with Mark's, according to which the three women purchased spices at the end of the sabbath day, but did not actually take them to the tomb until early the next morning. This suggests that in this part of his narrative Matthew represents the earliest tradition, which was later succeeded by the more popular account of the early Sunday morning visit.

Sabbath was discussed at 12.1. Most translators identify it as "the day of rest (for the Jews)." As for **first day of the week**, whether to translate literally or use "**Sunday**" (TEV) will depend on whether this identification will help readers or not.

The mention of **Mary Magdalene and the other Mary** ties the resurrection narrative closely to that of the death of Jesus (27.56) and of his burial (27.61).

And behold, there was a great earthquake; for an angel of the Lord descended from heaven and came and rolled back the stone, and sat upon it.

Suddenly there was a violent earthquake; an angel of the Lord came down from heaven, rolled the stone away, and sat on it.

"**Suddenly**" (TEV, GECL, NEB, NAB) is a valid way of translating **And behold**, which is one of Matthew's favorite transitional markers (see comment at 1.20).

Earthquake translates the same word used in 8.24 ("storm"); 24.7; 27.54.

The Greek text suggests that the coming of the **angel of the Lord** triggered the other events of this verse, and that all of them took place almost simultaneously: "And all at once there was a violent earthquake, for the angel of the Lord, descending from heaven, came and rolled away the stone and sat on it" (JB). Similarly GECL 1st edition has "Suddenly there was a violent earthquake, and an angel of God came down from heaven. He went to the tomb, rolled away the stone, and sat on it." Commentators note the similarity between the events described here and the words of Psalm 114.7: "Tremble, O earth, at the presence of the Lord . . . ."

Angel of the Lord was also used at 1.20. See comments there.

28.3	RSV	TEV

His appearance was like lightning, and his raiment white as snow.	His appearance was like lightning, and his clothes were white as snow.

Appearance (so NAB, NIV, Mft, AT), a word which appears only here in the New Testament, may also mean "face" (NJB, NEB, Brc). GECL translates "He shone like lightning." There are languages where the comparison may be rendered "shone brightly like lightning" or "was as bright as lightning."

Raiment simply means "**clothes**," as in TEV.

White, whether of lightning or of snow, is the "heavenly" color. In Daniel 7.9 the clothes of the "One who had been living forever" (TEV) are "white as snow," as is also the hair of the risen Lord (Rev 1.14). And of the angel who appeared to Daniel (10.6), it is said "His face was as bright as a flash of lightning" (TEV). Note also the similar descriptions found in Luke 9.29 and 24.4.

White as snow is obviously going to be a problem in areas where snow is unknown. Some translators, recognizing that this is simply a way of saying that his clothing was very white, either use a cultural substitution such as "white as egret feathers (or, as cotton)" or use whatever is the normal way in the language to say "very, very white."

28.4	RSV	TEV

And for fear of him the guards trembled and became like dead men.	The guards were so afraid that they trembled and became like dead men.

As RSV intimates, **for fear of him** comes first in the Greek sentence, while the second element is the verb **trembled** (translated "was stirred" in 21.10 and "shook" in 27.51). These are the expected reactions to the sudden appearance of a divine being, and both are intended to emphasize the tremendous fear that came over the guards. Some translations will say "the guards were so afraid," but others will have ". . . afraid of him," as in the text.

Guards does not translate the same noun used in 27.65,66; it is a noun made from the same stem as the verb "kept watch" in 27.36 and "keeping watch" in 27.54.

Became like dead men is perhaps an intended contrast to the "dead man" whose tomb they are guarding. He is alive, but they "lay there as dead men" (GECL). One vivid expression is "fell to the ground paralyzed with fear like dead men." It is almost essential in many languages to make it explicit that they fell to the ground, since otherwise it would seem they stood in fear without moving.

RSV	TEV
But the angel said to the women, "Do not be afraid; for I know that you seek Jesus who was crucified.	The angel spoke to the women, "You must not be afraid," he said. "I know you are looking for Jesus, who was crucified.

The angel had no message for the guards, but he did address **the women** with words of encouragement: **Do not be afraid**. The tense of the imperative is a form which would normally assume that the persons addressed were already afraid and are told to dispense with their fears. Moreover, the pronoun "you" is expressed in the Greek text, thus adding emphasis: " 'You,' he said, 'have nothing to fear . . . ' " (NEB).

Matthew includes **I know**, which is not found in the Marcan parallel (16.6). Matthew is also distinguished from Mark by having **Jesus who was crucified** in place of Mark's "Jesus of Nazareth, who was crucified" (16.6).

28.6   RSV   TEV

RSV	TEV
He is not here; for he has risen, as he said. Come, see the place where he[q] lay.	He is not here; he has been raised, just as he said. Come here and see the place where he was lying.

[q] Other ancient authorities read *the Lord*

Has risen: see "has been raised" of 14.2. The Greek is actually passive (see TEV), so that "has been raised" or "God has raised him" would be better than **has risen**.

As he said is not found in the Marcan parallel (16.6), but Mark later attaches it to the promise that Jesus will go ahead of his disciples to Galilee (16.7). Often translators have "as he said would happen" or possibly "as he said he would" (Brc).

Come, see is somewhat stronger than "see" of Mark (16.6).

28.7   RSV   TEV

RSV	TEV
Then go quickly and tell his disciples that he has risen from the dead, and behold, he is going before you to Galilee; there you will see him. Lo, I have told you."	Go quickly, now, and tell his disciples, 'He has been raised from death, and now he is going to Galilee ahead of you; there you will see him!' Remember what I have told you."

The adverb **quickly** is introduced by Matthew but not found in the Marcan parallel.

Whereas Matthew has **tell his disciples**, Mark has "tell his disciples and Peter" (16.7). In light of Matthew's interest elsewhere in Peter, it is noteworthy that he is not singled out here.

He has risen translates the same passive verb used in verse 6 (see comment at 14.2). Here Matthew adds **from the dead**, which is not explicitly mentioned in verse 6, but which may require explicit mention in many languages. Mark does not repeat this information but follows directly with "he is going before you to Galilee; there you will see him" (16.7). This statement is word-for-word the same in Matthew and Mark, but Matthew prefaces it with **and behold**, which is one of his favorite transitional formulas (see comments at 1.20).

TEV understands **and behold** to introduce the exact message in direct speech that the women are to give the disciples, so that the first two occurrences of **you** refer to the disciples. This can also be translated with indirect speech, as in "tell his disciples that he has risen from the dead, and that he is going before them to Galilee where they will see him." The third **you** refers to the women only. If the whole passage is in indirect speech, as in the RSV text, then the women are often included as those who should go to Galilee: "tell his disciples that he has risen from the dead, and that he is going before you (all) to Galilee where you will see him." But the TEV interpretation seems more likely. In either case, **I have told you** (Brc "That is the message I have for you") seems to be addressed to the women only.

For **he is going before you to Galilee**, see 26.32.

Lo (or "Behold"), **I have told you** confirms the angel's message; in place of this Mark has "as he told you" (16.7). In most translations this is rendered by a separate sentence.

28.8	RSV	TEV

So they departed quickly from the tomb with fear and great joy, and ran to tell his disciples.

So they left the tomb in a hurry, afraid and yet filled with joy, and ran to tell his disciples.

Departed translates a verb which technically means "go away from," suggesting that the women did not actually enter the tomb. Mark has "went out" (16.8), indicating that the women had been inside the tomb and now go out of it.

Quickly translates the same adverb used in verse 7. Matthew indicates that the women did precisely as the angel had commanded them.

Fear is the same noun used in verse 4; elsewhere in the Gospel it is found only in 14.26, when the disciples encounter Jesus walking on the water. Mark is even more dramatic in his use of "trembling and astonishment" (16.8). In place of Mark's second noun ("astonishment"), Matthew substitutes **great joy**; then he adds **and ran to tell his disciples** (Mark: "and they said nothing to any one, for they were afraid").

With fear and great joy is often rendered by a short sentence: "they were afraid but very happy."

If **tell** requires an object, translators can have "tell his disciples what the angel had said" or ". . . what had happened."

RSV	TEV
28.9	
And behold, Jesus met them and said, "Hail!" And they came up and took hold of his feet and worshiped him.	Suddenly Jesus met them and said, "Peace be with you." They came up to him, took hold of his feet, and worshiped him.

Mark's account concludes with the events of the previous verse, but Matthew adds an account of the appearance of Jesus to the women: **And behold, Jesus met them and said, "Hail!"** TEV translates **And behold** as "Suddenly" (see verse 2), and it represents **Hail** as "Peace be with you" (see comment at 26.49; 27.29).

Came up translates a verb which Matthew uses fifty-one times; only in 17.7 and 28.18 is it used with Jesus as subject; elsewhere Jesus is the one approached by the subject of the verb. "They approached him" or "went up to him" may be more natural in many languages.

Took hold of his feet is not intended to prove the reality of Jesus' resurrection body. Rather it is an act of worship to be taken in conjunction with the verb phrase **worshiped him**. The verb **worshiped** was first used of Jesus in 2.2. Here the translators may have "took hold of his feet in worship" or "worshiped him by taking hold of his feet."

RSV	TEV
28.10	
Then Jesus said to them, "Do not be afraid; go and tell my brethren to go to Galilee, and there they will see me."	"Do not be afraid," Jesus said to them. "Go and tell my brothers to go to Galilee, and there they will see me."

Do not be afraid translates the same construction used in verse 5.

Go and tell my brethren to go to Galilee, and there they will see me is now rendered as a command of the risen Lord himself; it was given as a statement by the angel in verse 7.

Brethren are not the biological brothers of Jesus, but rather his disciples (see verse 16). One way to translate is "my disciples, who are like brothers to me," but this is a little cumbersome. "My closest friends" has also been used, and "the ones I love like brothers" is another possibility.

28.11-15

RSV	TEV
	The Report of the Guard
11 While they were going, behold, some of the guard went into the city and told the chief priests all that had taken place. 12 And when they had assembled with the elders and taken counsel, they gave a sum of money to the soldiers 13 and said, "Tell people, 'His disciples came by night and	11 While the women went on their way, some of the soldiers guarding the tomb went back to the city and told the chief priests everything that had happened. 12 The chief priests met with the elders and made their plan; they gave a large sum of money to the soldiers 13 and said, "You

stole him away while we were asleep.' 14 And if this comes to the governor's ears, we will satisfy him and keep you out of trouble." 15 So they took the money and did as they were directed; and this story has been spread among the Jews to this day.

are to say that his disciples came during the night and stole his body while you were asleep. 14 And if the Governor should hear of this, we will convince him that you are innocent, and you will have nothing to worry about."

15 The guards took the money and did what they were told to do. And so that is the report spread around by the Jews to this very day.

SECTION HEADING: **"The Report of the Guard"** may be "What the guards reported" or "The guards tell what happened."

This narrative serves to explain the origin of the false rumor that the disciples of Jesus stole his body. It is constructed similarly to the story of the guard at the tomb (27.62-66), and it also possesses grammatical and stylistic features in common with that account. Both accounts open with a description of the setting (27.62 and 28.11) and close with an observation by the author (27.66 and 28.15). In the first account the chief priests and the Pharisees are the opponents of Jesus, and they employ direct discourse (27.63-64), while in the second account Jesus' foes are the chief priests and the elders, and they also use direct discourse (28.12-14). Of special interest is the attitude that dominates the two narratives: everything is reported in a matter-of-fact fashion, and in either story the narrator adds no negative comment against the evil plans of the Jewish leaders.

28.11   RSV   TEV

While they were going, behold, some of the guard went into the city and told the chief priests all that had taken place.

While the women went on their way, some of the soldiers guarding the tomb went back to the city and told the chief priests everything that had happened.

The women do as the Lord had commanded them and go on their way to tell Jesus' "brethren" of his resurrection and of his command for them to meet him in Galilee. **While they were going** may need some expansion. **They** is the women, for example, and **going** may require a destination: "While the women were on their way to the disciples."

Matthew once again introduces the word **behold** (see comments at 1.20) to draw attention to a significant aspect of the narrative: **some of the guard went into the city and told the chief priests all that had taken place**. It is significant that the **guard** (the same word used in 27.65-66) reports to **the chief priests** and not to Pilate. However, this is not as surprising as it may seem at first glance, since according to 27.65 the guard is apparently placed under the authority of the chief priests. **Guard** is a singular noun employed in a collective sense, and so the basis for "soldiers" of TEV.

In this context **all that had taken place** refers specifically to the events of verses 2-3; it does not include the dialogue between the angel and the women, nor does it tell of the women's departure to make the news known. Thus translators may have "everything that happened when the angel came to the tomb."

And when they had assembled with the elders and taken counsel, they gave a sum of money to the soldiers

The chief priests met with the elders and made their plan; they gave a large sum of money to the soldiers

In Greek the subject of the verb **had assembled** is not indicated, though it is evidently **"the chief priests"** (TEV) of verse 11. This information comes through clearly enough in RSV, since the last persons mentioned in the previous verse happen to be the chief priests.

Taken counsel (TEV **"made their plan"**) is the same construction used in 12.14.

A sum of money is translated **"a large sum of money"** by TEV and NIV, while NJB has "a considerable sum of money." With a slightly different but accurate emphasis, NEB translates "a substantial bribe," and NAB "a large bribe."

28.13 RSV TEV

and said, "Tell people, 'His disciples came by night and stole him away while we were asleep.'

and said, "You are to say that his disciples came during the night and stole his body while you were asleep.

By shifting **Tell people** into indirect discourse (**"You are to say that"**), TEV avoids the possible complication of a quotation within a quotation. It is almost comical that the soldiers are told to spread the rumor abroad that Jesus' disciples came during the night and stole his body while they were asleep. If they were asleep, how could they know what had happened to the body of Jesus? Moreover, as one commentator observes, "Above all, to ask them to say that they had fallen asleep while on watch and allowed what they were guarding to be stolen is asking them to sign their own death warrant." Matthew appears to have recorded this narrative with some degree of humor, emphasizing how foolish it is to believe the rumor current in his day that Jesus' disciples had stolen his body.

28.14 RSV TEV

And if this comes to the governor's ears, we will satisfy him and keep you out of trouble."

And if the Governor should hear of this, we will convince him that you are innocent, and you will have nothing to worry about."

And if this comes to the governor's ears (TEV **"And if the Governor should hear of this"**) translates a passive construction in Greek, literally "And if this should be heard by the governor." **This** refers to the news about the disciples having come and stolen the body of Jesus while the guards slept. It does not refer to the money being paid to the guards. Translators may have "this story." It is recalled that throughout the trial scene Matthew frequently referred to Pilate by his official title, **the governor** (27.2,11, 14,15,21,27); Mark, for whatever reason, avoids the use of the title.

In the construction **we will satisfy him**, the pronoun **we** is emphatic. GECL has "we will speak with him," and NAB "we will straighten it out with him"; TEV is more specific yet with "**we will convince him that you are innocent.**" It may be that the verb **satisfy** has the implied meaning "with money," in which case the full meaning is "we will pay him off" or "we will pay him what is necessary." But no translations seem to go in this direction.

Out of trouble translates a noun which is used in the New Testament elsewhere only in 1 Corinthians 7.32. NIV translates precisely as RSV, while NJB is similar with "see that you do not get into trouble." The meaning of TEV is the same, though the wording is somewhat different: "**you will have nothing to worry about.**"

28.15	RSV	TEV

So they took the money and did as they were directed; and this story has been spread among the Jews to this day.	The guards took the money and did what they were told to do. And so that is the report spread around by the Jews to this very day.

They is translated "**the guards**" by TEV, a technique adopted also by GECL, FRCL, and DUCL.

As they were directed (TEV "**what they were told to do**") is transformed into a nonpersonal construction by GECL: "as one had told them to do." One may also translate by supplying the agent of the passive verb: "what the chief priests had told them to do."

This story has been spread among the Jews to this day refers to the events of verses 11b-14. One must avoid the implication that **this story** includes as well the information that the soldiers took the money and did as they were told (verse 15a). In some cases it is helpful to say "this story about Jesus' disciples stealing his body" or "this story they told."

Spread is the same verb used in 9.31.

Among the Jews: RSV translates the Greek prepositional phrase as indicating location, but it may also carry the meaning of instrument (TEV "**by the Jews**"); in the final analysis the meaning is the same.

28.16-20

RSV	TEV
	Jesus Appears to His Disciples
16 Now the eleven disciples went to Galilee, to the mountain to which Jesus had directed them. 17 And when they saw him they worshiped him; but some doubted. 18 And Jesus came and said to them, "All authority in heaven and on earth has been given to me. 19 Go therefore and make	16 The eleven disciples went to the hill in Galilee where Jesus had told them to go. 17 When they saw him, they worshiped him, even though some of them doubted. 18 Jesus drew near and said to them, "I have been given all authority in heaven and on earth. 19 Go, then, to all peoples

disciples of all nations, baptizing them in the name of the Father and of the Son and of the Holy Spirit, 20 teaching them to observe all that I have commanded you; and lo, I am with you always, to the close of the age."

everywhere and make them my disciples: baptize them in the name of the Father, the Son, and the Holy Spirit, 20 and teach them to obey everything I have commanded you. And I will be with you always, to the end of the age."

SECTION HEADING: most translators find they can retain the form of the TEV heading, "**Jesus Appears to His Disciples.**" Otherwise it may have to be "Jesus goes to his disciples and they see him."

This final appearance of Jesus to his disciples, unique to the Gospel of Matthew, may conveniently be divided into two parts: (1) the setting (verses 16-18a) and (2) Jesus' instructions to his disciples (verses 18b-20). The grammar and style both reflect Matthew's hand at work, as do the theological concepts which run through the account.

28.16   RSV   TEV

> **Now the eleven disciples went to Galilee, to the mountain to which Jesus had directed them.**

> **The eleven disciples went to the hill in Galilee where Jesus had told them to go.**

Now is merely a transition marker introducing a new scene, and renders a Greek particle often translated "but."

The eleven disciples went to Galilee, to the mountain to which Jesus had directed them: the reference is to verse 10, according to which Jesus had told the women to inform his "brothers" to go to Galilee, where they would see him. The noun "disciple" is first used in 5.1, as is the word **mountain**. It is doubtful that any specific **mountain** is in mind; it is important to remember that in Jewish thought hills and mountains are places of divine revelation.

The mountain to which Jesus had directed them may be expressed as "the mountain that Jesus had told them they should go to."

28.17   RSV   TEV

> **And when they saw him they worshiped him; but some doubted.**

> **When they saw him, they worshiped him, even though some of them doubted.**

The verse says **when they saw him**, leaving it clear that Jesus appeared to them when they reached the mountain. In many languages this is not possible, so translators have had to begin this verse by saying "There they saw Jesus, and when they saw him . . . ."

Worshiped translates a verb frequently used in this Gospel (see 2.2; 28.9 for its first and most recent occurrences). **Him** is not found in all Greek manuscripts, but many languages will require that the verb be accompanied by an object indicating the one to whom their worship was directed.

But some doubted (so also NIV, Lu) appears in TEV as **"even though some . . . doubted."** NAB renders as though their doubt was something that took place prior to the resurrection appearance ("those who had entertained doubts"), although it follows with a footnote ("literally, 'some doubted' "). NJB offers the time perspective of NAB as a possibility in its alternative reading ("though some had hesitated"), but the translators confess that this has less grammatical support than the reading which they place in the text ("though some hesitated"). As a matter of fact, it is difficult to find any grammatical support for the interpretation of NAB; it appears rather to be an attempt to force a theological judgment on the text.

The clause is also difficult to interpret for other reasons. First, **some** may refer exclusively to the eleven disciples ("some of the disciples") or to others outside the group of the disciples ("some other disciples"). But even if the exegesis of RSV and TEV (**the eleven**) is accepted, then two possibilities still result: (1) "All eleven of the disciples worshiped Jesus, even though some of them had their doubts"; and (2) "Some of the eleven disciples worshiped Jesus, but others of them only doubted." If the alternative exegesis is followed, then once again two possibilities result: (1) "The eleven disciples worshiped Jesus, while a larger group of disciples who were there only doubted"; and (2) "The eleven disciples worshiped Jesus, as did some others in the larger group of disciples who were there, but others of them doubted."

The second major concern is that of the time perspective of the two events ("doubting" and "worshiping"), which Matthew almost with certainty regards as simultaneous. Moreover, since he specifically identifies only the eleven as the participants in the event, it is logical to conclude that he conceives of them all as both doubting and believing. The nearest grammatical antecedent to this construction is found in 26.66, where "they" in Greek is the same as **some** here: "They answered, 'He deserves death.' " This cannot possibly be taken to mean "Some of them answered"; it must mean "They all answered." On the basis of this grammatical pattern, one is forced to conclude: all eleven saw him, all eleven worshiped him, and yet all eleven doubted! Thus one can translate "When they saw him, they worshiped him, even though they were not completely sure that it was Jesus." In this same regard it is of interest to note that the only other occurrence of the verb "doubt" in Matthew's Gospel has the disciples as its subject (14.31). **Doubted** is often expanded to "doubted it was Jesus" or "were not sure it was really him."

It is also "them" (that is, the eleven) to whom the risen Lord announces his authority (verse 18), gives the commission (verses 19-20a), and grants the promise of his presence (verse 20b). It is this word that dispels doubt and evokes faith!

28.18	RSV	TEV

And Jesus came and said to them, "All authority in heaven and on earth has been given to me.

Jesus drew near and said to them, "I have been given all authority in heaven and on earth.

Jesus came translates the same verb used of Jesus in 17.7. TEV renders it as **"drew near,"** which is more natural in English.

All authority . . . has been given to me may need to be reformulated as an active construction with God as the expressed agent: "God has given me all authority" (GECL). Or, on the basis of verse 19, it may be even better to render "My Father (in heaven) has given me all authority."

Jesus first declares his **authority** in 7.29; see discussion there for the other places where similar declarations are made of Jesus. **All authority in heaven and on earth** may need to be expressed as "complete authority over all (living) creatures in heaven and on earth."

28.19   RSV   TEV

Go therefore and make disciples of all nations, baptizing them in the name of the Father and of the Son and of the Holy Spirit,	**Go, then, to all peoples everywhere and make them my disciples: baptize them in the name of the Father, the Son, and the Holy Spirit,**

Go . . . baptizing . . . teaching (verse 20) are each participles dependent upon the main verb **make disciples of**. But in such a construction it is not uncommon for the participles themselves to assume the force of an imperative. However, the command to **make disciples** is the primary command, while the commands to baptize and teach are ways of fulfilling the primary command. TEV, NJB, GECL, Lu, together with a number of other modern translations, translate all of the four verb forms as imperatives: "**Go . . . make . . . disciples . . . baptize . . . teach** (verse 20)" (TEV). Of the contemporary translations, RSV and NIV are in the minority as they follow the pattern set by KJV, which renders "baptizing" and "teaching" as participles.

All nations (TEV "**all peoples everywhere**") continues the concept of all-inclusiveness which is emphasized throughout verses 18b-20: "All authority . . . all nations . . . all that I have commanded . . . always."

Make disciples of is also used with a causative force in Acts 14.21; the only other occurrences of this verb in the New Testament are in Matthew 13.52 ("has been trained") and 27.57 ("was a disciple"). The notion of discipleship is integral to the Gospel of Matthew, where the noun "disciple" is used seventy-two times.

To **make disciples of all nations** has been translated by Brc as "make the people of all nations my disciples."

The disciples are to proceed with their work by **baptizing** the people of all nations. (Notice that in most languages one can baptize people, not nations.) "Baptism" was discussed at 3.1.

That baptism should be **in the name of the Father and of the Son and of the Holy Spirit** is stated only here in the New Testament. In fact a trinitarian formula is found elsewhere in the New Testament only in 2 Corinthians 13.14 (TEV 13.13), where it forms part of a benediction. Elsewhere in the New Testament baptism is done only "in the name of Jesus Christ" (Acts 2.38); "in the name of the Lord Jesus" (Acts 8.16).

In the name of means "by the authority of"; most translations retain the literal form, perhaps under the influence of church tradition. In some cases the phrase will have to be used with all three authorities, as in "in the name of the Father, in the name of the Son, and in the name of the Holy Spirit."

There will be languages where **the Father** will have to be "God the Father," but it would not be normal to render **the Son** by "Jesus the Son," if for no other reason than that it is Jesus himself speaking here. "God the Son" is certainly the way most churches understand this phrase, but it should not be added to the translation. (On the other hand "God the Father" will have been used by many throughout the Gospel of Matthew.)

For **Holy Spirit** see discussion at 1.18.

28.20 RSV	TEV
teaching them to observe all that I have commanded you; and lo, I am with you always, to the close of the age."	and teach them to obey everything I have commanded you. And I will be with you always, to the end of the age."

Teaching is best interpreted as the equivalent of an imperative (see comment at verse 19).

Some translations render **them** to include only those who have been baptized, and others make it refer to the people of all nations. Probably a reference to all people is more natural, since the command of Jesus does not say to baptize only some, and translators should not be specific in this verse in a way the text is not.

Observe is used of commandments in 19.17 and of instructions in 23.3; it is also the same verb translated "keep watch" in 27.36,54, and the participle "guards" (28.4) is also derived from this same verb. Here translators can say "to do all the things I have commanded you" or "to live according to my commandments to you."

Commanded is first used in 4.6 (translated "give . . . charge of"); it is found elsewhere in 15.4; 17.9; 19.7. Commentators note that the construction **all that I have commanded** is similar to one that is frequently employed in the Septuagint of God's commands to Israel (for example, Exo 7.2; 23.22; 29.35; 31.11; Deut 1.41; 4.2; 6.6). Translators can have either "everything I have commanded you" or "all the commands I have given you" (so Brc).

The expression **and lo** is not natural in contemporary English, so most translators drop it. But sometimes it is rendered as "And it will be" or "it will happen that."

I am with you always also has its roots in the Old Testament (see Exo 3.12; Josh 1.5,9; Isa 41.10; 43.5). It is often more natural to say "I will be with you always (or, at all times)."

The close of the age is the same expression used in 13.39. The period indicated here is that which extends from the time of Christ's resurrection-exaltation to the end of the world. Translators can have "until the end of the world (or, the end of time)."

Bibliography

Bible Texts and Versions Cited

Texts

The Greek New Testament. 3rd edition (corrected), 1983. K. Aland, M. Black, C. M. Martini, B. M. Metzger, and A. Wikgren, eds. Stuttgart: United Bible Societies. (Cited as UBS Greek New Testament.)

Novum Testamentum Graece. 26th edition, 1979; corrected, 1981. Erwin Nestle and Kurt Aland, eds. Stuttgart: Deutsche Bibelgesellschaft. (Cited as Nestle-Aland.)

Versions

Die Bibel in heutigem Deutsch: Die Gute Nachricht des Alten und Neuen Testaments. 1982. Stuttgart: Deutsche Bibelgesellschaft. (Cited as GECL.)

Die Bibel: Nach der übersetzung Martin Luthers, revidierter Text. 1975, 1978. Stuttgart: Deutsche Bibelstiftung. (Cited as Lu.)

The Bible: A New Translation. 1925. James Moffatt. New York: Harper and Brothers; London: Hodder and Stoughton. (Cited as Mft.)

La Bible de Jérusalem. 1973. Paris: Les Éditions du Cerf. (Cited as BJ.)

La Bible en français courant. 1982. Paris: Alliance Biblique Universelle. (Cited as FRCL.)

The Complete Bible: An American Translation. 1923. J. M. Powis Smith and Edgar Goodspeed. Chicago: University of Chicago Press. (Cited as AT.)

Dios Habla Hoy: La Biblia con deuterocanónicos. Versión Popular. 1979. New York: Sociedades Bíblicas Unidas. (Cited as SpCL.)

Groot Nieuws Bijbel: Vertaling in omgangstaal. 1983. Boxtel: Katholieke Bijbelstichting; Haarlem: Nederlands Bijbelgenootschap. (Cited as DUCL.)

Good News Bible: The Bible in Today's English Version. 1976, 1979. New York: American Bible Society. (Cited as TEV.)

889

Die Gute Nachricht: Das Neue Testament in heutigem Deutsch. 1967, 1971. Stuttgart: Württembergische Bibelanstalt. (Cited as GECL 1st edition.)

Die Heilige Schrift des Alten und Neuen Testaments. 1935. Zürich: Zwingli-Bibel. (Cited as Zür.)

The Holy Bible (Authorized or King James Version). 1611. (Cited as KJV.)

The Holy Bible: New International Version. 1978. Grand Rapids, Michigan: Zondervan Bible Publishers; London: Hodder and Stoughton. (Cited as NIV.)

The Holy Bible: Revised Standard Version. 1952, 1971, 1973. New York: Division of Christian Education of the National Council of the Churches of Christ in the United States of America. (Cited as RSV.)

The Jerusalem Bible. 1966. London: Darton, Longman & Todd. (Cited as JB.)

Kabar Baik: Alkitab dalam Bahasa Indonesia Sehari-hari. 1985. Jakarta: Lembaga Alkitab Indonesia. (Cited as INCL.)

The Living Bible. 1971. Translated by Kenneth Taylor. Wheaton, Illinois: Tyndale House. (Cited as LB.)

The New American Bible. 1970. Camden, New Jersey: Thomas Nelson, Inc. (Cited as NAB.)

The New American Standard Bible. 1973. La Habra, California: Lockman Foundation. (Cited as NASB.)

The New English Bible. Second edition, 1970. London: Oxford University Press and Cambridge University Press. (Cited as NEB.)

The New Jerusalem Bible. 1985. Garden City, NY: Doubleday. (Cited as NJB.)

The New Testament: A New Translation. Volume 1: The Gospels and the Acts of the Apostles, 1968. William Barclay. London and New York: Collins. (Cited as Brc.)

The New Testament in Modern English. 1972. Translated by J.B. Phillips. New York: Macmillan. (Cited as Phps.)

Perjanjian Baharu: Berita baik untuk manusia moden. 1976. Singapore: Bible Society of Singapore, Malaysia & Brunei. (Cited as MACL.)

La Sainte Bible: Traduite d'après les textes originaux hébreu et grec. 1978. Nouvelle version Segond révisée, deuxième édition. Paris: Alliance biblique universelle. (Cited as Seg.)

Traduction œcuménique de la Bible. 1972, 1975, 1977. Paris: Société Biblique Française et Éditions du Cerf. (Cited as TOB.)

The Translator's New Testament. 1973. London: British and Foreign Bible Society. (Cited as TNT.)

General Bibliography

Commentaries

Albright, W.F., and C.S. Mann. 1971. *Matthew: Introduction, Translation, and Notes* (The Anchor Bible). Garden City, New York: Doubleday. (Cited as AB.)

Allen, Willoughby C. Third edition, 1912. *A Critical and Exegetical Commentary on the Gospel According to S. Matthew* (International Critical Commentary). Edinburgh: T. and T. Clark.

Argyle, A. W. 1977. *The Gospel According to Matthew* (The Cambridge Bible Commentary on the New English Bible). Cambridge: Cambridge University Press.

Bruce, Alexander Balmain. n.d. *The Synoptic Gospels* (The Expositor's Greek Testament). Grand Rapids, Michigan: Eerdmans.

Carson, Donald A. 1984. *Matthew* (In: The Expositor's Bible Commentary 8, pages 1-599). Grand Rapids, Michigan: Zondervan.

Grundmann, Walter. Zweite Auflage, 1971. *Das Evangelium nach Matthäus* (Theologischer Handkommentar zum Neuen Testament). Berlin: Evangelische Verlagsanstalt.

Hill, David. 1972. *The Gospel of Matthew* (New Century Bible). Greenwood, South Carolina: Attic Press.

Johnson, Sherman E. 1951. "The Gospel According to Matthew." *The Interpreter's Bible*, volume 7. Nashville: Abingdon-Cokesbury.

Kee, Howard Clark. 1971. "The Gospel According to Matthew." *The Interpreter's One-Volume Commentary on the Bible*. Nashville: Abingdon.

Kingsbury, Jack Dean. 1977. *Matthew* (Proclamation Commentaries). Philadelphia: Fortress.

Lohmeyer, Ernst, and Werner Schmauch. 1958. *Das Evangelium des Matthäus* (Kritisch-exegetischer Kommentar über das Neue Testament). Göttingen: Vandenhoeck und Ruprecht.

McKenzie, John L. 1968. "The Gospel According to Matthew." *The Jerome Biblical Commentary.* Englewood Cliffs, New Jersey: Prentice-Hall.

Plummer, Alfred. 1960. *An Exegetical Commentary on the Gospel According to S. Matthew.* Grand Rapids, Michigan: Eerdmans.

Robinson, Theodore H. 1951. *The Gospel of Matthew.* The Moffat New Testament Commentary. London: Hodder and Stoughton.

Schniewind, Julius. 1971. *Das Evangelium nach Matthäus.* Das Neue Testament Deutsch. Göttingen: Vandenhoeck und Ruprecht.

Schweizer, Eduard. 1975. *The Good News According to Matthew.* Atlanta: John Knox.

Stendahl, Krister. 1972. "Matthew." *Peake's Commentary on the Bible.* London: Thomas Nelson and Sons.

Special Studies

Blair, Edward P. 1960. *Jesus in the Gospel of Matthew.* Nashville: Abingdon.

Bornkamm, Gunther, Gerhard Barth, and Heinz Joachim Held. 1963. *Tradition and Interpretation in Matthew.* Philadelphia: Westminister.

Davies, W. D. 1966. *The Setting of the Sermon on the Mount.* Cambridge: Cambridge University Press.

Franzmann, Martin H. 1961. *Follow Me: Discipleship According to Saint Matthew.* St. Louis: Concordia.

Jeremias, Joachim. 1972. *The Parables of Jesus.* Second edition. New York: Charles Scribner's Sons.

————. 1978. *The Prayers of Jesus.* Philadelphia: Fortress.

Johnson, Luke T. 1986. "The Gospel of Matthew." Chap. 8 in *The Writings of the New Testament.* Philadelphia: Fortress.

Kingsbury, Jack Dean. 1971. *The Parables of Jesus in Matthew 13: A Study in Redaction-Criticism.* Richmond, Virginia: John Knox.

————. 1978. *Matthew: Structure, Christology, Kingdom.* Philadelphia: Fortress.

Lohmeyer, Ernst. Zweite unveränderte Auflage, 1953. *Gottesknecht und Davidssohn.* Göttingen: Vandenhoeck und Ruprecht.

———. Vierte, unveränderte Auflage, 1960. *Das Vater-unser*. Göttingen: Vandenhoeck und Ruprecht.

Pregeant, Russell. 1978. *Christology Beyond Dogma: Matthew's Christ in Process Hermeneutic*. Philadelphia: Fortress; and Missoula, Montana: Scholars Press.

Schweizer, Eduard. 1974. *Matthäus und seine Gemeinde*. Stuttgart: KBW Verlag.

Stendahl, Krister. 1968. *The School of St. Matthew and Its Use of the Old Testament*. Philadelphia: Fortress.

Strecker, Georg. Dritte, durchgesehene und erweiterte Auflage, 1971. *Der Weg der Gerechtigkeit: Untersuchung zur Theologie des Matthäus*. Göttingen: Vandenhoeck und Ruprecht.

Walker, Rolf. 1967. *Die Heilsgeschichte im ersten Evangelium*. Göttingen: Vandenhoeck und Ruprecht.

Other Works

Aland, Kurt, ed. 1978. *Vollständige Konkordanz zum griechischen Neuen Testament. Band II: Specialübersichten*. Berlin und New York: Walter de Gruyter.

Arndt, William F., and F. Wilbur Gingrich. 1979. *A Greek-English Lexicon of the New Testament and Other Early Christian Literature*. Second edition, revised and augmented by F. Wilbur Gingrich and Frederick W. Danker. Chicago and London: The University of Chicago Press.

Blass, F., and A. Debrunner. 1961. *Greek Grammar of the New Testament and Other Early Christian Literature*. Chicago: University of Chicago Press.

Buttrick, G. A., ed. 1962. *The Interpreter's Dictionary of the Bible*. 4 vols. Nashville: Abingdon.

Crim, Keith, ed. 1976. *The Interpreter's Dictionary of the Bible*. Supplementary Volume. Nashville: Abingdon.

Metzger, B. M. 1971. *A Textual Commentary on the Greek New Testament*. London and New York: United Bible Societies. (Cited as TC-GNT.)

Moulton, W. F., and A. S. Geden. 1963. *A Concordance to the Greek Testament*. Fourth Edition Revised by H. K. Moulton. Edinburgh: T. and T. Clark.

Glossary

This Glossary contains terms which are technical from an exegetical or a linguistic viewpoint. Other terms not defined here may be referred to in a Bible dictionary.

ABSTRACT noun is one which refers to a quality or characteristic, such as "beauty" or "darkness."

ACTIVE. See **VOICE**.

ADJECTIVE is a word which limits, describes, or qualifies a noun. In English, "red," "tall," "beautiful," and "important" are adjectives.

ADVERB is a word which limits, describes, or qualifies a verb, an adjective, or another adverb. In English, "quickly," "soon," "primarily," and "very" are adverbs.

ADVERBIAL refers to adverbs. An **ADVERBIAL PHRASE** is a phrase which functions as an adverb. See **PHRASE**.

AGENT is that which accomplishes the action in a sentence or clause, regardless of whether the grammatical construction is active or passive. In "John struck Bill" (active) and "Bill was struck by John" (passive), the agent in either case is John.

ALLEGORY is a story in which persons (or other figures) and actions are used to symbolize spiritual forces, truths, human conduct, experience, etc. **ALLEGORICAL** interpretation of Scripture sees similar symbolic meaning in the historical parts of the Bible.

AMBIGUOUS (AMBIGUITY) describes a word or phrase which in a specific context may have two or more different meanings. For example, "Bill did not leave because John came" could mean either (1) "the coming of John prevented Bill from leaving" or (2) "the coming of John was not the cause of Bill's leaving." It is often the case that what is ambiguous in written form is not ambiguous when actually spoken, since features of intonation and slight pauses usually make clear which of two or more meanings is intended. Furthermore, even in written discourse, the entire context normally serves to indicate which meaning is intended by the writer.

AORIST refers to a set of forms in Greek verbs which denote an action completed without the implication of continuance or duration. Usually, but not always, the action is considered as completed in past time.

APPOSITION (APPOSITIONAL) is the placing of two expressions together so that they both refer to the same object, event, or concept; for example, "my friend, Mr. Smith." The one expression is said to be the **APPOSITIVE** of the other.

ARAMAIC is a language that was widely used in Southwest Asia before the time of Christ. It became the common language of many of the Jewish people in Palestine in place of Hebrew, to which it is related.

ARTICLE is a grammatical class of words, often obligatory, which indicate whether the following word is definite or indefinite. In English the **DEFINITE ARTICLE** is "the," and the **INDEFINITE ARTICLE** is "a" or ("an").

CAUSATIVE (CAUSAL) relates to events and indicates that someone or something caused something to happen, rather than that the person or thing did it directly. In "John ran the horse," the verb "ran" is a causative, since it was not John who ran, but rather it was John who caused the horse to run.

CHIASMUS (CHIASTIC) is a reversal of words or phrases in an otherwise parallel construction. For example: "I (1) / was shapen (2) / in iniquity (3) // in sin (3) / did my mother conceive (2) / me (1)."

CLAUSE is a grammatical construction, normally consisting of a subject and an predicate. An **INDEPENDENT CLAUSE** may stand alone. The **MAIN CLAUSE** is that clause in a sentence which could stand alone as a complete sentence, but which has one or more dependent or subordinate clauses related to it. A **SUBORDINATE CLAUSE** is dependent on the main clause, but it does not form a complete sentence. For **COORDINATE CLAUSE**, see **COORDINATE STRUCTURE**.

CLIMAX (CLIMACTIC) is the point in a discourse, such as a story or speech, which is the most important, or the turning point, or the point of decision.

COLLOQUIAL refers to informal language used widely in spoken conversation, but not normally used in formal writing on in speeches.

CONJUNCTIONS are words which serve as connectors between words, phrases, clauses, and sentences. "And," "but," "if," and "because" are typical conjunctions in English.

CONNOTATION involves the emotional attitude of a speaker (or writer) to an expression he uses, and the emotional response of the hearers (or readers). Connotations may be good or bad, strong or weak, and they are often described in such terms as "colloquial," "taboo," "vulgar," "old-fashioned," and "intimate."

CONSTRUCTION. See STRUCTURE.

CONTEXT (CONTEXTUAL) is that which precedes and/or follows any part of a discourse. For example, the context of a word or phrase in Scripture would be the other words and phrases associated with it in the sentence, paragraph, section, and even the entire book in which it occurs. The context of a term often affects its meaning, so that a word does not mean exactly the same thing in one context that it does in another context.

COORDINATE structure is a phrase or clause joined to another phrase or clause, but not dependent on it. Coordinate structures are joined by such conjunctions as "and" or "but," as in "the man and the boys" or "he walked but she ran"; or they are paratactically related, as in "he walked; she ran."

CULTURE (CULTURAL) is the sum total of the beliefs, patterns of behavior, and sets of interpersonal relations of any group of people. A culture is passed on from one generation to another, but undergoes development or gradual change.

DEFINITE ARTICLE. See ARTICLE.

DEPENDENT CLAUSE is a grammatical construction consisting normally of a subject and predicate, which is dependent upon or embedded within some other construction. For example, "if he comes" is a dependent clause in the sentence "If he comes, we'll have to leave." See CLAUSE.

DIRECT DISCOURSE, DIRECT QUOTATION, DIRECT SPEECH. See DISCOURSE.

DIRECT OBJECT is the goal of an event or action specified by a verb. In "John hit the ball," the direct object of "hit" is "ball."

DISCOURSE is the connected and continuous communication of thought by means of language, whether spoken or written. The way in which the elements of a discourse are arranged is called DISCOURSE STRUCTURE. DIRECT DISCOURSE (or, DIRECT QUOTATION, DIRECT SPEECH) is the reproduction of the actual words of one person quoted and included in the discourse of another person; for example, "He declared 'I will have nothing to do with this man.' " INDIRECT DISCOURSE (or, INDIRECT QUOTATION, INDIRECT SPEECH) is the reporting of the words of one person within the discourse of another person, but in an altered grammatical form rather than as an exact quotation; for example, "He said he would have nothing to do with that man."

DISTRIBUTIVE refers not to the group as a whole, but to the members of the group.

DIVINE PASSIVE is the use of the passive form of a verb in order to avoid mentioning God or the name of God. For example, "You will be blessed" uses the passive "be blessed" but may be understood to mean "God will bless you." See also VOICE, PASSIVE.

897

DYNAMIC EQUIVALENCE is a type of translation in which the message of the original text is so conveyed in the receptor language that the response of the receptors is (or, can be) essentially like that of the original receptors, or that the receptors can in large measure comprehend the response of the original receptors, if, as in certain languages, the differences between the two cultures are extremely great.

ELLIPSIS (plural, **ELLIPSES**) or **ELLIPTICAL EXPRESSION** refers to words or phrases normally omitted in a discourse when the sense is perfectly clear without them. In the following sentence, the words within brackets are **ELLIPTICAL**: "If [it is] necessary [for me to do so], I will wait up all night."

EMPHASIS (**EMPHATIC**) is the special importance given to an element in a discourse, sometimes indicated by the choice of words or by position in the sentence. For example, in "Never will I eat pork again," "Never" is given emphasis by placing it at the beginning of the sentence.

ESCHATOLOGICAL refers to the end of the world and the events connected with it. In this connection, the "world" is understood in various ways by various persons.

EUPHEMISM is a mild or indirect term used in the place of another term which is felt to be impolite, distasteful, or vulgar; for example, "to pass away" is a euphemism for "to die."

EXCLUSIVE first person plural excludes the person(s) addressed. That is, a speaker may use "we" to refer to himself and his companions, while specifically excluding the person(s) to whom he is speaking. See **INCLUSIVE**.

EXEGESIS (**EXEGETICAL**) is the process of determining the meaning of a text (or the result of this process), normally in terms of "who said what to whom under what circumstances and with what intent." A correct exegesis is indispensable before a passage can be translated correctly.

EXPLICIT refers to information which is expressed in the words of a discourse. This is in contrast to implicit information. See **IMPLICIT**.

FEMININE is one of the Greek genders. See **GENDER**.

FIGURE, FIGURE OF SPEECH, or **FIGURATIVE EXPRESSION** involves the use of words in other than their literal or ordinary sense, in order to bring out some aspect of meaning by means of comparison or association. For example, "raindrops dancing on the street," or "his speech was like thunder." **METAPHORS** and **SIMILES** are figures of speech.

FINITE VERB is any verb form which distinguishes person, number, tense, mode, or aspect. It is usually referred to in contrast to an **INFINITIVE** verb form, which indicates the action or state without specifying such things as agent or time.

FIRST PERSON. See **PERSON.**

FLASHBACK is a reference in a narrative to events prior to the time of the portion of the narrative under consideration.

FOCUS is the center of attention in a discourse or in any part of a discourse.

FUTURE TENSE. See **TENSE.**

GENDER is any of three grammatical subclasses of Greek nouns and pronouns (called **MASCULINE, FEMININE,** and **NEUTER**), which determine agreement with and selection of other words or grammatical forms.

GENITIVE case is a grammatical set of forms occurring in many languages, used primarily to indicate that a noun is the modifier of another noun. The genitive often indicates possession, but it may also indicate measure, origin, characteristic, separation, or source, as in "people of God," "pound of flour," "child's toy," or "Garden of Eden."

GREEKS, strictly speaking, were the inhabitants of Greece, corresponding to the Roman province of Achaia in New Testament times. In the New Testament, the term is used in a wider sense as referring to all those in the Roman Empire who spoke the Greek language and were strongly influenced by Greek culture.

HEBREW is the language in which the Old Testament was written. It belongs to the Semitic family of languages. By the time of Christ, many Jewish people no longer used Hebrew as their common language.

HENDIADYS is a figure in which a single complex idea is expressed by two words or structures, usually connected by a conjunction. For example, "weary and worn" may mean "very tired."

HISTORICAL PRESENT refers to the use of the **PRESENT TENSE** to refer to events that occurred in the past, as in "Moses sees the burning bush, hears the voice, and removes his shoes." This device often helps the events of the past seem more vivid for the reader or hearer.

HONORIFIC is a form used to express respect or deference. In many languages such forms are obligatory in talking to or about royalty and persons of social distinction.

HYPOTHETICAL refers to something which is not recognized as a fact but which is assumed to be true to develop an argument or line of reasoning.

IDIOM or **IDIOMATIC EXPRESSION** is a combination of terms whose meanings cannot be understood by adding up the meanings of the parts. "To hang one's head," "to have a green thumb," and "behind the eightball" are American English idioms. Idioms almost always lose their meaning or convey a wrong meaning when translated literally from one language to another.

IMPERATIVE refers to forms of a verb which indicate commands or requests. In "Go and do likewise," the verbs "Go" and "do" are imperatives. In most languages, imperatives are confined to the grammatical second person; but some languages have corresponding forms for the first and third persons. These are usually expressed in English by the use of "may" or "let"; for example, "May we not have to beg!" or "Let them work harder!"

IMPERFECT TENSE is a set of verb forms designating an uncompleted or continuing kind of action, especially in the past.

IMPERSONAL VERB is a third person singular verb that denotes an action by an unspecified agent; for example, "It is raining."

IMPLICIT (IMPLIED) refers to information that is not formally represented in a discourse, since it is assumed that it is already known to the receptor, or evident from the meaning of the words in question. For example, the phrase "the other son" carries with it the implicit information that there is a son in addition to the one mentioned. This is in contrast to **EXPLICIT** information, which is expressly stated in a discourse. See **EXPLICIT**.

IMPLY. See **IMPLICIT, IMPLIED**.

INCLUSIVE first person plural includes both the speaker and the one(s) to whom that person is speaking. See **EXCLUSIVE**.

INDEPENDENT CLAUSE. See **CLAUSE**.

INDICATIVE refers to forms of a verb in which an act or condition is stated as an actual fact rather than as a potentiality, a hope, or an unrealized condition. The verb "won" in "The king won the battle" is in the indicative form.

INDIRECT DISCOURSE, INDIRECT QUOTATION, INDIRECT SPEECH. See **DISCOURSE**.

INDIRECT OBJECT is the benefactive goal of the event or action specified by a verb. In "John threw Henry the ball," the direct object or goal of "threw" is "ball," and the indirect object is "Henry." See **DIRECT OBJECT**.

INFINITIVE is a verb form which indicates an action or state without specifying such factors as agent or time; for example, "to mark," "to sing," or "to go." It is in contrast to **FINITE VERB** form, which often distinguishes person, number, tense, mode, or aspect; for example "marked," "sung," or "will go." See **FINITE VERB**.

INTENSIVE refers to increased emphasis or force in any expression, as when "very" occurs in the phrase "very active" or "highly" in the phrase "highly competitive." The Hebrew language has a set of verb forms which indicate that the action of the verb is intensive.

INTERPRETATION of a text is the exegesis of it. See **EXEGESIS**.

IRONY (IRONIC, IRONICAL) is a sarcastic or humorous manner of discourse in which what is said is intended to express its opposite: for example, "That was a smart thing to do!" when intended to convey the meaning, "That was a stupid thing to do!"

KERNEL is a sentence pattern which is basic to the structure of a language. **KERNELS** may also be called "basic sentence patterns," out of which more elaborate sentence structures may be formed.

LITERAL means the ordinary or primary meaning of a term or expression, in contrast with a figurative meaning. A **LITERAL TRANSLATION** is one which represents the exact words and word order of the source language; such a translation is frequently unnatural or awkward in the receptor language.

MANUSCRIPTS are books, documents, or letters written or copied by hand. A **SCRIBE** is one who copies a manuscript. Thousands of manuscript copies of various Old and New Testament books still exist, but none of the original manuscripts. See **TEXT**.

MANUSCRIPT EVIDENCE (MANUSCRIPT SUPPORT) is also called **TEXTUAL EVIDENCE**. See **TEXT, TEXTUAL**. A group of manuscripts that are similar may be said to belong to a specific **MANUSCRIPT TRADITION**.

MASCULINE is one of the Greek genders. See **GENDER**.

METAPHOR is likening one object, event, or state to another by speaking of it as if it were the other; for example, "flowers dancing in the breeze." Metaphors are the most commonly used figures of speech and are often so subtle that a speaker or writer is not conscious of the fact that he is using figurative language. See **SIMILE**.

MIDDLE VOICE. See **VOICE**.

MODIFIER is a grammatical term referring to a word or a phrase which is used to modify or affect the meaning of another part of the sentence, such as an adjective modifying a noun or an adverb modifying a verb.

MODIFY is to affect the meaning of another part of the sentence, as when an adjective modifies a noun or an adverb modifies a verb.

NARRATIVE DISCOURSE is a text consisting of a series of successive and related events.

NEUTER is one of the Greek genders. See **GENDER**.

NOUN is a word that names a person, place, thing, or idea, and often serves to specify a subject or topic of discussion.

NOUN PHRASE. See **PHRASE.**

OBJECT. See **DIRECT OBJECT, INDIRECT OBJECT.**

ONOMATOPOEIA (ONOMATOPOEIC) is the use or invention of words that imitate the sounds of what they refer to; for example, "swishing," "bang!" or "bubble."

ORTHOGRAPHY (ORTHOGRAPHIC) refers to a system of writing and is often used in speaking of a similarity or difference in spelling.

PARAGRAPH is a distinct segment of discourse dealing with a particular idea, and usually marked with an indentation on a new line.

PARALLEL, PARALLELISM, generally refers to some similarity in the content and/or form of a construction; for example, "The man was blind, and he could not see." The structures that correspond to each other in the two statements are said to be parallel. **PARALLEL PASSAGES** are two separate biblical references that resemble each other in one or more ways.

PARTICIPIAL indicates that the phrase, clause, construction, or other expression described is governed by a **PARTICIPLE.**

PARTICIPLE is a verbal adjective, that is, a word which retains some of the characteristics of a verb while functioning as an adjective. In "singing children" and "painted house," "singing" and "painted" are participles.

PARTICLE is a small word whose grammatical form does not change. In English the most common particles are prepositions and conjunctions.

PASSIVE. See **VOICE.**

PERFECT TENSE is a set of verb forms which indicate an action already completed when another action occurs. For example, in "John had finished his task when Bill came," "had finished" is in the perfect tense. The perfect tense in Greek also indicates that the action continues into the present. See also **TENSE.**

PERSON, as a grammatical term, refers to the speaker, the person spoken to, or the person or thing spoken about. **FIRST PERSON** is the person(s) speaking (such as "I," "me," "my," "mine," "we," "us," "our," or "ours"). **SECOND PERSON** is the person(s) or thing(s) spoken to (such as "thou," "thee," "thy," "thine," "ye," "you," "your," or "yours"). **THIRD PERSON** is the person(s) or thing(s) spoken about (such as "he," "she," "it," "his," "her," "them," or "their"). The examples here given are all pronouns, but in many languages the verb forms have affixes which indicate first, second, or third person and also indicate whether they are **SINGULAR** or **PLURAL.**

PERSONIFY (PERSONIFICATION) is to refer to an inanimate object or an abstract idea in terms that give it a personal or a human nature; as in "Wisdom is calling out," referring to wisdom as if it were a person.

PHONOLOGICAL refers to the sounds of language, especially their formal similarities and differences.

PHRASE is a grammatical construction of two or more words, but less than a complete clause or a sentence. A phrase is usually given a name according to its function in a sentence, such as "noun phrase," "verb phrase," or "prepositional phrase."

PLAY ON WORDS in a discourse is the use of the similarity in the sounds of two words to produce a special effect.

PLURAL refers to the form of a word which indicates more than one. See **SINGULAR**.

POSSESSIVE refers to a grammatical relationship in which one noun or pronoun is said to "possess" another ("John's car," "his son," "their destruction"). (Obadiah/Micah) [In Greek this relation is generally marked by the **GENITIVE CASE**.

PREDICATE is the part of a clause which contrasts with or supplements the subject. The **SUBJECT** is the topic of the clause, and the **PREDICATE** is what is said about the subject. For example, in "The small boy ran swiftly," the subject is "The small boy," and the predicate is "ran swiftly." See **SUBJECT**.

PREPOSITION is a word (usually a particle) whose function is to indicate the relation of a noun or pronoun to another noun, pronoun, verb, or adjective. Some English prepositions are "for," "from," "in," "to," and "with."

PREPOSITIONAL refers to **PREPOSITIONS**. A prepositional phrase or expression is one governed by a preposition. "For his benefit" and "to a certain city" are prepositional phrases.

PRESENT TENSE. See **TENSE**.

PRONOMINAL refers to **PRONOUNS**.

PRONOUNS are words which are used in place of nouns, such as "he," "him," "his," "she," "we," "them," "who," "which," "this," or "these."

PROPER NOUN is the name of a unique object, as "Jerusalem," "Joshua," "Jordan." However, the same name may be applied to more than one object; for example, "John" (the Baptist or the Apostle) and "Antioch" (of Syria or Pisidia).

QUALIFY is to limit the meaning of a term by means of another term. For example, in "old man," the term "old" qualifies the term "man."

QUOTATION is the reporting of one person's speech by another person. See **DISCOURSE**.

READ, READING. See **TEXT, TEXTUAL.**

RECEPTOR is the person(s) receiving a message. The **RECEPTOR LANGUAGE** is the language into which a translation is made. For example, in a translation from Hebrew into German, Hebrew is the source language and German is the receptor language.

REFERENT is the thing(s) or person(s) referred to by a pronoun, phrase, or clause.

RELATIVE CLAUSE is a dependent clause which describes the object to which it refers. In "the man whom you saw," the clause "whom you saw" is relative because it relates to and describes "man."

RESTRUCTURE. See **STRUCTURE.**

RHETORICAL QUESTION is an expression which is put in the form of a question but which is not intended to ask for information. Rhetorical questions are usually employed for the sake of emphasis.

SCRIBE, SCRIBAL. See **MANUSCRIPT.**

SECOND PERSON. See **PERSON.**

SEMANTIC refers to meaning. **SEMANTIC** features are the distinctive features of the meaning of a term. For example, the central meaning of **MAN** has the components of human, adult, and male.

SEMITIC refers to a family of languages which includes Hebrew, Aramaic, and Arabic. Greek belongs to quite another language family, with a distinct cultural background. In view of the Jewish ancestry and training of the writers of the New Testament, it is not surprising that many Semitic idioms and thought patterns (called Semitisms or Hebraisms) appear in the Greek writings of the New Testament.

SENTENCE is a grammatical construction composed of one or more clauses and capable of standing alone.

SEPTUAGINT is a translation of the Hebrew Old Testament into Greek, made some two hundred years before Christ. It is often abbreviated as LXX.

SIMILE (pronounced SIM-i-lee) is a **FIGURE OF SPEECH** which describes one event or object by comparing it to another, using "like," "as," or some other word to mark or signal the comparison. For example, "She runs like a deer," "He is as straight as an arrow." Similes are less subtle than metaphors in that metaphors do not mark the comparison with words such as "like" or "as." See **METAPHOR**.

SINGULAR refers to the form of a word which indicates one thing or person, in contrast to **PLURAL**, which indicates more than one. See **PLURAL**.

STRUCTURE is the systematic arrangement of the elements of language, including the ways in which words combine into phrases, phrases into clauses, and clauses into sentences. Because this process may be compared to the building of a house or bridge, such words as **STRUCTURE** and **CONSTRUCTION** are used in reference to it. To separate and rearrange the various components of a sentence or other unit of discourse in the translation process is to **RESTRUC-TURE** it.

STYLE is a particular or a characteristic manner in discourse. Each language has certain distinctive **STYLISTIC** features which cannot be reproduced literally in another language. Within any language, certain groups of speakers may have their characteristic discourse styles, and among individual speakers and writers, each has his own style.

SUBJECT is one of the major divisions of a clause, the other being the predicate. In "The small boy walked to school," "The small boy" is the subject. Typically the subject is a noun phrase. It should not be confused with the semantic agent. See **PREDICATE**.

SUBJUNCTIVE refers to certain forms of verbs that are used to express an act or state as being contingent or possible (sometimes as wish or desire), rather than as actual fact. For example, in "If I were young, I would enjoy my health," "were" and "would" are subjunctive forms.

SUFFIX is a letter or one or more syllables added to the end of a word, to modify the meaning in some manner. For example, "-s" suffixed to "tree" changes the word from singular to plural, "trees," while "-ing" suffixed to "sing" changes the verb to a participle, "singing."

SYNONYMS are words which are different in form but similar in meaning, such as "boy" and "lad." Expressions which have essentially the same meaning are said to be **SYNONYMOUS**. No two words are completely synonymous.

SYNOPTIC GOSPELS are Matthew, Mark, and Luke, which share many characteristics that are not found in John.

TEMPORAL refers to time. A **TEMPORAL CLAUSE** is a dependent clause which indicates the time of the action in the main clause; for example, "when the bell rang, the students went home.

TENSE is usually a form of a verb which indicates time relative to a discourse or some event in a discourse. The most common forms of tense are past, present, and future.

TEXT, TEXTUAL, refers to the various Greek and Hebrew **MANUSCRIPTS** of the Scriptures. A **TEXTUAL READING** is the form in which words occur in a particular manuscript (or group of manuscripts), especially where it differs from others. **TEXTUAL EVIDENCE** is the cumulative evidence for a particular form of the text. **TEXTUAL PROBLEMS** arise when it is difficult to reconcile or to account for conflicting forms of the same text in two or more manuscripts. **TEXTUAL VARIANTS** are forms of the same passage that differ in one or more details in some manuscripts. Ancient texts that resemble each other may be said to belong to a specific **TEXTUAL TRADITION**. See also **MANUSCRIPTS**.

THIRD PERSON. See **PERSON**.

TRANSITION in discourse involves passing from one thought-section or group of related thought-sections to another. **TRANSITIONAL** expressions are words or phrases which mark the connections between related events. Some typical transitionals are "next," "then," "later," "after this," "when he arrived."

TRANSLATION is the reproduction in a receptor language of the closest natural equivalent of a message in the source language, first, in terms of meaning, and second, in terms of style.

TRANSLITERATE (TRANSLITERATION) is to represent in the receptor language the approximate sounds or letters of words occurring in the source language, rather than translating their meaning; for example, "Amen" from the Hebrew, or the title "Christ" from the Greek.

VERBS are a grammatical class of words which express existence, action, or occurrence, such as "be," "become," "run," or "think."

VERBAL has two meanings. (1) It may refer to expressions consisting of words, sometimes in distinction to forms of communication which do not employ words ("sign language," for example). (2) It may refer to word forms which are derived from verbs. For example, "coming" and "engaged" may be called verbals, and participles are called verbal adjectives.

VOCATIVE indicates that a word or phrase is used for referring to a person or persons spoken to. In "Brother, please come here," the word "Brother" is a vocative.

VOICE in grammar is the relation of the action expressed by a verb to the participants in the action. In English and many other languages, the **ACTIVE VOICE** indicates that the subject performs the action ("John hit the man"), while the **PASSIVE VOICE** indicates that the subject is being acted upon ("The man was hit"). The Greek language has a **MIDDLE VOICE**, in which the subject may be regarded as doing something to or for himself (or itself); for example, "He washed," meaning "He washed himself."

Index

This index includes concepts, key words, and terms for which the Handbook contains a discussion useful for translators.